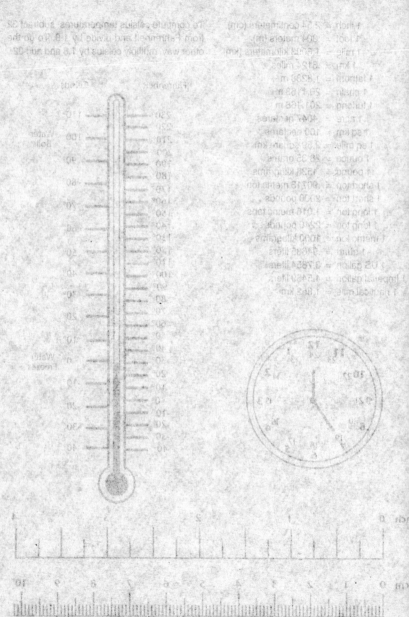

THE METRIC SYSTEM

1 inch = 2.54 centimeters (cm)
1 foot = .304 meters (m)
1 mile = 1.6093 kilometers (km)
1 km = .6124 miles
1 fathom = 1.8288 m
1 chain = 20.1168 m
1 furlong = 201.168 m
1 acre = .4047 hectares
1 sq km = 100 hectares
1 sq mile = 2.59 square km
1 ounce = 28.35 grams
1 pound = .4536 kilograms
1 short ton = .90718 metric ton
1 short ton = 2000 pounds
1 long ton = 1.016 metric tons
1 long ton = 2240 pounds
1 metric ton = 1000 kilograms
1 quart = .94635 liters
1 US gallon = 3.7854 liters
1 Imperial gallon = 4.5459 liters
1 nautical mile = 1.852 km

To compute celsius temperatures, subtract 32 from Fahrenheit and divide by 1.8. To go the other way, multiply celsius by 1.8 and add 32.

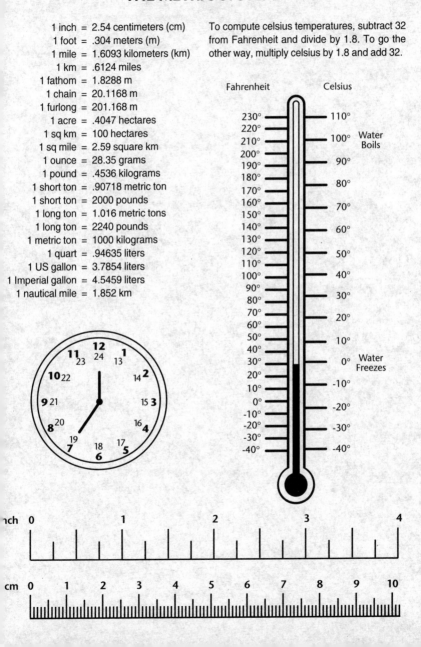

WYOMING
HANDBOOK

INCLUDING YELLOWSTONE AND GRAND TETON NATIONAL PARKS
THIRD EDITION

DON PITCHER

MOON
PUBLICATIONS INC.

WYOMING HANDBOOK
INCLUDING YELLOWSTONE AND GRAND TETON NATIONAL PARKS
THIRD EDITION

Published by
Moon Publications, Inc.
P.O. Box 3040
Chico, California 95927-3040, USA

Printed by
Colorcraft Ltd., Hong Kong

ISBN: 1-56691-085-4
ISSN: 1091-3386

Editor: Mike Sigalas
Map Editor: Gina Wilson Birtcil
Copy Editor: Gregor Krause
Production & Design: Rob Warner
Cartographers: Brian Bardwell, Chris Folks, Mike Morgenfeld, Rob Warner
Index: Gregor Krause

Front cover photo: Bison by river, Yellowstone National Park; by Glen Tig, Globe Trotter Photo Art.

Distributed in the USA and Canada by Publishers Group West
Printed in Hong Kong

Please send all comments,
corrections, additions,
amendments, and critiques to:

**WYOMING HANDBOOK
MOON PUBLICATIONS, INC.
P.O. BOX 3040
CHICO, CA 95927-3040, USA
e-mail: travel@moon.com**

Printing History
1st edition — July 1991
2nd edition — August 1993
3rd edition — April 1997

Wyoming seems to be the doing of a mad architect—tumbled and twisted, ribboned with faded, deathbed colors, thrust up and pulled down as if the place had beeen startled out of a deep sleep and thrown into a pure light.

—Gretel Ehrlich in The Solace of Open Spaces

God bless Wyoming and keep it wild.

—last entry in the diary of a girl
who died in the Tetons

CONTENTS

INTRODUCTION 1

The Land 5
   Geography; Climate

Flora and Fauna 8
   Vegetation; Wildlife; Bison

History 14
   Native Americans; Trappers and Explorers; The Oregon Trail;
   The Pony Express; The Overland Trail; Connecting the
   Coasts; Statehood; Cattle Country; Sheep; Energy Boom
   and Bust

Economy and Government 31
   Politics

ON THE ROAD 35

Outdoor Recreation 35
   Getting Into the Wilderness; Backcountry Safety

Accommodations and Food 42
   Lodging Choices; Camping; Food and Drink

Events and Activities 46
   Modern-Day Rendezvous; Rodeo

Information and Services 51
   Information Sources; Federal and State Offices; Services;
   Health and Safety

Transportation 57

SOUTHEAST WYOMING 61

Cheyenne 62
   History; Sights; Accommodations; Food; Entertainment and
   Events; Frontier Days; Other Events; Recreation; Shopping;
   Information and Services; Transportation

Curt Gowdy State Park 80

Pine Bluffs 81

Chugwater 83

Wheatland 84

Guernsey and Vicinity 88
   Hartville Area; Guernsey State Park; Glendo State Park

Fort Laramie National Historic Site 91
   History; Fort Laramie Today; The Town of Fort Laramie

Torrington 96
   Torrington Area

Lusk 101
   Legend of Rawhide; Heading North

MEDICINE BOW COUNTRY 105

Laramie 107
History; University of Wyoming; Wyoming Territorial Park;
More Laramie Sights; Accommodations; Food; Other
Practicalities; Pole Mountain Area

Medicine Bow Vicinity 123
Como Bluff; Medicine Bow; Shirley Basin; Hanna; Elk
Mountain; Arlington

Medicine Bow Mountains and Vicinity 128
Laramie Plains Vicinity; Snowy Range; Saratoga;
Encampment and Riverside; Sierra Madre; Little Snake River
Valley; Fort Fred Steele; Sinclair

Rawlins 145
History; Frontier Prison; Other Sights; Practicalities; Heading
North

SOUTHWEST WYOMING 152

The Red Desert 153
Killpecker Dunes Area

Rock Springs 156
History; Sights; Practicalities

Green River 162

Green River Vicinity 166
Little America

Flaming Gorge National Recreation Area 167
Access and Sights; Practicalities

Bridger Valley 170
Lyman; Mountain View; Piedmont; Fort Bridger

Evanston 173
History; Sights; Practicalities

Kemmerer 179
History; Sights; Practicalities

Fossil Butte National Monument 182

Kemmerer Vicinity 184
Oregon Trail Sights; Cokeville

Star Valley 185
Afton; Greys River Loop Road; Other Towns; Alpine; Snake
River Canyon

CENTRAL WYOMING 194

Douglas 195
History; Sights; Practicalities

Douglas Vicinity 202
Fort Fetterman; Thunder Basin National Grassland and
Vicinity; Laramie Mountains; Ayres Natural Bridge Park

Glenrock 207

Casper 209
History; Sights; Accommodations; Food; Entertainment;
Events; Recreation; Getting Malled; Information and Services;
Transportation

Casper Vicinity 222
Casper Mountain; Bessemer Bend; The "Lake District";
Oregon Trail Landmarks; North of Casper; Heading West

WIND RIVER MOUNTAINS COUNTRY . . . 235

Riverton 238

Riverton Vicinity 242
Shoshoni; Boysen State Park; Gas Hills; Hudson

Lander 243

Lander Vicinity 250
East On U.S. 287; Sinks Canyon and the Loop Road

Wind River Indian Reservation 253
Shoshone History; Arapaho History; Reservation Life;
Arapahoe and St. Stephens; Ethete; Fort Washakie;
West to Dubois

Dubois 264
History; Sights; Accommodations; Food; Fun and Games;
Other Practicalities; Dubois Vicinity; Over Togwotee Pass

Wind River Mountains 272
Green River Lakes Area; Bridger Wilderness; Fitzpatrick
Wilderness; Popo Agie Wilderness

South Pass Area 282
South Pass City; Atlantic City

Farson Area 289

Pinedale 290
Accommodations and Camping; Food; Entertainment and
Events; Recreation; Information and Services

Pinedale Vicinity 298
To Jackson Hole

JACKSON HOLE AND THE TETONS 301
History

Jackson 305
Sights; National Elk Refuge; Accommodations; Camping;
Food; Entertainment; Events; River Rafting; Fishing and
Boating; Other Summer Recreation; Winter Recreation;
Information and Services; Shopping; Transportation

Downhill Skiing and Snowboarding 338
Grand Targhee Ski Resort; Jackson Hole Ski Resort;
Snow King Resort

Cross-Country Skiing 342
Nordic Centers; On Your Own

Grand Teton National Park. 346
Geology; Wildlife; History; Touring the Park; Backcountry
Hiking; Mountain Climbing; Grand Teton Practicalities

Bridger-Teton National Forest 365
Teton Wilderness; Gros Ventre Wilderness

Targhee National Forest. 367
Jedediah Smith Wilderness

YELLOWSTONE NATIONAL PARK. 369

Geology 371
Volcanism; Geysers; Other Geothermal Activity

The Yellowstone Ecosystem. 373
Plants; Wildlife

Park History 377
Sheepeater Indians; Fur Trappers; Expeditions; Establishing
the Park; Roads and Railroads; The Army Years; The Park
Service Takes Over

Touring Yellowstone 385
South Entrance Road; West Thumb to Upper Geyser Basin;
Upper Geyser Basin; Midway and Lower Geyser Basins;
Madison Junction to West Yellowstone; Madison Junction
to Norris; Norris Geyser Basin; Norris Junction to Canyon;
Norris Junction to Mammoth; Mammoth Hot Springs Vicinity;
Mammoth to Tower Junction; Northeast Entrance Road;
Tower Junction to Canyon; Grand Canyon of the Yellowstone;
Canyon to Lake Junction; Yellowstone Lake; East Entrance
Road

Into the Backcountry 406
North Yellowstone Trails; South Yellowstone Trails

Winter in Yellowstone. 409

Yellowstone Practicalities 413
The Basics; Getting Around; Facilities and Services;
Campgrounds; Hotels and Cabins; Fishing and Boating;
Bicycling; Other Recreation; Greater Yellowstone Coalition;
Working in Yellowstone

Gateway Towns. 420
West Yellowstone; Gardiner; Silver Gate and Cooke City

BIGHORN BASIN 431

Shoshone National Forest 432
Wapiti Valley; Buffalo Bill State Park; Sunlight Basin;
South Fork Area; Beartooth Mountains; North Absaroka
Wilderness; Washakie Wilderness

Cody. 441
Buffalo Bill Historical Center; Other Sights; Accommodations;
Food; Events and Entertainment; Recreation; Other
Practicalities

Cody Vicinity 456
Heart Mountain; Heart Mountain Relocation Center; East to Powell

Meeteetse 458
Meeteetse Area

Powell 460
History; Sights; Practicalities; East to Lovell

Lovell 464
History; Practicalities

Bighorn Canyon National Recreation Area 466
Sights; Practicalities; Pryor Mountain Wild Horse Range

Greybull 471
Sights; Practicalities

Greybull Vicinity 473
Basin; Shell and Manderson; Medicine Lodge State Park

Worland 475
History; Sights; Practicalities

Ten Sleep 478

Thermopolis 480
Hot Springs State Park; Other Attractions; Practicalities

Wind River Canyon 486

POWDER RIVER COUNTRY 487

Big Horn Mountains 487
Cruisin' Through; Practicalities; Medicine Wheel; Cloud Peak Wilderness

Sheridan 497
History; Sights; Accommodations; Food; Other Practicalities

Sheridan Vicinity 505
Ranchester; Dayton; East of Sheridan; South of Sheridan; The Bloody Bozeman

Buffalo 514
History; Sights; Practicalities

Buffalo Vicinity 522
Lake Desmet; Kaycee; Hole-in-the-Wall Country

Gillette 526
History; Sights; Accommodations; Food; Other Practicalities; Heading South

THE BLACK HILLS 534

Newcastle 535
History; Sights; Practicalities

Newcastle Vicinity 539
Upton Area; Moorcroft; Keyhole State Park

Sundance 541
  Sights; Practicalities

Black Hills National Forest 544

The Northern Black Hills 545
  Aladdin and Vicinity; Hulett and Vicinity

Devils Tower National Monument 546
  History; Practicalities

BOOKLIST 551

INDEX 560

MAPS

INTRODUCTION

Mileage Map of Wyoming 57
Oregon Trail. 19
Wyoming Counties 4
Wyoming Geography 7
Wyoming, Historical 16
Wyoming Land Status 54-55
Wyoming State 2-3
Wyoming Vegetation 10

SOUTHEAST WYOMING

Cheyenne 64
Cheyenne, Downtown 68
Fort Laramie National Historic Site 92
Oregon Trail Country 90
Torrington. 98
Wheatland 85
Wyoming, Southeast 63

MEDICINE BOW COUNTRY

Laramie 108
Laramie, Downtown 113
Medicine Bow Country. 106
Medicine Bow Mountains 129
Pole Mountain Area 121
Rawlins 145
Snowy Range Trails. 131
Saratoga 135
University of Wyoming. 111

SOUTHWEST WYOMING

Evanston 175
Flaming Gorge National Recreation Area. 168
Green River 163
Kemmerer Area 180
Rock Springs. 157
Star Valley Area 187
Wyoming, Southwest 154

CENTRAL WYOMING

Casper 210
Casper Area 222
Casper, Downtown 213
Douglas 196
Laramie Mountains 206
"Lake District" 225
Wyoming, Central. 195

WIND RIVER MOUNTAINS COUNTRY

Big Sandy Area Trails 279

Dubois Area 265
Lander 245
Pinedale 291
Pinedale Area Trails. 275
Riverton 238
Sinks Canyon and South Pass Area . . . 283
Wind River Mountains Country 236
Wind River Mountains Wilderness Areas . 237

JACKSON HOLE AND THE TETONS

Grand Teton National Park and Vicinity . 348
Jackson 306
Jackson, Downtown. 307
Jackson Hole Vicinity 322
Jackson Hole and the Tetons. 302
Teton Hiking Trails 358

YELLOWSTONE NATIONAL PARK

Firehole River Area 391
Grand Canyon of the Yellowstone. . . . 401
Mammoth Hot Springs Area 397
Southern Yellowstone Trails 408
Upper Geyser Basin. 387
Yellowstone National Park 370
Yellowstone National Park Mileage . . . 371

BIGHORN BASIN

Bighorn Basin Area 433
Bighorn Canyon National Recreation Area 467
Cody 442
Powell. 461
Northern Shoshone National Forest . . . 434
Thermopolis 481
Worland 476

POWDER RIVER COUNTRY

Buffalo 516
Cloud Peak Wilderness Area 496
Fort Phil Kearny Area 512
Gillette 527
Medicine Wheel Area 493
Powder River Country 489
Sheridan. 498
Sheridan, Downtown 499

THE BLACK HILLS

Black Hills, The 535
Devils Tower 547
Newcastle 537

HANDBOOK SECTION DIVISIONS

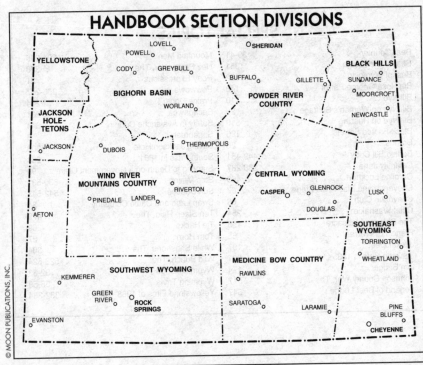

MAP SYMBOLS

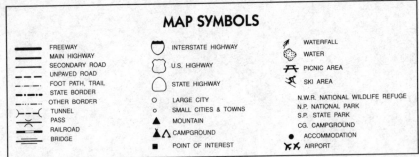

FREEWAY
MAIN HIGHWAY
SECONDARY ROAD
UNPAVED ROAD
FOOT PATH, TRAIL
STATE BORDER
OTHER BORDER
TUNNEL
PASS
RAILROAD
BRIDGE

INTERSTATE HIGHWAY
U.S. HIGHWAY
STATE HIGHWAY
LARGE CITY
SMALL CITIES & TOWNS
MOUNTAIN
CAMPGROUND
POINT OF INTEREST

WATERFALL
WATER
PICNIC AREA
SKI AREA
N.W.R. NATIONAL WILDLIFE REFUGE
N.P. NATIONAL PARK
S.P. STATE PARK
CG. CAMPGROUND
ACCOMMODATION
AIRPORT

SPECIAL TOPICS

Bear Country 39-41
Beaver Dick Leigh. 351
Best of Wyoming. 52
Big Nose George Parrot 148
Bill Nye 110
Bill Nye on Women's Suffrage 25
Bill Nye on Rustling 518
Black-Footed Ferrets 126
Brands 28
Buffalo Bill Cody 449-451
Calamity Jane 286-287
Caroline Lockhart 469
Cheyenne and Black Hills Stage 67
Cheyenne Club 66
Chief Washakie. 254
The Chinese Massacre 158
Francis E. Warren 65
Jackalopes. 197
Jackson Hole in 1835 301
Jim Bridger. 174
Johnson County War, The 517
Legend of Bear Lodge 547

Mountain Men 294-295
Nez Percé War, The. 378
Pony Expressions 21
Powwows 256-257
Prairie Dogs 204
Sacagawea 261
Safety in Avalanche Country 344
Sagebrush 8
Saving Jackson Hole 308
South Pass in 1861 284
Starving to Death on a Government Claim . . 99
Strip Mining 530-531
Sun Dances 542-543
Swan Land and Cattle Company 84
Ten Sleep Raid, The. 479
Tie Hacks 269
Tom Horn 27
White Shoshone, The 304
Wild Bunch, The 523-524
Wyoming Lingo 32-33
Wyoming Trivia 58-59
Yellowstone Fires of 1988, The 382-384

CHARTS

SOUTHEAST WYOMING
Cheyenne Accommodations 72-73
Cheyenne Area RV Parks. 74
Cheyenne Bed and Breakfasts. 71
Lusk Accommodations. 102
Torrington Accommodations 100
Wheatland Accommodations 86

MEDICINE BOW COUNTRY
Encampment and Riverside
Accommodations. 139
Laramie Accommodations 117
Rawlins Accommodations. 149
Saratoga Accommodations. 136

SOUTHWEST WYOMING
Alpine Accommodations 192
Green River Accommodations 162
Evanston Accommodations 176
Kemmerer and Diamondville
Accommodations 181
Rock Springs Accommodations . . . 159
Star Valley Accommodations 188

CENTRAL WYOMING
Casper Accommodations 216-217
Douglas Accommodations 199

WIND RIVER MOUNTAINS COUNTRY
Dubois Area Accommodations 267
Lander Accommodations. 247
Pinedale Accommodations 293
Riverton Accommodations 240

JACKSON HOLE AND THE TETONS
Grand Teton National Park Area
Accommodations 363
Jackson Hole Accommodations. . . 312-314
Jackson Hole Bed and Breakfasts. . . 316
Jackson Hole Public Campgrounds . 319-320
Jackson Hole Guest Ranches 318
Jackson Hole RV Parks 321

YELLOWSTONE NATIONAL PARK
Cooke City and Silver Gate
Accommodations. 429
Gardiner Accommodations 426
Yellowstone Campgrounds. 415
Yellowstone Accommodations 416

BIGHORN BASIN
Cody Accommodations 447-448
Greybull Motels. 472
Powell Accommodations. 462
Thermopolis Accommodations 484
Wapiti Valley Lodges and
Guest Ranches. 435-436
Worland Accommodations 477

POWDER RIVER COUNTRY
Buffalo Accommodations. 519
Gillette Accommodations. 528
Sheridan Accommodations. 502

THE BLACK HILLS
Newcastle Accommodations 538

ACKNOWLEDGMENTS

Travel writing has an image that goes well beyond reality, as I discovered during the updating of this book. When I mentioned what I was doing, it inevitably elicited one of two responses: "What a great job!" or "What ever possessed you to do something like this?" On more than one occasion while working on this new edition, I asked myself the latter of these questions. Fortunately, the benefits of rediscovering Wyoming's obvious and not-so-obvious charms always makes it worthwhile.

Many people helped me in producing this edition. I especially appreciate those who offered insights gleaned from a life's experience in their hometowns: the chamber of commerce volunteers and employees who endured a barrage of questions, the B&B owners who filled me with details of political intrigue and little-known local attractions, the government officials who offered tips on the most scenic backcountry trails, and the countless others whose advice ended up in this guidebook.

Very special thanks are due the following people for their generosity during the researching of this edition: Denny and Chris Becker, Irene Bridges, Taydie and Kent Drummond, Jesse O'Connor, and Ron and Bobbie Spahn. In addition, the following folks contributed in one way or another: Gary C. Anderson, Patricia A. Andrews, Dave Baker, Johan Bakker, Gina Baldwin, Karrie Ballard, Richard K. Bellingham, Thomas Bills, Gay Collar, Gina M. Costante, Craig Cope, Linda Couture, Aline Crausaz, Scotti Cunningham, T.H. Davies, Linda De Tavernier, Desirée Drane-Martin, Sharon Earhart, Alice Eddy-Sears, Wyn Edwards, Mel Furman, Scott Goetz, Nadine Gross, Glenn Hare, Cody Hartley, Dave Hauks, Daniel Hintzche, Alan Hirst, Diana Hood, Laurie Ideker, Daisy Kosine, Laurie Latta, Leah Leneman, Mark P. Madia, Helen Marbell, Edwin H. Maynard, Carol Mitchell, Karen R. Mobley, Connie Mock, Mesia Nyman, Denise Odde, Jane Pennell, Carole Perkins, Becky Schaffer, Mary Short, Skip Shoutis, Dr. Diana Skroch, C. Smith, Susan and Phil Smith, James Staebler, Cindy Stein, Dr. Joe Stickler, Cyndi Sullivan, Tom Thorne, Claudia Wade, Judy Walton, Ralph Weitz, Grace E. Willing, Judy Woodworth, Michael G. Yauck, Professor Mantz Yorke, Tom Thorne, and G. Walker. Thanks very much to everyone!

This book is the product of the staff at Moon Publications who saw it from computer bits and bytes to the printed word. Thanks especially to editor Gina Birtcil, designer Dave Hurst, and mapmaker Bob Race for their hard work. And I offer a very special thank you to Karen Shemet for supporting me through the sometimes trying experience of producing this new edition.

TELL US ABOUT YOUR TRIP

This book, like all travel guides, *is* out of date. The nature of the publishing business means that words in print were always written at some earlier time, and much can change in the two years between editions. Wyoming is not a static place; prices rise, businesses fail, restaurants change hands, and new places wait to be discovered. And sometimes I simply miss interesting sights entirely, or don't give them the coverage that they deserve. This third edition of *Wyoming Handbook* contains extensive revisions and additions—a number of which were suggested by readers of the second edition.

If you find any notable omissions, take offense at what is said, discover a new (or old) place worthy of mention, find inaccurate maps, or just want to rant and rave about this book, I'd be happy to hear from you. Although I try to respond to all letters and messages, you may need to wait awhile for a response since I'm often on the road. To reach me via the Internet, put "Wyoming Handbook" in the subject heading and send e-mail messages to me at: travel@moon.com. Send your snail-mail observations to:

Don Pitcher
c/o Moon Publications
P.O. Box 3040
Chico, CA 95927-3040

BOB RACE

INTRODUCTION

It's kind of funny how you get used to the country. When I go to town, the noises keep me awake. The coal trains, the sirens going down the road, even if they are a long ways away. People get used to that. We've had people come out here who couldn't sleep because it was so quiet. No noise to lull them to sleep or whatever. My nearest neighbor is five miles away. It takes all kinds of people to make the world go around. If everybody in the world wanted to be a rancher, I probably wouldn't, because there wouldn't be anyplace to live.

—*Ed Swartz, quoted in Steve Gardiner's* Rumblings From Razor City

The expansively rugged land called Wyoming resonates with the spirit of the American West. For anyone who has spent time in Wyoming, the state evokes vivid images: cattle standing in the lee of snow fences, children riding horses along dusty dirt roads, weather-beaten ranches lit by the slanting light of late afternoon, oil-cov-

ered roustabouts struggling with the furious machinery of a drilling rig, the sounds of drumming and singing at a powwow, and cow towns where the area code is larger than the population. Here is the original "Wild West," the real-life inspiration for countless Western novels, movies, and songs.

A frontier spirit pervades both Wyoming's landscape and its people, mixing the past and present so completely that it sometimes seems as though around the next bend you might see Chief Washakie's braves circling a massive herd of bison, or Butch Cassidy and the Sundance Kid shooting it out with lawmen, or a party of fur trappers setting out for the mountains. Officially known as "The Equality State" because it was the first to allow women to vote, Wyoming actually revels in another title, "The Cowboy State." License plates carry the state emblem: a cowboy, hat in hand, atop a furiously bucking bronco. A cowboy hat and boots are acceptable dress anywhere, and the unpolished individuality embodied in the cowboy remains the state's heritage, even for those whose only connection is country and western music.

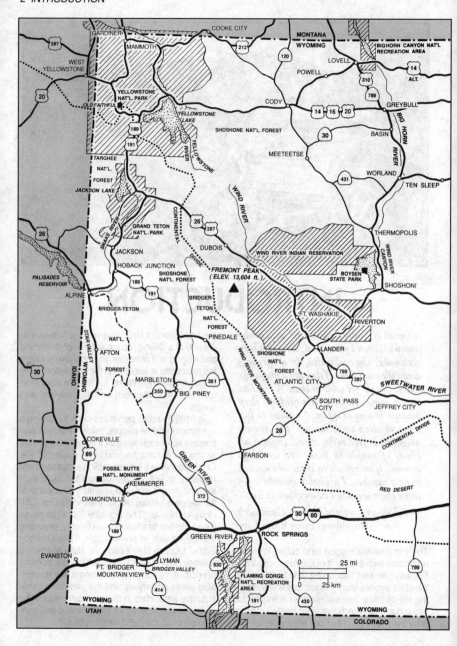

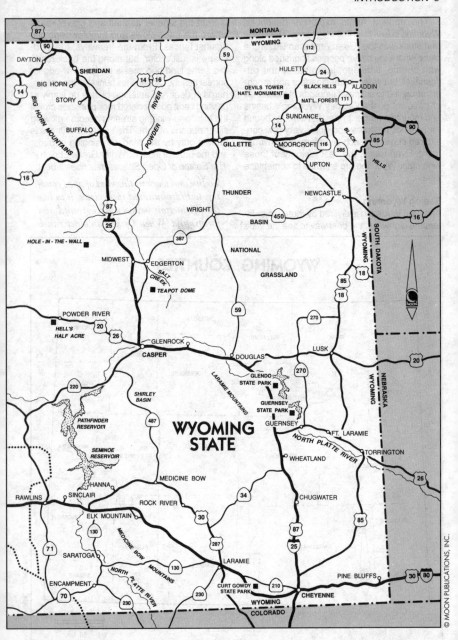

© MOON PUBLICATIONS, INC.

The earliest Anglo explorers described Wyoming in less than flattering terms. The image that stuck was the "Great American Desert," a place where the native peoples flourished along with buffalo, antelope, jackrabbits, and rattlesnakes but where homesteaders and ranchers struggled to survive. Hundreds of thousands of travelers pushed across Wyoming's basins and mountain ranges in the 19th century, bound for greener pastures and gold. Very few considered staying in such an unforgiving environment. Even today, the vast majority of those who enter Wyoming are en route to someplace else.

Seeing Wyoming

Although Wyoming is divided by three major interstate highways, the best way to see the state is from the smaller asphalt and gravel roads where the pace slows and tumbleweeds pile against fences. From the freeways, the landscape is just a blur, but along the back roads this same land becomes a thing of raw-edged, surreal beauty. Old ranches hunker in the valleys, herds of deer and antelope glance up warily at passing cars, oddly colored rock pinnacles crown the hills, and winding streams become glowing silver ribbons of light. The sense of stillness is broken only by the wind, the singing of birds, and the buzz of insects. Writer Gretel Ehrlich in *The Solace of Open Spaces* describes it best:

To live and work in this kind of open country, with its hundred-mile views, is to lose the distinction between background and foreground. When I asked an older ranch

WYOMING COUNTIES

SHERIDAN
CROOK
PARK
BIG HORN
CAMPBELL
JOHNSON
WESTON
TETON
WASHAKIE
HOT SPRINGS
NATRONA
NIOBRARA
FREEMONT
CONVERSE
SUBLETTE
LINCOLN
GOSHEN
PLATTE
SWEETWATER
ALBANY
UINTA
CARBON
LARAMIE

0   50 mi
0   50 km

© MOON PUBLICATIONS, INC.

hand to describe Wyoming's openness, he said, "It's all a bunch of nothing—wind and rattlesnakes—and so much of it you can't tell where you're going or where you've been and it don't make much difference.

On the back roads you'll find folks lifting a hand to wave as you pass. Small-town cafes serve downhome food, friendly motel owners greet tired travelers, and the pace of living slows measurably. You can almost feel the stress of city life dissipating. People leave their homes, cars, and bikes unlocked; they load up clothes in the laundromat and come back later to move them to the dryer. They pull in at the drive-up liquor store for a six-pack and a to-go cup. Unlike big cities, where waiting in lines becomes a way of life, the bank, grocery store, and post office queues are short or nonexistent. Try on a cowboy hat and boots, take a look around the local museum, or stop in for a beer at a country bar and joke with the locals. In a short while you'll gain an appreciation for Wyoming and the down-to-earth people who live here.

The Sky

In the vast open spaces of Wyoming, the sky takes on its own importance, sometimes making the land seem like an afterthought. The land changes slowly with the seasons—first a carpet of winter white, then the mud and first luminescent green buds of spring growth, followed by the verdant summer flowers, and finally the brilliance of fall cottonwood trees along a dry creekbed. But the sky follows the beat of another drummer, changing moment by moment throughout each day. Cottonball clouds float overhead, sending moving shadows across the landscape and coloring the sun's light. Storm clouds build on a summer afternoon, and in the distance a lightning bolt leaps to earth. Perhaps the most memorable times are the lingering sunsets, when colors seem to bounce back and forth across the sky, finally exiting as a fringe of color on the western horizon. At night, coyotes howl the same way they have for millennia, and an enormous panorama of stars arches above, undimmed by discordant city lights.

THE LAND

Covering nearly 98,000 square miles, Wyoming is America's ninth-largest state. The states of Connecticut, Delaware, Hawaii, Maryland, Massachusetts, New Hampshire, New Jersey, Rhode Island, Vermont, and West Virginia would all fit within Wyoming's borders with room to spare. With just 482,680 inhabitants in 1996—the smallest population of any state—Wyoming remains a remarkably undeveloped and unsettled place. Cattle outnumber people by nearly three to one. The population density averages fewer than five people per square mile, and in some counties there is nearly a square mile of land for each person. With an average elevation of 6,700 feet (and a range of 3,125 to 13,804 feet), Wyoming is the third-highest state in the nation. Only Alaska and Colorado are higher.

GEOGRAPHY

On the map, Wyoming is simply a gigantic trapezoidal chunk of earth. Its straight-line border (375 miles from east to west and 276 miles north to south) is an arbitrary human creation that encompasses a surprising diversity of country. The Continental Divide wanders diagonally across the state's mountains from the northwest corner to south-central Wyoming, forming the barrier that separates waters flowing into the Atlantic and Pacific Oceans. More than 71% of Wyoming's lakes, rivers, and streams drain into tributaries of the Missouri River, eventually reaching the Atlantic Ocean; most of the rest flow into tributaries of the Colorado and Columbia Rivers and thence to the Pacific Ocean. Small portions drop into the Great Basin (Salt Lake) or the Great Divide Basin (between Rock Springs and Rawlins), where the water evaporates or percolates into the ground

Wyoming's mountains generally trend northwest to southeast, but this gross overall pattern is broken up by smaller ranges. Northwest Wyoming is dominated by a complex mélange of mountains: the Absaroka, Teton, Gros Ventre, Wyoming, and Wind River Ranges. North-central Wyoming is divided by the Big Horn Mountains, while the Laramie Range and the Medicine

Bow Mountains dominate the south-central region. The far northeast corner holds the Black Hills. In among these ranges, the land spreads out in broad basins, including Bighorn Basin and Powder River Basin in the north, Wind River Basin in the west-central region, and the Green River, Red Desert, and Washakie Basins in the southwest. The eastern portion of Wyoming drops gently into the Great Plains.

CLIMATE

Sometimes I wish that Wyoming had more vegetation and less catarrh, more bloom and summer and fragrance and less Christmas and New Year's through the summer. I like the clear, bracing air of 7,500 feet above the civilized world, but I get weary of putting on and taking off my buffalo overcoat for meals all through dog days. I yearn for a land where a man can take off his ulster and overshoes while he delivers a Fourth of July oration, without flying into the face of Providence and dying of pneumonia . . . As I write these lines I look out across the wide sweep of brownish gray plains dotted here and there with ranches and defunct buffalo craniums, and I see shutting down over the sides of the abrupt mountains, and meeting the foothills, a white mist which melts into the gray sky. It is a snow storm in the mountains.

I saw this with wonder and admiration for the first two or three million times. When it became a matter of daily occurrence as a wonder or curiosity, it was below mediocrity. Last July a snow storm gathered one afternoon and fell among the foothills and whitened the whole line to within four or five miles of town, and it certainly was a peculiar freak of nature, but it convinced me that whatever enterprises I might launch into here I would not try to raise oranges and figs until the isothermal lines should meet with a change of heart.

—*Nineteenth-century humorist Bill Nye*

Wyoming's climate mirrors its diverse geography, ranging from arid deserts to cool mountain forests. The mountain ranges act as barriers to eastward-moving weather systems. Moist air is forced upward by the mountains, releasing rain or snow along the western slopes. By the time the clouds reach the east side, much of the water has been wrung out, creating a "rain shadow." Because of this, midwinter finds Togwotee Pass smothered under many feet of snow while Dubois, in the lee of the Absaroka Range, may have only a dusting on the ground.

Visitors to Wyoming discover weather typical of the West's high plains and mountains: hot, dry summers punctuated by fierce thunderstorms, and cold winters with a fair amount of snow. Conditions vary greatly throughout the state, however, with cooler summers and heavy winter snows in the mountains.

Extremes

Wyoming has a reputation for extreme conditions. Wintertime blizzards periodically lash the land, and strong winds pile the snow into huge drifts. Summertime thunderstorms—particularly in the mountains—can be an almost daily occurrence. Southeast Wyoming has an average of nine hailstorms a year—it's the hail capital of North America. Temperatures have been recorded from -66° F (Yellowstone National Park) to 114° F (the town of Basin). Precipitation shows a similar variation—high mountain ranges of northwest Wyoming see as much as 60 inches (mostly snow) a year, while parched desert areas in Bighorn Basin and Great Divide Basin receive only six.

Wyoming is well known for its wind. Through much of the state, the wind never seems to stop blowing, averaging more than 16 miles an hour along the eastern border. Buffalo Bill Cody, a man who symbolizes the West in the American conscience, once defended Wyoming when a friend complained of the wind: "You know where those winds come from? Well, this country up here is so close to paradise you can feel the breezes from heaven. That wind comes from the angels' wings. When they flap their wings the wind comes right down this valley."

Basin Weather

In the expansive basins that cover much of Wyoming, typical midsummer daytime temper-

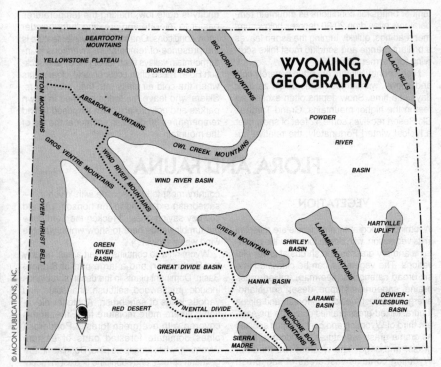

WYOMING GEOGRAPHY

BEARTOOTH MOUNTAINS
YELLOWSTONE PLATEAU
BIGHORN BASIN
BIG HORN MOUNTAINS
BLACK HILLS
TETON MOUNTAINS
ABSAROKA MOUNTAINS
POWDER RIVER
GROS VENTRE MOUNTAINS
WIND RIVER MOUNTAINS
OWL CREEK MOUNTAINS
BASIN
WIND RIVER BASIN
OVER THRUST BELT
GREEN MOUNTAINS
HARTVILLE UPLIFT
LARAMIE MOUNTAINS
GREEN RIVER BASIN
SHIRLEY BASIN
GREAT DIVIDE BASIN
CONTINENTAL DIVIDE
HANNA BASIN
RED DESERT
LARAMIE BASIN
DENVER-JULESBURG BASIN
WASHAKIE BASIN
MEDICINE BOW MOUNTAINS
SIERRA MADRE

© MOON PUBLICATIONS, INC.

atures are in the 80s and 90s, with nights dropping into the 50s and 60s. Low relative humidity makes the heat easier to take. The wettest months are April and May, with lots of sun in the summer. Afternoon thunderheads often build up, temporarily blocking the sun, but generally dropping more lightning than rain. Fall can be a most pleasant time of year, with shirt-sleeve days and cool evenings.

When winter arrives in November and December, it can do so with a vengeance, pushing the mercury well below zero. Snowfall is not great, totaling 15 to 60 inches over the winter months, but when combined with winds pushing 50 mph, it can look like a lot more. In places, snow fences extend for many miles beside the highways, attempting to blunt the blowing snow. Ground blizzards sometimes halt traffic along I-80 for days at a time. Locals joke that it only snows a couple of inches in December and then the snow blows back and forth across the state the rest of the winter until it is finally worn

out. Actually, winters are not all so bleak, and temperatures occasionally rise into the 50s. You can expect sun 60% of the time. Chinooks—warm downslope winds—are common in the winters along the eastern slopes of the mountains, particularly around Sheridan, Dubois, and Cody.

Mountain Weather

Many of the favorite sites in Wyoming—including Yellowstone and Grand Teton National Parks—lie primarily above 7,000 feet. Here, the weather is considerably cooler than in the basins. Summertime temperatures rarely top 80° F, while nights often dip into the 40s. Snow is possible at any time of the year. April and May are generally the wettest months. Spring comes late in the mountains, and high passes are often blocked by drifts until mid-July. Summer thunderstorms are common, especially in the northwest mountains, where they gather over the high peaks most afternoons. Mid-Sep-

tember brings fall conditions as mountain temperatures often drop 20-30 degrees below summer readings, quickly turning the aspen leaves a brilliant orange and sending most folks scurrying for warmer climes.

High-country winters are often severely cold and snowy, with temperatures below zero for days at a time. Snow depths often exceed six feet in the higher mountains. Grand Targhee Ski Resort receives some 42 feet of snow over a typical winter! Fortunately, the relative humidity is quite low, making the temperatures easier to tolerate and creating fluffy powder snow conditions. One surprising winter feature is the presence of temperature inversions in intermountain valleys such as Big Piney and Jackson Hole. These often occur on cold, clear nights when the cold air sinks into the valley floors. Skiers who leave the lodge bundled in down parkas and polypro are often surprised to find temperatures 30 degrees warmer at the top of the mountain.

FLORA AND FAUNA

VEGETATION

Wyoming's topography and climate are reflected in its vegetation, with dense forests in the mountains and dry grasses and shrubs at lower elevations. The vegetation can be classified into six broad categories (see map): mixed-grass prairie, sagebrush steppe, desert shrubland, evergreen forest, deciduous forest, and alpine tundra. Mixed-grass prairies dominate the eastern third of Wyoming and contain such species as grama grass, wheatgrass, junegrass, bluegrass, and sage. The western two-thirds of Wyoming contains vast areas of sagebrush steppe, a threadbare carpet of big sagebrush, wheatgrass, needle-and-thread grass, grama grass, tumbleweed, and other plants. This is the country most folks associate with Wyoming—sagebrush extending to the horizon. (An old cowboy saying goes, "I reckon the Lord done put tumbleweeds here to show which way the wind was a-blowin'.")

Wyoming also contains desert areas, notably the Red Desert and a large part of Bighorn Basin. Dominant plants in the desert shrublands include greasewood, saltbush, shadscale, and various kinds of sagebrush. At higher elevations, where more moisture falls, the land is covered with evergreen forests. Ponderosa pines dominate forested parts of eastern Wyoming, while lodgepole pine, Douglas fir, Engelmann spruce, and subalpine fir exist in mountains to the west. A few areas also have pinyon pine and juniper trees. Deciduous forests are scattered in small patches around Wyoming

SAGEBRUSH

Sagebrush is Wyoming's ubiquitous common denominator, a sweetly pungent bush found from the lowest deserts to 10,000-foot mountains. More sage grows here than anyplace else in North America. The volatile oils make it a last choice for cattle and act as a natural herbicide, preventing competition from other plants. Ranchers consider the plant less than worthless, but native animals such as sage grouse, antelope, and mule deer depend upon sage for survival. You won't even find sage grouse where sage doesn't grow.

The terms sagebrush and sage are generally used interchangeably in the West. Note, however, that the spice on your kitchen shelf is not the same as the Wyoming plant (Artemesia), and any attempt to cook with sagebrush is likely to leave you gagging. Sage has been in the West for some 25 million years and is well adapted to the poor soils and arid conditions of the desert. Sage survives by using its network of shallow roots to draw moisture from the ground as it percolates down. Wyoming actually has at least seven different species of sage. Some of these exist only on very specific sites: black sagebrush grows on windy ridges between 5,000 and 8,000 feet, where the soil is shallow and stony; alkali sagebrush grows in impermeable soils that are highly alkaline. The predominant species across much of Wyoming is big sagebrush, a bush that grows to three feet in height and often covers extensive areas.

consisting of cottonwoods along riverbottoms, aspens in the middle elevations, and bur oak in the Black Hills. Treeline in much of Wyoming is around 9,500 feet. Above this, one finds alpine tundra, where the dominant plants are low-growing herbs, grasses, and forbs.

WILDLIFE

When the first mountain men and explorers wandered into the vast land that became Wyoming, they found an incredible abundance of wildlife: herds of bison stretching to the horizon, antelope, elk, and deer grazing on the broad plains, and grizzly bears, wolves, coyotes, cottontails, and jackrabbits. Although wolves were poisoned to extinction, and only a few hundred bison and grizzlies remain, other animals fared better. Today, the two most common large mammals are mule deer and pronghorn antelope, both of which are found across much of the state. The sagebrush lands also provide cover for sage grouse, a large chicken-like bird (the males perform an elaborate X-rated mating display). In the mountains, one often hears the early-summer drumming of ruffed grouse. Rarest of Wyoming's animals is the endangered black-footed ferret (see the special topic "Black-footed Ferrets" in the Medicine Bow Country chapter for more on these).

Watchable Wildlife
Wyoming's undeveloped character makes it a Mecca for those who enjoy watching wild animals. Yellowstone National Park is a favorite place to look for bison, elk, coyotes, moose, mule deer, bighorn sheep, river otters, and trumpeter swans. Both black and grizzly bears also live here, though they're less commonly seen. Another popular place is the National Elk Refuge in Jackson Hole, the winter home for a herd of more than 10,000 elk. Excellent places to see bighorn sheep are the Whiskey Basin Habitat Area, near Dubois, and the Bighorn National Recreation Area. Wyoming has around 3,500 wild horses; watch for them at Bighorn National Recreation Area or in the Red Desert. Mountain goats live in the Beartooth Mountains along Wyoming's border with Montana. The high mountains of the Tetons and the Wind River Range have such animals as pikas and yellow-bellied marmots, while the sagebrush country abounds with deer, antelope, coyotes, jackrabbits, cottontails, and prairie dogs. Certainly the most distinctive Wyoming critter is the jackalope (see the special topic in the Central Wyoming chapter).

The Wyoming Game and Fish Department publishes *Wyoming Wildlife,* an attractive monthly publication available for just $10 a year. To subscribe, call (800) 548-9453. This same number gets you a catalog of other wildlife-related products and publications, including videos, T-shirts, caps, mugs, books, posters, and cards.

Rattlesnakes
Everyone's least favorite reptile is the prairie rattlesnake, a heavy-bodied venomous creature with a telltale rattle. Prairie rattlesnakes often reach nearly a yard in length (the longest was 57 inches!) and are found in the plains and foothills of eastern and central Wyoming, generally below 7,000 feet. They're especially common around rockpiles and in prairie dog towns. You *won't* find them in mountain country over 7,200 feet, in the Laramie area, in Yellowstone and Grand Teton National Parks, or in the southwestern desert country (with the exception of the lower Green River Valley area). Prairie rattlers feed primarily on ground squirrels, rabbits, chipmunks, prairie dogs, and other small rodents, but can also kill birds and lizards. They reproduce every other year, and large groups of rattlesnakes gather in dens to spend the winter months in a dormant state.

Prairie rattlesnakes usually offer a warning of their presence—hence the name—but not all the time. At times aggressive, their size and appearance will certainly send your blood pressure up, but the venom is actually less toxic than that of other rattlers and is usually only one-eighth the amount needed to kill a human. Because of this, snakebite fatalities are rare in Wyoming.

A smaller snake, the midget faded rattlesnake, dwells only in the lower Green River Valley country around the cities of Green River and Rock Springs, and in Flaming Gorge National Recreation Area. These snakes frequent rocky outcrops and, though smaller, they're more poisonous than the prairie rattlesnake. The status of midget faded rattlers is currently in question; some believe they've been entirely exterminated from Wyoming.

WYOMING VEGETATION

YELLOWSTONE

CODY

WORLAND

SHERIDAN

GILLETTE

JACKSON   DUBOIS

PINEDALE

RIVERTON

CASPER

ROCK SPRINGS   RAWLINS

WHEATLAND

EVANSTON

LARAMIE

CHEYENNE

EVERGREEN FORESTS

DECIDUOUS FORESTS

SAGEBRUSH STEPPE

MIXED GRASS PRAIRIE

ALPINE TUNDRA

DESERT SHRUBLAND

0   100 mi

0   100 km

© MOON PUBLICATIONS, INC.

The best defense against rattlers is to always use care when walking in their country and to keep your distance if you spot one. Be especially careful when clambering over rockpiles or walking through dense grasses and sage. Shake out sleeping bags, boots, and bedding, and wear tall leather boots rather than sneakers.

If someone is bitten by a rattlesnake, immobilize the area of the bite and immediately get him or her to a hospital or medical facility. If the bite is on an arm or leg, keep it below the level of the heart. Time is of the essence. Other treatments are possible for emergency situations when there is no chance of getting to a doctor in time, but the

potential for harm is great if you don't know what you are doing. Take a good first-aid class to learn how to handle these situations, or talk with your doctor about where to get and how to use suction pumps. Your best bet is always preventing a bite in the first place. For more on rattlers and other crawly things, see *Amphibians and Reptiles of Wyoming*, by George T. Baxter and Michael D. Stone (Cheyenne: Wyoming Game and Fish Department).

Pronghorn Antelope

One of the most commonly seen Wyoming animals is the antelope (biologists prefer the name

"pronghorn"). More than 400,000 live here, constituting half the world's pronghorn population. Antelope survive on plants that other animals avoid, notably sagebrush—perhaps Wyoming's most abundant plant. They are built for speed: oversized lungs and windpipes give them the ability to run for miles at 30 mph and to accelerate to twice that for short bursts. To watch for predators, they have the largest eyes by body weight of any mammal. Despite this speed, pronghorn have an innate inquisitiveness that makes them relatively easy to hunt, an attribute that nearly drove them to extinction by market hunting early in this century. Strict laws and careful management have brought antelope populations back.

Deer

Wyoming has almost as many deer as people. You can see two species along the state's roads: white-tailed deer—common in the Black Hills—and the larger mule deer, found across the state. Be especially careful when driving after dusk during the fall breeding season, since the hormone-crazed bucks tend to leap out in front of cars. Nearly everyone who has lived in Wyoming has hit a deer under these circumstances. Slow down at night, especially in areas posted with Deer Crossing signs.

Elk

A majestic member of the deer family, elk (many biologists prefer the term "wapiti") are a favorite with both tourists and hunters. Elk inhabit much of Wyoming, with the largest herds along the western mountains. More than 30,000 elk graze in Yellowstone National Park alone. With bulls weighing up to 900 pounds and cows up to 600 pounds, they are some of the largest antlered animals in the Americas.

Elk spend summers high in the mountains, feeding in alpine meadows and along forest edges. Mature bulls graze alone, but the cows and calves—generally born in late May and early June—group in large herds for protection. When the fall rutting season arrives, bulls attempt to herd the cows and calves around, mating with cows when they come into estrus and defending their harems from other bulls. During this time of year the bugling of bull elk is a common sound in the mountains, a challenge to

any bull within earshot. When a competitor appears, a dominance display often follows—complete with bugling, stomping, and thrashing of the ground—to show who is the baddest bull around. In a fight, bulls lock their massive antlers and try to push and twist until one finally gives in and retreats. These battles help ensure that the healthiest bulls produce the most offspring. Ironically, other bulls often wait in the wings for battles over harems to occur, then rush in to mate with the cows while the larger bulls are sparring. (When the cat's away . . . .) The snows of late fall push elk to lower-elevation winter ranges, notably at the National Elk Refuge in Jackson Hole, where they are fed. When spring comes, the bulls drop their antlers and immediately begin to grow new ones. The elk head back into the high country, following the melting snowline.

Elk and bison both are frequently infected with brucellosis, a bacterium causing spontaneous abortions. Brucellosis is transmitted to other animals by contact with the dead fetus, and can cause undulant fever in humans. Though the evidence is circumstantial at best for this, ranchers worry that brucellosis can spread from elk and bison to cattle, particularly around elk feeding grounds in western Wyoming. To lessen the incidence of brucellosis, state employees now routinely vaccinate elk at the feeding grounds, shooting them in the hindquarters with vaccine-loaded pellets.

BISON

The bison is the definitive frontier animal and Wyoming's state mammal—its outline graces the state flag. Weighing up to 3,000 pounds, these are the largest land mammals in the New World. Bison live 45 years or more, with females bearing calves until they are in their 40s. The calves weigh 30 to 40 pounds at birth and within minutes are standing and able to graze. Two races of bison exist: the plains bison, primarily east of the Rockies, and the mountain bison (sometimes called wood bison) in the higher elevations. Technically, these huge, hairy beasts are bison—the only true buffalo are the water buffalo of Southeast Asia—but the name buffalo is commonly used.

With their massive heads, huge shoulder humps, heavy coats of fur, and small posteriors, buffalo are some of the strangest animals in North America. They look so front-heavy as to seem unstable, ready to topple forward onto their snouts at any time. Despite this impression, buffalo are remarkably well adapted to life on the plains. A bison will use its strong sense of smell to find grass buried in a deep snowdrift and then sweep the snow away with a sideways motion of its head. The animals are also surprisingly fleetfooted, as careless Yellowstone photographers have discovered. In addition, the buffalo is one very tough critter. In 1907, a buffalo was pitted against four of the meanest Mexican bulls at a Juarez, Mexico, bullring. After knocking heads several times with the buffalo, the bulls fled and were saved only when bullfighters opened the chute gates to let them escape.

"Blackening the Plains"

When Europeans first reached the New World, they found massive herds of bison in the Appalachians and even more as they headed west. Daniel Boone hunted them in North Carolina in the 1750s; Pennsylvanians shot hundreds of buffalo that were invading their winter stores of hay. By 1820, settlers had nearly driven the buffalo to extinction in the east. But there were far more living to the west. As explorers, mountain men, and the first tentative settlers reached the "Great American Desert," they were awestruck by the numbers. Travelers told of slowly moving masses of buffalo blackening the plains and watched in astonishment as the herds stopped at rivers and literally drank them dry. A fair estimate of the original population of buffalo in North America is 75 million. Even in the middle 1860s, travelers through Wyoming's Wind River Valley reported seeing 10,000 bison at one time. A pioneer Kansas settler named William D. Street recalled a trip in which a herd roared past his camp for an entire night. The next morning, he climbed a nearby butte and saw buffalo covering the plains below. According to Street:

The herd was not less than 20 miles in width—we never saw the other side—at least 60 miles in length, maybe much longer; two counties of buffaloes! There might have been 100,000, or 1,000,000, or 100,000,000. I don't know. In the cowboy days in western Kansas we saw 7,000 head of cattle in one roundup. After gazing at them a few moments our thoughts turned to that buffalo herd. For a comparison, imagine a large pail of water; take from it or add to it a drop, and there you have it. Seven thousand head of cattle was not a drop in the bucket as compared with that herd of buffalo.

Indians and Buffalo

The Plains Indians depended heavily upon the buffalo for food and—like the proverbial hot dog, which "contains everything but the moo"—they used every part of the animal. Hooves were carved into spoons, skins became buffalo robes and covers for boats and tepees, rawhide was used for drumheads, calf skins became storage sacks, hair was turned into earrings, and horns were formed into cups and arrow points. Everything that remained—including the muzzle, penis, eyes, and cartilage—was boiled down to use as glue for arrowheads. The ubiquitous buffalo chips became a cooking fuel on the treeless prairies.

Hunting techniques varied depending upon the terrain. When possible, the Indians drove herds of bison into arroyos with no exits, over cliffs, or into deep sand or snow, making them easier to kill. The arrival of Spanish horses in the 16th century made it far easier to hunt bison. In a surround, mounted hunters attacked from at least two sides, creating chaos in the herd and allowing buffalo to be shot with arrows or guns.

BOB RACE

When whites first spread across the plains, they found the bison a plentiful food source, but also viewed the massive herds as a hindrance to agriculture and cattle raising. But these were not the only reasons whites wanted to destroy the buffalo. Killing off the bison would starve the Indians into submission and force them to take a more "civilized" way of life. General Philip Sheridan, commenting in support of white buffalo hunters, said

Instead of stopping the [white] hunters they ought to give them a hearty, unanimous vote of thanks, and appropriate a sufficient sum of money to strike and present to each one a medal of bronze, with a dead buffalo on one side and a discouraged Indian on the other. They are destroying the Indian's commissary, and it is a well-known fact that an army losing its base of supplies is placed at a great disadvantage. Send them powder and lead, if you will; for the sake of a lasting peace, let them kill, skin and sell until the buffaloes are exterminated.

This reckless slaughter did indeed endanger the Indians, but it also had an unwanted side effect: the Indians went on the warpath. The loss of their primary food source helped convince many Indians that their own extinction was next. The warriors who massacred Custer and his men at Little Big Horn had watched their people pushed to the brink of starvation by the destruction of the buffalo.

The Slaughter

Two factors propelled the slaughter to new heights in the 1870s: new railroads across the plains, and a sudden international demand for buffalo robes and hides. Buffalo meat proved to be a readily available food source for railway construction workers, and hunters such as "Buffalo Bill" Cody provided a steady supply, generally taking just the hindquarters and hump and leaving the rest on the plains. Hundreds of thousands were killed. Once the railroads were completed in 1869, a new "sport" appeared—shooting buffalo from the moving railcars and leaving them to rot on the prairie. Wealthy gentry from the East Coast and Europe also dis-

covered the joys of killing. One Irish nobleman had an entourage of 40 servants, with an entire wagon just for firearms; he killed 2,000 buffalo in a three-year carnage.

Conservationists tried to halt the buffalo slaughter through legislation in 1874, but President Grant's corrupt Secretary of the Interior, Columbus Delano, said, "I would not seriously regret the total disappearance of the buffalo from our western prairies, in its effect upon the Indians. I would regard it rather as a means of hastening their sense of dependence upon the products of the soil and their own labors." The legislation was pocket-vetoed by Grant.

In 1872, thousands of hide hunters spread through Kansas, Nebraska, and Colorado in search of buffalo. Over the next three years, they brought in more than three million buffalo hides, with Indians killing another 400,000 bison for meat and robes. Good hide hunters could bring down 25 to 100 buffalo in a typical day, keeping five skinners busy from sunup to sundown. One hunter, Jim White, killed at least 16,000 buffalo in his career. Only the hides, cured hams, and buffalo tongues (which could be salted and shipped in barrels) were saved. When Gen. Grenville M. Dodge toured Kansas in the fall of 1873, he noted that "the air was foul with a sickening stench, and the vast plain, which only a short twelvemonth before teemed with animal life, was a dead, solitary, putrid desert." Buffalo carcasses dotted the plains in such numbers that in later years bone pickers would collect massive piles of bones for knife handles, combs, and buttons or to be ground up for sugar refining, fertilizer, or glue.

When the buffalo of the central states approached extinction, hunters turned their attention elsewhere, reaching Wyoming, Montana, and the Dakotas in 1880. In 1882, more than 200,000 hides were taken, and another 40,000 the following year. By 1884, only 300 hides were shipped. The slaughter was nearly over; only a few private herds and scattered individual bison remained. The Indians who had once depended so heavily on buffalo for all the necessities of life were reduced to eating muskrats, gophers, and even grass. Some killed their horses, others stole settlers' cattle, and the rest had to beg the government for food. In only a couple of years, an entire culture had been devastated.

But the slaughter ruined the lives not just of the buffalo or the Indians; hide hunters often spiked buffalo carcasses with strychnine, returning later to skin the wolves that had come to feed on the meat. Coyotes, kit foxes, badgers, vultures, eagles, ravens, and anything else that ate the meat were also killed. With both the buffalo and the "vermin" out of the way, Wyoming and the West were safe for domestic sheep and cattle.

Protection

The first federal legislation protecting buffalo (only in Yellowstone National Park, however) did not pass until 1894. The following year, only 800 buffalo remained in all of North America, one-thousandth of one percent of their original numbers. Despite this dismal picture, the population has rebounded dramatically; today an estimated 65,000 bison roam across America. In Wyoming, small populations can be seen in Hot Springs State Park and Grand Teton National Park, while one of the few large wild populations remains in Yellowstone National Park.

A strong demand for buffalo meat has led some Wyoming ranchers to raise bison. It's a highly specialized ranching endeavor, since the animals can flatten most fences and standard roundup techniques don't work. Durham Buffalo Ranch near Wright has one of the largest private buffalo herds in the country: 3,500 head. Ranchers have discovered that bison are more efficient grazers than cattle, making it possible to produce more meat per acre, and they are less susceptible to disease. Perhaps someday the vast herds of bison may return to Wyoming's rangelands in the form of bison ranches.

HISTORY

Although Wyoming is a young state—only reaching the century mark in 1990—it seems to have more history per square inch than just about any other place in America. This history is a mixture of Indians and cowboys, settlers and outlaws, schemers and dreamers, railroad magnates and cattle barons, and plain folks clinging to plots of marginal farmland despite unbelievable odds. Wyoming's 19th-century frontier is a recurring theme in America's imagination, as revealed in countless books, songs, and movies. This rich treasure trove from the past is stored not just in the little-changed landscape, where the ruts from wagon trains are still visible and emigrant names remain carved in rocky buttes, but also in the cattle drives and rodeos and the weather-etched faces of sheepherders and cowboys working the range. It is hard to imagine a place with a richer past.

NATIVE AMERICANS

Humans have been in Wyoming for perhaps 25,000 years. The Plains Indians—comprising 27 different tribes—were found from the Mississippi River to the Rockies, and from Texas to central Canada. The lives of these people revolved around the buffalo; they followed the vast herds, migrating where the buffalo led. Because of this nomadic lifestyle, everything they had was pared to the minimum. Pottery, so common in the southwestern deserts, was replaced by woven baskets on the plains. The tepee, an easily portable lodge, offered protection from the elements, and clothing was warm yet not burdensome.

Days of Glory

Although many people view the Plains Indians as existing in a state of balance with their environment, there is ample evidence that things were changing even before whites first pushed their way onto the plains. The arrival of horses and guns in the 17th and 18th centuries created a time of plenty that has rarely been known among nomadic hunting tribes. Horses made it easier to follow and hunt the huge bison herds, and tribes that had been at least partially farmers turned entirely to hunting. Native populations grew rapidly with the abundance of food. The warrior also gained importance with the changing culture as raiding parties stole horses and attacked other tribes. Villages grew larger as families gathered for mutual protection from their enemies.

AMERICAN HERITAGE CENTER, LARAMIE, WY

The Sioux warrior Red Cloud proved a formidable military leader during the Plains Indian wars.

The turmoil that resulted led to a constantly changing situation in Wyoming during the 19th century, as the tribes each strove for control. It was this turbulent society that greeted the first Euro-American explorers. Whites were accustomed to well-defined land ownership, with definite boundaries within which one lived; here the territories were in a state of flux, with tribes claiming overlapping areas.

During the 1700s, Indians from the Great Lakes and Canadian plains had moved into what would become Wyoming. By the 1850s, the Sioux were in Powder River Basin, the Crow in Bighorn Basin, and the Cheyenne and Arapaho south of the North Platte River. The Shoshone and the Bannock—originally from the Great Basin—had moved into the Green River and Wind River valleys, while their relatives, the Utes, held the Sierra Madre and desert land to the west. Communication between these diverse tribes was possible in a sophisticated sign language.

Treaties

During the first half of the 19th century, American explorers, fur trappers, traders, and settlers began to push across Wyoming. As emigration westward increased in the 1840s, so did conflicts with Indians. Whites complained of random attacks and stolen horses. Indians complained of trampled grass, polluted water, and wasteful killing of bison. To deal with these problems, a great council was called at Fort Laramie in 1851, attracting 10,000 Indians from many different tribes. Indian agent Thomas Fitzpatrick was eager to gain permission for settlers to use the Oregon Trail across Indian lands in Wyoming. In exchange for gifts from the federal government in the form of annuities, the tribes agreed to stay within specified boundaries and to punish those who violated the accord or attacked white emigrants.

Father Pierre DeSmet drew up the boundaries, with allowances for hunting outside the "home" regions. The unstated long-term goal of the treaty was to transform the Indians from hunters into farmers. By developing a paternalistic system of dependency on the government, combined with educational programs and settlement, the Indians would—in theory—become like the whites. Violence erupted almost immediately among the tribes and between them and the Anglo emigrants. Soon, whites would be more concerned over how to dispossess the Indians of their land than how to get through it safely.

In 1861, the Fort Wise Treaty abrogated much of the Treaty of 1851, forcing the Arapaho and Cheyenne onto a desolate reservation at Sand Creek, Colorado, to get them away from the suddenly valuable land to the north. The treaty was signed by some leaders, but only after the starving individuals saw that they would not receive their annuities without affixing their Xs.

The Battle Begins

Colorado's Sand Creek Massacre of 1865 proved a turning point in the history of Indian-white relations. A small band of Arapaho attacked a family farm, brutally murdering the family. When the mutilated bodies were put on display in Denver, public outrage pushed Col. John M. Chivington—formerly a Methodist minister—to lead one of the most vicious and unwarranted attacks ever perpetrated by the Army. Two hundred Cheyenne and Arapaho died in the day-

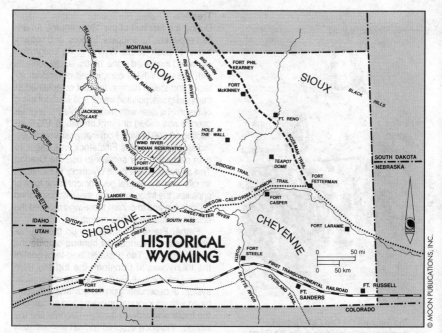

© MOON PUBLICATIONS, INC.

break attack on Chief Black Kettle's peaceful village.

The Indians—not just the Cheyenne and Arapaho, but also the Sioux—quickly retaliated by striking throughout Colorado and Wyoming, killing some 75 settlers around the Rock Creek Station (northwest of present-day Laramie) and destroying stage stations all along the Oregon Trail. Over the next several years, hundreds died on both sides. The main focus of Indian attacks was the Bozeman Trail through the lush Powder River country of the Sioux. The Army responded with an alternating series of military campaigns and peace overtures as the national mood flip-flopped between war and accommodation.

A major cause of these conflicts was the hysteria that gold created. Each new gold rush—California in 1849, Colorado in 1859, Montana in 1864, and finally the Black Hills in 1874—led to new incursions onto Indian lands. When whites found Indians standing in the way of development, they attempted to renegotiate the treaties or, failing that, to find some excuse to set them aside. Once gold had been found, the end

of Indian culture was almost a given. Senator John Sherman noted: "If the whole Army of the United States stood in the way, the wave of emigration would pass over it to seek the valley where gold was to be found."

Other factors also played critical roles in the destruction of the Indian way of life on the plains. Perhaps the most crucial was the loss of their primary food source, the buffalo. But many tribes were devastated as well by diseases brought by contact with Europeans, especially smallpox, cholera, whooping cough, and venereal diseases.

Cultural Mistrust

Many whites viewed the Indians with deep distrust. Writer James Chisholm reflected a typical frontier attitude, calling them "useless, strutting, ridiculous, pompous humbugs—lying, faithless, stealing, begging, cruel, hungry, howling vagabonds—cowardly, treacherous red devils." In 1869, Gen. Philip Sheridan took matters even further by claiming, "The only good Indian is a dead Indian."

The Indians themselves were not entirely innocent. Attacks on wagon trains were frequent, and many of the trappers, stagecoach drivers, and ranchers who settled in Wyoming were murdered and their bodies mutilated by the Sioux, Cheyenne, or Arapaho. Scalping—a practice introduced by white traders—became commonplace. Whites complained that the federal government was arming and feeding the Indians at the same time it was leading military campaigns against them.

Evicting the Indians

More than a thousand engagements were fought between Indians and whites in the late 19th century, killing at least 2,500 whites and twice as many Indians. On the plains, most of the battles involved the Sioux, Cheyenne, Arapaho, Kiowa, and Comanche tribes. The Shoshone under Chief Washakie always remained peaceful. The final drama came in the 1870s, beginning with the discovery of gold in the Black Hills of Dakota Territory. A flood of miners overwhelmed attempts by the government to keep them out of Sioux territory, and negotiations to purchase the land bogged down when Red Cloud demanded a $600 million payment.

In 1876, General Sheridan led a three-pronged invasion to forcibly evict the Sioux from the Powder River region. He hadn't counted on two problems: the large numbers of Indians ready to do battle, and the rashness of junior officer Col. George A. Custer. At Little Big Horn on June 25, 1876, all 225 of Custer's men were wiped out by a combined force of Indians led by Crazy Horse, Sitting Bull, and others. This massive Indian victory quickly became the rallying cry for whites anxious to "solve" the Indian problem by forcing them onto reservations. Within five years, the last of the tribes had given up the fight. The uprising that led to the infamous Wounded Knee Massacre of 1890 was a last dying gasp in the attempt to regain land that had once all belonged to Native Americans.

Those who had lived in this land for centuries had been evicted by new peoples from another world. Chief Washakie of the Shoshones described the painfulness of this change (quoted in *Chief Washakie*, by Mae Urbanek):

The white man, who possesses this whole vast country from sea to sea, who roams over it at pleasure, and lives where he likes, cannot know the cramp we feel in this little spot, with the undying remembrance of the fact, which you know as well as we, that every foot of what you proudly call America, not very long ago belonged to the red man. The Great Spirit gave it to us. There was room enough for all his many tribes, and all were happy in their freedom. But the white man had, in ways we know not of, superior tools and terrible weapons, better for war than bows and arrows; and there seemed no end to the hordes of men that followed them from other lands beyond the sea. And so, at last, our fathers were steadily driven out, or killed, and we, their sons, but sorry remnants of tribes once mighty, are cornered in little spots of the earth all ours of right—cornered like guilty prisoners, and watched by men with guns, who are more than anxious to kill us off.

TRAPPERS AND EXPLORERS

The first Europeans to explore Wyoming were in a party of Frenchmen led by François and Louis-Joseph Verendrye, who crossed northern Wyoming in 1743. During the winter of 1807-08, John Colter—a trapper and former guide for the Lewis and Clark Expedition—explored northwestern Wyoming in an attempt to develop the fur trade with Crow Indians. Colter was soon followed by other trappers in search of beavers. It was a hazardous business, with the constant threat of Indian attacks and the many natural hazards such as angry grizzlies, disease, and injuries. Help was hundreds of miles away. The era of the mountain-man lasted only until 1840, when demand for the furs plummeted, but the trappers' knowledge of the terrain proved invaluable. Many became guides for civilian and military expeditions, wealthy hunters, and government explorations of the West. The mountain passes they found (or, more likely, had been shown by Indians) provided a route for the exodus westward in the 1850s.

THE OREGON TRAIL

When God made man,
He seemed to think it best
To make him in the East
And let him travel West.

—from an Oregon Trail pioneer's diary

To 19th-century emigrants the Oregon Trail represented perhaps the best example of "Manifest Destiny"—the idea of an American nation reaching from the Atlantic to the Pacific. The Oregon Trail is actually a general term used to describe a whole series of wagon roads that headed west from Missouri. At different times, and over various paths, this route encompassed the Oregon Trail (to both Oregon and Washington), the California Trail (to the gold fields), the Mormon Trail (to Salt Lake City), and the short-lived Pony Express route. To emigrants it was not a trail but always "The Road."

Wyoming contains the least-changed and longest stretch (487 miles) of the Oregon Trail. From eastern Wyoming, the trail—actually a series of braided paths spreading across the river valleys—followed the North Platte and Sweetwater Rivers upstream to the Continental Divide at South Pass. Travelers chose this route because of abundant forage for stock, good water, and a gentle grade over the divide. As the only route that met all three criteria, the Oregon Trail became a national thoroughfare to the Promised Land of the West.

"Oregon Country" was not simply the area that would become the state of Oregon, but the entire region west of South Pass. Thus, the hills just beyond the Continental Divide in Wyoming became the "Oregon Buttes," and emigrants wrote of entering Oregon as they crossed the pass: "Today we entered Oregon. . . . We nooned beyond at a small spring and drank the waters of the Pacific!" (The vast land collectively called Oregon actually belonged to the British, but this legal nicety was quickly pushed aside by the influx of Americans.) West of South Pass, the route divided at the "Parting of the Ways." California- and Utah-bound travelers turned south to Fort Bridger, while those bound for Oregon and Washington headed due west on the Sublette or Lander Cutoff.

Origins

Americans emigrated west for a number of reasons: to escape a severe economic depression in the East and falling crop prices, to get out of the crowded and polluted cities, to find religious freedom in Utah, to search for gold in the mountains of California, or simply to join in a great adventure in a new and undiscovered land. (More than a few also headed west to get away from debts or the law.) The first whites to cross the Continental Divide on what would become the Oregon Trail were a party of fur trappers known as the Astorians. They rode horses over South Pass in 1812, but it was not until a decade later that trappers really moved deeply into this country. The first freight wagons rolled over the pass in 1830, en route to a mountain-man rendezvous on the Green River. By the early 1840s, emigration westward was getting easier and more inviting. Fort Laramie, in eastern Wyoming, and Fort Bridger, in southwestern Wyoming,

OREGON TRAIL

provided valuable way stations where travelers could rest up, repair their wagons, trade worn-out stock for fresh animals, and purchase food, whiskey, and supplies.

The turning point in the history of the Oregon Trail came in 1843, when the Applegate Wagon Train left Independence, Missouri, with 1,000 people, 120 wagons, and 5,000 head of livestock. It was the largest wagon train ever assembled. Under the leadership of Marcus Whitman (later killed in an Indian attack near present-day Walla Walla, Washington) and guided by mountain man Bill Sublette, the party made it all the way to the Columbia and Willamette Rivers by September. It had taken six long months to travel the 2,000 miles, but they had shown that the route was feasible. The gates of history had been cracked open, and they could never be closed again. Soon, the trickle westward turned into a flood tide.

Rolling West

Most travelers tried to depart Independence or St. Joseph, Missouri, in the spring, leaving as soon as the grass would support their stock. Typically, each evening found the emigrant just 15 miles farther down the trail, and it generally took five or six months to travel from Missouri to California or Oregon. They had to be over the mountains before the first snows of winter struck,

and those who erred—such as the infamous Donner Party of 1846—paid a high price.

Emigrants were forced to travel as light as possible to lessen the burden on oxen. Some traders grew rich on the castoffs from overburdened wagon trains, while others profited by operating toll bridges and ferries across the North Platte and Green Rivers. (Toll at the Green River crossing was sometimes an amazing $16 per wagon!) Guidebooks—there were several; this was a big business even in the 19th century—described the crossings and camping places and suggested provisions for the 2,000-mile journey. A wagon, harness, and eight oxen cost travelers around $400.

Because of the scarcity of wood, Oregon Trail travelers used dry grass, sagebrush, or buffalo chips for fuel. Meals were simple but hearty, often consisting of a few staples plus whatever game might be found along the trail. Today, when you drive across the state it is easy to see how trying an experience this must have been for the emigrants—gale-force winds, dust, and lightning combine with the parched ground, the deceptively long distances, and the lack of shade. Wyoming can be a harsh and unforgiving land; it is not a place to wander into unprepared. Perhaps a tenth of the people who set out on the Oregon Trail never made it to their destination, and fellow travelers noted in their diaries the

disturbing presence of graves—sometimes every 80 yards. Many died from diseases such as cholera, or from accidents and drownings; others were killed by early winter storms and Indian attacks. Few of the graves are marked.

At the peak of migration in 1850 (when California gold fever had struck America), some 55,000 men, women, and children pressed their way across the plains and mountains. It is easy to imagine the impact these wagons could have had with their thousands of cattle, horses, and mules. The grass quickly became overgrazed under this onslaught, and the already-scarce water badly polluted around popular campsites. Late-summer travelers were forced to range far and wide for better conditions, creating even more paths. The Indians who had lived here were shocked by the magnitude of the migration and began to realize not just what the whites were doing to their buffalo, but also how overwhelmed the native peoples would be by the newcomers. (The entire Plains Indian population probably numbered 40,000 individuals at its peak, and disease and war greatly reduced these numbers.)

Finale

By 1870, perhaps 350,000 people had traveled across Wyoming by wagon train, stagecoach, horseback, and foot. It was the greatest peacetime migration in history. For most of them, this country seemed a worthless stretch of sagebrush and a barrier to the green lands farther west. It took the railroad to change this. Completion of the transcontinental railroad in 1869 turned the Oregon Trail into an anachronism. Suddenly one could cross the nation easily, in days instead of months. The trail continued to be used by freighters and some pioneers even as late as the turn of the century, but the vast majority of travelers turned to rail travel. An era had ended.

The Trail Today

It has been more than 150 years since the first wagon train traveled along the Oregon Trail, but the mystique of the "great migration" continues to draw people from around the world. Much of the trail cuts across publicly owned land, and the tracks are readily visible in many places even after a century and a half. Explorers still discover artifacts strewn along the way. Visitors to Wyoming will enjoy delving into this rich past at such places as Fort Laramie, Oregon Trail Ruts, Register Cliff, Fort Caspar, Independence Rock, Devil's Gate, South Pass, Names Hill, and Fort Bridger. Hundreds of other lesser sights line the route, from the remains of old trading posts to countless emigrant graves. Portions of the Oregon Trail are described in greater detail in the Southeast, Central, Wind River Mountains, and Southwest chapters of this book.

A number of businesses attempt to re-create the days of the great migration with wagon trips along the historic Oregon Trail. **Historic Trail Expeditions,** tel. (307) 266-4868, and **Trails West,** tel. (307) 332-7801 or (800) 327-4052, both offer multi-day wagon train and horse trips along the Oregon Trail in Wyoming. **Western Encounters,** tel. (800) 572-1230, leads weeklong horseback rides on the Oregon Trail. **Great Divide Tours,** tel. (307) 332-3123 or (800) 458-1915, provides a wide range of horseback and wagon trips, including Oregon Trail rides. Five-to-seven-day treks cost $950-1,300 per person, which includes everything except sleeping bags.

THE PONY EXPRESS

On April 3, 1860, a lone rider galloped westward from the town of St. Joseph, Missouri. Nearly 2,000 miles away, another rider left the booming city of San Francisco, heading east. One of the most celebrated passages in American history had begun. Although it only lasted 18 months and was a financial disaster, the Pony Express caught the national imagination, proved that rapid mail service was possible even in the winter, and helped keep California in the Union.

The Pony Express was the brainchild of William H. Russell, one of the great wheelers and dealers of the late 19th century and director of the Central Overland California & Pike's Peak Express Company. Russell, along with partners Alexander Majors and William Bradford Waddell, managed the largest freighting company in the West, a business that at one time owned 50,000 oxen for its 3,500 wagons and employed 4,000 workers.

PONY EXPRESSIONS

We had had a consuming desire from the beginning, to see a pony-rider, but somehow or other all that passed us and all that met us managed to streak by in the night, and so we heard only a whiz and a hail, and the swift phantom of the desert was gone before we could get our heads out of the windows. But now we were expecting one along every moment, and would see him in broad daylight. Presently the driver exclaims: "

HERE HE COMES!"

Every neck is stretched further, and every eye strained wider. Away across the endless dead level of the prairie a black speck appears against the sky, and it is plain that it moves. Well, I should think so! In a second or two it becomes a horse and rider, rising and falling, rising and falling—sweeping toward us nearer and nearer—growing more and more distinct, more and more sharply defined—nearer and still nearer, and the flutter of the hoofs comes faintly to the ear—another instant a whoop and a hurrah from our upper deck, a wave of the rider's hand, but no reply, and man and horse burst past our excited faces, and go winging away like a belated fragment of a storm!

So sudden is it all, and so like a flash of unreal fancy, that for the flake of white foam left quivering and perishing on a mail-sack after the vision had flashed by and disappeared, we might have doubted whether we had seen any actual horse and man at all, maybe.

—*Mark Twain in* Roughing It

In 1855, the firm of Russell, Majors, & Waddell secured a monopoly to supply all U.S. government military posts west of the Missouri River. Because of Mormon raids on the supply wagons and the failure of the War Department to pay the company for its services, it was soon in financial trouble. To escape, the company needed the contract for mail service between California and St. Louis, a route then held by the Butterfield Overland Mail Company. Butterfield's route took mail along a circuitous 25-day trek through Texas and Arizona into southern California. With the nation slipping rapidly toward the Civil War—and Texas on the side of the South—there were fears that mail service would be halted and that California might join the Confederacy.

Express Mail

In 1859, the postmaster general signed a contract with Russell, Majors, & Waddell to operate coaches and horses along the central route to California. The Pony Express was born as a flamboyant symbol of the superiority of this route. Experienced young horsemen, some as young as 14 and none weighing more than 120 pounds, would ride the finest horses at a full gallop, carrying telegrams and mail through some of the most desolate land on earth. The trip was to take just 10 days.

Each horse had four mail pouches sewn into a leather *mochila,* which could be easily transferred between horses. (At $7.50 per half ounce, Pony Express mail was primarily urgent messages and newspapers.) Riders changed horses at relay stations—crude huts with station keepers and stock tenders—every 10 to 15 miles, continuing on for 75-100 miles before passing the precious package to another rider. After a short break, the rider would speed back to his home station with mail headed in the opposite direction. The whole operation required a military precision to keep the 119 relay and home stations stocked, make sure the horses were in good condition, and guard against attack. For their work, riders received $120 per month (including room and board).

The Demise

The threat of Indian hostilities became real when Nevada Piutes, angry after decades of abuse and the theft of their land, began attacking white settlements, killing 16 of the men working at the relay stations, taking 150 horses, and burning seven stations. A full-scale war was avoided, but it took more than a month to get the Express back into operation, at a cost of $75,000. Already a money loser, this helped ensure the collapse of the Pony Express. But it was not just money that brought down the Pony Express. Completion of the first continental telegraph line on October 24, 1861, also contributed; its mission replaced by a much more rapid means of communication, the Pony Express ended just two days later. Riders had delivered 34,753 pieces of mail, losing only one *mochila* (both horse and rider were killed) in 616 cross-country runs.

The Final Chapter

The story of the Central Overland California & Pike's Peak Express Company does not end here. By late 1860, a year before the Pony Express ceased operations, Russell, Majors, and Waddell's firm already teetered on the verge of bankruptcy (its employees nicknamed it "Clean Out of Cash and Poor Pay"). To stave this off, William Russell met with a clerk in the U.S. Dept. of the Interior and received $150,000 in bonds belonging to the Indian Trust Fund. Russell collected more than $870,000 in illegal government funds before being caught.

The whole house of cards came tumbling down when partner Alexander Majors declared bankruptcy and Russell's partner in crime, Godard Bailey, confessed. Russell spent Christmas of 1860 in prison, but he somehow managed to escape prosecution and he never repaid the money. With the start of the Civil War, Congress had greater concerns. In 1861, a joint agreement moved all western mail delivery to the central route, combining the forces of Butterfield's Overland Mail Company with the remnants of the Russell, Majors, & Waddell firm to avoid travel through the Confederate states. Later, Ben Holladay bought up the bankrupt firm and transformed it into the Overland Stage Line. Both Russell and Waddell died poor men. Years later, one of the Pony Express riders,

"Buffalo Bill" Cody, found Alexander Majors living in a tiny Denver shack. In a gesture typical of him, Cody put Majors on a cash retainer for the rest of his life.

THE OVERLAND TRAIL

Lesser known and shorter-lived than the Oregon Trail, the Overland Trail was established by Ben Holladay, owner of the Overland Stage Company. Although the Oregon Trail had served for many years as the primary route west, by the 1860s a need was developing for a new path. Increasing Indian attacks made the Oregon Trail dangerous, and the rapidly growing mining town of Denver was too far away. After Holladay was given the contract to deliver mail to the West, he quickly rerouted travel along a trail originally scouted by Jim Bridger.

The new route proved 60 miles shorter than the Oregon Trail, but it passed directly through the difficult desert country of western Wyoming rather than along the relatively lush North Platte and Sweetwater Rivers. Holladay established stage stations for changing teams every 10-15 miles, and built home stations where travelers could stop for meals or lodging every 50 miles. Conditions at these relay stations were primitive at best; one traveler described southwestern Wyoming's Sand Springs station as "roofless and chairless, filthy and squalid, with a smoky fire in one corner, and a table in the center of an impure floor, the walls open to every wind and the interior full of dust." But the stations were better than sitting outside in the blazing hot sun or the bitter winter winds.

The stages covered 100-125 miles in a 24-hour period but were extraordinarily expensive for the time: $500 from Atchison, Kansas, to San Francisco. Still, emigrants began using the new route instead of the Oregon Trail; in a single year (1864), some 17,584 men, women, and children used the Overland Trail, along with 50,000 head of livestock and 4,264 wagons.

Although the new route remained relatively free from attacks for several years, the 1865 Sand Creek Massacre sent Indians on the warpath throughout the plains. Stage stations were destroyed, stagecoaches were attacked, and many died on both sides. The attacks con-

railroad building on the Great Plains, from Harpers Weekly, 1875

tinued sporadically for the next two years. With completion of the transcontinental railroad in 1869, the Overland Stage rapidly faded in importance, and stagecoach service ended. The old Overland Trail continued to be used by wagons until the turn of the century.

CONNECTING THE COASTS

More than any other event, the completion of the transcontinental railroad led to the settlement and development of Wyoming. Most of its major towns and cities originated along the railroad lines. Not only did the railroad bring Wyoming within a couple of days of either coast, but it also led to the opening of coal mines to fuel the engines, hastened development of the logging industry (for railroad ties and mine props), and made it easy to ship cattle to market. Settlers could order most anything—Sears Roebuck even shipped prefabricated houses that filled two boxcars. It was no coincidence that Wyoming became a territory just as the railroad was being pushed across its southern border. An enduring impact from the railroad is a

checkerboard pattern of public and private land ownership along the Union Pacific's route across Wyoming.

Surveying the Route

The Union Pacific's route was planned by Gen. Grenville M. Dodge, a veteran of battles with the Sioux in the Powder River country. The traditional Oregon Trail route ran too close to Sioux country, was too far from the gold-mining city of Denver, and didn't have the rich coal deposits of southwestern Wyoming. The course Dodge chose headed almost straight across southern Wyoming, climbing the Laramie Mountains west of Cheyenne, then cutting through the Laramie Plains and the Red Desert before winding across the mountains of eastern Utah.

Despite Dodge's efforts to avoid direct confrontation with the Indians, and the government's diversionary tactic of building the Bozeman Trail through the Powder River country, the Arapaho did not take kindly to the presence of railroad surveying and construction parties in their traditional hunting grounds. They pulled up survey stakes, stole horses, and killed surveyors and loggers, forcing Dodge to request military

escorts. Three forts (Russell, Sanders, and Steele) were built in Wyoming to house these troops.

Working on the Railroad

To span the continent, the Union Pacific headed west from Omaha, while the Central Pacific worked east from Sacramento. By July 1867 tracklayers had reached the main division point, which would become Cheyenne, and headed on west to found Laramie, Rawlins, Green River, and Evanston. Most of the Central Pacific's workers were Chinese contract laborers, while those on the Union Pacific were a mixture of Americans and emigrants, especially Irishmen. Great competition grew between the two groups, and a record was set as the tracklayers worked across the searing heat of Wyoming's Red Desert: the men laid seven and a half miles of track in a single day. Laborers were paid an extraordinary $2.50 an hour, but the work was equally dangerous; some estimate that the transcontinental railroad was built at the cost of 10 men's lives per mile of track! Many were buried right in the roadbed. The tracklayers finally pushed their way into Utah and met workers of the Central Pacific at Promontory Point on May 10, 1869.

The railroad brought with it a gang of men who seemed to thrive on corruption, thievery, prostitution, gambling, drunkenness, and murder. As construction moved westward, temporary towns sprang up along the way; many were gone as soon as the tracks were out of sight. The entire procession of construction workers and hangers-on quickly became known as Hell-on-Wheels.

Worst of the temporary frontier towns was Benton, located a few miles east of present-day Rawlins. Those who passed through called it "nearer a repetition of Sodom and Gomorrah than any other place in America" and a "congregation of scum and wickedness . . . by day disgusting, by night dangerous." There was no grass, little water, and the alkali dust stood eight inches deep. Murders were a nightly affair at the 25 saloons and five dance halls. The big attraction was gambling, with hundreds of men crowding the big tent each evening, paying for whiskey, dance-hall girls, or roulette wheels. Before the short-lived settlement could disappear in the alkali dust—just three months after its founding—more than 100 men lay buried in boot hill.

Newspaper reporter James Chisholm described these men in less than appealing terms:

I often speculate on what will finally become of all that rolling scum which the locomotive seems to blow onward as it presses westward. Will they get blown clean off the continent at last into the Pacific Ocean? One is gradually surrounded by the same faces in each successive town, the same gamblers, the same musicians playing the same old tunes to the same old dance, the same females getting always a little more dilapidated. As the excitement dies out of one town, and the railroad leaves it behind in a kind of exhausted repose, these old familiar faces die out to reappear in a new state of existence.

A rolling newspaper press tagged along with the flotsam and jetsam across Wyoming, printing the weekly *Frontier Index* in each new camp. Its editor, Legh Freeman, angered the primarily northern-born workers by constantly showing his support for the Confederacy; he once labeled Gen. Ulysses Grant "the whiskey bloated, squaw ravishing adulterer, nigger worshipping mogul rejoicing over his election to the presidency." In Bear River City (long gone but near present-day Evanston), Freeman made the mistake of suggesting that several accused murderers then in jail should meet up with Judge Lynch. After a gang of vigilantes followed his suggestion by throwing a necktie party for the three, other ruffians destroyed the *Frontier Index* office and chased its editor out of town.

STATEHOOD

Because of its difficult climate, a paucity of good agricultural lands, and the lack of major deposits of gold, Wyoming was one of the last states to be settled. At various times, portions of Wyoming were parts of Indian country, Mexico, Louisiana, Missouri, Texas, Nebraska, Dakota, Idaho, Oregon, and Utah. In 1868, the Wyoming Territory was carved out of the Dakota Territory, a move

primarily intended to keep the Democratic voters building the Union Pacific Railroad from overwhelming the Republican power base in distant Yankton. The folks out west were equally happy to gain independence from such a tenuous governmental link. It was not until May 19, 1869, that an organized government was established in the new territory. The first census of Wyoming, in 1870, found just 9,000 people (Indians were not counted).

The word "Wyoming" comes from the Leni Lanape Indians of Pennsylvania; their word "mecheweami-ing" meant "at the Great Plains." The term was first applied to the land that would become Wyoming in 1865, when Ohio's J.M. Ashley introduced a bill to form a "temporary government for the territory of Wyoming." Newspaper editor Legh Freeman has been credited with popularizing the name and having it inserted in the bill that created the Wyoming Territory in 1868.

A triumvirate of politicians—Francis E. Warren, John B. Kendrick, and Joseph M. Carey—governed Wyoming for much of its first half century. Carey, a Republican turned Democrat, was a founder of both the powerful Wyoming Stock Growers Association and the Cheyenne Club. He was a strong proponent of Wyoming statehood and introduced the enabling legislation in the U.S. House. During the debate, he claimed a Wyoming population of something over 110,000 people, an exaggeration that helped sway enough House votes to pass the measure. (The next year, the U.S. census found just 62,555 people in Wyoming.) The act was signed into law by President Benjamin Harrison on July 10, 1890, making Wyoming the 44th state. Interestingly, this was the same year that the director of the U.S. Census Bureau declared that the "frontier of settlement" was no more.

The Equality State

Wyoming's first territorial legislature passed an act granting women the right to vote. The measure was signed into law by Gov. J.A. Campbell on December 10, 1869, making this the first government in the world to grant women the right to vote. (Technically, Wyoming was not the first state to allow women suffrage; New Jersey

---

BILL NYE ON WOMEN'S SUFFRAGE

There have been many reasons given, first and last, why women should not vote, but I desire to say, in the full light of a ripe experience, that some of them are fallacious. I refer more particularly to the argument that it will degrade women to go to the polls and vote like a little man. While I am not and have never been a howler for female suffrage, I must admit that it is much more of a success than prohibition and speculative science. . . . In Wyoming, where female suffrage has raged for years, you meet quiet, courteous and gallant gentlemen, and fair, quiet, sensible women at the polls, where

there isn't a loud or profane word, and where it is an infinitely more proper place to send a young lady unescorted than to the post office in any city in the Union. . . . All these things look hopeful. We can't tell what the Territory would have been without female suffrage, but when they begin to hang men by law instead of by moonlight, the future begins to brighten up. When you have to get up in the night to hang a man every little while and don't get any per diem for it, you feel as though you were a good way from home.

—*19th-century humorist Bill Nye*

widows already had limited voting rights.) The name "Equality State" comes from this bold step. It would be another 50 years before the 19th Amendment was finally passed, giving all women in America the right to vote. Not everyone looked upon women's suffrage as such a good step. In 1871, Democrats in the second territorial legislature repealed the measure, then came within one vote of overriding Governor Campbell's veto.

When the territory of Wyoming was seeking admission to the Union in 1890, the issue of giving women the right to vote—a measure included in Wyoming's new constitution—became a hotly contested topic. Alabama's Sen. John T. Morgan led the fight against admitting the new state, with the argument that the other half of the population would be polluted by politicians (such as himself?): "It is the immoral influences of the ballot upon women that I deprecate and would avoid. I do not want to see her drawn in contact with the rude things of this world where the delicacy of her senses and sensitivities would be constantly wounded by the attrition with bad and desperate and foul politicians and men."

Wyoming's status as the home of equal rights took another big step in 1925 after the death of Gov. William B. Ross. His wife, Nellie Tayloe Ross, was nominated to replace him and won the special election on a sympathy vote. She made no effort to get elected, noting, "I shall not make a campaign. My candidacy is in the hands of my friends. I shall not leave the house." She served ably as the nation's first woman governor and achieved considerable national attention. Despite a good record, Ross lost her bid for reelection, primarily because she was a Democrat in a heavily Republican state. In 1933, President Roosevelt appointed her as director of the U.S. Mint, a title she held for the next 20 years. She died in 1967 at the age of 101.

CATTLE COUNTRY

Hardly had the thunder of the Sioux ponies, along the Powder, the thunder of the cavalry died down, when over the southern horizon came a new army. An army of tossing horns, white in the sun; of lithe young men lolling in their saddles; riding at point,

on the flanks, on the drag. The Cowboy was coming to Wyoming.

—*Struthers Burt in*
Powder River Let 'er Buck

Opening the Range

Once the bison herds had been devastated and the Indians evicted, cattlemen found what seemed like a Garden of Eden in Wyoming: land, grass, and water were essentially free for the taking. The cattle industry began innocently enough. In December 1863, Tom Alsop was returning to Omaha with a train of 50 wagons when a snowstorm pinned them down near present-day Cheyenne. Alsop abandoned the oxen and wagons on the plains and led his men safely home on horseback. The following spring, they rode back to recover the freight, and were startled to discover that the cattle they had left to die of exposure had not only survived the winter but were thriving. The discovery soon attracted droves of ranchers.

The first cattle drive through Wyoming came in 1866, when a Montana merchant named Nelson Story decided that what the Virginia City miners needed was fresh beef. Heading south to Kansas with $10,000 sewn in the lining of his clothes, he filled a wagon with supplies, bought 3,000 Texas longhorns, hired 27 cowboys, gave them the finest Remington breech-loading rifles, and headed north for the gold fields (see "The Bloody Bozeman" under "Sheridan Vicinity" in the Powder River Country chapter for more on this notorious fort), Colonel Carrington forbade them from continuing north through Sioux country since they did not have the required 40 armed guards. (Some feel that Carrington actually hoped to requisition the cattle for his men; most of the Army's had already been stolen.) In response, an angry Story thumbed his nose at the government, heading north under cover of darkness. Discovering his departure, Carrington was forced to cave in, sending 15 soldiers along to bring Story's force up to the legal minimum. Although one man died, the rest of the men and cattle made it to Virginia City on December 9. Nelson Story had gained himself a place in history.

Millions of cattle headed into or through Wyoming in the 1870s and 1880s. Ranching looked like a can't-lose business; dump a couple

TOM HORN

The story of the outlaw Tom Horn will always remain something of a mystery. Over the years, Horn worked as a stage driver, an Army scout, a deputy sheriff, a Pinkerton investigator, and a stock detective for the Wyoming Stock Growers Association. When J.M. Carey (later Wyoming governor and senator) discovered that Tom Horn was out to murder, rather than bring in for trial, accused rustlers, he had Horn fired from the association. Other cattle barons quickly moved to hire him, however, paying $500 for each man murdered. Horn is generally blamed for ambushing and killing two ranchers (and suspected rustlers) in the Laramie Mountains in 1895, along with two others in Brown's Park, Colorado, five years later.

Wherever Horn went, a trail of dead men was left behind, but nobody was able to pin the blame on him until 1901, when a 14-year-old boy was shot in the back and killed in the Laramie Mountains. It was a case of mistaken identity, since the boy had been wearing his father's hat and clothes. The older man was later shot from ambush but survived. Horn was implicated in the boy's slaying by his trademark: a small stone placed under the victim's head.

Horn would probably have escaped even this heinous crime had he not bragged about it. (The confession would never hold up in court today; Deputy U.S. Marshal Joe LeFors had plied Horn with liquor and had a court stenographer listen through a crack in the door as he boasted of the slaying.) Horn had little money himself, but his supporters spent $100,000 in his defense, hiring the finest legal council, John W. Lacey, who had never lost any of his 50 previous murder trials (and who, not coincidentally, also represented the Wyoming Stock Growers Association and the Union Pacific Railroad).

Despite this, Horn was adjudged guilty and sentenced to hang. Horn's supporters tried to free him with a dynamite blast, and he later did briefly escape from jail, but on November 20, 1903, he was hanged before a large crowd at the corner of Pioneer and 19th Avenues in Cheyenne. Until the last minute, everyone expected a pardon, and many wealthy cattlemen feared what Horn might reveal about them, but in the end, his last words were to his friend T. Joe Cahill: "Joe, they tell me you are married now. I hope you're doing well. Treat her right."

thousand head of cows and calves on the range in spring and return a year later to round them up for market. What could be simpler? Investors from Omaha, New York, England, Scotland, and France quickly took note of the potential fortunes to be made.

By 1883, English and Scottish investors had poured some £6 million into Wyoming cattle and had turned Cheyenne into a country club for the European gentry. Some were more gullible than others; stories are still told of an Englishman who watched as the cattle he was buying were driven by to be counted, not noticing that the same cattle had come around the hill a couple of times before. The use of "book counts" also inflated the value of the herds; frequently, nobody bothered to make sure that numbers in the books equaled cattle on the range. The aristocrats were regarded with a mixture of humor and disdain by the hardened cowboys whose every other utterance was a swear word. One British lord rode up to a cowboy in his buggy, asking, "My good man, could you tell me where your master is?" The cowboy glowered back, spat out his tobacco, and said, "The son-of-a-bitch ain't been born yet!"

During the early years of ranching in Wyoming, cattle were allowed to roam at will and were not sorted out until the annual roundups. Sounds fine in theory, but in practice a few flaws showed up, notably the problem of mavericks. The term maverick refers to an unbranded calf or cow of questionable ownership, or, as writer Struthers Burt put it, "A calf whose mamma has died and whose father has run off with another lady cow." Unbranded calves were generally divvied up among the ranchers on the basis of which herd they were with, but when herds became mixed together, conflicts were inevitable. In addition, multiple roundups meant that the first cowboys on the scene could pretty much decide for themselves which calves were theirs. Some even went so far as to slit the tongues of calves so they could no longer suckle and would not follow their mothers, thus becoming instant mavericks.

BRANDS

Branding dates back to the Egyptian pharaohs, who branded not only their cattle, camels, and donkeys, but even their slaves. Slave branding was also practiced in America. The American tradition of cattle branding comes from the Spanish conquistadors and their vaqueros but was adapted to the spacious western plains. Because there were no fences, cattle belonging to various ranchers became intermixed, leading to inevitable questions of ownership, which brands helped answer.

Brands appear almost anywhere on an animal, and a given ranch may have a half-dozen or more for its cattle, sheep, and horses. An individual animal often has several different brands or marks. To make them easier to identify on the hoof, cattle are frequently distinctively marked by cutting a notch in the ear, slicing the skin that hangs under the cow's throat (the dewlap), or hacking a flap of hide (a wattle) so that it hangs loose from the neck.

In Wyoming, having a brand is something of a status symbol, and the Wyoming Brand Book lists more than 27,000 currently in use (one for every 17 residents!).

Not everyone who has a brand has stock; some are simply used for mailbox decorations on suburban ranchettes. The more complex ones aren't likely to appear on any cows since they become illegible as the scar heals. Brands that are hard to alter or of historic significance may sell for more than $5,000. Coming up with a design for a new brand can be a problem, since the state looks askance on brands that resemble others in the same area or that might be easily altered by rustlers (they still exist). One 19th-century rancher, fed up with having his brand suggestions rejected, wrote the brand department, demanding, "Send me a brand P.D.Q." They complied by giving him the brand PDQ. Reading brands is an art gained by years of experience. They are read from left to right, top to bottom, and outside to inside.

Branding usually takes place in the spring, before cattle and calves are driven into the higher pastures or set loose on the plains. A branding iron is heated to a dull red in a fire and then pressed against the calf as it is held down. Freeze branding is also often used. Most male calves are castrated at the same time.

Cattle Barons and Rustlers

To curb the temptations for such "sooners," the powerful Wyoming Stock Growers Association—an organization dominated by the wealthiest of the cattlemen—gained the authority to dictate when roundups could be held. The organization dominated the political landscape of Wyoming for many years; by the 1880s, a third of the state legislature belonged to the association. The 1882 Maverick Bill gave the association control over all cattle roundups in the territory, with proceeds from the sales of mavericks going into the association's coffers. It could blacklist cowboys as "rustlers" on the basis of hearsay, and cattle shipped without the association's permission risked being impounded by inspectors in Chicago or Omaha. Even worse, ranchers suspected of rustling (which seemed to include anyone except members) were sometimes ambushed and murdered by enforcers, the most notorious of whom was Tom Horn. Whole regions of Wyoming were terrorized by the practice of dry-gulching, in which suspected rustlers would be shot from behind and left in an out-of-the-way gulch.

Meanwhile, the big cattlemen—commonly called cattle barons—also ran into trouble, especially in the Powder River country. The fierce winter of 1886-87 devastated their herds; some lost all their cattle, while others had just 20 or 30 percent of the numbers from the previous year. Big ranching outfits also found themselves hemmed in by homesteading settlers who fenced the land. Fences created a hazard, since cattle often moved with the winter winds until they hit the fences and then piled up there to die.

The big cattlemen accused these "nesters" not only of fencing the land, but also of taking stray cattle for themselves. Using a "long rope" and a "running iron," they could easily alter the brands and soon have their own herd. The cattle barons decided to put an end to this thievery once and for all with the infamous Johnson County War of 1892, but the campaign proved a complete fiasco. Two men died on each side in pitched battles between the "barons" and the "rustlers." Although the invaders managed to escape prosecution, the small nesters and rustlers had won the day. From that time on, the range would increasingly be fenced in.

SHEEP

History

Cattle arrived in most parts of Wyoming a decade or so before the first sheep munched their way across the grazing lands, but by 1902 the rangeland was crowded with close to six million sheep. Cattlemen considered the public land their own—by right of previous use—although legally it was all open range owned by the government. As competition increased, cattlemen declared "dead lines," across which no sheep would be allowed. Conflicts quickly erupted, and the single herder and his dogs proved no match for a gang of cattlemen on horseback. Herders were murdered throughout the state, and the violence escalated into the infamous Ten Sleep Raid of 1909 (see the special topic in the Bighorn Basin chapter), in which three sheepmen were brutally murdered. After this, things quieted down as the land became increasingly settled and government policies divided up the areas. Some cattlemen even turned to raising sheep, but animosity still remains between sheepmen and cattlemen in some areas.

Times have not always been easy for herders. Alfred Mokler in *History of Natrona County* describes one horrific night:

> *During a severe storm the latter part of March 1895, Noel R. Gascho was with a band of sheep on the open range. The band became unmanageable and drifted with the storm. Gascho went with the sheep, which was the only thing to do. The snow came down in blinding sheets, the cold wind swept over the bleak prairie and hundreds of the sheep were frozen. Gascho said it seemed as though the blood in his veins and the marrow in his bones were frozen. He became numb and sleepy and to keep awake he would stick his legs with a knife blade. About midnight he caught one of the sheep, cut its throat and drank the blood. Then he set fire to the wool on the dead sheep and the greasy wool burned readily. Before daylight, he had burned six*

*sheep after he had cut their throats and
drank of their blood. This was all that
saved his life.*

Sheepherding

Over the years, the number of sheep in Wyoming
has steadily dropped; today there are around
790,000 at any given time. Sheep are generally
moved up into the mountains each spring to
graze in the high meadows and then brought
back down in the fall. A long drive along country
roads is a sight straight out of the history books.
Sheep are sheared in spring, generally just before
lambing season. By fall the lambs are big enough
to send to market, and the ewes are bred.

A good number of the first sheepherders in
Wyoming were from Europe's Basque region.
Many preferred to take sheep instead of a salary
and so gradually gained flocks of their own. The
frugal ones eventually became ranch owners in
their own right. The herding business has not
changed much over the years, however, and
herders still spend weeks at a time alone, seeing
nobody but the camp mover when he arrives
to help move the outfit to new feeding grounds.
Today many herders are Mexican immigrants,
although some Basque and American herders
are still around. The herder's life is a simple and
quiet one, with plenty of time for reflection. It
takes someone with the right temperament to be
a sheepherder.

The sheepherder's wagon—an early version
of the RV—was invented by James Candlish, a
Rawlins blacksmith, and later improved and
marketed by Casper's Schulte Hardware Company. The design proved an efficient one, and
herders still use the old wagons, though rubber
tires have replaced wagon wheels and the roof
is now tin instead of canvas. The layout is simple: a Dutch door opens into a small space filled
with a bed at the back with drawers underneath
and shelves above. A small woodstove near
the entrance is used for both heating and cooking. Almost every Wyoming museum seems to
have one tucked away in a corner, but many
more are still in use on the lonely high plains.

ENERGY BOOM AND BUST

Wyoming's first oil well was drilled in 1884, and
by 1908—the year of the first oil boom—pro-

duction approached 18,000 barrels per year.
Production continued to climb over the decades,
reaching a peak in 1970, when more than 155
million barrels were pumped. Since then, production has declined as older fields have become exhausted and low prices discourage further exploration. By 1995, production had fallen
to 86 million barrels. The decline in oil production
has been offset somewhat by dramatic increases in two other energy sources: natural
gas and coal. During the 1980s, both industries
nearly doubled their production levels in
Wyoming. Since then, gas production has remained high, while coal mining continues to
boom.

The Arab oil embargo of 1973 and subsequent price increases turned Wyoming upside
down. The oil-patch towns—particularly Casper,
Rock Springs, Evanston, and Green River—
turned into madhouses of pickup trucks, heavily muscled oil workers, honkytonk bars, strip
joints, fast-food outlets, and trailer courts. Drugs,
crime, prostitution, and gambling ripped across
the state. The population of Rock Springs doubled in two years. In the heady rush of new
workers and high-paying oil jobs, many towns
embarked on ambitious construction projects
such as schools and housing developments,
while trailer parks sprouted up across the
countryside. (Wyoming still holds top honors as
the state with the highest percentage of mobile
homes.)

This economic bubble collapsed with the sudden halving of oil prices in 1982, and Wyoming's
population actually dropped by almost three
percent during the 1980s. The hard-hit Douglas
area lost 20% of its population between 1985
and 1990. The bust left many towns struggling to
survive as unemployment skyrocketed, the state
government was forced into consolidation mode,
and local residents were left with a bloated set of
facilities. In the late 1980s and early '90s, the
economy rebounded, and recent years have
seen efforts to diversify. The inevitable booms
and busts associated with the energy and mining industries will affect Wyoming for the fore-
seeable future, but growing numbers of tourism
and service-sector jobs will help cushion the
blows next time around. The money may not
approach that of the $24-per-hour coal mining
jobs, but a sales position at Wal-Mart at least
pays the bills.

ECONOMY AND GOVERNMENT

Due to financial restraints, the light at the end of the tunnel will be turned off until further notice.

—sign in Hot Springs County Library

In the 1980s, Wyoming rode an economic bucking bronco as oil prices shot up and then suddenly dove, throwing this energy-rich state out of the saddle. During that decade the state's population actually declined and the economy floundered. Things have turned around more recently, thanks to the arrival of small industries, a stabilization in oil and gas prices, and communities' growing emphasis on tourism. During the 1990s, people are once again moving into Wyoming, but this time many come because they want to live or retire here, rather than simply make money. Unfortunately, the result is not always beneficial, since folks moving in with cash in the bank and telecommuting jobs drive up housing prices and put additional pressure on already crowded recreational areas. By 1996 the state's economy was growing slowly, and many towns—particularly those with tourism potential—were doing quite well.

Wyoming's economy is affected not only by private developments but also by the government. The federal government owns almost 47% of the land, while the state government holds another 10%—leaving 43% in private hands. The largest public land agency—the Bureau of Land Management (BLM)—owns nearly 18 million acres in Wyoming, but most of this exists in a checkerboard of small parcels with limited public access. The BLM manages only a few patches of wilderness scattered around Wyoming. The U.S. Forest Service has 8.7 million acres within nine national forests which cover the state's largest mountain ranges, and the National Park Service has another 2.3 million acres in five national parks, monuments, and recreation areas. Warren Air Force Base—the most important ICBM base in North America—is located in Cheyenne and represents the state's only major military installation. The military also owns land in other parts of Wyoming today, notably the Camp Guernsey training area north of Wheatland and a Naval

Petroleum Reserve at Teapot Dome. Partly because of all this federal involvement, Wyoming residents are on the receiving end of generous federal monies; the state is second only to Alaska in per-capita federal aid.

Working for a Living

Today, Wyoming's economy is based on several industries: oil and gas extraction, coal and trona mining, cattle and sheep ranching, and tourism. Of these, the most important financially is the oil and gas industry, which contributes more than 40% of the state's tax base and employs 18,000 people. Some 1,000 fields annually produce 86 million barrels of oil (sixth in the nation) and 800 million cubic feet of natural gas (fifth in the nation). Oil production—mainly in the Powder River and Bighorn basins—continues a long-term decline, while gas production—mainly in the southwest corner of the state—holds steady.

A quarter of the nation's coal reserves lie beneath Wyoming, and in recent years it has become the largest coal-producing state, outstripping (pun intended) West Virginia and Kentucky. Nearly all the 275 million tons extracted each year comes from enormous open-pit mines, primarily in the Powder River Basin. With perhaps a *trillion* tons of coal still below the surface, Wyoming is one of the largest energy storehouses anywhere on the planet. Vast deposits of trona (used primarily in glass and chemicals) occur in southwestern Wyoming, where mines produce 90% of the nation's supply. The state is also a major producer of bentonite, helium, and sulfur. Uranium was once an important industry—a third of America's reserves are in Wyoming—but since Three Mile Island production has dropped to almost nothing, although mines are being opened near Douglas.

Tourism has grown rapidly in recent years and now contributes more than $1 billion annually to the state's economy. It is particularly important in northwestern Wyoming, where Yellowstone and Grand Teton National Parks and other "lifestyle" attractions led to a 20% increase in Teton County's population from 1990 to 1995. Smaller levels of growth are taking place in other edge-of-the-mountain towns such as Cody,

WYOMING LINGO

Absaroka—Alternatively pronounced "ab-SOR-ka" or "ab-SOR-aka," the word means "People of the Large-beaked Bird" (hence the name Crow Indians). The Absaroka Mountains lie east of Yellowstone National Park.

Arapaho—The word is often spelled Arapahoe. An Indian tribe of Algonquin stock originally living on the Canadian plains, the Northern Arapaho now live on the Wind River Reservation. The name comes from a Crow Indian term meaning "Tattooed People." They call themselves simply "Our People."

bentonite—A special kind of clay that originates from volcanic ash, bentonite absorbs large amounts of water, increasing in volume by 30%. Bentonite is used in oil drilling, to line ponds, and even in candy bars. Wyoming is the nation's largest producer of this mineral.

booshway—the boss at a mountain-man rendezvous

buck and rail fence—Consisting of X-shaped supports and connecting poles, this is the classic fence of Jackson Hole, where the soils proved too rocky for ranchers to dig postholes. The abundant lodgepole pines made fine fences. Today, buck and rail fences are built more for beauty than function.

calcutta—The auctioning off of various rodeo teams or contestants; it's a popular way to wager on rodeo events. Rules vary.

cattle baron—a cattle owner with extensive holdings; primarily used during the heyday of the giant cattle spreads in the 1880s

chaps—pronounced "shaps," protective leather leg coverings; useful when riding horses through brush

chiselers—Ground squirrels, also called "ground cougars." The lemmings of Wyoming, they seem to delight in waiting till the last minute and then dashing toward car wheels. Lots of them get nailed on dirt roads all across the state.

coup—Pronounced "coo"; a Plains Indian word that signified great skill and daring, it involved striking an enemy in the midst of a battle or some other deed of valor. "Counting coups" was similar to gaining today's military medals of honor. Those with many coups wore warbonnets with many feathers.

coyotes—Fans of these ubiquitous critters call them "ky-O-tees," while those who regard them as "varmints" tend to pronounce the word "KY-oats."

creek—Everyone knows what it is, but old-timers in Wyoming pronounce the word "crik."

dead line—A line established by turn-of-the-century cattlemen who feared competition from sheep. Those herders who brought sheep across the imaginary line risked death and the destruction of their flocks.

dogger—A rodeo term used for steer wrestlers; it originated from Will Pickett, an early wrestler who threw steers to the ground by biting their lips in the manner of a bulldog. The name stuck, even though the lip-biting part didn't.

dogie—A motherless calf. A famous old cowboy poem begins:

As I walked out one morning for pleasure,
I spied a cowpuncher all riding alone;
His hat was throwed back and his spurs was a-jingling,
As he approached me a-singin' this song,

Whoopee ti yi yo, git along, little dogies,
It's your misfortune, and none of my own.
Whoopee ti yi yo, git along, little dogies,
For you know Wyoming will be your new home. . .

dog-trot—A type of log cabin common on old Wyoming ranches. Two cabins were connected by a breezeway, making a favorite place for dogs to hang out on hot summer days. This cabin style actually originated in the southern Appalachians.

dude—This is a term that has changed in meaning over the years. Writer Nathaniel Burt called the dude "any fancy-pants young man who wore a boutonniere and parted his hair in the middle." Later, the term came to mean a wealthy easterner vacationing on a western ranch, in contradistinction to "tourists," who were viewed as an inferior species. Today, Wyoming's many dude ranches are more proletarian. The wealthy elite generally prefer "guest ranches," which are really luxury resorts with a few horses thrown in.

emigrants—The dictionary defines emigrants as people who leave one place to settle elsewhere, in contrast to immigrants, who come into a new

place. Guess it all depends on your perspective, but for some reason folks heading west on the Oregon Trail were almost always called emigrants, not immigrants.

hazer—A rodeo term used in steer wrestling. It refers to a cowboy who rides beside the steer to keep it in position for the dogger.

hog ranch—An establishment of ill repute where booze, gambling, and loose women were the primary attractions. The most famous were located near military forts in Wyoming, notably Fort Fetterman and Fort Laramie. The name is generally attributed to the appearance of the women, but may also refer to the tiny, squalid rooms where they plied their trade. Author David Lavender called them places offering "the poorest whiskey and women in the west."

hooey—A tie used in calf-roping events at rodeos. Three of the calf's feet are wrapped with a piggin' string and completed with a half-hitch.

jackalope—an antlered jackrabbit found most commonly in the vicinity of Douglas, Wyoming, but proliferating throughout the West

maverick—An unbranded cow or calf of questionable ownership. The term originated from Samuel Maverick, owner of a two-million-acre Texas ranch in the 1840s. Because many of his cattle were never branded, cowboys coming across unbranded cattle on the open range would joke that they were Maverick's. Eventually the term was applied to all unbranded cattle.

piggin' string—a short piece of rope used to tie a hooey around the feet of a roped calf or steer at a rodeo

rendezvous—French for "appointed place of meeting." Between 1825 and 1840 the annual rendezvous was the big shindig for Rocky Mountain trappers, Indians, and traders. Modern-day versions try to re-create this trading and partying atmosphere.

runnin' iron—an improvised branding iron used by rustlers

rustler—A cattle thief or someone accused of taking cattle from the cattle barons; during the Johnson County War the term actually became a badge of honor in parts of Wyoming. "Packing a long rope" became the common term applied to folks who rustled.

sage hen—Another name for the sage grouse, a common bird across Wyoming. This was also a cowboy term for women.

scoria—A red rock commonly used on Powder River Basin roads. It was formed when coal beds caught fire and burned underground, baking adjacent shale and sandstone to create a bright red slag. The red comes from iron oxide. Clinker is another word commonly used for scoria.

Shoshone—An Indian tribe on Wyoming's Wind River Reservation. The word is also frequently spelled Shoshoni, and is generally pronounced with a long *e* at the end.

Sioux—The word was derived from a derogatory term meaning "enemy" or "snake" and used by the Chippewa Indians to describe the Indians who lived just to their west. The Sioux actually called themselves Dakota, meaning "alliance of friends."

trona—a mineral (sodium sesquicarbonate) used in glass, detergents, baking soda, and other products; mined in huge underground mines west of Green River

varmint—any animal you don't like; especially used for prairie dogs, ground squirrels, and coyotes

wapiti—Pronounced "WOP-a-tee." The Indian word for elk, it is occasionally used by biologists who consider it a more precise term.

Sheridan, Buffalo, Laramie, Pinedale, Dubois, Lander, and Saratoga. More than three million people come to enjoy the state's abundant recreational opportunities each year.

The state's most obvious industry, and the one that encompasses 90% of its land base, is agriculture. Surprisingly, however, grazing and farming employ less than six percent of the population. Wyoming is third in the nation in terms of sheep and lamb production and has 1.4 million cattle and calves. But it takes 30 acres to support a single cow (versus one acre per cow in parts of Nebraska!), which is why the average Wyoming farm is 3,761 acres—eight times the national average. Only four percent of the state is cultivated; primary crops are sugarbeets, barley, alfalfa hay, wheat, oats, and dry beans. These are mainly grown within Bighorn Basin and Wind River Basin, and along Wyoming's eastern plains.

The state has no truly large manufacturing plants, though every town has its own specialty, from cheesemaking to computer manufacturing. The services sector of the economy—from flipping burgers to running copy machines—is the unheralded source of real growth in Wyoming, though the wages are nothing to brag about.

POLITICS

During the campaign in those days there were always a great many "doubtful voters," and it sometimes required several quarts of liquor and an unlimited number of cigars to convince them.

—Alfred J. Mokler, describing the 1898 election campaign for Frank W. Mondell, running for U.S. Senate (he won)

Unlike in many states, where apathy reigns, Wyomingites take their right to vote seriously, with turnout during presidential election years sometimes topping 80% of registered voters. Wyoming has 64 elected state representatives (who serve two-year terms) and 30 state senators (elected for four-year terms). The elected statewide officials—governor, secretary of state, auditor, treasurer, and superintendent of public instruction—all stand for office every four years.

Republicans have controlled both houses of the legislature almost since statehood; Wyoming's congressional delegation has long been staunchly Republican, and in 1994, for the first time in nearly two decades, Wyoming voted in a Republican governor. Sierra Clubbers and liberals might want to keep a low profile in most parts of the state.

State Symbols

The Great Seal of the State of Wyoming is filled with symbolism. The two dates commemorate establishment of the territorial government (1869) and statehood (1890). The Roman numerals (XLIV) represent Wyoming as the 44th state to be admitted to the Union; the male figures represent the livestock and mining industries, while the central female figure stands for political equality. In early versions the woman was unclothed, but legislators quickly sensed the problems inherent in nudity on Wyoming's official emblem and rejected the design. After a swath of cloth made everything acceptable, the symbol was finally adopted by the state legislature in 1893. The state flag includes both this symbol and the outline of a bison.

Wyoming's best-known symbol is its bucking horse, a figure that has appeared on state license plates since 1936. The silhouette was created by artist Allen True of Denver and was reputedly inspired by the rodeo cowboy Albert ("Stub") Farlow. The bucking horse insignia had been used earlier by Wyoming soldiers during World War I.

Wyoming has all kinds of other official designations: the state flower (Indian paintbrush), bird (meadowlark), tree (cottonwood), stone (jade), mammal (bison), fossil (knightia, a fish), fish (cutthroat trout), and even a state dinosaur *(Triceratops)*. The state nickname seems to suffer from a split personality, being both "Equality State" and "Cowboy State."

ON THE ROAD

OUTDOOR RECREATION

Wyoming is famous for its great outdoors, with to-the-horizon vistas and an extraordinary variety of activities. The biggest attractions are Yellowstone and Grand Teton National Parks, but other National Park Service, Forest Service, Bureau of Land Management, and state park lands offer an array of adventures, from whitewater rafting to horseback riding to skiing.

Fishing and Hunting

Outstanding fishing opportunities abound throughout Wyoming, and a number of places—mostly in the Yellowstone area—have attained recognition as some of the finest in America. Cutthroat, brown, rainbow, brook, and lake trout are favorites of many anglers, but the state's waters also contain mountain whitefish, kokanee, grayling, channel catfish, smallmouth bass, largemouth bass, and others. Nonresident fishing permits cost $5 for one day, $20 for five days, $30 for 10 days, or $50 for a season. Resident fishing licenses are $9 for the year. Non-

resident youths (ages 14-19) pay $10 for a 10-day permit ($3 for resident youths). Kids under 14 don't need a license if they are with an adult who has a valid fishing license. A $5 conservation stamp is also required of all anglers except non-residents with one-day or five-day licenses and seniors. Get permits at most sporting-goods stores or at Game and Fish Dept. offices. Game and Fish produces an excellent free *Wyoming Fishing Guide,* with descriptions of the various river drainages, what fish you can catch in each, state record fish, and basic information on techniques, access, and maps. Note that the Wind River Indian Reservation and Yellowstone National Park have their own regulations and permits; see the appropriate sections of this book for details.

For detailed fishing and hunting information, contact the Wyoming Game and Fish Department at 5400 Bishop Blvd., Cheyenne, WY 82006, tel. (307) 777-7735 or (800) 842-1934. Report fishing violations and illegal fish stock-

ing by calling (800) 442-4331. Note that Wyoming game laws are enforced with a vengeance, so out-of-state hunters must be sure they know and obey the regulations thoroughly. Access to private land is often available only for a fee, and trespassers are subject to stringent prosecution.

Alpine Skiing
Downhill skiing enthusiasts will be pleased to find developed facilities at 11 different Wyoming locations. The finest are in the Jackson area: Jackson Hole, Grand Targhee, and Snow King. Other ski areas are Snowy Range (west of Laramie), Hogadon (near Casper), Yellowstone Mountain (west of Cody), and Antelope Butte (east of Greybull). More limited facilities can be found at High Park (east of Worland), Pine Creek (east of Cokeville), White Pine Ski Area (near Pinedale; may not be open), and Snowshoe Hollow (near Afton). See the appropriate chapters for descriptions.

Cross-Country Skiing
Skinny-skiers have an overwhelming choice of places to ski in Wyoming. The only developed Nordic areas are located around Jackson Hole, but all of the mountain ranges fill with deep snow and provide inexhaustible opportunities for discovery. See the special topic "Safety in Avalanche Country" for precautions to take while cross-country skiing in the backcountry.

Groomed ski trails are maintained in mountain country all over the state, with notable cross-country ski areas near the following towns: Afton, Buffalo, Casper, Cody, Douglas, Dubois, Encampment, Evanston, Jackson, Lander, Laramie, Pinedale, Saratoga, Sheridan, South Pass, Sundance, and Ten Sleep. In addition, Yellowstone and Grand Teton National Parks have world-class skiing, though the trails are not groomed. See specific chapters for details on all these places.

Snowmobiling
Wyoming has some of the most extensive snowmobile trails in America, covering more than 1,800 miles. The most popular snowmobile areas lie on National Forest lands in the mountains of northwestern Wyoming, and in the Medicine Bow Mountains, the Wind River Range, and the Big Horn Mountains, and the Laramie Range. Best-known is the 360-mile Continental Divide Snowmobile Trail, stretching from Lander around the Wind River Mountains and then north through Grand Teton National Park (this section is quite controversial) to Yellowstone.

Snowmobile trail maps and registration information are available from local visitor centers and the Wyoming Snowmobile Program, 2301 Central Ave., Cheyenne, WY 83002, tel. (307) 777-7550. The brochures can also be found in many visitor centers throughout the state. For trail conditions around the state, call the snowmobile hotline in Cheyenne at (307) 777-6503. See area-specific chapters and sections for snowmobile rental information.

GETTING INTO THE WILDERNESS

To get a real feel for Wyoming, you need to abandon your car, get away from the towns, and head out into the vast undeveloped public lands. Wyoming's most popular backcountry areas are in the Wind River, Medicine Bow, and Big Horn Mountains and the entire northwest corner of the state, including Yellowstone and Grand Teton National Parks. The Yellowstone region contains one of the largest nearly natural ecosystems and some of the most remote country in the Lower 48.

Many campers prefer to use horses for longer trips, but backpacking is very popular on the shorter trails, especially in the Wind River Mountains and the national parks. Backcountry permits are required only within Yellowstone and Grand Teton. It is, however, a good idea to check in at a local Forest Service ranger station to get a copy of the regulations since each place is different in such specifics as how far your tent must be from lakes and trails and whether wood fires are allowed. Be sure to take insect repellent along on any summertime trip since mosquitoes, deerflies, and horseflies can be quite thick, especially in July and early August.

A number of hiking trails, mostly two- or three-day hikes, are described for each of Wyoming's best-known backcountry areas. For more detailed hiking information on Yellowstone, Grand Teton, the Big Horns, or the Wind Rivers, see

STANDING BEAR

We did not think of the great open plains, the beautiful rolling hills, the winding streams with tangled growth as wild. Only to the white man was nature a wilderness, and only to him was the land infested with wild animals and savage people. To us it was tame. Earth was bountiful, and we were surrounded with the blessings of the Great Mystery. Not until the hairy man from the east came, and with his brutal frenzy, heaped injustices upon us and the families we loved, was it wild to us. When the very animals of the forest began fleeing from his approach; then it was that for us, the 'wild west' began.

—Sioux Chief Standing Bear

the Booklist at the end of this book. An overall guide is *The Hiker's Guide to Wyoming,* by Bill Hunger (Falcon Press, Helena, Montana). The National Park Service and the Forest Service can also provide specific trail information.

Horses

For many people, the highlight of a Wyoming vacation is the chance to ride horseback into wild country. Although a few folks bring their own horses, most visitors leave the driving to an expert local outfitter instead. (If you've ever worked around horses in the backcountry, you'll understand why.) Horse packing is an entirely different experience from backpacking. The trade requires years of experience in learning how to properly load horses and mules with panniers, which types of knots to use for different loads, how to keep the packstrings under control, which horses to picket and which to hobble, and how to awaken when the horses decide to head down the trail on hobbles at three in the morning. Add to this a knowledge of bear safety, an ability to keep guests entertained with campfire tales and ribald jokes, a complete vocabulary of horse-cussing terms, and a thorough knowledge of tobacco chew-

ing, and you're still only about 10% of the way to becoming a packer.

Dozens of outfitters are scattered across Wyoming, but you'll find concentrations in the Jackson Hole, Pinedale, Cody, Dubois, Sheridan, and Saratoga areas. For a listing of outfitters in a given region, contact local Forest Service offices. The **Wyoming Outfitters Association,** Box 2284, Cody, WY 82414, tel. (307) 527-7453, has a statewide listing.

Horse and Wagon Tours

A unique way to discover the old West is the not-for-profit **Outlaw Trail Ride** in mid-August. This six-day, 100-mile trip follows the Outlaw Trail from the Hole-in-the-Wall country of Butch Cassidy and the "Wild Bunch" to Thermopolis. You'll need to bring your own horse, bedroll, and gear, but meals are provided for a fee. There is a limit of 100 riders. Call (800) 443-6235 for information.

Great Divide Tours, tel. (800) 458-1915, has Oregon Trail wagon trips, a cattle drive along the Sweetwater River, treks into Hole-in-the-Wall country, and other adventures. More Wild West adventures are offered by **Historic Trail Expeditions,** tel. (307) 266-4868 (in Casper). They lead a wide range of Conestoga wagon and horse trips along the Oregon Trail and even a weeklong cattle drive into Hole-in-the-Wall country. **Trails West,** tel. (307) 332-7801 or (800) 327-4052, offers three-day wagon-train treks from South Pass along the old Oregon Trail. Shorter covered-wagon rides are offered by dude ranches and a number of chuck wagon cookout operations in the Jackson area.

Backcountry Ethics

Wyoming's wilderness areas represent places to escape the crowds, enjoy the beauty and peace of the countryside, and develop an understanding of nature. Unfortunately, as more and more people head into the backcountry, these benefits are becoming endangered. To keep the wild places wild, always practice "no trace" hiking and camping. This means using existing campsites and fire rings, locating your campsite well away from trails and streams, staying on designated trails, not cutting switchbacks, burning only dead and down wood, extinguishing all fires, washing dishes 200 feet from lakes and creeks, digging "catholes" at

least 200 feet from lakes or streams, and hanging all food well above the reach of bears. Your tent site should be 100 yards from the food storage and cooking areas to reduce the likelihood of bear problems. Wood fires are not allowed in many areas, so be sure to bring along a portable gas stove. And, of course, haul your garbage out with you. Burning cans and tinfoil in the fire lessens their weight (and the odors that attract bears), but be sure to pick them out of the fire pit before you depart. And make sure that fire is completely out. For detailed brochures on minimizing your impact and treating the land with respect, call (800) 332-4100.

Trail Etiquette

Because horses are so commonly used in Wyoming, hikers should follow a few rules of courtesy. Horses and mules are not the brightest critters on this planet and can spook at the most inane thing; even a bush blowing in the breeze or a brightly colored hat. Hikers meeting a pack string should move several feet off the trail and not speak loudly or make any sudden moves. If you've ever seen what happens when just one mule in a string decides to act up, you'll appreciate the chaos that can result from sudden noises or movements. Anyone hiking with a dog should keep it well away from the stock and not let it bark. Last of all, never walk close behind a horse, unless you don't mind spending time in a hospital. Their kick is definitely worse than their bite.

Range Etiquette

Wyoming's land-ownership pattern includes many areas where private and public lands are intermingled in a complex checkerboard pattern. This creates all sorts of problems for management of and access to public lands, and for private owners. The conflict is most apparent in grazing country, where many ranchers jealously guard their land from trespassers for any reason. There are places—most notably in the Hole-in-the-Wall country of northeastern Wyoming—where access to public lands is blocked by private landowners who have had problems in the past. A gate left open by a careless visitor or sheep sent running by a barking dog can quickly sour even the most generous rancher. Many of them are living a marginal existence already, so every little problem becomes

magnified, especially if created by a cityslicker—or even worse, a cityslicker with California license plates.

Private boundaries are not always marked by No Trespassing signs, so it's a good idea to use a detailed map (such as those sold at BLM offices throughout the state) to be sure you are walking on public land. This is a particularly big issue during the fall hunting season, when many ranchers require a hefty "trespass fee" for access. If you *do* hunt despite warning signs, don't expect any help from the state, since Game and Fish officers are very supportive of private-property rights. And since we're talking ethical issues, here's some more advice: never ask a rancher how many cattle he has; it's like asking someone how much money he earns.

BACKCOUNTRY SAFETY

Beaver Fever

Although Wyoming's lakes and streams may appear clean, you may be risking a debilitating sickness by drinking the water without treating it first. The protozoan *Giardia lamblia* is found throughout the state, spread by both humans and animals (including beaver). Although the disease is curable with drugs, it's always best to carry safe drinking water on any trip or to boil any water taken from creeks or lakes. Bringing water to a full boil is sufficient to kill Giardia and other harmful organisms. Another option is to use water filters available from backpacking stores. Note, however, that these may not filter out other organisms such as *Campylobactor jejuni*—bacteria that are just 0.2 microns in size. Chlorine and iodine are not always reliable, taste foul, and can be unhealthy.

Giardia lamblia

BEAR COUNTRY

Bears seem to bring out conflicting emotions in people. The first is an almost gut reaction of fear and trepidation: What if the bear attacks me? But then comes that other urge: What will my friends say when they see these great bear photos? Both of these reactions can lead to a multitude of problems in bear country. "Bearanoia" is a justifiable fear but can easily be taken to such an extreme that one avoids going outdoors at all for fear of meeting a bear. The "I want to get close-up shots of that bear and her cubs" attitude can lead to a bear attack. The middle ground incorporates a knowledge of and respect for bears with a sense of caution that keeps you alert for danger without letting fear rule your wilderness travels. Nothing is ever completely safe in this world, but with care you can avoid most of the common pitfalls that lead to bear encounters.

Brown and Black Bears

Old-timers joke that bears are easy to differentiate: a black bear climbs up the tree after you, while a grizzly snaps the tree off at the base. Black bears live in forested areas throughout Wyoming, but grizzlies exist only in Yellowstone National Park and surrounding country. Both grizzlies and black bears pose potential threats to backcountry travelers, although you are considerably more

likely to be involved in a car accident while driving to a wilderness area than you are to be attacked by a bear once you arrive.

Grizzlies once ranged across the entire Northern Hemisphere, from Europe across what is now Russia and through the western half of North America. When whites arrived, there were 50,000-100,000 grizzlies in what would become the Lower 48. Unfortunately, as white settlers arrived, they came to view these massive and powerful creatures (average adult males weigh 500 pounds) as a threat to themselves and their stock. The scientific name, *Ursus arctos horribilis,* says much about human attitudes toward grizzlies. They were shot, trapped, and poisoned nearly to the brink of extinction in the Lower 48, so that today they exist in only a few of the most remote parts of Montana, Wyoming, Idaho, and Washington. By 1975, when the Fish & Wildlife Service listed them as threatened, fewer than 1,000 grizzlies survived south of Canada. Since that time the population appears to have stabilized, with approximately 250 grizzlies in Wyoming's Greater Yellowstone Ecosystem.

Avoiding Bear Hugs

Bear encounters are rare but frightening. Avoid unexpected encounters with bears by letting them know you're there. Most bears hear or smell you long before you realize their presence, and hightail it away. Surprising a bear—especially a sow with cubs—is the last thing you want to do in the backcountry. Before heading out, check at a local ranger station to see whether there have been recent bear encounters. If you discover an animal carcass, be extremely alert since a bear may be nearby and may attack anything that appears to threaten its food. Get away from such areas. Make

(continues on next page)

BOB RACE

BEAR COUNTRY
(continued)

noise in areas of dense cover or when coming around blind spots on trails. Do not hike at night or dusk, when bears can be especially active. If you're unable to see everything around you for at least 50 yards, warn any hidden animals by talking, singing, clapping your hands, tapping a cup, or rattling a can of pebbles. Some people tie bells to their packs for this purpose, while others regard this as an annoyance to fellow hikers. In general, bells are probably of little value since the sound does not carry far, and they may actually serve to attract bears. If you think the bears might not be able to hear you, don't be shy—yell! It might seem a bit foolish, but yelling may prevent an encounter of the furry kind. (Unfortunately, it will probably scare off other animals, so you're not likely to see many critters. And other hikers may not appreciate the noise.) Safety is also in numbers: the more of you hiking together, the more likely a bear is to sense you and stay away.

At the Campsite

Before camping, take a look around the area to see if there are recent bear tracks or scat and to make sure you're not on a game trail. If possible, camp near a climbable tree. Bears are attracted to odors of all sorts including food, horse feed, soap, toothpaste, perfume, deodorants, and sexual smells. Keep your campsite clean and avoid such smelly foods as tuna, ham, sausage, and bacon; freeze-dried food is light and relatively odorless (though also tasteless). Store food in airtight containers or several layers of plastic bags, and be sure to hang all food and other items that bears may smell at least 12 feet off the ground and four feet from tree trunks. Bring 50 feet of rope for this purpose. Tie two cups or pots to it so you will hear if it's moved. Some Forest Service and Park Service wilderness areas provide food storage poles

at campsites. In the Teton and Bridger Wilderness Areas you can also rent bear-resistant backpacker food tubes or horse panniers from Forest Service offices. Camping stores in Jackson, Cody, and elsewhere sell similar containers. Your cooking, eating, and food storage area should be at least 50 yards away from your tent. Women should be especially cautious during their menstrual periods. Used tampons should be stored double-bagged in air-tight containers and packed out with all other garbage.

Encounters of the Furry Kind

Hunters and photographers are the main recipients of bear hugs. Never under any circumstances approach a bear, even if it appears to be asleep. Move off quickly if you see bear cubs, especially if one comes toward you—Mom is almost always close by. Dogs create dangerous situations by barking and exciting bears—leave yours at home. And, of course, never leave food around for bears. Not only is this illegal, but it also trains the bears to associate people with free food. Fed bears become garbage bears, and wildlife officials are eventually forced to destroy them. Remember, bears are dangerous wild animals. This is *their* country, not a zoo. By going in you accept the risk—and thrill—of meeting a bear.

If you do happen to encounter a bear and it sees you, try to stay calm and not make any sudden moves. Do not run, since you could not possibly outrun a bear; they can exceed 40 mph for short distances. If a good-sized tree is nearby, climb it as high as you can with safety and stay there until you're certain that the bear has left the area. If no tree is close, your best bet is to back slowly away. Sometimes dropping an item such as a hat or jacket will distract the bear, and talking also seems to have some value in convincing bears that you're a human. If the bear sniffs

the air, or stands on its hind legs, it is probably trying to identify you. When it does, it will usually run away. If a bear woofs and postures, don't imitate—this is a challenge. Keep retreating. Most bear charges are also bluffs; the bear will often stop short and amble off.

If a *grizzly* bear does attack, hold your ground and freeze. It may well be a bluff charge, with the bear halting at the last second. If the bear does not stop its attack, curl up face-down on the ground in a fetal position with your hands wrapped behind your neck and your elbows tucked over your face. Your backpack may help protect you somewhat. Remain still even if you are attacked, since sudden movements may incite further attacks. It takes a lot of courage to do this, but often a bear will only sniff or nip you and leave. The injury you might sustain would be far less than if you had tried to resist.

Many bear authorities now recommend against dropping to the ground if you are attacked by a *black* bear, since they tend to be more aggressive in such situations. If a black bear attacks, fight back with whatever weapons are at hand; large rocks and branches can be surprisingly effective deterrents. (This, of course, assumes you can tell black bears from brown bears. If you can't, have someone who knows—such as a park ranger—explain the differences before you head into the backcountry.) In the rare event of a night attack in your tent, defend yourself very aggressively. Do not play dead under such circumstances, since the bear probably views you as prey, and may give up if you make it a fight.

Protecting Yourself

Recently, cayenne pepper sprays such as "Counter Assault" (available in camping stores) have sometimes proven useful in fending off bear attacks. These "bear mace" sprays are effective only at close range. This is particularly true in open country where winds quickly disperse the spray or may blow it back in your own face. Another problem with bear mace is that you cannot carry it aboard commercial jets due to the obvious dangers should a canister explode. Though they *are* better than nothing, pepper sprays are not a cure-all or a replacement for caution in bear country. It's far better to avoid bear confrontations in the first place.

Hypothermia

Anyone who has spent much time in the outdoors knows the dangers of exposure to cold, wet, and windy conditions. Even at temperatures well above freezing, hypothermia—the reduction of the body's inner core temperature—can prove fatal. In the early stages, hypothermia causes uncontrollable shivering, followed by a loss of coordination, slurred speech, and then a rapid descent into unconsciousness and death. Always travel prepared for sudden changes in the weather. Wear clothing that insulates well and that holds its heat when wet. Wool and polypro are far better than cotton, and clothes should be worn in layers to provide better trapping of heat and a chance to adjust to conditions more easily. Always carry a wool hat, since your head loses more heat than any other part of the body. Bring a waterproof shell to cut the wind.

If someone in your party begins to show signs of hypothermia, don't take any chances—even if the person denies needing help. Get the victim out of the wind, strip off his clothes, and put him in a dry sleeping bag on an insulating pad. Skin-to-skin contact is the best way to warm a hypothermic person, and that means you'll also need to strip and climb in the sleeping bag. If you weren't friends before, this should heat up the relationship! Do not give the victim alcohol or hot drinks, and do not try to warm the person too quickly—it could lead to heart failure. Once the victim has recovered, get medical help as soon as possible.

Actually, though, you're far better off keeping close tabs on everyone in the group and seeking shelter *before* exhaustion and hypothermia set in.

ACCOMMODATIONS AND FOOD

LODGING CHOICES

Lodging in Wyoming covers the complete spectrum, from the very finest of luxury accommodations where a king would feel pampered, all the way down to flophouses so tawdry that even town drunks think twice. In general, visitors will find motel prices considerably lower than what they might pay in other parts of America. This is especially true in the smaller towns and places where the economy is weak. During the summer, rates at the mom-and-pop motels that line the streets of every Wyoming town start around $25 for one person and $30 for two people. Tack on another $5-10 for slightly fancier places with the AAA sign out front. Come wintertime, rates may drop 25% or more. In general, visitors will be very pleased with Wyoming motels. The low rates reflect a less-expensive economy, not shoddy conditions. Don't be scared off by a price that seems too low by New York standards!

The exception to these low rates is the northwest corner of the state—notably Cody and most egregiously Jackson. During peak summer or winter season in Jackson Hole, only a few places are less than $60 s or d. Also beware that rates for Cheyenne motel and hotel rooms skyrocket during Cheyenne Frontier Days (late July). Motel prices have a way of changing even in a given day. The law of supply and demand holds, and many owners raise prices as the evening progresses and the rooms start to fill up, when a convention comes to town, and on weekends.

For a complete listing of motels, hotels, bed and breakfasts, dude ranches, and camping places in Wyoming, request a copy of the free **Wyoming Accommodations Directory** from the Wyoming Division of Tourism and State Marketing, I-25 at College Dr., Cheyenne, WY 82002, tel. (307) 777-7777 or (800) 225-5996. The booklet lists lodging and campgrounds in every part of the state.

Throughout this book I have listed only two prices for most lodging places: single, or s (one person), and double, or d (two people in one bed). The lodging charts list peak-season prices and are arranged from least to most expensive. These prices are not set in concrete and will certainly head up over time. If a convention is in town or the motel is nearly full, they may rise; if the economy is tight, or if it's the off-season at a seasonal area, you may pay considerably less. Always ask to see the room before deciding to stay at one of the less-expensive motels—places that I consider more than adequate may be beneath your standards. If in doubt, you may want to choose one that gets the American Automobile Association seal of approval. The annual **TourBook** for Idaho, Montana, and Wyoming (free to AAA members) is a helpful guide to the better hotels and motels, offering current prices and accurate ratings. Members often get discounts on rates.

Hotels

Most of the historic hotels that once offered lodging for weary Wyoming travelers have either fallen to the wrecking ball or have been turned into residence flophouses. Only a few of these gems have been restored to their glory; they include Cheyenne's Plains Hotel, Cody's Irma Hotel, Jackson's Wort Hotel, and Saratoga's Wolf Hotel. Other interesting historic hotels that may or may not be up to your standards include Medicine Bow's Virginian Hotel and the Elk Mountain Hotel in the town of Elk Mountain. Yellowstone National Park offers some of the finest old-time luxury accommodations anywhere in America: Old Faithful Inn, Lake Hotel, and Mammoth Hot Springs Hotel. Of these, Old Faithful Inn is in a category all its own, and is perhaps the grandest hotel in any American national park. Don't miss this one!

Motels

The various motel chains—Best Western, Days Inn, Holiday Inn, La Quinta, Motel 6, and Super 8—all operate motels across the state, primarily in the larger towns. These cinder block monuments to the bigger-is-better school of lodging stand on the edges of towns, their towering

signs glaring eyesores (but visible at 75 mph from the freeway). Each chain publishes its own brochure listing locations and rates. Pick up a copy at a chain motel near your home or call their toll-free numbers.

If you're staying with the pricier chains, always be sure to ask about the sometimes substantial discounts such as AAA-member rates, senior discounts, corporate or government rates, business travel fares, military rates, or other special deals. Try not to take the first rate quoted at these places, especially if you're calling their 800 number; these "rack rates" are what they charge if they can get away with it. You may also get better prices sometimes by bargaining with clerks who are more likely to be able to dicker over price than the toll-free operators who are sitting in Alabama. Of course, if it's a big convention or festival weekend, you may have no choice. Note that the "free continental breakfast" offered at many of the big chain motels can be pretty meager, often just a pile of doughnuts and a pot of coffee.

Every town in Wyoming has its locally owned small motels, often run by an elderly woman with a yip-dog slightly larger than a small shrew (but twice as feisty). These motels vary widely in quality and price but tend to offer the best rates and friendliest service.

If you don't smoke and can't stand the stench of tobacco in motel rooms, be sure to ask about non-smoking rooms; many motels have them, though they may cost a few bucks more. Also, take a look around the motel to see if the railroad or a busy highway lies next door. If so, try to get a room on the opposite side of the motel, or prepare to put in earplugs. Another thing to watch for is the checkout time; at some places it's as early as 10 a.m.

Bed and Breakfasts

Bed and breakfasts are a relatively recent addition to Wyoming's lodging picture but more are appearing each year. These range from remote places where the accommodations are not unlike those at a guest ranch to historic Victorian homes in the center of town. Some of the best are found in Big Horn, Buffalo, Cheyenne, Cody, Douglas, Dubois, Jackson Hole, Lander, Laramie, Rawlins, Saratoga, and Wheatland. Get a detailed brochure listing many of the

state's B&Bs by writing to **Wyoming Homestay & Outdoor Adventures (WHOA),** 1031 Steinle Rd., Douglas, WY 82633.

A few of Wyoming's B&Bs don't allow kids and almost none allow pets or smoking inside. Most guest rooms have private baths, and if they don't one is probably just a few steps away. Bed and breakfasts, favorites of 30- and 40-something professional couples, are a fine way to get acquainted with a new area—a good choice if you're traveling alone, since you'll have opportunities to meet fellow travelers in the library, over tea, and at breakfast. Note, however, that often the single person rate differs little if at all from the price for couples.

One problem with B&Bs is that they sometimes get a bit too homey and lack the privacy afforded by motels. I've been in some where the owner sits by your table in the morning, feeling it his duty to hold a conversation. This may be fine sometimes, especially if you want to learn more about the local area, but it's not so great if you're looking for a romantic place or you just want to read the newspaper in peace. In some places the intense personal attention and strict rules (no hard-soled shoes, no noise after 10 p.m., and so on) get a bit much, making you feel less a guest than an intruder. In others, hosts serve breakfast at precisely 8 a.m. and guests who sleep in miss out. Other B&Bs are more flexible, and some even offer separate cottages or suites for honeymooners seeking privacy.

Dude Ranches

An old and respected Western tradition is the dude ranch, which began as a sideline to the business of raising cattle. Friends from back east would remember old Jake out there in wild Wyoming, where the buffalo roam and the antelope play, and would decide it was time for a visit. So off they would head, living in the rancher's outbuildings and joining in the chores. The "dudes," as they became known, soon told their friends, and Jake found his ranch inundated. After a couple of years of this the next step was obvious: get those eastern rascals to fork over some cash for the privilege of visiting. Pretty soon the dude ranching business was born. At its peak in the 1920s, dude ranching spread through much of Wyoming and the West. Dude

ranching saved many cattle ranches from extinction by providing a second source of income and simultaneously brought these magnificent lands to the attention of people who had the money to prevent their development (most notably Grand Teton National Park).

At the older ranches, generations of families have returned year after year to vacation in the "Wild West." Many dude ranches now call themselves guest ranches, a term that reflects both the suspicious way some people view the word "dude" and the changing nature of the business. Many city folks today lack the desire or skill to actually saddle up their own horses, much less push cattle between pastures. As a result, guest/dude ranches tend to emphasize grand scenery, horseback riding—the centerpiece of nearly every ranch—campfires, hearty meals, chuck wagon cookouts, sing-alongs, and evenings around the fireplace. Some folks even camp overnight out there in the fearful wilderness, where the coyotes howl and the mice chew into your stash of potato chips. A few ranches still offer the chance to join in on such activities as cattle drives, branding, pregnancy testing, shot-giving, calving, and roundups. For some folks it's a great chance to learn about the real West; others view it as paying good money to work as a cowhand.

Wyoming has literally dozens of dude ranches and ranch resorts offering accommodations ranging from spartan to so sumptuous that they bear absolutely no resemblance to ranch life. Not all dude

ranches are created equal—some are slick and modern with tennis courts and hot tubs while others are funky and old-fashioned with delightful rough edges. Dudes normally sleep in log cabins. Conditions inside can vary widely, but don't expect TVs or phones in the rooms. The cabins are usually located near a central lodge where meals are served family style. Many also have big libraries and outdoor games such as volleyball and horseshoes. Fishing and photography are other big attractions.

Dude ranch rates generally cost around $850-1,100 per person per week double occupancy, less for kids, surcharges for those staying by themselves. The price includes all meals, lodging, and horseback rides, but you'll usually pay more for features such as airport shuttles, rafting trips, guided fishing, beer and wine, or backcountry pack trips, not to mention local taxes and tips. The fanciest resorts, such as Lost Creek Ranch in Jackson Hole or Vee Bar Guest Ranch near Laramie, will set you back over $1,800 per person per week. Many guest ranches offer discounted rates in early June and late September, and for repeat guests. Some also have special adults-only weeks. Most require that you stay a week, or at least three nights, though a few places offer overnight accommodations. To really get into the comfortably slow pace of ranch life, try to set aside at least a week. Ask plenty of questions before you visit, such as what activities are available, what to bring in the

Horseback riding is a popular activity at many dude ranches.

CATHY CARLSON

way of clothing, what sort of meals to [...]
(vegetarians may have a hard time on [...]
ranches), whether there are additional cha[...]
whether they accept credit cards (many do[...]
what the living accommodations are like, a[...]
how many other guests will likely be there a[...]
the same time—some house up to 125, others
fewer than a dozen. Upon request the better
ranches will provide lists of references from previous clients. Note that it is considered proper to
tip the ranch hands, kitchen help, and others
who work hard to keep the ranch running; the
standard total is 10-15% of your bill. For many of
them, this is a way to fund their college education (or buy a winter in Belize).

An excellent source of detailed information
about guest ranches in Wyoming (and elsewhere) is *Kilgore's Ranch Vacations*, by Eugene Kilgore (Santa Fe: John Muir Publications).
The **Dude Ranchers' Association** was formed
in 1926 and includes only the most established
and authentic dude ranches in the nation. Call
(970) 223-8440 to request a copy of their magazine ($5) listing member ranches throughout
the West, including 33 in Wyoming.

CAMPING

Wyoming has dozens of public campsites scattered across the state, primarily on Forest Service and Park Service lands and in state parks.
Most of these have potable running water,
garbage pick-up, and outhouses but no showers.
The fee is generally $5-9 per night, and most are
open from early June to mid-September. After
that, many of the campgrounds remain open
(no charge) but do not have garbage pick-up
or running water. There is a 14-day limit on
camping at any site, so don't plan on moving
in permanently. It's generally legal to camp for
free on undeveloped Forest Service or BLM
land throughout the state, but check with local offices for any restrictions.

Many Forest Service campgrounds are now
on a reservation system; for an extra service
charge of $8.25 you can reserve a site up to a
year in advance. Call (800) 280-2267 for details. Budget cutbacks have forced the Forest
Service and Park Service to contract out the
management of many campgrounds. The ef-

Wyoming is [...] wn for its haute cuisine. This is c[...] ntry, the land of the free
and the home o[...] range, where juicy steaks
and the finest prime rib can be found in every
Podunk town in the state. (The two best steak
houses may well be in the don't-blink-or-you'll-
miss-it town of Hudson.) If you don't like that, try

dating no-smoking sections so if you don't enjoy a dose of cigarette smoke with your food you may just be out of luck.

...Wash
...k for a big
...t's pretty much
...accompanied by a
...these parts call coffee.
...ee, made only over an open
...d not available within 20 miles of
...en, is a potent medicine, not advised for
...en or the weak-kneed. Check local outfitters for the prescription.

Unfortunately, in Wyoming—as in the rest of the nation—the real dining-out kings are Mc-Donald's, Wendy's, Domino's, Dairy Queen, and all the other fast-food outlets that are turning regional differences into a bland mediocrity of frozen burgers and whipped-shortening "milk shakes." For Mexican fare, many locals head to the appropriately named Taco John's, a Wyoming chain that is—unfortunately—now being unleashed on other parts of the West.

Actually, Wyoming food is not quite as uni-formly bland as might be imagined, and travelers will discover several innovative and surprising-ly reasonable restaurants in Laramie, Jackson, Cody, and Dubois; fine Mexican eateries in Rawlins and Cheyenne; authentic Chinese food in Cheyenne and Casper; and nouvelle cuisine restaurants scattered around the state. The most creative (and pricey) food can probably be found in the tourist town of Jackson and the college town of Laramie. One more note about Wyoming restaurants: they can be quite smoky. In many towns there are no regulations man-

On the Town

No man, woman, or child should let a day pass without drinking a good glass of beer. Beer is an article of food and nourishing as bread if it is pure and free from adulter-ation.

—1892 ad for the Green River Brewery

In many Wyoming towns, drinking and carousing hold as much interest as eating, especially on Friday and Saturday nights. Every burg of any size has its resident country and western band, and saloon dance floors fill with duded-up cow-boys and cowgirls out for a night on the town. Many of these bands also play Eagles-style rock tunes for variety. The larger cities and tourist towns have several nightclubs, some with disc jockeys, others with basic rock and roll fare. Don't expect a steep cover charge to get in the door—most places are free.

In the last few years breweries and brew-pubs have begun to spread across Wyoming. Otto Brothers Brewery in Jackson Hole was the first, but at last count nine different places had opened in Buffalo, Jackson, Laramie, Lander, Sheridan, Gillette, and Cheyenne. A number of other startups are in the works, so look for new pubs soon in other towns, especially tourist towns such as Pinedale, Saratoga, and Cody.

EVENTS AND ACTIVITIES

During the summer months, every town in Wyoming has its own main event, generally centered on a morning parade, an afternoon rodeo, and an evening of country music and dancing. Rodeos are the definitive Wyoming activity, reflecting an enduring nostalgia for cat-tle and cowboys. Daily summertime rodeos can be found in Cody and Jackson, and twice-week-ly rodeos in Laramie and Casper. Riverton has weekly rodeos in the summer. Informal roping events go on all summer long around the state; ask locally for times. See "Rodeo Today," below, for more details.

Wyoming's most famous event is **Cheyenne Frontier Days**, a 10-day bash that fills every hotel for a hundred miles and makes Cheyenne streets look like a miniature Los Angeles. It starts the last full week of July each year. The centerpiece of Frontier Days is, of course, the rodeo, which at-tracts the nation's finest riders, but there are also parades, pancake feeds, art exhibits, and much more. Don't miss this one! The **Cody Stampede** (early July) is another very popular rodeo, pa-rade, and all-round chance to party. The **PRCA Rodeo Finals**—Wyoming's largest indoor rodeo—comes to Casper each October.

Tastes of History

The **Gift of the Waters Pageant** arrives in Thermopolis in early August. It celebrates Chief Washakie's gift of this wonderful hot spring to the federal government to be used by all people. *The Legend of Rawhide,* an outdoor play held each July since 1947, has a cast that seems to include half the town of Lusk. The story is based on the 1849 killing of a Sioux girl by a white gold-seeker and the Indians' retaliatory skinning-alive of the protagonist, hence the name.

For a more sanguine view of life in the early days, visit one of the many mountain-man rendezvous held around the state. The biggest and best are the **Fort Bridger Rendezvous,** held each Labor Day, and Pinedale's **Green River Rendezvous** in July. Also of note are those in Lander (early June), Riverton (early July), and Jackson (mid-July). A good time is had by all in an authentic and picturesque setting. (See below for more on rendezvous.)

Wyoming's largest powwows are the **Plains Indian Powwow** in Cody each June, Fort Washakie's **Eastern Shoshone Powwow and Rodeo** in early July, and the **Labor Day Powwow** in Arapahoe.

Other Events

Thousands of people flood the tiny settlement of Encampment for the **Woodchopper's Jamboree** in late June. Another big attraction is the **Wyoming State Fair,** held in Douglas during mid-August. County fairs are held in each of Wyoming's 23 counties during the summer. Casper's biggest event is the **Central Wyoming Fair and Rodeo** in early August.

Jackson Hole has a number of popular events through the year including the highly acclaimed **Grand Teton Music Festival** in July and the **Fall Arts Festival,** which attracts entries from all over the world. Jackson's annual **Elk Antler Auction** in late May attracts aphrodisiac (!) buyers from all over the globe. For something completely different, head to Chugwater in late June for the **Chugwater Chili Cook-off.** Bring along a bottle of Maalox.

All of these events—and many more—are described in greater detail in appropriate sections of this book. For a complete calendar of Wyoming events, contact the Wyoming Division of Tourism and State Marketing, I-25 at College Dr., Cheyenne, WY 82002, tel. (307) 777-7777 or (800) 225-5996.

MODERN-DAY RENDEZVOUS

In recent years, mountain-man rendezvous have become major summertime attractions in Wyoming. These are rather strange affairs, attracting both tourists and locals to gawk at guys in buckskin pants or breechcloths and women in tanned leather skirts. Unlike the original rendezvous, you won't see many Indians at these get-togethers. The participants are a mixture of Joe Blow Businessman who likes a little diversion, Wendy Waitress who dreams of simpler times, and a lot of folks who look like they're either Deadheads or Hell's Angels and find this a great way to live the simple life in a semi-legitimate way. More long hair, beards, braless women, and barefoot kids than you've seen in two decades.

Participants live in tepees, bake bread over fires, race horses bareback, and mug for tourists' clicking cameras. Lots of beef jerky, Indian tacos, and fry bread for sale. This isn't a good place for the animal-rights crowd, since many of the trade items at the modern rendezvous (as at the original ones) come from wild animals. Most of the people who attend rendezvous have something to offer: old beads, leather clothing, tomahawks, knives, moccasins, woven crafts, tanned hides, and lots of fox, coyote, rabbit, ermine, and other furs.

Events at rendezvous include black-powder shooting contests, storytelling, fiddle music, dancing, hide-tanning demonstrations, tomahawk and knife throwing, and footraces for the kids. In the evening, when all the gawkers head back to their air-conditioned motel rooms, the rendezvous really come to life with big campfires, more storytelling, carousing, drinking, and a raucous good time for all. But woe to the visitor who shows up after dark in modern-day civilian clothes!

RODEO

Sometimes I think life is just a rodeo. The trick is to ride and make it to the bell...

—*John Fogerty*

It may come as a revelation to many, but rodeo—in Wyoming, always pronounced "ROE-dee-oh"—is one of the most popular sports in America; more people watch professional rodeos than attend NFL football games! In Wyoming, where even the license plate is graced with a cowboy astride a bucking bronc, it's no surprise that rodeo is king. Every small town in the state has a rodeo of some sort during the summer, and the larger cities have world-class rodeos that attract hundreds of riders and ropers from the Professional Rodeo Cowboys Association (PRCA).

TODD CLARK

History

Although rodeo seems to have a few drops of the Spanish bullfight in its blood, and while many of the words—rodeo, bronco, lariat, arena, and honda—have Spanish origins, rodeo's true genesis was in the days of cowboys and cattle in the Wild West. Gradually, groups of cowboys got together to show off their riding and roping skills and to compete with neighboring outfits. Everyone argues over the official origin of rodeo, but credit is generally given to a bucking and roping competition between the Mill Iron and Hash Knife outfits who met near Deer Trail, Colorado, in 1869.

As the West began to be fenced in, the cowboy events moved into the nearby towns as organized "buckin' shows." Buffalo Bill Cody probably had more to do with popularizing the sport than any other person. For many years his Wild West Show traveled the world, providing a spectacle that included several of the events in present-day rodeos. Lander lays claim to the oldest rodeo in Wyoming; begun in 1893, the Lander Pioneer Days rodeo still comes around each July. By far the most famous Wyoming rodeo, the "Daddy of 'em All," is the Cheyenne Frontier Days, one of the top four rodeos in the world.

Rodeo Today

Over the years, rodeo has become more professional and less connected to the true cowboy. Many participants today come from cities and have never spent time herding cattle or working on a ranch; some of the finest have come from Harlem and the Bronx. Of course, many other cowboys still come from more traditional farming and ranching backgrounds, though they may work part-time at the local grocery store to fund their travels on the rodeo circuit. When they get enough money, they attend a weeklong rodeo school to pick up pointers from past champions.

Those who make it to the top do so the hard way. Grand Nationals winners are decided on the basis of rodeo earnings, which means that cowboys must compete almost continuously, flying from one rodeo to another and staying in cheap motels or living out of their RVs. Semipros and amateurs compete in the hundreds of smaller rodeos that dot Wyoming and the West, hoping to make it to the professional level. Most don't even come close, losing their stiff entry fees to more experienced competitors and taking home only bruises or broken bones.

The major rodeo events generally fall into two categories—riding and roping. Riding events include saddle bronc riding, bareback bronc riding, and bull riding; roping events include steer wrestling, calf roping, and steer roping. Women's barrel racing, clown bullfighting, and chuck wagon races complete the roundup. In most of the events, luck has much to do with who wins. Much of the scoring is based on the difficulty of the ride; consequently, the toughest broncs or bulls are favorites because they mean higher scores. Times for ropers depend upon the speed and behavior of the calf or steer they're trying to tackle.

Many rodeo riders are young, skinny-as-a-rail types, but ropers tend to be bulkier and older. The two groups don't mix much and generally have disparaging words to say about the "skinny cowboys on their rocking horses" or "those fat bulldoggers with no style and no skill."

But behind this bluster lies respect—and even more for competitors in a cowboy's own events. Hang around the chutes awhile and you'll discover a surprising generosity among fellow riders and ropers as they warn what to expect from a given bronc, help cinch down the straps, and joke over the new shiner from the horseshoe firmly planted in the bareback rider's face. They party together late into the night, looking for the rodeo queens and girls who like the smell of horse sweat. Small-time winners often spread the loot back among the losers, buying drinks and renting a motel room where everyone can sneak in for a night's rest. In *Rodeo! The Suicide Sport,* writer Fred Schnell tells a story that seems to epitomize rodeo life:

> *Once, when rodeo announcer Mel Lambert explained to the audience that a champion who had just made a good ride neither drank nor smoked and was a college athlete, Jim Shoulders, who has won 16 world titles, turned to a friend behind the chutes and said disgustedly, "Isn't that the worst crap you've ever heard? What the hell is rodeo coming to?"*

One thing newcomers soon notice about rodeo cowboys is the clothes they wear—long-sleeve shirts, cowboy hats, Wrangler jeans (never Levi's—the seam is in the wrong place for riding), and cowboy boots. As writer Mary S. Robertson noted, "In no other sport but rodeo do the players and the spectators dress alike." Interestingly, the PRCA actually has a rule requiring long-sleeve shirts and cowboy hats; apparently at one time too many riders and ropers were wearing baseball caps and T-shirts, so the more traditional attire was made mandatory. And, of course, there is one additional piece of attire worn by rodeo cowboys: the plate-sized silver and gold belt buckles. Top winners get these as awards for surviving a season of abuse; others buy them for flash and dash.

The Suicide Sport

A title occasionally used for rodeo is "the suicide sport." It is, unfortunately, all too true. Accidents are very common and rodeos always have an EMT ready to tend to the inevitable smashed legs, kicked-in ribs, and broken collarbones.

Many cowboys are crippled for life and at least several die each year in the sport, including two at Cheyenne Frontier Days in the 1980s. Even the nation's top riders and ropers can be killed. Most dangerous of all are the bull rides, but just watching a "dogger" leaping off his horse onto the horns of a speeding steer can give the crowd pause. Rodeos are criticized by animal-rights activists as unnecessarily cruel to animals—steers occasionally die from broken necks and broncs sometimes injure themselves (and their riders) by trying to jump out of the chutes—but the cowboys really do all they can to prevent injury to the animals they ride or rope.

Steer Wrestling

Steer wrestling, or bulldogging, involves leaping from a quarter horse onto the back of a 700-pound Mexican steer running at 25 miles an hour, grabbing his horns, and wrestling him to the ground. If you think that sounds easy, try it some time! Steer wrestling originated in 1903, when Bill Pickett, a black Texas cowboy (many early cowboys were black), jumped on the back of an ornery steer, grabbed its horns, bent over its head and bit the steer's lower lip like an attacking bulldog. Soon he was repeating the stunt for the 101 Ranch Wild West Show. Others copied this feat, and though the lip-biting part has long since disappeared, the name bulldogging has stuck.

Steer wrestling is a complex endeavor involving two men: a dogger and a hazer. When the steer hurtles into the arena, the two spur their horses in quick pursuit, with the hazer trying to force the steer to run straight ahead while the dogger gets into position to leap onto the steer's horns and wrestle him to the ground with his feet and head facing the same direction. Since they are competing with other doggers on time, every second counts. Good doggers can get a steer down in less than seven seconds.

Calf Roping

Calf roping originated in the Old West when ropers would pull down a calf and quickly tie it up for branding. Today, this is the most competitive of all rodeo events, and there is often big money for the winners. Calf ropers chase a 300-pound

calf on their expertly trained horses, rope it, and then quickly throw it on its side. The piggin' string is wrapped around three ankles and secured with a half-hitch ("hooey"), and then the calf is allowed to try to break free. If it can't within six seconds, the time stands and an untie man rides in to free the calf. Time is of the essence in calf roping, and a roper's horse is his most valuable asset. The best horses are in high demand and are often rented to other riders for a cut of any winnings.

Steer Roping

The most controversial of all rodeo contests is steer roping, an event banned from most rodeos because it is so hard on the animals. Cheyenne Frontier Days is one place where you can still see it. The procedure is essentially the same as calf roping, but with a much larger animal. When the 700-pound steer is jerked back by the rope and then thrown down with a thud, you can almost feel the impact. Fortunately, injuries to the tough old steers are uncommon.

Saddle Bronc Riding

When you say the word "rodeo," many people immediately think of saddle bronc riding. The oldest of all rodeo sports, it originated in cowboys' attempts to train wild horses. Rodeo saddle bronc riding is more complex than this, however; it requires a special "association" saddle and dulled spurs, and is played by very precise rules. It is a judged event, with points taken away for not being in the correct position or in control. The bronc is saddled up in the chute (a fenced-in enclosure along the edge of the arena) and the rider climbs on, grabbing a thick hemp rope in one hand and sinking his boots into the stirrups. When the gate opens the bronc goes wild, trying to throw the rider off. The smooth back-and-forth motion of a good saddle bronc rider makes it appear that he is atop a rocking chair. Rides only last eight seconds (leading to lots of ribald cowboy jokes); when the horn sounds, a pick-up man rides alongside the bronc and the rider slides onto the other horse.

Bareback Bronc Riding

Bareback riding is a relatively recent sport, having arrived on the scene in the 1920s. The rules are similar to those for saddle bronc riding but

the cowboy rides with a minimum of equipment—no stirrups and no reins. A small leather rigging held on by a leather strap around the horse is topped with a suitcase-like handle. A second wool-lined strap goes around the flank of the horse to act as an irritant so that he bucks more. The cowboy holds on with one hand and bounces back and forth in a rocking motion, an effort akin to trying to juggle bowling pins while surfing a big wave. Eight seconds later it's over and a pick-up man comes in to rescue the rider—if he hasn't been thrown to the ground.

Bull Riding and Rodeo Clowns

Bull riding is in a class of danger all its own. Unlike broncs, which just want that man off their back, bulls want to get even. When a bull rider is thrown off (and this is most of the time, even with the best riders), the bull immediately goes on the attack, trying to gore or trample him. Many bull riders are seriously injured and some die when hit by this 2,000 pounds of brute force. There are no saddles in bull riding, just a piece of thick rope wrapped around the bull's chest, the free end wrapped tightly around the rider's hand. A cowbell hangs at the bottom of this contraption to annoy the bull even more. When the chute opens, all hell breaks loose as the bull does everything it possibly can to throw his rider off—spinning, kicking, jumping, and running against the fence.

If the rider hangs on for the required eight seconds (style isn't very important), the next battle begins—getting out of the way of one very angry bull. Here the rodeo clowns come in. Dressed in bright red-and-white shirts and baggy pants, they look like human Raggedy Andy dolls. In reality they are moving targets. Clowns use every trick in the book—climbing into padded barrels that the bulls butt against, weaving across the arena, mocking the bulls with matador capes, and simply running for their lives to reach the fence ahead of the bull. Frequently, two clowns work in tandem to create confusion, one acting as the barrel man and the other as a roving target. The rodeo clown also plays another role, that of entertainer between events. A clown's stock of supplies includes rubber chickens, trick mules, pantomime jokes with the announcer, and anything else that might keep folks from getting restless.

In a few of the larger rodeos there are clown "bullfights" in which a clown is pitted against a bull in a specially constructed small arena. He taunts the bull in every possible way, running past and around him, touching him, and maybe even leaping over him—all the while trying to stay out of the way of those horns and hooves. These last only 45 seconds, but that seems like an eternity of danger. No wonder they call this the suicide sport!

Other Events

One of the funniest of all rodeo events is the **wild horse race,** a zany event that since 1897 has ended each day at Cheyenne Frontier Days. Twelve teams of three cowboys try to rope, saddle, and then race a collection of the wildest horses imaginable. If they manage to get on the broncs, their next problem is convincing the horses to run around the half-mile track in the right direction. It seems the definition of bedlam, with horses breaking loose and starting off in opposite directions, crashing into mounted riders and other horses. For sheer chaos, wild horse races would even put a Democratic Convention to shame!

Another crowd favorite at Frontier Days is the **chuck wagon race,** a Canadian invention with mostly Canadian teams. It is a confusing, fast-paced, chaotic, noisy, and dusty sport that involves four wagons, each pulled by four horses. Each team also has two "outriders," boys on horseback. At the sound of the starting gun, an outrider throws a 50-pound "cookstove" into the back of the chuck wagon and climbs back on his horse to chase the wagons. Then everyone takes off on a tight figure-eight course around several barrels and onto the half-mile circular track. The outriders ride in pursuit; they must cross the finish line near their chuck wagons. Needless to say, with four wagons pulled by 16 horses running at a full gallop and another eight horses running alongside, the race is both exciting and dangerous. When the wagons come around the last corner, the spectators in the stands are all on their feet, yelling and cheering.

Barrel racing—one of the only female-dominated events—is found at nearly every rodeo and consists of a triangular course around three barrels arranged a hundred feet apart. The event requires riding a fast horse in a set pattern around these barrels, trying not to knock any over. The fastest time wins.

Some rodeos also have what is called a **calf scramble**—featuring dozens of children from the stands chasing a calf to get a ribbon off its tail—and a **colt race,** in which young colts are let loose in a race toward their mares. Both are real crowd pleasers.

INFORMATION AND SERVICES

INFORMATION SOURCES

Chamber of commerce information centers are described for each town in this book. Large **state information centers** are located near Cheyenne, Evanston, Jackson, Laramie, Pine Bluffs, Sheridan, and Sundance. The telephone **area code** for all of Wyoming is 307. Throughout this book, summer is defined as Memorial Day weekend (the fourth weekend of May) to Labor Day (the first weekend of September)—except when otherwise noted.

For a helpful overall guide to Wyoming, along with a listing of events, chamber of commerce offices, and lodging and camping places, request a copy of the free *Wyoming Vacation Di-* *rectory* from the Wyoming Division of Tourism and State Marketing, I-25 at College Dr., Cheyenne, WY 82002, tel. (307) 777-7777 or (800) 225-5996. Both summer and winter versions are available. They also have free **state maps,** or pick them up at any local visitor center. A great way to check the pulse of Wyoming is to read the letters to the editor in the *Casper Star-Tribune,* the state's major paper. They fill several pages every day and are sometimes quite amusing.

On the Radio

If you like country and western music, you'll love traveling through Wyoming, where the radio dial is filled with country stations playing mournful songs about leaving small towns for greener

BEST OF WYOMING

I t isn't just the spectaculars of Wyoming—Yellowstone, the Tetons, Devils Tower—that make it wonderful. It's also the absence of such spectacles, the lack of "sights," the lack of people, the lack of civilization. This is a land of rutted dirt roads and a sky that envelops it all. The following places offer a cross section of Wyoming's delights. This highly selective list features just a few of the many places worth exploring; this book is filled with hundreds of others.

The "Biggies" Everyone Should See
Big Horn Mountains
Bighorn Canyon National Recreation Area
Buffalo Bill Historical Center, Cody
Devils Tower National Monument
Fort Laramie
Hot Springs State Park
Jackson Hole
National Museum of Wildlife Art, Jackson
Grand Teton National Park
Snowy Range
Wind River Mountains
Yellowstone National Park

Lesser-Known Places Well Worth a Visit
Ayres Natural Bridge
Black Hills
Casper Mountain
Castle Gardens
Flaming Gorge National Recreation Area
Fort Bridger
Fossil Butte National Monument
Frontier Prison, Rawlins
Guernsey State Park
Hells Half Acre
Independence Rock
Killpecker Dunes
Medicine Lodge State Park
Medicine Wheel
Oregon Trail Ruts, Guernsey
Sacagawea Cemetery, Fort Washakie
Sierra Madre Range
Snake River Canyon
South Pass City
St. Stephens Mission
Sunlight Basin
Trail Town, Cody
Vedauwoo Rocks
Wyoming Territorial Park

Interesting Offbeat Attractions
Accidental Oil Company, Newcastle
CallAir Museum, Afton
Charcoal kilns, Piedmont
Crimson Dawn Museum, Casper Mountain
Elk antler arch, Afton
Elk antler arches, Jackson

J.C. Penney house, Kemmerer
Jackalope statue, Douglas
Joss House, Evanston
Little America
Midwest-area pumpjacks
Mother Featherlegs monument, Lusk area
Star Valley Cheese factory, Thayne
Torrington Livestock Auction
World's "Oldest" Building, Como Bluff
Wright-area coal mines

Great Country Roads
Little Sandy Road (partly gravel) between
    Farson and Boulder
Sinks Canyon Road (partly gravel) between
    Lander and Atlantic City
Pass Creek Road (gravel) between Elk
    Mountain and State 130
State 24 between Devils Tower and Aladdin
State 70 between Encampment and Baggs
State 89 between Cokeville and Alpine
State 211 between Chugwater and Cheyenne
State 215 between Pine Bluffs and LaGrange
State 230 between Laramie and Encampment
State 296 (partly gravel) through Sunlight Basin
State 414 between Mountain View and Manila
State 487 through Shirley Basin
US 14 and 14A over the Big Horn Mountains
US 14-16 between Ucross and Gillette
US 14-16-20 between Cody and Yellowstone
US 16 between Worland and Buffalo
US 18-85 between Newcastle and Lusk
US 287 between Fort Washakie and Dubois
US 26-287 between Dubois and Moran Junction
US 212 between Cooke City and Red Lodge

Fascinating Small Towns
Aladdin	Meeteetse
Atlantic City	Saratoga
Buffalo	Sundance
Dayton	Ten Sleep
Dubois	Wilson
Elk Mountain	
Encampment	
Jay Em	
Hartville	
Medicine Bow	

pastures, hard times, loose women, and truck-driving men. My favorite has to be the one that begins: "You're the first thing that I thought of/when I thought I'd drink you off my mind." Pretty much says it all.

Wyoming Public Radio (FM 91.9) is based in Laramie, with repeaters throughout the state providing in-depth morning and evening news from National Public Radio, the BBC, the Canadian Broadcast Corporation, Wyoming news reports, and the "World Cafe" for eclectic music on weekday evenings. It's a vast improvement over the Rush Limbaugh broadsides, Top-40 hit stations, and recycled rock pabulum found elsewhere on the radio dial. In northern Wyoming's Bighorn and Powder River basins, you'll find National Public Radio coming to you via Montana's "Yellowstone Radio" instead.

Museums

For a complete listing of more than 225 museums and galleries, contact the Wyoming Arts Council, 2320 Capitol Ave., Cheyenne, WY 82002, tel. (307) 777-7742. The **Colorado Wyoming Association of Museums,** Box 18157, Denver, CO 80218, also publishes a helpful free brochure on local museums. The finest large museum—Cody's Buffalo Bill Historical Center—should not be missed, but a visit to the smaller and lesser known museums is also well worth your time. Some of the best museums and historical sites are found in Buffalo, Casper, Cheyenne, Douglas, Fort Bridger, Fort Laramie, Grand Teton National Park, Jackson, Lusk, Pinedale, South Pass City, and Thermopolis. See appropriate chapters for specifics.

FEDERAL AND STATE OFFICES

The U.S. government owns more than 30 million acres in Wyoming, primarily in national forests, national parks, and BLM lands. The State of Wyoming owns another 3.8 million acres, including more than 118,000 acres of state park lands. Addresses for **National Park Service** offices are:

Grand Teton National Park, Moose, WY 83012, tel. (307) 739-3399

Yellowstone National Park, Box 168, Yellowstone, WY 82190, tel. (307) 344-7381

Bighorn Canyon National Recreation Area, Box 487, Lovell, WY 82431, tel. (307) 548-2251

Devils Tower National Monument, Box 10, Devils Tower, WY 82714, tel. (307) 467-5283

Fossil Butte National Monument, Box 592, Kemmerer, WY 83101, tel. (307) 877-4455

Fort Laramie National Historic Site, Box 86, Fort Laramie, WY 82212, tel. (307) 837-2221

The **Forest Service** has ranger district offices in Afton, Big Piney, Buffalo, Cody, Douglas, Dubois, Encampment, Evanston, Greybull, Jackson, Kemmerer, Lander, Laramie, Lovell, Meeteetse, Moran, Mountain View, Newcastle, Pinedale, Powell, Saratoga, Sheridan, Sundance, and Worland. The following national forests cover parts of Wyoming:

Bighorn National Forest, 1969 S. Sheridan Ave., Sheridan, WY 82801, tel. (307) 672-0751

Black Hills National Forest, Box 680, Sundance, WY 82729, tel. (307) 283-1361

Bridger-Teton National Forest, Box 1888, Jackson, WY 83001, tel. (307) 739-5500

Flaming Gorge National Recreation Area, Box 278, Manila, UT 84046, tel. (801) 784-3445

Medicine Bow National Forest, 2468 Jackson St., Laramie, WY 82070, tel. (307) 745-2300

Shoshone National Forest, Box 2140, Cody, WY 82414, tel. (307) 527-6241

Targhee National Forest, 420 N. Bridge St., Box 208, St. Anthony, ID 83445, tel. (208) 624-3151

Wasatch-Cache National Forest, 8230 Federal Bldg., 125 S. State St., Salt Lake City, UT 84138, tel. (801) 524-5030

Local offices of the **Bureau of Land Management** are located in Buffalo, Casper, Cheyenne, Cody, Kemmerer, Lander, Mills, Newcastle, Pinedale, Rawlins, Rock Springs, and Worland. The main office is: **Wyoming State BLM Office,** 2515 Warren Ave., Box 1828, Cheyenne, WY 82003, tel. (307) 775-6256.

State parks and recreation areas in Wyoming include the following: **Bear River State Park** near Evanston, **Big Sandy State Recreation Area** near Farson, **Boysen State Park** near

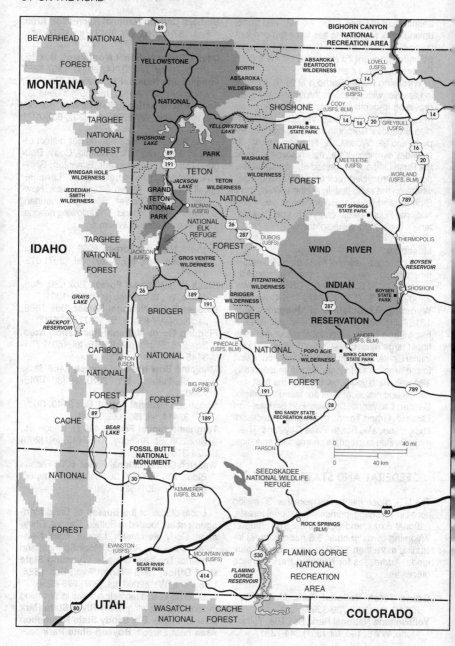

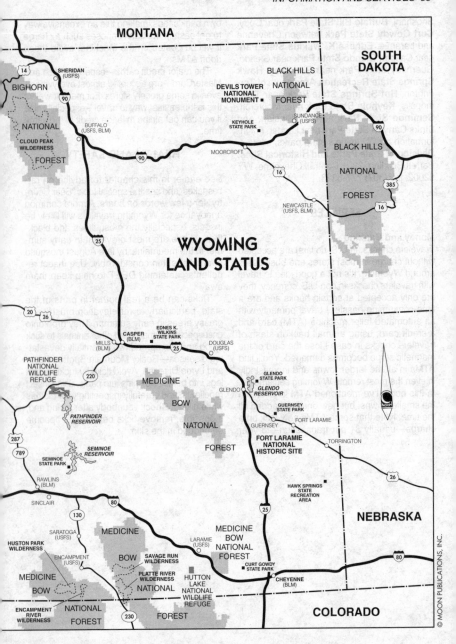

MONTANA

SOUTH DAKOTA

BIGHORN

NATIONAL

CLOUD PEAK
WILDERNESS

FOREST

SHERIDAN
(USFS)

BUFFALO
(USFS, BLM)

DEVILS TOWER
NATIONAL
MONUMENT

BLACK HILLS
NATIONAL
FOREST

KEYHOLE
STATE PARK

MOORCROFT

SUNDANCE
(USFS)

BLACK HILLS
NATIONAL
FOREST

NEWCASTLE
(USFS, BLM)

WYOMING
LAND STATUS

PATHFINDER
NATIONAL
WILDLIFE
REFUGE

MILLS
(BLM)

CASPER
(BLM)

EDNES K.
WILKINS
STATE PARK

DOUGLAS
(USFS)

MEDICINE

BOW

NATONAL

FOREST

GLENDO
STATE PARK

GLENDO
RESERVOIR

GLENDO

GUERNSEY
STATE PARK

GUERNSEY

FORT LARAMIE

FORT LARAMIE
NATIONAL
HISTORIC SITE

TORRINGTON

PATHFINDER
RESERVOIR

SEMINOE
RESERVOIR

SEMINOE
STATE PARK

RAWLINS
(BLM)

SINCLAIR

HAWK SPRINGS
STATE
RECREATION
AREA

NEBRASKA

SARATOGA
(USFS)

MEDICINE

HUSTON PARK
WILDERNESS

ENCAMPMENT
(USFS)

BOW

SAVAGE RUN
WILDERNESS

PLATTE RIVER
WILDERNESS

MEDICINE
BOW
NATIONAL
FOREST

LARAMIE
(USFS)

CURT GOWDY
STATE PARK

HUTTON
LAKE
NATIONAL
WILDLIFE
REFUGE

CHEYENNE
(BLM)

MEDICINE

BOW

ENCAMPMENT
RIVER
WILDERNESS

NATIONAL

FOREST

NATIONAL

FOREST

COLORADO

Shoshoni, **Buffalo Bill State Park** near Cody, **Curt Gowdy State Park** between Cheyenne and Laramie, **Edness K. Wilkins State Park** near Casper, **Glendo State Park** near Glendo, Guernsey State Park near Guernsey, **Hawk Springs State Recreation Area** south of Torrington, **Hot Springs State Park** near Thermopolis, **Keyhole State Park** near Moorcroft, **Seminoe State Park** north of Sinclair, and **Sinks Canyon State Park** near Lander. For information on Wyoming's state parks, contact: **Division of State Parks and Historical Sites,** Barrett Building, 2301 Central, Cheyenne, WY 82002, tel. (307) 777-6323.

SERVICES

Money and Banking

Travelers checks (in U.S. dollars) are accepted without charge in most stores and businesses around Wyoming. It's not a good idea to travel with travelers checks in non-U.S. currency; they are only accepted at certain banks and are a time-consuming hassle. I travel primarily with an automated teller machine (ATM) card and a credit card, using a small backup stash of travelers checks in case I lose the card or the magnetic stripe becomes damaged. You'll find ATMs in all the larger towns and increasingly in even the most remote Wyoming settlements. In this book, I've mentioned ATM locations in the smaller towns, but new ones are added all the time. Note that some ATMs now tack on a charge—usually $1 per transaction—to your own bank's fees, making this an expensive way to get cash. If the bank imposes such a charge it will be posted on the machine; avoid these ripoff ATMs.

The major credit cards—especially Visa and MasterCard—are accepted almost everywhere, even in some grocery stores. For many travelers this is the easiest way to travel—especially nice if you can get airline mileage credit at the same time.

HEALTH AND SAFETY

See earlier in this chapter for advice on rattlesnakes, and see the special topic "Bear Country" for a few words on bears. A more common annoyance for Wyoming travelers will likely be insects, especially the mosquitoes and blackflies. These are most prevalent in early summer in the mountains; by late August mosquito populations thin considerably. Use insect repellents containing DEET to help keep them away.

Ticks can be a real bother in parts of the state, particularly lower-elevation brushy and grassy areas in early summer. They drop onto unsuspecting humans and other animals to suck blood and can spread two potentially devastating diseases—Rocky Mountain Spotted Fever and Lyme Disease. Avoid ticks by tucking pant legs into boots and shirts into pants, using insect repellents, and carefully inspecting your clothes while hiking. Check your body after hiking and, if possible, remove ticks before they become embedded in the skin.

TRANSPORTATION

By Air

Commercial airline service to Wyoming is limited to the towns of Casper, Cheyenne, Cody, Gillette, Jackson, Laramie, Riverton, Rock Springs, Sheridan, and Worland. Three major airlines serve the state—United, Delta, and American—but most connections are via Denver or Salt Lake, even if you want to fly from one part of Wyoming to another. Deregulation at work!

By Car

Given the expanse and small population of Wyoming, it's no surprise that the automobile—the pickup truck in rural areas—is the primary means of transportation. Thousands of miles of paved and gravel roads cut across the state.

See Dan Lewis's *8,000 Miles of Dirt: A Backroad Travel Guide to Wyoming* (Casper: Hawks Book Co.) for descriptions of these interesting back roads. Be forewarned, however, that flying gravel is a constant problem, since drivers seldom slow down when meeting. This is even a problem on paved roads. Make sure your insurance pays for windshield repairs!

You can rent cars at all the larger towns, and those with airports generally have Hertz, Avis, and other national chains. See individual city descriptions in this book for local rental companies. You'll find four-wheel-drive vehicles available in some locations, including Jackson Hole. You may, however, pay dearly for a 4WD rental.

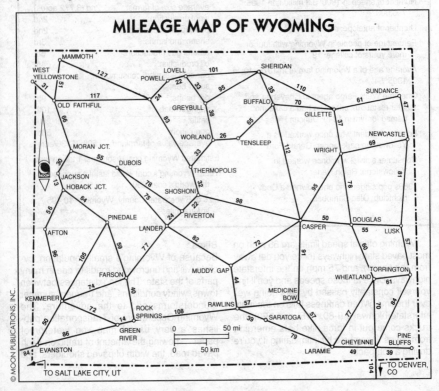

MILEAGE MAP OF WYOMING

WYOMING TRIVIA

Size: 62,664,960 acres or 97,914 square miles (ninth-largest state)

Lowest Point: 3,125 feet, where Belle Fourche River leaves Wyoming

Highest point: 13,804 feet, Gannett Peak

Number of people in 1996: 482,680

Number of people per square mile: 4.9

Racial mix in 1990
White: 427,061 (94.2%)
Hispanic (includes any race): . 25,751 (5.7%)
Native American: 9,479 (2.1%)
Black: 3,606 (0.8%)
Asian or Pacific Islander: . . . 2,806 (0.6%)
Other races: 10,636 (2.3%)

Number of cattle in 1995: 1,400,000

Number of sheep in 1900: 3.3 million; in 1995: 790,000

Number of antelope: 400,000

Percentage of people in Wyoming with four or more years of college: 19

Average age of a Wyoming farmer in 1975: 40; in 1995: 54

One-time Wells Fargo agent in Cheyenne and later restaurant critic who had a cake mix named for him in 1949: Duncan Hines

Former president who once worked as a Yellowstone park ranger: Gerald Ford

Consumer activist who once worked in Yellowstone: Ralph Nader

1960s pop singer who once owned a Cody nightclub: Glen Campbell

Retail chain founder who named his original Kemmerer shop the Golden Rule Store: J.C. Penney

Number of Democratic governors: 10

Number of Republican governors: 12

Number of years Democrats controlled both houses of the state legislature between 1890 and 1996: 4; controlled by Republicans: 102

World's largest piece of jade: a 3,366-pound nephrite jade boulder found near Lander in the 1940s

National rank in terms of:
coal production: 1st
trona production: 1st
bentonite production: 1st
mobile homes: . . 1st (on a per capita basis)
average size of farms: . . 2nd (3,772 acres)
wool production: 2nd
per-capita federal aid: 2nd
sheep and lambs: 3rd
natural gas production: . . : 6th
oil production: 4th
per-capita alcohol consumption: 8th
sugar beets: 8th
dry beans: 9th
spring wheat: 10th
cattle: 28th
population: 50th
average value of farmland: . . 50th ($136/acre)

Estimated Wyoming coal resources: 1 trillion tons

Years Wyoming's coal would last if it supplied all the world's coal: 230

Size of Sweetwater County, Wyoming: 10,495 square miles

Wyoming official speed limits are 65 mph on most paved state highways (once you get away from the towns), and 75 mph on the interstate highways. Drive at those speeds and you'll find yourself constantly passed by cars going well over the limit. When darkness falls on the main interstate highways (I-80, I-15, and I-90), the trucks come out in force, like bats emerging from caves. It can be a bit intimidating if you're driving a compact.

Bikes
Because of Wyoming's small population, cyclists will find uncrowded roads to ride in many parts of the state. The long distances between towns, windy conditions, and frequent summer thunderstorms add to the adventure. The Wyoming Department of Transportation publishes a very useful map—on waterproof paper—showing the amount of traffic on each paved road, the width of paved shoulders, and

Size of Rhode Island, Delaware, and Connecticut combined: 7,859 square miles

Number of Wyoming farms in 1920: 15,800; in 1994: 9,200

Percentage of water behind North Platte River dams in Wyoming used to irrigate Wyoming fields: 20%; used for Nebraska fields: 80%

Number of acres submerged by the Pathfinder dam: 22,000

Number of acres irrigated in Wyoming by the Pathfinder dam: 4,000

Cost of a trip from Cheyenne to Deadwood by stagecoach in 1880: $20 (first class)

Cost of the same trip by bus in 1990: $57

Number of "Peacekeeper" MX missiles in the Cheyenne area: 50; in the rest of the nation: 0

Nation's first national park: Yellowstone

Nation's first national monument: Devils Tower

Nation's first national forest: Yellowstone Timber Reserve (now Shoshone National Forest)

Nation's first polo field: north of Sheridan

"Oldest" building on earth: cabin built from dinosaur bones at Como Bluff

Oldest military building in Wyoming: Fort Laramie's "Old Bedlam"

First business west of the Missouri River: a fur trading post called Fort William (it later became Fort Laramie)

First American Legion post: in Van Tassell, Wyoming

First state to grant women full citizenship: Wyoming (in 1868, while still a territory)

First woman governor in America: Nellie Tayloe Ross (1925)

First artificially lit football game: in Midwest, Wyoming (1925)

First female voter: Louisa Gardner Swain ("Grandma Swain") voted in Laramie on September 6, 1870

World's first female jurors: in Laramie in 1870

World's first female prison chaplain: Mrs. May Slosson at the Laramie Penitentiary in 1899

World's first female fire lookout: Lorraine Lindaley, stationed at Medicine Bow Peak Lookout (west of Laramie) in 1921

profiles of the steeper road grades. Anyone touring on a bike will find this map immensely valuable. Get a copy by writing to Bicycle Coordinator, Box 1708, Cheyenne, WY 82003, or by calling (307) 777-4719.

Many thousands of miles of gravel and dirt roads provide excellent places to explore on mountain bikes; check at local bike shops for nearby routes. Get the BLM 1:100,000-scale area maps (available at most BLM offices for $4) before heading out. They show land ownership, contour lines, and all roads. On Forest Service lands, purchase equally detailed maps from local district offices. Mountain bikes can be rented in most of the larger towns, especially the tourist towns.

Rail Travel
Amtrak offers passenger train service three times a week across southern Wyoming. The Pioneer Line connects Seattle and Chicago with Wyoming stops in Evanston, Green River, Rock Springs, Rawlins, Laramie, and Cheyenne. Each train has a dining car, a lounge car, and sleeping cars (available by reservation only). For price and scheduling information, call Amtrak at (800) 872-7245. This is an excellent way to reach Wyoming and is helping revitalize the state's wonderful old train depots. One warning on Amtrak: don't expect on-time service. The trains often run far behind schedule.

Buses
Greyhound, tel. (800) 231-2222, covers the southern end of Wyoming along I-80 while **Powder River Trailways,** tel. (307) 266-1904 or (800) 442-3682, focuses on the northern and eastern parts of the state. Powder River has daily service to Cheyenne, Wheatland, Douglas, Casper, Buffalo, Gillette, Sheridan, Cody, Powell, Thermopolis, Worland, Greybull, and Lovell, as well as connections to major cities in surrounding states including Denver, Omaha, Billings, and Rapid City.

SANTA (Shoshone Arapahoe Nations Tran-

sit Authority), tel. (800) 439-7118, offers on-demand bus service to Riverton and Lander, with connections to Dubois, Jackson, Rock Springs, Rawlins, Pinedale, Cody, and Salt Lake City.

Winter Travel

During the winter months, Wyoming travelers need to take special precautions. Snow tires are a necessity, but you should also have on hand a number of emergency supplies including tire chains, a shovel and a bag of sand in case you get stuck, first-aid kit, booster cables, flares, flashlight, dehydrated food, water, an ice scraper,

and a sleeping bag. Call the Wyoming Highway Department at one of the following numbers for road and travel conditions: (800) 442-7850 (western—including Jackson Hole and Yellowstone), (800) 442-2535 (north-central), (800) 442-2555 (northeast), (800) 442-2565 (east-central), and (800) 442-8321 (southeast). If you can't reach any of these, call (307) 352-3000 for current road conditions anywhere in Wyoming. The state also publishes a map showing winter routes and even which roads get plowed first. Pick one up in visitor centers.

CATHY CARLSON

SOUTHEAST WYOMING

Southeast Wyoming is farming and ranching country, part of the vast prairie region that drapes America's heartland. In many ways, it is indistinguishable from western Nebraska or eastern Colorado—one long continuum of grass, grain, and grazing. Folks drive big American cars and Ford pickups. Instead of the saddleries and oil companies elsewhere in Wyoming, you'll find farm-equipment dealers and more feed caps than cowboy hats (they hold down better in the wind that seems to never stop blowing).

Buffalo roamed through southeast Wyoming for thousands of years, hunted by nomadic tribes of Plains Indians. Now sheep and cattle follow the same trails, and farmers grow wheat where Cheyenne Indian villages once stood. Alternating bands of wheat and fallow land give some areas a candy-striped appearance, while in others the expansive prairie extends in all directions. Old windmills, white farmhouses, hip-roofed barns, rusting retired farm machinery, and tall silos mark the old homesteads that became permanent farmsteads. The gravel roads cut straight across this gently rolling land with sudden right-angled jags around old homestead

boundaries. Drive out on these roads and the pace slows to country speed and meadowlarks call from the fenceposts. Folks raise a hand to wave as you pass and stop to chat on the crest of a hill. Tune in the radio and you're likely to hear country music, farm market reports, and Paul Harvey commentaries. This is Wyoming's most important agricultural region.

The capital city, Cheyenne, dominates the economy of southeast Wyoming, one of only two real cities in the state (the other is Casper). The other major settlements—Wheatland, Torrington, and Lusk—are small agricultural focal points and governmental centers for their respective counties.

Southeast Wyoming experiences typical high-plains weather. It is hot and windy in the summer, cold and windy in the winter. The wind—averaging over 13 mph—is a given; this is great country for kites, but not much fun when the gales of winter slice through like a knife. Partly because of this wind, however, Cheyenne has some of the cleanest air in the nation. Explore the back roads and you'll find busy cattle ranches, abandoned mining towns, remnants of many

historic trails, archaeological sites, dinosaur bones, and old sod homesteads. Hiking through the gently undulating plains is a delightful experience for vast expanses of this land remain almost unchanged from the time when bison roamed the great grasslands of the West.

CHEYENNE

As you drive west toward Cheyenne (pop. 53,000), the Colorado Rockies loom on the southwestern horizon like whitecaps in a sea of barely rolling plains, snow fences, stunted grass, and the highway slashing toward the boundary of sight. You catch quick glimpses of the great mountain ranges that ramble across Wyoming—like tantalizing flashes in a burlesque show. Gradually they grow larger, and finally you know that the Great Plains will soon be left behind. It's easy to imagine how this must have looked to the railroad passengers who passed this way in the 1860s, watching the mountains loom on the horizon as they rolled into Wyoming. Suddenly you're shaken into the present by the highway sign "Cheyenne Next 4 Exits." Suburban homes crowd over the gentle hillsides, and the state capitol gleams in the setting sun. You have arrived at Wyoming's political and transportation fulcrum.

The city of Cheyenne hunkers down in the southeastern corner of Wyoming, just 10 miles from Colorado and 40 miles from Nebraska. Its wide, tree-draped urban streets and graceful older homes form a gridwork through downtown, while suburbia spreads its tentacles into the surrounding prairie. Cheyenne is remarkably similar to (although smaller than) another state capital—Lincoln, Nebraska. For many visitors, it offers a taste of the West without leaving the Midwest. Folks in Casper or Cody view Cheyenne as the capital of eastern Wyoming and as a city whose ties are really closer to the markets of Denver or Omaha than to the sagebrush, oil, and coal of Wyoming. People in Cheyenne brush aside these criticisms. They know everyone else is just jealous.

As the state capital, the largest city, home to a strategic military base, a center for various governmental agencies, and a major transportation hub, Cheyenne is a big fish in the small pond called Wyoming. The city has one of the most stable and prosperous economies in the state. Its largest employer (nearly 5,000 people) is giant Francis E. Warren Air Force Base, but several thousand other folks work for the federal, state, and local government agencies around town. Railroad tracks of the Union Pacific and Burlington Northern Railroads head to the four points of the compass, and Cheyenne is right at the junction of two of the primary transportation routes across the Plains and the Rockies: I-25 and I-80. Some 800 folks work for Union Pacific, with hundreds more employed in light industry, communications, and shipping firms. Head out Dell Range Boulevard on the north side of town and you'll run into mile after mile of new developments, with national chains of all stripes moving in: Red Lobster, Burger King, Sam's Club, Kmart, Barnes & Noble, Target, Taco Bell, Boston Market, and more. The homogenization of America continues, even in Wyoming.

HISTORY

Like so many other Wyoming cities, Cheyenne is a creation of the railroad. It is the oldest of Wyoming's railroad towns, established as the Union Pacific raced westward in 1867. When Gen. Grenville M. Dodge was planning the new railroad's route, he decided to establish a major rail terminal in the plains just before the long climb over the Laramie Mountains. He named the new settlement Cheyenne, for the Indians who lived in this country. The word is from the Sioux Indian term "Shey an nah," meaning "People of a Strange Tongue." (Some have suggested a less complimentary origin for the word, the French term *chienne,* meaning "bitch.") While Dodge was there, Indians attacked a Mormon grading crew, killing two men. The graveyard was started before the first building was up. By November of that year the new town of Cheyenne had swollen to 4,000 people, earning the nickname "Magic City of the Plains." It was easily the largest town in Wyoming and has remained that way for much of the state's history.

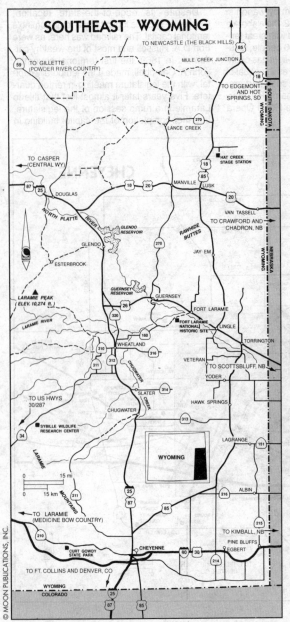

SOUTHEAST WYOMING

At first, Cheyenne consisted of the usual hell-on-wheels railroad settlement of tents and hastily erected buildings. Railroad workers and Army men from nearby Fort D.A. Russell turned the town into a rip-roaring place—every second building was a saloon and burlesque shows were the rage. At center stage stood a 36- by 100-foot tent housing Headquarters Saloon. Reporter James Chisholm noted:

The wildest roughs from all parts of the country are congregated here, as one may see by glancing into the numerous dance houses and gambling halls—men who carry on the trade of robbery openly, and would not scruple to kill a man for ten dollars.

Settling Down

Within a decade, however, Cheyenne had settled into a more urbane stage. The railroad provided access to the East, not only allowing cattle to be shipped but also keeping the town abreast of the latest fashions and furnishings and bringing news of world events. With the discovery of gold in the Black Hills, Cheyenne became the primary shipping center for supplies to the Black Hills and gold bullion from the smelters.

By the 1880s, Cheyenne had grown to a cosmopolitan small city of 14,000 people and was declared the wealthiest city per capita in the world. It was one of the first cities in the West to have electric lights—a power plant charged batteries during

the day and then delivered them by wagon in time for the evening's use. In 1882, the elaborate Cheyenne Opera House opened with great fanfare. With seating for up to 1,000 people, luxurious furnishings, and a huge 52-light gas chandelier overhead, it was regarded as the equal of any in New York and attracted such performers as Lily Langtry, Sarah Bernhardt, P.T. Barnum, Buffalo Bill Cody, and the Royal Opera Company.

Despite its edge-of-the-state location, Cheyenne was the logical place for Wyoming's territorial capital. The railroad was here, as were Fort D.A. Russell and most of the wealthy cattlemen. In 1869, the first territorial governor, John A. Campbell, made it the temporary capital, with the legislature meeting in rented quarters. Five years later it almost lost that title to Laramie in a rump session of the legislature, but after completion of the capitol building in

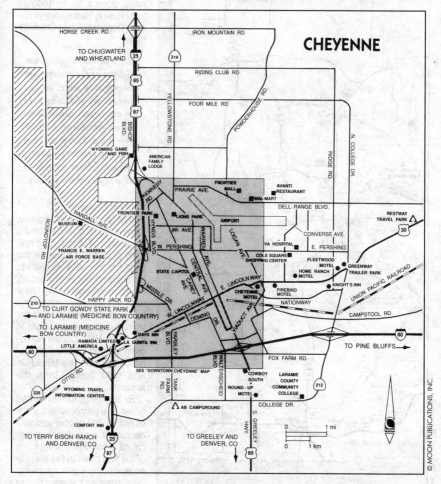

CHEYENNE

© MOON PUBLICATIONS, INC.

FRANCIS E. WARREN

WYOMING STATE MUSEUM

One of Wyoming's best-known politicians was Francis E. Warren (1844-1929). A lifelong Republican, Warren served as both a territorial and state governor before being elected to the U.S. Senate in 1890. One of the millionaire cattle barons, his ranch once held more than 100,000 sheep. This land later got him in trouble when he was charged with fencing public land for his own gain, but his friendship with President Theodore Roosevelt helped keep him out of prison. While territorial governor in the 1880s, Warren ardently agitated for statehood. His 37 years in the U.S. Senate made him one of its most powerful members, and newspapers labeled him the "Boss of Wyoming." Upon his death, Fort D.A. Russell was renamed in his honor.

1888 it became obvious that the governmental seat would remain in Cheyenne.

Rule of the Cattle Barons

Destruction of the once-vast herds of bison and the widespread slaughter of Indians who had lived in Wyoming suddenly opened up nearly all the territory to cattle grazing. At the time, Laramie County extended all the way to the border with Montana, so it was logical that Cheyenne became the focal point for hundreds of cattlemen who rushed in to make a killing on the booming cattle market. The most famous of these was Alexander Swan, founder of a spread so large that it required a special book to keep track of all its cattle brands. Other part-time residents included members of English nobility such as Moreton Frewen (nephew of Sir Winston Churchill) and Sir Oliver H. Wallop, seventh earl of Portsmouth.

Fort D.A. Russell

In 1862, President Lincoln approved creation of a military fort to guard the then-proposed transcontinental railroad against Indian attacks. When the railroad finally arrived—five years later—the Army established a fort near the new town of Cheyenne. Both the town and fort were officially established on the same day. Origi-

nally named for a Civil War general—David A. Russell—the new fort grew into America's largest cavalry outpost. Troops from the base were sent out to protect railroad survey and construction parties and later served as guards along the route. The **Cheyenne Depot,** commonly called Camp Carlin, was established adjacent to the fort, providing vital equipment for a dozen Army posts scattered throughout the Indian frontier. It was abandoned in 1890.

With the Indians' forced relocation to reservations, the role of Fort D.A. Russell changed and it became a training center and strategic garrison for the Rockies. New brick barracks and officers' quarters were completed in 1885, and the dusty parade ground was planted with grass and trees. Wyoming's Senator Francis E. Warren had long "brought home the bacon" by gaining political plums for his constituents and one of the biggest was continued support for the fort in Cheyenne. After his death in 1929, the fort was renamed **Francis E. Warren Air Force Base.** The base served as a training center and POW camp in WW II and was transferred to the newly created Air Force in 1947.

The fort's current role began in 1958, when the arrival of Atlas missiles made Warren the nation's first nuclear-missile base. The event was greeted with glee by Cheyenne's then

mayor, Worth Story, who exclaimed, "Cheyenne is proud to be the nation's number one target for enemy missiles." Today, the city enjoys a similar privilege as the only place in the nation where the 10-warhead "Peacekeeper" MX nuclear missiles are based. Cheyenne even has a Missile Drive. Warren Air Force Base houses 150 Minuteman III missiles—now rendered unlaunchable in the post-Cold War era—plus all 50 "Peacekeeper" MX missiles in existence, giving it 40% of the nation's intercontinental ballistic missiles (ICBMs) and making it one of the most important ICBM centers in America. The missiles are dispersed over a 150-mile radius in Wyoming, Colorado, and western Nebraska, creating an attractive bullseye target centered on Cheyenne. Missile silos are manned by two crew members working some 60 feet underground on 24-hour shifts. Each of these "capsules" controls 10 missiles in surrounding areas.

CHEYENNE CLUB

One of the most unusual organizations in frontier Wyoming was the Cheyenne Club, first established in 1880 as an exclusive English country club. With membership limited to 200, it included only the wealthiest of the cattlemen—men who quickly became known as cattle barons. Many came from aristocratic social backgrounds and were graduates of the finest universities on the East Coast and in Europe. Some were millionaires who summered in Cheyenne and then sailed back to Europe for winters. With the growing prosperity of the cattle business, the Cheyenne Club claimed the finest French-Canadian chef and steward in the country and was said to be the first club in America to have electricity. Dinner dress was always formal. Despite strict rules on behavior (no card cheating, pipe smoking, or profanity), one member did manage to shoot a hole through a painting of a cow and bull—he claimed it to be an abomination against purebred cattle. With the sudden economic bust that followed the harsh winter of 1886-87, the cattle barons were abruptly brought back to reality. Many went out of business, and the club quickly followed. The historic Cheyenne Club was razed in 1936.

The missiles are launched by steam (!) for the first 150 feet before the missile itself ignites, an event one hopes never occurs.

SIGHTS

A good introduction to Cheyenne is to take one of the **trolley tours** that depart from 16th and Capitol daily in the summer. These two-hour tours cost $7 ($4 for kids under 13) and include visits to several historic buildings, F.E. Warren Air Force Base, and the Old West Museum. Get tickets at the visitors bureau, 309 W. Lincolnway, on weekdays or the Wrangler Store, 1518 Capitol Ave., on weekends. Call (307) 778-3133 or (800) 426-5009 for specifics.

State Capitol

Capitol Avenue—one of the primary streets in Cheyenne—seems to symbolize the city's history. State government buildings line the street and at the ends are the two main reasons for Cheyenne's existence: the Union Pacific depot to the south and the State Capitol to the north. The Capitol is open Mon.-Fri. 8:30 a.m.-4:30 p.m. and offers free guided tours throughout the year. Call (307) 777-7220 for more info.

Wyoming's capitol falls in the tradition of ostentatious political structures and is modeled after the Capitol in Washington, D.C. The initial structure was authorized with a $150,000 appropriation from the territorial legislature in 1886. The cornerstone was laid on May 18, 1887, and the central portion was completed the following year, with the two wings added later. When completed in 1917, the building measured its present 300-foot length. The 146-foot-tall dome has been regilded four times, most recently in 1986. (Don't bother trying to climb up to steal any; the entire dome is covered with less than an ounce of gold.)

The capitol's central rotunda has a checkered marble floor with cherrywood staircases leading to the second story. Directly overhead is a beautiful blue stained-glass window imported from England. Interesting historical photographs line the second-floor walls. The senate chambers are in the west wing; the house meets in the east wing. You can view the legislature from the third-floor balconies when it is in ses-

CHEYENNE AND BLACK HILLS STAGE

With the 1874 discovery of gold in the Black Hills, a stampede of miners headed north in search of riches. A fierce competition quickly developed between Cheyenne, Wyoming, and Sidney, Nebraska, to be the jumping-off point for miners. With support for road construction from the Wyoming Territorial Legislature, a 300-mile stage route was soon laid out, and the first coach headed north on February 3, 1876. The Cheyenne and Black Hills Stage, Mail and Express Line had begun.

The line ran almost straight north from Cheyenne to the vicinity of present-day Lusk before veering into Dakota Territory and ending at Deadwood. Drivers made the trip in three days and three nights, with station stops every 15 miles that usually lasted less than three minutes—just long enough to change horses. It was a strenuous and tiring journey through Sioux Indian territory, over treacherous river crossings, and past hideouts of notorious road agents. On the long trip south from the mines, special armored coaches carried gold bullion in steel strongboxes, protected by four to six armed guards. Often they held up to $100,000 in gold dust and nuggets and sometimes as much as $350,000! Outlaws—including Frank and Jesse James and Big Nose George Parrot's gang—targeted these coaches, riding off with both the gold and the horses. One of the most infamous attack sites was near the Robber's Roost Stage Station, along the Cheyenne River north of Lusk. Here the stages were frequently attacked, sometimes every day.

The "Deadwood Coaches," such as the one used by Buffalo Bill in his Wild West Show, were actually the famed Concord coaches built by Abbott and Downing of Concord, New Hampshire. They could jam nine passengers inside (first and second class) for $15-20 a head and an equal number on top (third class) at $10 apiece. Riders on top sometimes had to get off and push the stage up hills. (Despite the attention given to stagecoaches, much of the traffic along the goldfields route was in freight wagons pulled by long strings of oxen.) Upon completion of the Chicago and Northwestern Railroad to Rapid City, traffic on the Cheyenne to Deadwood stage dropped, and the last coach ran on Feb. 19, 1887. In just 11 years, the stage line had carved out a big piece of history, and its closing marked the end of one of the most romantic chapters in the history of the West.

---

sion. Inside the legislative chambers are four Western murals painted by Allen T. True—designer of Wyoming's bucking-bronco symbol—along with others by Joseph Henry Sharp and Bill Gollings. Look upward in each chamber to see the large Tiffany stained-glass ceilings with the state seal.

From the outside, the capitol dome seems strangely tall; rumor has it that architects once voted it the nation's ugliest state capitol—although Alaska's would give it a run for this dubious honor. Out front stands a bronze statue of **Esther Hobart Morris,** the person incorrectly credited with making Wyoming the first state to grant women the right to vote. Directly behind the capitol building is the sparkling **Herschler Building,** named for the only Wyoming governor to serve three terms, Ed Herschler. It has an attractive interior atrium and houses the offices of various state agencies. In between the two buildings is an 18-foot-tall bronze statue by Edward Fraughton, *Spirit of Wyoming,* a bucking horse and rider that seem almost suspended in space. It is perhaps fitting that the two nicknames of Wyoming—"the Equality State" and "the Cowboy State"—are symbolized by statues on either side of the State Capitol. Wander around the flower-garnished grounds and you'll discover a monument to the Spanish-American War, a statue of a bison, and a copy of Philadelphia's Liberty Bell.

Historic Governors' Mansion
Located at 300 E. 21st St., tel. (307) 777-7878, the old governors' mansion is open year-round Tues.-Sat. 9 a.m.-5 p.m. There is no admission charge. A 10-minute video provides information about the house and its inhabitants including the nation's first woman governor, Nellie Tayloe Ross, who lived here from 1925 to 1927. The two-and-a-half-story brick building was completed in 1905 at a cost of $33,000; it is in the Georgian style with four Corinthian columns out front. Inside are furnishings from several periods. The current governor's mansion, completed in 1976, is near the intersection of Central Ave.

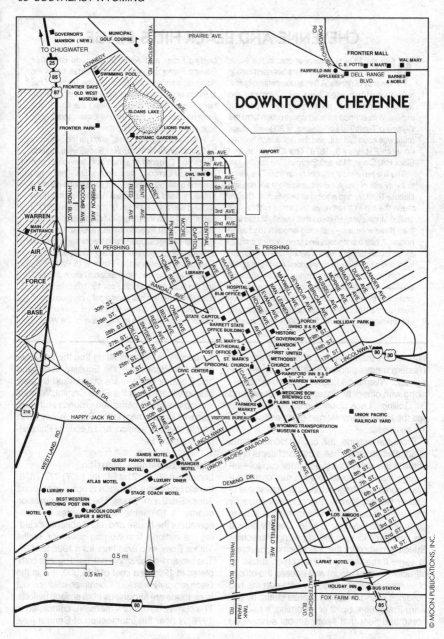

DOWNTOWN CHEYENNE

© MOON PUBLICATIONS, INC.

and I-25. Tours are offered only for groups; call (307) 777-7398 for appointments.

Frontier Days Old West Museum

Located right next to the rodeo grounds in Frontier Park, this is one of the nicest museums in Wyoming. It's open Mon.-Fri. 9 a.m.-5 p.m. and Sat.-Sun. 10 a.m.-5 p.m. year-round (daily 8 a.m.-8 p.m. during Frontier Days) and costs $3 for adults, $2 for seniors and ages 13-17, and free for kids under 13. Call (307) 778-7290 for details. The museum's focus is on Western heritage, with changing historical and art exhibits, early clothing, old films, Frontier Days displays—including a bronc-riding saddle that you can try out—and a special "Hole in the Wall" hands-on kids room. The museum is best known for its extraordinary collection of horse-drawn transportation of all types. More than 40 carriages—including many that appear in the annual Frontier Days parade—are displayed. The stars are a Cheyenne-to-Deadwood stage, a prairie schooner, sleighs, a buckboard (the name came from the lack of springs on the axles), and, of course, a surrey with a fringe on top. Be sure to check out the luxurious landau—sort of an early convertible. The gift shop sells various Frontier Days souvenirs and historical books. Out front is a sculpture of champion bull rider Lane Frost, who was killed during a 1989 ride at Frontier Days. A big Western Art Show and Sale takes place at the museum during Frontier Days.

Botanic Gardens

One of Cheyenne's lesser-known attractions is the fine city-run Botanic Gardens in Lions Park, tel. (307) 637-6458. Hours are Mon.-Fri. 8 a.m.-4:30 p.m. and Saturday and Sunday 11 a.m.-3:30 p.m.; no charge. Troubled kids, handicapped people, and seniors grow flowers and vegetables in the botanic gardens. Visitors find it a pleasant place to relax, especially during the winter, when the warmth and the showy flowers are delightful surprises. Inside the passively solar-heated greenhouse (look for the black metal drums filled with water) are three sections containing everything from vegetables to cacti. The central portion of the greenhouse has tall banana plants, tropical flowers, and a pond containing goldfish and turtles. The angel's trumpet, with its beautiful orange flowers, is the centerpiece. Upstairs is a small library with various gardening magazines and books. Outside are pleasant picnic tables and a gazebo set among the flower beds and shade trees.

F.E. Warren Air Force Base

For something different, try a visit to Wyoming's primary military base. The entrance to Warren Air Force Base is flanked by four missiles, but the buildings are surprisingly quaint—two- and three-story brick structures set back from the tree-lined streets. Some 220 of these buildings are on the National Register of Historic Places! Expansive green lawns give it a country-club feeling. This is essentially a self-supporting city, with childcare facilities, schools, stores, a veterinary clinic, and that old neighborhood standby, nuclear warheads. The only aircraft kept here most of the time are seven UH-1N "Huey" helicopters, but during Frontier Days jets take off constantly from the airport, suddenly screaming overhead in sharp climbs that bring gasps from the crowd.

The small **Warren Heritage Museum,** tel. (307) 775-2980, is open to the public Mon.-Fri. 8:30 a.m.-4 p.m. and Saturday 1-4 p.m., but you'll need to stop at the main gate for permission to enter. The museum actually consists of two buildings. One has a few artifacts such as sabers, uniforms, and other military memorabilia; more interesting is the adjacent building, which houses exhibits on missiles. These include photos of the early Atlas rockets and Minuteman I missiles, a model of the MX missiles the Air Force euphemisitically calls "Peacekeepers," and old launch-control equipment. A staff member here will tell you how the missiles are fired and where they are located—more or less. Grave gazers may want to visit the base cemetery, where soldiers and others have been interred since 1867. An interesting pamphlet available at the museum tells the stories of some who lie here. **Tours** of the F.E. Warren Base are usually given during Frontier Days, and group tours are available at other times; call (307) 775-3381 for details.

Historic Buildings

The **Whipple House,** located at 300 E. 17th St., is a wonderful Victorian home built in 1883 by Ithamar C. Whipple, a wealthy merchant,

cattleman, mayor, and state legislator. The home was later occupied by attorney and one-time Wyoming Territorial Supreme Court Justice John W. Lacey, who defended both the notorious outlaw Tom Horn and the equally infamous oilman Harry Sinclair. The building is on the National Register of Historic Places but is not presently open to the public. Cheyenne has several of Wyoming's most ostentatious and interesting churches. **St. Mark's Episcopal Church,** 1908 Central Ave., tel. (307) 634-7709, is the oldest, begun in 1886 but not completed until 1893. It has an exterior of red lava stones with traditional stained-glass windows, including one by Tiffany. This was the home church for many of the transplanted British and Scottish cattle barons, so it is fitting that the funeral for gunman Tom Horn, who worked for some of them, was held here in 1903. Two other impressive churches are **St. Mary's Catholic Cathedral,** 2107 Capitol Ave., tel. (307) 635-9261, built in 1907 of native standstone in the Gothic Revival style, and the **First United Methodist Church,** 18th and Central avenues, tel. (307) 632-1410, completed in 1894 and also made from sandstone. The previous Methodist church, on the same site, was where marshal, gunman, and gambler Wild Bill Hickok married a circus performer, Agnes Lake Thatcher, in 1876. The officiating clergyman wrote in the registry, "Don't think they meant it." Just five months later Wild Bill was shot in the back in a Deadwood saloon.

Railroad Paraphernalia

The railroad business reached its peak in the 1940s, when Cheyenne had the finest equipment and service anywhere in America. The railroad is still an important part of Cheyenne's economy, with freight trains rumbling through town day and night. Drop by the gorgeous old **Union Pacific Railroad depot** at the south end of Capitol Ave. to see one of the finest remaining depots in the West. Following a $6 million restoration, the depot has reopened as the **Wyoming Transportation Museum and Center,** tel. (307) 637-3376. Built of red and gray sandstone in 1886, the structure was for a time the largest building in the territory and the most elaborate depot between Omaha and San Francisco. (The depot was a reward to Governor Francis E. War-

ren for restoring order after the 1885 massacre of Chinese workers at the Union Pacific's vital Rock Springs coal mines.) It occupies an entire block, with clock tower and Romanesque arched openings adding a touch of class. Currently the building is used for gatherings, but a $20 million museum of transportation is in the works. It probably won't open till the year 2000, but the wonderful old building is worth visiting. Amazingly, Amtrak trains do not stop at this wonderful old depot, but rather 10 miles west of Cheyenne at the railroad siding called Borie.

Holliday Park, along E. 17th St., has a **Big Boy locomotive,** one of only 25 ever made and one of the largest steam locomotives ever built. It was used to haul freight over the mountain tracks between Cheyenne and Ogden, Utah. A couple of blocks east of here is a boxcar from the **French Merci Train,** given as a thank-you for food Americans gave the French after WW II.

Wyoming Hereford Ranch

In 1883, cattle barons Alexander and Thomas Swan, backed by European investors, formed the Wyoming Hereford Association, placing 400 purebred Hereford bulls and cows on a ranch near Cheyenne. This was the first real attempt to bring quality cattle to the state and was at one time the world's largest herd of thoroughbred cattle. Gradually other ranches followed this lead and the rangy longhorns of Texas were replaced by the more manageable Herefords—now the dominant breed in Wyoming. The 60,000-acre Wyoming Hereford Ranch has survived for more than a hundred years and has many historic structures in immaculate condition. A small visitor center houses awards and old photos, and out front you'll find monuments to prize bulls Prince Domino and Lerch, who sired many of the prize Herefords in America today. Prince Domino's memorial reads, "He lived and died and won a lasting name." How touching. You can wander around the showcase ranch and explore the red barns and other buildings. Wyoming Hereford Ranch is five miles east of Cheyenne off I-80. Call (307) 634-1905 for free tours. Since 1980, the ranch has been owned by a local surgeon, Dr. Sloan Hales, who lives in an enormous Tudor mansion just up the hill.

Other Sights

The fine **Wyoming State Museum,** in the Barrett State Office Building at 24th and Central, tel. (307) 777-7022, is closed for complete renovation, but is expected to reopen in 1998. During the renovation, small exhibits are held at the Wyoming Arts Gallery, 2320 Capitol Avenue.

Cheyenne has quite a number of interesting Victorian buildings. Stop by the visitors bureau for a brochure that takes you on a **walking tour** of historic downtown. Of particular note are the Victorian homes of "Cattle Baron's Row" on 17th Street. The **Wyoming Department of Game and Fish** at 5400 Bishop Blvd., tel. (307) 777-7735, has a small museum with wildlife dioramas, an aquarium with trout, and wildlife photographs; open Mon.-Fri. 8 a.m.-5 p.m. and Sat.-Sun. 9 a.m.-5 p.m. in summer and Mon.-Fri. 8 a.m.-5 p.m. the remainder of the year. No charge.

ACCOMMODATIONS

Motels and Hotels

Choose from more than two dozen different lodging places in Cheyenne; see the chart in this chapter for details on these. Generally space is not a problem, but when Frontier Days comes to town the rates often double or even triple (some places that cost $25 d in the winter months are $120 d during Frontier Days), and motels and campgrounds book up six months in advance. Obviously the quality doesn't suddenly improve quite this much; elsewhere this would be called price gouging, but the motels somehow get away with it. Even towns as far away as Torrington are affected by Frontier Days, so be sure to plan well ahead for accommodations. Be certain to take a look around before paying for a room at Cheyenne's cheaper motels, and also check the location. Motels near the rail-

CHEYENNE BED AND BREAKFASTS

Note: Accommodations are listed from least to most expensive. Add an eight percent tax to these rates. Area code is 307.

Bit-O-Wyo B&B; 470 Happy Jack Rd. (23 miles west of Cheyenne); tel. 638-8340, $45 s, $55-75 d; spacious three-story log home, four guest rooms, shared or private baths, indoor jacuzzi, full breakfast, kids welcome, open Memorial Day to Labor Day

Howdy Pardner B&B; five miles north of Cheyenne; tel. 634-6493; $45 s, $55 d; modern ranch house, country location, three guest rooms, shared or private baths, full breakfast, kids and pets welcome, friendly owners

The Storyteller Pueblo B&B; 5201 Ogden Rd.; tel. 634-7036; $45-50 s or d; contemporary home, Native American artifacts collection, fireplaces, three guest rooms, shared or private baths, full breakfast

Porch Swing B&B; 712 E. 20th St.; tel. 778-7182; $43-66 s or d; historic home with porch, antique-furnished, two small guest rooms, shared bath, full breakfast, AAA approved

Adventurer's Country B&B/Raven Cry Ranch; 15 miles east of Cheyenne; tel. 632-4087; $50-68 s, $55-75 d; modern ranch house with porches, country location, five guest rooms, private baths, three-room suite with jacuzzi tub for $125 d, full breakfast, kids welcome

A. Drummond's Ranch B&B; 399 Happy Jack Rd. (23 miles west of Cheyenne); tel. 634-6042; $60-75 s, $70-150 d; exceptional country home, mountain views, four guest rooms, private or shared baths, outdoor jacuzzi, terry robes, kids okay, AAA approved

Windy Hills Guest House; 393 Happy Jack Rd. (23 miles west of Cheyenne); tel. 632-6423; $75 s or d; attractive home, fine views, two guest rooms, private baths, mountain bikes, AAA approved

Rainsford Inn B&B; 219 E. 18th; tel. 638-2337; $75-95 s or d; large Victorian home, jacuzzi tubs, five guest rooms, private baths, full breakfast, AAA approved

CHEYENNE ACCOMMODATIONS

Note: Accommodations are listed from least to most expensive. Rates may be considerably lower in the off-season. Add an eight percent tax to these rates. Area code is 307.

Pioneer Hotel; 209 W. 17th St.; tel. 634-3010; $19 s or d; flophouse

Lariat Motel; 600 Central Ave.; tel. 635-8439; $22 s, $23 d; see rooms first

Home Ranch Motel; 2414 E. Lincolnway; tel. 634-3575 or (800) 999-7188; $24 s, $26 d

Round-Up Motel; 403 S. Greeley Hwy.; tel. 634-7741; $25 s, $27 d; kitchenettes and weekly rates available

Guest Ranch Motel; 1100 W. Lincolnway; tel. 634-2137; $26 s, $32 d

Ranger Motel; 909 W. Lincolnway; tel. 634-7995; $26 s, $32 d; see rooms first

Motel 6; 1735 Westland Rd.; tel. 635-6806 or (800) 466-8356; $27 s, $33 d; outdoor pool

Sands Motel; 1100 W. 16th St.; tel. 634-7771; $28 s, $35 d

Atlas Motel; 1524 W. Lincolnway; tel. 632-9214; $28 s, $35 d; kitchenettes available

Cheyenne Motel; 1601 E. Lincolnway; tel. 778-7664; $30-35 s or d

Sapp Brothers Big C Motel; six miles east on I-80 (exit 370); tel. 632-6600; $30 s, $34 d; no phones in rooms

Stage Coach Motel; 1515 W. Lincolnway; tel. 634-4495; $30-35 s, $37-40 d; AAA approved

Fleetwood Motel; 3800 E. Lincolnway; tel. 638-8908 and (800) 634-7763; $31 s, $37 d; outdoor pool, AAA approved

Plains Hotel; 1600 Central Ave.; tel. 638-3311 or (800) 341-8000; $32 s or d; historic five-story hotel, saunas, jacuzzis

Knight's Inn; 3839 E. Lincolnway; tel. 634-2171; $33 s or d

Firebird Motel; 1905 E. Lincolnway; tel. 632-5505; $35 s or d; outdoor pool

Terry Bison Ranch; eight miles south of Cheyenne on I-25 (exit 2); tel. 634-4171; $38 s or d in small rooms with bath down the hall; $79 for up to four in cabins with kitchenettes; extra charge for bison ranch tours, rodeos, chuckwagon dinners, horseback and wagon rides

road—and this includes nearly all the less-expensive places—may suffer from noise as freight trains rumble past at all hours. Bring earplugs.

Cheyenne is fortunate in having one of Wyoming's few surviving historic lodging places, the **Plains Hotel,** tel. (307) 638-3311 or (800) 341-8000. Built in 1911, the hotel was completely refurbished in 1986. For many years this was the political center of Cheyenne, with politicians repairing to the bar to discuss whatever politicians discuss. Note the tile mosaic of Chief Little Shield in the sidewalk along Central Avenue.

Also of interest is the **Terry Bison Ranch,** tel. (307) 634-4171, located eight miles south of Cheyenne along I-25, and just on the Wyoming side of the state line. This 27,500-acre dude ranch offers overnight visits as well as extended stays and runs one of the largest bison herds in the state.

Bed and Breakfasts

With the exception of Jackson, the Cheyenne area has more B&Bs—eight in all—than any other Wyoming city. Located right downtown, the **Porch Swing B&B,** tel. (307) 778-7182, is a cute cottage built in 1907 with a back porch for relaxing on a summer evening. The rooms are small and furnished with antiques. The very helpful hosts serve up a full breakfast. So do

Luxury Inn; 1805 Westland Rd.; tel. 638-2550; $37-41 s, $44-47 d; friendly, continental breakfast, low off-season rates, AAA approved

Frontier Motel; 1400 W. Lincolnway; tel. 634-7961; $40 s or d; see rooms first

Super 8 Motel; 1900 W. Lincolnway; tel. 635-8741 or (800) 800-8000; $41 s, $46 d

Quality Inn; 5401 Walker Rd.; tel. 632-8901 or (800) 876-8901; $44 s, $48 d; outdoor pool

Ramada Limited; 2512 W. Lincolnway; tel. 632-7556 or (800) 272-6232; $44 s, $56 d; indoor pool, jacuzzi, AAA approved

Lincoln Court Motel; 1720 W. Lincolnway; tel. 638-3301; $50 s, $55 d; outdoor pool, playground, privileges at jacuzzi and sauna next door, AAA approved

La Quinta Inn; 2410 W. Lincolnway; tel. 632-7117 or (800) 531-5900; $55 s, $63 d; outdoor pool, AAA approved

Days Inn; 2360 W. Lincolnway; tel. 778-8877 or (800) 325-2525; $60-62 s, $65-67 d ($120 s or d during Frontier Days); jacuzzi, sauna, limited exercise facility, continental breakfast, AAA approved

Comfort Inn; 2245 Etchepare Dr.; tel. 638-7202 or (800) 228-5150; $60-70 s or d ($125-175 s or d during Frontier Days); outdoor pool, continental breakfast, in-room VCRs, AAA approved

Fairfield Inn (Marriott); 1415 Stillwater Ave.; tel. 637-4070; $63 s, $70 d; indoor pool, jacuzzi, game room, continental breakfast, AAA approved

Little America Hotel; 2800 W. Lincolnway; tel. 634-2771 or (800) 445-6945; $66-82 s, $76-92 d; large outdoor pool, large rooms, quiet location, exercise facility, airport shuttle, AAA approved (four diamond)

Holiday Inn; 204 W. Fox Farm Rd.; tel. 638-4466 or (800) 465-4329; $73 s, $83 d; indoor pool, jacuzzi, sauna, airport shuttle, exercise room, AAA approved

Best Western Hitching Post Inn; 1700 W. Lincolnway; tel. 638-3301 or (800) 221-0125; $80-90s, $86-94 d ($200 s or d during Frontier Days!); indoor and outdoor pools, jacuzzi, sauna, airport shuttle, exercise room, AAA approved

those at the **Rainsford Inn B&B,** tel. (307) 638-2337, an elegant Victorian-era home in the heart of Cheyenne with five antique-furnished guest rooms, ceiling fans, and jacuzzi tubs.

The friendly **Howdy Pardner B&B,** tel. (307) 634-6493 is out in the country five miles north of Cheyenne—call ahead for directions. The hilltop ranch-style home offers three guest rooms and great views of the rolling plains. A full ranch breakfast is served. Located on the north side of town, **Storyteller Pueblo B&B,** tel. (307) 634-7036 is a modern home with Native American artifacts and three guest rooms run by friendly and dynamic folks in a quiet location. **Adventurer's Country B&B/Raven Cry Ranch,** tel. (307) 632-4087 is a modern ranch-style home located 15 miles east of Cheyenne. The emphasis here is on horseback riding; seven-day all-inclusive pack trips ($850 per person) are available to the Snowy Range.

In addition to these, three fine B&Bs are located halfway between Cheyenne and Laramie on Happy Jack Road (State 210): A. Drummond's Ranch B&B, tel. (307) 634-6042; Bit-O-Wyo B&B, tel. (307) 638-8340; and Windy Hills Guest House, tel. (307) 632-6423.

Campgrounds

See the "Cheyenne Area RV Parks" chart for local places to park for the night. The most complete local RV camping facility is **Restway Travel Park,** tel. (307) 634-3811 or (800) 443-2751. In addition to those listed, look for the brand-new **Cheyenne KOA,** tel. (307) 638-8840. Cheyenne's closest public campgrounds ($4) are in **Curt Gowdy State Park,** tel. (307) 632-7946 26 miles west on State 210. There are also campsites ($5) within the scenic Pole Mountain area of Medicine Bow National Forest.

CHEYENNE AREA RV PARKS

AB Campground; 1503 W. College Dr.; tel. 634-7035; $13 for tents; $18 for RVs; open March-Oct.

Greenway Trailer Park; 3829 Greenway St.; tel. 634-6696; $15 for RVs; showers for $3, open year-round

Hide a Way RV Park; 218 S. Greeley Hwy.; tel. 637-7114; $12 for tents or RVs; open year-round

Hyland Park RV Campground; I-25 at Missile Dr.; tel. 634-0517; $15 for RVs; no tents and no bathrooms; open May-Sept.

Jolly Rogers RV Park; 6102 E. U.S. 30; tel. 634-8457 or (800) 458-7779; $10 for tent spaces; $17 for RVs; open year-round

Restway Travel Park; 4212 Whitney Rd.; tel. 634-3811 or (800) 443-2751; $13 for tents; $16 for RVs; $3 showers for noncampers, outdoor pool, miniature golf, horseback rides, chuck wagon dinners, shuttle-bus service (fee charged) to Frontier Days; open year-round

Terry Bison Ranch; eight miles south of Cheyenne on I-25 (exit 2); tel. 634-4171; $11 for tents; $20 for RVs; bison tours, horseback rides, rodeos, and chuckwagon dinners available (extra charge); open year-round

T-Joe's RV Park; I-80 E. Service Rd. (Archer exit); tel. 635-8750; $13 for tents; $18 for RVs; open year-round

FOOD

The city of Cheyenne offers a surprisingly diverse choice of eateries. In addition to all the places listed below, the city is jammed with all the fast-food chains, particularly along E. Lincolnway.

Breakfast

One of the real treats in Cheyenne is **Lexie's,** 216 E. 17th St., tel. (307) 638-8712, a classy little downtown place with great breakfasts (and the best burgers in town). The place gets crowded with locals most days and serves three meals a day. The **A & B Cafe,** 2102 E. Lincolnway, tel. (307) 632-0343, and **Driftwood Cafe,** 200 E. 18th St., tel. (307) 634-5304, are also popular for breakfast. The huge **Little America** coffee shop, 2800 W. Lincolnway, tel. (307) 634-2771, is open 24 hours a day and offers better-than-average truck-stop food and a fine Sunday buffet brunch.

Coffee and Bakeries

Barnes & Noble Books, 1851 Dell Range Blvd., tel. (307) 632-3000, houses the only **Starbucks** coffeehouse in Wyoming. A smaller venue with good books and great espresso coffees is **Joe Pages Bookstore & Coffeehouse,** 207 W. 17th St., tel. (800) 338-7428. **Java Joint,** 1720 Capitol Ave., tel. (307) 638-7332, has tasty light lunches, and mochas, lattes, and other caffeine fixes. **Mary's Bake Shoppe,** 206 W. 16th St., tel. (307) 635-6279, is a little place with delicious breads, muffins, cookies, coffeecakes, pastries, and hand-dipped chocolates. **Bagel Makers,** 1821 Dell Range Blvd., tel. (307) 634-2200, has fresh bagels. Best pies in town? Try **Pie Lady Bakery & Cafe,** 3705 A E. Lincolnway, tel. (307) 637-8838. Find more sweets at **Cookie Jar Bakery,** 3219 Snyder Ave., tel. (307) 632-2488.

Lunch

Matilda's, 1651 Carey Ave., tel. (307) 635-4896, makes healthy sandwiches, salads, and homemade soups for lunch. Then you can ruin your diet with a fattening slice of carrot cake and a latte. For a taste of the East Coast, try a Philly steak sandwich or pierogie from **Little Philly,** 1121 W. Lincolnway, tel. (307) 632-6824. A downtown lunch and dinner favorite of many locals is **Albany Restaurant,** 1506 Capitol Ave., tel. (307) 638-3507. The cheapest meal in Cheyenne is the state government cafeteria in the **Herschler Building,** directly behind the capitol, where a filling lunch will set you back less than $5. The atrium is spacious and very pleasant. Open Mon.-Fri. 6 a.m.-4 p.m., with limited service after 1:30 p.m.

International Eats

Several places in town make very good south-of-the-border food. The best and most authentic is **Los Amigos,** 620 Central Ave., tel. (307) 638-8591, with daily lunch specials for less than $4, but **Estevan's Cafe,** 1820 Ridge Rd., tel. (307) 632-6828, also has quite good fare. **Cellar Restaurant,** 1607 ½ Carey Ave., tel. (307) 638-8976, serves Mexican food, chicken, steak, seafood, pasta—and the best margaritas in Cheyenne.

Wyoming is not known for its Asian food, but Cheyenne does offer two relatively authentic Chinese restaurants worth a visit: **Twin Dragon Restaurant,** 1809 Carey Ave., tel. (307) 637-6622, and **San Dong Chinese Restaurant,** 801 W. Pershing Blvd., tel. (307) 634-6613. Twin Dragon's lunchtime buffet is a very good deal and the restaurant always serves huge portions. **Dynasty Cafe,** 600 W. 19th St., tel. (307) 632-4888, has a big menu of reasonably priced Chinese and Vietnamese dishes and vegetarian specialties. Full family dinners start at just $7 per person.

Stuff yourself at **Avanti Restaurant,** 4620 Grandview Ave., tel. (307) 634-3422, where the all-you-can-eat Italian-American evening buffet is less than $8. **Pete's Pizza,** 1801 Warren Ave., tel. (307) 632-2267, claims to make "the world's best pizza," but most folks in Cheyenne seem to prefer **Pizza Hut,** 2215 E. Lincolnway, tel. (307) 635-4151.

Dinner

A popular Cheyenne eatery is **Applebee's,** located at 1401 Dell Range Blvd., tel. (307) 638-3434. Although it's part of a chain, the grilled specialties, crunchy munchies, and decadent desserts earn long waits most evenings. Get there early. **C.B. Potts,** 1650 Dell Range Blvd., tel. (307) 632-8636, has an eclectic menu that includes pasta, burgers, Tex-Mex food, salads, New York-style pizzas, great nachos, and buffalo wings. Try outstanding hearty barbecue pork and beef ribs at **Hickory House BBQ,** 2001 E. 11th, tel. (307) 638-1445.

Owl Inn, 3919 Central Ave., tel. (307) 638-8578, has been around since 1935 and is still a popular family dining establishment, famous for its homemade chicken noodle soup. It's also a good place for a quiet drink with friends. The big menu covers the spectrum from Cajun blackened redfish to fajitas to steak. **Poor Richard's,** 2233 E. Lincolnway, tel. (307) 635-5114, has Cheyenne's only Saturday brunch. The prime rib and seafood are excellent and reasonably priced, and the salad bar is one of the finest around. Enjoy a drink at the fireside lounge. **Carriage Court** at the Best Western Hitching Post Inn, 1700 W. Lincolnway, tel. (307) 638-3301, is the place to go for fresh fish or oysters, steaks, prime rib, and pasta. Entrées are in the $12-19 range. **Little Bear Inn,** five miles north on I-25, tel. (307) 634-3684, serves consistently fine steak, frog legs, shrimp, lobster, scallops, and other seafood. Another favorite steak place is **Cowboy South,** 312 S. Greeley Hwy., tel. (307) 637-3800. For prime rib, fly up to **Cloud 9 Restaurant** at the airport (300 E. 8th Ave.), tel. (307) 635-1525.

Brewpub

Medicine Bow Brewing Co., 115 E. 17th St., tel. (307) 778-2739, is Cheyenne's *in* place, with a young crowd and live music on weekends. They brew four types of beer on the premises, and the wide-ranging menu includes such pub faves as buffalo wings, nachos, fish and chips, calamari, burgers, pizzas, burritos, Philly cheese steak sandwiches, and Indian fry bread. Prices are reasonable, too. Get here on Wednesday from 5-6 p.m. for 25-cent beers. But be prepared for noise; the brewery can get mighty loud.

Grocers

The **Cheyenne Farmers Market** is held Saturdays 8 a.m.-1 p.m. during August and September in the big parking lot at 16th and Carey. This is the best place to get fresh fruits and vegetables. Cheyenne has several of the major national grocery chains, including Buttrey, Albertson's, and Safeway, and there are even three international grocers: **Gies Philippine Oriental Store,** 1623 E. Lincolnway, tel. (307) 635-7654; **International Groceries,** 1609 W. Lincolnway, tel. (307) 634-4888; and **Golden Dragon International Groceries,** 1605 Seymour Ave., tel. (307) 634-1686. The largest store in town—with a deli, seafood counter, bakery, and the best fruit selection—is the **Safeway,** tel. (307) 632-5171, in the Cole

Square Shopping Center at 19th and Converse. Another very good grocer is the locally owned **Dan's Country Market,** 1764 Dell Range Blvd., tel. (307) 635-4390. You'll find the best selection of beer and wine at **Town & Country Supermarket Liquors,** 614 S. Greeley Hwy., tel. (307) 632-8735.

ENTERTAINMENT AND EVENTS

All summer long, visitors gather at Lincolnway and Carey Streets to watch the **Cheyenne Gunslingers** put on a Hollywood-style shoot-'em-up. Hope I don't give anything away, but the good guys invariably win. It's pretty tacky, and bears absolutely no relation to Cheyenne's history. The "gunfights" take place at 6 p.m. on weekdays and at "high noon" on Saturdays (more frequently during Frontier Days). Also here at "Gunslinger Square" is a replica of the gallows used to hang Tom Horn (no mock hangings, alas) and a "Sody Saloon." A *sody saloon?* What would a real cowboy say?

The **Hell on Wheels Rodeo** takes place on Tuesday and Wednesday evenings June-Aug. at the Terry Bison Ranch, tel. (307) 634-4171, off I-25 eight miles south of Cheyenne. The cost is $5 for adults, $4 for seniors, and $1 for kids under 12.

During July and August, tourists fill the historic Atlas Theatre at 211 W. 16th St. to watch comic melodramas by the **Little Theatre Players.** The experience offers lots of audience participation, and popcorn, pizza, and beer are for sale. Call (307) 638-6543 or 635-0199 for tickets. For something more sedate, you may want to attend Sept.-May performances of the **Cheyenne Symphony Orchestra,** tel. (307) 778-8561.

Nightlife
Cheyenne is a hopping town when it comes to nightlife—especially during Frontier Days, when every country and western band this side of the Mississippi finds a place in town to play. **Cowboy South,** 312 S. Greeley Hwy., tel. (307) 637-3800, is the biggest and best country-music bar in Cheyenne. They also have happy hour specials on weeknights. Another favorite, especially with the Air Force crowd, is the similarly spacious **Cheyenne Club,** 1617 Capitol Ave., tel. (307) 635-7777. **Hitching Post Inn Lounge,** 1700 W. Lincolnway, tel. (307) 638-3301, and **Little Bear Inn,** three miles north of Cheyenne, tel. (307) 634-3684, are also popular country-western hangouts with nightly dancing. **Medicine Bow Brewing Co.,** 115 E. 17th St., tel. (307) 778-2739, has acoustic jazz, folk, or blues bands most weekends. For jazz music in a formal setting, visit **Players Restaurant,** 3307 Nationway, tel. (307) 637-7339. **Cellar Restaurant,** 1607 1/2 Carey Ave., tel. (307) 638-8976, has juke-joint jazz on Saturday nights and great margaritas. Also check **O'Brien's Tavern,** 222 W. 16th, tel. (307) 635-7581, and **Mingles,** 1318 Stillwater, (307) 632-9966 for rock music. **Les and Carol's Lamp Lounge,** 101 W. 6th, tel. (307) 635-7557, is a pool-shootin' locals' bar. If you're looking for tunes without the booze, **Joe Pages Bookstore & Coffeehouse,** 207 W. 17th St., tel. (800) 338-7428, often has live music. For something more risqué, head 10 miles south of town to the Wyoming-Colorado border, where **The Clown's Den,** tel. (307) 635-0765, features topless performers and nightly wet-T-shirt contests.

Movies
Local film houses are **Frontier Six Theatres,** tel. (307) 634-9499 in the Frontier Mall at 1400 Dell Range Blvd.; **Cole Square 3,** tel. (307) 635-2923 at 19th and Converse; and **Lincoln Movie Palace,** tel. (307) 637-7469, 1615 Central Street. The last of these is a classic place that opened in 1926 and today offers $2 movies.

FRONTIER DAYS

Cheyenne Frontier Days—the "Daddy of 'em All"—is Wyoming's largest and most famous annual event, with all sorts of entertainment from professional rodeos to parades. Festivities begin the last full week of July and continue for 10 action-packed days. There is something for everyone at this memorable event, but the rodeo is the main attraction for upwards of 300,000 visitors from all 50 states and many other nations. The largest number commute in from Denver, while others jam the campgrounds and motels for a hundred miles in all directions.

History

There are several versions of the origin of Cheyenne Frontier Days, the most plausible being that it was inspired when a Union Pacific employee, F.W. Angier, watched a group of cowboys from the Swan Land and Cattle Company trying to load an ornery horse into a railroad car. The spectacle sparked his imagination and when he suggested the idea of a Wild West buckin' and ropin' contest, others quickly jumped on the bandwagon. Just one month later (September 1897), the first Cheyenne Frontier Days celebration began. It was a rip-roaring success, with 15,000 people in attendance. In addition to various cowboy contests, Frontier Days included several events that you won't see today—a staged battle between Sioux Indians and the U.S. Cavalry, Pony Express demonstrations, and a mock stage holdup and hanging by vigilantes. Obviously, the production had been influenced by Buffalo Bill's Wild West Show, which was then touring Europe. Most amusing of all was the dog and hare event, where a rabbit was released to be chased by dogs. Unfortunately, the dogs in the race were quickly joined by many more from the stands so no winner was declared, although the loser was obvious. Cheyenne Frontier Days has grown over the years to a 10-day celebration (two weekends) and is regarded as one of the top four rodeos in the world (the others being the Salinas, California, Rodeo, Canada's Calgary Stampede, and Oregon's Pendleton Round-Up). Local enthusiasts call it the world's largest outdoor rodeo.

Activities

Frontier Days centers on the daily rodeos, with the nation's top rodeo cowboys showing their stuff. The rodeo has all the standard contests: bareback bronc riding, saddle bronc riding, Brahma bull riding, steer roping, calf roping, and steer wrestling. Other events include exciting and dangerous chuck wagon races, chaotic and amusing wild horse races, and a real crowd pleaser, the colt race (where young colts race toward their mares). With a purse of more than $400,000, the largest regular-season payoff in rodeo, Frontier Days attracts more than 1,000 contestants so many of the timed events must begin at 7 each morning!

Frontier Park is the center for all sorts of other activities during Frontier Days, including daily performances by the **Southern Plains Indian Dancers** and a **tepee village** on the south end of the parking lot. Each evening brings musical performances including the top names in country music. A large and well-run **carnival** provides stomach-churning rides, sugar and grease in all forms (cotton candy, candy apples, ice cream, corn dogs, burgers, and so on ad nauseam), plus thousands of stuffed animal prizes, stretched-out Coke bottles, velvet paintings, and other necessities. Other entertainment includes comedians, balloon "sculptors," magicians, square dances, chili cookoffs, and cloggers. After all this debauchery, try attending the **cowboy church services** held nightly at 7 p.m. on the rodeo grounds. Also in Frontier Park is the Cheyenne Frontier Days Old West Museum (described above), where the annual **Cheyenne Frontier Days Western Art Show and Sale** offers the chance to view or purchase works from more than 50 different Western artists.

Not everything happens in Frontier Park. On Monday, Wednesday, and Friday mornings during Frontier Days, a free **pancake feed** stuffs close to 10,000 folks. The feeding frenzy runs 7-9 a.m. Check out the cement mixer used (in theory at least) to stir up 3,600 pounds of pancake batter and the Boy Scouts trying to catch the furiously flying flapjacks. Visitors sit on bales of hay and are treated to performances by Native American dancers and musicians of all stripes. For many children, the four **parades** (held at 9:30 a.m. on both Saturdays, Tuesday,

and Thursday) are a special treat featuring the largest collection of horse-drawn vehicles in the nation. You'll see everything from popcorn wagons to hearses.

The first weekend of Frontier Days is also the time for **Fort D.A. Russell Days** at F.E. Warren Air Force Base. Events include a living history camp, mountain-man rendezvous, black powder shoot, tours of the base, and a hair-raising air show starring the **U.S. Air Force Thunderbirds.** Ride the shuttle bus to the base from Frontier Mall.

Specifics

For information on Frontier Days, including a schedule of events, call (307) 778-7222 or (800) 227-6336. Some of the night shows sell out well ahead of time so advance reservations are advised. Rodeo tickets cost $8-15 per person, while tickets to night shows are $15-20. A package ticket including rodeo entrance, a night show, and admission to the Old West Museum costs $26. Get tickets from the ticket office south of the main grandstand or by calling the 800 number. Entrance to the midway is $1 for adults, but persons holding tickets to Frontier Days events are admitted free. Parking costs $4 per vehicle in the huge lot along Carey and 8th Avenues. (Note, however, that overnight camping is not allowed here.) Because of the large number of participants in the calf-roping, steer-roping, and steer-wrestling contests, preliminary events are held each morning 7-10 a.m., with no entrance fee charged. The main rodeo events start promptly at 1:30 p.m. and last three hours. Information wagons are in various locations around the park.

OTHER EVENTS

In addition to Frontier Days, Cheyenne plays host to a number of popular events. In early January, the **Mountain States Circuit Finals Rodeo** takes place at Laramie County Community College southeast of downtown off State 212. **Super Day** in late June brings rides, games, a carnival, arts and crafts, and entertainment to Lions Park. Another popular event is the **Laramie County Fair,** held the first full week in August. It has all the usual fair activities, in-

cluding art and craft contests and 4-H competitions. **Oktoberfest** in September (September-fest?) features food and booze, crafts, polka bands, and dancing. The year winds down with a big **Christmas Parade, Craft Show, and Concert** in late November and early December. The nighttime parade includes 100 lighted entries, including horse-drawn wagons, cars, tractors, and floats. Call (307) 638-0151 for more info.

RECREATION

Enjoy one-hour horseback rides at **Blue Ribbon Horse Center,** 406 N. Fort Rd. (two miles west of Cheyenne), tel. (307) 634-5975, which also offers chuck wagon suppers. Horseback and wagon rides, chuck wagon dinners, fishing, and tours of the bison ranch are available at **Terry Bison Ranch,** eight miles south of town, tel. (307) 634-4171.

Swim or play on the water slide at Lions Park **indoor pool,** tel. (307) 637-6455. **Sloans Lake,** also in Lions Park, is a popular summertime swimming hole. The park also has a flower garden, an 18-hole **municipal golf course** (tel. 307-637-6418), picnic areas, playgrounds, ponds that turn into skating rinks in the winter, and several bison. The city is home to three other public golf courses: **Little America Golf Course,** tel. (307) 775-8400; **Prairie View,** tel. (307) 637-6420; and **Warren Air Force Base Golf Course,** tel. (307) 775-3556.

SHOPPING

Cheyenne is an automobile town, so most folks shop at one of the big malls scattered around the edges of the city. **Frontier Mall,** at 1400 Dell Range Blvd., is one of the state's largest, with more than 75 stores. Also impressive is **Cole Square Shopping Center** at 19th and Converse. Wal-Mart, Sam's Club, Target, and Kmart add to the town's shop-'til-you-plop allure.

Western Wear

Downtown Cheyenne has two of the largest Western clothing stores in the state: **Wrangler** (owned by Corral West), 1518 Capitol Ave., tel.

(307) 634-3048, and **Cheyenne Outfitters,** 210 W. 16th, tel. (307) 775-7550 or (800) 234-0432. Both are great places to pick up a cowboy hat or cowboy boots. The latter also publishes a national catalog for mail orders. Another place for quality Western wear and other gear is **Snubbing Post,** 1802 Dell Range Blvd., tel. (307) 638-6421. **Sierra Trading Post,** tel. (307) 775-8050, has a big factory outlet store at the Campstool exit off I-80 a few miles east of Cheyenne.

Outdoor Gear

Peoples Sporting Goods, 4516 Stillwater Ave., tel. (307) 638-8981, offers a wide variety of outdoor gear and topographic maps and rents skis in winter months. Rock climbers will want to visit **Fandango Outdoor Supply,** 217 W. 16th St., tel. (307) 637-3486. Get used gear of all sorts at **Play it Again Sports,** in the Cole Shopping Center at 19th and Converse, tel. (307) 637-4030. **Marv's Place Pawn Shop,** 223 W. 16th St., tel. (307) 632-7887, is run by a decidedly unique owner. His ads brag of offering the "worst free coffee in town." Give it a taste. For cheap clothes, stop by the large **Salvation Army Thrift Store** at 1401 E. Lincolnway, tel. (307) 637-8073.

Galleries

Cheyenne has quite a few art galleries of varying quality; two of the best are **Manitou Gallery,** 1715 Carey Ave., tel. (307) 635-0019, and **De-Selms Fine Art,** 215 W. 17th St., tel. (307) 632-0607. **Cheyenne Artists Guild,** tel. (307) 632-2263, is the state's oldest art guild (since 1949) and has a nonprofit gallery at 1010 E. 16th St. in Holliday Park. The **Wyoming Arts Council Gallery,** 2320 Capitol Ave., tel. (307) 777-7742, has changing exhibits throughout the year. **Frontier Antiques,** 216 W. 17th St., tel. (307) 635-5573, offers the most interesting collection of antiques in the area.

Books

Cheyenne has several of the largest bookstores in Wyoming. **City News,** at 18th and Carey streets, tel. (307) 638-8671, has many Wyoming titles; **Waldenbooks** in Frontier Mall, tel. (307) 634-7099, is another good-sized shop. But the largest shop in Cheyenne—in all of Wyoming, in fact—is **Barnes & Noble Books,** 1851 Dell Range Blvd., tel. (307) 632-3000. In addition to books and magazines, the store houses the only place with Starbucks coffee in the state. Barnes & Noble has frequent book talks, signings, and poetry nights. **Joe Pages Bookstore & Coffeehouse,** 207 W. 17th St., tel. (800) 338-7428, is a friendly small shop with books, espresso, live music, and poetry. For used books, head to **Book Rack,** 3583 E. Lincolnway, tel. (307) 632-2014. **Abundance,** 1809 Warren Ave., tel. (307) 632-8237, will fill new-agers' needs for crystals and metaphysical books.

INFORMATION AND SERVICES

You'll find the **Cheyenne Convention & Visitors Bureau** at 309 W. Lincolnway, tel. (307) 778-3133 or (800) 426-5009. Hours are Mon.-Fri. 8 a.m.-5 p.m., Saturday 10 a.m.-4 p.m., and Sunday noon-4 p.m., from Memorial Day to Labor Day (daily 8 a.m.-6 p.m. during Frontier Days) and Mon.-Fri. 8 a.m.-5 p.m. the rest of the year. The state also maintains a spacious **Wyoming Travel Information Center** at the College Dr. exit along I-25, tel. (307) 777-7777 or (800) 225-5996. It's so windy at this exposed site that the garbage cans are all set inside concrete pipes to keep them from blowing away! Open daily 8 a.m.-5 p.m. all year except Thanksgiving, Christmas, and New Year's.

You'll find **ATMs** all over Cheyenne, including in nearly all the banks. Laundromats include **Duds 'n Suds,** 1802 Dell Range Blvd., tel. (307) 632-4873; **Sparkling Brites,** 912 E. Lincolnway, tel. (307) 635-6881; **Easy Way Laundry,** 900 W. 16th St., tel. (307) 638-2177; **Lady Saver Self Service Laundry,** 117 W. 5th St., tel. (307) 632-2292; and **Tip Top Laundry,** 1900 E. 21st St., tel. (307) 638-9938.

Other practicalities include the expansive **Laramie County Public Library** at 2800 Central Ave., tel. (307) 634-3561, and the main **post office** at 4800 Converse Ave., tel. (307) 772-6580. For details on points to the south, see *Colorado Handbook,* by Stephen Metzger (Moon Publications).

Laramie County Community College, 1400 E. College Dr., tel. (307) 778-5222, offers both day and night classes for some 3,500 students.

Founded in 1968, the school focuses primarily on technical fields, although there are two-year degrees in everything from accounting to wildlife conservation. The 271-acre campus has 18 buildings, most built in the ugly concrete-box style common to the early 1970s.

TRANSPORTATION

Train

Amtrak offers train service west to Portland on Monday, Wednesday, and Friday, and east to Chicago via Denver on Sunday, Tuesday, and Thursday. Ironically, Cheyenne—the city built around the railroad and even today hosting the finest depot in Wyoming—receives no direct rail service. Because of inadequate tracking, trains now stop at the railroad siding called Borie, 10 miles west. It's just a brown trailer in the middle of nowhere, but a free shuttle bus provides service to and from downtown. Call (307) 788-3912 or (800) 872-7245 for schedules and tickets.

Bus

The bus depot is on S. Greeley Hwy. next to Subway. **Greyhound,** tel. (307) 634-7744 or (800) 231-2222, provides connections east and west along I-80 and south to Denver; **Powder River Trailways,** tel. (307) 635-1327 or (800) 525-0840, has daily bus service from Cheyenne north to much of northern and eastern Wyoming, with connections to a network linking you to anywhere else in the Lower 48.

Air

Cheyenne Airport is just south of Dell Range Blvd., with the entrance at the east end of 8th Avenue. **United Express,** tel. (800) 241-6522, has daily flights to Denver. Both **Denver Express,** tel. (303) 482-0505, and **Airport Express,** tel. (970) 482-0505, offer daily van service to Denver's new airport for $26 one-way or $39 roundtrip.

Cars and Taxis

At the Cheyenne airport you can rent cars from **Avis,** tel. (307) 632-9371 or (800) 831-2847; **Dollar,** tel. (307) 632-2422 or (800) 800-4000; **Econo-Rate,** tel. (800) 289-1417; **Enterprise,** tel. (307) 632-1907 or (800) 325-8007; and **Hertz,** tel. (307) 634-2131 or (800) 654-3131. **Affordable Rent A Car,** 701 E. Lincolnway, tel. (307) 634-5666, and **American West Rentals,** 120 Greeley Hwy., tel. (307) 634-0665, have used cars for better rates.

There are four local taxi companies to choose from: **A-A Taxi,** tel. (307) 634-6020, **A-1 Veterans Cab,** tel. (307) 634-4444; **Checker Cab,** tel. (307) 635-5555; and **Yellow Cab,** tel. (307) 633-3333.

CURT GOWDY STATE PARK

The 1,645-acre Curt Gowdy State Park is located 26 miles west of Cheyenne along State 210 (Happy Jack Road), the scenic "back way" to Laramie. The road rises slowly through the grasslands west of Cheyenne. At Curt Gowdy, the Granite Reservoir and Crystal Reservoir offer recreation for anglers, boaters, snowmobilers, and cross-country skiers. The small lakes, constructed between 1904 and 1910, are parts of Cheyenne's water supply—no swimming. An elaborate Rube Goldberg scheme completed in 1964 now carries 12 million gallons of water from the west and across the Continental Divide, the Sierra Madre, the Snowy Range, and the Laramie Range to get it to thirsty Cheyenne. In 1971, the two lakes at the eastern end were set aside as a state park and named for Wyoming native **Curt Gowdy.** Born in the town of Green River in 1919, Gowdy was a basketball player on the University of Wyoming's national championship team in 1943 and the long-time voice of the New York Yankees and Boston Red Sox. He later served as host of television's *The American Sportsman* for two decades and as a broadcaster of professional sporting events of all types including the World Series, the Olympics, and NFL games. Entrance to the park is $3 for non-Wyoming vehicles, $2 for cars with Wyoming plates. No entrance fees are collected in the winter months. Camping here costs $4 per day at any one of five sites. There's pleasant hiking in the surrounding pine-covered country-

side, but by late summer the lakes tend to get rather severely drawn down. There are some interesting granitic formations to explore and climb. Also in the park is the historic **Hynds Lodge,** a stone structure completed in 1923 and available for families and groups to rent in the summer. For details, call park headquarters at (307) 632-7946. An **ice fishing derby** takes place in mid-February at the park.

Lodging
The open country surrounding Curt Gowdy State Park boasts three bed and breakfasts well worth the drive from either Cheyenne or Laramie. An outstanding lodging option is **A. Drummond's Ranch Bed and Breakfast,** tel. (307) 634-6042, located just a mile and a half away from the park and offering vistas of the Vedauwoo Rocks and a private loft with a fireplace, a steam shower, terry cloth robes, and an outdoor jacuzzi. This is a very nice place to splurge, and a fun

place to meet the menagerie of pets: llamas, goats, horses, cats, dogs, and a goose. The Drummonds have an indoor arena for folks who bring their own horses (extra fee) and can serve lunch and dinner. For more on these three, see the "Cheyenne B&Bs" chart.

Another impressive place is **Bit-O-Wyo B&B,** tel. (307) 638-8340, a 4,800-square-foot log home with picture windows overlooking Table Mountain. Inside you'll find four guest rooms, full breakfasts, and an indoor jacuzzi. The singing family members are memorable. Bit-O-Wyo is open summers only and also has ranch vacations at $750 per person for a five-day stay that includes all meals and horseback riding.

Windy Hills Guest House, tel. (307) 632-6423, is a modern home with a deck overlooking Granite Lake and the nearby mountains. Inside are two guest rooms with private baths, a rock fireplace, and jacuzzi. Mountain bikes are available and a full breakfast is served.

PINE BLUFFS

Pine Bluffs (pop. 1,100) is a small agricultural and transportation center on Wyoming's eastern border. The local economy seems to be spiraling downwards, and most of downtown seems abandoned. Pine Bluffs feels like western Nebraska, with ponderosa pines crowding the long ridge south of town. The countryside is filled with silos, farm equipment, and rifle-racked pickup trucks while the airwaves contain market reports and hog futures. Wheat fields and irrigated potato fields surround Pine Bluffs. The spuds head to the potato-chip factory here (look for Rocky Mountain brand—the crunchiest chips anywhere—in Wyoming stores). The town itself is middle America, with spreading shade trees and quiet homes along the side streets.

Sights
The most interesting sight in Pine Bluffs is the ongoing **archaeological excavation** near a major Native American occupation site that dates back 8,000 years. Indians pitched their tepees atop the pine-covered bluffs here and headed down to the fertile valley below to hunt and collect berries. Their tepee rings are still visible. Each summer, University of Wyoming

students under the direction of Pine Bluff native Dr. Charles Reher arrive to slowly dig through the soil in search of a buried treasure trove of prehistory. The staff will be happy to answer your questions. The covered site, open Memorial Day to Labor Day, is a 10-minute walk from the tourist information center at the rest area on the south side of I-80. Also here are several painted tepee replicas; pick up the brochure describing the various designs. Several **nature trails** with interpretive signs depart from the rest area and loop to the top of the bluff. Pick up a brochure for details on these paths. You can also access the hills by car by following Beech Street south under the freeway and turning right on the dirt road at the crest of the hill. This is an excellent place to watch sunrises and sunsets or to enjoy a picnic lunch amid the pines.

The town of Pine Bluffs lies right along the great **Texas Trail;** at its peak in 1871, more than 600,000 cattle were trailed north from Texas past this point. Pine Bluffs became not just a watering place for the stock, but also a vital shipping point. For several years, more cattle were shipped from the railroad station at

Pine Bluffs than anywhere else in the world. A monument to the Texas Trail stands in the adjacent park. The free **Texas Trail Museum** at 3rd and Market Streets, tel. (307) 245-3713, houses a Conestoga wagon, old photos, and a small collection of homesteading and ranching items. Be sure to see the hand-crocheted snowflakes in the museum gift shop. It's open daily 9 a.m.-5 p.m. May-Sept., by appointment (stop by the town hall) at other times. Next to the museum are a caboose (these are becoming almost as common as sheep wagons in Wyoming museums) and several historic buildings— a one-room schoolhouse, an old church, and a railroad boardinghouse. The **University of Wyoming High Plains Archaeology Field Lab and Visitor Center** (try saying that one fast) is located at 2nd and Elm and is open daily during the summer. Inside are interesting archaeological displays and artifacts.

Lodging and Camping

Gator's Travelyn Motel, 515 W. 7th, tel. (307) 245-3226, has comfortable rooms for $28 s, $34 d (higher during Frontier Days). **Sunset Motel,** 315 W. 3rd, tel. (307) 245-3591, offers a few small somewhat run-down rooms for $22 s, $24 d. **Pine Bluff RV Campground,** tel. (307) 245-3665, is a half-mile east of town, and has tent spaces, no shade, but lots of wind for $12 and RV sites for $15. Showers cost an exorbitant $5 for noncampers; open mid-April to mid-October.

Food

Restaurant options are pretty slim in Pine Bluffs. Best bet is **Uncle Fred's Place,** 701 Parsons, tel. (307) 245-3443, where you'll find family meals and a salad bar. Locals also eat at the **Wild Horse Restaurant** in the Total station, 600 Parsons, tel. (307) 245-9365, but it's a cigarette smoker's heaven and a nonsmoker's hell—open 24 hours for your breathing enjoyment. The Total station also has an **ATM.** Get fast food from **Subway,** tel. (307) 245-3405, at the Ampride gas station/mini-mart on Parsons Street. Get groceries in **Texas Trail Market,** 3rd and Elm, tel. (307) 245-3302. This is a co-

operatively run store, as is the auto-repair shop at 700 Parsons and the local grain elevator. Socialism in a rock-ribbed Republican state!

Events and Entertainment

Pine Bluffs Trail Days comes around the first weekend in August with rodeos, barbecues, a parade, a melodrama, and dancing. A few mountain-man types rendezvous in the bluffs above town. There are also **calf and team roping** events at the rodeo grounds on most Sunday afternoons through the summer, with practice roping on Tuesday and Thursday evenings.

The primary hangout in Pine Bluffs is the local bowling alley, **Pine Bowl,** at 3rd and Pine, tel. (307) 245-3622. **Jim's Bar** and **Pal's Pub** occasionally have live music.

Other Practicalities

There's no chamber of commerce in town, but the state-run **Tourist Information Center** at the I-80 rest area has both local and statewide info. It is open late May to September. The **library** is at 108 E. 2nd, tel. (307) 245-3646, and Pine Bluffs has a free outdoor **swimming pool** (open summers only) at 200 E. 8th, tel. (307) 245-3783.

No bus service exists to Pine Bluffs; the nearest stops are in Cheyenne and Kimball, Nebraska.

North from Pine Bluffs

For a delightful break from busy I-80, drive north of Pine Bluffs along State 215 through the wheat and grasslands on the Wyoming/Nebraska border. The high plains landscape has a smattering of ponderosa pines capping the rocky bluffs, a handful of ranches, and to-the-horizon vistas. The road rolls past **Albin** (pop. 80) 18 miles north of Pine Bluffs, where an old sod house is the local claim to fame. **Albin Days** is held each July; call (307) 547-2206 for details. The nothing farm village of **LaGrange** (pop. 150) is approximately 25 miles northwest of Albin. Just to the north is 66 Mountain, so called because it supposedly has the number hidden in its profile. Stop in LaGrange each August for the **Mini Fair & Rodeo.**

CHUGWATER

Chugwater (pop. 230) was once headquarters for the giant Swan Land and Cattle Company, the greatest of Wyoming's cattle spreads during the 1880s. The town itself was founded in 1913 on land sold by the Swan Company. "Chugwater" has to have one of the strangest origins of any town name in America, coming from the Indian practice of driving buffalo over cliffs into the creek. The "chug" sound they made as they hit the water led Indians to call it "Water at the Place Where the Buffalo Chug." The prominent flat-topped mesa over which the bison were driven rises just north of town. When the railroad was built here thousands of buffalo bones were discovered at the base of these cliffs. Today Chugwater is undergoing a renaissance of sorts, with a small influx of new tourist-oriented businesses.

Sights
Chugwater is perhaps best known for **Chugwater Chili**, sold in stores throughout the Rockies or by mail order. Get a free taste at 210 1st St., tel. (307) 422-3345 or (800) 972-4454. The annual **Chugwater Chili Cook-off** is held at Diamond Guest Ranch the third Saturday in June and attracts upwards of 80 chefs and thousands of fire-breathing chili-eaters. Other events include a fiddle contest, bluegrass music, an auction, a barbecue, and country and western music. Call (307) 422-3564 or (800) 932-4222 for details on the cook-off.

Chugwater's free **museum** is located in an old bank building and contains an impressive collection of brands, aging farm machinery, and various homestead-era items. Out front is a turn-of-the-century caboose. Open Sat.-Sun. 1-4 p.m.; if it's closed, stop across the street at the **Chugwater Soda Fountain**, tel. (307) 422-3222, for access. The old-fashioned soda fountain also sells T-shirts, gifts, a few groceries, and liquor.

For an extraordinarily scenic drive, take State 211 from Chugwater to Cheyenne. The road is a mix of gravel and pavement and is longer than I-25 but is virtually free of traffic; it takes you through a majestic Wyoming landscape of grass and sage-carpeted hills, tree-lined creeks, magnificent old ranches, and herds of deer and antelope. Stop to listen to the meadowlarks on a spring day or to watch the clouds roiling overhead in this peaceful place.

Practicalities
The **Diamond Guest Ranch**, tel. (307) 422-3564 or (800) 932-4222, is located on a historic 75,000-acre cattle ranch 15 miles west of town and is very popular with families and retirees. The ranch was begun in 1884 and was for many years a breeding center for Clydesdale and Morgan horses. It has been a guest ranch since 1968 but retains many of the original buildings. All sorts of outdoor recreation is on offer here, including hayrides, horseback rides, fishing, dances, and an outdoor swimming pool. Also here are a restaurant and a bar. Campsites cost $14 for tents, $18 for RVs. Cabins cost $46-68 for up to eight people, and guest rooms are $46-55 s or d. Open mid-May to mid-October. Back in town, **Pitzer's Trailer Park**, tel. (307) 422-3421, has RV hookups for $10; open year-round.

Buffalo Lodge & Grill, 100 Buffalo Dr., tel. (307) 422-3248 or (800) 616-2668, has rooms in a new motel for $48 s, $40 d ($68 s, $70 d during Frontier Days). The premises include a small outdoor pool and a restaurant serving burgers, sandwiches, chicken, pasta, pork chops, and more. The modern building, however, seems quite out of character in cozy Chugwater.

Westridge Land and Cattle Co., tel. (307) 422-3251, 417 1st St., is a new steak house with reasonably priced dinners in a down-home atmosphere and polka music on Sunday nights, line dancing on Thursday nights, and country and western tunes Friday and Saturday nights.

The state has a rest area just south of Chugwater on I-25. **Powder River Trailways**, tel. (800) 442-3682, provides daily bus service north and south from Chugwater. The bus stops at the Sinclair station.

WHEATLAND

With a name like Wheatland (pop. 3,300), it should be pretty obvious that you're in farming country. Actually, wheat is not the primary crop grown here; sugar beets, dry beans, and barley are. And the largest local employer is the 1,650-megawatt, coal-fired Laramie River Station power plant, built in the 1980s five miles north of town and supplying electricity to a grid that feeds an eight-state area. Another substantial employer is a local marble quarry that mines dolomite in the Laramie Mountains and crushes it for use in everything from aquarium gravel to cattle feed. Don't let on that I told you, but Wheatland also has Minuteman III nuclear missiles out in the country near the power plant. Perhaps for this reason, the town boasts one of the highest number of churches per capita anywhere—23 different houses of worship crowd the town.

History

An early settler in this part of Wyoming called it "a desolate looking place, nothing but sagebrush, cactus, rocks, mudhole, rattlesnakes, and coyotes." It took water to change all this. Wheatland is a creation of the Wyoming Development Company, founded in 1883 by a number of individuals, including Senators Joseph M. Carey and Francis E. Warren. In one of the few successful applications of the famous Carey Act in Wyoming, the company built a dam on Big Laramie River and canals to carry the water to some 50,000 acres where homesteaders formed the Wheatland Colony. Today it remains the largest privately owned irrigation system in the nation. In 1905 the town of Wheatland was incorporated (the name won out over Wheatdale and Wheatridge) and became the hub of activity for the region—and later the Platte Coun-

SWAN LAND AND CATTLE COMPANY

The most famous of all Wyoming ranching operations was the Swan Land and Cattle Company, Ltd., founded in 1883 by Alexander and Thomas Swan with enormous financial backing from Scottish investors—£600,000 the first year and an additional £1.6 million over the next three years. At its peak in the mid-1880s, the company's holdings reached from its headquarters along Chugwater Creek westward for 120 miles to the North Platte River near Rawlins. More than 110,000 cattle ranged across this vast expanse. The company bought 550,000 acres of Union Pacific Railroad land (and therefore controlled the checkerboard of public land in alternating sections) and purchased government land along major creeks in the area. By doing this, it controlled access to water in this semiarid country, thus keeping others from settling on surrounding public lands. All told, the Swan Land and Cattle Company had its tentacles over nearly a million acres with more than 30 different ranches. The company had dozens of different brands, but locals knew it as the "Two Bar." Cowboys loved the company because

it always provided good working conditions and wages ($20 a month to start) and the best grub around.

In the mid-1880s, though, things began to turn sour and by 1886 the Scottish investors accused Alexander Swan of fraud and misrepresentation; the 110,000 cattle shown on the books did not all exist on the hoof. A lawsuit eventually led to Swan's firing. Even more devastating was the severe winter of 1886-87, which killed off thousands of the firm's cows and calves, pushing the company to the brink of bankruptcy. Amazingly, the reorganized company managed to survive for more than 50 years, though it began raising sheep instead of cattle after 1903. It was quite prosperous during World War I, when wool prices soared, but its fortunes gradually declined with the economy. By 1950, the vast operation had been entirely liquidated. Some folks claim that Steamboat, a wild bronc from the old Two Bar Ranch, was the inspiration for the bucking horse symbol found on Wyoming license plates. Many of the historic ranch's buildings are still intact, and the complex has been designated a National Historic Landmark.

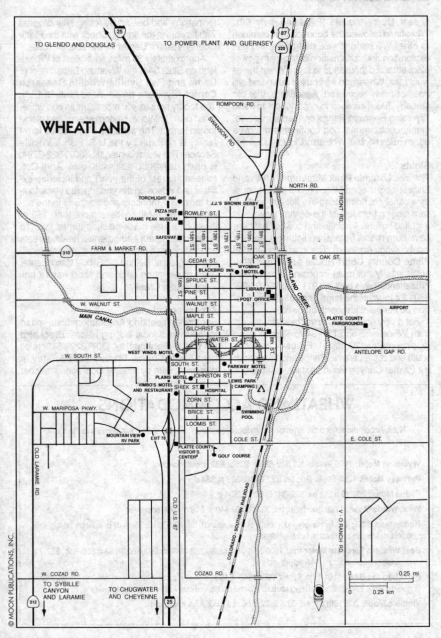

WHEATLAND

TO GLENDO AND DOUGLAS

TO POWER PLANT AND GUERNSEY

ROMPOON RD.

SWANSON RD.

NORTH RD.

FRONT RD.

TORCHLIGHT INN

J.J.'S BROWN DERBY

PIZZA HUT
LARAMIE PEAK MUSEUM

ROWLEY ST.

SAFEWAY

FARM & MARKET RD.

OAK ST.

E. OAK ST.

CEDAR ST.

WYOMING
MOTEL

BLACKBIRD INN

SPRUCE ST.

PINE ST.

LIBRARY

POST OFFICE

WALNUT ST.

W. WALNUT ST.

MAPLE ST.

MAIN CANAL

GILCHRIST ST.

CITY HALL

AIRPORT

PLATTE COUNTY
FAIRGROUNDS

WATER ST.

WEST WINDS MOTEL

ANTELOPE GAP RD.

W. SOUTH ST.

SOUTH ST.

PARKWAY MOTEL

PLAINS MOTEL

JOHNSTON ST.

VIMBO'S MOTEL
AND RESTAURANT

SHIEK ST.

LEWIS PARK
(CAMPING)

HOSPITAL

ZORN ST.

W. MARIPOSA PKWY.

BRICE ST.

SWIMMING
POOL

LOOMIS ST.

MOUNTAIN VIEW
RV PARK

EXIT 78

COLE ST.

E. COLE ST.

PLATTE COUNTY
VISITOR'S
CENTER

GOLF COURSE

W. COZAD RD.

COZAD RD.

V-O RANCH RD.

TO SYBILLE
CANYON AND LARAMIE

TO CHUGWATER
AND CHEYENNE

OLD LARAMIE RD.

OLD U.S. 87

COLORADO-SOUTHERN RAILROAD

© MOON PUBLICATIONS, INC.

0   0.25 mi

0   0.25 km

ty seat. During the late 1970s and early '80s, Wheatland followed the boom pattern common to other Wyoming towns: nearby oil and gas exploration and construction of the giant power plant attracted thousands to town. When things went bust, Wheatland was pulled down and still has not really recovered. Agriculture, that old standby, has increased in importance. In 1996 Wyoming Premium Farms opened a massive, highly controversial hog confinement farm a dozen miles north of Wheatland. Hold your nose.

Sights

The free **Laramie Peak Museum** on 16th and Elliot streets is open Mon.-Fri. 1-5 p.m. It houses a variety of homestead-era flotsam and jetsam ranging from turn-of-the-century tricycles to a stuffed vulture. A saddle and cowboy hat here have burn marks from when lightning struck a local cowboy (he lived). The marble-columned **Platte County Court House** at 9th and Walnut is easily the most imposing structure in Wheatland. It was built in 1911. Call (307) 322-9601 for tours of the huge **Laramie River Station** power plant just north of town.

For a very scenic loop drive, head southwest from Wheatland on State 34 to Tunnel Road (approximately 20 miles). Follow it over the south end of the Laramie Range and then return via Palmer Canyon Road past interesting rock formations and beautifully rolling hills covered with flowers in the spring. Check with the Platte County Visitor's Center for the specific route.

Approximately 30 miles southwest of Wheatland on State 34 is the Wyoming Department of Game and Fish **Sybille Wildlife Research Center** (Sybille is pronounced "suh-BEEL"). The facility houses elk, moose, mule and white-tailed deer, antelope, bighorn sheep, and black-footed ferrets. The separate black-footed ferret facility is now run by the U.S. Fish & Wildlife Service. The visitor center, tel. (307) 322-2784, is open daily 8:30 a.m.-4:30 p.m. April-Oct. (closed the rest of the year) and includes exhibits and videos on the endangered black-footed ferret. TV monitors show activity in the adjacent ferret facility, where more than 150 of these cute little black-masked furries live. To lessen the impact and potential health threats from introduced diseases, tours are only available for groups. Behind the Sybille visitor center is an observation deck and short nature trail along Sybille Creek.

Accommodations

See the "Wheatland Accommodations" chart for a listing of local lodging places. **Blackbird Inn Bed & Breakfast,** tel. (307) 322-4540, rates near the top of my list of places to stay in Wyoming. Run by friendly local schoolteacher

WHEATLAND ACCOMMODATIONS

Note: Accommodations are arranged from least to most expensive. Add a five percent tax to these rates. Area code is 307.

Wyoming Motel; 1109 9th St.; tel. 322-5383; $28 s, $33 d; outdoor pool

Parkway Motel; 1257 South Rd.; tel. 322-3080; $28 s, $34 d

Plains Motel; 208 16th St.; tel. 322-3416; $30 s, $34 d

West Winds Motel; 1756 South St.; tel. 322-2705; $40 s, $48 d; AAA approved

Homestead B&B; 431 E. Havely Rd. (south of Wheatland); tel. 422-3316; $50 s or d; country home, five guest rooms, shared baths, full breakfast

Best Western Torchlite Motor Inn; 1809 N. 16th St.; tel. 322-4070 or (800) 528-1234; $60-65 s, $67-71 d; outdoor pool, jacuzzi, AAA approved

Blackbird Inn B&B; 1101 11th St.; tel. 322-4540; $45 s, $55 d; historic place, wrap-around porch, four guest rooms and a suite with two rooms, shared baths, antique furnishings, full breakfast

Vimbo's Motel; 203 16th St.; tel. 322-3842; $66 s, $71 d; AAA approved

Dan Brecht, this 1910 Victorian has been lovingly restored. The wrap-around front porch is a fine place to sit on a warm summer day. Excellent full breakfasts are served during the summer, but even the continental breakfast offered the rest of the year will fill you up. **Homestead B&B,** tel. (307) 422-3316, is south of town in the wheat fields between Wheatland and Chugwater. The old homestead offers five guest rooms on a working farm.

Camping

You can camp for free at 40-acre **Lewis Park** right in town (with showers and RV hookups) or pay $12 for RV parking at **Mountain View RV Park,** tel. (307) 322-4858, 77 20th St. (just west of Exit 78). Open year-round. Camping is free at **Grayrocks Reservoir** northeast of Wheatland beyond the power plant. There are no RV hookups, but they do have coin-operated showers here. Additional free camping is available in undeveloped facilities at other nearby reservoirs and on Forest Service land in the Laramie Mountains west of Wheatland.

Food

For the best local breakfasts—especially the omelettes—head to **Breakfast Inn,** 86 16th St., tel. (307) 322-9302. **Granny's Goodie Shop,** 719 9th St., tel. (307) 322-5321, makes good sandwiches for lunch including cabbage burgers (!) and serves hot coffee and donuts for a quick breakfast. Pseudo-Mexican food comes to you courtesy of the Korean chefs at **El Gringo's,** 705 10th St., tel. (307) 322-4402. **Vimbo's Restaurant,** 203 16th St., tel. (307) 322-3725, is a star on the local scene with dependably good food, a big menu, and friendly waitresses. For fast food, eschew the Burger King and Arby's; head instead to **Casey's Drive In,** 1556 S St., tel. (307) 322-9616. In addition to very good burgers, Casey's cranks out full dinners of steak, prime rib, and seafood with homemade pies and cakes for dessert.

Wheatland's surprise is **J.J.'s Little Brown Derby,** 1707 9th St., tel. (307) 322-4257. Located in a 1950s-era trailer house with appropriately tacky decor, it has great food, reasonable prices, and huge portions. They always offer lunch specials, and the burgers and chicken-fried steak are famous. For something different, try the Friday night prime rib specials. Even the Burlington Northern freight train stops so the crew can come over for dinner! **Pizza Hut,** near the Torchlight Inn, is the only place open late most nights. Groceries are available at **Safeway** and **Jack and Jill Market.**

Recreation

Seven miles south of Wheatland, the century-old **Grant Ranch,** tel. (307) 322-2923, has guided horseback tours in the summer starting at a pricey $75 for a two-hour ride ($25 for kids under 12). Of more interest are the three-day cattle drives for $700 ($300 for kids), including all meals and lodging.

There is a fine outdoor **swimming pool** (tel. 307-322-9254) in Lewis Park, open only during the summer. Entrance costs 75 cents for adults, free for kids under six. The nine-hole **Wheatland Golf Course** is at 1253 Cole, tel. (307) 322-3675.

Events

Wheatland has a big fireworks show at the fairgrounds on the **4th of July. Summer Fun Fest and Antique Tractor Pull** takes place the second Saturday of July with live music, dancing, food and craft booths, and a tractor pull in Lewis Park. The **Platte County Fair and Rodeo** comes to town the second week of August and offers a street breakfast, barbecue, parade, rodeo, entertainment, and all the usual fun of a country fair. Most enjoyable of all is the pig wrestling.

Information, Services, and Transportation

The **Platte County Visitor's Center** is next to I-25 exit 78, tel. (307) 322-2322, and is open Mon.-Fri. 8 a.m.-5 p.m. and Sat.-Sun. 10 a.m.-5 p.m. June to Labor Day and Mon.-Fri. 8 a.m.-5 p.m. the rest of the year. Other practicalities include the **Platte County Library** at 904 9th St., tel. (307) 322-2689, and the **post office** at 852 Walnut St., tel. (307) 332-3287. Get fast cash from **ATMs** at Key Bank on 9th and Gilchrist, the Conoco station at 1650 South St., and the Mini-Mart at 1456 South Street.

Powder River Trailways, tel. (307) 322-2725 or (800) 442-3682, has daily bus service to Cheyenne and most of northern Wyoming. The buses stop at Videoland, 956 Maple Street.

GUERNSEY AND VICINITY

Guernsey (pop. 1,100) is a scenic railroad and ranching town along the once mighty North Platte River (the river is now just a trickle in late summer, thanks to all the upstream dams). Guernsey was named after Charles A. Guernsey, a prominent local rancher and legislator who came here in the late 19th century. The town is right in the heart of Oregon Trail country, with Fort Laramie just 11 miles east and numerous 19th-century historical markers. The Wyoming Army National Guard maintains Camp Guernsey, a large troop training facility just north of town.

Emigrant Trail Sights

The Oregon Trail ran just on the other side of the North Platte River from Guernsey. One mile south of town are some of the deepest Oregon Trail ruts anywhere along the historic route. A short trail leads uphill to four-foot-deep gouges cut into the soft sandstone. The paths of bull-whackers are visible alongside. The old wagon trail is easy to follow in both directions, and the surrounding landscape has probably changed little since the last wagon train rolled past. Perhaps better than any historic photos or written descriptions, these deep ruts serve as permanent reminders of the great westward migration. Not far away is a white obelisk marking the grave of Lucindy Rollins, one of the thousands who died on the hard road west.

The hundred-foot-tall Register Cliff is four miles south of Guernsey. Here the soft limestone made a perfect place for passing emigrants to carve their names, and thousands took the time to do so. The oldest—dating to the 1850s—are now behind a chain-link fence to keep folks from defacing them further. Hundreds of swallows nest on the cliff here. North of Guernsey, ruts of the historic Mormon Trail are visible along Emigrant Hill, where Mormon pioneers struggled to hoist their wagons up the steep slope.

Another important nearby site was Emigrants' Washtub, a warm springs where weary travelers stopped to bathe and wash clothes. The springs are an enjoyable place to relax even today and are a two-mile walk along a dry creekbed. Access is a bit tricky since you pass through private land along the way and need to watch out for old shells left behind from National Guard training exercises. Get access information from the visitor center.

Lodging and Camping

No bunkhouse accommodations are to be had at the Bunkhouse Motel, tel. (307) 836-2356, but nice motel rooms are $30 s, $37 d (friendly folks, too). Sagebrush Motel, tel. (307) 836-2331, charges $28-32 s or d. You can get pleasant riverside campsites near the Oregon Trail ruts at Larson Park; $5 for tents, $8 for RVs including showers. Showers are $2 for noncampers. Open April to mid-October.

Food

S & S Cafe, tel. (307) 836-9301, serves three meals a day with home-baked goods and good breakfasts. The best steaks in Guernsey are at Trail Inn, tel. (307) 836-2573. Burrito Brothers Mexican Food offers tasty Mexican food. Tummy Stuffer's on the east side of town has burgers, corn dogs, and surprisingly good homemade pizzas. It's the only place open after 8 p.m. Get groceries at B&F Super Foods.

Other Practicalities

Guernsey's small visitor center/museum at S.W. Wyoming and W. Sunrise Streets opens during the summer months. It's located right in front of the town swimming pool, which is also open summers. The Phillips 66 station has an ATM. The nine-hole Trail Ruts Golf Course provides a place to putt around, and there is a small library open Mon.-Saturday. Guernsey's airport is surprisingly large and well equipped, not because of any commercial service but because of the nearby National Guard training facilities.

Each 4th of July, the Old Timer's Rodeo comes to Guernsey, and offers all the standard small-town fun: a parade, a rodeo, a barbecue, a street dance, and fireworks. Labor Day brings a demolition derby and an arts-and-crafts fair.

HARTVILLE AREA

Six miles north of Guernsey on State 270 is the picturesque old mining community of Hartville (pop. 90). Established in 1884, it is the oldest incorporated town in Wyoming. The town is named for Colonel Verling Hart, an officer at nearby Fort Laramie and owner of a copper mine here. The Hartville Uplift—as it is known by geologists—is one of the most mineral-rich regions in Wyoming. Indians used its iron as pigment to make war paint. During the 1870s, prospectors found gold, silver, copper, onyx, and iron ore in these scenic pine- and juniper-dotted hills. Copper brought the first miners, but by 1887 it had been mostly mined out and they turned to iron ore. Hartville arose as a shopping, gambling, boozing, and whoring center for the miners; many of the historic stone and false-front buildings still stand.

Of note is the **Miners Bar**—the state's oldest drinking establishment. The cherrywood back bar was made in Germany in 1864 and shipped to Fort Laramie, then moved to Hartville in 1881. Also in Hartville is an old stone jail and **Venice Bar,** tel. (307) 836-2485, where homemade Italian dinners are served some Saturday evenings. This is a fun place to drop quarters in the jukebox and listen to the country tunes with locals. **Casino Night** in April brings roulette and poker games to Hartville.

The mining ghost town of **Sunrise** (closed to the public) is just a mile east of Hartville. An extraordinarily rich body of iron ore was discovered here in 1887, and a dozen years later the Colorado Fuel and Iron Corp. established an open-pit iron mine, a mine that would eventually reach 650 feet in depth, the largest glory hole in the world. It closed in 1984 and reclamation work has restored the gaping hole to a more natural contour. When the mine first opened, the company hired some 750 predominantly Italian and Greek emigrants to dig the ore, which was shipped to a smelter in Pueblo, Colorado. To house the workers, the clean, well-planned company town of Sunrise sprang up. The mine was closed in 1980 due to a lessened demand for ore, and its brick buildings now stand abandoned. Sunrise claims a minuscule footnote to history: *Ripley's Believe*

It or Not! noted that the town had the longest string of car garages in the world. They are still standing.

The Hartville area is part of the so-called **Spanish Diggings,** an extensive archaeological site that covers hundreds of square miles. Early settlers believed this to be the site of a Spanish gold mine—hence the name—but it is now known to have been used instead by Native Americans gathering flint for arrowheads. They mined quartzite, jasper, moss agate, and chalcedony here for perhaps 10,000 years. Stone flakes and countless old pits up to 15 feet deep and 50 feet across abound in this region. The material mined was carried all the way to the Missouri River. You'll find hundreds of tepee rings and rock chips here. One of the most important aboriginal places in Wyoming is in this area—an 11,000-year-old paleo-Indian site called **Hell Gap.**

The road north from Hartville (State 270) leads over pine-carpeted hills and then descends through rolling grassland with a backdrop of rocky buttes and antelope grazing beside old windmills. There are dramatic views of Laramie Peak from the hilltops. At **Manville** (pop. 130) the road meets U.S. 18/20, which leads to Lusk. There's not much in Manville other than a few old buildings including one of the smallest post offices in Wyoming, a water tower, a school, and a gas station/cafe/bar. The latter, called The Golden Spur, is notable for its "Porn O' Plenty" vending machine in the men's restroom.

GUERNSEY STATE PARK

Two state parks are found along the North Platte River in eastern Wyoming. Seven miles long and covering 6,538 acres, Guernsey is the smaller of the two but is far more interesting than its sister, Glendo State Park. The south entrance to Guernsey State Park is a mile northwest of Guernsey, and the road connects through to the Hartville area. The park surrounds Guernsey Reservoir, which is backed up behind a 105-foot-tall, 560-foot-long earthen dam completed in 1927. Originally, the dam stored 74,000 acre-feet of water, but half that capacity has been lost due to siltation. To reduce this problem, authorities now drain the reservoir each summer

OREGON TRAIL COUNTRY

© MOON PUBLICATIONS, INC.

after July 4th—killing off many of the fish and sometimes creating havoc with boaters, since it can take place with almost no warning. Don't bother bringing your fishing pole. Guernsey is surrounded by scenic grass-and-sage-covered hills topped with juniper and pine. The drive from Hartville through the park is a surprise after the open sage-and-grass country north of here. Pink-walled sandstone cliffs suddenly appear as the narrow, winding road (not for RVs) enters the canyon, hugs the cliffs as it passes the lake, and then climbs into the pines. There is a pleasant sandy beach five miles west along the southern shore and there are 19 different **campgrounds,** each costing $4 per night year-round. The water is quite warm, making this a popular swimming hole. Entrance to Guernsey State Park costs $3 for nonresident vehicles, $2 for folks with Wyoming plates, but fees generally aren't collected after mid-September. Call (307) 836-2334 for more information.

Other than the scenery, the main attractions in Guernsey State Park are the wonderful stone structures built by the Civilian Conservation Corps during the 1930s—some of the best examples of CCC craftsmanship in existence. **Guernsey State Park Museum**—built in 1936—is the finest of all, with an arched stone entrance facing impressive Laramie Peak 35 miles to the west. Inside are enormous hand-hewn timbers, wrought-iron light fixtures, and flagstone floors. This place was built to last! The free museum, tel. (307) 836-2900, is open daily 10 a.m.-6 p.m. May to Labor Day, closed the rest of the year, and houses 14 displays created by the CCC to illustrate the geology and human use of the surrounding country. Take a look at the historical slide show. Other park structures built of native materials include roads, overlooks, rock walls, culverts, bridges, picnic shelters, and the so-called "million-dollar privy" located on the

southwest side of the park. Drink in outstanding vistas from this area at sunset. Also within Guernsey State Park are eight miles of hiking trails and a short nature trail near the museum. Pick up a trail guide inside.

GLENDO STATE PARK

Located 25 miles east of Douglas and 32 miles north of Wheatland, 10,000-acre Glendo State Park surrounds Glendo Reservoir. A 167-foot-high earthen dam backs up water for 14 miles and generates some 24,000 kilowatts of electricity. This is one of the largest reservoirs on the North Platte River, and it has almost 80 miles of shoreline. Note, however, that drought years sometimes reduce the reservoir to little more than a puddle. The surrounding country is treeless and windy but the towering 10,272-foot summit of Laramie Peak dominates the skyline to the west. The surprisingly warm water at Sandy Beach makes this a favorite play area for families. Other attractions are the Red Cliffs, where cliff divers agonize over the long drop, and Muddy Bay, where anglers look for walleye (lunker walleyes here), perch, or trout. You can explore dozens of small coves by boat or float down the river below the dam. The wind can really blow, making for good windsurfing conditions but also creating hazards for folks who go out in small boats.

Practicalities

There are seven state park campgrounds ($4; open year-round) on the eastern end of Glendo Reservoir. Get permits from park headquarters, tel. (307) 735-4433, near the dam. Entrance is $3 for nonresident vehicles, $2 for Wyoming vehicles. The desolate and run-down town of **Glendo** (pop. 230) is just two miles from Glendo State Park, near the site of the old **Horseshoe Creek Stage Station.** Built by Mormons in the 1850s, the station was later burned by them to keep it out of government hands. A small **Glendo Historical Museum** next to the town office is open Mon.-Fri. 8 a.m.-noon and 1-4 p.m. and displays early settlers' gear, dinosaur bones, and rocks.

Lodging is available at **Howard's Motel,** 106 A St., tel. (307) 735-4252, for $20 s, $27 d. **Glendo Marina,** near the dam, tel. (307) 735-4216, has rustic motel accommodations overlooking the lake for $45 s or d, a restaurant, a small grocery store, and RV hookups ($13). Rent fishing boats here for $60 a day or pontoon boats for $125-150 a day. The marina is open year-round but the other facilities are closed in winter.

On Memorial Day weekend the **Hot Air Balloon Rally** takes place at Glendo. In addition to the balloons, it features a craft fair, games, a flea market, food booths, and a street dance. Call (307) 735-4543 for more info. The **Glendo Walleye Fishing Tournament,** tel. (307) 735-4216, comes around in early June, and a fireworks display takes place on the 4th of July.

FORT LARAMIE NATIONAL HISTORIC SITE

One of the most important historic sites in all Wyoming is old Fort Laramie, located three miles south of the town of the same name. The fort played a variety of roles as the West was developed: Indian trading post, emigrant way station, and military center. Fort Laramie stood at the crossroads of history. The budding territory's first school and post office opened here, and nearly every famous citizen of the frontier era—from Jim Bridger to Mark Twain—stopped in. Today Fort Laramie is one of the most popular stopping points for visitors who want a taste of the rich history of this region.

HISTORY

In 1834, trader William Sublette halted along the banks of the Laramie River near its confluence with the North Platte. With him were 35 mountain men, their pack animals weighted down with trade items for the annual rendezvous along the Green River. Sublette had a bold plan to build a permanent trading post here, one that would make it easier to bring supplies west and beaver furs and buffalo robes back east, a place where Indians and whites could parley and prof-

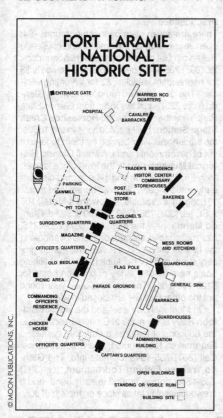

FORT LARAMIE
NATIONAL
HISTORIC SITE

ENTRANCE GATE

MARRIED NCO QUARTERS

HOSPITAL

CAVALRY BARRACKS

TRADER'S RESIDENCE

VISITOR CENTER / COMMISSARY STOREHOUSES

PARKING

SAWMILL

POST TRADER'S STORE

BAKERIES

PIT TOILET

LT. COLONEL'S QUARTERS

SURGEON'S QUARTERS

MAGAZINE

MESS ROOMS AND KITCHENS

OFFICER'S QUARTERS

OLD BEDLAM

FLAG POLE

GUARDHOUSE

PICNIC AREA

PARADE GROUNDS

GENERAL SINK

COMMANDING OFFICER'S RESIDENCE

BARRACKS

GUARDHOUSES

CHICKEN HOUSE

OFFICER'S QUARTERS

ADMINISTRATION BUILDING

CAPTAIN'S QUARTERS

OPEN BUILDINGS

STANDING OR VISIBLE RUIN

BUILDING SITE

© MOON PUBLICATIONS, INC.

During the next eight years, Fort Laramie emerged as a strategic center trade with the Indians; more than 10,000 buffalo robes were purchased each year. (Traders generally paid the equivalent of $1 per robe in the form of gunpowder, hatchets, tobacco, coffee, sugar, blankets, and, of course, liquor. The robes were sold in St. Louis for $4 each.) But its time as a trading post gradually gave way to a new role for the fort.

The Army Takes Over

Fort Laramie stood right along the main trail to Oregon and California. It was one-third of the way from Missouri to the Columbia River mouth and provided a much-anticipated break before the long, desolate trek over the Continental Divide. In 1843, nearly a thousand people passed the fort. The numbers increased each year, reaching a crescendo after gold was discovered in California in 1849. Soon thereafter, more than 50,000 emigrants were trudging into Fort Laramie each summer. They stopped to repair wheels at the carpentry and blacksmith shops, purchase food and whiskey at the store, or trade tired stock for fresh oxen and horses. The latter was the best deal for traders at the fort; all they had to do was put the oxen and horses they had gotten in trade (generally a two-for-one deal) out to pasture for a couple of weeks and then trade them as fresh stock to subsequent emigrants.

This great migration westward had its negative consequences. Indians complained that buffalo were being shot and forced away from their traditional migration routes and that the thousands of stock brought by the emigrants were destroying the grass. The inevitable conflicts began as young warriors halted wagon trains demanding "tolls" in the form of tobacco, coffee, or sugar. Quickly, this escalated into attacks against the emigrants, and a great hue and cry went up for protection from the "savages." Thus it was that Congress gave Fort Laramie the new role of military garrison mandated to protect the Oregon Trail.

In 1849, the Army purchased Fort Laramie for $4,000, establishing the first military post in what would become Wyoming. Some 180 men—both cavalrymen and infantrymen—were assigned to the post. A rapid expansion program was begun; the old adobe fort served as

it. He left behind a dozen men to begin work on what would become Fort William (named after its founder) and hurried west to the rendezvous. The men threw up a cottonwood stockade with blockhouses on the corners and a tunnel to the outer gate for trading with the Indians.

Over the next two years the post changed hands a couple of times. Changing its name to Fort Lucien, it became an important trade center for Pierre Chouteau's American Fur Company. By 1841, competition from another trading post—built just a mile away—forced the company to start again. This time they spent $10,000 building a whitewashed adobe fort near the already rotting old one. Fort John-on-the-Laramie was the official name given to the second fort, but this was quickly shortened to Fort Laramie.

temporary quarters while more elaborate facilities were built. The Army's Fort Laramie did not fit the Hollywood stereotype of a frontier fort—it had no log perimeter or blockhouses. The fort was instead laid out around a central parade ground, with clapboard and "lime grout" concrete buildings forming a loose perimeter. In case of attack, the Army was prepared to retreat to a single, heavily fortified building. Despite this general lack of protection and the fact that Indians once brazenly drove off the fort's horses, the fort was never attacked by Indians, and most soldiers never engaged in battle with the Indians.

Fort Laramie was essentially a male bastion, though a few officers' wives were present. The only exceptions were laundresses, hired generally on the basis of their physical appearance: the less attractive the better, so as to not appeal to the soldiers' prurient interests. A small group of Indians, derisively termed "Laramie Loafers," soon attached themselves to the fort, camping nearby and providing scouts, interpreters, errand boys, and paramours. Fort Laramie was not a pleasant place. The food was deplorable, discipline so strict that even the smallest infraction could land a man in the brig, and sanitary conditions were so bad that by 1880 it was getting hard to find a place to dig latrines that had not already been contaminated. The infrequent paydays turned into drunken brawls. No wonder so many men deserted their post and slipped off for the promising goldfields of California! The inevitable "hog ranches" also grew up near the fort and offered an escape from the day-to-day monotony of the soldiers' lives. In 1877, Lt. John G. Bourke described the "ranches" as

tenanted by as hardened and depraved a set of witches as could be found on the face of the globe. Each of these establishments was equipped with a rum-mill of the worst kind and each contained from three to half a dozen Cyprians, virgins whose lamps were always burning brightly in expectance of the coming of the bridegroom, and who lured to destruction the soldiers of the garrison. In all my experience I have never seen a lower, more beastly set of people of both sexes.

For the next four decades, Fort Laramie served as the nerve center for this part of the plains, providing troops and cavalry to retaliate against Indian attacks and serving as a meeting place for treaty arrangements when the political wind shifted toward negotiation instead of confrontation. The first of these treaties came in 1851, under the forceful leadership of Indian agent Thomas Fitzpatrick, a former mountain man. More than 10,000 Indians attended, representing the Sioux, Cheyenne, Arapaho, Shoshone, Crow, Gros Ventre, and Assiniboin tribes. The treaty consisted essentially of annual bribes (annuities) to be given to the Indians to compensate them for their losses to whites. The various tribes would be assigned to distinct territories but could hunt in other areas. After signing the treaty, a mountain of presents awaited—the first of the $50,000 in annuities for each of the next 50 years. Shortly thereafter, the federal government reneged on the promise, increasing the annual amount to $70,000 per year but cutting the time to just 10 years. Peace lasted but a short while.

Grattan Massacre

One of the few Indian-white conflicts to occur in the vicinity of Fort Laramie took place in 1854. It began innocently enough when a Mormon emigrant's lame cow wandered off and was butchered by a hungry Miniconjou Indian waiting for the government to dispense annuities. A hot-headed young lieutenant, John Grattan, was sent out to bring in the Indian. Unfortunately, Grattan's interpreter was drunk and began immediately shouting insults at the Sioux in whose village the man was camped. Grattan himself was anxious for a fight, hoping to gain a piece of fame, so when the Sioux refused to give up the man—offering instead to pay for the cow with two horses—Grattan would have nothing of it. His soldiers opened fire and were themselves immediately attacked by a vastly superior force of Sioux. All 29 soldiers died in the massacre that followed, and Fort Laramie stood in danger of being destroyed. But the Indians instead raided local storehouses for the promised annuities and headed out. The Army used the Grattan Massacre as proof that the Indians could not be trusted. In reality, the entire incident was an instance of utter stupidity on the part of the Army.

More Trouble

One of the least distinguished post commanders at Fort Laramie was the hard-drinking and ill-tempered Colonel Thomas Moonlight. In 1865, he publicly hanged two Sioux subchiefs who had brought in two white women captives for reward. Their bodies were left dangling in chains for several days, an act that brought condemnation from the Eastern press. In retaliation, the Sioux killed several soldiers and then managed to drive off most of the horses from Colonel Moonlight's cavalry. A sullen Moonlight led his almost horseless cavalry in the 120-mile hike back to the fort. Though shortly thereafter stripped of his command, Moonlight later served as the politically appointed territorial governor of Wyoming.

With the decline in importance of the Oregon Trail, Fort Laramie became a staging area for military expeditions against the Indians. In the Treaty of 1868, signed at the fort, the Sioux were guaranteed the Powder River country "as long as the grass shall grow and the buffalo shall roam." But the discovery of gold in the Black Hills abruptly changed the picture, and whites now wanted the land itself, not just a road through it. They eventually got it, but not before the massacre of Custer and his men at Little Big Horn in 1876. After this, with the Indians tucked away on reservations, most of the hostilities died down and the fort lost its strategic importance. The railroad had long since supplanted the Oregon Trail as the primary route west, and for the decade of the 1880s Fort Laramie served as a way station along the Cheyenne-to-Deadwood stage road. During this time the fort grew more genteel with the planting of trees and completion of numerous substantial homes.

The Army Departs

By 1889, it was clear that Fort Laramie had outlived its usefulness and it was ordered closed. The following year, the 35,000 acres of military land were opened to homesteaders and the buildings auctioned off. Because of the scarcity of wood in the area, many were stripped and hauled away to become cabins or other structures. Others remained on the site and were used as homes, businesses, or barns. For the next half century the historic fort slowly deteriorated, but in 1937 the state of Wyoming purchased the site and donated it to the federal government. The following year it was declared a national monument, to be managed by the National Park Service. A lengthy and difficult restoration process managed to stabilize the ruins and restore a dozen of the historic structures, but it was not until 1964 that the fort was restored to something approaching the conditions in the 1880s.

FORT LARAMIE TODAY

Each year nearly 90,000 visitors come to historic Fort Laramie for a rewarding traipse back in time. The clear, tree-lined Laramie River still flows close by, and the spacious parade ground engenders a feeling of this fort's importance, while the bleak, windswept setting speaks of its hardships.

Visiting the Fort

Buildings and grounds of the 830-acre Fort Laramie National Historic Site are open year-round 8 a.m. to sunset. Entrance costs $2 for adults, no charge for kids under 16 or seniors with Golden Age passes. There's no camping at the site but there is a pleasant picnic area. For a good orientation to Fort Laramie, head to the old commissary building, now the **visitor center/park headquarters,** tel. (307) 837-2221. Inside are excellent displays and historic photos, including a scale model of the fort, an 1876 Gatling gun, and many photos. The center is open daily 8 a.m.-7 p.m. mid-May through mid-September and daily 8 a.m.-4:30 p.m. the rest of the year. Videos about the fort and the old West are shown at scheduled times during the summer, by request the rest of the year. The bookstore has probably the most complete collection of historic books on the frontier anywhere in Wyoming. It also sells such authentic items as lye soap and hardtack. Ask about interpretive talks and tours and the dramatic firings of historic weapons.

If you're in the area in early July, be sure to drop by Fort Laramie for an **Old-Fashioned 4th of July Celebration** with all sorts of festivities. Many locals join in by dressing up in period clothing and taking part in activities including a fur trade camp.

Historical Buildings

By the time it was abandoned in 1890, Fort Laramie was approaching the size of a small town; 60 buildings of all types were scattered around the grounds. The remains of 21 of these are still visible—some simply lime-grout concrete ruins maintained in a state of arrested decay. A dozen have been completely restored and refurbished with authentic period pieces behind Plexiglas doors. The Park Service has an informative *Historic Buildings Guide* for 20 cents available at the visitor center. Several of the buildings are particularly noteworthy: the cavalry barracks, Old Bedlam, the bakery, and the guardhouse.

Most of the men who soldiered out of Fort Laramie lived under crowded conditions with little privacy. Sometimes this meant living in tents for long periods. The **cavalry barracks** on your left as you enter the fort were an improvement, but quarters were still tight. Walk up to the restored second floor to find row upon row of cots where an entire company of 60 men slept. Then try to imagine all the snoring and the smelly feet after being out on duty for weeks at a time! Baths were taken, in theory, every Saturday night in a half barrel.

The **post trader's store** just right of the entrance provided a break from the army's monotonous food and supplies. Built in 1849, it served not only the military but also the thousands of civilians who poured west along the Oregon Trail and the Indians who traded for various items. The store owner provided everything from essential food supplies to fresh oxen for weary emigrants. He also sold alcohol and benefited from the tons of excess belongings that many overburdened travelers cast aside to lighten their loads.

The officers enjoyed far better living conditions than the cavalry and infantry, including access to a pleasant officer's club and a hired cook. The 1884 **lieutenant colonel's quarters** has been restored to the era when Lt. Colonel Andrew Burt and his family lived here (1887-88). Inside you'll see a number of the family's original furnishings. Next door is the **post surgeon's quarters**, completed in 1875. The surgeon had a highly respected rank in the fort and was accorded the responsibility of gathering weather data as well as scientific specimens.

The surgeon dealt primarily with such problems as kicks by horses, injuries from brawls, frost-bitten fingers and toes, and venereal diseases. War wounds were far less common but when they did occur many could not be adequately treated and the men often died.

The oldest and most prominent building at Fort Laramie is **Old Bedlam**, an attractive clapboard structure that dominates the west end of the parade grounds. Built in 1849, it was the center of life at the fort. Old Bedlam served a variety of purposes when the military was here; initially the post headquarters, it later became a hotel of sorts for bachelor officers and housing for married officers and their families. The name apparently comes from the bedlam that existed with so many folks jammed together—particularly after payday, when parties raged. Old Bedlam is now refurbished to represent two different periods. Upstairs are displays representing the living quarters of Lt. Colonel William O. Collins, while the bachelor officers' quarters are downstairs.

Behind the attractive **Captain's Quarters** on the south end of the parade ground is a model of adobe-walled Fort John, which stood on this spot in 1841. The "bat house" near here was recently built in an attempt to keep bats from roosting in the Captain's Quarters. A footpath leads to the Laramie River. The old stone **guardhouse** on the east side of the fort could house up to 40 prisoners, ranging from soldiers who had violated minor conduct rules to those charged with murder. The basement jail had no furniture, toilet, or light, and no heat even in the dead of winter. Stop by the historic **bakery**—one of four built here at different times—for a taste of bread. One loaf of bread, along with greasy salt pork, beans, rice, and rotgut coffee, was the typical daily allotment for soldiers. Fresh vegetables were often unavailable for months at a time, and scurvy was a constant threat. In the field, the rations were even worse, generally consisting of salt pork, beans, and wormy hardtack.

One of the less-visited sights in the area is **Old Bedlam ruts**, two miles northwest of Fort Laramie. A gravel road leads to the location; get a map from park headquarters. The ruts (marked by posts) climb up into the gentle hills west of the old fort, offering a marvelous

panorama of a landscape that has not changed much in the last century. From here, it's easy to imagine emigrants looking back on the fort, their last touch with civilization for hundreds of miles. Laramie Peak is prominent to the west. Nearby is the grave of Mary Homsley, one of the thousands who died along the difficult trek west. The ruts can be traced all the way to Guernsey, where they grow even deeper. A similar series of ruts extends eastward from the fort. If you're heading to Wheatland from the fort, try the "back way" via Grayrocks Reservoir—the source of cooling water for the Laramie River Power Plant. The road is rough for the first eight miles or so, but it is paved beyond that and offers an enjoyable taste of the rugged countryside around the reservoir. Signs point the way to Wheatland.

THE TOWN OF FORT LARAMIE

The town of Fort Laramie (pop. 220) lies three miles north of the historic fort and across the North Platte River. Wyoming's oldest post office is here, dating back to the 1880s when the Army was occupying the nearby fort. A mile south of town is an **iron bridge** built in 1875. Though long superseded by a concrete span just upriver and not much to look at, the bridge bears historical importance. Funded by a $15,000 congressional appropriation, the bridge ensured the establishment of the Cheyenne-Deadwood Stage and Express through here. It

remained the major route north for many years thereafter. Note how much longer the old bridge is than the new one. Upstream dams have blocked the river flow, making it barely a third of the original width. A highway monument east of town along U.S. 26 notes the site of the **Grattan Massacre** (see above).

Practicalities

Recently restored by its English owners, the historic **Rose & Crown**, tel. (307) 837-3065, now contains a white-linen restaurant on the main floor, a cozy British pub with overstuffed furniture downstairs, and B&B accommodations upstairs for $85-90 s or d. The rooms feature private baths, and a full breakfast is served. The restaurant menu changes nightly but always includes English favorites and imported beers.

Fort Laramie Motel, tel. (307) 837-3063, offers quite basic accommodations for $25 s or d and kitchenettes for $5 extra. Open May-October. Pitch tents for free at the town park just across the railroad tracks on the south side of town (no showers). **Chuckwagon Campground,** tel. (307) 837-2828, is open April-Nov. only and charges $9 for tents, $12 for RVs. **Bennett Court Campground,** tel. (307) 837-2270, may also be open. **Pony Soldier RV Park,** tel. (307) 837-3078, five miles east of Fort Laramie and five miles west of Lingle, is open April-Oct. with tent spaces for $10, RVs for $13. It's a desolate place in a windblown field.

A small log-cabin **visitor center** on the main street is staffed daily May to mid-October.

TORRINGTON

Torrington (pop. 5,800) is a quiet farming town located just eight miles from the Nebraska border. It's the seat of Wyoming's most important agricultural county—Goshen, alias "The Land of Goshen." Lots of sugar beets, alfalfa, oats, dry beans, corn, and hay are grown here. The tree-lined North Platte River drifts lazily through town. Torrington's economy is relatively stable; the biggest local employer, a Holly Sugar factory, is on the edge of town and many productive farms are scattered in the surrounding countryside. Two long waterways—Fort Laramie Canal and the Interstate Canal—provide irrigation water

to much of this farmland. Trains filled with coal from Campbell and Weston Counties constantly rumble through toward the south and east, a stench from the sugar refinery hangs in the air, and the livestock auction is the big daily event. A walk along Main Street is a trek through the American heartland.

History

Although several hundred thousand emigrants passed through Goshen County on their way to Oregon, California, or Utah, none bothered to stop. The area was not settled until cattlemen

came in the 1880s, followed by homesteaders around the turn of the century including many from Russia and Germany. Many of the "soddies" and wooden shacks these emigrants built still stand in the fields throughout the county. Named for Torrington, Connecticut, the town was incorporated in 1907 as a ranching and farming center. Completion of the Interstate Canal in 1915 and the Fort Laramie Canal in 1924 brought North Platte River water, making it possible to grow a wide variety of crops. The Burlington Railroad arrived from the east in 1900 but it was not until 1926 that the Union Pacific built a line connecting Torrington with Pine Bluffs to the south. That year proved a pivotal one, for it brought a new train depot and the Holly Sugar plant. The town has grown slowly over the years and except for a brief flirtation with oil and gas in the 1970s has remained true to its farming and ranching roots.

Homestead Museum

Located right at the crossroads of the Oregon Trail, the Cheyenne-to-Deadwood stage route, the Mormon Trail, and the Texas Cattle Trail, the Homestead Museum seems to sit atop history. It is housed in the 1926 brick-and-masonry Union Pacific depot just south of town. The last train stopped at the depot in 1964. The museum, tel. (307) 532-5612, is open Mon.-Sat. 10 a.m.-5 p.m. and Sunday 1-4 p.m. during the summer and Mon.-Fri. 10 a.m.-4 p.m. in winter. Although it contains a substantial paleo-Indian collection, the museum focuses on the thousands of turn-of-the-century homesteaders who flocked to eastern Wyoming. The Yoder Ranch collection (artifacts from 1881 on) is particularly noteworthy. Other displays include items from the 4A Ranch and the Bordeau Trading Post near Fort Laramie, a homemade baseball bat from 1920, and a marvelous collection of old black-and-white photos. Sit down and spend some time looking through these pictures; they will quickly transport you back to a simple era when pioneers scratched out a hardscrabble life on the mixed-grass prairie in wooden or sod shacks. Once you're through

these, check out the box of freebies: pieces of old stone knives and scrapers from a nearby archaeological dig. The KKK robe displayed in the museum comes from the 1920s, when a vehemently racist and anti-Catholic spirit dominated much of rural America. Outside are an old homestead cabin, a windmill, and a caboose housing historic railroad photos and memorabilia.

Other Sights

Over 120,000 cattle are raised in Goshen County each year—more than in any other Wyoming county—so it is logical that Torrington should also be at the center of the state's livestock trade. Each year more than a quarter of a million cattle are marketed at Torrington's two livestock sales barns. These are fascinating places to visit, offering an authentic taste of ranching life. **Torrington Livestock Market,** on U.S. 26 at W. E St., tel. (307) 532-3333, has auctions every Friday beginning at 10 a.m., with additional Wednesday load lot auctions in the fall. **Stockman Livestock Auction,** tel. (307) 532-7079, is two miles south of Torrington on U.S. 85, then a half mile west on State 154. Here you'll find cattle sales every Thursday at 10 a.m.

Two miles west of town is the University of Wyoming's **College of Agriculture Research and Extension Center,** open to the public. Two-hour tours of nearby cattle ranches are available through a local women's group, the **Goshen County CowBelles.** Advance arrangements are necessary; call (307) 837-2510.

For a nice walk, saunter along the paved **Grassroots Trail,** built atop an old irrigation canal that slices along the northern edge of Torrington. A small **Botanical Park** occupies the corner of 1st Ave. and S. Main St. with paths and plants. South of Torrington a sign marks the **Cold Springs Campground** used by travelers on the Oregon Trail and later the site of a stage station and a pony express stop. A few miles east of town is a memorial marker to the party of Astorians who camped nearby in the winter of 1812.

TODD CLARK

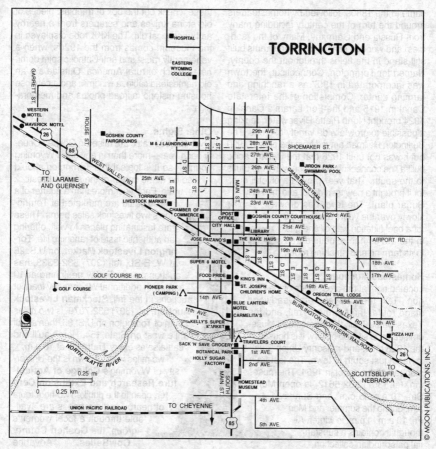

TORRINGTON

Eastern Wyoming College, 3200 W. C St., tel. (307) 532-7111, is one of the oldest junior colleges in the state, first established in 1948 as an extension of the University of Wyoming but now independent. The hilltop campus has 1,800 full- and part-time students studying in nearly 60 vocational and academic fields.

Accommodations and Camping

See the "Torrington Accommodations" chart for local motels. Note that noisy freight trains roll through Torrington at all hours of the night, so you may want to choose a place as far as possible from the tracks.

Camp for free in **Pioneer Park** along the North Platte River on the edge of town. It's open year-round but during the winter you'll need to get water elsewhere. **Travelers Court,** 750 S. Main, tel. (307) 532-5517, has shady riverside tent sites for $4 and RV sites for $12. The facilities are a bit run-down. Showers for noncampers cost $2. Open year-round.

Food

For reasonable breakfasts (try the buttermilk hotcakes) and fresh baked goods, head to **The Bake Haus,** 1915 Main St., tel. (307) 532-2982. Lots of locals hang out here in the morning,

STARVING TO DEATH ON A GOVERNMENT CLAIM

My name is Frank Taylor, a bachelor I am,
I'm keeping old batch on an elegant plan,
You'll find me out West in the county of Lane
A-starving to death on a Government claim.

Hurrah for Lane County, the land of the free,
The home of the bedbug, grasshopper and flea,
I'll sing of its praises and boast of its fame
A-starving to death on a Government claim.

My clothes they are ragged, my language is rough,
My bread is case-hardened and solid and tough,
But I have a good time and live at my ease
On common sop-sorghum and old bacon grease.

How happy am I when I crawl into bed,
With rattlesnakes rattling just under my head,
And the gay little bedbug, so cheerful and bright,
He keeps me a-going two-thirds of the night.

How happy am I on my Government claim,
I've nothing to lose and I've nothing to gain,
I've nothing to eat and I've nothing to wear,
And nothing from nothing is honest and fair.

Oh, come to Lane County, there's room for you all,
Where the wind never stops and the rains never fall,
Oh, join in the chorus and sing of her fame,
A-starving to death on a Government claim.

Oh, don't be downhearted, you poor hungry men,
We're all just as free as the pigs in the pen,
Just stick to your homestead and fight with your fleas,
And pray to your Maker to send some more breeze.

Now all you poor sinners, I hope you will stay
And chaw on your hardtack till you're toothless
*   and grey,*
But as for myself I don't aim to remain
And slave like a dog on no Government claim.

Farewell to Lane County, the pride of the West
I'm going back East to the girl I love best,
I'll stop in Missouri and get me a wife,
And live on corn doggers the rest of my life.

—Anonymous

and the Friday and Saturday night prime rib is another favorite. **Chuckwagon Cafe,** 2113 N. Main St., tel. (307) 532-2888, serves breakfast all day long and has great all-American stuff-yourself meals. The fare includes inexpensive burgers, steaks, roast turkey, a salad bar, and a dessert table. The Sunday all-you-can-eat buffets ($7) are especially popular. **Java Jar,** 1940 N. Main, tel. (307) 532-8541, has espresso coffees, soup served in bread bowls, and sandwiches.

Deacons Restaurant, 1558 S. Main St., tel. (307) 532-4766, opens Mon.-Sat. at 5:30 a.m. for dependably good meals. **Jose Paizano's,** 1918 Main St., tel. (307) 532-4822, cooks up Mexican and Italian dishes, including very good pizzas. For the chain version, try **Pizza Hut,** 1300 E. Valley Rd., tel. (307) 532-7007. **Peking Garden,** 2126 N. Main St., tel. (307) 532-8883, serves up Chinese food, and **Carmelita's,** 1250 S. Main, tel. (307) 532-8622, has Mexican meals and margaritas.

Kings Inn, 1555 S. Main St., tel. (307) 532-4011, has nightly dinner specials and happy hours in the lounge on weeknights. For reasonably priced steaks and seafood in an attractive setting, head to **Little Moon Lake Supper Club,** tel. (307) 532-5750, on the state line eight miles east on U.S. 26. Three grocers are in Torrington: **Kelly's Super Market** on S. Main, tel. (307) 532-3113, **Sack 'N' Save Supermarket,** 615 S. Main St., tel. (307) 532-2167, and **Food Pride Grocery Store,** 1542 S. Main, tel. (307) 532-3401.

Recreation
Torrington has an outdoor **swimming pool** (tel. 307-532-7798) in Jirdon Park, open summers only. Kids will love the 180-foot water slide. There is also an 18-hole municipal **golf course,** tel. (307) 532-2418, outside of town.

Entertainment and Events
Watch movies at **Wyoming Theatre,** 126

TORRINGTON ACCOMMODATIONS

Note: Accommodations are listed from least to most expensive. Add an eight percent tax to these rates. Area code is 307.

Maverick Motel; 1.5 miles W on US 26-85; tel. 532-4064; $30 s or d; kitchenettes, AAA approved

Oregon Trail Lodge; US 26 & F St.; tel. 532-2101; $20-28 s, $22-30 d

Blue Lantern Motel; 1402 S. Main St.; tel. 532-9986; $20 s, $25-30 d; very friendly, kitchenettes

Western Motel; 1.5 miles W on US 26-85; tel. 532-2104; $30-40 s, $36-46 d; clean

Super 8 Motel; 1548 S. Main St.; tel. 532-7118 or (800) 800-8000; $41 s, $47 d; exercise room, AAA approved

King's Inn; 1555 S. Main St.; tel. 532-4011; $46 s, $66 d; indoor pool, AAA approved

E. 20th Ave., tel. (307) 532-2226. **Broncho Bar,** 1924 Main St., tel. (307) 532-4285, is a classy place with live country music on weekends. Many locals also head over to the **Stateline Oasis,** tel. (307) 532-4990, next to the Nebraska line, for the chance to dance to rock or country and western tunes or to watch the strippers Tuesday through Thursday nights.

The biggest annual event in Torrington is the **Goshen County Fair,** held the second full week in August and presenting everything from a parade to pig wrestling. It's a good place to check out all the 4-H hogs and sheep on display.

Information and Services

The **Torrington Chamber of Commerce** office, 350 W. 21st Ave., tel. (307) 532-3879, is open Mon.-Fri. 8 a.m.-5 p.m. Other practicalities include the **public library** at 2001 E. A St., tel. (307) 532-3411, which sells a few used books, and the **post office** at 2145 Main St., tel. (307) 532-2213. Wash clothes at **M&J Laundromat,** 27th Ave and W. C St., tel. (307) 532-9993. Rent cars from **Platte Valley Motor Co.,** 510 W. Valley Rd., tel. (307) 532-2114.

TORRINGTON AREA

The town symbol for Torrington is the ring-necked pheasant—a fitting logo in this farming country. **Downar Bird Farm,** 17 miles south on U.S. 85, tel. (307) 532-3449, raises some 7,000 pheasants each year. It is run by the Wyoming Game and Fish Department, which releases the birds each fall for area hunters. This is basically a release-and-shoot operation, since the birds are let go in unfamiliar territory just in time for hunting season. The farm is an interesting place to visit and boasts 27 different pheasant breeds. The ring-necked pheasant so common in the Midwest, incidently, is a native of China.

The minuscule town of **Veteran** (pop. 20)—basically a post office and general store located 15 miles southwest of Torrington—was established by Iowa veterans of WW I. A prisoner-of-war camp was established here in WW II. The surrounding landscape is a mixture of grass, wheat, sage, and rocky buttes with cattle grazing the land and vultures circling above. **Hawk Springs State Recreation Area** lies to the south off U.S. 85 near the town of **Hawk Springs** (pop. 100). The only attraction here is the Longbranch Steakhouse/Saloon/Cafe.

Heading North

Ten miles northwest of Torrington is the prosperous farming crossroads called **Lingle** (pop. 490). Trains laden with coal roll through almost continuously. The small **Western History Center** in Lingle, tel. (307) 837-3052 or 837-2545, is open Mon.-Sat. 9 a.m.-4 p.m. and Sunday 1-6 p.m. The town has two fine places to eat but no lodging places. **Lira's,** tel. (307) 837-2826, offers authentic Mexican food that attracts folks from many miles around. Also here is **Stagecoach Cafe,** tel. (307) 837-2614, with Saturday night prime rib specials. Lingle's **Harvest Festival** takes place each August.

North of Lingle on U.S. 85, the irrigated pastures and green fields give way to endless prairies. This is a land of sandy hillocks carpeted with short grasses, similar to the sandhill country of western Nebraska which lies just a dozen miles eastward. Halfway between Lingle and Lusk, the road passes the near-ghost

town of **Jay Em** (pop. 15), named for the cattle brand of rancher Jim Moore. Just to the north lies his old Jay Em Ranch. A few people still live in the old wooden houses of Jay Em, and the post office becomes a meeting place each morning, but the town is otherwise deserted. It's a peaceful spot to stop and walk along nar-row Rawhide Creek among the cottonwood trees and tall grass. The town is a National Historic District and the rustic old buildings are a photographer's treat. Continuing north to Lusk, the country again opens into grassland, wind-mills, cattle, a few tree-topped hills, and small rocky buttes.

LUSK

Lusk (pop. 1,600) is the seat of Wyoming's least-populated county. Just 3,200 people live in rural Niobrara County—an average of almost 524 acres per person! It's remote grassland country here with long, straight highways heading out in the compass directions. The oil industry that once was so prominent has faded considerably in recent years, but ranching provides a rela-tively stable, albeit limited, economic base. The town itself has a quiet, Midwestern feel, with tree-lined streets and attractive older homes. Lusk's main attraction is the *Legend of Rawhide,* a July extravaganza.

History
The first settlers in this part of Wyoming were miners in search of copper, silver, and gold. They built a small settlement around the Silver Cliff Mine but moved a mile east when the Fremont, Elkhorn, and Missouri Valley Railroad arrived in 1886. Lusk was named for Frank Lusk, a local rancher who donated land for the new townsite. In 1917, oil was discovered along Lance Creek 20 miles north of here and almost overnight Lusk became a boomtown, reaching more than 10,000 residents during the peak years of oil produc-tion. Pipelines were built to the 200 producing wells and a refinery was added in Lusk. By the 1940s, Lance Creek had become Wyoming's largest oilfield. More recently, oil production has declined and the old standby of ranching has re-gained prominence. In 1984, the town succeed-ed in getting a women's correctional center built; this is now the second-largest employer in the county (after the local school district).

Lusk has seen its share of lust over the years. The Yellow Hotel brothel occupied a place of local importance until the late 1970s; rumor has it that the madam, Del Burke, was allowed to keep it open because she owned most of Lusk's water bonds! **Mother Featherlegs**—so named because she often rode horseback with her red pantaloons blowing in the wind—was a well-known 19th-century madam who was murdered in 1879, apparently for money. Some claim that a fortune in gold she had buried nearby still waits to be claimed. A granite marker southwest of Lusk notes the site of her old place of entertainment along the Cheyenne-Black Hills Stage Line; it's said to be the nation's only historical marker com-memorating a prostitute. Get here by heading two miles west of town on U.S. 18 and then turn-ing south at the rest area for another 11 miles. In 1990, Lusk locals swept into a Deadwood sa-loon and recovered her famous pantaloons, stolen from the historic site in 1964. Today, you'll find them on display at the town museum.

Sights
Lusk has one of the nicer historic collections in the state, the aptly named **Stagecoach Muse-um,** 342 S. Main St., tel. (307) 334-3444. It's open Wed.-Fri. 10 a.m.-8 p.m. and Sat.-Tues. 10 a.m.-5 p.m. from Memorial Day to Labor Day, Mon.-Fri. 10 a.m.-5 p.m. the rest of the year. Call (307) 334-2372 for access at other times. Admission is $2 for adults, free for kids under 12. Climb up the steep, narrow stairs to find the reason for its name—an old coach built by Ab-bott & Downing of Concord, New Hampshire, in 1863. Used for many years on the famed Cheyenne and Black Hills Stage and Express Line, the stagecoach is one of only two in exis-tence; its sister resides in the Smithsonian In-stitution. The museum also houses a treasure chest broken open during the Canyon Springs Stage robbery of 1879. It contained gold bul-lion from the Black Hills destined for Cheyenne.

Here, too besides the standard fare—an old buggy, a sulky, a dray wagon, covered wagons, and various Indian artifacts and arrowheads—you'll find such intriguing odds and ends as a 1950s iron lung, a two-headed calf, an antique bedpan collection, photos of Niobrara County's many one-room schoolhouses, and a 31-star 1876 U.S. flag. Try not to snicker at the kitschy collection of dolls dressed up as the wives of various presidents (including Barbara Bush as a busty Barbie doll). Out back is an old one-room log schoolhouse built in 1886. And, oh yes, the famous Mother Featherlegs pantaloons are next to the museum director's desk, where she can make sure they aren't stolen again by folks from Deadwood.

The city park at 14th and Linn contains a **homestead cabin** built in the 1880s and originally located at Running Water Stage Station. Another site of minor historical interest is on the east side of town along the railroad tracks. Here you'll find a **redwood water tank** built in 1886 to supply water for steam engines of the Chicago and Northwestern Railroad. It is one of only six still standing in the nation.

Accommodations

See the "Lusk Accommodations" chart for a list of local motels. Note that rates may be higher during the *Legend of Rawhide* and other events.

A couple of places offer unique true-West accommodations. **Mill Iron 7 Ranch,** tel. (308) 668-2148, is a working cattle ranch in the badlands 25 miles east of Lusk along the Wyoming/Nebraska border. There's no pretense here; guests stay in wall tents and eat with the ranchers. **Granite Creek Livestock Ranch,** tel. (307) 334-2372, is 14 miles southwest of Lusk near the old Cheyenne and Black Hills route. Guests stay in the big bunkhouse, a tent trailer, or private guest house and enjoy horseback rides, wagon tours of nearby canyons, fishing, and hiking. Three big meals are served each day.

Camping

BJ's Campground, 902 S. Maple St., tel. (307) 334-2462, has unshaded RV sites for $13; open year-round. **Prairie View Campground,** two miles west of Lusk on U.S. 18/20, tel. (307) 334-9904, isn't particularly attractive but has RV hookups for $13.

Food

You'll find the best breakfasts in town (and good burgers and shakes) at **The Diner,** 234 S. Main, tel. (307) 334-3606. **Fireside Inn,** 904 S. Main, tel. (307) 334-3477, has very good family-style meals, the Sunday brunch is a bargain, and the soup and salad bar offers an inexpensive way to

---

LUSK ACCOMMODATIONS

Note: Accommodations are arranged from least to most expensive. Add an eight percent tax to these rates. Area code is 307.

Hospitality House Motor Hotel; 201 S. Main; tel. 334-2120; $20 s, $24-28 d; upstairs rooms

Rawhide Motel; 805 S. Main; tel. 334-2440; $28 s, $32 d

Townhouse Motel; 565 S. Main; tel. 334-2376; $36-40 s or d; weekly rates available, AAA approved

Best Western Pioneer Court; 731 S. Main; tel. 334-2640 or (800) 528-1234; $40-56 s, $53-70 d; outdoor pool, AAA approved

Trail Motel; 305 W. 8th; tel. 334-2530 or (800) 333-5875; $42 s or d; outdoor pool, AAA approved

Covered Wagon Motel; 730 S. Main; tel. 334-2836 or (800) 341-8000; $55 s or $64 d; indoor pool, jacuzzi, sauna, exercise room, continental breakfast, AAA approved

Granite Creek Livestock Ranch; 14 miles southwest of Lusk; tel. 334-2372; $125-150 per person/day; ranch with rustic accommodations, three meals, horseback rides, wagon tours, fishing, hiking, open mid-May through August

pig out. **Little Diego's,** 206 S. Main St., tel. (307) 334-2132, serves notably authentic Mexican food. Even the tortillas are homemade.

The Pizza Place, 218 S. Main, tel. (307) 334-3000, is the local pizza joint, and a **Subway** sells sub sandwiches. **Cindy's Cafe,** on the south end of town, tel. (307) 334-3085, serves meals 24 hours a day. Lusk has a **Safeway** at 405 S. Main.

Recreation and Entertainment

Swim at the **Lusk Plunge** on the north side of the tracks during the summer. The **Lusk Municipal Golf Course,** tel. (307) 334-9916, has one of the best nine-hole golf courses in the state. Two miles west of town you can watch flicks in the summer at the old-fashioned **Lusk Drive-in Theatre.** Bowl at **Rawhide Lanes,** 326 S. Main St., tel. (307) 334-0159, or catch live country and western music at the downtown Fireside Inn's **Cowboy Bar,** 904 S. Main1, tel. (307) 334-3634.

Information and Services

The **Lusk Visitor Center** is housed in the museum at 342 S. Main St., tel. (307) 334-2950 or (800) 223-5875, and is open Mon.-Fri. 10 a.m.-5 p.m. Information may also be available May-Aug. in the caboose at Main St. and Griffith Boulevard. The local **library** is at 425 S. Main, tel. (307) 334-3490, and the **post office** is at 116 W. 3rd St., tel. (307) 334-3700. Wash clothes at **Econowash** on S. Main Street. Be prepared: Lusk has no ATM machine.

The **Niobrara County Fair** comes to Lusk in early August, but the major local event is the *Legend of Rawhide.*

LEGEND OF RAWHIDE

In 1946, the people of Lusk were looking for an event to attract visitors—something, say, along the lines of Cheyenne Frontier Days, only different. A local doctor, Walter Reckling, faintly remembered a tale that had been passed down for generations—the legend of Rawhide Buttes. It was one of the enduring yarns of the Old West, one with a thousand variations, claimed by half a dozen states. In the story, an emigrant wagon train headed west to the California goldfields

carrying a young man who boasted that he would shoot the first Indian he saw. He killed an innocent Indian girl—a princess, of course—and her tribe retaliated by attacking the wagon train and forcing the young man to surrender. He was skinned alive in revenge. Nobody has ever been able to substantiate the tale, but then again, nobody has proved it *didn't* happen, either.

Dr. Reckling managed to stir up considerable interest for the idea in Lusk and then found a local college student, Eva Lou Bonsell, who was studying theater in Colorado. She wrote a play to be pantomimed as a narrator described the scenes, and the *Legend of Rawhide* was off and running. The first production gained a measure of realism by being staged in the midst of a thunderstorm. The crowd of 10,000 loved it. The *Legend of Rawhide* made the covers of *Life* and *Look* magazines at various times and ran from 1946 to 1966. It was revived again in 1986. Today, the annual production is still a decidedly local affair, with a cast of 200 folks from the surrounding area. The spectacle has evolved over the years with the addition of 13 "soiled doves," Father DeSmet, Jim Bridger, some 15 wagons, and several dozen Indians on ponies. The skinning alive of bad guy Clyde Pickett is the gory climax. It's also quite a trick, but I won't give away the secret.

The *Legend of Rawhide* is put on the second weekend in July every year and begins at 8 p.m. on Friday and Saturday nights. Other activities include afternoon parades, an art show, square dancing, country music, and pancake breakfasts. For more information, call (307) 334-2950 or (800) 223-5875. The *Legend of Rawhide* attracts upwards of 3,000 visitors, so be sure to book motel rooms far ahead of your visit.

Whether or not the story is true, the **Rawhide Buttes** actually do exist; they are 10 miles south of Lusk. Some stories give a less interesting origin of the name Rawhide Buttes, claiming they were the site where raw buffalo hides were prepared for shipment east. A highway marker notes the Cheyenne and Deadwood Stage station that once stood here. Two miles west of Lusk on U.S. 18/20 is a historical marker along the Cheyenne-Deadwood Trail. The ruts are still visible for a ways here, and George Lathrop, one of the best-known stage drivers, is buried nearby.

HEADING NORTH

U.S. 18/85 heads due north from Lusk toward Newcastle, passing through mile after mile of rolling and windy grassland with scattered rocky buttes—a few wearing top hats of ponderosa pines. For the first dozen miles the road parallels the historic Cheyenne-Deadwood Stage Route. Bottomland creeks curl through with cotton-woods and willows on both sides. This is gorgeous big-sky country; the land seems almost an afterthought. It's about as remote a place as you'll find, with just a few ranches, windmills, and cattle for company.

Some 13 miles north of Lusk a sign marks the old **Fort Hat Creek Stage Station,** mistakenly built (in 1876) along Sage Creek, Wyoming, instead of Hat Creek, Nebraska! It's easy to see how the country could start to blend together here. The old stage station, on private land but right next to the road, is two miles east of here on a paved road and then one mile southwest on a gravel road. It is an impressive two-story log structure built in 1887 to replace the original buildings, which had burned. The small fort garrisoned 40 soldiers who would ride out to protect the Cheyenne-Deadwood Stage from attack. Hat Creek was typical of stage stations along the route. One writer of the time, Leander P. Richardson, noted: "At any of these places a traveler can purchase almost anything, from a glass of whiskey to a four-horse team, but the former article is usually the staple of demand."

Tiny **Lance Creek** (pop. 180) lies in the middle of Niobrara County and is surrounded by the Lance Creek oilfields. An oil boom peaked here during WW II; more recently production has declined and the community now ekes out a minimal survival. The Lance Creek area is famous as the site of discoveries of horned dinosaurs (Ceratopsians) and other fossils. Beginning in the 1880s, scientists found an incredible number of fossil plants, dinosaurs, and ancient mammals, including at least 75 different species of vertebrates, many of which were previously unknown. There are no signs or facilities to mark the location.

Halfway between Lusk and Newcastle is **Mule Creek Junction,** consisting of a state rest area and a combination gas station/cafe/junk-food shop. **Sage and Cactus Village,** tel. (307) 663-7653, is 2.5 miles north on U.S. 85, with eight tepees in a circle and a central fire each evening. This is a fun and down-to-earth experience—great for families. Rates are $30 s, $45 d, including a hearty break-fast. Open Memorial Day to Labor Day. A couple of miles north of this, U.S. 85 crosses Cheyenne River near the site of the aptly named **Robber's Roost Stage Station.** Here outlaws sometimes attacked the Cheyenne-Deadwood Stage when it slowed to cross the river. In an 1878 robbery attempt an outlaw was killed here by the shotgun messengers, but his partners managed to escape with the mail sacks.

DOVER PUBLICATIONS, INC.

DOVER PUBLICATIONS, INC.

MEDICINE BOW COUNTRY

West from Cheyenne, I-80 climbs a long, gentle ramp into the Laramie Mountains, reaches the highest point on its 3,000-mile trek across America, and then abruptly begins a steep descent onto the spacious Laramie Plains. A distinctly frontier feeling envelops this land: mountains rim the valley, and as you continue west the grass intermixes with more and more sagebrush. You are entering the real West of mountains, sage, and sky.

Medicine Bow Country consists of Albany County—with Laramie and the Laramie Plains at its center and the Laramie and Medicine Bow mountains on either side—and Carbon County, where Rawlins is the main town and the Sierra Madre mountains dominate the southern horizon. The name "Medicine Bow" has a convoluted origin. The mountains in southern Wyoming were considered a sacred place, and each year Indians gathered nearby to celebrate powwows and build bows from the cedar wood. The Indian term for "medicine" means something spiritually powerful—symbolized by the mountains, the cedar that made fine bows, and

the annual powwows. Whites combined the various tribal activities into "Medicine Bow" and applied the name to a river, a mountain range, a national forest, and a town.

The land is remarkably diverse in terms of both topography and vegetation. Laramie Basin contains the highest short-grass prairie in the world, some 7,200 feet above sea level. Three mountain ranges cross through this region: the Laramie Mountains, the Medicine Bow Mountains (also called the Snowy Range), and the Sierra Madre. Mountain slopes are covered with lodgepole pine, Engelmann spruce, and subalpine fir, while alpine meadows, tundra, and rock dominate the highest elevations. To the north and west of these mountain ranges, the country is a dry landscape of sage and desert.

History
For many centuries this land was filled with buffalo, elk, and deer, providing a rich home for wandering tribes of Indians. By the time whites arrived in large numbers, the area was claimed and fought over by many tribes including Oglala

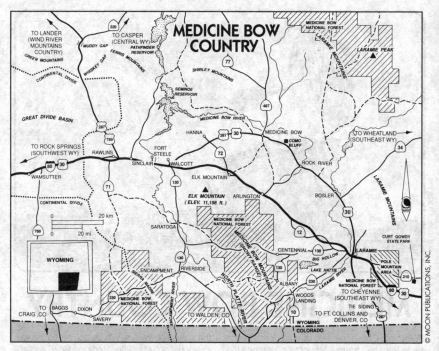

Sioux, Northern Arapaho, Eastern Shoshone, Northern Cheyenne, and White River Utes. Although mountain men long trapped in this part of Wyoming, it remained off the beaten path for many years, with emigrants preferring the Oregon Trail through the central part of the state. This began to change in 1862, when the Overland Trail opened across southern Wyoming. Ben Holladay's stage traversed the route, as did many thousands of emigrants who found it shorter and generally safer from Indian attack. As with the rest of southern Wyoming, the coming of the Union Pacific Railroad transformed this from a place to get through into a place to live. The railroad provided the region's lifeblood for many years. Later, Laramie gained the University of Wyoming and Rawlins the state penitentiary.

Economy

The economy of the Medicine Bow region is much like that of the rest of Wyoming—heavily dependent upon grazing and energy. More than 170,000 cattle and 75,000 sheep graze this land of sage and grass, mines near Hanna produce large amounts of low-sulfur coal, and wells in Carbon County pump more than 37 million cubic feet of natural gas each year. Other important pieces of the regional economy are the University of Wyoming, in Laramie, and tourism—particularly in the Snowy Range and Upper North Platte River Valley. Transportation has long been a vital factor in the region. Ben Holladay's stage and the Union Pacific Railroad were followed on this route eventually by I-80, the primary artery across America for truckers and travelers. The remote stretch of I-80 between Laramie and Elk Mountain is commonly called the "Snow Chi Minh Trail," a joking reference to the ceaseless blowing snow that sometimes shuts down traffic for days at a time during the winter. Gale-force winds have even been known to blow semis over!

LARAMIE

The countryside around Laramie (pop. 27,000) differs little from that in much of Wyoming—arid plains abruptly broken by rugged mountain ranges—but the town itself offers a real change of pace. True, Laramie does have rodeos, restaurants with names like the Cavalryman, and great country-western tunes at the ever-popular Cowboy Saloon, but it also seems to violate one's expectations of a Wyoming town. It has to be the only place in the state where the Chuckwagon Restaurant features espresso! Take a stroll along downtown's Ivinson Ave. and you'll discover a shop selling fancy chocolates from everywhere, flower shops, cafes, bookstores, and even an organic foods store complete with post-hippie decor. Nearby are vegetarian restaurants, bars that attract reggae or blues bands, and galleries filled with hand-crafted items from all over the planet. With the recent addition of the new American Heritage Center and the development of Wyoming Territorial Park, Laramie has been drawing an increasing number of visitors.

Laramie is one of my favorite cities in Wyoming, a place that has a sense of intelligence without being stultified, where culture mixes with fun and games. Tourist brochures call Laramie "Gem City of the Plains." It has the laid-back college-town feel of Chico, California, or Fort Collins, Colorado. The students add a playful, literary atmosphere—bikes on the streets, heady conversations over beers, rock concerts, and theatrical productions. Laramie has both crowded fast-food outlets and sophisticated restaurants offering more substantial fare. It's probably the only place in the state other than Jackson where a restaurant would dare carry wine descriptions on its menu: "An excellent varietal aroma of apples and butter. . . a full rich flavor and a nicely balanced, clean finish. . . ."

The Union Pacific Railroad splits Laramie into two distinct parts. The campus, the more stately older homes, and nearly the whole city lie on the east side; less pretentious quarters lie on "the other side of the tracks." Long freight trains roll through every few minutes at all hours

of the day and night piled high with double-deck containerized freight boxes destined for Chicago, Denver, or Las Vegas.

Located close to the Medicine Bow Mountains (hiking and skiing), Vedauwoo Rocks (rock-climbing), Lake Hattie (windsurfing), and the Colorado Rockies (John Denver?), Laramie is a haven for those who love the outdoors. The only problem is the midwinter wind, which makes life in this part of the state difficult. Temperatures may be relatively mild—in the low 20s—but add in a 30-mph wind and it feels like 20 below zero. Bitter gale-force winds can howl through for days on end in this open country.

HISTORY

The city of Laramie (and several other places in eastern Wyoming) has the name of a French-Canadian trapper who was killed by Indians in the mountains now also named in his honor. Nearly everything about the man is open to question. Jacques LaRamee (or was it Joseph De la Ramie?) was killed in 1820 (or 1821) by Arapahos (or another tribe), who stuffed his body under the ice in a beaver pond (or left his body in his cabin). Be that as it may, he attained a far more lasting legacy through his death than through anything he did while alive.

Fort Sanders

The first permanent settlement in the Laramie area was Fort Sanders, originally known as Fort John Buford, built in 1866. Located approximately two miles south of present-day Laramie, it served to protect emigrants and stagecoaches along the Overland Trail and, later, Union Pacific Railroad construction workers. At its peak, Fort Sanders housed nearly 600 soldiers. As with other posts on the frontier, desertions were rampant; 41 men went AWOL in a single month, taking with them whatever supplies they could grab. As the threat of Indian attacks lessened over the years, so did the value of Fort Sanders. It was abandoned in 1882.

The Union Pacific Arrives

Laramie City (as it was first called) was named and established by Gen. Grenville Dodge, the man in charge of planning the Union Pacific's route westward. The location was chosen because of a major spring that still produces millions of gallons of water, and because ties could be cut in the mountains to the west and brought down the Laramie River. The proximity of Fort Sanders also influenced the location. By the time the first train rolled into Laramie City on May 10, 1868, many "sooners" had already set up business in tents. The first passengers were

met with 23 saloons, one hotel, and no churches. Within three months, Laramie had 5,000 people.

Many of the earliest to arrive were the usual end-of-the-track types: hoodlums, gamblers, prostitutes, and others out to make a fast buck. When the tracks headed on westward, the riffraff stayed behind, kept busy by the soldiers. Within a short time, a saloon owner named Asa Moore gained the support of various gambling houses, brothels, and other bars to create a rump town government with himself as mayor. The man they appointed town marshall had re-

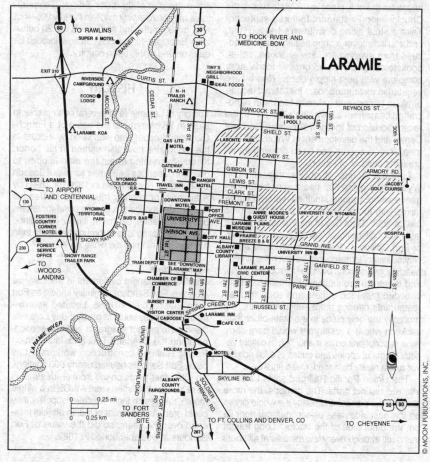

cently left Cheyenne after being acquitted on a murder charge, and his assistant was caught stealing mules. Laramie quickly became one of the wildest towns on the frontier, with murders occurring almost daily. Men who were arrested often faced trial in a back room of Asa Moore's saloon, where his men robbed and then killed them, burying their bodies out on the plains. Stories tell of up to 10 men disappearing in a single night.

Seeing that the law was in the hands of criminals, the more respectable citizens decided to put an end to the mayhem. More than 500 men joined a vigilante committee that swept into the saloons, brothels, dance halls, and casinos on the night of October 18, 1868. Three men died in gun battles (including a musician and a vigilante) and dozens of others were wounded. Another three were hanged by vigilantes, including the mayor, Asa Moore. The next day, outlaw Big Steve Young met the same fate, and more than a hundred crooks were piled into railroad cars and sent west. These actions calmed things down rather quickly, and thereafter Laramie City became something of a model town. It is perhaps fitting that four years later Laramie would be awarded the territorial prison.

For many years the main reason for the existence of Laramie was the presence of the railroad and the operations it established, including a roundhouse, an iron foundry, a tie-treating plant, machine shops, and a mill for reprocessing old rails. Gold discoveries in the Snowy Range to the west helped Laramie's economy grow, but the railroad remained the largest employer in Laramie until the 1950s, when it was supplanted by the university.

Women's Suffrage

Laramie was the site of two of the most notable events in the history of women's rights. On September 6, 1870, Louisa Gardner ("Grandma") Swain became the first woman in the nation to vote in an open and public election. A few months before this, a judge in Laramie established the world's first jury with women members. (Reporters noted that the female jurors hid behind heavy veils and held crying babies on their laps.) The women brought about a change in the jury system: breaks for boozing and gambling were ended, and smoking and chewing

women's suffrage, from Frank Leslie's Illustrated Newspaper

WYOMING STATE MUSEUM

tobacco in the jury box were also halted. The women also proved more likely to convict men of murder than their male peers, who regarded killing humans a less serious crime than rustling cattle. A stone monument near 1st and Garfield Streets marks the location where the first all-woman jury met.

The University

In 1886, Laramie received a gift from the state legislature that would eventually transform it from a cow town into a college town. Under the leadership of Col. Stephen W. "Father of the University" Downey, the legislature voted to establish the new University of Wyoming. It was part of a deal that carved up Wyoming: Laramie got the university, Cheyenne became the capital, Rawlins landed the prison, and Evanston got the state asylum. The bill was signed into law by Gov. Francis E. Warren in 1886, four years before Wyoming achieved statehood. The school opened the following year with a single

BILL NYE

Laramie lays claim to one of the most popular humorists of the 19th century, Edgar "Bill" Nye (1850-1896). Born in Maine and raised in Wisconsin, Nye arrived in Laramie in 1876 and soon began writing columns for a local newspaper. His sharp wit and wry sense of humor quickly showed through the news. Local Republicans backed him in publishing his own paper, the *Laramie Boomerang*—named for a flea-bitten gray mule that kept returning no matter how hard Nye tried to get rid of him. The paper first rolled off his "lemon-squeezer" press in 1881. When the news wasn't all that interesting, Nye would embellish it: "[I] write up things that never occurred with a masterly and graphic hand. Then, if they occur, I am grateful; if not, I bow to the inevitable and smother my chagrin."

Even Nye's appointment as Laramie City postmaster (a political plum gained because of his connection with the dominant Republican party) became grist for his humor mill. He wrote the postmaster general, noting, "I look upon the appointment, myself, as a great triumph of eternal truth over error and wrong. It is one of the epoches, I may say, in the Nation's onward march toward political purity and perfection. I do not know when I have noticed any stride in the affairs of state, which so thoroughly impressed me with its wisdom . . ." Nye only kept the position for a year.

In 1883, an attack of spinal meningitis forced him to leave high-elevation Laramie for a lower climate. By the time he departed, Nye's newspaper was in dire financial condition, but it managed to survive under new, more responsible, management. The *Boomerang* is still published today and is one of the state's few daily papers. The old livery stable where it was originally published is on the corner of Third and Garfield; Nye's office was on the second floor.

Bill Nye's witty *Boomerang* columns gained a national following, and by the 1890s he had become the best-paid humorist in America. Nye would eventually write 14 books of humor; *Bill Nye's History of the United States,* published in 1894, sold an incredible 500,000 copies. Unfortunately, the intense stress of life on the road helped shorten his life. Nye died of a stroke when just 45 years old.

Much of Nye's humor falls flat today, and its racial stereotypes are certainly dated, but some of the short pieces still have a delightful zing, particularly when he tweaks the noses of famous people such as Oscar Wilde (whom Nye called "Thou bilious pelican from o'er the sea") or a competing newspaper editor ("We have nothing more to say of the editor of the Sweetwater *Gazette.* Aside from the fact that he is a squint-eyed, consumptive liar, with a breath like a buzzard and a record like a convict, we don't know anything against him . . ."). The only book of Nye's works still in print is *Bill Nye's Western Humor,* a collection of his pieces published by the University of Nebraska Press.

The following commentary on Wyoming agriculture and "reclamation" efforts is typical of Nye's tongue-in-cheek writing:

I do not wish to discourage those who might wish to come to this place for the purpose of engaging in agriculture, but frankly I will state that it has its drawbacks. In the first place, the soil is quite course, and the agriculturist, before he can even begin with any prospect of success must run his farm through a stamp-mill in order to make it sufficiently mellow. This, as the reader will see, involves a large expense at the very outset. Hauling the farm to a custom mill would delay the farmer two or three hundred years in getting his crops in, thus giving the agriculturist who had a pulverized farm in Nebraska, Colorado, or Utah, a great advantage over his own, which had not yet been to the reduction works.

building—now called Old Main—built at a cost of $49,000. The new program had five professors and a co-ed student body of 42, who paid $7.50 each to attend. Over the years, the railroad gradually diminished in importance while the university added more and more to the local economy, until it became the biggest local employer. It remains so today. Because of the university, Laramie has never really experienced the economic booms and busts common to much of Wyoming.

UNIVERSITY OF WYOMING

Wyoming is the only state to have just one baccalaureate-granting institution. The University of Wyoming campus in Laramie thus gains the state's undivided financial support, much to the chagrin of the two-year colleges. The university lays claim to being the highest university campus in the nation—at 7,200 feet, it makes Denver's mile-high claim to fame look puny. Although not a major research institution, UW has respected programs in atmospheric sciences (ozone-depletion studies), coal production, aquatic toxicology, oil recovery technology, water management, agricultural research, and infrared as-

tronomy. Approximately 12,000 students attend the university under the tutelage of 2,000 faculty and staff members.

The university offers a wide spectrum of degree programs—98 at the undergraduate level and 97 at the graduate. It operates on a semester system, with a summer session open to visiting students. A summertime Elderhostel provides classes for folks over 60, and various noncredit classes are also offered throughout the year, covering the spectrum from ballroom dancing to LSAT preparation. For a copy of the school's *General Bulletin,* call the admissions office at (307) 766-5160 or (800) 342-5996, or write: University of Wyoming Admissions Office, P.O. Box 3435, Laramie, WY 82071. Find their Internet homepage at http://www.uwoy.edu.

Seeing the Campus

Begin your campus visit at the very helpful **University of Wyoming Visitor Information Center,** 1408 Ivinson Ave., tel. (307) 766-4075. It's open Mon.-Fri. 9 a.m.-5 p.m. and Saturday 9 a.m.-1 p.m. all year. Tours are only available for prospective students, but the center can provide maps and complete info on the school including lectures, films, concerts, dances, and other events open to the public. Right next door

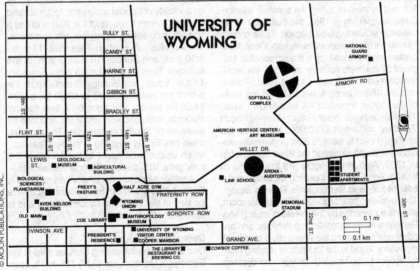

UNIVERSITY OF WYOMING

you'll find the historic **Cooper Mansion,** built in 1920 in the Mission Pueblo style and now on the National Register of Historic Places. An **information desk,** tel. (307) 766-3160, in the Wyoming Union building is open Mon.-Fri. 7:30 a.m.-7 p.m. in the school year and Mon-Fri. 8 a.m.-4 p.m. in the summer months. Check the ride board here if you're looking for or offering transportation. Also stop in the union for a listing of campus activities, stamps, cash from the ATM, or snacks. The main campus buildings center around **Prexy's Pasture,** where the school's first president grazed his personal cattle. Today Prexy's is a favorite place to relax on sunny days—and it's still legal to leave your horse here.

American Heritage Center

The newest addition to the UW campus is the controversial $19-million American Heritage Center. The center serves as a major research facility and an exhibition space for art and historical pieces. Designed by famed architect Antoine Predock, this multilevel conical building contains expansive art galleries and thousands of manuscripts, rare books, and artifacts from Wyoming and the West. The building was designed to represent the mountains surrounding Laramie and is oriented so that one small section is lit by the sun during the summer solstice. Since its opening in 1993, the building has received a decidedly mixed reaction. To be honest, I found it a big disappointment, with a wonderful central loggia ruined by a claustrophobic tangle of 32 concrete columns intended, the architect claimed, to resemble a forest. Nine oil paintings by Alfred Jacob Miller hang on the walls of the loggia, including his best-known work, *The Rendezvous Near Green River—Oregon Territory,* valued at $750,000. Miller was the only artist ever to witness a mountain-man rendezvous; he documented the West during a trip in 1837. Also in the loggia are the saddle of William Boyd, a.k.a. "Hopalong Cassidy," and a cast of Frederic Remington's *Bronco Buster.* This level also has the George Rentschler room, with nine paintings by the Western artist Henry Farney; a room with changing exhibits; and another one containing the university's rare book repository. Head to the fourth-floor reading room for access to the research collection of Western books, documents, and photographs, and to see the star attraction—Jack Benny's violin. The collection includes the papers of Buffalo Bill Cody, F.E. Warren, Jack Benny, and Irving Wallace. The fifth floor provides a dramatic view across Laramie to the Snowy Range and a look at historic photos on the walls. There's no charge to walk around the center, which is open Mon.-Fri. 7:30 a.m.-4:30 p.m. and Saturday 11 a.m.-4:30 p.m. in the summer, Mon.-Fri. 8 a.m.-5 p.m. and Saturdays noon-5 p.m. during the school year. Call (307) 766-2570 for more information.

Art Museum

The excellent University Art Museum, tel. (307) 766-6622, is housed in the same building as the American Heritage Center and encompasses nine large galleries, including an outdoor sculpture court. Exhibits change several times a year, so you aren't likely to see the same thing twice. Some of these are from the university's permanent collection of 6,000 paintings, pieces of sculpture, and other works of art. The permanent collection is mostly by 19th- and 20th-century artists, including paintings and drawings by Thomas Hart Benton, Charles M. Russell, Paul Gauguin, Andy Warhol, Thomas Moran, and Pablo Picasso. The museum puts on a variety of special programs, lectures, and other art events throughout the year and has a fine gift shop selling distinctive arts and crafts. The Art Museum is open Tues.-Sat. 11 a.m.-4:30 p.m. and Sunday 10 a.m.-3 p.m. in the summer, Tues.-Fri. 10 a.m.-5 p.m., Saturday 11 a.m.-5 p.m., and Sunday 10 a.m.-3 p.m. the rest of the year. Entrance is $3.50 for adults, $1.50 for seniors and ages 6-17, free for UW students, staff, and kids under six, and free for everyone on Sunday or Thursday. The museum often has Friday evening "Palette Pleasers," when visitors who come to the museum 5-7 p.m. get a 10% discount at local restaurants.

Another place to view artwork on campus is **Gallery 234,** which exhibits student pieces. It's located in the Wyoming Union building and is open Mon.-Fri. 8 a.m.-5 p.m.

Geological Museum

One of the more interesting campus sites is the Geological Museum, tel. (307) 766-4218, open

Mon.-Fri. 8 a.m.-5 p.m. and occasionally on weekends. Free tours are available. A life-size bronze *Tyrannosaurus rex* greets visitors at the entrance, while dinosaur bones surround the doorway. Inside the museum you'll find fossil and mineral displays from around the state. An enormous woolly mammoth skull found near Rawlins is one of the most impressive fossils, but the museum's centerpiece is a 75-foot-long, 15-foot-tall skeleton of an *Apatosaurus excelsus,* better known as a Brontosaurus. Excavated along Sheep Creek in Albany County, it's one of just five mounted specimens in the world. Also here is a cast of the largest *Allosaurus* skeleton ever found; it was excavated in 1991 near Shell, Wyoming.

Right next door to the Geological Museum is the **Wyoming Geological Survey Building,** which sells fun maps of all types and a number of good guides to the state's geology.

Other University Sights

The first campus building was **Old Main,** completed in 1887 and now housing the administrative offices. The prominent tower that once adorned the building was removed in 1915. Look for Wyoming's territorial seal over the west entrance. Head to the Anthropology Building to view the university's **Anthropology Museum,** representing a small portion of the department's extensive cultural collection. The museum (tel. 307-766-5136) is open Mon.-Fri. 8 a.m.-5 p.m. and focuses on the Plains Indians. A mammoth skull is here, along with a display on the Vore Site buffalo jump in northeastern Wyoming, where thousands of buffalo were trapped and killed.

In the Agriculture Building is the **Entomology Museum,** which houses thousands of insect specimens. Although primarily for research, it's open to the public. Also in the same building is the **Range Herbarium,** considered one of the most complete collections of grasses in the western states. It's open by request; tel. (307) 766-5263. At the even more impressive **Rocky Mountain Herbarium,** on the third floor of the Aven Nelson Building, tel. (307) 766-2236, you'll find one of the nation's largest plant collections—open to the general public only by prior arrangement. The **Terua P. Williams Botany Conservatory** next to the Aven Nelson Building

is open to the public. A planetarium at the university was heavily damaged by flooding but may reopen in the future; call (307) 766-6150 for the latest.

WYOMING TERRITORIAL PARK

In 1869, the territorial legislature voted to construct a penitentiary at Laramie. (Wyoming prisoners had previously been housed in the Detroit House of Correction at a cost of $1.25 a week.) The imposing three-story stone building in west Laramie off Snowy Range Road was dedicated to "evil doers of all classes and kinds"; fittingly enough, a bottle of bourbon was deposited in the cornerstone. It remained a prison until 1902, when the inmates were transferred to a new facility in Rawlins. After the prisoners were moved out, the building was turned over to the university for use as an experimental livestock farm; the cells became cattle stalls and the prison broom

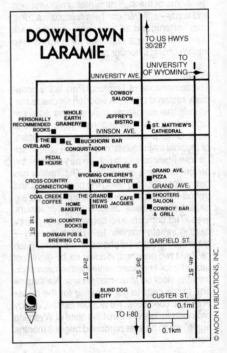

WYOMING TERRITORIAL PRISON CORPORATION

factory a sheep barn. In the 1980s, the university farm moved to a more modern facility elsewhere and the historic prison was officially established as Wyoming Territorial Park. Both state and local funds ($5 million worth) were used to transform the badly deteriorated buildings into one of the largest western-heritage parks in the Rockies. Some of the stuff here gets a bit cutesified and corny—children can help recapture a "prisoner" attempting an "escape"—but the park does offer a unique and fascinating way to step into Wyoming's frontier past.

Prison

The cornerstone of Territorial Park is the beautifully restored prison. A wooden stockade surrounds the sandstone building and adjacent broom factory where prisoners were forced to work. Other prisoners made candles, furniture, or musical instruments, or braided leather. Pick up a self-guided tour brochure as you enter the prison, or take a guided tour. The interior has been reconstructed using the original cells and period fixtures; modern additions include excellent short videos describing the prisoners' lives. The convicts who served time here—including inmate number 187, Butch Cassidy—glare down from giant photos on the walls. Each cell held two prisoners in a tiny six-by-eight-foot arched brick enclosure sealed with an iron door. Inmates slept on straw mattresses. Walk inside one of the cells to get a feeling for the claustrophobic conditions. No wonder Butch Cassidy promised to "never molest the state of Wyoming again" when he was pardoned after 18 months here!

Horse Barn

The old horse barn has been transformed into a museum and dinner theatre. Downstairs is the **National U.S. Marshals' Museum,** housing everything from frontier-era artifacts—including a bullet-riddled Wells Fargo cash box—to displays on the crack-cocaine busts of today. The Marshals Service is the oldest civilian law-enforcement agency in the world and was responsible for managing the Wyoming Territorial Prison. Visitors will enjoy finding John Wayne, Clint Eastwood, and Ronald Reagan in the film clips that feature Hollywood's version of Old West marshals. Here, too, you'll learn all sorts of lawman trivia. For instance, the five-pointed star worn by U.S. Marshals was derived from a pentacle worn by 17th-century soldiers and was supposed to make them bulletproof.

Upstairs you'll find a **dinner theater** where each evening a professional cast puts on a musical revue. It's pretty foolish, but the production and singing are first-rate, and the meal is well prepared. The Horse Barn Dinner Theatre runs every day except Monday, with lower-priced Saturday and Sunday matinees. The dinner theatre is also the scene of Monday evening talks by various historical speakers and folk artists.

Frontier Town

Just west of the prison lies an "end-of-the-tracks town" featuring simple wood and canvas buildings that come alive with living history characters such as Calamity Jane—played by her great-great niece—and fur trapper Jacques LaRamee. The old warden's house contains a variety of

period artisans at work including basket makers, wool spinners, lace makers, and an old photography studio. Frontier Town also has a print shop and a blacksmith (in real life the chairman of UW's language department) turning out authentic period items. Other buildings house a printing press that cranks out wanted posters, a saloon, a photo studio, a general store, a livery stable, and a depot (but no whorehouse). Stagecoach rides are available, and the amphitheater provides entertainment. The quarter-mile **Laramie River Interpretive Trail** follows the banks of the river near the prison, providing a place to relax and explore. Children will enjoy the chance to take part in a "dinosaur dig" where they'll find replica fossils along the river and learn about the 19th-century discoveries at nearby Como Bluffs. Kids can also try on period costumes and pet farm animals.

Practicalities

Wyoming Territorial Park, located west of town on Snowy Range Road, is open daily 9 a.m.-6 p.m. from Memorial Day to Labor Day. Entrance to the frontier town and the living history presentations are free but guided prison tours and entrance to the Marshals Museum costs $6 for adults, $5.50 for seniors, $3 for children, free for ages under eight. The 45-minute tours begin on the hour from 10 a.m. to 5 p.m. The dinner theater is $25 for adults, $24 for seniors, $16 for kids; evening performances run late May through September. The prison and Marshals Museum are open daily 10 a.m.-6 p.m. from mid-May through September, and Frontier Town is open daily 10 a.m.-6 p.m. Memorial Day to Labor Day. Everything is closed Oct.-April. A gift shop sells souvenirs and books. The entire park, including the old prison, is fully accessible. For more information, call (307) 745-6161 or (800) 845-2287. The park's e-mail address is wyoterpark@aol.com. (See "Events" below for additional park activities.)

MORE LARAMIE SIGHTS

Ivinson Mansion

Although its official name is the Laramie Plains Museum, this historic site is known to most folks as the Ivinson Mansion. Located at 603 Ivinson, the home is a delightful example of the Queen Anne style of Victorian architecture. Now on the National Register of Historic Places, it was built in 1892 for millionaire merchant-turned-banker and politician Edward Ivinson. That same year, Ivinson ran unsuccessfully for governor, intending to make his palatial new home the governor's mansion. After his death, the mansion became an Episcopal girls' school. When the school closed, locals managed to raise more than $74,000 to buy the mansion and turn it into a museum.

The Ivinson Mansion spreads over an entire city block with a carriage house out back and attractively landscaped grounds. Few of the original furnishings remain but much of the interior woodwork—including a freestanding stairway built without nails or screws—is still here. Ongoing restoration has vastly improved the building in recent years. The museum has been furnished with antiques, including some elaborate hand-carved furniture built at the Wyoming Penitentiary in 1901, handmade toys including a 160-year-old doll, a piano that arrived by covered wagon, and a number of Indian artifacts. More unusual are a quilt that took 60 years to complete (listed in *Ripley's Believe It or Not!*), a seven-headed shower that looks like a medieval torture device, and a square Steinway grand piano. The back carriage house has a small visitor center, carriages, old bikes, impressive fur coats, and two wonderful antique woodstoves. Also on the grounds is a one-room log schoolhouse built in 1924.

The museum, tel. (307) 742-4448, has hours that change through the season: Mon.-Sat. 9 a.m.-8 p.m. and Sunday 1-5 p.m. June-Aug.; Mon.-Fri. 10 a.m.-3 p.m. and Saturday 1-4 p.m. September to mid-October; Mon.-Sat. 1-4 p.m. mid-October to mid-December and February to mid-May; closed mid-December through January. Guided hour-long tours are given throughout the day, with the last one starting an hour before closing time; $4 for adults, $3 for seniors, $2 for students and children.

Downtown

Laramie's downtown buildings, many of them dating from the 19th century, are on the National Register of Historic Places. Along Ivinson Avenue, a major renovation turned what

had been a collection of sleazy flophouses and bars into a lively, attractive, and fun section of town. The chamber of commerce visitor center provides a city map that includes historical and architectural **walking tours. St. Matthew's Cathedral,** at the corner of 3rd and Ivinson, is one of Wyoming's more interesting churches. The limestone structure was built in 1868 and funded by Edward Ivinson.

Laramie has a number of small art galleries in addition to the those at the university. **Earth, Wind and Fire Gallery,** 220 S. 2nd St., tel. (307) 745-0227, has designer jewelry, Indian art, art prints, and fine pottery. Other noteworthy galleries include **French Creek Gallery,** 152 N. 2nd St., tel. (307) 721-4005; **Gallery West,** 121 Ivinson Ave., tel. (307) 742-3245; and **Artisans' Gallery,** 213 S. 2nd, tel. (307) 745-3983. If you're around on the first Friday of the month, join the evening **gallery walk,** which features artists and authors.

The **Wyoming Children's Nature Center and Museum,** 221 Grand Ave., tel. (307) 745-6332, is open Tuesday 9 a.m.-1 p.m., Wed.-Thurs. 1-5 p.m., and Saturday 10 a.m.-4 p.m. year-round—and also Friday 1-5 p.m. in the summer. This unique museum contains all sorts of fun hands-on exhibits for kids, including an art center and an Oregon Trail exhibit with a wagon, trading post, and gold panning. The nature center houses salamanders, turtles, a snake, and a crawl-through "beaver lodge." Admission is $2 for adults, $1 for kids, free for children under three.

On the grounds of the **Laramie Plains Civic Center** at 710 Garfield, you'll find **East Side School.** Built in 1878, this is the oldest stone schoolhouse in Wyoming. Inside the civic center theater are six murals painted in the early 1930s by noted artist Florence E. Ware.

Farther Afield

A granite monument to **Fort Sanders** stands two miles south of town on Fort Sanders Road (Kiowa Street). Not much remains of the fort other than the ruins of the old stone guardhouse and the powder house. One of Fort Sanders' wooden buildings was moved to LaBonte Park, at 9th and Canby Streets in Laramie and is now used as a recreation center. **Hutton Lake National Wildlife Refuge** lies six miles south of Laramie on State 230, then three miles south on County Road 37. It is a quiet, peaceful place to look for ducks, shorebirds, and migratory birds. The Wyoming/Colorado Scenic Railroad offered scenic excursions along the foot of the Snowy Range for many years but went out of business in 1995 and is not expected to return anytime soon. Ask locally whether anything has changed.

ACCOMMODATIONS

Motels

Space is generally not a problem at Laramie's motels, though you should reserve well ahead during graduation week (mid-May) and Cheyenne Frontier Days (mid-July), and on football weekends. The old rule of supply and demand holds here, so rates also rise considerably at these times. Long-term housing can be difficult to find here; if you're moving to Laramie, check with Golden Key Realty, 310 University Ave., tel. (307) 742-8131, for apartments.

Bed and Breakfasts

One of the homiest places to stay in Laramie is **Annie Moore's Guest House,** tel. (307) 721-4177 or (800) 552-8992, located just a few blocks from campus. Built in 1912, the home served for many years as a boardinghouse run by Annie Moore. After Moore's death in 1950, the home did duty as a sorority and later a fraternity house before being completely renovated in 1981. Today the B&B includes an attractive, sunlit, natural wood interior, a second-story sundeck, a spiral staircase, and six guest rooms. Even older is **Prairie Breeze B&B,** tel. (307) 745-5482, built in 1888 and now on the National Register of Historic Places. The house was once home to the university president and offers a gracious place to stay in Laramie.

Camping

The closest public campgrounds ($6) are in the scenic Pole Mountain portion of **Medicine Bow National Forest,** approximately 10 miles east of Laramie. Other public campsites are 30 miles west in the Snowy Range. See below for details on both areas. **Curt Gowdy State Park,** 22 miles east of Laramie on State 210 (Happy Jack Road), has campsites for $4. See the Southeast Wyoming chapter for more on this

LARAMIE ACCOMMODATIONS

Note: Accommodations are arranged from least to most expensive. Add an eight percent tax to these rates. Area code is 307.

Motel 6; 621 Plaza Lane; tel. 742-2307 or (800) 466-8356; $23 s, $29 d; outdoor pool

Motel 8; 501 Boswell Dr.; tel. 745-4856; $30 s, $39 d; kitchenettes, local calls 25 cents

Ranger Motel; 453 N. 3rd St.; tel. 742-6677; $32 s, $35 d; kitchenettes, weekly rates available

Downtown Motel; 165 N. 3rd St.; tel. 742-6671 or (800) 942-6671; $43 s, $50 d; AAA approved

University Inn; 1720 Grand Ave.; tel. 721-8855 or (800) 869-9466; $45 s, $45-59 d; see rooms first; kitchenettes, AAA approved

Sunset Inn; 1104 S. 3rd St.; tel. 742-3741 or (800) 308-3744; $45 s, $52 d in older rooms with no phones; $95 s, $100 d in new rooms; outdoor pool, jacuzzi, weekly rates available, kitchenettes, AAA approved

Annie Moore's Guest House B&B; 819 University Ave.; tel. 721-4177 or (800) 552-8992; $45-55 s, $55-65 d; comfortable historic home, six guest rooms, shared baths, continental/plus breakfast, no young children

Comfort Inn; 3420 Grand Ave.; tel. 721-8856 or (800) 228-5150; $65-125 s, $75-135 d; indoor pool, jacuzzi, fitness room, continental breakfast

Super 8 Motel; 1987 Banner Rd.; tel. 745-8901 or (800) 800-8000; $49 s or d

Travel Inn; 262 N. 3rd St.; tel. 745-4853 or (800) 227-5430; $50-55 s, $60-65 d; outdoor pool, AAA approved

Best Western Foster's Country Corner Motel; 1561 Jackson St.; tel. 742-8371 or (800) 526-5145; $54 s, $60 d; indoor pool, jacuzzi, sundeck, AAA approved

Best Western Gas Lite Motel; 960 N. 3rd; tel. 742-6616 or (800) 942-6610; $55 s or d; outdoor pool, AAA approved

Laramie Inn; 421 Boswell; tel. 742-3721 or (800) 642-4212; $58 s, $68 d; outdoor pool, AAA approved

Holiday Inn; 2313 Soldier Springs Rd.; tel. 742-6611 or (800) 526-5245; $60 s, $68 d; indoor pool, jacuzzi, free airport shuttle, AAA approved

Prairie Breeze B&B; 718 Ivinson Ave.; tel. 745-5482; $60-80 s or d; historic Victorian home, antique furnishings, four guest rooms, private baths, continental breakfast

Econo Lodge; 1370 McCue St.; tel. 745-8900 or (800) 424-6423; $89-99 s or d; indoor pool with water slide, AAA approved

park. The local private camping options are pretty miserable, unless you enjoy treeless gravel lots. **Riverside Campground,** I-80 at Curtis, tel. (307) 721-7405, charges $7 for tents, $12 for RVs, and is open year-round. Showers for noncampers run $3. **Laramie KOA,** 1171 Baker, tel. (307) 742-6553 or (800) 562-4153, charges $12 for tents and $18 for RVs. Showers cost $2 for noncampers; open year-round. **N-H Trailer Ranch,** 1360 N. 3rd., tel. (307) 742-3158, charges $12 for RV parking with hookups (no tent spaces) year-round. **Snowy Range Trailer**

Park, 404 S. Taylor, tel. (307) 745-0297, offers tent spots for $10, RV hookups for $17.

FOOD

If you like reasonable prices, creative cooking, and a wide selection (who doesn't?), you're bound to appreciate all that Laramie has to offer in the way of dining out. You'll discover some of the best food in Wyoming here, from thick, juicy steaks to nouvelle cuisine.

American

For earthy breakfasts, lunches, and dinners, visit **The Overland,** 100 Ivinson Ave., tel. (307) 721-2800, a very popular cafe with a wine list that includes more than 125 different selections. For traditional steaks and seafood, **The Cavalryman Supper Club,** 4425 S. 3rd, tel. (307) 745-5551, is considered the best around. Also well-liked is **Cowboy Bar & Grill,** 309 S. 3rd, tel. (307) 742-3141, where a fun atmosphere makes it popular with families. It serves good breakfasts and, later in the day, burgers and steaks. **The Fabulous '50s Diner,** 615 S. 2nd St., tel. (307) 742-5599, serves old-fashioned sodas, banana splits, malts, and two-fisted burgers in a retro setting complete with a 1936 Olds coupe, bopping Elvis tunes on the jukebox, and dancing waitresses.

You'll find inexpensive cafeteria food, pizza, ice cream, and deli food at the **University Cafeteria,** downstairs in the Wyoming Union building on campus. **CowBelle Cookouts** are put on by local ranches four times each summer. Just $7.50 gets you a tour of a ranch, a barbecued beef dinner, and entertainment. Call (307) 745-5767 for reservations.

International Eats

Several places offer Mexican food in town. The best are **El Conquistador,** 110 Ivinson Ave., tel. (307) 742-2377, and **Cafe Olé,** 519 Boswell Dr., tel. (307) 742-8383. **Chelo's,** 357 University Ave., tel. (307) 745-5139, is a tiny greasy spoon that locals rave over. Judge for yourself.

Two places offer decent Chinese food: **The Great Wall,** 1501 S. 3rd, tel. (307) 745-7966, and **The Mandarin,** 1254 N. 3rd, tel. (307) 742-8822. The latter serves up spicier and more authentic fare. **Grand Avenue Pizza,** 301 Grand Ave., tel. (307) 721-2909, bakes some of the best homemade pizzas in Wyoming.

Eclectic

Jeffrey's Bistro, 123 Ivinson Ave., tel. (307) 742-7046, is a personal favorite. The menu is on the light side and includes creative vegetarian specialties and great homemade bread served in a pleasant brick, oak, and brass atmosphere. Next door is **Sara's Bakery at the Bistro,** tel. (307) 742-0744, offering wonderful vegetarian salads, sandwiches, breads, pastries, and other

healthy fast food (is this a culinary oxymoron?). Both of these are well worth visits.

For a fine night on the town, locals head to **Cafe Jacques,** 216 Grand Ave., tel. (307) 742-5522, where the varied menu emphasizes high quality and nouvelle cuisine. Jacques presents an impressive wine list, too, and is the only place in town with cloth napkins. Highly recommended. Next door, with the same management and phone, is **Third Street Bar & Grill.** Lighter fare, lower prices, and a friendly bar make this a relaxing place to munch on the best burgers in town, tip one of the more than 75 choices of brew, and watch a ballgame. Despite their proximity, the two places attract completely different crowds.

Coal Creek Coffeehouse, 110 Grand Ave., tel. (307) 745-7737, is an enjoyable spot to meet friends over espresso in a pleasant, art-filled setting serving good sandwiches and desserts, too. More espresso coffee and pastries can be had at **Cowboy Coffee,** 1710 Grand Ave., tel. (307) 745-5288.

Tiny's Neighborhood Grill at Northridge Center, 1660 N. 4th St., tel. (307) 745-6334, serves very good salads, pizzas, sandwiches, and munchies. Popular for lunch, it also offers free delivery.

Brewpubs

Laramie is home to two very popular brewpubs. Located right across from campus, **The Library Restaurant and Brewing Co.,** 1622 E. Grand Ave., tel. (307) 742-0500, is a favorite of the college crowd, with reasonable prices and ample servings of food. For a more classy atmosphere, good beer and tasty pub grub, head to **Bowman Pub & Brewing Co.,** 320 S. 2nd St., tel. (307) 742-3349. It attracts a young and trendy crowd and always has at least half a dozen freshly brewed ales on tap. The diverse menu includes soft pretzels, buffalo burgers, pasta primavera, catfish gumbo, and an especially popular Highland Cottage Pie. There's cheap beer during the daily happy hour (4-6 p.m.). Bands play rock music at the Bowman on weekends. Highly recommended.

Bakers and Grocers

Australian bakers Allison and Kim Campbell crank out delicious homemade breads and pastries at

Home Bakery, 304 S. 2nd, tel. (307) 742-2721. In the 1800s, this building served as the second office of Bill Nye's *Boomerang* newspaper. A bakery has been on the premises since 1901. **The Chocolate Cellar,** 115A Ivinson Ave., tel. (307) 742-9278, sells imported chocolates. **Ideal Foods,** 1575 N. 4th, tel. (307) 742-2188, has a good deli counter and salad bar. Also try the **Buttrey Food,** 3112 E. Grand Ave., tel. (307) 742-8146, and **Safeway,** 554 N. 3rd, tel. (307) 721-5107. **Whole Earth Grainery and Truck Store,** 111 Ivinson, tel. (307) 745-4268, is a funky and friendly grocery with all sorts of organic produce, dried foods, teas, spices, and coffees. There are not many places like this in Wyoming!

OTHER PRACTICALITIES

Entertainment

You'll find plenty of night action in this youthful town. Laramie's oldest saloon—dating to 1890—is the **Buckhorn Bar,** 114 Ivinson Ave., tel. (307) 742-3554. Mounted heads of all types—including a two-headed calf—and an antique bear trap adorn the walls, students and bikers adorn the pool table and barstools. Notice the bullet hole in the mirror behind the bar—the result of a 1971 incident in which a man opened fire on the bartender (he missed). The Buckhorn is a popular place for TV sports; when school's in session, the back room thumps to rock or blues most weekends. The bar opens early, attracting the after-school college crowd. **Blind Dog City,** 201 Custer St., tel. (307) 721-5097, another very popular club, hosts live rock or blues nightly. Other places for rock, pop, or blues tunes are **Bowman Pub & Brewing Co.,** 320 S. 2nd St., tel. (307) 742-3349, and **Ranger Lounge,** 463 N. 3rd Ave., tel. (307) 745-9751. **Coal Creek Coffeehouse,** 110 Grand Ave., tel. (307) 745-7737, has live music some weekends.

For hot country-western music, duded-up cowboys, and fresh-faced cowgirls, saunter on down to **The Cowboy Saloon,** 108 S. 2nd, tel. (307) 721-3165. It's a spacious place with a big dance floor, two bars, and several pool tables. You'll find more country tunes (and free hors d'oeuvres on weeknights) at **Mulligan's,** 1115 S. 3rd, tel. (307) 745-9954. At the popular **Mingles,** 3206 Grand Ave., tel. (307) 721-2005,

you can shoot pool at any of the 14 tables. It's especially popular for happy hour. **Bud's Bar,** 354 W. University Ave., tel. (307) 745-5236, is a favorite with university alumni. Everyone goes there before and after university football or basketball games. Students hang out at "Club UDub"—the **Beergarden** in the basement of the Wyoming Union building, which has live music during the school year. The **Sports Bar & Grill,** at the Holiday Inn, 2313 Soldier Springs Rd.; tel. (307) 742-6611, also has two big-screen TVs, 17 smaller ones, pool tables, and draft beer from all over the globe.

Local movie houses are the **Fox 4 Theatres,** 505 S. 20th St., tel. (307) 742-2842, and the **Wyo Theatre,** 309 S. 5th St., tel. (307) 745-4442.

Events

Each year, the university puts on a **summer theater** with lighthearted productions at the Fine Arts Building. Call (307) 766-2198 for details. The university also has a summer music festival and in June and July **band concerts** are held at the Washington Park Bandshell on Wednesday evenings. A **Frontier Festival** in early June features an antique tractor pull, chuck wagon cooking, cowboy poetry and music at Wyoming Territorial Park. It's followed there by a **Mountain Man Rendezvous** on the 4th of July weekend with 50 costumed traders and trappers. Black powder shoots and tomahawk throws are featured attractions. The **U.S. Marshals Day & Posse Rendezvous** on the third weekend of July attracts marshals from around the country with special demonstrations by law-enforcement teams and an auction.

Laramie Jubilee Days rolls around in early July, bringing rodeos, parades, the biggest fireworks in Wyoming, live music, barbecues, a free pancake breakfast, a street dance, melo-dramas, an art fair, square dancing, a quarter-horse show, a carnival, art exhibits, and other activities to celebrate Wyoming's statehood. Call (307) 745-7339 or (800) 9445-5303 to order rodeo tickets.

The annual **Ranch Tour** includes visits to four local ranches in mid-July. Contact the chamber of commerce for specifics. The ever-popular **Albany County Fair** is held the first week of August, with 4-H contests and a popular demo-

lition derby. For something completely different, watch the **original-rules baseball games** held in early August. Players pitch underhanded and don't wear mitts. Each Halloween, the Wyoming Territorial Prison opens for spooky nighttime **haunted prison tours.**

Sports

The biggest attraction in Laramie comes each fall with the arrival of football season. Half the state seems to turn out to join in the festivities at War Memorial Stadium—tailgate parties, rooting sections, and rock-'em-sock-'em helmeted soldiers battling it out against other citadels of higher learning. Up to 30,000 fans crowd the stadium Saturday afternoons to cheer on the Wyoming Cowboys—better known as "the 'Pokes"—as in "Cowpokes." The football team has a mixed record over the years—a Cody rodeo announcer once joked that Nebraska and Wyoming were uniting so that Nebraska could share Yellowstone and Wyoming could have a real football team! Needless to say, the crowd did not appreciate the humor. The university also competes in a number of other sports—men's basketball is a primary draw. The athletic facilities are among the finest in the nation and include a modern 15,000-seat arena-auditorium for basketball games, concerts, and other events. For tickets, call (800) 442-8322.

Recreation

The public **swimming pool** is at 11th and Reynolds, tel. (307) 721-4426. **Single Tree Guest Ranch** on Herrick Lane west of Laramie, tel. (307) 745-5095, is the place to go for horseback ($15 an hour) and wagon rides ($10 an hour). Square dancers should check out the three-times-a-month dances in Laramie at **Quadra Dangle Square Dance Club,** 3905 Grays Gable Rd., tel. (307) 742-6008. **Jacoby Park Golf Course** on N. 30th, tel. (307) 745-3111, is an 18-hole public course. **Skyline Skate,** 15th St. at Skyline Dr., tel. (307) 745-7574, has rollerskating.

Rent skis and get details on local conditions from **Cross-Country Connection** 117 Grand Ave., tel. (307) 721-2851, or **Fine Edge Ski Shop,** 1657 Jackson, tel. 745-449. **West Laramie Fly Store,** 1657 Snowy Range Rd., tel. (307) 745-5425, is the place to go for fishing gear. Shallow **Lake Hattie,** 20 miles southwest

of Laramie on State 230, is a good place to swim or fish for kokanee or rainbow trout in the summer. Rent mountain bikes at **Pedal House,** 207 S. 1st St., tel. (307) 742-5533. The folks here are very knowledgeable about local cycling trails and also rent rollerblades and snowboards. **Use It Again Sports,** 407 S. 2nd St., rents and sells all sorts of used outdoor gear including sleeping bags, tents, backpacks, stoves, bikes, rollerblades, skis, and snowshoes.

Shopping

Get outdoor supplies from **Lou's Sport Shop,** 217 Grand Ave., tel. (307) 745-8484. For a different type of clothing, **The Hourglass,** 210 S. 2nd St., tel. (307) 745-3288, claims to have the largest selection of lingerie in the Rockies! More of the same at **The Sensuous She,** 106 Ivinson Ave., tel. (307) 721-5835. You can purchase some of the nicest stained-glass work anywhere at **The First Tree,** 113 Ivinson Ave., tel. (307) 745-5876.

Information and Services

The **Laramie Chamber of Commerce,** 800 S. 3rd St., tel. (307) 745-7339 or (800) 445-5303, is open Mon.-Fri. 8 a.m.-5 p.m. Look for the visitor center in the caboose on the south end of town open daily 9 a.m.-5 p.m. Memorial Day to Labor Day. The University of Wyoming also has its own visitor centers (see the earlier section on the university for location and hours). If you're heading out to the Medicine Bow mountains, be sure to stop by the **Forest Service Supervisor's Office** at 2468 Jackson St., tel. (307) 745-2300, for maps and up-to-date trail and campground information. The office is open Mon.-Fri. 7:30 a.m.-5 p.m. all year and Saturday 7:30 a.m.-4 p.m. June to mid-September. The 100,000-watt **Wyoming Public Radio** station KUWR (91.9 FM) is based in Laramie, with repeaters throughout Wyoming providing in-depth news and music sans commercials.

Libraries

Albany County Library is at 310 S. 8th, tel. (307) 745-3365, and its Wyoming Room has a big selection of historic books and other documents. Much more impressive are the eight university libraries which house more than 1.1 million volumes—including the most complete collection of Wyoming books in existence—plus

150,000 maps and 13,000 periodicals. Most of these publications are in the **William Robertson Coe Library,** tel. (307) 766-5312, which also has a map room, an extensive depository of government publications, and the American Heritage Center's outstanding collection of historic books about Wyoming and the West. Also of note are the **Geology Library,** in the Geology Building, tel. (307) 766-3374; the **Science and Technology Library,** in the Science Complex, tel. (307) 766-5165; and the **Law Library,** in the College of Law, tel. (307) 766-2210.

Bookstores

Laramie is home to several excellent bookstores. The spacious **University Bookstore,** in the student union, tel. (307) 766-3264, has many regional titles and travel books. **Chickering Bookstore,** 307 S. 2nd, tel. (307) 742-8609, is a small and friendly bookshop in downtown Laramie. **Personally Recommended Books,** 105 Ivinson, tel. (307) 745-4423, is a relaxing upstairs place to look over local literary favorites while enjoying fresh coffee or pastry. **The Grand News Stand,** 214 E. Grand Ave., tel. (307) 742-5127, has a big magazine selection and lots of books on Wyoming. **High Country Books,** 306 S. 2nd, sells both new and used books, rare titles, and some of the funniest Wyoming postcards anywhere. This is the place to find those obscure (by Wyoming standards) magazines such as *Yellow Silk* or *Vegetarian Times.* **Hastings,** 654 N. 3rd St. in Gateway Plaza, tel. (307) 745-0312, is a big chain store with books, CDs, software, and videos.

Transportation

Amtrak, tel. (307) 721-5096 or (800) 872-7245, operates from the Laramie depot at 1st St. between Sheridan and Kearney. Trains head west to Portland on Monday, Wednesday, and Friday, east to Chicago via Denver on Sunday, Tuesday, and Thursday. Built in 1923, the recently restored depot features a display of railroad photographs. Open daily 10 a.m.-5 p.m.

Laramie Airport is just west of town on State 130. **Mesa/United Express,** tel. (307) 742-5296 or (800) 241-6522, has daily flights from Laramie to Denver and Cheyenne, and **Airport Express,** tel. (970) 482-0505, offers daily van service to Denver's international airport for $31 one-way $46 roundtrip.

Rent **cars** at the airport from **Avis,** tel. (307) 745-7156 or (800) 331-1212; **Dollar,** tel. (307) 742-8805 or (800) 800-4000; **Enterprise,** tel. (307) 721-9876 or (800) 325-8007; or the locally owned **Laramie Auto Rental,** tel. (307) 742-8412 or (800) 982-5935. **Laramie Taxi Service,** tel. (307) 745-8294, provides local cab service.

Greyhound buses, tel. (800) 231-2222, stop at the Tumbleweed Express Gas Station on E. Grand at I-80. Buses operate daily in both directions along I-80.

POLE MOUNTAIN AREA

Heading east from Laramie on I-80, the freeway climbs steadily up into the second-growth ponderosa and lodgepole pine forests of the Pole Mountain area. It's a scenic land punctuated by unusual and colorful rock formations. For many years much of the land here belonged to the military and was used as a target and maneuver area for the Army's version of off-road vehicles—tanks. Amazingly, the land seems to show little sign of all this abuse today.

Ten miles east of Laramie is the Summit Rest Area at the highest point (8,640 feet) along I-80. A 12-foot-tall bronze bust of **Abraham Lincoln** looks over the freeway from atop a granite base. It was created by Robert I. Russin, former art

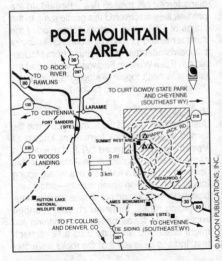

professor at the university and Wyoming's best-known sculptor. The old road through this pass was known as the Lincoln Highway—the first transcontinental highway—and the sculpture was placed in this area in 1959, the 150th anniversary of Lincoln's birth. The sculpture was moved to the present location in 1968 when the interstate highway came through. The **visitor center** here has information on nearby areas and is open daily 9 a.m.-7 p.m. mid-May through October. Also here is a small theater showing videos.

Choose from three Forest Service campgrounds (free to $6; open late May to October) in the Pole Mountain area or camp for free on land away from the roads. **Headquarters National Recreation Trail** extends five miles from the Summit Rest Area to the Headquarters Road. During the winter, Pole Mountain's groomed trails make it a popular cross-country ski area. Many others come to play on the tubing and tobogganing hill near Happy Jack Trailhead.

East of the summit, I-80 follows a long open plateau and then drops gradually into the short-grass prairie of southeastern Wyoming via "The Gangplank." The Colorado Rockies form a jagged southern horizon line. This crossing of the Laramie Range was discovered by Gen. Grenville Dodge in 1865. While exploring the railroad's new route, an attack by a party of Indians forced his men to flee eastward. In the process they discovered this gentle ramp to the plains of Cheyenne. Unfortunately, today the route is marked for miles by a domino-like line of billboards advertising everything from McDonald's to Giant Western Fireworks. It's too bad the billboards can't topple like dominoes to reveal the expansive grassland beyond!

Vedauwoo

Just five miles east of the summit you'll find the turnoff to strange rock formations known as Vedauwoo (pronounced "VEE-dah-voo"), a name meaning "earthborn" in Arapaho. In this area—considered a sacred place where young Indian men went on vision quests—oddly jumbled rocks form all sorts of shapes: mushrooms, balancing rocks, feminine curves, rounded knolls, lizards, faces, turtles, and anything you might dream up. Imagine it as a Rorschach test. Indians believed that the rocks were created by animal and human spirits. Today, Vedauwoo is considered one of Wyoming's best places for rock-climbing. Climbs go from a difficulty level of 5.0 all the way up to 5.14, with many easy places to practice crack climbs. Nonclimbers come just to view the rocks, ride mountain bikes along the dirt roads, hike in the countryside, or scramble up for marvelous vistas of the surrounding land. Vedauwoo Glen Road connects with Happy Jack Road for a nice loop trip. There are campgrounds right at Vedauwoo, but if freeway noise doesn't keep you awake, you can pull out on the side roads and pitch a tent.

Pyramid Power

Head two miles south from the Vedauwoo exit to one of the strangest monuments in Wyoming: a 60-foot-tall pyramid in the middle of nowhere. The monument commemorates Oakes and Oliver Ames, two of the most influential figures in the building of the transcontinental railroad. As a U.S. congressman, Oakes Ames gained passage of a bill that allowed the railroad to sell bonds equal to the amount loaned by the federal government—some $60 million. The company they established to handle this financing was the infamous Credit Mobilier of America. It later came to light that Oakes had bribed fellow congressmen with discounted railroad stock and greatly exaggerated construction costs for his own gain. A congressional investigation labeled Oakes "King of Frauds" and censured him. He died before he could stand trial, and the money was never recovered.

Despite this bit of infamy, the monument to the Ames brothers was built in 1882 at a cost of nearly $65,000. It was originally located at the highest elevation of the transcontinental railroad route, near the town of Sherman, a place where trains halted to check their brakes before the long descent on either side. In 1902, the tracks were rerouted a couple of miles to the south, leaving the grandiose pile of rocks by itself. Nothing remains today from the Sherman townsite except a cemetery. The Ames Monument seems to bring out two conflicting emotions: dismay at the obscenity of this monstrosity and amusement at the irony that so much money was wasted on a self-aggrandizing monument soon abandoned even by the railroad the Ames brothers had helped build.

MEDICINE BOW VICINITY

Two roads head west from Laramie. Most people follow I-80 straight to Rawlins, but U.S. 30/287 (the old Lincoln Hwy.) gets you there in about the same time and provides a strong flavor of the Old West. State Hwy. 34 heads northeast from U.S. 30 near the dot on the map called **Bosler,** climbing over the low mountains to Wheatland 50 miles away. It's a pretty drive with little traffic and is worth a detour to visit **Sybille Wildlife Research Center,** 26 miles up the road. This is where the endangered black-footed ferrets are raised. Two miles east of Sybille is the Johnson Creek Wildlife Habitat Management Area, a popular place for fishing. There are no trails, but hiking is easy in the open country here.

Rock River

This almost-ghost town of 180 is home to the small **Rock River Museum,** tel. (307) 378-2386; open Tues.-Sun. 10 a.m.-3 p.m. June-August. Inside you'll find exhibits on dinosaurs, a collection of phosphorescent rocks, and local memorabilia. A statue of a *Triceratops* stands in the town park. The town also has a bar, a motel, a general store/laundromat, a cafe, and a pretty red-doored church. **Longhorn Lodge Motel,** 362 N. 4th, tel. (307) 378-2555, charges $20 s, $25 d. **Dodge Creek Ranch,** tel. (307) 322-2345, is 35 miles northeast of Rock River, 40 miles southwest of Wheatland, on State 34. This cattle ranch specializes in weeklong vacations, with backpacking trips, fishing, photography, and other activities.

West of Rock River, the road sails through desolate treeless country, with sagebrush to the horizon and the impressive summit of Elk Mountain rising to the southwest. The Union Pacific Railroad parallels the highway most of the way, and antelope glance up at the passing trains. Anyone coming through in the winter will appreciate the miles of snow fences along the south side of the highway. Still, the snow streams over the roadway almost constantly.

COMO BLUFF

Halfway between the towns of Rock River and Medicine Bow on U.S. 30/287 is a long, low ridge known as Como Bluff. There isn't much to distinguish this from countless other buttes in the West, but paleontologists consider it one of the most important sites ever discovered, a place one author likened to Darwin's *Origin of the Species* in terms of its impact on scientific thought. This was the first large discovery of dinosaurs anywhere, and the first place *Diplodocus* dinosaurs—the largest ever found—were discovered. The mammals discovered here are prized around the world and include all but three of the 250 known Jurassic mammals found in North America. Combined, the dinosaur and mammal fossils from Como Bluff make up a major part of the collections of Yale's Peabody Museum, the Smithsonian Institution, the New York Museum of Natural History, the National Museum in Washington, D.C., and many others around the world.

History

In July of 1877, Professor Othniel Charles Marsh of Yale College received a letter from two Wyoming men calling themselves Harlow and Edwards. They told of finding

a large number of fossils, supposed to be those of the Megatherium, although there is no one here sufficient of a geologist to state for a certainty. We have excavated one (1) partly, and know where there is several others that we have not, as yet, done any work upon . . . We are desirous of disposing of what fossils we have, and also, the secret of the others. We are working men and are not able to present them as a gift, and if we can sell the secret of the fossil bed, and procure work in excavating others we would like to do so. We have said nothing to any-one as yet . . . We would be pleased to hear from you, as you are well known as an enthusiastic geologist, and a man of means, both of which we are desirous of finding—more especially the latter.

Marsh was in stiff competition with other paleontologists around the country, and his rival, Professor E.D. Cope from the Philadelphia

Academy of Sciences, had just scooped him on a major dinosaur discovery in Colorado. The letter from "Harlow and Edwards" piqued Marsh's curiosity. An assistant sent to investigate wrote that the find was indeed substantive and suggested that Marsh immediately hire the two discoverers—actually two railroad employees, William Reed and William Carlin—to keep them from revealing the secret to others. Reed would later work for many years as a collector for the University of Wyoming and eventually as an instructor in geology and curator of the Geology Museum on the Laramie campus.

Work began almost immediately and continued right through the blizzards of winter, but despite efforts to keep the find a secret, Professor Cope soon had his own men working at Como Bluff. The rivalry almost came to blows, and Marsh's men made it a point to smash any bones left behind after their digging was complete and to backfill the quarries with rocks, even if their rivals were working below. Excavations continued until 1889, by which time most of the finest specimens had been unearthed.

Today geology and paleontology classes still come to Como Bluff, but the quarries where the bones were found are now abandoned and can't be seen from the road. Como Bluff itself is visible a little over a mile north of U.S. 30 and a sign describes the site. Travelers will want to stop at **"the world's oldest building"** at Como Bluffs, a now-closed museum/gift shop built from dinosaur bones.

MEDICINE BOW

The little town of Medicine Bow (pop. 360) is the sort of place where headlines in the weekly *Medicine Bow Post* complain of dogs getting into garbage or barking at kids. For the most part it's a nondescript town with old box-like houses and newer box-like trailers. Medicine Bow is not unlike hundreds of places all over the West, but it was here that novelist Owen Wister had his legendary cowboy hero, the Virginian, face off with Trampas. Over a game of cards, Trampas calls the Virginian a "son-of-a-bitch," leading to the famous encounter in which the Virginian pulls his pistol and says, "When you call me that, smile!" It remains one of the

classic lines in American folklore. *The Virginian* became the prototype for the modern Western and was later made into three movies and a TV series.

History
The town of Medicine Bow began in the 1870s as a Union Pacific pumping station along Medicine Bow River and grew into a local supply point and minor Army garrison. It has always been a center for the ranchers who run thousands of head of livestock in the surrounding countryside, so it was a logical place for Wister to base his cowboy hero. During the 1930s,

---

Town, as they called it, pleased me the less, the longer I saw it. But until our language stretches itself and takes in a new word or closer fit, town will have to do for the name of such a place as Medicine Bow. I have seen and slept in many like it since. Scattered wide, they littered the frontier from the Columbia to the Rio Grande, from the Missouri to the Sierras. They lay stark, dotted over a planet of treeless dust, like soiled packs of cards. Each was similar to the next, as one old five-spot of cards resembles another. . . . Yet this wretched husk of squalor spent thought upon appearances; many houses in it wore a false front to seem as if they were two stories high. There they stood, rearing their pitiful masquerade amid a fringe of old tin cans, while at their very doors began a world of crystal light, a land without end, a space across which Noah and Adam might come straight from Genesis. Into that space went wandering a road, over a hill and down out of sight, and up again smaller in the distance, and down once more, and up once more, straining the eyes, and so away.

—From Owen Wister's
The Virginian

Medicine Bow prospered because it lay along the Lincoln Hwy. (U.S. 30) but, following completion of I-80, it lapsed into decay. The coal mines of Hanna (20 miles west) and uranium and oil explorations in Shirley Basin led to temporary energy booms, but the economy has now returned to its ranching base.

Sights

Medicine Bow's main attraction is the boxy, three-story **Virginian Hotel,** built in 1909—seven years after *The Virginian* came out. At the time, it was the largest hotel between Denver and Salt Lake City. It's still a marvelous building, so take a look around, even if you aren't planning on staying here. The Virginian's authentic old-time bar is one of the best in Wyoming. Just down the street is the modern **Diplodocus Bar**—alias "the Dip"—containing the largest jade bar in existence, cut from a 4.5-ton jade boulder discovered near Lander. Look down for the only hand-painted dance floor west of the Mississippi. While you're here for a beer, be sure to ask owner Bill Bennett to show his unusually intricate woodcarvings.

Across from the hotel is the **Medicine Bow Museum,** housed in the old wooden railroad depot (1913). Out front is a cabin built by Owen Wister—it stood in Jackson Hole until being moved here in 1976—and a petrified-wood monument to the novelist. The museum contains the typical things found in small-town museums—various homesteading items, a lamb warmer, a coyote scare made from sawdust and firecrackers, and old fire equipment. It's kind of like wandering through an old attic where you wonder how half the stuff was ever used. There's an old caboose on the side. The museum, tel. (307) 379-2383, is open daily 10 a.m.-5 p.m. Memorial Day through Labor Day, Mon.-Thurs. 10 a.m.-3:30 p.m. the rest of the year.

Five miles south of Medicine Bow is the remains of a giant **wind turbine** built in 1982 for the U.S. Department of the Interior. The largest wind generator in existence, it's located in one of the windiest spots in America. Originally there were two such windmills here, each producing five million kilowatt hours of electricity a year. Supporters envisioned an enormous wind farm with perhaps another 50, but these 400-foot-tall monsters proved unwieldy embarrassments

and were abandoned by the government when it discovered that repairs would be prohibitively expensive. One of the $6 million turbines was blasted over with dynamite and sold for $13,000 on the scrap market in 1988. The remaining turbine is now privately owned and produced electricity until a 1994 storm destroyed the blades. There is once again talk, this time from electrical utility companies, of constructing a windmill farm in the area.

Practicalities

Rooms at the historic **Virginian Hotel,** tel. (307) 379-2377, are remarkably inexpensive, starting at just $20 s, $22 d with a bath down the hall. You should, however, check them out first, since they definitely aren't to everyone's liking and can get noisy when downstairs bar patrons are in full swing. For $65 s or d, sleep in the two-bedroom suite where Owen Wister stayed. If you miss your TV and private bath, try a room in the annex next door for $38 s, $40 d. The downstairs restaurant provides good home cooking, and most Saturday nights will find country bands in the bar. **Trampas Lodge,** tel. (307) 379-2280, also has rooms with private baths and cable TV for $27 s, $30 d. Open May-Oct. only. Pitch your tent or park RVs at the town park. Groceries are available from **Bow Market,** pastries from **Pearle's Kitchen.**

Medicine Bow Days is the annual celebration in town, held at the end of June and including rodeos, parades, a picnic, foot races, live music, and dancing. The "highlight" is the hanging of Dutch Charlie at high noon. In 1879 and 1871, respectively, Dutch Charlie and Big Nose George were lynched for the murder of two deputies. (See the special topic "Big Nose George Parrot" in this chapter.)

SHIRLEY BASIN

State 487 heads north from Medicine Bow across the vast and remote Shirley Basin, some of the finest cattle rangeland in Wyoming. The road is smooth with wide shoulders (perfect for bikes), and the vistas are dramatic—colorful badlands, rolling hills covered with sage and grass, and cottonwood-lined creeks. There's lots of wildlife here, too—especially antelope

and deer, but also some of the largest remaining prairie-dog towns in existence. Because of this, Shirley Basin was the first area where the endangered black-footed ferret was released back into the wild. Ferret releases took place from 1991 to 1994. Despite high mortalities, many survived to reproduce. Severe flooding from a 1994 rain and hail storm unfortunately killed many prairie dogs in the basin; without sufficient food the ferret population plummeted to barely a dozen survivors. This, combined with the presence of sylvatic plague, has dimmed hopes for a successful reintroduction of ferrets to Shirley Basin, at least in the short term.

Extensive deposits of uranium have been discovered in Shirley Basin—some of the largest

BLACK-FOOTED FERRETS

On September 25, 1981, near Meeteetse, Wyoming, a dog walked up to its master with a strange creature in his mouth. It was a black-footed ferret, a sleek, black-masked animal last seen in 1972 and feared extinct. Biologists soon discovered that a nearby prairie dog colony housed the only living population of the ferrets, the world's rarest mammals. Ferrets eat prairie dogs and were once found in their colonies from Saskatchewan to Texas. The colonies were huge—one along the Cheyenne River in eastern Wyoming stretched for a hundred miles—but the prairie dogs went the way of many other animals, hunted and poisoned by settlers and their land taken over by plowed fields. Although still present in Wyoming, prairie dog colonies are now much smaller and more isolated. The population of ferrets declined with their shrinking food source.

With the discovery of ferrets living near Meeteetse, national attention focused on saving the population from extinction. A 1985 outbreak of canine distemper threatened to kill all the remaining wild ferrets, so all 18 survivors were captured and taken to the Wyoming Game and Fish Wildlife Research Unit at Sybille . After inoculations, an ambitious captive breeding program was begun. Only five of the animals actually reproduced, but the program proved so successful that the population was split up to reduce the chance that all might be killed in an accident such as a fire or disease. Ferrets are now raised not only at Sybille, but also at the National Zoo in Virginia, Henry Doorly Zoo in Omaha, Louisville Zoological Park, the Phoenix Zoo, Cheyenne Mountain Zoo in Colorado Springs, and the Metropolitan Toronto Zoo.

Begining in 1991, ferrets have been released to the wild in Shirley Basin (north of the town of Medicine Bow). Additional ferrets have since been set free in north-central Montana and southwest South Dakota, and there are plans to eventually release them in Wyoming at Thunder Basin National Grassland and in the Bighorn Basin. The Shirley Basin ferrets initially did very well, and reproduced in the wild but a combination of severe flooding and the presence of sylvatic plague set things back. As of 1996 a dozen or so survived in the basin, with similar numbers at the other release sites in Montana and South Dakota. Eventually, researchers hope to reestablish ferrets in at least 10 separate areas around the West.

Because of their relatively short lifespan (two to three years in the wild) and their susceptibility to diseases and to predators such as owls and coyotes, ferrets will almost certainly remain endangered for many years. Unfortunately, continued destruction of prairie dog colonies by "varmint hunters" and poisoning by ranchers has made it more and more difficult to find places to release wild ferrets. The habitat is becoming increasingly fragmented into "islands" separated by areas where the prairie dogs have been killed off.

The **Sybille Wildlife Research Center,** on State 34 halfway between Bosler and Wheatland, tel. 322-2784, is open daily 8:30 a.m.-4:30 p.m. April-Oct. (closed the rest of the year). Inside are exhibits and videos on the endangered black-footed ferret. TV monitors show activity in the adjacent ferret facility, home to more than 170 ferrets. Tours are available only for groups.

BOB RACE

and richest in the world—but low prices and an oversupply have all but halted the uranium-mining business. Ask in Medicine Bow for directions to the petrified forest. Nearly every yard in town has a piece out front.

HANNA

The town of Hanna (pop. 1,100) lies at the center of one of the state's major coal fields. There are lots of mobile homes and company housing in Hanna, but there is nothing particularly interesting about the town, unless you care to check out the miners memorials or the enormous Union Pacific snowplow. Near Hanna are two large coal mines: the Medicine Bow strip mine, 23 miles west, and the larger Cyprus Shoshone mine, five miles north. Mining has been a mainstay of the local economy since coal was discovered here in the late 1800s. Two disastrous explosions, in 1903 and 1908, killed 228 miners, but the mines remained open until 1954 and were reactivated in the 1970s. Two monuments commemorate the men who died. The mining ghost town of **Carbon**—established in 1868 as the state's first coal town—once stood a few miles east of here. The coal ran out in 1902, and today only a few ruins and the graveyard remain. **Hanna Basin Museum,** tel. (307) 325-6340, has local memorabilia.

Practicalities

Golden Rule Motel, tel. (307) 325-6525, charges $23 s, $25 d, for simple prefab rooms. Very friendly owners make this the de facto chamber of commerce office. **The Tucker Box,** 624 Madison, tel. (307) 325-6353, serves good breakfasts and lunches, or try **Jade Cafe,** tel. (307) 325-6355. Hanna's fine **recreation center** includes a sauna, a pool, a jacuzzi, and a gym. Groceries are available at **The Super Market.** Other businesses include a hardware store, two liquor stores, a video shop, and a bank—but there's no ATM.

ELK MOUNTAIN

The tiny settlement of Elk Mountain (pop. 200) stands just off I-80 halfway between Laramie and Rawlins. *Do* take this exit! Although almost within sight of the freeway, the town seems a world apart. Big cottonwoods line the quiet streets. The Medicine Bow River, home of blue-ribbon trout fishing, flows right through town. Several buildings are noteworthy: the small New England-style community church, the Elk Mountain Trading Company—one of the best old-time general stores in Wyoming—and an enormous log barn still in perfect condition after more than 100 years. Directly behind town is the rounded, snow-topped 11,156-foot summit of Elk Mountain, one of the most prominent natur-

*Rock Creek Stage
Station, 1861*

BUFFALO BILL HISTORICAL CENTER

al landmarks anywhere along I-80. Unusual clouds frequently hang off its peak, making it a valuable site for the University of Wyoming's atmospheric research program. Ask in town for access information; you'll need to get permission from local ranchers.

Elk Mountain Hotel, tel. (307) 348-7774, built in 1905, is an old-fashioned, slightly run-down hotel where the bath-down-the-hall rooms are $25 s, $35 d. The hotel also runs a bar and restaurant specializing in steaks, burgers, and seafood. You can also try the attractive **Noon Camp Cafe,** tel. (307) 348-7478. Still standing in Elk Mountain is **Garden Spot Pavilion,** a decrepit former dance hall that in the 1930s and '40s attracted the likes of Louis Armstrong, Tommy Dorsey, Glenn Miller, Louis Armstrong, and Lawrence Welk. Five miles west of town, a stone monument marks the site of **Fort Halleck,** a short-lived military post built in 1862 to guard the Overland Trail. With the arrival of the transcontinental railroad, it was abandoned in 1866 and its fixtures moved east to Fort Buford (later called Fort Sanders), near present-day Laramie.

Head south from Elk Mountain on Pass Creek Road (Road 404) for a wonderful round-the-mountain drive. The gravel road curves south past Elk Mountain, then west along the willow-lined Pass Creek to a junction with State 130, where you can continue to Saratoga. This little-traveled road offers open hills with wide vistas of the mountains and plains. While you listen to meadowlarks singing and wind rustling through the grass, you can watch—as the song says—the deer and the antelope play. Not even a line of telephone poles breaks the view, and seldom is heard a discouraging word.

ARLINGTON

Approximately 30 miles west of Laramie is a freeway crossroads with lots of history called Arlington. Stay at the **Arlington KOA,** tel. (307) 378-2350 or (800) 562-3705, where tents are $14.50, RVs $18; open May-October. Wagon rides depart from the Arlington Trading Post daily in the summer months—$25 for adults, $15 for ages 6-18, free for younger kids. Prices include a barbecue and entertainment. Call (307) 378-2459 for specifics. **Overland Trail Guest Ranch,** tel. (307) 378-2400, has two modern cabins with kitchenettes for $45 s, $50 d. This is primarily a hunting and fishing spot, with wintertime snowmobiling and cross-country skiing. Meals are also available.

In Arlington are several buildings from the **Rock Creek Stage Station,** which stood along the Overland Route, including a log cabin built around 1860—one of the oldest buildings in Wyoming. Also here, located on private land south of the freeway, is a combination blacksmith shop/dance hall/gambling palace. In 1865, Indians attacked a wagon train near the Rock Creek Stage Station and captured two girls, Mary and Lizzie Fletcher. Mary was eventually sold to a white trader, but Lizzie remained with the Arapahos for the rest of her life. It wasn't until 35 years later that Mary discovered her sister alive and living on the Wind River Reservation. Having grown accustomed to the Arapaho way of life and enjoying a high status in the community, Lizzie chose to stay in her home. She is buried next to her husband, Broken Horn, in the St. Stephen's Mission Cemetery.

MEDICINE BOW MOUNTAINS AND VICINITY

Medicine Bow National Forest is scattered over four disjunctive areas in Wyoming. The northern portion—the Laramie Mountains—is discussed in the Central Wyoming chapter; the Pole Mountain section is described under "Laramie" earlier in this chapter. The other two mountainous areas are west of Laramie: the Medicine Bow Mountains, locally called the Snowy Range, and the Sierra Madre. The Forest Service has controlled most of this land since 1902, although

the name and boundaries have changed over the years. Mining was the big attraction in the late 1800s, but the major gold and copper deposits were quickly mined out and logging became the primary use of this mountainous country. Between 1867 and 1940, millions of railroad ties were brought out of the Laramie and Medicine Bow mountains by tie hacks who logged almost every driveable creek they could find. The area provided ties for not only

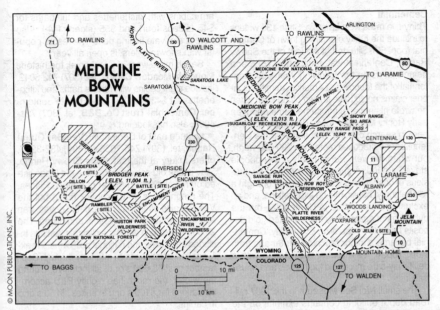

Wyoming but western Nebraska and Colorado as well. Logging for lumber is still important in the Medicine Bow National Forest but recreational use is increasing each year as more and more people discover this very scenic country. The supervisor's office for Medicine Bow National Forest is in Laramie; district offices are in Saratoga, Encampment, and Douglas. Pick up a copy of the Medicine Bow National Forest Map ($3) at any of these offices before heading out.

LARAMIE PLAINS VICINITY

Heading west from Laramie on State 130, you pass through some of the most desolate country in Wyoming, with flat grassland stretching in all directions, interrupted by mountains to the east, south, and west. An enormous windswept bowl here—**Big Hollow**—was created by howling winds during the last ice age. The only other place like this is in Russia. Laramie Basin is also unique in having the highest short-grass prairie in the world, some 7,200 feet above sea level. Eleven miles west of Laramie, State 130 crosses the historic **Overland Trail,** which carried emigrants, mail, and freight west between 1862 and 1868, when the railroad replaced it. The wagon ruts are still visible, with markers tracing the old route. As you approach the Medicine Bow Mountains, the highway dips down to sample the tree-lined beauty of Little Laramie Creek and then begins the long ascent to Snowy Range Pass.

Albany

State 11 heads south along Little Laramie Creek to the foothills town of Albany, passing rolling grass and sagebrush country with pine-topped hills. Old ranches are sprinkled around this gorgeous little valley. Rustic cabins with shared bath at the **Albany Lodge,** tel. (307) 745-5782, cost $35 s or d and even more rustic motel rooms are $25 s or d. The bar has hundreds of baseball caps tacked to the ceiling. On Saturday nights this is a popular place with tasty $13 prime rib dinners. A dirt road continues south from Albany to Woods Landing, but blowing snows often cause its closure in the winter. Albany is a very popular base for snowmobilers.

Centennial

Thirty-five miles west Laramie, State 130 widens to include the funky old mining town of Centennial (pop. 50). Situated at the foot of the Snowy Range, Centennial was founded in 1875 and gained its name the following year—the centennial of the founding of America. James Michener claims not to have known of the town when he wrote his novel of the same name about an early Rocky Mountain town. Prospectors came here in search of gold. That first year the Centennial Mine produced more than $90,000 worth, but when the vein ran out only a few people stayed around. A short boom created by infusions of cash from a Boston financier brought a fish hatchery, hotels, mining explorations, and an exclusive country club to Centennial, but the bubble burst again when the expected gold deposits failed to materialize. Eventually, Centennial became a minor ranching center and train stop. Today, it's a tourist way station with a devil-may-care mix of old log homes and house trailers.

The small **Nici Self Museum** in the 1907 railroad depot building contains exhibits on the area's mining and logging history and is open Sat.-Sun. 1-4 p.m. from July 4 through Labor Day, by appointment the rest of the year (tel. 307-742-7158 or 742-8612). Out front is a Union Pacific caboose and various old farm implements. Check out the "police car" as you roll through town.

Old Corral Motel, tel. (307) 745-5918 or (800) 678-2024, has rooms in the lodge for $40 s, $55 d in the summer without breakfast, $49-55 s or d winters with a full breakfast. Their restaurant, open for all three meals in summer but dinners only in winter, serves outstanding steaks in a comfortably rustic atmosphere and has live music on summer weekends. **Friendly Motel,** tel. (307) 742-6033, has rooms for $30 s, $36 d; open year-round. Across the road is **Trading Post Restaurant & Lounge,** tel. (307) 721-5074, where you'll find country, blues, or rock on Saturday nights. It also has two cabins for rent year-round: $35 d, $45 for four, including kitchen, but no phones or TVs. According to the waitress, the steaks are so good "They'll make your tongue slap your brains out."

Rainbow Valley Resort, tel. (307) 745-0368, two miles northwest of Centennial, offers modern cabins with kitchenettes and full baths for $45 (sleeps four) and $55 (sleeps five). Also here is a private fishing pond The resort, popular with snowmobilers, is open all year.

Seven miles west of Centennial, the historic **Mountain Meadow Cabins,** tel. (307) 742-6042, include eight cabins with private baths and kitchenettes for $43-68. Open June to late September. **Centennial Trust Co. B&B,** tel. (307) 721-4090, also has lodging.

Located east of Centennial, **Vee Bar Guest Ranch,** tel. (307) 745-7036 or (800) 483-3227, offers luxury at the foot of the Snowy Range. Stay in fine old cabins or in a fine old lodge listed on the National Register of Historic Places. The emphasis is on horseback riding but the Vee Bar also offers hay rides, cattle drives, trap shooting, archery, trout fishing, and hiking. The 26,000-acre ranch attracts a clientele that has included celebrities and national politicians. Weekly accommodations from mid-May through September cost $3,600 s or d, all inclusive. During the winter, the ranch has nightly B&B accommodations for $100 s or d in suites, $150 s or d in cabins.

SNOWY RANGE

In between the Laramie Plains and the valley created by the upper North Platte River lie the Medicine Bow Mountains, locally called the Snowy Range. The latter is an appropriate name; it can snow here at any time of the year; 10-foot drifts are not uncommon in the winter, and snow remains on high passes until late summer. The Snowy Range contains the **Savage Run Wilderness** (15,260 acres) and the **Platte River Wilderness** (22,749 acres), both lying along the southwestern end of the range just above the Wyoming-Colorado border. Most visitors simply enjoy the drive over the mountains and the chance to camp beside an alpine lake with a backdrop of 12,000-foot mountains. Numerous short hiking trails make this a favorite spot for locals.

The Forest Service has detailed forest maps and helpful brochures on these mountains at its Laramie office, 2468 Jackson St., tel. (307) 745-8971. You'll also find Forest Service **information centers** on both sides of the Snowy

SNOWY RANGE
TRAILS

TO SAND LAKE

DEEP LAKE

SHEEP LAKE

ROCK CREEK
KNOLL
(ELEV. 11,125 ft.)

SHEEP LAKE TRAIL

NORTH
TWIN
LAKES

QUEALY LAKE

QUEALY LAKE TRAIL

RESERVOIR
LAKE

NORTH GAP
LAKE TRAIL

GAP LAKES

BROWNS PEAK
(ELEV. 11,722 ft.)

TELEPHONE
LAKES

BROOKLYN
LAKE

BROOKLYN LAKE
GUARD STATION

OPEN AIR
CHAPEL

MEDICINE BOW
PEAK (ELEV. 12,013 ft.)

LEWIS LAKE

LIBBY
LAKE

SUGARLOAF
RECREATION
AREA

TO
CENTENNIAL

SUGARLOAF
MOUNTAIN
(ELEV. 11,398 ft.)

LOOKOUT
LAKE

LAKES
TRAIL

SNOWY
RANGE
PASS

LIBBY LAKE

MIRROR LAKE

LIBBY FLATS

MEDICINE BOW
OBSERVATION AREA

LAKE MARIE

TO SARATOGA AND ENCAMPMENT

130

0   1 mi

0   1 km

© MOON PUBLICATIONS, INC.

Range along State 130. One of these, located a mile west of Centennial, is open daily 8 a.m.-5 p.m. mid-May through October and Sat.-Sun 10 a.m.-3 p.m. in the winter. The other, the Brush Creek Work Center, tel. (307) 326-5562, is 20 miles east of Saratoga and is open daily 8 a.m.-5 p.m. Memorial Day through September.

Over the Top

The 40-mile drive on State 130 over the Snowy Range is one of the most dramatic in Wyoming and is designated a National Scenic Byway. The pass is closed by snow from late October to Memorial Day but remains open year-round to

just beyond the Snowy Range Ski Area on the east side and 20 miles up from the west side. Higher-elevation parts of the road are very popular with snowmobilers and cross-country skiers. West of Centennial, the highway climbs sharply through lodgepole and spruce forests to beautiful Snowy Range Pass at 10,847 feet (second-highest in the state).

Be sure to stop at **Sugarloaf Recreation Area,** just east of the pass. Sharp, glacially carved spires rise above the small lakes, and islands of stunted Engelmann spruce dot the alpine country. Trails head out to nearby lakes and flower-covered alpine meadows. At the

summit, a viewing platform provides panoramic vistas of Libby Flats, massive Medicine Bow Peak, and the valleys on both sides. Pull off at the Medicine Bow Peak Observation Point for a three-quarter-mile hike in to the picturesque remains of an old mine. Just west of here, **Mirror Lake** and **Lake Marie** are two of the most photographed spots in Wyoming, with a spectacular backdrop of steep mountain faces reflected in the dark blue lake waters. Campgrounds and picnic areas are all along here. A wheelchair-accessible path leads along one shore of Lake Marie, and the west parking lot acts as a trailhead for the path up **Medicine Bow Peak** (see below). On the western side of the pass, the highway drops steadily down through the forest, eventually reaching the rolling sage and grass of the Upper North Platte River Valley. Stop at the Brush Creek Visitor Center for directions to **Kennaday Peak Lookout,** one of the few fire lookouts still in use in Wyoming. It's open July to Labor Day and is accessible by high-clearance cars. No RVs.

Route 230

Another route west is State 230. While this highway is not as dramatic as the Snowy Pass trek, it's open year-round and is still quite scenic. The road curves around the southern end of the Snowys and passes through Woods Landing en route to the Colorado border. You'll find excellent fishing for brown trout along the Big Laramie River near the nearly abandoned settlement of Woods Landing. The mining ghost town of **Old Jelm** is four miles south of Woods Landing and contains a number of old clapboard buildings. Ask locally for permission to visit. The university's **Jelm Mountain Observatory** is up a five-mile dirt road from here. Call the university in advance (tel. 307-766-6150) for a tour of the largest infrared telescope in the continental United States. The **Guest House at Jelm,** tel. (307) 742-6081, is a three-bedroom log home for $65 d (more for additional people); open mid-May through November.

Woods Landing has a country store/gas station/bar, tel. (307) 745-9638, and is the only real settlement between Laramie and Encampment—a distance of 87 miles. There's excellent fishing in the Big Laramie River here. Beyond Woods Landing, State 230 dips south and

passes several mountain lodges including **Wyo-Colo Lodge,** just north of the state line, tel. (307) 742-4230, where rustic cabins with a shared bathhouse cost $20 s, $30 d; open year-round. Also here is a bar. The road continues into Colorado for nine miles along Colorado 127, then back north on Colorado 125 for another nine miles before again crossing into Wyoming on State 230. Much of this is open rangeland with hills on either side. Only a few abandoned cabins and fences mark the presence of humans on this vast landscape. The huge white hip-roofed barn of the Big Creek Ranch is one of the most beautiful in all Wyoming. Turn around for outstanding views of the Colorado Rockies. See Stephen Metzger's *Colorado Handbook* (Moon Publications) for details on sights to the south.

Campgrounds

Twenty-four different Forest Service campgrounds rent spots for $6-8 per site within the Snowy Range portion of Medicine Bow National Forest. Most of these are open June-Sept., but the season varies depending upon snow conditions and budget constraints. A few of the campgrounds—those with no water or trash pickup—are free. Because of heavy use during the summer, you should arrive at the most popular sites early in the day. Any of these campgrounds may be reserved by calling (800) 280-2267, but you'll need to pay an $8.25 reservation fee. In addition to the official campgrounds, dispersed camping is permitted in most areas as long as you're off the main roads—although not near Sugarloaf Recreation Area. Check with the Forest Service for specifics.

Mountain Lodges

Snowy Mountain Lodge, tel. (307) 742-7669, is just beyond the Snowy Range Ski Area seven miles west of Centennial. Built as a University of Wyoming science camp in 1927, the lodge includes cozy accommodations in log cabins at $45 s or d, $90 for up to eight, or in a bunkhouse at $15 per person. The bunkhouse is especially popular with groups of wintertime cross-country skiers looking for a cheap place in the mountains. In the winter you'll need to ski in or catch a snowcat ride from the lodge for the last third of mile; the road isn't plowed. The restaurant at

the lodge serves three solid meals a day and has a bar, pool table, jukebox, and recreation room. It's not a place to be pampered but a great place for folks who want to explore the nearby mountains by foot, bike, ski, or snowmobile.

Another delightful place is **Brooklyn Lodge B&B**, tel. (307) 742-6916, west of Centennial in the Snowy Range at an elevation of 10,200 feet. The log lodge is on the National Register of Historic Places and contains a living room with a large stone fireplace and a front porch overlooking a mountain meadow. Guests stay in one of two rooms for $75 s, $85 d (shared bath), with a minimum two-night stay on weekends, three nights on holidays. Room price includes a full breakfast; other meals are available with advance notice. This is a favorite spot for early summer weddings.

Historic **Medicine Bow Lodge,** just inside the western Forest Service boundary along State 130, tel. (307) 326-5439, has comfortable historic cabins for $65 per person per day including three meals and access to a hot tub. They offer summertime horseback rides and winter snowmobile tours. Cross-country skis are available for guests. Open all year except November and mid-April to mid-May, the lodge first opened in 1917; the main building is still in use.

Trails

The Medicine Bows are ideal for short one- to five-day hikes. The three-mile-long **Medicine Bow Peak Trail** climbs 1,600 feet to the summit of this 12,013-foot mountain, highest in southern Wyoming, for extraordinary vistas from the top. The trail leaves from the Lake Marie picnic area and is in exposed alpine terrain most of the way. You can make an approximately six-mile loop by following this route to the top and then dropping down the east side to the **Lakes Trail,** which takes you past rock-rimmed Lookout Lake—keep a lookout for marmots—and on to Mirror Lake. Your starting point is just down the road. Medicine Bow Peak can also be climbed via a shorter trail (four miles roundtrip) that leaves from the Lewis Lake Trailhead.

North Gap Lake Trail departs from the Lewis Lake parking lot in the Sugarloaf Recreation Area and follows a gentle grade past Gap Lakes, continuing on to Sheep Lake. Beyond these, hikers can continue north to Sand Lake, nine miles from your starting point, or loop back to State 130 via the **Sheep Lake Trail.** The latter route ends at Brooklyn Lake, where you can hitch a ride back to your starting point (or leave a vehicle beforehand). This entire area is crisscrossed with other alpine trails, some of which are not shown on topographic maps. Check with the Forest Service for details.

Platte River Trail, a five-mile-long path, parallels the river through North Gate Canyon, a long stretch of whitewater in the Platte River Wilderness. The banks are lined with ponderosa pines and Douglas firs. Access is from the south via Sixmile Gap Campground. The trail's on the western bank of the river but by late summer the river can sometimes be forded, allowing hikers to continue another 1.5 miles northward to Pickaroon Campground. **Savage Run Trail** crosses the wilderness area of the same name. Nine miles long, it follows Savage Run Creek, dropping 2,400 feet along the way. Access is too confusing to describe, but it's not that hard to find if you have a Medicine Bow National Forest map.

Snowy Range Ski Area

Located in the mountains 32 miles west of Laramie on State 130, the Snowy Range Ski Area has four lifts and 23 different runs. Outside of Jackson Hole, this is the best place to ski in Wyoming, with a good variety of skiing conditions, uncrowded slopes, and soft powder snow. Snowy Range is open mid-November through mid-April and charges $25 for adults ($20 per half-day), $12 for kids ages 6-12 and seniors ($10 per half-day). Children under six are free with a paying adult. The area is open daily 9 a.m.-4 p.m., with ski and snowboard rentals and lessons and guided snowmobile trips available. The lodge has cafeteria food, beer, and a fireplace. For more information, call (307) 745-5750 or (800) 462-7669.

Other Winter Sports

The Forest Service maintains dozens of miles of groomed Nordic ski trails in the mountains around Snowy Range Ski Area, with a wide variety of loops and longer treks available for those willing to strike out on their own. An overnight ski hut is available for rent (tel. 307-745-2300) near Little Brooklyn Lake. Snowmobiling is one of the most popular winter activities in the Snowy

Range, and parking lots on all sides of the range fill with vehicles on winter weekends. More than 200 miles of groomed trails follow summertime roads. For details on both cross-country skiing and snowmobiling, stop by the Forest Service offices in Laramie or Saratoga.

River Recreation

The North Platte River forms a major focal point for visitors staying in Saratoga or Encampment. The trout fishing is excellent and the scenery grand; no wonder they call this the "Good Times Valley!" Many travelers float downriver either on their own or with guides. Check with local Forest Service offices for river access information and a list of guides. In Saratoga, **Great Rocky Mountain Outfitters,** 216 E. Walnut, tel. (307) 326-8750 or (800) 326-5390, sells quality Orvis fly-fishing gear and can fill you in on the latest fishing and floating conditions. Rent rafts for $75 a day or canoes for $35. All-day fishing trips run $275 for two people; overnight camping and fishing trips and boat shuttles are also available. **Medicine Bow Drifters,**120 E. Bridge St., tel. (307) 326-8002, has scenic float trips for $60 per person for a minimum of four people and all-day float and fishing trips costing $275 for two people. Other companies with similar services include: **Platte Valley Outfitters,** 1st and Bridge streets, tel. (307) 326-5750; **Hack's Tackle & Outfitters,** 407 N. 1st St., tel. (307) 326-9823, **TA Outfitters,** tel. (307) 326-8455, and **Grand & Sierra Outfitters** in Encampment, tel. (307) 327-5200.

As the North Platte River enters Wyoming from Colorado it drops into **North Gate Canyon,** a class III and IV stretch of whitewater with several hairy sets of rapids. Beyond Sixmile Gap, the river broadens and becomes a gentler float. If you are a whitewater enthusiast, get here early—the water level drops after June. Check with the above places for guided whitewater trips in May and June.

SARATOGA

The friendly, laid-back town of Saratoga (pop. 1,900) is one of two towns in Wyoming—the other being Thermopolis—that center around hot springs. The name was borrowed from another well-known spa: Saratoga, New York. Wyoming's version of Saratoga straddles the North Platte River and putters along on a mixed economy. Louisiana Pacific Company has a large lumber mill in town, and many cattle graze in the beautiful river bottom country along the North Platte. Saratoga is also something of a bedroom community for coal miners who work in Hanna but prefer the country around Saratoga. Others commute as far as Rawlins to work.

Like many places in Wyoming, Saratoga has long depended upon various extractive industries for a livelihood and is only now discovering how attractive the land itself is. With mountains on both sides, "blue ribbon" trout fishing, river float trips, a free hot springs, a rich history, and lots of wildlife, it's certain that tourism will grow increasingly important. The elaborate new Rawlins National Bank shows that money is starting to pour into Saratoga. Each year more folks arrive and new businesses sprout up, creating concerns that Saratoga could go the way of other edge-of-the-mountains towns.

History

Indians called Saratoga Hot Springs "Place of the Magic Water"; it was a place of healing where various tribes could mingle without fear of attack. When whites arrived and first bathed here, the Indians noted that the waters boiled more violently than before, indicating an evil spirit. Thereafter most shunned the hot springs, but an 1874 smallpox epidemic forced some to return. Patients were soaked in the hot water in an attempt to boil out the disease and then dipped in the cold river water. When all the patients died, the Indians decided that whites had turned the waters from good medicine to bad medicine. The area was littered with the graves of smallpox victims. Thereafter, the Indians moved even farther from the hot springs.

In 1877, William H. Cadwell homesteaded near the springs, built a wooden bathhouse on the site, and offered hot baths, meals, and a place for travelers to stretch out for a night's sleep. People flocked here from all over the region—some even came from England to soak in the waters claimed to cure "rheumatism, eczema, paralysis, stomach trouble, kidney disease, nerves, and all forms of blood and skin disease." The copper-mining boom in the Sierra

TO SARATOGA LAKE AND I-80

DEER HAVEN RV PARK

CHATTERTON DR.

130

NORTH

VETERAN ST.

HUGUS AVE.

E. FARM AVE.

SARATOGA TRAILER CAMPER PARK

FARM AVE.

3RD

PIZZA HUT

E. ROCHESTER AVE.

ROCHESTER AVE.

RIVIERA LODGE

E. SARATOGA AVE.

6TH

7TH

5TH

4TH

2ND

1ST

SILVER MOON MOTEL

FAR OUT WEST BED AND BREAKFAST

SARATOGA AVE.

8TH

STATE ST.

HOOD HOUSE BED AND BREAKFAST

STUMPY'S EATERY

BUBBA'S BAR-B-QUE

MAIN AVE.

E. BRIDGE ST.

E. RIVER ST.

POST OFFICE

PLATTE

BRIDGE ST.

WOLF HOTEL

PIC PIKE COUNTY RD.

SPRING AVE.

ST.

CHAMBER OF COMMERCE

RIVER

SARATOGA INN

ELM AVE.

ST.

LIBRARY

SAGE AND SAND MOTEL

VETERAN ISLAND PARK

HICKORY AVE.

ST.

WALNUT AVE.

MAPLE AVE.

HOBO POOL

CYPRESS AVE.

SHIVELY AIRFIELD

MOUNTAIN VIEW AVE.

WILLOW AVE.

VETERANS ST.

RIVER

CEDAR AVE.

GREENWOOD AVE.

MUSEUM

CONSTITUTION AVE.

MEDICAL CENTER

HOLLY AVE.

MOON

SARATOGA

130

MYRTLE AVE.

HACIENDA MOTEL

VALLEY FOOD

0   0.25mi

0   0.25 km

TO RIVERSIDE AND ENCAMPMENT

FOREST SERVICE OFFICE

© MOON PUBLICATIONS, INC.

Madre brought prosperity as miners came to Saratoga to relax and freighters used it as a way station and supply center. A spur route from the Union Pacific line was built south to Saratoga in 1907 to haul ore from the mines, but when they closed shortly thereafter the town was forced to turn to other pursuits—becoming a ranching and logging center.

Sights

The main attraction in Saratoga is **Hobo Pool,** on the east end of Walnut Ave., where an outdoor concrete pool is fed by the odorless 117-128° F water of Saratoga Hot Springs. It's open 24 hours a day and is fully accessible. No charge, no alcohol, and no naked bodies allowed. A heated changing room has showers. A larger swimming pool—not mineral water—is open daily 11 a.m.-4 p.m. and 6-9 p.m. summers only; $2 per swim. The mineral baths attract both old and young, with more adventurous types sprinting down to the adjacent North Platte River to cool off. Other hot springs feed directly into the river, keeping some stretches open year-round. Because of this, **Odd Fellows Park** at River St. and Main Ave. is a good place to see ducks and geese at all times of the year.

Saratoga's wonderful **Wolf Hotel,** tel. (307) 326-5525, 101 E. Bridge St., was built in 1893 by a German emigrant named Frederick Wolf. Today it's a National Historic Landmark. The old brick building with steeply gabled windows served for many years as a stage stop along the road to the mines of the Sierra Madre. Restored with antique furnishings during the 1970s and '80s, the Wolf offers an enjoyable taste of the past.

Saratoga Museum, tel. (307) 326-5511, on the south end of town across from the airport, is housed in the old railroad depot. Inside are items from the region's ranching, logging, and sheepherding past, along with a hands-on archaeology exhibit. It's open daily 1-5 p.m. Memorial Day through Labor Day, by appointment the rest of the year. Outside you'll find an old Union Pacific boxcar and caboose, along with a newly built gazebo.

The **North Platte River** is one of the only rivers in the U.S. that flows predominantly north. From the Wyoming-Colorado border to the mouth of Sage Creek, 65 miles north, it is also the only "blue ribbon" trout fishery in southern Wyoming, with outstanding fishing for rainbow and brown trout. Studies have found over 4,200 catchable wild trout averaging 13-17 inches per

---

SARATOGA ACCOMMODATIONS

Note: Accommodations are arranged from least to most expensive. Add a seven percent tax to these rates. Area code is 307.

Wolf Hotel; 101 E. Bridge St.; tel. 326-5525; $26-31 s, $30-37 d in standard rooms; $52-69 s, $58-79 d in suites; historic 1893 hotel, antique furnishings

Silver Moon Motel; 412 E. Bridge St.; tel. 326-5974; $28-30 s, $34 d; kitchenettes

Sage and Sand Motel; 311 S. First St.; tel. 326-8339; $30 s, $38 d; kitchenettes

Riviera Lodge; 303 N. First St.; tel. 326-5651; $33-75 s, $38-75 d in newly remodeled motel rooms; $135 for up to six in two-bedroom condos with kitchenettes; riverside location

Hacienda Motel; 1/2 mile south of town; tel. 326-5751; $42 s, $52 d; AAA approved

Hood House B&B; 214 N. 3rd; tel. 326-8901; $50 s, $60 d; historic home, antique furnishings, four guest rooms, private or shared baths, full breakfast

Saratoga Inn Resort; E. Pic Pike Rd.; tel. 326-5261; $99-129 s or d; newly remodeled rooms or suites, hot springs, outdoor pool

Far Out West B&B; 304 N. 2nd St.; tel. 326-5869; $80 s, $95 d; five guest rooms and a three-bedroom house, private baths, full breakfast, kids welcome

mile in the river. See "River Recreation" above for details on floating and fishing the river. You can find Indian petroglyphs along the bluff above the river just north of Saratoga. Fish are raised at the **Saratoga National Fish Hatchery,** five miles north of town, tel. (307) 326-5662; open Mon.-Sat. 8 a.m.-4 p.m. Constructed in 1915, the hatchery produces fingerling cutthroat, rainbow, and brook trout for Wyoming rivers and lakes.

Accommodations

See the "Saratoga Accommodations" chart for lodging places in town. The classic **Wolf Hotel,** described above, offers a range of upstairs rooms, from simple ones with baths down the hall to very nice suites. Any of them offer a wonderful change from standard motel rooms. Two Saratoga B&Bs offer comfortable downtown accommodations in historic homes: **Hood House B&B,** tel. (307) 326-8901, and **Far Out West B&B,** tel. (307) 326-5869.

Brush Creek Guest Ranch, tel. (307) 327-5241 or (800) 726-2499, is a 6,000-acre cattle ranch that dates back to early in this century. Guests stay in the 7,000-square-foot main lodge or comfortable modern cabins, and the emphasis is on horseback riding, guided fly-fishing—it's an Orvis-endorsed lodge—hayrides, creekside barbecues, hiking, and wintertime cross-country skiing. Guests can help move the 500 head of cattle between pastures or simply relax on the big front porch overlooking the flower-filled yard. Rates for adults are $1,025 per person a week, all inclusive; open year-round.

Campgrounds

Saratoga Lake Campground, 1.5 miles north of town, has campsites around this small lake for $5-7.50 with RV hookups. Bike campers pay just $1. No trees or showers. It's open May-October. The closest Forest Service campground is 25 miles east, with many more campgrounds ($6-8) as you continue on State 130 over Snowy Range Pass. **Saratoga Trailer Camper Park,** 116 W. Farm Ave., tel. (307) 326-8807, has tent spaces for $8, RV sites for $12. Showers cost $2 for noncampers. Although right in town, the riverside location has lots of shade. More RV parking ($10) at **Deer Haven RV and Mobile Home Park,** 701 N. 1st St., tel. (307) 326-8746. It's $5 for tents, though I don't recommend tenting

here. **Saratoga Inn,** E. Pic Pike County Rd., tel. (307) 326-5261, offers RV sites for $18, which includes access to the outdoor pool and hot springs.

Food

Get espresso coffees and ice cream at the summer-only **Lollypops** on E. Bridge St., tel. (307) 326-5020, and fresh baked goods from **Classic Knead Bakery,** 113 W. Bridge St., tel. (307) 326-8932. For pizzas and lunchtime sandwiches, you won't go wrong at **Stumpy's Eatery,** 218 N. 1st, tel. (307) 326-8132, which has excellent pizzas and burgers. The first of the national chains reached Saratoga in 1996, when **Pizza Hut** opened along N. 1st Street.

Historic **Wolf Hotel** serves up a complete range of food from grilled cheese sandwiches to king crab. The bar is the local hangout and offers live country-western music periodically. **Saratoga Inn Restaurant** also serves fine steaks and seafood. This is a popular place for Sunday brunch, and its bar has live country, blues, or rock music on most weekends. The **Rustic Bar,** 124 E. Bridge, tel. (307) 326-5965, is known for its "fighting" mountain lion mounts. **River St. Deli,** 106 N. River St., tel. (307) 326-8683, has good sandwiches for lunch. A recent transplant from Jackson Hole is **Bubba's Bar-B-Que Restaurant,** with great barbecued spare ribs and chicken at 119 N. River St., tel. (307) 326-5427. Good pies, too. **Lazy River Cantina,** 110 E. Bridge Ave., tel. (307) 326-8472, has inexpensive Mexican food and a bar with darts and TV sports.

Get groceries at **Valley Foods** on the south end of town. The deli here has baked goods, or you can hang out with the locals over coffee and donuts at **Billy's Donuts** on W. Bridge Street. Actually the best place to find locals is the 7-Eleven, where Saturday mornings find the high school's entire junior and senior classes parked out front. It's obviously the place to be seen.

Events

The **Platte Valley Festival of the Arts** is held around July 4th each year and features a juried art show, a Wild West shootout, a parade, a barbecue, a melodrama, and the obligatory fireworks show. The **Saddle-Peddle-Paddle**

Triathlon takes place at the same time, with contestants competing on bikes, horseback, and canoes. At the end of August, the **Sierra Madre Mountain Man Rendezvous** brings mountain men and women to town. The **Ice Fishing Derby** each January is considered one of the top fishing derbies in the Lower 48. The following month brings **cutter races** and **draft-horse pulls**—which offer lots of excitement as two-horse teams race down the straightaway.

Shopping

Eaton's, 117 E. Bridge, tel. (307) 326-5314, is a delightfully funky and friendly old Western clothing store. The aisles are packed with so much stuff that you have to dig through them to find anything. **Whitney's Saddle Shop**, 107 W. Bridge, tel. (307) 326-5935, also sells quality Western clothing. **Blackhawk Gallery**, 100 N. 1st., tel. (307) 326-5063, sells Western artwork, and **Medicine Bow Mt. Gallery**, 117 W. Bridge St., tel. (307) 326-5513, has jade jewelry and local gifts. Bill Naylor of **Peg Leg Mountain Furniture**, 413 E. Bridge, tel. (307) 326-5022, makes unique lodgepole items, from walking sticks to bunk beds. Get regional books from **Bookends**, 106 N. 1st St., tel. (307) 326-5269.

Information and Services

The **Saratoga Chamber of Commerce**, 114 S. 1st St., tel. (307) 326-8855, is open Mon.-Fri. 9 a.m.-5 p.m. The Forest Service's new **Saratoga Ranger Station** is on the south edge of town, tel. (307) 326-5258; open Mon.-Fri. 7:30 a.m.-5 p.m. Stop here for information on tours of historic tie-hack camps. The **library** is at 503 W. Elm St., tel. (307) 326-8209, and the **post office** is at 105 Main Ave., tel. (307) 326-5611. A real surprise in Saratoga is the airport, with an 8,400-foot runway. It provides no commercial service, but during the summer and fall (especially on Labor Day weekend), wealthy businessmen—alias "the conquistadors"—flock here for a rendezvous at local dude ranches, jamming the tarmac with corporate jets and turning Shively Field into the third-busiest jetport in Wyoming. There's no bus service to Saratoga, but you can get cash from **ATMs** at Key Bank, 302 N. 1st St., and pretentious Rawlins National Bank at 217 N. 1st Street.

ENCAMPMENT AND RIVERSIDE

The small logging and tourism town of Encampment (pop. 500) lies in the gorgeous foothills of the Sierra Madre, country once home to thousands of copper miners. Today the area abounds with ghost towns from that era. Encampment's twin settlement of Riverside (pop. 80) lies just a mile to the east. This is a very popular area with hunters, who come for deer, antelope, and elk, and with photographers, who enjoy the colorful autumn leaves, and anglers, who cast about for trout. It's the sort of place where visitors roll into town and silently say to themselves, "I'd love to live here." The community is decidedly conservative: bumper stickers proclaim, "If you're out of work and hungry eat an environmentalist" and each fall finds the back roads crowded with gun-racked pickup trucks and silent, orange-capped hunters scanning the horizon for bucks. Back in town, the smokey bars fill each night with tales of the chase and old men winking at the waitresses over their Budweisers.

History

Encampment takes its name from the Grand Encampment of French-Canadian trappers who rendezvoused along the Encampment River in 1838. Miners had long suspected that the Sierra Madre contained a wealth of minerals, but it was not until 1896 that the first significant gold strike was made. It was another mineral, however, that transformed the region. Encampment itself began in 1897, when British sheepherder Ed Haggerty discovered a rich vein of copper in the Sierra Madre to the west. The mine he developed was named Rudefeha, a word concocted from the letters of the various partners' names—J.M. *Ru*msey, Robert *De*al, George *Fe*rris, and Ed *Ha*ggerty. In the first three months of digging miners recovered $300,000 worth of copper ore. Haggerty took his 10% share and returned to England.

As the wealth of the discovery became known, Chicago promoter and newspaperman Willis George Emerson purchased the mine and built a 16-mile-long aerial tram to haul the ore up over the 10,600-foot Continental Divide and then down to the Boston-Wyoming Smelter at

ENCAMPMENT AND RIVERSIDE ACCOMMODATIONS

Accommodations are listed from least to most expensive. Add a seven percent lodging and sales tax to these rates. Area code is 307.

Lazy Acres Campground & Motel; Riverside; tel. 327-5968; $22 s, $26 d in motel; $17 s or d in very rustic cabins

Vacher's Bighorn Lodge; 508 McCaffrey; tel. 327-5110; $27 s, $33 d; simple but well-maintained

Riverside Cabins; Riverside; tel. 327-5361; $28 s or d; rustic cabins; $33 for four-person cabin; $68 for up to eight in cabins with kitchenettes

Bear Trap Cafe; Riverside; tel. 327-5277; $28 s, $33 d for rustic cabins or modular motel rooms; open May-Nov.

Grand & Sierra B&B; 1016 Lomax; tel. 327-5200; $38-48 s, $48-58 d; newer home with trophy heads, hot tub, five guest rooms, shared or private baths, big game trophies, pool table, fireplace

Platts Rustic Mountain Lodge B&B; 12 miles south of Encampment; tel. 327-5539; $45 s, $65 d; cabin or lodge accommodations, full breakfast; weekly rates and guided trips available

Boondocks Bunkhouse; 211 W. 7th St.; tel. 327-5944; $50 s or d; bring your own bedding; weekly rates available

The Old Depot Inn B&B; Riverside; tel. 327-5277; $120 s or d; new house with antique furnishings, jacuzzi tub, porch, continental breakfast

Encampment (elevation 7,200 feet). The tram consisted of 304 wooden towers with buckets supported on thick steel cables. Each bucket held 700 pounds of ore and moved at four miles an hour. The tram could carry almost 1,000 tons of ore a day and was powered by water flowing through a four-foot wooden pipeline. Thousands of men flocked to the mines, creating almost overnight the settlements of Elwood, Battle, Copperton, Dillon, Halfway House, and Rambler. A railroad was completed from the smelter to the main Union Pacific line at Walcott in 1905, and by 1908 more than 23 million pounds of copper had been produced.

The main regional settlement was Encampment, located at the foot of the mountains and numbering 1,500 rough and hardened souls at its peak. By 1900, the town featured three general stores, two lodging houses, two hotels, two restaurants, and three lumber yards, along with nine saloons and two houses of prostitution. Nearby Riverside served as a shipping center for the mines. (Originally known as Dogget, the name was changed to Riverside after folks began calling it "Dog Town.") Another 1,500 people lived in the other mining towns. The mining boom came to an abrupt halt after two dis-astrous fires destroyed the concentrating mill, the smelter, the boiler room, and the powerhouse. Combined with falling copper prices, it forced the company into bankruptcy. Soon, all sorts of illegal actions surfaced, including overcapitalization and fraudulent stock sales.

All but a few diehards left the area, and what had once been the town of Grand Encampment was eventually reduced to simply Encampment. Logging, first for ties and mine supports and later for lumber, became an important part of the economy; today the R.L. Hammer Sawmill is the largest local employer. Tourism is becoming increasingly important in the area, and retirees are attracted to the slow pace, moderate prices, and beautiful setting.

Sights

Located on the south side of Encampment at 6th and Barnett Streets, the excellent **Grand Encampment Museum** includes items from the turn-of-the-century mining camps that filled the Sierra Madre. Displays include historic photographs, 19th-century clothing, Indian artifacts, Forest Service memorabilia, and even a folding bathtub from the 1890s. Teddy the (stuffed) dog greets visitors. Most interesting of all are

the 14 authentic historic buildings set up as a frontier town with wooden boardwalks. These include a tie-hack cabin, a bakery, a lookout tower, and a stage station. The transportation barn even houses Noah's Ark—though, alas, it's probably not the original one. Oddest of all is a two-story outhouse modeled after one used in the mining ghost town of Dillon. The lower level was used in summer, with the upper floor reserved for wintertime when the snows drifted many feet deep. The Australian term for privies—"long drop"—is especially fitting here! Also at the museum are parts of the 16-mile-long aerial tramway that brought ore from the Rudefeha mine.

This free museum is open daily 1-5 p.m. Memorial Day through Labor Day and Sat.-Sun. 1-5 p.m. Sept.-October. After that, you can see the museum by special appointment only—still for no charge; tel. (307) 327-5205. Retired locals provide informative tours throughout the day, and you can even buy bars of homemade soap inside the main building. On Memorial Day weekend the museum has turn-of-the-century living history demonstrations.

At the museum, pick up a copy of the local **walking tour** brochure, which describes some of the most interesting buildings in town. Be sure to also see the pretty white **Presbyterian Church** at 9th and Rankin. A three-quarter-mile trail leads to the **Indian Bathtubs,** natural geologic formations that collect rainwater. Indian hunters used them for bathing. Get to the start of the trail by heading one mile south of Riverside on State 230 and turning up Blackhall Road.

Lodging

Although popular with visitors all year, this area is doubly so during the fall hunting season; book ahead if you're coming through then. See the "Encampment and Riverside Accommodations" chart for local cabins, motels, and B&Bs. Twelve miles south of Encampment is **Platts Rustic Mountain Lodge B&B,** tel. (307) 327-5539, with a big log lodge offering dramatic vistas and a rustic cabin for more seclusion. Both are available on a nightly or weekly basis. They also offer horseback trail rides, fishing, pack trips, tours of the Red Desert, and that old favorite, "varmint" hunting.

Grand & Sierra B&B, tel. (307) 327-5200, also has distinctive features, including animal mounts lining the walls, a pool table, and a shag carpet on the floor. This is a hunter's paradise; when I last dropped by, someone was skinning beavers in the garage.

Camping

Pitch your tent for free—no RVs—on the south side of **Grand View Park** next to the museum. The nearest Forest Service campsite ($6; open June-Oct.) is **Bottle Creek Campground,** seven miles southwest of town on State 70. Five more campgrounds (free to $7) lie west of here in the Sierra Madre. Ask locally for directions to three BLM campgrounds: Bennett Peak, Corral Creek, and Encampment River, the latter being the closest. Bennett Peak costs $3, the others are free. **Lazy Acres Campground & Motel** in Riverside, tel. (307) 327-5968, has shady RV and tent sites for $10 and RV sites for $15. Showers for noncampers are $3. Open May-October.

Food

Eat at **Betty's Encampment Cafe,** 623 Freeman in Encampment, tel. (307) 327-5207. An interesting old two-story brick building at 706 Freeman houses both **Kuntzman's Cash Store** and the **Sugar Bowl,** tel. (307) 327-5271, which has an old-fashioned soda fountain with malts, subs, soups, and banana splits. **Bear Trap Cafe** in Riverside, tel. (307) 327-5277, serves standard American food. Riverside's **town park** is a great place for picnic lunches amid tall cottonwoods, but there's no camping.

Events

In early February, the **Sierra Madre Winter Carnival** includes dogsled and snowmobile races, snow sculptures, broom ball, a casino night, a melodrama, dances, and other activities. One of the most popular events in Wyoming is the **Woodchoppers Jamboree and Rodeo** at Encampment the third weekend of June. Begun in 1961, this is the state's largest loggers' show, with all sorts of events, including tree-felling, chainsaw log-bucking, hand-sawing, pole-throwing, and axe-throwing contests. Other activities include a fun amateur rodeo, a parade, a barbecue, and a melodrama featuring "dance hall

girls." The town erupts with lots of drunken and rowdy behavior at night, befitting such a festival. Both **Pine Lodge Saloon,** 518 McCaffrey, tel. (307) 327-5203, and the **Mangy Moose** in Riverside, tel. (307) 327-5117, have live music during the jamboree.

Information and Services

A small summer-only **information cabin** in Riverside is open Mon.-Fri. 9 a.m.-4:30 p.m., or get local info at the Grand Encampment Museum. Encampment's **city hall** is in the historic Opera House, a wooden building with a bell tower that looks like a lighthouse. The **Encampment Library** is on the east end of town at 202 Rankin Ave., tel. (307) 327-5775. The local place for clothing and other supplies is **Big R,** 614 McCaffrey, tel. (307) 327-5444. **Boondocks Giftshop,** tel. (307) 327-5944, has locally made items, pottery, crafts, and used books. The Encampment **post office,** tel. (307) 327-5747, sits on the corner of 6th and McCaffrey Streets.

SIERRA MADRE

The historic Sierra Madre cover a small section of Wyoming—a finger from the Medicine Bow Range that stretches south into Colorado. This is one of the lesser-known parts of the state. Worth a visit are the many mining ghost towns and historic mine sites, and quite a few miles of wilderness trails. The highest mountain in the range is 11,004-foot Bridger Peak, named for mountain man Jim Bridger. Before heading out, get maps ($3) and camping and hiking information from the Forest Service's **Hayden Ranger Station** at 204 W. 9th, tel. (307) 327-5481, in Encampment. Open Mon.-Fri. 7:30 a.m.-4:30 p.m. all year. Ask for the self-guided auto tour brochure available here.

Sights

Now entirely paved, Battle Highway (State 70) crosses the Sierra Madre from Encampment on the east to Baggs on the west, a distance of 57 miles. The smooth, wide-shouldered road is extraordinarily scenic, especially in the fall when the aspens turn golden. Lodgepole pines are the dominant trees at higher elevations. During the winter—generally November to mid-

June—State 70 is closed at the forest boundary, though snowmobilers and skiers may continue up the road. Approximately 10 miles west of Encampment the road reaches the Continental Divide at 9,916-foot Battle Pass. This is the location of **Battle,** one of many ghost towns capping the Sierra Madre. Battle is named for an 1841 fight between Indians and whites that took place near here.

A 4WD road good for mountain bikes heads north from the east side of the pass to the Bridger Peak summit and then down the western side to the Ferris-Haggerty mine site at the ghost town of **Rudefeha,** where remains of the tramway towers are still visible. A mile to the west you'll find the remains of **Dillon,** established after the company town of Rudefeha banned saloons; the saloon owners simply moved a short distance away and started anew and in no time at all Dillon was the largest town in the Sierra Madre. Many buildings remain here, hidden in the trees.

Two miles west of the Continental Divide on State 70 is a pullout overlooking pretty Battle Lake and a monument to **Thomas A. Edison.** While vacationing here in 1878, Edison was pondering over what substance to use as a filament for incandescent lights. One night he threw a broken bamboo fishing pole in the fire and was intrigued by the way the frayed pieces glowed. Carbonized bamboo would make a fine non-conducting filament for his bulbs. This tale has been passed down as fact through the years, but in reality Edison didn't come up with the idea until a year later. Maybe he remembered the old fly rod at that time.

The town of **Rambler** once stood along the lake shore, with the Doane-Rambler copper mine nearby. The mine operated from 1879 to 1902, producing a half million tons of copper. Another six miles west are a few remains from the settlement of **Copperton.**

Aspen Alley

The western slopes of the Sierra Madre are carpeted with extensive stands of quaking aspen trees that came up after fires swept this region during the mining era. These reach for many miles along State 70. A favorite of photographers is Aspen Alley, a half-mile stretch of fabulously flamboyant fall foliage. Get here by turn-

ing north onto Deep Creek Road (Forest Road 801). The colors generally peak in late September but this varies, so you may want to call ahead (try the Encampment Forest Service office, tel. 307-327-5481) to get there at the best time. Sandstone Campground (no charge; open June-Oct.) is just up the road; adventurous souls will enjoy the 50-mile drive north to Rawlins.

Once the gravel road emerges from the national forest, the land broadens into sage and grass before once again climbing over the Continental Divide. Stop here on a fall night and listen to the quiet. A few clouds hang on the western horizon. A few pickups churn clouds of dust up the road—en route to either hunting grounds or a bar. The night lies over the land like a blackened canvas splattered with stars. There aren't many places like this anymore.

Campgrounds

The Forest Service maintains five campgrounds (free to $7; open June-Oct.) in the Sierra Madre, all of which are located along the main road across the mountains, State 70. These campgrounds are not nearly as crowded as those in the Snowy Range to the east.

Huston Park Wilderness

The 31,300-acre Huston Park Wilderness straddles the Continental Divide just south of Battle Pass. It contains spruce, fir, aspen, and lodgepole forests, and open alpine country reaching to 10,500 feet. **Huston Park Trail** provides an enjoyable high-elevation trek along the Continental Divide. Not a developed trail, this 16-mile-long route is marked with rock cairns and blazed trees. Trailheads are located one mile south of the Battle townsite and 2.5 miles west of Hog Park Reservoir.

The nine-mile-long **Baby Lake Trail** is an enjoyable overnight trip through high meadows and along a mountain creek. Take in excellent vistas of the Snake River Valley from the Continental Divide. The trail is accessible from State 70 on both ends, but for the easiest hiking start from a trailhead at the end of a two-mile gravel road just south of Battle Pass. From here, the trail drops 2,600 feet in elevation to a second trailhead located off Forest Road 811 (near Lost Creek Campground).

North Fork Encampment Trail takes you

two miles up North Fork Creek to Green Mountain Falls. Get to the trailhead by driving west from Encampment to Bottle Creek Campground and then south on Forest Road 550 for 1.5 miles. This is one of the few waterfalls in the area.

Encampment River Wilderness

At just 10,400 acres, Encampment River Wilderness is one of the smallest and least-visited wilderness areas in Wyoming. The centerpiece is the Encampment River, with its narrow canyon, rushing rapids, quiet pools, and fine fishing. Despite the Encampment's current wilderness status, much of this land was logged over at the turn of the century to supply railroad ties and mine timbers for the Union Pacific Railroad. Old cabins and mines offer endless opportunities to explore. The well-maintained **Encampment River Trail** is a 15-mile-long path that follows this wild and scenic river through the heart of the wilderness. Roads provide access from either end, so the trail is easier to hike if you can shuttle a second vehicle to the other end. Start from a trailhead near the BLM's Encampment River Campground, located two miles south of Encampment. The trail follows the river, beginning in low-elevation sage-and-grass country and gradually climbing into dense lodgepole and spruce forests. The first five miles are considerably easier hiking than higher up, where the canyon narrows and becomes more rugged. The trail ends at Hog Park, near the Colorado state line.

Another off-the-beaten-path sight near the Encampment River Wilderness is an old abandoned fire tower at **Blackhall Mountain,** approximately 15 miles south of Riverside on Forest Road 409. The last several miles are narrow but passable. From the top are long vistas into the mountains of Wyoming and Colorado.

Winter Recreation

During the winter months the Forest Service maintains many miles of **cross-country ski trails** around the Bottle Creek Campground 5.5 miles west of Encampment and along the South Brush Creek 20 miles east of Saratoga. Call (307) 326-5258 for access details. The rustic **Green Mountain Cabin,** a popular spot for cross-country skiers, stands near the South

Brush Creek and Bottle Creek Trails. Rates are $20 for up to four people. The cabin has a woodstove, firewood, and basic supplies. Call the Trading Post in Riverside at (307) 327-5720 for details. Many forest roads in the Sierra Madre are used extensively by snowmobilers, with 26 miles of groomed trails and an equal amount of ungroomed trails. Contact Forest Service offices in Encampment and Saratoga for details.

LITTLE SNAKE RIVER VALLEY

The Little Snake River Valley is one of the most isolated parts of Wyoming; it lies right along the Colorado border, with the desolate Red Desert to the west and the Sierra Madre to the east. Three tiny towns spread out along the irrigated farmland that follows Savery Creek: Savery, Dixon (pop. 60), and Baggs (pop. 260). See Stephen Metzger's *Colorado Handbook* (Moon Publications) for details on sights south of the Wyoming line.

Savery
An unusual two-story log blockhouse built by mountain man Jim Baker is in Savery next to the **Little Snake River Museum.** The museum is open Wed.-Sun. 2-5 p.m. Memorial Day to Labor Day. Jim Baker and his wife lie buried a mile west of town. The museum houses Jim Baker's canoe and other historical items. Also on the museum grounds are a one-room schoolhouse from the Brown's Hill area and a cabin built in 1882 and moved here in 1987. The **Savery Store,** tel. (307) 383-2711, has groceries, supplies, and a campground.

Savery Creek Thoroughbred Ranch, near Savery, tel. (307) 383-7840, is a special riding ranch for those serious about horses. The owner spent extensive time in Europe, so the emphasis is upon both Western and English riding. Beautiful country surrounds the ranch, which offers gracious lodging in an antique-furnished home. The ranch only hosts six people at a time, allowing for personalized attention. Open May-September.

Dixon
Four miles west of Savery and seven miles east of Baggs, the small agricultural settlement of Dixon holds the **Little Snake River Valley Rodeo** each July. It also holds the **Cutting Horse Contest,** where cowboys work specially trained horses to move cattle.

Baggs
Named for rancher George Baggs and his wife Maggie, Baggs' isolated location and proximity to the state line made it a gathering place for outlaws. In 1900, following a $32,000 bank robbery in Winnemucca, Nevada, Butch Cassidy helped build a cabin here to serve as a refuge for his gang. The cabin, now called the **Gaddis-Matthews House,** still stands. Another noteworthy building is the **Bank Bar Club,** listed on the National Historic Register. Built as a bank, it later became a bar. Stay at **Drifters Inn,** tel. (307) 383-2015, for $31-35 s or $36-40 d.

FORT FRED STEELE

History
Fort Fred Steele—named for Civil War hero Maj. Gen. Frederick Steele—was built in 1868 as one of three Wyoming posts established to protect the transcontinental railroad from Indian attacks. Soldiers from the fort fought against the Utes in northern Colorado during their 1879 uprising against tyrannical Indian agent Nathan C. Meeker. The troops also helped reestablish peace after the 1885 anti-Chinese riots in Rock Springs.

After the fort was abandoned by the Army in 1886, civilians took over the buildings and turned this into a supply base for ranchers and sheepherders. It was headquarters for the Carbon Timber Company, which controlled the enormous tie market for the Union Pacific Railroad in the Rockies and owned nearly 25,000 acres of timberland. Lodgepole pine were felled in the Medicine Bow Mountains and floated down the North Platte River during high flows each spring. At Fort Steele, they were caught by a log boom and loaded onto railway cars or used in the sawmill or box factory. The tie industry remained important well into this century—300,000 ties were sent down the North Platte River in 1938 alone—but when the Union Pacific stopped using hand-hewn ties in 1940 the town of Fort Steele suffered. With the loss of its main indus-

try and the 1939 rerouting of the Lincoln Highway, all but a few people moved away.

Fort Steele Today

Fort Steele is now a 137-acre state park located nine miles east of Sinclair on I-80. A small visitor center in the old bridge tender's house contains many historical photos of the fort and the Carbon Timber Company. The park is open daily 9 a.m.-7 p.m. from late May to mid-September. Historical plaques are scattered over the grounds, but not much remains of what had been a substantial settlement: just a couple of clapboard buildings, some sandstone foundations and chimneys, and the walls of a house once owned by Fenimore Chatterton—Wyoming's governor from 1903 to 1905. Stone walls from the military quartermaster's corral remain just west of the parade grounds, but a disastrous arson fire on New Year's Eve 1976 destroyed two enlisted men's barracks that had stood here for more than a century. Just up the hill from the fort site is a square stone ordinance magazine (1881) with an adjacent cemetery containing the graves of civilians who died in the area. Only a few headstones remain. The slow-moving North Platte River right next to the fort is a great place for picnics—but there's no camping. Despite the paucity of historical buildings, there's something rather nice about the authenticity of the site. Stop in at dusk on a summer evening and you'll hear the distant rumble of freight trains while coyotes howl from nearby hills and the North Platte River rolls quietly away from this lonely place.

SINCLAIR

Sinclair (pop. 500) is one of the more distinctive small settlements in Wyoming. In 1923, the Producers Oil and Refining Company (Parco) established a 50,000-barrel-a-day oil refinery here, built a town to house its employees, and named the town Parco. When the Sinclair Oil Company bought the refinery in 1934, the town's name changed. Today, the refinery still lights up the night sky for miles around, and hundreds of giant oil tanks stand behind the facility. Interstate 80 passes right by Sinclair and most folks don't bother to stop except to fill up at the Burns Brothers Truckstop a mile east of town or at the Sinclair station in town. Actually, Sinclair is a pleasant little resting place and a nice spot for a shady picnic lunch.

Parco built the company town, including the large Parco Inn at the center, in Spanish-mission style with red-tile roofs and stucco walls. You'd think you were in southern California. An elaborate fountain and a nice small park stand across from the inn, now abandoned but listed on the National Register of Historic Places. A pair of Civil War-vintage cannons guard the water fountain from attack by marauding oil executives. They were brought here originally to blow holes in burning oil tanks, allowing the oil to drain into the surrounding dikes before the tanks could explode from the heat.

The **Sinclair/Parco Museum** is located in the old bank building and contains a number of local items, including the high point, a newspaper headlined "Nixon Resigns." Open summer weekdays; if it's closed stop at the town hall next door for access. The town also has a branch library and recreation center. Of note in Sinclair is **Su Casa Cafe,** tel. (307) 328-1745, which makes genuine Mexican food. There are no motels in town, but the road north of Sinclair leads to popular Seminoe and Pathfinder Reservoirs, where camping is available. (See the chapter on Central Wyoming for more information on these recreation areas.) Sinclair also has the nine-hole **Sinclair Golf Course,** tel. (307) 324-3918, site of the biggest 4th of July fireworks display in the area. The Burns Brothers Truck Stop has an **ATM** and a restaurant with trucker meals.

RAWLINS

The small city of Rawlins (pop. 9,300) sits right in the middle of southern Wyoming. To the east and south lie mountain ranges and rich grazing land; to the west is the Great Divide Basin and a vast expanse of desert country. During the late 1970s and early '80s, Rawlins was a hub of development as the "Oil Patch" blossomed and energy companies pumped petrodollars into the economy. But as in so many other Wyoming towns, the inevitable bust that followed was traumatic. Layoffs affected everyone in town in one way or another, and downtown Rawlins still shows signs of being down in the dumps with quite a few empty and boarded-up storefronts. Not everyone packed up and left, however. Most of the people who lived here before the oil boom stayed around when the bust hit, scraping by

on business brought in by freeway travelers, local ranchers, and the energy companies. Many Rawlins workers now commute 40 miles to work in the Hanna coal mines. With restoration of the old state prison, Rawlins is trying to broaden its limited tourism base. New businesses have started to spread over the east end of town, creating the now-standard mix of fast food, discount megamarts, gas stations, and chain motels.

HISTORY

Rawlins is named for Gen. John A. Rawlins, secretary of war under President Grant. In 1867, as the railroad route was being surveyed west-

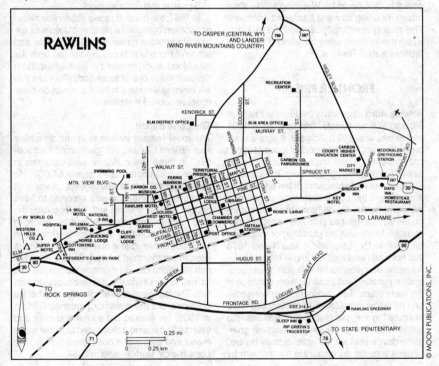

ward, the crew of Gen. Grenville Dodge met up with soldiers under Rawlins' command. When they discovered a clear, alkali-free spring at the base of a hill, Rawlins remarked, "If anything is ever named after me, I hope it will be a spring of water." Dodge immediately decided to name this Rawlins Spring. When a division point on the Union Pacific was established here in 1868, the town was also named Rawlins Spring. Its name was later shortened to Rawlins.

In 1886, the Wyoming Legislature appropriated $100,000 for a state penitentiary in Rawlins. Two years later, construction began with enormous slabs of sandstone cut and hauled by wagon from a quarry south of town. Because of inadequate funding the new prison was not completed and occupied until December 1901, some 13 years after it was begun. By that time the town had grown, and what had been a relatively remote location was now in central Rawlins. For the next eight decades this would be Wyoming's only state prison, housing its most hardened criminals. The prison was finally abandoned in 1981, when the inmates were transferred to a new facility south of Rawlins.

FRONTIER PRISON

Rawlins' main attraction is the Frontier Prison at 5th and Walnut streets, first opened in 1901 and in use until 1981. Actually, it was a state prison for all of its existence, but locals prefer to call it a frontier prison since construction began while Wyoming was still a territory. The imposing turret towers and stonework of the prison's exterior give it the oppressive appearance of a medieval castle. Inside, conditions for the inmates were almost as primitive—bordering on ghastly. There was no plumbing or electricity for the first 15 years, and it wasn't until 1978 that hot water was installed in one block of cells. A special dungeon house was built for uncooperative inmates, and beatings were common in the early years. Ten prisoners were hanged—one by fellow inmates—and another five were executed in the gas chamber in Rawlins, the last in 1965. The gallows were a uniquely gruesome device in which the victim actually hanged himself through an elaborate mechanism by

which his weight displaced a water counterbalance, thus releasing a trapdoor and leaving him hanging by a noose. It was built to hang notorious cattle detective and murderer Tom Horn in 1903 and moved into the prison later (Horn was never in this prison). The instrument did not always work; one man had to be strangled by the "humane" guards when he didn't die fast enough. Science marches onward: Wyoming's death-row inmates now face lethal injection instead.

The old prison was the scene of several escape attempts, including one in which four death-row inmates tunneled out as far as the west wall before being caught. The dirt was secreted away in the ceiling panels where it's still visible. Two other breakouts were successful—one involved 28 men—although nearly all the escapees were later caught or killed in the surrounding community. In later years the penitentiary housed 500 prisoners and employed 100 guards and other workers.

In 1987, the grade-B movie *Prison* was filmed on location here with a number of locals as extras. Parts of the movie set are still visible, and some of the prison floors are still red from the fake blood. If you missed it in the theaters, don't despair; this is one of those godawful flicks that will eventually make it to the 4 a.m. slot on some obscure cable-TV station.

The Lone Bandit

The most famous inmate to spend time here was William Carlisle, the "gentleman train robber." In three Union Pacific train robberies in Wyoming, Carlisle netted barely $1,000. He never robbed female passengers, never shot or injured anyone, and was reported to have bought gifts for children with the loot. After the third robbery, he was caught and sentenced to life in prison. Carlisle was sent to Rawlins in 1916 but escaped in a shirt crate three years later. In another train robbery Carlisle was shot and wounded but still managed to remain free for two weeks before a posse caught up with him. The last conviction landed him another life sentence, but the governor pardoned Carlisle in 1936. He walked out a changed man and eventually became a respected Laramie motel owner and author of a book about his life, *The Lone Bandit.* Carlisle died in 1964.

Practicalities

During the summer months, the prison is open daily 8:30 a.m.-5:30 p.m. with guided tours every hour. The motto: "No visitors locked inside since 1981." These excellent, hour-long tours cost $3.50 for adults, $3 for seniors or kids (children under six are free), $15 for families. During the rest of the year, tours are generally offered 8:30 a.m.-5:30 p.m. daily in the summer. Winter tours are by appointment but someone is generally here weekdays; call (307) 324-4422 for details. Ask for Mark Setright to get the most entertaining and educational tours. Be sure to bring a sweater or coat with you since the stone prison is a chilly place even in midsummer. For a scarier visit, ask about the nighttime flashlight tours offered most Friday and Saturday nights in summer ($5 per person) and on Halloween by reservation only. Not recommended for young children.

The Smell of Sage

Outlaw Mercantile in front of the old prison sells T-shirts, dream catchers, wallets, hatbands, paintings, and other items made by inmates at the new state penitentiary just south of Rawlins. A portion of the old prison now serves double-duty as a small museum housing photos and descriptions of various inmates and a souvenir shop selling postcards, books, and other items. One book well worth a look is *The Sweet Smell of Sagebrush.* This is a collection of stories by William Stanley Hudson, a man who served four separate sentences here for such crimes as horse stealing and passing stolen checks. It offers not only a glimpse of turn-of-the-century prison life but also a fascinating account of criminal logic. The title comes from his release from prison after serving his first sentence:

i thought little of those things that august day as i walked out from the damp prison air into the glorious sunshine of this enchanted land. i felt only a desire to get away somewhere out of sight. after walking towards the buisness part of town a short way, i turned and went straight out of town untill i reached the high sagebrush. the smell of the sage was that day sweeter to

me than a breath from a bed of rarest flowers. for an hour i was content to sit and breathe the pure mountain air and enjoy the warm sunshine.

Hudson's fate is unknown. After release from his fourth incarceration in 1921, he disappeared. Perhaps he was a reformed man. Or perhaps he learned enough to avoid getting caught again.

OTHER SIGHTS

Carbon County Museum

Housed in an old Mormon church at 9th and Walnut Streets, tel. (307) 324-9611, the Carbon County Museum is open Mon.-Fri. 10 a.m.-5 p.m. and 7-9 p.m., Sat.-Sun. 10 a.m.-5 p.m. June-Aug.; Mon.-Fri. 10 a.m.-5 p.m. in Sept.; and Mon.-Fri. 1-4 p.m. in May. Closed Oct.-April. No charge. The museum is a mixed bag, containing a few Indian relics, a 1920 hook-and-ladder truck, and various stage-station and Civil War artifacts. Easily the strangest object in the museum is a pair of two-tone shoes made from the skin of Big Nose George Parrot, a train robber and murderer. These were crafted by Dr. John E. Osborne, who also decided to saw open George's skull to see if the brains of desperadoes differed from those of common men. The skullcap became an ashtray now on exhibit at the Union Pacific Railroad Museum in Omaha. The bottom of the skull is also on display here, along with Big Nose George's death mask and a photo of the old whiskey barrel in which Osborne decided to store the body. The barrel wasn't discovered until 1950 when a construction crew found it while digging at an old Rawlins drugstore. Incidentally, this same Dr. Osborne went on to serve as Wyoming's governor from 1893 to 1895!

Looking for more criminals? Try **St. Joseph's Cemetery,** where two early train robbers are buried. Ask at the museum for the exact grave locations. Still more crooks? Try the state penitentiary, south of town; you'll meet real live ones there.

Buildings

Quite a number of interesting old sandstone buildings are scattered throughout downtown, built from stone quarried around Rawlins. Pick

BIG NOSE GEORGE PARROT

George Manuse, better known as Big Nose George Parrot, was a rustler from the Powder River country who joined up with Dutch Charley Burris and Frank James (of the James Gang) on an 1878 robbery attempt. The trio tried to derail a Union Pacific train by prying up a piece of track and waiting in ambush. Unfortunately for the outlaws, an alert UP employee discovered the missing rail before the train arrived, and a manhunt ensued. A posse tracked the gang into Rattlesnake Canyon and then stopped in a freshly deserted camp. As a deputy sheriff bent over to check the coals, he commented, "They're hot as hell." Immediately, a voice shouted from behind the bushes, "We'll show you how hot hell is." Two deputies were shot dead, and the three robbers escaped.

After the murders, the trio split up. Dutch Charlie was caught the following year and sent back via train to Carbon, Wyoming, for trial. But the trial never came; a group of masked men pulled him from the train and threw a noose around his neck. When Dutch Charlie was asked if he had any last words, one of the deputy's widows yelled out, "No, the son-

of-a-bitch has nothing to say!" and booted the barrel from under his feet. The newspaper noted, "the train was delayed only thirteen minutes by the operation."

In 1880, the law finally caught up with Big Nose George in Montana, and he too was hauled back to Rawlins in shackles. When the train pulled into town, 15 armed men forced the sheriff to release the prisoner to them and hauled him off to be hanged. Big Nose George managed to avoid his fate this time by reminding his would-be lynchers that "dead men tell no tales," but he confessed to and was convicted of the murders the following spring and was sentenced to hang. In an escape attempt shortly after the trial, George cracked the skull of a guard with his shackles before finally being subdued. When word of the escape attempt spread through Rawlins, a mob of masked men broke into the jail. Big Nose George was hauled out and lynched in the street, though it took two tries—the rope was too long the first time. The Rawlins jail register notes that Big Nose George Parrot "Went to join the angels via hempen cord on telegraph pole front of Fred Wolf's saloon."

up an informative walking-tour brochure of historic buildings from the chamber of commerce at 517 Cedar Street. Notable ones include the Shrine Temple at 5th and Pine (completed in 1909), the Elks Club at 4th and Buffalo (completed in 1909), and the Presbyterian church at 3rd and Cedar (built in 1882). The Union Pacific Railroad depot at 400 W. Front was built in 1901 of granite and brick and was in use until 1983. It's still in good condition, but for some reason Amtrak stops at the small shed next door! One of the most attractive buildings in Rawlins is the **Ferris Mansion** at 607 W. Maple, built for the widow of an early mining pioneer, George Ferris, and now open as a bed and breakfast. An old **steam locomotive** rests in Tully Park on Elm Street next to the hospital.

"Rockology"
The country around Rawlins is a geologist's and rock hound's paradise; jade; petrified wood, agate, and other minerals are here to be discovered. Of course, oil, gas, and coal are what geologists are most interested in around here.

The **Rawlins Uplift** (a thrust-faulted anticline) rises immediately north of town, providing a textbook example of stratigraphy. Plenty of fish and invertebrate fossils are here, too. As a side note, the paint known as "Rawlins Red" originated from iron oxide mined just north of town. The color is still used for barns and buildings in the eastern U.S., and this was the color originally chosen by General Rawlins to paint the Brooklyn Bridge (as Secretary of War, he approved the bridge plans).

PRACTICALITIES

Accommodations
Given its relatively small size, Rawlins has a surprising number of places to stay. Partly this is a legacy of the boom era, when tight housing conditions forced many workers into motels and mobile homes; partly it's attributable to the nightly influx of tired I-80 travelers. See the "Rawlins Accommodations" chart for a complete listing. If you plan to stay at one of the cheap motels,

take a look at the rooms first—some may not be up to your standards. One place that *exceeds* most people's standards is the **Ferris Mansion Bed and Breakfast,** tel. (307) 324-3961, a classic Victorian home built in 1903 and on the National Register of Historic Places. A grand oak stairway leads to the four upstairs guest rooms furnished with antiques, and the big front porch has an old-fashioned swing for slowing down. Owners are friendly, too. Be sure to ask about the ghost that periodically waters the mansion's houseplants.

Campgrounds
The nearest public campground (free; open June-Oct.) is at **Teton Reservoir,** 17 miles south of Rawlins. More public facilities ($4; open year-round) are in Seminoe State Park, 28 miles north of Sinclair. You'll find a trio of parking lot campgrounds in Rawlins. Expect to pay $10 for tents, $16 for RVs at **Western Hills Campground,** 2500 Wagon Circle Rd., tel. (307) 324-2592; **American President's Camp RV Park,** 2346 W. Spruce St., tel. (307) 324-3218; or **RV World Campground,** 2401 Wagon Circle Rd.,

---

RAWLINS ACCOMMODATIONS

Note: Accommodations are arranged from least to most expensive. Add a seven percent tax to these rates.

Golden West Motel; 822 W. Pine; tel. 324-4452; $19 s, $24 d; very plain, fridges and microwaves in rooms, weekly rates available

Ideal Motel; 1507 W. Spruce; tel. 324-3451; $20 s, $22 d; kitchenettes

Prairie Winds Motel; 713 W. Spruce; tel. 324-4561; $22 s, $28 d

Bucking Horse Lodge; 1720 W. Spruce; tel. 324-3471; $25 s, $30 d; kitchenettes

La Bella Motel; 1819 W. Spruce; tel. 324-2583; $25 s, $30 d

Cliff Motor Lodge; 1500 W. Spruce; tel. 324-3493; $26 s, $34 d; microwaves and fridges

Rifleman Motel; 1915 W. Spruce; tel. 324-2263; $27 s, $30 d; weekly rates available

Jade Lodge; 405 W. Spruce; tel. 324-2791; $27 s, $30 d; weekly rates available

Sunset Motel; 1302 W. Spruce; tel. 324-3448 or (800) 336-6752; $28 s, $32 d; kitchenettes $5 extra, AAA approved

Weston Inn; 1801 E. Cedar; tel. 324-2783; $29 s or d; outdoor pool

Bridger Inn; 1902 E. Cedar; tel. 328-1401; $30 s, $34 d

Rawlins Motel; 905 W. Spruce; tel. 324-3456; $30 s, $34 d; AAA approved

Key Motel; 1806 E. Cedar; tel. 324-2728; $32 s, $35 d

National 9 Inn; 1617 W. Spruce; tel. 328-1600 or (800) 457-7820; $35 s, $40 d

Sleep Inn; 1400 Higley Blvd.; tel. 328-1732 or (800) 753-3746; $46-51 s, $51-56 d; new motel, continental breakfast, AAA approved

Super 8 Motel; 2338 Wagon Cir.; tel. 328-0630 or (800) 800-8000; $49 s or d; exercise facility

Days Inn; 2222 E. Cedar; tel. 324-6615 or (800) 325-2525; $50-55 s, $55-60 d; indoor pool, continental breakfast, AAA approved

Ferris Mansion Bed and Breakfast; 607 W. Maple; tel. 324-3961; $58-65 s or d; restored Victorian mansion, antique furnishings, four guest rooms, private baths, full breakfast, no young children, open mid-March to mid-Nov., AAA approved

Best Western Cottontree Inn; 23rd & Spruce; tel. 324-2737 or (800) 662-6886; $63-71 s, $68-85 d; indoor pool, sauna, AAA approved

tel. (307) 328-1091 or (800) 478-9753—great places to swelter in the simmering heat of summer as you listen to the freeway traffic. Western Hills is open all year.

Food

Rawlins has a surprising number of good eateries. Start the day at **Square Shooter's Eating House,** 311 W. Cedar, tel. (307) 324-4380, serving standard American fare amidst the ambience of mounted animal heads (it's good for lunches and dinners, too). **5th St. Bistro,** 112 5th St., tel. (307) 324-7246, is a classy little eatery with daily lunch specials and fresh-baked breads. Very good sandwiches, soups, salads, and espresso. Closed Sunday and Monday.

One of Wyoming's dining-out gems is **Rose's Lariat** at 410 E. Cedar, tel. (307) 324-5261. The ads claim, "Best Mexican food in town. Ask anyone!" Some folks claim that this is one of the best and most authentic Mexican restaurants in Wyoming. Not to be missed, but be ready to wait in line at dinnertime. Another good dinner choice is **The Pantry,** 221 W. Cedar St., tel. (307) 324-7860, located in a building built in 1881. This is a fine, family-run place with reasonable prices and all-American food. Lots of grub for the buck. Housed in a historic home at 318 5th St., **Aspen House Restaurant,** tel. (307) 324-4787, serves steaks, seafood, chicken, pasta, and Asian specialties. The owner is Singaporean and brings an Eastern touch to the cookery. Open for lunch and dinner only. **Jo Mama's,** 1307 W. Spruce St., tel. (307) 324-6864, has Italian food including pasta, calzone, and pizza. For Chinese meals, head to **China Panda** 1810 E. Cedar, tel. (307) 324-2198.

For pizza, try **Cappy's,** 18th and W. Spruce, tel. (307) 324-4847, or **Pizza Hut,** 506 Higley Blvd., tel. (307) 324-7706. The latter usually has lunchtime specials. Get fast service and decent truckstop grub at **Gay Johnson's Restaurant,** two miles west of Rawlins, tel. (307) 324-3463, and **Rip Griffin's Truckstop,** I-80 at Higley Blvd., tel. (307) 328-2103. Get sandwiches from the deli counters at **Ideal Foods,** 1016 W. Spruce, tel. (307) 324-6040, and **City Market,** 602 Higley Blvd., tel. (307) 328-1421.

Entertainment and Events

The lounge at **Day's Inn,** 2222 E. Cedar, tel. (307) 324-6615, has Top-40 DJ tunes most nights and occasional rock bands. For live country music, traipse on down to **Golden Spike Inn,** 1617 W. Spruce St., tel. (307) 324-2271. Another place to try is **The Keg,** 307 E. Cedar, tel. (307) 324-9826.

The main local event is the **Carbon County Fair and Rodeo,** held the second full week of August each year. Attractions include livestock and farm exhibits, arts and crafts, parades, a carnival, a street dance, a pancake breakfast, and a demolition derby. On the second weekend of July, **Summerfest** includes a chili cookoff, booths, bed races, fireworks, stagecoach rides, and country music.

Recreation

The **Rawlins Family Recreation Center,** 1616 Harshman, tel. (307) 324-7529, has racquetball, basketball, and volleyball courts, a weight room, an indoor track, and other facilities. Swim at the high-school pool year-round or Washington Park pool in summer. **Galaxy Skate Center,** 3rd and Cedar, tel. (307) 324-7850, has evening skating. You can join the locals for bingo at the Moose Lodge.

Information and Services

The **Rawlins-Carbon County Chamber of Commerce** is next to City Hall at 519 Cedar St., tel. (307) 324-4111 or (800) 228-3547, and is open Mon.-Fri. 8 a.m.-5 p.m. year-round. **Carbon County Public Library** is at 3rd and Buffalo, tel. (307) 328-2618, and the **post office** is at 106 5th St., tel. (307) 324-3521. Wash clothes at **The Washboard,** 504 23rd, tel. (307) 324-2434. **Carbon County Higher Education Center,** 600 Higley Blvd., tel. (307) 328-9204, offers night classes and a variety of two-year degree programs. The **BLM district office** is at 1300 N. 3rd, tel. (307) 324-7171, and the **BLM Great Divide Resource Office** is at 812 E. Murray, tel. (307) 324-4841. **Cedar Chest Gallery,** 416 W. Cedar, tel. (307) 324-7737, is a gift shop and art gallery with a small collection of Wyoming books. The Frontier Prison also sells books on Wyoming. Find **ATMs** at Rawlins National Bank, 220 5th St.; Bank of Commerce,

3rd and Buffalo; and Rip Griffins Truck Stop, I-80 at Higley Boulevard.

Transportation
Amtrak, tel. (800) 872-7245, has train service heading west to Portland Monday, Wednesday, and Friday, and east to Chicago via Denver Sunday, Tuesday, and Thursday. Trains stop next to the old downtown depot. **Greyhound,** tel. (307) 324-5496 or (800) 231-2222, has bus service along I-80 in both directions but no direct connections between Rawlins and Casper or other cities in the northern part of Wyoming; the nearest connection is via Cheyenne or Rock Springs. Buses stop at McDonald's, 2225 E. Cedar Street. **SANTA** (Shoshone Arapahoe Nations Transit Authority), tel. (800) 439-7118, offers on-demand bus connections to Riverton, Lander, Dubois, Jackson, and Cody. Rent cars from **Kar Kraft,** 1111 E. Daley, tel. (307) 324-6352. No commercial air service to Rawlins.

HEADING NORTH

U.S. 287-State 789 points north from Rawlins into Wyoming's heartland, crossing the Continental Divide twice along the way as it dips into the Great Divide Basin and then back out again. Once inside the basin, the highway throws itself straight across this sandy land from point A to point B, with not much in between to deflect it. No need to touch the steering wheel here. The fences collect both tumbleweeds and bits of

miscellaneous junk. To the northeast the tilted face of 10,037-foot Ferris Mountain rises, but your sense of distance falters in the featureless desert land where only fences and a few gullies halt the relentless horizontal geography. Geologists love this place: long, eroded ridges and scarps in the distance which appear so parched of water that their barren slopes could be the bleached rib cages of some prehistoric monster. Some amazing badlands formations are here as well.

Forty miles north of Rawlins, the highway climbs through **Whiskey Gap** with Green Mountain to the west and the Ferris Mountains to the east. The gap got its name in 1862 when Maj. Jack O'Farrell caught his soldiers drinking from an illegal barrel of whiskey in a trader's wagon. The whiskey was dumped on the ground, but some flowed into a spring that one soldier later called the "sweetest water he had ever tasted." Another five miles north is the junction of U.S. 287-State 789 and State 220 at **Muddy Gap,** where you can gas up. The road diverges, with one fork leading northeast to Casper, passing the Oregon Trail landmarks of Devil's Gate and Independence Rock (see "Oregon Trail Landmarks" under "Casper Vicinity" in the Central Wyoming chapter) and the other heading northwest to Lander, with Split Rock and Jeffrey City along the way (see "East on U.S. 287" under "Lander Vicinity" in the Wind River Mountains Country chapter for more on Jeffrey City). In either direction you will find stereotypical Wyoming vistas—sagebrush, grass, cattle, and sky.

BOB RACE

SOUTHWEST WYOMING

Southwest Wyoming is the state's forbidden quarter, a place seen most frequently from Interstate 80. Most folks consider it a stark, barren, and worthless chunk of earth. In 1866, Gen. William T. Sherman wrote, "The Government will have to pay a bounty for people to like it up here." Others said people wouldn't come no matter how many incentives the government might offer. But despite the lack of trees, the broiling hot summers, and the wind-iced winters, people *have* settled here, primarily to extract the area's immense energy and mineral resources. Southwest Wyoming contains both the state's largest county (Sweetwater) and its smallest (Uinta), as well as Lincoln County, seemingly named for its L-shape. The Green River cuts across this part of Wyoming, eventually joining the Colorado River in Utah.

History
When whites first arrived in southwest Wyoming, they found the Shoshone and Ute Indians hunting buffalo and antelope in this desert country. The first mountain-man rendezvous took place here, and many of the vital emigrant routes

passed through—including the Oregon, Mormon, and Overland Trails—as did the Pony Express and the transcontinental telegraph. But it was the Union Pacific Railroad that opened the land to settlement. Completion of the railroad in 1869 brought about the establishment of Rock Springs, Green River, and Evanston, and coal mines were developed in the Rock Springs, Evanston, and Kemmerer areas to fuel these trains. Men of all nationalities came to work the mines, creating a racial diversity still visible.

Just as the coal mines began to close in the 1950s, enormous trona deposits were developed in western Sweetwater County, and many miners simply switched employers. Other mines extract phosphates and coal, and the natural-gas fields of Sweetwater and Uinta counties are the most productive in Wyoming. Southwest Wyoming has the world's biggest coal mine, biggest coke-producing plant, biggest trona mine, and biggest helium plant. Put all this together and it's obvious that despite the desert setting and small population, southwest Wyoming is in some ways the most industrialized part of the state.

THE RED DESERT

The eastern half of Sweetwater County contains a vast treeless area known as the Red Desert, so named because of the brick-red soil that stretches in all directions. It's not a place to be trifled with. Less than nine inches of precipitation falls each year, and summertime temperatures frequently top 100° F in this forbidding, lonely place—the largest stretch of unfenced land in the Lower 48. Some of the biggest remaining herds of wild horses roam here, along with desert elk and one of the last wild herds of bison. Antelope are found throughout this country, as are a few cattle and lots of sheep. The signs of humans are few and far between: dirt roads, oil and gas wells, and a few wind-scoured buildings.

Interstate 80 is most folks' sole acquaintance with the Red Desert—two double-wide rivers of asphalt cracking open the desiccated land. There are not many sights to see unless you pull off the main road and slow down. Despite its harshness, the Red Desert has a desolate beauty that grows on you. Pick what may seem the least interesting place, where the ramp ends at a cattle crossing and the road immediately turns to gravel. When you're far enough from the interstate that you can no longer hear the trucks, get out of your car and use all your senses to grasp this place. Feel the intensity of the sun on a blistering summer day. Look at the way the thin-crusted snow lies in the lee side of the sage in the winter, worn out by the constant wind. Listen to the "scree!" cry of the red-tailed hawk. Taste a couple of the pungent sage leaves; smell the rusty air as the first drops of a sudden shower pummel the road dust. Watch a herd of antelope bound away and then turn warily back to see who might be stopping in such a place. Or simply let the stillness of this vast land sweep over you, broken by the howl of a distant coyote. This is Wyoming.

The Red Desert lies within **Great Divide Basin,** a 90-mile-long region where the little water that falls never makes it to either ocean. Red Lake—a salty playa—fills with water during rare rainy spells, only to have it soak into the sandy soil or evaporate in the summer sun. The Continental Divide splits south of Great Divide Basin and then rejoins on its northern margin, leaving a bowl in the middle. Highway travelers on I-80 thus cross the Continental Divide twice.

Wamsutter

As you drive the 108 miles west from Rawlins to Rock Springs, the only town worth noting—and marginally so—is Wamsutter (pop. 250). Natural-gas wells sprinkle the country to west and south, and the town itself consists of a trashy collection of old trailer homes, oilfield equipment, and smashed-up trucks hauled here from I-80 accidents. This is a good place to read a romance novel and pretend you're somewhere else. Butch Cassidy's Hole-in-the-Wall gang robbed a Union Pacific train near here in 1900, and freight trains still roll by every few minutes, day and night.

Rest your head at the pleasant **Wamsutter Motel,** tel. (307) 324-7112, where rooms with kitchenettes are $26 s or d. The **Sagebrush Motel,** tel. (307) 328-1584, charges $24 s or d and also has RV parking, but the rooms are in trailer homes. The surrounding country is a rock hound's paradise, with petrified wood, tortilla agate—beautiful when polished—and fossils found on public lands in the area. Enjoy good home cooking at **Broadway Cafe,** tel. (307) 324-7830, or tip a beer at the **Desert Bar,** tel. (307) 324-4949.

Point of Rocks

At the Point of Rocks exit, 25 miles east of Rock Springs, the state has restored an Overland Stage station and adjacent stables built in 1862. Built from sandstone, the station served as a jumping-off point for a road to South Pass City during the gold-rush years. Get here by following the sign to the historical marker for the Overland Trail and then continuing another half mile over the railroad tracks and south to the stage station on a hillside overlooking the railroad and freeway. The historic stone building is well worth the brief side trip from I-80. The "town" of Point of Rocks has a gas station/restaurant/store/bar and several dozen trailer homes.

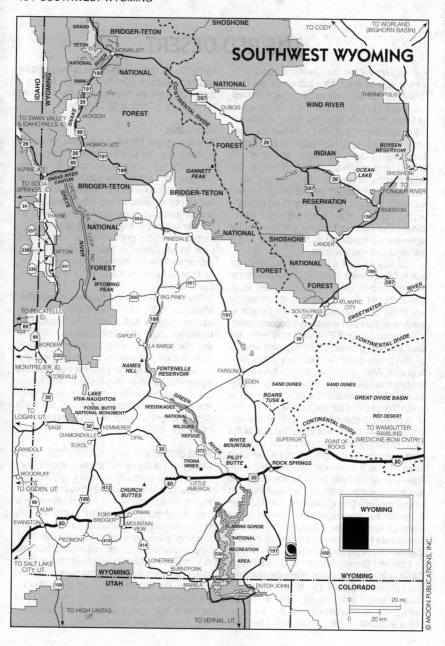

SOUTHWEST WYOMING

Coal is dug from the ground at two large strip mines not far from Point of Rocks. The Jim Bridger Mine feeds directly into the huge Jim Bridger Power Plant, built in the early 1970s to supply power for Utah and Wyoming. North of here are the **Natural Corrals,** an area where caves reach into the volcanic hills and often contain ice even in midsummer. Check with the Rock Springs Bureau of Land Management (BLM) office for directions and precautions.

KILLPECKER DUNES AREA

North of Rock Springs, White Mountain rises like a cresting wave over the valley through which U.S. 191 passes. Approximately 11 miles up is the turnoff to Tri-Territory Road, providing access to the Killpecker Sand Dunes, the largest active dunes in North America. The dunes—some topping 150 feet in height—extend eastward for 55 miles in a band that averages two to three miles wide but sometimes reaches 10. The constantly shifting dunes are formed from Eden Valley dirt that blows east on the prevailing winds. Signs point the way to most of the sights in the Killpecker Dunes area.

Petroglyphs and Boars Tusk

Follow gravel Tri-Territory Road 12 miles east from U.S. 191 and head left at the turnoff to **White Mountain Petroglyphs,** along a very rough four-mile track that ends at a low sandstone cliff. Avoid this road after rains and early in the year. Some 100 or so petroglyphs were carved into the soft rock by the Indian peoples who lived here in centuries past. Look closely to find elk, bison, horses, feather headdresses, and even a human footprint. Many petroglyphs relate to hunting. Because of the horses pictured here—horses didn't reach this region until the 16th century—it's likely that many of the petroglyphs are of relatively recent origin. Look up the cliff to find several large raptor nests. Juniper and sage poke up through the remote desert landscape.

Return to the main gravel road and turn left to get to other interesting sights. Six miles to the east, the road splits. Turn right to reach the ORV area of the dunes, left to visit **Boars Tusk** and dunes where vehicles are not allowed. Follow the latter road a mile and a half to an unmarked road that leads to the base of Boars Tusk, a 400-foot-high rocky spire—a volcanic plug—that local rock climbers love. The 2.5-mile side road to Boars Tusk may be passable in a high-clearance vehicle, but I'd recommend 4WD.

The Dunes

The dunes begin a mile and a half beyond the turnoff to Boars Tusk, 22 miles from U.S. 191. This fascinating area is most beautiful in the early morning or at dusk, when sunlight gleams off the sand. Because it is a wilderness study area, vehicles are not allowed off the roads. Animals are surprisingly common in the Killpecker Dunes, and even a cursory examination will reveal tracks of coyotes, deer, elk, birds, and insects. Small pools of water are on the lee side of some dunes. This is a great place to hike but be sure to come prepared for a desert climate: bring food and water, a compass, and a topographic map. The dirt roads are also fine for mountain biking. See the BLM office in Rock Springs for more details on this unusual area.

BOB RACE

Boars' Tusk

ROCK SPRINGS

As an energy and transportation center, Rock Springs (pop. 21,000) is western Wyoming's largest city. It's also Wyoming's whipping boy, the place people joke about and consider a local version of hell-on-earth. Despite recent renovation efforts, the city still doesn't offer much beyond a place to rest up on the way to somewhere else. Pull off the freeway and you'll find the standard grouping of fast-food eateries, chain motels, gas stations, and convenience stores. The rest of Rock Springs consists of a patchwork of dead-end streets, trailer parks, and split-level homes sprawling in various directions with the train tracks cutting through the middle of it all. The convoluted street system is a legacy of the coal-mining era, when paths taken by miners walking to work gradually evolved into a road network. Rock Springs makes the spiderweb streets of Boston look like a model of city planning.

Like most other mining and energy towns, Rock Springs has always experienced booms and busts. Most of the underground coal mines are closed, but they still create a hazard as they settle, dropping the buildings above as they go. The subsiding mines are perhaps a symbol of what happened to Rock Springs in the late 1980s as the energy-dependent economy collapsed and the oilfield workers fled for greener pastures, leaving a plague of abandoned businesses. In the last several years the citizens of Rock Springs have worked hard to clean up their image. Extensive restoration work on the historic city hall—now a museum—and along Front Street is helping transform downtown into a more likeable place, and the backfilling of old coal tunnels is helping reduce the subsidence problems.

HISTORY

Rock Springs began as a stage station along the Overland Trail but grew because of the Union Pacific's need for coal to run its trains. The Railway Act granted the Union Pacific rights to all coal along the transcontinental route. Al-

though nearly all of Sweetwater County is underlain with coal, in Rock Springs the coal was close to the surface and easily accessible; the mines actually ran beneath the tracks in many places. Eventually the mines spread over a mile in various directions, creating a honeycomb of tunnels under Rock Springs.

Water and Coal

Despite the fact that Rock Springs is named for flowing water, the lack of water has always been a problem. Rock Spring dried up once coal mining began, and Bitter Creek provided only muddy, bitter water. Killpecker Creek, a sometime stream that flows through Rock Springs, was named by soldiers who noted the alkaline water's rather painful biological effects when they visited the outhouse. Honest. In the early years, Rock Springs was so short on drinking water that it had to be brought by train from Green River. Baths were once-a-week events despite the coal dust that blackened everyone.

Coal mining brought workers from all over the globe; locals call it the 57-variety town. Many arrived from Great Britain or Ireland, but others included Chinese, Italians, Scandinavians, Austrians, Hungarians, Yugoslavians, and Czechs. It was an uneasy melting pot. They lived in company housing, riverbank dugouts, or shanties and used Bitter Creek—already notorious because of its undrinkable water—as the local cesspool and garbage dump. Rock Springs continued to expand as more mines were opened by the UP, and the Chinese Massacre of 1885 (see special topic) had only a minimal impact on production. By 1892, some 943,513 tons of coal were being hauled out by 1,500 miners.

Although various companies mined here, it was the Union Pacific Coal Co. that really owned Rock Springs and its miners. And it was the UP that was to blame for many of the problems: the filth, the poor housing, the lack of water, and the working conditions that spawned racial hatred. After Union Pacific engines switched from coal to diesel in the 1950s, the underground mines were closed and the economy began to fade. During another boom in the '70s,

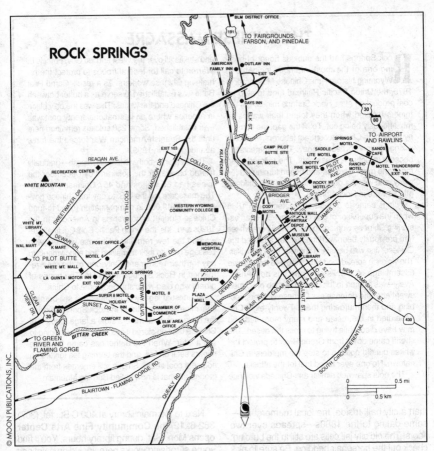

Rock Springs' population doubled, and by 1982 high-paying energy and construction jobs had made it the wealthiest city in the nation on a per-capita basis. With the crash in oil prices, however, many companies fled town and the economy went into a tailspin. More recently, the city has once again rebounded as coal and trona mining, a phosphate fertilizer plant, and gas and oil production bring steady jobs to Rock Springs. An open-pit mine located east of Rock Springs provides coal for the enormous Jim Bridger Power Plant—the largest power plant in Wyoming—while the Black Buttes strip mine in the same area feeds power plants elsewhere

in the nation. The latter may eventually spread its tentacles over 60 square miles of desert land. There are also two underground mines in the vicinity.

SIGHTS

The **Rock Springs Museum** in the old city hall, 201 B St., tel. (307) 362-3138, is open summers Mon.-Sat. 11 a.m.-7 p.m., and Wed.-Sat. noon-5 p.m. the rest of the year. There's no admission charge. Built in 1894, this attractive sandstone building looks more like a medieval castle

THE CHINESE MASSACRE

Rock Springs had the dubious honor of hosting one of the most infamous incidents in Wyoming history—the Chinese Massacre. In 1875, the Union Pacific Railroad tried to step up coal production at its Rock Springs mines, but the miners refused when they found their wages simultaneously being cut. To fill the gap, the company brought in Chinese contract laborers who were willing to work for less money. They immediately became targets of harassment. The railroad hired more and more Chinese and began turning whites away, and within a decade more than 500 Chinese miners were in Rock Springs.

Things came to a head on September 2, 1885 when the supervisor of one of the mines began assigning Chinese workers to locations where whites had previously been working. Whites attacked the Chinese, first with picks and shovels, then with rifles. The violence spread, and Chinatown—a ramshackle assemblage of shacks along what is now Ahsay Ave.—was burned to the ground. A mob of 60 men swept after the defenseless Chinese workers, robbing and then murdering them. Twenty-eight Chinese died in the melee and many more fled and may have died while trying to cross the desert. The sheriff came down from Green River to protect the whites but did nothing to stop the murders in Chinatown. No one ever faced trial for the attacks.

The riots spawned similar anti-Chinese violence and strikes all over the West and led Gov. Francis E. Warren to call for federal troops to protect the remaining Chinese workers. As a result, Camp Pilot Butte was established to serve as a buffer between the Chinese and the whites. This was the only place in America where an international treaty post was ever established. Some 250 soldiers remained here until the Spanish-American War forced the fort's abandonment in 1899.

The workers—both white and Chinese—gradually filtered back after the riots, and by December the mines had 85 whites and 457 Chinese workers. The massacre led the U.S. to pay the Chinese government $149,000 in compensation (used to fund Chinese student scholarships in America). In the 1920s and '30s, the Union Pacific Coal Co. finally rewarded the few remaining Chinese workers with passage back to their homeland and endowments to pay for their retirement. Only one of the men remained in Rock Springs all his life. The bones of others who died were shipped home to China.

An unusual legacy of the riots is a still-burning coal mine at Potter Street in Rock Springs. During the melee, several miners stole a large amount of Chinese tea and stored it in a mine tunnel, hoping to sell it later. When the authorities came for it, the miners set it on fire, and the burning tea ignited an adjacent coal seam. Smoke still emerges from the ground at what is now called Burning Mountain.

---

than a city hall. Inside, the local memorabilia—some dating to the 1880s—spreads over two floors. The old city jail cells are still in the building; check out the horsehair bedding. Be sure to pick up a copy of the excellent historical downtown walking-tour brochure while here. The building at 432 Main, now a copy center, was once a butcher shop. According to some historians, it was while working here and in other local meat shops that Robert LeRoy Parker ("Butch Cassidy") acquired his nickname "Butch." (Several other tales purport to explain how he got the name, but nobody really knows which one is true.) The walking tour details several other Cassidy hangouts, plus the beer garden where Calamity Jane "announced her appearances in town by emptying both of her six shooters and 'shouting verbal oaths well tarnished.'"

Next to the main library at 400 C St., tel. (307) 362-6212, the **Community Fine Arts Center** opens Mon.-Sat. during library hours. You'll find some surprising works here, including paintings by Conrad Schwiering, Hans Kleiber, Grandma Moses, and Norman Rockwell. Also here is a 1993 painting of the Chinese Massacre by Taylor Spence.

The site of **Camp Pilot Butte** (see the special topic "The Chinese Massacre") is now occupied by the Saints Cyril and Methodius Catholic Church at 633 Bridger, a major Slavonian center in the community. Only one of the original buildings remains—a soldiers' barracks now used as a parish school. Chinatown was just north of here. The second JCPenney store ever opened was housed in the building at 531 N. Front Street.

The **Reliance tipple,** five miles north of town on U.S. 191 and then two miles in on County Road 4-42, was used to load coal into railroad cars in the 1930s. Today the impressive structure is open for self-guided walking tours. A paved path passes several interpretive signs describing the facility.

The town of **Superior**—once home to 3,000 people, is now down to fewer than 280. Located 23 miles northeast of Rock Springs, this almost-ghost town contains many old buildings that are

fun to explore. It's where the movie *Growing up in Normal* was filmed.

Several miles northwest of Rock Springs is **Pilot Butte,** a prominent spire visible for miles in all directions and a milestone for emigrants along the Overland Trail. Get there via Gookin-White Road on the west side of town. You'll need a 4WD or a mountain bike unless you want to hoof it. Another interesting rock formation stands across from Plaza Mall on Dewar Drive.

ROCK SPRINGS ACCOMMODATIONS

Note: Accommodations are arranged from least to most expensive. Add a seven percent tax to these rates. Area code is 307.

Saddle Lite Motel; 1411 9th St.; tel. 362-1846; $20 s, $25 d; weekly rates available

El Rancho Motel; 1430 9th St.; tel. 362-3763; $20-25 s or d; fridges and microwaves

Cody Motel; 75 Center St.; tel. 362-6675; $24 s, $26 d

Knotty Pine Motel; 1234 9th St.; tel. 382-6600; $24 s, $31 d; kitchenettes

Motel Thunderbird (Sands Inn); 1556 9th St.; tel. 362-3739; $25 s, $32 d

Elk St. Motel; 1100 Elk St.; tel. 362-3705; $26 s, $28 d; fridges and microwaves, weekly rates available

Motel 8; 108 Gateway Blvd.; tel. 362-8200; $27 s, $34 d

Motel 6; 2615 Commercial Way; tel. 362-1850 or (800) 466-8356; $28 s, $34 d; outdoor pool, AAA approved

Springs Motel; 1525 9th St.; tel. 362-6683; $30-32 s, $34-36 d; AAA approved

Rocky Mt. Motel; 1204 9th St.; tel. 362-3443; $30-45 s or d; weekly rates available

Rodeway Inn; 1004 Dewar Dr.; tel. 362-6673 or (800) 228-2000; $40 s, $44-64 d; AAA approved

La Quinta Motor Inn; 2717 Dewar Dr.; tel. 362-1770 or (800) 531-5900; $44 s $52 d; outdoor pool, continental breakfast, AAA approved

American Family Inn; 1635 N. Elk St.; tel. 382-4217 or (800) 548-6621; $45 s or d; outdoor pool, jacuzzi, continental breakfast, AAA approved

Super 8 Motel; 88 Westland Way; tel. 362-3800 or (800) 800-8000; $45 s, $48 d; indoor pool, jacuzzi, AAA approved

Days Inn; 1545 Elk St.; tel. 362-5646 or (800) 329-7466; $47-57 s, $51-61 d; outdoor pool, microwaves and fridges, continental breakfast, AAA approved

Inn at Rock Springs; 2518 Foothill Blvd.; tel. 362-9600 or (800) 442-9692; $58 s, $64 d; indoor pool, jacuzzi, exercise facility, AAA approved

Comfort Inn; 1670 Sunset Dr.; tel. 382-9490 or (800) 228-5150; $61 s, $67 d; outdoor pool, jacuzzi, exercise room, continental breakfast, AAA approved

Holiday Inn; 1675 Sunset Dr.; tel. 382-9200 or (800) 465-4329; $62-64 s, $68-70 d; indoor pool, jacuzzi, AAA approved

Best Western Outlaw Inn; 1630 Elk St.; tel. 362-6623 or (800) 528-1234; $67-71 s, $72-77 d; indoor pool, atrium, AAA approved

Western Wyoming Community College, 2500 College Dr., tel. (307) 382-1600, is a two-year college in attractive brick buildings with fine views of town. Inside you'll find a small art gallery, a full-size *Tyrannosaurus rex* skeleton cast, an unexpected display of dinosaur bones, and a museum containing archaeological and natural-history collections. Check out the giant pendulum and the spacious atrium in the student center.

Wild Horses

More than 1,500 wild horses still run free in southwest Wyoming. Though they're often spotted east of Rock Springs along I-80, the best place to view them is along the west side of U.S. 191 approximately 28 miles north of Rock Springs. Other Wyoming places to see them are near Lander, Worland, Cody, and Lovell. The BLM has two offices in Rock Springs: 1993 Dewar Dr., tel. (307) 362-6422, and north of town on U.S. 191, tel. (307) 382-5350. Either of them can supply info on the Killpecker Dunes area. Contact the latter for information on adopting a wild horse from one of their Red Desert roundups or write the BLM at Box 1869, Rock Springs, WY 82901, for a brochure. Visiting hours at the wild-horse facility are Mon.-Fri. 10 a.m.-3 p.m.

PRACTICALITIES

Accommodations

Rock Springs has quite a number of reasonably priced places to stay; see the accommodations chart for specifics. As you're driving into Rock Springs on I-80, keep a watch for billboards proclaiming motel discount rates; sometimes you need to mention the ad to get the discount.

Camping

The nearest public camping is the free **Firehole Campground,** 27 miles southwest of Rock Springs in Flaming Gorge National Recreation Area, open mid-May to mid-Sept. By calling (800) 280-2267 and paying an $8.25 fee, you can reserve a spot ahead of time. A **KOA Kampground** two miles west of town on North Service Rd., tel. (307) 362-3063 or (800) 562-

8699, provides great scenic vistas of the oil storage tanks—and you won't need to worry about trees blocking the sun. If you still want to stop, tent sites cost $15, RVs $20. A pool and hot tub are here and it's open April to mid-October.

Food

Ask people in Rock Springs where they go for meals and they're likely to say, "Green River." Interestingly, the same question posed to someone from Green River elicits the response, "Rock Springs." Something strange is going on here. Rock Springs does have one place you should not miss: **Grub's Drive In,** 415 Paulson, tel. (307) 362-6634, where the thick shakes, grease-drenched—but exceptional—fried chicken, and homemade fries are favorites of both locals and visitors. This old-time family operation features Shamrock burgers which come loaded down with all the fixin's. You can almost feel your arteries clogging. The best place for a downhome breakfast in a greasy-spoon atmosphere is **Renegade Cafe,** 1610 Elk St., tel. (307) 362-3052. **Crueljacks Restaurant,** west of Rock Springs, tel. (307) 382-9018, has good truckstop food. **Killpeppers,** 1030 Dewar Dr., tel. (307) 382-8012, offers quality family cooking and good lunches at slightly higher prices.

For cheap lunches and a very pleasant atrium setting overlooking Rock Springs, head to the cafeteria at **Western Wyoming Community College,** 2500 College Drive. Three places in town offer decent Chinese-American fare in quantity: **Lew's Family Restaurant,** 1506 9th St., tel. (307) 382-9894; **Hong Kong House,** 1676 Sunset Dr., tel. (307) 382-5462; and **Sands Cafe and Bar,** 1549 9th St., tel. (307) 362-5633. The Sands has probably the best all-around meal deal in Rock Springs. Try **Santa Fe Trail,** 1635 Elk St., tel. (307) 362-5427, for distinctive Mexican and Native American cooking. Three excellent steak and seafood places operate off I-80 west of town: **Log Inn Supper Club,** tel. (307) 362-7166; **Ted's Supper Club,** tel. (307) 362-7323; and **White Mountain Mining Co.,** tel. (307) 382-5265. You won't go wrong at White Mountain Mining. The classiest place around is **T&J's North Park Dining,** at the White Mountain Golf Course, tel. (307) 362-3950. The surf-and-turf menu includes a Friday night prime rib and seafood buffet. **Fred's**

Breads, 601 Broadway, tel. (307) 362-9212, has good breads, bagels, cakes, and cookies, with an adjacent coffee shop.

Entertainment

In 1903, some 40% of the businesses in Rock Springs were bars; even during Prohibition, many "soft-drink parlors" dispensed Kemmerer moonshine. To produce this booze, 100 train cars of grapes arrived in Rock Springs within a two-month period. Quite a few places still offer nightlife, though many tend toward the sleazy side—particularly those along the railroad tracks. The best places for live country-western music are **White Mountain Mining Co.,** west of Rock Springs, tel. (307) 382-5265, and **Saddle Lite Saloon,** 1704 Elk St., tel. (307) 362-8704. **Killpeppers,** 1030 Dewar Dr., tel. (307) 382-8012, is the place for rock and pop bands. For exotic dancers, try **Mike's Astro Lounge,** 822 Pilot Butte Ave., tel. (307) 382-9876. Local movie houses are **White Mountain Theatres,** tel. (307) 362-8633, in the White Mountain Mall, and **Reel Theatres,** at two addresses: 618 Broadway, tel. (307) 362-2101, and 591 Broadway, tel. (307) 382-9707.

Events

Start the summer with rhymes and tunes at the **Cowboy Poetry & Music Festival** on the second weekend of May at the Sweetwater Events Complex. The **Red Desert Round Up,** held the last weekend of July, is the second-largest professional rodeo in Wyoming and the primary summertime event. It also features a Saturday-morning pancake breakfast followed by a parade. **Sweetwater County Fair** is held here in early August right after the Round Up. Auto-racing enthusiasts will find stock-car racing and other events all summer long at **Sweetwater Speedway.** If you're in the area the second weekend of July, be sure to ask about the **Desert Balloon Extravaganza,** which includes some 30 different hot-air balloons. In late August, the **Great Wyoming Polka & Heritage Festival** attracts polka dotties from all over the nation.

Recreation

The outstanding **Rock Springs Recreation Center,** 3900 Sweetwater Dr., tel. (307) 382-3265, has an indoor pool and gym, ice skating,

racquetball and tennis courts, a weight room, a sauna, and a jacuzzi. Entrance is $3.75 for adults, $1.25 for seniors, $2 for children. Out front are unique carved-brick sculptures. Similar facilities and prices are changed at the **civic center,** 410 N St., tel. (307) 362-6181. You'll find a third pool at Western Wyoming Community College. The 18-hole **White Mountain Golf Course,** tel. (307) 382-5030, lies three miles north of town.

Information and Services

The **Rock Springs Chamber of Commerce,** 1897 Dewar Dr., tel. (307) 362-3771, is open Mon.-Fri. 8 a.m.-5 p.m. year-round. The entryway is open 24 hours and has pamphlets on the area. The **library** at 400 C St., tel. (307) 362-6212, is open Mon.-Thurs. 10 a.m.-9 p.m. and Fri.-Sat. 10 a.m.-5 p.m. Inside, you'll find a good collection of Wyoming books. **White Mountain Library** at 2935 Sweetwater Dr., tel. (307) 362-2665, has the same hours and is a wonderful place to enjoy the view of White Mountain or stroll through a pleasant rock garden. There is a paperback book swap just inside the front door. For books, visit two places in the White Mountain Mall: **B. Dalton,** tel. (307) 382-4900, and **Hastings Books, Music, & Video,** tel. (307) 382-6610. You can also buy books at the **Campus Bookstore,** tel. (307) 382-1600, at the community college. The local **post office** is at 2829 Commercial Way, tel. (307) 362-9792.

Wash clothes at **Imperial Laundromat,** 1669 Sunset Dr., tel. (307) 382-2774; **Launderette,** 328 Paulson, tel. (307) 362-6108; or **9th Street Laundromat,** 1215 9th St., tel. (307) 382-6092.

Transportation

Amtrak trains arrive at the Rock Springs depot heading west to Portland on Monday, Wednesday, and Friday, and east to Chicago via Denver on Sunday, Tuesday, and Thursday. Call (800) 872-7245 for schedule information. The Rock Springs airport is eight miles east of town and has daily service to Denver on **Mesa/United Express,** tel. (800) 241-6522. Rent cars at the airport from **Avis,** tel. (307) 362-5599 or (800) 831-2847; **Enterprise,** tel. (307) 362-8799 or (800) 325-8007; **Hertz,** tel. (307) 382-3262 or (800) 654-3131; or **Wayne's Car Rental,** tel. (307) 362-6970.

Greyhound Bus, at 1655 Sunset Blvd. behind the Burger King, tel. (307) 362-2931, has I-80 service in both directions. **SANTA** (Shoshone Arapahoe Nations Transit Authority), tel. (800) 439-7118, offers on-demand bus connections to Riverton, Lander, Dubois, Pinedale, Jackson, and Cody.

GREEN RIVER

Green River (pop. 14,000) straddles the river of the same name and is a prosperous trona-mining and transportation town as well as the seat of Sweetwater County. Interstate 80 cuts a swath just north of town, plunging through tunnels beneath memorable badlands topography. The huge Union Pacific Railroad yard divides the town. Run-down buildings crowd the railroad tracks, but elsewhere Green River appears vibrant. Wander through the older parts of town to find small but tidy wooden frame homes, while ranch-style suburbs spread to the south. During the 1970s and '80s, Green River saw an enormous growth surge as the trona mines expanded their operations, as oil and gas explorations attracted thousands of roustabouts, and as a helium facility opened nearby. The population jumped from fewer than 5,000 in 1970 to almost 13,000 in 1980 and has held steady since then.

History

Green River was established in 1868 as workers constructed the Union Pacific Railroad across southern Wyoming. Three years later, Frederick Dellenbaugh described the town he found in less than flattering terms:

This place, when the railway was building, had been for a considerable time the terminus and a town of respectable proportions had grown up, but with the completion of the road through this region, the terminus moved on, and now all that was to be seen of those golden days was a group of adobe walls, roofless and forlorn. The present 'City' consisted of about thirteen houses, and some of these were of such complex construction that one hesitates whether to describe them as houses with canvas roofs, or tents with board sides.

In May of 1869, Major John Wesley Powell brought fame to the town when his expedition of 10 men climbed off the train at Green River City and began a long float down the Green and Colorado Rivers. According to one observer, while in Green River awaiting orders, Powell and his men "tried to drink all the whiskey there was in town. The result was a failure, as Jake Field persisted in making it faster than we could drink it." They made it all the way through the Grand Canyon in stout wooden boats. Seven men sur-

---

GREEN RIVER ACCOMMODATIONS

Note: Accommodations are listed from least to most expensive. Add a seven percent tax to these rates. Area code is 307.

Desmond Motel; 140 N. Seventh; tel. 875-3701; $28 s, $32 d

Mustang Motel; 550 E. Flaming Gorge; tel. 875-2468; $29 s or d; see rooms first

Flaming Gorge Motel; 316 E. Flaming Gorge; tel. 875-4190; $29 s, $33 d; kitchenettes for $33 s, $37 d; weekly rates available, see rooms first

Coachman Inn Motel; 470 E. Flaming Gorge; tel. 875-3681; $34 s, $38 d; AAA approved

Western Motel; 890 W. Flaming Gorge; tel. 875-2840; $33 s, $37-40 d; AAA approved

Super 8 Motel; 280 W. Flaming Gorge; tel. 875-9330 or (800) 800-8000; $37 s, $42 d; AAA approved

Sweet Dreams Inn; 1416 Uinta Dr.; tel. 875-7554; $49-79 s or d; new motel

GREEN RIVER

TO LYMAN AND EVANSTON
EXIT 89
TOLLGATE ROCK
REST AREA
374
HILLCREST
WESTERN MOTEL
DESMOND MOTEL
N 7th W
N 6th W
N 5th W
CASTLE ROCK
SUPER 8 MOTEL
N 2nd W
N 1st W
CENTER
N 1st E
N 2nd E
RAILROAD AVE.
COUNTY COURTHOUSE / MUSEUM
LIBRARY
TRUDEL'S GAST HAUS
TO ROCK SPRINGS
EMBERS RESTAURANT
N 2nd E
N 3rd E
N 5th E
30 80
EXIT 91
CENTER ST.
FLAMING GORGE MOTEL
WALKWAY
COACHMAN INN MOTEL
MUSTANG MOTEL
S 2nd E
4th E
FLAMING GORGE WAY
RIVER VIEW DR.
EXPEDITION ISLAND
UNION PACIFIC RAILROAD
POST OFFICE
ASTLE AVE.
CITY MARKET
GREEN RIVER
MANSFACE ROCK
UINTA DR.
EAST TETON BLVD.
RODEO ARENA
WILKES DR.
MONROE ST.
HOSPITAL
CLEARVIEW LANES
CHAMBER OF COMMERCE
SWEET DREAMS INN
SHOSHONE AVE.
WEST TETON BLVD.
HITCHING POST DR.
UPLAND WAY
BRIDGER DR.
COLORADO DR.
0   0.5 mi
0   0.5 km
RECREATION CENTER
TO FLAMING GORGE NAT'L. REC. AREA
530
WESTERN WYOMING COMMUNITY COLLEGE
TO SCOTT'S BOTTOM NATURE AREA/FMC PARK

vived; three who decided to hike out rather than face the treacherous rapids were never seen again. Powell returned to Green River in 1871 for a second voyage with a large contingent of scientists who helped map this region and later directed the U.S. Geological Survey.

Green River claims title to a minor legal footnote. In 1931, Green River passed an antipeddling ordinance that achieved national notoriety and inspired similar ordinances in many other towns and cities. The "Green River Ordi-

nance" declared uninvited peddlers or hawkers to be a nuisance punishable by a fine of $25 and up. The Fuller Brush Company unsuccessfully fought the ordinance all the way to the U.S. Supreme Court.

Trona Mining

Wyoming leads the world in the mining of an obscure but important mineral: trona. With processing, trona—sodium sesquicarbonate—becomes soda ash and is used in glass, deter-

gents, pulp and paper, metal refining, and baking soda. Trona is found in a few widely scattered places around the globe but mined commercially only in a thousand-square-mile area located 25 miles west of Green River. Most trona occurs in a 10-foot-thick bed some 1,500 feet underground. No chance of running out soon—there's enough here to supply the world for several thousand years. The mineral was deposited 50 million years ago when a saline lake developed, reaching 100 by 60 miles in size and up to 2,000 feet in depth. As the climate fluctuated, the lake periodically dried out, precipitating sodium salts. The trona deposits were first discovered in 1938, when an unsuccessful natural-gas well brought up core samples containing trona.

Today, the five major trona mines are the region's largest employers, producing over 15 million tons of trona and 8 million tons of soda ash annually. The world's largest trona mine is run by FMC Corporation and has 2,000 miles of tunnels, more than all the streets of San Francisco. Its tunnels are 14 feet wide and eight feet tall, big enough to use as two-lane roads. Miners get around by driving diesel-powered jeeps or electric golf carts through the maze. Mining methods include a continuous mining machine that grinds out six tons of trona a minute; a long-wall process in which hydraulic rams hold the roof up as it is being mined and then allow the walls to collapse behind after the ore is removed; and solution mining, by which the trona is dissolved underground and pumped to the surface. Once at the surface, trona is processed and sent out on railroad tank cars or in 100-pound bags of soda ash. The production is staggering: at FMC's plant alone the mine extracts more than 900 tons an hour.

Sights
Sweetwater County Historical Museum, in the county courthouse at 80 W. Flaming Gorge Way, tel. (307) 872-6435, is open Mon.-Fri. 9 a.m.-5 p.m. and Saturday 1-5 p.m. July and August, Mon.-Fri. 9 a.m.-5 p.m. the rest of the year. The exhibits change each year but always include photographs from the Powell expedition, turn-of-the-century home furnishings, mining exhibits, and an impressive *Tyrannosaurus rex* footprint found in a nearby coal mine. Pick up a

copy of the detailed *Self-Guided Tour of Historic Green River* from the museum for a walking tour of the town's oldest buildings.

The most distinctive feature of the country around Green River is **Castle Rock,** the stunning rocky pinnacle that rises above the freeway north of town. Other unusual buttes are **Tollgate Rock** on the northwest end of town and **Mansface Rock** behind the post office. The visitor center has a fascinating brochure describing the stories behind these and many other buttes in the area. **Expedition Island**—a National Historic Site—is where John Wesley Powell began his expeditions down the Green River. A small plaque memorializes these voyages of discovery.

Accommodations and Camping
See the "Green River Accommodations" chart for a listing of local motels. The closest public camping is at **Buckboard Crossing Campground** in Flaming Gorge ($10; open mid-May to mid-Sept.), 25 miles south of Green River on State 530. Call (800) 280-2267 for reservations ($8.25). **Tex's Travel Camp,** four miles west on State 374, tel. (307) 875-2630, open May-Sept., is right along the river and has some shade trees. Tenters camp for $14, RVs for $20; showers cost $5 for noncampers. If you are on a bike, ask about pitching a tent next to the chamber of commerce office.

Food
Some of the most popular local restaurants lie on the way east; see "Rock Springs" above for details. **Ember's Family Restaurant,** 95 E. Railroad Ave., tel. (307) 875-9983, has good breakfasts, home-style cooking, and delicious prime rib. Good sandwiches, lunch deals, and espresso can be had at the tiny **Grandma's Daily Grind,** 176 E. Flaming Gorge, tel. (307) 875-3931, or try **Roosters,** 375 Uinta Dr., tel. (307) 875-9052, for dinner specials on Tuesday and Friday nights.

The real surprise in Green River is **Trudel's Gast Haus,** 520 Wilkes Dr., tel. (307) 875-8040. Trudel Lopez, the cook, is German, but her husband, Armando, is Mexican, and the menu shares a similar eclecticism. Most of the time you'll find Mexican and American cookery, but

two Saturday nights a month Trudel's dishes up hearty German fare. Decidedly different and decidedly recommended. The best local pizza is at **Pizza Hut,** 615 E. Flaming Gorge Way, tel. (307) 875-4562. **China Gardens,** 190 N. 5th, tel. (307) 875-3259, has a good lunch buffet on weekdays.

Get groceries and baked goods at **City Market,** 400 Uinta Dr., tel. (307) 875-2577, or **Smith's Food Store,** 905 Bridger Dr., tel. (307) 875-6900. Both are open 24 hours.

Entertainment
Given its blue-collar base, it's no surprise that Green River has lots of bars. You'll find half a dozen along Railroad Ave., including **The Brewery,** 50 W. Railroad Ave., tel. (307) 875-9974, housed in an amusing castle built in 1900 as part of the Green River Brewery. **Wild horse Saloon,** 580 E. Flaming Gorge Way, tel. (307) 875-8550, has country-western or rock music on Friday and Saturday nights, as does **Finer Edge,** 950 W. Flaming Gorge Way, tel. (307) 875-6455. **The Other Place Restaurant,** in the Clearview Lanes Bowling Alley at 1410 Uinta Dr., tel. (307) 875-2695, has karaoke Thurs.-Sat. nights. **Mast Lounge,** 24 E. Flaming Gorge Way, tel. (307) 875-9990, is a biker hangout with rock music, go-go dancers, and striptease artisans. Watch movies at **Reel Theatres,** 699 Uinta Dr., tel. (307) 875-4702.

Events
Flaming Gorge Days, the last weekend of June, features a parade, a chili cookoff, country and rock concerts, mud bog races, horseshoe contests, a flea market, and other activities. On the **4th of July** Green River has rock and jazz concerts at the softball complex, along with the obligatory fireworks show. The **Flaming Gorge Classic Car Show** on Labor Day weekend attracts participants from throughout the Rockies, with cars and bands playing '50s and '60s music.

Recreation
The excellent **Green River Recreation Center,** 1775 Hitching Post Dr., tel. (307) 875-4772,

has an Olympic-size pool, a gym, a weight room, nursery services, even miniature golf in the summer months. Entrance costs $3 for adults, $1 for seniors, $2 for kids. During the winter, rent cross-country skis here to explore the nearby Uinta Mountains. **Fergy's River Rats,** tel. (307) 875-7743, offers Green River float trips and raft rentals. This is a rather gentle float. **Highland Desert Flies,** 218 Uinta Dr., tel. (307) 875-2358, sells Orvis fishing gear. Roll black balls down the lanes at **Clearview Lanes,** 1410 Uinta Dr., tel. (307) 875-2695.

Scott's Bottom Nature Area consists of a half-mile riverside nature path at FMC Park on the southeast edge of town. It's part of a greenbelt project that will eventually extend across town along the river. Call the Green River Parks and Recreation Dept. at (307) 872-0511 for details.

Information and Services
The **Green River Chamber of Commerce** office at 1450 Uinta Dr., tel. (307) 875-5711, is open Mon.-Fri. 8 a.m.-5 p.m. and Sat.-Sun. 8 a.m.-4:30 p.m. Memorial Day-Labor Day, Mon.-Fri. 9 a.m.-5 p.m. the rest of the year. Be sure to stop here to see the large relief map of Flaming Gorge and purchase Forest Service maps or local books. **Sweetwater County Library** is at 300 N. 1st East, tel. (307) 875-3615. Built over an old cemetery, it seems to be filled with ghosts. Librarians claim to have seen the ghosts, heard voices from empty rooms, and watched gates open on their own. The local **post office** is at 350 Uinta Dr., tel. (307) 875-4920. Wash clothes at **Liberty's Laundry,** 1315 Bridger Dr., tel. (307) 875-8134. There's a small bookstore in the Green River campus of **Western Wyoming Community College** on College Way, tel. (307) 875-2278. The school sits atop a hill just south of town, offering a fine view of the surrounding badlands. Find **ATMs** at First Bank, 285 Uinta Dr.; First Security Bank, 125 W. Flaming Gorge Way; and Key Bank, 10 Shoshone Avenue. **Greyhound** no longer stops in Green River except by special request, and there are no local taxis.

GREEN RIVER VICINITY

Little America

Find Little America approximately 20 miles west of Green River. From either direction along I-80, billboards announce, "Little America, only 350 [250, 150, 100 . . .] miles ahead!" And then, out in the desolate, windblown landscape, drivers suddenly come to this oasis of consumption where you can cozy up to cable TV or enjoy fresh produce trucked in from California. The repair bays can hold half a dozen tractor-trailers at once and often do. Ten bright red fuel tanks have "Little America" emblazoned on their sides, flanked by two emperor penguins, and a small town's worth of tidy brick buildings occupy the site: a gift shop, restaurant, grocery mart, and cafe.

Little America had its origins in the mind of S. M. Covey, a sheepherder who spent a fearful winter near here in the 1890s. Covey resolved to build a way station for travelers, a place to escape the blizzards and wind. Many years later he saw a photo of Admiral Byrd's "Little America" in Antarctica and was inspired in 1932 to create his own Little America, adding over the years a restaurant, a motel, and dozens of gas pumps (65 at current count—OK, one is a propane tank). He died in the 1960s and the operation was bought by Earl Holding. Other Little America stations are flung across the West—Cheyenne, Sun Valley, Flagstaff, Salt Lake City, and even San Diego—but this is the real thing, and the only one that rates a name on the map.

Little America Motel, tel. (307) 875-2400 or (800) 634-2401, has immaculate rooms for $53-72 s, $59-79 d. The coffee shop is always open and good; you'll find reasonably priced meals both here and in the restaurant. The pastries and pies are divine, and nearly everyone gets a 35-cent soft ice cream cone to go. But the real reason for Little America's existence is fuel to propel you on down the road. It's fitting that a place with such a patriotic name should be built to worship the internal-combustion engine.

Church Buttes

West of Little America, I-80 lies across colorful badlands country, passing a temple of a different kind—Church Buttes. Brigham Young and his Mormon pioneers held religious services under these churchlike spires in 1847. Take the Church Buttes exit from I-80 and head 5.5 miles north on a gravel road; you can't miss it. The area has quite a few gas wells.

Granger

The dinky town of Granger (pop. 130) is five miles north of Little America on U.S. 30, and contains the **Granger Stage Station.** The sandstone building was a stopping point on the Overland Trail, and housed such visitors as Mark Twain and Horace Greeley.

Seedskadee National Wildlife Refuge

The 13,812-acre Seedskadee National Wildlife Refuge is 37 miles northwest of the town of Green River on State 372. The word comes from the Shoshone Seeds-kee-dee, meaning "River of the Prairie Chicken." The refuge stretches 35 miles along the Green River and contains marshes and riparian areas that provide outstanding waterfowl and wildlife habitat. It's one of the finest birding areas in the state; over 200 species have been sighted. Canada geese are common, along with sandhill cranes, coots, shorebirds, great blue herons, and a variety of ducks. Good fishing here, and canoeists and rafters will see quite a few moose, deer, and antelope along the banks. This is a relatively gentle float trip, though you will need to watch for boulders placed in the channel to improve fish habitat. Camping is not allowed within the refuge, but you can camp upstream from the refuge at the BLM-run Weeping Rock and Slate Creek campgrounds. Refuge headquarters (tel. 307-875-2187) is just northwest of the intersection of State Highways 372 and 28.

FLAMING GORGE NATIONAL RECREATION AREA

Flaming Gorge National Recreation Area covers 94,308 acres of wild country, reaching 91 miles from the town of Green River into northeastern Utah. The region is named for the impressive canyon that Major John Wesley Powell described in his famous 1869 expedition down the river:

> *At a distance of from 1 to 20 miles a brilliant red gorge is seen, the red being surrounded by broad bands of mottled buff and gray at the summit of the cliffs, and curving down to the water's edge on the nearer slope of the mountain. This is where the river enters the mountain range—the head of the first canyon we are to explore, or rather, an introductory canyon to a series made by the river through the range. We name it Flaming Gorge.*

Flaming Gorge Reservoir backs up behind a 502-foot-high concrete arch dam, completed in 1964 and located 15 miles south of the Wyoming border. Each of the dam's three enormous generators produces 50,000 kilowatts of power. The reservoir also provides irrigation for Utah farmers and recreation for boaters, water-skiers, and anglers. Many osprey nest on the rocky pinnacles and cliffs around the edges, while below the dam is a river-runner's funhouse. The area attracts over two million visitors annually.

ACCESS AND SIGHTS

The landscape surrounding the Wyoming portion of Flaming Gorge is typical high-desert country, but once you cross into Utah, the road climbs into spectacularly rugged mountains covered with forests of juniper and pinyon, lodgepole, and ponderosa pine. This area was a favorite hideout of Butch Cassidy and other outlaws who operated out of nearby Brown's Hole. Flaming Gorge Reservoir is encircled by roads—total loop distance 160 miles—providing a pleasant overnight break from the grinding I-80 routine.

The main roads don't come particularly close to the dramatic gorge itself except at the dam, but side roads do provide access.

One of the most interesting ways to reach Flaming Gorge is via State 414 heading southeast from the town of Mountain View. The road climbs past colorful, eroded badlands topography—as though an enormous skeletal landscape were showing through—before emerging into wide-open spaces carpeted with grass and sage.

Then the road dips down along the Henrys Fork, where cottonwoods and willows border lush green pastures. Huge piles of hay crowd the pastures. Keep your eyes open for the many historic log structures. A sign notes the location of the first mountain-man rendezvous in 1825, when 120 trappers traded furs for supplies from the East. Butch Cassidy and other outlaws later frequented Uncle Jack's Cabin Saloon, which stood nearby. Today, tiny **Lonetree** is the "smallest town in the world with a parking meter"—it was brought in from Denver—and **McKinnon** has a little store and a post office, but that's about it till you reach Manila, Utah. This is the real West!

Flaming Gorge National Recreation Area is administered by the U.S. Forest Service. Get information and topo maps at the Ashley National Forest offices in Manila, Utah, tel. (801) 784-3228, or Green River, Wyoming, tel. (307) 875-2871. The Manila office is open daily 8 a.m.-4:30 p.m. in the summer. The Bureau of Reclamation and U.S. Forest Service maintain a year-round **Flaming Gorge Dam Visitor Center** atop the dam; open daily 8 a.m.-6 p.m. Memorial Day to Labor Day, daily 9 a.m.-5 p.m. the rest of the year. Guided dam tours are offered daily 9 a.m.-4:30 p.m. April-October; call (801) 885-3135 for specifics.

The **Red Canyon Overlook Visitor Center** is open daily 10 a.m.-4 p.m. Memorial Day to Labor Day only and offers breathtaking canyon views. Campfire programs are given on Friday and Saturday evenings in the summer. Check at the visitor centers for a current schedule of activities.

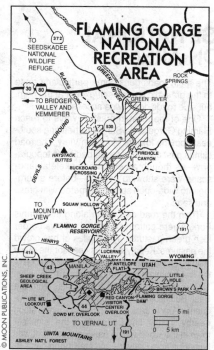

FLAMING GORGE NATIONAL RECREATION AREA

© MOON PUBLICATIONS, INC.

U.S. 191 heads south from the Rock Springs area over the dry sage-and-juniper landscape. Take the paved turnoff to **Firehole Canyon**, where there are some interesting geological treats, including the two fingerlike projections known as North and South Chimney Rocks. Look for sheepherders tending huge flocks nearby. Open May-Sept., the **Firehole Canyon Campground** costs $10, including showers. Call (800) 280-2267 for reservations ($8.25). A dirt road continues south along the canyon to the Wyoming border, or you can return to U.S. 191 to eventually reach the dam. Utah Hwy. 44 meets U.S. 191 near the dam and climbs through the scenic mountain country to the west before dropping down to the town of Manila, where it joins State 530 heading north.

Sheep Creek Geological Area is a side loop from the southwestern end of the National Recreation Area and has all sorts of craggy rock formations. It's a good place to witness a billion years of geologic history and to watch for

bighorn sheep. A road leads west from here to **Ute Mountain Fire Tower,** an old wooden lookout with grand vistas. Built in 1935 by the CCC, it's still in use today and is open Fri.-Mon. 9 a.m.-5 p.m. Memorial Day to Labor Day. **Swett Ranch,** located just south of Flaming Gorge Lodge, is another historic site and a good place to see deer and elk. Open Thurs.-Mon. 9 a.m.-5 p.m., Memorial Day-Labor Day. The Forest Service's **Flaming Gorge National Recreation Area District Office** in the town of Manila, Utah, is open Mon.-Fri. 8 a.m.-4:30 p.m. year-round; tel. (801) 784-3445. Just northeast of Manila and barely in Wyoming are a number of unusual Indian petroglyphs; ask at the Forest Service office for directions. As you continue north along the western side of Flaming Gorge along State 530, the road passes **Haystack Buttes,** a series of beehive-shaped rocky mounds, followed by the barren, eroded badlands of **Devils Playground,** where sagebrush, sand, and cactus extend as far as you can see.

PRACTICALITIES

Accommodations and Food
Because of the popularity of this area, it's a good idea to reserve a week or two ahead during the summer to be assured of a motel room—or in July if you need a place on Labor Day weekend. **Flaming Gorge Lodge** is four miles southwest of the dam, tel. (801) 889-3773, and has motel rooms for $52 s, $58 d, and one-bedroom condos with kitchens for $92 s, $98 d.

One of the nicest places in the area is **Red Canyon Lodge,** tel. (801) 889-3759, near Red Canyon Overlook nine miles southwest of the dam. Rustic cabins are $30-45 s, $40-55 d, and luxury units with kitchenettes are $100. Also here is a fine restaurant, horseback rides, mountain bike rentals, boat rentals—for East Greens Lake only—and a small store with limited groceries, souvenirs, and fishing tackle. Kids fish for free in a private lake on the grounds. The lodge is open daily April-Oct. and on weekends Jan.-March. In the winter months the lodge rents snowmobiles and offers the luxury log units for $80, which sleep four. Recommended.

The town of **Manila,** just three miles south of the Wyoming border on the west side of the

reservoir, has several lodging places. Cheapest is **Steinaker's Motel,** tel. (801) 784-3363, where rooms are $25 s, $28 d. Stop by the Chevron station to check in here. **Flaming Gorge Bunkhouse,** tel. (801) 784-3131, charges $28 s, $34 d for rooms and has a friendly cafe. **Vacation Inn,** tel. (801) 784-3259, has condos with kitchens for $50 s or d. Very clean and nice, it has fly-fishing gear and can accommodate pets, horses, and boats. **Niki's Inn,** tel. (801) 784-3117, is a modern and comfortable place to stay for $40 s or d. Niki's Inn Restaurant serves meals.

Get groceries and pizzas at the **Flaming Gorge Market,** tel. (801) 784-3392, in Manila and Mexican food at **The Hub,** tel. (307) 874-6103, located on State 530 just across the Wyoming-Utah border. The Hub also has a Sunday buffet breakfast and live music most weekends. **Spring Creek Camp Ranch B&B,** tel. (801) 880-8772, is 12 miles north of Dutch John off U.S. 191. Here visitors can take part in all sorts of Western adventures from guided horseback rides to cattle drives. For more on this area and points south see *Utah Handbook,* by Bill Weir and W.C. McRae (Moon Publications).

Camping

The Forest Service maintains 18 different roadside campgrounds in the Flaming Gorge National Recreation Area, generally running $10-12 per night though some are free. Most campgrounds are on the Utah side, particularly around the dam, and many open by mid-May and remain open to mid-September; a few are open year-round. The Red Canyon Campground is especially noteworthy, with spectacular canyon vistas. For an $8.25 service fee, you can make reservations for several of the campgrounds by calling (800) 280-2267. You can also camp for free in undeveloped parts of the Flaming Gorge NRA or in one of several boat-in camps. A **KOA Kampground** in Manila, Utah, tel. (801) 784-3184 or (800) 562-3254, offers tent sites for $13, RV sites for $18. Showers for noncampers cost $4. Open mid-April through October.

Hiking

Several trails are noteworthy in Flaming Gorge. **Little Hole Trail** follows the north bank of Green River from just below the dam to Little Hole, seven miles away. You may want to set up a car shuttle to save having to hike back the same way. The scenic five-mile **Canyon Rim Trail** connects Greendale Overlook with the Red Canyon Visitor Center. The trail is also accessible from the Skull Creek, Greens Lake, and Canyon Rim Campgrounds. The steep **Dowd Mountain-Hideout Canyon Trail** drops five miles from Dowd Mountain Overlook to Hideout Boat Campground; it's open to mountain bikes. The overlook itself is four miles off the main road. A helpful brochure describing these and other trails is available from the Forest Service offices in Manila or Green River.

If you want to explore further, head 30 miles west of Manila to the wonderful **High Uinta Wilderness.** This area is very popular with hikers and cross-country skiers from the Evanston and Green River areas and includes Kings Peak, the highest mountain in Utah. Several access roads come in from the north; see the Forest Service office in Evanston for details. A cautionary note for hikers in the Flaming Gorge area: rattlesnakes are common in the desert and can be deadly. Keep your eyes and ears open at all times.

Mountain Biking

Excellent opportunities exist for mountain bikers throughout the Flaming Gorge area but especially on trails in the more rugged southern end. Pick up a brochure describing the most popular routes Forest Service offices in Manila or Green River. Only the Little Hole National Recreation Trail is closed to bikes. Rent mountain bikes by the hour, day, or week from **Flaming Gorge Lodge,** four miles southwest of the dam, tel. (307) 889-3773, or **Red Canyon Lodge,** near Red Canyon Overlook nine miles southwest of the dam, tel. (801) 889-3759.

Fishing and Boating

Flaming Gorge Reservoir is famous for its monster fish, including a record 51-pound Mackinaw and a 33-pound world-record brown trout. In addition to these two species, anglers catch lake and rainbow trout, kokanee, and smallmouth and largemouth bass. **Flaming Gorge Fishing Derby** in mid-May is one of the biggest such events in Wyoming. Three places on the reservoir rent fishing and ski equipment and houseboats for $60-150 a day: **Buckboard Marina,** tel. (307) 875-6927; **Cedar Springs Marina,** tel.

(801) 889-3795; and **Lucerne Valley Marina,** tel. (801) 784-3483. At these spots you can also rent fishing gear or hire a fishing guide. Other fishing guides operate out of Manila and Dutch John; see the Forest Service office in Manila for a complete listing. Below the dam, the Green River's considered the finest fishing in Utah, with up to 20,000 trout per mile. If you have a Wyoming fishing license and plan to fish in the Utah part of Flaming Gorge—or vice versa—you'll need to purchase a special Flaming Gorge Reservoir Reciprocal Stamp for $10. Get them from the Forest Service office in Manila.

Float Trips

One of the most popular summertime activities is floating down the Green River below Flaming Gorge Dam. An entry station below the dam has safety information. The first several miles of the river are relatively gentle—although there are a half-dozen small rapids—and can be run without a guide, but life jackets are mandatory. Most folks put in just below the spillway and take out at Little Hole, seven miles downriver. Plan on three hours for the run. There's no overnight camping allowed along this stretch, but you'll find campsites below Little Hole. You can also continue on down the river to Gates of Lodore, 31 miles beyond Brown's Park. Check at the various visitor centers for details and pre-

cautions for these longer float trips.

Rent rafts ($45 for a six-person vessel) from **Flaming Gorge Recreation Services** in Dutch John, tel. (801) 885-3191; **Flaming Gorge Lodge,** four miles south of the dam, tel. (801) 889-3773; and **Flaming Gorge Flying Service** in Dutch John, tel. (801) 885-3338. All these companies offer guided fishing trips ($275 a day for two people) and shuttle services (from Little Hole, $40 for up to eight people). Flaming Gorge Recreation Service also has hot showers for $3. Note that varying releases from the dam may push the river up or down three to four feet in a matter of 15-30 minutes.

Winter Recreation

Snowplows keep the paved highway circling Flaming Gorge National Recreation Area clear throughout the winter, providing access to outstanding places for exploration. The Forest Service maintains **cross-country ski trails** at six areas along the Utah side of Flaming Gorge: Death Valley, Elk Park, Dowd Mountain, Canyon Rim, Lake Creek, and Swett Ranch. These vary greatly in length and difficulty; pick up a map from the Ashley National Forest offices in Manila (tel. 801-784-3228) or Green River (307-875-2871). **Snowmobiling** is also very popular in the Flaming Gorge area; you can rent machines from Red Canyon Lodge.

BRIDGER VALLEY

Beautiful Bridger Valley is a large splotch of green in the midst of desert country, nourished by numerous irrigation ditches off the Blacks Fork River. This was the first place in Wyoming to be farmed, having been settled by Mormons in 1853. (By the way, the various branches of the Green River—Smiths Fork, Blacks Fork, Henrys Fork, La Barge, and Hams Fork—are all named for trappers in Jedediah Smith's party of mountain men, who first spread over this country in 1824.) At the time these were considered the richest beaver-trapping waters ever discovered.

LYMAN

Lyman (pop. 1,900) consists of a wide main street and not a whole lot else. Named for a

Mormon leader, the town's initial settlers included many members of that religion. Lyman's pretentious town complex is the only building of note, more because of its size than for any architectural merit. Upstairs the small **Trona Mining Museum,** tel. (307) 787-6738, has exhibits on trona, how it's mined and processed, and its uses.

Stay at **Valley West Motel,** tel. (307) 787-3700, where comfortable rooms (including some with kitchenettes) are $33 s, $35 d. For meals, try **Golden Eagle Cafe,** tel. (307) 787-3822, or **Longhorn Restaurant,** or buy groceries at **Foodtown,** tel. (307) 787-3344. Just north of town, the **KOA Kampground,** tel. (307) 786-2762 or (800) 562-2762, has an outdoor pool. The charge is $14.50 for tents, $18.50 for RVs; open mid-May through October. **Greyhound,**

tel. (307) 787-6192, stops at Taco Time in Lyman. Wash clothes at **Valley West Laundry,** tel. (307) 786-4328. The town also has a public swimming pool, tel. (307) 787-6333.

Since this is a Mormon town, July 24 has a special meaning; it was on this date in 1847 that pioneers first reached Salt Lake City. Lyman's **Days of '47 Celebration** on this date includes a rodeo, a parade, and a dance.

MOUNTAIN VIEW

The town of Mountain View (pop. 1,200) is appropriately named; to the south, the Uintas form a rough-edged horizon. Mountain View is in the heart of farming and ranching country. There's not much to see in the town itself. You'll find the best food at the **V Drive Inn, Pizza Hut,** or the **Thriftway** grocery store. For entertainment . . . well, there's always the bowling alley. **Hoedown on the Smiths Fork** comes to Mountain View on Labor Day weekend and features polkas, bluegrass music, and cowboy poetry. The closest public campground is 22 miles away along the Wyoming-Utah line. For details, stop by the **Wasatch National Forest district office** in Mountain View, tel. (307) 782-6555. Mountain View also has a public **swimming pool,** tel. (307) 782-3525.

PIEDMONT

The ghost town of Piedmont is a rarely visited part of Wyoming but worth the seven-mile drive south from I-80. Take the LeRoy Road exit (mile 24), head west on County Road 128, and follow an old railroad grade south. Continue straight at the intersection and keep your eyes open for the herd of wild buffalo that roams this country. Established as a water and wood refueling station for the Union Pacific, Piedmont was also the scene of an incident in 1869 in which 300 railroad workers blocked a train carrying UP vice president Dr. Thomas Durrant en route to ceremonies at Promontory Point. The workers demanded $200,000 in back pay before they finally let Durrant proceed.

Around 1869, Moses Byrne built five **charcoal kilns** near Piedmont, each 30 feet high and 30 feet across and made of stone and mortar. Wood was sealed in the ovens and slowly burned until it turned into charcoal for Utah's Pioneer smelter. Three of these massive kilns still stand, like three oversized breasts emerging from the plains. A half-mile south are a dozen buildings from the ghost town of Piedmont, abandoned when the railroad tracks were moved farther north in 1901. The last store closed in 1940. A local legend claims that Butch Cassidy buried loot from one of his bank holdups near here. Treasure hunters still search for it. The father of Calamity Jane, gunned down in a saloon, lies buried in an unmarked grave in the small Piedmont cemetery.

FORT BRIDGER

The most interesting historic site in Southwest Wyoming is Fort Bridger, located in the town of the same name. The Uinta Mountains form a majestic backdrop to the south, and the Blacks Fork River winds through. The old fort is just three miles off I-80 and provides an easy diversion from the interstate-highway blahs.

History

Fort Bridger was built in 1843 by the famed mountain man Jim Bridger and his Mexican partner, Louis Vásquez. The location—right on the Oregon and Mormon Trails—quickly made this a vital stopping point for emigrants heading west to California, Oregon, or Salt Lake City. In a letter dictated to Vásquez, Bridger remarked

I have established a small store with a blacksmith shop, and a supply of iron in the road of the emigrants, on Black Fork of Green River, which promises fairly. They, in coming out are generally well supplied with money, but by the time they get there, are in want of all kinds of supplies, horses, provisions, smithwork, etc. They bring ready cash from the states, and should I receive the goods ordered, will have considerable business in that way with them, and establish trade with the Indians in the neighborhood, who have a good number of beaver among them.

The new "fort" consisted of a few crude log huts and a corral surrounded by a log stockade, while the lush riverside country provided pasturage for stock. Conflicts quickly developed between Bridger and the Mormon emigrants, who eyed his prosperous trade with envy and his good relations with the Indians as competition in their own efforts to turn them against the U.S. government. Under the pretext that Bridger was supplying weapons to Ute Indians, Brigham Young ordered Bridger arrested and sent 150 men to do the job. Bridger managed to escape, hiding in a nearby eagle nest while the men searched in vain. He finally fled with his Indian wife to Fort Laramie but lost all his merchandise, livestock, and buildings to the invaders. The Mormons then built their own base, **Fort Supply,** 12 miles south of Bridger's trading post, and established the first agricultural settlement in Wyoming. Soon Fort Supply had more than 100 log buildings surrounded by a palisade. In 1855, they purchased Fort Bridger from Vásquez—without Bridger's knowledge or consent—and added a variety of structures. When the so-called Mormon War began two years later, the Saints decided to leave nothing for the U.S. Army. They burned both forts and fled to Salt Lake City.

Jim Bridger leased his land to the Army in 1858 for $600 a year. The Army rebuilt the fort with room for 350 resident troops. A Pony Express station was established in 1860, followed later by an Overland Stage station. The fort was the site of the first newspaper published in Wyoming (1863) and also served as a base for Chief Washakie's band of Shoshone Indians until a treaty signed here in 1868 established the Wind River Reservation. Fort Bridger was abandoned by the military in 1890, and many of its buildings were sold at auction. Thirty years later, the state of Wyoming bought the site and has since restored or reconstructed many of the structures.

Sights

Fort Bridger, tel. (307) 782-3842, is open daily 9 a.m.-5:30 p.m. May-Sept., and Sat.-Sun. 9 a.m.-4:30 p.m. October to Thanksgiving and March-April. Closed Thanksgiving to February. Entrance costs $1 (free for ages under 18). A number of buildings are open to the public during the summer, but only the museum is open

the rest of the year. In June, July, and August the staff dresses in 1880s costumes and provides living-history demonstrations and historical information. Various activities take place throughout the year, including a mountain-man rendezvous (see below), a Labor Day soldiers association encampment in mid-June, and special moonlight tours in July when you meet various characters from the past (call several months ahead to book this popular tour).

The attractive grounds are sprinkled with aspen and cottonwood trees and beautifully restored buildings. First stop is the **museum and visitor center,** housed in the enlisted-men's barracks. Inside you'll gain an excellent glimpse into the past with a model of the old fort, displays of Army uniforms and weapons, Indian artifacts—including a bowl made from the hump of a buffalo—a chuck wagon, papoose board, and even a working telegraph on which to practice your Morse code. Be sure to look for Jim Bridger's old powderhorn, vest, and other items, including a photo of a "young" Jim Bridger created by computerized reverse aging. Visitors can watch a slide show on the fort's history.

The **Bridger-Vásquez Trading Co.** stands in one corner of the fort and is open summers when the museum is open (closed Oct.-April). This replica of Bridger's original trading post is open May-Sept. and is run by Dick and Sandy Gregory, who will be happy to talk about the trapper's life or to sell trade beads, furs, Indian sweetgrass, clothing, and even bull-scrotum bags. Be sure to ask how to use the fire steels.

Just south of the museum is a rock wall built by Mormons when they had the fort. Other buildings include a small commissary and two guardhouses. On the east side of the fort is the antique-filled **commanding officer's quarters,** built in 1884. Aspen trees line the alleyway connecting this building with the **log officer's quarters,** built in 1858. Look inside for the section from an aspen tree carved by Buffalo Bill Cody.

The **post sutler's complex** contains several furnished buildings including Wyoming's oldest schoolhouse (1860), the post trader's store, and five other structures. Not far away is the fenced-in grave of a local hero—Thornburgh the dog, who once saved a drowning boy and later warned the post of an Indian attack. A small human cemetery is near the commanding offi-

cer's quarters. Ongoing archaeological digs take place each summer. A display case in the museum houses items found in the dig, including buttons, trade beads, and other items.

Practicalities

The town of Fort Bridger contains the **Wagon Wheel Motel,** tel. (307) 782-6361, where rooms start for $28 s, $30 d. You can park RVs here for $15, but you'll find no showers or tent spaces. You'll find a restaurant on the premises, or you can get limited groceries at **Fort Bridger Cash Store,** tel. (307) 782-6744. **Jim Bridger Trading Post,** tel. (307) 782-6115, sells souvenirs, some groceries, and—if you're in the market—washing machines. **T.L.C. Horse Co.,** tel. (307) 786-2915, has summertime horseback rides by the hour or the day.

Fort Bridger Rendezvous

Each Labor Day weekend the largest modern-day mountain-man rendezvous in Wyoming comes to Fort Bridger. Tents and tepees sprawl across the fort grounds. Events include cannon shoots, muzzle-loading shoots, Indian dancing, Dutch-oven cooking contests, tomahawk throwing, live music, clothing contests, all sorts of trading, and food. Be sure to attend performances of *A Ballad of the West,* written by a great grandnephew of Jim Bridger. The rendezvous attracts 400 buckskinners, squaws, hunters, and pilgrims, and over 10,000 spectators.

Other summer events include a parade, a rodeo, and a dance on the **4th of July,** and **moonlight tours** of the fort grounds in July (call 307-782-3842 for reservations).

EVANSTON

West of Fort Bridger, I-80 begins a lengthy climb into the hills, leaving the desert behind as it heads toward the Utah border. The attractive, friendly town of Evanston (pop. 12,000) lies just six miles from Utah and only 80 miles from Salt Lake City. It's a typical small town, with a mixture of prosperity and difficulty. On the outskirts of Evanston, fireworks stands crowd the freeway off-ramps waiting to lure Utahans who create weekend traffic jams in pursuit of booze, bars, and betting. Evanston's economy depends upon gas and oil wells, tourists, ranching, and a state hospital. (In 1886, the territorial legislature offered Uinta County representatives the choice of either the university or the insane asylum. They chose the asylum.)

HISTORY

As the transcontinental railroad's construction crews raced across Wyoming in 1868, the settlement of Evanston was established as the last division point before the Wasatch Range. The town received its name from the railroad's surveyor, James A. Evans. By 1887, Evanston had 1,500 people, many of whom worked at the Union Pacific car and machine shops, at an ice plant, or on the tracks. Others logged railroad

ties in the mountains or raised sheep and cattle. Rich deposits of coal were discovered four miles north of Evanston, and several mines soon opened, creating the town of **Almy.** In 1869, hundreds of Chinese miners were hired as strikebreakers at the mines, creating tensions that would later erupt into race riots and force the temporary abandonment of Evanston's Chinatown. The Almy mines became notorious for deadly methane-gas explosions. At least 60 whites and uncounted Chinese miners were killed in blasts in 1881, 1886, and 1895. The mines closed in 1906, leaving many of the fires unextinguished; you can still see evidence of the smoldering fires. Many of the old mine buildings still stand at the townsite, but the town itself is long since abandoned.

The Overthrust Belt

Evanston lies at the center of the energy-rich Overthrust Belt, which extends from Canada to Mexico. This 40-mile-wide uplift was formed when two land masses smashed together, thrusting the western portion atop the eastern half and creating folds that trapped oil and gas. It was long believed to contain rich energy deposits, but hundreds of dry holes were drilled before one finally hit home. In 1976, the Yellow Creek Oil Field was discovered, producing both

JIM BRIDGER

Legendary figures fill the history of the West, but Jim Bridger ranks as the uncrowned king of the mountain men. Like many other 19th-century frontiersmen, Bridger never learned to read or write, but his deep knowledge of the mountains and Indians gained him the name "Old Gabe"—his skills were said to rival those of the angel Gabriel. Jim Bridger has 21 different Wyoming places named for him—more than any other individual.

Bridger was born in 1804 in Virginia, then moved with his family to Missouri. When both his parents died, he was sent off to apprentice with a blacksmith, but the wild country beckoned, and when William Ashley advertised for "Enterprising Young Men" to go into the Rockies to trap beaver, Bridger quickly joined up. He was on the first keelboat that headed out in 1822 and wintered that year on the Bear River of southern Idaho. When men began speculating on where the Bear River led, Bridger volunteered to find out, thus becoming the first white man to discover the Great Salt Lake. Bridger took any challenge in stride. When Ashley needed a volunteer to test the possibility of running furs down the Bighorn River, Bridger stepped forward. He nearly died taking his log raft through the wild waters of Bighorn Canyon, but the adventure added to his growing reputation.

Bridger entered the fur trading business in 1830 when he and four others bought the Rocky Mountain Fur Company from Ashley. They in turn sold the business to William Sublette five years later. Bridger

Jim Bridger

BUFFALO BILL HISTORICAL SOCIETY

continued to lead trapping parties until the last rendezvous in 1840 and then turned his attention to the growing tide of emigrants heading west to California and Oregon. Together with partner Louis Vásquez, Bridger built a trading post (Fort Bridger) along the Blacks Fork of the Green River. He later served as a scout for the U.S. Army in the Powder River, although his sage advice was often ignored.

Like many other mountain men, Jim Bridger had several wives. His first was a white Mormon woman, but when Jim refused to join her religion they separated. He later married three different Indian women, none of whom spoke English. The first two died early but the last one—daughter of the great Shoshone Chief Washakie—returned to Missouri with him.

Bridger's knowledge of sign language was legendary; he once kept an audience of Sioux and Cheyenne Indians in rapt attention for over an hour as he signed a lengthy adventure. In one of his yarns told to a naive British army captain, Bridger described how the Indians had him trapped in a canyon with his only escape up a 200-foot waterfall. When the captain insisted upon discovering how he escaped this predicament, Bridger wryly went on, "Oh bless your soul, Captain, we never did get out. The Indians killed us right there!" Partly because of such stories, few believed Bridger's true accounts of the geysers and hot springs he had found in Yellowstone or of the stream that split along the Continental Divide, with waters flowing in both directions. Bridger died on his Missouri farm in 1881 at the age of 77.

oil and natural gas and unleashing a boomtown atmosphere. Many more oil and gas fields have been discovered since then. Although Uinta County is Wyoming's smallest, it's easily the largest in terms of natural-gas production; more than a third of the state's output comes from here.

SIGHTS

Depot Square

A major renovation project in downtown Evanston has created an attractive central area with a fountain and open grassy lawns for relaxing. The

focal point is the old **Evanston Depot.** Built in 1900, it was one of the finest along the line and had separate waiting rooms for men and women. A 1944 Union Pacific dining car and caboose stand outside the depot, and Amtrak trains arrive twice daily at the Evanston station, heading west to Portland on Monday, Wednesday, and Friday and east to Chicago via Denver on Sunday, Tuesday, and Thursday. The nearby **Beeman-Cashin Implement Depot** is used for dances and community activities. Built around 1886 and restored in 1986, this unique wooden structure has no supporting posts.

Located in the old town library, the **Uinta County Museum,** tel. (307) 789-2757, is open

Mon.-Fri. 9 a.m.-5 p.m. year-round, plus Sat.-Sun. 10 a.m.-4 p.m. during the summer. Also of interest here are various Chinese items; including opium pipes, an impressive turn-of-the-century dragon, a Buddha figure, a gong, and lanterns; hundreds of historic photos; and various Indian artifacts. While here, pick up a walking-tour brochure of Evanston that details many of the older buildings in town. Outside the museum are various old wagons.

Joss House
Early in this century, Evanston had a prominent Chinatown located along the north side of the tracks. Life centered around the Joss House, a

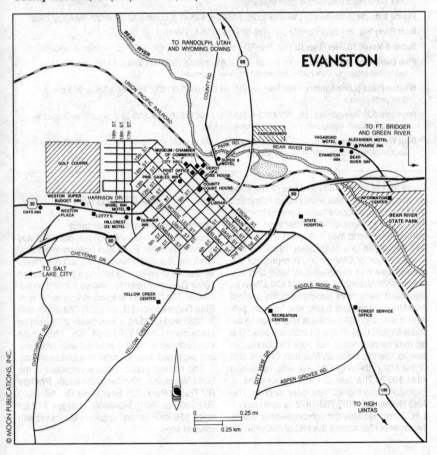

EVANSTON ACCOMMODATIONS

Note: Accommodations are listed from least to most expensive. Add a seven percent tax to these rates. Area code is 307.

Alexander Motel; 248 Bear River Dr.; tel. 789-2346; $20 s, $22 d; weekly rates available, no phones in rooms

Hillcrest DX Motel; 1725 Harrison Dr.; tel. 789-1111; $20 s, $25 d; no phones in rooms

Vagabond Motel; 230 Bear River Dr.; tel. 789-2902 or (800) 789-2902; $23 s, $27 d

Evanston Inn; 247 Bear River Dr.; tel. 789-6212 or (800) 443-1982; $24 s, $27 d; kitchenettes

Whirl Inn Motel (National 9 Inn); 1724 Harrison Dr.; tel. 789-9610 or (800) 621-9610; $25-27 s, $27-30 d

Weston Super Budget Inn; 1936 Harrison Dr.; tel. 789-2810 or (800) 255-9840; $25-39 s or d; outdoor pool, continental breakfast, access to jacuzzi

Prairie Inn; 264 Bear River Dr.; tel. 789-2920; $28-32 s, $38-42 d; continental breakfast, AAA approved

Bear River Inn; 261 Bear River Dr.; tel. 789-0791; $30-35 s, $35-40 d

Super 8 Motel; 70 Bear River Dr.; tel. 789-7510 or (800) 800-8000; $35 s, $41 d; continental breakfast

Pine Gables Inn B&B; 1049 Center St.; tel. 789-2069 or (800) 789-2069; $40 s, $47 d; historic place, four guest rooms, private baths, full breakfast, AAA approved

Weston Plaza (Lamplighter); 1983 Harrison Dr.; tel. 789-0783 or (800) 255-9840; $50 s, $55 d; outdoor pool, jacuzzi

Days Inn; 339 Wasatch Rd.; tel. 789-2220 or (800) 357-2220; $55-70 s, $60-75 d; jacuzzi, sauna, continental breakfast, kitchenettes available, AAA approved

Best Western Dunmar Inn; 1019 Lombard; tel. 789-3770 or (800) 654-6509; $66-78 s, $78-90 d; outdoor pool, exercise facility, AAA approved

Taoist temple built in 1894 and one of just three in the nation (the others were in San Francisco and New York). Pilgrims came from hundreds of miles away to worship here. After the Chinese workers returned to their homeland, the building was destroyed in a suspicious 1922 fire that leveled much of Chinatown. A replica of the Joss House was completed in 1990 and furnished with historic photos, an 1874 Chinese signboard, decorative panels from the original Joss House, and other items. Also here are pottery, coins, and other artifacts found during archaeological digs at the Chinatown site. The dig may be continuing; ask here for details. Be sure to see the video on Mormon Charlie and China Mary, the only Chinese who remained after 1922. The few Chinese-Americans in Evanston today moved here more recently. The Joss House, tel. (307) 789-1472, is open daily 7 a.m.-7 p.m. mid-May through September; ask at the museum for access the rest of the year.

PRACTICALITIES

Accommodations and Camping

You'll find quite a few inexpensive places to stay in town; see the "Evanston Accommodations" chart for specifics. Reserve ahead on summer weekends to be sure of having a place, and on Labor Day you'll need to reserve a month in advance. The homiest lodging in Evanston is at **Pine Gables Inn B&B,** tel. (307) 789-2069, built in 1883 and used as a European-style lodging place during the 1920s and '30s. The house was restored in 1981, furnished with antiques, and reopened as a delightful bed and breakfast.

The nearest public campgrounds are in the Uinta Mountains, 30 miles to the south. **Phillips RV Trailer Park,** 225 Bear River Dr., tel. (307) 789-3805 or (800) 349-3805, charges $12 for tents, $16 for RVs, and is open year-round with shaded sites.

Food

Meet Evanston cops over coffee and donuts at **Main Street Deli,** 1025 Main St., tel. (307) 789-1599. It also offers good breakfast bargains and soup, sandwiches, and cornbread that make for tasty lunches. **Legal Tender Dining Room** in the Dunmar Inn, 1601 Harrison Dr., tel. (307) 789-3770, is an attractive local establishment offering lunch specials and reasonably priced steak-house fare. **Last Outpost,** 205 Bear River Dr., tel. (307) 789-3322, grills buffalo burgers and great steaks in a rustic atmosphere and is a good family place. **Lotty's Family Restaurant,** 1925 Harrison Dr., tel. (307) 789-9660, has a big salad bar and buffet with all-you-can-stuff-in prime rib Fri.-Sun. nights. **Latte at Main,** 927 Main, tel. (307) 789-9184, has espresso, sandwiches, salads, and pastries. **Ulness Lefse,** 1005 Front St., tel. (307) 789-3393, has dessert potato lefse.

New Garden Cafe, 933 Front, tel. (307) 789-2882, offers very reasonably priced Chinese and American cooking, but you might want to peek in the kitchen before deciding whether to eat here. **Don Pedro's Family Mexican Restaurant,** 909 Front St., tel. (307) 789-2944, is the place to find outstanding and authentic Mexican fare including fajitas. Try more international eats at **Sorella's,** 123 10th, tel. (307) 789-8720, where the menu features delicious seafood and pasta, with ice-cream cocktails for dessert. Best pizza around is at **Pizza Hut,** 134 Yellow Creek Rd., tel. (307) 789-1372, though **Shakey's,** 350 Front St., tel. (307) 789-8281, offers lunch and dinner all-you-can-eat buffets. Be assured that Evanston also has most of the fast-food chains, including Subway, Little Ceasar's, Wendy's, Arby's, Domino's, KFC, and McD's. **Hamblin Park,** next to the fairgrounds on Bear River Drive, is a very pleasant place to enjoy a picnic lunch beneath tall cottonwood trees.

Entertainment

Evanston is jam-packed with liquor stores and lounges to quench the parched throats of Utahans who cross the border in droves. **Legal Tender Lounge** at Dunmar Inn, 1019 Lombard, tel. (307) 789-3770, has two bars—an upstairs disco and a downstairs saloon where you can dance to country-western bands on weekends—and draws mainly a young crowd. For rock tunes, try **Pete's Rock-N-Rye Club,** a long-time bar east of town on U.S. 30, tel. (307) 789-2135. Or just hang out in the relaxing atmosphere of **Kate's Bar,** 936 Main, tel. (307) 789-7662. Watch movies at **Evanston Valley Cinema,** 45 Aspen Grove Dr. E, tel. (307) 789-0522 or **Strand Theatre,** 1028 Main, tel. (307) 789-2974. **Whirl Inn Hide-Out Lounge,** 748 11th, tel. (307) 789-3383, has pool tables where you can join divorced men over a game.

Events

One of the most unusual Evanston events is **Chinese New Year,** featuring a parade, fireworks, and, of course, the dragon. With so few Chinese-Americans in Evanston today, many of the performers come from other ancestry. On summer weekends, **Wyoming Downs Racetrack,** 12 miles north of Evanston on State 89, tel. (307) 789-0511 or (800) 842-8722, has horse racing with pari-mutuel betting. This is particularly popular with folks from Salt Lake, since horse racing is illegal in Utah. From the Western Super Budget Inn race enthusiasts can also watch and wager off-track bets on races as far away as California. The **Evanston Rodeo Series** includes amateur rodeo events several times a month throughout the summer; call (307) 789-2757 for a schedule.

Mid-June brings a very popular **Chili Cookoff,** followed in late June by the 80-mile-long **High Uinta Bike Race.** The **Uinta County Fair** the first week of August includes a greased-pig contest, animal judging, carnival rides, music, and dancing. In mid-August, the **Muddy Medicine Fat Tire Bike Race** takes part on backcountry trails south of town.

The big event in Evanston is, predictably, the annual rodeo, here known as **Cowboy Days.** Labor Day weekend festivities pack all the motels in town as folks come from all over Wyoming, Idaho, and Utah to watch professional cowboys show their stuff at "the biggest little rodeo in the world." The three-day event also includes musical entertainment, dances, an arts-and-crafts fair, a parade, a pancake breakfast, a spaghetti dinner, and clowns.

Recreation

Bear River State Park covers 280 acres of land surrounding the Bear River Information Center

just south of I-80. There's no camping, but the park has two miles of mostly gravel trails that make popular hiking and biking paths in the summer and cross-country ski trails come winter. The park also has a small herd of bison. The paved **Bear Parkway** extends westward from the park for two miles along the river, and plans call for it to eventually continue to the west side of town. The Bear River—just a creek here—flows northward, eventually draining into Great Salt Lake. At 400 miles in length, it's the largest river in the Western Hemisphere that doesn't reach the ocean.

The excellent **Evanston Recreation Center,** 275 Saddle Ridge Rd., tel. (307) 789-1770, features a swimming pool, gyms, racquetball courts, a weight room, and a hot tub. Entrance costs $3 for adults, $1.50 for seniors and youths.

Cross-country skiers head to the **Lily Lake Touring Area,** 30 miles south of Evanston in the Uintas, with groomed trails and a yurt for overnight stays ($35 for up to eight people). Call (307) 789-7588 for details. You'll find more groomed trails in Bear River State Park and the Aspen Elementary School. In wintertime, a small, free ice rink opens at the Bear Parkway ponds. **Purple Sage Golf Course** is a nine-hole public course on Country Club Lane, tel. (307) 789-2383.

Information and Services

Evanston has two places to go for information. If you're entering the state from the west, stop at **Bear River Information Center** at Exit 6 just off I-80, tel. (307) 789-6540. The center has a wealth of statewide information, a pleasant picnic area, and short trails. It's open summers daily 8 a.m.-5 p.m. and winters daily 9 a.m.-5 p.m. The info center lies within Bear River State Park (see above). The **Evanston Chamber of Commerce,** 36 10th St., tel. (307) 789-2757 or (800) 328-9708, is inside the county museum and has more local info. Hours are Mon.-Fri. 9 a.m.-5 p.m. For details on westward destinations, see *Utah Handbook,* by Bill Weir and W.C. McRae (Moon Publications).

Uinta County Library is at 701 Main, tel. (307) 789-2770. The **Mountain View Ranger Station,** 1565 S. State 150, tel. (307) 789-3194, has maps of Wasatch National Forest but not much else. A tiny corner of the forest comes into Wyoming.

Get cash from **ATMs** at Key Bank, 849 Front St.; First Security Bank, 724 Front St.; First Bank, 748 Main Street. Get new and used books from **Book Nook,** 1008 Main, tel. (307) 789-6465. Wash clothes at **Sunfresh Laundro,** 116 Yellow Creek Rd., tel. (307) 789-1163. **Rocky Mtn. Lodgepole Furniture Co.,** 1049 Main St., tel. (307) 789-9042 or (800) 827-9042, creates rustically functional chairs, benches, beds, and other furnishings.

Transportation

Amtrak trains arrive at the Evanston depot twice a day. Call (800) 872-7245 for schedule information. **Greyhound** runs buses both east and west on I-80 and stops next to the McDonald's on 1st Street. Rent cars from **Evanston Motor Co.,** 2000 U.S. 30 W, tel. (307) 789-3145, or **Affordable Used Car Rental,** 101 U.S. 30, tel. (307) 789-3096. There's no commercial service at the airport. **F&M Taxi,** tel. (307) 789-0469, will take you around town.

North to Kemmerer

North of Evanston, U.S. 189 follows a long valley most of the way to Kemmerer. A hogback ridge hems you in to the east. Stop for a look back at the ragged snow-topped Uintas that form a southern horizon line. Near the junction with State 412 (36 miles up) is the small **Cumberland** cemetery, enclosed within a white picket fence. Turn down State 412 to see what's left of the ghost town of Cumberland. This was a booming coal-mining town between 1920 and 1935, with four underground mines going at once. Today all that remains are the sandstone Ziller ranch buildings—the old whorehouse and saloon—and the cemetery. The buildings are not open to the public.

KEMMERER

The twin towns of Kemmerer (pop. 3,000) and Diamondville (pop. 900) are at the center of the coal industry in southwestern Wyoming. Drive west of town and you'll even pass coal seams in the road cutbank. Kemmerer is the Lincoln County seat and is located on the Hams Fork River; Diamondville lies just a few yards south. The surrounding country is dotted with mining and energy plants of various types. The world's largest strip mine is several miles south, and a nearby Exxon plant is the world's largest manufacturer of helium and the state's largest consumer of electricity. Another major employer is the FMC coke plant, which provides coke for a phosphorous plant in Pocatello, Idaho. It, too, is the largest such operation in the world. Natural gas, oil, and sulfur are also very important locally, as are cattle and sheep ranching. Given this setting it should come as no surprise that this is a pickup-truck town. Either that or you better drive a Mustang with growling glaspak mufflers.

HISTORY

Coal Mining

Explorer John C. Frémont first chanced upon coal here in 1843, but it wasn't until 1881 that the Union Pacific opened the first underground mine. Things really began to boom when Patrick J. Quealy and his partner Mahlon S. Kemmerer established the Kemmerer Coal Company. Hundreds of men died in mine accidents; the worst was a 1923 explosion that killed 99 miners, mostly emigrants. The operation moved aboveground in 1950, and the Kemmerer mine became the Pittsburg & Midway Coal Company, now a subsidiary of Chevron. Located six miles south of Kemmerer along U.S. 189, it's the world's largest open-pit coal mine, an 800-foot-deep monstrosity. Two-thirds of the coal is used at the adjacent Pacific Power Naughton Plant, which produces 710 megawatts of power. The mine—the longest continuously operating mine in Wyoming—and the power plant are the largest employers in the region. Call (307) 828-2200 for tour information.

Moonshine and Shady Ladies

During the 1920s, Kemmerer became a national center for bootlegging and a major supplier for Chicago. Kemmerer "moon" was a favorite of speakeasies, and winemakers ordered grapes by the trainload. A 1931 bust near Kemmerer found 24,000 gallons of liquor. All this ended when Prohibition was repealed in 1933.

With all the coal miners, the ratio of men to women in Kemmerer was nearly 50 to one, prime pickings for the world's oldest profession. Into these conditions stepped Madam Isabelle Burns, fresh off the train from Salt Lake City with considerable experience in the "sporting" trade. She arrived in 1896 looking for somewhere to invest the $28,500 inheritance from her husband's suicide. With $5,000 in cash she bought a dance hall with enough convenient side rooms to house 50 prostitutes. In a short while, the Green House was a roaring success, allowing Madam Isabelle to build the most elegant house then in town—still standing at 301 Ruby Street. Because of the demand for "evening wear," Kemmerer's shoe store reportedly sold more high-heeled satin slippers than any shop west of the Mississippi. A nude painting of one of the Green House ladies with her brother (and lover) is now in the Golden Nugget Bar in Las Vegas. Madam Isabelle quit the business in 1926, left town, and married a New Orleans physician. Her business went on in fresh hands.

Several deaths took place at the Green House, leading to a grand conflagration when a man whose sons had been murdered there burned one of the women to death, igniting the building in the process and leaving it a pile of ashes. After the 1926 fire, it was replaced by the Southern Hotel. A newly elected sheriff finally shut things down in 1967, despite pleas from locals that the loss of all the Utah and Idaho clients would hurt business in town. For more on this tantalizing bit of history, see Ray Essman's *Only Count the Sunny Hours* (Winona, MN: Apollo Books).

TO ALTON
TO LAKE ALICE
233
232
30
COKEVILLE
PINE CREEK SKI AREA

KEMMERER AREA

TO BIG PINEY AND MARBLETON
LA BARGE
189
NAMES HILL
FONTENELLE RESERVOIR

LAKE VIVA NAUGHTON

NANCY HILL GRAVE

SEEDSKADEE NATIONAL WILDLIFE REFUGE
372
TO GREEN RIVER

233
189
240

FOSSIL BUTTE NATIONAL MONUMENT

30

89
TO EVANSTON AND SALT LAKE CITY, UTAH

DIAMONDVILLE
KEMMERER
OPAL
30

0   15 mi
0   15 km

189

MOON

TO EVANSTON, CARTER, AND LYMAN

TO GREEN RIVER

CUMBERLAND

© MOON PUBLICATIONS, INC.

SIGHTS

J.C. Penney

The most unusual sights in Kemmerer relate to **James Cash Penney,** founder of the JCPenney chain. Penney moved to Kemmerer in 1902 from Evanston to open a dry goods store in the booming mining town, and his Golden Rule Store quickly achieved a reputation for quality and honesty. By 1912 there were 34 Golden Rule stores; the following year their name was changed to JCPenney.

The **J.C. Penney Home** is a six-room cottage where Penney lived between 1903 and 1909. The house is right behind the chamber of commerce office downtown and is open

summers Mon.-Sat. 9 a.m.-6 p.m. and Sunday 1-6 p.m. During the rest of the year, ask at the JCPenney store for access. No admission charge. Guides are ready to show you around or put on a video about the company's history. The JCPenney "mother store" is also in Kemmerer, just a few doors up the street.

Museum

Kemmerer's **Fossil Country Frontier Museum,** 400 Pine Ave., tel. (307) 877-6551, is open Mon.-Fri. 9 a.m.-5 p.m. in summer and Mon.-Sat. 10 a.m.-4 p.m. the rest of the year; no admission charge. It contains a variety of art, mining, and archaeological exhibits, a walk-through underground coal mine exhibit, and dozens of kinds of barbed wire dating from the 19th cen-

tury. The small gift shop sells inexpensive fossil fish. The museum puts on evening **campfire chats** every Thursday at 7 p.m. June-Aug. at Archie Niel Park. This is a good way to learn about the natural and cultural history of the area.

The nicely restored **Lincoln County Courthouse** at Sage and Topaz streets was built in 1925 and contains a fine collection of fossils. Stop by the post office at Cedar and Sapphire streets to view the attractive **fossil murals** painted by WPA artists in 1938.

PRACTICALITIES

Accommodations and Campgrounds

See the "Kemmerer and Diamondville Accommodations" chart for local motels. The closest public camping ($5; open Memorial Day through September) is **Fontenelle Creek Campground,** 25 miles northeast of Kemmerer on U.S. 189 beside Fontenelle Reservoir. Three free campgrounds are located along the river below the Fontenelle dam. **Riverside Trailer Park,** 216 Spinel St., tel. (307) 877-3416, has RV spaces for $12, but it's a shadeless gravel lot (no tent sites). It's open mid-May to mid-October. Worse is **Foothills RV Park,** a field full of trailers on N. U.S. 189, tel. (307) 877-6634.

KEMMERER AND DIAMONDVILLE ACCOMMODATIONS

Note: Add a five percent tax to these rates. Area code is 307.

Antler Motel; 419 Coral St., Kemmerer; tel. 877-4461; $20-24 s, $24-30 d

Fossil Butte Motel; 1424 Central Ave., Kemmerer; tel. 877-3996; $25 s, $30 d

Energy Inn; Diamondville; tel. 877-6901; $34 s, $43 d; kitchenettes, AAA approved

Fairview Motel; 501 N. US 30; tel. 877-3938; $34 s, $38 d;

Dee's Apartments; 1325 Central Ave., Kemmerer; tel. 877-6226; $35 s or d; kitchenettes $45 s or d; well maintained, weekly rates available

---

Food

Polar King Drive In, U.S. 189, tel. (307) 877-9448, is the place for burgers as well as surprisingly good breakfasts. **Luigi's Supper Club,** 819 Susie Ave. in Diamondville, tel. (307) 877-6221, has good Italian-American cooking. There's a **Pizza Hut** in Diamondville, tel. (307) 877-6969. **Bon Rico's,** 12 miles south of town, tel. (307) 877-4503, is another favorite place to stuff yourself with steak or fish. Some locals also like **Lake Viva-Naughton Marina,** 16 miles north of Kemmerer on the reservoir, tel. (307) 877-9669, for seafood and steaks, but the atmosphere and cleanliness may leave something to be desired. Instead, I'd try the historic **Frontier Saloon & Restaurant,** north of town on State 233, tel. (307) 877-9922, in business since 1898. Try their great Saturday-night prime-rib specials. Other restaurants include **Tom's Place Cafe,** 1433 Central, tel. (307) 877-9412, and **Sagebrush Sue's Cafe,** 801 S. Main, tel. (307) 877-4007.

Entertainment

The **Stock Exchange Bar** downtown has a pool table and fills with locals most nights. **Luigi's Supper Club,** 819 Susie Ave. in Diamondville, tel. (307) 877-6221, sometimes has live music, as does **Bon Rico's,** 12 miles south of town, tel. (307) 877-4503. Luigi's has a photo of one of Kemmerer's many madams at the bar. On weekends, try **Lake Viva-Naughton Marina,** 15 miles north of Kemmerer, tel. (307) 877-9669, for country and '60s music on weekends. The **Frontier Theatre** shows movies every day.

Events

Kemmerer is one of nine stops in the **Rocky Mountain Stage Stop Sled Dog Race,** an event that attracts some of the nation's best mushers. Unlike other races such as the Iditarod, this one is run in nine 30-to 80-mile stages, with teams ending in a new town each night. The race begins in Jackson, stops for the night in Moran, Dubois, Pinedale, Lander, Atlantic City, Kemmerer, Box Y Guest Ranch (Greys River area), and Afton before ending at Alpine. The race is held over 10 days in early February and has a $100,000 purse.

Turn of the Century Days comes around the last weekend in July and includes a chili

cook-off, a carnival, a Little Buckaroo Rodeo, a parade, bed races, and other activities. The **Wyoming State Flatpick Guitar Contest & Music Festival** is held in Kemmerer on the third weekend of August with an outdoor barbecue, contests, and concerts from guitar, fiddle, banjo, and mandolin musicians. The "band scramble" is especially fun—musicians must play together without time to rehearse. Anglers may want to join in the **Ice Fishing Derby** on the third weekend of February or the **Open Water Fishing Derby** on the last weekend of June at Lake Viva-Naughton.

Recreation
Kemmerer Recreation Center, 1776 Dell Rio Dr., tel. (307) 877-9641, has an indoor pool, racquetball courts, a weight room, a jacuzzi, and a sauna. An outdoor pool (tel. 307-877-9641) in **Archie Neil Park** is open during the summer. Kemmerer's nine-hole golf course is north of town on U.S. 189, tel. (307) 877-6954.

Information and Services
The **Kemmerer Chamber of Commerce** is housed in a log cabin in Triangle Park at the center of town, tel. (307) 877-9761 (locals joke that Kemmerer is too small to have a town square, so it has a town triangle instead). It's open summers Mon.-Sat. 9 a.m.-5 p.m. and Sunday noon-4 p.m. and the rest of the year Mon.-Fri. 9 a.m.-2 p.m., plus additional weekend hours in September and October. Inside are displays of fossils and historical pictures, and you can buy local books and old Wyoming license plates. The office can also provide helpful information on nearby fossil-fish quarries and details on tours of industrial plants in the area. The **Rock & Wash**—a combination car wash and rock shop at 502 Coral, tel. (307) 877-3220—is a fun place to get petrified wood and other interesting rocks. See "Fossil Collecting" below for a list of places to get fish fossils. The new Forest Service **Kemmerer Ranger District,** 308 N. U.S. 189, tel. (307) 877-4415, is open Mon.-Fri. 8 a.m.-4:30 p.m. The **BLM office** is on N. U.S. 189, tel. (307) 877-3933, and is open Mon.-Fri. 7:30 a.m.-4:30 p.m. The **Lincoln County Library** is at 519 Emerald St., tel. (307) 877-6961. Get dollars from the **ATM** at Key Bank, 801 Pine Avenue.

FOSSIL BUTTE NATIONAL MONUMENT

Established in 1972, Fossil Butte is an 8,198-acre natural area managed by the National Park Service and located 14 miles west of Kemmerer. The dominant feature is a 1,000-foot-tall escarpment rising above the arid plains. Within this butte are millions of fossil fish, insects, snails, turtles, and plants. This is also one of the few places in the world where fossilized birds and bats have been found. The Green River Formation fossils were first collected by geologist Dr. John Evans in 1865.

Origins
Fossil Butte is not unlike countless other buttes throughout Wyoming: an exposed rocky cliff lit with the red, yellow, and buff colors representing millions of years of deposition and erosion. Despite the arid conditions today, this land once

Diplomystus are among the most common species found at Fossil Butte National Monument.

BOB RACE

supported a subtropical climate similar to that along the Gulf Coast. During the Eocene Epoch (50 million years ago), palm trees grew along the shore of a lake, now called Fossil Lake, whose waters teemed with fish, crocodiles, turtles, stingrays, and other animals. Over a period of two million years, changing salinity levels and variations in runoff from calcium-rich streams caused calcium carbonate to precipitate out. Dead animals and plants on the deep lake bottom were covered with a blanket of fine sediment. Eventually they were fossilized, and when the lake dried up the sedimentary deposits were gradually thrust upward by geological forces.

Visitor Center
The free **Fossil Butte Visitor Center,** tel. (307) 877-4455, is open daily 8 a.m.-7 p.m. June-Aug. and daily 8 a.m.-4:30 p.m. the rest of the year (closed Thanksgiving, Christmas, and New Year's). The visitor center 3.5 miles off U.S. 30 (follow the signs) houses a variety of displays on the area's geology, paleontology, and natural history. Here you can view two videos, one an orientation to the area and the second a lesson on fossil preparation. A variety of natural-history books awaits in the gift shop. On summer weekends, rangers lead informative walks originating at the visitor center. Evening campfire programs take place at the picnic area periodically in the summer; check the visitor center for specific times. Camping is not allowed at Fossil Butte, and the nearest lodging and private RV parks are in Kemmerer. You can, however, camp on nearby BLM lands; see their office in Kemmerer for details.

Hiking
The 2.5-mile **Historic Quarry Trail** on the south side of the monument provides access to an old fossil quarry site (600 feet up) and has various interpretive signs along the way. It is illegal to remove fossils or other items.

Fossil Lake Trail begins from a pleasant picnic area located three miles north of the visitor center. It provides an enjoyable 1.5-mile loop hike through open sage country and a grove of aspen trees. Many varieties of flowers are blooming in midsummer. Keep your eyes open for mule deer, coyotes, sage grouse, prairie dogs, and other animals on these paths. The visitor center has a brochure on these trails. Other than these two, you're on your own, although the open country makes hiking relatively easy.

Fossil Collecting
Although it's illegal to collect fossils within the national monument, several nearby areas permit it for a fee. These are only open in the summer months. The best known—its fossils are exhibited in the Smithsonian—is **Ulrich's Fossil Gallery,** tel. (307) 877-6466, located just outside the national monument. Out front are enormous dinosaur tracks found in a nearby coal mine. Ulrich's has a nearby quarry on state land where you can dig your own fish fossils for $55 (advance reservations required). You're allowed to keep a wooden pallet full of the most common species, although the state gets any rare specimens that turn up. The place also sells prepared fossils at the gallery. **Tynsky's Fossil Fish Shop,** next to the JCPenney store in Kemmerer, tel. (307) 877-6885, has fossil fish for sale, but their quarry is not open to the public. **Warfield Fossil Quarry,** tel. (307) 883-2445, 15 miles south of Kemmerer on U.S. 189, charges diggers $35 per day and is open Memorial Day through August. Both Tynsky's and Warfield are located on private land. **Severns Studio,** located five miles west of Kemmerer, tel. (307) 877-9402, also sells fish fossils.

KEMMERER VICINITY

OREGON TRAIL SIGHTS

Ten miles north of Kemmerer on State 283 are the still-noticeable ruts of the Oregon Trail's Sublette Cutoff. Thirteen miles to the west is the grave of a young emigrant, Nancy Hill. An 1852 letter written by her uncle describes how suddenly life could end on the treacherous journey west:

July the 6th. Since left off writing we have made slow progress in traveling on account of sickness and lame cattle. On last Friday & Saturday we layby on account of abe. He was very bad but is now in a fair way to get well. This day was called on to consign to the tomb one other of our company N.J. Hill. She was in good health on Sunday evening, taken unwell that knight worse in the morning & a corps at nine o'clock at knight. We had two doctors with her. They pronounced her complaining cholera but I believe it was nothing more than cholera with conjestion connecter.

Names Hill

At three well-known places in Wyoming, Oregon Trail travelers paused to carve their names into the rocks: Register Cliff, Independence Rock, and—westernmost of the three—Names Hill. The last of these is six miles south of the tiny oil and gas town of **La Barge** (pop. 600) near the

---

*There's roads and there's roads
And they call, can't you hear it?
Roads of the earth
And roads of the spirit
The best roads of all
Are the ones that aren't certain
One of those is where you'll find me
Till they drop the big curtain*

—Bruce Cockburn,
"Child of the Wind"

Lander Cutoff of the Oregon Trail. Hundreds of old names are carved in the sandstone cliff—along with far too many recent additions. A fence surrounds one carving that reads, "James Bridger 1844 Trapper." Its authenticity is dubious since Bridger could neither read nor write and always signed his name with an X. Maybe a companion carved it for Bridger while he watched? **Fontenelle Reservoir** lies just west of Names Hill and backs up behind a 137-foot earthen dam on the Green River. As you head north from here, the red and yellow badlands rise along the east side of the Green River while oil pumpjacks punctuate the land in all directions.

COKEVILLE

Cokeville (pop. 500) lies in a long, fertile valley along the Idaho border south of Star Valley. Directly behind the town is an impressive triangular mountain, **Rocky Point.** The ranching and farming country is punctuated with small white farmhouses, but many locals commute to work at the coal mine and power plant near Kemmerer. Nearly everyone is Mormon here. The town of Cokeville was founded in 1874 with the arrival of the Oregon Shortline Railroad and is named for the coal that was used to produce coke. By the turn of the century it had become the "sheep capital of the world" and claimed more millionaires per capita than anywhere on earth. Cokeville's proximity to the state line also made it a haven for outlaws—with Utah and Idaho just six miles away, lawbreakers found it easy to leave the posse behind as they fled to a different jurisdiction.

Practicalities

Valley Hi Motel, tel. (307) 279-3251, has rooms for $32 s, $42 d; **Hideout Motel,** tel. (307) 279-3281, charges $30 s or d and up. Get meals at **Texaco Cafe** (open 24 hours). A small **Cokeville Visitor Center,** tel. (307) 279-3223, is open for summer. **Hams Fork Campground,** $4, open Memorial Day through October, is the closest public campground, located 28 miles from Cokeville along the Smiths Fork Road.

Pine Creek Ski Area, six miles east of Cokeville, tel. (307) 279-3201, consists of a chairlift and rope tow with a 1,200-foot vertical rise. Rates are $14 for adults, $12 for kids. Ski rentals and instruction are available. It's open Tuesday, Saturday, and Sunday Jan.-March. The mountains east of Cokeville also contain many miles of groomed snowmobile trails during the winter.

Lake Alice

Take an enjoyable side trip to Lake Alice, a pristine mountain lake at the end of a 1.5-mile trail in Bridger-Teton National Forest. Three-mile-long Lake Alice was created many centuries ago when a mountain slid across the valley and dammed the creek. Water from the lake flows underground for more than a mile before emerging in springs. Get here by heading northeast from Cokeville on State 232 and bearing right at the Y 12 miles up where the pavement ends. The gravel road continues to the trailhead 34 miles from Cokeville, where you'll find the very nice **Hobble Creek Campground** ($5; open July-Oct.). There's good fishing both in the creek and at Lake Alice. The road into Lake Alice is generally closed by snow from October to late June. The country around here is some of the only unroaded land left in the Wyoming Range. The route to Lake Alice passes the **Kelly Guard Station,** which you can rent for $20 a night for up to five people Nov.-April. Access is by snowmobile or cross-country skis, approximately nine miles in. Call the Forest Service in Kemmerer, tel. (307) 877-4415, for specifics

Heading North

The drive north from Cokeville to Star Valley climbs from the sage and grass lowlands into lodgepole pine-covered mountains. It's a taste of the majestic mountain country that fills the northwest corner of Wyoming. **Canyon Inn Motel,** tel. (307) 849-0100, 24 miles north of Cokeville and just inside the Wyoming state line, has rooms for $29-39 s or d. Open May-December.

STAR VALLEY

West of the Wyoming Range, the mountains seem exhausted as they dip into a broad, fertile farming valley that stretches across the Idaho border. This is Star Valley, a place with closer ties to Idaho—in terms of geography, farming, sheep ranching, transportation, and even religion—than to Wyoming. Locals call it the "home of 5,000 people and 20,000 cattle." The valley reaches 10 miles across and 40 miles north to south; an early settler labeled it "The Star of all Valleys." Star Valley is a very pretty place; the Salt River—named for the salt deposits and saline springs along its banks—creates an oasis of greenery and the mountains make a grand backdrop. Irrigation ditches flow alongside the roads, barbed wire stretches between old lodgepole posts, and dairy cows graze in the velvet green farm fields. Spacious old ranches—built to house large Mormon families—alternate with more modern ranch-style homes. A single main road, U.S. 89, heads north the full length of Star Valley, with a network of side roads and scattered pinprick settlements. For details on the land just west of Star Valley, see *Utah Handbook* by Bill Weir and W.C. McRae (Moon Publications).

History

The **Lander Cutoff** of the Oregon Trail angles through the southern half of Star Valley, follows the Salt River as far as the Auburn area, and then cuts northwest along Stump Creek. The 250-mile trail—constructed in 1858 under the direction of Frederick W. Lander—was the first federal road built west of the Missouri River. Fur trappers had used the route for 45 years before Lander and his men, funded with a $300,000 appropriation from Congress, upgraded it for wagon travel. The Lander Cutoff saved Oregon-bound travelers more than 100 miles but also entailed climbing over a rugged 9,000-foot pass. You can see parts of the route along the south end of Greys River Road, where concrete posts and emigrant graves mark the way.

The first white settlers came to Star Valley from Idaho in the 1880s, fleeing laws restricting the number of wives a man could have. Polygamy, while outlawed by the federal government in 1882, was winked at by Wyoming authorities for many years. They needed all the settlers they could get—especially the conservative, hardworking Mormons. When Frank W.

Mondell was running for Congress in 1894, he came to Star Valley and found that the Afton mayor was a polygamist. Mondell noted,

> *We assured our friend we were not disposed to question the propriety of his family affairs and would be glad to accept his hospitality. Thereupon our party partook of a fine supper in the modest home of very pleasant and comely wife No. Three, and thereafter, leaving Miss Reel with her, the remainder of our party was comfortably housed in the larger homes of Wives One and Two.*

Polygamy has long since been outlawed, but a large brick LDS church still stands in every podunk town in Star Valley.

AFTON

The primary settlement in Star Valley is Afton (pop. 1,600), a typical small American town and the sort of place where parents complain of kids partying with kegs and making out on back roads while the high schoolers complain they've nothing to do. The local economy suffered in the early '90s as farmers struggled on fertile land in a marginal climate, but tourism began to kick in as the overflow from Jackson Hole spilled into Star Valley. Things are changing now, with ranchettes and summer homes sprouting in what had been farmland, and new real estate offices on the edge of town enticing more folks to move in. Look out, Afton—here comes the tourist onslaught.

Aviat, Inc., manufactures a variety of small aircraft in Afton, including the Pitts Specials, considered the finest aerobatics planes in existence; the Eagle homebuilt kit; and the Husky A-1, similar to the famous Super Cub. Quite a few other workers also commute to Jackson Hole—69 winding miles each way—where service jobs are plentiful. Tricon Timber had a lumber mill in Afton for many years, but it was bought out by Louisiana-Pacific in 1994. They then closed the mill, not for lack of timber but because it was cheaper to haul the logs all the way to Red Lodge, Montana. Money still rules this country.

Sights

Afton's best-known attraction is the world's largest **elk antler arch**, an 18-foot-high arch that extends over the main street. Built in 1958, it contains 3,011 antlers. At today's antler prices—they're prized as aphrodisiacs in Asia—the arch would be worth over $300,000!

In 1994, a new hangar was built on the south end of town to house the **CallAir Museum**. The museum honors a small aircraft manufacturing company that began in 1937 and lasted until 1962. Many CallAir planes are still in use all over the world, primarily as crop dusters. The founder, Reuel Call, later made money in the oil business with Maverick Country Stores and Flying J truck stops and invested $2 million to found this free museum. Inside you'll find various CallAir planes, other aircraft, historic photos, and even snowcars and snowplanes (forerunners of snowmobiles—snowplanes could reach speeds of 90 mph). You can watch workers restoring old planes, view educational videos,

Pitts Specials, made in Afton, are world-famous stunt planes.

BOB RACE

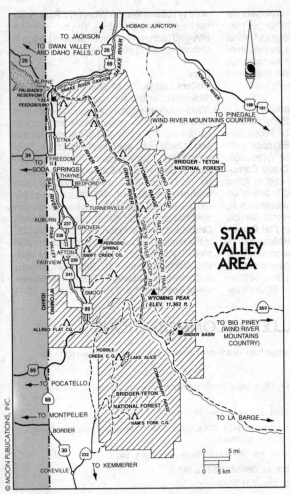

of its aircraft manufacturing facility, but you may want to drop by on weekdays between 11 a.m. and 3 p.m. just in case.

The small **Pioneer Museum** at 46 5th Ave., tel. (307) 886-3667, is open Mon.-Fri. 1-5 p.m. June-Aug., by appointment the rest of the year. No charge. Inside are various items collected by the Daughters of the Utah Pioneers, including a loom, a spinning wheel, and other miscellaneous memorabilia. The enormous **Afton Tabernacle**—LDS, of course—sits at the corner of Jefferson and 3rd and serves as a community focal point. This impressive sandstone building (architects call this a Middle English design) was begun in 1904 and received further additions in the 1940s.

Periodic Spring

Afton's most unusual sight is Periodic Spring, located in Swift Creek Canyon east of town (take 2nd Avenue). The six-mile drive is quite a contrast to wide-open Star Valley—it parallels a pretty tree-bordered creek and steep rocky slopes. The largest of only three intermittent springs known to exist, Periodic Spring is reached via a three-quarter-mile trail. The crystalline water of this spring emerges from the base of a cliff to feed Swift Creek, the water source for Afton, and is so pure that no chlorination is needed. When the spring is operating it seems as though there were a timer and an on-off switch buried in the mountain. Icy water gushes from a gaping opening in the cliff for approximately 18 minutes, then stops for an equal period. The Shoshones regarded this as a sacred place of healing and said that a powerful medicine man was able to turn the waters on

and get flying paraphernalia and books in the gift shop. There's even a kid-size plane for the younger set. The museum is open Mon.-Sat. 9 a.m.-6 p.m. April to mid-September, and Mon.-Fri. 10 a.m.-4 p.m. the rest of the year. There's no charge and you'll be treated to an informative tour of the facility. See "Events" below for details on the CallAir Fly-In. **Aviat,** 672 Washington, tel. (307) 886-3151, does not officially offer tours

and off by command. Today, hydrologists believe that a large underground chamber periodically fills with and then empties of water through a natural siphon in the porous limestone rock. The spring loses its intermittence in spring and flows constantly. Best time to see it in action is in late summer or early fall.

Accommodations and Campgrouds

See the "Star Valley Accommodations" chart for a complete list of local motels. The Forest Service has three campgrounds ($5; open mid-May to mid-September) in the Star Valley area. Closest is the attractive **Swift Creek Campground** only a mile and a half east of Afton (take 2nd Ave.—Periodic Spring is farther up the same road). Unfortunately, problems with local teenagers may lead the Forest Service to close this popular area. **Allred Flat Campground,** is right along U.S. 89 20 miles south of Afton. **Cottonwood Lake Campground** is a very nice place with lakeside sites and nearby hiking trails. It's seven miles up the Cottonwood Lake Road south of Smoot. RVers may want to pull into **Wagon Wheel RV Park** ($14), but it's a rather bleak place. You can also park RVs and pitch tents at **Silver Stream Lodge** in Grover, tel. (307) 883-2440.

Food

Colters Lodge, 355 N. Washington, tel. (307) 886-9597, is the best place for meals in Afton—good breakfasts, all-you-can-eat lunch buffets, and pasta, grilled steaks and chicken for dinner. The rustic Old West atmosphere and outside patio are added attractions. Recommended. Get standard American breakfasts at **Golden Spur Cafe,** 486 Washington, tel. (307) 886-9890, or the somewhat nicer **Elkhorn Restaurant,** 465 Washington, tel. (307) 886-3080. The latter also has good lunch specials and a big salad bar. **Red Baron Drive-In,** 838 Washington, tel. (307) 886-3745, is the hangout for folks who want burgers and fries. Try the lunchtime buffet at **Pizza Hut,** 228 Washington, tel. (307) 886-9794, or get a fast meal from **Subway** or **Taco Time. Homestead Restaurant,** just south of town, tel. (307)

STAR VALLEY ACCOMMODATIONS

Note: Accommodations are arranged from least to most expensive. Add a seven percent tax to the rates. Area code is 307.

Salt River B&B; Etna; tel. 883-2453; $25 s, $45 d; comfortable home, three guest rooms, private or shared bath, full breakfast

Horse Shoe Motel; Etna; tel. 883-2281; $33 s or d; open May-Nov.

Corral Motel; 161 Washington, Afton; tel. 886-5424; $34 s, $38 d; plaster "log" cabins from 1940s, very clean, kitchenettes, open April-Oct., AAA approved

Colters Lodge; 355 N. Washington; tel. 886-9891 or (800) 446-7005; $34 s, $40 d

Lazy B Motel; 219 Washington, Afton; tel. 886-3187; $35 s, $40 d

Swiss Mountain Motel; Thayne; tel. 883-2227; $38 s or d

Silver Stream Lodge; three miles north of Grover; tel. 883-2440; $39-42 s or d in cabins; kitchenettes $50 s or d; no TVs or phones, open Memorial Day-Oct.

Flat Creek Cabins; Thayne; tel. 883-2231; $42 for up to four in cabins with kitchenettes

Sunset Motel; Thayne; tel. 883-2462; $42 s, $45 d

Best Western Hi Country Inn; 3/4 mile south of Afton; tel. 886-3856 or (800) 528-1234; $45-65 s, $50-85 d; outdoor pool, jacuzzi, AAA approved

Mountain Inn; one mile south of Afton; tel. 886-3156 or (800) 682-5356; $50-65 s or d; very clean, outdoor pool, sauna, jacuzzi, AAA approved

886-3878, offers the area's finest prime rib. Try the double-fudge desserts. Get groceries at **Thriftway** just north of Afton, tel. (307) 886-5550.

Entertainment
For live country-western or rock music on Friday and Saturday nights, head to **Colters Lodge,** 355 N. Washington, tel. (307) 886-9597, where the young crowd hangs out, or **Valley Vineyard,** 967 Washington, tel. (307) 886-9215.

Events
Afton and nearby Box Y Ranch—in the Greys River area—are two of nine stops in the **Rocky Mountain Stage Stop Sled Dog Race,** an event that attracts some of the nation's best mushers. Unlike other races such as the Iditarod, this one is run in nine 30- to 80-mile stages, with teams ending in a new town each night. The race begins in Jackson and stops for the night in Moran, Dubois, Pinedale, Lander, Atlantic City, Kemmerer, Box Y Guest Ranch, and Afton before ending at Alpine. The race is held over 10 days in early February and has a $100,000 purse.

The **CallAir Fly-In/Star Valley Aviation Days** takes place the last Friday and Saturday of June and includes a free breakfast, aircraft and helicopter rides, tours of the Aviat plant, and radio-controlled model planes. The **Lincoln County Fair** is held in Afton in late July and early August, with all the country fair favorites: musical entertainment, a carnival, a parade, rodeos, 4-H agricultural exhibits, and lots more. Rodeos are also held several other times each summer; see the visitor center for specifics.

Recreation
Golfers will find a pair of nine-hole courses (one of these—Valli-Vu Golf Course—is free if you're staying at a local motel) and two 18-hole courses at Star Valley Ranch Resort in Thayne. During the winter the town operates **Snowshoe Hollow Ski Area,** tel. (307) 886-9831, a small area just east of Afton. The hill has a rope tow and snack bar. Stop by the Forest Service office for information on the many miles of groomed **cross-country ski trails** in Star Valley. The mountains to the east offer unlimited opportunities for further exploration by skiers, with snow

till the 4th of July some years. Popular groomed snowmobile trails are also available, and you can rent snowmobiles in Alpine.

Shopping
Get outdoor gear or rent cross-country skis in the winter from **Lone Pine Sports** at Washington and Nield String Rd., tel. (307) 886-9581. **Quiet Place Books,** 460 N. Washington, tel. (307) 886-5246, has religious titles (mainly LDS) and a smattering of other books and something they call espresso. For a real dose of Star Valley culture, drop by the **Hastings Store,** 422 Washington, tel. (307) 886-3503. Inside is a large selection of LDS books along with a world map showing where local kids have gone as Mormon missionaries (15% discount for outgoing missionaries). A **Wyoming Woolens** factory outlet store, tel. (307) 886-3135, is next to the factory on the north side of Afton. If you're driving north from Afton toward Jackson be sure to fill up with gas either here or in Thayne; it won't get any cheaper.

Information and Services
Afton's summer-only **visitor center** at 2nd and Washington, tel. (307) 886-3156 or (800) 426-8833, is open Tues.-Sat. 10 a.m.-6 p.m. Behind the center you'll find the University of Wyoming research and extension center and, directly across the road, the **Forest Service Greys River District Office,** tel. (307) 886-3166, dispenses local maps, natural history books, and info on nearby recreational opportunities Mon.-Fri. 7:30 a.m.-4:30 p.m. The **Star Valley Branch Library** at 261 Washington St., tel. (307) 886-3158, carries lots of genealogy titles. You'll find the **post office** at 31 W. 4th Ave., tel. (307) 886-3625. Get fast cash from **ATMs** at First Security Bank of Wyoming, 485 N. Washington, or First National Bank, 302 Washington.

GREYS RIVER LOOP ROAD

Star Valley is bordered on the east by two parallel mountain ranges: the Salt River and the Wyoming. The Greys River flows between them. Alongside it runs an 80-mile-long gravel road popular with vacationers, hikers, anglers, and hunters. The road begins a dozen miles south of

Afton and goes all the way to Alpine. Excellent fishing for cutthroat, rainbow, brown, and brook trout in the river, and good opportunities to see deer and moose along the way. All this country lies within Bridger-Teton National Forest. Considerable logging takes place in the mountains, and many thousands of sheep and cattle graze the open areas, but much of the land remains wild and beautiful. It is an almost unknown part of Wyoming. If you drive north along the Greys River Road you'll be able to watch the Greys grow from a small creek into a river. Kayakers often paddle the lower stretches of the river; see the Forest Service for specifics.

Another fascinating drive (great for mountain bikes) is to continue east through Snider Basin to the town of Big Piney on Forest Road 10128. The road parallels the still-visible Lander Cutoff of the Oregon Trail for a long distance, and a number of emigrant graves are noted along the way. Keep your eyes open for elk and deer on the slopes and beaver dams in Piney Creek. The high country is lodgepole-pine forests, passing into open sage land as you descend toward Big Piney. Note that this route can be confusing (signs are often missing) and sometimes muddy, so be sure to get a Forest Service map and current conditions before heading out from Afton. The **La Barge Guard Station** is located approximately 22 miles from the Afton end of the road and is available for rent ($20 a night for up to six people) Nov.-April. Access is by snowmobile or cross-country skis. Call the Forest Service in Kemmerer for specifics, tel. (307) 877-4415.

Camping

Camping ($3-5; open mid-June to mid-September) is available at seven places along the Greys River Road; nicest are ones at Murphy Creek and Forest Park. At other times of the year the campgrounds are open at no charge, but you'll need to bring in water and haul out your own garbage. You can also camp off the road for free in most parts of the national forest.

Recreation

More than 450 miles of trails cut across this country, including the 70-mile-long **Wyoming Range National Recreation Trail,** which climbs through beautiful alpine meadows and over narrow, rocky ridges. A side road off the Greys River Road leads to a two-mile trail that climbs

11,363-foot **Wyoming Peak,** tallest in the range. During the winter cross-country skiers will find four groomed ski trails and snowmobilers can cruise on 100 miles of groomed routes. See the Forest Service office in Afton for maps and recreation information, including a listing of permitted guides and outfitters. **Greysnest Mountain Retreat Camp,** tel. (307) 886-3511, has a rustic wall-tent camp 19 miles southeast of Alpine on Greys River Road. It offers meals, lodging, and horseback riding at $350 per person for five days.

OTHER TOWNS

Grover

Five miles north from Afton, the village of Grover is the home of **Papa's Playhouse,** tel. (307) 886-3356, where melodramas are performed Wed.-Sat. evenings from mid-June to Labor Day. The show is $6 for adults, $3 for kids; a "milk can meal" is $6 for adults, $4 for kids. The meal is prepared by placing ingredients for a stew in a milk can and cooking it the old-fashioned way—over an open fire.

Auburn

The town of Auburn, eight miles north and west of Afton, contains a small area of travertine terraces and hot springs on private land. The nearby countryside is filled with old log homes, cabins, and barns. A historic stone church, built in 1889, sits across from the tiny Auburn post office and is used for summertime productions by the **Star Valley Historical Theatre.** Call (307) 886-3640 for details. Not far away is the Davis Ranch, where Butch Cassidy and his gang holed up one winter. West of Auburn on County Road 134 is **Auburn Fish Hatchery,** where some 50,000 trout are raised annually. It's open daily 8 a.m.-5 p.m. The road to the hatchery parallels the Lander Cutoff of the Oregon Trail for several miles.

Thayne

Thayne's (pop. 390) claim to fame is the **cutter races,** a sport invented here in the 1920s. It's said that racing began with dairymen who used sleighs to haul milk to the local creamery. To avoid having to wait in line, there was often a race to get to the creamery ahead of other

farmers, and this sparring eventually grew into a competition that now encompasses seven western states. (The "world finals" are held in Pocatello, Idaho.) In a cutter race, horses pull chariots over a frozen field at breakneck speeds; the world record stands at 21.8 seconds for the quarter-mile run. Races are held in Thayne on most Saturdays between December and February.

Star Valley Cheese, tel. (307) 883-2510, is one of the most unusual eating places in Wyoming. The restaurant—an old-fashioned place straight out of the 1950s—serves reasonably priced burgers, homemade pies, ice cream, malts, shakes, and other fare and sells fresh cheeses from the coolers. It's open daily May-Oct. and is almost always filled with folks. Some 60,000 pounds of mozzarella, provolone, and Swiss cheese are made in the plant right behind the shop. Everything here gets the Star Valley label although the plant is now a part of Western Dairymen Cooperative. Well worth a stop.

Across the highway from Star Valley Cheese is **Star Valley Gift & Rock Shop,** tel. (307) 883-2028, selling fossils, gold, jade, and crystals. **JH Ranch Cafe,** tel. (307) 883-2357, has homemade breads and pastries and "The Thing." **Dad's Steak House,** tel. (307) 883-2300, offers live music on weekends and the best steaks in the area. This is also home to a small cutter-racing museum (the sport was established by "Dad" Walton). If you're heading north to Jackson Hole, fill your gas tank in Afton or Thayne. Prices only go up from here. In late July Thayne comes alive with three popular events on the same weekend: the **Little Britches Rodeo,** an "almost white-water" river race, and family dances. Call Town Hall at (307) 883-2668 for details.

See the "Star Valley Accommodations" chart for places to stay in and around Thayne. **Flat Creek RV Park** south of Thayne, tel. (307) 883-2231, charges $18 for RVs, $10 for tents. Showers cost $3. It's open year-round. A couple miles north of Thayne is **Star Valley Ranch Resort,** tel. (307) 883-2457, an obscenely elaborate place with several hundred summer homes, a restaurant, an RV park, two pools, two golf courses, and tennis courts. Ugly billboards announce its presence for miles in both directions. This is the sort of development that is ruining the West.

Bedford

The tiny farming and sheep-ranching settlement of Bedford lies near the center of Star Valley. On fall days you're likely to meet huge herds of sheep being driven down the main roads as they return from a summer in the mountains. **Preston Ranches/Range Riders,** tel. (307) 882-2742 or (800) 484-3932, has out-with-the-cattle operations where guests learn about cattle herding and ranch living. Meals, tents, and cots are provided, but you'll need a sleeping bag. There's a three-day minimum stay.

Freedom

Freedom (pop. 100), Star Valley's oldest settlement, straddles the Idaho-Wyoming border. The town was established by Mormons in 1879 and offered an escape from the Idaho Territory's efforts to ban polygamy. Arthur Clark named the town for his freedom to have multiple wives. Today, Freedom has a small country store just a few feet from the border where you can buy Idaho lottery tickets. **Horse Shoe Cafe** in Etna is a classic small-town eatery, filling with locals every day and deer hunters on cool fall mornings. Freedom is famous in gun circles for a small factory, **Freedom Arms,** tel. (307) 883-2468, which makes handguns, including the massive .454 Casull, the world's most powerful revolver—and one of the most expensive at $1,100 apiece. No surprise that Clint Eastwood owns one. Don't ever get on the wrong end of this deadly instrument. Visitors can watch a short video and view a gun display here. Free camping is available three miles west of Freedom, in Idaho, at the Forest Service's **Tincup Campground.**

Etna

Etna lies near the northern end of Star Valley and has a small country store and an outsized brick LDS church that looks big enough to house the entire population of 200. In late summer, the sweet scent of new-mown hay hangs in the air. **Etna Trading Co.,** (307) 883-2409, is an old-time country store. **Salt River B&B,** tel. (307) 883-2453, is a cozy in-town home with three guest rooms and a full breakfast. The owner is a quilter and sells locally made quilts here. They also serve lunch here in the summer months.

ALPINE

Located at the intersection of U.S. 26 and 89, the crossroads settlement called Alpine (pop. 220) is an ugly place with a quickly multiplying collection of businesses—fireworks stands, motels, restaurants, and bars strung out in all directions. It's a sad sight and all here because of the tourists en route to or from Jackson Hole. The area is called Lower Valley and borders on Palisades Reservoir. Approximately 1,000 elk gather each winter at the **Elk Feedground** a mile south of Alpine on U.S. 89. You can view the elk from the parking area here—they often approach parked cars rather closely. Best time to visit is in the mornings, when they are fed. For details on westward destinations, see *Utah Handbook,* by Bill Weir and W.C. McRae (Moon Publications).

Lodging and Camping
See the "Alpine Accommodations" chart for a list of local lodging places. Reservations are advisable during July and August, when everything

---

ALPINE ACCOMMODATIONS

Note: Accommodations are arranged from least to most expensive. Add a seven percent tax to the rates. Area code is 307.

Lakeside Motel; tel. 654-7506; $35 s, $40 d; kitchenettes $10 extra

Palisport Motel; tel. 654-7540; $39 s or d; open mid-May through Oct.

Three Rivers Motel; tel. 654-7551; $40 s, $45 d; kitchenettes $10 extra

Alpen Haus Hotel; tel. 654-7545 or (800) 343-6755; $47-92 s, $54-100 d; jacuzzi tubs in some rooms, AAA approved

Nordic Inn; tel. 654-7556; $63-73 s or d; classy place, jacuzzi, open late May to mid-Oct.

Best Western Flying Saddle Lodge; tel. 654-7561 or (800) 528-1234; $65-150 s or d; attractive rooms and cottages, outdoor pool, jacuzzi, open late May through Sept., AAA approved (four diamond)

---

fills up fast. **Palisport Campground,** tel. (307) 654-7540, has tent sites for $12, RV sites for $18; it's open mid-May to mid-October. You can also park RVs at **Alpen Haus Hotel;** tel. (307) 654-7545 or (800) 343-6755. There's lots of public camping nearby; see "Snake River Canyon" below or "Greys River Loop Road" above.

Other Practicalities
Contact **Alpine Riding & Rafts** at Alpen Haus, tel. (307) 654-9900, for horseback rides in the area and raft trips down the Snake River Canyon. Float trips can also be booked at **Nordic Inn,** tel. (307) 654-7556. Many similar operations are run in nearby Jackson.

    Lakeside Restaurant, tel. (307) 654-7507, features homemade food. **Bette's Cafe,** tel. (307) 654-7536, serves delicious, reasonably priced breakfasts and lunches on weekdays, dinners Fri.-Sun. nights. The real surprise in Alpine is **Brentoven's Restaurant,** where the chef—Brent Johnston—is not only talented in the kitchen but is also an international concert pianist. You'll find everything from fresh fruit crepes for breakfast to steak and venison for dinner. The bar has a fine wine selection, and owner Mike Clinger will be happy to discuss opera or tell you about his distinctive Colonial home located behind the Nordic Inn. The restaurant and inn are open only in the summer months. **Gunnar's Pizza,** tel. (307) 654-7778, has outside dining, pizzas including whole-wheat and deep-dish versions, and good sub sandwiches.

    Bar Nothin' Saloon, tel. (307) 654-7222, has live music on Friday and Saturday nights and is one of the most popular weekend hangouts in the Star Valley/Alpine area. Next door, the **Main Street Grill,** tel. (307) 654-7222, serves chicken, steaks, and Saturday-night prime rib.

Events
Alpine is the final stop in the **Rocky Mountain Stage Stop Sled Dog Race** (see "Events" under "Afton" earlier in this section for more on the race).

    Alpine Mountain Days in mid-June is the big summer celebration, with mountain men, a black powder shoot, arts and crafts, Dutch oven cookoff, Indian dancing, and other activities.

SNAKE RIVER CANYON

Above Alpine, the country abruptly changes as U.S. 89/26 enters Snake River Canyon, paralleling it all the way to Hoback Junction 23 miles away. In places the highway hangs high over the river with only a guardrail blocking the way—and sometimes not even that. This is a delicious way to enter Jackson Hole, offering numerous pullouts where you can view the roiling, rambunctious rapids of the sinuous Snake River as it slithers through millions of years of rocky cliffs. At sunset, the river glows a silver ribbon of light. A big, powerful river, the Snake eventually feeds into the Columbia in Washington. Riverbanks are lined with ancient cottonwoods while the higher slopes show lodgepole pines.

The whitewater of Snake River Canyon is a favorite of recreationists, and during the summer you're bound to meet cars with kayaks on their roofs and vans filled with happy rafters heading back to Jackson. See "Jackson Hole" for details on the many river-running options. River access is generally via the West Table Creek and Sheep Gulch boat ramps.

A half-dozen Forest Service **campgrounds** ($8, open late May to mid-September) are scattered all along the way. Many fill up early in the day during midsummer. Call (800) 280-2267 for advance reservations ($8.25 charge). The highway through the Snake River Canyon is currently being widened and relocated in a major multi-year construction project. Because of this, some campgrounds may be closed or moved. Check with Forest Service offices in Afton and Jackson for the latest. Undeveloped camping spots along the way are also used by many travelers.

Emigrant Train crossing the Platte in Early Days.

WYOMING STATE MUSEUM

CENTRAL WYOMING

The counties of Natrona and Converse enclose definitive Wyoming country: sage-and-grass-carpeted plains, desolate badlands, impressive tree-draped mountainsides, and the big, lazy North Platte River. This is grazing country; each year nearly a quarter of the sheep raised in Wyoming, and 120,000 cattle, come from these two counties. The dominant industry, however—and the one that dictates the region's economy—is oil. It means jobs for roughnecks in dozens of oil fields, but it also greases the wheels of city life, creating refinery and transportation jobs, government positions, and a wave of other effects in the local community as the wages pass on to construction workers, shop owners, and schoolteachers. Without oil, Casper—Wyoming's second-largest metropolitan area—would be little more than a cattle town crossroads on the way to Yellowstone.

The Land

Geographically, central Wyoming is quite diverse. The north portion is an open, expansive place. Driving across the long, straight highways that divide this land is like sailing a boat over an ocean of gentle rollers—the mountains are so far in the distance that they could well be islands. Golden eagles spin giant loops in the sky, and the coal black clouds of distant summertime thunderheads are pierced by brilliant slashes of lightning. The wind blows on, bending the grass as it passes in waves of motion, whirling the old windmills that pump water to sheep, cattle, and deer. This is rolling mixed-grass prairie and sagebrush country, with sharp ridges appearing suddenly, topped by narrow bands of ponderosa pine and juniper.

South of this rangeland lies the North Platte River, carving a slow curve first north, then east, and finally southeast toward Nebraska. Giant dams hold back the water for irrigation and electricity. A green stripe of riparian forests and irrigated fields borders the river. South of the Platte, the land changes again, with the Laramie Mountains rising in a rough-edged jumble of rugged canyons and pine-covered peaks. Elk stand along mountain meadows, bugling in the cool air of late fall. Pickup trucks slow as wild turkeys speed-walk across the gravel roads. Clear mountain brooks cascade down mountain

slopes. West of here, central Wyoming becomes drier and more desolate, wrinkled by the badlands of Hell's Half Acre and the barren crests of desert mountain ranges.

Casper dominates the central Wyoming economy with oil refineries, the only statewide newspaper, and the state's largest junior college and shopping mall. The towns of Douglas and Glen-

rock go their own ways, with a mixture of ranching, oil, coal, and tourism. Farther north, the tiny settlements of Midwest and Edgerton cap the vast Salt Creek Oil Field. Between these few outposts of civilization lie hundreds of square miles of sagebrush and grass, jackrabbits, and rattlers. Only the scattered roads, oil pumpjacks, windmills, and old ranch houses mark the presence of humans.

DOUGLAS

Douglas (pop. 5,200) epitomizes life in small-town America. It's the sort of place where the big summertime events are the state fair and weekly drag races, where a night on the town means joining a bowling league or doing the two-step at the LaBonte Inn, and where men hang out in the Corner Barber Shop to talk politics, repairing next door to the historic College Inn Bar for a beer. On both ends of Douglas are more modern slices of Americana—suburban ranch-style homes cover the hills. It's a friendly, conservative town with pickup trucks, dense American food, and an unusual history.

HISTORY

Douglas came into existence with the arrival of the Fremont, Elkhorn, and Missouri Valley Railroad. Platted in 1886, the town was named for Stephen A. Douglas, the senator from Illinois best known for his debates with Abraham Lincoln. It quickly boomed to 1,600 people that first year, boasting three newspapers, several restaurants and hotels, two dance halls, 12 stores, and 21 saloons (easy to see where priorities lay). Once the railroad construction had moved

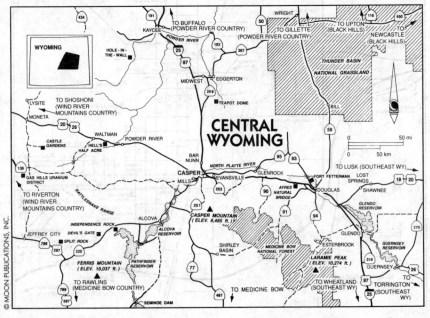

on down the line to Casper, the population dwindled and it became a sleepy little ranching center for the next 70 years. Only the late-summer state fair brought Douglas to life each year.

World War II

One of the strangest pieces of Douglas history is its prisoner-of-war camp, built in 1943 along the North Platte River. The camp contained 180 barracks-style buildings and housed up to 3,000 prisoners of war. The camp was surrounded by an electrified fence, watchtowers, German shepherds, and Army guards. One prisoner was shot by a guard and a few others escaped, but they

didn't get far in this remote country—2,000 miles from the sea. Though some of the prisoners at Douglas were German Nazi and SS officers, the majority were Italians, many of whom were happy to be away from the war.

The prisoners worked in local agricultural fields harvesting potatoes and sugar beets for $4 a day, or at a variety of art projects in the camp. Most impressive was the work of several Italian artists who painted the interior of the U.S. officers' club with 15 murals of Old West scenes. After the war, the prisoners returned home, though some have returned to visit in later years. The land was sold to Converse County for $1,

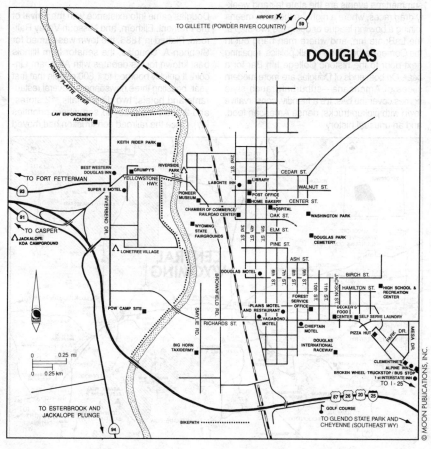

JACKALOPES

Definition: Jackalope—a mammal that moves by bounding, found originally in Converse County, Wyoming, but now distributed throughout the western states. It has the horns of an antelope, the body of a jackrabbit, and the stealth of both. First observed by trapper Roy Ball in 1829, the jackalope was later noted by cowboys and others after too little sleep, too many days in the saddle, and too much cheap whiskey. Nocturnal animals, jackalopes are never seen during the day. These powerful and vicious animals are reputed to attain speeds approaching 90 mph and often sing and mate during thunderstorms. The hornless does are commonly seen by tourists, while the bucks remain elusive. Westerners—particularly members of the militias—feel that the federal government is hushing up the true story of these dangerous critters to make cowboys look like liars.

Okay, I admit to liking plastic pink flamingos and tacky postcards, but jackalopes are another story. The first time you see a mounted jackalope specimen, it is mildly amusing, but with each tourist junk shop west of the Mississippi offering more jackalopes, the originality quickly fades. The town of Douglas takes credit for this harebrained idea, though its claim is a bit suspect. In the 1920s, a Douglas resident saw a jackalope mounted in a store in Buffalo, Wyoming. He described the creature to his grandson, Douglas Herrick, who was intrigued by the animal. In 1941, he attached the antlers of a deer to the head of a large jackrabbit he had shot and sold the specimen to the LaBonte Hotel. The rest is history. Douglas Herrick's son, Jim Herrick, follows in his father's footsteps, offering everything from fighting jackalopes to jackalope "love mounts" at Big Horn Taxidermy on Smylie Rd. (tel. 307-358-6523).

In 1960, the State of Wyoming gave the Douglas Chamber of Commerce "jackalope" as a registered trademark. Today you see jackalopes everywhere in Douglas: the town symbol contains one; an eight-foot-tall jackalope statue greets visitors at Jackalope Square; another statue has hopped atop the LaBonte Hotel; a roadside sign warns "Watch Out For Jackalope." You can buy cans of jackalope milk in the stores, "Rabbit Punch" at a local bar, and jackalope hunting licenses at several spots around town. And, of course, the critters multiply like rabbits on the shelves of local shops.

BOB RACE

and the barracks were dismantled or bought by locals who moved them to other parts of town. Today the POW camp site is an open meadow on the west bank of the North Platte south of Richards Street.

Boom and Bust
Like much of Wyoming, Douglas has watched its fortunes wax and wane over the years. In the 1950s, with the Cold War at fever pitch, prospectors combed Wyoming with Geiger counters, discovering major uranium deposits just north of Douglas. Others found oil, gas, and coal. A giant coal-fired power plant opened in nearby Glenrock, and by the late '70s the region was one of the most prosperous in the state. At the peak of the oil-and-uranium orgy of the early 1980s, the town of Douglas had doubled in size to over

10,000 people. But then the bust hit, and within a couple of years the population plummeted back to where it had been. Longtime locals had mixed feelings when the balloon suddenly burst—they were happy to see the rabble leave town but were also suddenly burdened with paying for all the new schools, roads, and other facilities ordered up in the heady heyday. Today, the economy of Douglas is back to its old mixture of energy and ranching, with some people commuting 60 miles each way to the busy coal mines near Wright while others work for the railroad or at a newly opened uranium mine northwest of town. Most folks are happy to live a simpler life. Of course, the next energy boom could be just around the corner.

SIGHTS

Pioneer Museum
The people of Douglas point with pride to their local museum, easily one of the finest in Wyoming. Located just inside the fairgrounds, the spacious and free museum, tel. (307) 358-9288, is open Mon.-Fri. 8 a.m.-5 p.m. and Saturday 1-5 p.m. (closed Sundays) June-September. After that it gets confusing: in April, May, and October the hours are Mon.-Fri. 8 a.m.-5 p.m.; in November, February, and March stop by on weekday afternoons. The museum is closed in December and January. The main room is filled with old rifles and saddles, including one that belonged to outlaw Tom Horn. Check out the special "running irons" used by rustlers to alter cattle brands. Fittingly enough, the rifle of Nate Champion—a rustler murdered in the Johnson County Wars—is also here. Above one doorway is a pole from the original transcontinental telegraph line; it's one of just six known to survive. Look around the other rooms and you'll discover the bison-fur mittens worn by Portugee Phillips on his ride to get help for Fort Kearny and an Army trumpet and bullets from the Custer battlefield.

The museum also contains hundreds of historic photos, a big doll collection, and a back room filled with impressive Indian artifacts including baskets, pottery, Sioux and Crow war clubs, a bow from the Custer battleground, and a tepee used in the movie Dances with Wolves. Downstairs are several wonderful old quilts and a collection of homestead items. The stairwell features the 64-inch-waist overalls that belonged to flamboyant C.B. Irwin, one of outlaw Tom Horn's closest friends. Irwin was a stockman, railroad detective, rodeo performer, and manager of Cheyenne Frontier Days. Outside is a schoolhouse constructed in 1886.

Douglas Railroad Interpretive Center
This in-progress center consists of seven train cars located outside the old Chicago Elk Horn Railroad depot (built in 1888 and now home to the chamber of commerce). The collection includes a steam locomotive, a dining car, a sleeper, a baggage car, a coach, a cattle car, and a caboose. They represent many different eras—the oldest is the 1884 caboose. A visitor center is still in the planning stages, but tours are available during the summer; see the chamber of commerce for details.

More Sights
The old officers' club from the Douglas POW camp is now an Odd Fellows Hall at 115 S. Riverbend Dr., tel. (307) 358-2421. Ask to take a look inside at the wall-to-wall murals painted by Italian artists who were prisoners during WW II. One of Wyoming's oldest churches is the Christ Episcopal Church, built in 1896 and now on the National Register of Historic Places. The attractive white structure is located at 411 Center, tel. (307) 358-5609. The Plains Complex, 628 E. Richards, tel. (307) 358-4489, has several historic structures hauled in from all over this part of Wyoming. Included are the old officers' quarters from Fort Fetterman and a POW-camp building. The ice-cream parlor served at various times as a barn, a boardinghouse, and a maternity center. Check out the doors on the ceiling of the ice-cream shop. The Douglas Park Cemetery, on the east end of Pine Street, has a number of interesting old graves, including that of horsethief and later saloon-keeper "Doc" Middleton. Also here is the grave of the outlaw George W. Pike, whose exploits managed to lead to at least two appearances in court annually for 15 consecutive years. His gravestone reads:

Underneath this stone in eternal rest
Sleeps the wildest one of the wayward
west
He was gambler and sport and cowboy
too

And he led the pace in an outlaw crew.
He was sure on the trigger and staid to
the end
But he was never known to quit on a
friend
In the relations of death all mankind is
alike
But in life there was only one
George W. Pike.

PRACTICALITIES

Accommodations

You have more than a dozen lodgings to choose from in Douglas; see the accommodations chart for specifics. In July and August you should book motel reservations up to two months ahead—especially for the weekend drag races

and state fair week. Several locals rent out rooms in their homes to visitors while the fair is going on; get a list from the chamber of commerce, tel. (307) 358-2950. More than a century old, **Carriage House B&B,** tel. (307) 358-2752, was originally built as a barn, then remodeled into a home in the 1950s. It offers three inexpensive guest rooms with private or shared baths.

Guest Ranches

Wagonhound Ranch B&B, tel. (307) 358-5439, is a working cattle ranch covering 16,000 acres of country in the foothills of the Laramie Mountains. Although primarily a guest ranch where folks stay for a week or more ($840 per person a week all inclusive), the ranch also has nightly rates and B&B accommodations. Lodging is in modern suites with fireplaces, whirlpool tubs, and wraparound decks overlooking a creek, or in

---

DOUGLAS ACCOMMODATIONS

Note: Accommodations are listed from least to most expensive. Rates may be considerably cheaper in the off-season, and higher during the state fair. Add a seven percent tax to these rates. Area code is 307.

Plains Motel; 628 E. Richards; tel. 358-4484; $24 s, $26 d; kitchenettes $2 extra, plain rooms

Vagabond Motel; 430 Richards; tel. 358-9414; $24 s, $26-32 d; basic, but clean and friendly

Four Winds Motel; 615 Richards; tel. 358-2322; $26 s, $28-38 d; heavy on the Christianity

First Interstate Inn; 2349 E. Richards; tel. 358-2833; $32 s, $39 d; AAA approved

Chieftain Motel; 815 Richards; tel. 358-2673; $34 s, $39-43 d; large rooms, AAA approved

Alpine Inn; 2310 E. Richards; tel. 358-4780; $35 s, $40 d; friendly

LaBonte Inn; 206 Walnut; tel. 358-9856; $38 s or d; can be noisy at night

Super 8 Motel; 314 Russell Ave.; tel. 358-6800 or (800) 800-8000; $38 s, $45 d; AAA approved

Carriage House B&B; 413 Center St.; tel. 358-2752; $40 s, $45 d; historic home, three guest rooms, private or shared baths, continental breakfast, kids welcome

Deer Forks Ranch; 24 miles southwest of Douglas; tel. 358-2033; $40 s, $80 d in guesthouse; $50 s, $100 d with full breakfast; two-night minimum stay, private baths, weekly rates available

Wagonhound Ranch B&B; 22 miles southwest of Douglas; tel. 358-5439; $50 s, $75 d with full breakfast; $140 pp/day with three meals and horseback rides; 16,000-acre cattle ranch, shared or private baths, weekly rates available, open May-Sept.

Best Western Douglas Inn; 1450 Riverbend Dr.; tel. 358-9790 or (800) 344-2113; $70 s, $78 d; indoor pool, jacuzzi, sauna, weight room

Cheyenne River Ranch; 50 miles northeast of Douglas off Hwy. 59; tel. 358-2380; $125 pp/day for adults, $80 pp/day for kids; working cattle ranch, full breakfasts, three-day minimum stay, outdoor pool, open May-Oct., AAA approved

a three-room home (for B&B guests only). Archaeological excavations are ongoing at an 8,300-year-old site here, and guests can take part in short cattle drives or fish in nearby ponds and creeks. Open May-Sept., with accommodations for a maximum of 12 guests.

Deer Forks Ranch, 24 miles south of Douglas, tel. (307) 358-2033, provides a fine chance to join in horseback riding and other activities on a working cattle and sheep ranch. It's a long ways out here and the road gets muddy when it rains, but the Laramie Mountain backdrop and friendly downhome owners make this a fun place. Guests stay in modern houses with kitchens or in the old ranch house and can ride horses ($30 per person per day extra) or simply relax in the country. The ranch also has RV hookups ($20) and a variety of weekly rates. They have a second ranch located in the rolling grasslands 25 miles east of Bill.

An excellent place to experience ranch life is **Cheyenne River Ranch,** tel. (307) 358-2380, 50 miles northeast of Douglas. This 8,000-acre working cattle and sheep ranch offers bed and breakfast accommodations as well as more traditional dude ranch stays. Guests get a chance to go on trail rides, feed orphan lambs, gather eggs, or simply sit back and relax in the country. Recommended.

Two Creek Ranch, tel. (307) 358-3467, is a 25,000-acre spread located eight miles south of Douglas. The place runs 600 cows with their calves over this land and takes on working dudes May-October. Guests ride horseback while helping out in calving, 75-mile cattle drives, branding, roundups, and other activities on the ranch. Prices are around $100 per person per night all inclusive, and last three to 11 days. This is the real thing, with guests sharing the home or bunkhouse; no hot tubs or swimming pools here.

Camping

Pitch tents or park RVs for free at **Riverside Park** along the North Platte River. The free showers have an amusing Western-decor bathroom covered with "branded" wood. Camping is limited to two nights, and the sprinklers come on at 8 a.m., so get up early! Two nearby camping places—Ayres Natural Bridge Park and the Laramie Mountains—are described under "Dou-

glas Vicinity," below. The RV crowd heads to **Jackalope KOA,** tel. (307) 358-2164 or (800) 562-2469, west of Douglas on State Hwy. 91. Rates are $15 for tents, $19 for RVs; open mid-March through October. **Lonetree Village Mobile Home Park,** 1 Lonetree Dr., tel. (307) 358-6669, also has RV parking for $10. During the state fair, camping is available on the fairgrounds; call (307) 358-2398 for specifics.

Food

With a few exceptions, restaurant food in Douglas is pretty standard Wyoming fare. For dependable food and big portions three downhome meals a day, you won't go wrong at **LaBonte Inn,** 206 Walnut St., tel. (307) 358-9856. Very good pies, too. The **Broken Wheel Truckstop,** just east of town, tel. (307) 358-4446, serves breakfast 24 hours a day. **Clementine's,** 1199 Mesa Dr., tel. (307) 358-5554, has all-you-can-eat lunch specials, steak and prime rib, pizza, and Mexican food served in a pleasant atmosphere. **Pizza Hut,** 1830 Richards, tel. (307) 358-3657, also has stuff-yourself lunch specials.

The **Plains Complex,** 628 E. Richards, tel. (307) 358-4489, has a so-so coffee shop (open 24 hours) and an old-fashioned ice-cream parlor. The best lunch spot in town is **Thru-the-Grapevine Coffee Co.,** 301 Center St., tel. (307) 358-4567, with homemade soup served in a breadbowl, sandwiches, salads, sweets, and espresso coffees.

Gilly's Supper Club, in the American Legion hall at 6th and Oak, tel. (307) 358-2317, is the fanciest place in town with good steak, a small salad bar, and classy decor. **Chute's Eatery,** in the Best Western, 1450 Riverbend Dr., tel. (307) 358-9790, has a soup and salad buffet and an all-you-can-eat Sunday brunch. The quality is variable. Get reasonable and tasty Mexican fare from **Santa Fe Cafe,** 1954 Richards St., tel. (307) 358-5933. Douglas also has the standard along-the-highway fare, including McDonald's, Arby's, Subway, Pizza Hut, and Kentucky Fried Chicken.

Douglas has three grocery stores: **Peyton Bolln Grocery,** 100 S. 3rd, **Decker Food Center,** 1100 Richards, and **Safeway,** 130 S. 4th. For fresh-baked pastries, head to **Home Bakery,** 119 N. 3rd, tel. (307) 358-9251.

Recreation

The **Douglas Recreation Center** at the high school 1701 Hamilton, tel. (307) 358-9750, houses, gyms, racquetball courts, and a weight room. A new **outdoor swimming pool** ($3 for adults, $2 for kids; open June-Aug.) is in Washington Park. Seven miles south of Douglas on Esterbrook Rd. (State 94) is **Jackalope Plunge Swimming Pool,** tel. (307) 358-2820, fed by the 86° F water of Douglas Warm Spring. No chlorine. This is a fun place to play volleyball, enjoy a picnic, or practice your diving. Entrance is $3 for adults, $2 ages under 12. It's open Memorial Day through Labor Day, closed the rest of the year. A couple of miles south of Jackalope Plunge, you can see ruts of the old Oregon Trail; ask at the chamber of commerce for directions.

An 18-hole **golf course,** tel. (307) 358-5099, is southeast of Douglas. (There are no sand traps here—the fierce winter winds kept blowing them away.) **Riverside Park,** along the western bank of the North Platte River, contains a two-mile-long paved bike path that makes for a pleasant evening stroll. Take along your fishing pole to try for trout, walleye, or channel catfish. If you have your own raft or canoe, the river provides pleasant, leisurely float trips; pick up a map of river access points from the chamber of commerce.

Entertainment

Chutes Lounge in the Best Western Douglas Inn, 1450 Riverbend Dr., tel. (307) 358-9790, has lounge-lizard tunes, a big-screen TV, and free hors d'oeuvres on weeknights. **LaBonte Lounge,** 206 Walnut, tel. (307) 358-5210, is the place for weekend bands. More country two-stepping takes place occasionally at the **Plains Complex,** 628 E. Richards, tel. (307) 358-4489. Farther afield, you can dance on summer weekends at **Esterbrook Lodge,** 32 miles south of Douglas. The historic **College Inn Bar,** 103 N. 2nd, tel. (307) 358-9976, is a favorite place for major-league drinking with the locals. Drop by on Wednesday nights for 50-cent draft beers. For movies, head to **Mesa Theatre,** 104 N. 3rd St., tel. (307) 358-6209.

Wyoming State Fair

In 1905, the Wyoming Legislature appropriated $10,000 for a Wyoming State Fair in Douglas. With land donated by the Chicago and North-western Railroad, the "Show Window of Wyoming" opened that summer, offering a variety of agricultural exhibits, horseback wrestling, Roman races, and concerts. To top it off, two cavalry soldiers added their own drama by putting on an impromptu gunfight. Later, auto polo and motorcycle-riding events were added, but the big hit was Professor Carver's High Diving Girl, who leapt with her horse off a 40-foot platform into a pool of water.

The Wyoming State Fair is held the entire third week of August each year, drawing thousands of visitors from all over the nation. The 113-acre fairgrounds is right next to town and includes a 4,300-seat grandstand, an arts-and-crafts building, a cafeteria, an arena, an open-air pavilion, livestock barns and stalls, and, of course, plenty of carnival rides, cotton candy, and stuffed-animal prizes in the midway. Keep yourself entertained at the market swine evaluation, the 4-H vegetable judging, the demolition derby, or the sheep-to-shawl contest. A free "people shuttle" (tractor-pulled wagon) takes folks around the fairgrounds. Other attractions include evening country-western concerts, the Miss Rodeo Wyoming contest, and a Saturday morning parade. Since this is Wyoming, the biggest events at the fair are the **PRCA rodeos** held the final three days.

Other Events

Both locals and visitors enjoy the **High Plains Oldtime Country Music Show & Contest** held in mid-April. Plenty of hot fiddle, guitar, and banjo players provide the entertainment. On the third weekend of June, **Jackalope Days** offers a street dance and beer garden, games, arts and crafts, bed races, and live music. The **Wyoming High School Rodeo Finals** take place that same weekend. **Fort Fetterman Days,** held the second weekend of July at the old fort, attracts a troop of soldiers and other period-attired folks for a festival featuring blackpowder contests, old-time music, folklore, crafts, living-history demonstrations, and games. The first weekend of August brings in a very popular **Senior Pro Rodeo.** All summer long, the grandiosely named Douglas International Raceway on the southeast edge of town hosts **drag races** of all types. Located on an old airport runway, it's considered one of the top quarter-mile strips in the nation. The biggest races come

in mid-July. In early August Douglas plays host to hundreds of motorcycle enthusiasts en route to the Sturgis Rally with a variety of hospitality tents and facilities.

Information and Services

The **Douglas Area Chamber of Commerce** is inside the old train depot at 121 Brownfield, tel. (307) 358-2950. Open Mon.-Fri. 9 a.m.-noon and 1-4 p.m. all year. Other services of note are the **Converse County Library**, 300 Walnut St., tel. (307) 358-3644, the **post office** at 129 N. 3rd St., tel. (307) 358-3106, and **ATMs** in the Converse County Bank, 322 Walnut St., and Key Bank, 240 S. 4th Street. **R-D Pharma-**

cy, 206 Center, tel. (307) 358-3266, sells Wyoming books. Visit the **Meadowlark Gallery** at 300 S. 4th St., tel. (307) 358-3808, for local arts and crafts. The Forest Service's **Douglas Ranger District Office,** 809 S. 9th St., tel. (307) 358-4690, has maps and info on both Medicine Bow National Forest and Thunder Basin National Grassland. Open Mon.-Fri. 7:30 a.m.-4:30 p.m.

Powder River Trailways, tel. (800) 442-3682, has daily bus service from Douglas to towns in northern and central Wyoming, continuing north to Billings or Rapid City and south to Cheyenne or Denver. Buses stop at The Plains Motel, 628 E. Richards.

DOUGLAS VICINITY

FORT FETTERMAN

Seven miles northwest of Douglas on State 93 is Fort Fetterman State Historic Site. The fort was named for Lt. Col. William J. Fetterman, who was killed by Indians in the Fetterman Massacre of 1866 (see the section on "Powder River Country"). Begun in 1867, this was the last fort built in the Rockies. With the signing of the Fort Laramie Treaty of 1868, Forts Casper, Reno, Phil Kearny, and C.F. Smith were all closed, leaving Fort Fetterman the only Army base in northern Wyoming. The hilltop location afforded commanding views along the infamous Bozeman Trail in both directions, but the location proved inhospitable. A report to headquarters the first winter noted "officers and men were found under canvas exposed on a bleak plain to violent and almost constant gales and very uncomfortable." Even after the buildings were completed the fort remained a dreaded, windswept, lonely place, and many soldiers deserted as soon as they could get to the nearest railroad. The regimen was strict, with daily parade drills and the prospect of long rides to fight Indians in the surrounding country. Soldiers called the place "Hell Hole," while the Sioux derisively labeled it "Fort Fetterman Reservation." Not far away stood the "Hog Ranch"—sin city on the plains—where gambling, drinking, and women offered a choice of ways to spend the $13 a month the calvarymen received.

Fort Fetterman served as a supply base for the Army during the mid-1870s, and both General Crook and Colonel MacKenzie led expeditions from here to attack the Sioux, but the fort itself was never the scene of any conflicts. After the battles had finally died down, the fort was abandoned in 1882. Instead of immediately disappearing, however, "Fetterman City" became the center of ranching and trade in the area. For a while, at least, it was a wide-open town with enough gunfights, hangings, whoring, gambling, and drunkenness to give *Miami Vice* a run for the money. In his novel *The Virginian,* Owen Wister used Fetterman as the basis for his rough-and-tumble town of "Drybone."

Alferd Packer

One of the characters attracted to Fetterman was a prospector who called himself John Swartz. When a waiter was slow in bringing water to his table at a local restaurant, he pulled a gun, saying, "Damn you, ain't you going to bring me that water?" Service quickly improved. The man turned out to be Alferd Packer, wanted for robbing, killing, and then eating his five mining partners in Colorado during the winter of 1875. (Packer called human breast meat the sweetest he'd ever eaten.) After escaping from a Colorado jail, he remained free for the next decade before finally being recognized in Fetterman City. The sheriff captured him at a nearby ranch and spent several nervous nights on

the long stage ride to Rock Creek before finally turning Packer over to Colorado authorities. Although convicted of murder, Packer managed to escape from prison again; his body was found in the Rockies in 1903.

The Fort Today

After the railroad arrived in 1886, Douglas became the new center for trade, and Fetterman quickly faded from the scene. Most of the buildings were torn down or moved to Douglas; only two of the original buildings remain: an adobe ordinance warehouse and a log officers' quarters. Inside the officers' quarters is a small state-run **museum** (free) which includes historic displays on the fort, Indian battles, and Fetterman City. The buildings are open daily 9 a.m.-5 p.m. from Memorial Day to Labor Day, by appointment only (tel. 307-358-2864) the rest of the year. Entrance is $2 per car. You can visit the grounds at any time. The surrounding country still exudes a sense of barren loneliness, and it's easy to see how much the soldiers must have hated this windswept post. Ask the museum staff to point out the faint tracks of the "Bloody Bozeman" Trail to the south.

Fort Fetterman Days, the second weekend of July, brings military demonstrations, Indian dancing, the firing of artillery pieces, old-time music, crafts, and games. Many of the participants dress in authentic 1870s costume.

THUNDER BASIN NATIONAL GRASSLAND AND VICINITY

Thunder Basin National Grassland is an expansive blend of high rolling plateaus, steep rocky escarpments, and gentle plains. It's one of the few places in Wyoming where mountain ranges are not visible, giving the countryside a North Dakota feel. The country seems to reach forever with virtually no traffic on some of the main routes across the grassland, especially State 450 between Wright and Newcastle. Most of the national grassland is covered with a mixture of western wheatgrass, blue grama grass, and big sagebrush, but some of the ridges have stands of ponderosa pine and juniper, while creek bottoms contain cottonwood trees or greasewood. Naturalists count 170 golden-eagle

nests on Thunder Basin—one of the biggest concentrations in Wyoming—along with abundant populations of sandhill cranes, turkeys, antelope, mule deer, elk, and coyotes. Many bald eagles winter here. Look out for the jackalopes, too; lots of the antlerless variety get hit by cars.

Thunder Basin National Grassland covers 1.8 million acres within Powder River Basin. The land is a checkerboard of private ranches and property belonging to the Forest Service, the BLM, and the state. The federal government owns 572,000 acres of the total, managed from the Forest Service office in Douglas. Get a copy of the detailed Thunder Basin map there for $3.

History

Thunder Basin came about during the glory days of the New Deal and remains today an enclave of pseudosocialism within the rock-ribbed Republican state of Wyoming. Although ranchers had grazed sheep and cattle in the area since the mid-19th century, the arrival of homesteaders caused the land to be divided into smaller parcels. In the arid mixed-grass prairies of eastern Wyoming, it was nearly impossible for a family to survive—the rains fell too infrequently for farming, and profitable cattle or sheep operations required more than 640 acres of grazing land.

Overgrazing, soil erosion, and five consecutive drought years in the 1930s combined to force many families off the land. Counties risked bankruptcy because of lost tax revenue. The Agricultural Adjustment Administration finally began purchasing homesteads in 1934, giving money to the counties in lieu of taxes. Programs were begun to reestablish grasses to protect the soil and to develop water sources for livestock, while private land ownership was consolidated into larger, more economically manageable units.

Management

Today, local ranchers use the grassland in a cooperative grazing scheme that allows 21,000 cattle and an equal number of sheep on the federal land. Improvements such as dams, wells, and fences are cooperatively developed. In addition to livestock grazing, practically every acre of Thunder Basin has been leased for petroleum

PRAIRIE DOGS

Prairie dogs are cat-sized rodents that live in underground communities and feed on roots and plants. Prairie-dog towns sometimes cover thousands of acres (a Texas colony was once 100 miles long and 250 miles wide), with burrow holes spaced every 50 feet or so. Two species dwell in Wyoming: white-tailed and black-tailed. The latter are found in at least 135 towns covering more than 16,000 acres within Thunder Basin National Grassland, while white-tailed prairie dogs are found in south-central and western Wyoming. Ranchers often complain of lost grazing range due to feeding and digging by the dogs and injuries to horses and cattle that step into the holes. Because of this, the Forest Service for many years systematically poisoned prairie-dog colonies for "range improvement." These practices devastated the population. At the turn of the century they occupied 700 million acres of western grasslands; today it is down to just two million acres.

Sightings of the endangered black-footed ferret on the national grassland helped end most of the poisoning in the 1970s, and prairie-dog populations have rebounded dramatically. Unfortunately, the Forest Service continues its poisoning program in some places. In addition, because prairie dogs are still considered varmints, "sport" hunters aren't limited on how many they can shoot—and they don't need a license. Meanwhile, the U.S. Fish & Wildlife Service is raising a covey of once-wild ferrets at a Sybille Canyon facility, hoping to someday return them to such places as the national grassland (see

the special topic "Black-Footed Ferret" in the Southeast Wyoming chapter for more). By trying to contain the prairie-dog population to small and fragmented areas, the hunters, Forest Service, and private ranchers may well be endangering the long-term survival of the black-footed ferret, one of the world's rarest mammals.

If you're interested in seeing prairie dogs, ask at the Douglas Forest Service office for a copy of their prairie-dog-town map. The largest area—covering at least eight square miles—is along Horse Creek in the Rochelle Hills. Smaller prairie-dog colonies lie along North Antelope Road. Use caution if you are hiking around prairie-dog colonies since the dogs are sometimes infected with the plague bacteria, cause of Europe's infamous "black death" in the 1300s. Fleas carry the disease, which is potentially deadly but relatively easy to halt with antibiotics.

BOB RACE

---

exploration. Currently, over 375 oil and gas wells pump from 58 oil fields. Vast deposits of subbituminous coal underlie almost the entire area, and there are six gigantic strip mines, including Black Thunder Coal Mine, the largest coal producer in the nation. Revenues from oil and coal development on the grassland come to nearly $25 million a year for the federal treasury (and severance taxes for the state of Wyoming), a figure unmatched anywhere else in the Forest Service system. Bentonite—a lubricant and absorptive clay used in everything from oil-drilling muds to candy bars—is also mined on the grassland, and major uranium deposits wait for the public to forget about Three Mile Island and Chernobyl.

Recreation

A network of over 775 miles of gravel and dirt roads crisscrosses Thunder Basin National Grassland, but you'll look in vain for developed trails, campgrounds, or other facilities. You may, however, camp for free anywhere on the public lands. A couple of areas are popular with hunters, birdwatchers, photographers, and others looking for a chance to get out and about.

The **Rochelle Hills** area, a forested volcanic escarpment near the corner of Converse, Campbell, and Weston counties, is one of the prettiest parts of the national grassland, though a recent fire has blackened some of the trees. A scenic gravel road takes you on a long loop north of the tiny settlement of **Bill** (the name

came from four early homesteaders, all of whom had the same first name) and then for 50 miles through the Rochelle Hills before dropping back to State 59 eight miles south of Wright. The Forest Service office in Douglas has an informative pamphlet describing the Rochelle Hills route. The Upton-Osage area also contains miles of ponderosa-pine-topped hills and many small ponds that attract birds. Another fascinating area is in the northern part of the grassland in the Soda Well/Weston area (30 miles north of Gillette on State 59). This is a fine place to camp or explore; see the Forest Service for access details.

Because of the patchwork quilt of land ownership on the grassland, many federal parcels are accessible only across private property, and you may need to get permission from the landowners first. Land ownership is changing now as the Forest Service attempts to consolidate its acreage to make it easier to manage; check with the service for current ownership. As with much of Wyoming's rangelands, you should be on guard for prairie rattlesnakes, especially around rockpiles and prairie-dog towns. Also, beware of thunderstorms and the lightning that can strike in this open country—this isn't called Thunder Basin for nothing. Because of the lack of drinking-water sources, carry plenty with you in your travels.

LARAMIE MOUNTAINS

The Laramie Peak portion of Medicine Bow National Forest lies approximately 30 miles south of Douglas, cutting from northwest to southeast along the Laramie Mountains. The mountains are draped with stands of ponderosa, lodgepole, and limber pine, and Engelmann spruce and subalpine fir at higher elevations. Lower elevations are dominated by grass and sagebrush. It's pretty but rugged country, with deep valleys dividing the high granitic ridges and peaks—several exceeding 9,000 feet. Deer, elk, antelope, and wild turkeys are commonly seen in the Laramie Mountains, and rainbow, brook, and brown trout are found in the creeks. Public and private lands intermingle here, with only a few large tracts of Forest Service property—the biggest being around Laramie Peak.

This impressive mountain, clearly visible from Douglas, served as a landmark for travelers along the old Oregon Trail, who called this country the Black Hills. There is some logging around Esterbrook and Albany Peak, especially in insect-killed forests, but Laramie Peak is de facto wilderness. The Medicine Bow National Forest **Douglas Ranger District Office** at 809 S. 9th St., tel. (307) 358-4690, has maps ($3) and additional information.

Esterbrook

The Esterbrook area, 32 scenic miles south of Douglas on State 94, began as a copper-mining town in 1886 but never really had much to show for its effort. Esterbrook is famed for an **old log church,** whose rear window frames snow-capped Laramie Peak. It's a very popular place for weddings. A fine campground (free; open June to mid-October) is close by, as is **Esterbrook Lodge,** offering small and very rustic cabins, RV hookups, a restaurant, and a bar with live music on summertime weekends. There's free camping at three other small Forest Service campgrounds (open June to mid-October) in the Laramie Mountains; see the map for access. The **Esterbrook Rendezvous** takes place in early August with a black powder shoot, live music, hayrides, food and craft booths, and a barbecue.

Hiking

Some of the finest hiking in central Wyoming is found along the **Laramie Peak Trail,** a five-mile (one-way) path that climbs to the top of the 10,272-foot peak. The trail begins right behind Friend Park Campground, 48 miles south of Douglas (via a rough gravel road). The first mile is relatively easy as the trail parallels Friend Creek, but after this it's a long, arduous climb. Two miles from the start is a pretty cascade; fill your water bottles here if you're hiking in late summer (water can be hard to find above this point). Periodic forest openings offer dramatic vistas as you continue up the mountain, gaining 2,800 feet along the way. On top find expansive vistas in all directions—including into Nebraska, Colorado, and South Dakota on a clear day. Communication buildings and towers are also here. The trail is generally free of snow by late June.

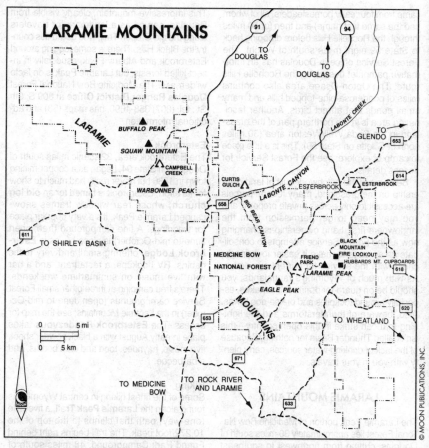

LARAMIE MOUNTAINS

TO DOUGLAS

91

TO DOUGLAS

94

TO GLENDO

653

LARAMIE

BUFFALO PEAK

SQUAW MOUNTAIN

CAMPBELL CREEK

WARBONNET PEAK

CURTIS GULCH

LABONTE CANYON

ESTERBROOK

ESTERBROOK

614

658

BIG BEAR CANYON

MEDICINE BOW

NATIONAL FOREST

611

TO SHIRLEY BASIN

BLACK MOUNTAIN FIRE LOOKOUT

HUBBARDS MT. CUPBOARDS

FRIEND PARK

LARAMIE PEAK

518

EAGLE PEAK

LARAMIE

MOUNTAINS

TO WHEATLAND

620

653

671

0 5 mi

0 5 km

TO MEDICINE BOW

TO ROCK RIVER AND LARAMIE

633

© MOON PUBLICATIONS, INC.

The two-mile-long **La Bonte Creek Trail** offers both pleasant hiking and good fishing for brook trout. The trailhead is at Curtis Gulch Campground, 38 miles south of Douglas. The path drops down a gorgeous steep-walled canyon (keep your eyes open for bighorn sheep and elk) and ends at a big-game refuge. Along the way are meadows, forests of poplar and Douglas fir, and flowers galore. Also near the Curtis Gulch Campground is a 4WD road/hiking trail that climbs for three miles up **Big Bear Canyon** to scenic Devils Pass.

Another good climb is up the 4WD road to **Black Mountain Lookout,** one of the last operating fire towers in Wyoming, open June-

September. You'll find great views down pristine Ashenfelder Creek. Get there by following Forest Road 633 south of Esterbrook Campground for six miles to the Laramie Peak Scout Camp. The 4WD road is just beyond this on the right.

The **North Laramie River Trail** starts approximately 20 miles west of Wheatland and descends for 3.5 miles into the North Laramie River Canyon, losing 1,000 feet in elevation along the way. There's good fishing in the river, and the remains of 15 buildings from a 1920s resort are fun to explore. Get to the trailhead by taking the El Rancho Exit from I-25 (between Glendo and Wheatland) and heading west on

Fish Creek Road to Fletcher Park Road. Continue on past Camp Grace to the intersection of Fletcher Park and Cow Camp Roads, where signs point the route to the trailhead.

Sunset Ridge Trail is a short 1.6-mile climb to a scenic view over the plains to the east. It originates from the Esterbrook Campground and gains 400 feet along the way before looping back down the hill.

Winter Recreation

Wintertime snow closes all roads over the Laramie Mountains, transforming the mountains into an excellent place for cross-country skiing, with many miles of scenic country and untracked snow. Over 20 miles of groomed trails surround the Esterbrook area, used primarily by snowmobilers, but also by skiers. A warming hut is also here. Pick up a map of snowmobile/ski trails from the Douglas ranger station.

AYRES NATURAL BRIDGE PARK

One of the most unusual geological formations in Wyoming lies 14 miles west of Douglas on I-25. Take Exit 151 and continue five miles south to tiny, 22-acre Ayres Natural Bridge Park, where the main attraction is a 100-foot-long, 50-foot-high rock arch over LaPrele Creek. This natural arch was formed when a meander bend in LaPrele Creek gradually eroded the base of the rock face, leaving the upper part of the cliff unscathed. Eventually the weakened rock gave way, and the creek flowed through the hole that had been created at the bend. The ancient creek bed is 300 feet away from the present creek and 50 feet higher.

History

For the Indians who first lived in this country, the natural bridge was a deadly place. A young brave had been struck by lightning and killed while hunting in the canyon; thus began a legend that an evil spirit lived below the bridge, ready to grab anyone who ventured into his lair. When white settlers realized this, they used the natural bridge as a place to escape from Indian attacks, knowing they would not be pursued across the arch. Early-day mountain men lived in caves here, and Mormon settlers built cabins nearby in the 1850s. It took an expedition by Dr. Ferdinand V. Hayden, director of the U.S. Geological Survey in 1869, to bring the rock arch to national attention. He found it odd "that so great a natural curiosity should have failed to attract the attention it deserves." In 1881, Alva Ayres bought the land and used the lush LaPrele Creek country as headquarters for a freighting business. The natural bridge and surrounding land were donated to Converse County in 1920 by Ayres' heirs.

Seeing the Bridge

Today, Ayres Natural Bridge offers a surprisingly beautiful side trip from I-25. Box elders and cottonwoods line LaPrele Creek, fluorescent green patches against the brilliant red sandstone and the rich blue sky. Along one face of the red-walled amphitheater that circles the park are carved the names of many visitors, some dating from the 1880s. This is a popular weekend picnic and swimming spot and a great place to watch birds or spend a quiet night at the small free **campground** (three-day limit). Ayres Natural Bridge Park is open daily 8 a.m.-8 p.m. April-October. A gate blocks the road during the winter, but you can walk in the last half mile. Call caretaker Ray Morton at (307) 358-3532 for more information.

GLENROCK

The podunk cattle-and-coal town of Glenrock (pop. 2,400) lies halfway between Casper and Douglas at the confluence of Deer Creek and the North Platte River. The town's name comes from Rock in the Glen, a large rocky outcrop just to the west. Deer Creek was a favorite camping spot along the Oregon Trail, a place to rest up, do a little fishing, and let the stock graze on the lush creekside grass. Starting in 1847, Mormon emigrants mined the coal visible along the north bank of the river; this proved to be the first coal mined in Wyoming. The first bridge to span the North Platte was built here in 1851 but was washed out in a flood the following year. Deer Creek Station was established in the 1850s, operating first as a trading post and later

as a relay terminal for the Overland Stage and a home station for the short-lived Pony Express. Later, when telegraph wires replaced the Pony Express, Deer Creek became a telegraph relay station. Indians burned the station to the ground in 1866 and it was never rebuilt.

Boom and Bust

Around the turn of the century, several underground coal mines opened, transforming the quiet settlement of Glenrock into a raucous mining town. They closed in 1916, just as oil was discovered west of Glenrock. Some 5,000 oil workers flooded the town along with a raft of less-honorable professionals. Two oil refineries were built, fed by 200 Big Muddy oil wells. One refinery closed in the 1920s and the other in the '50s. More oil was found in 1949 and again in 1973, leading to temporary booms. The massive coal-fired Dave Johnston Power Plant became one of the largest local employers when it opened in 1958, and the discovery of uranium 25 miles northeast of Glenrock attracted hundreds of people to the area when several large uranium mines opened. In the late 1980s the mines began to shut down, and Glenrock has experienced hard times. Downtown shows this decline in a number of boarded-up old storefronts.

Sights

Rock in the Glen, a half-mile west of Glenrock, has the carved names of a few of the 19th-century emigrants who passed by on the way to Oregon, California, or Utah. Several **graves** from this era are scattered around Glenrock, sad reminders of the thousands who never made it. One is that of A.H. Unthank, just east of the Dave Johnston Power Plant on Tank Farm Rd., who died of cholera just a week after carving his name in Register Cliffs near present-day Guernsey. Four miles west of town is the grave of Ada Magill, a young girl who died of dysentery in 1864 as her parents headed west in a wagon train. Stones were piled on top of the grave to keep wolves from digging up her body.

Glenrock City Park has a granite monument to **Dr. Ferdinand V. Hayden,** a physician who devoted his life to exploration of the West. Hayden helped found the U.S. Geological Survey and led the famed Hayden Yellowstone Expedition of 1870. The Indians considered Hayden a bit

wacky, calling him "Man-who-picks-up-stones-running." Hayden used the Deer Creek Station at present-day Glenrock as a base of operations for several of his expeditions around Wyoming, hence the monument—placed here in 1931 by his photographic partner on these trips, William H. Jackson.

The country around Glenrock is laced with energy projects of all types. Immediately west of town is the Big Muddy oil field, where more than 2.6 million barrels have been pumped out over the last 40 years. The giant **Dave Johnston Power Plant** is six miles east of Glenrock along the North Platte River. It's one of the largest coal-fired power plants in the Rockies, generating 810,000 kilowatts of electricity for the Pacific Northwest. A private railroad feeds the plant with coal from the Glenrock Coal strip mine 16 miles to the north.

Accommodations

Glenrock has two motels, a B&B, and a wonderful old hotel. **All American Inn,** 500 W. Aspen, tel. (307) 436-2772, has rooms starting at $26 s, $29 d. **Glenrock Motel,** 108 S. 3rd, tel. (307) 436-2722, charges $22 s, $26 d and up. **Hotel Higgins,** 416 W. Birch, tel. (307) 436-9212 or (800) 458-0144, is plain vanilla on the outside—red asbestos shingles on a building built in 1916—but the inside is a pleasant surprise. The entire hotel has been lovingly furnished with antique brass beds, wardrobes, lamps, and a ticking old grandfather clock. Rooms cost $46 s, $60-70 d including a full breakfast. For a taste of Western hospitality, stay just out of town at **Opal's Bed & Breakfast,** tel. (307) 436-2626. Rates are $40 s, $50 d including a full breakfast. The B&B has three guest rooms with private or shared bath.

Camping

Camping is free at **South Recreation Complex,** three miles south of Glenrock along the river. **Deer Creek RV Park,** on the east end of town, tel. (307) 436-8121, is open mid-April through October. Tent sites cost $8, RVs $14. Showers for noncampers are $3.

Food and Entertainment

The owners of the Higgins Hotel also run a fine gourmet restaurant here, **The Paisley Shawl,**

named after the delicate old·Scottish shawl—a family heirloom—in the dining room. The restaurant (open Tues.-Sat. only) has a statewide reputation for its lunches and its prime-rib, steak, and veal dinners. Unfortunately, the restaurant gets quite smokey sometimes. Get pizza at **Classic Cafe & Pizza,** 201 S. 4th, tel. (307) 436-2244. Other Glenrock eating establishments are **Four Aces Supper Club,** 316 W. Birch, tel. (307) 436-9010, and **Fort Diablo Steak House & Saloon.** tel. (307) 436-2288. Get groceries from **Williams' Town & Country Food Center,** 218 W. Cedar, tel. (307) 436-2344. At least one of the local bars (**Four Aces, El Diablo,** or **Deer Creek Lounge**) will have a country-western band on most weekends.

Information and Services
Stop by the **Glenrock Chamber of Commerce,** 217 W. Birch (inside First Insurance Agency), tel.

(307) 436-2564, for local information. You'll find a free indoor **swimming pool** at the monumental middle school (a heritage of early 1980s boomtimes), 225 Oregon Trail, tel. (307) 436-9201. Over at 518 S. 4th, tel. (307) 436-2573, the **Glenrock Library** houses a few dinosaur fossils found in the area. Golfers may want to check out the nine-hole **Glenrock Golf Course,** tel. (307) 436-9294.

The big annual event is **Deer Creek Days,** an early July carnival with parades, games, craft and food booths, a pancake breakfast, street dancing, and lots of drinking. For something tamer, visit the **Glenrock Livestock Exchange,** just east of town, tel. (307) 436-5327, where cattle, sheep, pigs, and even a few goats are auctioned off on Monday and Saturday during the summer months. This is an enjoyable way to learn about ranching and to rub shoulders with local cowboys.

CASPER

Wyoming's second-largest city, Casper (pop. 50,000) is in transition from an oil-dependent economy to a more diversified base. The city sprawls across both sides of the North Platte River and is surrounded by the outlying settlements of **Evansville** (pop. 1,500), **Mills** (pop. 1,600), and **Bar Nunn** (pop. 900), with more suburbs filling the intervening land. As "Oil Capital of the Rockies," the city has long been chained to the fortunes of oil. Casper sits at the center of several large oil fields and is home to two refineries and a giant tank farm. Oil-related manufacturing and service industries crowd the city; the Casper Yellow Pages contain almost 30 different types of oil-related listings—from oil and gas exploration companies to directional drilling outfits.

With its central location, substantial population, spacious convention facilities, and ties to the state's energy and ranching industries, Casper considers itself the true heart and soul of Wyoming. The only statewide newspaper, the *Casper Star-Tribune,* is based here, along with one of the state's premier medical centers. To Casperites, arch-rival Cheyenne is just a Nebraska city that happened to sneak into Wyoming. The rest of Wyoming, however, views

Casper with equal suspicion; in 1904 Casper aspired to become the state capital but failed miserably, coming in third behind Cheyenne and Lander in a statewide vote. A working-class town, Casper will never become a major tourist destination. Despite this, you'll find outstanding recreational opportunities on nearby Casper Mountain, at local reservoirs, and along the North Platte River, and a surprising variety of cultural activities centered around Nicolaysen Art Museum, Casper College, and the spacious Casper Events Center.

HISTORY

The Astorians
Although Casper is identified today with oil, the city began as a way station along the Oregon Trail. Seven of John Jacob Astor's fur traders led by Robert Stuart first traveled through this area in 1812 on their return from Oregon, arriving in late October. Knowing they could not make it back to St. Louis in their emaciated condition, the explorers constructed a rock-walled cabin (the first Anglo building in Wyoming) and covered it with buffalo hides. Game proved amaz-

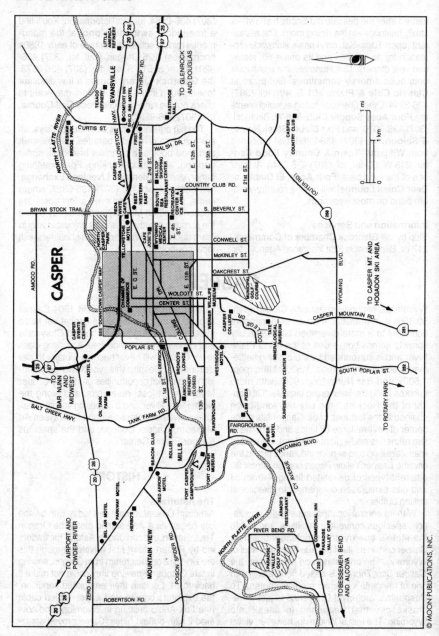

© MOON PUBLICATIONS, INC.

ingly plentiful. They returned from a hunting trip with 47 bison, 28 deer and bighorn sheep, and a bear! But five weeks later, a band of 23 Arapaho warriors appeared on their way to raid the Crow Indians farther north. Intimidated, the Astorians invited them in for a meal. They stayed for a day and a half, promising to return in two weeks. The Astorians quickly decided discretion was the better part of valor and moved to a new camp just across what is now the Nebraska border. They finally reached Missouri the following spring.

Ferries and Bridges

The route pioneered by the Astorians eventually became a virtual highway to the West. The North Platte River was one of the main barriers to this migration, with many emigrants choosing to ford near what is now Casper. In early summer, when the river ran dangerously high, people often died trying to cross. Others lost their wagon or watched as their oxen and horses were swept downriver. When Brigham Young's party of Mormon emigrants arrived here in 1847, they built a 23-foot-long raft and floated their wagons across. The Mormon ferry became Casper's first business venture, with gentiles charged $1.50 per wagon. Business boomed. By 1849, several different ferries were competing with the Mormon ferry, but there were still delays of up to a week as wagons waited in line to cross. (This has to rate as one of Wyoming's only recorded traffic jams.)

In 1852, a French-Canadian trader named John Reshaw built a long wooden toll bridge at present-day Evansville, charging $5 in gold per wagon—less when the river was low and folks would risk fording. To stifle competition, he bought the Mormon ferry for $300 and shut it down. Edwin R. Bird, an 1854 Oregon Trail pioneer, wrote of the toll bridge in his diary:

Here we found a good bridge far better than some I have seen at home. There is a store & other buildings connected with it. In the store saw two Frenchmen gambling. The owner of the bridge says he took in seventeen thousand dollars last season. He charges five dollars for a team & five cents a head for loose stock.

In 1859, another bridge was built six miles upriver by Louis Guinard to compete for the lucrative Oregon Trail traffic. Guinard's bridge must have been one of the most impressive structures along the entire 2,000-mile route. Built at a cost of $40,000, the bridge was 17 feet wide, 1,000 feet long, and supported by 28 log and rock cribs. It soon became the preferred crossing point along the North Platte; the old Reshaw bridge was torn down and the lumber used to build a fort—Platte Bridge Station—to protect the new bridge. Guinard made so much money at the toll station that he reportedly threw handfuls of gold into the river, exclaiming, "You have given me all my wealth; I now give back to you a tithe!"

Red Cloud's War

Platte Bridge Station served as a trading post for travelers, a Pony Express mail stop, and later a telegraph office. A volunteer force of up to 50 soldiers was posted to protect the telegraph and those traveling along the Oregon Trail from Indian and Mormon attacks. After a massacre of Indians at Colorado's Sand Creek in 1865, full-scale war broke out between Indians and whites. One of these battlegrounds that July was at Platte Bridge Station. Expecting a wagon train with vital supplies and ammunition, 20 men under the command of Lt. Caspar Collins left the fort to escort the expected convoy. Once across the bridge, the soldiers found themselves surrounded by Red Cloud and 3,000 of his Sioux warriors. In their flight back across the bridge, five soldiers died. Collins was killed when he stooped to rescue a fellow soldier and his horse

DOVER PUBLICATIONS, INC.

bolted, carrying him into the onrushing warriors. Other soldiers said that when last seen, he had his reins in his teeth and was firing pistols from both hands. His body was found two days later with 24 arrows in it.

A second battle occurred that afternoon—Custard's Wagon Train Fight. When the supply wagons of Sgt. Amos Custard came within sight of the fort, the soldiers tried to warn them with cannon fire. Three men from an advance guard made it to safety within the fort, and the others quickly corralled the three wagons together. Although they put up a fierce fight, within hours Red Cloud's men had killed and mutilated the 23 defenders and burned their wagons. In honor of Caspar Collins, Platte Bridge Station was renamed Fort Caspar. (Fort Collins, Colorado, is named for his father, William Collins.) Due to a never-corrected error by an Army telegraph operator—he typed a dot instead of a dot-dash—the town that eventually grew up nearby was misspelled Casper. Two years later, when most traffic on the Oregon Trail had been rerouted south to avoid conflicts with the Indians, Fort Caspar was abandoned. Shortly thereafter, the bridge and fort were burned by the Sioux.

Lawless Days and Nights

In 1888, the Fremont, Elkhorn, and Missouri Valley Railway extended its line up the North Platte River to the site of old Fort Caspar. A tent city quickly sprang up, followed by more permanent buildings. For the next 17 years the town of Casper lay at the end of the tracks. It was an exceptionally violent place; employees of the first grocery store surrounded their beds with sacks of flour for protection from stray bullets, and Casper's first public building was a jail. Even the mayor got in on the act, murdering his business partner in an 1890 gun duel on Main Street. The jury let him go free. When the ruffians became too much to tolerate, a street trial was held and those who refused to leave town faced the prospect of being strung up in a "necktie party." Pinned to the shirt of one murderer lynched by a vigilance committee was the following note: "Process of law is a little slow, so this is the road you'll have to go. Murderers and sinners, Beware! People's Verdict."

Oil Changes Everything

In 1851 Jim Bridger, Cy Iba, Kit Carson, and Basil Cimineau Lajeunesse discovered an oil spring just west of Casper at Poison Spider Creek. The oil was mixed with flour and sold as axle grease for wagon trains. By 1889, when the first oil well was drilled near Casper, it was clear that much more oil lay beneath the ground. Land speculators and claim jumpers flocked to Wyoming, and battles quickly broke out over who had staked the first claim; the winner generally had more burly men, guns, and lawyers. Soon the massive Salt Creek oil field, 40 miles north of Casper, was producing; wagons towed by teams of up to 20 horses hauled the oil back to Casper. A small refinery was built in 1895, the first in Wyoming. It was later replaced by more modern facilities including the now-closed Standard Oil plant, at one time the largest refinery on earth, handling 25,000 barrels of oil per day. Over time, Casper became a center for oil and refining in the Rockies.

Boom and Bust

Casper grew into a major industrial town with the development of Salt Creek and other oil fields. So many roustabouts flooded Casper that they had to sleep in shifts in the available tents, motels, garages, basements, or shacks. Dozens of illegal gambling houses and speakeasies helped make a trip to town memorable, and more than 2,000 prostitutes pursued their own boomtimes in the Sandbar district—prostitution was blatant here until the 1950s. Oil production peaked in the 1920s, but the crash of 1929 burst this economic bubble and cut the city's population in half within five years. World War II sent oil prices and Casper's economy soaring. An Army air base—home to 4,000 men—opened nearby; it's now the site of Casper's airport. In the late '50s, new technology—injecting water to force the remaining oil to wellheads—helped boost recovery dramatically at Salt Creek, and there followed another boom for Casper. The discovery of massive uranium deposits in the Pumpkin Buttes, Gas Hills, and Shirley Basin further fueled this growth.

The roller-coaster ride has continued in recent decades: down in the late '60s, back up in the '70s. When oil prices soared following the OPEC oil embargo in 1973, Casper experi-

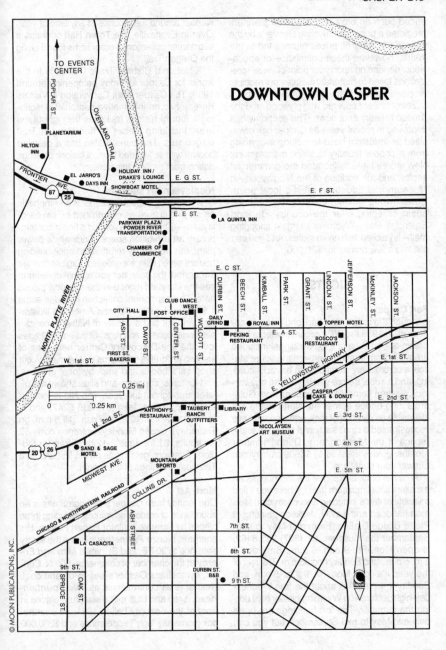

DOWNTOWN CASPER

enced such an orgy of growth that planners predicted a population rivaling Denver's by the year 2000. After oil prices plummeted in the 1980s, however, these optimistic—or apocalyptic, depending upon your point of view—predictions failed to materialize. Sales tax receipts dropped by half, many of downtown Casper's storefronts were covered with plywood, and the Amoco refinery shut down. The economy has improved in recent years as Casper has diversified its industrial base to include everything from a copper foundry to Mace manufacture. New stores have invigorated the commercial sector, and the addition of the Nicolaysen Art Museum has added an artistic focal point. Downtown is thriving, the suburbs are once again creeping over the countryside, and Eastridge Mall—Wyoming's largest shopping mall—is packed with chain stores. And you can still find a few homes for $20,000.

SIGHTS

Fort Caspar
Although the original fort had long since disappeared, in 1936 the WPA reconstructed a half-dozen of Fort Caspar's log buildings. Included are a blacksmith shop, an overland stage station, a commissary storehouse, a barracks building, and a sutler's store where you can buy various western items. Many supports from Guinard's long bridge across the North Platte are still visible as mounds of rock, and workers have reconstructed a small section of the span and a replica of the Mormon ferry. During summer months, guides dressed as 1860s cavalrymen answer your questions.

A newer brick building at the fort houses an excellent small museum (free), where you'll find a variety of items including a reconstructed Mormon handcart and a W.H. Jackson painting of Platte Bridge Station. From mid-May to mid-September the museum, tel. (307) 235-8462, is open Mon.-Fri. 9 a.m.-6 p.m., Saturday 9 a.m.-5 p.m., and Sunday noon-5 p.m. The rest of the year, it's open Mon.-Fri. 9 a.m.-5 p.m. and Sunday 1-4 p.m. Ask about the free Wednesday-night lectures on Wyoming history held during the summer. The fort buildings are open only mid-May to mid-September, but you can

wander around the grounds at any time of year. Over in Evansville, the **Town Hall** contains a substantial collection of other items found along the Oregon Trail.

A National Historic Trails Center is in the works for Casper and may be opening around 1999. The Casper Area Convention & Visitors Bureau has an informative pamphlet describing a tour of historic trail sites throughout the area, including places to find Oregon Trail wagon ruts. The bureau also has a detailed booklet with self-guided tours of historic buildings dating from early in this century.

Nicolaysen Art Museum
One surprising aspect of Casper is an emphasis on art and culture as exemplified by the Nicolaysen—"The Nic"—Wyoming's finest contemporary art exhibition space. Originally a power plant, this beautifully refurbished brick building houses seven different galleries. Exhibits change throughout the year, but you're unlikely ever to see the standard moose-in-the-meadow pieces here. The permanent collection includes some 1,900 drawings by German-American illustrator Carl Link and a variety of Native American paintings, pottery, and rugs. Children of all ages love the fine **Discovery Center** here, one of just two children's museums in Wyoming. A gift shop sells books and work by local artisans, and lectures, concerts, and slide shows are offered throughout the year. The Nic is located at 400 E. Collins, tel. (307) 235-5247, and is open Tues.-Sun. 10 a.m.-5 p.m. (till 8 p.m. on Thursday), closed Monday. Entrance costs $2 for adults, $1 for ages 2-12, and free for toddlers. Everyone gets in free on the first and third Thursday evenings of the month.

More Art
One legacy from Casper's oil boomtimes is an abundance of outdoor sculptures, including three pieces by Laramie sculptor Robert Russin. His energetic bronze **Prometheus** livens the library entrance at 307 E. 2nd St., while **Man and Energy** at the chamber of commerce, 500 N. Center, symbolizes Casper's ties to oil and coal. Neither is as controversial as **The Fountainhead,** a red and blue metal sculpture placed in front of the new city hall in 1981. Its unorthodox (some say "ugly") appearance and $230,000

price tag raised a few eyebrows—and blood pressures. A statue of Caspar Collins on horseback guards the Casper Events Center, and a monument to sheepherders stands in front of the Wyoming Wool Growers Building at 117 Glenn Road. Other places to see distinctive artwork are **West Wind Gallery,** 1040 W. 15th, tel. (307) 265-2655; **Artist's Choice,** 647 W. Yellowstone Hwy., tel. (307) 234-7000; **Daisy Patch Galleries,** 137 S. Center St., tel. (307) 234-8882; and the student art gallery at Casper College. **Windsong Studio,** 340 E. A St., tel. (307) 266-6456 or (800) 347-6456, is a great place to look for stained-glass and blown-glass pieces. They also offer a wide variety of classes and workshops to learn how to work with glass on your own.

Casper College

Casper College first opened its doors in 1945 and has grown into the state's largest junior college, with over 6,000 full- and part-time students. The college's brick buildings sprawl up a long hillside. Although many students live in dorms, most commute from around town, making for traffic jams in the parking lots and along adjacent city streets.

Casperites fought for many years to turn their college into a four-year school, but the university at Laramie successfully fended off those moves until 1987. In a joint venture, the University of Wyoming now offers a limited number of bachelor's degree programs at the Casper College campus. A fine 80,000-volume **library** on campus includes a rare-book room with unusual Wyoming titles. An **Elderhostel** program operates at Casper College during the summer, and the excellent **Fitness Center** is open to the public. In the College Center building you'll find a cafeteria, a small bookstore, and other facilities.

Visitors will enjoy stops at two Casper College museums. **Tate Mineralogical Museum,** tel. (307) 268-2574, is open Mon.-Fri. 9 a.m.-5 p.m. and Saturday 10 a.m.-3 p.m. during the summer and Mon.-Fri. 2-5 p.m. during the school year.

BRIAN BARDWELL

Entrance is free. Inside, you'll find one of the largest mineralogical collections in the Rockies, including several meteorites, various types of petrified wood, Indian artifacts, dinosaur fossils, and probably the largest collection of Wyoming jade anywhere. Polished stones are sold at a small gift shop here. **Werner Wildlife Museum,** 405 E. 15th, tel. (307) 235-2108, is open Mon.-Fri. 10 a.m.-5 p.m. from mid-May to early September and Mon.-Fri. 2-5 p.m. the rest of the year; no charge. The museum houses the usual stuffed critters from Wyoming— dozens of antelope heads, deer mounts, bears, bison, and many birds—along with several African trophies.

More Sights

The **Platte River Parkway** is a four-mile paved pathway along the river and a fine place to walk, rollerblade, or ride bikes. The chamber of commerce has a map of the route, or just look for it along the river. Eventually it will extend for almost 12 miles.

At the intersection of 1st and Poplar streets a wooden **oil derrick** stands as a monument to the city's heritage. One of Casper's minor claims to fame is having Wyoming's largest convention and performance center. Here you might run across a mining trade show, a concert by Pearl Jam or Reba McIntyre, wrestling tournaments, graduation ceremonies, conventions and trade shows, a cat-judging event, or even a monster-truck pull. Located on a hill overlooking the city, the **Casper Events Center** is a spacious, modern building with room for over 10,000 people. Call (800) 442-2256 for upcoming events.

The **Casper Planetarium,** 904 N. Poplar, tel. (307) 577-0310, is open daily during the summer, with programs starting at 4, 7, and 8 p.m. Admission costs $2, $5 for a family. **Dr. Spokes Cyclery & Museum,** 240 S. Center St., tel. (307) 265-7740, is a unique bike shop with an array of classic bikes and toy pedal cars arranged around the room. Some date back to the turn of the century.

ACCOMMODATIONS

Motels and Bed and Breakfasts

Casper motels cover the complete quality spectrum, from dumpy little hole-in-the-walls to an elaborate Hilton. In general you'll find prices in Casper to be among the cheapest in Wyoming. More than two dozen of the city's lodging establishments are listed in the accommodations chart. At the cheapest places, you'd better take a look at the rooms before plunking down any money. If you're driving into Casper along the interstate, keep a watch for billboards proclaiming discount motel rates; sometimes you need to mention the ad to get the discount.

Bessemer Bend B&B, tel. (307) 265-6819, offers modest accommodations in a tri-level home located 13 miles southwest of Casper near the Goose Egg Ranch. Friendly owners, reasonable prices, and a good chance to stay out in the country. The **Durbin St. Inn B&B,** tel. (307) 577-5774, built in 1917, serves full breakfasts to its guests in a large home with fireplaces and a patio.

Camping

The nearest public camping ($5-6) is in the pines on Casper Mountain, 10 miles south of Casper and 3,000 feet higher in elevation—well worth the drive (see "Casper Mountain," below, for details). Casper's three private campgrounds all have swimming pools. The **Fort Caspar Campground,** tel. (307) 234-3260, operates year-round on the river just beyond the old fort site. Sites run $11 for tents, $16 for RVs. **Casper KOA,** 2800 E. Yellowstone, tel. (307) 237-5155 or (800) 562-3259, charges $14 for tents, $18 for RVs; open late Feb.-November. It features an indoor pool and jacuzzi. **Antelope Run Campground,** in Bar Nunn at 1101 W. Prairie Lane, tel. (307) 577-1664, has tent sites for $12, RV

CASPER ACCOMMODATIONS

Note: Accommodations are listed from least to most expensive. Add a seven percent tax to these rates. Area code is 307.

Topper Motel; 728 E. A St.; tel. 237-8407; $20 s, $24 d; see rooms first, weekly rates

Red Arrow Motel; 308 S.W. Wyoming Blvd.; tel. 234-5293; $20 s, $22 d; see rooms first, weekly rates available

Bel Air Motel; 5400 W. Yellowstone; tel. 472-1930; $22 s or d; see rooms first, weekly rates available

Virginian Motel; 830 E. A St.; tel. 266-3959; $24 s, $28 d; see rooms first, no phones in rooms

Commercial Inn; 5755 CY Ave.; tel. 235-6688; $24 s, $29 d; kitchenettes $37 s or d; weekly rates available

Yellowstone Motel; 1610 E. Yellowstone; tel. 234-9174 or (800) 352-6551; $24-30 s, $28-38 d; kitchenettes $45-65 for up to six; local calls 25 cents

Parkway Motel; 5102 W. Yellowstone; tel. 234-2162; $25 s or d; marginal place, see rooms first, weekly rates available

Royal Inn; 440 E. A St.; tel. 234-3503 or (800) 967-6925; $26-29 s, $31-34 d; kitchenettes $37-46 s or d; outdoor pool, local calls 25 cents

Westridge Motel; 955 CY Ave.; tel. 234-8911 or (800) 356-6268; $26-35 s or d; AAA approved

Sand & Sage Motel; 901 W. Yellowstone; tel. 237-2088; $27 s, $32 d; kitchenettes for $32 s, $35 d; weekly rates available

Motel 6; 1150 Wilkins Circle; tel. 234-3903 or (800) 466-8356; $27 s, $33 d; outdoor pool

National 9 Inn Showboat; 100 W. F St.; tel. 235-2711 or (800) 524-9999; $29-34 s, $35-42 d; continental breakfast, AAA approved

sites for $16, including access to an indoor pool and jacuzzi. Showers for noncampers cost $3; open May-September.

FOOD

Casper has a wide range of dining options that will suit almost any taste and shows more diversity every time you visit. All the standard fast food greasers are here—from Taco Time to Hot Dog on a Stick—but so are a number of fine dining places.

Breakfast

For a homestyle, reasonably priced breakfast, visit **Paradise Valley Cafe**, 5755 CY Ave., tel. (307) 266-9914. On the other end of town is the **Red and White Cafe**, 1620 E. Yellowstone, tel. (307) 234-6962, a popular greasy-spoon hangout. A fine Sunday brunch place is **Circle T**

Restaurant, 7800 W. State 220, tel. (307) 237-0012—it has an extensive all-you-can-eat buffet.

Lunch

During the school year, visitors will find Casper's cheapest lunch eats at the **Casper College cafeteria.** Notable soup, sandwich, and salad places are **Cottage Cafe,** 116 S. Lincoln St., tel. (307) 234-1157, and **Cheese Barrel,** 544 S. Center, tel. (307) 235-5202 (which also serves good breakfasts). For the best sub sandwiches in Casper, head to **Mountain View Sub Shop,** 239 E. 1st St., tel. (307) 237-7999. More expensive than Subway or Blimpies, its well worth the price difference.

Steak and Seafood

The best local top-carnivore eateries are **Poor Boys Steak House,** in the Parkway Plaza Hotel at 123 W. E St., tel. (307) 235-1777, and **Duke's Steak House,** in the Shilo Inn at 739 Luker

Bessemer Bend B&B; 13 miles southwest; tel. 265-6819; $35 s, $45 d; riverside location, three guest rooms, shared bath, full breakfast, kids welcome

First Interstate Inn; Wyoming Blvd. at I-25; tel. 234-9125; $36 s, $41 d; AAA approved

Super 8 Motel; 3838 CY Ave.; tel. 266-3480 or (800) 800-8000; $40 s, $46 d; continental breakfast, AAA approved

Kelly Inn; 821 N. Poplar; tel. 266-2400 or (800) 635-3559; $40-46 s, $44-50 d; jacuzzi, sauna, AAA approved

La Quinta Motor Inn; 301 E. E St.; tel. 234-1159 or (800) 531-5900; $44-47 s or d; outdoor pool, continental breakfast, AAA approved

Parkway Plaza Hotel; 123 W. E St.; tel. 235-1777 or (800) 270-7829; $45 s, $48 d; outdoor pool, jacuzzi, weight room, AAA approved

Shilo Inn; 739 Luker Lane, Evansville; tel. 237-1335 or (800) 222-2244; $45-59s, $49-69 d; indoor pool, jacuzzi, sauna, steam room, fitness center, breakfast buffet, AAA approved

Best Western East; 2325 E. Yellowstone; tel. 234-3541 or (800) 675-4242; $54-84 s or d; indoor pool, continental breakfast, exercise facilities, AAA approved

Durbin St. Inn B&B; 843 S. Durbin; tel. 577-5774; $55-70 s, $65-80 d; 1917 home, five guest rooms, shared or private baths, full breakfast, smoking on first floor, no kids under age 14, AAA approved

Hampton Inn; 400 W. F St.; tel. 235-6668 or (800) 426-7866; $55-60 s, $63-68 d; sauna, outdoor pool, continental breakfast, airport shuttle, AAA approved

Comfort Inn; 480 Lathrop, Evansville; tel. 235-3038 or (800) 638-2657; $60-65 s, $70-75 d; indoor pool, jacuzzi, continental breakfast, AAA approved

Hilton Inn; I-25 and Poplar; tel. 266-6000 or (800) 916-2221; $61 s, $71 d; indoor pool, jacuzzi, exercise facility, airport shuttle, AAA approved

Holiday Inn; 300 W. F St.; tel. 235-2531 or (800) 465-4329; $65-71 s or d; indoor pool, jacuzzi, sauna, fitness center, atrium, airport shuttle, AAA approved

Lane, Evansville; tel. (307) 237-1335. **Dorn's Fireside,** 1745 CY Ave., tel. (307) 235-6831, is another popular beef-and-seafood house. In the same vein is **Goose Egg Inn,** nine miles southwest of Casper on State 220, tel. (307) 473-8838, where prime rib, seafood, and pan-fried chicken are house specialties well worth the drive. **Fat Boys BBQ,** 522 S.W. Wyoming Blvd. in Mills, tel. (307) 266-1414, cranks out excellent ribs. Packed with Casperites, **Herbo's,** 4755 W. Yellowstone, tel. (307) 266-2293, is one of the local restaurants where big servings win out over quality.

Italian

Casper has two decent Italian restaurants. **Anthony's,** 241 S. Center, tel. (307) 234-3071, is more centrally located, but the down-home **Bosco's,** 847 E. A St., tel. (307) 265-9658, really packs them in, particularly over the lunch hour. Recommended by locals. If you're looking for good pizza in Casper, give up. **Little Big Men Pizza (LBM),** 3350 CY Ave., tel. (307) 235-0786, turns out decent pizza. It's not going to make you forget the real thing, but it's still better than the various chains such as Godfather's and Pizza Hut.

Mexican

For Mexican food, everyone in Casper goes to **El Jarro's,** 500 W. F St., tel. (307) 577-0538. Be ready for a long wait most any evening. The El Jarro's phenomenon exists for a number of reasons: low prices, big margaritas, crispy chips, tangy salsa, and mass quantities of food. Besides, the bleached-blond hostesses and the beefy waiters (who gather around tables to sing "Happy Birthday" at least a dozen times each hour) make for lots of ogling. Be forewarned, however, that this is Americanized Mexican food—we're talking something that looks like mushroom soup over the chile rellenos! More critical locals call El Jarro's "El Horrible's." Find far more authentic Mexican fare at **La Costa** 400 W. F St., tel. (307) 266-4288, where the atmosphere is plain but the food is genuine. Also popular is **La Casacita,** 633 W. Collins, tel. (307) 234-7633, the oldest Mexican cafe in Casper; free delivery. **Cafe Jose's,** 1600 E. 2nd St., tel. (307) 235-6599, or 522 S.W. Wyoming Blvd. in Mills, tel. (307) 266-1414, has very good Tex-Mex fare, including fajitas.

Chinese

A real surprise in Casper is the large number of Asian restaurants that dot the town—eight places at last count. The food has suffered a bit from Americanization, but several of these places are tolerable. **South Sea Chinese Restaurant** has two locations: 2025 E. 2nd, tel. (307) 237-4777, and 116 W. 2nd, tel. (307) 265-9711, and offers the more authentic fare—though the no-smoking section is a joke. Also good is **Peking Chinese Restaurant,** 333 E. A, tel. (307) 266-2207. The **Mekong,** 144 S. Center, tel. (307) 237-6728, has a good reputation for its Vietnamese cuisine.

Coffee Shops

In Good Taste, 2113 E. 12th St., tel. (307) 577-6010, is the place to go for a latte fix or English teas. **Daily Grind Coffee House,** 328 E. A St., tel. (307) 234-7332, is an offbeat, homey spot for espresso coffees, pastries, and poetry on Thursday nights but at last check was struggling to survive. **Blue Heron Books & Espresso,** 201 E. 2nd St., tel. (307) 265-3774 or (800) 585-3774, is a pleasant downtown spot to browse books and enjoy a coffee. **Uncle Bruno's,** upstairs at Taubert's, 125 E. 2nd, tel. (307) 234-2500, also has espresso and pastries.

Bakeries and Groceries

First Street Bakers, 260 W. 1st St., tel. (307) 472-0255, bakes bagels, breads, and sweets, including enormous cinnamon buns. **Casper Cake and Donut,** 604 E. 2nd, tel. (307) 234-1180, is the other good bakery (with another shop in Eastridge Mall). Casper has a number of giant grocery stores scattered across the city, including Albertson's, Buttrey, Safeway, and Smith's; all have in-store bakeries and delis. If you're looking for fresh produce, be sure to check out the **Farmers Market** at the fairgrounds every Saturday morning during the summer.

ENTERTAINMENT

Movies

Casper's downtown movie theaters—**Rialto Theatre** at 1st and Center, tel. (307) 237-2416, and **America Theatre** at 119 S. Center, tel. (307) 235-5440—have some of the cheapest

flick-viewing to be found: $2 for all shows. Other movie houses include **Commonwealth Casper Theatres,** 2117 E. 12th St., tel. (307) 265-6061, and **Eastridge Mall Cinema Four,** 601 S.E. Wyoming Blvd., tel. (307) 234-5831.

Bar Hopping

See the *Casper Star-Tribune* for the latest on local nightlife. The biggest and best-known place for live music every night of the week is the **Beacon Club,** 4100 W. Yellowstone Hwy., tel. (307) 577-1503, with country tunes and a fun, trendy crowd. Dance lessons Tues.-Thurs. nights. Both **Bronco's Lounge,** 1200 W. Collins Dr., tel. (307) 266-5111, and the **Avalon Club,** 260 E. Yellowstone Hwy., tel. (307) 473-7544, offer Western dance bands most nights. Free dance lessons on Wednesday nights at Bronco's. **Club Dance West,** 225 N. Wolcott, tel. (307) 234-8811, has country music upstairs and rock or rap downstairs; open Friday and Saturday nights. **Drake's Lounge** in the Holiday Inn, 300 W. F St., tel. (307) 235-2531, has live top-40 music most evenings and free hors d'oeuvres on weeknights. There's more rock at **Moonlight Lounge,** 2305 E. 12th, tel. (307) 234-7787, and **Dillinger Bar,** 256 S. Center, tel. (307) 266-2330. Other places to check for musical entertainment and dancing are **Shilo Inn Motel,** 739 Luker Lane, tel. (307) 237-1335; **Colonial Lounge,** 4370 S. Poplar, tel. (307) 265-9988; **Goose Egg Inn,** 10580 Goose Egg Rd., tel. (307) 473-8838; **LBM Pizza,** 3350 CY Ave., tel. (307) 234-0786; and **Viking Restaurant and Lounge,** 2740 E. 3rd, tel. (307) 234-5386.

The Arts

Stage III Community Theatre, 4080 S. Poplar, tel. (307) 234-0946, puts on plays Sept.-July. The **Casper Symphony Orchestra,** tel. (307) 266-1478, Wyoming's only professional orchestra, presents winter performances.

EVENTS

Casper features a multitude of enjoyable events throughout the summer months, so there's bound to be something going on when you visit. Each Thursday evening from mid-June to mid-August the **Casper Municipal Band** performs free concerts at Washington Park on McKinley

and 8th streets. Join locals who sprawl out on the lawn and picnic to the big sounds. On the second weekend of June the **Cowboy State Games** are an Olympic-style multisport festival with teams from all over the state competing in everything from archery to wrestling. A winter version of the games takes place in February. On the third weekend of June the **Mountain Man Rendezvous** brings dozens of costumed mountain men and Indians to old Fort Caspar. See "Crimson Dawn," below, for the year's most unusual event, held atop Casper Mountain during the summer solstice (June 21). **Classicfest** takes place at the Events Center in late June and early July and features carnival rides, food booths, live music, and a crafts fair.

Casper's biggest annual event is the **Central Wyoming Fair and Rodeo** in early to mid-July. The various arts-and-crafts displays, farm animals, rodeos, and midway attract both locals and visitors. Rodeo events include exciting chuck wagon races and clown "bullfighting." For more laid-back action, try the twice-weekly rodeos at North 40, located 10 miles north of Casper on I-25. Call (307) 265-9619 for specifics. Each October, the **PRCA Rodeo Finals** are held at the Events Center. This is Wyoming's largest indoor rodeo.

Up on Casper Mountain the **Bear Trap Summer Festival** brings jazz and blues music during mid-July. For a glimpse of the city's past, come to Fort Caspar for the **Platte Bridge Encampment** the fourth weekend of July. It includes period fashion shows, living-history demonstrations, and military drills. The **Casper Troopers Drum and Bugle Corps**—one of the finest in the nation—often performs for the encampment. The corps has been performing together since 1957. Don't miss it! Call (307) 234-7005 for a schedule of performances.

Pari-mutuel horse racing comes to the fairgrounds later in August and lasts through Labor Day. The **Platte River Station Stage Bike Race** is held on Memorial Day weekend, with cyclists racing at speeds up to 65 mph in four different stages, including to Glenrock and back and along steep Garden Creek Road. The Nicolaysen Art Museum has an **Arts and Crafts Festival** on the first weekend of November with more than 75 artisans exhibiting their wares. It's a good place to shop early for Christmas.

RECREATION

The fine **Casper Recreation Center**, 1801 E. 4th St., tel. (307) 235-8383, provides racquetball and volleyball courts, a weight room, a gym, and a game room. Next door is **Casper Ice Arena**, tel. (307) 235-8484, with skating Aug.-April. Wyoming's largest roller-skating palace, **Wagon Wheel Roller Rink**, is in Mills at 305 Vanhorn Ave., tel. (307) 265-4214. Mountain bikers will find many miles of roads and trails on Casper and Muddy Mountains south of town. For maps and info, contact **Casper Wheelmen**, 548 E. A St., tel. (307) 577-9117, or **The Bike Stop**, 515 W. Collins, tel. (307) 577-0115. Rent bikes from **Mountaineer's Mercantile**, 8455 Casper Mountain Rd., tel. (307) 577-6004.

If you're looking for a little water activity, check out one of Casper's half-dozen **swimming pools**. Five outdoor pools, tel. (307) 235-8403, are scattered throughout the city and are open summers. The Paradise Valley pool also has a very popular corkscrew water slide. The indoor pool at Kelly Walsh High School is open on Wednesday evenings, and another indoor pool is at the YMCA, 315 E. 15th, tel. (307) 234-9187. Casper's high school was the first in the nation to have an indoor swimming pool, built in 1929.

Choose from three 18-hole golf courses in town: **Casper Municipal Golf Course**, tel. (307) 234-1037, **Paradise Valley Golf Course**, tel. (307) 234-9146, and **Casper Country Club**, tel. (307) 235-5777. Casper is one of the nation's windiest cities; winds averaging 13 mph make this a great place for kite flying, hang-gliding, and sailboarding. Pathfinder and Alcova Reservoirs are both popular sailboarding spots. **Mountain Sports**, 543 S. Center, tel. (307) 266-1136 or (800) 426-1136, sells quality outdoor gear and rents Windsurfers, downhill and cross-country skis, and rollerblades. While there, take a look at the various rock-climbing maps and books.

Looking for a taste of the Old West? **Historic Trails Expeditions**, tel. (307) 266-4868, leads a wide range of Conestoga wagon and horseback rides—from three hours to five days long—along the Oregon Trail and atop Casper Mountain.

River Recreation

The **North Platte River** flows right through the city of Casper, providing both the city's drinking water and a variety of recreational opportunities. The Platte's slow current and shallow depth—just two to four feet in most places—make for a gentle and scenic float trip with plenty of wildlife along the way: beaver, muskrats, ducks, geese, hawks, eagles, mule deer, and antelope. For a map and brochure describing public landings, camping, and parking areas along the 45-mile stretch of the Platte between Alcova Reservoir and Casper, contact the Bureau of Land Management at 1701 E. E St., (307) 261-7600.

Wyoming's Choice River Runners, 513 N. Lennox, tel. (307) 234-3870, rents canoes ($32 a day) and rafts ($55-65 a day), and provides shuttle boat service ($18-28). In addition, they offer scenic half-day float trips for $25 ($15 for kids) and guided drift fishing ($205 for two.) Fishing is excellent for both German brown and rainbow trout; locals call the North Platte one of the west's largest and finest trout fisheries. See the chamber of commerce for a listing of other local fishing guides. Two good fly-fishing shops are **Ugly Bug Fly Shop**, 316 W. Midwest Ave., tel. (307) 234-6905, and **Platte River Fly Shop**, 7400 Alcova Hwy. 220, tel. (307) 237-5997.

The 1,420-acre riverside **Edness Kimball Wilkins State Park**, six miles east of Casper on State 256, is perfect for quiet picnics among the cottonwoods, birdwatching (more than 200 species have been observed), and fishing. The park began as a rock quarry but has been gradually transformed into a delightful place to explore. No camping is allowed, but several trails—including a three-mile paved path—provide pleasant day hikes or bike rides, and the pond is a popular swimming hole. Entrance is $3 for nonresident vehicles, $2 for cars with Wyoming plates. Call (307) 577-5150 for more information.

GETTING MALLED

Casper is Wyoming's version of shop-till-your-car-dies. Sprawling suburbia, fast food, and a

half-dozen park-anywhere malls combine to make Casper indistinguishable from Modesto, California, or Columbus, Ohio. This is the sort of place where even the Highland Park Community Church is housed in what looks like an old Kmart store. **Eastridge Mall** is Wyoming's largest shopping mall, with 90 stores, including most of the big chains. If Norman Rockwell were alive today, he would be painting the high-school girls eyeing the hunks on parade and the over-60, post-heart attack crowd doing their fast walks around the mall.

Okay, so not all of Casper's stores are in shopping malls. Downtown at 125 E. 2nd St., tel. (307) 234-2500, is the impressive **Lou Taubert Ranch Outfitters,** a four-level department store with everything from cowboy boots (10,000 pairs in stock!) to gourmet coffee. It's a great place to try on a new cowboy hat. **Wyoming Products Limited,** 137 S. Center St., tel. (307) 266-2627, is a fun place to look for locally made crafts. **Mountain Sports,** 543 S. Center, tel. (307) 266-1136 or (800) 426-1136, has a good collection of outdoor supplies of all sorts, from windsurfing equipment to sleeping bags. Rent rollerblades here and pick up topo maps or local hiking and climbing books.

Bookstores

A number of places sell new books in Casper: **B. Dalton,** tel. (307) 247-0793, and **Waldenbooks,** tel. (307) 235-2046, in Eastridge Mall; **Ralph's Books** at Hilltop Shopping Center, tel. (307) 234-0308; **Blue Heron Books & Espresso,** 201 E. 2nd St., tel. (307) 265-3774 or (800) 585-3774; and **The Book Peddler** at Sunrise Shopping Center, tel. (307) 266-2021. **Westerner News,** 245 S. Center, tel. (307) 235-1022, sells history books, paperbacks, out-of-state newspapers, and all sorts of magazines. **Book Palace,** 134 S. Center St., tel. (307) 577-1325, offers a fine selection of used books and is a great place to browse. The **Book Nook,** 516 E. Yellowstone, tel. (307) 237-2211, and **Book Gallery,** 235 E. 1st St., tel. (307) 234-4412, also sell used titles.

INFORMATION AND SERVICES

The friendly **Casper Area Chamber of Commerce,** 500 N. Center, tel. (307) 234-5311 or (800) 852-1889, is the place to go for tourist paraphernalia. Between Memorial Day and Labor Day its open Mon.-Fri. 8 a.m.-6 p.m. and Sat.-Sun. 9 a.m.-6 p.m. The rest of the year, its hours are Mon.-Fri. 9 a.m.-5 p.m. Other Casper practicalities include the **Natrona County Library,** 307 E. 2nd, tel. (307) 237-4935, and the **post office** at 411 N. Forest Dr., tel. (307) 266-4000. **ATMs** are located in many places around Casper including nearly all the local banks. If you're into Christian music, Casper will fill you up with not just one but three radio stations offering preaching and countrified Christian tunes (or the mellow rock variety). You can also get the National Public Radio station based in Laramie.

TRANSPORTATION

Natrona County Airport is eight miles northwest of Casper on U.S. 20/26. **United Express/Mesa Airlines,** tel. (800) 241-6522, has commuter service (prop planes) to Denver, and **Delta/Sky West,** tel. (800) 221-1212, has daily service to Salt Lake City. The airport is an official Foreign Trade Zone.

Powder River Trailways, 123 W. E St. in the Parkway Plaza Hotel, room 1159, tel. (307) 266-1904 or (800) 442-3682, has daily bus service to towns in northern and central Wyoming, continuing north to Billings or Rapid City and south to Cheyenne and Denver. Call **RC Cab,** tel. (307) 235-5203, or **Rapid Cab,** tel. (307) 235-1903, for taxi service.

Rent cars from **Around Town Rent-A-Car,** tel. (307) 265-5667; **Avis,** tel. (307) 237-2634 or (800) 331-1212; **Budget,** tel. (307) 266-2251 or (800) 527-0700; **Enterprise,** tel. (307) 234-8122 or (800) 325-8007; or **Hertz,** tel. (307) 265-1355 or (800) 654-3131. You'll find the cheapest rates inside the Royal Inn at **Aries Car Rentals,** 440 E. A St., tel. (307) 234-3503 or (800) 967-6925.

CASPER VICINITY

CASPER MOUNTAIN

Scenic mountain country is just a hop, skip, and a jump away from Casper. When the thermometer tops 100° F in the summertime, Casper folks escape to the cool mountains just a 15-minute drive from town. Snow often lingers until July. Rotary Park, seven miles south of Casper on South Poplar St. (State 252), has a

number of official and unofficial trails that climb the steep canyon cut by Garden Creek. The creek drops 50 feet over **Garden Creek Falls**, one of the few waterfalls in this part of Wyoming. A viewpoint is just a short distance up the trail, or you can cross the bridge and follow a second path (actually a maze of routes) to the top of the falls, one mile up. Other trails head out to a ridge offering views of the surrounding country.

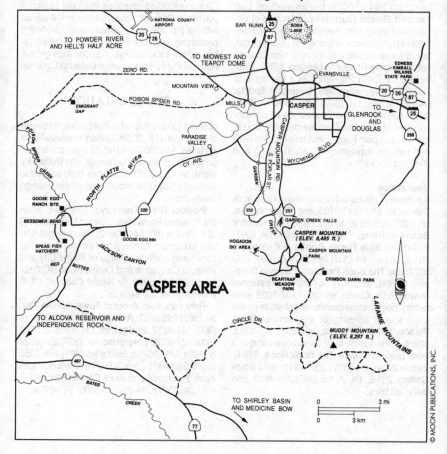

The steep, winding drive up Casper Mountain has turnouts offering panoramas that stretch all the way to the Big Horn Mountains 125 miles north. Casper Mountain's flattened 8,100-foot-summit is carpeted by ponderosa pine trees and pleasant grassy meadows. Several county parks—Casper Mountain, Crimson Dawn, Beartrap Meadow, and Ponderosa—are very popular getaways where deer and elk are found. The five **campgrounds** on Casper Mountain cost $5 per night; all are open year-round. Water is available only at Beartrap (the nicest) and Casper Mountain Campgrounds. Red Valley separates Casper Mountain from its neighbor five miles to the south, **Muddy Mountain.** The gravel road climbs up Muddy Mountain, where the BLM maintains a campground ($6; open mid-June through October), a self-guided nature trail, and other scenic paths. For more information on the various Casper Mountain parks, call (307) 234-6821. The short **Lee McCune Braille Trail** on Casper Mountain has 39 stations with plaques describing the natural world in braille and English. Even sighted people find the trail eye-opening. Nearby is a summer camp for the blind.

Hogadon Ski Area
First opened in 1959, the small, city-run Hogadon Ski Area is nine miles south of Casper near the top of the mountain. A family area, it includes hills ranging from the easiest bunny slope to black diamonds. Eleven different runs are fed by two chairlifts and a Poma lift, with a vertical rise of 600 feet. Ski rentals and lessons are available, and there's a cafeteria. The slopes are open to Telemarkers and snowboarders. Lift tickets cost $20 for adults, $17 for ages 12-18, $14 for ages 5-11, free for younger kids. Half-day rates are $13 for all age groups, and a Poma-only ticket costs $5. Hogadon is open Wed.-Sun. 9 a.m.-4 p.m. from Thanksgiving to early April. Call (307) 235-8369 for information and snow conditions.

Cross-Country Skiing and Snowmobiling
Casper Mountain often has surprisingly good powder conditions. Natrona County, tel. (307) 235-9311, maintains 28 km of groomed cross-country ski trails and a warming hut. Some trails are lit at night; daily passes cost $4. In addition, you'll find extensive undeveloped areas where more adventurous backcountry skiers can prac-

tice Telemarking. Rent cross-country skis from **Mountain Sports,** 543 S. Center, tel. (307) 266-1136; **Backcountry Mountain Works,** 4120 S. Poplar, tel. (307) 234-5330; **Sport N-Things,** 601 S.E. Wyoming Blvd., tel. (307) 237-5463 or (800) 249-5463; **Mountaineer's Mercantile,** 8455 Casper Mountain Rd., tel. (307) 577-6004; or **Dean's Sporting Goods,** 260 S. Center, tel. (307) 234-2788. Casper Mountain also has more than 52 miles of groomed snowmobile trails.

Crimson Dawn Museum
This is a place best experienced early in the morning, when the crimson light of dawn brushes across the ochre-colored earth and streams into the dark green forests. Come here alone to really feel the magic that captivated Neal Forsling almost 70 years ago. After growing up in Independence, Missouri—and nearly marrying Harry Truman—she headed west to Casper. There Neal married a lawyer, but a bitter divorce sent her fleeing to then-remote Casper Mountain with her two children, looking to start anew as a homesteader. She quickly fell in love with the country and later fell in love with local rancher Jim Forsling. They were married and settled into a fiercely independent life without electricity or running water and with but a few neighbors. The idyll was broken one bitterly cold winter day when Jim was skiing back from town with a backpack filled with supplies. Caught in a blizzard, he froze to death just a few miles from the cabin. He was 38 years old.

Neal adjusted to the loss by turning inward to grasp the spirit of the land, by painting out her emotions, and by opening outward to her own and neighboring children with stories. Over the years these grew into a complex series of fairy tales that detailed the good and evil witches, leprechauns, and trolls who inhabit these woods and fields. Midsummers' Eve was a special time when children and adults could enter this magical spirit world through her storytelling. In 1973, Neal Forsling gave her land and cabin to Natrona County for use as a park. She died a few years later and is buried nearby, but her extraordinary love for the earth is revealed in her small cabin, her mystical paintings, her fairy tales, and the trails that lead through the woods to shrines celebrating the good witches, magical creatures, and witty forest spirits who haunt this

land. Neal's philosophy is summed up by a sign in her cabin:

> *What I had, I lost*
> *What I saved, I spent*
> *What I gave, I have.*

Today, her old log home is a small museum (tel. 307-235-1303) open Sat.-Thurs. 11 a.m.-7 p.m. from mid-June until "the first big snow"—generally late September.

Eleanor Carrigen grew up on the mountain and spent countless childhood days with Neal Forsling, to whom she is related "by osmosis." She now leads tours of the turn-of-the-century cabin and tells delightful stories. Be sure to ask about the "chocolate war" between two of Forsling's suitors! Inside the cabin are several of Forsling's somewhat crude paintings—seemingly inspired by both Vincent van Gogh and Grandma Moses—which reveal her mystical sensibilities. A framed letter from Missouri friend Bess Truman hangs on one wall. You may want to purchase a copy of *Crimson Dawn,* a collection of Forsling's tales. And be sure to wander along the nearby woodland trails to enjoy the 20 shrines she created—my personal favorite is Sean the leprechaun. Get to the park by heading 12 miles south of Casper along State 251 and following the signs to Crimson Dawn.

On **Midsummer's Eve** (June 21), be sure to be in Crimson Dawn for a wonderfully mystical celebration of Casper Mountain's witches and spirits. The celebration has gone on every year since 1931. Visitors get to meet the local denizens in person and are invited to throw handfuls of the dark red earth into the bonfire; if it burns, your wish will come true. Hundreds of Casperites will also be there to celebrate, along with a handful of pompous protesters from Sunlight Ministries.

Joseph M. Carey

BESSEMER BEND

The bucolic Bessemer Bend area—10 miles southwest of Casper along State 220—abounds in history, both real and imagined. A lazy curve in the North Platte River, Bessemer Bend was an important 19th-century crossing point for wagon trains. Rock walls from a shelter built in 1812 by the Astorians are still visible on a knoll overlooking the river. Between 1860 and 1861, the Red Butte Pony Express station stood at the river bend, site of the longest of all Pony Express rides, a 320-mile gallop by Buffalo Bill Cody that lasted a grueling 21 hours and 40 minutes. The nearby Red Buttes were also where Custard's Wagon Train Fight took place (described above under "History" in the "Casper" section). Bessemer City sprang up along the bend in 1888, calling itself "Queen City of the Plains." It lasted only a couple of years, and when Casper was voted the Natrona County seat, Bessemer City quietly faded away. Many of its buildings were moved to Casper, and today Bessemer City is a just field of alfalfa.

Along the east side of the North Platte River at Bessemer Bend is the site of the famed **Goose Egg Ranch,** once one of Wyoming's largest cattle spreads. In *The Virginian,* Owen Wister used Goose Egg Ranch for a memorable scene in which two drunken cowboys switch blankets on a dozen babies while their parents are dancing, creating havoc when the ranch families drive home with the wrong children. Owned for many years by the Carey family—both father Joseph M. Carey and son Robert Carey served as governor and U.S. senator—it was later renamed the CY Ranch. The southern half of Casper is built on what was once CY land—hence CY Ave., one of the city's main thoroughfares. Ironically, the old Goose Egg ranch house died partly because

of the fame brought to it in *The Virginian.* The abandoned stone buildings gradually deteriorated as tourists chipped away for momentos. Fearing that the buildings might collapse, the owners finally tore down the ranch in 1951. John Wayne's oil field firefighter movie, *Hellfighters,* was filmed not far away in 1968.

Today folks come to Bessemer Bend to enjoy a steak at Goose Egg Inn or to watch wintering golden and bald eagles in nearby Jackson Canyon—named for famed Yellowstone photographer William H. Jackson. Another five miles down State 220 is **Dan Speas Fish Hatchery,** tel. (307) 473-8890, Wyoming's largest trout-rearing facility. It's open daily 8 a.m.-5 p.m.

THE "LAKE DISTRICT"

The 655-mile-long North Platte River rises in Colorado, heads north into Wyoming, and then curves a long lazy loop to the east, cutting across western Nebraska and finally joining the South Platte River near the city of North Platte. The entire basin covers 32,000 square miles and in Wyoming is fed by the Sweetwater, Medicine Bow, and Laramie Rivers. The name "Platte" is French for "Broad"; Indians called the river "Nebraska," meaning "flat." Both are appropriate titles along much of the river's path. Cottonwood trees line the banks, and the river offers an essential watering hole for wildlife. (Early settlers in Wyoming called the Platte "a mile wide and an inch deep," and "too thick to drink and too thin to plow.")

Once one of the most impressive rivers in the Plains states—at flood stage it ran 150 yards wide and 10-15 feet deep—the North Platte has been reduced to little more than a creek through much of Wyoming. Near Fort Laramie, where wagon trains in the 1850s found a treacherous crossing, the river today sometimes ceases to flow at all, lying in shallow puddles in the late summer sun. A look at the map makes it obvious what has happened to the water: agriculture has siphoned it all away.

Reclamation
Without irrigation, farming was difficult or impossible in much of the arid West, and the thousands of homesteaders who tried to survive on

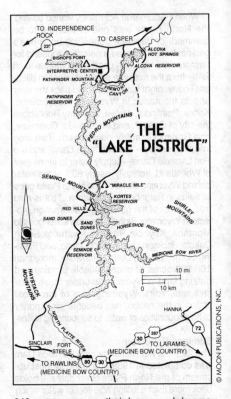

640 acres soon saw their hopes and dreams fizzle in the withering summer heat. Irrigation seemed natural for these desert lands. John Wesley Powell's idea of arid lands reclamation through dams and irrigation canals gradually gained favor, and by the 1890s Wyoming's politicians were claiming that irrigation could turn 12 to 15 million acres of the state into productive farmland. The Carey Act—named for Wyoming's Sen. Joseph M. Carey—tested these claims by having the federal government donate land to the states to be reclaimed by settlers. Wyoming became the first state to try out the new law, but only 10% of the two million acres in the program were finally patented. The costs were simply too high and the return too low; funding for the massive dams and irrigation canals could only come from the federal government. The Reclamation Act of 1902 was designed to do just that.

When Reclamation Act money started flowing, the North Platte was one of the first to be dammed (or damned, depending upon one's perspective). It seemed a potential godsend for farmers who had long used waterwheels to lift water from the river into adjacent irrigation ditches. Today, eight giant dams hold back the river and its tributaries in Wyoming: the Seminoe, Kortes, Pathfinder, Alcova, and Gray Reef above the city of Casper, and the Glendo, Guernsey, and Grayrocks farther downstream. Two long irrigation canals—the Interstate Canal and the Fort Laramie Canal—supply water to farms east of Wheatland. Ironically, nearly 80% of the water behind Wyoming dams on the North Platte goes to fields in neighboring Nebraska. This is also true at most of the other large reclamation projects in Wyoming: Bighorn Canyon water goes to Montana, Keyhole Reservoir water to South Dakota, Jackson Lake water to Idaho, and Flaming Gorge water to Utah. Meanwhile, more than 100,000 acres of once-valuable farming and grazing land in Wyoming lie under these massive reservoirs. Wyoming, one of the driest states in the nation, has become an exporter of huge quantities of water to surrounding states.

Seminoe Reservoir

The 295-foot-high concrete arch Seminoe Dam was completed in 1939 and is the farthest upstream of the North Platte River dams. It holds back more than a million acre-feet of water which drives a power plant that produces 45 megawatts of electricity. The reservoir is bounded by 3,821-acre **Seminoe State Park,** tel. (307) 328-0115, named for the nearby Seminoe Mountains, which in turn were named after the French trapper Basil Cimineau Lajeunesse—folks apparently had a hard time spelling his middle name. Entrance to the park costs $3 for nonresident vehicles, $2 if you're driving a Wyoming vehicle. The reservoir stretches almost 20 miles south of the dam through desolate, rocky mountains and gigantic dunes of white sand. Sandy beaches along the shoreline attract swimmers in late summer. Juniper and ponderosa pine trees dot the hills, while sagebrush, greasewood, yucca, and salt sage grow on the lower slopes. The steep 500-foot knife edge of Horseshoe Ridge is visible on the eastern shore. Golden eagles nest along the southern arm of Seminoe

BRIAN BARDWELL

Reservoir, and bighorn sheep and elk have been reintroduced. The area also abounds with sage grouse.

Seminoe has three state park **campgrounds** ($4, open year-round) along its northwest shore. Water and toilets are available. You can also camp for free on Bureau of Reclamation sand dunes along the lake's southern arm. The reservoir is popular for fishing (rainbow, brown, and cutthroat trout, and walleye) and water-skiing. Gas and limited provisions are available at Seminoe Boat Club. Access from Rawlins and Sinclair to the western shore of Seminoe is relatively easy via a 34-mile-long paved road, but the 70 miles of mixed pavement and gravel from Casper are a bit harder to take. The eastern shore is even less accessible.

An overlook at the dam site provides views into the steep rocky canyon and the dam that spans the chasm. North of this, the road drops steeply into the canyon and then climbs up through Morgan Creek Canyon, where big ponderosa pines, willows, and cottonwoods line the creek. A few miles beyond this, the road descends over a pass and then down through Hamilton Creek Canyon, finally emerging into open sagebrush country near the **Miracle Mile** of the North Platte River. You'll find free camping—among the cottonwoods that line the riverbank—and excellent trout fishing. More free camping is at Sage Creek Road, a half mile north of the river crossing. The name Miracle Mile—actually three miles of free-flowing river—

refers to this popular "blue ribbon" fishery, maintained by regulated flows from the 244-foot-high **Kortes Dam** power plant just upstream. In reality, the miracle is that any stretch of the North Platte still has anything resembling natural flows.

Pathfinder Reservoir

Pathfinder Reservoir is 30 miles southwest of Casper on State 220 and then another 10 miles in along County Road 409. In 1905, the federal government provided funds for this, the first dam in eastern Wyoming, to be built near the junction of the Sweetwater and North Platte Rivers. Proponents claimed that the reservoir would irrigate more than 700,000 acres, primarily in Wyoming, but, instead, only 130,000 acres were irrigated, nearly all in Nebraska.

Completed in 1909, Pathfinder Dam is considered an engineering marvel for its time and is listed on the National Register of Historic Places. The 214-foot-high arched structure is made up of large granite blocks quarried from adjacent hills and held together with cement and steel hauled by wagon teams from Casper, 45 miles away. (The trip sometimes took three weeks.)

Pathfinder is named for explorer John C. Frémont, "Pathfinder of the West." In 1842 he ventured down the river and—against the advice of his guides—decided to run the canyon below the present dam site (now Fremont Canyon). He and his men narrowly escaped alive, as Frémont described:

> *To go back was impossible; the torrent before us was a sheet of foam; and, shut up in the chasm by the rocks, which in some places seemed to almost meet overhead, the roar of the waters was deafening. . . the boat struck a concealed rock immediately at the foot of the fall, which whirled her over in an instant. . . . For a hundred yards below, the current was covered with floating books and boxes, bales of blankets, and scattered articles of clothing. . . . For a moment, I felt somewhat disheartened. All our books— almost every record of the journey—our journals and registers of astronomical and barometrical observations—had been lost in a moment.*

Pathfinder Reservoir splits into two arms, following the upstream path of the Sweetwater and North Platte Rivers. **Pathfinder National Wildlife Refuge** covers 16,807 acres of land around scattered parts of the reservoir and is home to many mammals and birds. Canada geese nest along the shore, and white pelicans nest on an island here. **Camping** is available at Pathfinder Mountain and Bishops Point ($5; April to mid-September), or you can camp for free along much of the lake's hundred-mile shore (except within the refuge). The deep-blue lake is a popular place for anglers in search of cutthroat, brown, and rainbow trout, or walleye. Sailboarders find some of Wyoming's finest sailing conditions. **Pathfinder Marina** has rental boats, fishing gear, gas, and a snack bar.

Not far from the dam is an old stone building that once housed the dam tender but is today used as an **interpretive center.** Summer hours are Saturday 11 a.m.-5 p.m. and Sunday 10 a.m.-4 p.m.; ask at the adjacent frame house for a peek inside at other times. A pleasant 1.5-mile loop trail crosses the dam, follows Fremont Canyon (lined with hundreds of cliff-swallow nests), and then re-crosses the river over an impressive swinging footbridge before returning to the interpretive center. The interpretive center has a brochure describing sights along the path.

The Lynching of Cattle Kate

Deep beneath the waters of Pathfinder Reservoir lies the site of one of the most infamous Wyoming lynchings. In 1889, James Averell and Ella "Cattle Kate" Watson operated a ranch here. Local cattle barons accused Averell of housing rustlers and operating a saloon and gambling house for them, with Cattle Kate running a sideline business in which cattle were exchanged for "personal favors." The charges were apparently a smokescreen put up by A.J. Bothwell and other large landowners who were angry that Averell and Watson had filed homestead claims on land being grazed by Bothwell's cattle. When Averell had the temerity to call the cattle barons "land sharks" in a letter to the Casper newspaper, they responded by sending a party out to eliminate the two. Averell and Watson were found hanging from a tree along the Sweetwater River. Later, the six men who

perpetrated the hanging escaped prosecution when the chief witness suddenly disappeared—apparently murdered by one of the lynching party. Bothwell went on to gain title to Averell and Watson's land, despite national newspaper complaints about "the barbaric lynching of a woman in Wyoming Territory."

Alcova Reservoir
Although much smaller than Pathfinder or Seminoe Reservoirs, Alcova is a favorite recreation spot for the people of Casper. Sailboarding, sailing, water-skiing, and ice fishing are all popular sports on this windy lake located 30 miles southwest of Casper. The upper portion of the reservoir reaches into famed **Fremont Canyon,** a mini-Grand Canyon whose red vertical cliffs rise 500 feet above the river. Access is via dirt roads from both sides. The water makes for exciting river-running if you have a kayak and the necessary skills. Golden eagles nest here. It's also very popular with rock climbers. You'll find dozens of climbs here, up to a rating of 5.12. For details, stop by Mountain Sports in Casper for a copy of Steve Petro's *Climber's Guide to Fremont Canyon and Dome Rock.* Anglers try their luck with the rainbow and cutthroat trout and walleye.

The name Alcova comes from **Alcova Hot Springs** (129° F water), so named because of its location within a series of coves. At the turn of the century, developers tried to turn the hot springs into a spa, but the propensity of Wyomingites to take baths but once a week made the venture a failure. The springs were covered by the reservoir, but an artesian well below the dam pours forth the naturally heated water. Bring your swimsuit!

The 265-foot-high Alcova Dam, part of the depression-era Kendrick Project, was completed in 1938; a 36-megawatt power plant was added in the 1980s. Facilities here include picnic areas, swimming beaches, four campgrounds ($5 for tents, $12 for RVs), and the **Alcova Lakeside Marina,** tel. (307) 472-6666, where you can rent boats and buy gas or supplies. Water leaves Alcova Dam and flows into small **Gray Reef Reservoir,** used to control the fluctuating discharges from Alcova and to generate more power. From here some of the water is diverted into the 62-mile Casper Canal to irrigate 24,000 acres of alfalfa, barley, oats, and corn west of Casper. A campground below Gray Reef Dam is a favorite place to launch canoes for a leisurely float down the river.

OREGON TRAIL LANDMARKS

Three of the most famous landmarks along the entire Oregon Trail lie within Natrona County: Independence Rock, Devil's Gate, and Split Rock. Travelers anticipated these landmarks, for they marked the start of a long, gentle approach to the Continental Divide 80 miles west. The route past these landmarks paralleled the Sweetwater River—a ribbon of lush grass in a rugged, desolate landscape. The names applied to adjacent mountains and creeks offer clues to the land's harshness: Rattlesnake Mountains, Poison Spider Creek, Greasewood Creek, Sulfur Creek, and Stinking Creek. Steamboat Lake, just a few miles north of Independence Rock, was a source of bicarbonate of soda used to bake bread. Cattle that drank the lake's putrid water died, while bread made with this baking soda took on a greenish cast. But along the Sweetwater, horses and oxen could find forage, firewood was available, and the clean mountain water offered a relief from the alkaline springs to the east. (The name Sweetwater arose when a mule team carrying sugar lost its load in the river.) Today, State 220 crosses the old Oregon Trail several miles east of its junction with U.S. 287 at Muddy Gap. The highway parallels the trail for the next 45 miles west.

Independence Rock
Head southwest from Casper along State 220 for 55 miles till the granitic dome of Independence Rock rises above the flat surrounding plain. Though not as spectacular or colorful, the setting seems reminiscent of Australia's Ayers Rock. Independence Rock is 1,950 feet long by 850 feet wide; its smoothly rounded top reaches to 193 feet. Travelers could not resist the chance to note their passing on this gigantic billboard; an estimated 50,000 names were carved, chipped, or painted on Independence Rock during the mid-19th century. Father Jean Pierre DeSmet, a famed Jesuit missionary, labeled it "the Great Register of the Desert." His initials, along with the names of Captain Bon-

August 16

Moved on up the creek saw the notable rock Independence with the names of its numerious visitors most of which are nearly obliterated by the weather & ravages of time amongst which I observed the names of two of my old friends the notable mountaneers Thos. Fitzpatrick & W. L. Sublette as likewise one of our noblest politicians Henry Clay coupled in division with that of Martin Van Buren a few miles further up the creek pases through the south point of ruged & solid looking granite rock by a verry narrow pass after passing which we entered a valy Surounded by low ruged mountains except to the West whare a defiel Shews itself the lower vally of this creek is well clothed with short grass the upper with sand & sage the mountains with short scattering pines but in many places nothing but the bear rock in large steep Surfaces made 8 miles & encamped for the night on a good plat of grass

—*Mountain man James Clyman describing Independence Rock in 1844*

neville, John C. Frémont, and many other explorers, were etched into the rock face.

Independence Rock apparently received its name from explorer and mountain man William Sublette, who arrived here on July 4, 1830, leading the first wagon train across the overland route. Oregon Trail emigrants tried to reach the rock around July 4 to be on schedule for Oregon. When the rock came into view, it was a source of rejoicing, for it offered a welcome place to rest alongside the Sweetwater River. During the heyday of migration along the Oregon Trail, dozens of wagon trains would find themselves at the rock on Independence Day, and the celebrations included patriotic flag-waving, the firing of guns, big dinners, and other festivities. Many people did not make it beyond Independence Rock; dozens of unmarked graves surround the rock.

Today, the state has a modern rest area next to Independence Rock with signs detailing the area's rich history. Hundreds of the original names carved into Independence Rock are still visible, though weathering and lichen have obliterated many more. Unfortunately, more recent travelers have added their names, sometimes covering up names over a hundred years old. Independence Rock can be climbed from a number of points along the perimeter, providing fine views of the surrounding countryside. Some of the oldest and best-preserved names are on top. An old road circles the rock, making for an interesting mile-long hike. You can spot names on all sides, and you're bound to see deer and other wildlife along the Sweetwater River. A small footbridge crosses the still-visible Oregon Trail route here.

Devil's Gate

Visible from Independence Rock and just seven miles to the southwest is another famed Oregon Trail landmark, Devil's Gate. Over the centuries, the Sweetwater River has gradually sliced a giant cleft through the Rattlesnake Mountains, leaving 370-foot cliffs on both sides of a 1,500-foot-long canyon. (An Indian legend offers an alternative origin for Devil's Gate: a gigantic tusked beast had roamed Sweetwater Valley, and when the Indians finally managed to mortally wound the animal it gouged out the nearby mountains in its death agony.) Devil's Gate was another favorite emigrant campsite. The cut is hard to miss, especially from the east—the direction of most Oregon Trail travelers. Today, the BLM maintains a historic site along State 220 with a short loop trail and signboards. At least 20 emigrant graves are nearby. The **Tom Sun Ranch**, visible from here, was established in 1872 by a French-Canadian trapper, Thomas De Beau Soleil (Thomas Sun). His original cabin is a National Historic Landmark, and the ranch is still owned by the Sun family. A small museum at the Sun Ranch is open by reservation only, tel. (307) 324-6925. The ranch also provides historical tours of the area.

Martin's Cove, just two miles northwest of Devil's Gate, is the site of the most disastrous experience along the Oregon and Mormon trails. In 1856, a group of 1,620 British converts to the Mormon religion sailed from Liverpool for Amer-

ica, intent upon reaching Salt Lake City before winter—total cost of the trip to Utah, including ship passage from England, was just $45 per person. The converts left Missouri in several groups; last to leave were 576 people under the direction of Edward Martin. They headed out in late August, crossing the North Platte at present-day Casper on October 19. Instead of the usual wagons, many of these poor emigrants pushed or pulled small handcarts that held their few possessions. Soon the weather turned bitterly cold, a blizzard dumped 18 inches of snow on them, and temperatures dropped to -14° F. The elderly and children died first; eventually even the strongest began to die. A rescue wagon from Salt Lake City finally arrived in late October, with rescuer Daniel W. Jones writing:

> *There were old men pulling and tugging their carts, sometimes loaded with a sick wife or children, women pulling along sick husbands; little children six to eight years old struggling through the mud and snow . . . The provisions we took amounted to almost nothing among so many people, many of them now on very short rations, some almost starving.*

The survivors were escorted 65 miles to Martin's Cove, a protected area near Devil's Gate. The company of foolhardy emigrants finally reached Salt Lake City in late November, but 145 members had died along the way. Another Mormon handcart company, led by James G. Willie, suffered a similar fate that same year, losing 67 people to the elements.

Split Rock

The final of the three geologic landmarks that lined the Oregon Trail through present-day Natrona County is Split Rock, a bite taken out of a solid granite mountain. The cleft was visible for two days as emigrants trudged along; it seemed to be a gunsight aimed toward the west. In the early 1860s, a Pony Express station, an overland stage station, a telegraph station, and a garrison of troops were located nearby. Today, Split Rock is noted at a turnout 10 miles west of Muddy Gap Junction along U.S. 287. Tourists sail past in minutes what took the emigrants

many long and treacherous days. See "Lander Vicinity" in the Wind River Mountains Country chapter for poins west of here on U.S. 287 including Jeffrey City and Ice Slough. If you're heading south to Rawlins on U.S. 287, see "Heading North" under "Rawlins" in the Medicine Bow Country chapter.

NORTH OF CASPER

Salt Creek Oil Field

Forty miles north of Casper is the Salt Creek Oil Field, considered the largest light oil field in the world. The 10-mile-long field covers a land of sage, sand, and rock that has produced over 600 million barrels of oil and 700 million cubic feet of gas. Much more oil has been found nearby. A drive up State 259 is a trip through a bizarre alien world of desert land carpeted with giant grasshopper-like electric pumpjacks spaced every couple hundred feet to the horizon. Actually, they look more like the little plastic ostriches sold in tourist shops—the ones that keep tipping down to a bowl of water to "drink." The pumpjacks don't run all the time, allowing the oil to accumulate in the well before pumping resumes. West of the company town of Midwest, things get even stranger, with an incredible grid of pumpjacks, dirt roads, power lines, and storage tanks crisscrossing the harsh land.

This famed oil field occupies a classic anticlinal structure that traps oil—hundred-foot cliffs

BRIAN BARDWELL

surround the field. Wyoming's territorial geologist, Samuel Aughey, discovered these unusual structures and brought the first speculators here to file placer claims in 1884. The first well in the area was drilled in 1889 by a Pennsylvania oilman, M.P. Shannon. The oil was hauled by horse-drawn wagon to Casper, 50 miles away. In 1904, Shannon sold his small Casper refinery and 105,000 acres of Salt Creek leases to European speculators for $350,000.

Four years later the real boom came when a Dutch-financed company struck black gold at 1,050 feet in the Salt Creek Field, spouting oil in a massive gusher. When the news hit, battles over land claims quickly escalated to the shouting and shooting stage. The Midwest Oil Company was formed and built the first pipeline to Casper in 1911 to feed the new Midwest refinery there. The Fransco Company added another refinery the following year, and Standard Oil of Indiana built a cracking plant to retrieve more gasoline from the crude.

As WW I steamed over the horizon, the field suddenly gained vital national importance; oil shipped to the allies from Salt Creek was considered an important factor in the defeat of Kaiser Wilhelm. After the war Standard Oil (now Amoco) bought out all of Midwest's Salt Creek properties, but the 14 remaining companies competed with each other for the crude, with oil derricks within spitting distance of each other.

Production declined as the companies attempted to pump the oil too fast, trying to get it before it flowed into neighboring wells. Finally, in 1939, Salt Creek became the first oil field in America to run as a unitized operation with joint management of the various wells for greater efficiency and conservation. Production in Salt Creek reached a peak in 1923 (when it produced five percent of the nation's oil), but the introduction of gas injection in the 1920s and water flooding in the 1950s helped push more oil to the wellheads. Today, more than 100 years after its discovery, workers have recovered just a third of the oil at Salt Creek. Culling the remaining oil will require more sophisticated techniques such as flooding with carbon dioxide. Even still, Salt Creek's current yield of 12,000 barrels a day accounts for two-thirds of Natrona County's oil production. It's Wyoming's third-largest producing field.

Midwest and Edgerton

The twin oil towns of Midwest (pop. 360) and Edgerton (pop. 160) lie near the center of the Salt Creek Field. A paved road north of Midwest leads to the Shannon Pool oil field, where oil was first discovered. Thousands of drill holes surround the towns, laced together by a grid of dirt roads, power lines, and pipes.

The company town of Midwest is named for Midwest Oil Company, now a part of Amoco. Its four straight streets contain rows of identical wooden houses built in the 1920s and now showing their age. The stench of sulfur from a gas-recovery plant south of town permeates the air. Midwest's golf course is dotted with oil pumps, and folks attending Mass at the Catholic church can hear the quiet, rhythmic "ker-thunk" of a pumpjack just a hundred feet away. Midwest was especially hard hit by the slide in oil prices in the '80s; assessed valuation plummeted from $9.2 million in 1987 to $1.5 million in 1989! The impact is obvious in a walk around town: peeling paint on the small wooden box houses, boarded-up buildings, aging cars, and a sense of defeat. Check out the small **Salt Creek Museum** in the town hall, tel. (307) 437-6513. Get groceries, booze, and gas at the general store.

The dumpy little town of Edgerton has a bit more to offer, with a grocery, a bank, two bars, a library, a gas station, and an old-time hardware store. For meals, try **Edgerton Cafe.** The only local lodging place is **Tea Pot Motor Lodge** in Edgerton, tel. (307) 437-6541, where rooms cost $30 s, $34 d. Buses from **Powder River Trailways,** tel. (800) 442-3682, stop here, heading both north and south. Edgerton claims a bit of baseball trivia: it was the first place in America to have a baseball game played under lights. The big local event—including dancing, food, a golf tournament, and more—comes in August, when both towns celebrate **Salt Creek Days.** Points northwest of Midwest and Edgerton are covered in the Powder River chapter.

Tempest in a Teapot

Twenty-five miles north of Casper along U.S. 87 is a distinctive butte, Teapot Rock. Until a 1962 windstorm knocked down the "spout" that bent away from one side, the rock resembled a teapot. In the first decades of this century, rapid growth in the oil industry sent prospectors and

speculators all over the west in search of black gold. To ensure adequate fuel supplies for the Navy's ships after WW I, the government set aside three large oil reserves—Elk Hills and Buena Vista in California, and Wyoming's Teapot Dome Oil Field (named for Teapot Rock).

In 1921 and 1922, Secretary of the Interior Albert B. Fall secretly leased Teapot Dome to Edward Doheny and Harry Sinclair, owners of Mammoth Oil Company—could anyone have ever come up with a more fitting name for a corrupt corporation? Although the action was technically legal, the $100,000 bribe paid by Doheny to President Harding's interior secretary was decidedly not legal, and Fall was forced to resign. The action brought a plethora of charges against the giant oil companies, and political cartoonists had a heyday with Teapot Dome. Interior Secretary Fall was convicted of accepting bribes and spent a year in prison. Harry Sinclair—for whom both the oil company and the Wyoming town are named—hired detectives to spy on a jury investigating Teapot Dome and was sent to jail in 1929 for contempt of court. He also spent three months in jail for refusing to testify before a Senate committee investigating the scandal. Today, the U.S. Navy still owns thousands of acres at Teapot Dome, and there are hundreds of oil wells a few miles east of the highway. A sign points out Naval Petroleum Reserve Number 3, but you won't find any historical signs mentioning this rather sordid piece of Wyoming history. The mailboxes and nearby white buildings of Teapot Dome Ranch mark the site of Teapot Rock.

HEADING WEST

Powder River

The tiny settlement of Powder River (pop. 50) lies along U.S. 20/26 where it crosses this famous river 35 lonely miles west of Casper. Not much is here today; writer James Conaway called the town "little more than a Texaco station and a bunch of pronghorn antelope looking at it." On the third weekend in July, however, several hundred people flock (pun intended) to town for the annual **Sheepherder's Fair**. It features dog trials, sheep roping and hooking, a lamb cook-

off, and sheepherding demonstrations of all sorts. Calcutta wagering goes on for most events, and a band plays country-western favorites late into the evening for a happy throng of dancers. Stay at **Tumble Inn Motel,** tel. (307) 234-4026.

Hell's Half Acre

Head west from Casper on U.S. 20/26 for 45 miles to one of the freaks of nature, Hell's Half Acre. Actually covering 320 acres, the area includes a strange collection of deeply eroded and colorful badlands surrounded by featureless sage-covered plains. Ancient coal deposits within the badlands caught on fire and burned for many years, and when explorer Captain Bonneville passed by in 1833, he labeled it Devils Kitchen because of these sulfurous fumes. The name Hell's Half Acre was a later title. Indians used these badlands as a buffalo trap, driving herds of them to their deaths over the canyon walls. In the late 19th century, after whites had slaughtered the bison to the brink of extinction, bone pickers gleaned thousands of these bones from Hell's Half Acre for eastern fertilizer plants. Archaeologists later discovered more bones here, along with arrowheads and other artifacts. Hell's Half Acre is well worth a stop, but be forewarned that a kitschy souvenir shop, cafe, motel (tel. 307-472-0018), and RV park detract from the view. It's a great place to meet busloads of tottering tourists from hell.

In 1996, the $90-million movie *Starship Trooper* was filmed at Hell's Half Acre. For the production, a space-station "city" was built on the south half of the badlands, a controversial action that led to considerable damage to the easily eroded slopes.

Lysite and Lost Cabin

This area is decidedly off the beaten track, located eight miles north of another nowheresville town, **Moneta** (pop. 10). At one time the main route into the Bighorn Basin and Yellowstone lay along the Lysite road, but with completion of a highway through Wind River Canyon in 1927, traffic bypassed this area. Slow-paced Lysite has an old-time country store and is the sort of place where horses are still a means of transportation. Lysite library is housed in a building slightly larger than a shoe box.

BOB RACE

with only the clothes on his back, decided sheep were a better bet, and gradually became a millionaire. Okie once ran 30,000 sheep through the surrounding country, gaining the title of "Sheep King." His mansion—called "The Big Tepee" by local Indians—was built in 1900 for $30,000 and filled with carved fireplaces, Asian chandeliers, imported furniture, stained-glass, and Persian prayer rugs. Surrounding it were a greenhouse filled with flowers tended by Japanese gardeners, a roller rink, a dance hall, and even an aviary housing 140 exotic birds. A power plant was built to supply electricity for Okie's town. In 1930, Okie drowned in a nearby reservoir while hunting ducks. The old mansion is not open to the public but is visible from the gate.

Castle Gardens

A remote and little-known archaeological site is Castle Gardens, located 21 miles south of Moneta on a gravel road and then another six miles east on a rough dirt road—not recommended for RVs or after rains, when the road turns into a quagmire. Signs at Moneta and at the turnoff keep you from getting lost. Castle Gardens is a desolate area with all sorts of odd sandstone formations: toadstools, spires, and various creatures seem to appear. It's easy to see how this would be a sacred spot for the Indians who came here centuries ago. Small juniper and limber pines grow amid the grey rocks and sand, creating a garden in the castles of Castle Gardens. There's no camping here, but you will find picnic tables and an outhouse.

Dozens of Indian pictographs (presumably Shoshonean in origin) have been sharply incised into the soft rock walls. They include many in the shield motif, believed to represent the round shields of Indian warriors. While they may be up to 900 years old, these figures are probably more recent than the pecked style of pictographs present in the Dinwoody Creek and Legend Rock areas. Castle Gardens' figures that show horses or tepees are clearly from the period after A.D. 1700. The most elaborate shield found here—the figure of a turtle painted green, yellow, and red—is now in the State Museum in Cheyenne. The remaining pictographs are protected by chain-link fences, but vandals have marred many of these priceless artifacts

Three miles to the east is Lost Cabin, named for a gold mine in the Big Horn Mountains. Miner Allen Hulburt and two partners discovered a stream filled with gold, but Indians killed his partners and partially burned their cabin. The dazed miner scooped up as much gold as he could carry and fled to Casper, where his tale pricked more than a few ears. Despite repeated efforts by Hulburt and others, the Lost Cabin mine was never again found. (This is only one of many such tales about the fabled mine.)

The flyspeck of a town called Lost Cabin is centered around the elaborate mansion of John B. Okie. He came to Wyoming as a cowboy

with graffiti. The site leaves you with mixed emotions: a multitude of questions about what the images represent, a feeling of closeness to the natural world in this remote and fascinating place, and an utter disgust for those who would destroy this cultural heritage.

West to Shoshoni

The 85 miles of highway (U.S. 20/26) that connect Casper with Shoshoni cross an almost featureless plain, a place that seems to define the word "bleak." With no trees in sight, the clouds throw moving shadows across a landscape of sage and grass. This is antelope country. Even the ranches are few and far between out here, and cattle take slow, desultory steps in the summer heat or brace against the bitter winds of winter. For many travelers this is pedal-to-the-metal country, a place to crank up the country tunes and sail on west.

BOB RACE

BOB RACE

WIND RIVER MOUNTAINS COUNTRY

The Wind River Mountains—Wyoming's highest and longest range—form a dramatic divide between two of the state's most important rivers. The east side drains into the Wind River, eventually reaching the Atlantic Ocean, and the western slopes drop into the Green River and eventually the Pacific. The name Wind River Mountains originated as a Crow Indian reference to the warm chinook winds that blow down the Wind River Valley.

The Land

This chapter covers Sublette and Fremont counties, named for two of the state's most famous explorers. Fremont County is a land of sharp contrasts. The eastern end consists of a spacious, arid landscape of sage, grass, and antelope, while to the west you'll find the fluorescent green of irrigated fields along the Wind River and the pastel badlands near Dubois. Along the southern and western borders rise the snow-crested Wind River and Absaroka Mountains.

At almost six million acres, this is Wyoming's second-largest county after Sweetwater.

The centerpiece of Fremont County is the Wind River Reservation, home to both the Eastern Shoshone and the Northern Arapaho peoples. Within the reservation itself lie the tiny towns of Fort Washakie, Ethete, and Arapahoe, as well as the larger non-Indian settlement of Riverton. Lander borders it on the south; farther south stand the historic mining towns of South Pass and Atlantic City. West of the reservation, the town of Dubois provides an entry point into the Absarokas, the Tetons, and Yellowstone.

The Wind River Valley is farming and ranching country, with nearly half of Fremont County's people employed in agriculture. Some 150,000 acres of alfalfa hay, feed and malt barley, sugar beets, and oats are under irrigation each year. This is Wyoming's second-biggest dairy county, eclipsed only by Park County, and it's home to the largest number of horses in the state. A sub-

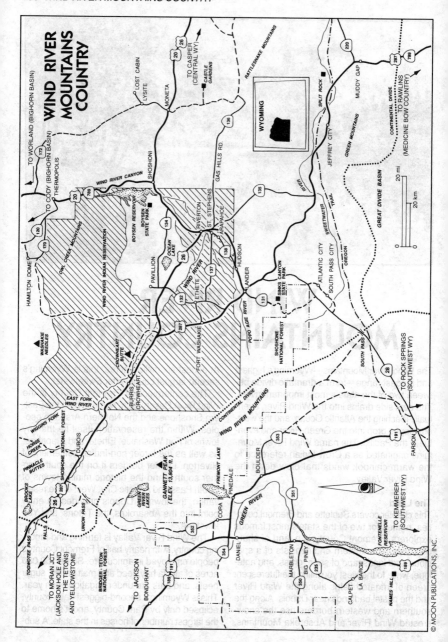

WIND RIVER MOUNTAINS COUNTRY

© MOON PUBLICATIONS, INC.

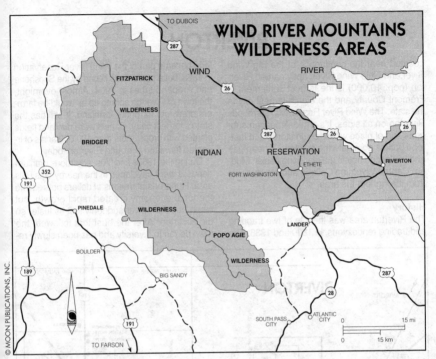

stantial amount of oil and natural-gas production takes place on the Wind River Reservation, where energy royalties bring in millions of dollars each year. Uranium was discovered in the Gas Hills area east of Riverton during the 1950s and spawned a major industry in the 1960s and '70s before plummeting when the Three-Mile Island accident of 1981 brought the dangers of nuclear power to the forefront. Today the main work in the uranium mines is an effort to clean up the abandoned sites.

Sublette County has just 4,500 individuals spread over 10,495 square miles. Cattle ex-

ceed people by a 16:1 margin, and you'll find only one town of any size—Pinedale—with a few folks living in the little burgs of Big Piney, Marbleton, Boulder, and Daniel. Not surprisingly, the big industry here is ranching, although the area's scenic beauty draws increasing numbers of tourists. You'll find magnificent vistas of the Winds all along the western front—far more dramatic than from the eastern side. Based in Riverton, the **Wind River Visitors Council,** tel. (800) 645-6233, has brochures with information on the entire area, including events, lodging, outdoor activities, and more.

RIVERTON

Located near the confluence of the Big Wind River and Little Wind River, aptly named Riverton (pop. 10,000) is the largest settlement in Fremont County and the eighth-largest city in the state. The Wind River Reservation surrounds Riverton on all sides. It's a mid-American suburbia sort of place where chain stores and fast-food outlets dominate the outskirts. Cheap gas and low-priced hotels make visiting easier. Modern Central Wyoming College attracts students from throughout the area.

History

The Riverton area was the site of two trapping and trading rendezvous, in 1830 and 1838. The land became part of the Wind River Reservation in 1868, but a portion was ceded by the Shoshone and Arapaho tribes in 1904. Almost overnight, the town of Riverton sprang up as would-be farmers drew lots for prime farmland. It still has the state's largest dairy. Canals were dug and fields planted with crops; more than 100,000 acres of irrigated farmland surround Riverton today.

During the 1960s and '70s, enormous uranium deposits were developed in the nearby Gas Hills area. Hundreds of millions of dollars poured into the local economy created rapid growth, but when nuclear power suddenly lost its luster so did Riverton. After the bust that followed, the town began to diversify and has been slowly re-

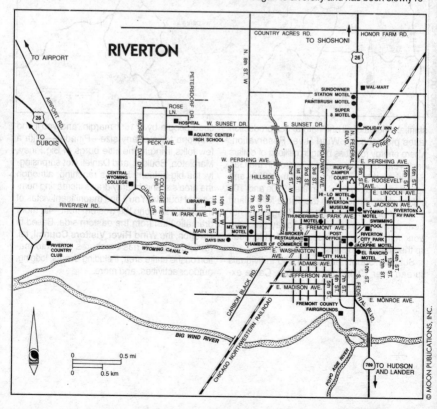

© MOON PUBLICATIONS, INC.

bounding. Today the largest private employer is DH Print, a manufacturer of computer printers. Other major employers are Bonneville Transloaders, a soda-ash hauling company; the Brunton Co., manufacturer of compasses, binoculars, and pocket transits; and various government agencies. The area is becoming increasingly popular with retirees.

Sights
The **Riverton Museum,** 700 E. Park Ave., tel. (307) 856-2665, is open Tues.-Sat. 10 a.m.-4 p.m. year-round; no charge. Local historical exhibits in this rambling, surprisingly large museum include a tepee containing a buffalo robe and powwow drum, an Indian cradle board with saddle, a model of the Carissa Mine at South Pass, various old farm and mining equipment, and an interesting exhibit on oil drilling. Take a gander at Desert Demon, a stuffed wild mustang that proved untamable—hence his current, more sedate, bullet-tamed condition. While here, also check out the photos of Leslie King, the father of former president Gerald R. Ford and a prominent Riverton-area rancher. (President Ford's parents were divorced, and his mother later married a Mr. Ford.) Gerald Ford worked as a Yellowstone National Park ranger after graduating from college in Michigan but is not known to have fallen into any geysers.

Riverton Livestock Auction, located on Fairgrounds Rd., tel. (307) 856-2209, is Wyoming's second-largest livestock auction barn, after Torrington. The monthly horse sales are the most enjoyable.

Accommodations
Riverton has some 15 different places to bed down for the night, all priced quite reasonably. See the "Riverton Accommodations" chart for specifics. For a taste of country living, **Cottonwood Ranch B&B,** tel. (307) 856-3064, is a working farm and ranch with three guest rooms in a family homestead. The ranch serves a full breakfast and welcomes kids.

Camping
The nearest public camping ($4; open year-round) is 20 miles north in **Boysen State Park. Rudy's Camper Court,** 622 E. Lincoln Ave., tel. (307) 856-9764, charges $16 for RVs, $9 for tents. Showers for noncampers cost $3.

Open year-round. **Owl Creek Kampground,** six miles northeast of Riverton on U.S. 26, tel. (307) 856-2869, has shady in-the-trees tent and RV sites for $15, showers for noncampers for $3. Open mid-May to mid-September. **Riverton RV Park,** 1618 E. Park Ave., tel. (307) 856-3913 or (800) 528-3913, has tent sites for $10, RV hookups for $18-20. Showers run $2 for noncampers; open year-round.

Food
One of the best local eateries is, surprisingly, **Airport Cafe,** at the airport, tel. (307) 856-2838, where homemade cinnamon rolls and pies are specialties. Fly out here for breakfast. The Thursday-night Navajo tacos at **Trailhead Restaurant,** 831 N. Federal Blvd., tel. (307) 856-7990, are worth a taste. For classy lunches and prime rib, steak, seafood, roast duck, and Mexican dinners, head to **Broker Restaurant,** 203 E. Main, tel. (307) 856-0555. **The Breadboard,** 124 E. Washington, tel. (307) 856-7044, makes good sub sandwiches. Get espresso, baked goods, and lunchtime sandwiches and bagels from **Split Rock Coffee & Bakery,** 108 S. 3rd E, tel. (307) 856-4334. For the drive-up version, stop by **Java Java,** 721 W. Main, tel. (307) 857-3999.

Bull Steakhouse, 1100 W. Main, tel. (307) 856-4728, has filet mignon, seafood, soup, a salad bar, and daily lunch specials. More than 200 Indian portraits line the walls. **Valley View Supper Club,** 4911 Valley View Rd., tel. (307) 856-2447, is another favorite for steaks and prime rib, but head to nearby Hudson (see "Hudson," below) for the very best steaks in this part of Wyoming. **Golden Corral,** 400 N. Federal Blvd., tel. (307) 856-1152, has a sprawling salad bar/buffet for stuff-it-in meals. **Trade Winds,** 302 N. Federal, tel. (307) 856-7666, serves Americanized Chinese dishes that locals rave over. **New China Restaurant,** 302 N. Federal Blvd., tel. (307) 856-7666, also enjoys popularity. You'll find all the fast-food chains on N. Federal Boulevard, or on the west end of Main Street. The cheapest meal deal in town is at Little Caesar's in the Kmart store on N. Federal, where you can get pizza by the slice. When everything else is closed, head to the always-open **Silver Spoon Cafe,** 1104 N. Federal Blvd., tel. (307) 856-4085. Get groceries at **Woodward's IGA,** 619 N. Federal and 906 W. Main, or **Smith's,** 1200 W. Main.

RIVERTON ACCOMMODATIONS

Note: Accommodations are listed from least to most expensive. Add a seven percent sales and lodging tax to these rates. Area code is 307.

Jackpine Motel; 120 S. Federal; tel. 856-9251; $25 s, $28 d; microwaves and fridges in rooms

Mountain View Motel; 720 W. Main; tel. 856-2418; $26 s, $28 d; kitchenettes $36 s or d; local calls 35 cents

El Rancho Motel; 221 S. Federal; tel. 856-7455; $28 s, $30 d; see rooms first

Thunderbird Motel; 302 E. Fremont; tel. 856-9201; $28-30 s, $30-36 d; quiet location, well-maintained, AAA approved

Wyoming Motel; 319 N. Federal; tel. 856-6549; $29 s, $32 d

Driftwood Inn; 611 W. Main; tel. 856-5811; $30 s, $34 d; kitchenettes $38 s or d; weekly rates available

Hi-Lo Motel; 414 N. Federal; tel. 856-9223; $30-32 s, $33-35 d; very clean, fridges and microwaves in rooms, weekly rates available

Paintbrush Motel; 1550 N. Federal; tel. 856-9238 or (800) 204-9238; $35 s, $38 d; clean and friendly, AAA approved

Tomahawk Motor Lodge; 208 E. Main; tel. 856-9205 or (800) 637-7378; $37 s, $42 d; clean and comfortable, AAA approved

Days Inn; 909 W. Main St.; tel. 856-9677 or (800) 325-2525; $35-45 s, $45-55 d; continental breakfast, AAA approved

Sundowner Station Motel; 1616 N. Federal; tel. 856-6503 or (800) 874-1116; $42-44 s, $44-46 d; outdoor pool, exercise room, sauna, very nice

Super 8 Motel; 1040 N. Federal; 857-2400 or (800) 800-8000; $44 s, $48 d; continental breakfast, AAA approved

Cottonwood Ranch B&B; 13 miles northwest; tel. 856-3064; $50 s, $55 d; working ranch and farm, three guest rooms, shared baths, full breakfast, children welcome

Holiday Inn; 900 E. Sunset; tel. 856-8100 or (800) 465-4329; $59 s or d; indoor pool, jacuzzi, exercise room, AAA approved

Entertainment

The local bowling alley—**StarLite Lanes,** 837 N. Federal, tel. (307) 856-5944—has country music nightly. **Good Time Charlie's Lounge,** 502 E. Main St., tel. (307) 856-4285, generally has rock bands on weekends. **Club El Toro,** tel. (307) 332-4627, in nearby Hudson also has live tunes. Watch movies at **Acme Theatre,** 312 E. Main, tel. (307) 856-3415. Central Wyoming College's **Peck Summer Theatre** produces plays both on campus and for dinner entertainment at local restaurants. Call (307) 856-5087 for upcoming productions.

Events

The **Wild West Winter Carnival** includes an ice-sculpture contest in Riverton and many other events at Boysen Reservoir. Summer kicks off with the **Mountain Man Rendezvous** the first weekend in July on the site of the 1838 rendezvous. Events include shooting matches, basket-making, beading, Indian dancing, a pow-wow, and other old-time activities. The **Riverton Rendezvous** occupies the next two weekends and includes a car show, a rodeo, and a **Hot Air Balloon Rally** (third weekend in July), where you're likely to see more than two dozen colorful balloons lifting off at sunrise. The event attracts celebrities from the ballooning world.

The **Fremont County Fair and Rodeo** comes to the Riverton Fairground in early August, with a carnival, parade, demolition derby, PRCA rodeo, musical entertainment, and fun

CATHY CARLSON

for all ages. Other **rodeos** are held every Tuesday night mid-June to August. In mid-August, the Riverton Museum sponsors a **Folk Festival** with demonstrations of pioneer skills and arts such as storytelling, old-fashioned cooking, and folk music. Meet all sorts of people in turn-of-the-century costumes and horse-drawn carriages. You can have more fun at the **Cowboy Poetry Roundup** in October, where the cowpokes spin tales at the largest cowboy poetry event in Wyoming.

Shopping
Books and Briar, 313 E. Main, tel. (307) 856-1797, a surprisingly nice bookshop in downtown Riverton, sells quite a few Wyoming and Indian titles. Also check out the bookstore on the CWC campus. **Wind River Trading Post,** 924 S. Federal Blvd., tel. (307) 856-6141, sells locally made beadwork and jewelry, and turquoise jewelry from Arizona. Royce Brown, a local Arapaho craftsman, makes miniature Indian war bonnets. Call **Lone Bear Crafts,** tel. (307) 856-1521, for details.

Recreation
Riverton has an outdoor summer-only pool in City Park at Main and Federal and an excellent indoor **Aquatic Center** at the high school on W. Sunset Dr., tel. (307) 856-4230. The Aquatic Center also has a sauna and a whirlpool. Both are free. The 18-hole **Riverton Country Club** is at 4275 Country Club Dr., tel. (307) 856-4779. **Central Wyoming College** offers nature

walks in the surrounding mountain country through the summer months; call (307) 856-9291 or (800) 735-8418 for details. Rent mountain bikes from **Out Sportin',** 310 E. Main, tel. (307) 856-1373 or (800) 371-1373.

The **Rails to Trails** project has created a 25-mile-long path along what was once a railroad grade. The route reaches from Riverton to Shoshoni, providing a fine place to mountain-bike or hike. Most of the path is gravel, but a portion through Riverton is paved.

Information and Services
Riverton Chamber of Commerce is in the old railroad depot at 1st and Main, tel. (307) 856-4801 or (800) 735-8418, and is open Mon.-Fri. 8 a.m.-5 p.m. The attractive 109-acre campus of **Central Wyoming College,** tel. (307) 856-9291 or (800) 442-1228, is on the west edge of town along U.S. 26. Founded in 1966, it offers two-year programs in more than 50 fields for nearly 1,000 full-time students. The impressive **Arts Center** houses a small gallery with changing exhibits. Riverton's modern **public library,** 1330 W. Park Ave., tel. (307) 856-3556, is open Monday, Tuesday, and Thursday noon-9 p.m., Wednesday 9 a.m.-9 p.m., and Friday and Saturday 9 a.m.-1 p.m. The college also has a good-sized library. For fast cash, you'll find **ATMs** at First Bank, 215 N. Broadway; Riverton State Bank, 616 N. Federal Blvd.; First Interstate Bank, 323 E. Main; and Key Bank, 123 E. Main. **Columbia/Riverton Memorial Hospital,** 2100 W. Sunset Dr., tel. (307) 856-4161, has emergency medical service.

Transportation
Riverton Airport, two miles northwest of town, has daily connections to Denver on **United Express,** tel. (800) 241-6522. There are no taxis in town, but you can rent cars at the airport from **Avis,** tel. (307) 856-5052 or (800) 831-2847, or **Hertz,** tel. (307) 654-3131 or (800) 654-3131.

SANTA (Shoshone Arapahoe Nations Transit Authority), tel. (800) 439-7118, has on-demand bus service throughout the area with connections to Jackson, Rock Springs (Greyhound and Amtrak connections), Rawlins, Pinedale, Cody, and Salt Lake City. They also operate a twice-daily scheduled shuttle connecting Riverton with Ethete, Hudson, and Lander.

RIVERTON VICINITY

SHOSHONI

During the late 1970s and early '80s Shoshoni (pop. 500) was a booming oil and uranium town, but the bust of the late 1980s left abandoned streets with tall grass and peeling paint and plywood windows on much of downtown. Tumbleweeds rolled down Main Street, and locals joked that no one wanted to be the last to turn out the lights because they were afraid of getting stuck with the electric bill! People are now starting to move back to Shoshoni, and things have begun to turn around a bit in the last few years. Locals point with pride to the (slightly) spruced-up center of town, three town parks, the new rodeo arena, and several cafes that have arrived of late. You still aren't likely to confuse Shoshoni with Jackson, but at least the town isn't as bleak as Jeffrey City. (See "Heading West" under "Casper Vicinity" in the Central Wyoming chapter for points east of Shoshoni, including the minuscule towns of Lysite, Lost Cabin, and Moneta.)

Practicalities

Shoshoni's main attraction is the **Yellowstone Drug Store,** tel. (307) 876-2539. During the summer months, scads of tourists stop here for ice-cream floats and ultra-thick malts at the old-time soda fountain. Peek in the windows of Gamble's across the street, a crowded, funky old store that was closed by the fire marshal several years ago. Also in Shoshoni is the interesting little **CU Rock Shop.** You can still see tepee rings northwest of town. Shoshoni is bordered on the north by Badwater Creek and on the south by Poison Creek. East of Shoshoni is an arid landscape of badlands topography.

Aside from Yellowstone Drug and the Rock Shop, Shoshoni's primary redeeming qualities are the reasonably priced accommodations and gas. **Desert Inn Motel,** 605 W. Second St., tel. (307) 876-2273, has rooms for $26 s, $332 d; and **Shoshoni Motel,** 503 W. Second, tel. (307) 876-2216, charges $25 s or d. **Boysen State Park** is just a few miles north of here, with camping facilities for $4 a night. You'll find rodeo ac-

tion during the summer months at Shoshoni's rodeo arena and the **Old Time Fiddlers' Contest** every Memorial Day.

Powder River Trailways, tel. (800) 442-3682, has daily buses from Shoshoni to northern and eastern Wyoming, with direct connections to other parts of America. **SANTA** (Shoshone Arapahoe Nations Transit Authority), tel. (800) 439-7118, offers on-demand bus service throughout the area, with connections all the way to Jackson, Rock Springs (Greyhound and Amtrak connections), Rawlins, Pinedale, Cody, and Salt Lake City.

BOYSEN STATE PARK

Established in 1956, Boysen State Park, tel. (307) 876-2796, surrounds a reservoir named for Asmus Boysen, a Danish emigrant who built the first dam here in 1907-08. When the water from his dam covered tracks of the Burlington Railroad, the railroad sued and had his dam blown up. The dam that now backs up the Wind River is a 230-foot-high earthen structure completed in 1961 and located at the entrance to Wind River Canyon. Boysen Reservoir is a motorboat playground popular with water-skiers and anglers (it's home to the biggest walleye in Wyoming—to 17 pounds). Its relatively warm waters attract swimmers to the beach near park headquarters.

Boysen Reservoir lies primarily within the Wind River Indian Reservation and is surrounded by open desert country. A nearly straight highway (U.S. 20) rolls north from Shoshoni over the arid hills and rocky buttes, providing a few good vistas across the lake. Southwest of Shoshoni, U.S. 26 crosses an arm of the reservoir. **Boysen Lake Marina,** on the north end near the entrance to Wind River Canyon, tel. (307) 876-2772, has a restaurant, a grocery store, and RV spaces. The reservoir is surrounded by 10 different state park campsites ($4; open year-round).

The **Wild West Winter Carnival** comes to Boysen (and Riverton) in mid-February, featuring souped-up snowmobile races, ice-fishing

contests, chariot races, ice sculptures, mountain-bike races, and even a "snodeo." The main event is the high-altitude speed run in which funny sleds—more like rockets with runners—reach speeds topping 160 mph.

GAS HILLS

The paved but almost-untraveled Gas Hills Road (State 136) leads east from the Riverton area to several now-closed open-pit uranium mines, including the Lucky McMine, discovered in 1953 by Neil and Maxine McNeice and mined for many years. Perhaps a third of the nation's uranium reserves remain in these arid hills. Today signs warn trespassers of the nuclear hazard in the abandoned mines. Dirt roads from the end of the pavement—approximately 45 miles east of Riverton—lead south to Jeffrey City, northwest to tiny Waltman, and east to Casper along Poison Spider Road. This is some of the most remote and desolate country you will ever find, with nary a tree in sight. The antelope love this sage-and-grass landscape. Castle Gardens can also be accessed from Gas Hills Road. A sign on the road—easy to miss—points out the turnoff. (See "Heading West" under "Casper Vicinity" in the Central Wyoming chapter for more.)

HUDSON

You could easily drive through Hudson (pop. 360) without paying any attention to this rather run-down little place, but that would be a mistake. Attractions include a multitude of shuttered shops, Riviera of Hudson Beauty Salon, and an aging Sinclair sign painted on the side of a brick building. Hudson has a distinct sense of decay, but off the main drag lie quiet, cotton-wood-lined streets, simple frame homes, and gardens filled with tall yellow sunflowers. This place overflows with character and characters.

Hudson was established in 1905 and became a major coal-mining center in the early part of this century before the mines closed. Most of those who settled here were European emigrants, and the town still maintains a strong ethnic flavor; the old fire truck says "Dago Red" on the front. Nowhere is this ethnic heritage as evident as in the two Slavic steakhouses that attract folks from all over the state. **Svilar's,** tel. (307) 332-4516, is the oldest, and its owners are staunchly Republican. Mama Bessie Svilar founded the restaurant in the 1920s to serve the hungry local miners, but it soon began drawing travelers out of their way to tiny Hudson. Restaurant critic Red Fenwick noted that Svilar's "put Hudson on the map in big red letters that dripped with gravy and honey and meat juices." Mama Svilar died in 1981, but the food is still great, and the bar remains a popular place for drinks.

Just across the road is **Club El Toro,** tel. (307) 332-4627, owned by the Vinich family and offering similarly fine steaks and other hearty fare. The homemade ravioli hors d'oeuvres are a specialty. The Vinich family also owns **Union Bar,** another very popular local hangout. El Toro has live country-western music on weekends. After stuffing yourself at Svilar's or Club El Toro, ask about the badlands country east of Hudson. You'll find some fascinating eroded formations just a few miles out.

SANTA, tel. (800) 439-7118, offers on-demand bus service throughout the area, with connections all the way to Jackson, Rock Springs (Greyhound and Amtrak connections), Rawlins, Pinedale, Cody, and Salt Lake City. The company also operates a twice-daily scheduled shuttle connecting Hudson with Ethete, Lander, and Riverton.

LANDER

Friendly Lander (pop. 7,200) lies along the banks of the Popo Agie River with the majestic Wind River Mountains rising just to the west. The town has a state training school for the mentally ill, which employs more than 600 people, and there are many jobs in government, ranching, and construction. Smaller and much more homey than nearby Riverton—where Kmart and Wal-Mart rule—Lander seems to epitomize the changing face of Wyoming. It is currently undergoing something of a rebirth as younger folks move in to raise families, opening

shops, restaurants, and small businesses oriented to those who love the outdoors. The relatively mild winters and lack of wind here make it an attractive place to retire, and Lander's proximity to the Popo Agie Wilderness makes it a jumping-off place for mountain treks into the high country. (See "Wind River Mountains" later in this chapter.) Lander is also the southeastern starting point for the 360-mile Continental Divide Snowmobile Trail, which reaches around the Wind Rivers and all the way to Yellowstone. I still can't figure out how it does it, but Lander somehow has managed to rope in some of the friendliest locals anywhere. It's a delightful town.

History
Lander began in 1869 when the Army established a small military post, Camp Augur (later Camp Brown), to protect Shoshones from attacks by the Sioux and Arapaho. Two years later the post was moved to Fort Washakie. The rich valley along the Popo Agie River proved easy to irrigate and grew ample crops to feed hungry miners in nearby South Pass. Settlers moved here from the dying gold mines of South Pass in the late 1870s, creating the crossroads settlement of Pushroot (named because the vegetables grew so well here). It was later renamed Lander, after Colonel Frederick W. Lander, who had surveyed the Oregon Trail's Lander Cutoff. One of the town's early denizens was the outlaw Butch Cassidy, who bought a ranch near Dubois and was often seen at Lander poker tables and dance halls. The town grew more rapidly once the railroad arrived in 1906, but it took local farmers a while to adjust. When the first train rolled into town, people crowded around, and the engineer jokingly yelled from his cab, "Stand back, I'm gonna turn around." The crowd scattered in fear. During the 1960s and '70s, Lander became a mining boomtown as hundreds of workers commuted to the Columbia-Geneva iron mine and mill near Atlantic City. The mine closed in 1983.

Sights
Lander's **Pioneer Museum** at 630 Lincoln St., tel. (307) 332-4137, is surprisingly large, given the size of the town, and is well worth a visit. It first opened in 1915, and the original log cabin still forms its core. The museum houses an outstanding collection of Indian artifacts, including buffalo robes, a sun-dance pole, beaded gloves, painted buffalo hides, and a squaw saddle. The skull of Harvey Morgan—a local farmer killed in an 1870 Indian raid in Deadman Gulch (east of Lander)—is also in the museum—with the 10-inch wagon bolt still gruesomely driven through it. A skilled marksman, he had fired more than 200 rounds from his rifle before his death. For something completely different, peek in the tiny wedding chapel, popular for spring nuptials. Another room, the One-Shot Antelope Hunt Memorial Room, is devoted to this bizarre sport and its own celebrities (see "Events," below, for details). Behind the main building you'll find a collection of farm wagons and machinery, and two cabins. One of these, the Sparhawk cabin, is said to have been used as a hideout by Butch Cassidy. It was moved here from Crooks Gap near Jeffrey City. The Pioneer Museum is open Mon.-Fri. 10 a.m.-5 p.m. and Sat.-Sun. 1-4 p.m. from June to mid-September. The rest of the year its doors are open Mon.-Fri. 1-5 p.m., Saturday 1-4 p.m., and by appointment at other times. No admission charge. A gift shop sells local books and used Wyoming horseshoes for good luck.

Accommodations
See the "Lander Accommodations" chart for local lodging options. A couple of the local B&Bs are noteworthy. Located in a quiet neighborhood a few blocks from downtown, **Blue Spruce Inn B&B**, tel. (307) 332-8235, is a large brick home built in 1920 and furnished with period pieces. It has four guest rooms with private baths and a rec room housing a dartboard and pool table. Friendly and helpful owners, too. **Piece of Cake B&B**, tel. (307) 332-7608 or (800) 251-6080, is a historic log home with two guest rooms and four cabins. Guests can enjoy the jacuzzi, borrow a mountain bike, or take part in one of their special package trips.

Head five miles north of Lander to **Edna's B&B**, tel. (307) 332-3175, where the 1889 ranch home provides modest accommodations and a delightful owner who grew up here. It's the real thing—a working cattle ranch in the foothills of the Wind River Mountains.

Located approximately nine miles northwest of Lander along the North Fork of the Popo Agie

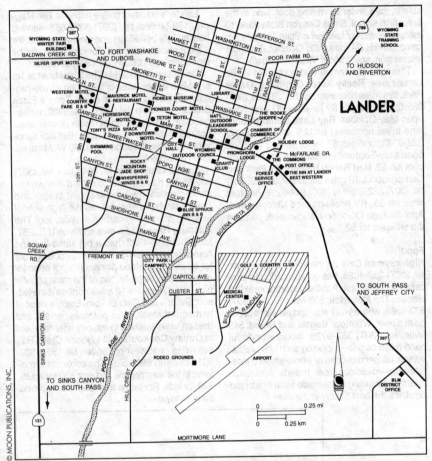

River, **Black Mountain Ranch Country Guest House**, tel. (307) 332-6442, has a spacious four-bedroom home with three baths, a full kitchen, and laundry. It's available for $450 per week.

At **Three Quarter Circle Ranch,** near Lander, tel. (307) 332-2995, dudes can join in the action on a 35,000-acre working cattle ranch. No swimming pools or golf courses at *this* ranch! Located at an elevation of 9,200 feet, **Allen's Diamond Four Ranch,** tel. (307) 332-2995, is 35 miles from Lander and offers horseback riding, fishing, and overnight trips to the nearby Popo

Agie Wilderness. The ranch offers basic accommodations with woodstoves and propane lights—no electricity. Guests bring their own sleeping bags and pillows. The ranch is open June-Sept. and can only accommodate 10 people.

Camping
Camping costs nothing at **Lander City Park**, 405 Fremont St., right along the banks of the Popo Agie River. Pitch tents on the shady grass here or park RVs in the lot. Local high schoolers often park here for a bit of extracurricular activity, so don't expect a quiet night. Showers are avail-

able at the Lander swimming pool, next to the junior high school. **Sinks Canyon State Park,** 10 miles southwest of Lander on State 131, has two campgrounds ($4) open May-October. (For more information, see "Lander Vicinity," below.)

Three private campgrounds operate in the Lander area. **Rocky Acres Camper & Trailer Park,** five miles northwest on U.S. 287, tel. (307) 332-6953, charges $9 for tents, $12 for RVs; open May-October. **Ray Lake Campground,** nine miles northwest on U.S. 287, tel. (307) 332-9333, charges $7 for tents, $13 for RVs; open May-September. Showers for noncampers run $2. **Hart Ranch Hideout RV Park and Campground,** 10 miles southeast on U.S. 287, tel. (307) 332-3836 or (800) 914-9226, has tent sites for $8, RV hookups for $13; open mid-April through October. Noncampers can use the showers for $2.

Food
Highwayman Cafe on the south end of town, tel. (307) 332-4628, has good sourdough pancakes for breakfast. Another favorite breakfast place is **The Maverick,** 808 Main St., tel. (307) 332-4868, where you'll also find excellent prime rib at dinner. **Wildflour Bagels and Bread,** 545 Main, tel. (307) 332-9728, bakes wonderful hand-rolled bagels—including such unusual flavors as jalapeño cheese or whole-wheat chocolate-chip—delicious fresh breads, and lunch specials, including homemade soup in a bread bowl. It's the best bakery in the area.

Lander's standout coffee house is **The Magpie,** 159 N. 2nd, tel. (307) 332-5565, serving healthy light breakfasts and lunches as well. It's a great place to hang out. For ice cream, stop by **Hooligan's,** 351 Main, tel. (307) 332-5050.

On weekends, head to **The Showboat** at 1st and Main for breakfast or lunch; the all-you-can-eat buffet is the best deal going. **Tony's Pizza Shack,** 637 Main, tel. (307) 332-3900, makes good pizzas using homemade dough; their breadsticks are a local favorite. Get deli sandwiches at **The Breadboard,** 1350 W. Main, tel. (307) 332-6090.

Judd's Grub Drive-In, 634 Main, tel. (307) 332-9680, has the best fast food in town (including an enormous one-pound burger and fresh strawberry shakes), as the high-school kids will attest, and carhop service, too. **The Hitching Rack,** half a mile south on U.S. 287, tel. (307) 332-4322, has a big salad bar and homemade soups. This is the place locals go out for steak and seafood dinners (it's not open for other meals). Actually, two of the most popular night-out places are 10 miles northeast in Hudson: Svilar's and Club El Toro. Enjoy a meal of barbecued steak, fried potatoes, salad, and dessert while listening to cowboy entertainment at **Outlaw Cookouts,** 2411 Squaw Creek Rd., five miles northwest of Lander, tel. (307) 332-3011 or (888) 668-8529. The cookouts are offered in the summertime and cost $30 for adults, $20 for kids. Roundtrip transportation is provided from town.

Main St., Lander, circa 1883

LANDER ACCOMMODATIONS

Note: Accommodations are arranged from least to most expensive. Add a seven percent tax to these rates. Area code is 307.

Pioneer Court Motel; 6th and Lincoln; tel. 332-2821; $28 s or d; kitchenettes $35-45 s or d

Maverick Motel; 808 Main St.; tel. 332-2821; $28 s, $30 d; comfortable rooms

Downtown Motel; 569 Main St.; tel. 332-5220; $29 s, $32 d; outdoor pool

Horseshoe Motel; 685 Main St.; tel. 332-4915; $29 s, $33 d

Teton Motel; 586 Main St.; tel. 332-3582; $29-31 s or d; kitchenettes $36 s or d; outdoor pool

Western Motel; 151 N. 9th; tel. 332-4270; $30 s, $37 d; kitchenettes $42 s or d

Edna's Bed & Breakfast; five miles north on US 287; tel. 332-3175; $30 s, $50 d; working cattle ranch, historic home, two guest rooms, shared bath, kids welcome, full breakfast

Silver Spur Motel; 340 N. 10th; tel. 332-5189 or (800) 922-7831; $39 s, $42 d; outdoor pool, kitchenettes $5 extra, AAA approved

Holiday Lodge (National 9 Inn); 210 McFarlane Dr.; tel. 332-2511 or (800) 624-1974; $40 s, $45 d; jacuzzi, kitchenettes $5 extra, AAA approved

Pronghorn Lodge (Budget Host); 150 E. Main St.; tel. 332-3940 or (800) 243-4678; $43 s, $47-53 d; jacuzzi, continental breakfast, exercise room, AAA approved

Whispering Winds B&B; 695 Canyon; tel. 332-9735; $45 s, $55 d; century-old ranch home, shared bath, kids welcome, full breakfast

The Inn at Lander (Best Western); 260 Grand View Dr.; tel. 332-2847 or (800) 528-1234; $47-75 s, $52-80 d; new motel, outdoor pool, jacuzzi, continental breakfast

Lander Llama Company; 2024 Mortimore Lane; tel. 332-5624 or (800) 582-5262; $65 for up to six people; make-your-own breakfast, rustic room with kitchenette on llama farm

The Blue Spruce Inn; 677 S. 3rd St.; tel. 332-8253; $65 s, $75 d; large 1920 house with veranda, four guest rooms, private baths, pool table, library, full breakfast, no kids under 12

Piece of Cake B&B; 2343 Baldwin Creek Rd.; tel. 332-7608 or (800) 251-6080; $75-85 s or d; historic home, two guest rooms and three cabins, private baths, fruit basket, full breakfast, jacuzzi

Outlaw B&B; 2411 Squaw Creek Rd. (five miles northwest); tel. 332-3011 or (888) 668-8529; $90 s or d; modern log cabin, log furniture, on cattle ranch near Wind River Mountains, children welcome, full breakfast

Located in an 1888 brick building that once housed a Chinese laundry, **Sweetwater Grille,** 148 Main, tel. (307) 332-7388 or (800) 714-7388, is one of the nicest places in the area, cranking out great upscale food three meals a day. The eclectic menu includes seafood—a specialty—chimichangas, burgers, pasta, Chinese dishes, steaks, and more. In the back you'll find **Popo Agie Brewing Co.**—the only brewery in Fremont County. It always has several fresh beers on tap, and you can get it to go in a refillable growler. Stop by on Friday and Saturday nights for live music. Definitely recommended.

China Garden, 140 N. 7th St., tel. (307) 332-7666, has good lunch specials, reasonable dinners, and vegetarian specials and if fairly authentic, too. **Big Noi Restaurant,** 280 N. U.S. 789, tel. (307) 332-3102, serves authentic Thai food and more standard American fare.

Recreation
When most folks think of recreation in Lander, they think of the wonderful mountain country just a few miles away (see "Popo Agie Wilderness" under "Wind River Mountains" below). **Wild Iris Mountain Sports,** 325 Main St., tel.

(307) 332-4541, sells books detailing local climbing areas including the **Wild Iris Climbing Area,** 29 miles south of Lander on Limestone Mountain. The climbing area has around 150 different climbs, with pitches from 5.7 to 5.14. Rent mountain bikes from **Desert Cycles,** 996 Lincoln St., tel. (307) 332-2237 or (800) 824-8318, or **Freewheel Ski & Cycle,** 258 Main St., tel. (307) 332-6616 or (800) 490-6616. If you can't get out, **The Gravity Club,** 221 S. 2nd St., tel. (307) 332-6339, has a great climbing wall, rents climbing shoes and other gear, and offers lessons.

Lander's Olympic-size **swimming pool,** 450 S. 9th, tel. (307) 332-2272, is open year-round. Entrance is $1.75 for adults, $1.25 for kids, free for seniors. You'll also find a weight room and hydrotherapy pool here. **Freewheel Ski & Cycle,** 149 Main, tel. (307) 332-6616, rents mountain bikes and cross-country skis. The 18-hole **Lander Golf and Country Club** is on Capitol Hill, tel. (307) 332-4653. During the winter, skate for free at City Park, where you'll also find a warming hut and skate rentals.

Western Encounters, tel. (307) 572-1230, offers weeklong horseback trips across various parts of Wyoming, including the Oregon Trail, Butch Cassidy's Hole-in-the-Wall country, the Great Divide Basin, and a cattle drive in the Big Horn Mountains. These cost $1,200-1,500 per person, including horses, meals, and equipment.

Great Divide Tours, 336 Focht Rd., tel. (307) 332-3123 or (800) 458-1915, provides a wide range of enjoyable horseback and wagon trips, including cattle drives, Oregon Trail rides, and trips into Butch Cassidy's Hole-in-the Wall lair. These excellent five- to seven-day treks cost $950-1,300 per person, including everything except sleeping bags.

NOLS

Because of its proximity to the glorious Wind River Mountains, Lander has become a center for the environmental movement in Wyoming. The best-known organization is the National Outdoors Leadership School (NOLS), located in a brick building at 288 Main St., tel. (307) 332-6973. Contact the school for a detailed catalog of classes. NOLS was established in 1965 to offer classes in wilderness living skills that would lead people to respect their environment and

that would go beyond the Outward Bound emphasis upon survival. Over the years, NOLS staff members have achieved a reputation as the purists in the field, emphasizing low-impact camping and respect for the land. The school publishes several excellent books on wilderness mountaineering, backcountry first aid, and minimizing your impacts.

Today the school offers classes all over the world lasting from two weeks to three months and covering everything from Rocky Mountain horse packing to a semester in Patagonia. These are *not,* however, glorified adventure travel; you'll need to carry your own gear, help with cooking and cleanup, and be willing to work hard. You can rent equiptment from NOLS for the classes. College credit is available for some courses, as is a limited amount of financial aid.

Other Environmental Groups

Also in Lander is the **Wyoming Outdoor Council,** an organization founded in 1967 that emphasizes conservation education and environmental lobbying, especially on such issues as wilderness, wildlife, growth impacts, and waste management. Tax-deductible memberships start at $25 a year. The council's address is 201 Main St., tel. (307) 332-7031.

The Nature Conservancy has its Wyoming state office at 258 Main St., tel. (307) 332-2971. Most of its 210,000 acres in Wyoming are conservation easements, land exchanges, or cooperative projects rather than preserves. It does, however, maintain three publicly accessible preserves: the Tensleep Preserve, Sweetwater River Project, and Red Canyon Ranch Preserve. All are described elsewhere in this book.

Entertainment

Sweetwater Grille, 148 Main St., tel. (307) 332-7388, has a popular brewpub and eatery with live jazz or folk bands on Friday and Saturday nights. The **One Shot Lounge,** 695 Main, tel. (307) 332-2692, occasionally offers rock and roll or karaoke. Also check **The Hitching Rack,** half a mile south on U.S. 287, tel. (307) 332-4322, and Hudson's **Club El Toro** for live bands. As a side note, the present **Stockgrower's Bar** at 202 Main, was—under another name—a

hangout for the outlaw Butch Cassidy. Built in 1886, it has country-western music some nights. Befitting its history, the bar's clientele tends toward the tough side. **Lander Bar,** 126 Main, tel. (307) 332-7009, has live or DJ music most weekends and an attractive outside deck. Watch flicks at **Grand Theatre,** 250 Main St., tel. (307) 332-3300.

Events

Lander hosts the **Wyoming State Winter Fair** the last weekend in January, with livestock exhibits, dog weight-pulling contests, horse shows, entertainment, and dancing.

Lander is one of nine stops in the **Rocky Mountain Stage Stop Sled Dog Race,** an event that attracts some of the nation's best mushers. Unlike other races such as the Iditarod, this one is run in nine 30-to 80-mile stages, with teams ending in a new town each night. The race begins in Jackson and stops for the night in Moran, Dubois, Pinedale, Lander, Atlantic City, Kemmerer, Box Y Guest Ranch (Greys River area), and Afton before ending at Alpine. The race is held over 10 days in early February and has a $100,000 purse.

On the second weekend of June the **Popo Agie Rendezvous** commemorates the 1829 rendezvous held near here. Activities include a mountain-man encampment, parade, art auction, buffalo barbecue, pack race, and all sorts of historical demonstrations and games. **Pioneer Days,** a three-day party around the 4th of July, is Lander's big event. It features a parade with dozens of floats, marching bands, vintage autos, and performers, along with a buffalo barbecue, Indian dancing, street dances, and evening fireworks. The primary event is the **rodeo,** the oldest paid rodeo anywhere on earth, first established in 1893. An **International Climber's Festival** attracts climbers to Lander the second weekend of July with slide shows and films, clinics, a trade fair, mountain-bike racing, and more. Call (307) 332-6339 for details.

The **One-Shot Antelope Hunt** attracts hunters in mid-September; teams of three head out to see how quickly they can bring down an antelope with just one shot. The governors of Wyoming and Colorado are "team captains," and celebrities sometimes participate, including Roy Rogers, Arthur Godfrey, and Chuck Yeager. All sorts of convoluted rules and ridiculous ceremonies make this akin to a fraternity initiation rite. Old men find strange ways to amuse themselves.

Getting Jaded

The Jeffrey City area (60 miles east of Lander) is world-famous for its nephrite jade, a mineral found only in Asia, British Columbia, and Wyoming. The jade comes from Crooks Mountain, and much of it was discovered in the 1930s and '40s by Bert Rhoads, who established **Rhoads' Jewelry,** 423 Main, tel. (307) 332-4439. His wife, Verla, discovered the largest piece of jade ever found—a 3,366-pound boulder that required heavy mining equipment to haul out. Wyoming jade varies greatly in value depending upon color and rarity. Some of it sells for around $7.50 a pound, but Wyoming emerald jade can sell for several thousand dollars per carat. Warning: Much of the jewelry sold as "Wyoming jade" actually comes from British Columbia. Buy only from reputable dealers.

Shopping

You'll find unusual homemade lodgepole beds, chairs, tables, and other furniture at **Mountain Breeze,** 875 Lincoln, tel. (307) 332-2160 or (800) 371-2738. **The Booke Shoppe,** 160 N. 2nd, tel. (307) 332-6221 or (800) 706-4476, has a fine selection of books on Wyoming and a friendly staff, and **Cabin Fever Books,** 163 S. 5th, tel. (307) 332-9580 or (800) 836-9580, offers both new and used titles. **Pioneer Pottery Gallery,** 162 N. 6th, tel. (307) 332-7234, sells high quality stoneware and porcelain pottery. **Camera Connection,** 329 Main St., tel. (307) 332-2432, is one of the most complete photo stores in Wyoming.

Stop by **Wild Iris Mountain Sports,** 325 Main St., tel. (307) 332-4541, for outdoor gear and climbing books, including guides to climbing areas in Fremont Canyon, Dome Rock, Sinks Canyon, and Wild Iris. Owners Todd Skinner and Paul Piana are world-renowned rock-climbers, and the shop is managed by another well-known climber, Amy Whisler (you see them on North Face posters). The bulletin board here is a good place to look for climbing partners or used gear.

Information and Services

The **Lander Chamber of Commerce** office is in the old railroad depot at 160 N. 1st St., tel. (307) 332-3892 or (800) 433-0662, and is open Mon.-Fri. 9 a.m.-8 p.m. in summer, Mon.-Fri. 9 a.m.-5 p.m. the rest of the year. Its e-mail address is: landercc@wyoming.com. The chamber rents taped audio tours of the Loop Road, describing sights along the way, for $6 plus a refundable deposit of $6.

The **BLM District Office** is at 125 Sunflower St., tel. (307) 332-7822, and the Forest Service's new **Washakie Ranger District Office** is at 333 E. Main, tel. (307) 332-5460; open Mon.-Fri. 8 a.m.-4:30 p.m. Stop here for Shoshone National Forest maps and hiking information, other maps and books, and lobby exhibits on the forest.

Lander's new **post office** stands at the junction of U.S. 287 and State 789, tel. (307) 332-2126. Unfortunately, it rests atop what was until recently Wyoming's only in-town prairie-dog

town. **Fremont County Library,** 2nd and Amoretti, tel. (307) 332-5194, is open Monday, Tuesday, and Thursday noon-9 p.m., Wednesday 9 a.m.-9 p.m., and Fri.-Sat. 9 a.m.-1 p.m. The closest commercial airport of any size is in Riverton. For fast cash, you'll find **ATMs** at First Bank, 505 Main St., and Key Bank, 303 Main Street. **Lander Valley Medical Center,** 1320 Bishop Randall Dr., tel. (307) 332-4420, has emergency medical services.

Rent cars from **Fremont Motors,** 161 State 789, tel. (307) 332-4355. **SANTA** (Shoshone Arapahoe Nations Transit Authority), tel. (800) 439-7118, offers on-demand bus service throughout the area, Riverton airport shuttles, and connections all the way to Jackson, Rock Springs (Greyhound and Amtrak connections), Rawlins, Pinedale, Cody, and Salt Lake City. It also operates a twice-daily scheduled shuttle connecting Lander with Ethete, Hudson, and Riverton.

LANDER VICINITY

EAST ON U.S. 287

A few miles east of Lander on U.S. 287, the highway passes an impressive vermilion sandstone butte. Near here is a beautiful, century-old red-rock barn that once stabled horses used on the stage route through here. In 1884, Wyoming's **first oil well** was drilled not far away. The site—now called the Dallas oil field—was known to Indians and described in Washington Irving's *Adventures of Captain Bonneville* as the "Great Tar Springs." Nineteenth-century emigrants used the oil to grease wagon axles, in lamps, and as a balm for their aches. Mountain man Osborne Russell described coming across the spring in 1837:

This spring produces about one gallon per hour of pure oil of Coal or rather Coal Tar the scent of which is often carried on the wind 5 or 6 mls. The Oil issues from the ground within 30 feet of the stream and runs off slowly into the water Camp stopped here eight days We set fire to the spring

when there was 2 or 3 Bbls. of oil on the ground about it, it burnt very quick and clear but produced a dense column of thick black smoke the oil above ground being consumed the fire soon went out.

As you continue eastward, the Wind River Mountains gradually diminish in magnitude. Stop to look up at them for a while. It is easy to see how the pioneers from the east—where a mountain is anything over 1,000 feet—would watch these mountains grow closer with each day's travel and wonder at their rugged crowns. It's also easy to see why they would choose to go around the southern end of this range—at South Pass—instead of crossing over it.

Along the Sweetwater

River Campground, tel. (307) 544-9318, sits at the junction of U.S. 287 and State 135 along the Sweetwater River. Open May-Sept., the campground has tent spaces for $7.50, bike camping for $2, RVs for $9. Showers cost $2 for noncampers. A mile west of the junction along U.S. 287 is the Nature Conservancy's **Sweetwater River Project,** a 4,500-acre natural area

that preserves 16 miles of riparian habitat along the Oregon Trail. For access, and information about guided hikes, contact the Conservancy in Lander at (307) 332-2971.

Ice Slough

Forty miles east of Lander, the highway passes a marker describing Ice Slough, one of many landmarks along this portion of the Oregon Trail. Dense grasses in a small marsh kept ice all through the summer, a real treat for emigrants on a hot summer day. In *Roughing It,* Mark Twain described Ice Slough as follows:

In the night we sailed by a most notable curiosity, and one we had been hearing a good deal about for a day or two, and were suffering to see. This was what might be called a natural ice-house. It was August, now, and sweltering weather in the day-time, yet at one of the stations the men could scrape the soil on the hill-side under the lee of a range of boulders, and at a depth of six inches cut out pure blocks of ice—hard, compactly frozen, and clear as crystal.

Jeffrey City

The bleak, almost-ghost town of Jeffrey City is a casualty of the bust that followed the uranium-mining boom of the 1970s. First called Home on the Range, the town was renamed for a Rawlins philanthropist, Dr. Charles W. Jeffrey. The town was built on the nuclear industry, and as a company town its survival was tied to the fortunes of Western Nuclear Company. By 1980, the population had swollen to 3,000. Today, weeds grow through the concrete sidewalks around empty bunkhouses with plywood-covered windows. Home on the Range Restaurant, Drillers' Delite Lounge, and Jeffrey City Grocery are all closed. Open still are Split Rock Bar & Cafe, Ore House Cafe, and the J.C. Motel—also called the Coats Motel—tel. (307) 544-9317, where rooms run $20 s, $24 d. The modern grade school looks rather forlorn in all this desolation. Ranching, oil, and gas keep Jeffrey City from drying up and blowing away. Rock hounds should ask for directions to the famed jade deposits around the city, but make sure you're on public land or have permission from landowners.

East of Jeffrey City lies definitive Wyoming country with rolling sage and grassland, a few weathered old homesteads, and distant mountains on all sides. A sign notes the turnoff to Cottonwood Campground ($4; open June-Oct.), a BLM facility six miles east of Jeffrey City and then eight miles south on Green Mountain Loop Road. You aren't likely to meet many folks here. (See the Central Wyoming chapter for more on the country east and north of Jeffrey City, including the Oregon Trail sites of Independence Rock, Devils Gate, and Split Rock, and the Indian pictographs at Castle Gardens.)

SINKS CANYON
AND THE LOOP ROAD

State 131 climbs south from Lander through fascinating Sinks Canyon and then over the mountains to Atlantic City. A popular loop trip is to follow this road to Atlantic City, returning to Lander via State 28, a total distance of 56 miles. Plan to spend at least a full day if you want to savor the many sights along the way. Locally known as the Loop Road, it is very popular with both visitors and residents. **Bighorn sheep** were transplanted into Sinks Canyon in 1987 and are common sights along the road, with a population of at least 50 sheep now. Rock-climbers practice their skills on the steep cliffs of the canyon. Of interest to climbers and geologists are the three different types of rock in a five-mile stretch: sandstone, limestone, and granite. You'll find several campgrounds here, lots of lakes, trails, and big mountain country. Get to State 131 by heading south on Lander's 5th Street. Sinks Canyon begins seven miles away.

The Sinks

The Popo Agie River (usually pronounced "po-PO-zha," but you'll hear lots of other versions) begins in the snowfields of the Wind River Mountains and drops northeast to its junction with the Wind River near Riverton. **Sinks Canyon State Park** contains one of Wyoming's geological wonders. Here the Middle Fork of the Popo Agie plunges into a cave (the "Sinks"), only to emerge again a half-mile down in a gigantic spring (the "Rise"). The river's name—Popo Agie—is a Crow Indian word meaning "Beginning of the Waters."

Apparently, the stream originally flowed above-ground—it still does during high spring runoff—but over time a cave formed in the water-soluble Madison Limestone that underlies this region, allowing the water to disappear into enormous underground caverns or convoluted passages from which it slowly drains. In 1983, researchers put dye in the Sinks. The dye did reappear at the rise, but not until two hours later! The water was also a few degrees warmer, and more water appeared than entered the cavern. Lots of fat rainbow and brown trout congregate in the pool at the Rise, waiting for visitors to toss them bits of food. A vending machine sells fish food (fish do not live by bread alone). No fishing allowed. Also keep your eyes open for the muskrat that lives in the spring here.

Sinks Visitor Center, tel. (307) 332-3077, houses displays of fish and animals, along with geological exhibits. Open daily 8 a.m.-7 p.m. during the summer only. The windows face down this steep-walled canyon, offering dramatic vistas. The cave into which the stream disappears is directly behind the visitor center. This area is a fine place to watch birds. Look for dippers—the odd birds that walk underwater—on the rocks above the Sinks.

Three campgrounds operate May-Oct. nearby: state-run **Sawmill Campground** and **Popo Agie Campground** ($4) and, just up the road, the Forest Service's **Sinks Canyon Campground** ($6). Get brochures at the visitor center for the mile-long **nature trail** near Popo Agie Campground. More interesting is the **Popo Agie Falls Trail,** which takes off from Bruce Picnic Ground a mile above Popo Agie Campground. This 1.5-mile trail climbs 600 feet in elevation to a series of attractive waterfalls, the largest being 60 feet. Horses and mountain bikes are allowed on the trail. During the winter, skiers enjoy groomed cross-country trails in the canyon.

Into the Mountains

Beyond the state park, the road turns to gravel and switchbacks steeply up the canyon's south face. The Owl Creek Mountains—50 miles to the north—are visible from the overlook. The road is usually open Memorial Day to mid-October and is washboarded in sections, so be ready for a buckin'-bronc ride and lots of traffic on summer weekends. The rough ride is made worthwhile by excellent vistas and several attractive lakes (enlarged by dams). This is primarily lodgepole and limber pine country, but around Louis Lake you'll discover some huge old Engelmann spruce and subalpine fir trees.

The Forest Service maintains five delightful campgrounds along the Loop Road: **Fiddler's Lake** ($6; open July to mid-Sept.), **Louis Lake** ($6; open July to mid-Sept.), **Popo Agie** (free; open July to mid-Sept.), **Sinks Canyon** ($6; open June-Oct.), and **Worthen Meadows** ($6; open July to mid-Sept.). Fiddler's Lake has fully accessible facilities and, at 9,400 feet, is the highest. Louis Lake is easily the most popular, made more scenic by a sharp granite cliff that rises directly behind the lake. There's good fishing for brown and Mackinaw trout, and moose are commonly seen around Louis Lake's margins. Other folks car-camp around Frye Lake or off the road. Hiking trails head west from Loop Road to the lake-dotted Popo Agie Wilderness (see "Wind River Mountains," below).

The newly refurbished **Louis Lake Lodge,** tel. (307) 332-5549 or (888) 422-2246, rents rustic four-person cabins with oil lanterns, handmade furnishings, and separate bathhouse for $60 per night or $350 per week and offers horseback rides, horse and llama packtrips, droppack trips, and rentals of fishing boats, sailboats, canoes, mountain bikes, backpacking gear, snowshoes, and cross-country skis. South from Louis Lake the road opens into a high plateau with limber pine trees and wide vistas south to the Oregon Buttes. Antelope are common in the sagebrush country, and moose are seen in the aspen stands along the road and in the marshes around Fiddler's Lake. The Loop Road meets State 28 beside the now-abandoned U.S. Steel iron-ore mine. From here you can continue back to Lander on the highway or visit the historic South Pass area (see below).

CATHY CARLSON

WIND RIVER INDIAN RESERVATION

At more than 2.2 million acres, the Wind River is one of America's largest Indian reservations. Home to both the Northern Arapaho and the Eastern Shoshone tribes, it reaches some 70 miles from north to south and 55 miles east to west. You'll find some of the most unforgettable vistas in Wyoming here: fabulous badlands on the western edge; the beautiful Wind River, where the cottonwoods glow a brilliant yellow in the cool fall air; deep green irrigated pastures where horses, sheep, and cattle graze; and desolate, wide-open spaces where only cactus, sagebrush, jackrabbits, and rattlesnakes grow. Bright yellow sunflowers add color to the roadsides in late summer, and horses seem to be everywhere. All this is backdropped by the enormous, snow-capped Wind River Mountains. The eminent guide Jim Bridger reportedly attempted to convince Brigham Young that this basin would be a far better home for the Mormons than the deserts around Salt Lake. Young refused to listen. It is just as well, for this was—and still is—Indian country.

The Wind River Reservation was the scene for the classic Zane Grey Western, *War Paint*, a film that featured Tim McCoy and hundreds of Arapaho and Shoshone Indians. Today, hundreds of people, both Indian and nonnative, come to watch a different form of entertainment—the many powwows that occur throughout the summer months on the reservation. The annual sun-dance ceremonies are more intense, spiritual events at which outsiders are only tolerated. The Shoshone and Arapaho peoples maintain separate sun dances and powwows; absolutely no cameras or tape recorders are allowed during the sun dances.

One of the most heated legal battles in recent Wyoming history focused on water from the Wind River. In 1989, the U.S. Supreme Court awarded the Shoshone and Arapaho tribes rights to nearly half the river's flow, based upon an 1868 treaty. The tribes then dedicated a substantial portion of the water to instream flows to develop a world-class fishery. Farmers dependent upon this water are angry that they may be left high and dry in some years, but the tribes counter that for years the farmers had done exactly the same thing to the local fish.

Don't bring the topic up in a Riverton bar.

Despite the close proximity of the reservation to Lander and Riverton, very little interaction goes on between Indians and nonnatives except in business situations. After more than 120 years, the various cultures—Arapaho, Shoshone, and Anglo—are still like oil and water. Whites regard the Indians as disorganized, drunken, and lazy. Indians view whites as pushy, materialistic, selfish, and disrespectful. Relations are not a whole lot better between the Shoshones and Arapaho, who still view each other with an animosity born of constant warfare during the 19th century.

Public Access

Although you can drive through with no problems, access to many parts of the reservation is controlled by Indian authorities, and trespassers may be fined. If you want to explore the reservation, pick up a copy of the fishing regulations from sporting goods stores in the towns of Lander, Riverton, and Dubois, or from the **Tribal Fish and Game Office** in Fort Washakie, tel. (307) 332-7207 (open Mon.-Fri. 8 a.m.-4 p.m.). These regulations detail not only fishing, but also hiking, boating, camping, and other recreation options on the reservation. For any of these activities you'll need a reservation fishing permit plus a recreation stamp. Nonresident rates total $15 for one day, $40 for one week. Restrictions apply, and a number of areas, including the entire northern end of the reservation, are closed to the non-Indian public. Access to some areas, including Moccasin Lake, Bull Lake, and some trailheads in the Fitzpatrick Wilderness, are only available if you hire an Indian outfitter, and the price is high—around $300 for groups of up to six people. Hunting by outsiders on the reservation is strictly verboten. The map that comes with the permit lists public camping areas on the reservation.

SHOSHONE HISTORY

Originally peoples of the Great Basin, the Shoshones first entered southwestern Wyoming in the 16th century, then gradually pushed north-

CHIEF WASHAKIE

The history of Wyoming during the 19th century is one of constant battles between Indians and the invading white settlers. Only one tribe—the Shoshone—provided an exception to this rule. The reason for this stems from Chief Washakie (pronounced "WASH-a-key"), a man whose life spanned the entire tumultuous century. Washakie was born around 1798 of Shoshone and Flathead parents. His birth name was Pina Quanah, but later in life he gained the name Washakie—literally, "The Rattler"—a reference to a rawhide buffalo rattle he used to scare Sioux ponies during his daring raids. Because his father was killed by the Blackfeet tribe, Washakie lived something of an orphan's existence, growing up among both the Lemhi and Bannock tribes. He eventually joined the Eastern Shoshones and quickly proved himself a fearless and extraordinary warrior.

In the 1830s, Washakie—fluent in sign language—met and became a close friend of famed mountain man Jim Bridger, and one of his daughters became Bridger's third wife. From Bridger, Washakie learned a few words of English and a realization that a union with whites against his enemies was wiser than trying to fight the countless hordes coming across the plains from the east. Around 1843, after the death of the previous chief, Washakie gained control over a band of Shoshones based in the Upper Green River. As their lifelong chief, he was recognized as an extraordinarily intelligent, kindhearted, and forceful leader. Because of his consistent support, Washakie was sought out by white settlers whenever trouble appeared with other tribes.

Chief Washakie

Washakie's people had been devastated over the years by smallpox, cholera, and other diseases, and they were no match for the Sioux, Cheyenne, and Arapaho. Because of this, he viewed an allegiance with whites as a way to drive back other tribes. When some of his young warriors began to complain that the old man was losing his warrior abilities and becoming a lackey, Washakie disappeared for a few weeks and returned with seven enemy scalps. The grumbling ended. Those who joined with others who attacked whites became instant outcasts.

In 1876, Washakie's Shoshones joined with General Crook against the Sioux and Cheyenne in the Battle of the Rosebud. The battle was a standoff, but Washakie's sage advice almost certainly prevented Crook's troops from facing what befell General Custer one week later. When President Chester A. Arthur visited Wyoming in 1883, he asked Chief Washakie to meet him at a reception in Fort Washakie. The proud chief demurred, instead insisting that the president come to him. They met in Washakie's tepee.

Chief Washakie died on the Wind River Reservation on February 22, 1900, and was buried with full U.S. military honors, the only Indian chief ever to be so honored. He was 102 years old and had led his people for over 60 years. With Washakie died the tradition of having one man as chief of the Shoshones. Although his name is not nearly as well known today as that of Red Cloud or Crazy Horse, Washakie deserves a place as one of the great warriors and peacemakers of history. A dozen different Wyoming places are named in his honor, including the Washakie Wilderness and Mount Washakie.

THERMOPOLIS MUSEUM

ward until they controlled most of the land now known as Wyoming, as well as territory all the way into Canada. As they moved onto the plains, and with the acquisition of the horse, Shoshone life changed drastically from a simple Stone Age culture of grubbing for roots and eating whatever they could catch by hand to a sophisticated buffalo-centered livelihood. Because Shoshone culture extended far to the south, they came into contact with Spanish traders

and were some of the first Indians to have horses. The Shoshone introduced horses to the northern plains region around 1700, forever transforming Plains Indian culture. To the trappers and traders who first encountered them, the Shoshone were known as "the Snakes," because of the serpentine hand signals they used to signify their tribal name. The word *Shoshone* refers to the simple willow-and-sagebrush lodges in which they lived before the great flowering of their culture in the 18th and 19th centuries. The Eastern Shoshone occupied western Wyoming, while their cousins the Western Shoshone lived in Idaho.

In the late 18th century, the expanding Shoshone culture was halted when their enemies—the Sioux, Crow, and Arapaho—forced the Shoshone west of the Laramie Mountains. The Wind River and Fort Bridger vicinities became wintering areas. After a spring sun dance and buffalo hunt, the various tribal members would move into the mountains of northern Utah to hunt, fish, and gather berries and roots. Each fall the entire tribe would gather in the Great Divide Basin and head across the Continental Divide for the fall buffalo hunt in the Wind River and Bighorn basins. Led by Chief Washakie, the Eastern Shoshone—unlike most other Plains Indians—maintained an unbroken friendship with the invading whites.

Onto the Reservation

The Shoshones were not recognized in the great Fort Laramie Treaty of 1851, and the Wind River Basin and Bighorn Basin where they had long lived were assigned to the Crows. The Fort Bridger Treaty of 1863 gave the Shoshones and Bannocks a reservation covering parts of Colorado, Utah, Wyoming, and Idaho. In 1868, this enormous, 45-million-acre spread was whittled down to just the Wind River region, and the Bannocks were given a separate Idaho reservation.

Several years later, the government lopped off 600,000 acres around the rich gold region of South Pass City, paying Chief Washakie $500 a year and $5,000 worth of cattle for five years—around four cents an acre. More land—Thermopolis Hot Springs—was ceded to the government in 1897 for $60,000, and in 1905 1.4 million acres were opened to homesteaders north of the Wind River. In exchange for the latter, the Shoshones and Arapaho received per-capita payments, schools, payment for water rights, and an irrigation system on what remained of their reservation. The reservation and adjacent lands are now some of the state's most important agricultural regions.

In 1878, Wyoming's territorial governor asked Chief Washakie if the destitute Arapaho—archenemies of the Shoshone—could be allowed to stay temporarily on the Wind River Reservation. Washakie's sympathetic heart finally gave in:

It is plain they can go no further now. Take them down to where Popo Agie walks into Wind River and let them stay until the grass comes again. But when the grass comes again take them off my reservation. I want my words written down on paper with the white man's ink. I want all you to sign as witnesses to what I have said. And I want a copy of that paper. I have spoken.

Despite this agreement, the "temporary" arrangement became permanent, and urgent pleas by Washakie went unheeded. Once again the government had abused its most loyal friend.

Many years after Chief Washakie's death, the Shoshones sued over this gross injustice. In 1937, the tribe was awarded $6.4 million for the land given to the Arapaho, minus the expenses for every building ever built by the government on the reservation and any services rendered. The cheapskate federal government even deducted $125 for a silver saddle given by President Grant to Chief Washakie as a token of appreciation! What was left amounted to a grand total of $2,350 per capita, distributed almost entirely in various Bureau of Indian Affairs (BIA)-run programs.

CATHY CARLSON

ARAPAHO HISTORY

The Arapaho—a Blackfeet Indian term meaning "Tattooed People"—always called themselves simply "Our People." They originally lived a farming life in what is now central Minnesota, but the arrival of whites on the East Coast created a domino effect among eastern Indians, pushing tribes westward on top of each other. Because of this pressure, the Arapaho, along with the Sioux and Crow, migrated onto the Great Plains in the late 18th century. They quickly adopted the nomadic life associated with Plains Indian culture, a life centered on the buffalo and made possible by the horse. Pressure from the Sioux—who numbered perhaps 25,000 individuals, versus 3,000 Arapaho—forced the Arapaho to join with the Cheyenne and move south to the Arkansas and Platte River regions.

Around 1830, the Arapaho split into northern and southern divisions, due in part to the establishment of Fort Laramie on the Laramie River in Wyoming and Bent's Fort on the Arkansas River in Colorado. For many years, the Northern Arapaho wintered in northern Colorado, scattering along the North Platte River with the coming of spring and then gathering again in late summer to hunt buffalo and prepare for winter. In the 1851 Fort Laramie Treaty, the Arapaho and Cheyenne tribes were assigned the area east of the Rockies between the Arkansas and North Platte Rivers, but as gold was discovered in the Rockies whites began to push the Arapaho off this land.

POWWOWS

The Indian "powwow" (an Algonquian term meaning "medicine man") is a colorful celebration of Native American culture that cuts across tribal boundaries. Nobody knows the exact origin of powwows, but they may have developed from the Grass Dance of the Omaha and Pawnee tribes, who passed the dance on to various Plains tribes. The dance was used as a way of communicating with the Great Spirit, and the rhythmic beat of the drum helped send prayers skyward. Buffalo Bill Cody first introduced Indian dancers to audiences all over America and Europe, and in 1887 the Ponca Tribe began the first Indian fair and powwow. Other tribes joined in, and powwows became increasingly popular with the coming of the 20th century. The creation of "fancy dancing" allowed more personalized costumes and dances. Women were allowed to dance and by the 1940s Indians began traveling long distances to join other tribal powwows.

Dancers perform to a beat set up by different groups of drummers, who sing a repetitious song as they beat out the rhythm. The chant evokes images of somber ceremonies far out on the plains and of a lost culture. The dances originated from different tribes but have been adapted using the more colorful synthetic fabrics and beads of today. Professional dancers travel a circuit throughout the western states, and even non-Indians take part in powwows. Contestants wear numbers sim-

CATHY CARLSON

ilar to those at track meets or rodeos and compete for cash awards.

After Cheyenne and Arapaho warriors began raiding white ranches in Colorado during the early 1860s, the governor demanded action. In the Sand Creek Massacre of 1864, a peaceful Cheyenne and Arapaho village was viciously attacked by U.S. cavalry soldiers under Colonel John M. Chivington. The action sparked a massive retaliation—Arapaho, Sioux, and Cheyenne warriors sacked Julesburg, Colorado, tore down miles of telegraph wire, stampeded cattle herds, and burned ranches and stage stations throughout the Rockies.

After this, the Arapaho shifted their living patterns and began spending winters along Wyoming's Powder River and summers in the Medicine Bow country to the south. They continued to attack Shoshones on the Wind River Reservation, emigrant trains along the Overland Trail, and miners around South Pass until the early 1870s, but gradually lessened their raids as the futility of their condition became more apparent.

The end came in the Bates Battle of 1874, when the Shoshones and the U.S. Army attacked the Arapaho, leaving them demoralized and without horses or supplies. In the late 1870s, many Arapaho served as Army scouts, and some even joined an Arapaho unit of the Army during the 1880s. Best-known of the Arapaho scouts was Friday, an orphan Arapaho boy adopted by mountain man and Indian agent Thomas Fitzpatrick and taught in eastern schools. He returned to his tribe and became their most important translator and a force for peace. It was probably Friday's friendship with Chief Washakie that led Washakie to finally tolerate Arapaho on his reservation.

CATHY CARLSON

Traditional and Fancy Dancing
Two main styles of powwow dance exist. In **traditional dancing,** the movements are slow and graceful, and dancers adhere to more authentic costumes and traditional dance steps. Male dancers wear bus-

tles of eagle feathers, representing the birds of prey that once gathered over battlefields to feed on dead warriors. They also wear head roaches made from porcupine guard hairs. **Fancy dancing** is more casual—sort of an anything-goes dance in which the steps are chosen by the individual dancers. It generally involves lots of spins, bows, and head movements. Men's costumes are equally free-form, with all sorts of gaudy additions, particularly colorful bustles added to the shoulders and arms. Women's costumes for both traditional and fancy dancing are not as showy as men's, although they do include bells, elk teeth (or plastic copies), and shell decorations on the dresses, along with shawls and necklaces of hairpipe.

Powwow Activities
The Wind River Reservation has a half-dozen powwows throughout the year, all but one of them held outdoors. Tepees are set up and the event becomes a joyful celebration of life and culture. These are three-day-weekend events involving not just singing and dancing, but also traditional games, parades, and a "giveaway ceremony." Activities last all day and late into the evening. Things generally begin with a festive parade that includes a military color guard and a powwow queen seated atop a car hood. Visitors are welcome at powwows and photos are not usually a problem, although this is less true at Arapaho powwows. For general information on powwows and other events on the reservation, call (307) 332-3040.

Onto the Reservation

With the buffalo gone and their way of life under constant pressure from white settlers and the deadly diseases they brought, the Arapaho were in desperate straits, shuttling from one temporary home to another. The government refused to set aside a separate reservation, insisting that they live with the Cheyenne in Oklahoma or the Sioux in South Dakota, far from their Wyoming home.

In 1878, the Northern Arapaho were shoe-horned onto the Wind River Reservation with their hated enemies in what was to be a "temporary" stay. Only 913 Arapaho—mostly women and children—remained from the tribe that had once been so powerful. (Interestingly, the Arapaho now outnumber the Shoshones on the reservation.) The two bands of Arapaho that settled on the Wind River Reservation were led by Chief Black Coal, whose people settled in present-day Arapahoe, and Chief Sharp Nose, whose people settled around present-day Ethete. Chief Sharp Nose served with the U.S. Army and later lobbied in Washington for the General Allotment Act of 1887, which issued parcels of land (160 acres to the head of a house, 80 acres to single persons over 18, 40 acres to those under 18) to everyone on the reservation. Sharp Nose even named one of his sons after General Crook, whom he fought alongside during the Sioux wars of the 1870s.

The two tribes continue to jointly occupy the Wind River Reservation, with the Arapaho holding the eastern half (the towns of Ethete and Arapahoe) and the Shoshones the west (the towns of Fort Washakie, Burris, and Crowheart). In 1891, the Arapaho were given equal rights on the reservation, despite Shoshone Chief Washakie's continued attempts to have them removed. Although Chief Washakie's son married an Arapaho woman there is still very little intermarriage between the tribes and almost no blending of the two cultures, even after more than a century.

RESERVATION LIFE

In the early reservation years every effort was made to break the spirit of the "savages" and make them into red-skinned Europeans (today's derogatory term is "Apples"—red on the outside, white on the inside). Even that most basic attribute—one's name—was taken away in the 1890s by the Commissioner of Indian Affairs. Thus, Yellow Calf became George Caldwell and Night Horse became Henry Lee Tyler. Even William Shakespeare and Cornelius Vanderbilt suddenly became tribal members! The effort was not entirely successful—William Shakespeare was credited with bringing Peyotism—an important Native American religion today—to the Wind River Reservation. Other measures helped weaken the culture, including the repression of native religious practices, indoctrination by Christian missionaries, prohibition of face painting, and the forced cutting of young boys' long black hair. Today, the nation is paying the price for these all-too-successful attempts to destroy Native American culture.

Most of the 5,200 Arapaho and 2,500 Shoshones live in housing built by the tribal council or in the hundreds of mobile homes that dot the reservation. From a non-Indian point of view, they are decidedly untidy, with junk of all sorts piled outside; but the folks who live here really don't care what outsiders think. You'll find older log cabins all over the back roads, their sod roofs collapsing and their log walls slowly returning to the earth. A number of missions are scattered throughout this area, marked by attractive log or stucco churches.

Oil and gas revenues from a number of major fields on the reservation provide millions of dollars each year in the form of monthly dividend payments. These royalties—along with various BIA assistance programs, ranching, farming, and tribal-owned businesses and leases—are the main source of income. A Business Council serves as the manager of tribal income. The Arapaho tend to emphasize communal sharing and oppose miscegenation much more than the Shoshones, who are more likely to marry whites and own private land.

Most people on the reservation are poor and many are unemployed, having lost their jobs when the uranium mines closed down and the oil companies left. Pawnshops in Lander and Riverton often acquire valuable cultural items from desperate individuals when the money runs out before the month does. For many on the reservation, sports are the way out. Every kid, it

seems, plays basketball; hoops hang outside all the trailer homes and government-built houses. For older folks, bingo is a major source of entertainment—there are games almost every night of the year.

Despair and Hope

The Wind River Reservation has severe problems with drugs and alcohol; a third of the children are born with fetal alcohol syndrome. Many young people—and older folks, too—die in alcohol-related car accidents or fights, and suicide and infant mortality rates are distressingly high. Despite all the problems, the Arapaho and Shoshone peoples take a genuine sense of pride in their cultural history. To attack the problems of alcoholism and the loss of cultural identity, young people learn their native tongue in special classes and take part in powwows, sun dances, and personal vision quests. The warrior tradition is expressed in a high enlistment in the nation's armed forces.

The reservation is a center for fine beaded clothing and moccasins much prized by collectors. Arapaho patterns are geometric in nature, with rectangles and triangles appearing frequently. Arapaho women generally use red, black, blue, yellow, orange, and white as the main colors, with mountains, tepees, and butterflies as common motifs. Eastern Shoshone patterns tend to be more circular, with the rose a popular theme.

ARAPAHOE AND ST. STEPHENS

The town of Arapahoe (known locally as Lower Arapahoe) is a small village on the southeastern edge of the reservation. It arose from animosity between the tribes, as a subagency through which annuities could be distributed to the Arapaho without their having to face the taunts of "beggar" or "dog eater" from the Shoshones at Fort Washakie. The town's prominent white water tower is visible for many miles. The **Northern Arapaho Powwow** (oldest on the reservation) is held here in early August, followed by the **Labor Day Powwow.**

St. Stephens Mission

In 1884, the St. Stephens Mission was established by Father John Jutz, a Jesuit missionary. Chief Black Coal consented to allow a mission to be built and later proved an ardent supporter of the school for Arapaho children. Until 1939, the Catholic Church operated a boarding school here. It was replaced by a day school that ran until the 1970s, when it became increasingly difficult to find priests and nuns to run the mission.

Visitors entering St. Stephens Mission pass a modern grade school built in 1983 and run by a private secular corporation with an entirely Indian leadership. The most interesting sight at the mission is **St. Stephens Church,** built in 1928. Its white stucco exterior is covered with colorful Arapaho geometric symbols. The excellent quarterly magazine *Wind River Rendezvous* is published by the mission and is available for just $10 a year; write to Box 278, St. Stephens, WY 82524. Although this is a religious organization, the magazine deals with all sorts of historical and social issues.

The **St. Stephens Mission Heritage Center,** tel. (307) 856-4330, contains a small museum and gift shop. Some of the most interesting items for sale are collector dolls dressed in Arapaho costume. Open Mon.-Wed. and Friday 9 a.m.-4 p.m. April-November. A nearby building houses the **Center for Native Arts and Humanities,** tel. (307) 856-8664, with art on display. Open Mon.-Fri. 9 a.m.-4 p.m.

A cemetery near the mission contains the graves of Chief Lone Bear, Francis Setting Eagle, and John Broken Horn, along with that of his wife, Sarah Broken Horn—a white woman (born Lizzie Fletcher) who had been captured as a child and raised as an Indian. (See "Arlington" under "Medicine Bow Vicinity" in the Medicine Bow Country chapter for more on this story.) The outlaw Butch Cassidy was a frequent visitor to Chief Lone Bear's camp.

BOB RACE

ETHETE

Ethete (pronounced "EEE-thuh-tee") is the primary Arapaho settlement on the reservation. People live in trailer homes scattered on small plots around town or in ticky-tacky box houses built by the BIA. (The prefabricated houses are known as the "Easter Egg Village" because of the bright colors.) Tepee poles lean against the barns, and the bright tribal colors and geometric patterns dominate the laundromat/video store. "Downtown" Ethete consists of a stoplight—the only one on the reservation—surrounded by a grocery store, a gas station, a community hall, a high school, and the above-mentioned laundromat. All this is entirely forgettable, but not nearby St. Michael's Mission. The **Ethete Community Powwow** is held in July and the annual **Ethete Celebration** in late July. In mid-July the Ethete powwow grounds come alive with the **Northern Arapaho Sun Dance** ceremony (no cameras allowed).

SANTA (Shoshone Arapahoe Nations Transit Authority), tel. (800) 439-7118, offers on-demand bus service throughout the area, with connections all the way to Jackson, Rock Springs (Greyhound and Amtrak connections), Rawlins, Cody, Pinedale, and Salt Lake City. They also operate a twice-daily scheduled shuttle connecting Ethete with Lander, Hudson, and Riverton.

St. Michael's Mission

Established in 1887 by Rev. John Roberts of the Episcopal Church, this mission is the town's reason for existence. When Chief Sharp Nose was asked for his approval to build here, the response was "*Ethete*," meaning "Good." The buildings here were constructed between 1910 and 1917 and are arranged in a circle around a grassy lawn. Most are built from cobblestones, with Arapaho designs on the doors, but the **Church of Our Father's House** is of log. Inside this fascinating building built in the shape of a cross are rustic handmade wooden benches and a central Arapaho drum. Altar seats are made of elk antlers, and the back window faces the great Wind River Mountains.

Across the circle is the **Arapaho Cultural Museum,** tel. (307) 332-2660, housing a small but remarkable collection of artifacts that in-

cludes beaded garments, medicine pouches, peace pipes, warbonnets, and more. It is open Mon.-Sat. 10 a.m.-6 p.m. mid-April to Labor Day and by appointment the rest of the year. No charge. If nobody is here, knock on the house next to the church to have someone let you in.

FORT WASHAKIE

Fort Washakie is the center of activity on the Wind River Reservation. The BIA compound is here (locals insist the initials stand for Boss Indians Around) and so is the tribal council headquarters. Fort Washakie was the home of Chief Washakie, the longtime leader of the Shoshones. Behind Chief Washakie's town are a series of dramatic escarpments and canyons, and through a gap in the hills you can peer into the mighty Wind River Mountains.

In 1869, the U.S. Army established a fort, Camp Augur (later Camp Brown), along the Popo Agie River to protect the Shoshones from attacks by Arapaho and Sioux warriors. The fort was later moved a dozen miles west and renamed Fort Washakie, making this one of the only forts ever named for an Indian chief. It remained open until 1909, when the threat of conflict between the Shoshones and Arapaho had diminished. A few buildings still stand, including a **stone guardhouse.** They are now used by the BIA.

Sights

Despite its minuscule size, Fort Washakie has an array of interesting sights. The **Shoshone Tribal Cultural Center,** tel. (307) 332-9106, is in the historic "White House" on the BIA compound. Built in 1913, it now serves as an information and heritage center. Upstairs are some historical photos and a video about powwows (get a powwow calendar here); downstairs is Chief Washakie's headdress, leather shirt, and decorated suitcase. Young people take cultural and Shoshone language classes here. It's open Mon.-Fri. 9 a.m.-4 p.m. year-round. Hourlong tours of the cultural center are available for a fee.

South Fork Road west from Fort Washakie passes the **Washakie Graveyard.** A substantial granite memorial notes that Washakie was "Always loyal to the government and his white brothers. A wise ruler." Directly across the road

SACAGAWEA

ictional books about Sacagawea (pronounced "sah-cah-jah-WEE-ah") describe her as a beautiful Indian maiden, a guide, a peacemaker, a heroine, and a mother—sort of the original Superwoman. Historian James Truslow Adams declared her one of the six most important women in American history. The reality is a bit less romantic but still fascinating. Sacagawea—her name meant "Bird Woman" in Shoshone—was born around 1788 in what is now eastern Idaho. As a child, she was captured by the Minnetaree tribe and later sold to a French-Canadian trapper and interpreter named Toussaint Charbonneau. He eventually made her one of his many wives.

The Lewis and Clark Expedition

In 1803, President Thomas Jefferson negotiated the Louisiana Purchase from the French. For the fire-sale price of $16 million he suddenly doubled the size of the young United States of America. Captains Meriwether Lewis and William Clark were selected to lead a secret exploration of this vast land. They left St. Louis in late 1804 and camped that first winter in North Dakota, where they met Sacagawea and her husband Charbonneau. Lewis and Clark didn't think much of the ill-tempered and untrustworthy Charbonneau but realized the value of having a Shoshone woman who was fluent in English and French. Charbonneau was hired, with the stipulation that his wife come along.

Over the winter, Sacagawea gave birth to a baby boy (Baptiste), and when the troupe headed out two months later, the child was on her back in a cradle board. Contrary to the romanticized novels, her role was not so much that of guide as interpreter, as one who knew the edible plants along the way, and as a symbol of the expedition's friendly intentions. When the expedition reached the Continental Divide, they met up with Sacagawea's sister and brother, whom she had not seen since being kidnapped six years before. The Shoshones agreed to provide guides and horses to cross the Rockies.

They reached the Pacific Ocean that fall and built a fort near the mouth of the Columbia River for winter quarters. They recrossed the mountains the following summer, and Sacagawea, Charbonneau, and their son returned to their old existence in Mandan country. The rest of the expedition party reached St. Louis on September 23, 1806, long after everyone but President Jefferson had given them up for dead. The trip proved a vital step in bringing the Northwest under the U.S. flag.

BOB RACE

Later Years

From here, Sacagawea's story becomes murkier. Some researchers claim she died in 1812 of "putrid fever" at Fort Mandan in North Dakota. This version is generally told by Dakota folks. Wyoming partisans prefer another story: that the woman who died so young was one of Charbonneau's other wives, and that Sacagawea continued to live for many more years. After leaving her abusive husband, she wandered all over the West—gaining the name Wad-ze-Wipe ("Lost Woman")—before finally ending up on the Wind River Reservation with her fellow Shoshones. She served a crucial role as translator for Chief Washakie in negotiations to establish the reservation and was often seen wearing one of the peace medals given out by Lewis and Clark. Sacagawea (or at least the Wyoming version) died on April 9, 1884, and was buried near Fort Washakie in a cemetery overlooking the Wind River. It wasn't until 25 years later that historians began to realize who the "Lost Woman" really was. The 13,569-foot Mt. Sacagawea in the Wind River Mountains is named for the remarkable woman who remained unrecognized much of her life.

is the **R.V. Greeves Art Gallery,** tel. (307) 332-3557, open by appointment only. Greeves is one of state's better-known sculptors; his *The Unknown* is in the Buffalo Bill Historical Center.

Continue another mile along this road (stay left at the Y and turn left again at the Full Gospel Revival Center's log church) to the **Sacagawea Cemetery,** perhaps the most beautiful cemetery in Wyoming. The remote setting offers views of the Wind River Mountains. When I last visited, the sun was playing behind darkly rumbling thunderheads atop the Wind Rivers while horses whinnied in the fields below. Sacagawea's gravesite (the Wyoming version) is marked by an impressive granite headstone, and one of her sons, John Baptiste, is buried alongside. A granddaughter and other descendants are up the hill. The graveyard also contains an old log church and a number of old bed frames over graves, a burial practice that was common for many years on the reservation.

The historic **Shoshone Episcopal Mission** is on Trout Creek Road, 1.5 miles southwest of Fort Washakie (turn east just beyond the Hines General Store), and was founded in 1883 by Rev. John Roberts, a Welsh missionary known as "White Robe." A boarding school for Indian girls was built in 1891. The two-story brick-and-stone building still stands, though the school closed in 1945. A simple log mission church is nearby.

Three miles east of Fort Washakie on the way to Ethete is **Chief Washakie Hot Springs,** where 110° F sulfur-rich water flows into a public swimming pool. This was a favorite place of Chief Washakie. Maybe these mineral waters are what helped him live to age 102! After a major remodeling, the pool is expected to reopen sometime in 1997; call the Cultural Center at (307) 332-9106 for the latest.

Arts and Crafts

Shoshone Tribe Arts and Crafts, tel. (307) 332-7330, sells handmade Indian beadwork, jewelry, garments, and other items from the reservation. Owned and operated by the Eastern Shoshone tribe, it's open Mon.-Fri. 8 a.m.-5 p.m. **Wind River Trading Co.,** next to Hines General Store, has dreadfully tacky beadwork, moccasins, and baskets. The setting is more elaborate than Shoshone Tribe Arts and Crafts, but much of this is not from the Wind River Reservation. A good place to find quality craftwork is the nursing home, Morning Star Manor. Other locals worth contacting for beadwork and art are Nathaniel Barney, Orlean Ute, and Vina Ingawanup, Stan DeVinney, Zella Guina, and Pauley Brooks; check with the cultural center for details.

Practicalities

El Ranchito, next to Hines General Store, sells delicious Indian tacos and Mexican food. Open weekdays only. Get fast food from the cafe (of sorts) inside the Texaco station. **Ray Lake Campground,** at the intersection of U.S. 287 and State 132, tel. (307) 332-9333, charges $7 for tents, $13 for RVs. Tepees are also available for rent, and the cafe has meals. Open May-September, it's run by friendly folks, and the remote country setting offers classic Wyoming scenery. There is no other lodging available on the reservation, although many places are available in nearby Lander, Riverton, and Dubois.

Events

In late June, Fort Washakie is home to the **Treaty Day Celebration,** which includes Indian games, dancing, and a feast. It is immediately followed by the **Eastern Shoshone Indian Days Powwow and Rodeo,** which attracts participants from all over the west. The all-Indian rodeo features bull riding, saddle bronc and bareback riding, calf roping, team roping, and the favorite—**Indian relay horse racing,** in which bareback riders rocket around the track in a chaos of flying dirt and colliding horses. Another Shoshone powwow is held in Crowheart the first week of June, and an Eastern Shoshone sun dance takes place near Winkleman Dome in late July. In late December, another Shoshone powwow is held at Fort Washakie, but this time inside the local gymnasium. The **Shoshone Tribal Fair** is held the last week of August and is a fine time to purchase quality handmade items—from jewelry to saddles—and to watch the cattle judging, exhibitions, and bareback relay races.

WEST TO DUBOIS

As you head northwest along U.S. 26/287, the Wind River Mountains and Absarokas grow ever closer, and the Wind River Valley begins to nar-

row. Crowheart Butte dominates the skyline to the north for many miles, and then you drop over a rise to discover a stunning landscape of red-rock badlands accented by the green of cottonwoods along the Wind River. For the next 20 miles, travelers are treated to a constantly changing panorama of gloriously colorful badlands topography, with 11,635-foot Ramshorn Peak rising in the distance. It's a geologist's dreamworld. Several reservoirs provide irrigation and recreation on the Wind River Reservation. Largest is **Bull Lake**, along the western margin. The Shoshones say that it is haunted by a supernatural water buffalo. The aquamarine waters of **Ocean Lake** are well-known for bass and crappie fishing. Other people come to swim or water-ski.

Crowheart Butte

The tiny settlement of **Crowheart** consists of an old-fashioned country store and gas station surrounded by irrigated fields and grazing cattle. A couple miles northeast of the store—and visible for many miles in any direction—is a regal summit, Crowheart Butte, looking like a pyramid whose top got caught in a giant lawn mower.

The name comes from an 1866 battle in the Wind River Valley. The Shoshones and Bannocks fought the Crows over hunting rights. The Crows had been "given" the valley in the Fort Laramie Treaty of 1851, while the Shoshones and Bannocks were "given" the same land in the 1863 Fort Bridger Treaty. Four days of intense fighting led to a standoff, and to prevent further bloodshed the chiefs declared a winner-takes-all fight near this butte. Charging each other on horseback with lances drawn, both were thrown in the collision, and the fight turned to a hand-to-hand struggle. In the battle, Shoshone Chief Washakie killed Crow Chief Big Robber and then reputedly ate the vanquished leader's heart (or at least carried it around on a spear). Thus the name, Crowheart Butte. When Chief Washakie was later asked about the story, he replied, "When a man is in battle and his blood runs hot, he sometimes does things that he is sorry for afterwards. I cannot remember everything that happened so long ago."

Crowheart Butte is regarded as something of a sacred place by local Indians and is used as a place of spiritual renewal for young men on a vision quest. A small rock shelter stands on the top for this purpose. Non-Indians are legally forbidden to climb Crowheart Butte, and legends claim that those who do so may disappear.

Broken Wheel Ranch

The Broken Wheel Ranch, located near Dinwoody Creek (10 miles west of Crowheart), offers an amusing taste of the Hollywood frontier. During the 1980s, Lee Kozell—a onetime Wyoming cowboy and retired Pittsburgh bartender—built this miniature Wild West town including a saloon, jail, church, general store, bank, and brothel. Get here by turning south on the dirt road just beyond Dinwoody Creek and following the road 1.5 miles to the buildings. The reservation land behind here is closed to the public except with written permission.

Whiskey Basin

The highway continues its slow and scenic climb to Dubois, crossing the cottonwood-lined Wind River three times en route. Approximately 25 miles west of Crowheart (five miles east of Dubois), a sign points the way to Whiskey Basin. Follow the gravel road two miles to the **Dubois State Fish Hatchery**, where rainbow, cutthroat, golden, brook, and brown trout as well as grayling are raised. Open daily 8 a.m.-5 p.m. The bucolic setting is hard to beat: a tree-lined creek surrounded by sage, mountains, and badlands. The road deteriorates as you continue, approaching 4WD status within a couple of miles as it follows Torrey Creek up past a string of four small lakes. (The lakes were created by retreating glaciers centuries ago, though small dams have enlarged them.) State Game and Fish **campsites** (free) are located along Ring and Trail Lakes. A very popular trailhead at the end of the road (12 miles) provides access to the primary route up to Dinwoody Glacier and 13,804-foot Gannett Peak. Keep your eyes open for the osprey nest at mile five. The Audubon Society has a field camp at mile eight.

You'll discover quite a few Indian **pictographs** on large boulders in the Trail Lake vicinity. The figures—some four feet tall—are elaborate otherworldly creations with horns and headdresses. They are believed to represent shamans performing ceremonies under altered states of consciousness. While their age is unknown, they

are probably at least 2,000 years old and of Athapaskan (a Canadian tribe) rather than Shoshonean origin. This is some of the oldest rock art in Wyoming.

During the winter months, **Whiskey Basin Habitat Area** contains the largest population of **Rocky Mountain bighorn sheep** anywhere on earth. At times more than 1,200 sheep congregate here because of the mild winters and the lack of deep snow. Best time to find them here is Nov.-Jan., when the rams are present, but some stick around till April. The lambs are born in late May and early June high up on rocky slopes. Bighorn sheep are also sometimes seen in the meadows along the highway or in the hills just above Dubois. Five-hour **winter wildlife tours** ($30 per person) of the Whiskey Basin Habitat Area are offered by the National Bighorn Sheep Interpretive Center in Dubois; call (307) 455-3429 for reservations.

DUBOIS

Approaching Dubois (pop. 1,100) from either direction, you drive through the extraordinary red, yellow, and gray badlands that set this country apart. The luxuriant Wind River winds its way down a narrow valley where horses graze in the irrigated pastures and old barns and newer log homes stand against the hills, and the tree-covered Absaroka and Wind River Mountains ring distant views. The town of Dubois consists of a long main street that makes a startlingly abrupt elbow turn and then points due west toward the mountains. The many log buildings and snatches of wooden sidewalks give the place an authentic frontier feel. Locals live in cabins, trailer homes, and simple frame houses. Dubois weather is famously mild; warm chinook winds often melt any snow that falls. Grand scenery reigns in all directions. Snowmobilers, hunters, and anglers have discovered that Dubois provides a good place to relax in Wyoming's "banana belt" while at the same time remaining close to the more temperamental mountains. The area basks in an average of 300 days of sunshine each year. By the way, Dubois is pronounced "DEW-boys"; other pronunciations will reveal your tenderfoot status. Locals sometimes jokingly call it "Dubious."

HISTORY

Dubois began in the 1880s when pioneer ranchers and more than a few rustlers—including Butch Cassidy—settled in the area, followed by Scandinavian hand-loggers who cut lodgepole for railroad ties. The town that grew up along the juncture of Horse Creek and the Wind River was first known as Never Sweat, but when citizens applied for a post office the Postal Service refused to allow the name and suggested Dubois instead—the name of an Idaho senator who just happened to be on the Senate committee that provided funding for the post office.

Dubois is a town in transition. For most of its existence, it served as a logging and ranching center. In 1987, the Louisiana Pacific sawmill shut down, throwing many loggers and mill-workers onto the unemployment rolls. Loggers blamed environmentalists and the Forest Service for sharply reducing the timber available; environmentalists countered that the company was simply using the reductions as an excuse to close an aging mill. After everyone ran out of mud to sling, they decided to look at what Dubois had to offer and discovered that, lo and behold, they just happened to be sitting in an almost-undiscovered recreational and retirement gold mine. In the last few years the town has leapt full-force into the tourism business and is starting to really grow. The transformation of Dubois to a visitor-oriented economy certainly has its downside—elaborate log summer homes are beginning to overrun the lush pastures on both ends of town, and the first national operation—a Super 8 Motel—has already arrived, along with the first condominiums. Will the factory outlets and fast-food chains be next, or can "industrial tourism" be kept away from this pretty little place? Stay tuned.

SIGHTS

National Bighorn Sheep Center

The National Bighorn Sheep Interpretive Center, 907 W. Ramshorn, tel. (307) 455-3429, houses interpretive displays on desert bighorn, Rocky

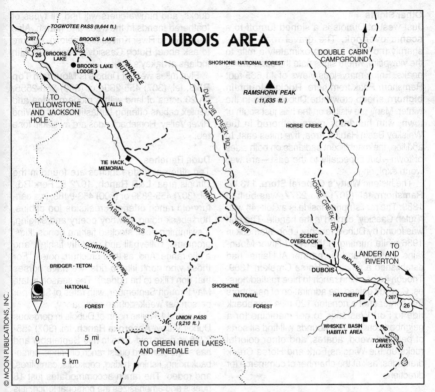

DUBOIS AREA

TOGWOTEE PASS (9,644 ft.)

BROOKS LAKE

BROOKS LAKE LODGE

SHOSHONE NATIONAL FOREST

TO DOUBLE CABIN CAMPGROUND

TO YELLOWSTONE AND JACKSON HOLE

FALLS

PINNACLE BUTTES

RAMSHORN PEAK (11,635 ft.)

HORSE CREEK

TIE HACK MEMORIAL

WARM SPRINGS RD.

DU NOIR CREEK RD.

WIND RIVER

HORSE CREEK RD.

SCENIC OVERLOOK

TO LANDER AND RIVERTON

CONTINENTAL DIVIDE

BRIDGER - TETON NATIONAL FOREST

DUBOIS

BADLANDS

SHOSHONE NATIONAL FOREST

HATCHERY

UNION PASS (9,210 ft.)

WHISKEY BASIN HABITAT AREA

TORREY LAKES

TO GREEN RIVER LAKES AND PINEDALE

0   5 mi
0   5 km

© MOON PUBLICATIONS, INC.

Mountain bighorn, stone sheep, and Dall sheep. The museum details how careful management has brought the population back from the brink of extinction and includes fine hands-on exhibits and interactive displays on how bighorns live, a diorama of a Sheepeater Indian trap, and mounted specimens around a 16-foot-high central "mountain." A theater shows videos on bighorn sheep and other topics, and a gift shop sells books and other items. The center is open daily 9 a.m.-8 p.m. from Memorial Day to Labor Day and Thurs.-Mon. 9 a.m.-4 p.m. the rest of the year. Entrance costs $2 for adults, 75 cents for kids under 13, $5 for families.

The center also offers **winter wildlife tours** of the Whiskey Basin Habitat Area just west of town (see "West to Dubois" under "Wind River Indian Reservation" earlier in this chapter). These five-hour van trips cost $30 per person and include binoculars and spotting scopes to watch the animals. They operate on weekends from mid-November through March. Reservations are recommended; call the center for details.

Museum

The **Dubois Museum** at 909 W. Ramshorn (right next door to the Bighorn Sheep Center), tel. (307) 455-2284, is open Mon.-Sat. 10 a.m.-5 p.m. and Sunday noon-5 p.m., May-Sept.; $1 for adults, 50 cents for kids under 12, $3 for the whole family. It houses exhibits on the Sheepeater Indians and various cultural artifacts, petrified wood, and displays on ranch life, natural history, and the tie hacks. Be sure to check out the hilarious photo of 1930s movie star Tim McCoy teaching golf to a skeptical group of Shoshone Indians! Out front are five historic log cabins. Behind the museum is the **Headwaters Community Arts and Conference Center**, where local artists display their works.

Other Sights

Just west of Dubois is a signed turnoff to a **scenic overlook.** The gravel road climbs sharply (no RVs) for approximately a mile to the viewpoint, where signs note the surrounding peaks. Enjoy marvelous views of 11,635-foot Ramshorn Peak from here. **Rocky Mountain bighorn sheep** crowd the Dubois area in the winter. Many are visible on the hills just south of town, with hundreds more gathered in the Whiskey Basin Habitat Area, five miles east. In addition, the magnificent badlands on both sides of town—but especially to the east—are well worth exploring.

The historic **Welty's General Store,** 113 W. Ramshorn, tel. (307) 455-2377, was built in 1889. The real surprise inside is a Colt .44 with "Butch Cassidy" carved in the handle. The gun was found by Dubois rancher Leon Warnock in 1936 while hunting in the Wind River Mountains. Cassidy and his partner Al Hainer had established a ranch up Horse Creek in 1889. Though he used the ranch to hide rustled horses, Cassidy gained the admiration of neighbors that winter after a nonstop 120-mile horseback ride to Fort Washakie to get medicine for a neighbor's child. Rock hounds will find all sorts of petrified wood, agates, and other colorful rocks up the Wiggins Fork and Horse Creek drainages; ask at the chamber of commerce for directions.

ACCOMMODATIONS

Motels and B&Bs

Dubois makes an excellent stopping point on the way to Yellowstone and Grand Teton National Parks, with lodging prices well below those in Jackson Hole. See the chart for Dubois-area motels and lodges. Of note is **Twin Pines Lodge,** tel. (307) 455-2600, built in 1939 and on the National Historic Register of Historic Places. Another very enjoyable place is **Jakey's Fork Homestead,** tel. (307) 455-2769, with B&B accommodations in a delightful century-old homestead four miles east of town. Located near the bighorn sheep refuge in Whiskey Basin, Jakey's Fork offers extraordinary views of both the Wind River Mountains and nearby badlands. Visitors will also enjoy the sheep, dogs, donkey, and ducks, and birdwatchers will find all types of feathered friends in the trees and marsh. Also here is Wind River Knives (see below). Be sure to ask about Butch Cassidy's encounter with Indians at Jakey's Fork.

Five miles west of Dubois is **Mountain Top B&B,** tel. (307) 455-2304 or (800) 353-2555, on 20 acres of land with a modern lodge and duplex cabins offering fantastic views of Wind River Valley. Horseback rides are available for a fee.

Dude Ranches

Ten different dude ranches are found in the Dubois area. **L&B Ranch,** 1072 E. Fork Rd., tel. (307) 455-2839 or (800) 453-9488, is a century-old ranch offering creekside log cabins, horseback riding, cowboy poetry and singing, a swimming pool, stocked fishing ponds, kids' programs, volleyball and pool, fly-fishing, and a rifle range. And, as their brochure notes, "For those who don't like to ride, we have horses that don't like to be ridden!" The season is late May through September, with rates of $875 per person per week, double occupancy.

Located 18 miles north of Dubois in gorgeous Dunoir Valley, **Absaroka Ranch,** tel. (307) 455-2275, is open mid-June to mid-September and has all the standard guest ranch offerings: horseback riding, fishing, hiking, cookouts, campfires, and rodeo. The ranch accommodates just 18 guests and emphasizes the personal touch. It is surrounded by National Forest land and has a comfortable main lodge, log cabins, and a redwood sauna.

Bitterroot Ranch, tel. (307) 455-2778 or (800) 545-0019, emphasizes horseback riding for experienced riders. They have purebred Arabian horses, cross-country jumping courses, pack trips, fly-fishing, and kids' programs. Both French and German are spoken here, attracting an international clientele. The ranch is open June to mid-September.

Mackenzie Highland Ranch, 16 miles west of Dubois on U.S. 26/287, tel. (307) 455-3415, has overnight and weekly accommodations in a rustic log lodge or in cabins. Trail rides, meals, and guided trips are offered, and in the summer graduate-level classes are offered through Sam Houston University. (See "Over Togwotee Pass," below, for additional area guest ranches.)

DUBOIS AREA ACCOMMODATIONS

Note: Accommodations are listed from least to most expensive. Add a seven percent sales and lodging tax to these rates. Area code is 307.

Black Bear Country Inn; 505 W. Ramshorn; tel. 455-2344 or (800) 873-2327; $40-46 s or d; fridges in rooms, kitchenette for $65 (sleeps five), jacuzzi, open May-Nov., AAA approved

Branding Iron Motel; 401 Ramshorn; tel. 455-2893 or (800) 341-8000; $28-31 s, $34-39 d; log cabins, kitchenettes $5 extra, AAA approved

Riverside Inn; three miles east; tel. 455-2337; $30 s, $40 d; quiet location

Chinook Winds Motel; half-mile east; tel. 455-2987; $33-55 s, $40-55 d; kitchenettes $65 (sleeps four), AAA approved

Jakey's Fork Homestead; four miles east; tel. 455-2769; $65 s, $70 d; newer home or historic sod-covered cabin available, beautiful country location, sauna, jacuzzi bath, two guest rooms and one cabin, shared bath, full breakfast, friendly owners, kids welcome, dinners available by request

Mackenzie Highland Ranch; 16 miles west of Dubois; tel. 455-3415; $65 s or d; old ranch, log lodge, four guest rooms with shared baths, cabins with shared or private baths

Rendezvous Motel; one mile west; tel. 455-2844 or (800) 682-9323; $40 s, $42 d for motel rooms with kitchenettes; $85 for up to five in two-story townhouse

Stagecoach Motor Inn; 103 Ramshorn; tel. 455-2303; $38 s, $46 d; outdoor pool, kitchenettes $60-90 d, very nice, AAA approved

Super 8 Motel; 1414 Warm Springs Dr. (two miles west); tel. 455-3694 or (800) 800-8000; $41 s, $45 d; new motel, jacuzzi, AAA approved

Trail's End Motel; 511 Ramshorn; tel. 455-2540; $36 s, $42 d; nice place, open mid-May through September, AAA approved

Twin Pines Lodge & Cabins; 218 Ramshorn; tel. 455-2600; $30 s, $35 d in cabins; $40 s, $50 d in historic lodge, open mid-May to mid-Nov., AAA approved

Wapiti Ridge Ranch; 17 miles west of Dubois; tel. 455-2219 or (800) 927-4844; $50 s, $70 d; motel rooms, full breakfast

Wind River Motel; 519 W. Ramshorn; tel. 455-2611; $24-55 s, $30-75 d; rustic cabins, motel rooms, and suites, open April-Nov.

Mountain Top B&B; five miles west of Dubois; tel. 455-2304 or (800) 353-2555; $95-105 s or d; new lodge and two duplex cabins on 20 acres, dramatic views, five guest rooms, private baths, jacuzzi, full breakfast

Camping

The closest public camping is at **Horse Creek Campground** ($6; open June-Oct.), 12 miles north of Dubois on Horse Creek Road. **Circle-Up Camper Court,** 225 W. Welty, tel. (307) 455-2238, charges $14 for tents (some shade), $19 for RVs. Kids love the tepees for $17 (sleep six; bring your own sleeping bag). Noncampers may use the showers here for $4. Open year-round, this is one of Wyoming's nicer private campgrounds. You can also park RVs at **Riverside Inn,** three miles east of town; tel. (307) 455-2337.

FOOD

Cowboy Cafe, 115 E. Ramshorn, tel. (307) 455-2595, has good home-style breakfasts with big helpings of biscuits and gravy. For a real artery-clogger, try the steak and eggs. For excellent lunchtime sandwiches, homemade soups, and salads, head to **Wild West Deli,** 128 E. Ramshorn, tel. (307) 455-3354.

Village Cafe/Daylight Donut, 515 W. Ramshorn, tel. (307) 455-2122, is an interesting

family place offering donuts and coffee in the mornings and steak dinners each evening. **Ramshorn Inn,** 202 E. Ramshorn, tel. (307) 455-2400, serves good charbroiled steaks and seafood, and **Rustic Pine Steakhouse,** 119 E. Ramshorn, tel. (307) 455-2772, is a carnivore's delight, with prime rib on Friday and Saturday nights and Mexican dishes for lunch. **Buckaroo Bar B-Q,** 318 W. Ramshorn, tel. (307) 455-2021, is the place to go for hickory-smoked barbecue meats.

The **Old Yellowstone Garage,** tel. (307) 455-3666, is the restaurant standout in Dubois, even attracting folks from food-happy Jackson. The menu changes nightly but is always a mix of authentic Italian cuisine and Western American influences: wood-oven pizzas, homemade pastas, steaks, and seafood. Especially popular is the $7 all-you-can-eat Sunday-night pizza feast. Slices are served from each pizza as it comes out of the oven, so you get to sample a wide variety of pizzas. The Italian wine collection here is certainly the most complete in the state. Most dinner entrées are in the $15-20 range. Reserve a week in advance to be sure of a dinner table or come at lunch for a lighter menu of pastas, salads, foccacia, and burgers. Highly recommended. The restaurant is closed November and April to late May, when owners David and Cinzia Gilbert head to their second home—in Italy.

Get groceries at **Ramshorn Food Farm,** 610 W. Ramshorn. For outstanding fresh-baked pastries, breads, and tasty hardtack made from a special Swedish recipe, be sure to stop by **Circle-Up Camper Court,** 225 W. Welty, tel. (307) 455-2238. **Dunloggin' Bakery,** 305 S. 1st St., tel. (307) 455-2445, is more than a bakery, serving three meals a day; closed Mondays. Everything is made fresh on the premises. For espresso coffees, head to **Pony Espresso,** 401 W. Ramshorn, tel. (307) 455-3939.

FUN AND GAMES

Entertainment

Dubois is a hopping place during the summer, especially on weekends. **Outlaw Saloon,** 204 W. Ramshorn, tel. (307) 455-2387, often has rock tunes, while both **Ramshorn Inn,** 202 E.

Ramshorn, tel. (307) 455-2400, and **Rustic Pine,** 119 E. Ramshorn, tel. (307) 455-2430, offer country-western bands. The Rustic Pine also has square dancing on Tuesday nights in July and August. This classic western bar has elk and moose heads, plenty of old wood, and a pool table. Check out the ashtrays, which note, "God spends his vacation here." Dudes from local ranches often invade Dubois one night of the week; ask around to avoid this night if you don't want to be overwhelmed with fellow visitors.

Events

Dubois is one of nine stops in the **Rocky Mountain Stage Stop Sled Dog Race,** an event that attracts some of the nation's best mushers. Unlike other races such as the Iditarod, this one is run in nine 30- to 80-mile stages, with teams ending in a new town each night. The race begins in Jackson and stops for the night in Moran, Dubois, Pinedale, Lander, Atlantic City, Kemmerer, Box Y Guest Ranch (Greys River area), and Afton before ending at Alpine. The race is held over 10 days in early February and has a $100,000 purse.

On Memorial Day weekend Dubois hosts a series of enjoyable cowboy **Pack Horse Races.** The town's **4th of July** weekend is the biggest local event. Dubois comes alive with a street dance, an ice-cream social, a parade, a western barbecue, fireworks, and rubber-ducky races down the river. A **National Art Show** comes to the arts center on the third weekend in July, attracting both professionals and amateurs. **Whiskey Mountain Buckskinners Wind River Rendezvous** on the second weekend of August includes some impressive black-powder marksmanship contests. Also don't miss the Dubois firemen's **buffalo barbecue** during rendezvous weekend.

Recreation

Rent **mountain bikes** from Double Bar J Guest Ranch 20 miles west of Dubois, tel. (307) 455-2681, or Sawmill Inn, near Union Pass, tel. (307) 455-2171. The Wind River flows right through Dubois, with good trout fishing even in midwinter; hot springs up-river keep it open year-round. The nine-hole **Antelope Hills Golf Course** is on the western end of Dubois. The Absarokas and

TIE HACKS

Many of the trees cut in Wyoming's forests between 1870 and 1940 went to supply railroad ties for an ever-expanding network of rails throughout the Rockies. The men who cut these ties—tie hacks—spent long, hard months in the mountains, working through the winter. Many of the woodsmen were emigrants from Sweden, Norway, Finland, Austria, and Italy. Tie hacks first felled a suitable lodgepole pine using a bucksaw, then limbed the tree and used a broadax to hew the tie into shape, finally peeling the remaining bark from the sides and cutting it to length. Hundreds of thousands of ties—each eight feet long and at least five inches on each side—were produced each year by tie hacks. Horses dragged the ties down to a creek bank or flume to await high spring flows, when thousands of ties could be sent downriver at once. The enormous log jams that resulted sometimes required dynamite to loosen. Downstream booms caught the logs where they could be hauled up and loaded onto railway cars.

Tie hacks found work in many parts of Wyoming, but especially in the Medicine Bow Mountains, Laramie Mountains, Sierra Madre, Big Horn Mountains, and Wind River Mountains, where major streams provided a way for the ties to reach the railheads. In the upper Wind River country, the industry spanned three decades, from 1914 to 1946, and more than 10 million ties were cut and floated downstream to Riverton, where they were used by the Chicago and Northwestern Railroad. A stone monument to the tie hacks stands along US 26/287 approximately 18 miles west of Dubois.

Wind River Mountains around Dubois are extremely popular with snowmobilers during the winter months, and several places rent "sleds" in town and nearby. Don't expect peace and quiet with all these machines roaring through the backcountry! More than 300 miles of trails head out in all directions. **Cross-country skiers** find trails near Falls Campground and Brooks Lake (both 23 miles west of town) and Cowboy Village Resort at Togwotee (40 miles west), and with an enormity of backcountry areas off-limits to snowmobiles.

Washakie Outfitting, tel. (307) 733-3602, offers dogsled day tours ($65 for two hours, $95 for half-day, $150 for all day) and overnight dogsled trips ($300 for adults; $200 for kids under 12). **Geyser Creek Dogsled Adventures,** tel. (307) 739-0165 or (800) 531-6874, has dogsled tours of the Brooks Lake area and longer trips all the way up to a three-day sled trip that includes overnight stops in a tepee and a yurt. All-day rates are $175-195 for adults, $95 for kids under age 10.

OTHER PRACTICALITIES

Shopping

Justin Bridges makes and sells high-quality handmade folding knives, sporting knives, and kitchen cutlery at **Wind River Knives** four miles east of town, tel. (307) 455-2769. Some of the handles are made from the horns of bighorn sheep, and each one is a work of art. You're welcome to tour the shop, even if you can't afford the $200 to $1,500 they cost. Most knives are custom made, and his waiting list is generally two years!

Trapline Gallery, 120 E. Ramshorn, tel. (307) 455-2800, sells Indian-crafted beadwork, jewelry, and artwork, as well as furs. **Horse Creek Traders,** 104 E. Ramshorn, tel. (307) 455-3345, has an impressive collection of antique trade beads for sale along with tacky antler carvings and Indian trinkets. A few doors down is a nice bookshop, **Two Ocean Books,** tel. (307) 455-3554. **Water Wheel Gift Shop,** 113 E. Ramshorn, tel. (307) 455-2112, also carries a selection of Wyoming titles. Purchase topographic maps at **Welty's General Store,** 113 W. Ramshorn, tel. (307) 455-2377, and fishing supplies from **Wind River Fly Shop,** tel. (307) 455-2140.

Information and Services

The **Dubois Chamber of Commerce,** 616 W. Ramshorn, tel. (307) 455-2556, is open Mon.-Fri. 9 a.m.-5 p.m. Memorial Day to Labor Day and Mon.-Thurs. 9 a.m.-3 p.m. the rest of the year. Ask for a self-guided tour maps of old logging flumes, tie-hack cabins, and other historic structures. Stop by the Forest Service's **Wind River**

Ranger District office at 1403 W. Ramshorn (one mile west of town), tel. (307) 455-2466, for maps of Shoshone and Bridger-Teton National Forests ($3) and info on local trails. They also have a listing of local horsepacking outfitters. Open Mon.-Fri. 8 a.m.-5 p.m. (See the chapter on Bighorn Basin for more on the Washakie Wilderness.) The Fitzpatrick Wilderness is described under "Wind River Mountains," below. Dubois does not have a hospital, but the **Dubois Medical Center,** 706 Meckem, tel. (307) 455-2516, has a physician's assistant. Wash clothes at the laundromat on W. Ramshorn across from Branding Iron Motel.

Transportation

SANTA (Shoshone Arapahoe Nations Transit Authority), tel. (800) 439-7118, offers on-demand bus service connections to Lander, Riverton, Jackson, Rock Springs (Greyhound and Amtrak connections), Rawlins, Cody, Pinedale, and Salt Lake City.

DUBOIS VICINITY

Anyone who loves the outdoors will discover an abundance of pleasures around Dubois. There's good fishing for rainbow, cutthroat, brown, and brook trout in the Wind River and for rainbow, brook, and Mackinaw trout in the many alpine lakes, plus lots of deer, elk, and bighorn sheep. Hikers and horse-packers will find hundreds of miles of Forest Service trails in the area. Photographers love the brilliantly colored badlands that frame Dubois on both the east and west sides. And each winter, hundreds of 'bilers climb on their sleds and cross-country skiers strap on their boards to enter the world of deep powder in the Absarokas.

Horse Creek Area

Horse Creek Road heads north from Dubois and provides scenic views of the Absarokas. **Horse Creek Campground** ($6; open June-Oct.) is 12 miles north. Forest Road 504 continues another five miles, providing access to the Washakie Wilderness via Horse Creek Trail. Forest Road 508 splits off near Horse Creek Campground and leads another 17 miles to **Double Cabin Campground** ($6; open June-

September). Several trails head into the wilderness from here; most popular are Frontier Creek Trail and the Wiggins Fork Trail. You'll find remnants of a petrified forest six miles up the Frontier Creek Trail, but they have been rather picked over by collectors. (It's illegal to remove petrified wood from a wilderness area.) For other Washakie Wilderness trails info, ask at the Dubois Ranger Station.

Operating as a dude ranch since 1920, **T Cross Ranch** is located 15 miles north of Dubois near Horse Creek and is open June to mid-September. Surrounded by the Shoshone National Forest, the ranch has weekly accommodations for $925-1,000 per person per week, including horseback riding, all meals, an overnight campout for kids, trout fishing, and a hot tub. Backcountry pack trips and other activities are also available. Lodging is in comfortable log cabins, and the main lodge has a big living room, spacious front porch, and massive stone fireplace.

Union Pass

The first road across the Absarokas headed through Union Pass southwest of Dubois. The pass forms a divide between the waters of the Columbia, Colorado, and Mississippi Rivers and marks the boundary of the Absaroka, Wind River, and Gros Ventre mountain ranges. Nearby is an interpretive sign and a nature trail through a flower-filled meadow. Union Pass Road (gravel) leaves U.S. 26/287 approximately nine miles northwest of Dubois and climbs across to connect with State 352 north of Pinedale. On the west side of the pass the road becomes rougher and should only be attempted in dry weather with high-clearance vehicles.

The country near here is popular with mountain bikers, cross-country skiers, and far too many wintertime snowmobilers. **Sawmill Lodge,** tel. (307) 455-2171, five miles up Union Pass Road, has condo-style cabins, a bar, a restaurant, winter snowmobile rentals, and a summertime RV park ($15). The cabins are $50 per person (including breakfast and dinner) in the winter, $40 d summers. Closed mid-April through May.

A beautiful 20-mile-long side road takes off from a couple of miles up Union Pass Road, heads along Warm Springs Creek, and eventu-

ally reconnects with U.S. 26/287. Find fantastic views of the Absaroka and Wind River Ranges along this route. The remains of an old tie-hack logging flume are visible and a warm spring (85° F) flows into the creek.

OVER TOGWOTEE PASS

The enjoyable drive west from Dubois first cuts through the colorful badlands, playing tag with the Wind River as it begins a long ascent to 9,644-foot Togwotee Pass (pronounced "TOE-go-tee"). The pass is named for a subchief under Chief Washakie. Togwotee was one of the last independent Sheepeater Indians—a branch of the Shoshones—and the man who led a U.S. government exploratory expedition over this pass in 1873. He even guided President Chester Arthur on his monthlong visit to Yellowstone in 1883.

Togwotee Pass is one of the most scenic drives imaginable, with Ramshorn Peak peeking down from the north for several miles until the road plunges into dense lodgepole forests (Shoshone National Forest) with lingering glimpses of the Pinnacle Buttes. At the crest it emerges into grass-, willow-, and flower-bedecked meadows with Blackrock Creek winding through. Whitebark pine and Engelmann spruce trees cover the nearby slopes. As the highway drops down the western side into the Bridger-Teton National Forest, another marvelous mountain range—the Tetons—dominates the horizon in dramatic fashion. Snow lies along the roadsides until early July; notice the high posts along the road used by wintertime snowplows. Togwotee Pass is a complete shock after all the miles of sagebrush and grassland that control the heartland of Wyoming. It's like entering another world—a world of cool, forested mountains and lofty peaks instead of the arid land with horizon-wide vistas.

Pinnacle Buttes and Brooks Lake

Dominating the view along U.S. 26/287 for perhaps 15 miles are the castlelike Pinnacle Buttes. Twenty-three miles west of Dubois, you'll come to the turnoff to Brooks Lake, elevation 9,100 feet. Take it, even if you don't plan on camping here. A five-mile gravel road leads to the cliff-rimmed lake, and a clear creek flows east and

south from here. The Forest Service's excellent **Pinnacles** and **Brooks Lake** Campgrounds run $9 a night; open mid-June to mid-September along the lakeshore. Facing the lake is historic Brooks Lake Lodge (see below). Back on the main highway, you'll want to stop at **Falls Campground** (also $9; open June to mid-September). Here, Brooks Creek tumbles into a deep canyon. Catch very impressive views of **Brooks Creek Falls** along the short trail beginning from the parking lot here. In wintertime, cross-country skiers will find an easy signed but ungroomed ski trail that heads out two miles from here. **Wind River Lake** ($3) is another five miles up the hill, just below the pass. It's a gorgeous place for picnics, with deep blue water and the sharp cliffs of Pinnacle Buttes behind.

Mountain Lodges

Fourteen miles west of Dubois, **Timberline Ranch**, tel. (307) 455-2513, has wintertime lodging in cabins and condo accommodations for $50 per person, including breakfast and dinner. It also rents snowmobiles and has a restaurant and bar. Open mid-December through March. In the summer, the ranch is home to a geology field camp.

Located 18 miles west of Dubois, **Triangle C Ranch**, tel. (307) 455-2225, was established as the first tie-hack camp in the region and now operates as a summertime guest ranch and wintertime snowmobiling and cross-country skiing center. There's a three-night minimum stay in the summer, with meals, horseback riding, and various trips included.

Pinnacle Buttes Lodge, 20 miles west of Dubois on U.S. 26/287, tel. (307) 455-2506, has motel rooms for $60 and cabins with kitchenettes for $90. The cabins and motel rooms sleep four people. Also here are an outdoor pool, jacuzzi, and camping spaces ($10 for tents, $21 for RVs). Open year-round.

Double Bar J Guest Ranch, 20 miles west of Dubois, tel. (307) 455-2681, has log cabin accommodations, horseback rides, mountain biking, fishing, evening barbecues, and a sauna. There's a three-day minimum stay in the summer, with rates of $148-173 per person per day, including meals. In the winter the ranch offers cross-country skiing and snowmobiling, and nightly rates of $102-131 s, $175-234 d, includ-

ing all meals. The restaurant here features fabulous desserts but is open on a limited basis for those who aren't guests.

Brooks Lake Lodge, tel. (307) 455-2121, provides some of the most incredible scenery in Wyoming, with a dual backdrop of Brooks Lake and the Pinnacles. The enormous great hall (on the National Register of Historic Places) is filled with big-game trophies from all over the world. Built from lodgepole logs in 1922, this classic Western lodge has long served travelers en route to Yellowstone. It was completely restored in the late 1980s and now has six guest rooms in the main lodge and six more private cabins in the trees. Guests can relax in the jacuzzi or explore the magnificent country nearby. Brooks Lake Lodge is 23 miles west of Dubois—or 33 miles east of Moran Junction—and then five miles in from U.S. 26/287 along Brooks Lake Road. It's open July to mid-September and then mid-December to mid-April. During the summer, lodging costs $175 a day per person (double occupancy), including meals, horseback

rides, canoes, and fishing. Cabin suites run $195 per person per day (double occupancy). You need to stay three nights minimum; weekly rates are available. Be sure to reserve far ahead to be sure of a space. Come winter, Brooks Lake Lodge is a popular ski-in or snowmobile-in destination for lunch or evening cocktails (Thurs.-Mon. only). Overnight winter accommodations are available for $125 per person per day in the lodge or $150 per person per day in cabins, including breakfast, dinner, and cross-country skis. Couples can stay here on Wednesday and Thursday nights for $450 per couple for two nights, including meals. Both **Washakie Outfitting,** tel. (307) 733-3602, and **Geyser Creek Dogsled Adventures,** tel. (307) 739-0165 or (800) 531-6874, offer dogsled tours of the Brooks Lake area. Adult rates are $95 for a half-day, $175-195 for all day. Special dinner rides and overnight trips are also available. (See the Jackson Hole and the Tetons chapter for info on Cowboy Village Resort at Togwotee, a few miles west of Togwotee Pass.)

WIND RIVER MOUNTAINS

The Wind River Mountains begin near South Pass and continue 100 miles northwest to Union Pass to form part of America's Continental Divide backbone. The range is visible for more than a hundred miles across the sagebrush country of central and southwestern Wyoming, its rugged snowcapped peaks gleaming in the light. The Shoshones traversed this range each spring and fall, and Sheepeater Indians hunted in the high country, but to most of the white pioneers whose wagon trains rolled across South Pass the peaks represented a forbidding, mysterious place. In 1868, writer James Chisholm offered a description of the range that still rings true today:

I think the best inspired painter that ever drew would fail in attempting to describe these mighty mountains. He may convey correctly enough an impression of their shape, their vast extent and sublime beauty. But there is something always left out which escapes all his colors and all his skill.

Their aspects shift and vary continually. Their very shapes seem to undergo a perpetual transformation like the clouds above them. There is a mystery like the mystery of the sea—a silence not of death but of eternity.

Today, the Wind River Mountains are considered Wyoming's premier backpacking area, offering perhaps 700 miles of trails. Much of the country is well above timberline, featuring glacially carved mountains and countless small lakes. Mountain climbers enjoy practicing moves on thousands of granitic precipices representing all degrees of difficulty. The Wind River Mountains contain Gannett Peak—at 13,804 feet the tallest in Wyoming—and all but one of the state's 15 other highest peaks. The 150 glaciers in the mountains all formed during the Little Ice Age, between A.D. 1400 and 1850. The glaciers that actually carved these mountains were far larger—so massive, in fact, that they covered the mountaintops to great depths and spilled over to create the hanging valleys, cirques, alpine lakes,

U-shaped valleys, and steep cliffs of today.

Three different Forest Service wilderness areas cap these mountains; the largest is Bridger Wilderness, on the western side of the Continental Divide (in Bridger-Teton National Forest); the other two are Popo Agie and Fitzpatrick Wilderness Areas east of the crest (in Shoshone National Forest). Add in the BLM's Scab Creek Wilderness Study Area for a total of more than 735,000 roadless acres. The lower elevations of the Wind Rivers are also U.S. Forest Service lands but are managed for other purposes—primarily timber harvesting and grazing. On the northeast border is the Wind River Reservation, which includes some of the high mountain country, but access is restricted. Contact the Tribal Fish and Game Office in Fort Washakie, tel. (307) 332-7207, to purchase a limited hiking, fishing, and camping permit.

Wildlife

Most of the streams and larger lakes in the Wind Rivers have been planted with rainbow, cutthroat, California golden, brook, German brown, or Mackinaw trout and grayling and mountain whitefish. Although grizzlies are only infrequently sighted, black bears are still in these mountains—mainly below treeline—and have caused considerable problems in recent years. Always hang food out of their reach; check with local Forest Service offices for current conditions and precautions. Other creatures—mosquitoes and biting flies—are more common annoyances in the mountains. Be sure to bring insect repellent during July and August, when they are at their worst. Other critters you're likely to see include bighorn sheep, moose, elk, mule deer, and coyotes. Pikas and yellow-bellied marmots are common in the high-country boulder fields.

Access

Three highways circle the Wind River Range: U.S. 26/287 on the northeast, U.S. 191 on the southwest, and State 28 on the southeast. The mountains are traversed by only one road, gravel Union Pass Road. Most people cross the relatively gentle southern slopes at South Pass or over Togwotee Pass to the northeast. You can gain access to the three wilderness areas from either side, but the high passes and long distances keep many hikers on one side or the other. See descriptions of the three different wilderness areas (below) for specific access points.

Most trails in the Wind Rivers are relatively free of snow by early July and remain so until mid-September, but the high passes may not open until late July. Because of the open country in the alpine, off-trail travel is relatively easy here but is advised only for experienced hikers who know how to read topographic maps and can take care of themselves in an emergency. Be prepared for the thunderstorms that often roll in during the afternoon; lightning is a real problem above timberline. It can snow at any time in this mountain country; night temperatures can drop below freezing even in midsummer. You won't find a lot of wood in many parts of the range, so be sure to bring a gas stove to cook on. In addition, wood fires are prohibited at many of the most heavily used sites.

Unlike the mountain country farther north, most of the people who head into the Winds do so on foot rather than atop a horse. Horses are used by a quarter of the people, and "spot-packing," in which horses carry supplies for base camps but everyone hikes in on foot, is a popular way to get into the backcountry without carrying everything on your back. Many outfitters offer these services; stop by local Forest Service offices for a list of outfitters. Most backcountry users do not need permits, but visitor permits (free) are required for groups using stock animals and organized groups like the Boy Scouts and schools.

More Info

Forest Service ranger stations in Lander (Popo Agie Wilderness), Dubois (Fitzpatrick Wilderness), and Pinedale (Bridger Wilderness) can provide information on their respective areas. An area map ($3) of Southern Shoshone National Forest covers the Fitzpatrick and Popo Agie Wilderness Areas, while a Pinedale area map ($3) covers the Bridger Wilderness. Maps, copies of backcountry use regulations, and lists of approved outfitters are available from Forest Service offices.

Below you'll find brief descriptions of the most popular hikes, but with literally hundreds of treks available in the Winds don't think these are your only options. In fact, to avoid the crowds you

should probably pick up a few topo maps and discover your own trails. The late Finis Mitchell's *Wind River Trails* (Salt Lake City: Wasatch Publications) is a folksy, inexpensive guide by a man who hiked this country from 1909 nearly until his death in the 1990s. Mitchell personally planted trout in dozens of high-country lakes during the 1930s and even had a mountain named for him. Pick up this guide if you plan to do any fishing. *Climbing and Hiking in the Wind River Mountains* by Joe Kelsey (San Francisco: Sierra Club Books) has accurate information on most of the hiking trails and describes hundreds of technical climbs. For a guide directed specifically to hiking, not climbing, see *Walking the Winds: A Hiking & Fishing Guide to Wyoming's Wind River Range*, by Rebecca Woods (Jackson, WY: White Willow Publishing). Topographic maps are available from sporting-goods stores in the surrounding towns.

GREEN RIVER LAKES AREA

The long drive to Green River Lakes is one of the most popular getaways in the Wind River Mountains. The road parallels the Green River as it first drifts northward then makes a U-turn to meander across southwestern Wyoming, eventually joining the Colorado River in Utah. Willows line the riverbanks in this open valley, while sagebrush and aspen cover the hills. Cattle and horses graze on the lush grasses. Get to Green River Lakes by heading to **Cora** (10 miles north of Pinedale) and then north on State 352. The first 26 miles of the road to Green River Lakes are paved and kept plowed all winter. Approximately 15 miles up, a sign points the way to **New Fork Lake,** located four miles away on a gravel road. Camp here at either **New Fork Lake Campground** (free; open June to mid-September) or the popular **Narrows Campground** ($5; open June to mid-September). Make reservations ($8.25 extra charge) at the Narrows by calling (800) 280-2667. **New Fork Trail** takes off from the Narrows Campground, providing one of many routes into the Winds.

At the Forest Service border, state maintenance ends and the road becomes gravel and gets rougher and more washboarded as you go the remaining 18 miles. Watch the weather,

since this upper portion can become a quagmire after heavy rains. It's especially a problem if you're towing a trailer. Fantastic scenery makes the trip worthwhile despite the road conditions. Look for some enormous "erratic" boulders a couple of miles up the road from here, evidence of the glaciers that once scoured this valley and carried the boulders along with them.

Just inside the Forest Service border, a signboard describes the tie drives that sent several hundred thousand railroad ties down the Green River between 1869 and 1871. They made it all the way to Green River City (130 miles away), where a boom caught them and they were loaded on railcars. The crew boss, Charles Deloney, later became first superintendent of the Yellowstone Preserve and opened the first store in Jackson. The Green River Lumber and Tie Company came here in the 1890s, employing at least 50 men who lived in the town of Kendall. The company only lasted until 1904, but you can still find the tall stumps in the second-growth forests nearby.

Approximately three miles beyond the Bridger-Teton National Forest border, a rough gravel road splits off and heads over Union Pass to Dubois. Although this route was used by Indians and mountain men, today it probably sees more use by snowmobiles in the winter than cars in summertime. The Forest Service's **Whiskey Grove Campground** ($5; open mid-June to mid-September) is just across the bridge at the site of the old logging town of Kendall.

Box R Ranch, near Cora, tel. (307) 367-2291, is a working cattle ranch with accommodations for 20 guests. Dudes get horseback rides, whitewater float trips, fishing, and the chance to head into the backcountry on pack trips and drop camps. It's open June to mid-September.

Kendall Warm Springs

Back on Green River Lakes Road, you pass Kendall Warm Springs 1.5 miles above the turnoff to the campground, its 85° F waters issuing from a few hundred feet up the hill. This is the only place in the world where you can find **Kendall dace.** Fully grown, they are just two inches long, or, as the Forest Service notes, shorter than their scientific name, *Rhinichthys osculus thermalis*. The water drops over a 12-

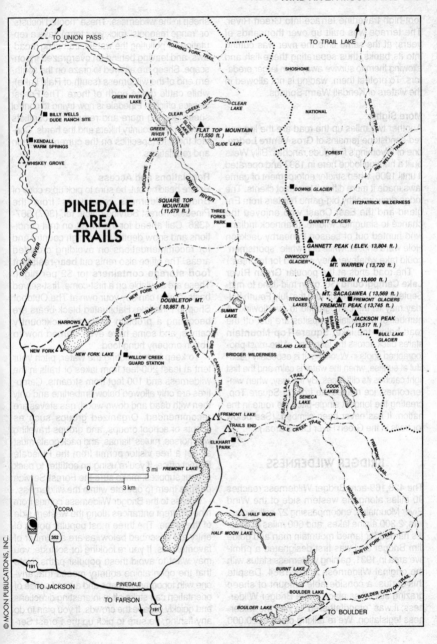

PINEDALE
AREA
TRAILS

TO UNION PASS

ROARING FORK TRAIL

TO TRAIL LAKE

SHOSHONE

NATIONAL

GREEN RIVER
LAKE

CLEAR CREEK TRAIL

CLEAR
LAKE

FOREST

GLACIER TRAIL

BILLY WELLS
DUDE RANCH SITE

KENDALL
WARM SPRINGS

WHISKEY GROVE

GREEN RIVER
LAKES

SLIDE
LAKE
TRAIL

FLAT TOP MOUNTAIN
(11,550 ft.)

SLIDE LAKE

INK WELLS TRAIL

DOWNS GLACIER

FITZPATRICK WILDERNESS

PORCUPINE TRAIL

SQUARE TOP
MOUNTAIN
(11,679 ft.)

THREE
FORKS
PARK

GREEN RIVER

CONTINENTAL DIVIDE

GANNETT GLACIER

GANNETT PEAK (ELEV. 13,804 ft.)

DINWOODY GLACIER

MT. WARREN (13,720 ft.)

MT. HELEN (13,600 ft.)

(NOT FOR HORSES)

MT. SACAGAWEA (13,569 ft.)

FREMONT GLACIERS

FREMONT PEAK (13,745 ft.)

JACKSON PEAK (13,517 ft.)

TITCOMB
LAKES

TITCOMB
BASIN
TRAIL

BULL LAKE
GLACIER

NEW FORK TRAIL

DOUBLETOP MT.
(10,867 ft.)

SUMMIT
LAKE

HIGHLINE TRAIL

ISLAND LAKE

INDIAN PASS TRAIL

BRIDGER WILDERNESS

NARROWS

NEW FORK

NEW FORK LAKE

DOUBLE TOP MT. TRAIL

PALMER LAKE TRAIL

PINE CREEK CANYON TRAIL

WILLOW CREEK
GUARD STATION

SENECA LAKE TRAIL

COOK
LAKES

SENECA
LAKE

COOK LAKES TRAIL

FREMONT LAKE

TRAILS END

ELKHART
PARK

POLE CREEK TRAIL

FREMONT TRAIL

FREMONT LAKE

0   3 mi

0   3 km

CORA

352

HALF MOON

HALF MOON LAKE

NORTH FORK TRAIL

TO JACKSON

PINEDALE

191

TO FARSON

BURNT LAKE

BOULDER LAKE

BOULDER LAKE

BOULDER CANYON TRAIL

TO BOULDER

© MOON PUBLICATIONS, INC.

foot-high travertine terrace into Green River. The terrace was built up over thousands of years; at the same time the river was cutting into its banks, thus separating these fish and allowing them to survive away from larger predators. To protect them, wading is not allowed in the waters of Kendall Warm Springs.

More Sights
Another two miles up the road are the log and red-sandstone remains of **Gros Ventre Lodge**, one of Wyoming's first dude ranches. Billy Wells built a hunting lodge here in 1897 and operated it until 1906, when stricter enforcement of game laws made it more difficult to attract clients. The lodge drew wealthy big-game hunters from England and the East Coast who enjoyed the chance to slaughter wildlife. (Bannock Indians who hunted out of season in nearby Jackson Hole were shot at, while rich white "sportsmen" could take whatever they wanted for trophies.)

The road ends at the popular **Green River Lake Campground** ($6; open mid-June to mid-September). Weekends and the July Fourth holiday may fill the campground to overflowing. A number of unofficial campsites are just off the road below the lake. **Square Top Mountain** stares back across the lake, one of the most photographed spots in Wyoming. It is especially beautiful at sunrise, when the water is calm and the first light catches its cliff faces. By the way, when winter comes, ice drapes the front of Square Top, creating the longest single-pitch ice route in the nation. It has never been climbed. (See below for trails in the Green River Lakes area.)

BRIDGER WILDERNESS

The 428,169-acre Bridger Wilderness reaches 90 miles along the western side of the Wind River Mountains, encompassing 27 active glaciers, 2,300 alpine lakes, and 600 miles of trails. It's named for famed mountain man and guide Jim Bridger and was first designated a primitive area in 1931, gaining wilderness status with the original Wilderness Act of 1964. Despite this status, a considerable amount of sheep grazing still takes place in the Bridger Wilderness; it was "grandfathered" in with the wilderness legislation. We're talking close to 20,000

sheep in the wilderness. These "hoofed locusts" or "range maggots" (pick your term) have a reputation for polluting the waters, trampling meadows, and leaving behind an overgrazed moonscape. Sheep are allowed to graze on the southern end of the wilderness (south of Raid Lake), while cattle graze north of there. The Forest Service office in Pinedale is now trying to control sheep grazing more and reduce the conflicts between backcountry hikers and the herds. Contact them for specifics on the current situation and regulations.

Regulations and Access
Before heading out, be sure to pick up a copy of Bridger Wilderness regulations from the Pinedale Forest Service office, tel. (307) 367-4326. Call ahead for the latest on trail conditions and snow depths in the high country and for recommendations on avoiding crowded areas. The office also rents out **bear-resistant food storage containers** for $2 per night. These are available on a first-come, first-served basis, or you can buy your own at The Outdoor Shop in Pinedale. Habituated black bears are becoming a problem in many backcountry camps, and some have even learned how to obtain properly hung food.

To keep from polluting the water, pitch your tent at least 200 feet from lakes or trails in the wilderness and 100 feet from streams. Campfires are only allowed below timberline and only then with dead and down wood; gas stoves are recommended. Organized groups such as scouts or school groups, and groups traveling with horses, mules, llamas, and pack goats must all get a free visitor permit from the Pinedale District office. If you're using an outfitter to pack in your supplies, make sure the Forest Service permits them to operate within the wilderness.

Access to the Bridger Wilderness comes from nine different entrances along the western side of the range. The three most popular points of entry are described below, as are a number of favorite trails. If you're looking for solitude, you may want to avoid these popular paths. Note that the open alpine country means that anyone with topographic maps and a good sense of orientation can strike off in interesting directions and quickly escape the crowds. If you plan to do any fishing, be sure to pick up the Forest Ser-

vice's guide to fishing lakes in the Bridger Wilderness, with details on which species are where.

Green River Lakes Trails

Easily the most scenic entry into the Winds is from Green River Lakes, located on the end of a paved-then-dirt road that leads north from Cora. The road ends at a campground ($6) facing onto Lower Green River Lake, where the unforgettable 11,679-foot summit of Square Top Mountain dominates the view.

For an easy five-mile day-hike, follow the trails that circle Lower Green River Lake (Highline Trail on the east and Lakeside Trail on the west). You'll have excellent views of Flat Top Mountain (not to be confused with Square Top Mountain) from the Lakeside Trail and of the Clear Creek Falls along the Highline Trail. Keep your eyes open for moose and osprey. An interesting side trip is the short hike to Upper Green River Lake, where Square Top proves even more startling. Another side trip heads up **Clear Creek Trail**—it takes off from the southeastern end of Lower Green River Lake, climbs two miles to a natural bridge, then continues an equal distance to Clear Lake. Some of this country was burned in a 1988 fire. Flat Top is relatively easy to climb; see Finis Mitchell's *Wind River Trails* for the route.

Those interested in longer hikes will find several trails in the Green River Lakes area. **Roaring Fork Trail** climbs up to Faler Lake, 14 miles away and 2,200 feet higher. The **Highline Trail** follows the northeast shore of Lower Green River Lake and then continues south to the uppermost headwaters of the Green River. From there, the trail stays in the alpine much of the way to its destination at the Big Sandy Trailhead on the southern end of the Bridger Wilderness. The total distance is 72 miles, but few people actually follow it that far, preferring to branch off to other sights. Another popular trek is up **Porcupine Trail** to Porcupine Pass and then down **New Fork Trail** to New Fork Lake (a total of approximately 17 miles). Porcupine Trail begins at the upper end of Lower Green River Lake, splitting off from Lakeside Trail.

Elkhart Park Trails

A paved road heads northeast from Pinedale along the eastern side of Fremont Lake, ending 15 miles later at Elkhart Park Trailhead (elevation 9,100 feet). The Forest Service generally has someone around to answer questions at the big parking area that fills with cars in July and August. An overlook along the way provides excellent vistas over Fremont Lake and Bridger Wilderness. The **Trails End Campground** at Elkhart Park ($5) is open from late June to mid-September.

Trails head out from Elkhart in two directions. **Pine Creek Canyon Trail** heads north, providing a relatively direct connection with Summit Lake (13 miles) and then down into Green River Lakes (30 miles total). Because of its steepness, it is not recommended for stock use. The main drawback to this trail is that it loses 2,000 feet by dropping into Pine Creek Canyon—elevation that you must regain to reach Summit Lake. You can make a nice loop by heading east from Summit Lake along the Highline Trail to Elbow Lake and Seneca Lake, where you follow the Seneca Lake and Pole Creek trails back to Elkhart Park. This loop takes you through some of the more scenic areas in the wilderness and covers approximately 31 miles.

The most popular destination from Elkhart is **Titcomb Basin**. Access from Elkhart Park is via a series of connected trails: the Pole Creek, Seneca Lake, Indian Pass, and Titcomb Basin Trails. Many hikers and climbers overnight at Island Lake, making for very crowded conditions much of the summer. It is 15 miles from Elkhart Park to Upper Titcomb Lake, a mountain cirque with abundant wildflowers. A side hike goes up through gorgeous Indian Basin to Indian Pass (three miles). Mountaineers can then descend to the Knife Point and Bull Lake glaciers within the Popo Agie Wilderness.

The valley above Titcomb Basin is open, giving climbers access to the west side of a whole row of peaks, including Mt. Helen (13,600 feet), Mt. Sacagawea (13,569 feet), Jackson Peak (13,517 feet), and **Fremont Peak** (13,745 feet). Climbers can tackle the last two without technical expertise, although Fremont does require some rough scrambling in places. It is most easily climbed from the southwest side; see a topographic map to find the route. Those with greater expertise will find many outstanding opportunities to test their skills on the cliff faces here. Warning: A number of folks have died climbing

Fremont Peak; use extreme caution when rock scrambling, and never push beyond your skills or ability.

Fremont Peak is named for **John C. Frémont,** the son-in-law of Senator Thomas Hart Benton, the biggest promoter of the Manifest Destiny that would lead Americans all the way to the Pacific. Because of this familial association, Frémont was given the task of exploring and mapping the western territories, work that brought him the nickname the "Great Pathfinder." Some of his ventures—such as floating through the wild waters of Fremont Canyon on the North Platte River, or crossing the Rockies in the dead of winter—were downright stupid, and his guides tried to stop him. Frémont's best asset was his wife, who painted his adventures in such a heroic light that his presidential ambitions were nearly realized.

In 1842, Frémont and his men climbed what appeared to be the highest mountain in the Wind River range, a summit they called Snow Peak (now Fremont Peak). From the west, it is obviously why Frémont and his men would mistake this for the highest: Gannett Peak (59 feet taller) is barely visible from a distance, hidden behind other summits. It was not until years later that the mistake was discovered. Frémont was led on his wilderness treks by men with far more experience—including Kit Carson and Tom Fitzpatrick—and his real role was to transfer their innate knowledge of the land onto maps. (Although most people believe Frémont did climb the peak bearing his name, others say he climbed another peak instead, or none at all. One of his scouts, Basil Lajeunesse, stated bluntly, "Frémont never ascended the peak." Perhaps that would account for the discrepancies between what Frémont described and what is actually there.)

Big Sandy Trails

One of the most popular entry points into the Bridger Wilderness is from Big Sandy Trailhead. Access is from a number of different directions, but all require long stretches of gravel road. Easiest access is from the north. From the town of Boulder, take State 353 where it turns west off U.S. 191 and follow it till it turns to gravel (16 miles). Bear left at the intersection a half-mile up and go another nine miles to another junction

(signed), where you again turn left and go seven more miles to the turnoff (left) to the Forest Service's Dutch Joe Guard Station and then on to Big Sandy Opening. The road ends at **Big Sandy Campground** (free; open mid-June to mid-September), where the trails begin. The Forest Service generally has someone stationed here. Note that the rough road into Big Sandy becomes slick and hazardous when it rains, so watch the weather reports closely. This is especially a problem if you're towing a trailer.

Big Sandy Lodge is just to the left near the end of Big Sandy Road (44 miles from Boulder) and provides guided trail rides and rustic log cabins ($45-55 s or d). The historic lodge (built in 1929) contains a trophy-filled lounge and two stone fireplaces. Meals, spot pack trips, and guided pack trips are also available, or you can stay by the week with everything included. There are no phones here, but you can leave messages at (307) 332-6782 in Lander; write the lodge at Box 223, Boulder, WY 82923, for more info and reservations. Open late May to mid-September.

A maze of trails departs from Big Sandy Opening. The **Highline Trail** heads north, extending across the Bridger Wilderness to Green River Lakes, and continues from there to Union Pass, 100 miles away. The trail connects with numerous others, including **Shadow Lake Trail,** a 2.5-mile route to this alpine lake. More adventurous types can continue up through Texas Pass and down to Lonesome Lake in the Cirque of the Towers, a distance of 15 miles. Another side route off the Highline Trail is the **Washakie Trail,** a path used by this famous Shoshone chief during his people's biannual migration between the Wind River Valley and the Green River country. This trail goes into the Washakie Lakes area of the Popo Agie Wilderness, where you can connect with the Bears Ears Trail (see below).

The most popular trail out of Big Sandy Opening is **Big Sandy Trail,** a 5.5-mile trek to crowded Big Sandy Lake, where it meets a spider web of trails and cairn-marked paths to other high-country lakes. Beyond the lake, **Big Sandy Pass Trail** climbs up North Creek and over Big Sandy Pass (shown as Jackass Pass on some maps) before dropping into Lonesome Lake and Cirque of the Towers (total distance 8.5

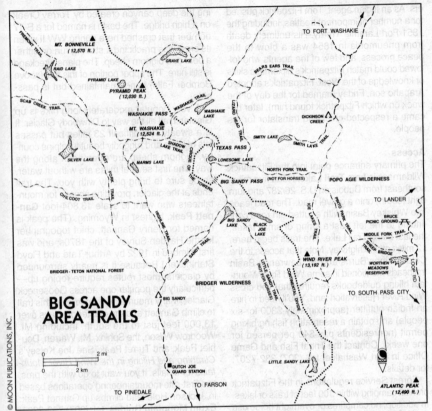

BIG SANDY AREA TRAILS

MT. BONNEVILLE (12,570 ft.)

FREMONT TRAIL

RAID LAKE

GRAVE LAKE

TO FORT WASHAKIE

BEARS EARS TRAIL

PYRAMID LAKE

PYRAMID PEAK (12,030 ft.)

LIZARD HEAD TRAIL

DICKINSON CREEK

WASHAKIE TRAIL

WASHAKIE LAKE

WASHAKIE PASS

SCAB CREEK TRAIL

MT. WASHAKIE (12,524 ft.)

SMITH LAKE

SMITH LAKE TRAIL

SHADOW LAKE TRAIL

SILVER LAKE

MARMS LAKE

TEXAS PASS

LONESOME LAKE

CIRQUE OF THE TOWERS

EAST FORK TRAIL

NORTH FORK TRAIL (NOT FOR HORSES)

POPO AGIE WILDERNESS

CHILCOOT TRAIL

BIG SANDY PASS

ICE LAKES TRAIL

PINTO PARK TRAIL

TO LANDER

BRUCE PICNIC GROUND

BIG SANDY LAKE

BLACK JOE LAKE

WIND RIVER PEAK (13,192 ft.)

MIDDLE FORK TRAIL

SHEEP BRIDGE

BIG SANDY TRAIL

WORTHEN MEADOWS RESERVOIR

LOOP RD.

BRIDGER-TETON NATIONAL FOREST

BRIDGER WILDERNESS

BIG SANDY

CONTINENTAL DIVIDE

LITTLE SANDY TRAIL (NOT FOR HORSES)

TO SOUTH PASS CITY

DUTCH JOE GUARD STATION

LITTLE SANDY LAKE

TO PINEDALE

TO FARSON

ATLANTIC PEAK (12,490 ft.)

0   2 mi

0   2 km

© MOON PUBLICATIONS, INC.

---

miles). Big Sandy Pass Trail is a long slog. A strenuous loop trip consists of the Big Sandy Trail-Big Sandy Pass Trail route combined with the Texas Pass-Shadow Lake Trail-Highline Trail route described above. Total distance is 24 miles.

FITZPATRICK WILDERNESS

The 198,838-acre Fitzpatrick Wilderness occupies the northeast side of the Wind River Mountains, sandwiched between the Bridger Wilderness just over the Continental Divide and the Wind River Indian Reservation to the east. The wilderness is a rugged landscape of rock and ice, with dozens of mountain lakes and cas-

cading mountain brooks. Wyoming's highest mountain, Gannett Peak, forms part of the western border, and 44 active glaciers crowd against the summits; the largest covers 1,220 acres. The Fitzpatrick is a favorite of folks with considerable backpacking or mountaineering experience.

Although long maintained as a primitive area, the Fitzpatrick Wilderness was officially established by Congress in 1976 and is named for Tom Fitzpatrick, a respected mountain man, guide, head of the Rocky Mountain Fur Company, Army scout, and Indian agent. To the Indians, he was "Broken Hand," a name received after he lost three fingers in a rifle accident while being pursued by Blackfeet Indians; despite this, he still managed to kill two of his attack-

ers. As an Indian agent, Tom Fitzpatrick pushed for a number of important treaties, including the 1851 Fort Laramie Treaty. His untimely death from pneumonia in 1854 was a blow to the peace process, and few of the agents who followed could match Fitzpatrick's diplomatic skills or knowledge of the West. Fitzpatrick's adopted Arapaho son, Friday (named for the day of the week on which Fitzpatrick found him), later became a respected chief and translator for his people.

Access

The primary entrance point into the Fitzpatrick Wilderness is from **Trail Lake.** Head five miles southeast from Dubois on U.S. 26/287 and turn right (south) onto a gravel road. The road leads into Whiskey Basin, with a rutted dirt road continuing to the left past a string of small lakes, the last being Trail Lake. The trails begin here, 12 miles off the highway. Note that access to the Cold Springs/Burris and St. Lawrence Basin trailheads mentioned in some Wind River Mountain hiking guidebooks requires that you cross Wind River Reservation land. You'll need to hire an Indian outfitter (approximately $300 for six people) and obtain a reservation fishing/hiking permit (nonresidents pay $40 per person for one week). Contact the Tribal Fish and Game Office in Fort Washakie, tel. (307) 332-7207, for details.

Forest Service regulations in the Fitzpatrick prohibit camping within 100 feet of trails or lakes. In addition, no campfires or overnight horse use is allowed above the confluence of Dinwoody and Knoll Lake Creeks. For details, contact the Forest Service office in Dubois, tel. (307) 455-2466.

Trails

Three major trails lead from Trail Lake into the high country. The **Whiskey Mountain Trail** climbs over the peak of the same name and then on to heavily used Simpson Lake, a dozen miles away. From here it's possible for experienced hikers to continue over a pass above Sandra Lake (another 3.5 miles) and then down into the Roaring Fork drainage of the Bridger Wilderness. The **Bomber Basin Trail** leads from Trail Lake Trailhead to Bomber Lake, eight miles away and 2,600 feet higher, cross-

ing the deep canyon created by Torrey Creek on a high bridge. The basin is named for a B-17 bomber that crashed here during WW II when its crew was practicing a strafing run on either a bear or a bighorn sheep. The plane wreckage is still here. The upper portion of this trail (above Bomber Falls) is not maintained but is passable.

A very popular moderately long hike is up **Glacier Trail** all the way to Dinwoody Glacier. It is a sweaty and difficult 23 miles but passes lots of lakes and ruggedly beautiful alpine country. Bighorn sheep are often seen along the way. The first several miles are without water, so be sure to bring plenty with you. The trail ends at the glacier, providing access for mountaineers who want to scale 13,804-foot **Gannett Peak,** highest in Wyoming. (The peak is named for Henry Gannett, chief topographer for the Hayden Survey of the 1870s, and was first climbed in 1922 by Arthur Tate and Floyd Stahlnaker.) Because it is nearly surrounded by glaciers, most routes require roping up—particularly the popular one across Gooseneck Glacier. Many mountaineers come up this trail to climb Gannett and the cluster of peaks over 13,000 feet just to the south, including Mt. Woodrow Wilson, the Sphinx, Mt. Warren, Doublet Peak, and Turret Peak. See Joe Kelsey's *Climbing and Hiking in the Wind River Mountains* for details. If you want to go with the pros, two first-rate mountaineering operations based in Jackson Hole lead climbs up Gannet Peak: **Exum Mountain Guides,** tel. (307) 733-2297, and **Jackson Hole Mountain Guides,** tel. (307) 733-4979.

POPO AGIE WILDERNESS

The Popo Agie Wilderness is a 101,991-acre parcel of magnificent mountain real estate with jagged peaks, deep valleys, and more than 240 lakes. At least 20 peaks rise above 13,000 feet; Wind River Peak is the tallest at 13,225 feet. Popo Agie was first established as a primitive area in 1932 and enlarged and reclassified as wilderness in 1984. The Popo Agie is bounded to the west by the Bridger Wilderness and to the north by the Wind River Indian Reservation. Access to the Popo Agie Wilderness is generally

from the east side, in the Lander vicinity, although it is possible to cross the Continental Divide from the Bridger Wilderness via several different passes. Camping is not allowed within 200 feet of trails, lakes, or streams. Anyone bringing in horses, mules, llamas, or pack goats will need to get a free livestock-use permit from the Forest Service office in Lander.

Dickinson Park Access

The primary jumping-off point into the Popo Agie Wilderness is the Dickinson Park area, northwest of Lander at an elevation of 9,300 feet. Get here by turning west on Moccasin Lake Road (paved) just south of Fort Washakie at the Hines Store. Stay right where the road turns to dirt and continue to Moccasin Lake/Dickinson Park junction, a total of 19 very rough and rutted miles. Turn left here and head another four miles to **Dickinson Creek Campground** (free; open July to mid-September), passing the Dickinson Park Work Center along the way. Note that you'll pass a "No Trespassing without Proper Tribal Travel Permit" sign on Moccasin Lake Road; it's okay to ignore this if you're en route to Dickinson Park.

Allen's Diamond Four Ranch, tel. (307) 332-2995, is near the Dickinson Park Campground and offers simple dude-ranch accommodations with three meals a day, horseback riding, fishing, and nature hikes. They also have guided horsepacking trips and spot pack trips. This is popular with those who want to hike while still enjoying the pleasures of a horse-packed base camp.

The **Bears Ears Trail** takes off from the end of a half-mile dirt road that turns west at the Dickinson Park Work Center and climbs quickly into the alpine before going over Adams Pass. It passes Bears Ears Mountain (look for the "ears") and follows through the alpine before dropping into the lake-filled headwaters of the South Fork of the Little Wind River, 14 miles away. Along the way are all sorts of connections to other trails, including a variety of loops.

From the Dickinson Campground trailhead, the popular **Smith Lake Trail** heads south and then west to Smith and then Cathedral Lakes (eight miles). The **North Fork Trail** splits off the Smith Lake Trail approximately a quarter-mile up. This trail will eventually (15 miles) take you straight to Lonesome Lake at the base of the soaring Cirque of the Towers. Unfortunately, the hike requires four different fordings of the North Fork of the Popo Agie River, a dangerous feat for your feet when the water is high. It's best to wait till late summer.

Loop Road Access

The Loop Road (State 131) cuts south from Lander through Sinks Canyon and then over the mountains to South Pass, providing a number of entry points into the Popo Agie Wilderness. **Middle Fork Trail** begins at **Bruce Picnic Ground,** 13 miles south of Lander on the Loop Road, and follows the Middle Fork of the Popo Agie River upstream to Sweetwater Gap (16 miles), where you enter the Bridger Wilderness. Many people use this trail to reach the Cirque of the Towers area via the Pinto Park and North Fork trails (total one-way distance approximately 23 miles). The **Tayo Creek Trail** splits off from the Middle Fork Trail approximately 13 miles up and continues another four miles to Tayo Lakes. **Sheep Bridge Trail** begins at **Worthen Reservoir,** 20 miles south of Lander on Loop Road, and heads west for three miles to its junction with the Middle Fork Trail. Many people use this to cut distance and elevation off their trek into the Tayo Lake or Cirque of the Towers areas. (It starts 1,200 feet higher than the Middle Fork Trail.)

Cirque of the Towers

This is one of the best-known and most-visited places in the Wind River Mountains, an incredible semicircle of pinnacles at the headwaters of the North Fork of the Popo Agie River. **Lonesome Lake** is in the center, backdropped by peaks with such names as Warbonnet, Pingora, Sharks Nose, Camels Hump, Lizard Head, and Watch Tower. All of these are well-known in the climbing community and attract folks from around the globe. Lonesome Lake is not so lonesome these days; on a typical day in early August you're likely to find a minitown of tents in the vicinity. The water quality suffers from all these people. To lessen the visual impact, some hikers bivouac behind the larger boulders rather than pitching a tent. Campers are required to camp at least a half-mile from the lake, and no campfires are allowed.

The most popular way to reach Cirque of the Towers is from the Big Sandy Opening Trailhead (see "Bridger Wilderness," above), but the longer North Fork Trail (described above) is also commonly used and does not require traversing any passes. The other popularly used route is the Sheep Bridge Trail (described above).

SOUTH PASS AREA

At the southern end of the Wind River Mountains, a broad, relatively gentle pass provides a corridor across the Continental Divide. This part of Wyoming is packed with history. Today, State 28 traverses South Pass, then climbs south and west from Lander, past beautiful **Red Canyon,** where maroon sandstone rocks rise like a backbone out of the sage and grass rangeland. The 34,000-acre **Red Canyon Ranch Preserve** is a working cattle ranch here maintained by the Nature Conservancy. It's a center for research on the ecological effects of different grazing techniques; call (307) 332-3388 for access information and guided walks.

West of Red Canyon, the highway passes just north of the almost-ghost towns of Atlantic City and South Pass before starting the long descent into the Green River Basin and the junction town of Farson. Winters on the pass are long, cold, and windy; the snow fences stretch for miles along the highway.

Gold was first mined here during the middle 1860s, and a long series of booms and busts followed. For a brief time in 1867-68, the **Sweetwater Mines** attracted national attention, and thousands of men (and a few women) flocked to the area. The land was officially part of the Wind River Reservation at the time, but legalities didn't matter much when gold could be found. South Pass was ceded by the Shoshones in 1878. Prospectors still head out each spring in search of the elusive mother lode, and various schemes to reopen the old mines surface periodically. Today the area is enjoyed by thousands of tourists and others attracted by the rich historical and recreational opportunities.

Over the Pass

South Pass was first discovered by the game animals who traversed this country and the Indian hunters who followed them. The first whites to traipse through were the Astorians, fur traders led by Robert Stuart in 1812. The first wagon

wheels rolled over South Pass in 1824, and between 1841 and 1866 more than 350,000 emigrants followed what had become the primary route west. Of all the sights along the Oregon Trail, South Pass must have been one of the most anticipated. West of here the waters flow to the Pacific Ocean, and the entire country became known as the Oregon Territory (hence the **Oregon Buttes** south of South Pass). Travelers took great pleasure in stopping at Pacific Springs, happy in the knowledge that its waters eventually reached the Pacific. An important stage and Pony Express station stood here; some of the buildings from a later ranch are still standing.

Today, State 28 traces a similar route across South Pass. Signboards denote various historic sites along the way. At the signboard that describes the Oregon Trail, a rough dirt road leads a mile back to the clear waters of Pacific Creek, where posts mark the historic route. Don't believe everything you read on the signs, however: the **Parting of the Ways** monument actually marks the South Pass City-Green River stage road where it intersects the Oregon Trail rather than the famous point where the Sublette Cutoff took Oregon- and California-bound travelers west while Mormon voyagers (and others in need of supplies) diverged southwest to Fort Bridger. The true Parting of the Ways lies 10 miles southwest of this marker. The highway west to Farson rolls up and down the sage-carpeted hills, cutting straight as a carpenter's plumb line. The Wind River Mountains dominate the northern horizon, while to the south the distant Killpecker Sand Dunes slide into view.

SOUTH PASS CITY

Located at 7,800 feet above sea level, South Pass City is one of Wyoming's highest settlements. Tall snow fences line the roads here in an attempt to halt the snow that blows all winter

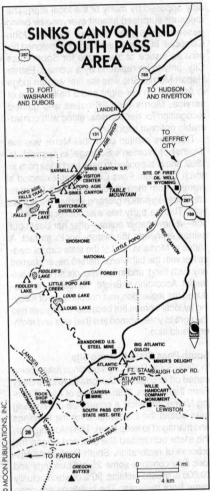

SINKS CANYON AND SOUTH PASS AREA

TO FORT WASHAKIE AND DUBOIS

TO HUDSON AND RIVERTON

287

789

131

LANDER

POPO AGIE RIVER

TO JEFFREY CITY

SAWMILL

SINKS CANYON S.P.

VISITOR CENTER

POPO AGIE SINKS CANYON

POPO AGIE FALLS TRAIL

SITE OF FIRST OIL WELL IN WYOMING

TABLE MOUNTAIN

LITTLE POPO AGIE RIVER

287

789

SWITCHBACK OVERLOOK

FRYE LAKE

FALLS

RED CANYON

SHOSHONE

NATIONAL

FIDDLER'S LAKE

FOREST

FIDDLER'S LAKE

LITTLE POPO AGIE CREEK

LOUIS LAKE

LOUIS LAKE

N

LANDER CUT-OFF

CONTINENTAL DIVIDE

ABANDONED U.S. STEEL MINE

BIG ATLANTIC GULCH

ATLANTIC CITY

MINER'S DELIGHT

ROCK SHOP INN

FT. STAMBAUGH LOOP RD.

ATLANTIC CITY

CARISSA MINE

WILLIE HANDCART COMPANY MONUMENT

SOUTH PASS CITY STATE HIST. SITE

LEWISTON

28

OREGON TRAIL

TO FARSON

OREGON BUTTES

0   4 mi

0   4 km

© MOON PUBLICATIONS, INC.

long. Although commonly called a ghost town, South Pass City never really died out. The town is now a State Historic Site, providing one of the most interesting and authentic historical settings in Wyoming.

Gold in the Hills

During the days of '49, many thousands of would-be miners streamed through South Pass on their way to California, little knowing that gold lay beneath their feet. Gold was first found in 1842, but its discoverer was killed by Indians; other miners faced similar fates. First to file a claim was Henry Reedal, who discovered what became known as the Carissa Lode in 1867. Shortly thereafter, the Miner's Delight Lode was discovered. The finds attracted an onslaught of miners, and by that fall the town of South Pass City had mushroomed into Wyoming's largest settlement, with nearly 3,000 residents.

The discovery of gold at South Pass helped propel the effort to make Wyoming a territory separate from Dakota, a move that took place the following year. At its rip-roaring peak, there was even an effort to make South Pass the Wyoming territorial capital. The town included six general stores, three butcher shops, several restaurants, two breweries, seven blacksmith shops, five hotels, and dozens of saloons and "sporting houses." In 1868, writer James Chisholm described his return to the town after an absence: "Late at night we arrived at Miner's Delight where everything was just as we had left it. The card table in the corner was in full blast. The parties whom we had left on a drunk were now sobering off and those we had left sober were getting on a drunk."

The Carissa Mine's shafts would eventually reach 400 feet down, and the mill would produce gold worth more than six million dollars. But this was primarily hard-rock mining, requiring large capital investments and long hours. The lack of water in this arid country meant that placer mining was possible only in the spring, while summers were spent toiling in the hard-rock mines for $5 a day. The Sweetwater mines were a short-lived bubble that burst almost as quickly as it grew. Instead of the hoped-for mother lode, miners found only small pockets of gold. Within five years most of the miners gave up and moved away. By 1875, fewer than a hundred people remained. But South Pass City refused to die. There were more booms (followed by busts) in the 1880s, 1890s, 1930s, and 1960s. Miners still come to these hills in search of gold.

Women's Suffrage

Given the rough mining crowd that jammed the streets of South Pass City, it seems odd to find the town at the center of the effort to

gain equal rights for women. In late 1869, the first territorial representative from South Pass City, William Bright, introduced a women's-suffrage bill before the first territorial legislature. It was a measure supported by his wife and a number of other South Pass women but prob-

---

SOUTH PASS IN 1861

In 1861, Mark Twain rumbled west through Wyoming on a stagecoach, a trip later made famous in his book *Roughing It*. At South Pass, Twain found that the pre-mining days settlement was not exactly a hubbub of activity:

Toward dawn we got under way again, and presently as we sat with raised curtains enjoying our early-morning smoke and contemplating the first splendor of the rising sun as it swept down the long array of mountain peaks, flushing and gilding crag after crag and summit after summit, as if the invisible Creator reviewed his gray veterans and they saluted with a smile, we hove in sight of South Pass City. The hotelkeeper, the postmaster, the blacksmith, the mayor, the constable, the city marshal and the principal citizen and property holder, all came out and greeted us cheerily, and we gave him good day. . . . South Pass City consisted of four log cabins, one of which was unfinished, and the gentleman with all those offices and titles was the chiefest of the ten citizens of the place. Think of hotelkeeper, postmaster, blacksmith, mayor, constable, city marshal and principal citizen all condensed into one person and crammed into one skin. Bemis said he was "a perfect Allen's revolver of dignities." And he said that if he were to die as postmaster, or as blacksmith, or as postmaster and blacksmith both, the people might stand it; but if he were to die all over, it would be a frightful loss to the community.

---

ably opposed by many of the local men. The measure surprised almost everyone by being passed and signed into law by Gov. John Campbell. In anger, the local judge resigned his post as justice of the peace for South Pass City, only to be replaced by a woman, Esther Hobart Morris. She was the first woman judge in America. In her eight and a half months of service, Morris tried 26 cases and gained recognition for her fairness, along with considerable national exposure.

The more exalted claim that Morris was the "Mother of Women's Suffrage" is suspect. In 1869, she is supposed to have held a tea party in which the South Pass City women extracted a promise from then-candidate William Bright to introduce legislation granting women the right to vote. The tea party tale was concocted by her son—a newspaper editor—after her death but gained entry into the history books as fact. A statue of Morris in front of the state capitol credits her with the bill. Morris herself never claimed any such thing, and in fact was not an active suffragist. According to Bright, the reason he introduced the legislation was not because of lobbying by local women but because "if Negroes had the right to vote, women like [his] wife and mother should also."

South Pass State Historic Site

In 1965, South Pass City's buildings risked being carted off to southern California's Knott's Berry Farm theme park. With the help of Alice "Flaming Mame" Messick, a committee of Wyoming folks outbid the Californians for the buildings and managed to keep them. The following year, the state purchased the site and began the process of restoration. South Pass State Historic Site contains some 25 old buildings and 30,000 authentic artifacts, 90% of which actually came from the area. The buildings are open daily 9 a.m.-6 p.m. May 15 through September; $1 for adults, free for kids under age 18. Call (307) 332-3684 for details. The rest of the year, visitors can wander the streets, but many items are in storage and the windows are covered with plywood.

On summertime weekends the old town comes alive with gold-panning and blacksmithing demonstrations by costumed oldtimers. Be sure to drop by the Morris cabin for fresh-baked cookies. The **Old-Fashioned 4th of**

Esther Morris

July celebration at South Pass is great fun, with country dancing, a barbecue, a pie-baking contest, horseshoe pitching, old-time music, exhibits, and lots of folks in old-time costumes.

Entrance fees ($1 per person) are collected at the **visitor center** in what was once an 1890 dance hall. Inside are interpretive displays and a book and gift shop. The small theater shows a 28-minute video on the area's rich history. Pick up a brochure here describing the buildings. A short way up the street is the **Smith Sherlock Co. Store,** where you can check out the old items or buy licorice candy, sarsparilla, and historical books. Next door is a small museum with historical photos.

Other interesting buildings that have been restored and furnished with original items include a blacksmith shop (with blacksmiths working on Sundays in the summer), a restaurant, butcher shop, hotel, miner's cabin, saloon, newspaper office, bank, school, and a dugout cave used to keep perishables cool. A gold mining exhibit on the hill behind town has a huge stamp mill, carts, and railroad track, along with other mining equipment. Gold panning demonstra-

tions are given periodically throughout the summer. **Sweetwater County Jail,** built in 1870, is the oldest nonmilitary government building in Wyoming, and the **"pest house"** was a place where patients with contagious diseases were left in isolation. Built in 1869, this is the state's oldest hospital, though the level of treatment wasn't always the finest.

The reconstructed **Esther Morris cabin** stands at the eastern end of the row of buildings. Out front is a granite marker from 1939 that credits her with originating women's suffrage. Next to it is a more recent disclaimer. Adding more insult to injury is the fact that the reconstructed cabin is now believed to be in the wrong place; the actual Morris cabin site is not far away, and this was the location of a print shop instead.

Just east of the Morris cabin is a half-mile **nature trail** along Willow Creek offering the chance to explore the Carie Shields Mine (it produced $35,000 worth of gold) and other mines, cabins, and mill sights. Be careful where you walk around these old structures. Along the creek you're likely to see all sorts of animals, from beavers and bighorn sheep to mule deer and moose. Pick up a trail map at the Smith-Sherlock Store. The state also has a 10-km **volksmarch trail** that is popular with the RV crowd.

Practicalities

Outside the State Historic Site is a cluster of old log cabins owned by a handful of locals. **CNL Clothier** makes authentic natural-fiber historic clothing including Old West military clothing, dresses, and cowboy gear. The 1880-style cowboy slicker is especially popular. Everything here is based upon careful research and uses patterns from original garments. The clothes are often used in museums and Hollywood movies. The shop also sells Wyoming history books and has snacks. Call (307) 332-6810 for a copy of their mail-order catalog.

Trails West, tel. (307) 332-7801 or (800) 327-4052, offers three-day covered wagon train rides along the Oregon Trail near South Pass. In the summer months, these trips leave every Tuesday morning and return on Thursday evening, providing two nights in tepees. The cost is $400 for adults, $300 for kids six to 12, $75 for younger children. A special overnight covered wagon trip on weekends costs $99 per person. These trips are about as authentic as you can get.

CALAMITY JANE

Calamity Jane—born Martha Jane Canary in 1852—is surely one of the most unusual characters to come out of the 19th-century West. In an era when the few women who found their way west almost invariably fell into one of three categories—housewife, washerwoman, or prostitute—Calamity Jane was all three, plus a lot more. At age 12, Martha Canary's family trekked west from Missouri to Montana. The trip took five months, and by the time they reached Virginia City she noted: "I was considered a remarkable good shot and a fearless rider for a girl of my age." Her mother died shortly after they arrived, and the family had a hard time surviving the harsh winter; Martha and her sisters were forced to beg on the streets. Her father died the following spring, and from that time on, Martha Canary was on her own. She landed in Miners Delight (near South Pass City) in 1870-71; here some claim she "entertained" men at Hyde's Hall Saloon. She certainly occasionally worked in "the sporting profession."

A Man's World

It was around this time that Calamity Jane gained her nickname. She claimed in a brief autobiography to have signed on as a scout for General Custer in Fort Russell, Wyoming, and to have soon thereafter "donned the uniform of a soldier. It was a bit awkward at first but I soon got to be perfectly at home in men's clothes." At other times she even masqueraded as a man and could by all accounts work, shoot, drink, and cuss as hard as the rough-edged men around her. While employed as a scout for General Crook's campaign near Sheridan she supposedly rescued the post commander, Captain Egan, from an Indian raid, helping him to safety. Egan then named her "Calamity Jane, the heroine of the plains." The name stuck for life.

Whether the story is true or not, Calamity Jane *did* live up to the sobriquet many times in later years. She was often found nursing men down with smallpox—she was immune to the disease—buying meals for the destitute, or assisting ill "soiled doves," even if it meant rolling a man for his money to pay the bills. She saved many lives at a time when life was short and cheap. This is not to suggest that Calamity Jane was the Mother Teresa of the Plains; the same woman who could care so much for others could also be loud and obnoxious when drunk—which was often. Her binges were legendary and

landed her behind bars on numerous occasions, including a monthlong stint in the Rawlins jail for a drunken brawl with one of her many husbands and an eight-day trip to the Laramie jail for drunkenness. Beer would never do: "Give me a shot of booze and slop her over the brim" was always the

Calamity Jane

YELLOWSTONE NATIONAL PARK

bartender's order. As a friend (Deadwood madam Dora DuFran) noted:

Her many friends—she had no enemies—would buy her drinks until she reached the howling stage. Then someone would steer her to the next saloon. Her time was limited in each one when that howling began. She would finally wind up by howling up and down Main Street. Even the law was paralyzed. Nothing could quell the howling completely, so some friend would escort her home with a quart of whiskey hugged to her breast to act as a night cap and put her to sleep. In the morning she would awaken with a hangover and start all over again. The only way to sober her up was to tell her someone was sick and needed her services. Not another drink would she take. Next day she would be ready for business.

In her autobiography, Calamity Jane said she married Clinton Burk in El Paso and went on to give birth to a girl "the very image of its father . . . but who has the temper of its mother." Nobody knows what became of the girl in later life, but Calamity went on to marry several other men. DuFran noted that "Jane had a very affectionate nature. There were very few preachers around to bother her, so whenever she got tired of one man she soon selected a new one." Calamity also alludes in her autobiography to an affair with famed gambler and gunfighter Wild Bill Hickok, and after her death a woman professed to be their illegitimate child raised by a wealthy East Coast family. Most folks put little stock in Calamity's relationship with Wild Bill, though the two did end up in Deadwood in 1876. A desperado shot Wild Bill in the back while he was seated at a gambling table; Calamity claimed to have helped capture the murderer.

Workin' and Boozin'

In later years, Calamity Jane seemed to spin her way across the west, stopping long enough to make money as a prospector, stagecoach driver, laundress, or some less seemly trade before getting the urge (or urging) to move on. Given the regimented

code of behavior under which women lived in her era, it's easy to see how her appearance caused such a stir. Newspapers trumpeted her arrival in town, and saloons attracted crowds as her exploits grew with each telling. Someone was always willing to buy a round of drinks for the chance to hear Calamity's tales. As a young woman she was certainly attractive, but the years of hard drinking and rough living were not especially kind. As author Ellen Mueller put it, however, "perhaps the men standing in a saloon dead broke and hankering for a drink would have found the woman beautiful who would get drinks 'on the house' for everybody."

Though she spent a brief period with Buffalo Bill's Wild West Show, Calamity Jane's biggest moment of glory came in an 1895 return to Deadwood after a 17-year absence. A masquerade ball was held in her honor, and the local newspaper noted that she was in great demand by the Dancers, many who were anxious to spend 25¢ to dance with her, just to have it to say they had danced with "Calamity Jane." She had a fair sized jag on board, and this, together with a vile cigar which she smoked, made her look anything but the beautiful woman which novelists and story writer have said so much about.

Calamity died in 1904, just 52 years old. Her deathbed plea was to be buried next to Wild Bill Hickock, who she said was the only man she had ever loved. Her funeral was one of the largest ever for Deadwood. Today, they lie next to each other at the Mt. Moriah Cemetery overlooking town. The testimony of fellow tough-living Dora DuFran again sums up her life best:

It is easy for a woman to be good who has been brought up with every protection from the evils of the world and with good associates. Calamity was a product of the wild and woolly west. She was not immoral; but unmoral. She took more on her shoulders than most women could. She performed many hundreds of deeds of kindness and received very little pay for her work. With her upbringing, how could she be anything but unmoral.

The Rock Shop, tel. (307) 332-7396, on State 28 one mile west of the turnoff to South Pass City, has a cafe, bar, gas station, and cabins, but no rocks for sale. The lodge is new, with eight modern cabins—running $55 for up to four people—and a full restaurant. Open year-round, this is a popular stopping point for snow-

mobilers on the Continental Divide Snowmobile Trail as well as cross-country skiers. **South Pass Cross-Country Ski Trails** take off from behind the Rock Shop, with a range of trails covering seven kilometers. The Wind River Nordic Ski Club maintains the trails, but they may not always be groomed.

ATLANTIC CITY

The funky, friendly little town of Atlantic City has dirt streets, old log and stone buildings, and a delightfully infectious country atmosphere. It's the sort of town where old-timers plunk themselves atop the Merc's barstools to talk cattle, football, and the old days; where many homes (and the church, too) still have outhouses; and where the big event is the volunteer fire department picnic (late August). Residents pile up huge stacks of firewood to make it through the long, cold winters. The snow can get deep here near the top of the Continental Divide (elevation 7,660 feet). One winter, the drifts topped 27 feet and the snowplows didn't get in for several weeks! Most residents like the quiet beauty that winter brings to Atlantic City and depend upon snowmobiles and skis to get around.

History

Atlantic City was formed in 1868 when gold mines had attracted thousands of miners to the Sweetwater Mining District. As miners arrived in South Pass, they spread out over the surrounding country in search of other gold deposits, founding the settlements of Atlantic City, Miner's Delight, and Lewiston at promising locations. As with most frontier towns, saloons vastly outnumbered churches in early Atlantic City. The first county sheriff owned a local brothel! **Fort Stambaugh** was established a few miles to the east in 1870 to protect miners from Sioux and Arapaho raids. It lasted only until 1878, and the buildings were auctioned off four years later.

In the 1880s, another miniboom hit as French capitalist Emile Granier built a 25-mile-long ditch from the Wind River Mountains to Atlantic City for hydraulic mining. The effort failed when the money ran out before gold could be found. Another boom hit in the late 1920s and '30s when a dredge worked its way down Rock Creek (leaving behind enormous piles of gravel). By the early 1960s, Atlantic City's population had been reduced to a handful of folks. Development of a U.S. Steel iron-ore (taconite) strip mine nearby brought prosperity after 1962, but the mine closed in 1983 and left behind a gaping pit now filled with water. Today Atlantic City depends upon tourism and summer homes.

But as a local brochure notes, "The wind of this old gold town always whispers of another boom on its way."

The Merc

Atlantic City's main attractions are its mining-era buildings, many dating from the turn of the century. The centerpiece is **Atlantic City Mercantile,** built in 1893 from adobe brick. Its false front is covered with old metal siding, and the interior is stuffed with stuffed heads, historic photos, mining artifacts, an old woodstove (usually in use), and a rich sense of the past. Pick up a brochure inside describing the town's many other historic buildings. The "Merc," tel. (307) 332-5143, rents A-frame cabins for $55 s or d during the summer and permits RV parking June-October. The bar often has live music on Friday nights, along with a piano where you can display your own musical talents at other times. The historic bar is more than 125 years old, and the mirror behind it suffers from a gunshot wound. The Merc's dinners are renowned throughout this part of Wyoming. In the front, you can munch on inexpensive but very good burgers. Back-room guests, on the other hand, are treated to an old-timey setting of oil lanterns and pine walls and a menu including aspen-grilled meats and seafood Thursday through Sunday, Mexican Mondays, Italian Tuesdays, and Wednesday-night seven-course Basque dinners. A bit on the pricey side—entrées around $25—but worth it. Reservations are advised for Friday and Saturday dinners.

More Buildings

The stone structure a block to the east of the Merc housed the **McAuley Store,** later Hyde's Hall. Calamity Jane once provided the entertainment in the saloon here. Up the hill is **St. Andrews Episcopal Church,** a rustic old log church built in 1913 and still used today. The **Gratrix Cabin,** a block east of the church, was built in the late 1860s and was home to Judge Buck Gratrix, a man who noted that he lived in three different counties, two territories, and one state while living in one place! One of the most attractive structures in Atlantic City is the mint-condition **Miner's Delight Inn.** Originally known as the Carpenter Hotel, the building was constructed in 1904 and run as a boardinghouse

for miners and others until 1961. It was a B&B for several years but is currently closed.

Nearby Sights

Rock Creek flows through Atlantic City, and on the west end of town the banks are lined with huge piles of boulders left behind by the gold-dredging operations of the '30s. Fort Stambaugh Road heads east from Atlantic City and follows a 12-mile loop past the site of Fort Stambaugh (not marked) and the ghost town of Miner's Delight. A side road leads to **Lewiston**, another abandoned gold-mining town. The loop road is a very scenic drive through open grassland and scattered patches of young aspen and lodgepole. (Miners wiped out previous stands.) Antelope are sure to be seen along the way. The settlement called **Miner's Delight** consists of a dozen log buildings in various states of decay. A small beaver pond and graveyard are also in Miner's Delight, with other old mining buildings visible just west of here.

The road west from Atlantic City to South Pass City passes more old gold mines, notably the **Duncan Mine** (two miles out) and the famous **Carissa Mine,** just before dropping down to South Pass City. Most of the mines and buildings are on private land, and many contain hazardous structures and shafts without covers. Watch your step!

A little over seven miles south of Atlantic City is a monument to the **Willie Handcart Company.** In 1856, a large group of Mormon emigrants led by James G. Willie was caught in a series of early winter storms and camped here awaiting help and provisions from Salt Lake City. Sixty-seven of them died before they could reach the promised land. This and the Mormon handcart monuments at Rocky Ridge and Rock Creek are described in a pamphlet available at South Pass State Historic Site.

Practicalities

Groceries are not available in either Atlantic City or South Pass, so stock up elsewhere. (See above for descriptions of Atlantic City Mercantile.) Also in town is **Sagebrush Saloon & Cafe,** which sometimes has live music. The big attraction here is the pool table.

The BLM maintains two attractive campgrounds ($4; open June-Oct.) in young aspen stands—very pretty in the fall—along the Fort Stambaugh Loop Road: **Atlantic City Campground** and **Big Atlantic Gulch Campground.** Big Atlantic Gulch doesn't have water.

Atlantic City is one of nine stops in the **Rocky Mountain Stage Stop Sled Dog Race,** an event that attracts some of the nation's best mushers. Unlike other races such as the Iditarod, this one is run in nine 30- to 80-mile stages, with teams ending in a new town each night. The race begins in Jackson and stops for the night in Moran, Dubois, Pinedale, Lander, Atlantic City, Kemmerer, Box Y Guest Ranch (Greys River area), and Afton before ending at Alpine. The race is held over 10 days in early February and has a $100,000 purse.

FARSON AREA

Farson (pop. 300) stands at the busy highway junction where State 28 and U.S. 191 greet each other. Locals live in trailer homes—the modern versions of log cabins—and work at a couple of local businesses. All around are long, straight roads, flat sagebrush desert, a few irrigated pastures, and antelope. It's a long way to anywhere else, so almost everyone stops here for a road break. In the simmering summer sun, **Farson Mercantile,** tel. (307) 273-9511, is crowded with people buying ice-cream cones to eat in the shade of the olive trees out front. Join the crowd; these are *huge* cones—"one scoop" is actually two or three scoops. The old brick two-story store is a classic country market. **Oregon Trail Cafe,** tel. (307) 273-9631, named for the historic trail, which passed right through the center of Farson, offers standard road grub, while at **Mitch's Cafe,** tel. (307) 273-9606, you're more likely to find locals atop the burlwood seats. **Sitzman's Motel,** tel. (307) 273-9246, charges $20-30 s, $30-40 d but is often full in midsummer and during the fall hunting season. Park RVs for free next to Farson Mercantile.

Heading South

Four miles south of Farson is tiny **Eden,** where irrigated green fields bring the arid landscape

alive. Of note here is the old **Oregon Trail Baptist Church,** with its brown log walls, quaint bell tower, and back window facing the Wind River Mountains. The view probably makes it hard to concentrate on the service. Kitty-corner across the road is the Eden Saloon, where the view may not be as great, but after a few beers it really doesn't matter. Bicentennial Park makes a shady place to enjoy a picnic. South of Eden, U.S. 191 cruises into the bleak Bad Lands Hills country on its way to Rock Springs. Killpecker Dunes rise on the eastern horizon.

Heading North
Immediately north of Farson, the highway crosses the Big Sandy River—little more than a creek much of the year, with Big Sandy Reservoir (free camping here) holding back much of its water for irrigation. Flat irrigated fields of hay surround Farson. As you continue north to Pinedale (58 miles), the jagged snow-topped crowns of the Wind River Mountains loom ever larger and the sagebrush grows more abundant on the arid landscape rolling away to the mountains. The highway crosses both the **Sublette Cutoff**—one of the original routes to Oregon Country—and the 1858 **Lander Cutoff,** the

first federal road west of the Mississippi. Tune in to KQSW (96.5 FM) for country tunes to speed you on your way.

A gravel road that begins two miles east of Farson and heads north along Little Sandy Creek and then northwest to Boulder is even more dramatic, passing along the foothills of the Winds. It's used for access to the Big Sandy Trailhead into the Bridger Wilderness. This is one of my favorite drives in Wyoming. Clouds often drape the distant mountains, but when they part—like curtains at a Broadway premier—they reveal the 13,000-foot crest of the Wind River Mountains in all its majesty. This is truly one of the classic western vistas, and the interplay of land, light, and sky creates an unforgettable scene.

The land knocks you out: mountains climb above the distant plain, crowning the eastern horizon with slanting patches of enormous rock faces and snow-mantled slopes, reflecting back the light from a westering sun. Antelope glance up as you drive past; a rough-legged hawk hunches down on a fence post; several horses paw the ground. Periodically a narrow set of pickup-truck tracks angles over the horizon to some remote ranch. In places like this, it is hard not to love the wildly beautiful state of Wyoming.

PINEDALE

Located in the upper Green River Valley, with the Wind River Mountains creating a dramatic backdrop, Pinedale (pop. 1,300) is surrounded by hay-filled meadows, grazing horses, and modern ranchettes. In addition to the economic mainstays of ranching and tourism, Pinedale is also a minor governmental center with BLM, Forest Service, Game and Fish, and Sublette County offices.

Pinedale is similar in many ways to its neighbor across the mountains, Dubois. Both towns were long dependent upon ranching and logging but are now starting to appreciate the visitors who come simply to enjoy the country. Pinedale has a solid core of downtown businesses, new log houses sprouting on the outskirts, and its first national chain operation (a Best Western motel). Residents fear that it could become "another Jackson," but the town has kept its Old West flavor without falling (yet) under the complete dom-

ination of the almighty tourist dollar. Wealthy people from all over the nation have bought up old ranches around Pinedale, turning them into summer homes; their small jets crowd the tarmac—if it can be called that—at the local airport. Most of these folks are corporate bigwigs, such as the head of PepsiCo, but others include John Barlow (former lyricist for the Grateful Dead) and James Baker III (former secretary of state).

History
The first inhabitants of the Upper Green River Valley were the Shoshone, Gros Ventre, Sheepeater, and Crow Indians who hunted buffalo, elk, and antelope in this rich country. Whites first came as explorers and fur trappers in the early 1800s, and by the 1830s this was the "capital" of the fur trade in the Rockies. Six different rendezvous were held along the Upper Green River. The first white settler arrived with his cattle in 1878, and

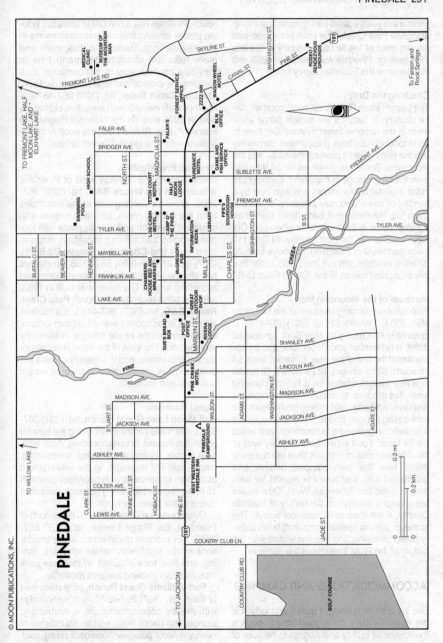

PINEDALE

© MOON PUBLICATIONS, INC.

TO FREMONT LAKE, HALF
MOON LAKE, AND
ELKHART LAKE

FREMONT LAKE RD.

MEDICAL
CLINIC

MUSEUM OF
THE MOUNTAIN
MAN

SKYLINE ST.

PINE ST.

WASHINGTON ST.

CANAL ST.

RODEO
RENDEZVOUS
GROUNDS

191

To Farson and
Rock Springs

FOREST SERVICE
OFFICE

WAGON WHEEL

ZZZZ INN

BLM
OFFICE

FALER AVE.

FALER'S

BRIDGER AVE.

MAGNOLIA ST.

GAME AND
FISH SERVICE
OFFICE

SUNDANCE
MOTEL

SUBLETTE AVE.

NORTH ST.

HIGH SCHOOL

TETON COURT
MOTEL

HALF
MOON
LODGE

FREMONT AVE.

FREMONT AVE.

B ST.

SWIMMING
POOL

TYLER AVE.

LOG CABIN
MOTEL

CAMP
THE PINES

FIFE'S
SOURDOUGH
HOUSE

LIBRARY

INFORMATION
KIOSK

TYLER AVE.

BUFFALO ST.

BEAVER ST.

HENNICK ST.

MAYBELL ST.

FRANKLIN AVE.

CHAMBERS
HOUSE BED AND
BREAKFAST

McGREGOR'S
PUB

MILL ST.

CHARLES ST.

WASHINGTON ST.

CREEK

LAKE AVE.

GREAT
OUTDOOR
SHOP

SUE'S BREAD
BOX

POST
OFFICE

MARILYN ST.

RIVERA
LODGE

PINE

SHANLEY AVE.

PINE CREEK
MOTEL

LINCOLN AVE.

MADISON AVE.

MADISON AVE.

STUART ST.

WILSON ST.

ADAMS ST.

WASHINGTON ST.

JACKSON ST.

AGATE ST.

JACKSON AVE.

JACKSON AVE.

TO WILLOW LAKE

ASHLEY AVE.

ASHLEY AVE.

CLARK ST.

COLTER AVE.

BONNEVILLE ST.

HOBACK ST.

PINE ST.

PINEDALE
CAMPGROUND

0.2 mi

0.2 km

LEWIS AVE.

BEST WESTERN
PINEDALE INN

COUNTRY CLUB LN.

191

TO JACKSON

JADE ST.

COUNTRY CLUB RD.

GOLF COURSE

0   0.2

0   0.2

within a few years a small trading center sprang up alongside Pine Creek. The town prospered with development of the tie-hack industry in the late 19th century. Pinedale was platted in 1899 and later became the Sublette County seat.

Catching the Drift
The Upper Green River is still very important cattle country; in fact, it's the largest range allotment in the national forest system. Get here in June to watch cowboys (locals more commonly use the term "riders") pushing the cattle into the mountains. Some are driven as far as 90 miles from the winter range in the desert. Cattle graze in the mountains all summer, watched over by a handful of riders who stay in cabins or trailers. Each fall, the cattle drift back down from their summer home in the mountains when cool October weather hits the high country. At Cora (10 miles northwest of Pinedale), cowboys from 20 different ranches sort out the 7,500 cattle that pile up against fences in the "Green River Drift."

Museum of the Mountain Man
Pinedale's outstanding Museum of the Mountain Man, 700 E. Hennick St., tel. (307) 367-4101, is open daily 10 a.m.-6 p.m. May-Sept., on special dates in November and December, and by appointment the rest of the year. Entrance costs $4 for adults, $3 for seniors, $2 for ages 5-12 (under age five free). Located on a hill overlooking town, this modern, spacious museum contains displays, artifacts, and memorabilia from the fur-trapping era. Jim Bridger's rifle is here, as are a covered wagon and a fascinating video about the fur trade. You'll learn about the daily lives of the different types of trappers (free vs. company men), how the men trapped beaver and processed furs, and how the market for hats helped open the American West. Downstairs are changing displays on the history of Sublette County. A gift shop sells historical books. The museum puts on special programs, living history demonstrations, and evening lectures on the history of the West throughout the summer

ACCOMMODATIONS AND CAMPING

See the chart for a listing of motels and lodges in the Pinedale area. It's a good idea to book a month ahead in July and August to be sure of

space. Pinedale has a number of attractive lodging places offering friendly and clean rooms in pleasant settings. Because of this, more and more folks are choosing to spend time in Pinedale on their way to Yellowstone, thus avoiding the crowds and high rates in Jackson. The **Log Cabin Motel,** tel. (307) 367-3579, is appropriately named, with attractive old cabins built in 1929 now on the National Register of Historic Places. **Rivera Lodge** is another friendly place with a range of different cabins.

Bed and Breakfasts
Located along the highway west of Pinedale, **Window on the Winds B&B,** tel. (307) 367-2600, offers a sweeping view of the mountains from the central room, plus a sunroom with jacuzzi. It's a warm and friendly place with four guest rooms and a filling breakfast. Right in town you'll find **Chambers House B&B,** tel. (307) 367-2168 or (800) 567-2168, an elegant two-story log home with four guest rooms and two sitting rooms. The home was built in 1933, and has been recently renovated. **Pole Creek Ranch B&B,** tel. (307) 367-4433, is a modern log home in the country with an outdoor jacuzzi, a barn, and corrals. Horse riding is available by arrangement. The view of the Wind River Mountains is impressive, and the friendly owners are quite religious. Horseback and covered wagon rides are also available.

Guest Ranches
Half Moon Lake Guest Ranch, tel. (307) 367-6373, has rustic cabins overlooking the lake for which it is named, horseback riding, pack trips, boat rentals, fishing, water skiing, windsurfing, meals, and RV hookups. In the wintertime it also offers cross-country ski packages over with 15 miles of groomed trails. The ranch restaurant opens to the public for lunch.

Overlooking the Green River 30 miles north of Pinedale, **Elk Ridge Lodge,** tel. (307) 367-2553, has modern guest-ranch accommodations by the night, with horseback rides, fishing, and float trips included. Wilderness pack trips and spot packing are also available.

Fort Williams Guest Ranch, eight miles east of town, tel. (307) 367-4670, is a rustic lodge with nightly accommodations, a restaurant, lounge, and dance floor, and an abundance of nearby outdoor activities: horseback riding, guid-

PINEDALE ACCOMMODATIONS

Note: Accommodations are listed from least to most expensive. Add a four percent tax to these rates. Area code is 307.

Teton Court Motel; 123 E. Magnolia; tel. 367-4317; $30 s, $35 d; nice place, kitchenettes $45 s or d, open May-Oct.

Pole Creek Ranch B&B; 244 Pole Creek Rd.; tel. 367-4433; $35 s, $50 d; rustic log home, mountain vistas, jacuzzi, three guest rooms, shared bath, Christian owners

Half Moon Lodge Motel; 46 N. Sublette; tel. 367-2851; $38-44 s, $46-56 d

Camp O' The Pines; 38 N. Fremont; tel. 367-4536; $40 s, $45 d; kitchenettes $5 extra, open May-Oct.

Wagon Wheel Motel; 407 S. US 191; tel. 367-2871; $40-60 s, $50-70 d; nice rooms, AAA approved

Pine Creek Inn; 650 W. Pine; tel. 367-2191 or (800) 213-3322; $42 s, $48 d

Sun Dance Motel; 148 E. Pine; tel. 367-4336; $44 s, $49 d; AAA approved

Lakeside Lodge Resort & Marina; four miles northeast on Fremont Lake; tel. 367-2221; $45 s, $50 d in rustic cabins with separate bathhouse; $50 s, $55 d in motel rooms; open May-Sept.

ZZZZ Inn; 327 S. US 191; tel. 367-2121; $45 s, $55 d; open May-Oct.

Rivera Lodge; 442 W. Marilyn; tel. 367-2424; $45-80 s or d; kitchenettes, variety of cabins, open May to mid-October

Log Cabin Motel; 49 E. Magnolia; tel. 367-4579; $48-80 s or d; historic log cabins, kitchenettes

Chambers House B&B; 111 W. Magnolia St.; tel. 367-2168 or (800) 567-2168; $50-90 s, $60-100 d; historic log home, four guest rooms, private or shared baths, full breakfast, children welcome

Green River Guest Ranch; 25 miles northwest of Pinedale; tel. 367-2314; $55 s or d; rustic log cabins, restaurant and bar, horseback rides and float trips available, closed April and November

Pinedale Inn (Best Western); 850 W. Pine St., tel. 367-6869 or (800) 528-1234; $55-75 s, $65-85 d; new motel, indoor pool, jacuzzi, fitness center, continental breakfast, AAA approved

Window on the Winds B&B; one mile west on US 191; tel. 367-2600; $58 s, $68 d; full breakfast, four guest rooms, shared bath, very nice, children and pets welcome, AAA approved

Fort Williams Guest Ranch; eight miles east; tel. 367-4670; $65 s or d; open May-Oct., horseback riding, fishing, and pack trips available

Elk Ridge Lodge; 30 miles north; tel. 367-2553; $70 d for lodging; $120 per person includes meals, horseback rides, fishing, and float trips

ed pack trips, spot packing, and fly-fishing. Open May-October.

Green River Guest Ranch, 25 miles northwest of Pinedale, tel. (307) 367-2314, has horseback rides, evening cookout rides, pack trips, spot pack trips, guided fishing and float trips, wintertime snowmobile rentals, and tours. Guest stay by the night in comfortably rustic cabins with baths. Also here is a restaurant and bar.

Flying A Ranch, tel. (307) 859-8228, is a historic 1920s ranch with luxuriously restored log cabins with kitchenettes, woodstoves, and an outdoor jacuzzi. Guests get three big meals,

horseback riding, mountain biking, trout fishing, and hiking for entertainment. Open mid-June through September; adults only. The secluded and historic **DC Bar Guest Ranch,** tel. (307) 367-2268, offers fishing and pack trips.

Camping

The closest public camping is at **Fremont Lake Campground** ($6; open late May to mid-September; call 800-280-2667 for reservations), seven miles northeast of Pinedale along the lake. Even if you aren't staying here or planning any wilderness hikes from the trailheads, *do*

MOUNTAIN MEN

The era of the fur trapper is one of the most colorful slices of American history, a time when a rough and hardy breed of men took to the Rockies in search of furs and adventure. Romanticized in such films as *Jeremiah Johnson,* the trappers actually played but a brief role in history and numbered fewer than 1,000 individuals. Their real importance lay in acting as the opening wedge for the West, a vanguard for the settlers and gold miners who would follow their paths—often led by these same mountain men.

The Fur Business

Fashion sent men into the Rockies in the first place, since the waterproof underfur of a beaver could be used to create the beaver hat, all the rage in the early part of the 19th century. Beavers in the eastern U.S. were soon trapped out, forcing trappers to head farther and farther west. Several companies competed for the lucrative fur market, but John Jacob Astor's American Fur Company proved the most successful. In 1811, Astor sent a party of men across the Rockies to the mouth of the Columbia to build a trading post and then set up a chain of posts across the West. The men—known as the Astorians—were probably the first whites to follow the route that would later become the Oregon Trail.

John Jacob Astor's trappers went head to head against the Rocky Mountain Fur Company, which was owned at various times by some of the most famous mountain men—Jedediah Smith, David Jackson, William and Milton Sublette, Jim Bridger, Thomas Fitzpatrick, and others. Competition for furs became so intense that Astor's men began following Jim Bridger and Tom Fitzpatrick to discover their trapping grounds. After trying unsuccessfully to shake the men tailing them, Bridger and Fitzpatrick deliberately headed into the heart of Blackfeet country, where Indians killed the leader of Astor's party and managed to leave Bridger with an arrowhead in his shoulder that was not removed until three years later.

A large number of Indians (particularly from the Flathead and Nez Percé tribes) were also involved in the fur trade, and a standard Indian trade value was 240 beaver pelts for a riding horse. In the mountains, anything from the world back east had considerable value. Guns sold for $100 each, blankets for $40 apiece, tobacco for $3 a pound, and alcohol (often diluted) for up to $64 a gallon. After just two years of such trading, William Ashley retired with an $80,000 profit. Control of the fur market continued to change hands as the Rocky Mountain Fur Company and the American Fur Company competed with each other and with a mysterious company headed by Capt. Benjamin Bonneville, which some believe was a front for the U.S. Army to explore the West.

Most of the men who trapped in the Rockies were hired and outfitted by the fur companies, but others worked under contract and traded furs for over-priced supplies. Many men found themselves in debt to the company at the end of a season. At the top of the heap were the free trappers, men who worked either alone or with others but who sold their furs to whomever offered the highest prices. Some men—primarily those who brought trade goods to the rendezvous—became rich in the process. Others, such as John Colter, Jim Bridger, James Beckwourth, Jedediah Smith, Thomas Fitzpatrick, and Kit Carson, would achieve fame for their rich knowledge of the land and their ability to survive insurmountable odds. Many trappers married Indian women, learned sign language and various Indian tongues, and lived in tepees.

Trappers worked through the fall and spring when the pelts were their finest; most winters were spent in the lower valleys with fellow trappers or friendly Indians. In his *Journal of a Trapper 1834-1843,* Osborne Russell described a campfire scene among fellow mountain men:

A large fire was soon blazing encircled with sides of Elk ribs and meat cut in slices supported on sticks down which the grease ran in torrents The repast being over the jovial tale goes round the circle the peals of loud laughter break upon the stillness of the night which after being mimicked in the echo from rock to rock it dies away in the solitary. Every tale puts an auditor in mind of something similar to it but under different circumstances which being told the "laughing part" gives rise to increasing merriment and furnishes more subjects for good jokes and witty sayings such as Swift never dreamed of Thus this evening passed with eating drinking and stories enlivened with witty humor until near Midnight all being wrapped in their blankets lying around the fire gradually falling to sleep one by one until the last tale is "encored" by the snoring of the drowsy audience The Speaker takes the hint breaks off the subject and wrapping his blanket more closely about

him soon joins the snoring party—The light of the fire being supersed by that of the Moon just rising from behind the Eastern Mountains a sullen gloom is cast over the remaining fragments of the feast and all is silent except the occasional howling of the solitary wolf on the neighboring mountain whose senses are attracted by the flavors of roasted meat but fearing to approach nearer he sits upon a rock and bewails his calamities in piteous moans which are re-echoed among the Mountains.

A good trapper could take in upwards of 150 beaver in a year, worth $4-6 apiece. It was an arduous job, and the constant threat of attacks by the Blackfeet Indians made it even more difficult. The great letting-go came with the summer rendezvous, an event anticipated for months ahead of time.

The Rendezvous

William H. Ashley, founder of the Rocky Mountain Fur Company, was one of the most important figures in the fur trade. In 1822, he ran an ad in a St. Louis paper that read:

To Enterprising Young Men. The subscriber wishes to engage ONE HUNDRED MEN, to ascend the river Missouri to its source, there to be employed for one, two or three years.—For particulars enquire of Major Andrew Henry, near the Lead Mines, in the County of Washington, (who will ascend with, and command the party) or to the subscriber at St. Louis.
—Wm. H. Ashley.

Ashley's company of men—along with $10,000 in supplies—made it up into the Yellowstone River country, where he left them the following year, promising to resupply them in 1825 on the Henrys Fork near its confluence with the Green River, along the present-day Wyoming-Utah border. Thus began the first rendezvous. They would take place every summer until 1840. Ashley failed to bring booze that first summer and the rendezvous only lasted two days. In future years, however, the whiskey flowed freely and the festivities lasted for weeks.

The rendezvous—a French word meaning "appointed place of meeting"—was a time when both white and Indian trappers could sell their furs, trade for needed supplies and Indian squaws (the women had little say in the matter but most took consider-

able pleasure in the arrangement), meet with old friends, get rip-roaring drunk, and engage in storytelling, gambling, gun duels, and contests of all sorts. Horse racing, wrestling bouts, and shooting contests were favorites—Kit Carson killed Shunar, a big French bully, in a duel during one of the Green River rendezvous. Debauchery reigned supreme in these three-week-long affairs, and by the time they were over, many of the trappers had lost their entire year's earnings.

During the heyday of the fur trade, a common saying was "all trails lead to the Seedskeedee [Green River]." Six rendezvous were held here in the 1830s, others were held in the Wind River/Popo Agie River area, on Ham's Fork of the Green River, and in Idaho and Utah. Sites were chosen where there was space for up to 500 mountain men and 3,000 Indians, plenty of game, ample grazing for the thousands of horses, and good water. Not coincidentally, all were held in Shoshone country rather than farther east or north, where the hostile Sioux, Blackfoot, and Crow held sway. Despite such precautions, over half of Ashley's men were scalped by Indians.

Changing Times

The end of the rendezvous system—and most of the Rocky Mountain fur trapping—came about for a variety of reasons: overtrapping, the financial panic of 1837, and the growing use of other materials—particularly the South American nutria and Chinese silk—for hats. In addition, permanent trading posts such as Fort Laramie drew Indians away from the mountains to trade for buffalo robes instead of beaver furs. By 1840, when the last rendezvous was held on the banks of the Green River near present-day Pinedale, it was obvious there would be no more. One of the longtime trappers, Robert Newell, said to his partner, Joseph Meek:

We are done with this life in the mountains—done with wading in beaver dams, and freezing or starving alternately—done with Indian trading and Indian fighting. The fur trade is dead in the Rocky Mountains, and it is no place for us now, if ever it was. We are young yet, and have life before us. We cannot waste it here; we cannot or will not return to the States. Let us go down to the Wallamet and take farms.

take the 15-mile (paved) drive from Pinedale to road's end, where you'll find the free Upper Fremont Lake Campground. The rugged crest of the Wind River Mountains forms a dramatic vista

along the way. **Half Moon Lake Campground** ($3; open June to mid-September) is on the northwest shore of Half Moon Lake, 10 miles northeast of Pinedale. A dozen other Forest Ser-

the Summer
Rendezvous

THE SUMMER RENDEZVOUS.

YELLOWSTONE NATIONAL PARK

vice and BLM campgrounds are dotted all along the western side of the Wind River Mountains.

Pinedale Campground, 204 S. Jackson Ave, tel. (307) 367-4555, charges $10 for tents, $16 for RVs; open mid-April through October. Showers for noncampers are $3. This is ye olde parking lot masquerading as a "campground." **Lakeside Lodge Resort & Marina** at Fremont Lake, four miles northeast of town, tel. (307) 367-2221, charges $8 for tents and $16 for RVs. Open May-September.

FOOD

Reflecting its proximity to Jackson, Pinedale's food prices are higher than in most parts of the state—but so is the quality. Travelers will find a good mix of fare, from traditional steak houses to more yuppified eateries.

Breakfast and Lunch
Start your day at **Fife's Sourdough House** on Fremont Ave., tel. (307) 367-2698, where the menu includes sourdough waffles and pancakes, tasty homefries, and SBC coffee. Breakfast is served till 2 p.m.; after that, try their sandwiches and sourdough-crust pizzas. Another popular breakfast spot is **Patio Grill,** 35 W. Pine, tel. (307) 367-4611, in existence for more than three decades with consistently good family breakfasts. The **Wrangler Cafe,** 310 E. Pine St., tel. (307) 367-4233, is famous for a dessert menu that in-

cludes 21 different types of pie. **Sue's Bread Box,** 423 W. Pine (behind the post office), tel. (307) 367-2150, serves earthy breakfasts and deli lunches with homemade soups and sourdough bread. Be sure to get one of the monstrous cinnamon rolls. **Home of the Range Espresso,** next to Faler's at 219 E. Pine, tel. (307) 367-4165, has a drive-up coffee shack. For a filling lunchtime pizza buffet, head to **Wind River Rendezvous Pizza,** 4 Country Club Lane, tel. (307) 367-6760.

Dinner
A favorite of both locals and visitors, **McGregor's Pub,** 25 N. Franklin Ave., tel. (307) 367-4443, specializes in prime rib, steak, and seafood but also has good lunches served on an outside deck in the summer. **Patio Grill,** 35 W. Pine St., tel. (307) 367-4611, has a local reputation for consistently good meals and a spotlessly clean facility. Located next to the Cowboy Bar, **Della Rose Restaurant,** 120 W. Pine, tel. (307) 367-2810, has family meals, fresh-baked pastries, and gourmet coffees.

Stockman's Steak Pub, 117 W. Pine, tel. (307) 367-4563, has the finest steaks in Pinedale, a good salad bar, veal, seafood, and chicken. Eight miles east of town on Fall Creek Road is **Fort Williams Guest Ranch,** tel. (307) 367-4670, which has thick steaks, beans, and other hearty fare served Thurs.-Mon. May-October. A great place for a meal with a view is **Lakeside Lodge Resort and Marina;** four miles northeast of Pinedale on Fremont Lake; tel.

(307) 367-2221. Fine food and stunning vistas of the Wind River Mountains.

Calamity Jane's, in the Corral Bar at 30 W. Pine, tel. (307) 367-2469, is the place to go for delicious burgers and fries, grinders, Mexican food, and pizzas. But it's a bar, so the atmosphere might not be for everyone. Open summers only, **King Cone Drive In,** 513 S. U.S. 191, tel. (307) 367-6404, is famous (infamous?) as "Home of the Road Kill Burger." Best sundaes in town. **Sweet Tooth Saloon,** 128 W. Pine St., tel. (307) 367-4724, is an old-fashioned ice-cream parlor.

Groceries

Get groceries at **Faler's Thriftway,** 341 E. Pine, tel. (307) 367-2131. Inside is a deli, plus one of the largest collections of critter heads anywhere. The city park is a pleasant place for picnic lunches.

ENTERTAINMENT AND EVENTS

Entertainment

Both **Cowboy Bar,** 104 W. Pine, tel. (307) 367-4520, and **Stockman's Bar,** 16 N. Maybell Ave., tel. (307) 367-4562, have live country-western tunes most weekends. The latter attracts a younger crowd. **Fort Williams Guest Ranch,** eight miles east of Pinedale, tel. (307) 367-4670, is a popular place to unwind in a cozy atmosphere; open May-Oct. only. **The Place Restaurant & Bar,** tel. (307) 367-2314, in Cora (10 miles northwest of Pinedale) has a pool table surrounded by mounted animal heads.

Events

Pinedale is one of nine stops in early February's **Rocky Mountain Stage Stop Sled Dog Race,** an event that attracts some of the nation's best mushers with a $100,000 purse. The race begins in Jackson and ends at Alpine.

The main event in Pinedale is **Green River Rendezvous Rendezvous Days,** held the second Sunday in July. Established in 1936, this is one of the oldest celebrations of the mountain-man rendezvous era and commemorates the raucous activities of the 1830s on nearby Horse Creek. The highlight is the rendezvous pageant, which attracts more than 2,000 visitors, and

there are all sorts of other activities including fur and bead trading, living-history demonstrations, a parade, live music, a crafts fair, art shows, a traditional buffalo barbecue featuring foods similar to those eaten at the original rendezvous, shoot-out skits, and rodeos.

All summer long visitors can watch roping events on Tuesday nights at the fairgrounds. In early August comes the annual **Fremont Lake Sailing Regatta.** The **Sublette County Championship Rodeo** in early September is the last big event of the year.

RECREATION

Summer Recreation

Golfers will enjoy Pinedale's 18-hole **Rendezvous Meadows Golf Course.** Stop by the Pinedale Ranger District office at 29 E. Fremont Lake Rd., tel. (307) 367-4326, for maps ($3) and hiking info on trails in the nearby Bridger Wilderness or a listing of fishing guides and permitted wilderness outfitters. **Horseback rides** are available from Fort Williams Guest Ranch, tel. (307) 367-4670; Elk Ridge Ranch, tel. (307) 367-2553; DC Bar Guest Ranch, tel. (307) 367-2268; Boulder Lake Lodge, tel. (307) 367-2961 or (800) 788-5401; **Wyoming Rivers & Trails,** tel. (307) 537-5666; and Pole Creek Ranch B&B, tel. (307) 367-4433. The **Great Outdoor Shop,** 332 W. Pine, tel. (307) 367-2440, sells quality outdoor gear of all sorts and topo maps.

On the Water

The east slope of the Wind River Mountains contains several large lakes created when glaciers retreated after the last major ice age some 10,000 years ago. The terminal moraines they left behind acted as dams, although some have been enlarged with human-created dams in recent years. The lakes are very popular with anglers. **Fremont Lake** is Wyoming's second-largest natural lake, reaching 12 miles in length, a half-mile across, and up to 600 feet deep. It's just three miles northeast of Pinedale and is famous for Mackinaw that approach 40 pounds. Fremont has three Forest Service campgrounds along its shore (free to $6; one accessible only by boat). Rent fishing boats, canoes, or a pon-

toon boat from **Lakeside Lodge Resort & Marina,** tel. (307) 367-2221, open May through early September. It also has a restaurant and accommodations here.

Other lakes of note are **Half Moon Lake, Willow Lake,** and **Boulder Lake.** (See "Green River Lakes Trails" under "Wind River Mountains" earlier in this chapter for info on the Green River and New Fork Lakes.) All of these lakes have Forest Service campgrounds—$3 for Half Moon, free for Willow, New Fork, and Boulder Lake campgrounds—and trails that lead into the Bridger Wilderness.

The lakes and streams near Pinedale offer outstanding fishing for cutthroat, rainbow, brook, Mackinaw, golden, and brown trout, plus grayling and whitefish. A number of local outfitters offer float-fishing trips down the Green River; see the chamber of commerce for a listing. Canoeists or kayakers will also enjoy floating stretches of the Green. The Forest Service office has details. Swim at Pinedale's Olympic-sized **indoor pool,** tel. (307) 367-2832, at the high school on the corner of Hennick St. and Tyler Avenue.

Winter Recreation

Cross-country skiers should pick up a copy of the **Skyline Drive Nordic Touring Trails** map from the Forest Service or chamber of commerce office in Pinedale. The 60 km of trails are marked but not always groomed. More adventurous skiers will find all sorts of places to explore in the Bridger Wilderness just a few miles east of Pinedale. Rent cross-country skis from the **Great Outdoor Shop,** 332 W. Pine, tel. (307) 367-2440. The

White Pine Ski Area was scheduled to open in 1997 but may or may not have the finances to do so. Call (307) 367-6606 for the latest.

The lower elevations of the Wind River Mountains are also extremely popular with snowmobilers; trails head out right from town. See the chamber of commerce for a list of local snowmobile outfitters. The 360-mile **Continental Divide Snowmobile Trail** passes right by Pinedale, continuing north to Yellowstone and around the Wind River Mountains to Lander.

INFORMATION AND SERVICES

An **information kiosk** on Pine St. near Fremont Ave. is open daily 9 a.m.-5 p.m. April-October. The Forest Service's new **Pinedale Ranger District Office** is located at 29 E. Fremont Lake Rd., tel. (307) 367-4326, and is open Mon.-Fri. 8 a.m.-4:30 p.m., and Saturday 9 a.m.- 4 p.m. in the summer months. Find the **BLM Office** at 431 W. Pine St., tel. (307) 367-4358. **Moosley Books,** 7 W. Pine St., tel. (307) 367-6622, sells books; the town **library** at 40 S. Fremont Ave., tel. (307) 367-4114, loans them. Wash clothes at **Highlander Center Laundromat** on Pine St., and get cash from the **ATM** at 1st National Bank of Pinedale.

Sublette Stage, tel. (307) 537-5403, the local taxi company, provides taxi service to trailheads, car shuttles, and vans to Jackson and Rock Springs. Drivers en route to Jackson should fill up in Pinedale; gas prices only get higher from here north.

PINEDALE VICINITY

Boulder

A dozen miles south of Pinedale is Boulder (pop. 70), consisting of the turn-of-the-century **Boulder Store,** adjacent **Basecamp Restaurant,** and newly built **Boulder Inn Motel,** tel. (307) 537-5480, where rooms go for $55-70 s, $65-70 d. A mile north of Boulder is **Wind River View Campground,** tel. (307) 537-5453, with tent sites for $15, RV hookups for $17; open mid-May to mid-September. There's no shade on this exposed site, but the mountain views are noteworthy.

Located 12 miles up State 353, **Boulder Lake Lodge,** tel. (307) 367-2961 or (800) 788-

5401, is a small place with modern guest rooms for $50 s or d. It serves family-style meals (extra charge) and offers horseback rides by the hour or day, pack trips, and drop trips. Open Memorial Day through October. Halfway between Pinedale and Boulder are two roadside telephone poles topped by active osprey nests.

Daniel

Head 11 miles west of Pinedale and then another mile south on U.S. 189 to tiny Daniel, where the country bar makes some of the best

Bloody Marys in Wyoming. A roadside marker north of Daniel notes the site of **Fort Bonneville,** built in 1832 to serve as a fur-trade center run by Captain Benjamin Bonneville. It lasted only a year but gained the nickname "Fort Nonsense" because of the severely cold and snowy winters that made life difficult for Bonneville's men. The fort consisted of two blockhouses guarding a perimeter of tall log posts.

Two miles south and then 2.5 miles east of Daniel on a dirt road is a monument to **Father Pierre Jean DeSmet,** who performed mass during the 1840 rendezvous at this site. A small shrine marks the site and is used during a commemorative mass each July. Pinckney Sublette, one of four brothers from the famous family of trappers, is also buried nearby. The access road cuts through barren sage and grass country, but the vista changes abruptly as you reach the tiny chapel. Below you the Green River twists its way through a lush landscape of grass, cattle, and cottonwoods. It's pretty easy to see why the rendezvous was held in this area! Get here for a summer sunrise, when it is easy to imagine the multitude of Indians and mountain men spread out below for the annual festivities. A short distance beyond the monument are the red log barn and white log home of the historic Quarter Circle 5 Ranch a definitive Wyoming spread.

The **David Ranch,** tel. (307) 859-8228, offers a chance to sample the cowboy life. Guests stay in comfortable log cabins and enjoy ranch-style meals in the main house. Days are spent on horseback rides, herding cattle, participating in cattle drives, or taking backcountry pack trips. The guest ranch is open mid-May to mid-September.

Big Piney

An oil boomtown in the late 1970s, Big Piney (pop. 500) has faced hard times more recently. The town is not entirely as it may first appear, however. Along Main Street many of the buildings are either run-down or boarded up, but attractive homes line the suburban neighborhoods, and a modern brick high school lies at the town's west end. Stay at **Big Piney Motel,** tel. (307) 276-3352, for $33-42 s or d. The historic **Frontier Hotel,** tel. (307) 276-3329, charges just $20 s, $22 d, but take a look at the rooms first. No TV or phones. **Lain's Sports Center & Motel,** tel.

(307) 276-3303, has dirt-cheap rates of $18 s, $25 d, for dumpy old trailers. **Sage Cafe,** tel. (307) 276-3068, serves good all-American fare and has a nice salad bar. **Ye Olde Pizza Parlor,** tel. (307) 276-3546, makes fine pizzas. **Erickson's Cafe** is the local greasy spoon, where you'll meet most everyone in town sometime during the day.

The main annual event is the **Big Piney Chuck Wagon Days** on the Fourth of July. Festivities include a rodeo, a parade, fireworks, and a free barbecue. Big Piney is also home to the **Sublette County Fair** held in early August each year. One of the attractions here is the Little Buckaroo Rodeo for children, complete with those ever-wild Shetland ponies. Other rodeos take place throughout the summer at the fairgrounds.

The town has a library and a Forest Service **district office,** tel. (307) 276-3375, where you can find out about the route west into the Wyoming Range. A fine-arts center and public swimming pool can both be found in the high school on the west side of town.

Marbleton

Marbleton (pop. 700), just a couple hundred yards up U.S. 189 from Big Piney, consists of a few old log buildings. **Marbleton Inn,** tel. (307) 276-5231, offers excellent dinners and the finest lodging accommodations in the area ($37 s, or $43 d). **Country Chalet Inn,** tel. (307) 276-3391, has pleasant rooms for $34 s, $40 d. Backpackers and campers will be happy to know that the **Laundry Basket Laundromat** in Marbleton has hot showers for $1. The **Waterhole,** tel. (307) 276-9977, is the center of nightlife in the area and puts on a popular cowboy open golf tournament.

Heading North

North of Marbleton, the enormous Wind River Mountains become more visible and the highway crosses the **Lander Cutoff,** its ruts now barely visible across the sagebrush. Built in 1858 by Col. Frederick W. Lander and his soldiers, it served two purposes: it was a shorter route to California and Oregon and a way to bypass the Mormon communities in Utah. The route offered good grazing and water as well as abundant game, and it quickly became the preferred route to California and Oregon.

TO JACKSON HOLE

U.S. 189/191 provides a scenic route to Hoback Junction and Jackson Hole, crossing the Green River and then slowly climbing into the hills. Aspens begin to appear on the hilltops, and willows line the creeks. The 11,000-foot-tall Gros Ventre Mountains are visible to the northwest. Gradually, lodgepole pine and aspen begin to replace the sagebrush. At **the Rim,** the road enters Bridger-Teton National Forest. West of here, the land drains into the Hoback River, which joins the Snake River at Hoback Junction 40 miles away. The road curves gradually down through this mountainous country, crossing the Hoback River again and again.

Bondurant

The spread-out town of Bondurant (pop. 100) straggles along the road through a gorgeous mountain valley, its pastures dotted with enormous piles of hay, creekside willows, and grazing horses. The Gros Ventre Mountains form a dramatic backdrop, but the developments consist of just a few scattered log homes. Bondurant is named for Sarah Ellen and Benjamin Franklin Bondurant, the first settlers here. Between 1907 and 1927 they ran a popular dude ranch and had as pets all sorts of wild animals: antelope, elk, even young bears. **Smiling S Motel,** tel. (307) 733-3457, charges $35-50 s or d; campground rates are $10 for tents, $18 for RVs. Showers for noncampers cost $3. Open late May through September; no TVs or phones. On the west end of "town," **Elkhorn Bar and**

Trading Post, tel. (307) 733-8358, has a general store and country watering hole.

Hoback Canyon

A few miles west of Bondurant, the road clings to the walls of Hoback Canyon as it passes the high face of Battle Mountain, site of one of the few conflicts between Indians and whites in this part of Wyoming. It was here in 1895 that whites from Jackson Hole attacked Bannock Indians who had been hunting "out of season" along the Hoback River. Just before you reach Hoback Junction, a sign describes John Hoback, the trapper and guide who led the Astorian trappers of Wilson Price Hunt through here in 1811.

Granite Hot Springs

Just west of Battle Mountain on U.S. 189/191 is the turnoff to Granite Hot Springs. *Do* take this very scenic side trip! A washboarded gravel road follows Granite Creek for 10 miles, affording impressive views of the Gros Ventre Range and a 50-foot waterfall. The road ends at a parking lot just a short walk from the hot springs. The pool (93-112° F) was built in 1933 by the CCC and is open 10 a.m.-8 p.m. during the summer, 10 a.m.-5 p.m. in winter (closed fall and spring). The cost is $5.50 for adults, $3.50 for kids. Suits and towels can also be rented. Granite Canyon Road is not plowed in winter but is groomed for use by both snowmobilers and cross-country skiers. A nearby campground ($8) is open late June through early September, or you can camp along the road to the hot springs. Call (800) 280-2267 for campground reservations ($8.25 extra fee).

BOB RACE

JACKSON HOLE AND THE TETONS

Jackson Hole is one of the most-visited slices of wild country in North America. Each year more than two million travelers pass through, stop to enjoy the energetic town of Jackson or camp under the stars in Grand Teton National Park, to hike flower-bedecked trails into the mountains or ride sleighs among thousands of elk, to raft down the Snake River or ski at one of the local resorts, or simply stand in wonderment at the view from Snake River overlook. Many continue on north to Yellowstone National Park, another place on everyone's must-see list. Drive north from Jackson toward Yellowstone and you'll quickly discover why so many people are attracted to this place. The Tetons act as a magnet, drawing your eyes away from the road and forcing you to stop and absorb some of their majesty. Welcome to one of the world's great wonderlands.

In the lingo of the mountain men, a "hole" was a large valley ringed by mountain ranges. Jackson Hole, on Wyoming's far western border, is justifiably the most famous of all these intermountain valleys. Although Jackson Hole reach-

JACKSON HOLE IN 1835

This Valley is called "Jackson Hole" it is generally from 5 to 15 mls wide: the southern part where the river enters the mountain is hilly and uneven but the Northern portion is wide smooth and comparatively even the whole being covered with wild sage and Surrounded by high and rugged mountains upon whose summits the snow remains during the hottest months in Summer. The alluvial bottoms along the river and streams inter sect it thro. the valley produce a luxuriant groth of vegetation among which wild flax and a species of onion are abundant. The great altitude of this place however connected with the cold descending from the mountains at night I think would be a serious obstruction to growth of most Kinds of cultivated grains. This valley like all other parts of the country abounds with game.

—From *Journal of a Trapper 1834-1843*, by Osborne Russell.

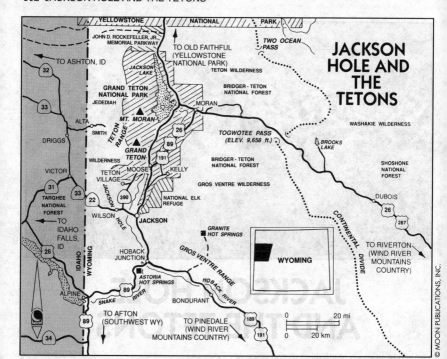

JACKSON
HOLE AND
THE
TETONS

TO ASHTON, ID

YELLOWSTONE   NATIONAL   PARK

JOHN D. ROCKEFELLER, JR.
MEMORIAL PARKWAY

TWO OCEAN
PASS

TO OLD FAITHFUL
(YELLOWSTONE
NATIONAL PARK)

JACKSON
LAKE

GRAND TETON
NATIONAL PARK

TETON WILDERNESS

BRIDGER - TETON
NATIONAL FOREST

JEDEDIAH

MORAN

WASHAKIE WILDERNESS

MT. MORAN

TOGWOTEE PASS
(ELEV. 9,658 ft.)

BROOKS
LAKE

SMITH

GRAND
TETON

SHOSHONE
NATIONAL
FOREST

WILDERNESS

BRIDGER - TETON
NATIONAL FOREST

MOOSE

KELLY

TETON
VILLAGE

GROS VENTRE WILDERNESS

DUBOIS

NATIONAL ELK
REFUGE

WILSON

JACKSON

GRANITE
HOT SPRINGS

WYOMING

TO RIVERTON
(WIND RIVER
MOUNTAINS
COUNTRY)

HOBACK
JUNCTION

GROS VENTRE RANGE

ASTORIA
HOT SPRINGS

HOBACK RIVER

SNAKE RIVER

BONDURANT

TO AFTON
(SOUTHWEST WY)

TO PINEDALE
(WIND RIVER
MOUNTAINS COUNTRY)

0   20 mi
0   20 km

CONTINENTAL DIVIDE

© MOON PUBLICATIONS, INC.

TO IDAHO
FALLS, ID

TARGHEE
NATIONAL
FOREST

IDAHO
WYOMING

DRIGGS

VICTOR

ALTA

TETON RANGE

ALPINE

32

33

31

33   22

390

26

89

191

26

89

189

191

34

26

287

es an impressive 40 miles north to south and up to 10 miles across, the magnificent range of mountains to the west is what defines this valley. Shoshone Indians who wandered through this country called the peaks Teewinot ("Many Pinnacles"); later explorers would use such labels as Shark's Teeth or Pilot Knobs, but the name that stuck came from lonely French-Canadian trappers who arrived in the early 1800s: les Trois Tetons, (literally, "Three Tits").

Contrary to what you may have been told, Jackson Hole is *not* named for Michael Jackson. The valley, originally called Jackson's Hole, was instead named for a likable trapper, David E. Jackson, one of the men who helped establish the Rocky Mountain Fur Company. When Jackson and his partners sold out in 1830, they realized a profit of over $50,000. Jackson's presence remains in the names of both Jackson Hole and Jackson Lake. Eventually, more polite folks began calling the valley Jackson Hole, in an attempt to end the ribald stories associated with

the name Jackson's Hole. (It's easy to imagine the jokes with both Jackson's Hole and the Tetons in the same place.) By the way, in 1991, a group calling itself the Committee to Restore Decency to Our National Parks created quite a stir by suggesting that Grand Teton National Park be renamed. A letter sent to the Park Service and various members of Congress noted: "Though a great many Americans may be oblivious to this vulgarity, hundreds of millions of French people around the world are not! How embarrassing that these spectacular, majestic mountains are reduced to a dirty joke overseas. . . ." After a flurry of letters in response, the hoax was revealed; it was a prank by staff members of *Spy* magazine.

HISTORY

The first people to cross the mountain passes into Jackson Hole probably arrived while the

last massive glaciers were still retreating. Clovis stone arrowheads—a style used 11,000 years ago—have been found along the edges of the valley. These early peoples were replaced in the 16th and 17th centuries by the Shoshone, Bannock, Blackfeet, Crow, and Gros Ventre tribes, who hunted bison from horses. When the first fur trappers tramped up the river valleys into Jackson Hole, they found Indian paths throughout the valley.

John Colter

Transport yourself back to the early 19th century, a time when people from the new nation called America saw the world west of the Mississippi River as just a blank spot on the map. In 1803, Thomas Jefferson purchased the Louisiana Territory from France, and to learn more about this gigantic piece of real estate he sent Meriwether Lewis and William Clark on a military expedition to the Pacific coast, a trip that took nearly two and a half years. Although the expedition skirted around Wyoming—heading across Montana instead—it proved the opening wedge for the settlement of the West and, indirectly, the discovery of Jackson Hole. On the return trip, the party met two fur trappers en route to the upper Missouri River. One of Lewis and Clark's respected scouts, John Colter, was allowed to join the trappers, "provided no one of the party would ask or expect a Similar permission."

After a winter of trapping with his partners, Colter headed alone down the Platte River, but before he could get back to civilization he met up with a company of trappers led by Manuel Lisa. They were on their way to the Rockies, determined to cash in on the huge demand for beaver

furs by trapping the rich beaver streams that Lewis and Clark had described. Wealth beckoned, and John Colter gladly turned around again, guiding Lisa's men up to the mouth of the Big Horn River, where they built a small fort. From there Colter was sent on a mission: contact Indians throughout the region, trading beads and other items for beaver furs.

His wanderings in the winter of 1807-08 were the first white exploration of this region. A map produced by William Clark in 1814 and based upon Colter's recollections shows an incredible midwinter journey around Yellowstone and Jackson Lakes, across the Tetons twice, and up through Jackson Hole. He did not get back to the fort until the following spring, telling tales of huge mountain ranges and a spectacular geothermal area that others quickly laughed off as "Colter's Hell." (In 1931, an Idaho farmer claimed to have plowed up a stone carved into the shape of a human face, with "John Colter 1808" etched into the sides. There is evidence that it was a hoax—carved by a man anxious to obtain a horse concession with Grand Teton National Park. He got the concession after donating the rock to the park museum.)

Colter went on to become one of the most famous of all mountain men, and his later harrowing escape from the Blackfeet in Montana has become the stuff of legend: after being captured and stripped naked, he was forced to literally run for his life and somehow managed to outdistance his pursuers for six miles before hiding in a pile of logs until dark. He walked barefoot the 300 miles back to Manual Lisa's fort, surviving on roots and tree bark. Shortly thereafter, Colter was reported to have thrown

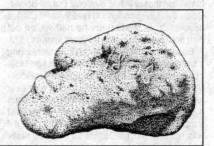

the "Colter Stone," with Colter's name inscribed on one face and the date 1808 on the other

JACKSON HOLE MUSEUM AND TETON COUNTY HISTORICAL SOCIETY

THE WHITE SHOSHONE

The quiet little Jackson Hole settlement of Wilson is named after one of the West's most fascinating characters, "Uncle Nick" Wilson. Born in 1842, Wilson grew up in Utah, where he made friends with a fellow sheepherder, an Indian boy, and learned to speak his language. Then, suddenly, Nick's life took a strange twist. The mother of Chief Washakie (from Wyoming's Wind River Reservation) had recently lost a son, and in a dream she had been told that a white boy would come to take his place.

Unable to convince her otherwise, Washakie sent his men out to find the new son. They came across Nick and offered him a pinto pony and the chance to fish, hunt, and ride horses all he wanted. It didn't take much persuading, and for the next two years he lived as a Shoshone, learning to hunt buffalo, use a bow and arrow, and answer to his new name, Yagaiki. He became a favorite of Chief Washakie, but when word came (falsely) that Nick's father was threatening to attack the Shoshones with an army of men to retrieve his son, the chief reluctantly helped Nick return home.

At age 18, Nick Wilson became one of the first Pony Express riders, a job that nearly killed him when he was struck in the head during a Paiute Indian attack. A doctor managed to remove the arrow point, but Wilson remained in a coma for nearly two weeks. Thereafter, Wilson always wore a hat to cover the scar, even inside buildings. He went on to become an Army scout and a driver for the Overland Stage before returning to a more sedate life of farming. Many years later, in 1889, Nick Wilson led a party of five Mormon families over steep Teton Pass and down to the rich grazing lands in Jackson Hole. The town that grew up around them became Wilson. In later years, "Uncle Nick" recounted his adventures in *The White Indian Boy.*

his hat on the ground, declaring, "I'll be damned if I ever come into [this country] again." He returned to St. Louis, married, and established a farm near that of fellow explorer Daniel Boone. Colter lived long enough to give William Clark a description of the country he had visited but died from jaundice just three years later, in 1813.

Because of the abundance of beavers along tributaries of the Snake River, Jackson Hole became an important crossroads for the Rocky Mountain fur trade. No rendezvous was ever held in the valley, but many of the most famous mountain men spent time here. They first trapped beavers in Jackson Hole in 1811, but it was not until the 1820s that fur trapping really came into its own as mountain men fanned through the wilderness in search of the "soft gold." This search continued for the next two

decades, finally dying out when overtrapping made beavers harder to find and silk hats replaced fur hats. After the last rendezvous in 1840, most of the old trappers headed on to new adventures, the best becoming guides for those en route to Oregon and California. Because Jackson Hole was not close to the Oregon Trail or other routes west, the area remained virtually deserted until the late 19th century.

Settlers

The first Jackson Hole homesteaders arrived in 1884, followed quickly by others coming to escape the law. The settlers survived by grazing cattle, harvesting hay, and acting as guides for rich hunters from Europe and eastern states. Gradually they filled the richest parts of the valley with homesteads. Conflicts soon arose be-

tween the Bannock Indians, who had been hunting in Jackson Hole for more than a hundred years, and the new settlers who made money guiding wealthy sportsmen.

By 1895, Wyoming had enacted game laws prohibiting hunting during 10 months of the year. Claiming that the Indians were taking elk out of season, Constable William Manning and 26 settlers arrested a group of 28 Indians (mostly women and children) who had been hunting in Hoback Canyon. When the Bannocks attempted to flee, an elderly Indian was shot four times in the back and died. Most of the others escaped. Settlers in Jackson Hole feared revenge and called in the cavalry, but the Indians who had been hunting in the area all returned peaceably to their Idaho reservation. Astoundingly, *The New York Times* headlined its report of the incident, "Settlers Massacred—Indians Kill Every One at Jackson's Hole—Courier Brings the News—Red Men Apply the Torch to All the Houses in the Valley." Although none of this was true, the attack by whites succeeded in forcing the Indians off their traditional hunting grounds, an action eventually upheld in a landmark U.S. Supreme Court case.

Jackson Hole Comes of Age
By the turn of the century, the settlements of Jackson, Wilson, Kelly, and Moran had all been established. The towns grew slowly; people survived by ranching, guiding, and engaging in the strange new business of tending to wealthy "dudes" from back east. Eventually, tourism would vastly eclipse raising cattle in importance, but even today Teton County has nearly as many cattle as people. Jackson, the largest town in Jackson Hole, was established in 1897 when Grace Miller (wife of a local banker known derisively as "Old Twelve Percent") bought a large plot of land and planned a townsite. In an event that should come as no surprise in "The Equality State," Jackson became the first town in America to be entirely governed by women. The year was 1920, and not only was the mayor a woman (Grace Miller), but so were all four council members, the city clerk, the treasurer, and even the town marshal. They remained in office until 1923.

Over the years Jackson has grown, spurred on by the creation of Grand Teton National Park and the development of Jackson Hole Ski Resort. During the 1980s Jackson Hole began to really boom as tourists flooded the region and wealthy families built elaborate second homes and golf courses. Although much of the area is public land and will remain undeveloped, rapid growth on private land threatens to turn Jackson Hole into another Aspen or Vail. The latest joke is that the billionaires are buying land so fast that they're driving the millionaires out of Jackson Hole.

JACKSON

The town of Jackson (pop. 6,000) lies near the southern end of Jackson Hole, hemmed in on three sides by Snow King Mountain, the Gros Ventre Range, and East Gros Ventre Butte. At 6,200 feet in elevation, Jackson experiences cold snowy winters, wet springs, warm sunny summers, and gorgeous falls. Jackson is quite unlike any other place in Wyoming; on a typical summer day an onrush of more than 35,000 tourists flood the town. Sit on a bench in the town square on a summer day and you're likely to see cars from every state in the Union. Tourists dart in and out of the many gift shops, art galleries, fine restaurants, Western-style saloons, and trendy boutiques. The cowboy hats all look as if the price tags just came off. This sure isn't Rock Springs!

In other parts of Wyoming, Jackson is viewed with a mixture of awe and disdain—awe over its booming economy but disdain that Jackson is not a "real" town, just a false front put up to sell things to outsiders. Yes, Jackson is almost wholly dependent upon the almighty tourist doll but as a result it enjoys a cultural richnes ing in other parts of the state. Besi don't like all the commercial f easy to escape to a campsi the wonderful countrysid National Park or Bri

Keep your e you're likel pending as

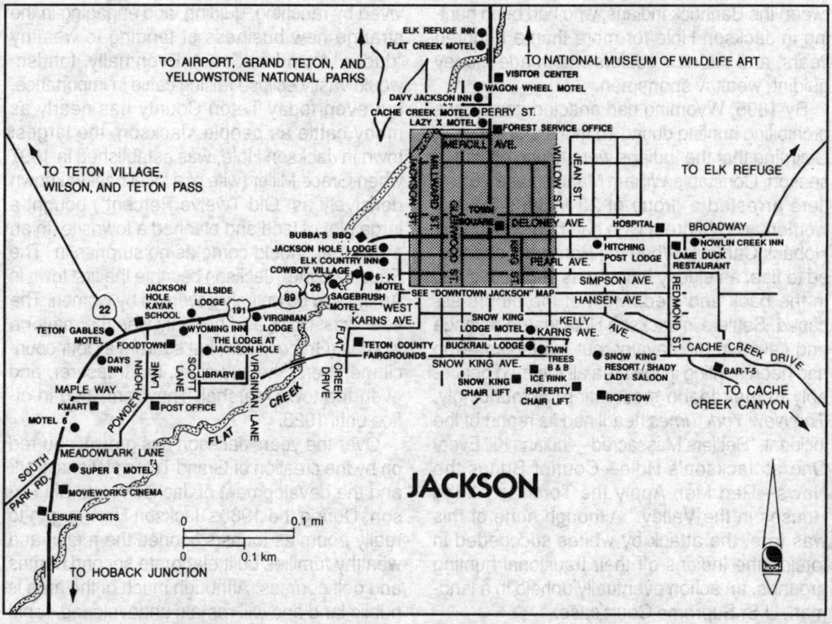
JACKSON
TO AIRPORT, GRAND TETON, AND YELLOWSTONE NATIONAL PARKS
TO NATIONAL MUSEUM OF WILDLIFE ART
ELK REFUGE INN
FLAT CREEK MOTEL
VISITOR CENTER
WAGON WHEEL MOTEL
DAVY JACKSON INN
CACHE CREEK MOTEL
PERRY ST.
LAZY X MOTEL
FOREST SERVICE OFFICE
MERCILL AVE.
JEAN ST.
WILLOW ST.
TO ELK REFUGE
TO TETON VILLAGE, WILSON, AND TETON PASS
JACKSON ST.
MILLWARD ST.
GLENWOOD ST.
TOWN SQUARE
DELONEY AVE.
HOSPITAL
BROADWAY
KING ST.
BUBBA'S BBQ
JACKSON HOLE LODGE
ELK COUNTRY INN
COWBOY VILLAGE
6 - K MOTEL
HITCHING POST LODGE
PEARL AVE.
NOWLIN CREEK INN
LAME DUCK RESTAURANT
SIMPSON AVE.
SEE "DOWNTOWN JACKSON" MAP
HANSEN AVE.
REDMOND ST.
JACKSON HOLE KAYAK SCHOOL
HILLSIDE LODGE
22
191
89
26
SAGEBRUSH MOTEL
WEST
KARNS AVE.
SNOW KING LODGE MOTEL
KELLY AVE.
KARNS AVE.
TETON GABLES MOTEL
FOODTOWN
WYOMING INN
VIRGINIAN LODGE
THE LODGE AT JACKSON HOLE
TETON COUNTY FAIRGROUNDS
BUCKRAIL LODGE
TWIN TREES B & B
CACHE CREEK DRIVE
DAYS INN
HORN
LANE
SCOTT LANE
LIBRARY
VIRGINIAN LANE
FLAT CREEK DRIVE
SNOW KING AVE.
SNOW KING CHAIR LIFT
ICE RINK
RAFFERTY CHAIR LIFT
SNOW KING RESORT / SHADY LADY SALOON
BAR-T-5
MAPLE WAY
POWDER
KMART
POST OFFICE
CREEK
FLAT
ROPETOW
TO CACHE CREEK CANYON
MOTEL 6
MEADOWLARK LANE
SOUTH PARK RD.
SUPER 8 MOTEL
MOVIEWORKS CINEMA
LEISURE SPORTS
0 0.1 mi
0 0.1 km
TO HOBACK JUNCTION
MOON

1983), attorney Gerald Spence (of Karen Silkwood and Imelda Marcos notoriety), former Wyoming governor Clifford Hansen, Yvon Chouinard (mountaineer and founder of Patagonia), Connie Stevens, Charles DuPont, and members of the Rockefeller family.

SIGHTS

Town Squar

One of

a leisurely ride around town ($3.50 for adults; $2.50 for kids). During the summer, "cowboys" put on a free **shoot-out** for throngs of camera-happy tourists. The shoot-out starts every night except Sunday at 6:30 p.m. With stereotypical players and questionable acting, the "mountain law" system seems in dire need of reform. Most folks love the sham; Kodak and Fuji love it even more.

National Museum of Wildlife Art

Jackson is the proud home of the magnificent National Museum of Wildlife Art. The $10-million facility opened in 1994 and is located two miles north of town along U.S. 26/89, directly across from the National Elk Refuge. The irregularly shaped museum is built from Arizona sandstone and resembles nearby rock outcroppings. Its exterior gets mixed reviews—ome folks hate it, others love it—but the inter-or is a marvelous 51,000-square-foot space using 12 galleries, including a hands-on kids' ce, a video theater, the Rising Sage Cafe ious lunches), a 200-seat state-of-the-art rium, and a gift shop. As visitors enter

the main gallery, a larger-than-life bronze mountain lion crouches above, ready to pounce.

The museum collection features pieces by Carl Rungius, George Catlin, Albert Bierstadt, Karl Bodmer, Alfred Jacob Miller, N.C. Wyeth, Conrad Schwiering, John Clymer, Charles Russell, Robert Bateman, and many others. Of particular interest are the reconstructed studio of John Clymer and the Rungius Gallery, where you'll find the largest collection of his paintings in the nation. Also of note is the exhibit on the

American bison, which documents these once vastly abundant animals and their slaughter. Six galleries contain changing exhibitions of photography, painting, and other art. Spotting scopes in the lobby and the cozy members' lounge (open to the public) are useful for watching residents of the adjacent National Elk Refuge. During the winter, come to the museum to purchase tickets for sleigh rides on the refuge.

Admission to the museum costs $4 for adults, $3 for seniors and students, $10 for families; kids under six get in free. It is open

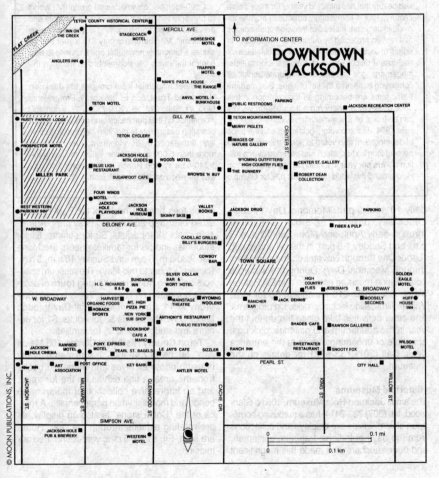

DOWNTOWN JACKSON

SAVING JACKSON HOLE

In recent decades the town of Jackson has boomed as expensive homes have spread across old ranchlands, huge retailers such as Kmart have moved in, and oil companies have salivated over oil and gas wells on nearby Forest Service land. Today, despite the fact that 97% of the land in Teton County is in the public domain, the 70,000 acres of private land that remain are rapidly being developed, and Jackson Hole is in grave danger of losing the wild beauty that has attracted visitors for more than a century. This is immediately obvious to anyone arriving in Jackson. Instead of the wide open spaces that remain protected by public land ownership, the edges of Jackson are falling under a proliferation of real-estate offices, chain motels, fast-food outlets, megamarts, gas stations, and elaborate banks, all competing beneath a thicket of signs. Summertime traffic jams are becoming all too common in this once-quiet place where more than 35,000 visitors can be found on a summer afternoon.

In 1994, Jackson voters got fed up with the pace of development and voted to scrap the town's two percent lodging tax, which had provided over a million dollars per year in funding to promote Jackson Hole around the world (and to help pay for Olympic skier Tommy Moe's condo). Supporters of the measure said that not collecting the tax would slash Jackson's promotion budget, thus possibly slowing growth. The long-term effects are unclear, but don't expect as many glossy publications emerging from the Jackson Hole Visitor Council; without funding, they were out of existence at the end of 1996.

The **Jackson Hole Alliance for Responsible Planning,** 40 E. Simpson St., tel. (703) 733-9417, is a 1,500-member environmental group that works to preserve the natural areas of Jackson Hole and prevent the town from becoming just another trashy tourist mill. Membership is only $15 a year and includes a bimonthly newsletter and a chance to help control the many developments that threaten the valley.

Another influential local group is the **Jackson Hole Land Trust,** 555 E. Broadway, Professional Bldg. #1, Suite 228, tel. (703) 733-4707, a nonprofit organization that purchases land and obtains conservation easements to maintain ranches and other land threatened by development. It now protects more than 6,000 acres in the valley, including the 1,740-acre Walton Ranch, visible along the highway between Jackson and Wilson.

---

daily 10 a.m.-5 p.m. Memorial Day through Labor Day; daily 9 a.m.-5 p.m. December through early April; and Mon.-Sat. 10 a.m.-5 p.m. and Sunday 1-5 p.m. in the fall and spring (Labor Day through November and early April through Memorial Day). During the winter, a combination museum entrance and Elk Refuge sleigh ride costs $10 for adults, $5 for kids. Wildlife films, slide lectures, talks, kid programs, and other activities take place throughout the year in the auditorium and galleries; pick up a schedule of upcoming events at the entrance desk. Call (307) 733-5771 for details on the museum.

Historical Museums

The small **Jackson Hole Museum,** 105 N. Glenwood, tel. (307) 733-2414, has a surprising homespun charm. Inside are displays and collections from the days of Indians, trappers, cattlemen, and dude ranchers who made this magnificent valley their home. Check out the Paul Bunyan-sized bear trap and the old postcards. Admission costs $3 for adults, $2 for seniors, $1 for students, and $6 for families. Hours are Mon.-Sat. 9:30 a.m.-6 p.m. and Sunday 10 a.m.-5 p.m. (closed October to mid-May). The museum sponsors hourlong **historical walking tours** of Jackson's downtown on Tuesday, Thursday, and Saturday at 11 a.m. from Memorial Day through Labor Day. The cost is $2 for adults, $1 for seniors and students, and $5 for families.

Teton County Historical Center, 105 Mercill Ave., tel. (307) 733-9605, is a research facility housing photo archives and many old books from the area, a fine exhibit on the fur trade, and an impressive collection of Indian trade beads and mountain-man paraphernalia. A replica of the "Colter stone" is also on display, as are rotating exhibits through the year. Hours are Mon.-Fri. 8 a.m.-5 p.m. year-round; free admission.

Art in Jackson Hole

Artists have long been attracted by the beauty of Jackson Hole and the Tetons. Mt. Moran, the 12,805-foot summit behind Jackson Lake, is named for Thomas Moran, whose watercolors helped persuade Congress to set aside Yellowstone as the first national park. The late Conrad Schwiering's paintings of the Tetons have attained international fame—one was even used on the Postal Service's Wyoming Centennial stamp in 1990. Ansel Adams's photograph of the Tetons remains etched in the American consciousness as one of the archetypical wilderness images. A copy of the image was included in the payload of the *Voyager II* spacecraft currently en route out of our solar system. Today many artists live or work in Jackson Hole, making this the art center of the Rockies, ranking with New York, San Francisco, Santa Fe, and Scottsdale.

More than 30 galleries crowd the center of Jackson, covering the spectrum from Indian art collections of questionable authenticity to impressive photographic exhibits and shows by nationally acclaimed painters. Unfortunately, many of these galleries offer recycled ideas now manufactured in mass quantity with every cliché thrown in. Particularly egregious examples are the southwestern-style pastel pottery, the elk-antler lamps, and the paintings of noble-looking mountain men and Indians set against a Grand Teton backdrop. The local free newspapers provide a complete rundown of current exhibitions and displays, along with maps showing gallery locations. Stop by the visitor center for info on upcoming **gallery walks** featuring many of the local galleries.

Several galleries are worth a visit; most notably the outstanding National Museum of Wildlife Art (described above). The non-profit **Art Association,** 260 W. Pearl, tel. (307) 733-6379, has art classes of all types throughout the year and displays changing exhibitions by local artists in its gallery; open Mon.-Fri. 9:30 a.m.-4:30 p.m. **Fiber & Pulp,** 170 E. Deloney, tel. (307) 734-2599, has workshops and short training sessions on such topics as bookbinding, silk painting, Polaroid dye transfers, rubber-stamping, and mask-making.

One of the largest private galleries is **Wilcox Gallery,** a mile north of town on U.S. 26/89, tel.

(307) 733-6450, which features works from prominent Western painters and sculptors. **Wapiti Gallery,** 90 N. Center St., tel. (307) 733-1732, emphasizes western paintings and sculpture, both contemporary and traditional. **The Robert Dean Collection,** 172 Center St., tel. (307) 733-9290, specializes in authentic, high-quality Indian art and jewelry; open summers only. **Rawson Galleries,** 50 King St., tel. (307) 733-7306, features both traditional and avant-garde watercolors, etchings, and other artwork. **River Rock Gallery,** 170 E. Deloney, tel. (307) 733-9181, features fine pottery and invitational exhibitions. Jack Dennis' **Wyoming Galleries,** 50 E. Broadway, tel. (307) 733-7548, specializes in wildlife and traditional landscape paintings. More unusual is **Center Street Gallery,** 172 Center St., tel. (307) 733-1192, where the emphasis is on brightly colored contemporary and abstract art. The **Hennes Studio & Gallery,** 5850 N. Larkspur Dr. (off Spring Gulch Rd.), tel. (307) 733-2593, features the oil and watercolor paintings of the Tetons by Joanne Hennes. Her commissioned works hang in the Moose Visitor Center and Jenny Lake Lodge.

Many nationally known photographers live or work in Jackson Hole, exhibiting their prints in Jackson galleries. Two photographers have noteworthy galleries. Tom Mangelsen's **Images of Nature Gallery** at 170 N. Cache, tel. (307) 733-9752, displays a selection of his outstanding wildlife and landscape photos, and **Light Reflections,** 35 E. Deloney, tel. (307) 733-4016, includes many of Fred Joy's large-format visions of the American West.

For a different kind of art, **Dancer's Workshop,** downstairs in the Pink Garter Plaza at 49 W. Broadway, tel. (307) 733-6398, offers dance classes—including very popular country-western barn dances—along with performances by the Three Rivers Dance Company.

Snake River Institute

Each summer, the Snake River Institute offers innovative workshops and seminars to explore the connections between art, history, cultures, and communities in the American West. The programs last one to five days and cover such diverse topics as poetry, painting, and photography workshops, building a house from straw

bales, journal writing, wildflowers, historic dude ranches, quilts, and fossils. Classes are taught by respected poets, writers, photographers, and scientists; tuition starts around $325 for a three-day workshop. Also available are special children's classes and interdisciplinary workshops for teachers. In early October, the institute offers a weekend symposium of readings, workshops, and other activities. Snake River Institute is headquartered in the historic Hardeman Homestead in Wilson. Contact the institute at Box 7724, Jackson, WY 83001, tel. (307) 733-2214, for more information and a class brochure. Its e-mail address is snakeriverinst@wyoming.com.

BOB RACE

NATIONAL ELK REFUGE

Just a couple miles north of Jackson is the National Elk Refuge, winter home for thousands of these majestic animals. During the summer, these elk range up to 65 miles away to feed on grasses, shrubs, and forbs in alpine meadows. But as the snows descend each fall, the elk move downslope, wintering in Jackson Hole and the surrounding country. The chance to view elk up close from a horse-drawn sleigh makes a trip to the National Elk Refuge one of the most popular wintertime activities for Jackson Hole visitors.

History

When the first ranchers arrived in Jackson Hole in the late 19th century, they moved onto land that had long been an elk migration route and wintering ground. The ranchers soon found elk raiding their haystacks and competing with cattle for forage, particularly during severe winters. The conflicts reached a peak early in this century when three consecutive severe winters killed thousands of elk, leading one settler to claim that he had "walked for a mile on dead elk lying from one to four deep."

Fortunately, a local rancher and hunting guide, Stephen N. Leek, had been given a camera by one of the sportsmen he had guided, George Eastman (founder of Kodak). Leek's disturbing photos of starving and dead elk found a national audience and helped pressure the state of Wyoming to appropriate $5,000 to buy hay in 1909. Two years later the federal government began purchasing land for a permanent winter elk refuge, a refuge that would eventually cover nearly 25,000 acres. Today it's administered by the U.S. Fish and Wildlife Service. Famed biologist, illustrator, and conservationist Olaus Murie came to Jackson Hole in 1927 to begin his studies of the elk, remaining here until his death in 1963. With his wife Margaret "Mardie" Murie, they chronicled their adventures in Wapiti Wilderness (Boulder: Colorado Associated University Press). Conservationist Mardie Murie still lives in Moose, holding near-sainthood status among Wyoming conservationists.

Today more than 10,000 elk—two-thirds of the local population—spend November through May on the refuge. Because development has reduced the elk habitat in the valley to a quarter of its original size, refuge managers try to improve the remaining land by seeding, irrigation, and prescribed burning. In addition, during the most difficult foraging period, the elk are fed pelleted alfalfa paid for in part by sales of elk antlers collected on the refuge. During this time, each elk eats more than seven pounds of supplemental alfalfa a day, or 30 tons per day for the entire herd. Elk head back into the mountains with the melting of snow each April and May; during the summer months you'll only see a few on the refuge.

Visiting the Refuge

The National Elk Refuge, tel. (307) 733-9212, is primarily a winter attraction, although it's also an excellent place to watch birds and other wildlife in summer. Trumpeter swans nest and

winter here. The refuge has staff members on duty year-round in the Wyoming State Information Center. Begin your wintertime trip to the refuge from the National Museum of Wildlife Art, two miles north of Jackson on Hwy. 26/89. Purchase your sleigh ride tickets here—$8 for adults, $4 for ages 6-12, free for kids under age six. A combination museum entrance and sleigh ride is $10 for adults, $5 for kids—a great deal. No reservations are taken for the sleighs, and rides are given on a first-come, first-served basis. The museum shows a slide show about the refuge while you're waiting for a shuttle bus to take you downhill to the delightful **horse-drawn sleighs.** These sleighs offer a unique opportunity to ride among the thousands of elk without disturbing them—people on foot would scare them. Sleighs run daily 10 a.m.-4 p.m. between late December and late March, heading out as soon as enough folks show up for a ride—generally just long enough for the early-comers to finish watching the slide show. The rides last for 45-60 minutes, so be sure to bring along warm clothes: the wind can get bitterly cold. A tour of the National Elk Refuge will certainly be a highlight of any wintertime visit to Jackson Hole. In December and January the bulls have impressive antlers that they start to shed by the end of February. Lots of sparring goes on January and February.

Special START (Southern Teton Area Rapid Transit) buses connect Jackson with the Elk Refuge and the Museum of Wildlife Art for just $1 each way; call (307) 733-4521 for details. If you don't want to wait for a bus, **All Star Transportation,** tel. (307) 733-2888 or (800) 378-2944, and **Buckboard Cab,** tel. (307) 733-1112, both offer shuttle service to the museum from Teton Village ($36 roundtrip for up to four) and downtown Jackson ($10 roundtrip for up to four).

Four miles north of town and next to the elk refuge is the **Jackson National Fish Hatchery,** tel. (307) 733-2510, which rears a half-million cutthroat and lake trout annually. Open daily 8 a.m.-4 p.m. year-round.

ACCOMMODATIONS

As one of the premier centers for tourism in Wyoming, Jackson Hole is jam-packed with more than 70 different motels, hotels, and B&Bs, plus many more condominiums and guest ranches. See the charts for a complete listing with prices, addresses, and phone numbers. Other lodging can be found just to the north within Grand Teton National Park (see the "Grand Teton National Park Area Accommodations" chart later in this chapter).

Because of their popularity, lodging places in Jackson command premium prices—a marked contrast to rates in other parts of Wyoming. With a few exceptions, you can expect to pay a minimum of $60 s or d during the peak visitor seasons of July-Aug. and late December to early January. Peak season rates at most motels are in the $80-100 s or d range. Rates can drop up to 40% in the off-season, so if you can visit March-May or late September to mid-December, you'll save a lot of cash. In the town of Jackson, the highest rates are usually in July and August, while at Teton Village skiers send lodging prices to their peak between mid-December and early January.

Because of Jackson Hole's popularity, reservations are highly recommended. For midsummer, make reservations at least two months ahead—longer if you really want to be certain of a place—and during the Christmas-to-New Year's period you should probably reserve six months in advance to ensure a spot.

Hostel
Jackson's least-expensive lodging option, the **Bunkhouse,** tel. (307) 733-3668 or (800) 234-4507, is located in the basement of the Anvil Motel at 215 N. Cache. Right in town, it almost always has space. The hostel costs just $15 per person and includes a TV room and a kitchen with a refrigerator and microwave but no stove. Sleeping rooms have 22 well-maintained beds with clean linen and adjacent storage lockers (bring your own lock). Though men's and women's showers and restrooms are separate, the sleeping space is coed. Unlike a youth hostel, the Bunkhouse has no curfew. Check in after 3 p.m. and be out by 11 a.m. Folks who aren't staying here can use the showers for $5.

Budget Motels
Hillside Lodge, tel. (307) 733-3391, has old-fashioned motel rooms and even better deals during the off-season. Hillside is definitely not for everyone, so see the rooms first. **Hostel X,** tel.

JACKSON HOLE ACCOMMODATIONS

Note: Accommodations are listed from least to most expensive. Add a six percent tax to these rates. See the text for other lodging options including condos, cabins, and houses. The "Jackson Bed and Breakfasts," "Jackson Hole Guest Ranches," and "Grand Teton National Park Accommodations" charts list additional nearby lodging places. Area code is 307.

Bunkhouse; 215 N. Cache; tel. 733-3668 or (800) 234-4507; $15 pp; hostel with kitchen

Hillside Lodge; 945 W. Broadway; tel. 733-3391; $35 s or d; kitchenettes $45 s or d; very plain rooms

Hostel X; Teton Village; tel. 733-3415; $38 s or d in summer; $44 s or d in winter; very plain, no phones or TV in rooms, central lounge with TV and games, ski wax room

Motel 6; 1370 W. Broadway; tel. 733-1620 or (800) 466-8356; $40 s, $46 d; outdoor pool, reserve six months ahead for midsummer

Alpine Motel; 70 S. Jean St.; tel. 733-2082; $52-66 s, $66-70 d; outdoor pool, kitchenettes available

49'er Inn (Quality Inn); 330 W. Pearl; tel. 733-7550 or (800) 451-2980; $52-160 s, $56-164 d; large jacuzzi, sauna, exercise room, AAA approved

Hoback River Resort; Hoback Jct. (12 miles south of Jackson); tel. 733-5129; $55-58 s or d in motel rooms with decks; $80-110 s or d in cabins with kitchens (no maid service); very nice riverside place, three-night minimum stay for cabins, free airport shuttle

The Cottages at Snow King; 470 King St.; tel. 733-3480; $56-74 s or d; kitchenettes available

El Rancho Motel (Budget Host); 240 N. Glenwood; 733-3668 or (800) 234-4507; $65-93 s or d, kitchenettes, jacuzzi

Pony Express Motel; 50 S. Millward St.; tel. 733-3835 or (800) 526-2658; $66-77 s or d; year-round outdoor pool, AAA approved

Sagebrush Motel; 550 W. Broadway; tel. 733-0336; $68 s or d; kitchenettes $78-88 s or d; motel and cabin-style rooms

Elk Country Inn; 480 W. Pearl; tel. 733-2364 or (800) 483-8667; $68 s or d; cabins and motel rooms, kitchenettes $74 s or d

Camp Creek Inn; 16 miles south of Jackson near Hoback Jct.; tel. 733-3099 or (800) 228-8460; $70 for up to six in A-frame cabins; continental breakfast, quiet location, no TVs or phones in rooms

Buckrail Lodge; 110 E. Karns Ave.; tel. 733-2079; $70-95 s or d; AAA approved, outdoor jacuzzi, cedar log units, closed mid-Oct. through April

Wagon Wheel Village; 435 N. Cache; tel. 733-2357 or (800) 323-9279; $73 s, $78 d; jacuzzi, modern log cabins, kitchenettes available, free airport shuttle, open May-Sept., AAA approved

Hitching Post Lodge; 460 E. Broadway; tel. 733-2606 or (800) 821-8351; $74 s or d; two-bed kitchenettes for $139 s or d; log cabins, outdoor pool, jacuzzi, continental breakfast, fridges and microwaves, AAA approved

Antler Motel; 50 W. Pearl Ave.; tel. 733-2535 or (800) 522-2406; $74-102 s or d; hot tub

Elk Refuge Inn; one mile north of town on U.S. 89; tel. 733-3582 or (800) 544-3582; $77 s, $82 d; kitchenettes $98 s or d, AAA approved

Rawhide Motel; 75 S. Millward; tel. 733-1216 or (800) 835-2999; $78 s, $83 d; large rooms with lodgepole pine furnishings

Wilson Motel; 292 E. Pearl; tel. 733-2956; $79 for up to four people; outdoor pool, kitchenettes available

Horseshoe Motel; 285 N. Cache; tel. 733-2287; $79 s or d

Teton Gables Motel; 1140 W. Broadway; tel. 733-3723; $80 s or d

Pioneer Motel; 325 N. Cache; tel. 733-3673; $80 s, $85 d; microwaves and fridges, homemade quilts

Stagecoach Motel; 291 N. Glenwood; tel. 733-3451; $80 s, $85 d

Anvil Motel (Budget Host); 215 N. Cache; tel. 733-3668 or (800) 234-4507; $80-84 s or d; outdoor jacuzzi

Teton Inn; 165 W. Gill St.; tel. 733-3883 or (800) 867-4667; $80-100 s or d

Prospector Motel; 155 N. Jackson; tel. 733-4858 or (800) 851-0070; $80-105 s or d; jacuzzi, AAA approved

Super 8 Motel; 750 South U.S. 89; tel. 733-6833 or (800) 800-8000; $81 s, $100 d

Crystal Springs Inn; Teton Village; tel. 733-4423; $84 s or d; fridges

Trapper Inn; 235 N. Cache; tel. 733-2648 or (800) 341-8000; $78 s, 85-95 s or d; two- and three-bedroom suites for $154-195 d; two jacuzzis, AAA approved

Flat Creek Motel; one mile north of town on U.S. 89; tel. 733-5276 or (800) 438-9338; $85 s or d; hot tub, sauna, kitchenettes $115 s or d

Ranch Inn; 45 E. Pearl St.; tel. 733-6363 or (800) 348-5599; $85 s or d; kitchenette suites $134-165 d; indoor and outdoor jacuzzis

Anglers Inn; 265 N. Millward St.; tel. 733-3682 or (800) 867-4667; $85-95 s or d; newly remodeled, fridges and microwaves, AAA approved

Old West Cabins; 5750 S. U.S. 89 (six miles south of Jackson); tel. 733-0333; $85-160 s or d; rustic log cabins, kitchenettes

Golden Eagle Motor Inn; 325 E. Broadway; tel. 733-2042; $88 s or d; suites (sleep six) $118-135; outdoor pool, AAA approved

Cache Creek Motel; 390 N. Glenwood; tel. 733-7781 or (800) 843-4788; $88-95 s or d; full kitchens, jacuzzi, AAA approved

Village Center Inn; Teton Village; tel. 733-3155 or (800) 735-8342; $88-98 s or d for studio and loft units; $130 for two-bedroom units (sleep four); all rooms with full kitchens

Sundance Inn; 135 W. Broadway; tel. 733-3444; $89 s or d; continental breakfast

Four Winds Motel; 150 N. Millward St.; tel. 733-2474 or (800) 228-6461; $89 s or d; AAA approved

Western Motel; 225 S. Glenwood; tel. 733-3291 or (800) 845-7999; $89-99 s or d; outdoor pool

Virginian Lodge; 750 W. Broadway; tel. 733-2792 or (800) 262-4999; $95 s or d; outdoor pool, jacuzzi, AAA approved

Jackson Hole Lodge; 420 W. Broadway; tel. 733-2992 or (800) 604-9404; $100 s or d for motel rooms; $175-250 for one- and two-bedroom condos with kitchens; large indoor pool, two jacuzzis, sauna, game room, AAA approved

Painted Buffalo Inn; 400 W. Broadway; tel. 733-4340 or (800) 288-3866; $105 s, $115 d; indoor pool, continental breakfast, AAA approved

Alpenhof Lodge; Teton Village; tel. 733-3242 or (800) 732-3244; $109-185 s or d; outdoor pool, jacuzzi, sauna, ski lockers, game room, AAA approved

The Inn at Jackson Hole (Best Western); Teton Village; tel. 733-2311 or (800) 842-7666; $109-229 s or d; outdoor pool, three jacuzzis, sauna, kitchenettes available, AAA approved

Parkway Inn (Best Western); 125 N. Jackson St.; tel. 733-3143 or (800) 247-8390; $110-135 s, $110-135 d; newly remodeled rooms furnished with antiques, indoor pool, jacuzzi, saunas, exercise gym, AAA approved

(continues on next page)

JACKSON HOLE ACCOMMODATIONS
(continued)

Cowboy Village Resort; 120 Flat Creek Dr.; tel. 733-3121 or (800) 962-4988; $114-134 s or d; cabins and suites, two outdoor jacuzzis, kitchenettes in all rooms, AAA approved

Sojurner Inn; Teton Village; tel. 733-3657 or (800) 445-4655; $139 s or d; outdoor pool, indoor and outdoor jacuzzis, sauna, closed mid-April to mid-May and mid-Oct. through November, AAA approved

Days Inn; 1280 W. Broadway; tel. 739-9010 or (800) 833-5343; $149-209 s or d; continental breakfast, jacuzzi, sauna, in-room safes, microwaves and fridges, AAA approved

Wort Hotel; 50 N. Glenwood St.; tel. 733-2190 or (800) 322-2727; $165-295 s or d; historic hotel with large rooms, two jacuzzis, fitness room, AAA approved (four diamond)

Snow King Resort; 400 E. Snow King; tel. 733-5200 or (800) 522-5464; $170-180 s or d for motel rooms; $200-340 for suites; $220-420 d for one- to four-bedroom condos; outdoor pool, jacuzzi, game room, indoor ice rink, sauna, airport shuttle, fitness room, concierge, free airport shuttle, AAA approved

The Lodge at Jackson Hole (Best Western); 80 S. Scott Lane; tel. 739-9703 or (800) 458-3866; $179 s or d; new three-story lodge, indoor and outdoor pools, jacuzzis, sauna, continental breakfast, fridges and microwaves, AAA approved

Wyoming Inn (Red Lion); 930 W. Broadway; tel. 734-0035 or (800) 844-0035; $179-219 s or d; new motel, large rooms, continental breakfast, jacuzzi, some rooms with fireplaces and jacuzzis, free airport shuttle, AAA approved

Davy Jackson Inn; 85 Perry Ave.; tel. 739-2294 or (800) 584-0532; $185-215 s or d; luxurious new inn, full breakfast and evening beverages, jacuzzi in gazebo, steam showers, fireplaces, AAA approved

Rusty Parrot Lodge; 175 N. Jackson; tel. 733-2000 or (800) 458-2004; $190-225 s or d; $450 d for suites; jacuzzi, full breakfast, handcrafted pine furniture, goose down comforters, some rooms with fireplaces and private jacuzzis, free airport shuttle, AAA approved (four diamond)

Spring Creek Resort; Gros Ventre Butte (four miles west of Jackson); tel. 733-8833 or (800) 443-6139; $200 s or d in hotel; $375-650 for one- to three-bedroom condos (sleep up to six); hilltop location on private pond, outdoor pool and jacuzzi, tennis courts, all rooms with fireplaces, kitchens, and pine furnishings, free airport shuttle, AAA approved (four diamond)

Rancho Alegre Lodge; 3600 S. Park Loop Rd.; tel. 733-7988; $350-750 s or d for suites; luxurious New England-style lodge, antique furnishings, gourmet breakfast

Inn on the Creek; 295 N. Millwood; tel. 739-1565 or (800) 669-9534; $149-189 s or d; suites for $379 s or d; new lodge, continental breakfast, outdoor jacuzzi, creekside patio, guest lounge, down comforters, some rooms with balconies, in-room jacuzzis, and fireplaces

(307) 733-3415, offers small, plain-vanilla rooms (no TV or phones) and a central area with a TV lounge and books. Because of its Teton Village location at the foot of Jackson Hole Ski Resort, Hostel X is very popular with skiers on a budget; reserve three months ahead for midwinter rooms. Hostel X also has Ping-Pong and pool tables, and a ski wax room. Jackson's best deal for standard motel rooms is—predictably—**Motel 6,** tel. (307) 733-1620 or (800) 466 8356, where the winter rates are an even better bargain.

Twelve miles south of Jackson in Hoback Junction, **Hoback River Resort,** tel. (307) 733-5129, has large motel rooms and cabins for up to six people on attractive grounds along the Hoback River. The rates are reasonable, and the rooms are very clean and well maintained. But the location—away from busy downtown Jackson—is the real draw here.

Mid-Priced Lodging
Most Jackson motels fall in the $70-100 s or d

range, with pricing factors being location, type of room, quality of furnishings, and amenities such as pools and hot tubs. Several good AAA-rated midrange motels are: **Buckrail Lodge,** tel. (307) 733-2079, **Golden Eagle Motor Inn,** tel. (307) 733-2042, and **Trapper Inn,** tel. (307) 733-2648 or (800) 341-8000. See the chart for a complete listing.

Top-End Lodging

It should come as no surprise that toney Jackson Hole has a number of elaborate, pricey, and sumptuous places to stay. The oldest and best known is the **Wort Hotel,** tel. (307) 733-2190 or (800) 322-2727, but several other places offer equally high standards (and prices). Some of the most dramatic vistas of the Tetons are from the luxurious **Spring Creek Resort,** tel. (307) 733-8833 or (800) 443-6139, high atop Gros Ventre Butte west of town. Located on a 50-acre spread, **Rancho Alegre Lodge,** tel. (307) 733-7988, offers the most stratospherically expensive Jackson lodging, charging up to $750 for a suite with two bedrooms (one with a king bed), a jacuzzi, private deck, and 25-foot cathedral ceiling. In the works as this was being written was Amanlodge, a luxurious lodge atop Gros Ventre Butte. It's expected to open by 1998.

Bed and Breakfasts

For those who can afford it, Jackson's many fine B&Bs are a delightful way to relax in comfort at the homes of locals. The chart, "Jackson Hole Bed and Breakfasts" describes each place. Be sure to reserve space far ahead during the peak summer season, though you might get lucky at the last minute if someone cancels. **Jackson Hole Bed & Breakfast,** tel. (307) 734-1999 or (800) 542-2632, offers one-stop B&B shopping—reservations for 14 local B&Bs and the latest on availability.

A personal favorite—it gets high marks from all who visit—is **Teton Treehouse B&B,** tel. (307) 733-3233, a gorgeous four-story hillside home. It really does feel like living in a treehouse and is a great place for birdwatchers. Decks provide impressive views across the valley below, and you can soak in the outdoor hot tub each evening and enjoy a big breakfast while the owners regale you with stories of Jackson Hole. Another recommended place is **Wild-**

flower Inn, tel. (307) 733-4710, a spacious log house with bright guest rooms set on three acres of country land. Four of the five rooms have their own private decks, and the earthy breakfasts are often served outside next to a pond. Wildflower's hot tub is located inside a plant-filled solarium. The owner/builders of Wildflower are an Exum climbing guide and former ski instructor. You'll find equally outdoorsy owners at **The Alpine House,** tel. (307) 739-1570 or (800) 753-1421, where both were Olympic skiers. The house has small but comfortable rooms and a hard-to-beat location: just two blocks from Jackson's town square.

For quiet downtown accommodations, **The Huff House Inn,** tel. (307) 733-4164, is another fine option. Built in 1917, this was for many years the home of one of Jackson's first doctors, Charles Huff. The rooms are well maintained and attractive, or you can stay in four cottages with cathedral ceilings, king-size beds, and jacuzzi tub baths.

A newly built home surrounded by aspens and pines, **Nowlin Creek Inn,** tel. (307) 733-0882 or (800) 533-0882, has five large, brightly lit guest rooms and a separate log cabin from 1925. From the front porch you can look across to the National Elk Refuge, but it's just six blocks to the center of Jackson. The Western decor—including a mix of old and new—reflects the owners' strong artistic sensibilities.

Out near Teton Village, **The Painted Porch,** tel. (307) 733-1981, was built in 1901 in Idaho and moved here many years later. Surrounded by a white picket fence and aspen trees, the rambling red farmhouse contains four attractive guest rooms, each with its own personality—from frilly lace to cowboy culture. One of the most impressive local B&Bs is **Bentwood,** tel. (307) 739-1411, an extraordinary log home with Western styling and English antiques. It's on the expensive side, but the rooms are luxurious; each has its own jacuzzi tub and fireplace.

Condominium Rentals

Condominiums provide one of the most popular lodging options for families and groups visiting Jackson Hole. These privately owned places are maintained by a number of local real-estate management companies and range from small studio apartments to spacious five-bedroom

JACKSON HOLE BED AND BREAKFASTS

Moose Meadows B&B; Wilson; tel. 733-9510 or (800) 652-9510; $65-135 s or d; ranch-style home on five acres, outdoor jacuzzi, four guest rooms, private or shared bath, full breakfast, children welcome, three-night minimum stay in summer

Teton View B&B; Teton Village Rd.; tel. 733-7954; $80-95 s or d; three guest rooms, private baths, deck facing Tetons, full breakfast

H.C. Richards B&B; 160 W. Deloney; tel. 733-6704; $92 s or d; downtown location, old-fashioned and cozy, three guest rooms, private baths, full breakfast, afternoon tea

Don't Fence Me Inn; Teton Village Rd.; tel. 733-7979; $100-125 s or d; custom log house on six acres, five guest rooms, private baths, full breakfast

The Huff House Inn; 240 E. Deloney Ave.; tel. 733-4164; $120-185 s or d; historic downtown Jackson home, five guest rooms and four luxurious cottages, private baths, jacuzzi, full breakfast

The Sassy Moose Inn; 3859 Miles Rd. (near Teton Village); tel. 733-1277 or (800) 356-1277; $99-129 s, $109-139 d; modest log house, five guest rooms, private baths, jacuzzi, full breakfast

The Painted Porch B&B; 3755 N. Moose-Wilson Rd.; tel. 733-1981; $110-170 s or d; restored turn-of-the-century farmhouse on three acres, four guest rooms, antiques, private baths, full breakfast, children welcome, two-night minimum stay

The Alpine House; 285 N. Glenwood; tel. 739-1570 or (800) 753-1421; $115 s or d; downtown location, seven guest rooms, private baths and balconies, healthy full breakfast, evening wine and cheese, AAA approved

Twin Trees B&B; 575 S. Willow; tel. 739-9737 or (800) 728-7337; $115 s or d; comfortable home at base of Snow King Mt., jacuzzi, three guest rooms, private baths, healthy full breakfast, no kids under 15, two-night minimum stay

Nowlin Creek Inn; 660 E. Broadway; tel. 733-0882 or (800) 533-0882; $115-200 s, $125-210 d; five guest rooms, private baths, three-night minimum stay June-Sept., outdoor jacuzzi, full breakfast, children welcome, AAA approved

Teton Treehouse B&B; Wilson; tel. 733-3233; $125-160 s or d; spacious open-beam home up 95 steps (not accessible for people with disabilities), six guest rooms, private baths, outdoor jacuzzi, decks with impressive vistas, healthy full breakfast

Wildflower Inn; Teton Village Rd.; tel. 733-4710; $140-150 s or d; jacuzzi, five guest rooms, private baths, handcrafted log beds, log house, healthy full breakfast, children welcome

Bentwood; Raven Haven Rd. (near Teton Village); tel. 739-1411; $145-165 s or d; very impressive custom log home, five guest rooms, private baths with jacuzzi tubs, fireplaces, full breakfast, children welcome

houses. All are completely furnished (including dishes) and have fireplaces, cable TV, phones, and midstay maid service. The nicest also include access to pools and jacuzzis and have balconies overlooking the spectacular Tetons. Many of the condominiums are in Teton Village, right next to the ski area; others are scattered around Jackson Hole.

During the winter holiday season, expect to pay $150 per night for studios (one or two people). Two-bedroom units (up to four people) cost $250-370 per night, and full four-bedroom and loft condos (these sleep eight) will set you back a lofty $550-650 per night. Summer and off-peak rates are approximately 40-50% lower, with spring and fall rates 50-75% less than peak season prices. In fall or spring, condos offer a real bargain for traveling families. Minimum stays of between two and seven nights are required throughout the year.

If you have the luxury of time, do a little comparison shopping before renting a condo. Things

to ask include whether you have access to a pool and jacuzzi, how close you are to the ski slopes, how frequent the maid service is, and whether the units include such amenities as free washing machines. Also be sure to find out what beds are in the rooms, since couples might not enjoy sleeping in twin bunk beds.

The following companies manage condos in Jackson Hole; contact them for details on price and availability: **Alpine Vacation Rentals,** tel. (307) 734-1161 or (800) 876-3968; **Ely & Associates,** tel. (307) 733-8604 or (800) 735-8310; **Teton Village Property Management,** tel. (307) 733-4610 or (800) 443-6840; **Jackson Hole Property Management,** tel. (307) 733-7945 or (800) 443-8613; **Jackson Hole Racquet Club Resort,** tel. (307) 733-3990 or (800) 443-8616; **Mountain Property Management,** tel. (307) 733-1684 or (800) 992-9948; **MTA Resorts,** tel. (307) 733-0613 or (800) 272-8824; **Snow King Resort Condominiums,** tel. (307) 733-5220 or (800) 522-5464; **Jackson Hole Lodge,** tel. (307) 733-2992 or (800) 642-4567; **Real Estate of Jackson Hole,** tel. (307) 733-6060 or (800) 443-6130; **Black Diamond Vacation Rentals,** tel. (307) 733-6170 or (800) 325-8605; **Accommodations in Jackson Hole,** tel. (307) 733-3039 or (800) 422-2927; **Owners Resorts & Exchange;** tel. (800) 748-4666; **Vine Suites,** tel. (307) 733-2888 or (800) 378-2944; and **Spring Creek Resort,** tel. (307) 733-8833 or (800) 443-6139. The largest of these companies—and good places to begin your search—are Jackson Hole Racquet Club Resort, Teton Village Property Management, Jackson Hole Property Management, Spring Creek Resort, and Snow King Resort Condominiums.

Cabin and Home Rentals
A number of Jackson Hole places offer log-cabin accommodations for a taste of old-time living. These are generally rented for several days or a week at a time and are favorites of families and groups. They may or may not have TVs and phones.

Twin Creek Cabins, five miles northeast of Jackson, tel. (307) 733-3927, has seven log cabins with kitchenettes, woodstoves, and impressive Teton vistas. They are rented by the week for $624-1,412; the largest ones sleep eight. **Mad**

Dog Ranch Cabins, on Teton Village Rd., tel. (307) 733-3729 or (800) 992-2246, has modern two-bedroom cabins with sleeping lofts, woodstoves, and a jacuzzi and rent for $129-149 per night. They sleep up to six people. **Split Creek Ranch,** nine miles north of Jackson, tel. (307) 733-7522, has log lodge units for $58 s, $64 d; kitchenettes run $79 s or d. A honeymoon cottage with a fireplace and private jacuzzi runs $180 d. Evening campfires are a favorite of guests. (See the "Grand Teton National Park Area Accommodations" chart for additional cabin rentals.)

Home rentals are available from: **Redmond Guest House,** tel. (307) 733-4003; **Elk Antler,** tel. (307) 733-3649; **Harley Varley Lodge,** tel. (307) 733-7072 or (800) 342-0833; **Jackson Hole Rental Residence,** tel. (307) 733-7503; **Steven's Guest House,** tel. (801) 565-2698; **Pearl St. Guest House,** tel. (307) 733-2833; **Andrei Moskowitz Vacation Home,** tel. (212) 721-2280.

Guest/Dude Ranches
Jackson Hole is a natural place for dude ranches and is home to several of the best-known and most luxurious ones in the state. A chart in this chapter describes nine within Jackson Hole. All offer horseback riding, hiking, cowboy cookouts, and kids' programs that make them perfect for families looking to rough-it in style. For an extra fee ranches will arrange river rafting, guided fishing, and backcountry pack trips. Two recommended old-time favorites lie within beautiful Buffalo Valley: **Turpin Meadow Guest Ranch,** tel. (307) 543-2496 or (800) 743-2496, and **Heart Six Ranch,** tel. (307) 543-2477. Both have comfortable accommodations and friendly staffs. **Triangle X Ranch,** tel. (307) 733-2183, is another recommended dude ranch with a long heritage and excellent kids' programs; it's been in the same family for more than six decades. It lies within Grand Teton National Park in a hard-to-beat setting. Jackson Hole's most elaborate guest ranch is **Lost Creek Ranch,** tel. (307) 733-3435, where the food is gourmet quality and the main lodge's patio overlooks the massive Teton range. Amenities here include such nontraditional items as a swimming pool and tennis courts, in addition to more standard horseback riding and fishing. It's all a bit too Disneyesque for my tastes, but for a mere $3,735 d per week you, too, can be pampered.

JACKSON HOLE GUEST RANCHES

The Cottonwoods Ranch; Gros Ventre River Rd. (40 miles northeast of Jackson); tel. 733-0945; small main lodge and five rustic cabins, separate bathhouse, five-night minimum stay, 4WD access only, no phones, radios, or TVs

Crescent H Ranch; Wilson; tel. 733-3674; fly-fishing, horseback riding, seven-night minimum stay

Darwin Ranch; Gros Ventre Valley north of Jackson; tel. 733-5588; small and remote high-elevation ranch, comfortable cabins, horseback riding, pack trips, very good fly-fishing, open year-round

Diamond D Ranch; Buffalo Valley, 45 miles north of Jackson; tel. 543-2479; Teton views from cabins, horseback riding, kids' programs, pack trips, wildlife tours, daily and weekly rates

Gros Ventre River Ranch; 18 miles northeast of Jackson; tel. 733-4138; small guest ranch, Teton vistas, log cabins or homestead house, horseback riding, cookouts, one mile of riverfront for fly-fishing, canoeing, mountain biking, wintertime cross-country skiing and snowmobiling, one-week minimum stay, open May-Oct. and Dec.-March.

Heart Six Ranch; Buffalo Valley, 45 miles north of Jackson; tel. 543-2477; classic family dude ranch, log cabins, kids' programs, cookouts, nature programs, rodeo, six-night minimum stay, open June to mid-Oct.

Lost Creek Ranch; 21 miles north of Jackson; tel. 733-3435; elaborate showplace ranch with Teton vistas, modern log cabins, horseback rides, pack trips, outdoor pool, tennis courts, one-week minimum stay

Moose Head Ranch; Moose; tel. 733-3141; inside Grand Teton National Park, modern log cabins, horseback riding, trout ponds, fly-fishing lessons, family atmosphere, five-night minimum stay, open mid-June through Aug.

R Lazy S Ranch; 13 miles northeast of Jackson; tel. 733-2655; historic dude ranch, log cabins, dorms for kids and teens, horseback riding, children's programs, swimming and trout ponds, fishing, one-week minimum stay, open mid-June through Sept.

Red Rock Ranch; northeast of Jackson near Gros Ventre Wilderness; tel. 733-6287; comfortable log cabins with wood stoves, horseback riding, cattle drives, pack trips, kids' programs, fishing pond, swimming pool, jacuzzi, one-week minimum stay, open June to mid-Oct.

Spotted Horse Ranch; near Hoback Jct. 14 miles south of Jackson, tel. 733-2097 or (800) 528-2084; modern log cabins along Hoback River, horseback riding (including Appaloosas), fishing, cookouts, jacuzzi, sauna

Trail Creek Ranch; Wilson; tel. 733-2610; horseback riding, swimming pool, cookouts, one-week minimum stay

Triangle X Ranch; Moose; tel. 733-2183; classic ranch with fantastic Teton views, horseback riding, kids' programs, float trips, family-oriented ranch, one-week minimum stay, open May-Oct.

Turpin Meadow Guest Ranch; Moran; tel. 543-2496 or (800) 743-2496; historic 1920s guest ranch, impressive Teton vistas, modern cabins, jacuzzi, cookouts, horseback riding, kids' programs, pack trips, natural history programs, four-night minimum stay

CAMPING

Both the National Park Service and the U.S. Forest Service maintain campgrounds around Jackson Hole. The "Jackson Hole Public Campgrounds" and "Jackson Hole RV Parks" charts show 26 public campgrounds and 11 private RV parks within 50 miles of Jackson. For more specifics on public sites, contact Bridger-Teton

National Forest in Jackson at 340 N. Cache, tel. (307) 739-5500, or Grand Teton National Park in Moose, tel. (307) 739-3603. In addition to these sites, many people camp for free in dispersed sites on Forest Service lands; see the Forest Service for restrictions.

None of the private RV parks in Jackson itself is really noteworthy; "parking lots" would be a better term. Seventeen miles south of town, **Astoria Mineral Hot Springs RV Park,** tel. (307) 733-2659, is along the river and has a naturally heated outdoor mineral pool with 95° F water. It's illegal to park RVs overnight on Jackson streets, and the ordinance is strictly enforced by the police.

FOOD

Jackson stands out from the rest of Wyoming on the culinary scene: chicken-fried steak may be available, but it certainly isn't the house speciality! You won't need to look far to find good food; in fact, the town seems to overflow with impressive (and even more impressively priced) eateries. At least 70 local restaurants do business here—in a town that the Census Bureau says contains just 4,500 people! To get an idea of what to expect at local restaurants, pick up a copy of the free **Jackson Hole Dining Guide** at the visitor center or local restaurants. It includes

---

JACKSON HOLE PUBLIC CAMPGROUNDS

Many Forest Service (FS) campgrounds can be reserved ($8.25 extra) by calling (800) 280-2267; they are noted by the word "reservable" below. National Park Service (NPS) campsites are available on a first-come, first-served basis only.

Jenny Lake Campground; 20 miles north of Jackson; open mid-May to late Sept.; $10; NPS; tents only; fills by 8 a.m. in midsummer

Signal Mountain Campground; 32 miles north of Jackson; open early May to mid-Oct.; $10; NPS; on Jackson Lake; fills by 10 a.m. in midsummer

Colter Bay Campground; 40 miles north of Jackson; open mid-May to late Sept.; $10; NPS; on Jackson Lake; coin-operated showers, fills by noon in midsummer

Pacific Creek Campground; 46 miles north of Jackson; open June-Nov.; free; FS; 12 miles up Pacific Creek Rd.

Lizard Creek Campground; 48 miles north of Jackson; open early June to early Sept.; $10; NPS; on Jackson Lake; fills by 2 p.m. in midsummer

Snake River Campground; 55 miles north of Jackson; open June 15-Sept. 10; $10; NPS; off U.S. 89/287 near Flagg Ranch; fills by 2 p.m. in midsummer

Sheffield Creek Campground; 55 miles north of Jackson; open mid-June to mid-Nov.; free; FS; off Hwy. 89/287 near Flagg Ranch

Curtis Canyon Campground; seven miles northeast of Jackson; open early June to mid-Sept.; $7; FS; six miles of gravel road, reservable

Gros Ventre Campground; 10 miles northeast of Jackson; open May to early Oct.; $10; NPS; along Gros Ventre River; often fills by evening in midsummer

Atherton Creek Campground; 18 miles northeast of Jackson; open early June-Oct.; $8; FS; five miles up Gros Ventre Rd. (dirt) near Gros Ventre River, reservable

Red Hills Campground; 22 miles northeast of Jackson; open early June-Oct.; $5; FS; four miles up Gros Ventre Rd. (dirt) along Gros Ventre River, reservable

Crystal Creek Campground; 23 miles northeast of Jackson; open early June-Oct.; $5; FS; five miles up Gros Ventre Rd. (dirt) near Gros Ventre River, reservable

(continues on next page)

JACKSON HOLE PUBLIC CAMPGROUNDS

(continued)

Hatchet Campground; 40 miles northeast of Jackson; open June to mid-Nov.; $5; FS; in Buffalo Valley

Blackrock Bicycle Campground; 40 miles northeast of Jackson; open mid-June through Oct.; free; FS; bikes only, three miles off U.S. 26/287 in Buffalo Valley, no potable water

Angles Campground; 45 miles northeast of Jackson; open June-Nov.; free; FS; near Togwotee Mountain Lodge

Box Creek Campground; 46 miles northeast of Jackson; open mid-June through Nov.; free; FS; off Buffalo Valley Rd., no potable water

Turpin Meadow Campground; 48 miles northeast of Jackson; open June-Oct.; $5; FS; in Buffalo Valley

Cabin Creek Campground; 19 miles south of Jackson; open late May to mid-Sept.; $8; FS; along Snake River, reservable

Elbow Campground; 22 miles south of Jackson; open mid-June to mid-Sept.; $8; FS; along Snake River, reservable

East Table Creek Campground; 24 miles south of Jackson; open early June to mid-Sept.; $8; FS; along Snake River, reservable

Station Creek Campground; 25 miles south of Jackson; open mid-June to mid-Sept.; $8; FS; along Snake River, reservable

Hoback Campground; 22 miles southeast of Jackson; open early June to mid-Sept.; $8; FS; along Hoback River, reservable

Kozy Campground; 30 miles southeast of Jackson; open early June to mid-Sept.; $5; FS; along Hoback River, reservable

Granite Creek Campground; 35 miles southeast of Jackson; open late June to mid-Sept.; $8; FS; near hot springs, nine miles up Granite Creek Rd. (gravel), reservable

Trail Creek Campground; 20 miles west of Jackson; open mid-June to mid-Sept.; $6; FS; west of Teton Pass

Mike Harris Campground; 21 miles west of Jackson; open mid-June to mid-Sept.; $6; FS; west of Teton Pass off State 22

sample menus and brief descriptions of most local establishments. If you don't find a place to your liking among those listed below, be assured that all the major fast-food outlets line Jackson's streets, ready to grease your digestive tract. And if you just want to eat in, call **Mountain Express,** tel. (307) 734-0123, which will deliver meals from more than a dozen local restaurants to your place in Jackson or Teton Village.

Breakfast

The best breakfast place in Jackson isn't in Jackson. **Nora's Fish Creek Inn** in Wilson, tel. (307) 733-8288, attracts a full house each morning with great, reasonably priced food, friendly waitresses,

and an authentically rustic atmosphere. Nora's also serves tried-and-true lunches and dinners at very good prices. Highly recommended. Ask President Bill Clinton—he ate here in 1995. Also very popular for breakfast and lunch is **Jedediah's House of Sourdough,** 135 E. Broadway, tel. (307) 733-5671, where, as the name implies, sourdough pancakes are the specialty. The old-time crowd heads to Jackson's greasy spoon for breakfast and other meals: **LeJay's Sportsman's Cafe,** 72 S. Glenwood St., tel. (307) 733-3110. Open 24 hours a day, this is the place to go when no other restaurant is open and your stomach is demanding all-American grub. Be ready for clouds of cigarette smoke. Another long-time breakfast

and lunch favorite is **The Bunnery,** 130 N. Cache, tel. (307) 733-5474, but the quality and service have suffered of late.

Lunch

One of the most popular noontime spots in Jackson is **Sweetwater Restaurant,** 85 King St., tel. (307) 733-3553, where the lunch menu includes dependably good salads, homemade soups, and a variety of earthy sandwiches. For dinner, try mesquite-grilled lamb or the spinach-and-feta vegetarian casserole. Recommended. **Pearl Street Bagels,** 145 Pearl St., tel. (307) 739-1218, serves home-baked bagels and espresso. Open daily till 6 p.m. in the summer. Get delicious sub sandwiches on tangy homemade bread at **New York City Sub Shop,** 25 S. Glenwood St., tel. (307) 733-4414. Fastest sandwich makers in

the business. Across the street, **Anthony's Little Italy,** 70 S. Glenwood St., tel. (307) 733-9717, has homemade subs made on sourdough rolls. **Hot or Not Deli,** 75 E. Pearl St., tel. (307) 733-3354, serves hot and cold sandwiches of all types, fresh salads, soups, desserts, and espresso. It's one of the best delis in Jackson.

If you're in search of a substantial vegetarian breakfast or lunch, try the cafe at **Harvest Organic Foods,** 130 W. Broadway, tel. (307) 733-5418. The organic salad and soup bar is a very popular lunch break for locals. Great sandwiches and baked goods, too. **Jackson Drug,** established in 1912 and in the same place since 1937, has a very popular soda fountain that serves homemade ice cream. It's located right on town square at 15 E. Deloney Ave., tel. (307) 733-2442.

JACKSON HOLE RV PARKS

Note: rates quoted for RVs are for full hookups. Rates do not include six percent state and local taxes. Area code is 307.

Astoria Mineral Hot Springs; near Hoback Jct. (17 miles south of Jackson); tel. 733-2659; $22 for RVs; $18 for tents; hot springs pool, playground, open May to early Sept.

Colter Bay RV Park; 30 miles north of Jackson near Moran; tel. 543-2855; $25 for RVs; no tents; evening nature programs, open late May to early Oct.

Elk Country Inn; 480 W. Pearl; tel. 733-2364 or (800) 483-8667; $30 for RVs; no tents

Flagg Ranch Village Campground; Rockefeller Parkway (55 miles north of Jackson); tel. 733-8761 or (800) 443-2311; $25 for RVs; $17 for tents; evening ranger programs, open May-Sept.

Grand Teton Park KOA; 36 miles northeast of Jackson on U.S. 26/287; tel. 733-1980 or (800) 562-3948; $26 for RVs; $18 for tents; hot tub, game room, playground, bike rentals, simple cabins available, evening summertime nature programs, open year-round

Lazy J Corral; Hoback Jct.; tel. 733-1554; $23 for RVs; no tents, open mid-May to mid-Oct.

Lone Eagle Campground; 15 miles south of Jackson near Hoback Jct.; tel. 733-1090 or (800) 321-3800; $32 for RVs; $20 for tents; package rates available, outdoor pool, hot tub, simple cabins and tepees available, open May to mid-Sept.

Snake River Park KOA; Hoback Jct.; tel. 733-7078 or (800) 562-1878; $30 for RVs; $23 for tents; simple cabins available, open mid-April to early Oct.

Teton Village KOA; Teton Village Rd.; tel. 733-5354 or (800) 562-9043; $30 for RVs; $23 for tents; game room, playground, simple cabins available, open May to mid-Oct.

Virginian RV Park; 750 W. Broadway; tel. 733-7189 or (800) 262-4999; $30-35 for RVs; no tents, outdoor pool, game room, open May to mid-Oct.

Wagon Wheel RV Park & Campground; 525 N. Cache; tel. 733-4588; $21 for RVs; $18 for tents; open May-Sept.

JACKSON HOLE VICINITY

GRAND TETON

NATIONAL PARK

JENNY LAKE

TO COLTER BAY, MORAN, AND ROCKEFELLER PKWY.

BRIDGER - TETON

NATIONAL

FOREST

ALASKA BASIN

MOOSE VISITOR CENTER

ANTELOPE FLATS RD.

TETON SCIENCE SCHOOL

ATHERTON CREEK

GROS VENTRE SLIDE

LOWER SLIDE LAKE

RED HILLS

TO GRAND TARGHEE SKI AREA AND IDAHO FALLS, ID

DEATH CANYON

GRANITE CANYON

PHELPS LAKE

JACKSON HOLE AIRPORT

KELLY

CRYSTAL CREEK

GROS VENTRE RIVER

RENDEZVOUS MOUNTAIN (10,927 ft)

JACKSON HOLE SKI AREA

TETON VILLAGE

GOLF COURSE

GROS VENTRE

FISH HATCHERY

33

MOOSE WILSON RD.

SPRING CREEK NORDIC CENTER

NATIONAL

22

JACKSON HOLE RACQUET CLUB

390

26

89

ELK

REFUGE VISITOR CENTER

CURTIS CANYON

GROS VENTRE

TRAIL CREEK

COAL CREEK

WILSON

REFUGE

WILDERNESS

TETON PASS (8,431 ft)

SPRING CREEK RESORT

SPRING CREEK GULCH RD.

EAST GROS VENTRE BUTTE

WEST GROS VENTRE BUTTE

JACKSON

GRANITE HOT SPRINGS

TARGHEE

NATIONAL

189

BRIDGER - TETON

191

SNAKE

RANGE

NATIONAL

FOREST

GROS

VENTRE

GRANITE

CREEK

RANGE

FOREST

IDAHO

WYOMING

HOBACK JUNCTION

ASTORIA HOT SPRINGS

HOGBACK

189

RIVER

RIVER

26

WILLOW CREEK

191

BONDURANT

PALISADES RESERVOIR

89

SNAKE

GRAND CANYON

ALPINE

0   10 mi

0   10 km

TO AFTON (SOUTHWEST WY)

TO PINEDALE (WIND RIVER MOUNTAINS COUNTRY)

© MOON PUBLICATIONS, INC.

Cafes and Espresso Places

Climbers and ski bums wear their Vuarnets to the oft-crowded **Shades Cafe,** 82 S. King St., tel. (307) 733-2015. The tiny log cabin has a summer-only patio on the side, and delicious salads, quiches, burritos, and espresso coffees. It's a great place to hang out, though it does close early in the fall, winter, and spring. Teton Village has a second (winter-only) Shades Cafe, tel. (307) 733-7091. Also in Teton Village is **Village Cafe,** tel. (307) 733-5998, where you'll dis-

cover very good breakfasts, baked goods, sandwiches, lasagna, burritos, coffees, and microbrewed beer. Open summers and winters only. **Betty Rock Cafe and Coffeehouse,** 325 W. Pearl, tel. (307) 733-0747, is a popular espresso place with tasty soups and salads.

The National Museum of Wildlife Art, two miles north of Jackson on U.S. 26/89, houses a delightfully bright little place with dramatic vistas across the National Elk Refuge. Called **Rising Sage Cafe,** tel. (307) 733-8649, its lunch menu

includes panini, pita and hummus, homemade soups served in a bread bowl, salads, and espresso. It's open the same hours as the museum. **Charlie's Jackson Hole Coffee Company,** 49 W. Broadway (upstairs in Pink Garter Plaza), tel. (307) 733-9192 or (800) 771-9192, has espresso and sweets, along with a computer terminal for Internet access.

Sugarfoot Cafe, 145 N. Glenwood, tel. (307) 733-9148, is an attractive little cafe housed within one of Jackson's oldest buildings—it was originally a saddle shop. The menu always includes delicious pastas and seafood, plus smoked pork chops, roasted chicken, and other specials. Entrées with salad go for $13-18. Sugarfoot is open for dinners only Jan.-March and July-Sept. (closed the remainder of the year).

American

The most popular locals' eatery is **Bubba's Bar-B-Que Restaurant,** 515 W. Broadway, tel. (307) 733-2288. Each evening the parking lot out front is jammed with folks waiting patiently for a chance to chew the marvelous barbecued spare ribs, savor the spicy chicken wings, or fill up at the impressive salad bar. Lunch is a real bargain at this four-stars place, with specials under $5.

Get great all-American burgers at the '50s-style **Billy's Burgers,** 55 N. Cache, tel. (307) 733-3279. This is the same location as the more upscale Cadillac Grille. When President Clinton visited Jackson in 1995, he ate at the Cadillac but ordered his burgers from Billy's. I'm told that Clinton called it the best burger he'd ever eaten—and this is coming from a man who knows his burgers. The Billy burger is a half-pound monster. Not on the menu, but recommended if you aren't ravishingly hungry is the one-third-pound Betty burger. Ask for it.

Next door to Billy's and the Cadillac is the **Million Dollar Cowboy Steakhouse,** tel. (307) 733-4790, with "casual Western elegance" and great steaks, from porterhouse to filet mignon. Also popular is **Gun Barrel Steakhouse,** 862 W. Broadway, tel. (307) 733-3287, where the mesquite-grilled steaks and wild game are served up in a hunting lodge atmosphere of trophy game mounts (they came from a wildlife museum that previously occupied the site). You'll find lots of historic guns and other Old West

paraphernalia around the Gun Barrel too, making this an interesting place to explore even if you aren't eating here. It's a bit on the pricey side, with dinner entrées for $12-18.

Head three miles south of town on U.S. 89 to find some of the finest steaks in Jackson Hole at the **Steak Pub,** tel. (307) 733-6977. Dinners are served in a rustic log-cabin setting. Another recommended place is **Camp Creek Inn,** 16 miles south of Jackson in Hoback Canyon. The cozy fireplace and rustic setting make this a good place to get away from the Jackson Hole crowds. Very good steaks and prime rib, and "no mercy" one-pound burgers enough to fill anyone. **Horse Creek Station,** 10 miles south of Jackson, tel. (307) 733-0810, serves delicious smokehouse meats including pork chops, baby back ribs, chicken, prime rib, and brisket in an Old West atmosphere with stuffed animal heads on the walls. A very popular place with both locals and ski bums is the **Mangy Moose** in Teton Village, tel. (307) 733-4913, where you'll find a big salad bar and fair prices on steak, pasta, chicken, and seafood.

Wilson's **Stagecoach Bar,** tel. (307) 733-4407, makes delicious nachos, burgers, and other pub grub. Get chicken atchaflaya, seafood gumbo, crawfish and shrimp etouffee, fried catfish, and other Cajun specialties at **The Acadian House,** 180 N. Millward, tel. (307) 739-1269.

Pasta and Pizza

One of the tried-and-true local restaurants is **Anthony's Italian Restaurant,** 62 S. Glenwood St., tel. (307) 733-3717. Prices are very reasonable, and vegetarians will find several good menu items. Dinners come with homemade soup, salad, and fresh garlic bread—guaranteed to fill you up and then some.

Several pizza places stand out in Jackson. You'll find **Calico Italian Restaurant & Bar,** tel. (307) 733-2460, in a garish red and white building three-quarters of a mile north on Teton Village Road. The menu has gone a bit upscale of late, but prices are still reasonable. During the summer, be sure to get a side salad, fresh from the big house garden; kids will love the two-and-a-half-acre lawn. The bar at Calico is a very popular locals' watering hole. **Mt. High Pizza Pie,** 120 W. Broadway, tel. (307) 733-3646, is a favorite downtown place with free delivery in Jackson.

From mid-September through April, Mt. High's $5.25 stuff-yourself lunchtime pizza buffet (Mon.-Fri. 11:30 a.m.-1:30 p.m.) is the best meal deal in Jackson. Get delicious gourmet pizzas and calzone—baked in a wood-fired oven—at Jackson Hole Pub & Brewery (described below under "Breweries and Wine Shops").

Continental/Nouvelle Cuisine

If you want fine continental dining and aren't scared off by entrees costing $17-27, Jackson has much to offer. In a plethora of fine European restaurants, one stands out: **Stiegler's**, tel. (307) 733-1071, in the Aspens on Teton Village Road. The menu has names big enough to eat—you could start with leberknödel suppe, before a main course of chicken breast aux trois citrons, followed by a topfen palatschinken. The dense Austrian cuisine is simply outstanding, but the portions are small. If you enjoy German cooking, particularly beef, lamb, and game, head to the **Alpenhof**, tel. (307) 733-3462, in Teton Village. The Alpenhof Bistro next door has a lighter and less-expensive dinner menu.

Gouloff's, across from the Aspens on Teton Village Rd., tel. (307) 733-1886, features "Teton cuisine" such as pistachio-nut chicken, elk medallions, and seafood lorenzo. Very nice. **The Range**, 225 N. Cache, tel. (307) 733-5481, serves excellent fixed-price nouvelle-cuisine dinners, making this a favorite of out-on-the-town locals. For views so spectacular they make it difficult to concentrate on your meal, don't miss **The Granary**, tel. (307) 733-8833, located atop East Gros Ventre Butte west of Jackson. This is also a very popular place for evening cocktails, and its Sunday brunch is the best around.

An excellent in-town continental restaurant is **The Blue Lion**, 160 N. Millward St., tel. (307) 733-3912. The front patio makes for delightful summertime dining. Try the tempeh crepes or Sicilian chicken. Jackson's most popular nouvelle-cuisine restaurant is **Cadillac Grille**, 55 N. Cache (on the square), tel. (307) 733-3279. The food is artfully prepared and includes a constantly changing menu of seafood, grilled meats, and game. The art-deco decor of the Cadillac helps make it one of the most crowded tourist hangouts in town. Portions tend toward the small side, however.

One of Jackson's newest gourmet eateries is **Snake River Grill**, 84 E. Broadway, tel. (307) 733-0557, with an expensive menu of lamb, chicken, seafood, and other specialties. It's owned in part by one of Jackson's best-known residents, Harrison Ford. **Jenny Lake Lodge**, inside Grand Teton National Park, is famous for gourmet American cuisine served in an elegantly cozy log lodge. The Sunday dinner buffet is legendary. Open June-Sept. only; call (307) 733-4647 for reservations (required).

South of the Border

Get very good Mexican fast food at **The Merry Piglets**, 160 N. Cache, tel. (307) 733-2966, including their specialty, the cheese crisp. **Cafe a Mano**, 45 S. Glenwood, tel. (307) 739-2500, has healthy fast food for a good price, including New Mexico-style burritos, tacos, quesadillas, and salads. Top them off with a choice of salsas from the big salsa bar. Early in the day, stop in for a coffee and New Orleans-style beignets.

Mama Inez, 380 W. Pearl, tel. (307) 739-9166, has fill-you-up servings of authentic Mexican cooking, including chimichangas, fajitas, and enchiladas. The largest and most popular Mexican restaurant is **Vista Grande**, tel. (307) 733-6964, on the road to Teton Village. The biggest drawing cards here are the pitchers of margaritas; the food is reasonably priced but nothing special.

Chinese Food

Chinatown Restaurant, 850 W. Broadway, tel. (307) 733-8856, makes good Chinese dishes—particularly the mu shu vegetables, lemon chicken, and their pot stickers—and offers bargain-priced lunch specials. The always-busy **Lame Duck Chinese Restaurant**, 600 E. Broadway, tel. (307) 733-4311, serves Chinese, Japanese, and other Asian specialties. The food is a bit less traditional than Chinatown's.

Breweries and Wine Shops

Prior to Prohibition in 1920, nearly every town in Wyoming had its own brewery, making such local favorites as Hillcrest, Schoenhofen, and Sweetwater. After repeal of "the noble experiment," breweries again popped up, but competition from industrial giants such as Anheuser-Busch and Coors forced the last Wyoming operation—Sheridan Brewing—out of business in

1954. It was another 34 years before commercial beermaking returned. In 1988, Charlie Otto started a tiny backyard operation in Wilson, **Otto Brothers Brewery,** tel. (307) 733-9000. It still cranks out handcrafted Teton Ale, Old Faithful Ale, Moose Juice Stout, and seasonal brews, which you'll find on tap at many Jackson-area bars and restaurants and in 22-ounce returnable bottles. Or take some home in a "growler," a half-gallon refillable bottle available at local liquor stores. The little downtown-Wilson brewery is open for tours and tasting Mon.-Fri. 10 a.m.-4 p.m., and a small shop in the log cabin out front sells classy T-shirts and glasses.

Jackson Hole Pub & Brewery, 265 S. Millward, tel. (307) 739-2337, opened in 1994 and is the opposite of low-key Otto Brothers. Owned by a former New York securities analyst, the brewery is housed in a spacious old warehouse that has been beautifully remodeled. Production now exceeds 3,500 barrels per year, and a bottling line produces beer for sale outside the brewpub. The beer—particularly the Snake River Zonker Stout—has received numerous awards at national beer festivals. The brewpub's bar generally has nearly a dozen Snake River beers on tap, with Zonker Stout, Snake River Lager, and Snake River Pale Ale always available. The lunch and dinner cafe menu includes delicious thin-crust wood-fired pizzas and calzone, a bruschetta appetizer, daily pasta specials, sandwiches, and salads. Great food and a lively, bright atmosphere.

The most complete local wine and beer shops are **Teton Liquors West,** next to Westside Store in the Aspens along Teton Village Rd., tel. (307) 733-5038; **The Liquor Store,** next to Albertson's at 520 W. Broadway, tel. (307) 733-4466; and **Dornan's** in Moose, tel. (307) 733-2415.

Groceries and Bakeries
Get groceries from the always-crowded **Albertson's,** 520 W. Broadway, tel. (307) 733-9222, or from **Food Town** next to the Pamida store at 970 W. Broadway, tel. (307) 733-0450.

For health foods, head downtown to **Harvest Organic Foods,** 130 W. Broadway, tel. (307) 733-5418, or to **Here & Now Natural Foods,** 1925 Moose-Wilson Rd., tel. (307) 733-2742.

Located along Fish Creek in Wilson, **Patty-Cake Patisserie,** 1230 N. Ida Lane, tel. (307) 733-7225, is a full bakery with wonderful sweets, a fine deli, and espresso coffees. In Jackson, get fresh baked goods at **Harvest Bakery & Cafe,** 130 W. Broadway, tel. (307) 733-5418.

ENTERTAINMENT

Nightlife
Barflies will keep buzzing in Jackson, especially during midsummer and midwinter, when visitors pack local saloons every night of the week. At least one nightclub always seems to have live tunes; check Jackson's free newspapers to see where. Cover charges are generally only a couple of bucks on the weekends, and many times you'll get in free.

The famous **Million Dollar Cowboy Bar,** on the west side of town square, tel. (307) 733-2207, is a favorite of cowboys and wannabe cowboys. The four pool tables at the front are almost always in use. Inside the Cowboy you'll discover burled lodgepole pine beams, display cases with stuffed dead bears and other cuddly critters, bars inlaid with old silver dollars, and saddles for barstools. Until the 1950s, the Cowboy was Jackson's center for illegal gambling. Bartenders kept a close eye on Teton Pass, where messengers used mirrors to deliver warnings of coming federal revenuers, giving folks at the bar time to hide the gaming tables in a back room. Today the dance floor fills with honkytonking couples as the bands croon lonesome cowboy tunes six nights a week. Looking to learn swing dancing? Every Thursday you can join a free beginners' class at 7:30 p.m., then dance up a storm when the band comes on at 9.

Just across the square is **Rancher Spirits & Billiards,** where the atmosphere is a bit more relaxed and the music closer to countrified rock. A few genuine cowboys still frequent it. Upstairs you'll find a big room filled with pool aficionados; it's the biggest billiard hall in Wyoming. **J.J.'s Silver Dollar Bar and Grill,** in the Wort Hotel at 50 N. Glenwood St., tel. (307) 733-2190, offers a setting that might seem more fitting in Las Vegas: gaudy pink neon lights curve around a bar inlaid with 2,032 (count 'em!) silver dollars. It tends to attract an older crowd. You'll have to sing your own tunes at the Silver Dollar since bands don't play here. Four blocks away, at 385 W. Broadway, tel. (307) 733-3853, is **Spirits of the West,** which attracts the young "skids" (ski kids) crowd. No cowboy hats in sight. Spirits has music and comedy some nights, along with karaoke and open-mike nights. **Gun Barrel Steakhouse,** 862 W. Broadway, tel. (307) 733-3287, has live country bands once a week or so, and they always have 18 draft beers on tap—more than anyplace else in Wyoming.

Jackson Hole Pub & Brewery, 265 S. Millward, tel. (307) 739-2337, has live jazz on Tuesday nights and periodically features blues or bluegrass bands. A fun place to relax. **Shady Lady Saloon,** in the Snow King Resort at 400 E. Snow King Ave., tel. (307) 733-5200, has live music or DJ tunes most nights.

Three other popular bars are in Teton Village. Right next to the tram, the **Mangy Moose Saloon,** tel. (307) 733-4913, attracts a hip skier, outdoorsy crowd with reggae, blues, or rock bands most nights of the week during the summer and winter. It's Jackson Hole's jumpingest pick-up spot. At **The Sojourner,** tel. (307) 733-3657, you can sip a beer and munch on the free hors d'oeuvres while watching basketball games on the wide-screen TV. **Dietrich's Bistro,** in the Alpenhof, tel. (307) 733-3242, has mellow music along with free tortillas and salsa during the winter.

Over in Wilson, **The Stagecoach,** tel. (307) 733-4407, is the place to be on Sunday nights 5:30-10 p.m. (Wyoming bars close their doors at 10 p.m. on Sunday.) In the early '70s, when hippies risked getting their heads shaved by rednecks at Jackson's Cowboy Bar, they found the 'Coach a more tolerant place. Today tobacco-chewing cowpokes show their partners slick moves on the tiny dance floor as the Stagecoach

Band runs through the country tunes one more time—the band has performed here every Sunday since February 16, 1969! For more entertainment, try a game of pool on one of the three tables, or a tasty buffalo burger. Out in Moose, **Dornan's,** tel. (307) 733-2415, has a Monday night Hootenanny where local musicians get together to jam. Join the onstage fun if you have musical talent (or can pretend).

Live Theater and Movies

In addition to the bar scene, summers bring a number of lighthearted acting ventures to Jackson. For musicals with an Old West theme—such as *Paint Your Wagon*—head to **Jackson Hole Playhouse,** 145 W. Deloney, tel. (307) 733-6994. Productions of such Broadway comedies as *Fiddler on the Roof, You Can't Take it with You,* and *The Pirates of Penzance* play at the **Mainstage Theatre,** 50 W. Broadway, tel. (307) 733-3670. These are family favorites; reservations are strongly recommended.

Watch flicks at **Teton Theatre,** 120 N. Cache, tel. (307) 733-6744; **Jackson Hole Twin Cinema,** 295 W. Pearl St., tel. (307) 733-4939; or **MovieWorks Cinema Four-plex,** 860 S. U.S. 89, tel. (307) 733-4939. Mainstage Theatre also has a screen and shows the cheapest matinees in town.

Chuck Wagon Shows

Folks also flock to the all-you-can-eat barbecue cookouts and western musical performances at three nearby ranches. Reservations are strongly suggested in midsummer. **Bar T-5,** 790 Cache Cr. Rd., tel. (307) 733-5386 or (800) 772-5386, is the most rustic of the lot, with a wagon train ride to the peaceful site of the cookout along Cache Creek; it charges $26 for adults, $21 for ages 9-14, $18 for ages 4-8, and free for kids under three. Entertainment in this family-run operation includes "singing cowboys, Indians, and mountain men." **Bar J,** on the Moose-Wilson Rd. near Teton Pines, tel. (307) 733-3370 or (800) 905-2275, is known for its first-rate musicians who perform winters in Tucson, Arizona. The meal and entertainment take place indoors and cost $13 for adults, $5 for kids under eight, and free for tots.

A/OK Corral, 10 miles south of Jackson near Hoback Jct., tel. (307) 733-6556, has two-hour horseback or covered wagon rides that end at an outdoor cookout where you chow down on

steak suppers or big ranch breakfasts. These dinners are $35 for adults with the horseback ride, $24 with a covered wagon ride. For kids, a covered wagon ride and dinner is $16. Breakfasts cost $18-26 for adults, $12 for kids.

Located in beautiful Buffalo Valley, 40 miles northwest of Jackson, **Box K Ranch,** tel. (307) 543-2407 or (800) 729-1410, has 20-minute covered wagon rides that take you to a cowboy steak cookout with low-key entertainment. Dinners are $22 for adults, $17 for kids under 12. Breakfast cookouts cost $12 for adults, $9 for kids.

Green River Outfitters, tel. (307) 733-1044, has combination trail rides and cookouts in the Gros Ventre Mountains 35 miles south of Jackson. These cost $110 per person, including guided horseback rides, roundtrip transport from Jackson, and a barbecued steak lunch.

EVENTS

Jackson Hole is packed with entertaining events almost every day of the year. Some of these are little homegrown affairs, such as the county fair or the annual spring cleanup, while others attract people from near and far. Of particular note are the Rocky Mountain Stage Stop Sled Dog Race, the Pole-Peddle-Paddle Race, the Elk Antler Auction, the Grand Teton Music Festival, and the Jackson Hole Fall Arts Festival. (In addition to these listed below, see "Grand Targhee Ski Resort" under "Downhill Skiing and Snowboarding" later in this chapter for year-round events on the other side of the Tetons.)

Winter and Spring

Kick the year off by watching (or participating in) the annual **torchlight ski parades** at all three local ski areas. They take place on Christmas and New Year's Eves at Grand Targhee, Christmas Day and New Year's Eve at Jackson Hole Ski Resort, and New Year's Eve at Snow King. Each January and February local Shriners hold horse-drawn **cutter races**—essentially a wild chariot race on a quarter-mile of sheer ice—at Melody Ranch six miles south of Jackson. Call (307) 733-3316 for more info.

The **Rocky Mountain Stage Stop Sled Dog Race** began in 1996 and proved to be an immediate hit. Unlike other races such as the Iditarod,

this one is run in nine 30- to 80-mile s teams ending in a new town each nigh the Tour de France, it's the total time that in this stage race. The race starts in Jacks stops for the night in Moran, Dubois, Pinedal Lander, Atlantic City, Kemmerer, Box Y Guest Ranch (Greys River area), and Afton and ends at Alpine. Already, the race has attracted some of the top names in dog mushing, including Alaskans Susan Butcher, Libby Riddles, Rick Swenson, and Dee Dee Jonrowe. The Rocky Mountain Stage Stop Sled Dog Race is held over 10 days in early February and has a $100,000 purse. Call (307) 733-3316 for details.

Ski races take place all winter long, ranging from elegant "Powder Eight" Championships in mid-February to blazingly fast freestyle cross-country races. (Volunteer to work one of the gates at a downhill race and you get to ski free the rest of the day.) The ski season ends in early April with the **Pole-Pedal-Paddle Race,** combining alpine skiing, cross-country skiing, cycling, and canoeing in a wild, tough competition. It's the largest such event in the West and great fun for spectators and contestants—many of whom dress up in goofy costumes. Call (307) 733-6433 for details.

The second weekend of May brings the Jackson **Spring Cleanup,** where the main attraction for visitors is a cattle drive through the center of town. Call (307) 733-3316 for more info. Then comes one of the favorites. On the third Saturday in May, the world's only public **elk antler auction** takes place on the town square, attracting hundreds of buyers from all over the globe. Local Boy Scouts collect three tons of antlers from the nearby National Elk Refuge each spring, with the proceeds helping to fund feeding of the elk. This may sound like an odd event, but the high demand for antlers in the insatiable (pun intended) South Korean and Chinese aphrodisiac markets have made antlers worth more than $14 per pound, so the bidding is highly competitive. There's more than a touch of irony in the Boy Scouts making money from the sale of sexual stimulants! Call (307) 733-3086 for more info.

Summer

Memorial Day weekend brings **Old West Days,** complete with Indian dancing, cowboy poetry, a street dance, a western barbecue, rodeos, a

vous, and other festivi-
5 for details. The **Fourth**
vent, with a parade and
show from Snow King

Saturday nights in the
watch bucking broncs, rodeo clowns, and hard-riding cowboys at the **Jackson Rodeo** on the Teton County Fair Grounds. Kids get to join in the calf scramble. The rodeo starts at 8 p.m. and costs $7 for adults, $5 for ages 4-12, $22 for the whole family; call (307) 733-2805 for details.

In existence for more than 35 years, the outstanding **Grand Teton Music Festival** is held at Teton Village. Performances of classical and modern works by world-renowned symphony musicians are the highlight of this extravaganza. The concerts are held June-Aug. each year; call (307) 733-3050 for a schedule of events and price information.

The last weekend of July brings an always-fun **Teton County Fair,** tel. (307) 733-5289, The demolition derby gives a bang-up finale to the festivities. In early September, the **Jackson Hole One-Fly Contest** attracts anglers from all over, including a number of celebrity competitors. For details, call (307) 733-3270.

Fall

Jackson Hole is at its most glorious in the fall, as aspens and cottonwoods turn a fire of yellow against the Tetons. Many of the tourists have fled back home, leaving locals and hardier visitors to savor the cool autumn nights. The major autumn event is the **Jackson Hole Fall Arts Festival,** featuring exhibits at the National Museum of Wildlife Art and local galleries, concerts, art demonstrations, dance performances, theater productions, and other events from mid- to late September. The annual Arts for the Parks National Art Competition (not for amateurs; the purse is $50,000) during the festival attracts thousands of paintings representing scenes from America's national parks. Also fun is a "quick draw" in which artists paint, draw, and sculpt while you watch; the pieces are then auctioned off. For more info and a schedule of the many events, call (307) 733-3316. At the tail end of the Arts Festival comes **Quilting in the Tetons,** a week of exhibits, classes, and quilting demonstrations. Call (307) 733-3087 for details.

RIVER RAFTING

Jackson Hole's most popular summertime recreational activity is running Wyoming's largest river, the Snake. Each year more than 125,000 people climb aboard rafts, canoes, and kayaks to float down placid reaches of the Snake or to blast through the boiling rapids of Snake River Canyon. (As an aside, the name "Snake" comes from the Shoshone Indians, who used serpentine hand movements as sign language for their tribal name—a motion trappers misinterpreted as a snake and applied to the river flowing through Shoshone land.)

Many different rafting companies offer dozens of different raft trips each day of the summer, so it generally isn't necessary to make reservations until the day you plan to go. Prepare to get wet. You may want to ask around to determine the advantages of each company—some are cheaper but require you to drive a good distance from town; others offer more experienced crews; still others provide various perks such as fancy meals, overnight camps along the river, or boats with fewer people. Also be sure to ask if you get to do any of the paddling or not. Note that this is pretty far from being a wilderness experience, especially in mid-July, when stretches of the river looks like a Los Angeles freeway with traffic jams of rafts, kayaks, inner tubes, and other flotsam and jetsam. The rafting companies generally operate from mid-May to late September. Get a complete listing of floating and boating outfits along with descriptive brochures at the Wyoming State Information Center in Jackson. Excellent maps of the Grand Canyon of the Snake River (printed on plastic) are sold at the Forest Service office at 340 N. Cache. In addition to the rapids, these describe the geology of the area and other features.

Float Trips

The gentlest way to see the Snake is by taking one of the many commercial float trips. Along the way, you'll be treated to stunning views of the Tetons and glimpses of eagles, ospreys, beavers, and perhaps moose or other wildlife along the riverbanks. Many local rafting companies offer five- or 10-mile scenic float trips along the quiet stretch within Grand Teton National Park, generally putting in at Deadman's

Bar or Schwabacher Landing and taking out in Moose. Prices run $30 for adults and $20 for children. Roundtrip transportation from Jackson is included by most companies. A wide variety of special voyages are also available, including overnight camping, fish and float, and even bike and float trips.

Call one of the following raft companies for details, or pick up one of their slick brochures at the visitor center or from their tiny offices scattered around town: **Barker-Ewing Float Trips,** tel. (307) 733-1800 or (800) 365-1800; **Flagg Ranch Rafting,** tel. (307) 543-2861 or (800) 443-2311; **Fort Jackson Float Trips,** tel. (307) 733-2583 or (800) 735-8430; **Grand Teton Lodge Float Trips,** tel. (307) 543-2811; **Heart Six Ranch,** tel. (307) 543-2477 or 739-9477; **Lewis & Clark Expeditions,** tel. (307) 733-4022 or (800) 824-5375; **Signal Mountain Lodge,** tel. (307) 733-5470 or 543-2831; **Solitude Float Trips,** tel. (307) 733-2871; and **Triangle X Float Trips** tel. (307) 733-5500. **O.A.R.S.,** tel. (800) 346-6277, offers unique overnight float trips on the Snake River at $245 for adults, $227 for youths. The organization also leads two- to five-day sea kayaking and hiking trips around Jackson Lake. Note that a few of these operators are regarded as "training grounds" for other companies; recommended rafting outfits with a good record include Barker-Ewing, O.A.R.S., Solitude, and Triangle X.

Whitewater Trips

Below Jackson, the Snake enters the wild Snake River Canyon, a stretch early explorers labeled "the accursed mad river." The usual put-in point for whitewater "rapid transit" trips is West Table Creek Campground, 26 miles south of Jackson. The take-out point is Sheep Gulch, eight miles downstream. In between the two, the river rocks and rolls through the narrow canyon, pumping past waterfalls and eagle nests and then over the two biggest rapids, Big Kahuna and Lunch Counter, followed by the smaller Rope and Champagne rapids. For a look at the action from the highway, stop at the paved pull-out at milepost 124, where a trail leads down to Lunch Counter. Whitewater trips last around three and a half hours (including transportation from Jackson) and cost around $30 for adults, $25 for children. Longer voyages including overnight trips cost approximately $110 for

adults and $80 for [...] rates early or late i[...] nies include roundtri[...] son. Don't take your [...] it's waterproof; banksi[...] be happy to sell you pic[...] record of your run.

For details on whitewate[...]ntact one of the following companie[...]er-Ewing **Whitewater,** tel. (307) 733-10[...] or (800) 448-4202; **Dave Hansen Whitewater,** tel. (307) 733-6295; **Jackson Hole Whitewater,** tel. (307) 733-1007 or (800) 648-2602; **Lewis & Clark Expeditions,** tel. (307) 733-4022 or (800) 824-5375; **Mad River Boat Trips,** tel. (307) 733-6203 or (800) 458-7238; **Sands Wild Water,** tel. (307) 733-4410 or (800) 358-8184; and **Lone Eagle Whitewater,** tel. (307) 733-1090 or (800) 321-3800. Recommended companies with good safety records and training include Barker-Ewing, Dave Hanson, and Sands.

Float It Yourself

Grand Teton National Park in Moose, tel. (307) 739-3602, has useful information on running the park portions of the river; ask for a copy of *Floating the Snake River.* Note that life jackets, boat permits ($5), and registration are required to run the river through the park, and that inner tubes and air mattresses are prohibited. Floating the gentler parts (between Jackson Lake Dam and Pacific Creek) is generally easy for even novice boaters and canoeists, but below that point things get more dicey. The water averages two or three feet deep, but it sometimes exceeds 10 feet and flow rates are often more than 8,000 cubic feet per second, creating log-jams, braided channels, strong currents, and dangerous sweepers. Peak flows are between mid-June and early July. Inexperienced rafters or anglers die every year in the river. Flow-rate signs are posted at most river landings, the Moose Visitor Center, and the Buffalo Ranger Station in Moran. If you're planning to raft or kayak on the whitewater parts of the Sna[...] River, be sure to contact the Bridger-Te[...] tional Forest office in Jackson, tel. ([...] 5500, for additional information.

Rent rafts of various sizes [...] from **Riding and Rafts** in A[...] 9900, or in Jackson fro[...]

(...07) 733-3040. The latter also
...uttle service for rafters for a fee.

FISHING AND BOATING

Fishing

Jackson Hole has some of the finest angling in Wyoming, with native Snake River cutthroat (a distinct subspecies) and brook trout in the river and Mackinaw (lake trout), cutthroat, and brown trout in the lakes. The Snake is a particular favorite of beginning fly-fishing enthusiasts. Many local companies offer guided fly-fishing float trips down the Snake River and other area waterways, or you can fish from the riverbanks with lures or flies. Two people should expect to pay $285 a day ($220 per half-day) with guide, rods and reels, lunch, and boat. Your fishing license and flies are extra.

The visitor center has a listing of more than 20 local fishing guides and outfitters, and its racks are filled with brochures from the various companies. Note that Wyoming fishing licenses are valid within Grand Teton National Park but not in Yellowstone.

Jackson has several excellent fly-fishing shops. Stop by **Jack Dennis' Outdoor Shop,** 50 E. Broadway, tel. (307) 733-3270 or (800) 522-5755, and pick up a copy of the free *Western Fishing Newsletter* for descriptions of local fishing areas and what lures to try. **Westbank Anglers,** 3670 Teton Village Rd., tel. (307) 733-6483 or (800) 922-3474, is another nationally known fly-fishing dealer with a slick mail-order catalog, excellent fishing clinics, and float trips. Both **High Country Flies,** in the Wyoming Outfitters store at 165 Center, tel. (307) 733-7210, and **Orvis Jackson Hole,** 485 W. Broadway, tel. (307) 733-5407, offer fly-fishing classes and sell quality gear. Rent fis... g rods, fly rods, float tubes, and ... ...sure Sports,** 1075 ... ...040, Jack Dennis,

$175 per person; with two students they are $85 per person. Beginners may want to start out with one of the three-hour "rubber duckie" inflatable kayak river trips for $30. In addition, the school has sea kayak tours of Yellowstone Lake. Teton Aquatics, at the same address and phone, rents canoes ($30 a day), sea kayaks ($40 a day for singles, $60 a day for doubles), whitewater kayaks ($30 a day), inflatable kayaks ($40 a day), and rafts ($50-60 a day), all with paddles and roof racks included. Also available for rent are scuba equipment and life jackets. Their free brochure describes conditions on various stretches of the Snake River.

The folks at **Rendezvous River Sports,** 1033 W. Broadway, tel. (307) 733-2471 or (800) 733-2471, teach kayaking roll clinics ($60) and a wide range of kayaking classes from beginner to advanced levels, including rescue clinics. A two-day class costs $160; five days of instruction runs $320; private lessons are also available. Rent sea kayaks or whitewater kayaks for $45 per day.

Leisure Sports, 1075 South U.S. 89, tel. (307) 733-3040, rents rafts, canoes, kayaks, inflatable kayaks, and all sorts of other outdoor equipment. They can also provide a shuttle service for rafters. **Adventure Sports** in Moose, tel. (307) 733-3307, also rents canoes and kayaks.

Windsurfing

Jackson Lake is a popular sailboarding place with moderate winds (perfect for beginners) and an impressive Teton backdrop. **Leisure Sports,** 1075 Hwy. 89 S, tel. (307) 733-3040, rents windsurfing equipment, wetsuits, and roof racks. Advanced windsurfers looking for stronger wind conditions head to Slide Lake east of Kelly or to blow-me-down Yellowstone Lake.

OTHER SUMMER RECREATION

Horsin' Around

Think of the Wild West and one animal always comes to mind—the horse. A ride on Old Paint gives city slickers a chance to saunter back in time to a simpler era and to simultaneously learn how ornery and opinionated horses can be. In Jackson Hole you can choose from brief half-day trail rides in Grand Teton National Park all the way up to weeklong wilderness pack trips into

the rugged Teton Wilderness. The visitor center has a brochure listing more than a dozen local outfitters and stables offering trail rides and pack trips.

For short rides by the hour or day ($14-18 an hour or $60-85 a day), try **Jackson Hole Trail Rides** in Teton Village, tel. (307) 733-6992; **Snow King Stables,** behind Snow King Resort, tel. (307) 733-5781; **Spring Creek Resort,** Spring Gulch Rd., tel. (307) 733-8833; **A/OK Corral,** in Hoback Jct., tel. (307) 733-6556; **Mill Iron Ranch,** Horse Creek Rd., tel. (307) 733-6390; **Lone Eagle Resort,** near Hoback Jct., tel. (307) 739-2508; **Bridger-Teton Outfitters,** south of Hoback Jct., tel. (307) 739-4314; or **Cowboy Village Resort at Togwotee,** 48 miles northeast of Jackson, tel. (307) 543-2847 or (800) 543-2847. Many of these also offer combination horseback rides and barbecue cookouts for an extra fee. Rides of all sorts are also available in Grand Teton National Park at **Jackson Lake Lodge** and **Colter Bay Corral;** call (307) 733-2811 for specifics. **Riding & Rafts,** in Alpine, tel. (307) 654-9900, offers unguided horse rentals for $12 an hour; it's the only place for do-it-yourselfers in the area.

For two- to six-day covered wagon trips in the mountains around Jackson Hole, contact **Bar T-5,** tel. (307) 733-5386 or (800) 772-5386, or **Wagons West,** tel. (307) 886-9693 or (800) 447-4711. Starting at 8 p.m. on Wednesday and Saturday evenings in the summer, the **Jackson Rodeo** brings rootin'-tootin' rodeo action to the Teton County Fair Grounds. Call (307) 733-2805 for details.

Llamas offer a unique way to experience the backcountry while learning about these fascinating and friendly animals. Local outfitters include **Jackson Hole Llamas,** tel. (307) 733-1617; **Black Diamond Llama,** tel. (307) 733-2877; and **Rendezvous Llamas,** tel. (307) 739-1639.

Mountain Biking

Jackson Hole offers all sorts of adventures for cyclists, particularly those with mountain bikes. **Teton Cyclery,** 175 N. Glenwood St., tel. (307) 733-4386; **Hoback Sports,** 40 S. Millward St., tel. (307) 733-5335; **Leisure Sports,** tel. (307) 733-3040, 1075 South U.S. 89; **Wilson Backcountry Sports,** in Teton Village, tel. (307) 733-5228; **Teton Village Sports,** in Teton Village, tel. (307) 733-2181 or (800) 874-4224; and **Ad-**

ven...
all re...
$25 p...
also r...
and rep...

Adve...
local mo...
plastic-co...
Jackson H...
fice or loca...
bikes are n...
Teton Nation...
ness areas. ...in the season, check...Lake Road inside the park; in Ap...s plowed but closed to cars. Great for an easy and very scenic mountain-bike ride.

Local mountain-bike tours (one includes a chair-lift ride to the top of Snow King) are available from **Fat Tire Tours/Hoback Sports,** tel. (307) 733-5335, for $35-40 per day. **Teton Mountain Bike Tours,** tel. (307) 733-0712 or (800) 733-0788, offers scenic half- or all-day bike trips through Grand Teton and Yellowstone National Parks as well as Bridger-Teton National Forest and the National Elk Refuge. These are for all levels of ability, with prices starting at $30 for a three-hour ride.

Alpine Slide and Scenic Rides

During the summer, kids love to race down the 2,500-foot-long **Alpine Slide** at Snow King Mountain right on the edge of Jackson. Rides cost $7 for adults, $6 for ages 6-12, and free for younger kids who ride with adults. Snow King's main **chairlift** is also in operation during the summer, taking folks for a 20-minute ride to the summit of the 7,751-foot mountain for $7 ($5 for kids under 13, $6 for seniors). The chairlift operates daily 9 a.m.-6 p.m. On top is a short nature trail and panoramic views of the Tetons. Call (307) 733-5200 for details on either ride.

Out in Teton Village, you can ride the **aerial tram** to the top of Rendezvous Mountain (10,450 feet) for $15 ($13 for seniors, $7 for ages 13-17, $5 for ages 6-12, free under age six). The ride takes 12 minutes and rises over 4,000 feet in elevation. Open daily late May-September, this is a spectacular way to reach the alpine. On top are a small gift and snack shop and naturalists who lead free summertime hikes into nearby Rock Springs Bowl. Call (307) 733-2292 or (800)

...s are available ... Over in Alta, for ... Targhee **chairlift** to ... mit of Fred's Mountain, ... on stands just seven miles ... operates Tuesday and Thurs.- ... y and August.

...orts

After decades of debate, the citizens of Jackson have finally built a marvelous recreation center, complete with a gymnasium, lap pool, and aquatics complex that includes a corkscrew water slide and jacuzzis. Entrance is $5.50 for adults, $4.25 for ages 13-17, $3 for younger kids, and $14.50 for families. They also offer a wide range of courses and activities here. Located at 155 E. Gill St., the **Teton County Recreation Center** is open daily; call (307) 739-9025 for details.

Relax in the warm waters of **Astoria Mineral Hot Springs,** 17 miles south of Jackson near Hoback Junction, tel. (307) 733-2659, for $5; open Memorial Day to Labor Day only. More out of the way is the wonderful hot mineral pool (105° F) at **Granite Hot Springs,** tel. (307) 733-6318. Head south to Hoback Junction and then up Hoback Canyon to the turnoff for Granite. The pool is another 10 miles along a dirt road—a total of 35 miles from Jackson—and costs $5.50 for adults, $3.50 for kids. It's open daily 10 a.m.-8 p.m. in the summer.

Jackson Hole Golf & Tennis Club, a mile north of town, tel. (307) 733-3111, has an 18-hole golf course (rated one of the 25 best in America), a swimming pool, and tennis courts. The Arnold Palmer-designed 18-hole **Teton Pines Country Club,** on Teton Village Rd., tel. (307) 733-1773, is Jackson Hole's second golf spot. **Jackson Hole Athletic Club,** 875 W. Broadway, tel. (307) 733-8830, has a gymnasium with Nautilus and other equipment and offers exercise classes. Rent golf clubs and tennis rackets from Jackson Hole Golf & Tennis Club, Teton Pines, or Leisure Sports, 1075 Hwy. 89 S, tel. (307) 733-3040. And for the truly serious golfer, Snow King Resort has a miniature golf course.

Teton Rock Gym, 1116 Maple Way, tel. (307) 733-0707, has an indoor climbing wall, free weights, and aerobic machines. See "Moun-

tain Climbing" in the "Grand Teton National Park" section for other athletic options.

If you're feeling flush with cash, both **Rainbow Balloon Flights,** tel. (307) 733-0470 or (800) 378-0470, and **Wyoming Balloon Co.,** tel. (307) 739-0900, offer one-hour hot-air balloon flights for $175 per person. **Jackson Hole Paragliding,** tel. (307) 739-8620, has classes in paragliding from introductory to advanced levels.

Hiking and Photo Treks

The **Teton County Parks and Recreation Department,** based in the recreation center at 155 E. Gill, tel. (307) 733-5056, leads summertime hikes for adults every Tuesday and Thursday for $5 and senior walks on Fridays for $1. They also provide Wednesday and Friday outings for kids—swimming, hiking, and more—for $3, and can rent out volleyballs, horseshoes, croquet sets, and other toys. (See "Jackson Hole Museum," above, for details on guided historical walks around downtown Jackson.) Nature walks into the mountains around Jackson are also offered by **The Hole Hiking Experience,** tel. (307) 733-7155, and **Sunrise/Sunset Wildlife Tours,** tel. (307) 733-2623. For a free version, Grand Teton National Park offers its own guided walks and nature talks throughout the year (see "Grand Teton National Park" for details). **Wilderness Exposure,** tel. (307) 733-1026, **Great Plains Wildlife Institute,** tel. (307) 733-2623; and **Firehole Photographic,** tel. (307) 733-5733, specialize in wildlife safaris and photography expeditions within Grand Teton National Park.

WINTER RECREATION

For details on the many skiing and snowboarding opportunities in and around Jackson Hole, see "Downhill Skiing" and "Cross-Country Skiing" later in this chapter.

Ice Skating

Each winter, the town of Wilson floods a hockey-rink-sized part of the town park for skating. A warming hut stands next to the rink. Jackson maintains a smaller ice rink along Gill Ave., plus a broomball rink in Snow King Ballpark. All of these are free to the public and lighted 6-10 p.m. Snow King Resort, tel. (307) 733-5200 or

(800) 522-5464, has a wintertime indoor ice-skating rink; entrance is $5 for adults, $3 for kids age 12 and under. They also offer lessons and skate rentals ($2), or you can rent skates from **Jack Dennis' Outdoor Shop,** 50 E. Broadway, tel. (307) 733-3270, or **Leisure Sports,** 1055 S. U.S. 89, tel. (307) 733-3040.

Snowshoeing

Grand Teton National Park has excellent naturalist-led snowshoe hikes several times each week during the winter months. Snowshoes are provided at no charge, and no experience is necessary. These generally depart at 2 p.m. from the visitor center in Moose, but for specifics call (307) 739-3399. Reservations are required.

Rent snowshoes from **Skinny Skis,** 65 W. Deloney Ave., tel. (307) 733-6094; **Teton Mountaineering,** 170 N. Cache, tel. (307) 733-3595 or (800) 850-3595; **Jack Dennis' Outdoor Shop,** 50 E. Broadway, tel. (307) 733-3270; **Gart Sports,** 485 W. Broadway, tel. (307) 733-4449; **Wilson Backcountry Sports,** Wilson, tel. (307) 733-5228; **Leisure Sports,** 1055 S. U.S. 89, tel. (307) 733-3040; and **Grand Targhee Ski Resort,** Alta, tel. (307) 353-2300 or (800) 827-4433.

Sleigh Rides

Three companies now offer romantic dinner horse-drawn sleigh rides in the Jackson Hole area mid-December through March. Make reservations well in advance for these popular trips. **Jackson Hole Ski Resort,** tel. (307) 733-6657, picks up Teton Village guests for a romantic 30-minute ride to a rustic log cabin where they are served a complete prime-rib dinner before heading back to civilization. Prices are $47 for adults, $29 for children under 11. **Spring Creek Resort,** tel. (307) 733-8833 or (800) 443-6139, picks guests up and carries them on an hourlong sleigh ride to the top of Gros Ventre Butte where they dine at the Granery Restaurant. The cost is $45 for adults, $30 for kids under 12. No sleigh rides on Mondays. **Bar T-5,** 790 Cache Cr. Rd., tel. (307) 733-5386 or (800) 772-5386, also has dinner sleigh rides with cowboy entertainment and a full meal, for $47 for adults, $20 for kids under 11. Dinner sleigh rides are also offered at Grand Targhee (see "Grand Targhee Ski Resort" under "Downhill Skiing and Snowboarding" earlier in this chapter for details). If you

don't have the cash for one of these rides, take a daytime sleigh ride at the National Elk Refuge (described under "Jackson" earlier in this chapter.

Dogsledding
Jackson Hole Iditarod Sled Dog Tours, tel. (307) 733-7388, was founded by Iditarod musher Frank Teasley and offers all-day trips into Grand Teton National Park, up the Gros Ventre River, and out to Granite Hot Springs. Full-day trips cost $225 per person; half-day rides are $125 per person. **Washakie Outfitting,** tel. (307) 733-3602, leads a variety of dogsled tours from Cowboy Village Resort at Togwotee, 48 miles north of Jackson. Full-day rides cost $199 for adults, $99 for kids. Shorter rides and combination dog sled and snowmobile rides are also offered, as are overnight dogsled trips.

Snowmobiling
One of Jackson Hole's fastest-growing—and most controversial—wintertime activities is snowmobiling. Hundreds of miles of packed and groomed snowmobile trails head into Bridger-Teton National Forest as well as Yellowstone and Grand Teton national parks. Some of the most popular places include the Togwotee Pass area 48 miles north of Jackson, Cache Creek Road east of town, and Granite Hot Springs Road 25 miles southeast. More than a dozen different Jackson companies offer guided all-day snowmobile trips into Yellowstone and elsewhere; expect to pay $125-150 per day (includes breakfast and lunch). You can also rent machines for self-guided trips. The visitor center has a listing of local snowmobile-rental companies and maps of snowmobile trails.

After years of contentious debate, the 360-mile-long **Continental Divide Snowmobile Trail** now passes through the heart of Grand Teton National Park, connecting the Yellowstone road network with snowmobile trails that reach all the way to Atlantic City at the southern end of the Wind River Mountains. Unfortunately, this means that even more snowmobiles will roar into two of America's great national parks. Don't be a part of this desecration; instead, enjoy these parks in quieter, less hurried ways such as on snowshoes or cross-country skis.

INFORMATION AND SERVICES

Information Sources

Anyone new to Jackson Hole should be sure to visit the impressive **Wyoming State Information Center** at 532 N. Cache, tel. (307) 733-3316. Hours are daily 8 a.m.-8 p.m. between June 15 and Labor Day, Mon.-Fri. 8 a.m.-5 p.m. and Sat.-Sun. 10 a.m.-2 p.m. the rest of the year. The information center is a two-level, sod-roofed wooden building with displays on local history and sights, a blizzard of free leaflets extolling the merits of local businesses, and an upstairs rear deck overlooking the National Elk Refuge. Ducks and trumpeter swans are visible on the marsh in the summer, and elk in the winter. The information center is staffed by folks from the Jackson Hole Chamber of Commerce, along with personnel of the Fish & Wildlife Service and Forest Service during the summer months. Check out posters over the entrance from some of the 15 movies filmed in Jackson Hole, including *Shane, Any Which Way You Can, Big Trail, Bad Bascomb, Big Sky, The Far Horizons, Spencer's Mountain, Jubal, Mountain Man,* and *Rocky IV.*

In addition to the main information center, you'll find **information kiosks** at the airport, the Pink Garter Plaza on the corner of W. Broadway and Glenwood, and at the Mangy Moose in Teton Village.

If you're looking for general information before coming to Jackson Hole, contact the **Jackson Hole Chamber of Commerce,** 555 E. Broadway, tel. (307) 733-3316. They have publications on chamber members and may also be able to provide more complete travel information. A large local travel agency, **Jackson Hole Central Reservations,** tel. (800) 443-6931, also produces a free vacation-planner brochure.

Bridger-Teton National Forest has a small **visitor center,** tel. (307) 739-5500, in the log cabin next to the forest office at 340 N. Cache. Summer hours are Mon.-Fri. 8 a.m.-5:30 p.m. and Saturday 8 a.m.-4:30 p.m. The rest of the year it's open Mon.-Fri. 8 a.m.-4:30 p.m. This is the place to get detailed forest maps ($3.75, or $5 for waterproof versions) and info on the Teton and Gros Ventre Wilderness Areas.

Services

Jackson's new main **post office** at 1070 Maple Way near Powderhorn Lane, tel. (307) 733-3650, is open Mon.-Fri. 8:30 a.m.-4:30 p.m., and Saturday 10 a.m.-1 p.m. Other post offices are downtown at 220 W. Pearl Ave., tel. (307) 739-1740, in Teton Village, tel. (307) 733-3575, and in Wilson, tel. (307) 733-3335.

For medical attention, head to **St. John's Hospital,** 625 E Broadway, tel. (307) 733-3636, or to **InstaCare of Jackson,** 545 W. Broadway, tel. (307) 733-7003, for non-emergency treatment.

Get fast cash from **ATMs** all over town—in banks, Albertson's, downtown in front of Sirk Shirts, at the airport, and in Teton Village and the Aspens. Note that many local ATMs charge an extra $1 "service charge"; at last check, the one at Key Bank, 120 W. Pearl, did not. Jackson has four different banks, several with ludicrously ostentatious structures. Most egregious of the lot is Jackson State Bank, whose new stone structure on the south end of town stands as a bloated monument to money.

Year-round, you'll find public lockers at **The Storage Stable,** 3800 S. U.S. 191, tel. (307) 733-6876, and at Jackson Hole Ski Resort during the winter. Wash clothes at **Soap Opera Laundry,** 850 W. Broadway, tel. (307) 733-5584; **Ryan Cleaners,** 545 N. Cache, tel. (307) 733-2938; or **The Laundromat** near the corner of W. Broadway and Millward Street.

Books and Newspapers

The brand-new **Teton County Library** on Virginian Lane at Snow King Ave., tel. (307) 733-2164, opens in 1997 and is three times the size of the cozy old log cabin that housed the library for more than fifty years. Inside you'll find a substantial collection of books about Wyoming and the West. Hours are Monday, Wednesday, and Friday 10 a.m.-5:30 p.m., Tuesday and Thursday 10 a.m.-9 p.m., Saturday 10 a.m.-5 p.m., and Sunday 1-5 p.m.

Unlike many Wyoming towns where the book selection consists of a few romance novels in the local drugstore, Jackson is blessed with two fine bookstores: **Teton Bookshop,** 25 S. Glenwood, tel. (307) 733-9220, and the large **Valley Bookstore,** 125 N. Cache, tel. (307) 733-4533. The latter sometimes has author signings and

readings. The **Moose Visitor Center,** tel. (307) 739-3399, and **Colter Bay Indian Arts Museum,** tel. (307) 543-2467, in Grand Teton National Park both sell natural history books and maps.

Jackson has not just one but two thick local newspapers, each produced in tabloid format: the *Jackson Hole News* and the *Jackson Hole Guide.* Both of these publish weekly editions with local news for 50 cents, along with Mon.-Fri. free papers found in shops in Jackson, Wilson, and Teton Village. The *Guide* represents more traditional Wyoming views (i.e., it's strongly Republican) while the *News* is usually more liberal.

Living in Jackson Hole

Jackson Hole is becoming an increasingly popular place to live and work, a fact that angers many long-time residents who came here to escape crowds elsewhere. The surrounding country is grand, with many things to do and places to explore, and you're likely to meet others with similar interests. Jobs such as waiting tables, operating ski lifts, driving tour buses, cleaning hotels and condos, and construction work are generally plentiful—the unemployment rate generally hovers around three percent—but the wages are not high. Check local classified ads or stop by the Wyoming Job Service Center, 545 N. Cache, tel. (307) 733-4091, to get an idea of available jobs. The best jobs are those that offer either such perks as free ski passes or give you lots of free time to explore the area.

Unfortunately, because of Jackson Hole's popularity, finding a place to live is quite difficult, especially during the peak summer and winter tourist seasons. Workers even drive in from Afton, 70 miles away! Land prices (and consequently housing costs) have been rising at an astronomical rate, pushing the average rent to $640, with a typical two-bedroom tract home selling for around $300,000. Many homes sell for $1-3 million, and the very finest log mansions fetch over $5 million each! A few Jackson-area restaurants include inexpensive housing as a way to lure workers, but this is the exception; many employees are forced to live under less-than-ideal conditions such as sleeping in tents during the summer or jamming into too-small apartments. The best times to look for a place to live are in April and November. Check the papers as well as local laundromat and grocery-store bulletin boards for apartments or cabins. The "Trash and Treasure" morning program on radio station KMTN (97 FM) is another place to try.

SHOPPING

If you have the money, Jackson is a great place to buy everything from artwork to mountain bikes. Even if you just hitchhiked in and have no cash to spare, it's always fun to wander through the shops and galleries surrounding the town square. The corporate chains and factory outlets have moved into Jackson in a big way within the last few years, with many of the standards to choose from, including The Gap, Eddie Bauer, The Nature Company, Pendleton, Ralph Lauren Polo, London Fog, J. Crew, Scandia Down, and Benetton.

Buy used clothing and other items at **Browse 'N Buy Thrift Shop,** 139 N. Cache, tel. (307) 733-7524, and **Orville's,** 285 W. Pearl, tel. (307) 733-3165. Orville's has old Wyoming license plates for just a buck—a big hit with European tourists. **Snooty Fox,** 70 S. King, tel. (307) 733-0019, is a new and consignment boutique with quality clothing and accessories for surprisingly reasonable prices.

Outdoor Gear

Outdoor enthusiasts will discover several excellent shops in Jackson. Climbers, backpackers, and cross-country skiers head to **Teton Mountaineering,** 170 N. Cache, tel. (307) 733-3595 or (800) 850-3595, for quality equipment, maps, and travel guides. This is America's oldest climbing shop. It also rents tents, sleeping bags, backpacks, ice axes, cook stoves, climbing shoes, cross-country skis, and other gear. Check the bulletin board for used items. **Jack Dennis' Outdoor Shop,** 50 E. Broadway, tel. (307) 733-3270 or (800) 522-5755, is a large upscale store that sells fly-fishing and camping gear in the summer and skis and warm clothes during the winter. They also rent almost anything: tents, stoves, lanterns, cookware, sleeping bags, fly rods, waders, float tubes, backpacks, skis, and more. **Skinny Skis,** 65 W. Deloney Ave., tel. (307) 733-6094, has more in

the way of high-quality clothing and supplies, especially cross-country ski gear. Rent tents, sleeping bags, climbing shoes, ice axes, rollerblades, baby carriers, and backpacks here. Another place to rent outdoor gear of all types—including volleyball sets, fishing gear, tents, and tarps—is **Leisure Sports,** 1075 South U.S. 89, tel. (307) 733-3040. **Moosely Seconds,** 150 E. Broadway, tel. (307) 733-7176, has outdoor gear at good prices, including seconds from Patagonia, Grammici, Lowe, and other companies. **Gear Revival,** 1260 Huff Lane, tel. (307) 739-8699, sells used outdoor gear of all types. The least expensive place to buy rugged outdoor wear, cowboy boots, and cowboy hats is **Corral West Ranchwear,** 840 W. Broadway, tel. (307) 733-0247.

Wyoming Woolens, an Afton-based local manufacturer of colorful high-quality outdoor clothing, operates a retail shop near the square at 20 W. Broadway, tel. (307) 733-2991. Despite the name, nearly everything here is made from high-tech fabrics such as Polartec fleece; some of these garments are made using recycled plastic bottles. Wyoming Woolens also produces a mail-order catalog; call (800) 732-2991 for a copy. For high-quality, handmade Lycra and Polarplus clothing, or if you're in need of tent or backpack repairs, visit **Columbine,** tel. (307) 733-7179, a small shop in Pink Garter Plaza at 49 W. Broadway. Highly recommended. In the same building you'll find **Cowboy Cooking & Supply Co.,** tel. (307) 733-2530 or (800) 733-2531, with old-fashioned cast iron ware for horsepacking camps, including a handy swivel camp grill for cooking over an open fire.

TRANSPORTATION

Access to Jackson Hole has become easier in recent years with several airlines and summer-only daily bus service. Most summer visitors arrive by car, though a few more adventurous souls pedal in on bikes. If you're looking for or offering a ride, the local radio station, KMTN (97 FM), tel. (307) 733-5686, has a daily ride-finder announcement at 11:20 p.m. Other folks call in with rides on the station's 9:30 a.m. "Trash and Treasure" show.

By Air
At one time, Jackson was considered virtually impossible to get to, but today daily jet service brings visitors from all over the world. Jackson Hole Airport is eight miles north of Jackson in Grand Teton National Park. The only commercial airport within any national park, it is a source of considerable tension, as plans to expand the runway conflict directly with the park's management for natural-resource values. The airport is served by **Delta,** tel. (800) 221-1212; **American,** tel. (800) 433-7300; **United Express,** tel. (800) 241-6522; **Horizon Air,** tel. (800) 547-9308; and **Skywest,** tel. (800) 453-9417. Delta and Skywest route all their flights through Salt Lake City, Horizon through Seattle and Boise, and United Express through Denver. American Airlines flights go via Salt Lake City, but during the winter they also offer direct service to Chicago. **Satellite Aero,** tel. (307) 739-1999 or (800) 328-3444, provides air charter service anywhere in the nation. **Jackson Hole Aviation,** tel. (307) 733-4767 or (800) 437-5387, has scenic flights over the valley.

Airport Shuttles and Taxis
Both **All Star Transportation,** tel. (307) 733-2888 or (800) 378-2944, and **Alltrans,** tel. (307) 733-4325 or (800) 443-6133, provide airport shuttle service to and from motels in Jackson ($8 per person) and Teton Village ($15 per person one-way, $21 roundtrip). These prices are higher if the shuttles are carrying fewer than three people. Both companies meet all commercial airline flights, but after 7 p.m. you should make advance reservations to be sure of an airport pick-up. Make outgoing reservations a day in advance. For taxi service ($16 to town, $21 to Teton Village for one or two people), call **A-l Taxi,** tel. (307) 733-5089; **Airport Taxi,** tel. (307) 733-1700; **Alltrans,** tel. (307) 733-1700 or (800) 443-6133; **Buckboard Cab,** tel. (307) 733-1112; **Tumbleweed Taxi,** tel. (307) 733-0808; or **Jackson Hole Transportation,** tel. (307) 733-3135.

Car Rentals
Most of the national chains offer rental cars in town or at the airport: **Alamo,** tel. (307) 733-0671 or (800) 327-0400; **Avis,** tel. (307) 733-3422 or (800) 831-2847; **Budget,** tel. (307) 733-

2206 or (800) 527-0700; **Dollar,** tel. (307) 733-0935 or (800) 800-4000; **Eagle,** tel. (307) 739-9999 or (800) 582-2128; **Hertz,** tel. (307) 733-2272 or (800) 654-3131; **National,** tel. (307) 733-0735 or (800) 227-7368; **Rent-A-Wreck,** tel. (307) 733-5014 or (800) 637-7147; **Thrifty,** tel. (307) 739-9300 or (800) 367-2277; and **Ugly Duckling,** tel. (307) 733-3040 or (800) 843-3825. The best deals (if you don't mind used cars) are generally from Rent-A-Wreck, 1250 S. Carol Lane. Most of these companies also offer 4WD cars and minivans. Note that peak-season car rental rates in Jackson are on the high side, with the smallest Geo Metros going for $35 per day. Reserve cars at least a month ahead during the summer and two months ahead for midsummer or Christmas to New Year's.

START Buses

Local buses are operated by Southern Teton Area Rapid Transit and serve Jackson and Teton Village most of the year. This is Wyoming's only true public bus system, though recent budget problems have thrown its continuation into question. START fares are $1 within town and $2 to Teton Village (seniors and children under eight are free). Discount coupons are available for multiple rides (winter only). During the summer, buses run seven days a week, approximately every two hours. Winter schedules offer more frequent service to Teton Village. Minimal bus service operates between mid-April and mid-June and between early September and early December. Pick up bus schedules and route maps in the visitor center. Hours of operation are generally 7 a.m.-11 p.m. Buses stop near most Jackson hotels and motels and are equipped to carry skis (in winter) and bikes (in summer) on outside racks. START buses do not run to the airport or to Wilson. Call (307) 733-4521 for more information.

Buses and Tours

Greyhound buses don't come even close to Jackson; the nearest stopping places are Evanston, West Yellowstone, and Idaho Falls. The closest Amtrak stations are in Evanston and Rock Springs. **Jackson Hole Express,** tel. (307) 733-1719, has direct luxury bus service between Salt Lake City and Jackson, with on-

board TV and restroom. Rates are $40 one-way, $65 roundtrip. **SANTA** (Shoshone Arapahoe Nations Transit Authority), tel. (800) 439-7118, offers on-demand bus service between Jackson and other points, including Rock Springs (Greyhound and Amtrak connections), Rawlins, Cody, Pinedale, Dubois, Lander, and Salt Lake City.

Grand Teton Lodge Company, tel. (307) 733-2811 or (800) 628-9988, offers twice-daily summer shuttle buses between Jackson and Jackson Lake Lodge for $12.50 one-way (plus a $4 park entrance fee), and on to Colter Bay Village for an additional $2.50 one-way. Buses depart from the Homewood parking lot on the corner of Gill and Cache and stop at the airport and Jenny Lake upon request. They also offer narrated bus tours of Grand Teton National Park on Monday, Wednesday, and Friday for $17 ($12 for kids under 12) and of Yellowstone National Park on Tuesday, Thursday, and Saturday for $40 ($25 for kids). Tours depart from Jackson Lake Lodge at 8:30 each summer morning.

Daily summertime bus tours of Grand Teton and Yellowstone National Parks and historical tours of Jackson Hole are available from **Gray Line,** 332 N. Glenwood, tel. (307) 733-4325 or (800) 443-6133. These six- to 10-hour tours cost $40-43 (including park entrance fees). Gray Line's four-day tours of the parks cost $349 per person, while five-day trips are $470 per person, including lodging. Gray Line also has one-way service between Yellowstone and Jackson for $25 in either direction; reserve ahead to schedule a pick-up in Jackson, Grand Teton, or Yellowstone. This is not a separate service from the tours; you are picked up by the regular tour buses, so you get part of a tour at the same time. In Yellowstone, travelers can connect with other buses to West Yellowstone, Gardiner, Montana, or Cody. During the winter, Gray Line has daily bus runs to Flagg Ranch for $25 each way, arriving in time to meet the snowcoach departures for Yellowstone. Reservations are required. Both **Buckboard Cab,** tel. (307) 733-1112, and **All Star Transportation,** tel. (307) 733-2888 or (800) 378-2944, also offer shuttles to Flagg Ranch in the winter months.

Sublette Stage, tel. (307) 367-6633, has taxi service to Pinedale ($83 for up to three passengers) and Rock Springs ($175 for up to three

people). Other companies offering guided van tours of Jackson Hole and surrounding areas include **Buckboard Cab,** tel. (307) 733-1112, **Callowishus Park Touring Company,** tel. (307) 733-9521; **Jackson's Hole Adventure,** tel. (307) 654-7849 or (800) 392-3165; **All Star**

Transportation, tel. (307) 733-2888 or (800) 378-2944; **Tours West,** tel. (307) 734-8311; and **Outdoor Adventures,** tel. (307) 739-9443 or (800) 642-8979. **Wild West Jeep Tours,** tel. (307) 733-9036, leads 4WD tours to more remote places around the valley.

DOWNHILL SKIING AND SNOWBOARDING

Until recently, Jackson Hole was primarily a summertime resort, filled with carloads of screaming kids, French tourists snickering at the name "Grand Teton," and adventurous young people streaming into the mountains. As access has become easier and the facilities more developed, many people have discovered the wonders of a Jackson Hole winter, especially one centered around a week on the ski slopes. Three very different ski resorts attract the crowds: Grand Targhee for downhome, powder-to-the-butt conditions; Snow King for steep, inexpensive, edge-of-town slopes; and Jackson Hole for flashy, world-class skiing. All three places have rental equipment, ski schools, and special programs for kids. Snowboarders and Telemarkers are welcome on the slopes. This mixture, along with an incredible abundance of developed and wild places to ski cross-country, combine to make Jackson Hole one of the premier ski destinations in America.

See your travel agent for package trips to any of the Jackson-area resorts. For daily ski reports—including downhill and Nordic areas and backcountry reports—listen to KMTN (FM 97) at 7:15, 8:15, 8:25, and 9:15 every morning. Hot tip: If you plan to spend more than a couple of days in the area, it may well be worth your while to join the **Jackson Hole Ski Club,** tel. (307) 733-6433. In return for a $25 annual membership, you receive an impressive number of premiums, including half-price lift tickets and lessons, various freebies, and discounts at more than 100 local stores. Join up at any local ski shop.

The three Jackson area ski resorts now offer a special **Jackson Hole Ski Three** pass for $210 per person. Ski Three gives you a book of five lift vouchers good at all three ski areas, providing a great chance to expand your skiing and

snowboarding options. In addition to the standard ticket, at Jackson Hole Ski Resort Ski Three includes a daily tram pass, at Grand Targhee you get either roundtrip bus service from Jackson or a ski lesson, and at Snow King they throw in a dinner at Rafferty's Restaurant. You must redeem Ski Three vouchers within seven days after you use the first ticket.

Ski and Snowboard Rentals

Rent or buy downhill skis and snowboards from: **Hoback Sports,** 40 S. Millward St., tel. (307) 733-5335; **Gart Sports,** 485 W. Broadway, tel. (307) 733-4449; **Jack Dennis' Outdoor Shop,** 50 E. Broadway, tel. (307) 733-3270; **Wildernest Sports,** Teton Village, tel. (307) 733-4297; **Teton Village Sports,** tel. (307) 733-2181 or (800) 874-4224; **Wilson Backcountry Sports,** Wilson, tel. (307) 733-5228; or **Leisure Sports,** 1055 S. Hwy. 89, tel. (307) 733-3040. Rentals are also available at all three ski areas. Snowboarders head to **Boardroom of Jackson Hole,** 245 W. Pearl, tel. (307) 733-8327, **Lowrider Board Shop** in Teton Village, tel. (307) 733-4505, and **Phat Fred's,** in Alta, tel. (307) 353-2300 or (800) 827-4433, for the latest gear.

GRAND TARGHEE SKI RESORT

Grand Targhee was long considered something of a hick ski area, the sort of place where folks skied in overalls and headed back to their farms to feed the cows. The food was dreadful, the lodging facilities were funky at best, and the lift operators wore cowboy hats with plastic covers. But skiers also discovered that Targhee had some of the most incredible snow in the universe. With an annual snowfall of 504 inches (42 feet!)—most of which is champagne powder—Targhee became the secret spot where

powder hounds got all they could ever want. *Snow Country Magazine* consistently ranks it as having the "best snow in North America." In fact, the resort guarantees its snow: if you find conditions not to your liking, you can turn in your ticket before 11 a.m. and get a "snow check" good for another day of skiing.

New owners took over in 1987 and began transforming Targhee into a first-class ski area—remodeling the facilities, adding new restaurants and services, and inaugurating snowcat skiing. But some things haven't changed: lift operators still wear cowboy hats, the slopes are still beautifully groomed and uncrowded, and the friendly customer service still gets high marks—despite the fact that the place has just four lifts. On the drawing boards are all sorts of new developments and a land swap with the Forest Service that have brought major controversy and even litigation by locals anxious to keep their peaceful way of life.

The biggest drawback to Grand Targhee is the same thing that makes it so great—the weather. Lots of snow means lots of clouds, and because it snows so much there are many days when the name cynics apply—"Grand Foghee"—seems more appropriate. Many folks who have returned to Targhee year after year have still not seen the magnificent Grand Teton backdrop behind the ski area! Be sure to bring your goggles.

Nuts and Bolts

Targhee has three double chairlifts and one surface lift on the prosaically named Fred's Mountain. The top elevation is 10,200 feet, with the longest run dropping 2,200 feet in almost three miles. Although only 300 acres are groomed, the remaining 1,200 acres of ungroomed powder mean that you'll always find track-free skiing (bring your snorkel). And if that isn't enough, try snowcat skiing ($195 per day including lunch and guide; $170 if you overnight at Targhee) on adjacent Peaked Peak. You'll get six to 10 runs each day. Lift tickets at Grand Targhee cost $36 a day ($28 per half-day) for adults and $22 per day for children ages 14 and under and seniors (free under age five and over age 69).

Fully 70% of Targhee's groomed runs are intermediate, but advanced skiers will find an extraordinary number of deep-powder faces to explore. Snowboarders can play at the permanent half-pipe. The ski school offers lessons for all abilities, and children's programs make it possible for parents to leave their kids behind. Cross-country skiers enjoy the Nordic center (see "Cross-Country Skiing" below). Rental skis and snowboards are available at the base of the mountain. The ski area usually opens in mid-November and closes in late April, though some years you may be able to ski even into July. Lifts operate 9:30 a.m.-4 p.m. daily. Call (800) 827-4433 for more on Grand Targhee.

Food and Lodging

At Targhee you can stay in motel-style rooms in Targhee and Teewinot lodges as well as condominium accommodations in Sioux Lodge. Nightly rates are $110-145 s or d during the holiday season, but a wide variety of ski and lodging package deals are also available, such as five nights lodging and four days skiing for $418-507 s, $836-1,014 d during the holiday season. A heated outdoor pool and hot tub are available for lodge residents. Call Targhee at (307) 353-2300 or (800) 827-4433 to get brochures detailing all these options. **Alta Outdoor Lodge,** tel. (307) 353-2582, has additional B&B accommodations in a new home with a spectacular view of the Tetons, a fireplace, and a hot tub. Rates in the four guest rooms with private or shared bath are $65-85 s or d including a full breakfast.

At the base of Grand Targhee you'll find a cafeteria and several restaurants. Especially noteworthy is **Skadi's,** where the gourmet meals led *Snow Country Magazine* to rate it second in the nation among on-mountain restaurants. You can also take a horse-drawn sleigh on a 15-minute ride to a Mongolian-style yurt for a home-cooked steak or chicken dinner. The price is $30 ($15 for kids ages 14 and under).

Grand Targhee's social center is the **Trap Bar,** with live music most nights. Other shops here sell groceries, ski equipment, and clothing. For another diversion, try **dog sledding,** at $55 ($30 for kids) for an hourlong ride. On Christmas and New Year's, be sure to stay around for the impressive **torchlit ski parade** down the mountain. A **Kid's Club** at Targhee provides supervised fun activities for children.

Getting There

Grand Targhee is located 42 miles northwest of Jackson on the western side of the Tetons in Alta, Wyoming. Get there by driving over Teton Pass (occasionally closed by winter storms), north through Victor and Driggs, Idaho, and then east back into Wyoming. The **Targhee Express** bus makes daily wintertime trips (90 minutes each way) to Grand Targhee from Jackson and Teton Village. Buses leave Jackson at 7:30 a.m. and return by 6:30 p.m. for a roundtrip fare of $15 per person (higher rates if the bus isn't full). Targhee Express riders also get a break on ski lift tickets, but you'll need to purchase the tickets when you reserve space for the shuttle bus. Reservations are required; make them at least one day in advance by calling (307) 733-3101 in Jackson, (800) 827-4433 at Targhee.

Summer Activities

Not far from Grand Targhee are several popular summertime hiking trails (see "Jedediah Smith Wilderness" under "Targhee National Forest" later in this chapter). The resort itself is a popular place to relax in the summer and offers many activities. You can rent mountain bikes, ride horses, enjoy hayride dinners, practice moves on the climbing wall, enjoy the spa and pool, or ride the chairlift. A nine-hole golf course is just down the road. Evening brings movies, lectures, hayrides, and campfire sing-alongs. Each 4th of July, balloon enthusiasts come to Targhee for the **Teton Valley Hot Air Balloon Festival.** A cross-country mountain-bike race during the Balloon Festival attracts everyone from beginners to pros. Lots of music during the summer includes the **Rockin' the Tetons Music Festival** in mid-July, when nationally known rock, blues, and reggae musicians perform. It's followed in mid-August by the equally popular **Targhee Bluegrass Festival.**

JACKSON HOLE SKI RESORT

Just 12 miles northwest of Jackson is Jackson Hole Ski Resort, the largest and best-known Wyoming ski area. A true skier's mountain, Jackson Hole is considered the most varied and challenging of any American ski area. The powder is usually deep (average snowfall is 38 feet!),

lift lines are short, the slopes are uncrowded, and the vistas are unbelievable. First opened in 1965, Jackson Hole Ski Resort has become one of the nation's favorite ski areas. The mountain has one unusual feature that occurs in midwinter: a temperature inversion frequently develops over the valley, meaning that when it's bitterly cold at the base of the mountain, the top is 15-20° F warmer. Skiers often remain on the upper slopes all day to enjoy these warmer temperatures.

Superlatives

A recent magazine article referred to Jackson Hole Resort as a place "where the skiing gets tough and the tough go skiing." The slopes are *steep* here; half the runs are in the advanced category, including several of the notorious double-diamonds. And yes, those death-defying cliff-jumping shots are real; on the tram ride up, check out the infamous Corbett's Coulair, a rocky gully that requires a leap of faith and suicidal urges. With an unsurpassed 4,139-foot vertical drop (longest in the U.S.), 2,400 acres of terrain spread over two adjacent mountains, runs that may exceed four miles in length, and 24 miles of groomed trails, Jackson Hole is truly a resort of superlatives.

Actually, the mountain is so large that even rank beginners will find plenty of bunny slopes on which to practice. Rendezvous Mountain (10,450 feet) is where experts strut their stuff, while adjacent Aprés Vous Mountain (8,481 feet) is primarily for those who like friendlier slopes. Intermediate skiers could spend all day exploring the various runs here. The most enjoyable way to the top of Rendezvous Mountain is aboard one of the 63-passenger aerial tram cars. Powered by 500-horsepower engines, they climb nearly 2.5 miles in 12 minutes, offering jaw-dropping views across Jackson Hole. Three quad chairlifts, a triple chairlift, three double chairlifts, and two Poma lifts spread over the rest of the terrain, and you can ski down 60 different named trails.

There is a negative side to Jackson Hole Ski Resort—in addition to the sky-high prices. In the early 1990s an ownership battle reached the courts, and management of the resort took a back seat, leading to complaints about deteriorating facilities and poor service. Things have im-

proved considerably since then, and the resort's 20-year master plan (if approved by the Forest Service) will include an investment of $50 million to add seven new lifts, several trails, a new base facility, three restaurants, and extensive snow-making capabilities. Most noticeable of these is a planned gondola that may be operational by winter of 1997.

Tommy Moe—gold and silver medalist at the 1994 Lillehammer Winter Olympics—is now Jackson Hole's official "ski ambassador"; in return, he received a Teton Village condo and lots of cash. (Moe is actually from Alaska, but Alyeska Resort there didn't offer nearly as much.) You can often spot Tommy on the slopes in winter. Jackson's director of skiing (he headed the ski school here for 30 years) is Pepi Stiegler, the Austrian winner of a silver medal in the 1960 Olympics and a gold medal in the 1964 Olympics.

Services and Rates
Get to Teton Village from the town of Jackson by hopping on the START bus ($2 each way). This is the only inexpensive part of a visit to Jackson Hole Resort, since prices for lift tickets approach the stratosphere. Single-day tickets for all lifts (including the tram) are $46 for adults ($35 per half-day) and $25 ($19 per half-day) for kids under 14 and seniors. Multiday all-lift tickets—the most common kind bought—are $287 a week for adults or $154 a week for kids. Lifts are open 9 a.m.-4 p.m. daily (last tram departs at 3:30 p.m.) from early December till early April.

Skis and snowboards can be rented in Jackson or Teton Village. The ski school offers a special Kinderschule program for children, and beginning snowboarders can learn from the pros. Jackson Hole Resort even has special steep snowboarding and steep skiing camps, where you learn from such extreme fanatics as Stephen Kogh—first person to snowboard the Grand Teton—and Doug Coombs, a former World Extreme Skiing Champion. You can ski with Olympian Pepi Stiegler Mon.-Fri. at 1:30 p.m.; meet him at the top of Casper lift. Ski hosts are scattered around the mountain, ready to provide information and tours of the slopes every hour on the hour from the top of Rendezvous Mountain. Racers and spectators will enjoy NASTAR events each Sunday, Tuesday, Thursday, and Saturday, along with various other

events throughout the winter. If you're looking for untracked powder, **Jackson Hole Guide Service** at (307) 739-2663 or (800) 450-0477 leads small groups of folks into parts of the mountain off-limits to mere mortals. Powderhound skiers with a ton of cash will find unparalleled outback conditions accessed via **High Mountain Heli-Skiing,** tel. (307) 733-3274.

Teton Village, a Swiss-style resort at the base of the mountain, has lodges, condominiums, espresso, restaurants, bars, shops, a small grocery, ski and snowboard rentals, storage lockers, a liquor store, car rentals, a Kids' Ranch childcare center, and even a travel agency for escapes to Hawaii. On-the-mountain facilities include a restaurant and a ski shop in Casper Bowl and a snack bar at the top of the tram. The Caspar Restaurant features a barbecue picnic most days and is a popular place to break for lunch and meet up with friends. For more information on Jackson Hole Ski Resort, call (307) 733-2292 or (800) 450-0477. For recorded snow conditions, call (307) 733-2291 or (888) 333-7766. The messages are changed each morning before 5 a.m. Reach them via e-mail at info@jacksonhole.com, or their Internet web page at http://www./jacksonhole.com/ski.

SNOW KING RESORT

Rising directly behind the town of Jackson, Snow King Resort's ski runs make up in difficulty what they lack in size. From below, the mountain (7,871 feet tall) looks impossibly steep and narrow. High atop the big chairlift, the vista provides a panoramic tour of Jackson Hole. Jackson's "town hill," Snow King was the first ski area in Wyoming (opened in 1939) and one of the first in North America. The original chapter of the National Ski Patrol was established here in 1941. In the 1990s, Snow King has undergone a major facelift that brought a new triple chairlift, a snowboard park, expanded night skiing—it now covers three-quarters of the mountain—and a new base lodge and indoor ice rink.

You'll find more than 500 acres of skiable terrain at Snow King, with the longest run nearly a mile in length. A triple chair, two double chairs, and a Poma lift climb up the mountainside. Prices for lift tickets at Snow King are well below those at other Jackson Hole resorts: $25 a day ($18

per half-day) for adults and $16 per day ($10 per half-day) for kids under 15 and seniors. Hours of operation are 9:30 a.m.-4:30 p.m., with **night skiing** (Mon.-Sat. 4:30-8:30 p.m.) available on the lower sections of Snow King for an additional $12 for adults and $8 for kids and seniors. With some of the best snowmaking in Wyoming, the resort usually opens by Thanksgiving and remains open till early April.

Hoback Sports rents skis at the foot of the mountain. There's a ski school, and guided Nordic tours down the back side of the mountain are available. At the base of Snow King you'll discover an elaborate lodge, two restaurants, the Shady Lady Saloon, and a variety of other facilities, including an indoor ice rink. Jackson's town square is only seven blocks away and START buses ($1 in town, $2 from Teton Village) offer frequent service. For more info on Snow King Resort, call (307) 733-5200 or (800) 522-5464 (outside Wyoming), or contact them over the Internet at http://www.snowking.com.

CROSS-COUNTRY SKIING

For many Jackson Hole residents the word "skiing" means heading across frozen Jenny Lake or Telemarking down the bowls of Teton Pass rather than sliding down the slopes of the local resorts. Jackson Hole is becoming a national center for cross-country enthusiasts and offers an impressive range of conditions from flat-tracking along summertime golf courses where gourmet restaurant awaits you to remote wilderness settings where a complete knowledge of snow crystal structure, avalanche hazards, and winter survival techniques are essential. Beginners will probably want to start out at one of the five nearby Nordic centers, progressing to local paths and the more gentle lift-serviced ski runs with experience. More advanced skiers will quickly discover the incredible snow in the surrounding mountains.

Ski Rentals
Rent (or buy) cross-country skis at **Skinny Skis,** 65 W. Deloney Ave., tel. (307) 733-6094; **Teton Mountaineering,** 170 N. Cache, tel. (307) 733-3595 or (800) 850-3595; **Jack Dennis' Outdoor Shop,** 50 E. Broadway, tel. (307) 733-3270; **Gart Sports,** 485 W. Broadway, tel. (307) 733-4449; **Wilson Backcountry Sports,** Wilson, tel. (307) 733-5228; and **Leisure Sports,** 1055 S. U.S. 89, tel. (307) 733-3040; . **All the local Nordic centers also rent equipment.**

NORDIC CENTERS

Jackson Hole Nordic Center
Nordic skiing enthusiasts will find three different developed facilities near Jackson and others at Grand Targhee and near Togwotee Pass. Largest is Jackson Hole Nordic Center, tel. (307) 739-2629, with 25 km of groomed trails—both set track and skating lanes—covering a wide range of conditions. Call (307) 733-2291 for the snow report. Located in Teton Village, this is the best place to try cross-country skiing. Fees are $8 a day for adults or $4 a day for children and seniors. Cross-country, skating, and telemarking equipment are available for rent. Hours are daily 8:30 a.m.-4:30 p.m. After 12:30 p.m., your alpine lift ticket at Jackson Hole Ski Resort is good at the Nordic center, too (but, hey, it better be—for $46!). The center offers a wide spectrum of lessons and naturalist-led tours of Grand Teton National Park or trips to Teton Pass for the more adventurous.

Teton Pines Cross-Country Ski Center
Located three miles north on Teton Village Rd., tel. (307) 733-1005, Teton Pines includes 13 km of groomed track (both diagonal-stride skiing and skating) on a summertime golf course. Rates are $7 a day for adults, $5 a day for children. Ski rentals and guided tours within Grand Teton National Park are available. Hours are daily 9 a.m.-5 p.m. The clubhouse here has a pricey restaurant for gourmet aprés-ski lunches and dinners.

Spring Creek Resort Nordic Center
Located three miles north of State 22 on Spring Gulch Rd., Spring Creek, tel. (307) 733-1004 or (800) 443-6139, is open 9:30 a.m.-5 p.m. daily. If you're staying in town, you can catch

BOB RACE

the free shuttle bus at the Wort Hotel; call the Nordic center for specifics. Guests of the Wort Hotel or Spring Creek Resort ski free. The center has 20 km of gentle groomed trails with skating lanes—perfect for beginners. Rates are $7 a day for adults, $5 a day for seniors, $4 a day for children, and $18 a day for a family. Ski rentals and lessons are available.

Cowboy Village Resort at Togwotee
Farther afield is Cowboy Village Resort at Togwotee, 48 miles northeast of Jackson, tel. (307) 543-2847 or (800) 543-2847, open daily 8:30 a.m.-5 p.m. Just a couple of miles above the lodge, U.S. 26/287 heads over the Continental Divide at 9,658 feet, so expect to find luxuriously deep powder. Teton Wilderness lies just north of here, and when you face west the Teton Range offers up a jagged horizon line. Cowboy Village Resort at Togwotee maintains 10 km of groomed single-track trails covering a variety of terrain. They start directly behind the lodge, and are generally groomed on Friday so weekend skiers have fresh conditions. No charge, and you can ski at any time. A donation is requested to cover the grooming costs. Ski rentals are only available for guests of Cowboy Village or Cowboy Village Resort at Togwotee. The lodge is a pleasantly rustic place to stay the night or enjoy a dinner before returning to Jackson. Extremely popular with the snowmobile crowd.

Brooks Lake Lodge
Drive another 10 miles over Togwotee Pass to Brooks Lake Lodge, tel. (307) 455-2121, for some of the most incredible scenery and cross-country skiing in the West. Brooks Lake Lodge is five miles in on a machine-packed road, making a perfect destination for day-trips. Once there, you'll find another five km of groomed trails (no charge) plus access to the nearby Teton Wilderness, where skiers can escape the snowmo-

biles. At the lodge—closed Tuesday and Wednesday—you can relax and enjoy lunch or spend the night. Advance reservations required.

Grand Targhee Nordic Center
Located on the west side of the Tetons, Grand Targhee Nordic Center, tel. (307) 353-2300 or (800) 827-4433, has 10 km of groomed cross-country ski trails covering rolling terrain. Trail passes are $7 a day for adults and $4 a day for seniors and kids. Lessons, ski rentals, and a variety of tours are also available. Hours are daily 9 a.m.-4:30 p.m. Guests with Targhee lodging packages can ski free on the cross-country tracks.

ON YOUR OWN

Nordic skiers who would rather explore Jackson Hole and the mountains that surround it o their own will discover an extraordinary range of options, from beginner-level treks along old roads to places where only the most advanced skiers dare venture. Because Jackson has so many cross-country fanatics (and visiting enthusiasts), trails are quickly broken along the more popular routes, making it easier for those who follow. For complete coverage of all these options, pick up a copy of the free winter outdoors guide *Trailhead* at Skinny Skis, 65 W. Deloney Ave., tel. (307) 733-6094. If you're heading out on your own, be prepared for deep snow (four feet in the valley) and temperatures that often plummet far below zero at night.

The **Teton County Parks and Recreation Department,** in the new recreation center at 155 E. Gill, tel. (307) 733-5056, leads a variety of all-day cross-country ski outings every Tuesday (early December to late March) for $5 per person. Bring your own skis and a lunch. The department also has full-moon ski tours once a month in the winter.

Jackson Hole Mountain Guides, tel. (307) 733-4979, runs wintertime ski tours, avalanche courses, ski mountaineering, rock- and ice-climbing classes, and overnight trips to the Mt. Glory ski hut on Teton Pass. Longer trips, such as a six-day Teton Crest tour, are also available. Over on the west side of the Tetons, **Rendezvous Ski Tours,** tel. (208) 787-2906, main-

tains three Mongolian-style yurts in the backcountry, located three to four hours of skiing apart. The huts can sleep up to eight and have kitchens, bunks, sleeping bags, and woodstoves.

Jackson Area

Even rank beginners will enjoy exploring several local spots. Get to **Moose-Wilson Road** by heading a mile north of Teton Village to where

the plowing ends. The nearly level road continues for two scenic miles across a creek and through groves of aspen. For more adventure, turn off at the Granite Canyon trailhead and follow the trail toward the canyon. Conditions get more difficult as you progress, and avalanches are a potential hazard farther up.

The closest place to Jackson for on-your-own cross-country skiing is **Cache Creek Canyon** at the east end of Cache Creek Drive,

SAFETY IN AVALANCHE COUNTRY

Backcountry skiing is becoming increasingly popular in the mountains surrounding Jackson Hole. Unfortunately, many skiers fail to take the necessary precautions. Given the enormous snowfalls that occur, the steep slopes the snow piles up on, and the high winds that accompany many storms, it should come as no surprise that avalanches are a real danger. Nearly all avalances are triggered by the victims. If you really want to avoid avalanches, ski only on groomed ski trails or "bombproof" slopes which, because of aspect, shape, and slope angle, never seem to slide. Unfortunately, this isn't always possible, so an understanding of the conditions that lead to avalanches is imperative for backcountry skiers. The Forest Service produces a useful booklet called *Basic Guidelines for Winter Recreation*, available in many of their offices around Wyoming. The best way to learn about backcountry safety is from an avalanche class such as those taught by the **American Avalanche Institute**, Box 308, Wilson, WY 83014, tel. (307) 733-3315; **Jackson Community Education**, tel. (307) 733-7425; or **Jackson Hole Mountain Guides**, tel. (307) 733-4979. Failing that, you can help protect yourself by following these precautions when you head into the backcountry:

• Before leaving, get up-to-date avalanche information by calling the 24-hour **Forest Service Avalanche Forecast** at (307) 733-2664. If they say the avalanche danger is high, try skiing on the flats instead.

• Be sure to carry extra warm clothes, water, high-energy snacks, a dual-frequency avalanche transceiver (make sure it's turned on and know how to use it!), a lightweight snow shovel (for digging snow pits, emergency snow shelters, or excavating

avalanche victims), first-aid supplies, a Swiss Army knife, a topographic map, an extra plastic ski tip, a flashlight, matches, and a compass. Many skiers also carry that cure-all, duct tape, wrapped around a ski pole. Let someone know exactly where you are going and when you expect to return. It's also a good idea to carry special ski poles that extend into probes in case of an avalanche.

• Check the angle of an area before you ski through it; slopes of 30-45 degrees are the most dangerous; lesser slopes do not slide as frequently.

• Watch the weather; winds over 15 mph can pile snow much more deeply on lee slopes, causing dangerous loading on the snowpack. Especially avoid skiing on or below cornices.

• Avoid the leeward side of ridges, where snow loading can be greatest.

• Be aware of gullies and bowls; they're more likely to slip than flat open slopes or ridgetops. Stay out of gullies at the bottom of wide bowls; these are natural avalanche chutes.

• Look out for cracks in the snow, and listen for hollow snow underfoot. These are strong signs of dangerous conditions.

• Look at the trees. Smaller trees may indicate that avalanches rip through an area frequently, knocking over the larger trees. Avalanches can, however, also run through forested areas.

• Know how much new snow has fallen recently. Heavy new snow over older weak snow layers is a sure sign of extreme danger on potential avalanche slopes. Most avalanches slip during or immediately after a storm.

• Learn how to dig a snow pit and how to read the various snow layers. Particularly important are the very weak layers of depth hoar or surface hoar that have been buried under heavy new snow.

where the plowing ends at a parking lot. Snow-mobiles and other skiers have packed the route. For a longer trip, take the Rafferty ski lift at Snow King and then ski west through the trees and down to Cache Creek, returning via the road. Ask at Snow King Resort for specifics. Another popular local place is along the **Snake River dikes,** where State 22 crosses the river (a mile east of Wilson). The dikes extend along both sides of the river for several miles, making for easy skiing. It's also a good place to watch ducks, moose, and other critters or just to listen to the river rolling over the rocks. More flat, easy skiing is on Moose-Wilson Road just north of Jackson Hole Ski Resort.

Grand Teton National Park Area

A bit farther afield, but well worth the detour, are several trails in Grand Teton National Park. Orange markers denote the paths, but these are not machine-groomed, just tracks laid down by other skiers. Park at the Cottonwood Creek bridge (the road isn't plowed beyond this), and head out for **Jenny Lake** (nine miles roundtrip) or **Taggart Lake** (three miles roundtrip). Just three miles south of Moose on Moose-Wilson Road, you may also want to try the trail to **Phelps Lake** (five miles roundtrip). Or, if you have more ambition and skill, longer routes could take you far up into the canyons of the Tetons. Be sure to stop at the Moose Visitor Center for current conditions and a copy of their trail map. Overnight ski tourers must also register here.

For unsurpassed vistas of the Tetons, try skiing to the top of 8,252-foot **Shadow Mountain,** 14 miles northeast of Jackson. (The name comes from the shadows of the Tetons that fall across the mountain's face each evening.) From the town of Kelly, drive another five miles north to a parking area (the road isn't plowed beyond this) and then ski up the nearby Forest Service road that snakes up Shadow Mountain. It's fair-ly steep in places and 10 miles roundtrip. Snow-mobilers also use this road.

Granite Hot Springs

One of the most popular ski- and snowmobile-in sites is **Granite Hot Springs,** tel. (307) 733-6318, a delightful 105° F hot-spring-fed pool on Forest Service land. Get there by driving 25 miles southeast of Jackson into Hoback Canyon and then skiing 10 miles in from the signed parking area. The route is not difficult, but due to the distance it isn't recommended for beginners unless they are prepared for a 20-mile roundtrip trek. The pool ($5.50 for adults, $3.50 for kids) is open 10 a.m. to an hour before dark. Bring your swimsuit. Ask the attendant about places to snow camp nearby.

Teton Pass

Locals head to 8,429-foot Teton Pass when they really want to test their abilities. The summit parking area fills with cars on fresh-snow mornings as everyone from advanced beginners to beyond-advanced mountaineering skiers heads out for a day in the powder or a week of wilderness trekking in the Tetons. Snow depths of eight feet or more are not uncommon in mid-winter. (The snow once became so deep on the pass that it took plows two weeks to clear the road!) The slopes around Teton Pass cover the full spectrum, but be sure you know your own ability and how to avoid avalanches. There are avalanche chutes all over here.

Before heading out, check the above-mentioned Skinny Skis *Trailhead Guide* for specifics on Teton Pass or talk to folks at Skinny Skis or Teton Mountaineering. This is the backcountry, so you won't see any signs at the various bowls; ask other skiers if you aren't sure which is which. Avalanches do occur in some of these bowls, and it's possible to get lost up here during a storm, so be prepared. Skiers frequently ski the five miles down old Teton Pass Road.

GRAND TETON NATIONAL PARK

Grand Teton National Park remains one of the preeminent symbols of American wilderness. The Tetons rise abruptly from the valley floor, their bare triangular ridges looking like broken shards of glass from some cosmic accident of creation. With six different summits topping 12,000 feet, plus some of the finest climbing and hiking in Wyoming, the Tetons are a paradise for lovers of the outdoors. They have long been a favorite of photographers and sightseers and once even appeared in an ad promoting Colorado tourism! The Tetons change character with the seasons. In summer the sagebrush flats are a garden of flowers set against the mountain backdrop. When autumn falls on the land, the cottonwoods and aspens become swaths of yellow and orange. Winter turns everything a glorious, sparkling white, set against the fluorescent blue sky.

GEOLOGY

Building a Mountain Range

The precipitous Teton range contains perhaps the most complex geologic history in North America. Although the Tetons are ancient by any human scale, they are the youngest mountains in the Rockies, less than 10 million years old (versus 60 million years for the nearby Wind River Mountains). The Tetons are a fault-block range, formed when the earth's crust cracked along an angled fault. Forces within the earth have pushed the western side (the Tetons) up, while the eastern portion (Jackson Hole) dropped down like a trapdoor. Geologists believe the fault could slip up to 10 feet at a time, producing a violent earthquake. All this shifting has created one of the most dramatic and asymmetric mountain faces on earth.

Unlike typical mountain ranges, the highest parts are not at the center of the range but along the eastern edge, where uplifting continues. The western slope, which drops gently into Idaho, is much less dramatic, though the views are still very impressive. This tilting-and-subsidence process is still going on today. The town of Wilson in Jackson Hole now lies 10 feet below the level of the nearby Snake River; only riverside dikes protect the town from flooding.

As the mountains rose along this fault, millennia of overlying deposits were stripped away by erosion, leaving three-million-year-old Precambrian rock jutting into the air above the more recent sedimentary deposits in the valley. Because of this shifting and erosion, sandstone deposits atop Mt. Moran match those 24,000 feet below Jackson Hole.

Rivers of Ice

In counterpoint to the uplifting actions that created the general outline of the Tetons, erosional forces have been wearing them down again.

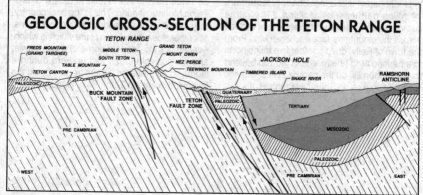

GEOLOGIC CROSS~SECTION OF THE TETON RANGE

REDRAWN FROM U.S.G.S. MAP OF THE GRAND TETON NATIONAL PARK

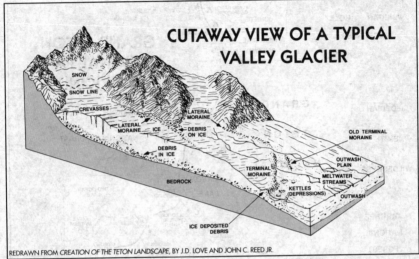

CUTAWAY VIEW OF A TYPICAL VALLEY GLACIER

SNOW

SNOW LINE

CREVASSES

LATERAL MORAINE

LATERAL MORAINE   ICE   DEBRIS ON ICE

DEBRIS IN ICE

BEDROCK

TERMINAL MORAINE

KETTLES (DEPRESSIONS)

OLD TERMINAL MORAINE

OUTWASH PLAIN

MELTWATER STREAMS

OUTWASH

ICE DEPOSITED DEBRIS

REDRAWN FROM *CREATION OF THE TETON LANDSCAPE,* BY J.D. LOVE AND JOHN C. REED JR.

Glaciers—created when more snow falls than melts off—have proven one of the most important of these erosional processes. After a period of several years and under the weight of additional snow, the accumulated snow crystals change into ice. Gravity pulls this ice slowly downhill, creating what is essentially a frozen river that grinds against whatever lies in the way, plucking loose rocks and soil and polishing hard bedrock. This debris moves slowly down the glacier as if on a conveyer belt, eventually reaching its terminus.

When a glacier remains the same size for a long period, large piles of glacial debris accumulate at its end, creating what glaciologists call a terminal moraine. One of these, Jackson Lake, was created when a huge glacier dumped tons of rock at its snout. After the glacier melted back, this terminal moraine became a natural dam for the waters of the Snake River. Similar mounds of glacial debris dammed the creeks that formed Jenny, Leigh, Bradley, Taggart, and Phelps Lakes within Grand Teton National Park.

Streams flowed from the ends of the glaciers, carrying along gravel, sand, silt, and clay. The cobbles and sands from these glacial streams were dropped on the flat valley below, while the finer silts and clays continued downstream, leaving behind soils too rocky and nutrient-poor to support trees. Only sagebrush grows on this flat plain today, while the surrounding hills and mountain slopes (which were spared this rocky deposition) are covered with lodgepole and subalpine fir forests. Trees can also be found covering the silty terminal moraines that ring the lakes.

Other reminders of the glacial past are the "potholes" (more accurately termed "kettles") that dot the plain south of Signal Mountain. These depressions were created when large blocks of ice were buried under glacial outwash. Only a dozen or so small glaciers remain in the Tetons; the largest is the 3,500-foot-long Teton Glacier, visible on the northeastern face of Grand Teton. For a more detailed picture of Teton geology, read *Creation of the Teton Landscape,* by J. D. Love and John C. Reed, Jr. (Moose: Grand Teton Natural History Association).

WILDLIFE

Grand Teton National Park is an excellent place to look for wildlife. Moose are often seen in the willow meadows along Jackson Lake, south of the settlement of Moose, and along the Snake River. Herds of pronghorn antelope are common on the sagebrush flats near Kelly. Elk (park biologists prefer the term "wapiti") are frequent

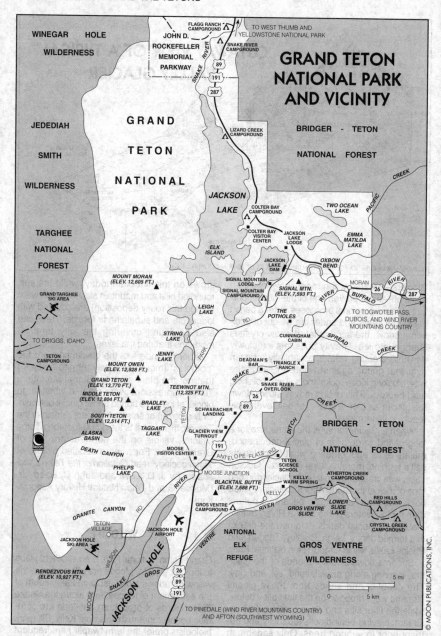

WINEGAR HOLE WILDERNESS

JOHN D. ROCKEFELLER MEMORIAL PARKWAY

FLAGG RANCH CAMPGROUND

TO WEST THUMB AND YELLOWSTONE NATIONAL PARK

SNAKE RIVER

SNAKE RIVER CAMPGROUND

89
191
287

GRAND TETON NATIONAL PARK AND VICINITY

LIZARD CREEK CAMPGROUND

JEDEDIAH

SMITH

WILDERNESS

BRIDGER - TETON

NATIONAL FOREST

PACIFIC CREEK

GRAND

TETON

NATIONAL

PARK

JACKSON LAKE

COLTER BAY CAMPGROUND

TWO OCEAN LAKE

TARGHEE

NATIONAL

FOREST

COLTER BAY VISITOR CENTER

JACKSON LAKE LODGE

EMMA MATILDA LAKE

ELK ISLAND

JACKSON LAKE DAM

OXBOW BEND

MORAN

26

RIVER

287

GRAND TARGHEE SKI AREA

MOUNT MORAN (ELEV. 12,605 FT.)

SIGNAL MOUNTAIN LODGE

SIGNAL MOUNTAIN CAMPGROUND

SIGNAL MTN. (ELEV. 7,593 FT.)

RIVER

BUFFALO

TO TOGWOTEE PASS, DUBOIS, AND WIND RIVER MOUNTAINS COUNTRY

LEIGH LAKE

THE POTHOLES

SPREAD

TO DRIGGS, IDAHO

TETON CAMPGROUND

STRING LAKE

RD.

CUNNINGHAM CABIN

CREEK

MOUNT OWEN (ELEV. 12,928 FT.)

JENNY LAKE

PARK

DEADMAN'S BAR

TRIANGLE X RANCH

SNAKE

GRAND TETON (ELEV. 13,770 FT.)

MIDDLE TETON (ELEV. 12,804 FT.)

TEEWINOT MTN. (12,325 FT.)

SNAKE RIVER OVERLOOK

CREEK

SOUTH TETON (ELEV. 12,514 FT.)

BRADLEY LAKE

TETON

26

SCHWABACHER LANDING

89

ALASKA BASIN

TAGGART LAKE

DITCH

DEATH CANYON

GLACIER VIEW TURNOUT

BRIDGER - TETON

PHELPS LAKE

MOOSE VISITOR CENTER

191

ANTELOPE FLATS RD.

NATIONAL FOREST

MOOSE JUNCTION

TETON SCIENCE SCHOOL

ATHERTON CREEK CAMPGROUND

RIVER

BLACKTAIL BUTTE (ELEV. 7,688 FT.)

KELLY WARM SPRING

KELLY

LOWER SLIDE LAKE

RED HILLS CAMPGROUND

GRANITE CANYON

RD.

GROS VENTRE CAMPGROUND

RIVER

GROS VENTRE SLIDE

CRYSTAL CREEK CAMPGROUND

TETON VILLAGE

JACKSON HOLE AIRPORT

NATIONAL

GROS VENTRE

JACKSON HOLE SKI AREA

WILSON

VENTRE

ELK

WILDERNESS

RENDEZVOUS MTN. (ELEV. 10,927 FT.)

SNAKE

GROS

REFUGE

JACKSON HOLE

26
89
191

0   5 mi

0   5 km

TO PINEDALE (WIND RIVER MOUNTAINS COUNTRY) AND AFTON (SOUTHWEST WYOMING)

© MOON PUBLICATIONS, INC.

sights in fall as they migrate down from the high country to the elk refuge near Jackson, but they can also be seen in the park during the summer. (Grand Teton is the only national park outside Alaska that allows hunting. The rules are pretty strange, however, requiring elk hunters to become temporarily deputized park rangers before they head out!) Grizzlies are currently found only on the park's northern margins, but black bears are present in wooded canyons and riverbottoms.

Bison (buffalo) are commonly seen in the Moran Junction area. They were present historically (hence the name Buffalo River) but had been extinct for perhaps a century when eight bison were released into Grand Teton National Park in 1969. The population grew slowly for the first decade until they discovered the free alfalfa handout at the elk refuge north of Jackson. With this winter feed, the population has grown to 100 animals—much to the chagrin of the elk-refuge managers. A public hunt has been instituted to control bison numbers. Other animals to look for are bald eagles and ospreys along the Snake River and trumpeter swans and Canada geese in ponds and lakes. The best times to see animals are in the early morning or at dusk.

HISTORY

Once the wonders of Yellowstone came to widespread public attention, it took only a few months for Congress to declare the area a national park, but the magnificent mountain range to the south proved an entirely different story. Early on, there were suggestions that Yellowstone be expanded to include the Tetons, but it would take decades of wrangling before Jackson Hole would finally be preserved.

"Damning" Jackson Lake

Jackson Lake represents one of the sadder chapters in the history of northwestern Wyoming. Jackson Lake Dam was built in the winter of 1910-11 to supply water for Idaho potato and beet farmers. The town of Moran was built to house construction workers for Jackson Lake Dam and at one time included more than a hundred ramshackle structures. Nothing remains of the town. The 70-foot-tall dam increased the size of the natural lake, flooding out more than 7,200 acres of trees and creating a tangle of floating and submerged trunks and stumps. To some, the dam seemed like the serpent in the Garden of Eden, a symbol of the development that would destroy the valley if not stopped. The trees remained in Jackson Lake for many years, creating an eyesore until the Park Service and the CCC finally launched a massive cleanup project in the 1930s. The dam was completely rebuilt in 1988-89, and while the lake now looks quite attractive, it remains yet another example of how Wyoming provides water for farmers in surrounding states. Late in the fall—especially in recent dry years—the lake can drop to a large puddle with long stretches of exposed bottom at the upper end. Fortunately, Idaho irrigators did not succeed in their planned dams on Jenny, Leigh, and Taggart Lakes.

Dudes and Development

Because of the rocky soils and long winters, Jackson Hole has always been a marginal place for cattle ranching, and only in the southern end of the valley are the soils rich enough to support a decent crop of hay. It was this poor soil and harsh climate that saved Jackson Hole from early development and forced the ranchers to bring in dudes to supplement their income. (One old-timer noted, "Dudes winter better than cattle.")

The first Jackson Hole dude ranch, the JY, was established along Phelps Lake by Louis Joy. It was quickly followed by the Bar BC Ranch of Struthers Burt, an acclaimed East Coast author who had come west as a dude but learned enough to go into the business for himself. The dude ranchers were some of the first to realize the value of Jackson Hole and to support its preservation. Burt proposed that the valley and mountains be saved not as a traditional park but as a "museum on the hoof," where ranching and tourism would join hands to stave off commercial developments. The roads would remain unpaved, all homes would be log, and Jackson would stay a frontier town.

The movement to save Jackson Hole coalesced in a 1923 meeting at the cabin of Maude Noble. Horace Albright, superintendent of Yellowstone National Park, was there, along with

local dude ranchers, businessmen, and cattlemen eager to save the remote valley from exploitation. To accomplish this goal, they proposed finding a wealthy philanthropist who might be willing to invest the two million dollars that would be needed to buy the land. Fortunately, one of Struthers Burt's friends happened to be Kenneth Chorley, an assistant to John D. Rockefeller, Jr. Burt used this contact to get Rockefeller interested in the project.

Rocky to the Rescue
In 1926, Rockefeller traveled west for a 12-day trip to Yellowstone. Horace Albright used the chance to take him on a side trip into Jackson Hole and to proselytize for protection of the valley. What they saw portended badly for the future: the Jenny Lake dance hall, roadside tourist camps and hot dog stands, rusting abandoned cars, and a place that billboards proclaimed "Home of the Hollywood Cowboy." Rockefeller was angered by the prospect of crass commercial developments blanketing Jackson Hole and quickly signed on to the idea of purchasing the land and giving it to the Park Service.

To cover his tracks as he bought the land, Rockefeller formed the Snake River Land Company—if ranchers had known that the Rockefeller clan was behind the scheme, they would have either refused to sell or jacked up the price. Only a few residents—mostly supporters—knew of the plan. The local banker, Robert Miller, served as land-purchasing agent, although even he opposed letting the Park Service gain control of the valley. Miller used his position to buy out ranches with delinquent mortgages at his Jackson State Bank and then resigned, claiming the whole thing was part of a sinister plot to run the ranchers out and halt "progress." In 1929, Congress voted to establish a small Grand Teton National Park that would encompass the mountains themselves—which stood little chance of development—but not much else. Conservationists knew that without preservation of the valley below, the wonderful vistas would be lost.

A National Battleground
Rockefeller and Albright finally went public with their land-purchasing scheme in 1930, releasing a tidal wave of outrage. Antipark forces led by Sen. Milward Simpson (father of recently re-

tired Sen. Alan Simpson) spent the next decade fighting the park tooth and nail, charging that it would destroy the economy of Jackson Hole and that ranchers would lose their livelihood. Rockefeller's agents were falsely accused of trying to intimidate holdouts with strong-arm tactics. Congress refused to accept Rockefeller's gift, and local opposition blocked the bill for more than a decade.

Finally, in 1943, President Roosevelt made an end run around the antipark forces; he accepted the 32,000 acres purchased by Rockefeller, added 130,000 acres of Forest Service land, and declared it the Jackson Hole National Monument. The move outraged those in the valley, prompting more hearings and bills to abolish the new national monument. Wyoming's politicians attacked Roosevelt's actions. A bill overturning the decision was pocket-vetoed by the president, but for the next several years, the Wyoming delegation kept reintroducing the measure.

Things came to a head when Wallace Beery—a Reaganesque Hollywood actor—threatened to "shoot to kill" park officials. Beery—who had to use a stepladder to climb on his horse—organized a cattle drive across the monument. Unable to find anyone to fire on in the new monument, his cadres sat on a creek bank and drank a case of beer, cussing out the damn bureaucrats. So much for the Wild West.

By 1947, the tide had turned as increasing postwar tourism revitalized the local economy. Finally, in 1950, a compromise was reached granting ranchers lifetime grazing rights and the right to trail their cattle across the park en route to summer grazing lands. The new-and-improved Grand Teton National Park had finally come to fruition.

Postmortem
Some of the early fears that Rockefeller would use the new park for his own gain seem at least partly justified. His descendants still own the old JY Ranch and use Phelps Lake as something of a semiprivate playground, while most of the other dude ranches have long since been taken over by the Park Service. Rockefeller also built the enormous Grand Teton Lodge along Jackson Lake and facilities at Colter Bay Village and Jenny Lake, leading some to accuse

BEAVER DICK LEIGH

Around 1863, Richard "Beaver Dick" Leigh became the first white man to attempt a permanent life in Jackson Hole. An Englishman by birth, Beaver Dick lived in a log cabin with his Shoshone wife, Jenny, and their four children, scraping out the barest existence by hunting, trapping, and guiding. As guide for the 1872 Hayden Survey of the Jackson Hole area, Beaver Dick gained the respect of the surveyors who named Leigh Lake for him and Jenny Lake for his wife. Today a local bar denigrates this remarkable man by calling itself Beaver Dick's and using a cartoonish image of him in its ads. The real man was nothing like this, and reading his diaries and letters is a lesson in how difficult life was for early Wyoming settlers. On one terrible Christmas in 1876, Beaver Dick watched his entire family—Jenny, their newborn baby, and the four other children—all slowly die from smallpox. Their deaths left him badly shaken, as he related in a letter to a friend:

i got Dick in the house and to bed and Tom went over to get Mr. Anes. Wile Tom and Anes was sounding the ice to see if a horse could cross my wife was struck with Death. she rased up and looked me streaght in the face and then she got excited . . . and she sade she was going to die and all our childron wold die and maby i wold die . . . she was laying very quiet now for about 2 hours when she asked for a drink of water. i was laying downe with one of my daughters on eatch arme keeping them quiet because of the fevor. i told Anes what she wanted and he gave hur a drink and 10 minuts more she was ded . . . i can not wright one hundreth part that pased thrue my mind at this time as i thaught deth was on me. i sade Jinny i will sone be with you and fell asleep. Tom sade i ad beene a sleep a half hour when i woke up everything was wet with presperation i was very weak. i lade for 10 or 15 minuts and saw William and Anne Jane had to be taken up to ease themselves every 5 minuts and Dick Juner very restlas . . . Anne Jane died about 8 o clock about the time every year i used to give them a candy puling and thay menchond about the candy puling many times wile sick . . . William died on the 25 about 9 or 10 o clock in the evening . . . on the 26th Dick Juner died . . . Elizabeth was over all danger but this, and she caught cold and sweled up agane and died on the 28 of Dec about 2 o clock in the morning. this was the hardist blow of all . . . i shall improve the place and live and die near my famley but i shall not be able to do enything for a few months for my mind is disturbed at the sights that i see around me and [the] work that my famley as done wile thay were liveing.

But the human spirit is remarkably resilient. Beaver Dick later married a Bannock girl, raised another family, and guided for others, even meeting Theodore Roosevelt on one of his hunting trips. Beaver Dick Leigh died in 1899 and was buried on a ridge overlooking Idaho's Teton Basin.

Beaver Dick and Jenny Leigh with their children

YELLOWSTONE NATIONAL PARK

the family of attempting to monopolize services within the park. The company, Rockresorts, was finally sold in 1986 to CSX Corporation.

Looking back on the controversial creation of Grand Teton National Park, it's easy to see how wrong park opponents were. Teton County has Wyoming's most vibrant economy, and millions of people arrive each year to enjoy the beauty of the undeveloped Tetons. As writer Nathaniel Burt noted, "The old enemies of the park are riding the profitable bandwagon of unlimited tourism with high hearts and open palms." Park opponents' claims that the Park Service would "lock up" the land ring as hollow as similar antiwilderness claims today by descendants of the same politicians who opposed Grand Teton half a century ago. Without inclusion of the land purchased by Rockefeller, it is easy to imagine the valley covered with all sorts of summer home developments, RV campgrounds, souvenir shops, motels, billboards, and neon signs. Take a look at the town of Jackson to see what might have been.

TOURING THE PARK

Grand Teton National Park has fewer "attractions" than Yellowstone—its big sister to the north—and an easy day's drive takes you past the road-accessible portions of Grand Teton. The real attractions are the mountains and the incomparable views one gets of them from Jackson Hole. This is one backdrop you will never tire of seeing.

Roads

Grand Teton is bisected by the main north-south highway (U.S. 26/89/191) and by the road heading east over Togwotee Pass (U.S. 26/287). Both of these routes are kept open year-round, although wintertime plowing ends at Flagg Ranch, just south of the Yellowstone boundary. In addition, a paved park road cuts south from Jackson Lake Dam to Jenny Lake and Moose. Only the southern end of this is plowed in winter; the remainder becomes a snowmobile and cross-country ski route. South of Moose, a narrow, winding road connects the park to Teton Village, nine miles away. It is rough dirt in places (no trailers or RVs) and is closed in winter. The following tour takes you past the points of in-

terest along the main roads. The route follows a general clockwise direction beginning and ending at the **Moose Visitor Center**, tel. (307) 739-3399. Before heading out, step inside the center for an introduction to the park and a look at the natural history videos, books, and oil paintings. A large three-dimensional map here reveals the lay of the land.

Menor's Ferry Area

Just inside the South Entrance to Grand Teton National Park, a side road leads to **Chapel of the Transfiguration** and **Menor's Ferry.** The rustic log church (built in 1925) is most notable for its dramatic setting. The back window faces directly toward the Tetons, providing ample distractions for worshippers. The bell out front was cast in 1842. Nearby Menor's Ferry is named for William D. Menor, who first homesteaded here in 1894 and later built a cable ferry to make it easier to cross the river. His old whitewashed house still stands. You can cross the river in a reconstructed version of the old ferry when the water level is low enough; check out the ingenious propulsion mechanism that uses the current to pull it across. For many years, Menor's ferry served as the primary means of crossing the river in the central part of Jackson Hole. Wagons were charged 50 cents, while those on horseback paid 25 cents. (William Menor's brother, Holiday, lived on the opposite side of the river, but the two often feuded, yelling insults across the water at each other and refusing to acknowledge one another for years at a time.) Also here is the half-mile **Menor's Ferry Trail;** a brochure describes historic points of interest along the path. Bill Menor's cabin houses a small country store that sells the old fashioned supplies he stocked at the turn of the century.

Menor sold out to Maude Noble in 1918, and she ran the ferry until 1927, when a bridge was built near the present one in Moose. Her cabin now houses an excellent collection of historical photos from Jackson Hole. Maude Noble gained a measure of fame in 1923 when she hosted the gathering of residents to save Jackson Hole from development (see above for park history).

Taggart and Bradley Lakes

Heading northwest beyond the Menor's Ferry area, the main road climbs up an old river bench (created by flooding from the rapid melting of

the glaciers) and passes the trailhead to the turquoise waters of **Taggart Lake.** The land around here was burned in the 1,028-acre Beaver Creek lightning fire of 1985, and summers find a riot of wildflowers. A very popular day-hike leads from the parking area here to Taggart Lake and then back via the Beaver Creek Trail, a distance of four miles roundtrip. A side loop to **Bradley Lake** adds another two miles to this. These trails provide a fine way to explore the dam-like glacial moraines that created these lakes. You can also continue beyond Bradley Lake on a trail that climbs to beautiful Amphitheater Lake, the primary access point for climbs up Grand Teton. (Climbers generally begin from Jenny Lake, however.)

Jenny Lake Area

The most loved of all the Grand Teton lakes is Jenny Lake, nestled at the foot of Cascade Canyon and surrounded by a luxuriant forest of Engelmann spruce, subalpine fir, and lodgepole pine. Jenny Lake is named for Jenny Leigh, the Shoshone wife of Beaver Dick Leigh (see special topic). A one-way loop road leads south past Jenny and String Lakes, providing excellent views of the **Cathedral Group:** Teewinot, Grand Teton, and Mt. Owen. This is the most popular part of the park, and day-hikers will find a plethora of trails to sample (and crowds to contend with. Paths lead around both Jenny and String lakes, while another nearly level trail follows the east shore of Leigh Lake to several pleasant sandy beaches. String Lake is narrow but very pretty and makes a fine place for canoeing or swimming.

One of the most popular attractions in the area is **Inspiration Point,** located on the west side of Jenny Lake. It's two miles by trail from the Jenny Lake Ranger Station, or you can ride one of the summertime shuttle boats that cross the lake every 20 minutes or so for $4 roundtrip ($2.25 for kids, free for ages under six). Scenic boat cruises and fishing boat rentals are also available; call (307) 733-2703. From the boat dock on the west side, the trail climbs a half mile to **Hidden Falls** and then another quarter mile to Inspiration Point, which overlooks Jackson Hole from 400 feet above Jenny Lake. Many day-hikers continue up Cascade Canyon (see "Backcountry Trails" below). If you miss the last boat back at 6 p.m., it's a 2.5-mile hike around the lake to the parking area.

Jenny Lake Lodge sits on the northeast end of the lake and is one of the finest lodging places in Jackson Hole; President Clinton and his family stayed here when they visited in 1995. The gourmet meals are justly famous here, but be sure to make advance reservations by calling (307) 733-4647.

Signal Mountain Area

As the road approaches Jackson Lake, a paved but narrow side road (no RVs or trailers) turns east and leads to the summit of Signal Mountain, 800 feet above Jackson Hole, for fine panoramic views of the Tetons, Jackson Lake, the Snake River, and the long valley below. To the south are **The Potholes,** a hummocky area created when huge blocks of ice were left behind by retreating glaciers. The melting ice created depressions, some of which are still filled with water. Signal Mountain was burned by a massive 1879 fire and offers a good opportunity to see how Yellowstone may look in a century.

Signal Mountain Lodge hugs the southeast shore of Jackson Lake and includes a full range of facilities, including cabins, campsites, a restaurant, and a bar. Just east of the lodge is **Chapel of the Sacred Heart,** a small Roman Catholic church. The road then crosses **Jackson Lake Dam,** which raises the water level by 39 feet, alters the river's natural flow, and inundates a large area upstream. Many conservationists fought to have Jackson Lake excluded from the park, concerned that it would establish a bad precedent for allowing reservoirs in other parks. Nevertheless, once you get away from the dam, the lake seems relatively natural today.

Along Jackson Lake

A pullout near Jackson Lake Junction provides views over **Willow Flats,** where moose are frequently seen, especially in the morning. Impressive **Jackson Lake Lodge** was built in the 1950s with the $5 million financial backing of John D. Rockefeller, Jr. The building tops a bluff overlooking the flats. Architects are not thrilled about the design (one author termed it "the ugliest building in Western Wyoming"), but the 60-foot-tall back windows frame an unbelievable view of the Tetons and Jackson Lake. A historic U.S.-Soviet diplomatic meeting was held here in 1989 between Soviet Foreign Minister

Eduard Shevardnadze and Secretary of State James Baker III. Immediately across from the lodge is a trail leading to **Emma Matilda** and **Two Ocean** Lakes. It is 14 miles roundtrip around both lakes, with lots of wildlife along the way, including moose, trumpeter swans, pelicans, and ducks. You may have to contend with large groups on horseback.

Colter Bay

Colter Bay Village is one of the most developed parts of the park, with a full marina, stores, a gas station, restaurants, and acres of parking. The main attraction here is the visitor center, which houses the **Colter Bay Indian Arts Museum,** tel. (307) 739-3594. Open daily 8 a.m.-5 p.m. mid-May to Memorial Day, daily 8 a.m.-8 p.m. from Memorial Day to Labor Day, and daily 8 a.m.-5 p.m. for the rest of September; no charge. The museum is closed Oct.-April. Inside is the extraordinary David T. Vernon collection of Indian pieces, the finest of its kind in any national park (and certainly one of the best anywhere in Wyoming). The collection spreads through several rooms on two floors and includes exquisitely beaded buckskin dresses, moccasins, kachina dolls, masks, ceremonial pipes, warbonnets, shields, bows, a blanket that belonged to Chief Sitting Bull, and other decorated items. Indian craft-making demonstrations are given daily Memorial Day to Labor Day. This museum is not to be missed!

A mostly level trail leads from the marina out to **Hermitage Point** before looping back again, a distance of nine miles roundtrip. Along the way you pass beaver ponds and willow patches where trumpeter swans, moose, and ducks are commonly seen. Get a map of Colter Bay trails from the visitor center. Shorter loop paths include the two-mile **Lakeshore Trail** and the three-mile **Swan Lake-Heron Pond Trail.**

North to Yellowstone

North of Colter Bay, the highway cruises along the shore of Jackson Lake for the next nine miles, providing a number of fine vantage points across to the Tetons. The burned area on the opposite shore was ignited by lightning in the 1974 Waterfalls Canyon Fire, which consumed 3,700 acres. By late fall each year, Idaho spud farmers have drawn down water in the lake, leaving a long, barren shoreline at the upper end.

Shortly after the road leaves the upper end of Yellowstone Lake, a signboard announces your entrance into **John D. Rockefeller, Jr. Memorial Parkway.** This 24,000-acre parcel of land was transferred to the National Park Service in 1972 in commemoration of Rockefeller's unstinting work in establishing Grand Teton National Park. The land forms a connection between Grand Teton and Yellowstone and is managed by Grand Teton National Park. Much of this area was severely burned by the 1988 Huck Fire, which began when strong winds blew a tree into power lines. Despite immediate efforts to control the blaze, it consumed 4,000 acres in the first two hours and later grew to cover nearly 200,000 acres, primarily within the Forest Service's Teton Wilderness.

On the northern end of Rockefeller Parkway is **Flagg Ranch,** where facilities include a store, a gas station, a new lodge and cabins, a restaurant, and a campground. During the winter, this is the jumping-off point for snowcoach and snowmobile trips into Yellowstone, and snowmobiles are available for rent. **Grassy Lake Road** takes off just north of Flagg Ranch and continues 52 miles to Ashton, Idaho. It's a scenic drive, but don't attempt this narrow and rough dirt road with a trailer or an RV. This route provides a shortcut to the Bechler River area of Yellowstone and is a popular wintertime snowmobile route. Huckleberry Hot Springs, a short hike north from the Grassy Lake Road bridge over the Snake River, was the site of a public swimming pool until 1983, when the facility was razed by the Park Service. The hot springs are accessible via an unmaintained trail, but you'll need to wade Polecat Creek to reach them. Although they remain popular with hikers and cross-country skiers, it's worth noting that the springs may pose a risk from dangerously high radiation levels.

Jackson Lake to Moran Junction

Heading east and south from Jackson Lake, the road immediately passes **Oxbow Bend,** where the pullout is almost always filled with folks looking for geese, ducks, moose, and other animals. The oxbow was formed when the meandering river cut off an old loop. The calm water here is a delightful place for canoes, though the mosquitoes can be a major annoyance in midsummer. Come fall, photographers

line the shoulder of the road for classic shots of flaming aspen trees with Grand Teton and **Mt. Moran** in the background. Mt. Moran is the massive peak with a flattened summit, a skillet-shaped glacier across its front, and a distinctive black vertical diabase dike that looks like a scar from some ancient battle. It rises 12,605 feet above sea level. The peak is named for Thomas Moran, whose beautiful paintings of Yellowstone helped persuade Congress to set aside that area as the world's first national park.

At **Moran Junction** you pass the park's Buffalo Entrance Station and meet the road to Togwotee Pass and Dubois. A post office and school are the only developments here. The epic Western *The Big Trail* was filmed nearby in 1930, starring an actor named John Wayne in his first speaking role. (Wayne had never ridden a horse before this.) An interesting side trip is to head east from Moran on U.S. 26/287 for three miles to **Buffalo Valley Road.** This narrow, scenic road leads to Turpin Meadow, a major entryway into the Teton Wilderness (see "Bridger-Teton National Forest" later in this chapter). Very pretty—especially in early summer when flowers carpet the fields. Buck and rail fences line the road and the pastures are filled with horses and cattle. Purty country. Beyond Turpin Meadow, the road turns to gravel and climbs sharply uphill, rejoining the main highway a couple of miles below Cowboy Village Resort at Togwotee. The Blackrock Ranger Station of Bridger-Teton National Forest is eight miles east of Moran Jct. on U.S. 26/287. Next door is historic **Rosie's Cabin,** built early in this century by Rudolph Rosencrans, an Austrian emigrant who was the first forest ranger in this part of the Tetons.

Moran Junction to Moose

Heading south from Moran, U.S. 26/89/191 immediately crosses the Buffalo River (a.k.a. Buffalo Fork of the Snake River), where bison were once abundant. With a little help from humans, bison have been reestablished and are now often seen just south of here along the road. The turnoff to the **Cunningham Cabin** is six miles south of Moran Junction. The structure actually consists of two sod-roofed log cabins connected by a covered walkway called a "dogtrot." Built around 1890, it served first as living quarters and later as a barn and smithy. A park brochure describes the locations of other structures on the property.

Pierce Cunningham came here as a homesteader and with his wife Margaret settled to raise cattle. Although this was some of the better land in this part of the valley, the soil was still so rocky that they had a hard time digging fencepost holes. Instead, they opted to build the buck-and-rail fences that have become a hallmark of Jackson Hole ranches. Cunningham Ranch gained notoriety in 1893 when a posse surrounded two suspected horse thieves who were wintering at Cunningham's place while he was away. Vigilantes shot and killed George Spencer and Mike Burnett in an example of "mountain justice." Later, however, suspicions arose that hired killers working for wealthy cattle barons had led the posse and that the murdered men may have been innocent. **Spread Creek** is just north of the Cunningham cabin, gaining its name by having two mouths, separated by a distance of three miles.

The highway next rolls past **Triangle X Ranch,** one of the most famous dude ranches in Jackson Hole. Although it's on park land, the Turner family has managed Triangle X for over 60 years. (One of the owners, John Turner, was President Bush's director of the Fish and Wildlife Service.) Stop by just after sunup to watch wranglers driving 120 head of horses up from the lower pastures. It's a scene straight out of a Marlboro ad. Southwest from Triangle X, the road climbs along an ancient river terrace and passes hidden **Hedrick Pond** where the 1963 Henry Fonda movie *Spencer's Mountain* was filmed. Although the book on which it was based was set in Virginia, the producers found the Tetons a considerably more impressive location. Trumpeter swans are sometimes seen on the pond. Several turnouts provide very popular photo-opportunity spots, the most famous being **Snake River Overlook.** Ansel Adams's famous shot of the Tetons was taken here and has been repeated with less success by generations of photographers. Throughout the summer, a progression of different flowers blooms in the open sagebrush flats along the road, adding brilliant slashes of color. They're prettiest in late June; in the high country, the peak comes a month or more later than elsewhere.

Just north of Snake River Overlook is the turnoff to **Deadman's Bar.** An extremely steep dirt road (4WD recommended) drops down to one of the primary river-access points used by river rafters. The river bar received its name from an incident in 1886. Four German prospectors entered the area, but only one—John Tonnar—emerged. Bodies of the other three were found along the Snake River, and Tonnar was charged with murder. The jury in Evanston believed his claim of self-defense, and he was set free, an act that so angered locals that they vowed to take care of future Jackson Hole criminals with a shotgun. A skull from one of the victims is on display in the Jackson Hole Museum. Another popular put-in for river runners is **Schwabacher Landing,** located at the end of a one-mile gravel road that splits off just north of the Glacier View Turnout. This is a pleasant place for riverside picnics.

Blacktail Butte Area
A mile north of the turnoff to Moose, Antelope Flats Road heads east along Ditch Creek. Blacktail Butte lies just south of here, a timbered knoll rising over the surrounding sagebrush plains. It's a favorite of rock-climbers. Keep your eyes peeled for the much-photographed old farm buildings known as **Mormon Row.** The farmland here was homesteaded by predominantly Mormon settlers in the early 1900s but was later purchased by Rockefeller's Snake River Land Company and transferred to the Park Service. A few of the buildings are still occupied, but most are abandoned and gradually collapsing under the heavy winter snows. The road to Mormon Row is filled with potholes.

Teton Science School
Hidden away in a valley along upper Ditch Creek is Teton Science School, a fine hands-on school for both young and old. Founded in 1967 as a summer field-biology program for high-school kids, it has grown into a year-round program with classes that run the gamut from elementary-school level all the way up to intensive college courses and adult seminars. Summertime visitors will enjoy their one- to five-day seminars on such diverse subjects as entomology for fly-fishers, edible and medicinal plants, river channels, and the wolves of Yellowstone. The

school's excellent monthlong wilderness EMT course ($1,635 per person) is one of the few programs of its kind in the nation. During the winter, TSS offers a **winter speaker series** at Snow King Resort in Jackson covering a spectrum of scientific, environmental, and social issues. In the spring and fall, it hosts **fireside chats** at the TSS library, where speakers talk about environmental issues. Call for details as dates vary each year.

The school is based at the old Elbo dude ranch (started in 1932), which includes two small dormitories, a central kitchen, dining area, and other structures. At the main building, visitors will find the large **Murie Collection** of birds, mammal skulls, and other natural-history specimens, including casts of animal tracks used by famed wildlife biologist Olaus Murie in producing his *Peterson's Guide to Animal Tracks.* It's open to the public, but call ahead to be sure it is not being used by a class. Check out the grizzly scat! Get a copy of the course catalog by contacting TSS at Box 68, Kelly, WY 83011, tel. (307) 733-4765.

Kelly Vicinity
The small settlement of **Kelly** borders on the southeastern end of Grand Teton National Park and has some log homes and a cluster of Mongolian-style yurts—certainly the most unusual dwellings in Wyoming. The Park Service's **Gros Ventre Campground** is three miles west of here. Gros Ventre Road leads east from the Kelly area, passing **Kelly Warm Spring** on the right. Its warm, clear waters are a favorite place for local kayakers to practice their rolls. A short distance up the road and off to the north are the collapsing remains of the *Shane* **cabin,** where a scene from the classic 1951 Western was filmed. Beyond this, the road enters Bridger-Teton National Forest and the Slide Lake area, where there is a Forest Service campground.

Gros Ventre Slide
One of the most impressive geologic events in recent Wyoming history took place in the Gros Ventre (pronounced "GROW-vont"—"Big Belly" in French trapper lingo) Canyon, named for the Gros Ventre Indians of this area. Sheep Mountain, on the south side of the canyon, consists of sandstone underlain by a layer of shale that becomes slippery when wet. Melting snow and

heavy rains in the spring of 1925 lubricated this layer of shale, and on June 23 the entire north end of the mountain—a section 2,000 feet wide and a mile long—suddenly slid a mile and a half downslope, instantly damming the river below and creating Slide Lake. A rancher in the valley, Guil Huff, watched in amazement as the mountain began to move, galloping his horse out of the way as the slide roared within 30 feet of him. Huff's ranch floated away on the new lake several days later.

For two years folks kept a wary eye on the makeshift dam of rock and mud. Then, on May 18, 1927, the dam suddenly gave way, pushing an enormous wall of water through the downstream town of Kelly. Six people perished in the flood, and when the water reached Snake River Canyon nine hours later it filled the canyon to the rim with boiling water, trees, houses, and debris. Today a smaller Slide Lake still exists, and the massive landslide that created it more than 65 years ago remains an exposed gouge visible for miles around. Geologists say that, under the right conditions, more of Sheep Mountain could slide. Dead trees still stand in the upper end of Slide Lake.

Gros Ventre River

Above Slide Lake, the road turns to gravel (unplowed in winter), becoming quite rutted in spots. Surprising scenery makes the bone-jarring route easier to take. The landscape here is far different from that of the Tetons, with the road passing colorful badlands hills rising sharply above the Gros Ventre River. Two more campgrounds (Red Hills and Crystal Creek) are four miles above Slide Lake. The road continues another 15 beautiful miles along the river, getting rougher at the upper end. The Gros Ventre Wilderness lies immediately south of the road and you'll encounter quite a few trailheads along the way. On the way back down the Gros Ventre River valley you will discover some fine views across to the Tetons.

BACKCOUNTRY HIKING

The precipitous Tetons that look so dramatic from the roads are even more impressive up close and personal. Grand Teton National Park is laced with 200 miles of trails, and hikers can choose anything from simple day-treks to week-long trips along the crest of the range. Unlike nearby Yellowstone, where most of the country is forested, the Tetons contain extensive Alpine scenery. This means, however, that many of the high passes won't be free of snow until late July and may require ice axes before then. Check at the visitor centers or Jenny Lake Ranger Station for current conditions.

The most popular hiking area centers on the crest of the Tetons and the lakes that lie at its feet, most notably Jenny Lake. **Teton Crest Trail** stretches from Teton Pass north all the way to Cascade Canyon, with numerous connecting paths from both sides of the range. Three relatively short (two to three days) loop hikes are described below. For more complete descriptions of park trails, see *Teton Trails* by Bryan Harry (Moose: Grand Teton Natural History Association) or *Hiking the Teton Backcountry* by Paul Lawrence (San Francisco: Sierra Club Books). Get topographic maps at the Moose Visitor Center or Teton Mountaineering in Jackson.

Regulations

The hiking trails of Grand Teton National Park are some of the most heavily used paths in Wyoming, and strict regulations are enforced. Backcountry-use permits (free) are required of all overnight hikers, and you'll need to specify a particular camping zone or site for each night of your trip. Get permits and detailed backcountry brochures from the visitor center in Moose or Colter Bay or at the Jenny Lake Ranger Station. Get there early in the morning during the summer for permits to popular trails. A limited number of backcountry permits may be reserved in advance (Jan. 1 to May 15 only) by writing the Permits Office, Grand Teton National Park, P.O. Drawer 170, Moose, WY 83012. For faster service, send a fax to (307) 739-3438. Grizzlies are only found in the northern end of Grand Teton, but you still need to hang all food, since black bears roam throughout the park, particularly in the forested areas along the lakes, where special boxes are provided for food storage. Campfires are not allowed at higher elevations, so be sure to bring a cooking stove. Bikes are not allowed on trails anywhere in the park.

TETON HIKING TRAILS

MOUNT MORAN

JACKSON LAKE

LEIGH LAKE

PAINTBRUSH DIVIDE

HOLLY LAKE

PAINTBRUSH CANYON TRAIL

LAKE SOLITUDE

STRING LAKE

JENNY LAKE LODGE

TO JACKSON LAKE DAM

GRAND TARGHEE RESORT

FREDS MOUNTAIN

CASCADE CANYON TRAIL

INSPIRATION POINT

JENNY LAKE

TO ALTA AND DRIGGS

TETON

HIDDEN FALLS

JENNY LAKE

MT. OWEN TEEWINOT MOUNTAIN

TABLE MOUNTAIN

JEDEDIAH SMITH WILDERNESS

DISAPPOINTMENT PEAK

LUPINE MEADOWS

ALASKA BASIN TRAIL

GRAND TETON

AMPHITHEATER LAKE

TIMBERED ISLAND

SNAKE RIVER

DEVIL'S STAIRS

MIDDLE TETON

BRADLEY LAKE

ALASKA BASIN

SOUTH TETON

TAGGART LAKE

CLIMBERS RANCH

GRAND TETON NATIONAL PARK

TO MORAN

TETON CREST TRAIL

DEATH CANYON TRAIL

VALLEY TRAIL

JACKSON HOLE

MOOSE-WILSON RD.

MENOR'S FERRY

DITCH CREEK

FOX CREEK PASS

WHITE GRASS RANGER STATION

MOOSE VISITOR CENTER

DORNAN'S

PHELPS LAKE

OPEN CANYON TRAIL

J Y RANCH

BLACKTAIL BUTTE

GRANITE CANYON TRAIL

TO JACKSON

RENDEZVOUS MOUNTAIN

JACKSON HOLE SKI AREA

TRAMWAY

AIRPORT

GROS VENTRE

NATIONAL

TO TETON PASS

TETON VILLAGE

390

26

89

191

ELK

REFUGE

0   2 mi

0   2 km

© MOON PUBLICATIONS, INC.

Cascade Canyon to Paintbrush Canyon

One of the most popular hikes in Grand Teton is this 19-mile loop trip up Cascade Canyon, over Paintbrush Divide, and down Paintbrush Canyon (or vice versa). The trip offers a little of everything: hiking through dense forests, magnificent views of Grand Teton, alpine lakes, and flower-covered meadows. This trip is best done in late summer, since a cornice of snow typically blocks Paintbrush Divide until late July. Most folks do this as an overnight trip, but it's possible to do the entire loop in a single (very long) day if you're in good shape. Be sure to bring plenty of water along.

Begin at the String Lake trailhead and head south around Jenny Lake, stopping to enjoy the views (and crowds) at Inspiration Point before heading up along Cascade Creek. The trail splits at the upper end of this canyon; turning left takes you to Hurricane Pass and the Teton Crest Trail where you'll discover fine views of the back side of Grand Teton. Instead, turn right (north) and

head up to beautiful Lake Solitude. Behind you, Teewinot, Mt. Owen, and Grand Teton are framed by the glacially carved valley walls. Above Lake Solitude, the trail climbs sharply to Paintbrush Divide and then switchbacks even more quickly down into Paintbrush Canyon. The trail eventually leads back to String Lake. Be sure to stop at beautiful Holly Lake on the way down.

Amphitheater Lake

A relatively short but very steep hike begins at the Lupine Meadows trailhead just south of Jenny Lake. It is only five miles to the cirque of Amphitheater Lake but 3,000 feet higher, making this the quickest climb to the Teton treeline. Many folks day-hike this trail to savor the wonderful vistas across Jackson Hole along the way. Camping is available at Surprise Lake a half-mile below Amphitheater. More adventurous folks may want to climb **Disappointment Peak,** the 11,618-foot summit directly in front of Grand Teton. (It was named by climbers who mistakenly thought they were on the east face of Grand Teton.) If you plan to do so, first talk to the climbing rangers at Jenny Lake—and only attempt it if you're able to handle a few areas of class 3 moves.

Rendezvous Mountain to Death Canyon

This 23-mile-long loop hike is different in that much of the way is downhill. Begin at the Jackson Hole tram in Teton Village, where a $15 ticket takes you to the top of Rendezvous Mountain. From the summit, the trail leads down to a saddle, across the South Fork of Granite Creek, and up to Teton Crest Trail. Head north on this trail to Marion Lake—a popular camping site—and then over Fox Creek Pass. The trail splits, and the right fork drops sharply down into scenic Death Canyon, named when a member of a survey party disappeared here in 1903. At the lower end of Death Canyon, cliffs rise nearly 3,000 feet on both sides. The trail forks at Phelps Lake, and from here you can either hike back to Teton Village via the Valley Trail or head to the trailhead at White Grass Ranger Station, 1.5 miles northeast of Phelps Lake. Note: If you reverse the direction of this hike you can save your money, since there is no charge for riding the tram down to Teton Village.

MOUNTAIN CLIMBING

The Tetons are considered some of the premier mountaineering country in the nation, with solid rock, good access, and a wide range of climbing conditions. Hundreds of climbing routes have been described for the main peaks, but the goal of many climbers is Grand Teton, better known as "the Grand." At 13,770 feet, this is Wyoming's second-highest summit, exceeded only by 13,804-foot Gannett Peak in the Wind River Mountains.

First to the Top

In the climbing trade, first ascents always rate highly, but the identity of the first to have scaled Grand Teton has long been a matter of debate. The official record belongs to the party of William Owen (as in nearby Mt. Owen), Bishop Spalding (as in nearby Spalding Peak), John Shive, and Frank Petersen, who reached the summit in 1898. Today, however, it appears that they were preceded by two members of the 1872 Hayden Expedition: Nathaniel P. Langford (first superintendent of Yellowstone National Park) and John Stevenson. In addition, another party made it to the top in 1893. Owen made a big deal out of his climb and spent 30 years trying to work himself into the record books by claiming the Langford party never reached the top. The whole thing got quite nasty, with Owen even accusing Langford of bribing the author of a history book to gain top honors. In 1929, Owen convinced the Wyoming Legislature to declare his party the first on top. Few people believe it today, and the whole thing looks pretty foolish since even seven-year-old kids have made it to the top. Several thousand people climb the Grand each summer, many with no previous climbing experience (but excellent guides and a couple days of training). And just to prove that it could be done, in 1971 one fanatic actually skied the Grand (he's the ski-school director at Snow King Resort), followed in 1989 by a snowboarder. Both lived to tell the tale.

Getting There

Most climbing takes place when the snow has melted back between mid-July and late September. Overnight mountain climbing or off-trail hiking requires a special permit available from

the **Jenny Lake Ranger Station** (staffed June to mid-September). There's no need to register if you're climbing or doing off-trail hiking for the day only, just for overnight trips. In the winter months, register at the Moose Visitor Center. The climbing rangers—one of the most prestigious and dangerous jobs in the park—are all highly experienced mountaineers and can provide specific route information for the various summits. Call (307) 739-3604 for additional climbing info.

Many climbers who scale Grand Teton follow the Amphitheater Lake Trail from Lupine Meadows to its junction with the Garnet Canyon Trail. This leads to the **Lower Saddle,** which separates Grand Teton and Middle Teton. Exum and the Park Service have base camp huts and steel storage boxes here, along with an outhouse. Other folks pitch tents behind boulders in this extraordinarily windy mountain gap. See Park Service handouts for camping restrictions and recommendations in this fragile alpine area where heavy use by 4,000 climbers each year has caused considerable damage. The final assault on the summit of Grand Teton requires technical equipment and expertise. No motorized drills are allowed for the placement of climbing bolts. Mountaineers can stay at **Climbers' Ranch,** near Taggart Lake, for $6 a night including bunk accommodations with showers and covered cooking areas; bring your own sleeping bag and food. The ranch is open mid-June to mid-September only. Call (307) 733-7271 for reservations.

Climbing Schools

Jackson Hole is blessed with two of the finest climbing schools in North America: **Jackson Hole Mountain Guides,** 165 N. Glenwood, tel. (307) 733-4979, and **Exum Mountain Guides,** tel. (307) 733-2297, with a summertime office at the south end of Jenny Lake near the boat dock. Both are authorized concessions of the National Park Service and the U.S. Forest Service and offer a wide range of classes, snow training, and climbs in the Tetons and elsewhere—even as far away as Alaska and the Himalayas. Exum has been around since 1931, when Glenn Exum pioneered the first solo climb of what has become the most popular route to the top of the Grand, the Exum Route. Exum is the only guide service permitted to guide all Teton peaks and routes throughout the year. Exum's base camp is located in the busy

Lower Saddle area, while Jackson Hole Mountain Guides' base camp is 450 feet lower in elevation in a more secluded location.

During midsummer, expect to pay around $675 (including food, gear, and shelter) for an ascent of Grand Teton; this includes two days of basic and intermediate training followed by a two-day climb up the Grand and back. Rates are lower before mid-July and in September. Basic and intermediate climbing schools cost around $60-85 per day. Also available are more advanced classes and climbs in the Tetons, the Wind River Mountains, Devils Tower, and other precipices. In addition, both companies offer many winter classes, including avalanche safety, ice-climbing, guided backcountry skiing and snowboarding, and winter ascents of Grand Teton. Jackson Hole Mountain Guides also offers an intensive (and expensive) three-week summer climbing camp for students ages 15 to 18. If you're planning to climb the Grand during the peak summer season, be sure to make reservations several months in advance to be assured of a spot.

On Your Own

If you already have the experience and want to do your own climbing, the most accessible local spot is **Blacktail Butte,** just north of Moose near Ditch Creek. The parking lot here fills on warm summer afternoons as hang-dogging enthusiasts try their moves on the rock face. Get climbing gear at **Moosely Seconds Mountaineering** in Moose, tel. (307) 733-7176 or (800) 669-7176, or in Jackson at **Teton Mountaineering,** 170 N. Cache, tel. (307) 733-3595 or (800) 850-3595. Both stores rent climbing boots ($5 a day). **Teton Rock Gym,** 1116 Maple Way, tel. (307) 733-0707, has an indoor climbing wall where you can practice your moves. For more detailed info on local climbing, see Leigh N. Ortenburger's two-volume tome, *A Complete Guide to the Teton Range* (Palo Alto, CA: self-published).

GRAND TETON PRACTICALITIES

The Basics

As of this writing, entrance to Grand Teton National Park is $20 per vehicle, $4 for individuals entering by bicycle, foot, motorcycle, snowmobile, or bus. The pass covers both Yellowstone

and Grand Teton National Parks and is good for seven days. If you're planning to be here longer or to make more visits, get an annual pass covering both parks for $40 or the Golden Eagle Passport, which is good for all national parks, for $25 a year. A Golden Age Passport for all national parks is available to anyone over 62 for a one-time fee of $10, and people with disabilities can get a free Golden Access Passport. Both of these also give you 50% reductions in camping fees. Note that entrance fees will probably be higher than those quoted here since the Park Service has proposed an increase to help provide much-needed funding. Call (307) 739-3600 for additional park information.

Visitor Centers

Grand Teton National Park headquarters is located in the settlement of Moose near the southern end of the park. **Moose Visitor Center,** tel. (307) 739-3399, is open every day except Christmas 8 a.m.-5 p.m. (till 7 p.m. in midsummer). **Colter Bay Visitor Center,** tel. (307) 739-3594, is open daily 8 a.m.-5 p.m. from mid-May through September, with midsummer hours to 7 p.m. **Jenny Lake Visitor Center** is open daily 8 a.m.-7 p.m. from early June to early September; **Flagg Ranch Information Station** is open daily 9 a.m.-6 p.m. between early June and early September and mid-December to mid-March.

The **Grand Teton Natural History Association** operates bookstores in the visitor centers and in the store at Menor's Ferry, and provides a mail-order service for books about the park. For a free catalog, contact them at P.O. Box 170, Moose, WY 83012, tel. (307) 739-3403.

Visitors receive a copy of *Teewinot,* the park newspaper, at the entrance stations. It lists park facilities and services, along with interpretive programs, nature walks, and other activities. Family favorites for generations are the evening campfire programs held at campground amphitheaters throughout the summer.

Boating and Fishing

Canoeists will discover several excellent places to paddle within Grand Teton, particularly the Snake River Oxbow Bend and String and Leigh Lakes. Boaters within Grand Teton will need to purchase a permit; seven-day permits cost $10 for motorboats, $5 for nonmotorized craft. Motorboats are only allowed on Jackson Lake, Jenny Lake (seven-and-a-half-horsepower max), and Phelps Lake. Sailboarding, water-skiing, and sailing are permitted on Jackson Lake. (For info on floating the Snake River through the park, see "River Rafting" under "Jackson" earlier in this chapter.) Marinas are located at Colter Bay Village, tel. (307) 543-2811, Signal Mountain, tel. (307) 733-5470, and Leeks Marina, tel. (307) 543-2494.

At **Signal Mountain** you can rent water-ski boats and skis, lifejackets, deck cruisers, fishing boats, pontoon boats, and canoes. **Colter Bay Marina** has scenic cruises, motorboat and canoe rentals, and fishing guides to take you to the hot fishing spots. Scenic boat cruises ($10.50 for adults, $6 for kids under 12) are available at Colter Bay Marina, as are cruise-and-dine trips.

Grand Teton National Park anglers must have a valid Wyoming state fishing license. Pick up a handout describing fishing creel and size limits from park visitor centers. (For more on fishing and river rafting within the park, see the appropriate sections under "Jackson.")

O.A.R.S., tel. (800) 346-6277, offers unique multi-day sea kayaking and hiking trips around Jackson Lake—perfect for beginning kayakers and families. Two-day trips cost $190 for adults, $99 for kids; three-day kayak trips run $290 for adults and $199 for kids. O.A.R.S also has combination trips that include kayaking on the lake and rafting down the Snake River.

Winter Recreation

In the winter months, when snow covers the land, Grand Teton National Park draws cross-country skiers, snowshoers, and snowmobilers. **Cross-country skiers** will enjoy a number of trails within the lower reaches of the park; the high country is dangerous due to extreme avalanche hazards. Park ski trails are not machine-groomed but are generally well packed by other skiers. After a new snowfall you'll need to break trail as you follow the orange markers. See above for more information on cross-country skiing areas in the park or pick up a brochure describing ski trails from the Moose Visitor Center. If you're planning to camp overnight in the park, you'll need to get a free permit here as well. Skiers and snowshoers are not allowed

on the Continental Divide Snowmobile Trail for safety reasons. Unfortunately, snowmobiles are allowed on the Teton Park Road, so your peace and solitude may be broken by the roar of distant machines.

Park rangers lead two-hour **snowshoe hikes** from late December through March and provide snowshoes at no charge. They depart from the Moose Visitor Center at 2 p.m. several times a week; reservations are required. Call (307) 739-3399 for details on these and other winter activities in the park.

After years of rancorous debate, the 360-mile-long **Continental Divide Snowmobile Trail** now cuts through 33 miles of Grand Teton National Park, providing a link between the Wind River Mountains and Yellowstone National Park. Within Grand Teton it is generally open from early January to mid-March and essentially parallels U.S. 26/287 from the east park boundary to Moran Junction and then along U.S. 89 north to Yellowstone. A spur trail connects the trail with other snowmobile routes along the Teton Park Road and up Signal Mountain. Snowmobiles are only allowed on designated routes, and specific regulations are enforced within the park. Get a copy of the park snowmobiling handout from the Moose Lake Visitor Center, or call (307) 739-3612 for recorded info on the Continental Divide Snowmobile Trail. Flagg Ranch, tel. (307) 543-2861 or (800) 443-2311, runs a snowmobile shuttle service between Flagg Ranch and the Hatchet Campground (east of Moran Junction). (For details on snowmobile rentals and tours in the Jackson area, see "Winter Recreation" under "Jackson" earlier in this chapter.)

Lodging

Several places provide comfortable lodging in and around Grand Teton National Park (see the "Grand Teton National Park Area Accommodations" chart for specifics) or you can stay in nearby Jackson. Built on a grand scale, **Jackson Lake Lodge,** tel. (307) 543-2855 or (800) 628-9988, has a spacious central lounge with 60-foot-high windows fronting on the Tetons and two stone fireplaces at either end of the room. It's located on a bluff above Willow Flats and features an outdoor pool, restaurants, and shops. **Jenny Lake Lodge,** tel. (307)

733-4647 or (800) 628-9988, offers four-star log-cabin accommodations right at the base of the Tetons. It's a marvelous honeymoon or big-splurge place, and the price includes horseback rides, bikes, breakfast, and a six-course dinner.

Colter Bay Village, tel. (307) 543-2811 or (800) 628-9988, has rustic log cabins of varying sizes with baths, plus simple canvas-and-log tent cabins with outdoor grills and picnic tables, woodstoves, and bring-your-own-bedding bunks. Restrooms are nearby, and the showers are coin-operated. Guests at the tent cabins can rent sleeping bags and other camping supplies. The experience isn't even remotely like staying at Jenny Lake Lodge! **Signal Mountain Lodge,** tel. (307) 733-5470 or 543-2831, has accommodations that range from simple log cabins to lakefront apartments with kitchenettes, while **Flagg Ranch,** tel. (307) 733-8761 or (800) 443-2311, has motel units and newly built cabins. **Cowboy Village Resort at Togwotee,** tel. (307) 543-2847 or (800) 543-2847, just west of Togwotee Pass on U.S. 26/287, is a favorite place for mountain-bike tours, fly-fishing, horseback rides, and backcountry pack trips during the summer and snowmobiling and cross-country skiing when the snow flies.

Camping

Grand Teton National Park has six different campgrounds: Colter Bay, Lizard Creek, Gros Ventre, Signal Mountain, and Jenny Lake. See the "Jackson Hole Public Campgrounds" chart for details of these and nearby Forest Service campgrounds. Accommodations at all park campgrounds cost $10 and are on a first-come, first-served basis with no reservations. By mid-afternoon in the peak summer season all park campgrounds may well be full. The largest—and last to fill—is Gros Ventre, near the town of Kelly. The most scenic location—and quickest to fill—is Jenny Lake. All Grand Teton National Park campgrounds are closed in the winter. Showers and a laundromat are available in Colter Bay Village. In the winter, limited tent camping and RV parking ($5; restrooms and water but no hookups) is available near the Colter Bay Visitor Center. Call (307) 739-3603 for additional campground information. In addition to the public campgrounds, park conces-

GRAND TETON NATIONAL PARK AREA ACCOMMODATIONS

Note: Accommodations are arranged from least to most expensive. Add a six percent sales tax to these rates. Many more places are available in nearby Jackson. Area code is 307.

Buffalo Valley Ranch; Moran; tel. 543-2477 or 739-9477; $25 s or d; rustic cabins

Colter Bay Village; Jackson Lake; tel. 543-2811 or (800) 628-9988; $29-104 s or d for rustic log cabins (open late may to early Oct.); $24 s or d for simple canvas and log tent cabins (open June to early Sept.), AAA approved

Flying Heart Ranch; Moran; tel. 733-6452; $55-125; open June-Sept., three-night minimum stay

Hatchet Motel; eight miles east of Moran Jct. on US 26/287; tel. 543-3413; $60 s, $65 d; very nice rooms, open Memorial Day-Sept., AAA approved

Signal Mountain Lodge; Jackson Lake; tel. 733-5470 or 543-2831; $68-150 s or d; motel rooms, apartments, and log cabins along Jackson Lake, some with kitchenettes and fireplaces, open mid-May to early Oct., AAA approved

Circle JP Ranch; 19 miles northeast of Jackson near Kelly; tel. 733-7711 or (800) 247-3893; $75 s or d; $90-160 for up to four; two guest cabins, next to park and forest lands, wood stoves, kitchens, three-day minimum stay, open mid-May to mid-Oct.

Cowboy Village Resort at Togwotee; 16 miles east of Moran Jct. on US 26/287; tel. 543-2847 or (800) 543-2847; summer rates: $109-145 s or d in rooms or log cabins; winter rates: $146 s, $236-288 d for rooms or log cabins with breakfast and dinner; sauna, jacuzzis, summer naturalist programs, free airport shuttle, closed mid-April through May, AAA approved

Flagg Ranch Village; Rockefeller Parkway; tel. 733-8761 or (800) 443-2311; $91-120 s or d; motel rooms, suites, and new cabins, open mid-May to mid-Oct. and mid-Dec. to mid-March, AAA approved

The Inn at Buffalo Fork B&B; Moran; tel. 543-2010 or (800) 260-2010; $125-165 s or d; new country inn, gorgeous Teton vistas, five guest rooms, private baths, full country breakfast, outdoor hot tub, AAA approved

Dornan's Spur Ranch Cabins; Moose; tel. 733-2522; $125-175; new one- and two-bedroom log cabins sleep up to six, lodgepole pine furniture, full kitchens, open year-round

Jackson Lake Lodge; Jackson Lake; tel. 543-2855 or (800) 628-9988; $95-450 s or d in rooms, suites, or cottages; spacious lodge with incredible Teton vistas, large outdoor pool, horse rides, no TVs or radios, open mid-May to mid-Oct., AAA approved

Luton's Log Cabins and Lodge; off US 26/287 east of Moran Jct.; tel. 543-2489; $112-180 s or d; new one- and two-bedroom duplex log cabins, full kitchens, AAA approved

Budges' Slide Lake Cabins; six miles east of Kelly; tel. 733-9061; $190 for up to eight people; secluded lakeside cabins, full kitchens, woodstoves

Jenny Lake Lodge; Jenny Lake; tel. 733-4647 or (800) 628-9988; $265-480 s, $335-480 d; price includes breakfast and dinner plus bikes and horseback rides, very nice cabins, cozy Old West main lodge; no TVs, radios, or phones; open mid-May to early Oct., AAA approved

sionaires maintain seasonal RV parks at Colter Bay Village and Flagg Ranch. Grand Teton Park KOA is a few miles west of Moran. (See "Jackson Hole RV Parks," for details on these and others to the south.)

Restaurants

Summertime restaurants and other eateries are located at Colter Bay Village, Signal Mountain, Flagg Ranch, Jenny Lake, Jackson Lake Lodge, and Leeks Marina. One of the restaurants at Jack-

son Lake Lodge features poolside dining on warm summer nights, or dining in the Mural Room, where 60-foot windows face the Tetons. Of particular note is the marvelous old **Jenny Lake Lodge,** where the service and setting are impeccable and the meals—especially the Sunday-night buffets—sumptuous. Lunch is a la carte; breakfast and dinner are fixed price. Jenny Lake Lodge is open June-Sept., and reservations are required; call (307) 733-4647. This is a dress-up place, so a jacket is recommended for dinner.

An old favorite with a more egalitarian setting is **Dornan's Chuck Wagon Restaurant,** tel. (307) 733-2415, offering very reasonable meals every summer since 1948. These include all-you-can-eat pancake breakfasts ($5.50), lunchtime sandwiches, and old-fashioned chuck wagon dinners of BBQ ribs, beef stew, mashed potatoes, and other filling fare ($10.50). In the winter, Dornan's has popular Friday and Saturday night dinners; reservations are required.

Services
The little settlement of Moose has several businesses in addition to Dornan's Restaurant. **Adventure Sports,** tel. (307) 733-3307, rents mountain bikes, canoes, and kayaks, and **Fish Moose** sells and rents fishing supplies and camping equipment. **Moosely Seconds,** tel. (307) 733-7176, offers good deals on hiking and climbing gear. Across the road are **The Trading Post,** tel. (307) 733-3471, with year-round groceries, good deli sandwiches, fresh baked goods, and camping supplies. **Dornan's Wine Shoppe** has more than 1,700 different wines—the biggest selection of wine and beer in Jackson Hole. Also here is the small Moose Bar, a gift shop, and an **ATM** for cash. You'll find a second ATM at Jackson Lake Lodge.

Colter Bay General Store, tel. (307) 733-2811, has a good choice of groceries and supplies, and in summer smaller general stores and convenience stores operate at Signal Moun-

tain, Flagg Ranch, and Jenny Lake. The stores at Moose and Flagg Ranch are open in both summer and winter seasons (mid-May to mid-October, and mid-December to mid-March).

Gas is available year-round at Moose and Flagg Ranch and summers only at Colter Bay Village and Jackson Lake Lodge. You'll find gift shops at Signal Mountain, Flagg Ranch, Jackson Lake Lodge, Moose, and Colter Bay Village; horseback rides ($18 an hour, or $45 for a half-day) at Jackson Lake Lodge and Colter Bay Village. Post offices are located at Colter Bay Village (summer only), Moran, Moose Junction, and Kelly.

Transportation
Grand Teton Lodge Company, tel. (307) 733-2811 or (800) 628-9988, has twice-daily summer shuttle buses connecting Jackson with Jackson Lake Lodge for $12.50 one-way (plus a $4 park entrance fee), and on to Colter Bay Village for an additional $2.50 one-way. Buses depart from the Homewood parking lot on the corner of Gill St. and N. Cache in Jackson and stop at the airport and Jenny Lake upon request. They also offer narrated bus tours of Grand Teton National Park on Monday, Wednesday, and Friday for $17 ($12 for kids under 12) and of Yellowstone National Park on Tuesday, Thursday, and Saturday for $40 ($25 for kids). Tours depart from Jackson Lake Lodge at 8:30 in the morning.

Daily summertime bus tours of Grand Teton and Yellowstone National Parks are available from **Gray Line,** 332 N. Glenwood, tel. (307) 733-4325 or (800) 443-6133. These six- to 10-hour tours cost $40-43 (including park entrance fees). Gray Line's four-day tours of the parks cost $349 per person and five-day trips are $470 per person, including lodging. (See "Transportation" under "Jackson" earlier in this chapter for info on other transportation and tours in the Jackson Hole area.)

BRIDGER-TETON NATIONAL FOREST

Bridger-Teton ("the B-T") National Forest is the second largest in the Lower 48, stretching southward for 135 miles from the Yellowstone border and covering 3.4 million acres. Portions of the forest are described elsewhere (see "Bridger Wilderness" and "Greys River Area"). In Jackson Hole, the two areas of most interest for recreation are the Teton Wilderness and the Gros Ventre Wilderness. Because of its extensive wilderness areas, the B-T has more outfitters than any other national forest in the nation. Much of the remaining land managed by the Forest Service is multiple-use, meaning lots of logging, cattle grazing, and oil and gas leasing.

The Bridger-Teton National Forest **visitor center** in Jackson, tel. (307) 739-5500, is next to the Supervisor's Office at 340 N. Cache. Summer hours are Mon.-Fri. 8 a.m.-5:30 p.m. and Saturday 8 a.m.-4:30 p.m. The rest of the year it is open Mon.-Fri. 8 a.m.-4:30 p.m. If you're planning a trip into surrounding Forest Service lands, be sure to stop by to pick up the forest map ($3.75, or $5 for plastic maps) and to ask for other publications on camping and sights. Ranger stations are in Jackson at 340 N. Cache, tel. (307) 739-5400, and nine miles east of Moran Junction, tel. (307) 543-2386.

TETON WILDERNESS

The Teton Wilderness covers 585,468 acres of mountain country, bordered to the north by Yellowstone National Park, to the west by Grand Teton National Park, and to the east by the Washakie Wilderness. Established as a primitive area in 1934, it was declared one of the nation's first wilderness areas upon passage of the 1964 Wilderness Act. The Teton Wilderness offers a diverse mixture of rolling lands carpeted with lodgepole pine, spacious grassy meadows, roaring rivers, and dramatic mountains. Elevations range from 7,500 feet to the 12,165-foot summit of Younts Peak. The Continental Divide slices across the wilderness, with headwaters of the Yellowstone River draining the eastern half and headwaters of the Buffalo and Snake Rivers flowing down the western side.

One of the most unusual places within Teton Wilderness is **Two Ocean Creek**, where a creek abruptly splits at a rock and the two branches never rejoin. One branch becomes Atlantic Creek, and its waters eventually reach the Atlantic Ocean, while the other becomes Pacific Creek and its waters flow to the Snake River, the Columbia River, and thence into the Pacific Ocean! Mountain man Osborne Russell described this phenomenon in 1835:

On the South side about midway of the prairie stands a high snowy peak from whence issues a Stream of water which after entering the plain it divides equally one half running West and other East thus bidding adieu to each other one bound for the Pacific and the other for the Atlantic ocean. Here a trout of 12 inches in length may cross the mountains in safety. Poets have sung of the "meeting of the waters" and fish climbing cataracts but the "parting of the waters and fish crossing mountains" I believe remains unsung yet by all except the solitary Trapper who sits under the shade of a spreading pine whistling blank-verse and beating time to the tune with a whip on his trap sack whilst musing on the parting advice of these waters.

Two natural events have had a major effect on the Teton Wilderness. On July 21, 1987, a world-record high-elevation tornado created a massive blowdown of trees around the Enos Lake area. The blowdown covered 10,000 acres, and trails are only now being rebuilt through this incredible jackstraw pile (since this is a wilderness area, chainsaws cannot be used). In 1988, extreme drought conditions led to a series of major fires in Yellowstone and surrounding areas. Within the Teton Wilderness, the Huck and Mink Creek Fires burned (in varying degrees of severity) approximately 200,000 acres. Over half of the wilderness remained untouched. Don't let these incidents dissuade you from visiting; this is still a marvelous and little-used area. Herds of elk graze in

alpine areas, and many consider the Thorofare country abutting Yellowstone National Park the most remote place in the Lower 48. This is prime grizzly habitat, so be very cautious at all times. Poles for hanging food have been placed at most campsites, and also have bear-resistant boxes or barrels. Local Forest Service offices have brochures showing the locations of these poles. You can rent bear-resistant backpacker food tubes or horse panniers for $2 per day from the Blackrock Ranger Station, tel. (307) 543-2386. It's a good idea to make reservations for these prior to your trip.

Access

Three primary trailheads provide access to the Teton Wilderness: Pacific Creek on the southwestern end, Turpin Meadow on the Buffalo Fork River, and Brooks Lake just east of the Continental Divide. Campgrounds are at each of these trailheads. Teton Wilderness is a favorite of Wyoming people, particularly those with horses, and in the fall elk hunters come here from across the nation. Distances are so great that few backpackers head into this wilderness area. No permits are needed, but it's a good idea to stop in at the **Blackrock Ranger Station,** tel. (307) 543-2386, nine miles east of Moran Junction on U.S. 26/287, for topographic maps and info on current trail conditions, bear problems, and regulations, and a list of outfitters offering horse trips. Unfortunately, the USGS maps fail to show the many trails built and maintained (or not maintained) by private outfitters. These can make hiking confusing. A few of the many possible hikes are described below.

Whetstone Creek

Whetstone Creek Trail begins at the Pacific Creek Trailhead, located on the southwest side of Teton Wilderness. An enjoyable 20-mile roundtrip hike leaves the trailhead and follows Pacific Creek for 1.5 miles before splitting left to follow Whetstone Creek. Bear left when the trail splits again another three miles upstream and continue through a series of small meadows to the junction with Pilgrim Creek Trail. Turn right here and follow this two more miles to Coulter Creek Trail, climbing up Coulter Creek to scenic Coulter Basin and then dropping down along the East Fork of Whetstone Creek. This rejoins

the Whetstone Creek Trail and returns you to the trailhead, passing many attractive small meadows along the way. The upper half of this loop hike was burned in 1988; some areas were heavily scorched, while others are quite patchy. Flowers are abundant in the burned areas, and this is important elk habitat.

South Fork to Soda Fork

A fine loop hike leaves Turpin Meadow and follows South Buffalo Fork River to South Fork Falls. Just above this, a trail splits off and climbs to Nowlin Meadow (excellent views of Smokehouse Mountain) and then down to Soda Fork River, where it joins the Soda Fork Trail. Follow this trail back downstream to huge Soda Fork Meadow (a good place to see moose and occasionally grizzlies) and then back to Turpin Meadow, a distance of approximately 23 miles roundtrip. For a fascinating side trip from this route, head up the Soda Fork into the alpine at Crater Lake, a six-mile hike above the Nowlin Meadow-Soda Fork Trail junction. The outlet stream at Crater Lake disappears into a gaping hole, emerging as a large creek two miles below at Big Springs. It's an incredible sight.

Cub Creek Area

The Brooks Lake area just east of Togwotee Pass is a very popular summertime camping and fishing place with magnificent views. Brooks Lake Trail follows the western shore of Brooks Lake and continues past Upper Brooks Lakes to Bear Cub Pass. From here, the trail drops down to Cub Creek, where you'll find several good campsites. You can make a long and very scenic loop by following the trail up Cub Creek into the alpine country and then back down along the South Buffalo Fork River to Lower Pendergraft Meadow. From here, take Cub Creek Trail back up along Cub Creek to Bear Cub Pass and back out to Brooks Lake. Get a topographic map before heading into this remote country. Total distance is approximately 33 miles roundtrip.

GROS VENTRE WILDERNESS

The 287,000-acre Gros Ventre Wilderness was established in 1984 and covers the mountain

country just east of Jackson Hole. This range trends mainly in a northwest-southeast direction and is probably best known for Sleeping Indian Mountain (maps now call it Sheep Mountain), the distinctive rocky summit visible from Jackson Hole. Although there are densely forested areas at lower elevations, the central portion of the wilderness lies above timberline, and many peaks top 10,000 feet. Tallest is Doubletop Peak at 11,682 feet. The Tetons are visible from almost any high point in the Gros Ventre, and meadows line the lower-elevation streams. Elk, mule deer, bighorn sheep, moose, and black bears are found here, and a few grizzlies have been reported. The Forest Service office in Jackson has more info on the wilderness, including brief trail descriptions and maps.

Access and Trails

A number of roads provide good access to the Gros Ventre Wilderness: Gros Ventre River Road on the northern border; Flat Creek, Curtis Canyon, and Cache Creek Roads on the western margin; and Granite Creek Road to the south. Note that hikes beginning or ending in

the Granite Creek area have the added advantage of nearby Granite Hot Springs, a great place to soak tired muscles.

An enjoyable two-day trip begins at **Jackpine Creek Trailhead** on Granite Creek Road, 35 miles southeast of Jackson. Follow Jackpine Creek Trail up to Shoal Lake and then loop back down via the Swift Creek Trail. The distance is approximately 16 miles roundtrip but involves gaining and then losing 4,000 feet of elevation. Another good hike is to follow **Highline Trail** from the Granite Creek area across to Cache Creek, a distance of 16 miles. This route passes just below a row of high and rugged mountains, but since it isn't a loop route, you'll need to hitchhike or arrange a car shuttle back. Plan on three days for this scenic hike. A third hike begins at the **Goosewing Ranger Station,** located 12 miles east of Slide Lake on Gros Ventre River Road. Take the trail from here to Two Echo Park (a fine camping spot) and then continue up to Six Lakes. You can return via the same trail or take the Crystal Creek Trail back to Red Rock Ranch and hitch back to Goosewing. The trail distance is approximately 23 miles roundtrip.

TARGHEE NATIONAL FOREST

The 1.8 million-acre Targhee National Forest extends along the western face of the Tetons and then south and west into Idaho. Much of the forest is heavily logged, but two wilderness areas protect most of the Wyoming portion of the Targhee.

JEDEDIAH SMITH WILDERNESS

The 116,535-acre Jedediah Smith Wilderness lies on the west side of the Teton Range, facing Idaho but lying entirely within Wyoming. Access is primarily from the Idaho side, although trails breach the mountain passes at various points, making it possible to enter from Grand Teton National Park. This area was not declared a wilderness until 1984. A second wilderness area, the 10,820-acre **Winegar Hole Wilderness** (pronounced "WINE-a-gur), lies along the southern border of Yellowstone National Park.

Grizzlies love this country, but hikers will find it uninteresting and without trails. In contrast, the Jedediah Smith Wilderness contains nearly 300 miles of paths and some incredible high-mountain scenery.

A number of mostly gravel roads lead up from the Driggs and Victor areas into the Tetons. Get a map ($3) showing wilderness trails and access points from Targhee National Forest ranger station in Driggs, Idaho, tel. (208) 354-2431, or from the Forest Service offices in Jackson. (Driggs is also home to the delightfully amusing Spud Drive-In, here since 1953.) Be sure to camp at least 200 feet from lakes and 50 feet from streams. If you plan to cross into Grand Teton National Park from the west side, be sure you have a camping permit in advance.

Hidden Corral Basin

Located at the northern end of the wilderness, Hidden Corral Basin provides a fine loop hike.

Locals (primarily horse parties) crowd this area on late summer weekends. Get to the trailhead by driving north from Tetonia on Idaho 32 to Lamont, then turn north on a gravel road. (The Tetonia area—Pierre's Hole—offers outstanding views of the Tetons, particularly at sunset. The three dominant peaks are more obvious from this side.) Follow it a mile and then turn right (east) onto Coyote Meadows Road. The trailhead is approximately 10 miles up, where the road dead-ends. An eight-mile trail parallels South Bitch Creek (the name Bitch Creek comes from the French word for a female deer, *biche*) to Hidden Corral, where you may see moose. Be sure to bring a fishing pole to try for the cutthroats.

Above Hidden Corral you can make a pleasant loop back by turning north onto the trail to Nord Pass and then dropping down along the Carrot Ridge and Conant Basin Trails to Bitch Creek Trail and then on to Coyote Meadows, a distance of 21 miles roundtrip. Note that this is grizzly country, so be sure to hang all food. By the way, Hidden Corral received its name in the outlaw days, when rustlers would steal horses in Idaho, change the brands, and then hold them in this natural corral until the branding wounds healed. The horses were then sold to Wyoming ranchers. Owen Wister's *The Virginian* describes a pursuit of horse thieves through Bitch Creek country.

Alaska Basin

The most popular hiking trail in the Jedediah Smith begins at Teton Canyon Campground ($6) and leads up into the flower-bedecked meadows of Alaska Basin. Great country, but don't expect a true wilderness experience (too many other hikers). Get to the campground by following the Grand Targhee Ski Area signs

east from Driggs, Idaho. A gravel road splits off to the right approximately six miles beyond the little settlement of Alta. Follow it to the campground. (If you miss the turn, you'll end up at the ski area.) For an enjoyable loop, follow Alaska Basin Trail up the canyon to Basin Lakes and then head southwest along the Teton Crest Trail to the Teton Shelf Trail. Follow this back to its junction with the Alaska Basin Trail, dropping down the Devils Stairs—a series of very steep switchbacks. You can then take the Alaska Basin Trail back to Teton Campground, a roundtrip distance of approximately 19 miles. You could also use these trails to access the high peaks of the Tetons or to cross the mountains into Death Canyon within Grand Teton National Park (permit required). Campfires and horse camping are not allowed in Alaska Basin.

Moose Meadows

For a somewhat less crowded hiking experience, check out the Moose Meadows area on the southern end of the Jedediah Smith Wilderness. Get to the trailhead by going three miles southeast of Victor on State 22. Turn north to Moose Creek Road and follow it to the trailhead at Nordwall Campground. The trail parallels Moose Creek to Moose Meadows, a good place to camp. You'll need to ford the creek twice, so this is best hiked in late summer. At the meadows, the trail dead-ends into Teton Crest Trail, providing access to Grand Teton National Park through some gorgeous alpine country. A nice loop can be made by heading south along this trail to flower-covered Coal Creek Meadows. A trail leads from here past 10,068-foot Taylor Mountain (an easy side trip with magnificent views), down to Taylor Basin, through lodgepole forests, and then back to your starting point. This loop hike will take you 15 miles roundtrip.

BOB RACE

YELLOWSTONE NATIONAL PARK

The words "national park" seem to stimulate an almost Pavlovian response: Yellowstone. The geysers, canyons, and bears of Yellowstone National Park are so intertwined in our collective consciousness that even our cartoons use the park as a model—Jellystone Park, where Yogi Bear and Boo Boo are constantly out to thwart the rangers. Yellowstone brings out the child in everyone.

On a map, Yellowstone appears as a gigantic box wedged so tightly against the northwest corner of Wyoming that it squeezes over into Montana and Idaho. The park measures 63 by 54 miles and covers 2.2 million acres, making it the largest national park in the Lower 48. The United Nations has declared Yellowstone both a World Biosphere Reserve and a World Heritage Site.

The Setting
Yellowstone evokes a torrent of emotions in anyone with a knowledge of and a concern for the natural world. Here was the birthplace of the national-park movement, a place so unusual that those who first wandered through it were afraid to tell others lest they be labeled liars. In the Yellowstone backcountry, one can still walk for days without seeing more than a handful of other hardy hikers, and the wildlife, geysers, and canyons continue to bring smiles to the faces of young and old alike. Americans love Yellowstone, the nation's crown jewel. One source estimates that nearly a third of the U.S. population has visited the park, and each year more than three million people roll through the gates. As visitation has risen in recent years, more and more folks have begun to suggest some sort of limits on numbers to preserve the experience and protect the park. Don't-tread-on-me Westerners consider the idea of limits an example of environmental extremism for the elite.

More than any other national park, Yellowstone seems to provide the oddities of nature, creating, as historian Aubrey L. Haines noted, "a false impression that the park is only a colossal, steam-operated freak show." During midsummer, a trip into Yellowstone can be something less than a natural experience. Thousands of behemoth land yachts clog the potholed roads

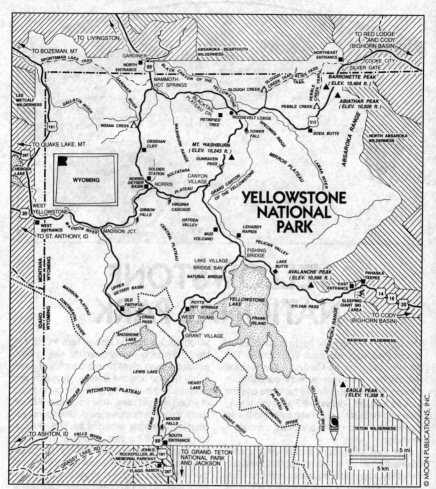

and crowd the parking lots. Throngs of visitors circle Old Faithful Geyser waiting for an eruption, while dozens of others cluster around bewildered elk to get photos for their scrapbooks. Although less than three percent of the park is developed, Yellowstone contains more than 2,000 buildings of various types, ranging from graceful historic hotels to one-hour photo shops. In some spots, these developments have grown to the point that the natural world seems simply a backdrop to the human world that pulls visitors in to buy T-shirts or to watch park slide shows on geysers or wildlife.

From day one, Yellowstone National Park was set up for what Edward Abbey called "industrial tourism." The park came into being in part because of a railroad promoter who hoped to gain from its development, and it grew to maturity on a diet of roads, hotels, and curio shops. Finally, in the 1960s and '70s, America began to

take a second look at this heritage and ask questions about what mattered more: providing a public playground or preserving an area that is unique on this planet. The inherent conflict between the need for public facilities and services in Yellowstone and the survival of a functioning ecosystem has come to the fore in recent years in such issues as wolf reintroduction, grizzly management, nearby mining developments, and fire suppression.

GEOLOGY

Yellowstone is perhaps the world's preeminent place to view geological processes, for here the forces that elsewhere lie deep within the earth seem close enough to touch. The forces are palpable not only in the geysers and hot springs but also in the lake that fills part of an enormous caldera, the earthquakes that shake the land, the evidence of massive glaciation, and the deeply eroded Grand Canyon of the Yellowstone.

VOLCANISM

The geologic history of Yellowstone centers around volcanism. The Absaroka Mountains along the park's eastern border were created by volcanic activity some 50 million years ago, but the park itself was most influenced by three violent explosions. Molten lava pushing from below bulged the land upward into an enormous dome. Eventually this pressure became too great, sending ash and rock blasting from fissures around the dome's margins. Afterward, the dome began to reform as more magma was forced in. This process has been repeated three times over the last two million years, with the last eruption approximately 600,000 years ago. The magnitude of this most recent event is beyond the realm of imagination: 240 cubic miles of ash were blasted into the atmosphere! This eruption—perhaps the largest ever to occur on earth—ejected 20 times more material than the massive Krakatoa eruption of 1883, an explosion heard 3,000 miles away! Undoubtedly, ash from the eruption affected the global climate for years to follow.

After this eruption, the magma chamber collapsed into a gigantic, smoldering pit reaching 28 by 47 miles and perhaps several thousand feet deep. Over time, additional molten rock pushed up from underneath and flowed as thick lava over the

YELLOWSTONE NATIONAL PARK MILEAGE MAP

89 TO LIVINGSTON 61 MI

NORTH ENTRANCE — GARDINER
5 mi
MAMMOTH HOT SPRINGS — 18 mi
MONTANA
WYOMING
NORTHEAST ENTRANCE
212
TO CODY 58 MI
TOWER-ROOSEVELT
29 mi
21 mi
19 mi
NORRIS JUNCTION
12 mi — CANYON VILLAGE
WEST YELLOWSTONE
14 mi
WEST ENTRANCE
14 mi
MADISON JUNCTION
16 mi
16 mi
LAKE JUNCTION
TO CODY 58 MI
14
OLD FAITHFUL — 17 mi
21 mi
27 mi
EAST ENTRANCE
16 20
WEST THUMB
22 mi
SOUTH ENTRANCE
191
89
287
0   20 mi
0   20 km
TO JACKSON 57 MI

MONTANA / WYOMING
IDAHO / WYOMING

© MOON PUBLICATIONS, INC.

land. Two resurgent domes—one near Old Faithful and the other just north of Yellowstone Lake—are still rising at nearly an inch per year. The one north of Yellowstone Lake is raising the lake's outlet and causing the water level to increase an inch a year, flooding trees along the margins. Yellowstone's volcanism is far from dead, and scientists believe another eruption is possible or even likely, though nobody knows just when it might occur.

Yellowstone is one of the hottest places on the planet; Firehole Basin has underground temperatures 700 times the global average. Geologists now believe that the source of this heat (and of the volcanism) is an enormous plume of superheated magma just below the surface. The earth's crust is gradually moving over this plume—a little like somebody pulling a piece of cloth across a candle. The plume has gradually shifted to the northeast over the millennia, leaving behind such places as Craters of the Moon in Idaho. A similar situation is believed to exist in the chain of Hawaiian Islands.

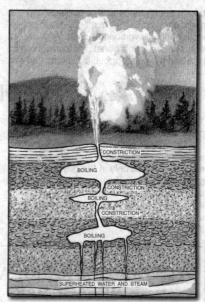

BOB RACE

GEYSERS

Yellowstone is famous for geysers, and geyser-gazers will not be disappointed. At least 60% of the world's geysers are in the park, easily the largest and most diverse collection of geysers in existence! Yellowstone's more than 300 geysers are spread over nine different basins, the largest being Upper Geyser Basin.

Geysers need three essentials to exist: water, heat, and fractured rock. The water comes from snow and rain falling on this high plateau, while the heat comes from the molten rock close to the earth's surface. Massive pressures from below have created a ring of fractures around the edge of Yellowstone's caldera.

How They Work

Geysers operate because dense cold water sinks while less-dense hot water rises. The periodic eruption of geysers is due to constrictions in the underground channels that prevent an adequate heat exchange with the surface. Precipitation slowly moves into the earth, eventually contacting the molten rock. Because of high pressures at these depths, water can reach extreme temperatures without vaporizing (as in a pressure cooker). As this superheated water rises back toward the surface, it emerges in hot springs, fumaroles, mudpots, and geysers. The most spectacular of these phenomena are geysers. Two general types of geysers exist in Yellowstone. Fountain geysers (such as Great Fountain Geyser) explode from pools of water and tend to spray water more widely, while cone-type geysers (such as Old Faithful) jet out of nozzle-like formations.

In a geyser, steam bubbles upward from the superheated source of water and expands as it rises. These bubbles block the plumbing system, keeping hot water from reaching the surface. Eventually, however, pressure from the bubbles begins to force the cooler water above out of the vent. This initial release triggers a more violent reaction as the sudden lessening of pressure allows the entire column to begin boiling, explosively expelling steam and water to produce a geyser. Once the eruption has emptied the plumbing system, water gradually seeps back into the chambers to begin the process anew. Some of Yellowstone's geysers have enormous underground caverns that fill with

water; in its rare eruptions, massive Steamboat Geyser can blast a million gallons of water into the air!

Preserving the Geysers
Unfortunately, some of Yellowstone's geysers have been lost because of human stupidity or vandalism. At one time, it was considered great sport to stuff logs, rocks, and even chairs into the geysers for a little added show. Others poured chemicals into them to make them play. As a result of such actions, some geysers have been severely damaged or destroyed, and a number of hot springs have become collection points for coins, rocks, sticks, and trash. It shouldn't be necessary to point out that such actions ruin these thermal areas for everyone.

OTHER GEOTHERMAL ACTIVITY

Although geysers are Yellowstone's best-known features, they make up only a tiny fraction of perhaps 10,000 thermal features in the park. **Hot springs** appear where water can reach the ground surface relatively easily, allowing for a dissipation of the heat that builds up in the chambers of geysers. When less groundwater is present, you may find **mudpots** (also called paint pots), while the driest shoot only steam through **fumaroles** or steam vents. Probably the best examples of these different forms are at Fountain Paint Pot in Lower Geyser Basin, where geysers and hot springs are found in the wetter lower areas paint pots and fumaroles sit atop a small hill.

The colors in Yellowstone's hot springs come from a variety of sources, including algae and bacteria as well as various minerals, particular-

ly sulfur, iron oxides, and arsenic sulfide. The algae and bacteria are highly temperature-specific and help to create the distinct bands of colors around many hot springs. Interestingly, many of these algal species are found only in hot springs, though they exist around the world. Above 190° F, even these hot-water bacteria and algae cannot survive, so the hottest springs may appear a deep blue due to the water's ability to absorb all wavelengths of light except blue, which is reflected back into our eyes.

Terminology
A couple of other terms are worth learning before heading out to see the sights of Yellowstone. **Sinter** (also called "geyserite") is a chemical composed primarily of silica. The silica is dissolved by hot water deep underground and brought to the surface in geysers or hot springs. At the surface the water evaporates, leaving behind the light gray sinter, which can create large mounds (to 30 feet high) around the older geysers. The rate of accumulation is very slow, and some of the park's geysers have obviously been active for many thousands of years. The other chemical that is sometimes deposited around Yellowstone's hot springs and geysers is **travertine,** consisting of calcium carbonate that has been dissolved underground. (See "Mammoth Hot Springs" below for more on this process.)

A Note of Warning
The surface around many of the hot springs and geysers is surprisingly thin, and people have been killed by falling through into the boiling water. Stay on the boardwalks in developed areas, and use extreme caution around backcountry thermal features.

THE YELLOWSTONE ECOSYSTEM

For most of its existence, Yellowstone has been regarded as an island of nature surrounded by a world of human development. Unfortunately, this attitude has led to all sorts of problems. Despite its size, Yellowstone alone is not large enough to support a viable population of all the animals that once existed within its borders. In recent years, there have been increasing calls to

treat the park as part of the larger Greater Yellowstone Ecosystem—14 million acres of land at the juncture of Wyoming, Montana, and Idaho. Within surrounding lands, conflicts between development and preservation are even more obvious than within the park itself. Logging is one of the most obvious of these, and along the park's western border aerial photos reveal a

At this place there is also large numbers of hot Springs some of which have formed cones of limestone 20 feet high of a Snowy whiteness which make a splendid appearance standing among the ever green pines Some of the lower peaks are very serviceable to the hunter in preparing his dinner when hungry for here his kettle is always ready and boiling his meat being suspended in the water by a string is soon prepared for his meal without further trouble . . . . Standing upon an eminence and superficially viewing these natural monuments one is half inclined to believe himself in the neighborhood of the ruins of some ancients City whose temples had been constructed of the whitest marble.

—*Mountain man Osborne Russell, describing the Firehole River area in 1839*

perfectly straight line, with lodgepole trees on the park side and enormous clearcuts on the Forest Service side. One of these was the largest timber sale ever made outside of Alaska! Add to this encroachment in the forms of housing developments, oil and gas drilling, mining activities, and a grizzly bear and wolf theme park, and the future looks difficult for the Yellowstone ecosystem, especially with continuing cuts in the park budget. Despite all these impacts, Yellowstone remains one of the largest intact temperate-zone ecosystems on the planet.

PLANTS

Yellowstone National Park is primarily a series of high plateaus ranging 7,500-8,500 feet in elevation. Surrounding this gently rolling expanse are the Absaroka Mountains along the east side and the Gallatin Range in the northeast corner. Elevations are lowest along the northern end of the park, where the Yellowstone River and other streams cut through. Here one finds open country with sagebrush, grasses, and shrubs, along with patches of aspen and Douglas fir. Farther south on the central plateaus are found the extensive lodgepole pine forests that cover 60% of the park.

At higher and cooler elevations, lodgepole forests grade into groves of Engelmann spruce and subalpine fir and eventually into stands of whitebark pine—an important food source for grizzlies. At timberline (approximately 10,000 feet), even these trees give way and only low-growing forbs, grasses, and shrubs survive. Not all areas follow this simple elevational gradient, however. The park contains extensive wet meadow areas in the Bechler and upper Yellowstone River areas. Other broad openings are found along the Gardner River, in Pelican Valley, and in Hayden Valley.

WILDLIFE

Yellowstone is world-famous for its wildlife and provides a marvelous natural setting in which to view bison, elk, moose, coyotes, antelope, bighorn sheep, and other animals. One of the easiest ways to find wildlife is simply by watching for the brake lights, the cars pulled half off the road, and the cameras all pointed in one direction. Inevitably, you'll find an elk or a bison placidly munching away, oblivious to the chaos that surrounds it. Be sure to bring binoculars for your trip to Yellowstone. A spotting scope is very helpful in finding distant bears and wolves.

Because of the constant parade of visitors and the lack of hunting, many of Yellowstone's animals appear to almost ignore the presence of people, and it isn't uncommon to see visitors approach them without respecting the animal's need for space. Although they may appear tame, these really are wild animals, and attacks are not uncommon. Those quiet bison can suddenly erupt with an enormous ferocity if provoked by photographers who come too close. Stay at least 25 yards away from bison and elk and at least 100 yards away from bears.

The Park Service has a free brochure showing where you're most likely to see wildlife in Yellowstone. Get it at any visitor center. The best time to view wildlife is generally in the early

morning and evening hours. Mosquitoes are a special treat and can be found almost anywhere in Yellowstone before mid-August. Fall is the best time to avoid these friendly critters.

Trumpeter swans—beautiful white birds with eight-foot wingspans—are a fairly common sight in Yellowstone, particularly on the Madison and Yellowstone Rivers. Many trumpeter swans winter in the hot-springs area. Another large white bird is the awkward-looking and bulbous-billed white pelican, common on Yellowstone Lake. Bald eagles and osprey have also managed comebacks in recent years and can be seen along the Yellowstone River.

Killing the Predators
Wildlife has always been one of the big drawing cards at Yellowstone, and early on there were constant charges of mass slaughter by poachers and market hunters. It was not until 1894 that Congress passed the Lacey Act, finally making it illegal to hunt within the park. Unfortunately, predators such as wolves, coyotes, mountain lions, and wolverines were regarded as despoilers of the elk, deer, and moose and became fair targets for poisoning and shooting by early park managers. The campaign proved all too successful, devastating the wolf and mountain-lion populations. One consequence of this is that bison and elk numbers have grown artificially high within Yellowstone. Artificial feeding of elk in Jackson Hole has also contributed to the high populations.

Bears
During the park's early years, bears were commonly viewed as either pets or nuisances. Cubs were tethered to poles in front of the hotels and other bears fed on the garbage piles that grew up around the hotels and camps. Older folks still recall the bear feeding grounds at the garbage dumps, where visitors might see 50 bears pawing through the refuse. These feeding shows continued until 1941, but it wasn't until 1970 that the park's open-pit dumps were finally sealed off and the garbage cans bear-proofed. Unfortunately, rather than gradually reducing the food available at the dumps to wean bears from the sites, they were shut down abruptly. The dumps had artificially maintained bear populations above their natural levels, and their clo-

sure brought almost immediate consequences; between 1970 and 1972 a total of 137 grizzlies died in confrontations with humans in the park or surrounding areas.

Today there are believed to be 200 to 250 grizzlies in the Greater Yellowstone Ecosystem, approximately the same as in the 1960s, when many lived on garbage dumps and campers' coolers, and more than in the early '80s. Both black and grizzly bears are found throughout Yellowstone, but the days of bear jams along the park roads are long past, since rangers actively work to prevent bears from becoming habituated to people. Most bears have returned to their more natural ways of living, although problems still crop up with bears wandering through campgrounds in search of food. You're more likely to encounter a bear in the backcountry areas. Some places—especially around the north end of Yellowstone Lake in Pelican Valley—are off-limits to hiking much of the year for this reason.

One unusual aspect of the Yellowstone grizzlies was just discovered in recent years—the surprising importance of moths as a food source. Millions of army cutworm moths congregate on Yellowstone's high alpine slopes during the summer, when they feed on nectar from the abundant flowers. Bears are attracted to this food source because of the insect's abundance and high fat content. Researchers have sometimes seen two dozen bears feeding on a single slope!

Safety in grizzly country is always a concern, but statistically you are far more likely to be hurt in a traffic accident than mauled during your visit to Yellowstone. There were just 21 bear-caused injuries between 1980 and 1995—one injury for every 1.9 million visitors! (For more on staying safe around grizzlies, see the special topic "Bear Country" in the On the Road chapter.)

The **Yellowstone Grizzly Foundation,** 104 Hillside Court, Boulder, CO 80302, tel. (303) 939-8126, is an excellent nonprofit organization dedicated to conserving grizzlies within the Yellowstone Ecosystem. You can also reach the foundation over the Internet at http://www.desktop.org/ygf. Established by Steve and Marilynn French—who have been studying grizzly bears since 1983—the foundation empha-

sizes non-intrusive observations. A recent groundbreaking project collected hair samples as bears crawled under barbed wire. DNA analysis of these hairs led to a new understanding of how grizzly bears in Yellowstone are related to other bears. It turns out that more than 90% of Yellowstone grizzlies originated from the same maternal lineage, a fact that may have important ramifications for management. The research also showed that the grizzlies of Yellowstone differ markedly from Alaskan grizzlies such as those found at the "Grizzly Discovery Center" zoo in West Yellowstone.

Bison

When Yellowstone was established in 1872, perhaps 1,000 mountain (wood) bison ranged across this high plateau. Sport and meat hunting—legal until 1894—and later poaching reduced the population, and by 1902 perhaps only 25 remained. That year, plains bison were brought in from private ranches in Montana and Texas to help restore the Yellowstone herd, and today there are over 3,000 buffalo in the park, making this the largest free-ranging herd of bison anywhere on earth. Unfortunately, interbreeding between the mountain and plains bison means that the animals in Yellowstone today are genetically different from the original inhabitants. The population of bison is still artificially high, though the reintroduction of wolves may have an impact in the future. A favorite time to see bison is late May, just after the new calves have been born. Their antics are always good for laughs. Be sure to use caution around bison; many people have been gored when they've come too close.

Bison (and elk) are carriers of brucellosis, a disease that causes cows to abort calves and the source of undulant fever in humans. Brucellosis is spread when a contaminated fetus is licked by other animals, a situation that is unlikely given the timing of bison movements. In 1985, Yellowstone's bison began wandering north into the Gardiner area for the winter. Montana and Wyoming are certified as "brucellosis-free" states, and although there is absolutely no evidence that wild bison have ever transmitted the disease to cattle, ranchers feared that the bison might threaten Montana's brucellosis-free status. A highly controversial "hunt" during the late 1980s let hunters shoot bison when they wandered outside the park; later, Montana state workers did the killing. As of this writing, the Park Service was working with other agencies to develop a new bison management plan to reduce contact with cattle and prevent the possible spread of the disease. (Ironically, the park's more numerous elk also carry brucellosis. Although they are hunted outside Yellowstone, nobody seems anxious to kill all the elk that wander across Yellowstone's borders.)

Wolves

The wolves are back! One of the most exciting developments for visitors to Yellowstone has been the successful reintroduction of wolves to the park, making this one of the few places in the Lower 48 where they can be viewed in the wild. Wolves once ranged across nearly all of North America, but white settlers regarded them—along with mountain lions, grizzly bears, and coyotes—as threats to livestock and unwanted predators upon game animals. Even in Yellowstone wolves were hunted and poisoned by both the Army and the Park Service. By 1940, the wolf was probably gone from the park, though a few turned up briefly again in the early 1970s.

Until 1995, wolves could only be found in parts of Canada, Alaska, northern Minnesota, Isle Royale, and Glacier National Park. With a more enlightened attitude in recent years, ecologists and conservationists began pushing for the reintroduction of wolves to Yellowstone, considered one of the few remaining areas in the Lower 48 that could support a viable wolf population. Without wolves, it was argued, elk, deer, and bison populations had grown too high, potentially throwing the entire ecosystem out of balance. Wolves also played a beneficial evolutionary role by taking primarily the weak, sick, or old prey—the easiest to chase down.

The proposal to return wolves to Yellowstone set off a firestorm from ranchers (with the ardent support of Wyoming's Republican senators) who feared that wolves would wander outside the park to destroy sheep and cattle. Opponents said hundreds of livestock would be killed each year around the park and that the reintroduction cost might reach $1.8 million per wolf, a figure sharply disputed by supporters who insist that the total cost will equal that of a

single postage stamp per U.S citizen. Despite these dire predictions, the Park Service began reintroducing wolves in 1995, initially releasing 14 gray wolves from British Columbia. Additional wolves were set free the following spring, with continued releases expected until the program establishes 10 packs of wolves in the Greater Yellowstone area. So far, things have gone better than anyone predicted. In 1995 one wolf was killed by federal officials after attacking sheep on a ranch, and two others were illegally shot and killed—apparently by ranchers—but the other wolves are doing fine, with five denning pairs in the spring of 1996. The program appears so successful that recovery goals may be exceeded well before the target date of 2002. All released wolves are radio collared to help biologists monitor their movements and to determine when they wander outside the park.

The return of the wolf to Yellowstone has created a buzz of excitement for visitors who stand for hours waiting for a glimpse of a distant wolf. The lucky ones get a closer view as wolves wander by and get to watch them play, interact with other animals, or hunt elk. So far, the best place to look for wolves is the open terrain of Lamar Valley (especially near Slough Creek), but wolves may be seen anywhere in the park. Best time to go looking is early in the morning or near dusk. And, yes, you may well hear their plaintive cry from your campground late at night. Binoculars or spotting scopes are very helpful for roadside wolf watching; do not follow the wolves around since this may disturb them and affect their survival. Denning activity takes place April-June, with active denning areas closed to humans; check with the Park Service for currently closed areas.

PARK HISTORY

Yellowstone National Park has a rich and fascinating history that reaches back through thousands of years of settlement. The most thorough source for history is *The Yellowstone Story,* an excellent two-volume set by former park historian Aubrey L. Haines.

SHEEPEATER INDIANS

Yellowstone has been inhabited by people for at least 11,000 years, although the tribes changed over the centuries. By the mid-19th century, the country was surrounded by Blackfeet to the north, Crow to the east, and Shoshone and Bannock to the south and west. These tribes all traveled through Yellowstone and hunted here periodically, but only the Sheepeater Indians actually lived on this high plateau. The Sheepeaters were of Shoshone stock, a simple and timid people who hunted bighorn sheep (hence the name) but also depended on other animals, fish, roots, and berries. They built temporary shelters called wickiups made of aspen poles covered with pine boughs, a few of which still exist in Yellowstone. Because they did not have horses, the Sheepeaters used dog travois to carry their

few possessions from camp to camp. Summers were spent in high alpine meadows and along passes where they hunted migrating

Sheepeater Indian in wickiup

game animals or gathered roots and berries. They wintered in protected canyons.

The Sheepeaters were smaller than other Indians and have achieved an aura of mystery since so little is known of their way of living. Yellowstone was at the heart of their territory, but with the arrival of whites came devastating diseases, particularly smallpox. The survivors joined their Shoshone brothers on the Wind River Reservation or the Bannock Reservation in Idaho. The last of the tribe left Yellowstone in the 1870s.

FUR TRAPPERS

The word "Yellowstone" appears to have come from the Sioux Indians, who called the river "Mi tse a-da-zi," a word French-Canadian trappers translated into "Rive des Roche Jaune"—literally, "Yellow Rock River." The Indians called it this because of the yellowish bluffs along the river mouth (not, as some claim, because of the colorful Grand Canyon of the Yellowstone). The term "Yellow Stone" was first used on a map

THE NEZ PERCÉ WAR

One of the saddest episodes in the history of Yellowstone took place in 1877 and involved the Nez Percé (pronounced "NAY-pur-SAY") Indians of Oregon's Wallowa Valley. When the government tried to force the people of Chief White Bird and Chief Joseph onto an Idaho reservation so that white ranchers could have their lands, they stubbornly refused. A few drunken young men killed four whites, and subsequent raids led to the deaths of at least 14 more. The Army retaliated but was turned back by the Nez Percé. Rather than face government reinforcements, more than 1,000 Nez Percé began an 1,800-mile flight in a desperate bid to reach Canada. A series of running battles followed as the Indians managed to confound the inept Army using their geographic knowledge and battle skills. The Nez Percé entered Yellowstone from the west, and a few hotheads immediately attacked vacationing tourists and prospectors. Two whites were killed in the park, others were kidnapped, and one man nearly died from his wounds.

The Nez Percé exited Yellowstone two weeks after they arrived, narrowly missing an encounter with their implacable foe, Gen. William T. Sherman, who just happened to be vacationing in Yel-

Chief Joseph in October 1887, immediately after his surrender at Bear Paw Mountain, Montana

lowstone at the time. East of the park, the Indians plotted a masterful escape from two columns of Army forces, feinting a move down the Shoshone River and then heading north along a route that left their pursuers gasping in amazement—straight up the narrow Clarks Fork Canyon, "where rocks on each side came so near together that two horses abreast could hardly pass." Finally, less than 40 miles from the international border with Canada, the Army caught up with the Nez Percé, and after a fierce battle the tribe was forced to surrender (although 300 did make good their escape).

Chief Joseph's haunting words still echo through the years: "Hear me, my chiefs, I am tired; my heart is sick and sad. From where the sun now stands, I will fight no more forever." Despite promises that they would be allowed to return home, the Nez Percé were hustled onto reservations in Oklahoma and Washington while whites remained on their ancestral lands. Chief Joseph spent the rest of his life on Washington's Colville Reservation and died in 1904, reportedly of a broken heart. Yellowstone's Nez Percé Creek, which feeds the Firehole River, is named for this desperate bid for freedom.

One of the publications resulting from reports of mass slaughters by poachers. Note that the "elk" actually have moose antlers!

made in 1798. When the Lewis and Clark Expedition traveled through the country north of Yellowstone in 1804, the Indians told them tales of this mysterious place: "There is frequently heard a loud noise like thunder, which makes the earth tremble, they state that they seldom go there because children Cannot sleep—and Conceive it possessed of spirits, who were adverse that men Should be near them." (This certainly was not the attitude of all the native peoples, for the park had long been inhabited.) The first white man to come through Yellowstone was John Colter, a former member of the Lewis and Clark Expedition who wandered through the region in the winter of 1807-08. A map based on Colter's recollections shows Yellowstone Lake ("Eustis Lake"), along with an area of "Hot Spring Brimstone."

As fur trappers spread through the Rockies in the 1820s and '30s, many discovered the geysers and hot springs of Yellowstone, and stories quickly spread around the rendezvous fires. The word of the trappers was passed on to later settlers and explorers but not entirely believed. After all, mountain man Jim Bridger described not just petrified trees, but petrified birds singing petrified songs! His tales of a river that "ran so fast that it became hot on the bottom" could well have referred to the Firehole River. When Bridger tried to lead a party of military explorers into Yellowstone, they were stymied by deep snows. Still, the word gradually got out that something very strange could be found in this part of the mountains. Little remains today from the mountain-man era, although in 1880 the letters "J.O.R. Aug. 19, 1819" were found carved in a tree near the Upper Falls of the Yellowstone, and later a cache of iron beaver traps similar to those used by the Hudson's Bay Company was discovered near Obsidian Cliff.

EXPEDITIONS

National attention finally came to Yellowstone with a series of three expeditions to check out the wild claims of local prospectors. In 1869, David E. Folsom, Charles W. Cook, and William Peterson headed south from Bozeman, finding the Grand Canyon, Lake Yellowstone, and the geyser basins. When a friend pressured them to submit a description of their travels for publication, the *New York Tribune* refused to publish it, noting that the paper "had a reputation that they could not risk with such unreliable material."

Their adventures led another group of explorers into Yellowstone the following year, but this time money was the motive. Jay Cooke's Northern Pacific Railroad needed investors for a planned route across Montana. A good public-relations campaign was the first step, and it happened to coincide with the visit of a former Montana tax collector named Nathaniel P. Langford who had heard of the discoveries of Folsom, Cook, and Peterson. The collection of 19 soldiers and civilians headed out in August of 1870 under Gen. Henry D. Washburn. They were thrilled by what they discovered and proceeded to name the geysers—Old Faithful, Castle, Giant, Grotto, Giantess—names that became permanently attached to them. The joy of the trip was marred when one man—Truman

Everts—became separated from the others and then lost his horse. He was not found until nearly a month later, by which time he weighed just 50 pounds. Evert's rescuer did not even recognize him as human. He survived and recovered.

With the return of the Washburn Expedition, national newspapers and magazines finally began to pay attention to Yellowstone, and Langford began lecturing in the East on what they had found. One of those listening was Dr. Ferdinand V. Hayden, director of the U.S. Geological Survey. Hayden asked Congress to fund an official investigation. With the help of Representatives James G. Blaine (coincidentally a supporter of the Northern Pacific Railroad) and conservationist Henry M. Dawes, Congress appropriated $40,000 for an exploration of "the sources of the Missouri and Yellowstone Rivers." Thus began the most famous and influential trip into Yellowstone, the 1871 Hayden Expedition. The troop included 34 men, an escort of cavalry, painter Thomas Moran, and photographer William H. Jackson.

ESTABLISHING THE PARK

When Hayden returned to Washington to prepare his report, he found a letter from railroad promoter Jay Cooke. In the letter, Cooke proposed that "Congress pass a bill reserving the Great Geyser Basin as a public park forever—just as it has reserved that far inferior wonder the Yosemite valley and big trees." (Abraham Lincoln had established Yosemite earlier as a state park.) In an amazingly short time, a bill was introduced to set aside the land, and Hayden rushed to arrange a display in the Capitol rotunda of geological specimens, sketches by Moran, and photos by Jackson. The bill easily passed both houses of Congress and was signed into law on March 1, 1872, by President Ulysses S. Grant. The first national park had come into existence, a culmination not just of the discoveries in Yellowstone but also of a growing appreciation for preserving the wonders of the natural world.

Congress saw no need to set aside money for this new creation, since it seemed to be doing fine already. Besides, it was thought that Jay Cooke's new railroad would soon arrive, making

it easy for thousands of vacationers to explore Yellowstone. In turn, concessionaires would build roads and hotels and pay the government franchise fees. The park was placed under the control of the Secretary of the Interior, with Nathaniel P. Langford as its unpaid superintendent. Meanwhile, the planned railroad fizzled when Jay Cooke & Co. declared bankruptcy, precipitating the panic of 1873.

ROADS AND RAILROADS

Because of the difficult access, fewer than 500 people visited in each of Yellowstone's first few years as a park, most to soak in tubs at Mammoth Hot Springs. Not a few decided to take home souvenirs, bringing pickaxes and shovels for that purpose. Meanwhile, hunters—including some working for the Mammoth Hotel—began shooting the park's abundant game. Two brothers who had a ranch just north of the park killed 2,000 elk in a single year. Superintendent Langford did little to stop the slaughter and only bothered to visit the park twice. Finally, in 1877, the Secretary of the Interior fired him, putting Philetus W. Norris in charge instead. Norris proved a good choice, despite a knack for applying his name to everything in sight. (Most of his attempts at immortality have been replaced by other titles, but Norris Geyser Basin, Norris Road, and even the town of Norris, Michigan, remain.)

Norris oversaw construction of the first major road in Yellowstone, a rough 60-mile route built in just 30 days to connect Upper Geyser Basin with Mammoth and the western entrance. All of this was precipitated by the raids of the Nez Percé Indians earlier that summer and threats that the Bannock Indians would strike next. In addition, Norris began, but never completed, the Queen's Laundry, a bathhouse that is considered the first government building built for the public in any national park. The log walls are still visible in a meadow near Lower Geyser Basin.

By 1882, Norris had managed to alienate the company that helped found the park, the Northern Pacific Railroad. The company announced plans to build a railroad line to the geysers and construct a large hotel, "being assured by the

Government of a monopoly therein." Norris's opposition led to his being fired and replaced by railroad man Patrick H. Conger. Soon, however, the scheme began to unravel. The Yellowstone Park Improvement Company—whose vice-president happened to be construction superintendent for the Northern Pacific's branch line into Gardiner—had planned not just a lodging monopoly, but also a monopoly on all transportation, timber rights, and ranching privileges in the park. Later it was discovered that the company had contracted for 20,000 pounds of venison (killed in the park) to feed the construction crews. As one newspaper writer commented, "It is a 'Park Improvement Company' doing this, and I suppose they consider it an improvement to rid the park, as far as possible of game."

Finally, in 1884 Congress acted by limiting the land that could be leased—thus effectively ending the railroad's plans—and adding funding to hire 10 assistants to patrol Yellowstone. Unfortunately, they neglected to include any penalties for the poachers and despoilers other than expulsion, so even the few assistants who did decent work found the culprits quickly returning. The problems were myriad. Cooke City miners were fishing with spears, seine nets, and even dynamite. Guides were throwing rocks into the geysers, squatters had ensconced themselves on prime land in Lamar Valley, and visitors were leaving fires unattended and breaking off specimens from the geysers.

Superintendent Conger was later replaced by Robert E. Carpenter, a man about whom historian Hiram Chittenden noted, "In his opinion, the Park was created to be an instrument of profit to those who were shrewd enough to grasp the opportunity." Carpenter lobbied Congress to remove lands from the park so that the Northern Pacific could construct a railroad along the Yellowstone River to Cooke City. In return, friends promised to locate claims in his name along the route so that he too might profit from the venture. The land grab fell apart when the Senate vetoed the move, and Carpenter was summarily removed from office. Not long thereafter, Congress flatly refused to fund the civilian administration of Yellowstone, and the secretary of the interior was forced to call in the military in 1886. It proved a fortuitous step.

THE ARMY YEARS

The Army finally brought a semblance of order, eliminating the political appointees who viewed Yellowstone as a place to get rich. That first year, a temporary fort—Camp Sheridan—was thrown up and a troop of soldiers arrived, but it wasn't until 1891 that work began on a permanent Fort Yellowstone at Mammoth. By 1904, the fort consisted of some 26 buildings housing 120 men. The soldiers had clear objectives—protecting wildlife (or at least bison and elk) from poachers, fighting fires, stopping vandalism, and generally achieving order out of chaos. These goals were accomplished with a fervor that gained widespread respect, and in a way that would later influence the organization of the National Park Service. One of the major accomplishments of the soldiers was completion of the Grand Loop Road, which passes most of Yellowstone's attractions. The basic pattern was completed by 1905.

Fort Yellowstone was a favorite station for soldiers, and it was considered something of an honor to be sent to such a setting. The life of the soldiers was not always easy, however, and a number died in the bitter winters or in accidents. A series of 16 soldier stations—actually little more than large cabins—was established around the park, and each was manned year-round, usually by four soldiers.

Before the arrival of cars, many visitors to Yellowstone were wealthy people from the east coast or Europe intent upon doing the grand tour of western sights. The railroads (Northern Pacific to the north, Union Pacific to the west, and the Burlington to the east) deposited them near park borders, where they were met by carriages, Tallyhos (26-passenger stagecoaches), and surreys. In 1915, there were some 3,000 horses in use within the park! Most "dudes" paid approximately $50 for a six-day tour that included transportation, meals, and lodging at the hotels. They paid another $2.50 for the privilege of sailing across Lake Yellowstone on the steamship *Zillah*. By contrast, another group, the "sagebrushers," came to Yellowstone in smaller numbers, arriving in their own wagons or hiring a coach to transport them between the "Wylie Way" campgrounds. These seasonal tent

THE YELLOWSTONE FIRES OF 1988

Many will long remember the summer of 1988 as the year fire seared Yellowstone National Park. TV reporters flocked to the park, pronouncing the destruction of America's most famous national wonder as they stood before trees turned into towering torches and 30,000-foot clouds of black smoke. Newspaper headlines screamed, "Park Sizzles," "Winds Whip Fiery Frenzy Out of Control," and "Firestorms Blacken Yellowstone." Residents of nearby towns complained of lost tourism dollars, choking smoke, and intentionally lit backfires that threatened their homes and businesses; Wyoming politicians berated the Park Service's "Let Burn" policy; President Reagan expressed astonishment that fires were ever allowed to burn in the national parks, though the policy had been in place for 16 years. Perhaps the most enduring image is from a forest that had been blown down by tornado-force winds in 1984 and then burned by the wind-whipped fires of 1988. The media ate it up, with one headline reading, "Total Destruction: Intense Heat and Flames from the Fires in Yellowstone Left Nothing but Powdered Ash and Charcoal Near Norris Junction." Unfortunately, the real story behind the fires of '88 was lost in this media feeding frenzy.

A Century of Change

In reality, these fires were not unprecedented; we were just fortunate enough to witness one of the incredible spectacles of nature, which may not occur again for another 300 years. When Yellowstone National Park was established in 1872, most of the land was carpeted with a mixture of variously aged lodgepole-pine stands established following a series of large fires. Fewer large fires, partly due to unusually moist summer weather conditions and partly to a fire-suppression policy in effect until 1972, meant that by the 1980s a third of the park's lodgepole stands were more than 200 years old. Yellowstone was ripe to burn.

Since the early 1950s, Smokey the Bear had drummed an incessant message: "Only You Can Prevent Forest Fires." Forest fires were viewed as dangerous, destructive forces that had to be stopped to protect our valuable public lands. Unfortunately, this immensely effective and generally valid ad campaign convinced the public that all fires were bad. Ecological research has shown not only that this is wrong, but that putting out all fires can sometimes create conditions far more dangerous than if fires had been allowed to burn in the first place. Fire, like the other processes that have affected Yellowstone—cataclysmic volcanic explosions, geothermal activity, and massive glaciation—is neither good nor evil. It is simply a part of the natural world that national parks are attempting to preserve. Unfortunately, national parks are no longer surrounded by similarly undeveloped land, so when fires burned in Yellowstone and surrounding Forest Service lands they also affected the surrounding towns and the people who make a living from tourism or logging.

Fire in Lodgepole Forests

Fire has played an important role in lodgepole-pine forests for thousands if not millions of years, and as a result the trees have evolved an unusual adaptation. Some of the cones are serotinous, with a resin that melts under the heat of forest fires. The

Yellowstone fire

BOB RACE

parent trees are killed, but a new generation is guaranteed by the thousands of pine seeds released to the bare, nutrient-rich soil underneath the blackened overstory. Within five years the landscape is dotted with thousands of young pines, competing with a verdant cover of grasses and flowers.

Although some animals are killed in the fires (including, in 1988, 257 of Yellowstone's 30,000 elk), and others die from a lack of food immediately after a fire, the early decades following a fire create conditions that are unusually rich for many animals. Wildlife diversity in lodgepole forests reaches a peak within the first 25 years as woodpeckers, mountain bluebirds, and other birds feed on insects in the dead trees, and elk and bears graze on the lush grasses.

As the forest ages, a dense stand of trees forms, keeping light from reaching the forest floor and making it difficult for understory plants to survive. These trees eventually thin themselves out, creating openings in the forest, but after 200-300 years without fire the lodgepole forests become a tangle of fallen trees that are difficult to walk through, are of limited value to many animals, and burn easily. They also become susceptible to attacks by bark beetles, such as those that killed thousands of acres of trees in Yellowstone during the 1980s—creating even more potential fire fuel.

Yellowstone in 1988

Yellowstone's 1988 fires were due not just to the heavy fuel loading from aging forests but also to weather conditions that were the driest and windiest on record. The winter of 1987-88 had been a mild one, and by spring there was a moderate to severe drought in the park, lessened only by above-normal rainfall in April and May. Since 1972, when Yellowstone Park officials first began allowing certain lightning fires to burn in backcountry areas, the acreage burned totaled less than two percent of the park. (Mistakenly called a "let burn" policy, the natural fire program actually involved close monitoring of these lightning-ignited fires to determine when and if a fire should be suppressed. All human-caused fires were immediately suppressed, as were any that threatened property or life.)

When the first lightning fires of the 1988 season began in late May, those in the backcountry areas were allowed to burn, as fire management officials anticipated normal summer weather conditions. Many went out on their own, but when June

and July came and the rains failed to materialize, the fires began to spread rapidly. Alarmed park officials declared them wildfires and sent crews to attempt to put them out. (Ironically, the largest fire, the North Fork/Wolf Lake Complex, was started by humans, and although firefighters immediately attacked the blaze, it consumed more than 500,000 acres.) As the summer progressed, more and more firefighters were called in, eventually totaling over 25,000 personnel, at a cost exceeding $120 million. Firefighters managed to protect many park buildings but had little effect on the forest fires themselves. Experts say that conditions in the summer of 1988 were so severe that even if firefighters had immediately responded to all the natural fires, it might have made little difference. Yellowstone has experienced these massive fires in the past and will again in the future, no matter what humans do.

Out of Control

Firefighters found the weather worsening with each passing hour. Winds blew steadily at 20-40 miles an hour, and gusts to 70 mph threw firebrands two miles in front of the firefront, across firelines, roads, and even the Lewis River Canyon. Fuel moisture in the large logs approached that of kiln-dried wood. By mid-August, more than 25 fires were burning simultaneously all over the park and surrounding national forests, with many joining together to create massive complexes such as the Clover-Mist Fire, the Snake River Complex, and the North Fork/Wolf Lake Complex. On a single day—September 7—more than 100,000 acres burned, and 20 out of the more than 400 buildings in the vicinity of Old Faithful were torched. The fires seemed poised to consume the remainder of Yellowstone, but four days later the season's first snow carpeted the park. Within a few days firefighters had the upper hand.

A Transformed Landscape

Nearly 800,000 acres (36% of the park) had been burned by the fires, and so had another 600,000 acres on adjacent Forest Service lands. Of the park total, 41% were canopy fires in which all the trees were killed, and another 35% were a mixture of ground fires and canopy fires. The remainder were lighter burns. The fires are out, the land is slowly recovering, and the park's natural-fire program was replaced after the fires by a somewhat more conservative version. *(continues on next page)*

THE YELLOWSTONE FIRES OF 1988
(continued)

Visitors to Yellowstone today will see enormous expanses of blackened trees in some parts of the park, while in other areas they find a complex mosaic of burned and unburned forest land. Once you grow accustomed to the burned areas and understand that they are a part of the natural process, they actually add interest to the park. Get out of your car and walk through the burned areas and you'll discover dense carpets of young lodgepole trees, along with impressive displays of wildflowers, forbs, and grasses in midsummer. Vistas that were long blocked by dense forests are now more open. The Park Service has placed informative signboards at seven sites around Yellowstone describing the fires and the changes they brought about. The Grant Village Visitor Center houses a special display and film on the fires.

camps were scattered around the park, providing an inexpensive ($35 for a seven-day tour) way to see the sights. Even as early as 1908, Yellowstone was being seen by 18,000 visitors a year.

The Northern Pacific was still intent upon carving Yellowstone into a money-making resort, even going so far as to propose an electric railroad, to be powered by a dam at the falls of the Yellowstone River. Fortunately, equally powerful forces—notably Gen. Phillip Sheridan and naturalist Joseph Bird Grinnell—saw through their designs and thwarted each attempt to bring railroads into Yellowstone. Still, the Northern Pacific's interests were represented by its indirect control of many of Yellowstone's hotels, stagecoaches, wagons, and other vehicles used to transport tourists.

All this changed when the first car was allowed through the gate on August 1, 1915. (Entrance fees were a surprisingly stiff $5 for single-seat vehicles and $7.50 for five-passenger cars.) Almost immediately, it became clear that horses and cars could not mix, and motor buses replaced the old coaches. From then on, the park would be increasingly a place for "autoists." Interestingly, within a year the park would come under the jurisdiction of the newly created National Park Service.

THE PARK SERVICE TAKES OVER

After years of Army control, supporters of a separate National Park Service finally had their way in 1916. The congressional act created a dual role for the new park system: to "conserve the scenery" and to "provide for the enjoyment of the same," a contradictory mandate that would later lead to all sorts of conflicts. The first couple of years were tenuous, as management flip-flopped between the Army and civilians, with the final changeover coming in 1918 and ending three decades of military supervision. The management of Yellowstone fell on the shoulders of two men, Horace M. Albright and his mentor, Stephen Mather, both of whom had been heavily involved in lobbying to create the new agency. Mather became the Park Service's first director, while Albright served as superintendent at Yellowstone and later stepped into Mather's shoes to head the agency.

Albright quickly upgraded facilities to meet the influx of motorists who demanded more camping facilities but also cabins, lodges, cafeterias, and bathhouses. Forty-six camps were constructed (only 12 survive today), fulfilling Albright's dream of "a motorist's paradise." The focus of the new Park Service was clearly visitation rather than preservation. Albright assembled a first-rate force of park rangers and instituted the environmental education programs that have been the agency's hallmark ever since.

As the automobile took over Yellowstone, the railroads gradually lost their sway. The last passenger train to the park's gateway towns stopped in 1961. In the 1950s, the Park Service initiated "Mission 66," a decade-long project to upgrade facilities and add more lodging. By the late '60s, a growing appreciation for the nat-

ural world was shifting public opinion away from such developments, and the 1973 master plan scaled back proposed developments. In recent years such issues as wolf reintroduction, grizzly management, snowmobile use, and the fires of 1988 have attracted widespread attention. The

1990s have been a time of budget cuts, which have had a noticeable effect throughout Yellowstone, from the pothole-filled roads to the lack of seasonal rangers and the closing of museums and campgrounds. One hopes that this is not allowed to continue.

TOURING YELLOWSTONE

Yellowstone is perhaps the most accessible national park. Nearly all the famous sights are within a couple hundred feet of the Grand Loop Road, a 142-mile figure-eight through the middle of the park. For all too many visitors, Yellowstone becomes a checklist of places to visit, geysers to watch, and animals to see. The Park Service has done its part by putting signs and labels on everything, right down to the smallest hot springs. All this tends to inspire an attitude that treats this great national park as a drive-through zoo where the animals come out to perform, and the geyser eruptions are predicted so everyone can be there on time. If you're one of this crowd, give yourself a giant kick in the rear and take a walk, even if it is just around Upper Geyser Basin where you see something beyond Old Faithful. Whatever you do, *don't* see Yellowstone at 45 miles an hour; that's like seeing the Louvre from a passing train.

The following loop tour of Yellowstone begins in the south and traces a clockwise path around the Grand Loop (with side trips). Although it is possible to follow this sequence (or some variation) the entire distance, a far better way to learn about Yellowstone is to stop for a while in the places that are the most interesting to you and really explore them, rather than trying to see everything in a cursory way. If you have the time, the entire park is well worth visiting, but if you have only a day or two, pick a couple of spots and see them right. Be sure to at least spend time at Grand Canyon of the Yellowstone and Norris Geyser Basin. And don't just check out the views everyone else sees; find a nearby trail and do a little exploring on your own. If you are planning a trip to the area, try to set aside a bare minimum of three days in Yellowstone.

SOUTH ENTRANCE ROAD

The South Entrance Station consists of several new log structures right along the Snake River. Just 1.5 miles beyond the entrance is an easily missed turnout where you can walk down to 30-foot-high **Moose Falls.** Beyond this, the road climbs up a long, gentle ramp to Pitchstone Plateau, passing green forests of lodgepole pine. Stop at a turnout to look back at the majestic Tetons. Abruptly, this gentle country is broken by the edge of **Lewis River Canyon,** with rhyolite walls that drop 600 feet on either side. Anyone who has not been to Yellowstone since the fires of 1988 will be shocked by the scene here— blackened remains of trees seem to extend in all directions. The Snake River Complex of fires joined together to leap a quarter-mile across this canyon, revealing the futility of bulldozer-cut firebreaks in trying to halt an inferno under the high wind conditions and severe drought that existed.

The road parallels the river for the next seven miles. Nearly everyone stops at 37-foot-high **Lewis Falls.** Camping is available at the south end of **Lewis Lake.** (The lake, falls, river, and canyon are all named for the Lewis and Clark expedition's Meriwether Lewis.) Lewis Lake is the park's third-largest body of water (after Yellowstone and Shoshone Lakes) and is popular with boaters and anglers. The clear waters contain brown trout and Mackinaw. Approximately four miles north of Lewis Lake, the highway tops the Continental Divide, but the point (7,988 feet above sea level) is not particularly noticeable. This is one of three such traverses roads make within Yellowstone.

Lewis Lake Hikes

Two trailheads are a mile north of Lewis Lake, providing access east to Heart Lake and west to

Shoshone Lake through country burned in the fires of 1988. The four-mile-long **Dogshead Trail** offers a direct route to Shoshone Lake, while the **Lewis Channel Trail** takes a scenic trek via the Lewis River channel, which connects Shoshone and Lewis Lakes. It's seven miles to Shoshone Lake on this path. The path is popular with anglers who come to the channel for brown and cutthroat trout during the fall spawning season. The trail to Heart Lake begins on the opposite side of the road and south a few hundred feet. (See "Into the Backcountry" later in this chapter for hikes in the Heart Lake and Shoshone Lake areas.) Canoeists sometimes paddle across Lewis Lake and then portage to Shoshone Lake.

Grant Village

The newest Yellowstone development is Grant Village, built to replace facilities at Fishing Bridge, an area of vital grizzly habitat. Unfortunately, instead of one bad development, Yellowstone now has two—Fishing Bridge still exists (although some of the buildings are gone). Grant Village was completed in the 1980s, but unlike some of the more historic places, where a natural rusticity prevailed, Grant Village has less charm than most Kmarts. A steak house restaurant juts out along the shore of Yellowstone Lake, and the Grant Village Hotel forms a chintzy condo backdrop. Other facilities include a campground, a store, a gas station, and a post office. Much of the area around here was consumed in the 1988 Snake River Fire; unfortunately, it missed this scar on the Yellowstone landscape.

Grant Village Visitor Center, tel. (307) 242-2650, is open daily 8 a.m.-7 p.m. Memorial Day to Labor Day and daily 9 a.m.-5 p.m. in the spring and fall. Inside, find informative exhibits and a slide show film on the fires of 1988.

West Thumb

If you look at a map of Yellowstone Lake, it's possible to imagine the lake as a giant hand with three mangled fingers heading south and a gnarled thumb extending west. Thus the name West Thumb. This portion of Yellowstone Lake is the deepest (to 390 feet) and is actually a caldera that filled with water after erupting 200,000 years ago. There is still considerable heat just below the surface, as revealed by **West Thumb Geyser Basin.** A short loop trail leads through the steaming hot springs and pools. Just offshore is **Fishing Cone Geyser,** where tourists once caught fish and then plopped them in the cone to be cooked. The water is no longer hot enough for this stunt, and besides, it's illegal. The **West Thumb Information Station** is open daily 9 a.m.-5 p.m. May-Sept. and has a small bookstore.

WEST THUMB TO UPPER GEYSER BASIN

Heading west from West Thumb, the highway climbs over the Continental Divide twice. Most of these forests escaped the 1988 fires. A couple miles beyond the unmarked eastern crossing is a turnout at **Shoshone Point** where you catch glimpses of Shoshone Lake and the Tetons. In 1914, highwayman Ed Trafton held up 15 stagecoaches as they passed by this point carrying tourists. He got away with $915.35 in cash and $130 in jewelry but made the mistake of allowing his photo to be taken in the process. He was caught the following year and spent five years in Leavenworth. When he died, a letter in his pocket claimed that he had been Owen Wister's model for the Virginian. Others suspected that he was more likely to have been Wister's model for the villain, Trampas.

DeLacy Creek Trail provides access to Shoshone Lake and begins at the picnic area between the two passes. It's three miles to the lake, which is circled by more trails. The western crossing of the Continental Divide is at **Isa Lake,** a tiny pond that empties into both the Atlantic and Pacific oceans through its two outlet streams. This is Craig Pass.

Approximately 14 miles beyond West Thumb, pull off to see the Firehole River as it drops over **Kepler Cascades.** Just to the east, a wide and partly paved trail (actually an old road) leads 2.5 miles to **Lone Star Geyser.** This is a popular route for bikers in the summer and skiers in the winter. (There's no bike traffic beyond the geyser, however.) Lone Star Geyser erupts every three hours from a distinctive nine-foot-high cone, with eruptions generally reaching 45 feet and lasting for 30 minutes. Hikers can also get to Lone Star via the Howard Eaton Trail out of Old Faith-

UPPER GEYSER BASIN

Map labels: TO FAIRY FALLS TRAILHEAD · MORNING GLORY POOL · TO BISCUIT BASIN AND MYSTIC FALLS · RIVERSIDE GEYSER · GROTTO GEYSER · GIANT GEYSER · DAISY GEYSER · CHROMATIC POOL · PUNCH BOWL SPRING · BEAUTY POOL · SOLITARY GEYSER · TO MADISON JCT. · FIREHOLE RIVER · GRAND GEYSER · OBSERVATION POINT · CRESTED POOL · CASTLE GEYSER · LION GEYSER · GEYSER HILL · GIANTESS GEYSER · BEEHIVE GEYSER · CHINESE SPRING · BLACK SAND BASIN · IRON SPRING CREEK · SERVICE STATION · STORE · OLD FAITHFUL · OLD FAITHFUL LODGE · OLD FAITHFUL INN · VISITOR CENTER · RANGER STATION · PHOTO STORE · CLINIC · SNOW LODGE · SERVICE STATION · STORE · TRAIL TO MALLARD LAKE · POST OFFICE · HOWARD EATON TRAIL · TO WEST THUMB

0   0.2 mi
0   0.2 km

© MOON PUBLICATIONS, INC.

ful. For a longer hike, you can continue south from Lone Star on **Shoshone Lake Trail** to Shoshone Lake, eight fairly easy miles from the main road. (See "Into the Backcountry" later in this chapter for other Shoshone Lake hikes.)

UPPER GEYSER BASIN

As you approach Old Faithful from either direction, the two-lane road suddenly widens into four, and you are confronted with what has to be one of the only cloverleafs in the entire national-park system. Welcome to Upper Geyser Basin, home of Old Faithful, some 400 buildings of all sizes, and a small town's worth of people. For many folks, this is the heart of Yellowstone, and a visit to the park without seeing Old Faithful is like a baseball game without the national anthem. If you came to Yellowstone to see the wonders of nature, you're going to see more than your share here, but you'll probably have to share your share with hundreds of other folks. Fortunately, the Upper Geyser Basin contains

the largest concentration of geysers in the world, and the adventurous will even discover places almost nobody ever visits. But be very careful—the crust can be dangerously thin around some of the hot springs and geysers, and people have been badly scalded and even killed by missteps. Stay on the boardwalks.

Old Faithful

The one sight seen by everyone who comes to Yellowstone is Old Faithful Geyser, easily the most visited geyser in the world. Its fame is second only to that of Iceland's Geysir (meaning "gusher" in Icelandic). Old Faithful is neither the tallest nor the most frequent geyser in Yellowstone, but it always provides a good show, is highly accessible, and is relatively predictable. Eruptions reach an average of 130 feet in the air. Contrary to the rumors, Old Faithful never erupted "every hour on the hour," but for many years its periodicity was a little over an hour. It has slowed down in recent years and is now averaging around 75-90 minutes. In general, the longer the length of the eruption, the longer the interval till the next eruption. Check at the visitor center for the latest prognostications on this and other geysers in the basin.

An almost level paved path circles Old Faithful, providing many different angles from which to view the eruptions, although none of these is particularly close to the geyser. Along the north side is **Chinese Spring,** named in 1885 for a short-lived laundry operation. Apparently, the washman had filled the spring with clothes and soap, not knowing that soap can cause geysers to erupt. One newspaper correspondent claimed—though the tale obviously suffered from embellishment and racism—that,

The soap awakened the imprisoned giant; with a roar that made the earth tremble, and a shriek of a steam whistle, a cloud of steam and a column of boiling water shot up into the air a hundred feet, carrying soap, raiment, tent and Chinaman along with the rush, and dropping them at various intervals along the way.

Old Faithful provides a textbook example of geyser activity. The first signs of life are when water begins to splash out of the vent in what is called preplay. This splashing can last up to 20 minutes, but it's generally only a couple minutes before the real thing. The water quickly spears into the sky, reaching 100-180 feet for two to five minutes before rapidly dropping down. During a typical eruption, between 3,700 and 8,400 gallons of water are sent skyward.

On any given summer day, the scene at Old Faithful is almost comical. Just before the predicted eruption time, the benches encircling the south and east sides are jammed with hundreds of people waiting expectantly for the geyser to erupt, and with each tentative spray the camera shutters begin to click. Listen closely and you'll hear half the languages of Europe and Asia. Once the action is over, there is a mad rush back into the visitor center, the stores, and Old Faithful Inn, and within a few minutes the benches are empty. A story is told of two concessionaire employees who once decided to have fun at Old Faithful by placing a large crank atop a box and putting the contraption near the geyser. When they knew it was ready to erupt, they ran out and turned the crank just as Old Faithful shot into the air. Their employer failed to find humor in the prank. Both were fired.

Geyser Hill Area

Upper Geyser Basin is laced with paved trails that lead to dozens of nearby geysers and hot springs. The easiest path loops around Geyser Hill, just across the Firehole River from Old Faithful. Here are 40 different geysers. Check at the visitor center to get an idea of current activity, and while there pick up the Upper Geyser Basin map (25 cents), which describes most of them. Several geysers are particularly noteworthy. When it plays, **Beehive Geyser** (it has a tall, beehive-shaped cone) vents water as high as 180 feet into the air. Such eruptions may be up to 10 days apart, however. **Lion Geyser Group** consists of four different interconnected geysers with varying periods of activity. Listen for the roaring sound when Lion is ready to erupt. **Giantess Geyser** is active only a few times a year, but the eruptions are spectacularly powerful, sending water 100-200 feet skyward. **Doublet Pool** is a stunningly beautiful deep-blue pool that is a favorite of photographers. Not far away is **Sponge Geyser,** which rockets water up to 229 millimeters into the air

> *From the surface of a rocky plain or table, burst forth columns of water of various dimensions, projected high in the air, accompanied by loud explosions, and sulphurous vapors, which were highly disagreeable to the smell . . . The largest of these wonderful fountains, projects a column of boiling water several feet in diameter, to the height of more than one hundred and fifty feet . . . After having witnessed three of them, I ventured near enough to put my hand into the water of its basin, but withdrew it instantly, for the heat of the water in this immense couldron, was altogether to great for comfort, and the agitation of the water, disagreeable effluvium continually exuding, and the hollow unearthly rumbling under the rock on which I stood, so ill accorded with my notions of personal safety, that I retreated back precipitately to a respectful distance.*
>
> *Yellowstone's first "tourist,"*
> *Angus Ferris in 1833*

(nine inches). It's considered the smallest named geyser in Yellowstone, a title achieved by sending up a spurt of water big enough to be mopped up with a sponge.

The two-mile-long **Observation Point Loop Trail** splits off shortly after you cross the bridge on the way to Geyser Hill and climbs to an excellent overlook where you can watch eruptions of Old Faithful. This is also a good place to view the effects of the 1988 North Fork Fire. Another easy trail splits off from this path to **Solitary Geyser**—actually just a pool that periodically burps four-foot splashes of hot water. This is not a natural geyser. In 1915, the hot spring here was tapped to provide water for Old Faithful Geyser Bath, a concession that lasted until 1950. The lowering of the water level in the pool completely changed the plumbing system of the hot springs and turned it into a geyser that at one time shot 25 feet in the air. The system still hasn't recovered, although water levels have been restored for more than 40 years.

More Geyser Gazin'

Another easy, paved path follows the Firehole River downstream, looping back along the other side for a total distance of three miles. Other trails head off from this loop to the Fairy Falls Trailhead, Biscuit Basin, and Black Sand Basin. The loop is a very popular wintertime ski path, and portions are open to bikes in the summer. Twelve-foot-high **Castle Geyser** does indeed resemble a ruined old castle. Because of its size and the slow accretion of sinter (silica) to form this cone, it is believed to be somewhere between 5,000 and 50,000 years old. Castle sends up a column of water and steam 90 feet into the air and usually erupts every 10-12 hours. Check at the visitor center for current activity.

Daisy Geyser is farther down the path and off to the left. It is usually one of the most predictable of the geysers, erupting to 75 feet approximately every 90-115 minutes. The water shoots out at a sharp angle and is visible all over the basin, making this a real crowd pleaser. Just east of Daisy is **Radiator Geyser,** which isn't much to look at (eruptions to two feet) but was named when this area was a parking lot and the sudden eruption under a car led people to think its radiator was overheating. A personal favorite, **Grotto Geyser,** is certainly the weirdest of all the geysers, having formed around a tangle of long-petrified tree stumps. It is in eruption a third of the time, but most eruptions only reach 10 feet.

Look for **Riverside Geyser** across the Firehole from the path and not far below Grotto. This beautiful geyser arches spray 75 feet over the river and is one of the most predictable, with 20-minute-long eruptions approximately every seven hours. The paved trail crosses the river and ends at **Morning Glory Pool.** For many years, the main road passed this colorful pool, and it became something of a wishing well for not just coins but trash, rocks, logs, and other debris. Because of this junk, the pool began to cool, and the beautiful blue color is now tinged by brown and green algae, despite efforts to remove the debris.

Turning back at Morning Glory, re-cross the bridge and head left where the path splits at Grotto Geyser. **Giant Geyser** is on the left along

390 YELLOWSTONE NATIONAL PARK

the river. Years may pass between eruptions of Giant but when it does go, the name rings true, since the water often reaches 200 feet. Cross the river again and pass **Beauty Pool** and **Chromatic Pool**, which are connected below the ground so that one declines as the other rises. Very pretty. **Grand Geyser** is a wonderful sight. The water column erupts in a towering burst of power every 7-15 hours, with a series of bursts lasting 9-12 minutes and reaching up to 200 feet. When Grand isn't playing, watch for eruptions of nearby **Turban** and **Sawmill** Geysers. Cross the river again just beyond Grand Geyser and pass **Crested Pool** on your way back to Castle Geyser. The pool contains deep-blue water that is constantly boiling, preventing the survival of algae.

Black Sand Basin
Just a mile west of Old Faithful is Black Sand Basin, a small cluster of geysers and hot springs. Most enjoyable is unpredictable **Cliff Geyser,** which often sends a spray of hot water 25-30 feet over Iron Spring Creek. Three colorful pools are quite interesting in the basin: **Emerald Pool, Rainbow Pool,** and **Sunset Lake. Handkerchief Pool** is now just a small spouter but was famous for many years as a place where visitors could drop a handkerchief in one end and then recover it later at another vent. In 1929, vandals jammed logs in the pool, destroying this little game. The pool was covered with gravel in subsequent eruptions of Rainbow Pool.

Biscuit Basin and Mystic Falls
Located three miles north of Old Faithful, this basin is named for biscuitlike formations that were found in one of the pools; they were destroyed in an eruption following the 1959 Hebgen Lake earthquake. From the parking lot, the trail leads across the Firehole River to **Sapphire Pool** and then past **Jewel Geyser,** which typically erupts every 10 minutes to a height of 15-20 feet. The boardwalk follows a short loop through the other sights of Biscuit Basin. From the west end of the boardwalk, a one-mile trail leads to where the Little Firehole River cascades 70 feet over **Mystic Falls.** You can switchback farther up the trail to the top of the falls and then connect with another trail for the loop back to Biscuit Basin (3.5 miles roundtrip).

This is a very nice short hike and can be lengthened into a trip to **Little Firehole Meadows** and back via the Fairy Creek Trail to Midway Geyser Basin (14 miles roundtrip). Bison are often seen in the meadows.

Old Faithful Inn
Despite its proximity to one of the great sights of the natural world, it is impossible not to love Old Faithful Inn, a place that contains perhaps the most winsome interior of any American building. It is said to be the largest log structure of its kind in existence. Designed by Robert Reamer and built in the winter of 1903-04, the inn has a steeply angled roofline reaching seven stories high, with gables jutting out from the sides and flags flying from the roof. Open the rustic old front door and you enter a world of the past dominated by a massive four-sided stone fireplace (500 tons of native stone were used) and a central space that arches 85 feet overhead. Four overhanging balconies extend above, each bordered by posts made from gnarled lodgepole burls found within the park. Above the fireplace is an enormous clock designed by Reamer and built on the site by a blacksmith. Reamer also designed the two wings that were added in 1913 and 1928.

On warm summer evenings, visitors stand out on the porch where they can watch Old Faithful erupting, sit at the old handcrafted tables to write letters, and play the piano in the corner. It's enough to warm the heart of even the most cynical visitor. A good restaurant is on the premises, as is a rustic but comfortable bar, a gift shop, and a fast-food eatery. Free 45-minute **tours** of Old Faithful Inn are given daily at 9:30 a.m., 11 a.m., 2 p.m., and 3:30 p.m. from mid-May to late September. Meet at the fireplace in the lobby. Old Faithful Inn closes during the winter months; it would be hard to imagine trying to heat such a cavern when it's 40° below zero outside!

Another building of interest is **Old Faithful Lodge.** Built in 1928, this is the large stone-and-log building just south of the geyser of the same name. The giant fireplace inside is a joy on frosty evenings.

Old Faithful Services
The Park Service's **Old Faithful Visitor Center,** tel. (307) 545-2750, is generally open mid-April to early November, and mid-December to mid-

March. Hours vary throughout the year, but it's generally open daily 8 a.m.-7 p.m. from Memorial Day to Labor Day and daily 9 a.m.-5 p.m. at other times. Films about Yellowstone are shown throughout the day. The center has a good selection of books, maps, and other publications and posts predictions for six of the major geysers (including Old Faithful) during the summer. The staff can provide you with all sorts of other info, from where to see bighorn sheep to where to find the restroom.

Backcountry permits are available from the ranger station; food, supplies, and postcards can be purchased at either of the two Hamilton Stores. Old Faithful Inn has a gift shop, a restaurant, a snack bar, a lounge, and an **ATM;** cafeteria meals are available at Old Faithful Lodge. Other facilities include two gas stations, a post office, a photo shop, and a clinic. See "Yellowstone Practicalities" later in this chapter for lodging details. Note that camping is *not* available in the Old Faithful area, and it's illegal to stay overnight in the parking lots. The closest campgrounds are in Madison (16 miles north) and Grant Village (19 miles southeast).

MIDWAY AND LOWER GEYSER BASINS

Heading north from Upper Geyser Basin, the road follows the Firehole River past Midway and Lower Geyser Basins, both of which are quite interesting. This stretch of the river is very popular with fly-fishing enthusiasts, and several side roads provide access to a variety of hot springs.

Midway Geyser Basin

Midway is a large and readily accessible geyser basin with a loop path leading to most of the sights. Climb the hill across the road for fine views of the basin and its colorful pools. **Excelsior Geyser** is actually an enormous hot spring that pours 4,000 gallons per minute of steaming water into the Firehole River. The water is a deep turquoise-blue. During the 1880s, this was a truly spectacular geyser, with explosions that reached 380 feet in the air and were almost as wide. These violent eruptions apparently damaged the plumbing system that fed them, and

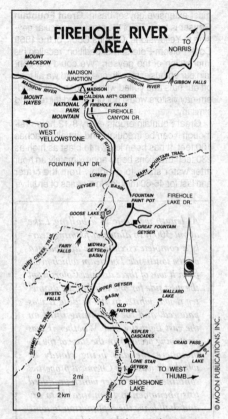

the geyser was dormant for nearly a century until smaller eruptions took place in 1985. At 370 feet across, **Grand Prismatic Spring** is Yellowstone's largest hot spring. The brilliant reds and yellows around the edges of the blue pool are from algae and bacteria that can tolerate temperatures of 170° F. It's difficult to get a good perspective on this spring from the ground; see aerial photos to really appreciate its beauty. There are additional geysers just south of here near a trailhead to Fairy Falls. The first mile of this trail is part of the old Fountain Flat Drive and is open to bikes.

Firehole Lake Drive

This road (one-way heading north) goes three miles through Lower Geyser Basin, the park's

most extensive geyser basin. **Great Fountain Geyser** is truly one of the most spectacular geysers in Yellowstone. Charles Cook, of the 1869 Cook-Folsom-Peterson Expedition, recalled his impression of the geyser: "We could not contain our enthusiasm; with one accord we all took off our hats and yelled with all our might." Modern-day visitors would not be faulted for reacting similarly.

Great Fountain erupts every 8-12 hours (although it can be irregular) and usually reaches 100 feet. It has been known to blast as high as 230 feet! Eruptions begin approximately an hour after water starts to overflow from the crater and last for 45-60 minutes in a series of eruptive

---

At length we came to a boiling Lake about 300 ft in diameter forming nearly a complete circle as we approached on the south side The steam which arose from it was of three distinct Colors from the west side for one third of the diameter it was white, in the middle it was pale red, and the remaining third on the east light sky blue Whether it was something peculiar in the state of the atmosphere the day being cloudy or whether it was some Chemical properties contained in the water which produced this phenomenon I am unable to say and shall leave the explanation to some scientific tourist who may have the Curiosity to visit this place at some future period—The water was of deep indigo blue boiling like an imense caldron running over the white rock which had formed the edges to the height of 4 or 5 feet from the surface of the earth sloping gradually for 60 or 70 feet. What a field of speculation this presents for chemist and geologist.

—Mountain man Osborne Russell describing Grand Prismatic Spring in 1839

---

cycles. Eruption predictions are posted at the geyser. While you're waiting, watch the periodic eruptions of **White Dome Geyser** just a hundred yards down the road. Because of its massive 30-foot cone, this is believed to be one of the oldest geysers in the park. Eruptions generally occur every 15-30 minutes and spray 30 feet into the air.

Another mile down, the road literally cuts into the mound of **Pink Cone Geyser,** which now erupts every six to 15 hours and reaches a height of 30 feet. The pink color comes from manganese oxide. Just up from here at the bend in the road is **Firehole Lake,** which discharges 3,500 gallons of water per minute into Tangled Creek, which then drains across the road into **Hot Lake.** The short **Three Senses Nature Trail** gives blind visitors (and sighted ones too) a chance to touch, smell, and hear the world of the geysers and hot springs. **Steady Geyser** is unusual in that it forms both sinter (silica) and travertine (calcium carbonate) deposits. It is located along the edge of Hot Lake and, true to its name, erupts almost continuously, though the height is only five feet. Firehole Lake Drive continues another mile to its junction with the main road right across from the parking area for Fountain Paint Pot. (In the winter, Firehole Lake Drive is popular with skiers but is closed to snowmobiles.)

Fountain Paint Pot

Always a favorite of visitors, Fountain Paint Pot seems to have a playfulness about it that belies the immense power just below the surface. Pick up a trail guide (25 cents) as you head up the walkway. During the summer, rangers are often here to offer additional information. **Silex Spring** is off to the right as you walk up the small hill and is colored by different kinds of algae and bacteria. The spring has been known to erupt as a geyser (to 20 feet) but is currently dormant. The famous Fountain Paint Pot is a few steps up the boardwalk and consists of colorful muds that change in consistency throughout the season depending upon soil moisture. The pressure from steam and gases under the Paint Pot can throw gobs of mud up to 20 feet into the air. Just north of here are fumaroles that spray steam, carbon dioxide, and hydrogen sulfide into the air. Continuing down the boardwalk,

you come upon an impressive overlook above a multitude of geysers that change constantly in activity. Some of the largest geysers in the park are here—including Morning Geyser, which erupts to over 150 feet. The most active is **Clepsydra Geyser,** in eruption much of the time. **Fountain Geyser** is usually active every 11 hours or so and can occasionally reach 80 feet. Very impressive. The rest of the loop trail passes dead lodgepole pines that are being petrified as the silica is absorbed, creating a "bobby socks" appearance.

Fountain Flat Drive

Fountain Flat Drive provides access to meadows along the Firehole River and is a great place to see bison and elk. The paved road ends after a mile at a parking area, but hikers and cyclists (or skiers and snowmobilers in winter) can continue another four miles to its junction with the main road again. Look for **Ojo Caliente**—a small hot springs with a big odor—right along the river. Several more hot springs are upstream from here. Beautiful 200-foot-high **Fairy Falls** can be reached by hiking the road three miles beyond the parking area (or one mile from the south entrance) to a junction at the end of the meadow. Here it's another 1.5 miles to the falls. This makes a pleasant afternoon walk and can be combined with a scenic loop back along the west edge of the meadow for a roundtrip distance of 6.5 miles. A side trip takes you to **Imperial Geyser,** which now shoots water approximately six feet in the air almost continuously. Fountain Flat Drive may be closed to cars in 1997 for bridge and road work but will remain open to folks on foot or bike.

Firehole Canyon Drive

This one-way road (south only) curves for two miles through Firehole Canyon, where dark rhyolite cliffs rise 800 feet above the river. The road begins just south of Madison Junction and was intensely burned in the 1988 North Fork Fire, giving the canyon's name a dual meaning. **Firehole Falls** is a 40-foot drop that is worth stopping to see, as is **Firehole Cascades** a bit farther up. Kids of all ages enjoy the swimming hole (warmed by hot springs) a short distance up the road.

MADISON JUNCTION TO WEST YELLOWSTONE

At Madison Junction, the Gibbon and Firehole Rivers join to form the Madison River, a major tributary of the Missouri River. The 14-mile drive from Madison Junction to the West Entrance closely parallels this scenic river in which geese, ducks, and trumpeter swans are almost always present. Bison and elk are other critters to watch for in the open meadows. The 406,359-acre North Fork Fire of 1988 ripped through most of the Madison River country, so be ready for many blackened trees, but also expect to see many flowers in midsummer. The river is open only to fly-fishing and is considered one of the finest places in the nation to catch trout (though they can be a real challenge to fool). On warm summer evenings, you're likely to see dozens of anglers casting for wily rainbow and brown trout and mountain whitefish. **West Entrance** is the busiest of all the park entry stations, handling roughly half of the 2.5 million people who enter Yellowstone each year. The tourist town of West Yellowstone, Montana (see "Gateway Towns" later in this chapter) is right outside the boundary.

Madison Canyon is flanked by mountains named for two photographers who had a marked influence on Yellowstone. To the north is 8,257-foot **Mount Jackson** (as in William H. Jackson, whose photos helped bring the area to national attention), and to the south is distinctive, 8,235-foot **Mount Haynes,** named for the man who held the park photo concession for nearly four decades. These mountains and the surrounding slopes were created by rhyolite lava flows.

MADISON JUNCTION TO NORRIS

The **Madison Information Station** near Madison Junction is open daily 8 a.m.-7 p.m. Memorial Day to Labor Day and daily 9 a.m.-5 p.m. in the spring and fall and has a small bookstore. Directly behind Madison Junction Campground is 7,560-foot **National Park Mountain,** named in honor of a fabled incident in 1870. Three explorers were gathered around the campfire, dis-

cussing the wonders that they had found in this area, when one suggested that rather than letting all these wonders pass into private hands, they should be set aside as a national park. Thus was born the concept that led to the world's first national park. The tale was passed on as the gospel truth for so long that the mountain was named in honor of this evening. Unfortunately, the story was a fabrication. Cynics may read something into the fact that National Park Mountain was torched by the fires of 1988.

North of Madison Junction, the road follows the Gibbon River nearly all of the 14 miles to Norris. It crosses the river five times and hangs right on the edge through Gibbon Canyon. The pretty, 84-foot-high **Gibbon Falls** is approximately five miles up the road and situated right at the edge of the enormous caldera that fills the center of Yellowstone. The 1988 fires consumed most of the trees around the falls. Another five miles beyond this, the road emerges from the canyon into grassy **Gibbon Meadows,** where elk and bison are commonly seen. The prominent peak visible to the north is 10,336-foot Mount Holmes. On the west end of Gibbon Meadows is a barren area that contains **Sylvan Springs Geyser Basin.** No maintained trail leads to this small collection of pools and springs, but hikers sometimes head across the north end of the meadows at the Gibbon River Picnic Area. The path is wet most of the summer.

An easy half-mile trail leads to **Artist Paint Pots,** filled with colorful plopping and steaming mud pots and hot springs. This is a nice place to escape the crowds. The forest was burned in the North Fork Fire, so it's also a good place to see how the lodgepole pine trees are regenerating. Just south of the parking area for Artist Paint Pots is a trail to **Monument Geyser Basin,** where there isn't much activity, but the tall sinter cones form all sorts of bizarre shapes, including Thermos Bottle Geyser. The mile-long hike climbs 500 feet and provides good views of the surrounding country. Another attraction is **Chocolate Pots,** found along the highway just north of Gibbon Meadows. The reddish-brown color comes from iron, aluminum, and manganese oxides. Just before you reach Norris, the road crosses through the appropriately named **Elk Park.**

NORRIS GEYSER BASIN

Although Old Faithful is more famous, many visitors to Yellowstone find Norris Geyser Basin more interesting. Norris sits atop the junction of several major fault lines, providing conduits for heat from the molten lava below. Because of this, Norris is considered the hottest geyser basin in North America, if not the world; a scientific team found temperatures of 459° F at 1,087 feet underground and was forced to quit drilling when the pressure threatened to destroy its drilling rig! Because of considerable sulfur (and hence sulfuric acid) in the springs and geysers, the water at Norris is quite acidic; a majority of the world's acid geysers are here. The acidic water kills lodgepole trees in the basin, creating an open, nearly barren place. Norris Basin has been around at least 115,000 years, making it the oldest of any of Yellowstone's active geyser basins. It is a constantly changing place, with small geysers seeming to come and go on an almost daily basis.

The paved trail from the oft-crowded parking area leads to **Norris Museum,** built of stone in 1929-30. The small museum houses exhibit panels on hot springs and geothermal activity and is generally open daily 8 a.m.-7 p.m. from Memorial Day to Labor Day, with reduced hours in mid-May and September. (Budget cuts have forced its closure in the past; see the current park newspaper for its current status.) Pick up a detailed brochure (25 cents) describing the various features at Norris. Ranger-led walks are given most days. From the museum, the Norris Basin spreads both north and south, with two rather different trails to hike. Take the time to walk along both; you won't regret it. The Norris Campground is only a quarter mile from the geyser basin.

Porcelain Basin

Just behind the museum is an overlook that provides an impressive view across Porcelain Basin. The path drops down into the basin, passing hissing steam vents, bubbling hot pools, and small geysers along the way, including **Dark Cavern Geyser,** which erupts several times an hour to 20 feet. **Whirligig Geyser** is another one that is often active, spraying a fan of water.

(Watch your glasses and camera lenses in the steam; silica deposits can be very hard to remove.) For an enjoyable short walk, follow the boardwalk around the mile-long loop. Stop to admire the bright colors in the steaming water, indicators of iron, arsenic, and other elements, along with algae and cyanobacteria.

Back Basin

A mile-long loop trail takes you to the sights within the Back Basin south of the museum. Before heading out, check at the museum for the latest on geyser activity. Most people follow the path in a clockwise direction, coming first to **Emerald Spring,** a beautiful green pool with acidic water just below boiling. A little ways farther down the path is **Steamboat Geyser.** Wait a few minutes and you're likely to see one of its minor eruptions, which may reach 40 feet. On rare occasions, Steamboat erupts with a fury that is hard to believe, blasting over 300 feet into the air—more than twice the height of Old Faithful—making this the world's tallest geyser. Eruptions can last up to 20 minutes, enough time to pour out a million gallons of water! The explosions have been heard up to 14 miles away. Steamboat's unforgettable eruptions cannot be predicted; a 50-year span once passed between eruptions, while at other times they may occur several times a year.

The path splits just below Steamboat; on the right is **Cistern Spring,** whose deep blue waters are constantly building deposits of sinter and have flooded the nearby lodgepole-pine forests, killing the trees. If you turn left where the trail splits, you come to **Echinus Geyser,** a personal favorite. (The name—Greek for "spiny"—comes from the sea-urchin-like pebbles around the geyser; they are a result of sinter accumulation.) Echinus erupts every 35-75 minutes and is well worth waiting for. Watch the pool closely, since explosions of steam and water generally begin once it has filled, with acidic water (pH 3.5) reaching 40-60 feet. Eruptions generally last 6-14 minutes but sometimes up to an hour or more. Unlike Old Faithful, this is one geyser where you can get up close and personal. Bench-sitters may get splashed, although the water is not hot enough to burn. Continue along this trail to see many more hot springs and steam vents. **Porkchop Geyser** was in contin-

uous eruption for several years but in 1989 self-destructed in an explosion that threw rocks more than 200 feet away, leaving behind a bubbling hot spring.

NORRIS JUNCTION TO CANYON

The dozen miles from Norris Geyser Basin to Canyon cut across the center of the park on the high Solfatara Plateau. This stretch of road is best known for what looks like a scene from an atomic blast, with the blackened remains of a forest seemingly blown down by the ferocity of the 1988 North Fork Fire. This is the place the news media focused on after the fires, making it appear as if it were typical of the park as a whole. In reality, the lodgepole pines were all uprooted in a wild 1984 windstorm that flattened many miles of forest both here and farther south in the Teton Wilderness. The dead trees dried out over the next four years, and when the wind-whipped fires arrived they went up in a holocaust. In 50 years, this may well be a meadow. **Virginia Cascades Road** is a 2.5-mile-long, one-way road that circles around this blow-down area and provides a view of the 60-foot-tall Virginia Cascade of the Gibbon River. Back on the main highway heading east, keep your eyes open for elk and bison as the road approaches Canyon. Also note the thick young forest of lodgepole pines that was established after a fire burned through in 1955.

NORRIS JUNCTION TO MAMMOTH

The park road between Norris and Mammoth Hot Springs provides a number of interesting sights, although much of this country burned in the 1988 North Fork Fire. Just beyond the highway junction is the Norris Soldier Station, built by the Army in 1897 and modified in 1908, one of just three still standing in the park. It now houses the small **Museum of the National Park Ranger,** tel. (307) 544-7353, with displays on the history of park rangers. The museum is open daily 9 a.m.-6 p.m. in the summer (though budget cuts may keep it closed). Just up the road is **Frying Pan Spring** (named for its shape), where the water is actually not that hot. The bubbles

are from pungent-smelling hydrogen sulfide gas. **Roaring Mountain** is a bleak, steaming mountainside four miles north of Norris. In 1902, the mountain erupted into activity with fumaroles that made a roar audible at great distances. It is far less active today.

Stop at **Obsidian Cliff** to see the black glassy rocks formed when lava cooled very rapidly. One mountain man (not, as many sources claim, Jim Bridger) told tales of "Glass Mountain," where his shots at an elk kept missing. When he got closer, he found he had actually been firing at a clear mountain of glass. The elk was 25 miles away, but the mountain was acting as a telescope to make the animal appear close. Obsidian Cliff was an important source of rock Indians used in making arrowheads and other tools. Obsidian points made from this rock have even been found in the Ohio River Valley. North of here the countryside opens up along Obsidian Creek at **Willow Park,** one of the best places to see moose, especially in the fall.

Approximately 13 miles north of Norris, the road passes Indian Creek Campground and the basalt columns of **Sheepeater Cliffs**, named for the Indian inhabitants of these mountains. North of this, the country opens into Gardners Hole, where you get a fine gander at 10,992-foot Electric Peak nine miles to the northwest. At **Golden Gate** the road suddenly enters a narrow defile, through which flows Glen Creek. Stop to look over the edge of **Rustic Falls** and to note how the road is cantilevered over the cliff edge. Acrophobics should *not* stop here. Instead, have someone else drive, close your eyes, and say three Hail Marys.

Bunsen Peak is the 8,564-foot volcanic cone visible just south of Mammoth. Any chemistry student will recognize the name, for Robert W. Bunsen not only first explained the action of geysers but also invented the Bunsen burner. Bunsen Peak looks like a chemistry experiment run amok. The North Fork Fire of 1988 swept through this area in a patchy mosaic, leaving long strips of unburned trees next to those that are now just blackened telephone poles. Trails lead up to the top of Bunsen Peak from both the east and west sides. The west trail (two miles) begins at the entrance to **Bunsen Peak Road,** just south of Rustic Falls. This rough and *very* steep one-way dirt road (six miles) circles

around the east side of the mountain. It's closed to trailers and RVs. The road begins a quarter-mile south of Golden Gate. From the road you are treated to views of 150-foot-high **Osprey Falls.** A trail to the falls was wiped out by a landslide; hopefully it will be rebuilt in the near future. This side road is well off the beaten track, but scenic.

If you take the steep main road rather than the Bunsen Peak Road, you will soon come to the **Hoodoos,** a fascinating jumble of travertine boulders leaning in all directions. The rocks were created by hot springs thousands of years ago and toppled from the east face of Terrace Mountain. Just before Mammoth, you'll see the turnoff for Upper Terrace Drive on the left. This half-mile loop road provides access to the upper end of Mammoth Hot Springs.

MAMMOTH HOT SPRINGS VICINITY

Mammoth Hot Springs lies near the northern border of Yellowstone and contains park headquarters, a variety of other facilities, and colorful hot springs. The Mammoth area is an important wintering spot for elk, antelope, deer, and bison. During the fall, a bull elk and his harem can be seen wandering across the green lawns while lesser males bugle challenges from behind the buildings. The bugling can keep you awake at night if you're staying in the Mammoth Hotel. The town of Gardiner, Montana, is just five miles away.

Origins

Mammoth Hot Springs consists of a series of multihued terraces down which hot, mineral-laden water trickles. This water originates as snow and rain that falls on the surrounding country, although some is believed to come from the Norris area, 20 miles to the south. As it passes through the earth, the water comes in contact with volcanic magma containing massive amounts of carbon dioxide, which is absorbed by the water to form carbonic acid. The now-acidic water passes through and dissolves the region's sedimentary limestone, and the calcium carbonate remains in solution until it reaches the surface at Mammoth. Once at the surface, the carbon dioxide begins to escape into the at-

mosphere, reducing the acidity and causing the lime to precipitate out, forming the travertine terraces that are so prominent here. As the water flows over small obstructions, more carbon dioxide is released, causing accumulations that eventually grow into the lips that surround the terrace pools. The rate of accumulation of travertine (calcium carbonate) is astounding: more than two tons a day at Mammoth Hot Springs. Some terraces grow by eight inches a year. The first explorers were fascinated by these terraces; mountain man Jim Bridger noted that they made for delightful baths. A later operation—long since ended—coated knickknacks by dipping them in the hot springs!

The springs are constantly changing as underground passages are blocked by limestone deposits, forcing the water into new directions. As a result, old dried-out terraces stand on all sides as new ones grow each day. Areas that

were active just a few years ago may now be simply gray masses of crumbling travertine rock. One of the most interesting aspects of the hot springs here are the colors, results of the many different species of algae and bacteria that live in the water. Various factors, including temperature and acidity, affect the survival of different species: bright yellow algae lives in the hottest areas, while cooler waters are colored orange and brown by other algae.

Visiting the Springs

Mammoth Hot Springs covers a steep hillside and consists of a series of colorful springs in various stages of development or decay. Road access is either from below or above (Upper Terrace Drive), with a boardwalk/staircase connecting the two. Pick up a Park Service brochure (25 cents) for more on the springs. The most interesting of the springs is **Minerva Terrace.**

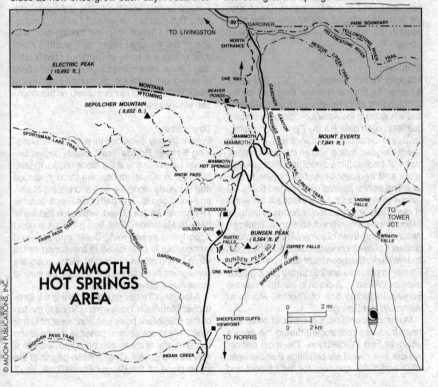

MAMMOTH HOT SPRINGS AREA

© MOON PUBLICATIONS, INC.

The springs change constantly, and nearby terraces that were active just a few years ago are now simply a bland mass of gray rock. At the bottom of Mammoth Hot Springs and off to the right is a 37-foot-tall mass of travertine known as **Liberty Cap** for its faint similarity to the caps worn by Revolutionary War soldiers. The spring that created this no longer flows.

Directly across the road is **Opal Terrace,** one of the most active of all the springs. It began flowing in 1926 and has continued to expand over the years until it now threatens the lush lawns of a house built in 1908 and designed by Robert Reamer (of Old Faithful Inn fame). All the water flowing out of Mammoth terraces quickly disappears into underground caverns. In front of the Mammoth Hotel are two sinkholes from which steam often rises. Caverns above the terraces were once open to the public but later were closed when it became apparent that they contained poisonous gases. Dead birds are sometimes found around one of the small pools in this area appropriately named Poison Spring.

Buildings

Albright Visitor Center, tel. (307) 344-2263, is named for the first National Park Service superintendent at Yellowstone, Horace Albright, and is housed in the Army's old bachelor officers' quarters, open daily 8 a.m.-7 p.m. from Memorial Day to Labor Day and daily 9 a.m.-5 p.m. the rest of the year. Inside, find an information desk, racks of books, films about the park, wildlife talks, and frequent ranger-led walks to surrounding sights. Spread over the two floors are various exhibits, but the real treats are the works of two artists who had major hands in bringing Yellowstone's magnificent scenery to public attention. Twenty-three of painter Thomas Moran's famous Yellowstone watercolors line the walls, and his studio has been recreated in one corner. Equally impressive are 26 classic photographs taken by William H. Jackson in the 1871 Hayden Survey, including one of Thomas Moran at Mammoth Hot Springs.

Mammoth contains a number of other historic structures constructed during the Army's tenure at Fort Yellowstone. The most distinctive are in a row of six buildings built between 1891 and 1909, quarters for the officers and captains. Most of the grunt soldiers lived in barracks just behind here, one of which is now the park administration building. The U.S. Engineers Department was housed in an odd stone building (across from the visitor center) with obvious Asian influences.

Most of the **Mammoth Hot Springs Hotel** was built in 1937, although one wing survives from a hotel built in 1911. Step inside to see the large map of the United States built from 15 different types of wood. Mammoth also features a Hamilton Store, a post office, a gas station, a restaurant, a fast-food eatery, and horseback rides. Mammoth Campground is just down the road.

North to Montana

The main road north from Mammoth Hot Springs follows the Gardner River. (Both this and the misspelled town of Gardiner are named for a ruthless trapper from the 1820s, Johnson Gardner.) The river is a favorite of fly-fishing enthusiasts, and a turnoff notes the "boiling river" section of the Gardner River, well worth a stop. Just before the town of Gardiner (see "Gateway Towns" later in this chapter), look for a herd of pronghorn antelope. Sometimes during the winter you can spot bighorn sheep on the mountain slopes nearby.

Day Hikes

For a relatively easy loop hike, try the five-mile-long **Beaver Ponds Trail,** which begins between Liberty Cap and the stone house. It gains 500 feet in elevation, passing through spruce and fir forests along the way and ending at several small ponds. The path then drops down to join the old Gardiner Road, which you can follow back to Mammoth. This trail provides a good opportunity to see mule deer, antelope, and moose, but is best hiked in the spring or fall when temperatures are cooler. Black bears are sometimes seen along the way, so be sure to make noise while you walk.

A longer (12 miles roundtrip) hike is the **Sepulcher Mountain Trail,** which climbs to the top of this 9,652-foot peak just northwest of Mammoth. There are several possible routes to the top, and any of these can be combined into a very nice loop hike. One of these begins at the same place as the Beaver Ponds Trail. You'll

find many flowers in the expansive meadows on the south side of Sepulcher Mountain (named for several strange rocks at its summit). From Mammoth, it is a 3,400-foot elevation gain, so be ready to sweat. Before heading out, check at the visitor center to see if there are any major bear problems in the area.

MAMMOTH TO TOWER JUNCTION

The 18-mile drive from Mammoth to Tower Junction takes visitors through some of the driest and most open country in Yellowstone. Two waterfalls provide stopping places along the way. Beautiful **Undine Falls** is a 60-foot-high double falls located just north of the road. Just up the road is a gentle half-mile path to **Wraith Falls,** where Lupine Creek cascades 90 feet. Look for ducks and trumpeter swans in **Blacktail Pond,** a couple of miles farther east.

Blacktail Plateau Drive, approximately nine miles east of Mammoth, turns off from the main road. The rough seven-mile dirt road is a one-way route that loosely follows the Bahnock Trail, a path used from 1838 to 1878 by the Bannock tribe on their way to buffalo-hunting grounds east of here. Their travois trails are still visible. Much of the road is through open sagebrush, grass, and aspen country, where you're likely to see deer and antelope. The trees are very pretty in the fall. On the east end, it drops back into a forest burned by a severe crown fire in 1988. Look for aspen and lodgepole seedlings among the abundant summertime flowers.

The Park Service has developed a two-thirds-mile boardwalk **Children's Fire Trail** approximately six miles east of Mammoth Hot Springs. Trailside exhibits describe the natural world. A half-mile beyond where Blacktail Plateau Drive rejoins the main road is the turnoff to the **petrified tree.** The 20-foot-tall stump of an ancient redwood tree (50 million years old) stands behind iron bars. A second petrified tree that used to stand nearby was stolen piece by piece over the years by thoughtless tourists. The **Tower Ranger Station,** originally occupied by the U.S. Army, is just before Tower Junction where the road splits, leading to either Northeast Entrance Road or Canyon.

NORTHEAST ENTRANCE ROAD

Of the five primary entryways into Yellowstone, Northeast Entrance is the least traveled, making this a nice place to escape the hordes in midsummer. It is also one of the few places in Yellowstone where one sees tall mountains. The road heads east from Tower Junction and immediately enters **Lamar Valley,** an area of grass and sage along the sinuous Lamar River. Osborne Russell, who trapped this country in the 1830s, described it with affection:

We descended the stream about 15 mls thro. the dense forest and at length came to a beautiful valley about 8 Mls. long and 3 or 4 wide surrounded by dark and lofty mountains. The stream after running thro. the center in a NW direction rushed down a tremendous canyon of basaltic rock apparently just wide enough to admit its waters. The banks of the stream in the valley were low and skirted in many places with beautiful Cotton wood groves. Here we found a few Snake indians comprising 6 men 7 women and 8 or 10 children who were the only Inhabitants of this lonely and secluded spot. They were all neatly clothed in dressed deer and Sheep skins of the best quality and seemed to be perfectly contented and happy. . . . We stopped at this place and for my own part I almost wished I could spend the remainder of my days in a place like this where happiness and contentment seemed to rein in wild romantic splendor surrounded by majestic battlements which seemed to support the heavens and shut out all hostile intruders. . . . There is something in the wild romantic scenery of this valley which I cannot . . . describe; but the impressions made upon my mind while gazing from a high eminence on the surrounding landscape one evening as the sun was gently gliding behind the western mountain and casting its gigantic shadows across the vale were such as time can never efface from my memory.

This is still one of the best places in Yellowstone to view bison. Elk and mule deer are also commonly seen, and the reintroduction of wolves has added another dimension to wildlife viewing here. The valley contains a number of small ponds created when the retreating glaciers left large blocks of ice that formed "kettles." Erratic glacial boulders are scattered along the way. There are campgrounds at Slough Creek and Pebble Creek. They are the last to fill in the park, but even these fill quickly in July and August. Very good fishing in Slough Creek.

Yellowstone Institute

The nonprofit Yellowstone Institute is housed within Lamar Valley's historic Buffalo Ranch, where turn-of-the-century efforts were made to protect and breed bison. Plains bison were brought here and kept in pens at night and herded during the day. After 1915, they were allowed to roam freely during the summer, although all the park's bison were rounded up and driven here for the winters. After 1938, the roundups ended, but hay was fed them every winter in Lamar Valley. Finally in 1952, even this was halted.

The old Buffalo Ranch bunkhouse is now headquarters for the Yellowstone Institute. Instructors lead more than 80 different environmental classes in the summer months and a few in winter. Most last two to five days and typically cost $100-225 per person. Courses cover the spectrum from Yellowstone bats to horsepacking explorations of the Nez Percé Trail. Participants generally stay in newly constructed log cabins ($10 per person per day extra) at the ranch and cook their own meals in the kitchen. The institute is funded in part by the Yellowstone Association, and $10 discounts are available to association members. For a brochure, call the Yellowstone Institute at (307) 344-7749 (June-Aug. only) or 344-2294 (year-round). The mailing address is Box 117, Yellowstone National Park, WY 82190.

Specimen Ridge

Just east of Yellowstone Institute is a turnout across from Specimen Ridge, where explorers discovered the standing trunks of petrified trees that had been buried in volcanic ash and mudflows some 50 million years ago. Over the centuries, the trunks literally turned to stone as silica entered the wood. The process was repeated again and again over the centuries as new forests gradually developed atop the volcanic deposits, only to be buried by later flows. Scientists have found 27 different forests on top of each other, containing walnut, magnolia, oaks, redwood, and maple—evidence that the climate was once more like that of today's central states. Erosion eventually revealed the trees, many of which are still standing. This is one of the largest areas of petrified trees known to exist.

There is no trail to the petrified forest, but during the summer rangers lead hikes into the area. Check at the Mammoth Visitor Center for upcoming treks. Mark Marschall's *Yellowstone Trails* provides a description of the 1.5-mile route if you want to try it on your own. A lesser-known petrified forest in the northwest corner of Yellowstone is accessible via U.S. 191.

Northeast Entrance

At the east end of Lamar Valley, U.S. 212 continues northeast up Soda Butte Creek and between the steep rocky cliffs of Barronette Peak (10,404 feet) and Abiathar Peak (10,928 feet). Stop at **Soda Butte,** where you'll find a small travertine mound similar to those at Mammoth. Although the springs are no longer very active, the air still reeks of hydrogen sulfide, the "rotten egg" gas. South of Soda Butte and several miles up a backcountry trail is **Wahb Springs,** found within Death Gulch. Here poisonous gases are emitted from the ground, killing animals in the vicinity. Early explorers reported finding dead bears who had wandered into the area and been overcome by the fumes.

Above Pebble Creek Campground, the road squeezes through chilly **Icebox Canyon** and into the lodgepole-pine forests. It follows the creek all the way to the edge of the park, crossing into Montana two miles before the park border. The **Northeast Entrance Station** is a classic log building built in 1935 and now designated a National Historic Landmark. The twin towns of Silver Gate and Cooke City (see "Gateway Towns" later in this chapter) are just up the road.

TOWER JUNCTION TO CANYON

Right at the junction of the roads to Canyon, Mammoth, and Lamar Valley is **Roosevelt Lodge,** built in 1920 and named for President Theodore Roosevelt, who camped a few miles south of here when he visited in 1903. President Roosevelt remained a lifelong supporter of Yellowstone and helped push through legislation that clamped down upon the rampant destruction of its wildlife. The Roosevelt area is a favorite of families, many of whom return each year. It has the rough-edged flavor of a hunting lodge and a peacefulness that you won't find at Old Faithful. Inside the lodge are two giant stone fireplaces. Lodging in rustic cabins, food, a gift shop, and horseback rides are available.

Stop at the overlook to **Calcite Springs,** two miles southeast of the junction, where a walkway provides dramatic views into the canyon, with steaming geothermal activity far below. The cliff faces contain a wide strip of columnar basalt, some of which overhangs the highway just south of here.

At **Tower Fall,** Tower Creek plummets 132 feet before joining the Yellowstone River. The towerlike black rocks of the area are made of basalt, a volcanic material. Nearby are a campground and a Hamilton Store. Tower Fall overlook is just a couple hundred paved feet from the parking area, or you can follow the path a half mile down the switchbacks to the canyon bottom, where the vista is far more impressive and a rainbow is sometimes visible. Be prepared to get wet in the spray. A ford of the Yellowstone River—used by Bannock Indians in the 19th century—is just a quarter-mile away. For more than a hundred years, a huge boulder stood atop Tower Fall; the water and gravity finally won in 1986.

Continuing south, the road climbs along Antelope Creek and eventually switchbacks up the aptly named Mae West Curve. The North Fork Fire swept through this country in 1988, leaving a blackened forest but abundant summertime flowers and verdant grasses. A popular trail to

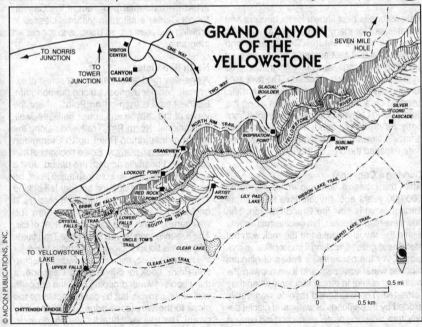

GRAND CANYON OF THE YELLOWSTONE

© MOON PUBLICATIONS, INC.

Mt. Washburn splits off just above Mae's curves, and you can drive up the first mile on old Chittenden Road. Park your car and hike the remaining three miles to the top. This is one of the nicest day-hikes in the park, providing a fine opportunity to see and photograph bighorn sheep. Many wildflowers bloom in midsummer, and hikers discover fantastic vistas from the lookout tower on top. Another popular three-mile trail up Mt. Washburn begins at the Dunraven Pass Picnic Area.

Dunraven Pass (8,859 feet) is named for the Earl of Dunraven, who visited the park in 1874 and whose widely read book *The Great Divide* brought Yellowstone to the attention of wealthy European travelers. This is the highest point along any park road. Look for whitebark pines near the road, and be sure to stop just south of here for a view across to the distant Grand Canyon of the Yellowstone.

GRAND CANYON OF THE YELLOWSTONE

Yellowstone is best known for its geysers and animals, but for many the Grand Canyon is its most memorable feature. The 20-mile-long canyon is 4,000 feet across and has colorful yellow, pink, orange, and buff cliffs that drop as much as 1,200 feet on either side. The river itself tumbles abruptly over two massive waterfalls, sending up a roar audible for miles along the rims. Grand Canyon is accessible by road from both the north and south sides, with equally amazing views. The lodgepole forests around here escaped the fires of 1988.

Carving a Canyon

After the massive volcanic eruptions some 600,000 years ago, rhyolite lava flows came through what is now the Grand Canyon. The flows eventually cooled, but geothermal activity within the rhyolite weakened the rock with hot steam and gasses, making it susceptible to erosion. Over the centuries, a series of glaciers blocked water upstream and then allowed the water in this lake to empty suddenly when they retreated. The weakened rhyolite was easily eroded by these floods of water and glacial debris, thus revealing pastel yellow and red canyon

walls colored by the thermal activities. The **Lower Falls** are at the edge of the thermal basin, above rock that was not weakened by geothermal activity. The **Upper Falls** are at a contact point between hard rhyolite that does not erode easily and a band of rhyolite that contains more easily eroded volcanic glass. Today, the canyon is eroding more slowly, having increased in depth only 50 feet over the last 10,000 years.

Canyon Village

Canyon Village on the north rim is a forgettable shopping mall in the wilderness, complete with various stores and eating places, a post office, a gas station, cabins, and a campground (RVs only). Horseback rides are available nearby. **Canyon Visitor Center,** tel. (307) 242-2550, includes films, slide shows, and exhibits on the geology and natural history of the area. Hours are daily 8 a.m.-7 p.m. Memorial Day to Labor Day and daily 9 a.m.-5 p.m. during the spring and fall. The visitor center is open mid-May to late September. Throughout the summer, an **artist-in-residence program** at the Canyon Visitor Center auditorium features classes in drawing and painting, art walks, and special art programs.

North Rim Vistas

A one-way road takes visitors to a series of extremely popular overlooks along the north rim. Farthest east is **Inspiration Point,** where the views of the canyon and Lower Falls are, well, inspirational. **North Rim Trail** leads along the rim from Inspiration Point up to Chittenden Bridge, three miles away. Some sections of this scenic and nearly level path are paved. Just a couple hundred feet up from Inspiration Point, be sure to look for the 500-ton boulder left behind 15,000 years ago by the retreating glaciers. It originated at least 15 miles north of here and was carried south atop the moving river of ice. The five-mile-long **Seven Mile Hole Trail** takes off near this boulder, providing fantastic views for the first mile or so, minus the crowds at Inspiration Point. Look for **Silver Cord Cascade,** a thin ribbon of water dropping over the opposite wall of the canyon, but be careful not to go too close to the very loose edge. It's a long way down! The trail switchbacks steeply down to

the Yellowstone River, passing odoriferous thermal areas en route. Many anglers come to Seven Mile Hole (it's seven miles downriver from Lower Falls) while other folks come to relax along the river. Save your energy for the strenuous 1,400-foot climb back up.

The one-way road continues westward to overlooks at **Grandview** and **Lookout Point.** From Lookout Point, a half-mile trail drops several hundred feet to **Red Rock Point** for a closer view of Lower Falls. Farthest west along the one-way North Rim Road is the trail to the **Brink of the Lower Falls.** It's half a mile long and paved, descending 600 feet to a viewing area where you can peer over the 308-foot precipice (twice the height of Niagara Falls). Not recommended for anyone suffering from vertigo. Just south of where the one-way road rejoins the main highway is a turnoff to the **Brink of the Upper Falls,** where a short walk takes you to an over-the-edge view of the 109-foot-high Upper Falls.

A party of prospectors wandered north into this country in 1867, following the Yellowstone downriver without suspecting the canyon below. A. Bart Henderson wrote in his diary of strolling down the river and being

very much surprised to see the water disappear from my sight. I walked out on a rock & made two steps at the same time, one forward, the other backward, for I had unawares as it were, looked down into the depth or bowels of the earth, into which the Yellow plunged as if to cool the infernal region that lay under all this wonderful country of lava and boiling springs.

South Rim Vistas
The south rim is lined with more dramatic views into Grand Canyon. Cross the Chittenden Bridge over the Yellowstone River (otters are sometimes seen playing in the river below) and continue a half-mile to Uncle Tom's parking area, where a short trail leads to views of the Upper Falls and Crystal Falls. More unusual is **Uncle Tom's Trail,** which descends 500 feet to Lower Falls. The trail is partly paved but steep and includes 328 metal steps before you get to the bottom. Good exercise if you're in shape. It was named for "Uncle" Tom Richardson who, with

the help of wooden ladders and ropes, led paying tourists to the base of the falls around the turn of the century. Because there was no bridge, Uncle Tom also rowed his guests across the river near the present Chittenden Bridge. After his permit was revoked in 1903, visitors had to make do on their own.

A mile beyond Uncle Tom's parking area, the road ends at the parking area for **Artist Point,** the most famous of all Grand Canyon viewpoints. A short paved path leads to an astounding point where one can look upriver to the Lower Falls or down the opposite direction into the canyon. Look for thermal activity far below. The point is apparently where artist Thomas Moran painted a number of his famous watercolors. **South Rim Trail** begins at the Chittenden Bridge and follows along the rim to Artist Point (two miles), providing more viewpoints along the way. The least-traveled part of this trail continues eastward another 1.5 miles to Sublime Point, with many fine looks into the canyon. Watch for loose rocks on the edge; it's a long way down on this side, too!

CANYON TO LAKE JUNCTION

Hayden Valley
Just a few miles south of Canyon, the country abruptly opens into beautiful Hayden Valley, named for Ferdinand V. Hayden, leader of the 1871 expedition into Yellowstone. Reaching eight miles across, this relatively level part of the park was once occupied by an arm of Yellowstone Lake. The sediments left behind by the lake, along with glacial till, do not hold sufficient water to support trees. As a result, the area is occupied primarily by grasses, forbs, and sage. This is one of the best areas in the park to see wildlife, especially bison and elk. The Yellowstone River wanders across Hayden Valley, and streams enter from various sides. The waterways are excellent places to look for Canada geese, trumpeter swans, pelicans, and many kinds of ducks. Although they are less common, grizzly bears sometimes can be found feeding in the eastern end of the valley. Because of the bears, hikers need to be especially cautious when tramping through the grasses and shrubs, where it is easy to sur-

prise a bear or to be likewise surprised. On the north end of Hayden Valley, the road crosses **Alum Creek,** named for its highly alkaline water, which could make anything shrink. In the horse-and-buggy days, Yellowstone wags claimed that a man had forded the creek with a team of horses and a wagon, but came out the other side with four Shetland ponies pulling a basket!

Mud Volcano Area

Shortly after the road climbs south out of Hayden Valley, it passes one of the most interesting of Yellowstone's many thermal basins. On the east side of the road, a turnout overlooks **Sulphur Caldron,** where a highly acidic pool is filled with sulfur-tinted waters and the air is filled with the odor of hydrogen sulfide gas. Directly across the road is the Mud Volcano area, where a two-thirds-mile loop trail provides what could be a tour through a very bad case of heartburn. Pick up a Park Service brochure (25 cents) from the box for descriptions of all the bizarre features. The area is in a constant state of flux as springs dry up or begin overflowing, killing trees in their path. One of the most interesting features is **Black Dragons Caldron,** where an explosive spring blasts constantly through a mass of seething black mud. The wildest place at Mud Volcano is **Dragon's Mouth,** which the Park Service notes is named for "the rhythmic belching of steam and the flashing tongue of water as it strikes out from the cavernous opening." It's easy to imagine the fires of hell not far below this. The waters are 180° F. During the winter months, the Mud Volcano area is a good place to see elk or bison.

Along the Yellowstone

South of Mud Volcano, the road parallels the Yellowstone River. At **LeHardy Rapids** a boardwalk provides an overlook where early summer visitors see blush-red spawning cutthroats. In late summer, this part of the Yellowstone River is a very popular fly-fishing spot—some call it the finest stream cutthroat fishing in the world—and a good place to view ducks and swans. Earlier in the year, it's open only to the bears that gorge on the cutthroats. By the way, the Yellowstone River is the longest free-flowing (undammed) river in the Lower 48.

YELLOWSTONE LAKE

When first-time visitors see Yellowstone Lake, they are stunned by its magnitude. The statistics are impressive: 110 miles of shoreline, 20 miles north to south and 14 miles east to west, with an average depth of 139 feet and a maximum depth of 390 feet. This is North America's largest mountain lake. Yellowstone Lake can seem a sheet of glass laid to the horizon and just a half-hour later it's a roiling ocean of whitecaps and wind-whipped waves. The changeable waters can be dangerous to those in canoes or small boats; a number of people have drowned. The water is covered by ice at least half of the year, and breakup does not come until late May or early June. Even in summer, water temperatures are often only in the 40s. David Folsom, who was part of an exploration party traveling through the area in 1869, described Yellowstone Lake as an

inland sea, its crystal waves dancing and sparkling in the sunlight as if laughing with joy for their wild freedom. It is a scene of transcendent beauty which has been viewed by few white men, and we felt glad to have looked upon it before its primeval solitude should be broken by the crowds of pleasure seekers which at no distant day will throng its shores.

Fishing Bridge

The area around famous Fishing Bridge (built in 1937) was for many years a favorite place to catch cutthroat trout. Unfortunately, these same fish are a major food source for grizzlies, and this area is considered some of the most important bear habitat in Yellowstone. Conflicts between bears and humans led to the death of 16 grizzlies here. To help restore grizzly populations, the Park Service banned fishing from Fishing Bridge in 1973 and tried to move the developments to the Grant Village area. Lobbying by folks from Cody (worried lest they lose some of the tourist traffic) has kept some of the facilities at Fishing Bridge from closing. Remaining facilities include an RV park run by AmFac Parks & Resorts, a Hamilton Store, and a gas station. **Fishing Bridge Visitor Center,** tel. (307) 242-

2450, has exhibits of Yellowstone birds and animals and geology and is open daily 8 a.m.-7 p.m. Memorial Day to Labor Day and daily 9 a.m.-5 p.m. in spring and fall. A nice loop path is the **Elephant Back Mountain Trail,** which begins a mile south of Fishing Bridge Junction. This four-mile (roundtrip) trail climbs 800 feet, providing panoramic views across Yellowstone Lake and into Pelican Valley.

Lake Yellowstone Hotel

Lake Hotel, the oldest extant park hostelry, was built in 1889-91 by the Northern Pacific Railroad and originally consisted of a simple boxlike structure facing Yellowstone Lake. The hotel was sold to Harry Child in 1901, and two years later Robert Reamer—the architect who designed Old Faithful Inn—was given free reign to transform this into a more attractive place with distinctive Ionic columns added out front. It is the second-largest wood-framed building in North America and requires 500 gallons of yellow paint each year to keep it in shape. During the 1960s and '70s the hotel fell into disrepair under the management of General Host Corporation. Finally, in disgust, the Park Service bought out the concession and leased it to another company. Major renovations in the 1980s transformed the dowdy old structure into a luxurious grand hotel with much of the charm it had when President Calvin Coolidge stayed here in the 1920s. Today, Lake Hotel is one of the nicest lodging places in the park, with fine vistas out over the lake and comfortable quarters. Relax with a drink in the sunlit Sun Room. Free 45-minute **tours** of historic Lake Hotel are given every day at 7:30 p.m. (6:45 p.m. after mid-August) from early June to late September.

Be sure to take a walk along the lakeshore out front of the hotel, where the Absaroka Range forms a backdrop far to the east. The highest mountain is Avalanche Peak (10,566 feet). Almost due south is the 10,308-foot summit of Mt. Sheridan, named for Gen. Philip Sheridan, a longtime supporter of expanding the park to include the Tetons. Watch for the big white pelicans catching fish on the lake. Just east of Yellowstone Hotel is the **Lake Ranger Station,** built in 1922 and now on the National Register of Historic Places. Inside the octagonal main room

is a massive fireplace, exposed log rafters, and rustic light fixtures. Not far away is **Lake Lodge,** another rustic log structure. Inside is a reasonably priced cafeteria, and out back are row upon row of very plain cabins. A Hamilton Store stands nearby.

To West Thumb

The highway south from Lake Junction to West Thumb follows the lakeshore nearly the entire distance. A campground and a boat harbor are at **Bridge Bay,** as are a ranger station and a marina store. Immediately south of Bridge Bay is a turnoff to **Natural Bridge.** The mile-long road ends at a 59-foot-high natural span carved by the waters of Bridge Creek. Hikers will discover a three-mile trail that leaves from the campground and climbs to the rock bridge. Back on the main road, keep your eyes open for Canada geese and trumpeter swans as you drive south. **Gull Point Drive,** a two-mile-long side road, offers views of **Stevenson Island** just offshore; farther south, **Frank Island** and tiny **Dot Island** become visible. The small **Potts Hot Springs Basin** just north of West Thumb is named for fur trapper Daniel T. Potts, one of the first white men to explore the Yellowstone country.

EAST ENTRANCE ROAD

Heading east from Fishing Bridge, the road follows the shore of Yellowstone Lake past country that escaped the fires of 1988. Three miles east of the bridge are Indian Pond and the trailhead for **Storm Point Trail,** a pleasant three-mile hike (roundtrip). This loop trail is essentially level and goes past a large colony of yellow-bellied marmots before reaching Storm Point, where waves pound against the rocks. The trail is often closed because of grizzlies. North of here, Pelican Valley is considered even more important grizzly habitat and is closed to all overnight camping and to travel between 7 p.m. and 9 a.m. Even daytime use is not allowed during early summer. Before venturing out on the Storm Point Trail or into Pelican Valley, check at the Lake Ranger Station for bear info.

At **Steamboat Point** the road swings out along the shore, providing excellent views across the lake and of a noisy fumarole. For

an even better view (don't miss this one!), take the **Lake Butte Overlook** road, which continues one mile to a small parking area a thousand feet above the lake. This is a fine place to watch sunsets and to get a feeling for the enormity of Yellowstone Lake. Back on the main highway and heading east, Yellowstone Lake is soon behind you and visible in only a few spots as the road climbs gradually, passing scenic **Sylvan Lake,** a nice place for picnics. Just up the road is tiny Eleanor Lake (little more than a puddle) and the trail to 10,566-foot **Avalanche Peak.** This two-mile-long unmarked trail begins across the road on the east side of the creek and climbs steeply. It emerges from the forest halfway up, with the top gained via a scree slope. At the summit, you can see most of the peaks in the Absarokas and in the Tetons 70 miles away.

Immediately east of Eleanor Lake, the main road climbs to 8,541-foot **Sylvan Pass,** flanked by Hoyt Peak on the north and Top Notch Peak to the south. Steep scree slopes drop down both sides. East of Sylvan Pass, the road drops quickly along Middle Creek (a tributary of the Shoshone River), providing good views to the south of Mounts Langford and Doane. **East Entrance Ranger Station** was built by the Army in 1904. For many years, the road leading up to Sylvan Pass from the east took drivers across Corkscrew Bridge, a bridge that literally looped over itself as the road climbed steeply up the narrow valley. (For more on the scenic country east of here, see "Wapiti Valley" in the "Bighorn Basin" chapter.) The road continues on to Cody but is undergoing extensive reconstruction as part of a multi-year project, so be prepared for delays.

INTO THE BACKCOUNTRY

The vast majority of Yellowstone visitors act as though they were chained to their cars with a hundred-yard tether, as if by getting out farther than that they might miss some other sight down the road. For the two percent or so who *do* abandon their cars, Yellowstone has much to offer beyond the spectacular geysers and canyons for which it is famous. Although many parts of the Yellowstone backcountry are heavily visited, regulations keep the sense of wildness intact by separating campsites and limiting the number of hikers. And if you head out early or late in the season, you'll discover solitude just a few miles from the traffic jams.

Much of Yellowstone consists of rolling lodgepole (or burned lodgepole) forests. With a few exceptions, anyone looking for dramatic alpine scenery would probably be better off heading to Grand Teton National Park or the Wind River Mountains. Despite this, the backcountry is enjoyable to walk through, and many trails lead past waterfalls, geysers, and hot springs. Besides, this is one of the finest places in America to view wildlife—including grizzlies and wolves—in a natural setting. Before August, when they start to die down, you should also be ready for the ubiquitous mosquitoes. The fires of 1988 have created some problems for backcountry

hikers. Blackened trees leave soot on clothes and gear, while the burned trees are a potential hazard during windstorms.

Rules and Regulations

A free backcountry-use permit is required of each overnight party and is available in person at the various ranger stations within 48 hours of your hike. You can also make advance reservations for a $15 fee; get forms at park ranger stations or by writing the Backcountry Office, Box 168, Yellowstone National Park, WY 82190. You'll need to specify exactly where you plan to camp each night and will be given a lengthy rundown on what to expect and what precautions to take. Hikers stay only at designated campsites, most with pit toilets, fire rings, and bear poles. Wood fires are not allowed in many areas and are discouraged elsewhere, so be sure to have a gas stove for cooking. Bear management areas have special regulations that may include seasonal restrictions, be for day-use only, or specify minimum group sizes. Pets are not allowed on the trails within Yellowstone, and special rules apply for those coming in with horses, mules, burros, and llamas. Because of wet conditions and the lack of forage, no stock animals are permitted before July.

For a description of backcountry rules, bear safety, and suggestions for hiking and horse-packing, pick up a copy of the free park pamphlet *Beyond Road's End* at any ranger station or by writing the Backcountry Office. Those interested in horse-packing or llama trips should contact the park at tel. (307) 344-7381 for a list of some 35 different outfitters authorized to operate in Yellowstone. They offer everything from day-trips to weeklong adventures deep into the backcountry.

More Info

I have selected a few two-to-four-day backcountry hikes covering various parts of Yellowstone. The park has over 1,200 miles of trails, so this is obviously a tiny sampling of the various hiking options. In addition, a number of day-hikes are described above in conjunction with adjacent sights. A fine small guide to park trails is *Hiking the Yellowstone Backcountry,* by Orville E. Bach, Jr. (San Francisco: Sierra Club Books), but your best bet is Mark C. Marschall's excellent *Yellowstone Trails,* published by the Yellowstone Association and available at park visitor centers. These centers also sell the best topographic park maps, produced by Trails Illustrated, tel. (800) 962-1643. They feature all the major trails and show the severity of burn from the 1988 fires—a considerable help when planning hiking trips.

NORTH YELLOWSTONE TRAILS

Sportsman Lake Trail

The land west of Mammoth is some of the most rugged in Yellowstone, with a number of peaks topping 10,000 feet. Several trails cut westward across this country, one of the most interesting being the Sportsman Lake Trail. It begins at Glen Creek Trailhead five miles south of Mammoth and follows Glen Creek for four miles before dropping into the Gardner River drainage. You'll need to ford the river twice; before late summer it can be dangerously deep, so do this hike later in the season. A spur trail makes it possible to climb **Electric Peak,** the 10,992-foot rocky summit just north of here; see Marschall's *Yellowstone Trails* for specifics. Beyond the river fords, the main trail climbs to

Electric Divide and then drops to Sportsman Lake. West of here the trail splits and you can either continue to the right and reach U.S. 191 (total distance 24 miles) or follow the Fan Creek and Fawn Pass Trails back to the Mammoth area (approximately 40 miles roundtrip). Warning: This country overflows with grizzly activity, and parties of four or more are required for travel here. Off-trail travel is prohibited.

Pebble Creek Trail

This 12-mile-long path cuts through a part of Yellowstone that is far away from the geysers and canyons for which the park is famous. The crowds don't come here, but the country is some of the nicest mountain scenery in the park. Pebble Creek Trail connects with the Northeast Entrance road at both ends, making access easy. You can start from either end, but if you begin from the Warm Creek Picnic area (1.5 miles west of the entrance station), it's all downhill after the first steep climb. Best time to hike this trail is in late summer when the water levels are down (there are two fords) and the mosquitoes have abated. Lots of alpine flowers and grand mountain scenery along the way. Halfway down the valley, **Bliss Pass Trail** splits westward and crosses Pebble Creek (quite deep till late summer) before climbing 1,400 feet to the pass and then dropping down 2,700 feet to **Slough Creek Trail.** The latter takes you into Slough Creek Campground.

SOUTH YELLOWSTONE TRAILS

Shoshone Lake

Shoshone Lake—the largest lake in the Lower 48 without direct road access—is probably the most visited part of Yellowstone's backcountry. Although its shoreline is dotted with more than 20 campsites, nearly every site fills up on midsummer nights. Access to Shoshone Lake is primarily from trailheads along the South Entrance Road and the road between West Thumb and Old Faithful. Paths circle Shoshone Lake, although they are away from the shoreline much of the distance. You may see moose or elk along the way. On the west end of the lake, hikers are delighted to find **Shoshone Geyser Basin,** an area filled with small geysers, beautiful pools,

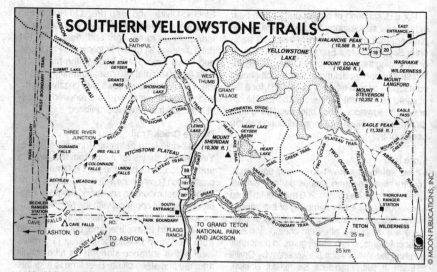

SOUTHERN YELLOWSTONE TRAILS

© MOON PUBLICATIONS, INC.

and bubbling mudpots. **Minute Man Geyser** is the most notable one here, with a distinctive five-foot-tall cone and eruptions 10-40 feet into the air. Befitting its name, it often erupts every one to three minutes.

Heart Lake

The Heart Lake area is another extremely popular backcountry (and day-hiking) area, offering easy access along with all sorts of sights: a pretty lake, hot springs, and impressive mountain vistas. **Heart Lake Trail** begins just north of Lewis Lake six miles south of Grant Village. The trail is fairly easy, climbing slowly for the first 5.5 miles and then dropping down the other side to Heart Lake (2.5 more miles) along the severely burned Witch Creek drainage. This creek is fed almost entirely by the hot springs and geysers scattered along it.

At Heart Lake Ranger Station the trail splits. Turning right, hike a half-mile to the **Mt. Sheridan Trail,** which heads west and then climbs 2,850 vertical feet in a distance of 3.5 miles. A fire lookout at the summit provides views across Yellowstone Lake and south to the Tetons. At the base of Mt. Sheridan and just to the north is another small thermal area that contains **Rustic Geyser** (eruptions to 50 feet every half hour or so, but irregular) and **Columbia Pool,** among other attractions. Be very careful when walking

here due to the overhanging rim at the pool edge. Although many people simply hike to Heart Lake for an overnight trip, there are many longer hikes one could take out of here. A complete loop around the lake is approximately 33 miles roundtrip but requires two river fords that are at least to your knees in late July. Check with the rangers for current conditions. The Heart Lake area is prime grizzly habitat and is usually closed until the first of July. Do not take chances in this country.

Bechler River

The southwest portion of Yellowstone is known as Cascade Corner, a reference to its many tall waterfalls; more than half of the park's falls are here. This country escaped the fires of 1988, but a 1995 lightning-caused blaze burned 8,400 acres. Primary access is from either the Bechler Ranger Station (pronounced "BECK-ler") or the Cave Falls Trailhead, both of which are well off the beaten path and must be reached via Cave Falls Road from the Idaho side. It's 26 miles in from Ashton, Idaho, the last 10 on a gravel road. (Grassy Lake Road provides a narrow and rough connection from Flagg Ranch to Ashton.) All hikers must register at the Bechler Ranger Station, even if they are heading out from Cave Falls Trailhead (three miles farther down the road). Cave Falls itself is a very wide but not particularly

tall drop along the Falls River. It's named for a cave on the west end of the waterfall. The Forest Service has a campground ($5) here.

A maze of trails cuts across the Bechler country, leading to the many waterfalls and other attractions. One very popular hike goes from Bechler Ranger Station to the Old Faithful area (or vice versa), a distance of 32 miles. From Bechler, the trail cuts across expansive Bechler Meadows and then up narrow Bechler Canyon, passing Colonnade, Ouzel, and Iris falls along the way. Many people stop overnight in Three River Junction before punching on up to the Continental Divide. Beyond this, the trail cuts above Shoshone Lake and on to Lone Star Geyser and the trailhead at Kepler Cascades. It's best to hike this route in late summer or early fall after the meadows have dried out a bit and the mosquitoes are down to a dull roar. Midsummer finds standing water and the ever-friendly leeches, although it is possible to skirt around the meadows.

The Thorofare

If any part of Yellowstone deserves the title untamed wilderness, it has to be the Thorofare. Situated along Two Ocean Plateau and cut through by the upper Yellowstone River, this broad expanse of unroaded country reaches from Yellowstone Lake into the Teton Wilderness south of the park. This is some of the most remote country in the Lower 48—more than 30 miles in any direction from the nearest road. Because of the distances involved, it's best to traverse the Thorofare via horseback. Access is from the Heart Lake area, via the Thorofare Trail, or from the Teton Wilderness. The **Thorofare Trail** begins at Nine-Mile Trailhead on the East Entrance Road and hugs the shore of Yellowstone Lake for the first 17 miles. This stretch was spared from the fires of 1988 and provides some incredible opportunities for sunsets over the lake. Canoeists sometimes paddle along the lakeshore and camp. Because of grizzly activity, off-trail travel is prohibited until mid-August, and you need to be very cautious along streams, where bears may be fishing for spawning cutthroats. Longer trips are also possible, but they require deep fords and may not even be possible till late summer. Check at the Lake Ranger Station for current conditions.

WINTER IN YELLOWSTONE

During Yellowstone's first 75 years as a park, winter visitation was almost unknown. The only people in the park were winterkeepers who spent months at a time with no contact with the world outside. This began to change in 1949, when snow-plane tours were first offered from the West Entrance. The planes could only hold two people—the driver and a passenger—so visitation barely topped 30 people that winter. In 1955, snowcoaches were permitted to come into Yellowstone, and more than 500 people arrived that winter, though few stayed overnight. The first snowmobiles arrived in 1964, when they were still a novelty. With the increasing interest in cross-country skiing and snowmobiling, the park opened Old Faithful Snow Lodge in the winter of 1971-72. Since then, winter use has rocketed seven-fold; today, over 140,000 people visit Yellowstone Park each winter. On busy days, more than 2,000 snowmobiles roar into the park through the West Yellowstone gate, spewing choking blue smoke that creates localized pollution worse than in some of the nation's major cities. While these numbers pale in comparison to summer visitation, some worry that snowmobilers and skiers could adversely affect the park's wildlife at a time when it is already under great stress.

Approximately three-quarters of Yellowstone's winter use consists of people who come in on quick day-tours of the park via snowmobile and then spend the night back in one of the gateway towns. To see Yellowstone right, however, it's best to spend more time, either snow camping or staying at Mammoth or Old Faithful. Winter transforms Yellowstone into an extraordinarily beautiful place where the fires and brimstone of hell meet the bitter cold and snow of winter. The snow often averages four feet in depth but can exceed 10 feet on mountain passes. The snow is usually quite dry, although late in the season conditions deteriorate as temperatures rise. Early in the winter or after major storms, backcountry skiing can be very difficult due to

YELLOWSTONE NATIONAL PARK

the Schwatcha Winter Expedition (U.S. Army) of 1887 at Obsidian Cliff

the deep powder. Temperatures generally fall in the 10-30° F range during the day, while nights frequently dip well below zero. (The record is -66° F, recorded on February 9, 1933.) Winds can make these temperatures feel even colder, so visitors should come prepared for extreme conditions.

The thermal basins are a real winter treat. Hot springs that are simply colorful pools in summer send up billows of steam in the winter, coating the nearby trees with thick layers of ice and turning them into "ghost trees." The geysers put on astounding displays as boiling water meets frigid air; steam from Old Faithful can tower 1,000 feet into the air! Bison and elk gather around the hot springs, soaking up the

heat and searching for dried grasses, and eagles are often seen flying over the heated waters of Firehole River. The bison are perhaps the most interesting to watch as they swing their enormous heads from side to side to shovel snow off the grass. Grand Canyon of the Yellowstone is another place transformed by the snow and cold. Although the water still flows, the falls are surrounded by tall cones of ice, and the canyon walls lie under deep snow.

Roads

Most of Yellowstone's roads officially close to cars when the first heavy snows block the passes, and by the first of November things are generally shut down all over except for the 56 miles between Mammoth and Cooke City. Roads don't open for cars again until mid-May and sometimes not until early June. The roads are open to snowmobiles and snowcoaches from mid-December to mid-March. The rest of the winter you'll only find skiers and park personnel on the snow-covered roads. During the winter, the most popular (and crowded) times to visit Yellowstone are around Christmas and New Year's and over the Presidents' Day weekend in February. If you plan to arrive at these times, make reservations six months to a year in advance. The rest of the winter, you should probably reserve at least three months ahead.

Accommodations and Services

During the winter, only two places offer lodging inside the park. **Mammoth Hotel,** tel. (307) 344-7311, is the only one accessible by road, but **Old Faithful Snow Lodge and Cabins** (same reservations number) provides accommodations and proximity to many miles of skiing trails. See the lodging chart for rates. Mammoth also offers multinight package deals in the winter months, with 30% discounts on transportation and food after three nights. Each has a restaurant, a lounge, and a gift shop. For a fee, Mammoth also offers a variety of special events, ice skating, and hot tubs.

Warming huts are located at Old Faithful, Madison, Canyon, West Thumb, Fishing Bridge, and Indian Creek (near Mammoth Hot Springs). All contain restrooms and snack machines (except at Indian Creek), and all (except at Old Faithful) are open 24 hours. Those at Mammoth

and Canyon also have snack bars offering hot chili or soup, and rangers are usually available at Canyon to answer questions. The Mammoth general store is open for groceries and supplies, but supplies are not available at Old Faithful.

Only the Mammoth and Old Faithful visitor centers are open during the winter season. Free ranger-led activities include evening programs at Mammoth and Old Faithful. AmFac Parks & Resorts offers guided ski and snowmobile tours and provides wildlife bus tours from Mammoth Hot Springs Hotel; call (307) 344-7311 for details. In addition, the Yellowstone Institute (described in "Northeast Entrance Road" under "Touring Yellowstone," above) offers a number of outstanding winter classes. Check the winter edition of *Yellowstone Today* for details. The only wintertime campground is at Mammoth Hot Springs, tel. (307) 344-7311, where temperatures are milder and the snow lighter. The Mammoth Clinic is open weekdays in the winter. Three-hour winter wildlife bus tours to the Lamar Valley depart from Mammoth, and cost $13 ($6.50 for kids).

Snowcoaches

The easiest and most enjoyable way to get into Yellowstone in the winter is on the ungainly snowcoaches, machines that look like something the Norwegian Army might have used during WW II. Most were actually made by a Canadian company, Bombidier. The windows fog up (hence the spray bottles of antifreeze), and they can be noisy. Despite their ancient condition and spartan interior, these beasts still work well and can carry 10 passengers along with gear (two suitcases per person) and skis. The more modern ones (Hagglunds) based at Mammoth are actually not nearly as comfortable as the older models on the bumpy snowpacked roads, and the separate back compartment makes communication with the driver/guide difficult.

A variety of snowcoach tours are available through AmFac Parks & Resorts, tel. (307) 344-7311. Rates to Old Faithful Snow Lodge are $36 one-way from Flagg Ranch (where the plowing ends just south of Yellowstone), $32 one-way from West Yellowstone, and $36.50 one-way from Mammoth. Snowcoach tours depart from Old Faithful for the Firehole River/Fountain Flats area (two and a half hours; $13 roundtrip), and West Thumb Geyser Basin (two and a half hours; $13). All snowcoach tours and transportation are half-priced for kids ages 2-11 and free for toddlers. See below for combination snowcoach and cross-country-skiing trips. For any of these trips, be sure to make reservations well in advance. During the winter, **Gray Line,** tel. (307) 733-4325 or (800) 443-6133, has daily bus runs from Jackson to Flagg Ranch for $25 one-way, arriving in time to meet the snowcoach departures for Yellowstone.

Three West Yellowstone-based companies offer snowcoach day-trips into the park: **Yellowstone Alpen Guides,** tel. (406) 646-9591; **Moonlight Enterprises,** tel. (406) 646-7276; and **Yellowstone Expeditions,** tel. (406) 646-9333 or (800) 728-9333. Yellowstone Expeditions runs converted vans jacked up above tracks and skis. Their excellent tours ($490 per person double occupancy for four days, up to $805 per person double occupancy for eight days) include housing in tent cabins, with yurts providing a central kitchen and social area. The price also includes food, sleeping bags and bedding, roundtrip transportation from West Yellowstone to the base camp near Canyon, a sauna, and backcountry ski guides. The company also offers special winter photography workshops. Recommended.

Cross-Country Skiing

Skis provide the finest way to see Yellowstone in the winter. Rent them at shops in Jackson, Cody, West Yellowstone, Gardiner, and Pahaska, or in the park at Old Faithful and Mammoth. (Snowshoes can also be rented at from Mammoth and Old Faithful, both of which sell ski wax and a few other ski supplies.) The Old Faithful area is the center for skiing within Yellowstone, with trails circling the Upper Geyser Basin and leading to nearby sights. You'll find similar ski trails (marked but not groomed) in the Tower

BOB RACE

Fall, Canyon, Northeast, and Mammoth areas. Get free ski-trail maps at the visitor centers.

Skiers sometimes assume that they can't possibly cause problems for Yellowstone's wildlife, but studies show that elk and bison often move away from skiers, which forces the animals to expend energy they need to survive through the bitterly cold winters. It's best to stay on the trails and to keep from skiing into areas where elk or bison may be disturbed by your presence.

AmFac Parks & Resorts, tel. (307) 344-7311, operates **skier shuttles** ($8-9 roundtrip) from Mammoth to Tower Junction, Blacktail Plateau, and Indian Creek and Golden Gate areas. A similar skier shuttle (via snowcoach) is available from Old Faithful to Fairy Falls or the Continental Divide area for $7.50. The latter is a one-way service that allows you to ski back to the lodge. A variety of other guided snowcoach-and-ski trips are also available. In addition, park naturalists sometimes lead ski trips from Old Faithful to nearby sights.

Yellowstone's roads are heavily traveled by snowmobiles and snowcoaches, making for all sorts of potential conflicts. Be sure to keep to the right while skiing. Most trails are identified by orange metal markers on the trees. If you're planning a longer backcountry trip, pick up a use permit at one of the ranger stations. A thorough understanding of winter camping and survival is imperative before you head out on any overnight trip. For more on skiing and winter visitation in the park, see *Cross-Country Skiing in Yellowstone Country* by Ken and Dena Olsen and Steve and Hazel Scharosch (Casper: Abacus Enterprises).

Snowmobiles

Winter snowmobile use in Yellowstone has risen rapidly in recent years, with almost three-quarters of winter visitors aboard them. It's not uncommon to meet long lines of machines ripping down the roads at any time of the day, disrupting Yellowstone's pristine winter silence with their noise and choking blue smoke (two-stroke engines produce far more pollutants than cars).

Despite the fact that the five national forests surrounding Yellowstone have many hundreds of miles of groomed trails and thousands of square miles of terrain open to the machines, Yellowstone's 180 miles of roads have become the focus of this mechanized winter onslaught. In 1996, a Colorado-based group, the Biodiversity Legal Foundation, sued the Park Service in an attempt to ban snowmobiling in Yellowstone. Meanwhile, folks in the towns surrounding Yellowstone push for ever-increasing snowmobile access to the park and are convinced it's all part of a greenie plot by the Park Service to keep the public out. Something has to give here, and the Park Service is currently trying to get control over the situation while simultaneously attempting to survive budget cuts as winter use keeps increasing.

If you really *must* come into Yellowstone by snowmobile, please show a few courtesies and precautions. In particular, stay on the roads and stay well away from the bison and elk commonly found along or on the roads. This is a highly stressful time of the year for them already, without being harassed by a steady stream of machines. If skiers are on the road, slow down and give them a wide berth as you pass. The speed limit (45 mph) is enforced, and one of the most bizarre Yellowstone sights is a park ranger waiting in a speed trap with his radar gun, ready to catch speeding sleds. Park rangers lead half-hour snowmobile tours from the Canyon warming hut on weekends.

Snowmobiles are available for rent from all four sides of the park. They can also be rented at Mammoth and Old Faithful within the park. You'll need a valid driver's license to drive snowmobiles into Yellowstone. Contact the chamber of commerce in West Yellowstone, Jackson, Cody, or Gardiner for a listing of companies. Snowmobile rentals cost $70-150 per day, with the lowest rates generally out of West Yellowstone. Snowmobile suits run another $10-12 a day. Most 'bilers join guided tours through the park. You can purchase gas inside the park at Mammoth Hot Springs, Canyon, and Old Faithful.

YELLOWSTONE PRACTICALITIES

THE BASICS

As of this writing, entrance to Yellowstone was $20 per vehicle, $4 for individuals entering by bicycle, foot, motorcycle, snowmobile, or bus. The pass covers both Yellowstone and Grand Teton National Parks and is good for seven days. If you're planning to be here longer or to make more visits, get an annual pass covering both parks for $40 or the Golden Eagle Passport, which is good for all national parks, for $25 a year. A Golden Age Passport for all national parks is available to anyone over 62 for a one-time fee of $10, and people with disabilities can get a free Golden Access Passport. Both of these also give you 50% reductions in camping fees. Note that entrance fees will probably be higher than those quoted here since the park has proposed an increase to help provide much-needed funding.

Upon entering the park, you'll receive a Yellowstone map and a copy of *Yellowstone Today,* a quarterly newspaper that describes facilities and services and provides camping, fishing, and backcountry information. This is the best source for up-to-date park information. It's also packed with enough warnings to scare off a platoon of Marines. Examples include cautions against falling trees, bathing in thermal pools (infections and/or amoebic meningitis), unpredictable wildlife, improper food storage, letting your kids wander, steep roads, rock climbing, scalding water, driving while intoxicated, and theft. And, oh yes, "swimming is generally discouraged." If you're planning a trip to Yellowstone, call the park at (307) 344-7381 to request a copy of another free publication, *Yellowstone Guide.*

Visitor Centers

The Park Service maintains visitor centers in five different places: Mammoth Hot Springs, Old Faithful, Canyon, Fishing Bridge, and Grant Village. All of these sell maps and natural-history books covering the park and surrounding areas. You'll also find smaller information stations at Madison and West Thumb (hours and seasons are listed in "Touring Yellowstone" above). Park interpreters (most folks call them rangers, but the real rangers actually do more law enforcement than education) and volunteers offer slide shows, films, guided walks, kids' programs, campfire talks, and other activities at the various campgrounds and visitor centers. These are always favorites of visitors, and on summer days you can choose from more than two dozen different Yellowstone activities (assuming Republicans don't axe Yellowstone's budget even more). Look for a complete listing of the many daily events in the Discover Yellowstone section of the free *Yellowstone Today* paper you receive upon entrance to the park.

Yellowstone Association

Founded in 1933, the Yellowstone Association is a nonprofit organization that serves an educational and scientific role in the park by producing books and pamphlets, helping fund the Yellowstone Institute, and assisting in the visitor centers. Members receive a 15% discount on books. Contact the association for membership information ($25 and up) and a listing of Yellowstone books, at Box 117, Yellowstone National Park, WY, 82190, tel. (307) 344-2293.

GETTING AROUND

Pothole Park

Yellowstone's roads are a constant source of irritation to travelers. In recent years they have deteriorated very rapidly as budget cuts leave less and less money for basic maintenance. Much of the roadbed was built at the turn of the century, when horses and carriages were the primary means of travel. Increasing traffic and larger vehicles have helped contribute to the rapid deterioration of park roads. Drivers and cyclists are confronted with roads that would make any New Yorker feel right at home: mile after mile of potholes and ruts. The extent of the damage is hard to believe until you try driving through Yellowstone. A 20-year road reconstruction program began in the 1990s, but

the park only has money to rebuild approximately eight miles per year, so don't expect any fast improvements. A stretched-thin budget means that even temporary patching and asphalt overlays are completed on a slower schedule. Check with the park for the latest on the road situation and construction delays, and write your Congresspersons to ask them to better fund Park Service maintenance.

The speed limit on all park roads is a strictly enforced 45 mph, although during the summer you're not likely to approach this speed, since long lines of traffic form behind monstrous RVs. Most roads in Yellowstone close with the first heavy snows—generally around the first of November—and usually open again by mid-May. They reopen in sections; the roads connecting Mammoth to West Yellowstone open first, and Dunraven Pass is plowed last. Only the road between Mammoth and Cooke City is kept plowed all winter long. The roads are groomed for snowmobiles (snow conditions permitting) by mid-December. If you're planning a trip early or late in the season, call the park (tel. 307-344-7381) for current road conditions.

Gas stations are located at Old Faithful, Canyon Village, Mammoth Hot Springs, Fishing Bridge, Grant Village, and Tower Junction, while repair services are available at all of these except Mammoth Hot Springs and Tower Junction.

Buses and Tours

During the summer, most people come into Yellowstone in private cars or RVs, but there *are* other ways of getting around; **4x4 Stage,** tel. (406) 388-6404 or (800) 517-8243, offers daily shuttle van service around the park ($10 per person) and on to Gardiner, West Yellowstone, Cooke City, and Bozeman, with by-request connections to other places. The scheduled service is offered June to mid-September; the rest of the year the company provides taxi service; call 24 hours in advance for reservations.

From mid-May to late September, **AmFac Parks & Resorts,** tel. (307) 344-7311, offers full-day bus tours from Canyon Lodge, Lake Hotel, Old Faithful Inn, Fishing Bridge RV Park, and Grant Village. Tours of either the upper or lower loops run $23-25 for adults, $12-13 for kids (free for kids under age 12). A longer Grand

Loop tour (not recommended unless you're into sensory overload and more than 10 hours of riding around) costs $26 for adults, $13 for kids. The Grand Loop tour is only available from Mammoth or Gardiner.

Similar loop tours ($30) are available out of West Yellowstone, Montana, from **Gray Line,** tel. (406) 646-9374, or **Yellowstone Tours,** tel. (406) 646-7337. More Yellowstone tours leave out of Cody ($41) aboard **Powder River Tours** tel. (307) 587-5544 or (800) 442-3682, and Jackson ($36) aboard **Gray Line,** tel. (307) 733-4325 or (800) 443-6133. Gray Line also has one-way service between Yellowstone and Jackson for $25 in either direction. They can pick you up at many places along the road system, but you need to schedule this in advance. This is not a separate service from the Gray Line tours; instead you are picked up by the regular tour buses, meaning that you get a portion of the tour at the same time.

Gardiner-based **Adventurer Tours,** tel. (406) 848-7078 or (800) 336-6219, offers van tours of the park with a different focus each day. The Bozeman Hostel offers a **Hostel Express** van, which takes folks from Bozeman, Montana, through Yellowstone, and on to their yurt hostel in Cooke City for the night, then returns to Bozeman the following day. The $60 cost includes lodging; food and entrance fees are extra. Call (800) 364-6242, for details.

You can rent self-guided car **audio tours**—complete with the latest CD technology—for $25 a day from the various park hotels. These plug into your cigarette lighter and play through the FM radio. See "Sea Kayaking" below for another type of park tour.

FACILITIES AND SERVICES

Shopping and Gifts

Nearly every road junction in Yellowstone has some sort of general store, gas station, gift shop, or other facility. **Hamilton Stores** are the most interesting, since they tend to be located in rustic old log structures and staffed by friendly retired folks and fresh college kids. Here you'll find all the standard tourist supplies and paraphernalia, groceries, camping equipment, books, and fishing supplies. You'll find jewelry, pottery,

and other mass-produced items at the Indian Handicrafts Shop within Old Faithful Inn.

Food

Restaurants are located at Mammoth Hot Springs, Lake Yellowstone Hotel, Old Faithful Inn, Old Faithful Snow Lodge, Grant Village, Roosevelt Lodge, and Canyon Lodge and offer reasonably priced and fairly good meals. Typical menus include steak, burgers, seafood, pasta, chicken, and vegetarian dishes. The chocolate pecan pie at Mammoth Hot Springs is noteworthy, as are the breakfast buffet and lunchtime soup and salad bar at Old Faithful Inn. Dinner reservations (tel. 307-344-7901) are required at Old Faithful Inn, Lake Yellowstone Hotel, Mammoth Hot Springs Hotel, Grant Village, and Canyon Lodge. Roosevelt Lodge offers an "Old West" barbecue dinner, while the Lake Lodge, Old Faithful Lodge, and Canyon Lodge dish up cafeteria food. Get box lunches from any of these places. In addition, fast-food eateries (not the chains) and/or delis are found at Mammoth, Old Faithful, Lake, and Canyon. General stores carrying at least a few groceries are at Mammoth, Canyon, Old Faithful, Grant Village, and Lake; the biggest selection is at Canyon.

Other Services

For a complete directory of the many other Yellowstone visitor services, see *Yellowstone Today*, which you get upon entering the park. **Medical facilities** include clinics at Old Faithful and Mammoth Hot Springs and a small hospital at Lake. Call 911 for emergencies. Check at any visitor center for a schedule of church services.

Exchange **foreign currency** Mon.-Fri. 8 a.m.-5 p.m. at front desks in the various park hotels. You'll discover **ATMs** inside Old Faithful Inn, Lake Yellowstone Hotel, and Canyon Lodge. **Post offices** can be found at Old Faithful, Lake Village, Canyon Village, and Grant Village. Find coin-operated **washers and dryers** at Fishing Bridge RV Park, Lake Lodge, Canyon Village campground, and Grant Village Campground and **public showers** at Fishing Bridge RV Park, Old Faithful Lodge, Canyon Village campground, and Grant Village Campground. One-hour **film processing** labs (print film only) operate at Old Faithful, Canyon, and Mammoth.

CAMPGROUNDS

Tent camping in Yellowstone's early days left a bit to be desired. One 1884 tourist noted that during the height of the summer season, "the principle upon which the beds are populated is said to be the addition of visitors so long as they may arrive, or until the occupants 'go for their guns.' The plan is simple, and relieves the authorities of responsibility." It's still crowded in the park, but generally not this bad!

Camping is available at a dozen sites scattered along the road network (though recent

---

YELLOWSTONE CAMPGROUNDS

Note: Call (303) 297-2757 for reservations at Bridge Bay, Canyon, Grant Village, and Fishing Bridge Campgrounds.

Bridge Bay; open late May to late Sept.; $12.50; fills early, showers, reservable

Canyon; open early June to early Sept.; $12.50; fills early, showers

Fishing Bridge RV Park; open mid-May to mid-Sept.; $22; fills early, hard-sided RVs only, showers

Grant Village; open late June to early Oct.; $12.50; fills early, showers

Indian Creek; open early June to mid-Sept.; $8

Lewis Lake; open early June to early Nov.; $8; fills early

Madison; open May to early Nov.; $12.50; fills early

Mammoth; open year-round; $10; near residential area

Norris; open mid-May through Sept.; $8; fills early

Pebble Creek; open early June through Sept.; $8

Slough Creek; open late May to early Nov.; $8

Tower Fall; open mid-May through Sept.; $8; fills early

budgetary cuts may force closures of some of these); reservations are available for the largest campgrounds: Bridge Bay, Canyon, Grant Village, Madison, and Fishing Bridge RV Park. Call AmFac Parks & Resorts at (307) 344-7311 for reservations. The other seven campgrounds are on a first-come, first-camp basis. See the chart for fees and dates of operation; only Mammoth Campground remains open year-round. Roadside or parking-lot camping is not allowed, and rangers *do* enforce this prohibition.

During July and August, all campsites in Yellowstone fill *before noon*, so get there early! The busiest weekends are—not surprisingly—around July 4 and Labor Day. Yellowstone's most popular campgrounds fill up even in late fall and early summer. When everything else is packed, folks head to campgrounds on surrounding Forest Service lands or to motels in the gateway towns. (See "Shoshone National Forest" in the Big Horn Basin chapter for areas east of Yellowstone and "Jackson Hole Campgrounds" in the Jackson Hole and the Tetons chapter for areas to the south.) Other campgrounds, both public and private, are described under the various park gateways—Cody, Jackson, Dubois, West Yellowstone, Gardiner, Silver Gate, and Cooke City.) The farther you get from

Yellowstone, the more likely you are to find space. If you reach Nebraska, you should have no trouble at all. Campers can take showers at Old Faithful Lodge, Grant Village Campground, Lake Lodge, Fishing Bridge RV Park, and Canyon Village Campground.

HOTELS AND CABINS

See the "Yellowstone Accommodations" chart for specifics on lodging places within Yellowstone National Park. **AmFac Parks & Resorts,** tel. (307) 344-7311, is Yellowstone's official lodging concessionaire. They operate everything from extremely basic cabins with four thin walls starting for $24 d to luxury suites with parlors for up to $342. Following a fine old Yellowstone tradition, none of these rooms have phones, radios, or TVs. What they do offer is the chance to relax in comfortable accommodations and explore the magical world outside. Most of these are open early June to mid-September. During the winter months, only Mammoth Hot Springs Hotel and the Old Faithful Snow Lodge remain open inside the park.

Try to book rooms at least six months ahead to be assured of a space. If you can't get through

---

YELLOWSTONE ACCOMMODATIONS

Note: These lodging rates are for one or two people. Extra persons are $8 each; children under 12 stay free. The least-expensive rooms and cabins have bathrooms nearby but not in the rooms. Call TW Recreational Services AmFac Parks & Resorts at (303) 297-2757 for reservations.

Canyon Lodge & Cabins; open June to early Sept.; $93 in new hotel rooms, $48-84 in cabins

Grant Village; open late May to late Sept.; $68-84 for hotel rooms

Lake Lodge Cabins; open early June to mid-Sept.; $43-84 for cabins

Lake Yellowstone Hotel and Cabins; open mid-May through Sept.; $84-125 for hotel rooms, $342 for suites, $63 for cabins

Mammoth Hot Springs Hotel and Cabins; open mid-May to early Oct. and approximately Dec. 20 to Mar. 2; $47-65 for hotel rooms, $226 for suites, $34 for cabins, $63 for cabins with hot tubs

Old Faithful Inn; open early May to late Oct.; $47-210 for hotel rooms, $289 for suites

Old Faithful Lodge Cabins; open mid-May to mid-Sept.; $22-38 for cabins

Old Faithful Snow Lodge and Cabins; open early May to early Oct. and mid-Dec. to early March; $47-53 for hotel rooms, $63-84 for cabins

Roosevelt Lodge Cabins; open early June through Aug.; $24-63 for cabins

to their reservation number, try calling on evenings or weekends. Operators are available daily 7 a.m.-8 p.m. May-Oct., and daily 8 a.m.-6 p.m. the rest of the year. You can also write AmFac Parks & Resorts, P.O. Box 165, Yellowstone, WY 82190. Several hundred more motels and other lodging places operate outside park boundaries in the towns of Jackson, Cody, West Yellowstone, Gardiner, and Cooke City and elsewhere. (See appropriate sections of this book for details.)

Hotels

At the turn of the century, most visitors to Yellowstone stayed in park hotels rather than roughing it on the ground. Three of these wonderful old lodging places remain: Old Faithful Inn, Lake Yellowstone Hotel, and Mammoth Hot Springs Hotel. Built in 1903-04, the classic **Old Faithful Inn** is easily the most interesting place to stay inside Yellowstone—if not in all of Wyoming. In the older section of the inn you'll find small rooms with thin walls and a bath down the hall, but the grand central space makes it all worthwhile. If you're able to get a room here during your visit to the park, do so; you won't regret it! If you can't get through at AmFac's main reservation number, try calling the inn directly at (307) 545-4600. Hot tip: the best views of Old Faithful Geyser are from Old Faithful Inn suites 176 and 177.

Lake Yellowstone Hotel is another fascinating old building with a magnificent view across Yellowstone Lake. The hotel was recently restored to its 1920s grandeur, and all the rooms have private baths (see Upper Geyser Basin for details). Two long-established Yellowstone hotels have comfortable accommodations (with or without private baths) available both summer and winter: **Mammoth Hot Springs Hotel** and **Old Faithful Snow Lodge.** In addition to these, you can stay in hotel-style accommodations with private baths at **Canyon Lodge** and **Grant Village.** (For more information on both the inn and the hotel, see "Upper Geyser Basin" under "Touring Yellowstone" earlier in this chapter)

Cabins

Cabin units are scattered around several of the developed areas within Yellowstone, including Canyon, Lake Yellowstone, Mammoth Hot Springs, Old Faithful, and Roosevelt Lodge.

Some of these are rustic bare-bones places with a separate bathhouse; others are quite comfortable and may even have private hot tubs. Don't get your hopes too high on these cabins; most are simple box-like structures lined up behind the hotels in row after identical row.

FISHING AND BOATING

Catching the Big Ones

In the early years of the park, fish from Yellowstone Lake were a specialty at the various hotels, and because there was no limit on the take up to 7,500 pounds of fish were caught each year. By the 1970s, Yellowstone Lake had been devastated by overfishing, and new regulations were needed. Beginning in 1973, bait fishing was banned, Fishing Bridge was closed to anglers, and catch-and-release rules were put into place. Because of these regulations, Yellowstone National Park has achieved an almost mythical status when it comes to fishing—the average cutthroat caught in Yellowstone Lake measures 18 inches. Increased fish populations have also been a boon for wildlife, especially grizzlies, bald eagles, and osprey. The most commonly caught fish in Yellowstone are cutthroat, rainbow, brown, and brook trout and mountain whitefish. Grayling are found in the Madison, Firehole, and Gallatin Rivers, while lake trout swim in Shoshone, Lewis, Heart, and Grebe Lakes.

Several good books—available in local stores and visitor centers—provide tips on fishing Yellowstone waters. Two of the best are *Yellowstone Fishing Guide* by Robert E. Charlton, and *Freshwater Wilderness: Yellowstone Fishes and Their World* by John Varley.

Trouble in Paradise

Above the falls on the Yellowstone River (and in Yellowstone Lake), the only trout—until recently—was the native cutthroat. In 1994, lake trout (Mackinaw) were discovered in Lake Yellowstone, and biologists fear that tens of thousands may now survive here. A $10,000 reward is offered for the idiot who planted them in the lake. A highly aggressive species, lake trout feed upon and compete with the prized native cutthroat, threatening to devastate the population.

Cutthroat spawn in the shallow waters of the lake's tributary streams, where they are caught by grizzly bears, bald eagles, and other animals. Lake trout spawn in deeper waters inaccessible to predators, and because of this fewer cutthroat and more lake trout could affect the survival of grizzlies and eagles. Eradication of the lake trout is virtually impossible, but the Park Service uses gill nets to catch them, and it's open season on fishing for lake trout in Yellowstone Lake. However, while there are no size or possession limits on lake trout caught in Yellowstone Lake, any lake trout you catch here must be kept and shown to rangers to help in determining the population size.

Another problem is fast becoming a grave threat to rainbow trout throughout the Rockies. Whirling disease, a devastating parasite-caused brain illness, has killed more than 90% of the rainbow trout in parts of the Madison River outside Yellowstone, and biologists fear it could enter the park. The disease is spread in part when mud or water is brought in from contaminated areas on waders, boats, and boots. Be sure to clean up thoroughly before departing an infected area.

Fishing Regs

In most parts of Yellowstone, the fishing season extends from Memorial Day weekend to early November, but check the regulations for specifics. Note that the Hayden Valley and certain other waters are closed to fishing entirely, often to prevent conflicts with bears. Only artificial lures are allowed, lead is not allowed, and a catch-and-release policy (with exceptions) is in effect for cutthroat and rainbow trout and grayling. Many of the fish are caught over and over again; a typical fish may be caught 45 times in its life! Barbless hooks are preferable for catch-and-release fishing since they cause less damage and are easier to remove. Anglers don't need a state fishing license but must obtain a special Yellowstone National Park permit from a visitor center or ranger station; state fishing licenses aren't required in the park. The adult fishing fee is $10 for a 10-day permit, $20 for a season permit. Kids ages 12-15 get permits for free, and younger children do not need a permit. Park offices also have copies of current fishing regulations.

Boating

Bridge Bay Marina runs hourlong scenic **boat tours** of Yellowstone Lake ($8 for adults, $4 for children), **motorboat rentals** ($20 per hour), and **guided fishing trips** ($40-54 an hour for up to six people). Rent 16-foot **rowboats** for $23 a day, and **outboard boats** for $22 an hour.

The best Yellowstone Lake fishing is from boats rather than from the shoreline. If you're bringing your own boat or canoe to Yellowstone, pick up a park permit ($10 for motorized and $5 for nonmotorized vessels for a seven-day permit) at the Lake Ranger Station or Grant Village Visitor Center. Boat slips are available at Bridge Bay Marina for $7 a night. All streams are closed to watercraft with the exception of the Lewis River between Shoshone and Lewis Lakes. Motorboats are allowed only on Lewis Lake and parts of Yellowstone Lake.

Sea Kayaking

Three companies offer guided sea kayak trips on Yellowstone lakes. **Snake River Kayak & Canoe School,** tel. (307) 733-3127 or (800) 529-2501, charges $130 per person per day for multi-day sea kayak tours around Yellowstone Lake. **Greater Yellowstone Sea Kayaking Tours,** tel. (307) 733-2471 or (800) 733-2471, has five-day tours of Yellowstone Lake for $700 per person and four-day tours of Shoshone and Lewis Lakes for $500 per person. They can also do customized trips of any length for approximately $150 per person per day. The prices for both companies include transportation from Jackson, kayaking and camping gear, and all meals. Based in Jackson, **Wilderness Exposure Expeditions,** tel. (307) 733-1026, offers guided canoe and sea kayak paddling trips around Yellowstone Lake and Shoshone Lake. These last four or five days, cost $755-985 per person, and include guides, canoes, meals, and some camping gear but not sleeping bags or transport to the lakes.

BICYCLING

Cycling provides a unique way to see Yellowstone up close, but, unfortunately, park roads tend to be narrow and have little or no shoulders, making for dangerous conditions. These prob-

lems are exacerbated early in the year by high snowbanks, so bikes are not allowed on some roads. Call (307) 344-7381 for current road conditions. Many stretches are filled with potholes; the Park Service says more than 80% of the roads are "structurally deficient." If you're planning a cycling trip through Yellowstone, be sure to wear a helmet and high-visibility clothing. A bike mirror also helps.

The best times to ride are in the morning before traffic thickens or late in the afternoon before the light begins to fade. The best roads to ride (less traffic and better visibility and shoulders) are the Northeast Entrance Road (Tower to Cooke City), Canyon to Lake, and Lake to Grant Village. You'll find a couple of short bike/hiking trails in the Old Faithful and Midway Geyser Basin areas, but the other roads are all open to cars. Bikes are not allowed on backcountry trails or boardwalks. For more on cycling in the park, get Gene Colling's *The Bicyclist's Guide to Yellowstone National Park,* (Helena, Montana: Falcon Press).

Backroads, tel. (800) 462-2848, has six-day cycling tours of Yellowstone during the summer. These are offered as either camping trips ($798 per person including meals) or trips where you stay at local inns and B&Bs ($1,290 per person including meals). A sag wagon carries your gear, bike rentals are available, and you can choose your own pace.

OTHER RECREATION

During the summer months AmFac Parks & Resorts, tel. (307) 344-7311, offers a variety of recreational opportunities in Yellowstone. **Horseback rides** are available at Mammoth Hot Springs, Canyon Lodge, and Roosevelt Lodge for $17 for one hour, $27 for a two-hour ride. Roosevelt also has daily **stagecoach rides** ($6 adults, $5 kids) and **Old West dinner cookouts** combined with a stage or horseback ride for $28-41 for adults, $17-30 for kids. Advance reservations are required; get tickets from any hotel or lodge in the park.

Hot Springs Bathing

Many people are disappointed to discover that there are no places in Yellowstone where you can soak in the hot springs. Not only is this illegal, but it can also be dangerous, since temperatures often approach boiling and bathers can cause severe damage to these surprisingly fragile natural wonders. Legal bathing pools are found in cold-water streams that have hot springs feeding into them. You're not allowed to enter the source pool or stream itself. Locations of these legal bathing streams are not publicized, but you may be able to get information by asking around within the park. Thirty miles north of Yellowstone is **Chico Hot Springs** in the little burg of Pray, Montana. If you're staying in the Mammoth Hot Springs area of Yellowstone, a side trip to Chico may be worthwhile. The large outdoor pool is a great place to relax, the gourmet restaurant serves some of the best dinners anywhere around, and the classic old hotel is a favorite. Call (406) 333-4933 or (800) 468-9232 for more information.

GREATER YELLOWSTONE COALITION

The most important environmental group involved with protecting Yellowstone and the surrounding public lands from development is the Greater Yellowstone Coalition. This private nonprofit organization is involved in all sorts of controversies within the 10-million-acre Greater Yellowstone Ecosystem—from wolf reintroduction to timber harvesting and mineral development. It represents some 4,000 members and publishes a quarterly newsletter detailing various issues. Membership costs $25 and up; write GYC, Box 1874, Bozeman, MT 59771, tel. (406) 586-1593, or reach them via e-mail at gyc@desktop.org.

WORKING IN YELLOWSTONE

Park Service Jobs

During the summer months, Yellowstone National Park provides several thousand jobs for both young and old. Most of these are with the concessionaires, but the Park Service also hires

a cadre of park rangers, interpretive staff, maintenance workers, and backcountry rangers. Get applications from: National Park Service, Seasonal Employment Unit, 18th and C St. NW, Room 2229, Washington, D.C. 20240. In recent years budget cuts have forced the Park Service to reduce its hiring of seasonal workers and increase the use of volunteers. Today, fully a third of the educational programs offered in the park are led by unpaid volunteers. If you want to join the ranks of the employed but unpaid, contact the **Student Conservation Association** at Box 550C, Charlestown, NH 03603. For both paid and volunteer positions, you need to apply early, before mid-January. Paid Park Service positions require U.S. citizenship.

Concessionaire Jobs

The park's two main concessionaires, Hamilton Stores and AmFac Parks & Resorts, employ several thousand folks each year. Most employees of these companies are either college students (who live in dorm-style accommodations) or retired folks (who live in their RVs). Don't expect high pay; entry positions start at around minimum wage, with meals and lodging deducted from this.

Hamilton Stores is the oldest privately owned concession in the entire national park system, having been around since 1915. They employ approximately 1,000 folks annually and accept applications after January 1 each year. If you can start in April or May you're considerably more likely to be hired. To receive an application form, call (800) 385-4979 or download info and an application via the Internet at: http://www.cool-works.com/showme/bearsrus. You can contact the Hamilton Stores personnel department directly in the winter months at 1709 W. College St., Bozeman, MT 59715, tel. (406) 587-2208, or in summer at Box 250, West Yellowstone, MT 59758, tel. (406) 646-7325.

AmFac Parks & Resorts is in charge of lodging, restaurants, bus tours, boat rentals, horse rides, and similar services within Yellowstone. It hires more than 3,500 people each summer. For more info and an application, call (307) 344-5324 or write AmFac Parks & Resorts, Human Resources Dept., Yellowstone National Park, WY 82190. It's best to apply early in the year (December and January are best) for summer jobs. The more competitive winter positions often go to those with previous work experience in the park.

GATEWAY TOWNS

Yellowstone National Park is most commonly entered via one of several Wyoming or Montana towns. The Wyoming entry points—Cody, Dubois, and Jackson—are described in other chapters. The four towns listed below are in Montana but lie just across the border and are important gateways into the park. Note that the area code for all these Montana towns is 406. For details on the great state of Montana, see *Montana Handbook,* by W.C. McRae and Judy Jewell (Moon Publications).

WEST YELLOWSTONE

West Yellowstone, Montana, is the definitive Western tourist town. With a year-round population of only 1,000 (three times that in the summer) but more than 50 motels, it's pretty easy to

see what makes the cash registers ring. The West Entrance gate—most popular of all Yellowstone entrances—lies just a couple hundred feet away. The town looks nicer than it did a few years back but still isn't particularly attractive; motels, restaurants, T-shirt stores, and gift shops crowd the streets.

West Yellowstone is surrounded by the Gallatin (GAL-a-tin) National Forest, and Targhee National Forest is only a few miles to the south. "West," as the town is known locally, began in 1908, when the first Union Pacific Yellowstone Special rolled into town from Salt Lake City. From here, stagecoaches took tourists into the park. The historic stone depot and a neighboring dining hall still stand, although the last passengers stepped off the train in 1959. Hamilton Stores—one of the primary Yellowstone concessionaires—has its summer offices in West Yellowstone.

Sights

Museum of the Yellowstone, 124 Yellowstone Ave., tel. (406) 646-7814, is a stone-and-log structure located right along the main highway into the park. Entrance is $5 for adults; $4 for seniors, students, and kids; and $14 for families. Kids under eight get in free. It's open daily 8 a.m.-10 p.m. May-Oct. and offers a good collection of regional books for sale. The museum houses exhibits on how the railroads helped establish Yellowstone National Park, on the Yellowstone fires of 1988, black and grizzly bears, mountain men, and the U.S. cavalry. Videos and movies about Yellowstone are shown in the theater. The extensive Plains Indian collection includes artifacts rarely seen in museums today, including a Blackfoot medicine bundle and other sacred items. A grand old park bus parked out front was last used in 1959.

Right next door is another wonderful stone structure (built in 1925) that served until the late 1950s as an elegant Union Pacific Dining Lodge. The building has a spacious dining hall containing an enormous fireplace, a 45-foot-tall vaulted ceiling, and handmade light fixtures.

Family-run **Eagle's Store,** on the corner of Canyon and Yellowstone, tel. (406) 646-9300, is well worth a stop. Built in the 1920s, this historic log building contains all the standard tourist knickknacks, quality Western clothing, and a delightful old-fashioned soda fountain (open summer only).

In the early 1990s, a massive $50 million project covering 67 acres transformed the town of West Yellowstone. Included are a grizzly and wolf theme park, an IMAX theatre, a resort hotel, cabins, a restaurant, fast-food joints, an RV park, and a post office. The centerpiece is the **Grizzly Discovery Center,** 201 S. Canyon St., tel. (406) 646-7001 or (800) 257-2570, home to seven Alaskan and Canadian grizzlies and 10 captive-born gray wolves. Not all the bears are visible at any given time, but visitors are bound to see at least one in the pseudo-natural habitat. The center also shows films about bears and is open daily all year—8:30 a.m.-8:30 p.m. in the summertime. Entrance costs $6.50 for adults, $3 for ages 5-16, free for kids under five. This profit-making center attracts throngs of visitors who might otherwise never

see a grizzly or wolf but remains quite controversial. Scientists note that the bears here are genetically quite distinct from those in Yellowstone, and anyone who has spent time around grizzlies in the wild will be dismayed to see them in captivity, even in a facility less oppressive than traditional zoos.

Fronting the Grizzly Discovery Center is **Yellowstone IMAX Theatre,** tel. (406) 646-4100, where you can watch the big-budget production of *Yellowstone* on the 60- by 80-foot screen. The theatre is open daily 9 a.m.-9 p.m. May to mid-October, with reduced hours the rest of the year. Admission is $6.50 for adults, $4.50 for ages 3-11, and free for younger children. The 35-minute movie presents Yellowstone history and geology complete with stirring music and a cast of dozens. If you haven't seen IMAX flicks before, hold onto your seat—lots of jaw-dropping scenes here. The movie packs in the crowds on summer days, but the film seems like a Disneylandish version of reality, ignoring many of the things you're likely to see in the park—such as burned forests, crowds of visitors, and potholed roads—and putting history into a pretty little box. Reality wasn't—and isn't—quite like this. Even more disconcerting is that this glorification of the park stands right next to the park. To me it symbolizes the make-a-buck attitude that holds Yellowstone up as an attraction while developing a massive complex on its very margin. The lobby houses a Taco Bell outlet, Starbucks espresso stand, gift shop, and tour-booking office.

Hostel

Budget travelers will be happy to discover the **West Yellowstone International Hostel** (not affiliated with AYH) in the historic Madison Hotel, 139 Yellowstone Ave., tel. (406) 646-7745 or (800) 838-7745. Built in 1912 and on the National Register of Historic Places, the hostel has a very friendly owner and a rustic downstairs lobby but no kitchen. Rates are $15 per person in dorm rooms, $30 d and up for a private hotel room. It's open late May through mid-October only; both nonsmoking and smoking rooms are available. Make reservations a few days ahead in midsummer or get here before evening to be sure of a space in the dorms.

Motels

The proximity to Yellowstone makes the town of West Yellowstone a popular stopping place for vacationers in both summer and winter. It is also a fairly pricey place to stay, with most rooms costing $50 and up during the peak summer season. Every street is lined with motels, so I won't try to list all of them, but if you're a member of AAA, check its *TourBook,* which includes at least 18 of the best. (Rates are often substantially lower for AAA members, too.) Be aware that during the summer everything fills up by early afternoon, so get there early or make advance reservations. To be certain of a place in July or August, make reservations by April! Motels can be full on weekends even in late September, so be sure to call ahead. Panorama West, tel. (800) 227-8483, makes reservations for motels in West Yellowstone, Gardiner, Cody, and other Yellowstone-area towns for a $4 service fee.

Two recommended budget-end places (no phones in the rooms, however) are: **Al's Westward Ho Motel,** 16 Boundary St., tel. (406) 646-7331, where rooms are $40-48 s or d (kitchenettes $3 more), and **Alpine Motel,** 120 Madison Ave., tel. (406) 646-7544, where rooms go for $44 s, $45-52 d. Both these are open May-Oct. only. For inexpensive year-round lodging, head to **Lazy G Motel,** 123 Hayden, tel. (406) 646-7586, where nice rooms start for $40 s, $48 d; **Pony Express Motel,** 4 Firehole Ave., tel. (406) 646-7644, with quiet rooms for $46 s or d; or **Golden West Motel,** 429 Madison Ave., tel. (406) 646-7778, with newly remodeled rooms costing $44 s or d. You'll find excellent new accommodations at **Brandin' Iron Motel,** 201 Canyon St., tel. (406) 646-9411 or (800) 231-5991. Rooms cost $63 s, $69 d, with access to whirlpools and a hot tub.

One of the best lodging places in West Yellowstone is the block-long **Stage Coach Inn,** 209 Madison Ave., tel. (406) 646-7381 or (800) 842-2882, owned by Hamilton Stores. Rooms go for $72-110 s, $79-116 d, and include access to a sauna and hot tubs. The impressive lobby is a treat. If you're willing to drive the extra seven miles west of town, **Lionshead Super 8 Lodge,** tel. (406) 646-9584 or (800) 843-1991, has quality rooms, a very nice country setting, and a sauna and hot tub. Rooms start at $50 s,

$54 d. It's very popular with the retirement crowd, who park RVs in the "campground." The most elaborate place in town is the new and ludicrously named **West Yellowstone Conference Hotel Holiday Inn Sunspree Resort,** 315 Yellowstone Ave., tel. (406) 646-7365 or (800) 646-7365, with rooms for $124-200 s or d. Facilities include an indoor pool, exercise room, sauna, and jacuzzi.

Families may prefer renting a fully furnished condo from **Yellowstone Townhouses** on Horse Rd., tel. (406) 646-9331; **Yellowstone Village,** tel. (406) 646-7335 or (800) 276-7335; or **Lodgepole Townhouse,** tel. (406) 646-9253. Expect to pay around $100 for one-bedroom units and $140 for two-bedroom units. **Sportsman's High Bed & Breakfast,** 750 Deer St., tel. (406) 646-7865 or (800) 272-4227, is in an attractive home eight miles west of town. Very nice accommodations with a big breakfast cost $95 d. The same people also rent five vacation homes and cabins for $110-225 for families.

Camping

The closest public camping (RVs only) is at **Baker's Hole** ($10; open late May to mid-September) three miles north of West Yellowstone. Tent campers will need to go to **Hebgen Lake,** eight miles north of town, where six different camping areas are strung westward along the lake; the farthest is 23 miles from West Yellowstone. Rates range from free (at the undeveloped sites) to $10 a night. Baker's Hole Campground and four others are reservable (additional $8.25 fee charged) by calling (800) 280-2267. In addition, the Forest Service maintains three public-use cabins ($20 a night) in the country around here; check at the ranger station for details.

West Yellowstone has a dozen private campgrounds, but most of these are just RV parking lots. The nicest are **Rustic RV Campground,** 634 U.S. 20, tel. (406) 646-7387, and **Wagon Wheel RV Park,** 408 Gibbon Ave., tel. (406) 646-7872. Expect to pay around $12 for tents, $15 for RVs at either place. Noncampers can shower for $3. Both campgrounds are open mid-April to mid-October. **Canyon Street Laundromat,** 312 Canyon, tel. (406) 646-9733, also has hot showers for $1.

Food

West Yellowstone has quite a number of good eateries. For breakfast, run on over to **Running Bear Pancake House,** 538 Madison Ave., tel. (406) 646-7703, but be ready for a long wait in midsummer. Other good breakfast places are **Silver Spur Cafe,** 111 Canyon St., tel. (406) 646-9400, and **Rustler's Roost Restaurant,** 234 Firehole Ave., tel. (406) 646-7622. For lunch or dinner, try the pizzas (best in town) or a "steak bomb," made with thinly sliced sirloin topped with mushrooms and Swiss cheese. **Gusher Pizza and Sandwich Shoppe,** Madison and Dunraven, tel. (406) 646-9050, is a family place with fast service, the best reubens in town, and decent pizzas (frozen crust, alas). **Pete's Rocky Mountain Pizza,** 104 Canyon St., tel. (406) 646-7820, has more pizza along with Italian and even Mexican specialties.

Totem Restaurant, 115 Canyon St., tel. (406) 646-7630, has the best prime rib around. Pig out cheaply at tiny **Mike's Cafe,** 38 Canyon, tel. (406) 646-9462, where they serve all-American faves: burgers, sandwiches, barbecue ribs, steak, and chicken. Fine German cooking can be had at **Alice's Restaurant,** seven miles west of town, tel. (406) 646-7296, where the rainbow trout is a specialty.

Ernie's Bighorn Deli, 406 Highway Ave., tel. (406) 646-9467, makes unbeatable sandwiches for lunch, while **Three Bear Restaurant,** 205 Yellowstone Ave., tel. (406) 646-7811, has the best salad bar in town. The upscale dinner menu includes shrimp, halibut, trout, chicken, and steaks. **Coachman Restaurant,** downstairs in the Stage Coach Inn, 209 Madison Ave., tel. (406) 646-7381, has a good salad bar. **Bullwinkles,** 19 Madison Ave. W, tel. (406) 646-7974, cranks out steak sandwiches, burgers, pork chops, salads, and homemade pastries.

For a sweet treat, head to **Arrowleaf Ice Cream Parlor,** 29 Canyon St., tel. (406) 646-9776, home of "2001 flavors." Get delicious gourmet coffee and fresh baked goods—including monster cinnamon rolls—at **Nancy P's,** 29 Canyon St., tel. (406) 646-9737. It's open summers only. **Market Place,** 22 Madison Ave., tel. (406) 646-9600, is the local grocery store.

Entertainment

During the summer, **Playmill Theatre,** 124 Madison Ave., tel. (406) 646-7757, offers light-hearted comedies and musicals; it's a favorite of families. For country and western and rock bands (winters only), try **Stage Coach Inn,** 209 Madison Ave., tel. (406) 646-7381. Another place with occasional live rock or country music is **Iron Horse Saloon,** inside the new West Yellowstone Conference Hotel at 315 Yellowstone Ave., tel. (406) 646-7365. **Lionshead Super 8 Lodge,** seven miles west of town, tel. (406) 646-9584, offers square dancing with callers from all over the nation and even provides the outfits.

Summer Recreation

Horseback trail rides and Western cookouts are available from a number of ranches in the surrounding area: **Parade Rest Guest Ranch,** tel. (406) 646-7217; **Diamond P Ranch,** tel. (406) 646-7246; **320 Ranch,** tel. (406) 995-4283 or (800) 243-0320; **Lone Mountain Ranch,** tel. (406) 995-4644; **Bar N Ranch,** tel. (406) 646-7229; **Firehole Ranch,** tel. (406) 646-7294; and **Jacob Island Park Ranch,** tel. (208) 662-5567. Unguided horse rentals are also available at **Lone Rider Stable,** eight miles west of town, tel. (406) 646-7900. Rent mountain bikes from **Yellowstone Bicycle and Video,** 132 Madison Ave., tel. (406) 646-7815.

You'll find five different **fly-fishing shops** in town, a reflection of the sport's importance in the Yellowstone area: **Arrick's Fishing Flies,** 125 Madison Ave., tel. (406) 646-7290; **Bud Lily's Trout Shop,** 39 Madison Ave., tel. (406) 646-7801; **Eagle's Tackle Shop,** 3 Canyon St., tel. (406) 646-7521; **Jacklin's,** 105 Yellowstone Ave., tel. (406) 646-7336; and **Madison River Outfitters,** 117 Canyon St., tel. (406) 646-9644.

Get outdoor gear—including tents, cross-country skis, and mountaineering equipment—from **Bear Essentials,** 121 Madison Ave., tel. (406) 646-4969.

Winter Recreation

West Yellowstone is infamous for its bitterly cold winters, when the thermometer can drop to 50 degrees below zero. Fortunately, it doesn't always stay there, and by March the days have often warmed to a balmy 20 degrees above. In

424 YELLOWSTONE NATIONAL PARK

November, West becomes a national center for cross-country skiers, with the U.S. Nordic and biathlon ski teams training here. Both the 25-km Rendezvous Trail and the 10-km Riverside Trail take off right from town. They are groomed with both diagonal stride and skating tracks from early November through March. You can also ski the snowpacked streets in winter. In mid-March the **Yellowstone Rendezvous,** a nationally known Nordic ski race, attracts more than 500 participants. Find many more places for flat tracking or Telemarking in adjacent Yellowstone National Park and the Gallatin and Targhee National Forests. Rent skinny skis at **Bud Lilly's Trout Shop,** 39 Madison Ave., tel. (406) 646-7801, **Madison River Outfitters,** 117 Canyon St., tel. (406) 646-9644, or **Alpenguides,** 555 Yellowstone Ave., tel. (406) 646-9591. A different sort of tour is offered by **Klondike Dreams Sled Dog Tours,** tel. (406) 646-4004, where half-day trips are $75 for adults, $55 for kids under 10.

The chamber of commerce trumpets West as the "snowmobile capital of the world," and each day between November and late March hundreds of 'bilers show up to roar through Yellowstone's entrance or across thousands of acres of adjacent Forest Service lands. More than 20 different tour and snowmobile rental companies operate out of West Yellowstone. Rentals run $70-150 per day (tours are more expensive); see the chamber of commerce for a list and a map of local trails. Hundreds more folks bring in their own "crotch rockets" to ride on Yellowstone National Park roads and across Gallatin and Targhee National Forest lands. The **World Snowmobile Expo** is held here the third weekend in March and includes races, demos, and other activities. Snowcoach tours of Yellowstone are available through **Moonlight Enterprises,** tel. (406) 646-7276, **Yellowstone Alpen Guides,** tel. (406) 646-9591, and **Yellowstone Expeditions,** tel. (406) 646-9333.

Information and Services
The **West Yellowstone Chamber of Commerce office** at 30 Yellowstone Ave., tel. (406) 646-7701, is staffed during the summer and winter months by Forest Service and Park Service volunteers who can provide info on the great outdoors. Office hours are a bit convolut-ed: daily 8 a.m.-8 p.m. in the summer (Memorial Day to mid-October); Mon.-Fri. 8 a.m.-5 p.m. mid-October to mid-December and mid-March to mid-May; and daily 8 a.m.-6 p.m. mid-December to mid-March and mid-May to Memorial Day. West Yellowstone's new post office is at 209 Grizzly Ave., tel. (406) 646-7704. The **Hebgen Lake Ranger District Office** is just north of town on U.S. 191/287, tel. (406) 646-7369. Get maps of Gallatin National Forest and info on the **Madison River Canyon,** where a magnitude-7.1 earthquake hit in 1959. It caused a massive landslide that killed 28 people, created Quake Lake, and caused cracks in Hebgen Dam. The quake also dramatically affected Yellowstone's geysers and hot springs. The site of the slide is approximately 20 miles north and west of West Yellowstone on U.S. 287. It's marked with various signs.

You'll find **ATMs** inside the Stage Coach Inn, 209 Madison Ave., and West Yellowstone Conference Hotel, 315 Yellowstone Avenue. Wash clothes at **Canyon Street Laundromat,** 312 Canyon St., tel. (406) 646-9733; **Econo-Mart Laundromat,** 307 Firehole Ave., tel. (406) 646-7887; or **Swan Cleaners & Laundromat,** 520 Madison Ave., tel. (406) 646-7892.

Books
The Book Peddler, 106 Canyon St., tel. (406) 646-9358 or (800) 253-2855, is an attractive bookstore with many Montana, Wyoming, and Yellowstone titles. Sip a cup of espresso while you read. **Bookworm Books,** 14 Canyon, tel. (406) 646-9736, another large bookshop with both new and used titles including many first editions, is open till midnight in the summer! The local **library** is at 200 Yellowstone Ave., tel. (406) 646-9017.

Transportation and Tours
West Yellowstone has some of the highest gas prices anywhere around; fill up before you get here! **4x4 Stage,** tel. (406) 388-6404 or (800) 517-8243, offers scheduled service between West Yellowstone and the park ($10) and onward to Gardiner, Cooke City, and Bozeman airport. You can charter the vans for service to other points in the vicinity, including Jackson Hole. The scheduled service is June to mid-September; the rest of the year the company

offers taxi service; call 24 hours in advance for reservations. **City Taxi,** tel. (406) 587-1135, also has taxi service to the West Yellowstone area.

Two companies offer all-day tours of Yellowstone from June through September. **Gray Line,** 633 Madison Ave., tel. (406) 646-9374 or (800) 523-3102, has daily "lower loop" park tours and "upper loop" tours three times a week for $36 including park entrance fees. They also have Quake Lake ($36) and Jackson Hole ($46) tours from West Yellowstone as well as lodging-tour packages. **Buffalo Bus Lines,** 429 Yellowstone, tel. (406) 646-9564 or (800) 426-7669, has narrated loop tours of Yellowstone for $33 per person (plus the park entrance fee). On odd days they circle the park's upper loop; on even days they take you to sights along the lower loop road.

Greyhound Bus, tel. (406) 646-7666 or (800) 231-2222, has daily summertime runs between Bozeman and Salt Lake City, with a stop in West Yellowstone at the corner of Firehole Ave. and Electric Street.

Sky West Airlines, tel. (800) 453-9417, has service to West Yellowstone airport from Salt Lake City, and **Northwest Airlines** tel. (800) 225-2525, flies in from Bozeman and Salt Lake City. Note that these only operate June-Sept.; the rest of the year the closest airport is in Bozeman or Jackson Hole. Get taxi service to Bozeman airport from 4x4 Stage or City Taxi (see above) for approximately $25 per person one-way, $45 roundtrip.

Rental cars are available through **Budget,** tel. (406) 646-7882 or (800) 527-0700; **Big Sky Car Rentals,** tel. (406) 646-9564 or (800) 426-7669; and **Travelers,** tel. (406) 646-9332 or (800) 548-9551. Big Sky has the cheapest rates.

GARDINER

The little tourism town of Gardiner, Montana (pop. 800), lies barely outside Yellowstone's northwest entrance and three miles from the Wyoming line. The Yellowstone River slices right through town. Park headquarters at Mammoth Hot Springs is just five miles away, and the large warehouses of park concessionaire AmFac Parks & Resorts dominate the vicinity.

Gardiner is the only year-round entrance to Yellowstone, and the Absaroka-Beartooth Wilderness lies just north of here. Also nearby is the 33,000-acre ranch of the Church Universal and Triumphant (CUT). Led by Elizabeth Clare Prophet, CUT has been involved in all sorts of end-of-the-world fantasies and has built bomb-shelter developments within grizzly-bear habitat (one shelter can house 756 people), stockpiled weapons, constructed fences that block elk migrations, and proposed geothermal projects that could affect Yellowstone's hot springs. CUT is not exactly popular with the townsfolk of Gardiner.

Gardiner was founded in 1883 when the Northern Pacific Railroad extended a line to the edge of Yellowstone, making it the first major entryway into the park. A reporter of that era described Gardiner as having "200 hardy souls, with 6 restaurants, 1 billiard hall, 2 dance halls, 4 houses of ill-fame, 1 milk man and 21 saloons." Today, the most distinctive structure in town is the monumental stone park entryway—similar to France's Arc de Triomphe—which was for many years the primary entry point into Yellowstone. Built in 1903, **Roosevelt Arch** was dedicated by President Theodore Roosevelt, a man regarded by many as Yellowstone's patron saint. A tablet above the keystone is inscribed, "For the Benefit and Enjoyment of the People." (The arch was actually built to offset the park visitors' initial disappointment at finding the rather ordinary country in this part of Yellowstone!)

Accommodations
Gardiner has 17 different lodging places, including a number with comfortable Old-West cabins; see the accommodations chart for specifics. Be sure to reserve ahead anytime in the summer; rooms may be hard to find even in mid-September. One of the nicest—if you have the bucks—is **Yellowstone Inn B&B,** tel. (406) 848-7000, consisting of two beautifully restored stone-walled houses (built in 1903) and a cottage. A full breakfast is served, and guests will enjoy the outdoor jacuzzi. Also of note is **Yellowstone Suites B&B,** tel. (406) 848-7937 or (800) 948-7937, another turn-of-the-century stone house that features attractive woodwork and hardwood floors, a veranda, a jacuzzi, and

continental breakfasts. Families and groups may want to check out the four spacious cabins at **Above the Rest Lodge,** tel. (406) 848-7747, one of which sleeps up to 14 people. Each has a full kitchen and a washer and dryer. Farther afield but worth a visit if you're heading north is **Chico Hot Springs,** located 30 miles north of Gardiner. The classic old hotel sits adjacent to a hot springs-fed pool, and the restaurant is an attraction in its own right. Dinner reservations required. Call (406) 333-4933 or (800) 468-9232 for more information.

Camping

Public camping is available five miles away within Yellowstone National Park at **Mammoth Campground** ($10; open year-round) or in Gallatin National Forest in the undeveloped **Eagle Creek Recreation Area** (free; open mid-June through October), two miles northeast of Gardiner on Jardine Road. Two other Forest Service campgrounds are farther up this road.

Park RVs at **Rocky Mountain Campground,** tel. (406) 848-7251, for $21 ($16 for tents), open May-October. Showers for noncampers cost

GARDINER ACCOMMODATIONS

Note: Accommodations are listed from least to most expensive. Add a four percent tax to these rates. The area code is 406.

Mile Hi Motel; tel. 848-7544; $40-48 s or d; open mid-May to mid-Oct.

Gardiner Town Motel; tel. 848-7322; $42 s or d; old place, see rooms first

Hillcrest Cottages; 200 Scott St.; tel. 848-7353; $45-50 s, $56-70 d; cozy cottages with kitchenettes

Jim Bridger Court; tel. 848-7371; $50 s or d; comfortable cabins, kitchenettes, open mid-May to mid-Oct.

Blue Haven Motel; tel. 848-7719; $50 s or d; cabins, kitchenettes $10 extra

Wilson's Yellowstone River Motel; tel. 848-7303; $50-70 s or d; open May-Oct., AAA-approved

Yellowstone Suites B&B; 506 4th St.; tel. 848-7937 or (800) 948-7937; $60-85 s or d; historic stone home, jacuzzi, veranda, three guest rooms, shared or private baths, continental breakfast, no kids under 12

Comfort Inn; 107 Hellroaring Rd.; tel. 848-7536 or (800) 228-5150; $60-185 s or d; continental breakfast, AAA-approved

Yellowstone Village Motel; tel. 848-7417 or (800) 228-8158; $64-69 s or d; indoor pool, sauna, AAA-approved

Yellowstone Inn B&B; tel. 848-7000; $64-104 s or d; beautiful historic inn, full breakfast, jacuzzi, nine guest rooms, shared or private baths

Westernaire Motel; tel. 848-7397; $75 s or d; very nice

Absaroka Lodge; tel. 848-7414 or (800) 755-7414; $80 s or d; immaculate two-bedroom suites with kitchenettes for $90 s or d, overlooks Yellowstone River

Best Western by Mammoth Hot Springs; tel. 848-7311 or (800) 829-9080; $84-89 s, $84-99 d; indoor pool, sauna, jacuzzi, AAA approved

Maiden Basin Inn; five miles west of Gardiner; tel. 848-7080 or (800) 624-3364; $85-105 s or d; new place, jacuzzi, kitchenettes, AAA-approved

Super 8 Motel; tel. 848-7401 or (800) 800-8000; $90 s or d; indoor pool

Above the Rest Lodge; tel. 848-7747; $100-250 for one- to three-bedroom cabins, full kitchens, impressive views

$3.50, and a public laundromat is on the site. Campsites are also available in crowded, along-the-river sites at **Yellowstone RV Park,** tel. (406) 848-7251, open June-October on the northwest end of town.

Food
Bear Country Restaurant has a popular break-fast buffet for $5. **K Bar Club,** tel. (406) 848-9995, doesn't look like much either outside or inside, but the from-scratch pizzas are very good in this lo-cals' hangout (not for kids since this is a bar). Families head to **Outlaw's Pizza,** in the Outpost Mall on the northwest end of town, tel. (307) 848-7733, for standard pizzas, pasta, and calzone, and a small salad bar. The mall also houses **Deedee's Chicken Basket,** tel. (307) 848-7771, where you can get a complete picnic lunch to go; call the night before to have it ready to pick up.

Town Cafe, tel. (406) 848-7322, has sand-wiches, burgers, and a big salad bar. Better food is upstairs in the Town Loft (summer only), where you can enjoy the vistas while you eat. **Sawtooth Deli,** tel. (406) 848-7600, has subs, grilled sand-wiches, soups, and espresso. Closed March and April. **Yellowstone Mine Restaurant** in the Best Western, tel. (406) 848-7336, offers very good but overpriced meals. Best steaks around. The most distinctive food in town is, surprisingly, at **Corral Drive Inn,** tel. (406) 848-7627, where Helen and her sons serve up the biggest, juiciest, and messiest (get a handful of napkins) ham-burgers anywhere around. Stop for groceries, fresh baked goods, and deli items at **Food Farm,** tel. (406) 848-7524, on the northwest end of town.

Entertainment and Events
The big annual event in town is the **Gardiner Rodeo,** which comes around in mid-June. More fun times come with **Buffalo Days** in late Au-gust, which brings an arts and crafts fair, live music and dancing, and plenty of barbecued buf-falo, beef, and pork. Look for live bands on week-ends at the **Two Bit Saloon,** tel. (406) 848-7743.

Recreation
During the summer, three rafting companies offer whitewater trips from Gardiner down the Yellowstone River: **Yellowstone Raft Compa-ny,** tel. (406) 848-7777; **Montana Whitewater,**

tel. (307) 763-4465 or (800) 799-4465; and **Ab-saroka Rafting Adventures,** tel. (406) 848-7414 or (800) 755-7414. Rates are approxi-mately $29 for adults, $19 for kids for half-day trips, and $65 for adults, $44 for kids for a full-day whitewater rafting trip. Yellowstone Raft Company also has guided fishing trips costing $235 a day for two people.

Wilderness Connection, tel. (406) 848-7287, has horseback trips into Yellowstone. In win-ter, rent cross-country skis from **Trailhead Sporting Goods,** tel. (406) 848-7712, or **Park's Fly Shop,** tel. (406) 848-7314. **Yellowstone Mountain Bike,** 220 W. Park St. (next to Saw-tooth Deli), tel. (406) 848-7600, offers bike rentals and tours. Open summers only.

Information, Services, and Shopping
The **Gardiner Chamber of Commerce,** on Park at 3rd (near Bear Country Restaurant), tel. (406) 848-7971, has local info but is only open Tues-day, Wednesday, and Friday 10 a.m.-3 p.m. If it's closed, check the bulletin board in the center of town. The **Gardiner District Office** of Gallatin National Forest, tel. (406) 848-7375, has maps and info on the 930,584-acre **Absaroka-Beartooth Wilderness.** The portion around Gardiner is lower in elevation and covered with forests, while farther east are the alpine peaks of the Beartooth Mountains. The **post office** is on the corner of Main and 3rd streets, tel. (406) 848-7579. Get fast cash at the **ATM** inside the Exxon station just north of the river or from the First Interstate Bank on the northwest end of Gardiner. Wash clothes at **Arch Laundrette,** just downhill from Cecil's Restaurant on Park Street. **High Country Books and Gifts,** on Park St. next to Cecil's Restaurant, tel. (406) 848-7707, has a good selection of Western books, along with espresso coffee. **Yellowstone Gallery & Frameworks,** tel. (406) 848-7306, sells quality pottery, jewelry, and artwork.

Transportation and Tours
4x4 Stage, tel. (406) 388-6404 or (800) 517-8243, offers scheduled service between Gar-diner and the park ($10) and onward to Cooke City, West Yellowstone, and Bozeman airport. You can charter the vans for service to other points in the vicinity, including Jackson Hole.

The scheduled service runs June to mid-September; the rest of the year the company offers taxi service. Call 24 hours in advance for reservations. From mid-May through September, **AmFac Parks & Resorts,** tel. (307) 344-7311, offers full-day bus tours of Yellowstone. Rates are $26 adults, $13 for ages 12-16, and free for kids under 12 (park entrance fees are extra). These are a bit exhausting, since you leave at 8:15 a.m. and don't get back till 6:15 p.m.

SILVER GATE AND COOKE CITY

A couple of miles after you exit Yellowstone's northeast corner along U.S. 212, the road widens slightly as it passes through two historic gold-mining towns: Silver Gate and the larger Cooke City (originally called Shoofly), Montana. The towns are just a couple miles apart and almost within spitting distance of the Wyoming line. The area code—406—for Silver Gate and Cooke City is larger than the combined population of both settlements! Although they also depend upon tourism, these relatively quiet, homespun places lack the hustle and bustle of West Yellowstone and have a more authentic *Northern Exposure* feel. Quite a few ex-hippies have moved in over the last few years. Most establishments are built of log, befitting the mining heritage, and evidence of the old mines abounds, including abandoned open pit mines that still leach acidic waste.

Both towns depend almost entirely on tourism and are crowded during the peak summer season. Cooke City now has legal slot-machine poker and keno gambling at All Seasons Hotel. Because the road is plowed all the way into Cooke City, this is a popular winter staging area for snowmobilers and skiers heading into the Beartooth Mountains. The Beartooth Highway across 10,947-foot Beartooth Pass is closed by the first of November (often earlier) and doesn't open again until June.

The country around both Silver Gate and Cooke City was torched in the Storm Creek Fire of 1988, leaving charred hills just a couple hundred feet to the north and prompting alterations in the road signs to read "Cooked City." Pilot and Index Peaks are the prominent rocky spires visible along the highway east of Cooke City. Dramatic Abiathar Peak juts out just south of Silver Gate.

Recreation
The **Absaroka-Beartooth Wilderness** is accessible from Cooke City or various other points to the east along the gorgeous Beartooth Highway. One of the more unusual sights is **Grasshopper Glacier,** eight miles north of Cooke City and four thousand feet higher. It's accessible by car and foot. The glacier contains the remains of a swarm of locusts that was apparently caught in a snowstorm while flying over the mountains. (See "Beartooth Mountains" under "Shoshone National Forest" in the Bighorn Basin chapter for more on this wilderness.)

Cooke City Bike Shack, tel. (406) 838-2412, is the center of outdoor activity for the adventure/greenie crowd, renting mountain bikes, tents, sleeping bags, and backpacks in the summer, and snowshoes Telemark and cross-country skis, transceivers, and other equipment in the winter. The store also offers summer bike tours and wintertime ski tours and lessons. Backcountry skiers and snowboarders can catch the store's snowcat ($12) for a five-mile ride up into the high country at Daisy Pass, gaining 2,100 feet of elevation along the way. This makes for a great day of skiing and a fun downhill run back to town. Pick up a map of groomed cross-country ski trails and snowmobile routes and call (406) 838-2341 for the latest on backcountry avalanche conditions before heading out. **All Seasons Inn and Casino,** in Cooke City, tel. (406) 838-2251, rents snowmobiles in the winter.

Beartooth Plateau Outfitters, tel. (406) 445-2293 or (800) 253-8545, offers horseback pack trips into the Absaroka-Beartooth Wilderness and sells fly-fishing tackle at its shop in Cooke City.

Accommodations and Camping
Cooke City and Silver Gate have quite a few old-fashioned cabins which provide a delightful Old West feeling; see the accommodations chart for specifics. As with other towns surrounding Yellowstone, advance reservations are always a good idea in mid-summer. The least-expensive option is **Yellowstone Yurt Hostel,** (800) 364-6242, where the lodging is cheap and unique. Nothing fancy here, but it's open summers (possibly longer), with bunks, hot showers, and a kitchen. Heading east from Cooke City, you'll find five Forest Service campgrounds ($5; open July through early Septem-

COOKE CITY AND SILVER GATE ACCOMMODATIONS

Note: Accommodations are listed from least to most expensive. Add a four percent tax to these rates.

Yellowstone Yurt Hostel; Cooke City; tel. (406) 838-2349 or (800) 364-6242; $10 pp; bunk accommodations in yurt, kitchen, open June-Sept.

Park View Cabins; Silver Gate; tel. (406) 838-2371; $30-32 s or d, $47-52 s or d with kitchenettes; attractive cabins, open May 15 through Sept.

Range Riders Lodge; Silver Gate; tel. (406) 838-2359; $35 s or d; upstairs rooms with bath down the hall, open Memorial Day to Labor Day

High Country Motel; Cooke City; tel. (406) 838-2272; $40-58 s or d; kitchenettes $10 extra, motel units and cabins

Big Moose Resort; three miles east of Cooke City; tel. (406) 838-2393; $40 s or d, $60 for up to seven; kitchenettes, open June-Sept.

Whispering Pines Lodge; Silver Gate; tel. (406) 838-2228; $42 s or d, $47 s or d in rustic creekside cabins with kitchenettes, open late May to mid-Sept.

Grizzly Lodges; Silver Gate; tel. (406) 838-2219; $45 s or d in motel rooms, kitchenettes $55 s or d, sauna, hot tub, open late May to Oct. and Christmas-New Year

Hoosier's Motel; Cooke City; tel. (406) 838-2241; $45-50 s or d; AAA-approved, open mid-May through October

Antler's Log Cabins; Cooke City; tel. (406) 838-2432; $45-55 s or d; cabins, some with kitchens and lofts, sauna, hot tub, open late May to Oct.

Alpine Motel; Cooke City; tel. (406) 838-2262; $50 s or d

Bearclaw Cabins; Cooke City; tel. (406) 838-2336; $52 s or d

Pine Edge Cabins; Silver Gate; tel. (406) 838-2222; $58 s or d; attractive log cabins with kitchenettes, open mid-May to mid-Oct.

All Seasons Mine Co. Hotel; Cooke City; tel. (406) 838-2251 or (800) 527-6462; $60-65 s or d; indoor pool, jacuzzi, video casino, AAA-approved

Pine Tree Cabins; Cooke City; tel. (406) 838-2213; $65 s or d; cabins with kitchens, full breakfast

Elk Horn Lodge; Cooke City; tel. (406) 838-2332; $65 for up to four people; cabins, kitchenettes

Beartooth Plateau Lodge; Cooke City; tel. (406) 445-2293 or (800) 253-8545; $75 for up to seven; kitchen

---

ber) within 10 miles. The closest—Soda Butte— is just a half-mile up the road.

Food

An old Cooke City favorite, **Joan and Bill's Restaurant,** tel. (406) 838-2280, serves family-style food, homemade pies, and enormous cinnamon rolls. Despite its popularity, you're likely to find better meals across the street at **Beartooth Cafe,** tel. (406) 838-2475, which serves good sandwiches, all-American dinners, and more than 130 kinds of beer. Also in Cooke City, **Pine Tree Cafe,** tel. (406) 838-2213, has reasonable prices, three meals a day, and locally famous milk shakes. Good pizza is available at Cooke City's **Miner's Saloon,** tel. (406) 838-2214. Over in Silver Gate, **Log Cabin Cafe,** tel. (406) 838-2367, is a consistent favorite, with trout, pasta, barbecued beef, steaks, and homemade soups. Get groceries, quality T-shirts, and gifts (including Indian jewelry and imported items from all over the globe) in the old red **Cooke**

City General Store, built in 1886, tel. (406) 838-2234 (open summers only). **Summit Provisions,** tel. (406) 838-2248, in Silver Gate, also has supplies. **Cooke City Bike Shack,** tel. (406) 838-2412, cranks out espresso.

Other Practicalities

Drinking appears to be the most popular local sport, but several local places occasionally have live music on weekends. The twin towns have a fun fireman's picnic and fireworks on the **4th of July.** Try **Miner's Saloon, Elkhorn Saloon,** or

Hoosiers for a start. You'll find a laundromat in Cooke City and local artwork at the **Blain Gallery.**

4x4 Stage, tel. (406) 388-6404 or (800) 517-8243, offers scheduled summertime service between Cooke City and Gardiner with connections to the park ($10) and onward to West Yellowstone and Bozeman. Call 24 hours in advance for reservations. **Hostel Express,** tel. (800) 364-6242, runs bus tours between the Bozeman Hostel and Yellowstone, overnighting in Cooke City.

BOB RACE

BIGHORN BASIN

Bighorn Basin is an enormous intermountain desertscape reaching almost 100 miles north to south and 50 miles east to west. Mountain ranges rim the basin—the Absarokas (pronounced "ab-SOR-kas") rise as a western border, the Owl Creek Mountains line the southern horizon, and the snowcapped Big Horns gleam in the east. The basin's rolling desert hills are topped with oil pumpjacks, and the wind blows incessantly. Cactus and sagebrush struggle up through a hardened surface of small rocks, and rugged badlands buttes rise above dry creekbeds. The countryside looks like southern Nevada.

Much of the basin gets less than 10 inches of precipitation per year—in some places just half that, and even in midwinter there isn't much snow on the ground. Three lazy rivers—Big Horn, Greybull, and Shoshone—create long green corridors through this desolation, offering an oasis in the dry desert country. Because of the lack of water, this was one of the last parts of Wyoming to be settled, and most of the towns did not spring up until the 1890s, when passage of the Carey Act brought a flood of irrigation speculators, investors, and farmers.

Canals have created wide swatches of irrigated green around the towns and along the rivers. Much of this water comes from the Buffalo Bill Reservoir just west of Cody and a series of canals supplying water to sugar beet and barley farms along the Big Horn and Greybull Rivers.

In the early part of this century boomtimes came to the basin with discoveries of oil and natural gas at Grass Creek and Byron. Along with cattle and sheep ranching (important since the 1880s), these industries still dominate the economy of Bighorn Basin. To most tourists, the basin (with the exception of Cody) is a place to get through on the way to Yellowstone or the Black Hills. Locals, however, call it a retirement haven and offer as proof the dry, sunny climate (more than 300 days of sun per year), relatively mild winters, cheap housing, low crime rate, and proximity to the recreational wonderlands of Yellowstone and the Absaroka and Big Horn Mountains. (In case you're confused, the word "Bighorn" is used for the national forest, canyon, and the basin, while "Big Horn" is the correct spelling for the river, the mountain range, the town, and the county.)

SHOSHONE NATIONAL FOREST

Shoshone National Forest encompasses 2.4 million acres and extends along a 180-mile strip from the Montana border to the Wind River Mountains. Sagebrush dominates at the lowest elevations, but as you climb, lodgepole, Douglas fir, Engelmann spruce, and subalpine fir cover the slopes. Above 10,000 feet, the land opens into alpine vegetation and barren rocky peaks. The supervisor's office is in Cody at 808 Meadowlark Ave., tel. (307) 527-6241; ranger stations are in Cody, Dubois, Powell, Meeteetse, and Lander. Forest maps ($3) are available at any of these.

More than half the forest lies inside wilderness boundaries; the Absaroka-Beartooth, North Absaroka, and Washakie Wilderness Areas cover much of the country east of Yellowstone National Park, while the Wind River Mountains contain the Fitzpatrick and Popo Agie Wildernesses. (See the "Wind River Mountains" sections of the Wind River Mountains Country chapter for more.) More than 1,500 miles of trails offer hiking and horseback access to much of this country. Shoshone has more than 50 campgrounds, most costing $7-9 per night during the summer. Once the water has been shut off for the winter months (generally Oct.-April), you can camp for free but will have to haul out your own trash. Space is generally available even at the busiest times of year. In addition, free dispersed camping is possible at undeveloped sites throughout the forest, with the exception of heavily traveled U.S. 14/16/20, where you must be a half mile off the road.

Though they are uncommon, black bears roam throughout the forest, and grizzlies are found within the northern portions, including the North Absaroka and Washakie Wilderness Areas. Be sure to take the necessary bear precautions anywhere in the backcountry. Bears also sometimes wander into campgrounds along U.S. 14/16/20 near Yellowstone National Park. Actually, you are more likely to encounter mosquitoes, deer flies, and horse flies in midsummer, so be sure to bring insect repellent.

History

Shoshone is America's oldest national forest. On March 30, 1891, President Benjamin Harrison signed a proclamation creating Yellowstone Timber Reserve adjacent to Yellowstone National Park. At first this title meant very little, but in 1902 President Theodore Roosevelt appointed rancher and artist A.A. Anderson to control grazing and logging and catch poachers. His strong management almost got him lynched. Three years later under Gifford Pinchot, the forest reserves were transferred to the Department of Agriculture and renamed national forests. Part of the credit for the surprising expanse of wilderness areas on the Shoshone goes to Buffalo Bill. By bringing people into the area to hunt, fish, and explore, he helped create what one author called a "dude's forest." In addition, the Buffalo Bill Dam (which he vociferously supported) prevented logs from being sent down the North Fork of the Shoshone River and thus made logging less important.

WAPITI VALLEY

Wapiti Valley provides one of the most popular and scenic routes into or out of Yellowstone National Park. President Theodore Roosevelt came here often and called it "the most scenic 50 miles in the U.S." Along the way are numerous lodges and resorts, private summer homes, Forest Service campgrounds, RV parks, and hiking trails. The fishing is great in the North Fork of the Shoshone River, which the road parallels for the entire 52 miles from Yellowstone to Cody. After Sylvan Pass, the highway drops through high forests and past an array of volcanic pinnacles and cliffs as the country becomes drier and more open. Cottonwoods line the gradually widening river, and Douglas firs intermix with sage, grass, and rock at lower elevations. Two wilderness areas—North Absaroka and Washakie (see below)—border the highway, and trailheads are scattered all along the valley. Many mountain resorts and dude ranches line the road between Yellowstone and Cody; most offer both food and lodging in rustic but scenic settings, and all have horseback

rides. Eleven different Forest Service camp-grounds ($8) provide more rustic living along the North Fork.

There's just one drawback to U.S. 14/16/20: it'll be undergoing a massive reconstruction until the year 2000, both inside Yellowstone and east of the entrance. Be ready for delays of up to 20 minutes outside the park and additional 30-minute delays inside Yellowstone. For the latest construction status, call the Cody Country Chamber of Commerce at (307) 587-2777.

Pahaska Tepee

Just 2.5 miles from Yellowstone's East Entrance, Pahaska Tepee was built around the turn of the century to house Buffalo Bill's guests and others on their way to the park. (Pahaska—pronounced "pa-HAZ-ka"—was Buffalo Bill's nickname, a Crow Indian word meaning "Long Hair.") Come winter, the road is not plowed beyond Pahas-ka, and the town becomes a very popular place to rent snowmobiles and cross-country skis for trips into Yellowstone. The ski center here has 12

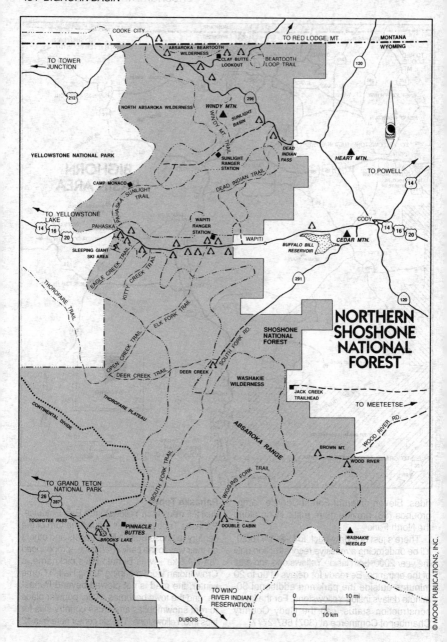

COOKE CITY

TO RED LODGE, MT

MONTANA
WYOMING

TO TOWER
JUNCTION

212

ABSAROKA - BEARTOOTH
WILDERNESS

CLAY BUTTE
LOOKOUT

BEARTOOTH
LOOP TRAIL

120

296

NORTH ABSAROKA WILDERNESS

WINDY MTN.

SUNLIGHT
BASIN

YELLOWSTONE NATIONAL PARK

SUNLIGHT
RANGER
STATION

DEAD
INDIAN
PASS

HEART MTN.

TO POWELL

14

CAMP MONACO

DEAD INDIAN TRAIL

TO YELLOWSTONE
LAKE

14
16
20

PAHASKA

SLEEPING GIANT
SKI AREA

WAPITI
RANGER
STATION

WAPITI

BUFFALO BILL
RESERVOIR

CODY

14 16
20

CEDAR MTN.

291

120

EAGLE CREEK TRAIL

KITTY CREEK TRAIL

ELK FORK TRAIL

SOUTH FORK RD

SHOSHONE
NATIONAL
FOREST

NORTHERN
SHOSHONE
NATIONAL
FOREST

THOROFARE TRAIL

OPEN CREEK TRAIL

DEER CREEK TRAIL

DEER CREEK

WASHAKIE
WILDERNESS

JACK CREEK
TRAILHEAD

CONTINENTAL DIVIDE

THOROFARE PLATEAU

TO MEETEETSE

WOOD RIVER RD

ABSAROKA
RANGE

BROWN MT.

WOOD RIVER

SOUTH FORK TRAIL

WIGGINS FORK TRAIL

WASHAKIE
NEEDLES

TO GRAND TETON
NATIONAL PARK

26
287

TOGWOTEE PASS

PINNACLE
BUTTES

BROOKS LAKE

DOUBLE CABIN

TO WIND
RIVER INDIAN
RESERVATION

DUBOIS

© MOON PUBLICATIONS, INC.

0   10 mi

0   10 km

WAPITI VALLEY LODGES AND GUEST RANCHES

These lodges and dude ranches are arranged by their distance from Cody on U.S. 14/16/20. (Subtract these numbers from 52 to determine the mileage from Yellowstone's East Entrance.) Most of these offer family style meals and barbecue cookouts (extra charge except for weekly stays) and along with fishing, hiking, and other outdoor recreation nearby. The lodges generally do not have TVs or phones in the rooms. Add a six precent tax to these rates. Area code is 307.

Pahaska Tepee Resort; tel. 527-7701 or (800) 628-7791; 50 miles west of Cody; $86-99 s or d in small rooms; $129 for up to four in cabins with kitchenettes; historic main lodge, jacuzzi, horseback rides and pack trips available, winter cross-country skiing and snowmobiling, open May-Oct. and Dec.-March, see rooms first

Shoshone Lodge; 48 miles west of Cody; tel. 587-4044; $58-64 s, $68-72 d; $80 s, $90 d for kitchenettes; classic lodge, modern log cabins, horseback rides and pack trips available, open mid-May through Oct.

Crossed Sabres Ranch; 43 miles west of Cody; tel. 587-3750; $900 per person/week for all-inclusive package; turn-of-the-century lodge, modernized cabins, jacuzzi, horseback rides, pack trips available, open late May through Sept.

Goff Creek Lodge; 41 miles west of Cody; tel. 587-3753 or (800) 859-3985; $90 s or d for deluxe log cabins; $95 d for lodging with three meals and horseback rides, pack trips available, open year-round, AAA approved

Elephant Head Lodge; tel. 587-3980; 40 miles west of Cody; $68-82 s or d; log cabins, horseback rides and pack trips available, open May-Sept., AAA approved

Absaroka Mountain Lodge; 40 miles west of Cody; tel. 587-3963; $49-70 s, $53-76 d; cabins, horseback rides and pack trips available, chuck wagon barbecues, open May-Nov., AAA approved

Blackwater Creek Ranch, 37 miles west of Cody; tel. 587-5201; $800 per person/week; log cabins with fireplaces, outdoor pool, jacuzzi, pool table, horseback rides and pack trips available, open June to mid-Sept.

Sweetwater Wilderness Lodge; 30 miles west of Cody; tel. 527-7817; $1,200 per person/week; guest ranch, horseback rides, winter snowmobiling

Cody's Ranch Resort; 25 miles west of Cody; tel. 587-6271; $85-105 s or d; $1,050 per person/week for all-inclusive stays; log cabins, jacuzzi, open year-round, horseback rides, wagon rides, and pack trips available, winter cross-country skiing and snowmobiling, AAA approved

Rimrock Dude Ranch; 25 miles west of Cody; tel. 587-3970; $1,000 per person/week all inclusive; classic old dude ranch, log cabins, horseback rides, pack trips available (white mules!), open late May-Sept.

Bretche Creek Ranch; 25 miles west of Cody; tel. 587-3844; $975 per person/week all inclusive; non-profit educational center and cattle ranch, lodging in rustic tent cabins, hot tub, horseback rides, cattle wrangling, no electricity, open June-Sept.

The Lodge at June Creek; 24 miles west of Cody; tel. 587-2143; $72-80 s or d; rustic log cabins, horseback rides and pack trips available, open year-round, AAA approved

Mountain View Lodge; 23 miles west of Cody; tel. 587-2081; $21 s, $25 d in motel rooms; $79 s or d in log cabins; kitchenettes, horseback rides available, open late May to early Sept.

Trail Inn; 23 miles west of Cody; tel. 587-3741; $56 s or d; rustic cabins with baths, horseback rides available, open May-Sept.

(continues on next page)

WAPITI VALLEY LODGES AND GUEST RANCHES
(continued)

Wise Choice Inn; 22 miles west of Cody; tel. 587-5004; $50 s or d; jacuzzi, horseback rides available, open mid-April to mid-Nov., AAA approved

Rand Creek Ranch; 20 miles west of Cody; tel. 527-4623; $66 s or d, $120 for up to six; modern log cabins, three-night minimum stay, horseback rides and pack trips available, open June-Sept.

Yellowstone Valley Inn; 18 miles west of Cody; tel. 587-3961 or (800) 234-2902; $37 s, $65 d; motel, outdoor pool, no phones in rooms, kitchenetes, horseback rides available, open May-Sept.

Wapiti Lodge; 18 miles west of Cody; tel. 587-6659; $35-70 s or d; cabins with kitchens, shared or private baths, open year-round

Elk Valley Inn; 18 miles west of Cody; tel. 587-4149; $39-69 s, $49-89 d; outdoor pool, paddle boats, kitchenettes, horseback rides available, open May-Sept.

Trout Creek Inn; 15 miles west of Cody; tel. 587-6288 or (800) 341-8000; $66 s, $70-75 d; motel rooms, outdoor pool, continental breakfast, kitchenettes, horseback rides available

Red Pole Ranch; 14 miles west of Cody; tel. 587-5929 or (800) 326-5928; $50-100 s or d; log cabins, kitchenettes, horseback rides and pack trips available, open July-Sept.

---

km of groomed ski trails over widely varied terrain. Buffalo Bill's original lodge is a two-story log building with many of the original furnishings, including an old buffalo skull over the stone fireplace. It's no longer used and is in need of repairs but is open for tours during the summer. On one of Buffalo Bill's many hunting treks with European royalty, he led the Prince of Monaco into the North Fork country. **Camp Monaco,** 15 miles up the Pahaska-Sunlight Trail from Pahaska Tepee, was named in his honor. Unfortunately, the old aspen tree inscribed with the words "Camp Monoco" was killed when the Clover-Mist Fire burned through here in 1988. (See the "Wapiti Valley Lodges and Guest Ranches" chart for a listing of other places to stay in the valley.)

Yellowstone Mountain Ski Area
This small family ski area, just four miles from Yellowstone's East Gate, has a chairlift and T-bar providing a vertical rise of 500 feet. The lifts run from November to early April and cost $18 for adults, $8 for kids. The ski area rents both Nordic and alpine skis. For more info, call (307) 587-4044. The **North Fork Nordic Trails,** tel. (307) 527-7701 or (800) 225-5996, begin at Yellowstone Mountain and cover 40 km of groomed cross-country ski trails, which continue to the edge of Yellowstone.

Down the Road
Below Yellowstone Mountain the road passes a whole series of delightfully weird volcanic rock formations. Signs point out several of the most obvious. Stop at a rock memorial to 15 firefighters who were killed in the Blackwater Fire of 1937. The picnic area here has a special pond for anglers with disabilities. Eight miles farther is the historic **Wapiti Ranger Station.** Built in 1903, it was the nation's first Forest Service ranger station. A summer-only **visitor center** has a short video on grizzlies. Three campgrounds are nearby.

Next up is a parking area at **Holy City,** an impressive group of dark red volcanic rocks with the Shoshone River cutting away at their base. Try to pick out Anvil Rock, Goose Rock, and Slipper Rock here. The highway leaves Shoshone National Forest and then passes the scattered settlement called **Wapiti**—an Indian word meaning "elk"—20 miles east of Cody. As you might guess, a large elk herd winters in this valley. An unusual volcanic rock ridge near here is locally called Chinese Wall. The eastern half of the road between Cody and Yellowstone passes the northern shore of Buffalo Bill Reservoir, cutting through three tunnels along the way.

BUFFALO BILL STATE PARK

Located six miles west of Cody on U.S. 14/16/20, **Buffalo Bill Reservoir** is a very popular place for local boaters and fishermen. Buffalo Bill State Park, tel. (307) 587-9227, encompasses the reservoir and includes a campground ($4; open May to mid-September). Entrance to the park is $3 for non-resident vehicles. An impressive **Buffalo Bill Dam visitor center** atop the dam has interesting historical displays and impressive views into the canyon that drops 350 feet below you. The center, tel. (307) 527-6076, is open daily 8 a.m.-8 p.m. May-Sept., closed the rest of the year. Be sure to take the time to walk across the dam. Fishing is good for rainbow, cutthroat, brown, and Mackinaw trout. The lake also offers some of the finest windsurfing conditions anywhere, with constant 30 mph winds; *Outside Magazine* once rated it among the country's 10 best spots. The water's cold—you'll need a wetsuit till mid-June.

History

In 1899, Buffalo Bill Cody acquired the rights to build canals and irrigate some 60,000 acres of land near the new town of Cody. With passage of the Reclamation Act of 1902, the project was taken over by the Reclamation Service and an enormous concrete-arch dam was added to provide water. The 328-foot-high dam was begun in 1904 and required five long years to finish. It cost nearly $1 million and when finally completed was the tallest dam in the world. Seven men died along the way—including a chief engineer—and the first two contractors were forced into bankruptcy as a result of bad weather, floods, engineering difficulties, and labor strife. A lack of sand and crushed gravel forced them to manufacture it from granite, and 200-pound boulders were hand-placed into the concrete to save having to crush more gravel.

Originally named Shoshone Dam, the impoundment was renamed in honor of Buffalo Bill in 1946. A hydroelectric plant and a 25-foot addition to the top were completed in 1993, bringing the total dam height to 353 feet and increasing water storage by 50 percent. The dam irrigates more than 93,000 downstream acres through the Shoshone Reclamation Project, making it one of the only Wyoming irrigation schemes that actually benefits the state's farmers to a large extent.

SUNLIGHT BASIN

The **Chief Joseph Scenic Highway** (State 296), is a 46-mile route through a magnificent Wyoming landscape. Popularly known as Sunlight Basin Road, it is now entirely paved and remains open year-round, providing access for backcountry skiers and snowmobilers to the beautiful Beartooth Pass area. The highway begins 17 miles north of Cody along State 120, with Heart Mountain prominent to the southeast, and climbs sharply up from the dry east side, passing a red butte en route to **Dead Indian Pass,** named for an incident during an 1878 fight between Bannocks and the U.S. Army. After the battle, Crow scouts found a wounded Bannock here and killed him, burying the body under a pile of rocks. Other tales claim that the name came from the body of an Indian propped up as a ruse to trick the Army during Chief Joseph's attempted escape to Canada in 1877. Chief Joseph *did* lead the Nez Percé through this country, avoiding the cavalry by heading up Clarks Fork Canyon, a route the

> *Winter looks like a fictional place, an elaborate simplicity, a Nabokovian invention of rarefied detail. Winds howl all night and day, pushing litters of storm fronts from the Beartooth to the Big Horn Mountains. When it lets up, the mountains disappear. The hayfield that runs east from my house ends in a curl of clouds that have fallen like sails luffing from sky to ground. Snow returns across the field to me, and the cows, dusted with white, look like snowcapped continents drifting.*
>
> —Gretel Ehrlich in
> The Solace of Open Spaces

Army had considered impassable. An overlook on top of Dead Indian Pass provides extraordinary panoramic vistas of the rugged mountains and valleys. The river forms a boundary between the volcanic Absarokas to the south and the granitic Beartooth Mountains to the north.

West of the overlook, the road switchbacks down hairpin turns into remote and beautiful Sunlight Basin. A gravel side road leads seven miles to **Sunlight Ranger Station,** built in 1936 by the CCC. This is some of the finest elk winter range anywhere and the home of a number of scenic old guest ranches. Back on the main road, a bridge (highest in Wyoming) spans deep, cliff-walled **Sunlight Gorge.** Sorry, no bungee jumping allowed. The highway then continues northwest past Cathedral Cliffs and through the scenic ranching and timbering valley of the Clarks Fork, offering views into the 1,200-foot-deep gorge. Part of the area burned by the 1988 Clover-Mist Fire is visible near Crandall Ranger Station. This area contains the only large herd of mountain goats in Wyoming. Eventually you reach the junction with U.S. 212, the Beartooth Highway (see "Beartooth Mountains" below for a description of this beautiful route).

Camping and Hiking

The Forest Service's Lake Creek, Hunter Peak, and Dead Indian Campgrounds (all $9 in the summer but open year-round) are found along Chief Joseph Scenic Highway. **Dead Indian Trail** (just uphill from free Dead Indian Campground, also open year-round) goes two miles to a fine overlook into Clarks Fork Canyon. Also of interest is **Windy Mountain Trail** which climbs 10,262-foot Windy Mountain. It starts from a trailhead four miles east of the Crandall Ranger Station (interesting old log buildings), is approximately seven miles one way, and gains 3,700 feet in elevation. Windy Mountain can also be climbed from the other side near the Sunlight Ranger Station. Trailheads into the North Absaroka Wilderness are at the Crandall Ranger Station and beyond the Little Sunlight Campground (free; open year-round) on Forest Road 101.

River Running

Clarks Fork of the Yellowstone River (named for William Clark, of the Lewis and Clark expe-

dition) is Wyoming's only designated Wild and Scenic River. Experienced kayakers will find a couple of great stretches of class IV-V whitewater in the upper Clarks Fork. However, use considerable caution—there are several big drops. Be sure to pull out before dangerous Box Canyon, which is considered unrunnable. Find more class IV waters farther down the river. Check with the Forest Service for specifics.

Guest Ranches

Seven D Ranch, 774 Sunlight Rd., tel. (307) 587-9885, is a family-oriented guest ranch offering horseback rides, cookouts, fly-fishing, hiking, and pack trips. The setting is spectacular—it's where some of the Marlboro ads are shot—and the cabins are comfortable and cozy. Open June-Sept. (adults only in September). Rates are $915-1,275 per person per week all inclusive.

K Bar Z Guest Ranch, 377 Crandall Rd., tel. (307) 587-4410, has nightly log cabin accommodations ($65 d) and weekly rates that include all meals and horseback rides ($650 per person). Pack trips, cookouts, and guided fishing trips are also offered, as are wintertime snowmobile rentals. The ranch has a sauna and hot tub and is open May-December.

Hunter Peak Ranch, tel. (307) 587-3711, is located on the banks of the Clarks Fork River, and offers lodging in rustic log cabins or motel-type rooms. Rates are $75 s or d per night or $375 s or d per week, with extra charges for meals, horseback rides, and pack trips. The main lodge was built from hand-hewn logs in 1917. Open May-December.

Other Services

Painter Estates RV Resort, 21 miles southeast of Cooke City on Chief Joseph Hwy., tel. (307) 527-5248, is open year-round. Not far away along the Clarks Fork River is **Cary Inn Restaurant,** tel. (307) 527-5510, serving three meals a day.

SOUTH FORK AREA

South Fork Road heads southwest from Cody and follows the South Fork of the Shoshone River for 42 miles to the edge of the Washakie

Wilderness (described below). It's a beautiful drive through definitive Western country with tree-covered mountains and the rich valley below.

Lodging

Several dude ranches and guest houses operate along the South Fork River. The **Flying T Ranch,** tel. (307) 587-2666 or 587-9019, a working cattle ranch 16 miles southwest of Cody, has a rustic log cabin (built in 1913) available. The cabin rents for $40 s or d, including a make-your-own breakfast; open May-October.

Located 17 miles southwest of Cody, **Hidden Valley Ranch,** tel. (307) 587-5090, is located 17 miles southwest of Cody and has an outdoor pool and jacuzzi and the standard trail rides, wagon train cookouts, and pack trips. Rates are $975 per person per week; open May-November. Very well run.

Castle Rock Ranch, tel. (307) 587-2076 or (800) 356-9965, also 17 miles southwest of Cody, offers an attractive central lodge with magnificent vistas from the tall windows. Guests stay in log cabins containing handmade furniture and woodstoves or fireplaces; facilities include an outdoor pool and a sauna. The ranch emphasizes not only horseback riding and fly-fishing but also less-traditional ranch activities like windsurfing, mountain biking, and even rock-climbing. Special kids' programs are offered. Rates are $805-1,200 per person per week; open June-September.

Diamond 88 Ranch, tel. (307) 587-3222, is a working buffalo ranch 19 miles southwest of Cody. Guests can rent a modern two-bedroom log home with a full kitchen for $100 s or d, $125 for up to five. Tours ($10 for adults, $5 for kids) of the 125-buffalo herd include a chance to see bison in an authentic setting. Sample buffalo meat, or watch hide tanning and skull cleaning demonstrations. (Sounds fascinating, but I'll pass).

The **Double Diamond X Ranch,** tel. (307) 527-6276 or (800) 833-7262, is a family-oriented dude ranch near the South Fork River 34 miles southwest of Cody. Guests take part in horseback rides, cookouts, square dances, and pack trips (extra charge). The facilities here include comfortable log cabins or lodge accommodations, an indoor pool and jacuzzi, and a tennis court. Rates are $965-1,460 per person per week all inclusive; open year-round.

BEARTOOTH MOUNTAINS

Spectacular Beartooth Scenic Byway (U.S. 212) connects Cooke City and Yellowstone National Park with the historic mining town of Red Lodge, Montana. Along the way, it passes through the Beartooth Mountains on a road built by the CCC in the 1930s. A small corner (23,750 acres out of a total of 945,334) of the **Absaroka-Beartooth Wilderness** lies in Wyoming north of the highway—the rest is right across the Montana border. Some have called this the most scenic route in America. If you like alpine country, hundreds of small lakes, and towering rocky spires, you're going to love this drive. Be sure to take a few casts for the brook, cutthroat, and rainbow trout in the lakes and streams.

The road sails across a high plateau and then over **Beartooth Pass,** 10,947 feet above sea level, the highest highway pass in Wyoming and one of the highest in America. As the road crosses into Montana, it passes Beartooth Mt. and begins a rapid elevator ride down folded ribbon curves into Red Lodge. On top, keep your eyes open for moose, mule deer, mountain goats, bighorn sheep, marmots, and pikas. Be ready for strange weather at this elevation, including snow at any time of year. The highway is closed with the first heavy snows (generally in September) and doesn't open till June.

Recreation

You'll find lots to see and do in the Beartooths. Majestic rock faces rise in all directions, the most obvious being Beartooth Mt., Pilot Peak, and Index Peak. Twenty-three miles east from Cooke City is the turnoff to an old fire lookout tower at **Clay Butte** (three miles off the main road). Although no longer used, the tower offers a chance to see even more of the surrounding countryside. There are four developed campgrounds ($9) along this stretch of State 212, and more once you drop into Montana. **Beartooth Lake** and **Island Lake** Campgrounds border alpine lakes with marvelous cross-country hiking opportunities all around but are only open from early July through Labor Day. (Be

sure to bring a compass, topo map, and warm clothes.) The trees are whitebark pine and Engelmann spruce. **Top-of-the-World Store** (gas, food, and limited accommodations) lies between the two campgrounds along the highway.

The **Beartooth High Lakes Trail**—actually a series of trails—connects Island Lake, Beartooth Lake, Beauty Lake, and many smaller alpine ponds and puddles. A good place to start is from the boat ramp at Island Lake; see topographic maps for specific routes. This is a very popular late-summer area for day-hiking or for access to the Beartooth Wilderness.

Beartooth Loop National Recreation Trail is a popular hiking path just two miles east of Beartooth Pass. This 15-mile loop traverses alpine tundra and passes several lakes and a century-old log stockade of unknown origins.

NORTH ABSAROKA WILDERNESS

The 350,488-acre North Absaroka Wilderness is one of the lesser-known wild places in Wyoming. The wilderness abuts Yellowstone National Park to the west and is bordered by the Sunlight Basin and Beartooth highways to the north and U.S. 14/16/20 to the south. North Absaroka Wilderness is primarily used by hunters who arrive on horseback. The few hikers tend to be quite experienced with backcountry travel and willing to tolerate the lack of trail signs and the steep and frequently washed-out paths. Much of the wilderness is relatively inaccessible, and snow may be present on passes until mid-July. Ask at the ranger stations for current trail conditions, and be sure to get topographic maps before heading out. Large populations of grizzly and black bears, bighorn sheep, moose, and elk are found in the Absaroka Mountains, and golden eagles are a common sight. The tough landscape is of volcanic origin, and the topsoil erodes easily, turning mountain creeks into churning rivers of mud after heavy summer rainstorms.

Hikes
The enormous 1988 Clover-Mist Fire that began in Yellowstone burned through a large portion of the North Absaroka Wilderness, so be prepared for blackened forests. Pick up a map of burned

areas from the Forest Service in Cody if you want to avoid these spots. Many hikers begin from trailheads near the Crandall Ranger Station along the Chief Joseph Scenic Highway. The **North Crandall Trail** is the most popular, a 16-mile hike up the North Fork of Crandall Creek. It is primarily used by horsepackers and offers great views of Hurricane Mesa along the way. Another popular wilderness path is **Pahaska-Sunlight Trail,** an 18-mile trek that begins at Pahaska Campground on U.S. 14/16/20 and heads north through historic Camp Monaco to Sunlight Basin.

WASHAKIE WILDERNESS

Covering 704,529 acres, Washakie Wilderness is one of the largest chunks of wild land in Wyoming. Named for Shoshone Chief Washakie, it lies between U.S. 14/16/20 (the road connecting Yellowstone and Cody) and U.S. 26/287 (Dubois area). To the west are Yellowstone National Park and Teton Wilderness. The Washakie is a land of deep narrow valleys, mountains of highly erodible volcanic material, and step-like buttes. The mountains—a few top 13,000 feet—are part of the Absaroka Range. About half of the land is forested. One of the unique features of Washakie Wilderness is a petrified forest, a reminder of the region's volcanic past.

Hikes
There are numerous trails through the Washakie Wilderness, but most require that you either return the same way or end at a location far from your starting point. Several trails stretch into Yellowstone National Park and are popular with extended horsepacking trips. The most popular Washakie Wilderness hikes are from U.S. 14/16/20 in Wapiti Valley. Most folks use them for short day-hikes or horseback rides rather than attempting longer backcountry treks.

Kitty Creek Trail leaves from the Kitty Creek summer home area, nine miles east of Yellowstone. Low-clearance vehicles will need to park along the highway. The trail follows the creek past two large scenic meadows to Flora Lake, 6.5 miles and 2,500 feet higher. This is the shortest hike in the area and one of the most popular.

The 21-mile-long **Elk Fork Trail** starts at Elk Fork Campground and crosses Elk Creek several times en route to remote Rampart Pass at nearly 11,000 feet. It is steep and rocky in the higher elevations. West of the Continental Divide you enter the Teton Wilderness. For the really ambitious, the Open Creek and Thorofare Trails continue on into Yellowstone National Park.

Deer Creek Trail departs from the free Deer Creek Campground, 42 miles southwest of Cody on State 291 (South Fork Road). The trail switchbacks very steeply uphill at first and after two miles reaches an attractive waterfall. Continue another eight miles from here to the Continental Divide and the Thorofare portion of the Teton Wilderness. This is probably the quickest route into this remote country and is popular with both horsepackers and hikers.

South Fork Trail takes off from the South Fork Guard Station across the creek from Deer Creek Campground. (Take a signed spur road to get there.) It climbs up along South Fork Creek to Shoshone Pass on the Continental Divide (9,858 feet). From here you can continue on a number of trails to the south, rambling over three more passes to eventually reach Double Cabin Campground, 27 miles north of Dubois. Another long hike into Washakie Wilderness leaves from this campground and follows the **Wiggins Fork Trail** up into a connecting series of paths: Absaroka, Nine Mile, East Fork, and Bug Creek Trails. It ends back at Double Cabin Campground. Total length is 60 miles. Along the way you're likely to see hundreds of elk in the high country as well as bighorn sheep. You won't see many other hikers.

CODY

The city of Cody (pop. 8,800) marks the transition point between the forested mountains of northwest Wyoming and the barren deserts of Bighorn Basin. It's a favorite stopping place for Yellowstone tourists. The park is just 52 miles due west, and other magnificent country spreads in all directions—the Beartooth Mountains and Sunlight Basin to the north, the Absaroka Range and Wapiti Valley to the west and south. Established as an agricultural and tourism center, Cody retains both roles today, though tourism seems to be gaining in importance with each passing year. The town is one of the few places in Wyoming that continued to grow through the 1980s; only Jackson Hole exceeds Cody as a tourism center. Not surprisingly, both are gateways to the national parks that dominate northwest Wyoming. Cody is also home to a number of medium-size companies, including oil, mining, and logging operations.

Cody itself has a number of attractions, including the justly famous Buffalo Bill Historical Center, Trail Town, and other local sights. The Shoshone River flows right through town, providing scenic float trips. Lots of events crowd the summer calendar, from nightly rodeos to parades and powwows; biggest of all is the annual Cody Stampede in July. The town also takes pride in a long list of artists that includes

Charles Cary Rumsey and Harry Jackson. Famed abstract expressionist Jackson Pollock was born here, but achieved his reputation in New York and never returned to his birthplace.

History
Just west of Cody are the Absaroka Mountains, named for the Native Americans who first lived here. They called themselves the Absaroka, or "Children of the Large Beaked Bird." Whites interpreted this as crow, and the natives have been called Crow Indians ever since. Explorer John Colter passed through this region in 1808 while recruiting Indians to supply beaver furs. When Colter returned to the semblance of civilization called Fort Manual Lisa, everyone laughed at his tales of a spectacular geothermal area along the "Stinkingwater River." Soon everyone was calling it "Colter's Hell." But the geysers were real; they still steam along the Shoshone (formerly the Stinkingwater) just west of present-day Cody. Other mountain men came later, followed by miners who found copper and sulfur in Sunlight Basin. The first real settler in the area was a Prussian, Otto Franc, who developed a large cattle spread at the famous Pitchfork Ranch. (Franc is said to have helped finance the Cattleman's Association during the Johnson County War.

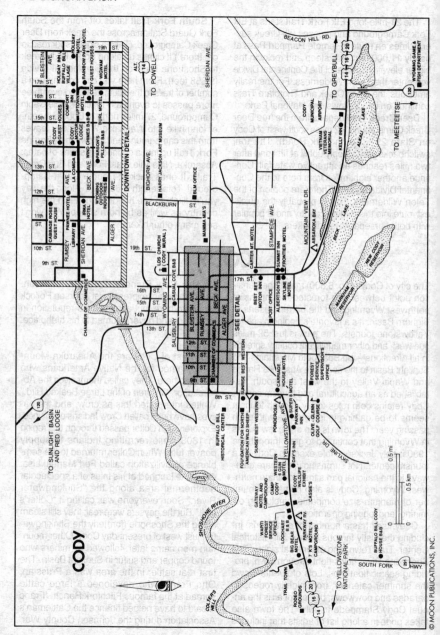

© MOON PUBLICATIONS, INC.

He was later murdered, and some blamed men affiliated with the homesteaders.)

In 1895, William F. "Buffalo Bill" Cody and two partners began plans for the Shoshone Land and Irrigation Company, with headquarters along the Shoshone River just west of the present city of Cody. Cody had spent much time in the Bighorn Basin, guiding parties of wealthy sportsmen and exploring the country, and was convinced that a combination of tourism and irrigated farming could transform this desert land. At the urging of Buffalo Bill, the Chicago, Burlington, & Quincy Railroad arrived in 1901, bringing in thousands of tourists who continued west up Shoshone Canyon to Yellowstone by stagecoach. Oil was first discovered near Cody in 1904, and Park County is now the second-largest oil producer in the state. Marathon Oil Company has its Rocky Mountain headquarters in Cody and is one of the town's largest employers. Also important are a wallboard manufacturing plant, a lumber mill, and a producer of ranch products.

BUFFALO BILL HISTORICAL CENTER

Each year, more than 300,000 people visit Cody's main attraction, the Buffalo Bill Historical Center. This is the largest and most impressive museum in Wyoming and the finest Western museum in the world. Author James Michener labeled it "one of the top four museums in America." The collection focuses on the Western frontier and includes thousands of artifacts and works of art spread through more than 237,000 square feet of space. The center actually houses four separate museums, a research library, the boyhood home of Buffalo Bill, and two sculpture gardens.

The original Buffalo Bill Museum opened in 1927 in what is now the chamber of commerce log cabin. Opening in 1959, the Whitney Gallery of Western Art formed a nucleus for the current museum location; later additions included the Buffalo Bill Museum, the Plains Indian Museum, and a new Cody Firearms Museum (completed in 1991). Other facilities at the Buffalo Bill Historical Center include a large gift shop and bookstore, a cafe, and a downstairs exhibition space. The **Harold McCracken Research Library** has thousands of historical photos and books, including more than 300 volumes about Buffalo Bill—mostly dime novels and comic books. Check the calendar of events at the historical center for activities ranging from historical talks to cowboy singing (also see "Events" below). Of note is the **Summer Institute in Western American Studies,** an in-depth two-week history course offered by the Historical Center during June.

The complex is open daily 7 a.m.-8 p.m. June-Aug.; daily 8 a.m.-8 p.m. in May and September, daily 8 a.m.-5 p.m. in October. April hours are Tues.-Sun. 8 a.m.-5 p.m., and in March and November hours are Tues.-Sun. 10 a.m.-3 p.m. The museum is closed Dec.-February. An admission pass costs $8 for adults, $6.50 for seniors, $4 for ages 13-21, and $2 for children ages 6-12. Children under six get in free. The admission is good for two days, so be sure to keep your receipt; it may well take you two days to really see this massive collection! Recorded audio tours are available for special exhibitions. Tours are generally offered only for school groups and VIPs, but the Historical Center often has summertime demonstrations, and the helpful docents can provide additional info. Call (307) 587-4771 or (800) 227-8483 for more on the museum.

Outside
Before heading inside, stop to view Buffalo Bill's **boyhood home,** a tiny yellow building built in 1841 by Isaac Cody. The house stood in LaClarie, Iowa, for almost a century. In 1933 it was sawn in half, loaded on two railcars, and hauled to Cody to be reassembled and refurbished. The house is on your left as you face the museum. Flanking the museum on the opposite side is **The Scout,** a dramatic, larger-than-life statue of larger-than-life Buffalo Bill. This huge bronze piece was created by New York sculptress Gertrude Vanderbilt Whitney and was unveiled in 1924. Her family later donated 40 acres of surrounding land to the Buffalo Bill Museum. Directly in front of the historical center are three colorfully painted **tepees,** a treat for kids. Once you enter the museum, ask for directions to the **Visitor's Lounge** where a 10-minute orientation video provides a fine introduction.

Buffalo Bill Museum

The Buffalo Bill Museum is a real joy. In it, the life of Buffalo Bill Cody is briefly sketched with all sorts of memorabilia from his Wild West Show including the famous Deadwood Stage, silver-laden saddles, enormous posters, furniture, guns, wagons, and clothing. Be sure to look for "Lucretia Borgia," the Springfield rifle that helped William Cody gain his nickname. Also here are some of the gifts given to Buffalo Bill by European heads of state (including a fur carriage robe from Czar Alexander II) and by Wild Bill Hickok and Sitting Bull. Original film footage from the Wild West Show runs continuously, offering a fascinating and sometimes unintentionally comical glimpse into the past. Amazingly choreographed marching soldiers, fake Indian battles, sign-language conversations, and bucking broncos make it easy to see how the Wild West Show could have inspired Western movies. Downstairs from the Buffalo Bill Museum are changing exhibits.

Whitney Gallery of Western Art

The Whitney Gallery contains a stunning collection of masterworks by such Western artists and sculptors as Charles Russell, Frederic Remington, Carl Bodmer, George Catlin, Thomas Moran, Albert Bierstadt, Alfred Jacob Miller, Edgar Paxson, N.C. Wyeth, and others. The studios of Frederic Remington and W.H.D. Koerner have been re-created, and Gertrude Vanderbilt Whitney's *The Scout* is visible from a large window on the north end. The collections of both "cowboy artist" Charles Russell and Frederic Remington—best known for his paintings of battles during the Indian wars—are the most complete here; the museum has more than a hundred of each man's paintings. Next to the Whitney Gallery is **Joseph Henry Sharp Garden** where you'll find the "Absarokee Hut" filled with the painter's paraphernalia.

The **Kriendler Gallery of Contemporary Western Art** is upstairs from the entrance to the Whitney Gallery, and contains a diverse collection of pieces, including several with a delightfully whimsical twist. Well worth the detour.

Cody Firearms Museum

The new Cody Firearms Museum contains one of the most comprehensive collections of Amer-

ican firearms in the world, including everything from 16th-century matchlocks to self-loading semi-automatic pistols. Start your visit by viewing "Lock, Stock, & Barrel," a 10-minute video program that describes the history of guns and how they work; it's interesting even for those who are not gun fanatics. In fact, the entire firearms collection is remarkably informative and well worth taking time to view.

The museum now contains more than 5,000 weapons, but these aren't just rows of guns in glass cases. Some of the more unusual weapons include a 10-shot repeating flintlock rifle made for the New York Militia around 1825 and a double-barrel knife-pistol. There are all sorts of displays to explore, including a colonial gun shop, a western stage station, a turn-of-the-century firearms factory, and a truly extraordinary collection of embellished arms. One of the most lavish is an intricately carved flintlock sporting carbine presented by Empress Elizabeth I of Russia to King Louis XV of France. The Boone and Crockett Club's collection of trophy animal heads is here, including an elephant-sized moose. All told, more implements of destruction than you're likely to see at a gathering of Montana milita members.

Plains Indian Museum

The largest exhibition space in the historical center encloses the Plains Indian Museum, with items from the Sioux, Cheyenne, Blackfeet, Crow, Arapaho, Shoshone, and Gros Ventre tribes. At first it may seem incongruous that a museum featuring the man once called the "youngest Indian slayer of the plains" should include so much about the culture of Indians, but Cody's later maturity forced him to the realization that Indians had been severely mistreated and that their culture was of great value. His Wild West Shows re-created some semblance of that lost society, if only for show. Some of the more important items here were given to Buffalo Bill by various Indian performers over the years, and the collection of artifacts is now one of the finest in America. Included are an extraordinary painted buffalo robe from 1890 which depicts the Battle of Little Big Horn, elaborately decorated baby carriers, ghost-dance dresses, leather garments, war bonnets, medicine pipes, and even a Pawnee grizzly claw necklace. The

moccasin collection fills an entire wall, and one room holds a Sioux camp as it might have appeared in the 1880s. Be sure to check out the exhibit on 10,000-year-old Mummy Cave, discovered in 1957.

OTHER SIGHTS

Trail Town
Point your horses toward the mountains and head 'em two miles west of town to a unique collection of historic buildings at Trail Town, tel. (307) 587-5302. The site is open daily 8 a.m.-7 p.m. mid-May to mid-September only; $3 entrance (free for kids under 12). This was the original location of "Cody City" in 1895. Trail Town is the creation of Bob and Terry Edgar. (In 1957 Bob Edgar discovered Mummy Cave— one of the most important archaeological finds in the West.) The Edgars bought the old Arland and Corbett trading post that had stood here since the 1880s and began dragging in other historic Wyoming cabins. Some were transported whole, others were disassembled and then put back together at Trail Town. Twenty-two buildings dating from 1879 to 1901 and 100 wagons are currently on the site.

For those who love history, Trail Town is an incredible treasure trove without the fancy gift shops and commercial junk that tag along with most such endeavors. This is the real thing, low-key and genuine. Probably the most famous building here is a cabin from the Hole-in-the-Wall country that Butch Cassidy and the Sundance Kid used as a rendezvous spot. Also at Trail Town is the oldest saloon from this part of Wyoming, complete with bullet holes in the door, and a cabin where Jim White—one of the most famous buffalo hunters—was murdered in 1879. The log home of Crow Indian scout Curley stands along main street too. (Curley was the only one of General Custer's command who escaped alive from the Battle of the Little Big Horn.) Inside the old Burlington Store are a black hearse, arrowheads, a cradleboard, and items from fur traders. The bodies of buffalo hunter Jim White, Belle Drewry ("The Woman in Blue"), and several other historic figures have been reinterred in a small graveyard at Trail Town. Most famous is **John "Liver Eating"**

Johnson, the mountain man portrayed by Robert Redford in the film *Jeremiah Johnson.* (Redford was here for the reburial in 1974.) A memorial to explorers John Colter and Jim Bridger stands near the graveyard. Trail Town provides a fine contrast to the glitzier Buffalo Bill Historical Center.

Irma Hotel
Pick up a copy of the **Cody Historic Walking Tour** ($1) brochure at the visitor center. It offers an informative introduction to local buildings and their history. One of the most interesting is the Irma Hotel, named for Buffalo Bill Cody's daughter. It was built in 1902 to house tourists arriving by train and was one of three way stations to Yellowstone built by Cody. It has long been one of the finest hotels in Wyoming. The luxurious saloon has a French-made $100,000 cherrywood bar given to Buffalo Bill by Queen Victoria. Many famous people have gathered here over the years.

Harry Jackson Studios
Harry Jackson's gallery at 602 Blackburn Ave., tel. (307) 587-5508, contains the works of this prolific and diverse artist. Born in Chicago in 1924, Jackson hitchhiked west at the age of 14 to become a cowboy. A harrowing stint in the Marines during WW II changed his life, leading him to become a painter. Upon his return home, he moved to New York where he became close friends with Jackson Pollock and Bill DeKooning. Harry Jackson's works have evolved over the years, covering the palette from abstract expressionist paintings, collages, and cubist studies to his more recent sculptures of traditional Old West figures—cowboys and Indians. His sculptures contain distinctively painted surfaces. The sculptures are his best-known works, including the monumental *Sacajawea* at the Buffalo Bill Historical Center and *Horseman* in Beverly Hills. Jackson's pieces have been exhibited throughout the U.S. and in Italy (where his works are cast). The studio is open Mon.-Fri. 10 a.m.-7 p.m. mid-June through September, and Mon.-Fri. 8 a.m.-5 p.m. the rest of the year. Sharon St. Clair leads excellent tours of the studio—with lots of fun stories—for $3 per person (family discounts available). Jackson himself divides his time between Cody and Italy. All bronzes

(but not his paintings) displayed here are for sale, but they're only for serious art patrons willing to spend thousands of dollars.

Other Art Galleries

The **Simpson Gallagher Gallery,** 1115 13th St., tel. (307) 587-4022, is one of the finest in Cody, with works that go well beyond the standard cliches. **The Jordan Gallery,** 1349 Sheridan Ave., tel. (307) 587-6689, is also worth a visit, with quality cowboy and Indian memorabilia and with rare books on the West. Of less interest but possibly worth a peek are two shops with predictable artworks: **Big Horn Gallery,** 1167 Sheridan Ave., tel. (307) 587-6762, and **Kilian Gallery,** 1361 Sheridan Ave., tel. (307) 527-5380. **Two Bears at the Irma,** 1192 Sheridan Ave., tel. (307) 587-9400, has Indian jewelry and kitschy jackalope mounts. **Shoshone River Pottery,** 1725 E. Sheridan (next to Buffalo Bill Village), offers a wide choice of pottery. Next to the chamber of commerce office at 836 Sheridan Ave. is the **Cody Country Art League,** tel. (307) 587-3597, with paintings, sculptures, and crafts for sale, plus workshops and judged art shows.

Et Cetera

The **Foundation for North American Wild Sheep** has its national headquarters at 720 Allen Ave., tel. (307) 527-6261 (just south of Buffalo Bill Historical Center). Open Mon.-Fri. 8 a.m.-5 p.m., the building isn't particularly interesting. A favorite of wealthy trophy hunters, this nonprofit group funds wild sheep research and conservation. The place is a bit bizarre, with oversized bronze rams and a recording that plays out front when nobody's around.

Cedar Mountain, the 7,889-foot-tall summit overlooking Cody from the west, is where Buffalo Bill had wanted to be buried. A winding 4WD trail climbs to the top, but there's no public access at present. Also here is **Spirit Mountain Cave,** one of the first national monuments ever designated (1909). A lack of interest caused the designation to be withdrawn, but the caverns are still on public land. Spelunkers can get permission to enter from the BLM office in Cody.

Southeast of Cody near Beck Lake is the **Wyoming Vietnam Veterans Memorial,** a black granite memorial modeled after the one in Washington. It contains the names of 137 Wyoming men who were killed or declared missing in action. The **Cody Wildlife Exhibit,** 433 Yellowstone Hwy., tel. (307) 587-2804, has a rather nice display of more than 400 mounted American and African wildlife—all sorts of record-sized critters, from a 17-foot-tall giraffe to a 2,800-pound buffalo. Admission costs $4 ($1 for kids under age seven). You might also want to check out **Old West Miniature Village and Museum,** 142 W. Yellowstone Ave., tel. (307) 587-5362. Entrance is $3; open daily 8 a.m.-10 p.m. May-Sept. and daily 10 a.m.-6 p.m. the rest of the year.

If you're really desperate for something to do, visit the **Cody Mural** on the domed ceiling of the LDS church at 1719 Wyoming Ave., tel. (307) 587-3290. Tours are available daily 8 a.m.-8 p.m. during the summer. No, it isn't the Sistine Chapel. The mural (painted in 1951) offers a rosy-tinted version of Mormon Church history.

ACCOMMODATIONS

Motels and Hotels

The tourist town of Cody is jam-packed with lodging facilities, but be ready to pay more than just about anyplace in Wyoming except Jackson Hole. Budget accommodations are nonexistent during the summer, though rates plummet with the first cold nights of fall. A youth hostel is definitely needed! Most of the year, lodging in Cody is not a problem as long as you check in before 4 p.m., but during July and August you should reserve a week ahead—and longer for the Cody Stampede (early July). See the "Cody Accommodations" chart for rates at the town's motels, hotels, and bed and breakfasts. Mountain lodges are listed in the section on Shoshone National Forest, and the chamber of commerce has a listing of more than 30 guest ranches in the area. Families may want to stay in one of the eight homes, cottages, and suites managed by **Cody Guest Houses,** tel. (307) 587-6000 or (800) 587-6560, including a beautiful three-bedroom Victorian home with a jacuzzi tub. Weekly rates are also available.

CODY ACCOMMODATIONS

Notes: Accommodations are listed from least to most expensive. Add a six percent tax to these rates. Area code is 307.

MOTELS AND GUEST HOUSES

Pawnee Hotel; 1032 12 St.; tel. 587-2239; $28 s, $32 d; refurbished old hotel

Best Bet Motor Inn; 1701 17th St.; tel. 587-9009; $33 s, $35 d; open June-Sept.

Gateway Motel and RV Park; 203 Yellowstone; tel. 587-2561; $35 s, $40 d; motel rooms and rustic cabins, no phones in rooms, open May-Sept.

Rainbow Park Motel; 1136 17th St.; tel. 587-6251 or (800) 341-8000; $39 s, $42 d; kitchenettes $10 extra, AAA approved

Holiday Motel; 1807 Sheridan Ave.; tel. 587-4258 or (800) 341-8000; $39 s, $42 d; AAA approved

Wigwam Motel; 1701 Alger Ave.; tel. 587-3861; $42 s or d; kitchenettes, on busy street

Uptown Motel; 1562 Sheridan Ave.; tel. 587-4245; $48 s, $52 d; kitchenettes $5 extra, comfortable rooms

Skyline Motor Inn; 1919 17th St.; tel. 587-4201 or (800) 843-8809; $48 s, $54 d; outdoor pool, AAA approved

Western 6 Gun Motel; 433 Yellowstone; tel. 587-4835; $50 s or d; kitchenettes, open May-Dec.

Carriage House Motel; 1816 8th St.; tel. 587-2572 or (800) 531-2572; $50 s or d; attractive 1920s cabins, no phones, open April.-Oct., AAA approved

Big Bear Motel; 139 W. Yellowstone (two miles west of Cody); tel. 587-3117 or (800) 325-7163; $52 s or d; outdoor pool, no phones in rooms, AAA approved

7 K's Motel; 232 Yellowstone; tel. 587-5890 or (800) 223-9204; $54 s or d; outdoor pool, no phones in rooms, kitchenettes, open mid-May to mid-Sept.

Carter Mountain Motel; 1701 Central Ave.; tel. 587-4295; $55 s or d; kitchenettes

Frontier Motel; US 14/16/20 E; tel. 527-7119; $56 s, $62 d; kitchenettes, open May-Sept.

Summit Inn; 1714 Stampede; tel. 587-4040; $59 s, $63; open June-Sept.

Irma Hotel; 1192 Sheridan Ave.; tel. 587-4221 or (800) 745-4762; $59-82 s, $65-88 d; motel and historic hotel rooms

Super 8 Motel; 730 Yellowstone; tel. 527-6214 or (800) 800-8000; $67 s or d

Kelly Inn; US 16 and 26th St. (one mile east of Cody); tel. 527-5505 or (800) 635-3559; $69 s, $82 d; sauna, jacuzzi, exercise room, AAA approved

Burl Inn; 1213 17th St.; tel. 587-2084 or (800) 388-2084; $70 s, $75 d; new motel, kitchenettes

Best Western Sunrise; 1407 8th St.; tel. 587-5566 or (800) 528-1234; $75 s, $75-89 d; outdoor pool, continental breakfast, open May-Oct.

Cody Motor Lodge; 1455 Sheridan Ave.; tel. 527-6291; $75 s, $79 d

Parkway Inn; 720 Yellowstone; tel. 587-4208; $75 s, $85 d; outdoor pool, nice place, open June-Sept.

Comfort Inn; 1601 Sheridan Ave.; tel. 587-5556 or (800) 527-5544; $75-119 s, $85-125 d; outdoor pool, continental breakfast, AAA approved

Buffalo Bill Village Resort; 1701 Sheridan Ave.; tel. 587-5544 or (800) 527-5544; $80 s or d; 1920s log cabins, outdoor pool, kitchenettes, open May-Sept., AAA approved

Days Inn; 524 Yellowstone Ave.; tel. 527-6604 or (800) 325-2525; $85-115 s, $95-125 d; new motel, indoor pool, jacuzzi, continental breakfast, AAA approved

(continues on next page)

CODY ACCOMMODATIONS
(continued)

Cabbage Rose Guest House; 1126 Bleistein Ave.; tel. 587-4984; $90-100 s or d; small historic home, two bedrooms, antiques, full kitchen

Holiday Inn; 1701 Sheridan Ave.; tel. 587-5555 or (800) 527-5544; $93-120 s, $99-126 d; outdoor pool, AAA approved

Cody Guest Houses; 1401 Rumsey Ave.; tel. 587-6000 or (800) 587-6560; $95-250 s or d; eight homes, cottages, and suites with kitchens, self-serve continental breakfast, AAA approved

Best Western Sunset; 1601 8th St.; tel. 587-4265 or (800) 624-2727; $97 s, $100-107 d; very nice motel, indoor and outdoor pools, jacuzzi, fitness facility, AAA approved

BED & BREAKFASTS

Casual Cove B&B; 1431 Salisbury; tel. 587-3622; $55-65 s or d; renovated 1908 home, three guest rooms, private baths, full breakfast, no kids under 12

Wind Chimes Cottage B&B; 1501 Beck Ave.; tel. 527-5310 or (800) 241-5310; $65-70 s or d in house; $130 for cottage (sleeps five); large house, period decor, four guest rooms, private baths, full breakfast, kids welcome

Rockwell Ranch B&B; 43 Juby Hill Rd. (five miles east of Cody); tel. 587-8223; $68 s, $75 d; newer log home on 60-acre ranch with horses, two guest rooms, shared bath, full breakfast, open May-Oct.

Parson's Pillow B&B; 1202 14th Ave.; tel. 587-2382 or (800) 377-2348; $80 s, $85 d; historic church building, furnished with antiques, four guest rooms, private baths, full breakfast, kids okay

Lockhart B&B Inn; 109 Yellowstone; tel. 587-6074 or (800) 587-8644; $82 s or d; seven guest rooms, full breakfast, see rooms before staying here

Buffalo Bill's Cody House B&B; 101 Robertson St. (two miles southwest of town); tel. 587-2528; $90 s or d; turn-of-the-century home of Buffalo Bill Cody, antique furnishings, four guest rooms, private baths, full breakfast, kids welcome, AAA approved

Bed and Breakfasts

Several historic buildings are now part of the Cody B&B scene, offering a taste of the genteel past. **Parson's Pillow B&B,** tel. (307) 587-2382 or (800) 377-2348, probably the most interesting, enjoys a good central location. Completed in 1902, this served for many years as an Episcopal Church. Today it's an attractive and well-maintained B&B with antique furnishings. Another friendly place is **Wind Chimes Cottage B&B,** tel. (307) 527-5310 or (800) 241-5310, with three guest rooms in the main house, plus a cottage for families. This is a nice place to stay, with filling country-style breakfasts and attractive rooms.

Buffalo Bill's Cody House B&B, tel. (307) 587-2528, was built for Buffalo Bill Cody at the turn of the century and is furnished with antiques. The building, a fairly simple two-story box with a big front porch and spacious grounds,

sits two miles out of town near Cedar Mountain. The **Lockhart B&B Inn,** tel. (307) 587-6074 or (800) 587-8604, includes what was once the home of novelist and flamboyant newspaper editor Caroline Lockhart (see the special topic). Unfortunately, it's really nothing special today and the facilities have received complaints.

Guest Ranches

The mountains around Cody are crowded with dude ranches and lodges. Twenty places west of town are listed in the "Wapiti Valley Lodges and Guest Ranches" chart. One of the most distinctive of these is the nonprofit **Bretche Creek Ranch,** tel. (307) 587-3844, offering classes in ecology, ornithology, photography, poetry, and other topics. Housing is very plain—canvas-roofed tent cabins—and the ranch lacks electricity, but guests can explore the 7,000-acre working cattle ranch and even help move cows.

BUFFALO BILL CODY

For many people today, the name "Buffalo Bill" brings to mind a man who helped slaughter the vast herds of wild bison that once filled the west. But William F. Cody cannot be so easily pigeonholed, for here was one of the most remarkable men of his or any other era—a man who almost single-handedly established the aura of the "Wild West." More than 800 books—many of them the dime-store novels that thrilled generations of youngsters—have been written about Cody. In many of these, the truth was stretched far beyond any semblance of reality, but the real life of William Cody contains so many adventures and plot twists that it seems hard to believe one person could have done so much.

Young Cody

Born to an Iowa farm family in 1846, William Cody started life as had many others of his era. His parents moved to Kansas when he was six, but his abolitionist father, Isaac Cody, soon became embroiled in arguments with the many slaveholders. While defending his views at a public meeting, Isaac Cody was stabbed in the back and fled for his life. When a mob learned of his father's whereabouts, the eight-year-old Will Cody rode on his first venture through enemy lines, galloping 35 miles to warn of the impending attack. Three years later, when Isaac Cody died of complications from the stabbing, 11-year-old Will Cody became the family's breadwinner. There were four other children to feed. Will quickly joined the company of Alexander Majors, running dispatches between his Army supply wagons and giving his $40 monthly wages to his mother. In Cody's autobiography he claimed to have killed his first Indian on this trip, an action that gave him the then-enviable title "youngest Indian slayer of the plains."

On his first long wagon trek west, the Army supply wagons were attacked by Mormon zealots who took all the weapons and horses, forcing Cody to walk much of the thousand miles back to his Kansas home. It was apparently on this walk that Cody met Wild Bill Hickok. At Wyoming's Fort Laramie, young Will sat in awe as famed scouts Jim Bridger and Kit Carson reminisced about their adventures. The experience was a turning point in Cody's life; he resolved to one day become a scout. Cody's next job offered excellent training: he became a rider for the Pony Express. At just 15 years of age he already was one of the finest riders in the West and a crack shot with a rifle. On one of his Pony Express rides Cody covered a total of 320 miles in just 21 hours and 40 minutes—the longest Pony Express ride ever. The Civil War had begun, and at age 18 Cody joined the Seventh Kansas Regiment, serving as a scout and spy for the Union Army.

After the Civil War, Will Cody tried his hand at the hotel business and then briefly joined Gen. George Custer as a scout before returning to Kansas to do a little land speculating along the route of the newly built railroad. He and a partner bought land and laid out a town they named Rome. For a short while it boomed, but when a man came to Rome and offered Cody the chance to own a small part of Cody's own town, he laughed at the offer, not knowing that the offer came from the president of the railroad's townsite company. Three days later the entire town of Rome—including all its buildings— moved east to a new location at a site selected by the railroad company. Cody had laughed at the wrong man.

Buffalo Hunter and Scout

In 1867, Cody found work hunting buffalo to supply fresh meat for the railroad construction crews, a job that soon made him famous as "Buffalo Bill" and paid a hefty $500 a month. With 75 million bison spread from northern Canada to Mexico, and herds so vast that they took many days to pass one point, it seemed impossible that they could ever be killed off. Cody was one of the best hunters in the West; in just eight months, he slaughtered 4,280 buffalo, often saving transportation by driving the herd toward the camp and dropping them within sight of the workers. Cody's name lives on in the jingle: "Buffalo Bill, Buffalo Bill; never missed and never will; always aims and shoots to kill; and the company pays his buffalo bill . . ."

After this stint, Cody finally got the job he wanted—chief scout for the U.S. Army in the West, a job packed with excitement and danger. Conflicts with Indians had reached a fever pitch as more and more whites moved into the last Indian strongholds. Cody worked as scout for Gen. Philip Sheridan, providing information on the Indians' movements, leading troops in pursuit of the warriors, and joining in the battles, including one in which he supposed-

(continues on next page)

BUFFALO BILL CODY
(continued)

ly killed Chief Tall Bull. His men considered Buffalo Bill good luck, since he managed to keep them out of ambushes.

During the Indian campaigns, the writer/preacher/scoundrel Ned Buntline began writing of Cody's exploits for various New York papers, giving Buffalo Bill his first taste of national acclaim. Soon Buntline had cranked out several romantic novels loosely based on Cody's adventures. America had a new national hero. European and Eastern gentry began asking Cody to guide them on buffalo hunts. On the trips, Cody referred to them as "dudes" and to his camps as "dude ranches"—perhaps the first time anyone had used the terms for such hunters. One of Wyoming's most unusual businesses had begun. Cody's incredible knowledge of the land and hunting impressed the men, but they were stunned to also discover in him a natural showman. In 1872, the Grand Duke Alexis of Russia came to the U.S. and was guided by Cody on a hunt that made national headlines and brought even more fame to the 26-year-old. On a trip to New York in 1872, Cody met Buntline again and watched a wildly distorted theater production called *Buffalo Bill*. Amazingly, Cody adjusted quickly to the new surroundings. Dressed in the finest silk clothes but with his long scout's hair under a Western hat, Cody suddenly entered the world of high society.

In a short while, Cody was on the stage himself, performing with Ned Buntline and fellow scout Texas Jack in a play called *Scouts of the Plains*. Although meant to be serious, the acting of all three proved so atrocious that the play had audiences rolling in the aisles with laughter. A New York reviewer called the play "so wonderfully bad it was almost good. The whole performance was so far aside of human experience, so wonderful in its daring feebleness, that no ordinary intellect is capable of comprehending it." Audiences packed the theaters for weeks on end. But Cody was suddenly called back west, for the Sioux were again on the warpath.

Shortly after Cody had returned to guide Gen. Eugene Carr's forces, they learned of the massacre of Custer's men at the Battle of the Little Big Horn. In revenge, Carr's men set out to pursue Indians along the border between Nebraska and Wyoming. Under Cody's guidance, they surprised a group of warriors at War Bonnet Creek. Cody shot the chief, Yellow Hand, and immediately scalped him, raising the scalp above his head with the cry "first scalp for Custer!" (Cody later claimed that he scalped the chief because he was wearing an American flag as a loincloth and had a lock of yellow hair from a white woman's scalp pinned to his clothing.) The Sioux immediately fled. If Cody had been famous before, this event propelled him to even more acclaim. It

Buffalo Bill with Indian children, 1913 (this photo was probably taken during the filming of The Indian Wars*)*

became the grist for countless dime-store novels and was embellished in so many ways over the years that the true story will never be known.

The Wild West Show

Buffalo Bill's days in the real Wild West were over, and he returned to staging shows, eventually starting his famed Wild West extravaganza. This was unlike anything ever done before—an outdoor circus that seemed to transport all who watched to the frontier. One newspaper remarked that Cody had "out-Barnumed Barnum." There were buffalo stampedes, cowboy bronc riding, Indian camps, a Deadwood stage and outlaws, crack shooting by Annie Oakley, and, of course, Buffalo Bill. At its peak in the late 1890s, the show made Cody more than a million dollars in profit each year.

Amazingly, Sitting Bull and Buffalo Bill became good friends. Cody, who had earlier bragged of his many Indian killings, changed his attitude, eventually saying, "In nine cases out of 10 when there is trouble between white men and Indians, it will be found that the white man is responsible." Cody's other attitudes also continued to evolve. He criticized the buffalo hidehunters of the 1870s and 1880s for their reckless slaughter and later became an ardent supporter of game preserves and limitations on hunting seasons.

The Wild West Show became one of the most popular events anywhere in America and Europe, attracting crowds of up to 40,000 people. Queen Victoria was a special fan (although rumors of an affair are probably false). At the peak of his fame around the turn of the century, Buffalo Bill was arguably the world's best-known man. Cody, however, continued to drink heavily. One day, an obviously drunken Buffalo Bill insisted that his cowboys ride Monarch, a massive and dangerous bison in the entourage. When they refused in front of thousands of spectators, Cody himself climbed on top and was immediately thrown to the ground. He spent the next two weeks in a hospital. For the next decade the show continued to tour but gradually lost its novelty as other forms of entertainment, especially movies, came along. Cody used his money to buy the 40,000-acre TE Ranch in northwestern Wyoming near Yellowstone National Park. For him the Bighorn Basin was paradise. The town that he helped establish here was named Cody in his honor, and he backed the massive Shoshone irrigation project.

A Sad Farewell

Unfortunately, Buffalo Bill seemed to have no comprehension of how to save his wealth. He was a notoriously soft touch and would give money to almost anyone who asked. As his fortune slipped away and his show became more dated, Cody was finally forced to join up with H.H. Tammen, the crooked owner of the Denver Post. Tammen used the aging Cody's fame to attract people to his own circus. He forced Cody's Wild West Show into bankruptcy in 1913, sold off all the incredible collection of historical artifacts that had been amassed over the years, and left workers to find their own way home. Buffalo Bill was heartbroken but, still trusting Tammen, agreed to join his circus almost as a sideshow act.

Three years later, Cody died while visiting his sister in Denver and was buried on Lookout Mountain near Denver. Cody had wanted to be buried on Cedar Mountain above the town of Cody, but even this wish was denied by Tammen, who apparently paid Cody's widow Louisa $10,000 for the privilege of choosing the burial site (and to use the funeral parade to the burial site as an advertisement for his circus troop). When rumors came that folks from Wyoming intended to dig up Cody's body and take it back to its rightful burial place, Tammen had tons of concrete dumped on top of the grave.

Despite the unhappy ending to Buffalo Bill's life, there are few individuals who lived such a diverse and adventure-filled life and who could count so many people as their friends, from the lowliest beggar to the richest king. Cody's life spanned one of the most remarkable eras in American history, and his impact on American culture is still felt today, not just in the image of the West that he created, which lives on in hundreds of Western movies, but also in the Boy Scouts (an organization inspired partly by his exploits), in the city of Cody, and even in the dude ranches that dot Wyoming.

Late in life, Cody was asked how he wanted to be remembered. He replied: "I don't want to die and have people say 'Oh, there goes another old showman.' When I die I want the people of Wyoming who are living on the land that has been made fertile by my work and expenditure to remember me. I would like people to say, 'This is the man who opened up Wyoming to the best of civilization.'"

Other guest ranches are described in the Sunlight Basin and South Fork sections.

Campgrounds and RV Parks

The closest public campground ($4) is 11 miles west in Buffalo Bill State Park. Find many more campgrounds ($8) in Shoshone National Forest, but the nearest is 28 miles west of town in Wapiti Valley.

You'll find eight private RV park/campgrounds in Cody. The best are: **Ponderosa Campground,** 1815 8th St., tel. (307) 587-9203, where tent sites are $12, RVs $21; open mid-April to mid-October; and **7 K's RV Park,** 232 Yellowstone Ave., tel. (307) 587-2532 or (800) 223-9204, where tent sites cost $12, RVs sites $20. Open mid-May to mid-September. Both of these have shade trees. **Cody KOA,** two miles east on U.S. 14/16/20, tel. (307) 587-2369 or (800) 562-8507, opened in 1964 as the first franchised KOA. Tent sites cost $18, RVs $25. Open May-Sept., with an outdoor pool and free pancake breakfasts. **Camp Cody,** 415 Yellowstone Ave., tel. (307) 587-9730 has RV hookups for $20 but no tent spaces. It's open year-round and has an outdoor pool.

Other park-it places are **Gateway Campground,** 203 Yellowstone Ave., tel. (307) 587-2561; **Parkway RV Campground** 132 W. Yellowstone, tel. (307) 527-5927; **River's View RV Park,** 109 W. Yellowstone Ave., tel. (307) 587-6074 or (800) 377-7255; and **Absaroka Bay RV Park,** U.S. 14/16/20 South, tel. (307) 527-7440 or (800) 557-7440. Absaroka's notable for a complete lack of shade; it's located on a windy hill to add to the fun. You can also park RVs at several of the Wapiti Valley lodges (see the chart), including Elk Valley Inn, tel. (307) 587-4140, Mountain View Lodge, tel. (307) 587-2081, Rand Creek Ranch, tel. (307) 527-4623, and Yellowstone Valley Inn, tel. (307) 587-3961 or (800) 234-2902. Noncampers can take showers for a fee at Gateway Campground, 7 K's, or Ponderosa Campground.

FOOD

Because Cody is a tourist town, it's no surprise to find many fine places to eat, covering the spectrum from buffalo burgers to Chinese won tons. Of course, Cody also has all the faves—Arby's, Taco John's, Subway, McDonald's, Taco Bell, and more.

Breakfast and Lunch

If you're just looking for a jolt to begin your day, plug in at **Caffe Espresso,** a popular basement hole-in-the-ground with lattes, pastries, pastas, and sandwiches. It sometimes has live guitar music and is located at 1272 Sheridan Ave., tel. (307) 527-4444. Another place to try is **Cody Coffee Company & Eatery,** 1702 Sheridan Ave., tel. (307) 527-7879.

A good breakfast and lunch place is **RJ's Cafe,** 148 W. Yellowstone, tel. (307) 527-4420. Big portions and reasonable prices, too. **Granny's,** 1550 Sheridan Ave., tel. (307) 587-4829, is not particularly noteworthy but stays open 24 hours a day and serves breakfast anytime.

Maxwell's, 937 Sheridan Ave., tel. (307) 527-7749, serves homemade lunches, including pizza, pasta, and salads. **Patsy Ann's Pastry & Ladle,** 1243 Beck Ave., tel. (307) 527-6297, creates very good sandwiches, homemade soups, and pastries (including great sticky buns). **Silver Dollar Bar & Grill,** 1313 Sheridan Ave., tel. (307) 587-3554, makes the best hamburgers and other cowboy grub in town, served in a Western atmosphere. Guaranteed to fill you up. **Pizza on the Run,** 1453 Sheridan Ave., tel. (307) 587-5550, sells hot slices for folks on the run.

Dinner

Proud Cut Saloon, 1227 Sheridan Ave., tel. (307) 587-7343, is a fine old-time Wyoming bar and restaurant offering unusual sandwiches at lunchtime and outstanding steak and prime rib for dinner. It's the real thing, with rustic Old West decor. **Irma Hotel,** 1192 Sheridan Ave., tel. (307) 587-4221, a long-time favorite of locals and visitors alike for lunch and dinner, offers a big salad bar. In existence since 1922, **Cassie's Supper Club,** 214 Yellowstone Ave., tel. (307) 527-5500, is famous locally for its steaks, prime rib, and shrimp. The Wednesday lunchtime Mexican specials are especially popular.

International Eats

You'll find outstanding Northern Italian cuisine at **Franca's,** 1374 Rumsey Ave., tel. (307) 587-5354. The menu changes through the week,

with a fixed-price dinner each evening ($20-30). Try the house specialty: Tortelloni Verdi al Mascarpone. Completely authentic, right down to the chef. Another upscale place with Italian lunches and dinners is **Mamma Mia,** 1905 E. Sheridan Ave., tel. (307) 587-5711. Prices are around $10-14 for dinner entrées.

La Comida, 1385 Sheridan Ave., tel. (307) 587-9556, serves very good Mexican food for reasonable prices. **Zapata's,** 325 W. Yellowstone Ave., tel. (307) 527-7181, offers food with a New Mexican flavor. For Chinese food, visit **Hong Kong Restaurant,** 1244 Sheridan Ave., tel. (307) 587-6420.

Grocers and Bakeries

Cody's grocers include an **IGA** at 1526 Rumsey, tel. (307) 587-6289, and a huge **Albertson's,** 1825 17th St., tel. (307) 527-7007. For natural foods and Wyoming-made gifts, head to **Whole Foods Trading Co.,** 1243 Rumsey, tel. (307) 587-3213.

Peter's Bakery, 1191 Sheridan Ave., tel. (307) 527-5040, bakes breads, cookies, bagels, and turnovers. It's a great place for sub sandwiches and soups. You won't want to go back to Subway after this; the bread they use is made from scratch, not pulled from the freezer.

EVENTS AND ENTERTAINMENT

Cody calls itself "Rodeo Capital of the World," and it packs the calendar with nightly summertime rodeos, plus the famous Cody Stampede. The rodeo grounds are a mile west of town on U.S. 14/16/20.

Cody Nite Rodeo

Almost everyone who passes through Cody between June and August makes sure to attend one of the evening rodeos. After more than 50 years of operation, the Cody Nite Rodeo is still one of the best in a state filled with rodeos. A favorite is always the calf scramble featuring kids from the stands. The best performances are on Friday and Saturday nights, when you'll see events sanctioned by the Professional Rodeo Cowboys Association (PRCA). The show begins at 8:30 p.m. Tickets cost $9 for adults and $4 for children; call (307) 587-5155 for ticket in-

formation. The **Cody Trolley Company,** tel. (307) 587-9327, operates buses between downtown Cody and the rodeo.

Cody Stampede

Independence Day sets the stage for Cody's main event, the Cody Stampede, held July 1-4. Established in 1922, the Stampede attracts thousands of visitors from all over the nation. Parade fans are treated to one each morning (including a kiddie parade), with dozens of marching bands, mountain men, vintage autos, floats, cowboys, and tons of free candy. Special PRCA rodeo performances, a street dance, art shows, running events, fireworks, and a carnival complete the schedule.

More Events

The **Cowboy Antiques and Collectibles Show** in mid-June offers the chance for collectors to purchase quality old cowboy gear. It's considered the finest such event in the nation. **Cowboy Songs and Range Ballads** is a unique Western musical festival held the second weekend of April. You'll hear true cowboy music (not country-western), poetry, and stories from cowboys, ranchers, and folklorists.

Frontier Festival, held in early June at the Buffalo Bill Historical Center, is a celebration of the many turn-of-the-century skills that were needed to survive on the frontier. Included are demonstrations of horsepacking, hide tanning, gunsmithing, rawhide braiding, weaving, and other homegrown talents. Various contests, musical performances, and booths make this an enjoyable and popular event.

Held in the Robbie Powwow Garden in front of the Buffalo Bill Historical Center in late June, the **Plains Indian Powwow** attracts several hundred participants from all over the Rockies and Canada vying for $10,000 in prize money. It includes daylong singing and dancing in tribal regalia and various dance competitions. Visitors can purchase Indian arts and crafts and taste Indian tacos and fry bread. Also in late June is the **Cody Old West Show and Auction,** where you can purchase antiques and other items from Wyoming's early years.

The **Yellowstone Jazz Festival** in mid-July attracts both regional and national jazz groups. The **Buffalo Bill Art Show & Sale** in mid-Sep-

tember is the biggest art event of the year. It features exhibitions, a symposium, receptions, and an auction.

Music and Entertainment

The downtown City Park bandshell is the place to be on Friday evenings during the summer; free musical performances start at 6 p.m. **Cassie's,** 214 Yellowstone Ave., tel. (307) 527-5500, offers Wednesday night country swing dance lessons and country-western and mellow rock tunes nightly throughout the summer. Hang around the bar long enough and you can join in that old Cassie's favorite, barroom brawling. **Angie's,** at the Silver Dollar Bar, 1313 Sheridan Ave., tel. (307) 587-3554, sometimes has rock bands and comedians. The big dance floor fills up on weekends. **Maggie's Supper Club,** 1901 Mountain View Rd. tel. (307) 527-5001, has Guinness and Harps on tap and dartboards.

Park Drive In, on the east end of Big Horn Dr., tel. (307) 587-2712, is one of the few drive-in theaters left in Wyoming. Open Thurs.-Sun. only. For the indoor version, head to **Cody Theatre,** 1171 Sheridan Ave., tel. (307) 587-2712.

RECREATION

River Rafting

One of the most popular summertime activities in Cody is floating the class I and II Shoshone River. Beware, however, that even with these mild conditions, you should plan on getting soaked in the rapids. Prices vary, depending upon trip length and whether it includes lunch, but expect to pay around $18 ($15 for kids) for a six-mile run (90 minutes) or $24 ($20 for kids) for a 13-mile (three-hour) float. For details, contact **Wyoming River Trips,** 1701 Sheridan Ave., tel. (307) 587-6661 or (800) 586-6661; **River Runners,** 1491 Sheridan Ave., tel. (307) 527-7238 or (800) 535-7238; **Cody Boys River Trips,** 720 Yellowstone (at the Parkway Inn), tel. (307) 587-4208; or **Red Canyon River Trip,** 1220 Sheridan Ave. (inside the Making Tracks store), tel. (307) 587-9496. Wyoming River Trips are the most experienced folks in Cody; they also offer inflatable kayak trips for those who want to run the rapids on their own power.

If you want to try rafting or kayaking on your own, you'll find several miles of very technical class IV water with some class V drops below the dam and above DeMaris Springs. Above the dam are stretches of class I and II water with good access from the main highway. Ask locally for flow conditions before heading out since snowmelt and dam releases can dramatically affect water levels. The rafting companies offer half-day whitewater trips down the North Fork above the reservoir for $40-45 per person. These trips only run late May through July, when the water level is high.

Most folks put in three miles west of Cody off Demaris Street. Just upstream from the put-in point is DeMaris Springs, a part of **"Colter's Hell"** (on private property and not open to the public). The area was once far more active, with hot springs bubbling out of the river and sulfurous smoke rising all around. People actually died from the poisonous gas. Today the geothermal activity has lessened, but the air still smells of sulfur and small hot springs color the cliff faces. Miners worked over nearby hillsides in search of sulfur; the diggings are still apparent. It's also pretty obvious why they first called this the Stinkingwater River.

Trail Rides

Horseback rides are available from **Gateway Motel and Campground,** 203 Yellowstone, tel. (307) 587-2561, and **Cedar Mountain Lodge,** 1192 Sheridan Ave., tel. (307) 587-2248. Many of the lodges in Wapiti Valley (see "Shoshone National Forest," above) also offer horseback rides as well as longer backcountry pack trips. The chamber of commerce office has a complete listing of more than 60 outfitters and guides in the Cody area.

More Recreation

Rent mountain bikes from **Olde Faithful Bicycle,** 1362 Sheridan Ave., tel. (307) 527-5110 or (800) 775-6023, which also offers mountain-bike tours. Swim at the **outdoor pool,** 1240 Beck Ave., tel. (307) 587-5254, or the **Stock Natorium,** 9th St. and Beck Avenue. The 18-hole **Olive-Glenn Golf and Country Club,** 802 Meadow Lane, tel. (307) 587-5688, is a PGA championship course. The club also has an indoor pool (tel. 307-587-5551) for lap swimming.

Outdoor Gear

For quality backcountry equipment—especially if you travel by horse—be sure to drop by **Wyoming Outdoor Industries,** 1231 13th St., tel. (307) 527-6449 or (800) 725-6853. You won't find Goretex jogbras here, just tough equipment for backcountry use, including folding woodstoves, pack saddles, bear-resistant panniers, and wall tents. They also have a mail-order catalog.

Sunlight Sports, 1251 Sheridan Ave., tel. (307) 587-9517, is the main outdoors shop in town, with tents, climbing equipment, clothes, topographic maps, and more. It also rents cross-country and downhill skis during the winter and is the place to go for details on ice climbing in the South Fork area.

OTHER PRACTICALITIES

Shopping

As you might expect from a tourist town, Cody has more than its share of shops dealing in clunky jewelry, crass T-shirts, and fake Indian trinkets, along with trendy boutiques and real estate offices. Fortunately, it's also home to a number of places with a bit more class.

Corral West Ranchwear, 1202 Sheridan Ave., tel. (307) 587-2122, has a large collection of big game heads and a couple of stuffed nine-foot-tall bears. Oh, yes, they also sell inexpensive Western wear. The **Branding Iron,** 1131 Sheridan Ave., tel. (307) 587-4582, is another good place to purchase shirts, boots, and hats that would make a cowboy proud. Get fancy Western duds at **Custom Cowboy Shop,** 1286 Sheridan Ave., tel. (307) 527-7300.

Cody Rodeo Company, 1291 Sheridan Ave., tel. (307) 587-5913, sells cowboy gear and rodeo memorabilia in a fun atmosphere. Decorations include a turn-of-the-century backbar from Hardin, Montana, and a **stuffed bull** that stood in front of the Irma Hotel for many years. Get your picture taken atop the bull for $6. Another fun place is **Crafty Quilter,** 1262 Sheridan Ave., tel. (307) 527-6305, which sells handmade quilts. **North Fork Anglers,** 1438 Sheridan Ave., tel. (307) 527-7274, has anything you might need for fly-fishing, including professional fishing guides and fly-tying clinics. You'll find

topo maps at **Cody Newsstand,** 1121 13th St., tel. (307) 587-2843.

Books

The **Park County Library** is at 1057 Sheridan Ave., tel. (307) 587-6204. New books are available at **Cody Newstand,** 1121 13th St., tel. (307) 587-2843, and **The Thistle,** 1243 Rumsey, tel. (307) 587-6635. **Wyoming Well Book Exchange and Oilfield Supply,** 1902 Sheridan Ave., tel. (307) 587-4249, is the oddest combination in town: bodice-buster novels and oil drilling equipment!

Information and Services

The **Cody Country Chamber of Commerce,** 836 Sheridan Ave., tel. (307) 587-2297, is open Mon.-Sat. 8 a.m.-7 p.m. and Sunday 10 a.m.-3 p.m. from Memorial Day to Labor Day, Mon.-Fri. 8 a.m.-5 p.m. the rest of the year. This log building housed the original Buffalo Bill Museum from 1927 to 1969 and was built as a replica of Cody's TE Ranch. It's on the National Register of Historic Places.

The BLM's **Cody Resources Office** is at 1002 Blackburn Ave., tel. (307) 587-2216. The Forest Service has two local offices: the **Shoshone National Forest Supervisor's Office** at 808 Meadowlark Ave., tel. (307) 527-6241, and the **Wapiti Ranger District Office** at 203 W. Yellowstone, tel. (307) 527-6921.

Get fast cash at **ATMs** scattered throughout Cody, including one inside the Buffalo Bill Historical Center and another in the Wal-Mart store. Watch out for extra charges on some machines—look for the warning notice. Wash clothes at **Skippy's Laundromat,** 728 Yellowstone Ave., tel. (307) 527-6001; **Eastgate Laundry,** 1813 17th St., tel. (307) 587-5355; and **Quick Coin-Op Laundromat,** 930 12th St., tel. (307) 587-6519.

Transportation

Yellowstone Regional Airport is just east of town on U.S. 14/16/20. **Skywest/Delta,** tel. (307) 587-9740 or (800) 221-1212, has year-round service to Salt Lake City, and **Mesa/United Express,** tel. (307) 527-6443 or (800) 241-6522, connects with Denver during the summer. **Spirit Mountain Aviation,** tel. (307) 587-6732, offers scenic flights and charter service.

Rent cars at the airport from **Avis,** (800) 331-1212, **Hertz,** tel. (800) 654-3131, **Rent-A-Wreck,** tel. (307) 587-4993 or (800) 535-1391, or **Farabee's 4x4 Rentals,** tel. (307) 587-6991.

Powder River Trailways, tel. (800) 442-3682, stops at Daylight Donuts, 1452 Sheridan Ave., with service to northern and eastern Wyoming and connections to other parts of America.

Tours

In the summer, daily lower-loop tours of Yellowstone National Park—$53 for adults, $25 for kids under 12—are available through **Powder River Transportation/Grub Steak Expeditions** at Buffalo Bill Village, 1701 Sheridan Ave., tel. (307) 527-6316, or (800) 527-6316. You can stay overnight in Yellowstone and return on a

later bus for no extra charge, transfer to Gray Line buses (tel. 307-733-4325 or 800-443-6133) to continue to Jackson, or catch the vans of 4x4 Stage (tel. 406-388-6404 or 800-517-8243) for Gardiner, West Yellowstone, Cooke City, and Bozeman. Powder River Transportation also has tours of Sunlight Basin, the Meeteetse area, Wapiti Valley, and the South Fork, plus multi-day trips to other destinations. **Wyoming Touring Adventures,** tel. (307) 587-5136, offers personalized automobile trips of Yellowstone, Sunlight Basin, and other areas around Cody.

SANTA (Shoshone Arapahoe Nations Transit Authority), tel. (800) 439-7118, offers on-demand bus connections to Riverton, Lander, Dubois, Jackson, Pinedale, Rock Springs (Greyhound connections), Rawlins, and Salt Lake City.

CODY VICINITY

See earlier in this chapter for Wapiti Valley, Buffalo Bill Reservoir, Sunlight Basin, and the wonderful mountain country west of Cody. For details on sights to the north, see *Montana Handbook,* by W.C. McRae and Judy Jewell (Moon Publications).

HEART MOUNTAIN

Halfway between Cody and Powell is Heart Mountain, so named because its twin summits faintly resemble the traditional valentine. The mountain is visible for many miles in all directions. Geologists scratch their heads over this seemingly upside-down mountain. The Heart Mountain detachment fault stretches for over a hundred miles, cutting southwest from near Cooke City, Montana. To the east are enormous blocks of land that have slid onto the top of more recent deposits, reversing the normal situation in which older rocks lie beneath more recent ones. Scientists know that these limestone and dolomite blocks moved around 45 to 50 million years ago, but none have been able to adequately explain how entire mountains, including Heart, could have slid for dozens of miles.

HEART MOUNTAIN RELOCATION CENTER

For Americans of Japanese ancestry, Heart Mountain might as well have been called Broken Heart Mountain. After the Japanese attack on Pearl Harbor in 1941, Japanese-

> *When my earthly trail is ended*
> *And my final bacon curled*
> *And the last great roundup's finished*
> *At the Home Ranch of the world*
> *I don't want no harps nor halos,*
> *Robes nor other dressed up things—*
> *Let me ride the starry ranges*
> *On a pinto hawse with wings!*
>
> *Just a-ridin, a-ridin'—*
> *Nothing I'd like half so well*
> *As a-roundin' up the sinners*
> *That have wandered out of hell,*
> *And a-ridin'*
>
> —Charles Badger Clark, Jr.

Heart Mountain Japanese relocation camp, circa 1940s

Americans found their patriotism under increasing suspicion, and the following spring President Roosevelt signed an executive order establishing the War Relocation Authority to move them away from the coasts. The authority built 10 remote "relocation centers" to imprison anyone of Japanese ancestry; one such center went up just east of Heart Mountain and housed 10,767 Japanese-Americans (two-thirds of them born in America). The camp became Wyoming's third-largest settlement. It took just 62 days to complete the 468 barracks, 40 laundry-toilet buildings, Buddhist and Christian churches, high school, fire station, recreation hall, power station, mess hall, hospital, sewage plant, administrative offices, and numerous other structures. (No environmental impact reports on this baby!) Barbed wire surrounded the perimeter, and military police manned nine guard towers with high-beam searchlights and machine guns.

Camp Life

Most of the Japanese-Americans took the forced relocation with remarkable aplomb, realizing the futility of any escape attempt. It almost seemed the patriotic thing to do; "shikata-ga-nai" ("I guess it cannot be helped") became the accepted phrase. Although life in the camp maintained a sense of normalcy—some kids came to enjoy their peaceful high-school years

and the picnics in Yellowstone—the camp was far from idyllic. Three or four people were jammed into each room, furniture was minimal, people had to share communal bathhouses, and the winter winds blew through the uninsulated tar paper buildings. Local folks resented the Japanese-Americans but appreciated the cheap farm labor that they provided while Wyoming's sons were off fighting the Germans and Japanese.

After the War

With the war's end in 1945, the camp was closed and the internees were given $25 and a one-way bus ticket home (or rather, to what remained; many found their homes ransacked). Over the next four years the 740 acres of land was opened to homesteading, and the barracks were sold two for $1. Most of the buildings ended up as temporary homes for the new settlers. None of the Japanese-American internees remained in the area, and most have little desire to even visit what seemed such a desolate, godforsaken place. They would rather try to forget. See Gretel Ehrlich's *Heart Mountain* for a fictional treatment of life inside the camp.

The Camp Today

Today the only reminders of the Heart Mountain Relocation Center are three buildings, the largest of which is the old hospital heating plant

with its tall brick chimney. A couple of plaques also mark the camp's site, one noting the more than 600 men who left Heart Mountain facility to join the U.S. Army in Europe. Twenty-one internees and a camp teacher died while fighting in Europe.

The site is 11 miles east of Cody on U.S. 14A. Barley fields now surround the former camp, while Heart Mountain stands guard over the western flank. The nonprofit **Heart Mountain Relocation Center Memorial Association,** Box 774, Ralston, WY 82440, works to preserve the memory of this painful era. Efforts are underway to preserve the remaining buildings and to eventually open a visitor center and museum.

EAST TO POWELL

The historic **Eagles Nest Stage Station** stands east of the relocation camp as you head toward Powell. The log cabins and barns were built a century ago by the Lanchbury family, which homesteaded here. Their ranch served as a stage station midway between Meeteetse (then the largest town in Bighorn Basin) and Red Lodge, Montana. Today, a fifth generation of the Lanchburys lives in the restored buildings of historic Eagles Nest. If you're looking for trivia, stop in the tiny settlement of **Ralston** to see the railroad bridge over a highway bridge, atop a creek. This odd collection made it into *Ripley's Believe It or Not!*

MEETEETSE

Along the western edge of Bighorn Basin is a charming little ranching center called Meeteetse (pop. 390). The name is a Crow Indian word meaning "Meeting Place of the Chiefs." The Absarokas rise gently to the south and west of Meeteetse, and the Greybull River flows right through town, cottonwood trees on either side. To the north, the highway crosses a rolling land of sage and greasewood, while to the south are rugged badlands. Meeteetse has wooden sidewalks and hitching rails, cattle drives right down Main Street, and not just one but three free museums.

History
One of the oldest towns in Bighorn Basin, Meeteetse was first settled in the early 1880s by homesteaders and wealthy European cattle barons. By 1890 it was the largest community in the basin. Several original buildings are still standing, including the impressively large **Meeteetse Mercantile,** built in 1899 and still stocked with everything you might need to survive. Imagine it as an early-day Wal-Mart. The last wild black-footed ferrets (see the special topic "Black-footed Ferrets" in the Southeast Wyoming chapter) were discovered just a dozen miles to the west at the famed Pitchfork Ranch. They were captured in 1987 after an outbreak of canine distemper threatened to kill all the remaining wild ferrets. Bronze ferret statues guard River-

side Park in town, but it may be quite a while before living ferrets return. As in other parts of Wyoming, Meeteetse is starting to undergo changes brought on by tourism and new residents, including a new golf course, an RV park, and a spiffed-up downtown.

Museums
Town Hall Museum, tel. (307) 868-2423, built in 1900, is filled with cowboy paraphernalia of all sorts and a nice collection of old china dolls and historic photographs. It's open Mon.-Sat. 10 a.m.-5 p.m. and Sunday 1-4 p.m. from mid-May to early September and by appointment at other times. The museum is the place to go for local info. Find more historical items at **Meeteetse Archives,** located in the old Hogg, Cheeseman, and MacDonald's Bank (1901). Hours here are Mon.-Fri. 10 a.m.-4 p.m. year-round.

The **Charles J. Belden Museum,** tel. (307) 868-2264, is open daily 9 a.m.-5 p.m. from Memorial Day to Labor Day (closed the rest of the year). Inside are hundreds of classic cowboy photographs that Charles Belden took at the 30,000-acre Pitchfork Ranch in the 1930s and '40s, along with a few Marlboro shots from the 1980s taken on the ranch. Well worth a look.

Accommodations
Oasis Motel, 1702 State St., tel. (307) 868-2551, has motel rooms for $25 s, $35 d; cabins

with kitchenettes for $35 s, $45 d; campsites for $9; and RV spots for $14. Open year-round. **Vision Quest Motel**, 2207 State St., tel. (307) 868-2512, charges $40 s, $45 d. Located kitty-corner from the Meeteese Archive, **Doc Bennett's B&B**, 2005 Warren St., tel. (307) 868-2486, is an attractive older home with three guest rooms for $75-100 s or d, including a full breakfast. Also in town, **Broken Spoke B&B**, 1947 State St., tel. (307) 868-2362, isn't a traditional B&B, but does have two simple rooms over the cafe of the same name for just $25 s, $35 d. Guests are served a full breakfast downstairs.

The Ranch at Meeteetse, tel. (307) 868-9266, offers dude ranch accommodations (three-day minimum stay) with horseback riding and fishing, an indoor pool, and a hot tub. It costs $700 per person per week all inclusive.

The 91,000-acre **High Island Guest Ranch** in Hamilton Dome, tel. (307) 867-2374, provides a chance to take part in cattle drives each spring and fall, May brandings, wilderness pack trips, and other cowpoke adventures on a working ranch in a gorgeous setting. This is the real thing, with dudes staying in canvas tents along the trail (bring your sleeping bag) and cabins or bunkhouses at the ranch. Visits are by the week only; open mid-May to mid-October.

Grub and Booze
Elkhorn Bar has the best local burgers and a meeting spot for local folks, especially on weekend evenings, when country bands play. **Outlaw Cafe** at the Cowboy Bar also has good pizzas and steaks and old photos from early-day Meeteetse. Be sure to ask the bartender at the Cowboy for the "true" origins of the word Meeteetse. More food can be had at **Lucille's Cafe**, tel. (307) 868-9909.

Other Practicalities
The **Forest Service District Office** is at 2044 State St., tel. (307) 868-2379. The town **swimming pool** is in the high school. The nine-hole **Antelope Ridge Golf Course** opens in 1997 with an adjacent RV park.

Come to Meeteetse on **Labor Day weekend** for a small-town parade, races, games, a country rodeo, a barbecue, a street dance, and crafts fair. Great fun.

MEETEETSE AREA

The excellent **Wood River Valley Ski Touring Park** (free) is 22 miles southwest of town on Wood River Road. Meeteetse Recreation District, tel. (307) 868-2603, runs the park and provides ski rentals in town. The cross-country ski area includes 25 km of groomed trails, wonderful mountain scenery, a warming hut, and a cabin with a woodstove for overnight stays (no charge, but reserve ahead). **Wood River Lodge**, tel. (307) 868-9211 or (800) 228-9211, has year-round accommodations nearby. Stay in modern rooms for $50-100 s or d.

The drive up Wood River Road is also enjoyable at other times of the year, providing the chance to see moose and elk in the bottomlands. Two free Forest Service **campgrounds** (open June-Nov.) are available near the end of the road. From here you can hike into the Washakie Wilderness along any of several different trails.

A 4WD road continues on to **Kirwin**, a gold and copper mining town that started in the 1880s and survived until the early 1960s. The abandoned town was given to the Forest Service in 1992 by the Mellon Foundation. It's a fascinating place to explore, with an old hotel, several cabins, and a mine shafthouse. Amelia Earhart was having a summer home built near here shortly before her 1934 disappearance during her around-the-world flight. The cabin was never finished.

Another historic place—**Palatte Ranch**—is at the end of a gravel road paralleling the Greybull River. The ranch was once owned by A.A. Anderson, first superintendent of the Yellowstone Timber Reserve (now Shoshone National Forest). The recently restored **Anderson Lodge**—a classic log home—is on the National Historic Register; check with the Forest Service office in Meeteetse for access.

Legend Rock Petroglyph Site
One of the finest sites for Indian rock art in all Wyoming lies between Meeteetse and Thermopolis in the foothills of the Owl Creek Mountains. Head 31 miles southeast of Meeteetse on State 120 (or 21 miles northwest of Thermopolis) and turn right at Hamilton Dome Road

(if you're coming from Thermopolis, turn left at the second Hamilton Dome turnoff). After five miles, turn right onto the gravel Cottonwood Creek Road. Continue two miles to the second cattle guard and follow the road a short distance to a parking area in front of a gate. The petroglyphs are a half-mile walk down from here. (If you want to drive down the hill, borrow the key from the Hot Springs State Park office in Thermopolis, tel. 307-864-2176.) The total distance from State 120 to the petroglyph site is eight miles.

At least 283 petroglyphs have been found on the nearby sandstone cliffs in a variety of styles. There are deer, bison, elk, various human figures, and even a "flying" rabbit. Owl Creek flows not far away, and oil pumpjacks dot the nearby hills (Hamilton Dome is one of the most impor-

tant oil fields in Bighorn Basin). The rock art is believed to have been associated with shamanism and ritual healing and may date back for 2,000 years.

West of Legend Rock is **Anchor Dam,** a major engineering blunder. The dam has never held much water, despite repeated attempts to seal the lake bottom at a cost of millions of dollars; the water simply seeps into the porous limestone beneath.

Northwest of Meeteetse is another important Indian site, the **Great Arrow,** a 58-foot-long arrow made from rocks and placed atop a long hogback ridge. Of unknown age, the arrow points toward the Medicine Wheel in the Big Horn Mountains 70 miles to the northeast. (See "Big Horn Mountains" in the Powder River Country chapter for more on Medicine Wheel.)

POWELL

One of the most pleasant settlements in Bighorn Basin is Powell (pop. 5,700), a clean and prosperous farming, oil, and college town halfway between Cody and Lovell. Declared an All-America City in 1994, Powell sits at the center of a rich farming region where sugar beets, dry beans, and malting barley (grown for Coors and Anheuser-Busch) are raised. Because these crops are harvested at different times of the year, many farmers grow all three. The big elevators of Powell Bean Growers Association and Baker Bean & Feed border the railroad tracks on the south edge of town. A dozen miles to the north is the giant Elk Basin oil field. First discovered in 1915, it had 150 wells pumping more than 4,200 barrels a day within five years. The field has proven a major factor in the growth of the northern Bighorn Basin, though production is gradually declining as the supply is exhausted.

HISTORY

Powell was named for Maj. John Wesley Powell (1834-1902), the famed one-armed explorer of the Colorado River and an early director of the U.S. Geological Survey. His 1889 report on the agricultural potential of Western desert lands had asserted the value of irrigation in "reclaim-

ing" these areas and proposed a system of dams and canals funded by the government. One of the earliest of these was the mammoth Shoshone Project, involving Buffalo Bill Dam and a series of canals to feed water to the fields along the Shoshone River. Powell is right at the center of all this irrigation, and homesteaders flocked here in the first two decades of this century. The town sprang up at a campsite used by workers on the Shoshone Project. With the arrival of the Chicago, Burlington and Quincy Railroad (now Burlington Northern), Powell became an agricultural shipping point.

Earl Durand

Folks still talk about "Tarzan of the Tetons," a local kid gone bad. Earl Durand was a crack shot and a mountain man of sorts. He had once traveled by horse and foot to Mexico, and bragged that he could survive on practically anything, even raw bobcat meat. Durand hated being cooped up inside buildings, so when he was arrested for poaching in 1939, he escaped the Cody jail. Five people died in the shooting rampage that followed, and the murders attracted intense national attention. The climax came when Durand robbed a Powell bank and suddenly found himself surrounded. A 17-year-old kid shot—but didn't kill—Durand as he

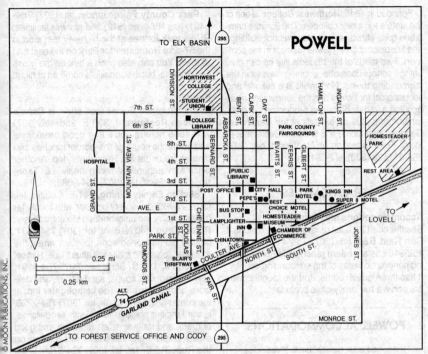

came out of the bank with a screen of hostages. Sensing the futility of the situation, Durand went back inside and committed suicide. Powell's Homesteader Museum has lots of old newspaper clippings on this sad story, and the incident inspired *The Legend of Earl Durand,* a minor 1974 movie starring Slim Pickens, Peter Haskell, and Martin Sheen. The story still touches raw nerves in Powell—almost 60 years later—with old-timers complaining of the strident news reports that cast such a negative light on local people.

SIGHTS

The free **Homesteader Museum,** on the corner of 1st and Clark Streets, tel. (307) 754-9481, is open Tues.-Fri. 1-5 p.m. May-Sept. and Friday and Saturday 10 a.m.-noon and 1-5 p.m. the rest of the year. The museum captures the hardscrabble life of turn-of-the-century

homesteaders in the northern Bighorn Basin. You'll find interesting old photographs, a beautiful collection of dryhead agate, some Indian artifacts, a century-old porcelain doll, and a German grandfather clock, chairs, and bench covered with carved bears. There's lots more junk to check out, but be sure to take the time to watch the videotape detailing the history of the nearby Heart Mountain Relocation Center (see "Cody Vicinity" earlier in this chapter). An adjacent building is filled with horse-drawn machines and old tractors, while outside are a caboose and various pieces of old farm equipment.

The chamber of commerce offers tours of the farms and ranches around Powell, providing a good way to learn about irrigation systems, dairy farms, feed lots, sheep breeding, and crop production. These unusual tours cost $33 for a half-day, $53 for all day, including transportation, a guide, and lunch. Call (307) 754-3483 or (800) 325-4278 for advance reservations.

Founded in 1946, **Northwest College** is one of the state's top junior colleges. The 95-acre campus is quite attractive, with modern brick buildings and fluorescent green lawns (at least in the summer). Two-thirds of the students live on campus, but the school does offer evening classes in the surrounding towns. Northwest is a cultural and social center for Powell and the surrounding area, bringing a variety of theater productions and entertainment, plus art exhibits at the **Northwest Gallery** (open Mon.-Fri. 8 to 5 from September to May). For information on Northwest, call (307) 754-6111 or (800) 442-2946.

PRACTICALITIES

Accommodations and Camping
See the chart for a list of local lodging options. **I Can Rest B&B** tel. (307) 754-4178 or (800) 452-9462, is a modern ranch-style home offering panoramic vistas of the surrounding country. It has three guest rooms, and the friendly owners serve a full family-style breakfast.

POWELL ACCOMMODATIONS

Note: Add a six percent tax to these rates. Area code is 307.

Best Choice Motel; 337 E. 2nd St.; tel. 754-2243; $35-55 s or d; open Feb.-Oct.

Best Western King's Inn; 777 E. 2nd St.; tel. 754-5117 or (800) 528-1234; $63-73 s or d; outdoor pool, steam baths, AAA approved

Lamplighter Inn; 234 1st St.; tel. 754-2226; $46 s or d

Park Motel; 737 E. 2nd St.; tel. 754-2233; $45 s, $55 d; kitchenettes $65 d

Super 8 Motel; 845 E. Coulter; tel. 754-7231 or (800) 800-8000; $53 s or d, AAA approved

I Can Rest B&B; 1041 Lane 11 (two miles southwest of Powell); tel. 754-4178 or (800) 452-9462; $50-70 s or d; $105 s or d for suite with jacuzzi tub; panoramic views, four guest rooms, shared or private bath, full breakfast, no kids

---

Park County Fairgrounds, tel. (307) 754-5421, has RV sites ($12) and shower facilities. RVers park for free at the highway rest area in the 57-acre **Homesteader Park** on the east end of town. You can also pitch a tent on the grass here for free, but the sprinklers come on at night.

Food
At the top of the Powell food chain is **Pepe's Mexican Restaurant,** 333 E. 2nd, tel. (307) 754-4665, where you'll find good breakfasts and authentic south-of-the-border lunches and dinners for under $6. Recommended. Another place with authentic Mexican meals is **El Tapatio,** 112 N. Bent, tel. (307) 754-8085.

Skyline Family Dining, 141 E. Coulter, tel. (307) 754-2772, is very popular with locals for breakfast. Try the chicken-fried steak for dinner. **Powell Drug,** 140 N. Bent, tel. (307) 754-2031, has an old-fashioned soda fountain where the root beer floats and malts still attract kids. **Hansel & Gretel's,** 113 S. Bent, tel. (307) 754-2191, serves spaghetti, soups, sandwiches, and delicious homemade pies. The **Lamplighter Inn,** at the corner of 1st and Clark, tel. (307) 754-2226, is the fanciest place in town, with sandwiches, burgers, and daily specials for lunch and good steaks, chicken, and seafood for dinner. **Pizza on the Run,** 215 E. 1st, tel. (307) 754-5720, is the local pizza joint, and **Chinatown,** 151 E. Coulter, tel. (307) 754-7924, has Chinese to eat in or take out. Easily the least-expensive meal deal in Powell is the **Student Union Cafeteria** on the Northwest College campus.

For sweets, head to **Powell Bakery,** 242 N. Bent St., tel. (307) 754-2971, or **Linda's Sandwich and Ice Cream Shoppe,** 121 N. Bent St., tel. (307) 754-9553. **Raven's Wing Gallery,** 109 N. Bent, tel. (307) 754-9830, is Powell's espresso shop, with Western art on the walls, the smell of coffee in the air, and—occasionally—poetry coming from the stage. Get groceries at **Blairs Market,** 311 W. Coulter Ave., tel. (307) 754-3122, or **Food Basket IGA,** 421 N. 1st, tel. (307) 754-3602. Blairs features a good deli and bakery.

Entertainment
Since this is a college town, you can always find live music on weekends. Try **Bent Street Station,** 117 S. Bent, tel. (307) 754-3384, for

rock or country tunes. **American Legion** on E. 1st, tel. (307) 754-3411, sometimes has bands. Northwest College's **Pub,** in the Student Union Building, is a popular student hangout before 10 p.m. **Time Out Lounge** has live country-western music some nights and sports on the TVs most of the time. For movies, drop by **Vali Cinema,** 204 N. Bent St., tel. (307) 754-4211, or, for the outdoor version, **Vali Drive-In Theatre,** 1070 Rd. 9, tel. (307) 754-5133.

Events
In early June the **Tour of Heart Mountain** bike race circles the mountain in a 100-mile marathon. It's followed by a popular **Foxtrotter Horse Show and Sale** on Father's Day weekend. The last full week of July brings the **Park County Fair,** with parades, horseshoe pitching contests, 4-H shows, a demolition derby, tractor pulls, a horse pull, dancing, headline acts, and a carnival. All summer long, **stock car races** take place every other Saturday afternoon at the fairgrounds and always attract a big crowd. The end of summer is marked by **Happy Days Celebration** in early September, with live music, a street dance, food booths, a quilt show, an antique car show, and games. **Sheepman's Holiday** in mid-October features sheep events of all sorts, including sheepdog trials. If you happen to be in the area in early December, stop by for **Country Christmas,** a three-day festivity with activities and craft exhibits as well as a live nativity scene.

Recreation
Attractive **Homesteader Park** has a number of modern recreation facilities, including a kids'll-love-it green frog slide at the wading pool. In winter, there is a free ice arena here with skate rentals and a warming hut. The public **swimming pool** ($1.25) is in the high school. The 18-hole **Powell Country Club** is five miles east of Powell, tel. (307) 754-3039. **Classic Lanes,** 162 N. Clark, tel. (307) 754-2422, is the local bowling alley.

Heart Mountain Land & Cattle Adventures, tel. (307) 754-4320, has five-day cowboy adventures throughout the summer, giving dudes the chance to drive cattle, brand calves, camp in the mountains, and eat at a real chuck wagon. Trips cost $200 per person per day (less in May).

Shopping
Mountain Man Moccasin Co., 265 N. Bent (downstairs from Powell Office Supply), tel. (307) 754-9779 or (800) 734-9779, makes high-quality leather moccasins from deerskin or elk leather. Powell Office Supply is at the same address and sells books and topographic maps. More books are for sale at the **Northwest College Bookstore,** tel. (307) 754-6308. **Paper Trail Books,** tel. (307) 754-5346, has a small basement shop at 207 N. Bent St., with new and used titles.

Get camping and hiking supplies at **War Surplus** (there always seems to be a surplus of wars, so you might as well buy a couple while you're in town), 130 N. Bent, tel. (307) 754-2694.

Information and Services
The **Powell Valley Chamber of Commerce,** 111 S. Day, tel. (307) 754-3494 or (outside Wyoming) (800) 325-4278, is open Mon.-Fri. 8 a.m.-5 p.m. Relax with a book at the modern **Powell Public Library,** 217 E. 3rd, tel. (307) 754-2261, or the **John Hinkley Memorial Library** on the Northwest College campus, tel. (307) 754-6207. (No, it isn't named for the man who shot President Reagan.) The **Shoshone National Forest District Office** is 2.5 miles west of town, tel. (307) 754-2407. Open Mon.-Fri. 8 a.m.-4:30 p.m. **ATMs** are located inside the Food Basket IGA and Blairs grocery stores; Key Bank, 105 E. 2nd St.; and First National Bank of Powell, 245 E. 1st Street.

Powder River Trailways, tel. (307) 754-3914 or (800) 442-3682, stops at Accents & Accessories, 127 N. Bent St., with daily service throughout northern and eastern Wyoming, and connections to other parts of America.

EAST TO LOVELL

A tangle of roads wanders through the country between Lovell and Powell, tying together a cluster of agriculture and oil settlements established by Mormon emigrants. **Cowley** (pop. 530) has a number of impressive old sandstone buildings. You can find Ancient Indian petroglyphs north of town in Blue Wash. The Cowley rodeo arrives in July. **Byron** (pop. 530) has quite a

few old log buildings and is surrounded by dairy farms. Check out the "roadkill" burger (with three patties) at **Half Fast Diner.** Just two miles south of the Montana border on U.S. 310, **Frannie** (pop. 150) straddles the line between Park and Big Horn Counties. Residents say it's "The Biggest Little Town in Wyoming because it takes two counties to hold the people." Stop by **Frannie Tack Shop,** tel. (307) 548-2344 or (800) 552-8836, to see the saddles or get repairs on canvas or leather items. **Deaver** has a population of 180 folks but no attractions of note. The dot of a place called **Garland** (pop. 50) is home to a wonderful old schoolhouse (now used as a church) that was built in the early 1900s.

Just east of Lovell, the pungent odors of sulfur and oil hang in the air, and the dry badlands are punctuated by oil pumpjacks. More than 117 million barrels of oil and 13 million cubic feet of gas have been produced in the Byron Oil Field since its discovery in 1918. The other business here is farming. Much of this desert land is now under irrigation, and the lush green farmlands are filled with sugar beets, beans, malting barley, alfalfa, and corn. A sign along U.S. 14A notes the **Sidon Canal,** built in 1900 by Mormon settlers of the Bighorn Basin. The 37-mile-long canal was entirely self-financed with land donated by the government, and transports water from the Shoshone River to 20,000 acres of farmland. Mormons claim that Prayer Rock, a large impediment to the canal's construction, was miraculously split as a result of their supplications.

LOVELL

The sleepy little burg of Lovell (pop. 2,200; pronounced "LOVE-ul") calls itself the "City of Roses," a title that comes from Dr. William Horsley, who lived here from 1924 till his death in 1971. Horsley loved roses and in the course of a lifetime of cultivating them became one of the nation's foremost authorities. The "Rose Doctor's" enthusiasm rubbed off on others, and today gardens all over town are packed with roses. Oil fields crowd around Lovell, and a Georgia Pacific wallboard plant and two bentonite plants are substantial local employers, but farming is king. The Western Sugar factory stands on the edge of town, providing jobs for workers and a market for local farmers who contract with the plant to grow sugar beets. In late fall, huge mounds of straw-covered beets pile up beside the factory and the rancid/sweet odor of cooking beets fills the air. Stray beets, spilled from overloaded farm trucks, lie along the highway for miles. Lovell doesn't offer much for tourists—it's one of the few midsize towns in Wyoming without a museum—and is known for its insular attitudes toward outsiders, but the surrounding country includes wonderful Bighorn Canyon National Recreation Area and the Big Horn Mountains. A state-run fish rearing station at Tillett Springs, 17 miles north of Lovell, raises cutthroat and rainbow trout.

Like most towns in the northern Bighorn Basin, Lovell is dominated by Mormons. An enormous brick LDS church fills an entire block along the main drag and is often mistaken for an imposing office building. Although Lovell has wide, clean streets crowded with summertime flower boxes, the downtown has quite a few empty storefronts.

HISTORY

The town of Lovell has its roots in the enormous ML Ranch, founded in 1880 by Anthony L. Mason and Henry Clay Lovell (see below for more on the ranch). In 1900, Mormon settlers moved to the remote Bighorn Basin (partly to escape prosecution for polygamy) and working on the Burlington Railroad and developing irrigation projects. The area boomed with the discovery of natural gas and the opening of various factories. A few years later, German emigrants provided labor for the farm fields and then settled down to acquire their own land. Yellowtail Dam on the Big Horn River was built in 1965, and the surrounding land became a national recreation area the following year.

Lovell is said to have the lowest crime rate in Wyoming, but nowhere in the tourist brochures

does the city mention the history of two of its most prominent doctors. A few years before his 1971 death, Dr. William Horsley, the famed "Rose Doctor," was forced to resign from the local hospital following a series of homosexual incidents with boys. But another respected physician, Dr. John Story, gained considerably more notoriety for his actions. Story arrived in 1958 to practice general medicine, joined the local Baptist church, and became a strong conservative community leader. Unfortunately, over the next 25 years he also raped or molested dozens (some say hundreds) of women and girls in his office. A combination of strict Mormon upbringing, sexual ignorance, shame, and fear prevented the victims from talking, and the few who did speak up were called liars. Finally, in 1983, the charges began to surface. The trial turned Lovell inside out. Despite intense pressure from local and state politicians (then-Governor Herschler called the victims' testimony "hogwash"), Story was convicted in April 1985 on several rape charges and is currently serving a 20-year sentence in the Wyoming State Penitentiary. Jack Olson's harrowing book, *Doc*, describes this sorry chapter in recent Wyoming history.

In 1996, a new chapter was added to the Lovell doctor saga when Dr. L. Stan Naramore was convicted of murdering one elderly patient and attempting to murder another (he gave them paralyzing drugs). Naramore was a physician at the Lovell hospital in 1993 and '94 but committed the crimes while working in Kansas.

· PRACTICALITIES

Accommodations

Stay at one of four places in Lovell. Cheapest is **Western Motel**, 180 W. Main St., tel (307) 548-2781, where rooms are $28 s, $34 d, and kitchenettes $50 for up to six people. **Horseshoe Bend Motel**, 375 E. Main St., tel (307) 548-2221 or (800) 548-2850, has kitchenettes for $36 s, $38 d, including access to an outdoor pool. **Super 8 Motel**, 595 E. Main St., tel (307) 548-2725 or (800) 800-8000, charges $37 s, $41 d. **Cattleman Motel**, 470 Montana Ave., tel (307) 548-2296 or (800) 845-2296, has rooms for $41 s, $44 d and kitchenettes available.

The **TX Ranch**, a 10,000-acre cattle ranch, offers a unique chance to take part in ranch life. It isn't a dude ranch, and visitors end up joining in cattle drives, branding calves, and doing roundups. Call (406) 484-2583 for details. The **Schively Ranch**, tel. (307) 548-6688 or (406) 259-8866, is a similar operation consisting of two ranches on the eastern side of the Pryor Mountains. Guests can take part in a 50-mile cattle drive each April or help in ranch chores at other times. A good way to learn about the real West.

Camping

The best campsites in the Lovell area lie within nearby Bighorn Canyon National Recreation Area (see below); closest is Horseshoe Bend Campground, 14 miles from Lovell. In town, camp for free (including showers) at **Lovell Camper Park** on Quebec Ave. north of Main Street. It's a quiet place surrounded by cottonwoods. RVers can pay to stay at **Camp Big Horn RV Park**, 595 E. Main St. (behind the Super 8 Motel), tel. (307) 548-2725. The price is $7 for tents, $12 for RVs; open year-round.

Food

Rose Bowl Cafe, 483 Shoshone Ave., tel. (307) 548-7121, is popular for breakfast and lunch; try one of the huge cinnamon rolls. For pizzas, head to **Pizza on the Run**, 214 Main St., tel. (307) 548-2206. The nicest local eatery is **Big Horn Restaurant**, 605 E. Main St., tel. (307) 548-6811, where locals and visitors come for a dinner out or to enjoy a leisurely breakfast. Also worth a visit is **Our Home Town Restaurant**, 43 E. Old Main St., tel. (307) 548-7112. Get groceries and deli food at **Red Apple Supermarket**, 9 E. Main St., tel. (307) 548-9907, which also houses a War Memorial.

Information and Services

For local info, visit the **Lovell Information Center** 287 E. Main, tel. (307) 548-7552. Hours are Mon.-Fri. 8:30 a.m.-12:15 p.m. and 1-5 p.m. from Memorial Day to Labor Day and Mon.-Fri. 8:30 a.m.-12:15 p.m. the rest of the year. There's a big indoor **swimming pool** ($1) and other recreation facilities on the southwest end of town. The Bighorn National Forest

Medicine Wheel Ranger District Office, 604 E. Main, tel. (307) 548-6541, is open Mon.-Fri. 8 a.m.-noon and 12:30-4:30 p.m. Stop here for information on the Medicine Wheel. Wash clothes at **Mustang Laundry,** 340 Montana Avenue. The town **library** is at 3rd St. and Oregon Ave., tel. (307) 548-7228, and the **post**

office is at 167 W. 3rd, tel. (307) 548-7605. Rent cars from **Murphey Ford,** 80 E. Main, tel. (307) 548-6546.

The big annual event in Lovell is **Mustang Days,** held the last full week in June. Activities include parades, fireworks, barbecues, a follies show, and a rodeo.

BIGHORN CANYON NATIONAL RECREATION AREA

Just east of Lovell is one of America's lesser-known but most stunning sights, Bighorn Canyon. Over the eons, the Big Horn River has slowly carved out a 2,200-foot-deep chasm through the desert country. Since 1967, when water backed up behind the 525-foot-tall Yellowtail Dam, the canyon has lain under a deep blanket of water—water that provides 250,000 kilowatts of electricity for the western U.S. and irrigates thousands of acres of Montana farmland. The dam itself is—as the raven flies—more than 20 miles north of the Wyoming-Montana border, but its impact reaches 70 river miles upstream, creating Big Horn Lake.

The Setting
The 120,000-acre Bighorn Canyon National Recreation Area is managed by the National Park Service. Entrance costs $5 per vehicle per day; an annual pass is $30. Separate facilities on both ends of the recreation area are linked by a circuitous 180-mile route that takes you through Billings, Montana. (A shorter route includes 18 miles of gravel road.) Because of the distances, most road-bound visitors come to either the Montana side or the Wyoming side but not both. Boaters can traverse the entire reach of the canyon.

Attractions accessible only from Montana include the dam itself (daily tours available through the summer), tel. (406) 666-2412, a short nature trail, and the site of two Bozeman Trail features: Fort C. F. Smith and the Hayfield Fight (both on private land). For details on sights north of the Wyoming border, see *Montana Handbook,* by W.C. McRae and Judy Jewell (Moon Publications).

From the Wyoming side, things are consid-

erably more interesting, even though some of the sights actually lie across the Montana border. A paved road extends 27 miles along the western side of the recreation area, with a rough dirt road continuing 15 more miles to the Crow Indian Reservation. Along the way are a couple of campgrounds, the historic Bad Pass Trail, two old ranches, magnificent Bighorn Canyon, and a good chance to see bighorn sheep and wild horses. The road cuts through impressive red and gray badlands carpeted by juniper, sagebrush, and mountain mahogany.

SIGHTS

Devil Canyon Area
The pièce de résistance of Bighorn Canyon National Recreation Area is **Devil Canyon Overlook,** where Devil Canyon joins Bighorn Canyon. From the overlook, the earth drops suddenly away. More than a thousand feet below, motorboats look like miniature toys in a bathtub. A real treat in the canyon is the chance to see **bighorn sheep** up close; more than 200 of these majestic animals live in the national recreation area. Although the more impressive rams tend to hang out in remote parts of the Pryor Mountains in the summer, you can spot ewes and lambs along the road between the state line and Layout Creek. The rams are more likely to be seen during the Nov.-Dec. rutting season, but some will probably be visible until late May.

Precipitous Bighorn Canyon was known as **Bad Pass** by the Indians. The trail they used to reach the buffalo herds followed the canyon rim for many miles and was marked by rock cairns. Some of these cairns are still visible be-

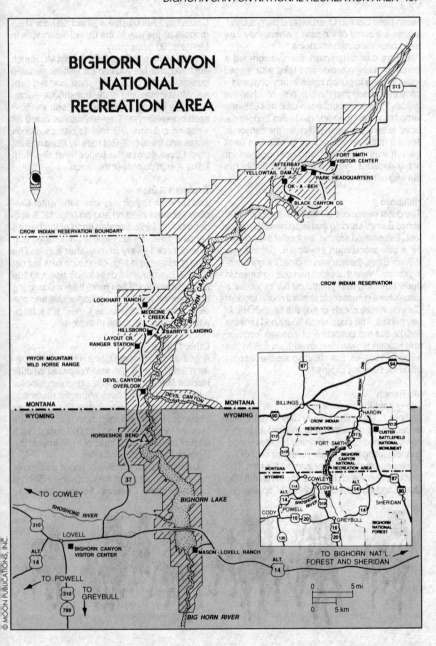

tween Devil Canyon Overlook and Barry's Landing, as are some of the caves where they wintered near the canyon bottoms.

Before it was dammed, the river offered a torrent of rushing rapids and falls, with jagged rocks waiting to punch holes in any boat and a canyon so deep that the sun only reached the bottom for a few hours each day. In 1825, the famed mountain man and guide Jim Bridger decided to take a wooden raft down the canyon to see if it could provide a way to ship furs back east. It was a feat that was not matched for many decades, when a motorboat finally ran the wild currents.

Hillsboro

The ghost settlement of Hillsboro is about a mile above Barry's Landing and is accessible only by foot. Established around the turn of the century by a self-proclaimed physician, Grosverner William Barry, the site was originally a gold-mining center. When that didn't pan out, he turned to dude ranching and promoted his ranch as a place where guests could cruise through Bighorn Canyon in motorboats or ride the English Hackney horses. The dude ranch flourished until the 1930s, but the collection of antique furniture and paintings was destroyed by a fire in the winter of 1947-48. Still standing are the old post office and various cabins.

ML Ranch

The great ML Ranch was founded in 1883 by Anthony L. Mason and Henry Clay Lovell. Lovell trailed herds of cattle up from Kansas to this newly opened country, building his main headquarters along the Bighorn River just east of the community that was later named for him. The vast unfenced ranch became known as the "Big Outfit" and employed hundreds of cowhands. Grazed by 25,000 cattle, it stretched from Thermopolis all the way to the Crow Reservation in Montana, 90 miles away.

Most of the buildings from the old ML Ranch are now gone, but you can still visit the restored bunkhouse, the blacksmith shop, and two cabins. Most interesting is the bunkhouse—actually three cabins connected by dogtrots (covered breezeways). The end cabins acted as sleeping quarters, the middle one as a cook shack and mess hall. Get here by heading east from Lovell across the bridge over Big Horn Lake. A sign points out the ranch.

Lockhart Ranch

The Lockhart Ranch was where the writer Caroline Lockhart lived off and on from 1926 until her death in 1962. Located north of the Barry's Landing area, it's accessible via a rutted 2.5-mile dirt road—very muddy after a rain. The road is passable in high-clearance cars but not RVs. A quarter-mile path leads down to the ranch, where you'll find more than a dozen log buildings set among the cottonwoods and box elder trees along Medicine Creek. It's a fascinating and bucolic place to explore.

Other Sights

Adjacent to the Bighorn Canyon National Recreation Area is the 19,424-acre **Yellowtail Wildlife Habitat Management Unit,** a popular place for hunters and birdwatchers. Many dirt roads and trails crisscross the area, and wildlife of all types abounds. During fall migration, the wetlands here are jammed with up to 10,000 ducks. Get a map of the roads and trails of Yellowtail at the Bighorn Canyon Visitor Center.

Caves create a latticework under portions of the recreation area. On the east side of Bighorn Lake is **Bighorn Caverns.** Access is limited to

BOB RACE

CAROLINE LOCKHART

The West overflows with famous men, and women sometimes get unjustly shunted aside in the accolades. One of the most interesting was Caroline Lockhart (1871-1962), a woman who began her career as an actress but turned quickly to journalism as a writer for a Boston newspaper. Using the pen name "Suzette," she became one of the country's first woman newspaper reporters, a job that led her into all sorts of adventures, from entering a circus cage with a lion that had killed his trainer the previous day to testing the Boston Fire Department's new fire nets by jumping out of a fourth-story hotel window. When she heard of a "Home for Intemperate Women" where the women were being severely mistreated, Caroline decided to investigate by posing as a derelict. She got her story all right, but it took considerable convincing from her editor to get her out. "Release!" shouted the matron running the house. "We can't! She's not cured yet." One of her most lasting impacts was the creation of Mother's Day. Although Anna Jarvis came up with the concept, Lockhart made it a real-

ity by tirelessly pushing the idea in the newspapers.

In 1904, Miss Lockhart took a bold step. After an interview with Buffalo Bill Cody in the town named for him, she decided to move to Wyoming. She purchased the local newspaper, the *Cody Enterprise,* and quickly made a name for herself as a crusader against prohibition and "game hogs" (hunters who killed everything in sight). She founded the Cody Stampede, the big annual event in Bighorn Basin, and later wrote several novels about the West, including *The Lady Doc,* a book that managed to ruffle local feathers with its too-close-to-the-truth descriptions of real-life Cody people. Lockhart's witty, humorous, and insightful writing gained her a national reputation.

In 1924, she sold the *Cody Enterprise* and bought a 7,000-acre ranch in the country along the Bighorn River north of Lovell, dividing her time between her Cody home (now the Lockhart Bed and Breakfast) and her ranch. She died at the age of 92. Today her old ranch lies within Bighorn Canyon National Recreation Area.

experienced spelunkers and requires 4WD vehicles; get the gate key and directions at the Bighorn Canyon Visitor Center. This cave is adjacent to **Horsethief Cave.** Although closed to the public, **Natural Trap Cave** is of biological value. Located 35 miles northeast of Lovell, a 12- by 15-foot opening drops into the 65-foot-deep cavern. Over the centuries many animals—from prehistoric horses to rabbits—have fallen in.

PRACTICALITIES

Camping
There are three campgrounds in the southern half of Bighorn Canyon. Folks in RVs park at **Horseshoe Bend** ($5). It has water, toilets, and covered picnic tables but just a lone tree for shade. The rocky surface, minimal shade, and windy conditions make this a rather bleak place for anyone in a tent. The drive to Horseshoe Bend passes lovely red sandstone badlands. Campfire programs are generally offered at Horseshoe Bend amphitheater on Saturday evenings in the summer.

Barry's Landing Campground has fewer sites but is a much nicer place to stay. No charge, but bring your own water. RVers can park for free above the boat ramp. Firewood is usually available at both Horseshoe Bend and Barry's Landing. In addition, you can pitch a tent at the free **Medicine Creek Campground,** though you'll need to hike in along a two-mile dirt road or float in by boat.

Backcountry camping is available throughout the southern end of the recreation area; check at the visitor center for current restrictions and access information. Also be sure to avoid trespassing on the nearby Crow Indian Reservation.

Hiking
Although there are only a few trails in Bighorn Canyon, the open badlands country makes hiking relatively easy. Some trails lead to spectacular canyon rim overviews. Best times are in the fall or in February and March, when temperatures are milder and you're less likely to meet a rattler. Prairie rattlesnakes and black widow spiders are both common in this desert

country, so be aware, especially when exploring old buildings.

Crooked Creek Nature Trail, a short path with self-guiding brochures, takes off from the Horseshoe Bend campground. In addition to this, a two-mile trail (actually an old prospecting road) follows the canyon rim from Barry's Landing to the Medicine Creek Campground. You can also hike the mile-long dirt path to the ghost town **Hillsboro,** described above. Ask at the visitor center for other interesting places to hike in Bighorn Canyon.

On the Water

Most visitors come to Bighorn Canyon to play on the water. You'll see lots of people tooling around in powerful boats, towing water-skiers, trolling for fish, or windsurfing. Fishing is the biggest attraction; walleye, rainbow, and brown trout, yellow perch, ling, crappie, and catfish are commonly caught. Note that because the lake straddles the state line, you need to purchase fishing licenses for both Wyoming and Montana if you plan on fishing both sides of the border. Launch ramps are at Barry's Landing and Horseshoe Bend, plus Ok-A-Beh Marina at the north end of the lake. Swimmers hang out at the Horseshoe Bend beach, the only place with a lifeguard (check with the visitors center to see when they're on duty).

Horseshoe Bend Marina, tel. (307) 548-7230, is open daily 8 a.m.-8 p.m. in summer and rents inner tubes, canoes, fishing boats, paddle boats, and pontoon boats. You can buy boat gas, food, and beer here as well. The cafe offers sandwiches, burgers, and weekend specials. Open late May to early October. One of the best ways to see the canyon is from below, aboard a pontoon tour boat from **Bighorn Canyon Boat Tours** at the marina. Led by experienced guides, these trips provide continuous vistas of the magnificent canyon walls for the entire trip. One-hour trips to Devil Canyon are $10 for adults, $8 for kids under 14. Longer two-and-a-half-hour tours to Barry's Landing and back are $16 for adults, $12 for kids. Bring your camera!

Ok-A-Beh Marina, tel. (406) 665-2216, on the Montana end has limited fishing supplies, food, boat gas, and boat rentals.

Information

For a good orientation to the area, stop by **Bighorn Canyon Visitor Center,** tel. (307) 548-2251, just east of Lovell along U.S. 14A. It's open daily 8:15 a.m.-5 p.m. all year (except Thanksgiving, Christmas, and New Year's Day). Opened in 1976, this solar-heated center is an attraction in itself; 70% of its heat comes directly from the sun. Inside are a three-dimensional relief map of the canyon, displays on local animals, books and topo maps for sale, and a 14-minute movie on Bighorn Canyon. The visitor center also loans out free 45-minute cassette tapes (and recorders) that provide an informative tour of Bighorn Canyon. Check the notice board for other talks or hikes in the recreation area, including the weekend **campfire programs** at Horseshoe Bend Campground (summer only). Summertime canoe tours of the canyon may be available; call a week ahead for specifics. Be sure to pick up a copy of *Canyon Echoes* the free visitor guide with current information. Ranger stations are found at Horseshoe Bend and Layout Creek. The **Ewing-Snell Historical Site** at Layout Creek has a recently restored one-room schoolhouse.

PRYOR MOUNTAIN WILD HORSE RANGE

Bordering on the western side of Bighorn Canyon is 47,000 acres of rugged country set aside in 1968 as the nation's first wild horse preserve. (Two other wild horse ranges now exist, in Nevada and Colorado, and there are another 3,000 wild horses in the Red Desert of southwestern Wyoming.) Managed by the BLM, Pryor Mountain's desert country contains three herds; periodic roundups keep the population near the carrying capacity of 121 horses. Many of the horses remain out of sight in remote box canyons, but you're likely to see some relatively tame ones along the road between Horseshoe Bend and Layout Creek Ranger Station.

Most "wild horses" of the West are of mixed origin. Some are primarily domestic horses that were released into the wild by local ranchers, others can trace at least some of the bloodlines to Spanish mustangs brought to the New World

in the 16th century. Recent studies of wild horses found that the mustangs at Pryor Mountain are the most strongly Spanish of any feral horse herd in America, with little intermixing from more recent breeds. This purity is exhibited in the distinctive colors that include roan, sorrel, black, blue, tan, and grulla. Most have dark manes and tails. Other common characteristics are dark leg bandings and a dark line running down the back.

Prior to protection of the wild horses, many were rounded up for use on ranches or for the glue factory. After 1971, when it became illegal to harass or kill wild horses, their numbers began to grow rapidly. Each year's colt crop increases the herd by 20%, creating competition with native deer and bighorn sheep. Today, the BLM controls numbers through its adopt-a-horse program, removing 25-50 horses every other year from Pryor Mountain and offering them to the public. For details on acquiring a wild horse, contact the BLM at 810 E. Main St., Billings, MT 59105, tel. (406) 657-6262.

GREYBULL

For travelers en route to Yellowstone, the crossroads town of Greybull (pop. 1,800) is a splotch of irrigated green surrounded by desert country. Greybull lies at the junction of Shell Creek and the Big Horn River and at the intersection of U.S. Highways 14 and 16-20. As such, it is both an agricultural center and a commercial center. Most of the town lies along the western shore of the river behind a long levee; barren rocky bluffs line the opposite bank. There are bentonite processing plants just north of town, oil pumpjacks farther afield, and irrigated farms along the river. Tip: if you're heading west to Cody and Yellowstone, fill up your tank here. Gas prices get more expensive as you approach the mountains.

History
The land around Greybull was first settled in the 1880s by stockmen, with several hundred Mormon homesteaders moving in a decade later to dig irrigation ditches and establish the minuscule farming settlements of **Burlington** (pop. 190) and **Otto** north of the Greybull River. Nearby **Emblem** was established by 600 German farmers in the late 1890s. A diversion of the Greybull River was begun in 1895, the first reclamation project under the Carey Act. Originally called Germania, the name was changed to Emblem (a reference to the American flag) during the anti-German hysteria of World War I.

The word Greybull comes from a huge albino buffalo that once roamed this country. The animal was sacred to the Indians, who noted it in pictographs still visible on the sandstone bluffs lining the river. The town is a creation of the Burlington Railroad in 1909-10, but much of its growth has been fueled by oil and gas developments in the surrounding country. Completion of U.S. 14 across the Big Horn Mountains in the 1930s brought tourists and led to Greybull's development as a way station for folks heading east to the Black Hills or west to Yellowstone. Beginning in 1934, scientists excavated a dozen complete skeletons of dinosaurs near Greybull, and in 1991 one of the largest Allosauruses ever found was excavated.

SIGHTS

Greybull Museum
The local museum is in the same building as the library (325 Greybull Ave., tel. 307-765-2444). It's open Mon.-Fri. 10 a.m.-8 p.m. and Saturday 10 a.m.-6 p.m. June-Sept., Mon.-Fri. 1-5 p.m. in the spring and fall, and Monday, Wednesday, and Friday 1-4 p.m. in the winter. No charge. Inside are agate collections and polished petrified wood pieces, a fine fossil collection that includes one of the largest fossil ammonites ever found, fossil turtles, and dinosaur bones. Also here are various Indian arrowheads and other historical artifacts, including a New England church made from royal icing!

Aerial Firefighting Museum
Big Horn County Airport, atop a hill just north of town, is the home of Hawkins & Powers Aviation, a major source of planes used to drop fire retardant on forest fires throughout the West.

During the summer fire season it's often a center of intense activity, with 11 air tankers and seven helicopters based here. Included are five of the six PB4Y-2s still flying—in World War II, these planes played an important role in routing the Japanese from Southeast Asia. Hawkins & Powers planes have appeared in a number of movies, including the Steven Spielberg firefighting film *Always*. A Museum of Flight and Aerial Firefighting includes a dozen planes on loan from the Forest Service on display just north of a state rest area adjacent to the airport. A small cabin contains a seasonal visitor reception and gift shop, and a larger building is in the works. Access to the planes is $2.50 for adults, $1 for kids, and free for children under age six. Open Mon.-Fri. 8 a.m.-6 p.m. and Sat.-Sun. 10 a.m.-6 p.m. in the summer and Mon.-Fri. 8 a.m.-5 p.m. the rest of the year, when the visitor center moves to the Hawkins and Powers office. You can also just check out the planes through the fence.

Other Sights

Find an attractive flower garden in the shape of the Wyoming state flag at the west end of Greybull Avenue. The **Greybull Livestock Auction** is held just north of town every Friday. And if you are really bored, head to the city park to find picnic tables, a jogging track, and the chimney of the first house built in Greybull.

Five miles northeast of Greybull is **Devil's Kitchen**, a fascinating arroyo filled with brilliantly colored badlands and many fossils. Get a map from the chamber of commerce and follow it closely; the last turnoff is easy to miss. **Sheep Mountain,** a 15-mile-long hogback of eroded land just north of Greybull, is a favorite of geologists, who marvel at this fossil-packed anticline. Photographers love the vivid reds, browns, and yellows of this desert landscape.

Two other places may be of interest: **Greybull Wildlife Museum,** 420 Greybull Ave., has a small collection of stuffed critters, and the old-fashioned **Probst Western Store,** 547 Greybull Ave., tel. (307) 765-2171, has a fine selection of cowboy hats, boots, and Western clothes.

PRACTICALITIES

Accommodations and Camping

See the "Greybull Motels" chart for a listing of local motels. **Green Oasis RV Park,** 540 N. 12th Ave., tel. (307) 765-2524, has tent sites for $9, RV sites for $15. Showers for noncampers cost $2. Open mid-May to September. **Greybull KOA,** 333 N. 2nd Ave., tel. (307) 765-2555 or (800) 562-7508, charges $17 for tent sites, $22 for RVs. Showers cost $3 for noncampers. Open May to mid-October, with trees and an outdoor pool.

GREYBULL MOTELS

Note: Motels are arranged from least to most expensive. Add a seven percent tax to these rates. Area code is 307.

Antler Motel; 1116 N. 6th Ave.; tel. 765-4404; $30-35 s or d; kitchenettes, open April-Oct., AAA approved

K-Bar Motel; 300 Greybull Ave.; tel. 765-4426; $32-44 s, $36-44 d; AAA approved

Sage Motel; 1135 N. 6th Ave.; tel. 765-4443; $35 s, $38 d; AAA approved

Three Chief Motel; 625 N. 6th Ave.; tel. 765-4626; $35 s, $45 d

Historic Hotel Greybull; 602 Greybull Ave.; tel. 765-2012 or (800) 417-1115; $40-50 s or d; restored 1915 hotel, eight guest rooms, private or shared bath, continental breakfast

Wheels Inn Motel; 1324 N. 6th Ave.; tel. 765-2105 or (800) 676-2973; $43 s $63 d; newly remodeled

Greybull Motel; 300 N. 6th Ave.; tel. 765-2628; $45 s or d

Yellowstone Motel; 247 Greybull Ave.; tel. 765-4456; $50 s, $56 d; outdoor pool, AAA approved

Restaurants and Bars

MJ's Cafe at the Greybull KOA, 333 N. 2nd Ave., tel. (307) 765-2555, is easily the most popular local eatery. Good food at a good price and in quantity. Locals drop by for breakfast, for the lunch-time salad bar, and to enjoy prime rib specials on the weekend. **Lisa's Restaurant,** 200 Greybull Ave., tel. (307) 765-4765, serves both Mexican and American fare and fills up most evenings. **Parker Cafe,** 536 Greybull Ave., tel. (307) 765-2152, has working-class food at reasonable prices, while **Wheels Inn Restaurant,** 1336 N. 6th Ave., tel. (307) 765-2456, is open 24 hours a day and serves up standard American fare. **Uptown Cafe,** 536 Greybull Ave., tel. (307) 765-2152, is another local favorite. **Pizza on the Run,** 427 Greybull Ave., tel. (307) 765-4454, has pizza by the slice or pie. Drive up to the **Dairy Freez,** 601 N. 6th Ave., tel. (307) 765-4718, for fast food, and get groceries at **Ron's Food Farm,** 909 N. 6th, tel. (307) 765-2890.

Entertainment and Events

For live music, head to **Hanging Tree Lounge,** 1040 N 6th Ave., tel. (307) 765-9986, **Smokehouse Saloon** 562 Greybull Ave., tel. (307) 765-2232, or **Silver Spur,** 445 Greybull Ave., tel. (307) 765-2300. The Smokehouse has a 19th-century backbar. Greybull's big annual event is **Days of '49** (1949 that is), held the second weekend in June. There's a top-notch rodeo, a parade, a barbecue, dancing, and a demolition derby.

Recreation

A marvelous old log building built in the 1920s houses the **Greybull Roller Rink,** at 527 S. 1st Ave., tel. (307) 765-2761. Less impressive but equally popular is the bowling alley, **Bighorn Lanes** at 141 N. 6th St., tel. (307) 765-2431. Swim and take showers at the **pool** across from the high school on 6th Avenue.

Information and Services

The **Greybull Chamber of Commerce,** tel. (307) 765-2100, has a small kiosk next to the library at 325 Greybull Avenue. It's open Mon.-Fri. 9 a.m.-12:30 p.m. and 1:30-4:30 p.m. and Saturday 10 a.m.-noon and 2-4 p.m. in the summer, Mon.-Fri. 9 a.m.-noon and 1-4 p.m. and Saturday 10 a.m.-noon and 2-4 p.m. in the winter. Ask here for directions to the Indian pictograph of the albino bison. The staff can also provide information on the major dinosaur digs (*Allosaurus, Diplodocus,* and *Stegosaurus)* taking place just north of town and maps of the 4WD roads on Sheep Mountain.

The Forest Service's **Paintrock District Office** is at 1220 N. 8th St., tel. (307) 765-4435. The **Greybull Public Library** is at 325 Greybull Ave., tel. (307) 765-2551. Find the local **post office** at 119 N. 7th St., tel. (307) 347-3321, and an **ATM** at 1st Interstate Bank, 601 Greybull Avenue. Wash clothes at **Coin-Op Laundromat** next to A&M on N. 6th Avenue.

Powder River Trailways, tel. (800) 442-3682, has daily bus service from Greybull to Billings, Montana, eastern Wyoming, and elsewhere in America. Buses stop in front of the chamber of commerce office on Greybull Avenue.

GREYBULL VICINITY

BASIN

South of Greybull, the highway parallels the Big Horn River. Sharp bluffs rise along the eastern side of the river, and cottonwoods and willows crowd the banks. As you head away from the broad river valley, the endless hills are covered with dry grass, sage, and greasewood. It's a plain-Jane, arid landscape. Eight miles away lies the pleasant town of Basin (pop. 1,200). After a stretch of rough going in which the town seemed on its way to extinction, Basin has bounced back a bit. The town putters along on its status as Big Horn County seat and the presence of an impressive state retirement center and a couple of publishing-related businesses, including Wyoming's largest book wholesaler, Wolverine Distributing.

Basin is a relaxing place to retire after a long day of driving. Established in 1896, the town has always been an agricultural center, with both farming and ranching in the surrounding land. In 1897, a bitter custody battle for the

county seat split voters between Basin City, as it was then known, and the older town of Otto. Basin City won by 38 votes.

Practicalities
Camping is free in the town park, but you'll have to pitch tents on the dirt. The **Lilac Motel,** 710 W. C St., tel. (307) 568-3355, has a quiet location and kindly owner. Rates are just $21 s, $26 d. Decent breakfasts are offered at **Big B Restaurant,** 602 S. 4th St., tel. (307) 568-2246, and very good steak and seafood at **Outpost Lounge,** 151 N. 4th St., tel. (307) 568-2134. For books, stop by **Big Horn County Library,** 103 W. C St., tel. (307) 568-2388. Wash clothes at the laundromat on D and 4th Streets, and get groceries from **Wheeler's Market,** 114 S. 4th, tel. (307) 568-2325. There is an outdoor **swimming pool** at the high school but no ATMs in town.

Stockman's Bar, 105 S. 4th St., tel. (307) 568-9942, has live country music a couple of times a month. Each August, Basin hosts the **Big Horn County Fair and Bean Festival** (pretty strange combination!), with livestock judging, a rodeo, a barbecue, and other activities.

Powder River Trailways, tel. (800) 442-3682, has bus service from Basin to northern and eastern Wyoming and onward to other parts of America.

SHELL AND MANDERSON

Shell Valley is farming and ranching country, its lush irrigated hayfields contrasting sharply with the arid landscape to the west. Tiny Shell has a country store/bar. Be sure to stop at the **Old Stone School** here, built in 1903 and used as a one-room school until the early 1950s. It is now run as an excellent little art gallery, bookstore, and information center, tel. (307) 765-4384. **Kedesh Ranch,** three miles east of Shell on U.S. 14, tel. (307) 765-2791 or (800) 845-3320, has log cabins with fine views. The dude ranch centers around horseback riding, fishing, cookouts, and hayrides but also takes guests on trips to explore nearby petroglyphs and dinosaur digs. Open June to mid-October, with weekly stays only. **Trapper's Rest B&B,** tel. (307) 765-9239 or (800) 826-8872, three miles southeast of Shell, has a rustic two-bedroom cabin (no

running water) and a large tepee for $40 s or d, including a full breakfast. The setting is peaceful and quiet, with a tree-lined trout stream nearby.

Shell Creek Guest Ranch, tel. (307) 765-2420, has dude ranch accommodations in new quarters including a central ranch house and hot tub. Guests take part in horseback rides, chuck wagon dinners, campfires, wagon rides, barbecues, fossil hunting, fishing, and more. Lodging-only rates are $65 per day for two adults and two kids, or you can stay for a week for $890 per person all inclusive.

State 789 heads south from Basin to dinky Manderson (pop. 90). **Harmony Ranch Cottage,** two miles east of here, tel. (307) 568-2514, has a country cottage for rent that sleeps six or seven. South of here the road splits and continues on both sides of Big Horn River to Worland. The main road (on the east side of the river) plays tag with the irrigation ditch much of the way, passing eroded desert bluffs to the east and flat farm country closer to the river. A thin strip of trees runs right down the middle; in fall they look like skeletons against the skyline. Lots of barley, sugar beet, and hayfields.

MEDICINE LODGE STATE PARK

Twenty-one miles east of Manderson on State 31 is the ranching center called **Hyattville,** really not much more than a waste spot in the road. Get to Medicine Lodge State Park by heading north out of town and turning right onto Cold Springs Road. After four miles, turn left again at the "Medicine Lodge" sign and follow the gravel road 1.5 miles to the park. The main attraction is a 750-foot-long low cliff that served as a backdrop to 10,000 years of Indian settlements. The cliff is covered with dozens of petroglyphs. A small log **visitor center,** tel. (307) 469-2234—built almost a century ago as a cowboy bunkhouse—is open Mon.-Fri. 8 a.m.-5 p.m. and Sat.-Sun. 9 a.m.-8 p.m May to Labor Day. Inside are displays on the area's incredibly rich archaeological history. Beginning in 1973, researchers uncovered some 60 cultural levels and thousands of artifacts and bones here. It's considered one of the most significant archaeological sites in the West. Ask at the visitor center to pick fruit from the old apple trees next

door. A three-quarter-mile **nature trail** begins nearby, and the old 4WD roads make for fine mountain-biking. Just a few hundred feet away is a very pleasant creekside **campground** (free) with restrooms and water and good fishing for brown trout in the creek.

Staying on Cold Springs Road—instead of turning off to Medicine Lodge State Park—takes you 15 miles to Paint Rocks Lakes, a jumping-off point for Cloud Peak Wilderness (described under "Big Horn Mountains" in the Powder River Country chapter). North of Hyattville, another interesting place awaits folks willing to do a bit of adventuring. **Trapper Canyon**, located on public land, has colorful walls rising 1,200 feet above Trapper Creek. Access is pretty tough and requires 4WD vehicles; check with the BLM office in Worland for details.

WORLAND

The prosperous farming town of Worland (pop. 6,000) depends upon a mixture of agriculture (primarily malt barley and sugar beets), sheep and cattle ranching, oil production, and manufacturing. Sheep glean plowed fields near town, and the Holly Sugar Company's plant on the southwest edge of Worland provides economic stability, keeping more than 15,000 acres in beets. Also important is a major aluminum can factor, which produces three million cans a day, and a Pepsi bottling plant that fills many of these. The town itself has a pleasant Midwestern feel with nightly baseball games through the summer, tree-bordered streets and simple homes in the center, and suburban ranch-style homes spreading across the surrounding countryside. The slow Big Horn River twists its way along the edge of Worland, but just a few miles farther west is desert country with dry rocky buttes, sagebrush, and sheep.

HISTORY

Worland is named for Charlie "Dad" Worland, one of the first homesteaders in this part of the Bighorn Basin and the manager of a stage station and saloon built along the old Bridger Trail in 1900. It wasn't much to look at—a cave dug into the riverbank, with log walls out front. His bar quickly acquired the nickname "The Hole-in-the-Wall." A cigar box just behind the bar served as the local bank, and anyone needing money could borrow it and leave behind an I.O.U. Other folks settled around Dad Worland, and A.G. Rupp added a general store nearby, also built into the side of the bank to save precious timber. Ray Pendergraft in *Washakie: A Wyoming*

County History, relates the following story about early Worland:

> *Once a compactly-built man rode into the settlement, refreshed himself at Worland's saloon, then went on to Rupps for some supplies. On one wall of the store was a poster, complete with a picture. It read, "$5,000 Reward, Dead or Alive Robert Leroy Parker, alias Butch Cassidy." The visitor examined it. "It's not a very good likeness," he told Rupp. Rupp examined the poster, looked at the man, and readily agreed. "You don't want it up there do you, Mr. Rupp?" the man politely asked. "No, I don't," replied Mr. Rupp. "I'll take it down for you," the man said, did so and went on about his selection of supplies.*

Originally located on the western side of the Bighorn River, Worland moved to the other side after the Chicago, Burlington, and Quincy Railroad announced plans to build along the east bank. The nucleus of Worland, 10 buildings, was slid across the river on the ice during the winter of 1905-06. The following year, construction was finished on the 54-mile-long Big Horn irrigation canal, opening some 30,000 acres to agriculture. It had been begun almost 20 years earlier. A new sugar beet processing plant in 1917 attracted more farmers and workers from the Midwest and many Germans and Ukrainians. The discovery of oil in the Hidden Dome field in that same year brought boom times as speculators flooded the area. Oil and agriculture, especially sugar beets, have remained important ever since, although oil pro-

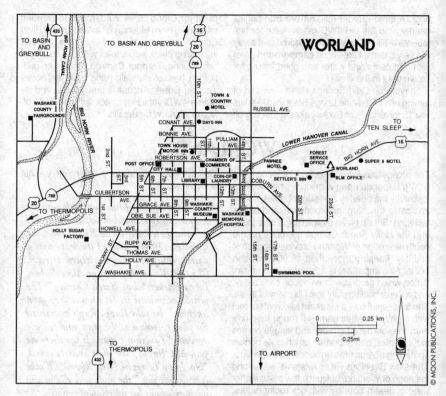

WORLAND

TO BASIN
AND
GREYBULL

TO BASIN AND GREYBULL

433

16
20
789

BIG HORN CANAL

BIG HORN RIVER

WASHAKIE
COUNTY
FAIRGROUNDS

TOWN &
COUNTRY
MOTEL

10th ST

RUSSELL AVE.

CONANT AVE.
BONNIE AVE.

DAYS INN

TO
TEN SLEEP

LOWER HANOVER CANAL

TOWN HOUSE
MOTOR INN

11th ST

PULLIAM
AVE.

14th ST

789
20

2nd ST

POST OFFICE
CITY HALL

ROBERTSON AVE.

CHAMBER OF
COMMERCE

BIG HORN AVE.

16

TO THERMOPOLIS

3rd ST
5th ST
6th ST

LIBRARY

COIN-OP
LAUNDRY

12th ST
13th ST

COBURN AVE.

20th ST

23rd ST

FOREST
SERVICE
OFFICE

WORLAND

SUPER 8 MOTEL

BLM OFFICE

PAWNEE
MOTEL

SETTLER'S INN

CULBERTSON
AVE.

1st ST

GRACE AVE.

8th ST
9th ST

WASHAKIE
COUNTY
MUSEUM

OBIE SUE AVE.

HOWELL AVE.

WASHAKIE
MEMORIAL
HOSPITAL

15th ST

17th ST
16th ST

HOLLY SUGAR
FACTORY

RAILWAY ST

RUPP AVE.
THOMAS AVE.
HOLLY AVE.
WASHAKIE AVE.

SWIMMING POOL

TO
THERMOPOLIS

432

TO AIRPORT

0   0.25 km
0   0.25mi

© MOON PUBLICATIONS, INC.

duction has declined since the 1950s as the fields have been pumped out.

SIGHTS

The **Washakie County Museum and Cultural Center,** 1115 Obie Sue Ave., tel. (307) 347-4102, is housed in an old Mormon church and is open Tues.-Fri. 9 a.m.-5 p.m. and Saturday 1-3 p.m. in summer and Tues.-Fri. 10 a.m.-4 p.m. the rest of the year. Inside this spacious multi-room museum are Indian artifacts from cave sites near Ten Sleep, a re-creation of the A.G. Rupp Store, old photos, an array of cowboy and ranch equipment, other historical items, and a fine geology and fossil collection. The museum's highlight is a Sheepeater Indian lodge constructed in the 1860s from 130 poles. It was

moved here from its original location near Soapy Peak. Kids will enjoy the hands-on exhibits such as the corn sheller and grinder. Local art shows and traveling exhibits can also be found here.

Next to the County Court House at the corner of Big Horn Ave. and 10th Street is a fountain fed by a 4,330-foot-deep **artesian well** located 23 miles north of Worland. The well flows at an impressive 14,000 gallons per minute and with sufficient pressure to push water all the way to Worland. Also on the courthouse grounds is a grotesque 15-foot-tall **Indian statue** carved out of wood by Peter Toth and placed here in 1980. **Pioneer Square,** just across the road, has unusual metal sculptures depicting pioneer settlers.

West of Worland in the Painted Desert, you'll find some of the most interesting badlands country in Wyoming. Of particular note are the

Gooseberry Badlands on BLM land near Squaw Teats and just off State 431. The BLM has developed a fascinating nature trail through the hoodoo formations here; pick up a descriptive handout from their office in Worland. There's plenty of eroded country to explore, including arches and a variety of bizarrely carved shapes. The bones of a prehistoric horse, *Eohippus*, have been found here.

PRACTICALITIES

Accommodations and Camping
See the chart for a complete listing of local lodging places. No public campgrounds are near Worland (although you can pitch a tent on nearby BLM lands), but the private **Worland Campground**, 2401 Big Horn Ave., tel. (307) 347-2329, has shady tent sites for $12, RV spaces for $16-18. Showers for noncampers cost $4. Open May-October.

Food
Maggie's Cafe, 541 Big Horn Ave., tel. (307) 347-3354, has very reasonable breakfasts and lunches, including homemade soups and breads. Things can get pretty chaotic at times. Get good breakfasts and lunchtime sandwiches (homemade bread) at **The Office**, 1515 Big Horn Ave., tel. (307) 347-8171. Good salads and specials, too. **Ranchito Mexican Food**, 1010 Big Horn Ave., tel. (307) 347-8501, serves

authentic south-of-the-border fare. Recommended. **Ram's Horn Cafe**, 629 Big Horn Ave., tel. (307) 347-6135, is also popular, serving three all-American meals a day.

Pizza Hut, 1927 Big Horn Ave., tel. (307) 347-2434, and **Pizza on the Run**, 1214 Big Horn Ave., tel. (307) 347-2453, are the local pizza joints. **Antone's Supper Club**, three miles east of town on U.S. 16, tel. (307) 347-2301, has great deals on sirloin steaks and a Wednesday night smorgasbord. **Harry's Steak House**, 1620 Big Horn Ave., tel. (307) 347-9261, is the fanciest place in town and grills the best steaks. Another option is the **Elks Club**, 604 Coburn Ave., tel. (307) 347-4401, where the service tends to be slow but you get all-American food for a reasonable price.

Stop by **Rolling Pin Bakery**, 105 N. 15th St., tel. (307) 347-2763, for fresh breads, cookies, and donuts. **Jon's IGA Foodliner**, 221 N. 10th St., tel. (307) 347-3628, **Rich's Foodtown**, 612 S. 12th St., tel. (307) 347-3001, and the **Worland Food Farm**, 420 N. 10th St., tel. (307) 347-9820, are the places to go for groceries and deli food.

Events and Entertainment
The big annual event in town is the **Washakie County Fair** in early August. It includes a parade, country music, and the standard country-fair fun. In early September, the **Sugar Beet Festival** has food booths, arts and crafts, contests, and even a sugar beet carving contest. The two-day **Sauger Derby** is a popular fishing

---

WORLAND ACCOMMODATIONS

Note: Accommodations are listed from least to most expensive. Add a six percent tax to these rates. Area code is 307.

Pawnee Motel; 1735 Big Horn; tel. 347-3206; $30 s, $40 d; thin walls

Town House Motor Inn; 119 N. 10th St.; tel. 347-2426; $31 s, $36 d

Town & Country Motel (Econo Inn); 1021 Russell St.; tel. 347-3249; $35 s, $38 d

Days Inn; 500 N. 10th St.; tel. 347-4251 or (800) 329-7466; $38-42 s, $42-50 d; very nice, continental breakfast, AAA approved

Super 8 Motel; 2500 Big Horn; tel. 347-9236 or (800) 800-8000; $41 s, $45 d; AAA approved

Best Western Settler's Inn; 2200 Big Horn; tel. 347-8201 or (800) 528-1234; $46 s, $52 d; continental breakfast, AAA approved

event held in the Big Horn River each September or October.

The Office Lounge/Other Room, 1515 Big Horn Ave., tel. (307) 347-8171, has rock or country bands most weekends, or try **RJ's Saloon** 607 Big Horn Ave., tel. (307) 347-8891. **Little Chicago (Ram's Horn),** 629 Big Horn Ave., tel. (307) 347-6135, is another popular bar and occasionally has live music.

Information and Services

The **Worland Chamber of Commerce** office, tel. (307) 347-3226, sits in front of the county courthouse at 120 N. 10th St. and stays open Mon.-Fri. 8 a.m.-noon and 1-5 p.m. The **Washakie County Library** is at 1019 Coburn Ave., tel. (307) 347-2231. The Bighorn National Forest **Tensleep Ranger Station** is at 2009 Big Horn Ave., tel. (307) 347-8291, and is open Mon.-Fri. 8 a.m.-4:30 p.m. Staff can provide details on mountain-bike trails and hiking in the Cloud Peak Wilderness. The **BLM Worland District Office** at 101 S. 23rd St., tel. (307) 347-9871, is open Mon.-Fri. 7:45 a.m.-4:30 p.m. Stop here for information on scenic back roads and nearby places to hike or mountain-bike. For emergency medical treatment, head to **Washakie Memorial Hospital,** 400 S. 15th St., tel. (307) 347-3221.

There is a community **swimming pool** ($1.75) at the high school, 1706 Washakie Ave., tel. (307) 347-4113, and an 18-hole **Municipal Golf Course,** tel. (307) 347-2695, next to the airport. Roller skate at **Wheels Skate Palace,** 1115 Big Horn Ave., tel. (307) 347-8808. Wash clothes at **Coin-Op Laundry** at 1401 Big Horn Avenue. For cash, find **ATMs** at the Conoco Station at 944 Big Horn Ave. and at Key Bank, 120 N. 7th Street.

Transportation

Powder River Trailways, tel. (800) 442-3682, has daily bus service to Billings, Montana, and to northern and eastern Wyoming, with connections to the rest of America. It stops at Daylight Donuts, 400 N. 10th Street. **SANTA** (Shoshone Arapahoe Nations Transit Authority), tel. (800) 439-7118, offers on-demand bus connections to Riverton, Lander, Dubois, Jackson, Pinedale, Rock Springs, Rawlins, Pinedale, and Salt Lake City.

The airport is two miles south of town and is served by **United Express,** tel. (800) 241-6522, with daily flights to Denver. Rent cars from **Big Horn Chevrolet,** 545 N. 10th Ave., tel. (307) 347-4229, **Worland Ford,** 500 Big Horn Ave., tel. (307) 347-4236, or **Western Motors,** 910 Pullman Ave., tel. (307) 347-2441.

TEN SLEEP

Ten Sleep (pop. 320) has one of the most picturesque settings in all Wyoming. The drive in from Worland offers a traipse across dry desert badlands crowded with oil pumpjacks and then up into rolling grass and sagebrush country with the tree-covered Big Horn Mountains marking the distant horizon. Great views from atop the long hills before the road descends sharply into a lush green valley cut through by Nowood and Tensleep creeks. Because of its mountain valley location, the town of Ten Sleep offers an escape from the oppressive summer heat of Bighorn Basin. This verdant valley is one of the few places in Wyoming where apple, peach, and pear trees grow. Rustic log buildings fill this tiny ranching and tourism center. Take away the cars and the asphalt and it's easy to imagine Ten Sleep as the location for some Hollywood film about the Green Valley.

The name Ten Sleep comes from the Sioux Indians who frequently stopped in this valley during their travels between a permanent camp along the Clarks Fork River in Montana and another one along the Platte River. Halfway between the two was Ten Sleeps, so named because they measured distances in the number of nights it took to get to a place. The town of Ten Sleep was established as a trading center for the Scottish and Irish sheepmen who came here in the 1890s.

Sights

The main sights in Ten Sleep are the comfortable, slow-paced town itself and its pretty setting. **Pioneer Museum** behind the Flagstaff Cafe has local artifacts and is open daily in the summer. An old sheriff wagon sits on main street ready to haul off the bad guys. Ask locally for di-

THE TEN SLEEP RAID

Cattlemen have always viewed sheep with disdain, regarding them as despoilers of the range, "locusts with hooves" or "range maggots." Cattle reached Wyoming's grazing lands first, and when sheep began to arrive in large numbers around the turn of the century, the cattle owners fought back with intimidation and violence. In many places, the cattlemen declared a "dead line," and any sheep or sheepherder that came into that area risked being killed. (One such line existed in Jackson Hole; even today the county has just 300 sheep as opposed to 12,000 cattle.) Despite these threats, sheep ranching was simply too lucrative to pass up; by 1889, Bighorn Basin was overrun with more than 387,000 sheep—and boasted fewer than 22,000 cattle.

Perhaps 10,000 sheep throughout the state were killed by cattlemen; some flocks were driven over cliffs, others were dynamited or attacked by dogs, and thousands more died from gunshots. Many of Wyoming's sheepherders were viciously attacked, and at least 16 were murdered. The most notorious of all these incidents took place along Spring Creek near Ten Sleep in 1909. Joe Emge, a hotheaded cattleman turned sheepman, announced plans to trail his sheep across the dead line set up in the Nowater Creek area. One April night just after the sheep had reached the grazing grounds, at least half a dozen masked men burst into the camp and murdered Emge, his partner, and a herder. The killers set the wagons afire and shot many sheep before disappearing into the night, leaving a grisly scene to be discovered the next morning.

The investigation pointed directly at a local cattleman, and after testifying before a grand jury one of the suspected raiders was found dead. Officials judged it a suicide, but many suspected that the cattleman had been waylaid by others seeking to silence anyone who might tell the truth. Eventually, two men broke the silence and fingered five others, including several prominent ranchers. All five were convicted and spent from three years to life in prison for the murders. Like the Johnson County War two decades earlier, this incident helped turn many people against the cattlemen. Sheep continued to grow in importance for a while—Wyoming became the largest wool producer in the country—but overgrazing, the severe winter of 1911-12, and the removal of a wool tariff the next year led to a long decline. Even today, though, Wyoming is America's third-largest producer of wool.

---

rections to the Indian pictographs on the Walt Patch Ranch. Drop into the **Ten Sleep Saloon,** tel. (307) 366-9208, or the **Big Horn Bar,** tel. (307) 366-9222, for a cold one with local ranchers. Ten Sleep Saloon has a bar inlaid with 5,052 pennies and 233 nickels; the bartender claims that they started out with inlaid silver dollars but this is all they had left after the taxes!

Just west of Ten Sleep is the turnoff to **Castle Gardens,** a scenic area of wind-carved sandstone badlands in all sizes and shapes. It's a 12-mile drive via a dirt road. Castle Gardens has picnic tables, though more often than not they've been used by gun enthusiasts for target practice and are somewhat the worse for the experience.

Tensleep Canyon

Six miles east of town, U.S. 16 passes the entrance to the 10,000-acre **Tensleep Preserve** managed by The Nature Conservancy. The preserve follows a 12-mile stretch of Canyon Creek and is a great place for day hikes and to watch for rare species such as peregrine falcons and Cooper's hawks. Formerly a girl-scout camp, the preserve has comfortable camping in wall tents, delicious meals, and guided explorations of the canyon. The cost is $70 per person per day all-inclusive. The preserve has all sorts of other activities through the year; for details, call (307) 366-2671 between mid-April and mid-December, or (307) 332-2971 the rest of the year.

Shortly beyond the turnoff to the Tensleep Preserve, the highway climbs up spectacular Tensleep Canyon toward 9,666-foot Powder River Pass in the Big Horn Mountains. **Wigwam Fish Rearing Station,** run by the Wyoming Game and Fish Dept., is five miles east of town. Another six miles up is the turnoff to **Ten Sleep Fish Hatchery.** Both of these are open daily for tours. (See the Powder River Country chapter for sights east of here as U.S. 16 climbs over the majestic Big Horns.)

Accommodations

Log Cabin Motel, tel. (307) 366-2320, has rooms for $32 s or d and RV parking for $8. If you're camping elsewhere, take showers at the laundromat here for $3. The nicest local lodging place is **Valley Motel,** tel. (307) 366-2321, where rooms cost $28 s, $36 d. Pitch your tent at **Flagstaff Camp,** tel. (307) 366-2250, for $8 ($15 for RVs); open May-October. You can also stay at any of a dozen campgrounds ($8-9) in Bighorn National Forest east of town or at Tensleep Preserve. You can reserve a place in Middle Fork and South Fork Campgrounds by calling (800) 280-2267 ($8.25 reservation fee).

Food and Information

Flagstaff Cafe, tel. (307) 366-2330, has great breakfasts, burgers, and steaks. The other local eatery is **Mountain Man Cafe,** housed in a building built in 1914. It still has the original tin ceiling. **Ten Sleep Mercantile** sells groceries. Quite a lot of fruit grows in the country around town; ask locally to see who might have some for sale. There's usually a bowl of fresh fruit at the **Senior Center,** tel. (307) 366-2210, which acts as the local information center. Hours are Mon.-Fri. 7 a.m.-3 p.m. year-round. Stop by on Wednesday nights to join in the bingo games.

Events and Recreation

Come to Ten Sleep on the **4th of July** for a very popular rodeo, a parade, outdoor dances, and a kids' sheep ride. **Ten Sleep Celebration Days** (second weekend in July) brings a junior rodeo, an ice cream social, races, and family events of all types. **Ten Sleep Trail Rides,** tel. (307) 366-2267, offers horseback rides or overnight backcountry trips.

THERMOPOLIS

The town of Thermopolis (pop. 3,400) lies on the southern edge of the Bighorn Basin surrounded by the Owl Creek Mountains. It's one of two towns in Wyoming established because of a hot springs; the other is Saratoga. Thermopolis comes from the words *thermae* (Latin for "hot springs") and *polis* (Greek for "city"). It is a fitting title, since the world's largest hot springs are the centerpiece of Thermopolis. Hot Springs State Park is right in town, encompassing both a wonderful public bathhouse and several commercial endeavors. The economy of Thermopolis was for a long while dependent upon oil and ranching, but tourism has become increasingly important. There are abundant reasons for travelers to stop here.

Thermopolis came into existence with the 1896 purchase of Big Springs from the Shoshone and Arapahoes. Streets were laid out wide enough for a 16-mule team to turn around in the middle of the block—something still obvious today, though you don't often see mule teams on the streets. Because of their medicinal value, the hot springs attracted many people, and the town became a health center, particularly for those suffering from arthritis and polio. There was not much timber around here, so the first lodging place, the Sage Brush Hotel, was made from a wooden frame laced with sagebrush and covered with a thatched roof of more sage.

HOT SPRINGS STATE PARK

History

Shoshone legend tells of a young warrior and his lover who were standing in the Wind River Canyon when an eagle feather—earned in battles with the enemy—blew out of his hair and wafted down the canyon. They raced after it and found it floating in an enormous hot spring with steam gushing from its mouth. The springs were a gift from the Great Spirit.

Originally a part of the Wind River Reservation, Big Springs and 10 square miles of surrounding land were sold to the United States government in 1896 for the bargain-basement price of $60,000. The treaty was signed by Shoshone Chief Washakie and Arapaho Chief Sharp Nose. In it, Washakie stipulated that some of the water must remain free to all people and that a campground be set aside for Indians: "I, Washakie, chief of Shoshones, freely give to the great white father these waters, belov'd by my people; that all may receive that great bless-

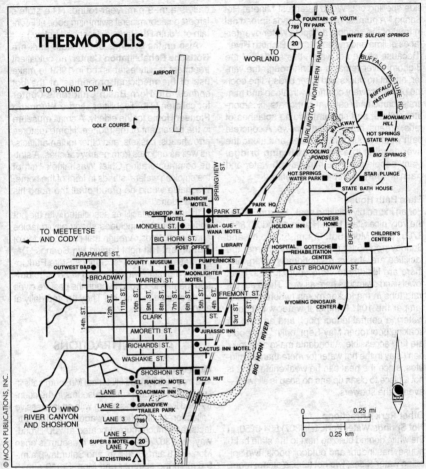

THERMOPOLIS

© MOON PUBLICATIONS, INC.

ing of bodily health in the bathing." Thus was established Wyoming's first state park. (See "Events" below for the annual Gift of the Waters Pageant.)

Today the park is the third-most-popular attraction in Wyoming; only Yellowstone and Grand Teton National Parks attract more visitors. The park includes a variety of facilities: a state-run bathhouse, two commercial establishments, a senior center, a rehabilitation center, and even a small herd of buffalo. Adjacent is the Holiday Inn spa facility. Park headquarters is the A-

frame structure at the corner of Park Street and U.S. 789. Just behind here is an impressive travertine cone created when workers put in a vent pipe.

Big Springs

Big Springs flows at a rate of approximately 2,575 gallons per minute at 135° F and is considered the largest hot springs in the world. The springs are located at the base of a small butte; just in case there might be some confusion, someone has placed white rocks along the hill-

side spelling out "World's Largest Mineral Hot Spring." A number of cooling ponds spread out in front of the springs, dropping water over terraces of lime and gypsum to the Bighorn River. (Because of the hot water, this stretch of the Bighorn River remains open through the winter, attracting ducks and other birds.) The cooling ponds are very colorful, with algae and minerals (particularly calcium carbonate, bicarbonate, sulfate, and sodium) adding splashes of reds, greens, browns, and yellows. A concrete path winds around the terraces and along the river, leading to a scenic **swinging bridge.** Many people drink the mineral-rich water and claim an array of medicinal benefits.

State Bath House

For an incredibly relaxing soak, be sure to visit the very nice State Bath House, tel. (307) 864-3765, open Mon.-Sat. 8 a.m.-5:30 p.m. and Sunday noon-5:30 p.m. No entry charge, the facilities are always exceptionally clean, and there are lockers to store your clothes. Rent towels and swimsuits here as well. There are private tubs in the locker rooms (where you can temper the 104° F mineral water with cooler water), a central indoor pool, and an outdoor soaking pool (open May-Sept. only). The pools are fully accessible. Attendants make sure folks don't stay in the hot water for more than 20 minutes, since the heat can be weakening. This is not a place to clean up and no soap is allowed—even in the showers.

Other Park Attractions

Hot Springs Water Park, tel. (307) 864-9250, in the white domed building next to the state bathhouse, has indoor and outdoor pools, two spiraling water slides, two hot tubs, a steam room, a sauna, and a mineral spa. Adults pay $7, kids $3, and seniors $5. Open daily 9 a.m.-9 p.m. all year. Massages are also available.

Even bigger is **Star Plunge,** tel. (307) 864-3771, also in the state park, with indoor and outdoor pools, two fast water slides, a steam room, two hot tubs, and tanning booths ($5 extra). The 500-foot-long outdoor slide is one of the three longest in the nation. Admission to Star Plunge costs $7 for adults, $5 for seniors, and $2 for kids under four. Towels, swimsuits, and inner tubes can also be rented. It's open

daily 9 a.m.-9 p.m. year-round. (The state's largest outdoor mineral swimming pool, at Fountain of Youth RV Park, is described below.)

Also on the grounds of the state park are **Gottsche Rehabilitation Center,** an outpatient treatment facility established in 1959 to make use of the medicinal properties of the hot springs, **Big Horn Basin Children's Center** for children with disabilities, and a **Wyoming Pioneer Home** for the elderly. A small **museum** in the basement of the Pioneer Home features arrowheads, baskets, and other Indian artifacts, as well as antiques from nearby ranches. A statue commemorating Chief Washakie's "gift of the smoking waters" stands in front of the home. Washakie would be proud of all the good his gift has done.

In addition to facilities associated with the hot springs, the park includes shady picnic tables and playgrounds. A rough trail cuts to the top of **Monument Hill** right behind Big Springs. The northeast portion of Hot Springs State Park includes a pasture where a herd of 20 or so **buffalo** roam. A loop road through the pasture gives you a chance to drive by. They are fed daily at 8:30 a.m.

OTHER ATTRACTIONS

Museum

The free Hot Springs Historical Museum calls itself "one of the best small museums in the country" and lives up to this billing with an impressive collection of old photos, wagons, Indian artifacts, and much more. Located at 700 Broadway, tel. (307) 864-5183, the museum is open Mon.-Fri. 8 a.m.-6:30 p.m. and Saturday 8 a.m.-5 p.m. in the summer and Mon.-Sat. 9 a.m.-5 p.m. the rest of the year. Entrance costs $2 for adults, $1.50 for seniors, $1 for ages 5-17, $5 for families. Kids under five get in free.

The museum sprawls through two floors of the main building and across the street to include an agriculture building, an old schoolhouse, a petroleum building, and a caboose. The main museum houses various displays of frontier life: a newspaper shop, dentist's office (complete with frightening tools), blacksmith shop, and general store. The cherrywood bar from the Hole-in-the-Wall Saloon is particularly popular; here mem-

bers of the famous outlaw gang tipped their glasses with sympathetic locals.

The Indian artifact collection downstairs is very impressive, not just because of the thousands of arrowheads but also because it includes an elk hide painted by Shoshone Chief Washakie. Outside, the 1920 Middleton Schoolhouse comes complete with old desks; check out the amusing letters from present-day schoolchildren. Kids of all ages love traipsing through the old Burlington Northern caboose and trying to figure out how the agriculture building's amazing 1926 Case threshing machine worked. The petroleum building houses exhibits on drilling for and refining oil, including old gusher photos and a gigantic power unit once used to pump oil before the arrival of electric pumps.

Wyoming Dinosaur Center

In 1992, three Germans formed a prospecting company to search for fossils in the Bighorn Basin. With the help of an American fossil expert they located a promising site just out of Thermopolis and in 1993 discovered a *sauropod* (a plant-eating dinosaur from the Jurassic Period). Realizing that many more dinosaurs lay below the surface, they purchased the land and began digging, later unearthing the most complete skeleton of a *brachiosaur* ever found and many more species. The discoveries led to the creation of the Wyoming Dinosaur Center, tel. (307) 864-2997, housed in a warehouse-type metal building on the eastern edge of town. The facility contains skeletons and casts from dinosaurs found not only nearby but also in Russia, Germany, and China. These include flying dinosaurs and marine reptiles. Although this is a for-profit venture with a gift shop selling miniature dinosaur figures, T-shirts, and fossils of various types, it's not just a gee-whiz exhibit to wow the

kids—the emphasis is heavily on science. Visitors can watch workers prepare specimens in the lab or take a tour of the Warm Springs Ranch dig site two miles away where excavations continue every summer. There's no chance of running out of specimens; the deposit contains an estimated 100,000 bones. The hourlong tours include a shuttle-bus ride from the Dinosaur Center and a presentation on digging techniques and local geology. Tours cost $10 for adults and $7 for kids and seniors and are free for children under five. Entrance to the Dinosaur Center is $6 for adults, $3.50 for kids and seniors, free for children under five. It is open daily 8 a.m.-8 p.m. May-Sept. and daily 10 a.m.-5 p.m. the rest of the year. Call (307) 864-2997 for more information.

PRACTICALITIES

Accommodations

Because of the popularity of Thermopolis during the summer, it's a good idea to reserve ahead (or check in during the afternoon) to be assured of a place. See the chart for specific motel and hotel rates. The fanciest lodging in town is **Holiday Inn,** tel. (307) 864-3131 or (800) 465-4329, located right in Hot Springs State Park. It's very popular with busloads of blue-haired Gray Line tourists and includes racquetball courts, a weight room, swimming pool, hot mineral jacuzzi, soaking tubs, saunas, massages, and more. Most of these cost extra. The walls are lined with big-game trophy mounts and skins and pictures of great white hunters standing over their deceased quarry. Owner Jim Mills killed most of the animals hanging around here. It's either appealing or appalling, depending upon your perspective.

Unfortunately, the most interesting lodging place in Thermopolis, Plaza Inn, went out of business in 1995. Hopefully it will reopen in the future. **Outwest B&B,** tel. (307) 864-2700, is housed within a turn-of-the-century Queen Anne home with stained-glass windows, an ornate staircase, and a screened balcony. The four guest rooms have shared baths and include a full breakfast. **Broadway Inn B&B,** tel. (307) 864-2636, is a turn-of-the-century brick hotel that has been restored and turned into a five-room

bed and breakfast. It has comfortable rooms and full breakfasts. **Faye's B&B,** tel. (307) 864-5166, is a newer home with four guest rooms.

Campgrounds

The closest public camping is 17 miles south in Wind River Canyon (see below). **Fountain of Youth RV Park,** two miles north of Thermopolis on U.S. 20, tel. (307) 864-9977, boasts Wyoming's largest mineral swimming pool, fed by what was intended to be an oil well. In 1918, C.F. Cross began drilling, but instead of hitting oil he struck hot mineral water, blowing the pipe casing out of the ground. Eventually a small travertine cone formed around the old casing. The "Sacajawea" well still flows at a rate of 1.3 million gallons per day. Not surprisingly, this is a very popular place with the "snowbird" RV crowd. The Labor Day breakfast in the pool is a favorite event. Open mid-April to mid-October, it costs $18 for RVs. **Grandview RV Park,** 122 U.S. 20 S, tel. (307) 864-3463, has tent spaces for $11, RV sites for $14. Showers for noncampers cost $3. Open mid-March to mid-October. **Latchstring RV Park,** on the south edge of town, tel. (307) 864-5262, charges $14 for tents, $18 for RVs; open May to mid-October. **Country Campin',** tel. (307) 864-2416, lives up to its name with a country location seven miles northeast of Thermopolis along the Big Horn River. Tent spaces are $14, RV hookups $16; tepee rentals are also available.

Food

Some of the best lunches and dinners in Thermopolis can be found at **Pumpernick's,** 512

THERMOPOLIS ACCOMMODATIONS

Note: Accommodations are listed from least to most expensive. Add a seven percent tax to the rates. Area code is 307.

Cactus Inn; U.S. 20; tel. 864-3155; $28 s, $36 d; kitchenettes $40 s or d

Bah-Gue-Wana Motel; 401 Park St.; tel. 864-3119; $28-30 s, $31-33 d; kitchenettes, no phones in rooms

Coachman Inn; U.S. 20; tel. 864-3141; $30 s, $40 d

Rainbow Motel; 408 Park St.; tel. 864-2129 or (800) 554-8815; $32 s or d; kitchenettes

El Rancho Motel; 924 Shoshoni; tel. 864-2341; $32 s, $37 d; AAA approved

Jurassic Inn; 501 S. 6th; tel. 864-2325; $39 s or d; continental breakfast, fridges in rooms, dinosaur gift shop

Outwest B&B; 1344 Broadway; tel. 864-2700; $40 s, $50 d; restored Victorian home, four guest rooms, shared baths, full breakfast

Roundtop Mt. Motel; 412 N. 6th; tel. 864-3126 or (800) 584-9126; $49 s or d for motel rooms; $52 s or d for cabins with kitchenettes, very nice

Faye's B&B; 1020 Arapahoe; tel. 864-5166; $50 s, $65 d; four guest rooms, shared or private bath, full breakfast

Best Western Moonlighter Motel; 600 Broadway; tel. 864-2321 or (800) 528-1234; $56-80 s, $59-80 d; indoor pool, AAA approved

Super 8 Motel; Lane 5, US 20 S; tel. 864-5515 or (800) 800-8000; $65 s, $69 d; new motel, indoor pool, jacuzzi, continental breakfast

Broadway Inn B&B; 342 Broadway; tel. 864-2636; $65-75 s or d; $95 for four in a two-room suite; turn-of-the-century hotel, five guest rooms, private baths, full breakfast

Holiday Inn of the Waters; Hot Springs Park; tel. 864-3131 or (800) 465-4329; $92 s or d; indoor pool, jacuzzi, sauna, exercise facility, racquetball courts, health club, AAA approved

Broadway, tel. (307) 864-5151. Try the pita-pocket sandwiches for lunch, or the homemade desserts. If you're in search of fresh deli sandwiches and soups, head to **Spatol's Deli-catessen,** 500 Broadway, tel. (307) 864-3960. Very good. **Manhattan Cafe,** 526 Broadway, tel. (307) 864-2501, has spicy barbecued beef rib and excellent malts. The **Sideboard Restaurant,** 109 S. 6th, tel. (307) 864-5335, offers standard American meals and a salad bar. In addition, Thermopolis has several fast-food places including Pizza Hut, McDonald's, Taco John's, and Subway.

Legion Supper Club, at the golf course on Airport Hill, tel. (307) 864-3918, is the local steak and seafood spot. Pricey, but good. The Sunday brunch buffet is especially popular. **The Safari Club,** in the Holiday Inn, tel. (307) 864-3131, has reasonably priced buffet breakfasts and dinners. Interesting atmosphere but variable food. Get groceries at **Consumers' Thriftway,** 600 S. 6th, tel. (307) 864-3112, or **Don's IGA,** 225 S. 4th, tel. (307) 864-5576. Don's also has a small deli and bakery. **Upper Crust Bakery,** 517 Broadway, tel. (307) 864-3665, has baked goods, sweets, and espresso coffees.

Entertainment
Mac's Bar, 506 Broadway, tel. (307) 864-3763, has live music on weekends, and the **Safari Club** at the Holiday Inn sometimes has a band. The **Little Broadway Theater** puts on amusing melodramatic performances during the summer months. Call the chamber of commerce at (307) 864-3192 for details and ticket reservations.

Events
The **Gift of the Waters Pageant** held the first weekend in August at Hot Springs State Park—commemorates the transfer of Big Springs to the federal government in 1896. The pageant has been presented every summer since 1950, with a cast that includes both local residents and Shoshone from the Wind River Reservation in full regalia. A tepee camp is set up near the hot springs for the festivities. Other events during Gift of the Waters include Indian dancing and a parade. **Hot Springs County Fair** is also held the first weekend of August, with all the standard agricultural and ranching exhibits. In mid-August, **Ranch Days Rodeo** is a competition in which local ranches vie with one another.

A unique way to discover the Old West is the **Outlaw Trail Ride** in mid-August. This week-long, 100-mile trip follows the "Outlaw Trail" from the Hole-in-the-Wall country of Butch Cassidy and the Sundance Kid to Thermopolis. This isn't for dudes—you'll need to bring your own horse, bedroll, and gear—but you'll find excellent meals provided here. A trail ride fee covers food, horsefeed, nightly entertainment, and more. Call (307) 864-2287 for information on this authentic not-for-profit adventure.

Recreation
Most of the playing takes place around the many pools in Thermopolis, including those in the state park, but there are other things to do as well. Rent clunker **bikes** from the Holiday Inn, tel. (307) 864-3131. The nine-hole **Legion Golf Course,** tel. (307) 864-5294, is on Airport Hill north of town. **Roundtop Mountain,** the distinctive butte that dominates the Thermopolis area, is an enjoyable but fairly steep hike. Take 7th Street to Airport Hill and turn on the first left. After the cemetery, turn right onto a gravel road that takes you to the trailhead.

Shopping
For a good selection of books, CDs, and tapes, stop by **The Wherehouse,** 107 N. 5th St., tel. (307) 864-5702. The **Wild Bunch Gallery,** 105 N. 5th St., tel. (307) 864-2208, sells limited-edition prints and original paintings. Note the swastikas embedded in the bricks above the Andreen Consignment Shop at 509 Broadway; they're actually Indian symbols from a pre-Nazi era.

Information and Services
The **Thermopolis Chamber of Commerce,** tel. (307) 864-3192 or (800) 786-6772, has its office in the museum at 700 Broadway. Open Mon.-Fri. 8 a.m.-8 p.m. and Saturday noon-6 p.m. in the summer and Mon.-Fri. 9 a.m.-5 p.m. the rest of the year. A summer-only **Welcome Wagon** is on the corner of 6th and Broadway. The **Hot Springs County Library** is located at 344 Arapahoe St., tel. (307) 864-3104. Wash your clothes at **Wishy Washy Laundromat** at 630 Shoshoni; open 24 hours a day in the summer. Get cash from the **ATM** at Don's IGA on 4th and Warren.

Transportation
SANTA (Shoshone Arapahoe Nations Transit Authority), tel. (800) 439-7118, offers on-demand bus connections to Riverton, Lander, Dubois, Jackson, Pinedale, Rock Springs (Grey-

hound connections), Rawlins, and Salt Lake City. **Powder River Trailways**, tel. (800) 442-3682, has scheduled bus service from Thermopolis to northern and eastern Wyoming and onward to other parts of America.

WIND RIVER CANYON

South of Thermopolis, the highway cuts across lush irrigated farm fields. Turn around and you'll see the steep slopes of Roundtop Mountain dominating the vistas. The highway bridges the Big Horn River and then, four miles south of town, abruptly enters magnificent Wind River Canyon. At this point the river's name changes just as abruptly. Lewis and Clark had named the Big Horn River, Crow Indians the Wind River. Early explorers somehow concluded that they were two separate waterways and in the confusion Wind River Canyon became the "Wedding of the Waters." Above this point the river is called the Wind, below it the Big Horn. A bit confusing.

Floating and Fishing
Many people float the Big Horn River, putting in at the Wedding of the Waters and taking out in Thermopolis. It's an enjoyable, leisurely drift with nice scenery and excellent fishing for rainbow trout (average size 15 inches). A special permit (available at Coast to Coast Hardware in Thermopolis) is required to fish in the canyon above Wedding of the Waters since it is part of the Wind River Indian Reservation.

Wind River Canyon Whitewater, tel. (307) 864-9343, leads exciting raft trips through the canyon during the summer, with the biggest water generally in June and July. These daily trips range from a quick two-hour drenching ($29 per person) to overnight trips with meals ($99-189 per person). The company also offers fishing trips and sells reservation fishing per-

mits and conservation stamps. See the chamber of commerce in Thermopolis for a listing of other fishing outfitters. **Canyon Sporting Goods,** 1002 Shoshoni in Thermopolis, tel. (307) 864-2815, sells fishing, boating, and camping gear.

Geologic History Lesson
The drive through Wind River Canyon is one of the most dramatic in Wyoming; U.S. 20 clings to the eastern bank of the river, and canyon walls rise up to 2,500 feet overhead. Tracks of the Burlington Northern Railroad (built in 1913) parallel the river on the other side, threading in and out through several tunnels. This place is a geologist's dream, slicing through rocks that grow progressively older as you continue south, with the oldest dating back to the Precambrian era, 2.7 billion years ago. A succession of roadside signs notes the various geologic formations, and the Thermopolis Chamber of Commerce can provide you with a descriptive log of the canyon's complex geology. At the upper end, the road quickly climbs past Boysen Dam and into the open country of Boysen State Park (see "Riverton Vicinity" in the Wind River Mountains Country chapter). Within the canyon you'll find two attractive **campgrounds,** Upper and Lower Wind River State Park ($4). The river flows right alongside, and there are many big old cottonwoods, but highway noise may keep you awake. Free tours of **Boysen Powerplant,** tel. (307) 864-3772, are available Mon.-Fri. 8 a.m.-4 p.m.

DOVER PUBLICATIONS, INC.

POWDER RIVER COUNTRY

Powder River country is the most historically interesting part of a state overflowing with history. For the Indians who made this their home, the basin was paradise, a place of massive bison herds and abundant forage for horses. Because of this richness, the area became a confrontation point between various Indian tribes and later between Indians and invading whites along the Bozeman Trail. Still later, the clashes were among the whites: cattlemen versus homesteaders, outlaws against lawmen. Today, the clashes have faded into memory, but the rich country remains. Coal, cattle, and sheep rule.

The Powder River Basin stretches from the crest of the Big Horn Mountains to the Black Hills and then south to Casper. The three largest settlements—Gillette, Sheridan, and Buffalo—dominate the region's economy. Sheridan and Buffalo provide gateways to the magnificent Big Horn Mountains, a recreation paradise capped by barren alpine peaks. Rolling grassland predominates across the Powder River Basin, accented by steep-sided buttes and lush riversides. The land is grazed extensively by cattle and sheep, though alfalfa and wheat are grown in many places. Oil and coal resources are vital to the economy of the area, especially around Gillette, making this the most important energy region in Wyoming. Despite the many large coal mines, the land remains relatively untouched. Nearly everyone chooses to live in the cities and smaller settlements, leaving enormous open expanses of land.

BIG HORN MOUNTAINS

Sandwiched between two broad basins—Bighorn to the west and Powder River to the east—are the majestic Big Horn Mountains. To the early explorers, this 70-mile-long range was the Shining Mountains, a name inspired by its snowcapped peaks, some topping 13,000 feet.

The Indians called it "Ahsahta," meaning "The Big Horns," after the Rocky Mountain bighorn sheep found here. Eventually, whites applied the name to all sorts of places in the region. The mountain country here is carpeted primarily with lodgepole and ponderosa pine, and En-

gelmann spruce and subalpine fir at higher elevations. While much of the country here is not as rugged as the mountains on the western border of Wyoming, the Big Horns do contain many rocky peaks above 9,000 feet, with 13,175-foot Cloud Peak crowning the skyline. Hundreds of small lakes reflect this dramatic scenery within the Cloud Peak Wilderness.

Nearly the entire range lies within **Bighorn National Forest,** a 1.1 million-acre chunk of public land set aside by President Grover Cleveland in 1897. Forest headquarters is in Sheridan at 1969 S. Sheridan Ave., tel. (307) 672-0751; additional district offices are in Lovell (tel. 307-548-6514), Worland (tel. 307-347-8291), Buffalo (tel. 307-684-7981), and Greybull (tel. 307-765-4435). Any of these can provide detailed forest maps ($4) and listings of permitted local outfitters.

This is multiple-use country, with logging, grazing, and recreation the primary attractions. Commercial logging has gone on within the forest for almost a century, and old tie flumes are still visible near Dayton. At one time, vast numbers of sheep grazed the Big Horns, totaling perhaps half a million. More than 50,000 sheep and 30,000 cattle still graze in these mountains, and sheepherder camps are common sights in the high meadows.

Most visitors simply drive through the Big Horns on one of the three scenic highways, but the country is well worth stopping to savor, especially if you're a fan of waterfalls. There are many campgrounds, more than 630 miles of hiking trails, and good fishing for rainbow, cutthroat, brook, and brown trout. Come winter, this is a popular destination for snowmobilers as well as cross-country and downhill skiers. There's quite a bit of wildlife to see here, too. Bighorn sheep have been reintroduced to the area and now number around seventy; all are located on the west side of the mountains. No grizzlies here, but quite a few black bears live in these mountains, especially on the northeastern slopes. Also look for mule and white-tailed deer, elk, and moose. (The moose are not native; they were transplanted from Jackson Hole beginning in 1948.)

CRUISIN' THROUGH

Three paved highways cut across the Big Horn Mountains, providing popular connections between Yellowstone and the Black Hills. U.S. 14 and 16 are both kept plowed through the winter, while U.S. 14A generally closes Nov.-May. All three have National Scenic Byway status, something that becomes more obvious with each mile you travel.

Highway 16
U.S. 16 climbs across the southern end of the range from Ten Sleep to Buffalo and is the easiest way across the Big Horns. More than a dozen Forest Service campgrounds line the route. This was the original "Black and Yellow Trail," first proposed in 1912 as a link between Chicago, the Black Hills, and Yellowstone. The first caravan of automobiles made it over the old sheepwagon track the following year, reaching Yellowstone after 18 hard days on the road. By the 1920s, the highway was marked with poles with alternating black and yellow bands. For many years, this was the main route to Yellowstone. East from Ten Sleep, U.S. 16 parallels cottonwood-lined Tensleep Creek, climbing past impressive red and yellow cliffs. A cross and marker commemorate Gilbert Leigh, an Irish nobleman who fell to his death while hunting here in 1884 (he was caught in an October snowstorm and, unable to see his way, slipped over the cliff). Eventually the switchbacks take you up to **Meadowlark Lake,** a popular winter destination for both cross-country skiers and 'bilers. The dirt road to **High Park Lookout Tower** is two miles east of here. Look for flower-bedecked **St. Christopher's Chapel of the Big Horns** as this side road climbs to the fire tower (not in use). Great views from the top. East of here, the road winds over Powder River Pass, providing breathtaking views into Cloud Peak Wilderness.

Highway 14
Open all year, U.S. 14 offers an equally impressive passage over the Big Horns between Greybull and Dayton. Above the dot of a town called Shell the road passes a remarkably phallic rocky butte, then catches Shell Creek and winds with it through the deep red rocks of dramatic **Shell Canyon,** past Shell Falls and the Antelope Butte Ski Area, before topping out at Granite Pass. (The name "Shell" appears repeatedly throughout the local topography thanks

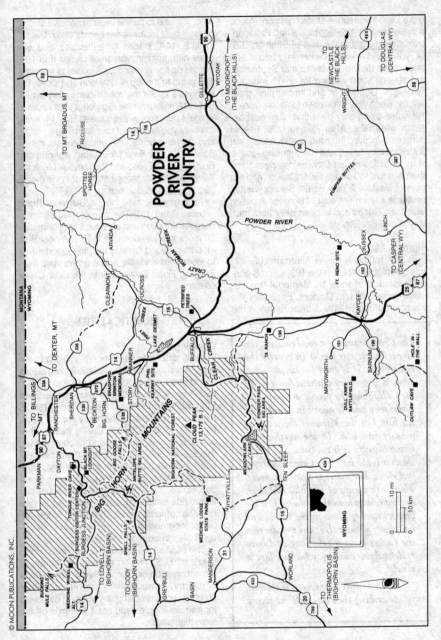

to the fossil invertebrate shells commonly found in the rocks.) At 120-foot-high **Shell Falls,** approximately eight miles east of Shell on U.S. 14, you'll find a visitor center with books and maps open daily mid-May to mid-September and several short walking trails with interpretive signs. Douglas fir and limber pine grow nearby. Keep your eyes open for water ouzels, the water-loving gray birds that often nest beneath waterfalls. After joining U.S. 14A at Burgess Junction, the road continues to Twin Buttes, Sibley Lake, and the amusing jumble of rocks called Fallen City, before zigzagging sharply down to Tongue River Canyon and the town of Dayton. A new Forest Service **visitor center** is a few miles east of Burgess Junction near Twin Buttes and is open daily from mid-May to mid-September.

Highway 14A

U.S. 14A (officially this is Alternate U.S. 14) was completely rebuilt in the 1980s and is generally cleared of snow by Memorial Day, remaining open till mid-October. Engineers like this road, modeled after similar routes in the Alps. It's said to be the most expensive stretch of road built in America. Locals claim the "A" in "U.S. 14A" stands for adventure, and with three different runaway truck ramps and 10% grades on some stretches it's easy to see why. The climb to the top is *very* long and steep, but the views make the tough climb worthwhile. U.S. 14A rises over the Big Horns from Lovell to Burgess Junction, where it meets U.S. 14. Along the way you're treated to miles of open sage-and-grass country with timbered islands on Bald and Little Bald Mountains, spectacular Bucking Mule Falls, and the famous Medicine Wheel. Watch for moose and deer in the meadows near Burgess Junction.

An enjoyable side loop is **Burgess Road** (Forest Road 15). The gravel road starts at Burgess Junction and continues approximately 20 miles to a junction with U.S. 14A near Bald Mountain. Along the way are fine opportunities to view deer and elk, and a grand vista from Burgess Road Overlook into the Lake Creek country.

PRACTICALITIES

Camping

With 35 different campgrounds ($8-10) in the area, you should have no trouble finding places to commune with nature. Most are above 5,000 feet in elevation, making for welcome escapes from summertime heat. Reservations ($8.25 extra) are available for the many popular spots by calling (800) 280-2267. During weekends in July and August, campgrounds along the main roads are frequently filled (get there before 2 p.m.), but harder-to-reach campgrounds usually have space. Forest Service offices in Sheridan, Buffalo, Greybull, Worland, and Lovell can all provide details on dates, cost, and access to these camping places. In addition to the official campgrounds, you can camp in undeveloped sites throughout the forest for free.

The BLM's Five Springs Campground (free) is just off U.S. 14A on the western border of the national forest. Scenic **Five Springs Falls** is nearby. In addition to the official campgrounds, you can camp anywhere in the forest for free, as long as you are a half-mile off the main highways.

> *The Crow country is a good country; the Great Spirit has put it in exactly the right place. It is good for horses—and what is a country without horses? On the Columbia, the people are poor and dirty; they paddle about in canoes and eat fish. On the Missouri the water is muddy and bad. To the north of the Crow country it is too cold, and to the south it is too hot. The Crow country is just right. The water is clear and sweet. There are plenty of buffalo, elk, deer, antelope, and mountain sheep. It is the best wintering place in the world and has plenty of game. Is it any wonder that the Crows have fought long and hard to defend this country, which we love so much?*
>
> *—Crow Chief Arapooish, describing the Powder River Basin.*

The historic **Muddy Guard Station** was constructed by the Civilian Conservation Corps in the 1930s and is now available for rent to the public. The log building has propane lights and a woodstove but no running water or electricity. It sleeps up to five and rents for $40 per day. Located 25 miles west of Buffalo on U.S. 16, this unique cabin is open year-round; call (307) 684-7981 for reservations.

Lodging and Food

Scattered throughout the Big Horns are seven mountain lodges, all of which have bars and restaurants. **Bear Lodge Resort,** at Burgess Junction (8,300 feet in elevation), tel. (307) 655-2444, is open year-round with older motel rooms ($44 s or d) and bring-your-own-linen rustic cabins ($23 for up to eight, plus $3 for showers). They also have a hot tub and rent mountain bikes in the summer and snowmobiles in the winter. If you're staying elsewhere, take a shower for $4. Pitch a tent for $5, park RVs for $8. The bar is a great place to shoot a game of pool and occasionally has live country music on weekends. The gift shop has a few groceries.

Arrowhead Lodge, tel. (307) 655-2388 or 672-4111, four miles east of Burgess Junction on U.S. 14, offers very basic cabins with kitchenettes starting for $25 s or d and motel rooms starting for $37 s or d. It's open year-round. Park RVs for $15 a night. If you aren't staying here you can use the showers for $2.

Ranger Creek Guest Ranch, tel. (307) 655-9420, is five miles south of U.S. 14 on Forest Rd. 17 (near the Antelope Butte Ski Area). Facilities on this small ranch include a central lodge and rustic log cabins with woodstoves and a central bathhouse. Daily rates are $50 s or d, $90 per person with three meals and horseback riding. Weekly rates are also available, as are fishing trips into wilderness camps.

Deer Haven Lodge, 18 miles east of Ten Sleep on U.S. 16, tel. (307) 366-2449, charges $28 s or d, $48 for up to four in plain-Jane cabins with woodstoves and a separate bathhouse; bring your own towels. They also have older motel rooms that sleep four for $48. Closed November and April.

Meadowlark Lake Resort, 22 miles east of Ten Sleep (42 miles west of Buffalo) along U.S. 16, tel. (307) 366-2449 or (800) 858-5672, has undergone a major transformation in recent years and is now the nicest resort in the Big Horns. The resort is open all year, and its restaurant serves three meals a day—breakfast all day long. Lodging includes rustic cabins with a central bathhouse ($33 s or d), motel rooms with private baths ($44 s or d), and cottages with kitchenettes ($40-67 s or d). Meadowlark also rents row boats, canoes, and a pontoon boat for the lake, and mountain bikes to explore the country. In the winter the lodge rents snowmobiles and cross-country skis for use on nearby trails. It has a restaurant, lounge, and gift shop; open year-round. Horseback rides are available in the summer at nearby Willow Park.

Lodge in the Pines, 14 miles west of Buffalo on U.S. 16, tel. (307) 680-8545 or 684-5204, has basic cabins ($28-75) that sleep up to four. Kids and seniors can throw in a line at the fishing pond.

South Fork Inn, 16 miles west of Buffalo on U.S. 16, tel. (307) 684-9609, also has a wide variety of cabins, and rents mountain bikes. They also offer horseback rides and drop camp trips. Open June-Sept. only.

Snowshoe Lodge, tel. (307) 765-2669 or 568-2960, is located six miles south of U.S. 14 and southwest of Antelope Butte Ski Area. You can stay year-round in the lodge for $60 s, $120 d with dinner, wine, and breakfast. The lodge also has a hot tub and double-deck porches. More-rustic accommodations include cabins at $40 for up to eight—no linen—and sheep wagons for $30 s or d—no linen.

Skiing and Snowmobiling

The Big Horns provide some of the finest snow in Wyoming, with groomed cross-country ski trails at **Sibley Lake,** 15 miles of trails and a warming hut off U.S. 14; **Willow Park,** 23 miles of trails near Meadowlark Lake; and **Pole Creek,** 13 miles of trails and a warming hut off U.S. 16. Trail descriptions are available from local Forest Service offices. The rest of the forest makes for outstanding skiing most of the winter, but you'll need to break your own trail. Snowmobilers will find trails throughout the forest; get a route map from chamber of commerce offices. **Meadowlark Resort,** tel. (307) 366-2424, rents snowmobiles and cross-country skis, and **Deer Haven Lodge,** tel. (307) 366-2449, rents snowmobiles.

Antelope Butte Ski Area, tel. (307) 655-9530, is a small family ski area 60 miles west of Sheridan and 35 miles east of Greybull on U.S. 16. It has two chairlifts and a platter lift; the vertical rise is 1,000 feet from a base elevation of 8,400 feet. It's open Wed.-Sun. and holidays 9:30 a.m.-4 p.m. mid-November through March. Lift tickets cost $20 for adults, $18 for seniors, $12 for ages 7-15, and free for young-uns. Rent skis, boots, and poles here for just $12, or take lessons from the ski school. The lodge serves light meals. Cross-country skiers will enjoy the five km of groomed trails that take off from the parking lot.

Powder Pass Ski Area, 35 miles east of Ten Sleep and 45 miles west of Buffalo on U.S. 16, tel. (307) 347-9831, is another small ski area with a double chairlift, a Poma lift, and rope tow serving an 800-foot vertical rise. It's open mid-December to early April with lifts running 9 a.m.-4 p.m. Wed.-Sun. and holidays. Get food, drinks, and ski rentals at the base lodge. Tickets cost $15 for adults, $10 for ages 7-15, and free for under age seven.

Hikes and Sights
You'll find plenty to see and do in the Big Horns, including Medicine Wheel and the Cloud Peak Wilderness (see below). Stop by the Forest Service office in Sheridan, Buffalo, Worland, Greybull, or Lovell for descriptions of other hiking trails.

Several trails take off from Sheep Mountain Road on U.S. 14A approximately 30 miles east of Lovell and three miles east of the turnoff to Medicine Wheel. **Littlehorn Trail** parallels the Little Bighorn River for 18 miles. Along the way you'll see 1,600-foot canyon faces and water fountaining off the limestone cliffs of Leaky Mountain. The trailhead is two miles up Sheep Mountain Road. A half-mile farther up the road is the trailhead for **Porcupine Falls,** a 200-foot-tall cascade accessible via a half-mile path. Along the way the trail passes a 1930s-era gold mine. Much of the area here was burned in a 1988 forest fire.

One of the not-to-be-missed places in the Big Horns is spectacular **Bucking Mule Falls,** a 600-foot cascade dropping into Devil Canyon. The trailhead for Bucking Mule Falls lies 11 miles off U.S. 14A on Sheep Mountain Road,

and the waterfall is a three-mile roundtrip hike. You can also do an 11-mile loop hike by following the trail to the falls and then continuing south to Porcupine Campground.

Black Mountain Lookout, west of Dayton on U.S. 14, offers surprisingly dramatic vistas from the top of a 9,300-foot peak. This old Forest Service fire lookout is open to the public and sits at the end of a one-mile trail. Get there by turning south on Forest Road 202 when it leaves U.S. 14 two miles west of the Fallen City area and follow it four miles to the trailhead.

The trailhead for **Tongue River Canyon** is 3.5 miles southwest of Dayton to the end of Tongue Canyon Road. This loop trail climbs up the canyon and then back again for a total of 14 miles, offering glimpses of the old McShane brothers' tie flume—built in 1894 and stretching for 26 miles—the fast-flowing blue-ribbon fishing stream (cutthroat, rainbow, brook, and German brown trout), and canyon walls reaching a thousand feet into the air. Ambitious hikers may want to continue all the way to Burgess Junction. Locals float down parts of the river during the spring, when water levels are high.

Tongue River Cave is near the trailhead and stays open all year. With well over a mile of passages, it's one of Wyoming's most popular caves but has been considerably vandalized with broken formations, trash, and graffiti. Because of its size, inexperienced spelunkers can become lost, so ask locally for someone willing to act as a guide. More than 100 other caves honeycomb this country; see the Forest Service for locations and precautions.

Another trail worth exploring if you want an out-of-the-way adventure is the **Little Bighorn River Canyon Trail** starting west of Ranchester along the Wyoming-Montana border. Contact the Forest Service in Sheridan for directions and details on this multi-day trek.

An enjoyable waterfall is **Big Goose Falls.** Follow Forest Road 26 (it starts approximately five miles south of Burgess Junction on U.S. 14) to Big Goose Ranger Station, then continue on via Forest Road 296 to the end. The falls are about five miles below the ranger station along the East Fork of Big Goose Creek. They include plunge pools and water-sculpted rocks.

One of the most interesting drives in the Big Horns slices through **Crazy Woman Canyon.**

Several stories exist for the origin of the canyon's name. One claims it's named for an Indian squaw who went insane while living alone in her tepee here. Another version says it came from a white settler who was pushed to insanity when Indians murdered and scalped her husband. Soldiers from Fort Laramie reportedly found her wandering the area. Either way, it wasn't exactly a soothing name for migrants on the old Bozeman Trail! Nevertheless, the canyon cut by cascading Crazy Woman Creek is a stunning one with steep cliffs on both sides. A very rough gravel road (high-clearance vehicles are recommended; this isn't for trailers or RVs) heads down the canyon from Crazy Woman Campground (25 miles west of Buffalo on U.S. 16; $9, open mid-May through September). You can follow the road all the way to the mouth of the canyon and then on to State 196. The canyon drive is actually more interesting (and easier on your brakes) if you do it from Buffalo westward, but be ready for a long and very difficult drive in either direction. **Crazy Woman Canyon Tours,** based at the Donut Shop in Buffalo, tel. (307) 684-5446, offers 4WD treks into this country.

MEDICINE WHEEL

High atop a windswept mountain plateau sits one of the best-known and least-understood archaeological sites in America, the Medicine Wheel. Measuring 80 feet across, this uneven "wagon wheel" of stones seems ready to roll over the nearby slopes. Twenty-eight rock spokes radiate out from a central hub, with six smaller rock cairns scattered around the rim. A variety of lesser-known rock structures surround the Medicine Wheel on nearby slopes, including an arrow that supposedly points southwest to another "wheel" near Meeteetse 70 miles away, a large rectangle of stones, and more than 50 tepee rings. An ancient cairn-marked travois trail continues northwest from Medicine Wheel over the Big Horn Mountains.

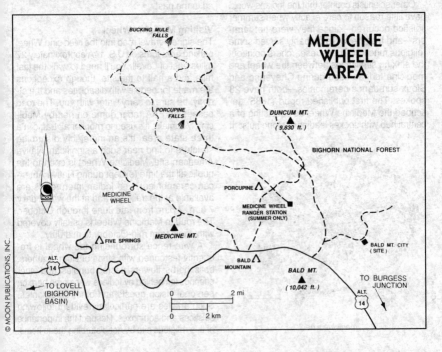

Origins and Purpose

Medicine Wheel's origins are hidden in the depths of time. White prospectors from the nearby gold-mining camp of Bald Mountain City (now entirely gone) discovered the Medicine Wheel around 1885. Carbon-14 dating of wood fragments found in one of the cairns yielded the date A.D. 1760, but some artifacts associated with the site may date back 11,000 years.

Prevailing theories about the purpose behind the Medicine Wheel fall into two schools: it was either an astronomical observatory or a site for sacred ceremonies. One of the most interesting theories was suggested by astronomer John Eddy in a 1977 *National Geographic* article. He noted that the 28 spokes are equal to the number of days in the lunar month and that two of the cairns served as horizon markers for sunrise and sunset, with the other four cairns marking the rising of three of the brightest stars. These could have signaled the summer solstice. Interestingly, similar alignments occur on a stone wheel in Saskatchewan, Canada.

Other scientists counter that the Indians would have little reason to care exactly when summer solstice occurred—since they were not farmers—and that the rocks probably served some religious function. These researchers point out the striking similarities between the wheel and medicine lodges used during Cheyenne and Sioux sun-dance ceremonies—both have 28 spokes. The first published report (1885) described the Medicine Wheel as consisting of a central hub with spokes leading to stone huts: "It

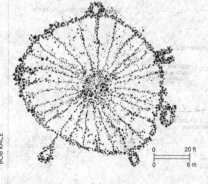

medicine wheel

is said that these smaller huts were, during religious ceremonies, occupied by medicine men of different tribes, while the larger hut in the center was supposed to be the abode of Manitour." Various later reports attributed it to the Crow, Sheepeater, Arapaho, and Cheyenne tribes. University of Montana anthropologist Gregory Campbell considers the wheel a source of religious power to Native Americans and notes that it is a place where "powerful events come to the fore" for those who search for strength.

Regardless of its origins or earliest uses, the Medicine Wheel *was* used in historical times—and is still used today—as a place for prayer, meditation, renewal, and vision quests. Chief Joseph of the Nez Percé fasted here, and Shoshone Chief Washakie was said to have gained his "medicine" here. Because of the Medicine Wheel's location and the importance of ceremony in Native American life, it certainly was—and is—a sacred site, whether or not it served any astronomical function. Its origins and original purpose, however, remain shrouded in the past.

Visiting Medicine Wheel

The signed gravel road into the Medicine Wheel parking area turns off U.S. 14A approximately 27 miles east of Lovell. You'll need to walk the last mile and a half to the site, though exceptions are made for people with disabilities and the elderly; be sure to carry water with you. The road passes an FAA radar dome on nearby Medicine Mountain; it's used to monitor air traffic in a three-state area. It's an incredibly disturbing structure to find near such a significant Native American site. Medicine Wheel is open to the public all the time (except during Native American ceremonies), and Indian interpreters are available at the trailhead and at the wheel daily 7 a.m.-7 p.m. from late June through October. The road to Medicine Wheel is usually covered with snow from mid-October to mid-July.

A wire fence surrounding the wheel is frequently festooned with strips of cloth, feathers, bells, herbs, flowers, sacred bundles, and other offerings left behind by Indians who come here on personal vision quests and other ceremonies. Such articles are particularly evident following solstices and equinoxes. Respect the importance of this religious site by not disturbing these items.

It is obvious why this mountain was chosen for the Medicine Wheel. The surrounding open country has scattered pine, juniper, and spruce, and the ridge drops off a 150-foot precipice just 50 feet away. From its 9,956-foot elevation, a vast panorama stretches to include the Bighorn Basin, the Wind River, the Absaroka Range, and the Pryor Mountains. Medicine Wheel is also a good place to look for hawks wheeling through the sky, especially red-tailed and kestrels.

CLOUD PEAK WILDERNESS

Although maintained as a primitive area since 1932, the 189,000-acre Cloud Peak Wilderness did not receive official wilderness status until 1984. It's named for 13,175-foot **Cloud Peak,** a rocky mountain visible for a hundred miles in all directions. At one time this entire range was glaciated, and reminders abound in the sharpened peaks, broad U-shaped valleys, and multitude of lakes in glacial tarns. There are even a few small patches of glacial ice. The Big Horns still get plenty of snow, leaving many hiking trails in the high country blocked until July. One oddly named mountain in the wilderness is **Bomber Mountain,** just south of Cloud Peak. An Air Force B-17 bomber crashed here in 1943, killing all 10 men on board. It was not found for two years. For the sad but fascinating story, see *The Bomber Mountain Crash: A Wyoming Mystery* by R. Scott Madsen (Buffalo, WY: Mountain Man Publishing).

With more than 140 miles of trails and thousands of acres more above timberline, hiking and horse-packing opportunities abound throughout Cloud Peak. Bears are not usually a problem in the Cloud Peak Wilderness. Backcountry users must fill out registration cards, available at the trailheads or local Forest Service offices. Be sure to camp at least 100 feet from water sources and trails and hang all food out of reach of black bears. Use existing campsites whenever possible to lessen your impact. The Forest Service produces a free map/guide to the wilderness area, which lists additional precautions.

For complete trail and historical info on the wilderness, get Kenneth Melius' book *Cloud Peak Wilderness: Trail Guide, History, and Photo Odyssey* (Pierre, SD: Tensleep Publications). *The Hiker's Guide to Wyoming,* by Bill Hunger (Helena, MT: Falcon Press), also features a number of hikes within Cloud Peak Wilderness. Be sure to purchase topographic maps before heading out.

Check with the Forest Service office in Sheridan, Buffalo, Lovell, Greybull, or Worland for a list of permitted outfitters and wilderness regulations and a list of important corrections and additions to Melius' guidebook. Be sure to always practice "no trace" camping; if you don't know what this means, pick up a handout from any of the Forest Service offices.

Access into Cloud Peak Wilderness is via several entry roads along U.S. 16 on the southern border—most of the use comes from this side—and from the north (U.S. 14) at Cross Creek and Ranger Creek Campgrounds and Twin Lakes Picnic Ground. Other entrance points surround Cloud Peak, but many require long hikes up 4WD roads to get to the wilderness boundary.

Trails

The **Stull Lakes-Coney Lake Trail** is one of the shortest hikes into the lake country of Cloud Peak. It climbs three miles from the Twin Lakes Picnic Ground, passes Stull Lake, and ends in the alpine country surrounding Coney Lake. Watch for elk and deer in late summer.

An excellent 21-mile loop hike begins at **Paintrock Lakes Trailhead** on the west side of the wilderness. This route traverses a wide variety of country, from dense timber to rocky mountain passes and small glaciers. The path climbs to a trail junction 1.5 miles west of Cliff Lake. From here, turn left and follow the trail to Geneva Pass (10,300 feet). The trail drops down to Lake Geneva and then follows East Fork Creek to the junction with the Edelman Trail. This path leads over Edelman Pass, around Emerald Lake, and then back down to the Edelman Trailhead, just 1.5 miles by road from your starting point. You'll find all sorts of other hikes and side trips in this area.

Another loop trip takes you to **Lake Solitude.** Begin at the Battle Park Trailhead approximately 15 miles north of Meadowlark Lake. Take the road to Tyrell Ranger Station and turn left after a

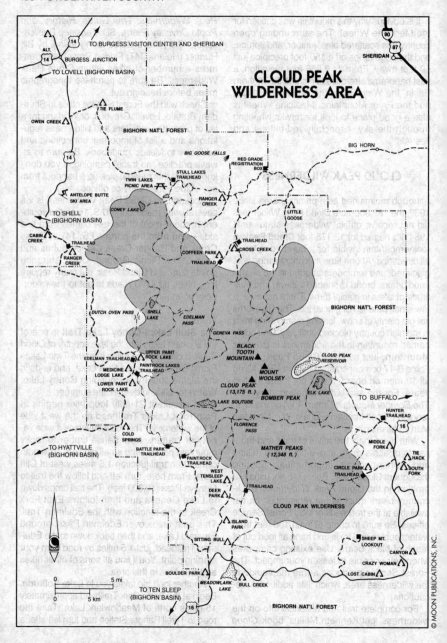

CLOUD PEAK WILDERNESS AREA

TO BURGESS VISITOR CENTER AND SHERIDAN

BURGESS JUNCTION

TO LOVELL (BIGHORN BASIN)

SHERIDAN

BIG HORN

TIE FLUME

OWEN CREEK

BIGHORN NAT'L FOREST

BIG GOOSE FALLS

RED GRADE REGISTRATION BOX

ANTELOPE BUTTE SKI AREA

TWIN LAKES PICNIC AREA

STULL LAKES TRAILHEAD

RANGER CREEK

LITTLE GOOSE

TO SHELL (BIGHORN BASIN)

Coney Lake

TRAILHEAD

CABIN CREEK

TRAILHEAD

RANGER CREEK

COFFEEN PARK

TRAILHEAD

CROSS CREEK

TRAILHEAD

DUTCH OVEN PASS

SHELL LAKE

EDELMAN PASS

BIGHORN NAT'L FOREST

GENEVA PASS

BLACK TOOTH MOUNTAIN

CLOUD PEAK RESERVOIR

UPPER PAINT ROCK LAKE

PAINTROCK LAKES TRAILHEAD

EDELMAN TRAILHEAD

MEDICINE LODGE LAKE

LOWER PAINT ROCK LAKE

MOUNT WOOLSEY

CLOUD PEAK (13,175 ft.)

BOMBER PEAK

ELK LAKE

LAKE SOLITUDE

Coney Lake

TO BUFFALO

HUNTER TRAILHEAD

COLD SPRINGS

FLORENCE PASS

TO HYATTVILLE (BIGHORN BASIN)

BATTLE PARK TRAILHEAD

PAINTROCK TRAILHEAD

MATHER PEAKS (12,348 ft.)

MIDDLE FORK

TIE HACK

SOUTH FORK

CIRCLE PARK TRAILHEAD

WEST TENSLEEP LAKE

TRAILHEAD

DEER PARK

CLOUD PEAK WILDERNESS

ISLAND PARK

SHEEP MT. LOOKOUT

CANYON

SITTING BULL

CRAZY WOMAN

LOST CABIN

BOULDER PARK

MEADOWLARK LAKE

BULL CREEK

TO TEN SLEEP (BIGHORN BASIN)

BIGHORN NAT'L FOREST

0   5 mi

0   5 km

© MOON PUBLICATIONS, INC.

mile, continuing up the rough gravel road to the trailhead. The trail climbs up Paint Rock Creek past Grace Lake and Lake Solitude to Mistymoon Lake. Beyond this you can either return on the same route or follow the trail down a steep valley to the water-lily-filled Lily Lake. Continue downhill to the Paintrock Trailhead on Forest Road 24, and turn right (northwest), following the road a mile back to your starting point. The loop is approximately 17 miles roundtrip.

The easiest—and probably busiest—route to the top of **Cloud Peak** takes off from West Tensleep Trailhead on Forest Road 27. Plan on a strenuous 10 hours for the 11-mile climb up and back. This is not a developed trail and will require considerable rock hopping, but the spec-

tacularly desolate scenery makes it worthwhile. Be prepared for sudden weather changes, and carry an ice ax into August. For detailed route instructions up Cloud Peak, get a topographic map and a copy of Bill Hunter's trail guide.

The **Elk Lake Loop** (19 miles roundtrip) begins at Hunter Trailhead on the southeast side of the wilderness and involves lots of climbing. Follow the old jeep trail to Soldier Park, a scenic grassy meadow. Turn north at the trail junction and follow the path to Elk Lake. Along the way are some outstanding views across the alpine terrain to Cloud Peak. Turn left at Elk Lake, head up over a pass, and then south to North Clear Creek Trail. Follow it downhill to Soldier Park and back to the trailhead.

SHERIDAN

The attractive and vibrant small city of Sheridan (pop. 14,800) has plenty to see, several fine restaurants, great country in the nearby Big Horn Mountains, and a genuine sense of history. At just 3,745 feet above sea level, it claims the lowest elevation of any Wyoming town, making for hot summers. The country around Sheridan was settled by a broad mixture of Europeans—everyone from British lords to Polish coal miners. Their heritage carries on in such events as an annual polka festival and weekly polo matches at Big Horn Equestrian Center, the oldest polo club in the nation (see "South of Sheridan" under "Sheridan Vicinity," below). Locals brag that Sheridan has a wealth of things to do and a surprising cultural richness without the crowds of Yellowstone and Jackson Hole. The town is, however, changing, losing some of the hard-edged cowboy feel from the past and gaining more yuppified Western wear boutiques, galleries, antique stores, and eateries all the time.

HISTORY

Sheridan, like other towns in the Powder River Basin, was built on coal, cattle, farming, and the railroad. In 1882, John D. Loucks took a liking to the country here and decided to establish a town, drawing up a plat on a piece of brown

wrapping paper. He named the new place for his commanding officer during the Civil War, Gen. Philip Sheridan, and immediately set about getting others to come. For several years Sheridan competed with nearby Big Horn City for the county seat, a title that ensured survival. Finally, in 1885, Sheridan promoters offered cowboys at the fall roundup free lots in the town. When most accepted, Sheridan finally had enough folks to incorporate. Almost overnight (literally, in some cases), businesses in Big Horn City moved to Sheridan, sometimes bringing their buildings along with them.

When the Burlington and Missouri Railroad reached Sheridan in 1892, the town suddenly changed. Now ranchers could get their cattle to market more easily and visitors could stay in the sumptuous Sheridan Inn. Dryland farming became more profitable as investors built large grain mills and a sugar-processing plant. The first underground coal mines opened in 1883, but it was not until 1903 that the Burlington Railroad began using the coal in its engines. For the next several decades these "black diamonds" were mainstays of the local economy. Sheridan soon had 1,500 people, wooden sidewalks, 30 saloons, six churches, and two opera houses. Small mining towns—Dietz, Acme, Kooi, Model, Riverside, and Carneyville—opened in the surrounding countryside, inhabited by thousands of European emigrants; newspa-

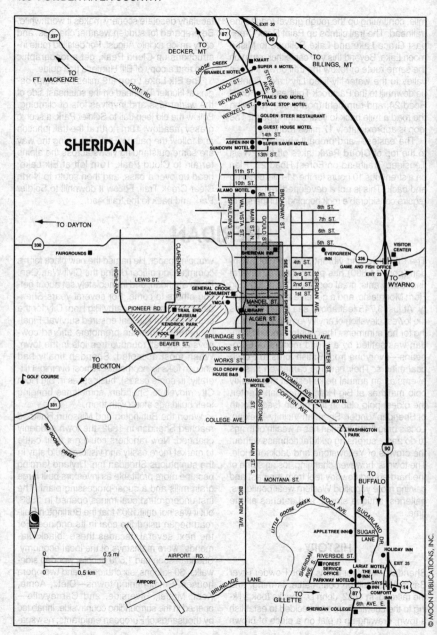

SHERIDAN

TO DECKER, MT

TO FT. MACKENZIE

TO BILLINGS, MT

GOOSE CREEK

FORT RD.

KMART
SUPER 8 MOTEL
BRAMBLE MOTEL

KOOI ST.

STEVENS AVE.

SEYMOUR ST.
TRAILS END MOTEL

WENZELL ST.
STAGE STOP MOTEL

GOLDEN STEER RESTAURANT
GUEST HOUSE MOTEL

14th ST.
SUPER SAVER MOTEL

ASPEN INN
SUNDOWN MOTEL

13th ST.

11th ST.

10th ST.

ALAMO MOTEL
9th ST.

BROADWAY

VAL VISTA ST.

SPALDING ST.

MAIN ST. N

GOULD ST.

8th ST.
7th ST.
6th ST.
5th ST.

EVERGREEN
INN

VISITOR
CENTER

GAME AND FISH OFFICE
EXIT 23

TO WYARNO

336

TO DAYTON

330

FAIRGROUNDS

CLARENDON AVE.

LEWIS ST.

HIGHLAND

PIONEER RD.

GENERAL CROOK
MONUMENT
YMCA

TRAIL END
MUSEUM
KENDRICK PARK
POOL

BLVD.

BEAVER ST.

BRUNDAGE ST.

LOUCKS ST.

WORKS ST.

OLD CROFF
HOUSE B&B

SHERIDAN INN

SEE "DOWNTOWN SHERIDAN" MAP

4th ST.
3rd ST.
2nd ST.
1st ST.

SHERIDAN AVE.

MANDEL ST.
LIBRARY
ALGER ST.

GRINNELL AVE.

WATER ST.

TRIANGLE
MOTEL

WYOMING AVE.

COFFEEN AVE.

ROCKTRIM MOTEL

GLADSTONE ST.

COLLEGE AVE.

WASHINGTON
PARK

TO BECKTON

GOLF COURSE

331

BIG GOOSE CREEK

MAIN ST. S

MONTANA ST.

90

TO BUFFALO

TO BECKTON

BIG HORN AVE.

LITTLE GOOSE CREEK

AVOCA AVE.

SUGARLAND DR.

0   0.5 mi

0   0.5 km

AIRPORT RD.

AIRPORT

BRUNDAGE
LANE

TO GILLETTE

APPLE TREE INN

SUGAR
LANE

RIVERSIDE ST.

SHERIDAN AVE. S

FOREST SERVICE
OFFICE
PARKWAY MOTEL

LARIAT MOTEL
THE MILL INN
DAYS INN
COMFORT INN

HOLIDAY INN

EXIT 25

14

87

6th AVE. E.

SHERIDAN COLLEGE

© MOON PUBLICATIONS, INC.

EXIT 20

87

90

pers often featured ads in both Polish and English. Electric streetcars were added in 1911, with frequent interurban service to the surrounding coal mines.

World War II brought prosperity as local mines operated at full tilt and new technology allowed construction of the first open-pit mine. After the war, however, trains shifted to diesel and homes began burning less-polluting natural gas, so that by 1953 the last of the old coal towns had died. With increasing demand for western coal in the 1970s, Sheridan's population boomed again. Recent years have seen the closing of some nearby strip mines and the crossing of many workers into Montana to work in the Decker and Spring Creek strip mines there, although a long strike in the Decker mine has split the community. Sheridan now depends upon a mixture of mining, ranching, government jobs, and tourism.

SIGHTS

Trail End State Historic Site
Located on spacious grounds overlooking Sheridan, Trail End Historic Center, 400 Clarendon Ave., tel. (307) 674-4589, is the city's best-known attraction. Managed by the state, it's open daily 9 a.m.-6 p.m. June-Aug. daily 1-4 p.m. in the fall and spring, and closed mid-December to mid-March. No charge. This was the home of John B. Kendrick, a wealthy rancher and a powerful Democratic politician. Born in Texas in 1857, Kendrick was raised as an orphan. He became a ranch hand by age 15 and, after trailing cattle north to Wyoming, fell in love with the country and took a job as a ranch foreman. At age 34, he married the 17-year-old Eula Wulfgen, and they lived on a ranch in southeastern Montana for the next 18 years.

Over the years Kendrick acquired more than 200,000 acres of land in Wyoming and Montana grazed by tens of thousands of his cattle. He personally financed local homesteaders, friends, former employees, and relatives. Politics beckoned once Kendrick was

firmly established as a rancher and businessman, and he served first as governor, then as a U.S. senator until his death in 1933. One paper called him "the craftiest politician the state has ever produced." Kendrick helped expose the Teapot Dome Scandal and gained funding for the massive Kendrick Project, a series of dams and irrigation canals on the North Platte River.

Shortly before entering politics, Kendrick selected the site for his end-of-the-trail mansion high atop a hill overlooking Sheridan. Begun in 1908, Trail End took five years to complete and served primarily as a summer home since politics kept Kendrick

DOWNTOWN SHERIDAN

5th ST.
SILVER SPUR CAFE
SHERIDAN INN
VAL VISTA ST.
4th ST.
3rd ST.
HISTORIC STREET CAR
SHERIDAN CENTER MOTOR INN
MAIN ST.
GOULD ST.
2nd ST.
1st ST.
GOOSE CREEK
BROADWAY
DOW ST.
X - L MOTEL
THE CHOCOLATE TREE
LIBRARY
BIG HORN MT. SPORTS
MANDEL ST.
SANFORD'S
ALGER ST.
SHERIDAN STATIONERY
CITY HALL
BROOKS ST.
GRINNELL AVE.
KING'S SADDLERY
MINT BAR
SCOTT ST.
CIAO BISTRO
THE BOOK SHOP
BEST OUT WEST MALL
BRUNDAGE ST.
0   0.25 mi
0   0.25 km
LOUCKS ST.
POST OFFICE

© MOON PUBLICATIONS, INC.

away the rest of the year. The mansion is in the Flemish Revival style, with curvilinear gables on the third-floor windows, a red-tile roof, hardwood floors, mahogany walls, and exposed-beam ceilings. Many of the sumptuous original furnishings (including a 25-foot-long Kurdistan rug) are still inside. Look for photos of several of Kendrick's ranches upstairs.

The house cost $165,000 in an era when typical homes went for less than $1,000. Its 18 rooms include a third-floor ballroom with a loft where musicians could play without interfering with the dancers below. The built-in central vacuum system still works. Heating Trail End sometimes required up to a ton of coal each day. Out back is a sod-roofed **log cabin** recently reconstructed and moved onto the grounds. Built in 1878, this historic structure served at various times as Sheridan's first post office, a school, a store, a law office, and a bank.

Sheridan Inn

Built in 1893, Sheridan Inn was considered by many to be the premier hotel between Chicago and San Francisco. Visitors included Presidents Theodore Roosevelt, Taft, and Hoover and other celebrities such as Will Rogers and Ernest Hemingway. Architect Thomas Kimball modeled the Inn after a Scottish hunting lodge, with dormer windows on all 62 rooms; *Ripley's Believe it or Not!* labeled it "The House of 69 Gables," a name that has stuck through the years. Inside, carpenters have added hand-hewn ponderosa pine beams, three large cobblestone fireplaces, the Buffalo Bill Bar (imported from England), elegant oak furnishings, and the first electric lights in Sheridan. Col. William F. (Buffalo Bill) Cody was later a part-owner of the hotel and used the veranda to audition performers for his Wild West Show. It was operated as a hotel until 1965 and later as a restaurant and bar.

Located on the corner of 5th and Broadway, the inn is a registered National Historic Landmark. A local nonprofit group is restoring the Sheridan to its original status as a classy lodging, eating, and drinking establishment. Admission is $3 for adults, $2 for seniors, and free for children under 12. Call (307) 674-5440 for details. Visitors get a 45-minute guided tour of this fascinating old building—if they get Linda Fauth, they may be treated to a much longer tour sup-

plemented by all sorts of fun details. Be sure to ask about Kate Arnold, who lived here for 65 years and whose ashes are buried in an upstairs wall. Her ghost still shows up periodically to make sure the inn is well managed. An interesting booklet about Miss Kate is sold in the gift shop.

The historic Sheridan Inn is open daily 9 a.m.-8 p.m. from Memorial Day to Labor Day and Mon.-Fri. 9 a.m.-5 p.m. the rest of the year. Tall, 100-year-old cottonwoods guard the front, and the huge porch wraps around the sides. Try to see if you can find all 69 gables.

King's Saddlery

Well worth a stop is King's Saddlery, 184 N. Main St., tel. (307) 672-2702 or (800) 443-8919, a Sheridan-area fixture for 50 years. When you step inside the doors the smell of leather is almost overwhelming. The long, narrow shop has handmade saddles, leatherwork, ropes, spurs, chaps, belt buckles, cowboy hats, and various other tack for horses. Be sure to take a look at the miles of ropes in the back room. Many top rodeo cowboys drop by to buy their lariats, and King's sells 40,000 feet of high-quality ropes a year.

The free **King's Western Museum** in the back contains hundreds of gorgeous saddles—including a 17th-century Japanese saddle and American saddles dating from before the Civil War—along with rifles, spurs, chaps, tools, old wagons, and carriages. It's one of the finest collections of cowboy memorabilia anywhere. Also here is an impressive collection of Indian artifacts including an amazing beaded pottery vase and bridles made a century ago. King's Saddlery is fittingly named: both Queen Elizabeth and the king of Saudi Arabia have visited, and both President Clinton and ex-Prez Reagan own King's leather belts. King's Saddlery is open Mon.-Sat. 8 a.m.-5 p.m. The store also has a mail-order catalog.

Fort Mackenzie

Built in 1902, Fort Mackenzie never really served much of a military function. Pushed through Congress by Wyoming's powerful Senator Francis E. Warren, the fort was ostensibly built as a base to put down any Indian uprising on nearby reservations, since the last major Indian battles

had occurred 20 years earlier. It was named for Gen. Ranald S. Mackenzie, a veteran of the Civil War and various Indian battles. Over the decades, the size of the fort shrank from 6,280 to 342 acres, and the last troops departed during WW I. In 1922, it became a 339-bed hospital for mentally-ill vets. You're welcome to walk around the grounds and admire the old brick buildings, but check in at the administration building first.

Sheridan County Library

Sheridan's excellent library at 320 N. Brooks, tel. (307) 674-8585, is open Mon.-Thurs. 9 a.m.-9 p.m. and Fri.-Sat. 9 a.m.-6 p.m. One section encloses a small collection of Indian artifacts and items from early settlers. The Wyoming Room has an extensive collection of old books, maps, and paintings, including a mural of the Wagon Box Fight; upstairs you'll find more historical exhibits and current artwork and a model of the Medicine Wheel. On the walls of the library are 11 paintings by Bill Gollings (1878-1932), a self-taught, but accomplished, cowboy artist.

Other Sights

A historic marker on the corner of West Dow and Alger Streets commemorates **General Crook's campsite.** In 1876 the general camped here at the junction of Big and Little Goose Creeks with 1,325 men and 1,900 pack animals after being forced to a stalemate by Sioux and Crow warriors on the Rosebud River. The fight took place just eight days before Custer would die at nearby Little Big Horn.

Directly across from the Sheridan Inn is the old red Sheridan **train depot,** built in 1892 and now housing a bar. Nearby is a huge Chicago, Burlington, and Quincy Railroad **locomotive.** Downtown on 3rd and Gould Streets is a Sheridan **streetcar** from the early 1900s. History and architecture buffs should pick up a copy of the guide to Sheridan's **Main Street Historic District** at the visitor center. One of the buildings included—the **Mint Bar,** 151 N. Main St., tel. (307) 674-9696—offers a genuine taste of the west. Cartoonist Linda Barry's description of the Mint says it all: "Stuffed animal heads galore. Taxidermied fish galore. Burlwood carpentry galore."

ACCOMMODATIONS

Motels and B&Bs

Most of Sheridan's motels lie along Coffeen Ave. and Main Street. See the "Sheridan Accommodations" chart for specific rates. During the off-season—through early May—you're likely to find lower prices, down to $20 a night at the budget motels. The **Mill Inn** is unique in that it's located within a historic flour mill, lending a new meaning to the term "hitting the sack.")

Several excellent bed and breakfasts are located in the country near Sheridan, including Spahn's Big Horn Mountain B&B in Big Horn (see "South of Sheridan" under "Sheridan Vicinity," below). **Old Croff House B&B,** tel. (307) 672-0898, is a pleasant in-town home built in 1917 with three guest rooms and a spacious suite. The big front porch has an old-fashioned wicker swing for a relaxing evening.

Five miles east of town is, **Ranch Willow B&B,** tel. (307) 674-1510 or (800) 354-2830, a gorgeous turn-of-the-century ranch home on 550 acres. The rooms are well appointed with handmade furniture, and breakfast includes fresh ranch eggs and organically grown ingredients. Bring your own horse to ride in the indoor arena.

Dude Ranches

Sheridan is surrounded by several classic dude ranches. The first in the area was run by the Hilman family, who took in their first paying dudes in 1889. It operated until the 1930s. Famous **Eaton's Ranch,** 18 miles west of Sheridan, tel. (307) 655-9285 or 655-9552, is one of the oldest and best-known dude ranches in America. The three Eaton brothers—Howard, Alden, and Willis—began ranching in North Dakota in 1879 but soon found themselves overwhelmed by visiting friends from the east. Eventually one offered to pay, and thus was born the first dude ranch. Initially these "dudes" (a term that both Buffalo Bill and Howard Eaton took credit for using first in this context) stayed wherever they could find space, eating the cowboy's grub and joining in on chores. In 1904, the brothers bought a ranch along Wyoming's Wolf Creek that would eventually grow to 7,000 acres. Third-, fourth-, and fifth-generation members of the Eaton fam-

SHERIDAN ACCOMMODATIONS

Note: Accommodations are arranged from least to most expensive. Add an eight percent tax to these rates. Area code is 307.

X-L Motel; 402 N. Main St.; tel. 674-4722; $24 s or d; no phones in rooms, weekly rates available

Parkway Motel; 2112 Coffeen Ave.; tel. 674-7259; $24 s, $30 d; kitchenettes $34 s or d

Stage Stop Motel; 2167 N. Main St.; tel. 672-3459; $28 s, $32 d

Super Saver Motel; 1789 N. Main St.; tel. 672-0471; $28 s, $34 d

Triangle Motel; 540 Coffeen; tel. 674-8031; $30 s or d; see rooms first

Lariat Motel; 2068 Coffeen Ave.; tel. 672-6475; $30 s, $32 d; clean and inexpensive

Aspen Inn; 1744 N. Main St.; tel. 672-9064; $32 s, $40 d; see rooms first

Guest House Motel; 2007 N. Main St.; tel. 674-7496 or (800) 341-8000; $33 s, $39 d; AAA approved

Rock Trim Motel; 449 Coffeen Ave.; tel. 672-2464; $32 s, $40 d; kitchenettes $44 s or d; AAA approved

Alamo Motel; 1326 N. Main St.; tel. 672-2455; $34 s, $41 d

Apple Tree Inn; 1552 Coffeen Ave.; tel. 672-2428 or (800) 670-2428; $36 s, $42 d; jacuzzi, sauna

Bramble Motel; 2366 N. Main St.; tel. 674-4902; $40 s, $43 d

Evergreen Inn; 580 E. 5th St.; tel. 672-9757 or (800) 771-4761; $40 s, $48 d; outdoor jacuzzi

Sundown Motel; 1704 N. Main St.; tel. 672-2439; $42 s or d; outdoor pool, see rooms first

Trails End Motel; 2125 N. Main St.; tel. 672-2477 or (800) 445-4921; $44-52 s, $48-58 d; indoor pool

Mill Inn; 2161 Coffeen Ave.; tel. 672-6401; $52 s, $65 d; continental breakfast, AAA approved

Best Western Sheridan Center Motor Inn; 609 N. Main St.; tel. 674-7421 or (800) 528-1234; $58-68 s, $66-76 d; indoor and outdoor pools, sauna, jacuzzi, continental breakfast, free airport shuttle, AAA approved

Days Inn; 1104 E. Brundage Lane; tel. 672-2888 or (800) 329-7466; $60-75 s, $60-80 d; indoor pool, jacuzzi, continental breakfast

Super 8 Motel; 2435 N. Main St.; tel. 672-9725 or (800) 800-8000; $61 s or d;

Little Goose Coop Guest House; 637 Val Vista; tel. 672-0886; $65 s or d, $15 a piece for additional guests; house sleeps six, full kitchen, washer and dryer

Ranch Willow B&B; 501 Hwy. 14 (five miles east of Sheridan); tel. 674-1510 or (800) 354-2830; $70-80 s or d; 1901 ranch home, four guest rooms, private baths, full breakfast

Comfort Inn; 1450 E. Brundage Lane; tel. 672-5098 or (800) 228-5150; $70-100 s or d; continental breakfast, AAA approved

Old Croff House B&B; 508 W. Works; tel. 672-0898; $65-90 s or d; 1917 home, two guest rooms and a suite, shared or private baths, continental breakfast, kids welcome, open June-Sept.

Holiday Inn; 1809 Sugarland Dr.; tel. 672-8931 or (800) 465-4329; $79-125 s, $96-125 d; atrium, indoor pool, sauna, jacuzzi, exercise room, free airport shuttle, AAA approved

ily still run the ranch. The ranch accommodates 125 dudes in modernized guest cabins and attracts many families who return year after year. The emphasis—not surprisingly—is on horseback rides; Eatons' is one of the few dude ranches where experienced riders can head out on their own (with permission from the ranch). Other facilities include an outdoor pool, trout fishing, and a nearby nine-hole golf course. Open June-Sept. with a one-week minimum stay in summer; $950 per person per week double occupancy ($100 extra for the best cabins).

Located high in the Big Horn Mountains 30 miles southwest of Sheridan, **Spear-O-Wigwam Dude Ranch,** tel. (307) 674-4496 (summers) or 672-0002 (winters), has operated since 1923. This classic dude ranch—Ernest Hemingway wrote *A Farewell to Arms* while staying here—has comfy log cabins, a large lodge with a stone fireplace, a hot tub, pool tables, and horseback rides or overnight trips into the nearby Cloud Peak Wilderness. There's a three-night minimum stay, and adult rates are $850 per person per week, double occupancy. Open mid-June to mid-September.

Camping
Camp for free in town at **Washington Park** (close to Little Goose Creek but also along the busy main drag) but for one night only—water sprinklers enforce this every afternoon, so get your tent down in time! Many more campgrounds ($8-10) operate within nearby Bighorn National Forest; see above for details. **Bighorn Mountain KOA**, 63 Decker Rd., tel. (307) 674-8766 or (800) 562-7621, has quiet tent sites for $15, RV sites for $20. Noncampers may shower for $3.50 (before 4 p.m. only). It's open May to early October, and has a pool and jacuzzi. **Bramble Motel RV Park;** 2366 N. Main; tel. (307) 674-4902, charges $15 for RV hookups; no tent spaces available.

FOOD

Breakfast
Sheridan has a broad choice of eateries. The **Silver Spur Cafe**, 832 N. Main St., tel. (307) 672-2749, only serves breakfast and lunch but it serves up the best downhome cowboy food in town—at reasonable prices, too. **Ritz Sporting Goods**, 135 N. Main St., tel. (307) 674-4101, is home to the local coffee klatch most mornings and has a lunch counter for burgers, French dips, and chili dogs. Get an espresso fix to jumpstart your day at **The Coffee House**, 123 N. Main St., tel. (307) 674-8619.

Lunch and Dinner
Sheridan's finest lunches and dinners are found at **Ciao Bistro**, 120 N. Main St., tel. (307) 672-2838. Wonderful sandwiches, salads, mini-pizzas, desserts, and fresh-baked breads. Get here early for lunch to avoid the lines, and make reservations for dinner. This is one of the few places east of Jackson Hole where you're likely to find radicchio on the menu! Another place that gets crowded for lunch is **The Chocolate Tree**, 423 N. Main St., tel. (307) 672-6160, where the menu includes very good sandwiches, salads, daily specials, and decadent chocolates. **Melinda's**, 57 N. Main St., tel. (307) 674-9188, has fresh baked goods and tasty light lunches. Closed Mondays.

Another noteworthy local eatery is **Golden Steer Restaurant**, 2071 N. Main St., tel. (307) 674-9334, where you'll find consistently good steaks, seafood, and prime rib. The best local burgers are—surprisingly enough—at **Dairy Queen**, 544 N. Main St., tel. (307) 674-9379. The **Sheridan Inn**, tel. (307) 674-5440, serves meals, and has popular Friday night barbecues on the front lawn. A great place to meet locals on a summer evening.

Little Big Men Pizza, 1424 Coffeen Ave., tel. (307) 672-9877, has reasonable pizza, burger, and salad meal deals including all-you-can-eat lunch and dinner smorgasbords, but **Ole's Pizza**, in the mall next to the Holiday Inn, tel. (307) 672-3636, is better and cranks out tangy barbecue ribs; very popular with families. Fill up on barbecued buffalo, chicken, and ribs during the evening chuck wagons at **Bighorn Mountain KOA**, 63 Decker Rd., tel. (307) 674-8766.

Ethnic Eats
Get fairly authentic Chinese cookery at **Golden China Restaurant** in the T&C Shopping Center at Brundage and Coffeen, tel. (307) 674-7181. **A.E. Suk**, 2004 N. Main St., tel. (307) 672-0357, has an Asian buffet lunch every day and the cheapest breakfasts around. **Pablo's**, 1274 N. Main, tel. (307) 672-0737, serves reasonably priced Mexican food and has a full bar.

Brewpub
Sanford's Grub, Pub & Brewery, 1 E. Alger Ave., tel. (307) 674-1722, is a trendy pub with all sorts of flotsam and jetsam from garage sales tacked along the walls and rock tunes blasting over the speakers. The bar claims to have the largest beer selection in Wyoming with more than 130 brews including 37 on tap. Several of these are made in the brewpub on the premises.

The place also has a big, diverse menu, making this a very popular place to hang out with friends.

Grocers

In addition to the standard mega-marts—Safeway, Decker's Market, Warehouse Foods, and Buttery Foods—you'll find holistic groceries in Sheridan at **Nanci's Natural Foods,** 38 S. Main St., tel. (307) 674-8344.

OTHER PRACTICALITIES

Entertainment

During the summer months, **WYO Theater,** 42 N. Main St., tel. (307) 672-9084, has live musical shows five nights a week, and the Kendrick Park bandshell is home to free Tuesday night **concerts in the park.** The bands range from polka to jazz. **Carriage House Theater** at Trail End, tel. (307) 672-9886, presents plays throughout the year. Ask at the visitor center about the annual **Shakespeare in the Park** performance put on by a Missoula-based troupe in late June.

Enjoy live rock 'n' roll on weekends at **LBM Pizza,** 1424 Coffeen Ave., tel. (307) 672-9877, or watch sports on the big-screen TV. **Golden Steer,** 2071 N. Main St., tel. (307) 674-9334, often has golden oldies from the '50s. Both the **Brass Banjo** at the Holiday Inn, 1809 Sugarland Dr., tel. (307) 672-8931, and **Sutton's Tavern,** 1402 N. Main St., tel. (307) 672-5213, have DJs spinning dance CDs most nights. The Brass Banjo also has rock bands on weekends, and the bar at **Sheridan Inn,** tel. (307) 674-5440, has music on Friday and Saturday nights. Pool and darts are at the **Caboose Bar** in the old depot across from the Sheridan Inn.

Events

The **Sheridan Wyo Rodeo** comes around in July each year, bringing with it not just professional rodeo cowboys at the "world's largest one go-round rodeo" but also a parade down Main Street, a pancake breakfast, the Wyoming Chili Cook-off, country-western bands, and street dances. Call (307) 672-9083 for specifics. In early August, visit the **Sheridan County Fair,** followed by the **Sheridan County Rodeo** later in the month. This rodeo, for the younger set,

even includes stick-horse races for those under age four! **Big Horn Mountain Polka Days** is a fun Labor Day weekend event which attracts hundreds of polka enthusiasts. Oom-pa-pa! During the winter, **"Chariot Races"** are held at the Soldier Creek Complex on 5th Street.

Recreation

Kendrick City Park has a small game preserve with various native critters such as bison and elk. Swim at the **outdoor swimming pool** (summer only) in the park, and feel like a kid again on the 90-foot-long waterslide. Admission is $2.25 for adults, $1.50 for ages 13-17, and $1.25 for children under 12. There's another pool at the **YMCA,** 417 N. Jefferson, tel. (307) 674-7488, plus racquetball and tennis courts and weight machines. Golfers will want to try out the 18-hole **Kendrick Golf Course** three miles west of town, tel. (307) 674-8148.

Sheridan has an abundance of outdoor shops lining Main Street. **Big Horn Mountain Sports,** 334 N. Main St., tel. (307) 672-6866, has a big choice of outdoor gear and topographic maps. Much of this gear can also be rented, including cross-country skis, snowboards, snowshoes, tents, sleeping bags, backpacks, rollerblades, fly rods, and float tubes. The staff teaches classes in skiing, kayaking, sailboarding, fly-tying, fly-fishing, and rock-climbing. **Back Country Bikes,** tel. (307) 672-2453, inside Big Horn Mountain Sports, rents mountain bikes. **Ritz Sporting Goods,** 135 N. Main St., tel. (307) 674-4101, also sells a range of camping and outdoor supplies. The **Outdoor Groove** bike shop at 251 N. Main St., tel. (307) 672-8186, rents mountain bikes, water skis, wakeboards, snowboards, and downhill and cross-country skis. **Fly Shop of the Big Horns,** 227 N. Main St., tel. (307) 672-5866, has Orvis gear, classes in fly-casting and fly-tying, and guided fishing trips on the Big Horn and Platte Rivers. Rent float tubes and fins here.

Shopping

You'll find a fine selection of Wyoming titles at **The Book Shop,** 122 N. Main St., tel. (307) 672-6505, and **Sheridan Stationery,** 206 N. Main St., tel. (307) 672-8080. The Book Shop also has monthly poetry readings and other literary events. Several Sheridan art galleries are

worth a peek including **Gallery 348,** tel. (307) 672-6120, in the Best Out West Antiques & Collectibles Mall at 109 N. Main St.; **Medicine Wheel Gallery,** 109 N. Main St., tel. (307) 672-0124; and **Golden Crown Art Gallery,** 50 N. Main St., tel. (307) 674-7676. The **Custom Cowboy Shop,** 321 N. Main St., tel. (307) 672-7733, has quality boots, hats, saddles, and tack. See also the famous King's Saddlery, described above. **Everything's Hand Made,** 2161 Coffeen Ave., tel. (307) 674-6742, is a gift and souvenir shop with Wyoming-made jewelry, foods, and other items.

Information and Services
The **Sheridan Visitor Center/State Information Center,** tel. (307) 672-2485 or (800) 453-3650, is located in the rest area at the 5th St. exit of I-90. Inside are various historical displays, a 3-D map, and a panoramic view of the Big Horns from the windows. The center is open daily 8 a.m.-7 p.m. mid-May to mid-October, and Mon.-Fri. 8 a.m.-5 p.m. the rest of the year. A small kiosk visitor center in Washington Park opens daily 4-8 p.m. during the summer. The **Wyoming Game & Fish Department Visitor Center** (tel. 307-672-2790) is directly across the road and contains a number of professionally produced and informative wildlife and fish displays. Hours here are Mon.-Fri. 8 a.m.-5 p.m. year-round. It's only 25 miles from Sheridan to the Montana border via I-90. For details on sights to the north, see *Montana Handbook,* by W.C. McRae and Judy Jewell (Moon Publications).

The **Bighorn National Forest Supervisors Office** at 1969 S. Sheridan Ave., tel. (307) 672-0751, provides forest maps ($4) and info Mon.-Fri. 8 a.m.-5 p.m. The 2,000-student **Sheridan College,** tel. (307) 674-6446, is one of the largest two-year schools in the state. Founded in 1948, it offers degrees in both academic and technical fields. The **Special Collections** room of the college library (tel. 307-674-6446) has a variety of Indian artifacts, including vests, moccasins, pipes, and weapons.

ATMs are in many places around Sheridan, including First Interstate Bank, 4 S. Main St.; Key Bank, 2 N. Main St.; First Bank, 203 S. Main St.; and First Federal Savings Bank, 462 Coffeen Avenue. Wash clothes at **Econ-O-Wash Laundry,** 19 E. 5th St., tel. (307) 672-7899, **Super Saver Laundromat,** 1789 N. Main St., tel. (307) 672-0471, or **Sugarland Laundromat,** in Sugarland Village, tel. (307) 672-5736. If you are heading west over the mountains or south to Buffalo, fill up with gas in Sheridan; prices are usually lower.

Transportation
Sheridan airport is just southwest of town. **United Express,** tel. (800) 631-1500, has daily flights between Sheridan and Denver. Next to Evergreen Inn, **Powder River Trailways,** 580 E. 5th, tel. (307) 674-6188 or (800) 442-3682, has daily bus service to Billings, Montana, and most towns in eastern Wyoming. Rent cars at the airport from **Avis,** tel. (307) 672-2226 or (800) 331-1212, or **Enterprise,** tel. (307) 672-6910 or (800) 325-8007, or in town from **Sheridan Motor,** 1766 Coffeen Ave., tel. (307) 672-3411.

SHERIDAN VICINITY

RANCHESTER

The little village of Ranchester (pop. 700) calls itself "The town where the handshake's stronger and the smile lasts longer." This seems true enough.

Historic Sights
Connor Battlefield State Historic Site is right in Ranchester city park. It's a very pleasant place with picnic tables, camping ($4), and tall cotton-

wood trees along the Tongue River (so named because of a tonguelike rock along a tributary). Good fishing for brown trout. A cable footbridge leads across the river. Despite this bucolic setting, the park has a gruesome history representing one of the worst massacres in the Powder River Basin. The massacre took place in 1865, during a time of hit-and-run battles throughout the plains set off by the massacre of the Cheyenne at Sand Creek in Colorado and continued in dozens of Indian attacks upon settlers and emigrants. Red Cloud had just struck against Platte Bridge Sta-

tion (see "Casper" in the Central Wyoming chapter) a few weeks before, killing 28 men, and the Army was eager to avenge that raid as well as attacks along the Bozeman Trail.

Gen. Patrick E. Connor—a proponent of the shoot-first, ask-questions-later school of military diplomacy—attacked Indian villages throughout the West, killing 200 Shoshone in an 1863 Utah attack and then rampaging through Nevada and Idaho. Connor's 1865 expedition to the Powder River included nearly a thousand soldiers and 179 Pawnee and Winnebago scouts. Most of the effort was a failure as Indians kept ahead of the ponderous military wagons, but on August 29 Connor's men came upon Chief Bear's Arapaho village along the Tongue River. Connor ordered his men, "You will not receive overtures of peace or submission from the Indians, but will attack and kill every male Indian over 12 years of age." In a pell-mell rush, Connor's men slaughtered 63 men, women, and children, destroyed 250 lodges along with much of their winter supplies, and captured more than 1,100 ponies. Eight troopers died. No one ever determined whether the Arapaho they encountered were the same ones who had been attacking along the Bozeman Trail. The expedition ended when the government realized the expedition was costing over a million dollars a month for transportation alone. A chastened Connor stashed his supplies at Fort Connor (later renamed Fort Reno) and returned to Fort Laramie.

Four miles west of here on U.S. 14, another monument marks the **Sawyer Fight.** Here, two days after Connor attacked the Arapaho along the Tongue River, Arapahoes retaliated against a 100-man roadbuilding expedition led by Col. James Sawyer. Three of his men were killed and the rest were pinned down for nearly two weeks before finally being rescued by Connor's troops.

Practicalities

Stay at the clean and friendly **Western Ranchester Motel,** tel. (307) 655-2212 or (800) 341-8000, for $32-38 s, $36-40 d. It also has an outdoor pool. The **Historic Old Stone House B&B,** 135 Wolf Creek Rd., tel. (307) 655-9239, was built in 1899 by local cattle baron Samuel H. Hardin. The stone house occupies a hilltop south of Ranchester and has four guest rooms with pri-

vate baths ($60 s, $70 d), a suite with a jacuzzi tub ($135 s or d), plus two separate guest houses ($90-100 s or d). A full breakfast and afternoon tea are served. **Lazy B Campground,** has RV sites for $10. Lodging is also available at **Double Rafter Ranch,** 18 miles northwest of Ranchester (near the Montana state line), tel. (307) 655-9362. Bed-and-breakfast accommodations in a two-bedroom cottage cost $100 for up to six people.

Ranch House Restaurant, tel. (307) 655-9527, serves up family fare, and **Kelly's Kitchen,** tel. (307) 655-9016, has ice cream and fast food. Head to **DD's Bar & Lounge,** tel. (307) 655-9818, for live music on some weekends. Get groceries at **Buckhorn Groceries,** tel. (307) 655-9766, and cash from the **ATM** at Ranchester State Bank. The local mini-mall has a laundromat. Children will enjoy the kid-designed wooden playground of forts and slides at the elementary school.

Ranchester Days in early August features a horseshoe tournament, a horse-drawn parade, arts-and-crafts booths, and a street dance.

DAYTON

The village of Dayton (pop. 600) contains the little log-cabin studio of water colorist **Hans Kleiber** (1887-1966), now used as a combination museum and visitor center. Kleiber was known as "Artist of the Big Horns," and his works are internationally collected today. Inside are his press, art books, and several of his etchings. The museum is open daily in the summer and closed the rest of the year. Dayton's old **bell tower,** built in 1910 to warn of fires, is now in the city park.

Accommodations

Foothills Campground and Motel, tel. (307) 655-2547, has cabins for $21 s or d (kitchenettes for $4 more). Camp along the river here for $10, park RVs for $14. Noncampers can shower for $2. The campground is open May-October.

Built as a hotel in 1904 and completely renovated in 1995, **The White Horse B&B,** 306 Main St., tel. (307) 655-9441, has three guest rooms with private baths. Rates are $60-70 s, $70-80 d, including a full breakfast.

Food and Shopping

Dayton Mercantile, tel. (307) 655-2214, was built in 1898 and is now run as a gift shop and restaurant. The interior is filled with local handicrafts, quilts, dolls, and jewelry. The cafe here features homemade sandwiches, soups, breads, and especially good pies. Try a sarsaparilla float. They offer homecooked lunches and dinners with evening specials in the summer. Meals are also available at **The Branding Iron,** tel. (307) 655-9054.

Summerhouse Books, tel. (307) 655-2367, has both new and used books for sale, and **The Red Barn,** sells antiques and gifts. **Dreamcatcher Gallery,** tel. (307) 655-2275, has framed jewelry, Western art prints, and gifts. The **Spirit of the West Gallery,** tel. (307) 655-9769, sells predictable bronze sculptures of cowboys, Indians, and critters by local sculptor Mike Flanagan. Former Vice President Dan Quayle owns one, which should tell you something about these pieces.

Events and Recreation

Dayton Days, held the last weekend in July, has the usual country favorites, including a parade, food and craft booths, a firefighters' water fight, Indian dancing, and a street dance. Fishermen will find blue-ribbon trout fishing along the Tongue River. Dayton also has an outdoor **swimming pool** open June-Aug. next to the Kleiber cabin. The nine-hole **Horseshoe Mountain Golf Course** in Dayton includes some unique hazards: horse-hoof-sized potholes.

EAST OF SHERIDAN

Some of the prettiest plains country in Wyoming lies along U.S. 14, a quiet, scenic road that curls through mile after mile of ranchland and winter wheat. The road heads southeast from Sheridan, gradually narrowing as it climbs through rugged hills and down a long green valley filled with fine ranches and modern homes.

Ucross

At the crossroads called Ucross, a huge red barn ("Big Red") dominates the view at the 22,000-acre Ucross Ranch. The ranch is headquarters for the nonprofit Ucross Foundation, tel. (307) 737-2291, an important artist retreat sponsored by grants from Apache Oil Corporation. Each year some 60 selected artists enjoy a two- to eight-week residency program that includes individual work spaces, a printmaking studio, a gallery, and royal-treatment living accommodations. It's all to give time for artists to focus on ideas, theories, and works. Author E. Annie Proulx wrote both *Postcards* and *The Shipping News* while staying here; the latter won her a Pulitzer Prize in 1992. Ucross also houses a conference center. Drop in for a tour of the immaculate buildings or to check out gallery exhibitions.

The **art gallery** at Ucross is open Mon.-Fri. 9 a.m.-4 p.m. and Sat.-Sun. 11 a.m.-3 p.m. and features rotating exhibits throughout the summer. Big Red was headquarters for the enormous Pratt and Ferris Cattle Co., a spread that extended 35 miles along Clear Creek. At one time, more than 35,000 calves were branded each fall, and the huge barn could hold 30 teams of horses. The "U Cross" was their brand.

Ucross is also home to **The Ranch at Ucross,** tel. (307) 587-5555 or (800) 447-0194, a luxurious guest ranch that frequently attracts tour buses during the summer. Call to make sure the buses won't be there if you plan to overnight. Guests stay in condo-type rooms or modern cabins for $95 s, $115 d. The price includes a full breakfast and access to the outdoor pool, with an extra charge for horseback rides. All-inclusive rates with three meals a day plus horseback riding are also available. If you're in the area around **July 4th,** stick around for food, games, live music, and a spectacular fireworks display.

Clearmont Area

The 20 miles east from Ucross are some of the most distinctive in Wyoming. The road parallels cottonwood-bordered Clear Creek, winding its way down the grassy hillsides. The Big Horn Mountains form a dramatic western backdrop, and large ranches dot the countryside with stone buildings and spreading old trees. It's easy to see why the Sioux fought so hard to keep this country out of white hands!

The largest settlement between Gillette and Sheridan, **Clearmont** is a pleasant place with a bit over 100 folks. **Red Arrow Motel,** tel. (307)

758-4455, has rooms for $40 s or $55 d, a cafe, and a bar complete with pool table. Stop by the small Clearmont General Store for crafts and homemade quilts. Clearmont has a pretty little town park, tall deciduous trees lining the handful of streets, and a combination library/community center.

East from Clearmont is minuscule **Leiter**, with a motel and a bar but nothing else. Halfway between Clearmont and Leiter is the **RBL Bison Ranch**, tel. (307) 758-4387 or (800) 597-0109, where daily tours are available May-Sept. for $5 per person. This is a great chance to see buffalo up close—and even feed them. Afterwards you can feed on them at the restaurant, which serves buffalo burgers and steaks. The ranch has rather plain bunkhouse accommodations—communal showers—for $48 s or d, or $78 d with breakfast (now *that's* an expensive breakfast!). Park RVs for $16, pitch a tent for $12. Accommodations and the restaurant close Nov.-March.

The highway crosses the Powder River at the little settlement called **Arvada** and then heads east to Spotted Horse. **Powder River Experience**, tel. (307) 736-2402, offers ranch vacations on a 24,000-acre spread south of Arvada. Guests ride horseback and join in short cattle drives or other ranch activities. You can stay by the night or the week in the two guest houses with shared or private baths; meals and lodging are included.

Spotted Horse

At Spotted Horse—named for a minor Cheyenne chief—the combination country store/gas station/saloon/cafe is worth a stop, if only to hang out with locals in the bar. Hard times show in the faces of local ranchers. The bar has a jukebox, a few fast-food items on the menu, and cold beer. Its walls are carpeted with an amusing collection of old junk, historic photos, and cheesecake biker shots.

The 1811 overland expedition of the Astorians passed through the Spotted Horse area. During the 1930s, tourists en route to Yellowstone posed on a stuffed bucking bronc in the back paddock, but once I-90 was completed business plummeted. The area's economy has suffered a long decline, and other tiny burgs nearby—Recluse, Arvada, and Leiter—appear on the verge of extinction. **Cow Camp**, tel. (307)

> *May your horse never stumble*
> *Your spurs never rust*
> *Your guts never grumble*
> *Your cinch never bust*
> *May your boots never pinch*
> *Your crops never fail*
> *While you eat lots of beans*
> *And stay out of jail*
>
> —*from a sign in Spotted Horse*

687-1210, is a 40,000-acre ranch on the Wyoming/Montana border 20 miles north of Recluse, offering five-day cattle drives, brandings, round-ups, and trail rides May-October.

Southeast from Spotted Horse, the highway curves toward the coal mines of Gillette. The red scoria rock of the highway points through summer-green grass. (Also called clinker, this rock was created when coal burned underground, baking adjacent shale and sandstone to a bright red. Similar red roads exist all over Powder River Basin.) Old windmills pump water for cattle and sheep. From atop the hills a landscape of fences, phone lines, plowed fields, bales of hay, and horses spread out in all directions. The sun darts between cottonball clouds as a lone cyclist pumps up the road, swerving around the smashed jackrabbits and passed by pickup trucks with gun racks and tipped-back cowboy hats. This is the true West, not the region cutesified for the tourists. Red-sided buttes rise above the rolling plains. The new ranch houses—trailer homes—stand next to aging farmsteads and collapsed log cabins; imported pickups sit in the driveways and satellite dishes guard the front yards. If you like grass and sky, brilliant starry nights, antelope, haystacks, and oil wells, you'll love this place. Stop for a while and listen to the silence broken only by the meadowlarks and the wind. God's country.

SOUTH OF SHERIDAN

Although I-90 cuts south of Sheridan toward Buffalo, U.S. 87 offers a much more interesting route, taking you through rolling ranch coun-

try and past cottonwood-lined draws. Along the way are the little settlements of Big Horn and Story and the historically rich country around old Fort Phil Kearny and the Bozeman Trail. The area's beauty has long attracted wealthy corporate executives and politicians, who come here to relax as gentlemen ranchers in ostentatious homes.

Big Horn

Tiny Big Horn was founded in 1879 by O.P. Hanna (local Indians called him "Big Spit" because of his tobacco chewing), a ceaseless promoter who sent glowing accounts of "Big Horn City" to various newspapers. A reporter decided to investigate and found the town consisted primarily of a few outlaws, including "Big Nose" George Parrott and Jesse James' outlaw brother, Frank. A few homesteaders and settlers did take the bait, however: by 1884 Big Horn City had a hotel, three stores, two blacksmith shops, three saloons, a newspaper, a school, a church, and even a college of sorts. Over the years, most of the businesses moved to Sheridan, but still here is **Big Horn Mercantile,** built in 1882 and considered the oldest business in northern Wyoming. Take a look inside for the photo of Queen Elizabeth, who visited this historically British area in 1984. From the same era is **Bozeman Trail Inn,** tel. (307) 672-9288, where you'll find one of the oldest bars in Wyoming.

A historic 1881 blacksmith shop houses the **Bozeman Trail Museum.** Open Saturday and Sunday 11 a.m.-6 p.m. June-Aug. and by appointment at other times, the museum displays various local memorabilia, old photos of the town, and a small gift shop. The ceiling is "branded" with local cattle brands. No admission charge. The town park next door makes a pleasant picnic spot.

The **State Bird Farm,** tel. (307) 674-7701, on Bird Farm Rd., raises more than 13,000 pheasants each year. These birds are released around Wyoming shortly before the fall hunting season, just in time to get shot as "wild game." The farm also has show birds including over a dozen species of pheasants, as well as peacocks, turkey, chukkar, and guinea hens.

Certainly the last thing one might expect to find in Big Horn is a polo field, but the English tradition lives on at **Big Horn Equestrian Cen-**ter south of town on Bird Farm Road. Polo games are held on Sundays at 11 a.m. and 1 p.m. during the summer. These are informal events with changing teams and players of varying abilities. Polo games began on the Polo Ranch a couple miles west of Big Horn and moved to the present equestrian center in the 1980s. The Polo Ranch itself is hard to miss, with an enormous white barn and immaculate white picket fences. The place positively reeks of money. The current owner is an executive with American Standard, the toilet-fixture company. The Polo Ranch was formerly owned by ex-U.S. Senator Malcolm Wallop, the grandson of Sir Oliver H. Wallop, seventh earl of Portsmouth (who served in the Wyoming Legislature before returning to England to sit in the House of Lords). Oliver Wallop and the two Moncrieffe brothers (see below) bought Western horses for the British Army during the Boer War, shipping 20,000 of them overseas. To test the ponies, the British purchasing officer would ride them the length of a polo field. Malcolm Moncrieffe trained a team on this field and later competed with them in England. Thus began what is believed to be the oldest polo club in America.

Blue Barn B&B, tel. (307) 672-2381, was built as a barn in the early part of this century and was completely remodeled in 1993, transforming it into a bed and breakfast with three fine guest rooms with private baths ($75-90 s or d). The country location, plant-filled atrium, and tasty breakfast add to the allure. Owners Carol and Sam Mavrakis also operate Ritz Sporting Goods in Sheridan, so they can help you with fly-fishing trips and other activities. Kids are welcome.

Located in the cool pine forests seven miles west of Big Horn, **Spahn's Big Horn Mountain Bed & Breakfast,** tel. (307) 674-8150, is one of the finest B&Bs in the state. The beautiful three-story log home was built by Ron Spahn, a former geologist and lawyer who runs the place with his wife Bobbie, a nurse. Enjoy a full breakfast on the porch, where the view extends for a hundred miles across Powder River Basin—all the way to Montana. It's a great place to watch distant lightning storms. Guests stay in three rooms inside the main house ($65-110 s or d) or in one of two cabins ($80-120 s or d) just a short walk away. The cabins are perfect for fam-

ilies or honeymooners. Plan on spending several days here; there's lots to do nearby, and the country is grand.

The big annual event in Big Horn is the **Cowboy Round-Up** held the second weekend of June at the equestrian center. It features polo matches, working horse competitions, stock dog trials, cowboy music and poetry, crafts demonstrations, and more. Call (307) 674-8582 or (800) 453-3650 for more information. The **4th of July** fireworks show in Big Horn is the biggest in the Sheridan area.

Bradford Brinton Memorial Museum
In 1892, two Scottish brothers, William and Malcolm Moncrieffe, built a spacious two-story ranch house along Little Goose Creek. It became headquarters for their Quarter Circle A Ranch. A businessman and lover of the West, Bradford Brinton bought the ranch in 1923 and enlarged the home to 20 rooms, furnished it with fine furniture and lined the walls with his art collection. Bradford's sister Helen owned the house after his death in 1936, and upon her own 1960 passing the building became a museum honoring her brother. The museum, tel. (307) 672-3173, is open daily 9:30 a.m.-5 p.m. from mid-May to early September and closed the rest of the year, with guided tours of the home and a creekside cabin. A donation is requested. Step inside to taste the genteel life and to view works by some of the west's best-known artists, many of whom were friends of Bradford Brinton. The collection includes over 600 works by such artists as John James Audubon, Hans Kleiber, Charles M. Russell, Frederic Remington, and Will Gollings. Also here are impressive Indian handicrafts, a Jefferson peace medal given to an Indian chief, books, and historic documents. The log lodge of Bradford Brinton sits right along Little Goose Creek, filled with big game trophies. Here, too, is a small gallery with high-quality art for sale. Horses are still raised on the 600-acre ranch, and the rural setting is most enjoyable: mountains rise on two sides and big old cottonwoods border the drive. Get here by heading five miles west on State 335 from the junction with U.S. 87. Follow the signs.

For a panoramic view of the surrounding country, follow State 335 west from the Bradford Brinton Memorial Museum. The road turns to gravel after three miles and then continues into the Big Horn Mountains as **Red Grade Road** (Forest Road 26). The route's a bit rough and too steep for RVs but it provides outstanding vistas after just a couple of miles. The road eventually connects with U.S. 14, but bring along a Forest Service map.

Story
The town of Story (pop. 650) is surprisingly different from nearby Sheridan and Buffalo. The road winds more than a thousand feet above the valley floor to the pine-covered slopes of the Big Horns. Locals and visitors come up to escape the hot summer air, enjoy the restaurants, and look for deer, elk, moose, and wild turkeys. Story is the site of "Piney Island," a stand of timber used to build nearby Fort Phil Kearny in 1866. The town was named for Nelson Story, the first man to trail cattle north across the Powder River Basin. **Story Fish Hatchery,** established in 1907, raises trout for Wyoming lakes and streams. The visitor center has interpretive exhibits and is open daily 8 a.m.-5 p.m. in the summer; tel. (307) 683-2234.

Lodore Supper Club and Lounge, tel. (307) 683-2355, which opened in 1919, is still a popular steak and seafood restaurant. For good fish and chips and a menu that covers the spectrum from frog legs to enchiladas, head to **Tunnel Inn,** tel. (307) 683-9921. **Wagonbox Inn,** tel. (307) 683-2444 or (800) 308-2444, serves some of the best and most innovative food in the area, with prime rib, steaks, chicken, fish, and a substantial wine list. On weekend nights, folks come here for live music. The Wagonbox has cozy cabins (sleep 2-6) for $55-95 and shared-bath bunkhouse accommodations for $30 s or d including a sauna. Reserve a month ahead for midsummer visits. Showers for those not staying here are $5. Next door to the Wagonbox, **North Piney Horse Corral,** tel. (307) 683-2838, has trail rides and pack trips.

Piney Creek General Store, tel. (307) 683-2400, is an old-fashioned country store with a great little deli that serves homemade soups, creative sandwiches, and other treats. Worth a stop.

Piney Creek Inn B&B, tel. (307) 683-2911, has accommodations in a rambling log house on five quiet wooded acres. Stay in one of three guest rooms (private or shared baths) in the

house for $45 s, $50-60 d, or in a log cabin that includes a kitchenette and spiral staircase for $85 s or d. A full breakfast is included, and guests will enjoy the hot tub and large deck. The folks here also set up tours of the area, trail rides, and a variety of ranch activities.

Ed and Sali Smyth's **Line Camp Gallery** on Rosebud Lane, tel. (307) 683-2213, exhibits Western artwork. **Piney Creek Pottery,** across from Tunnel Inn, tel. (307) 683-2181, sells pottery and other artwork.

Located on a thousand-acre spread, **Rafter Y Ranch,** tel. (307) 682-2221 (summers) or 437-6934 (winters), has space for just 17 dudes in comfortable log cabins. It's a fine place to ride horses or just relax in the foothills of the Big Horns. Open late June through August with a minimum stay of four days.

THE BLOODY BOZEMAN

The discovery of gold in Montana during the 1860s triggered an avalanche of miners and businessmen. The fastest route to the Virginia City goldfields headed northwest from Bridger's Ferry (near present-day Douglas) through the Powder River Basin, and then west across Montana. One of the pioneers who scouted and constantly promoted the "Montana Road" was John M. Bozeman (as in Bozeman, Montana). Before being killed by Indians on the Yellowstone River in 1867, he led several groups up the Bozeman Trail, as the route became known. Hundreds of others would die along Bozeman's route to the goldfields. Guide Jim Bridger knew that the Sioux would never stand for whites in their Powder River country—a place they had recently wrested from the Crows, the Shoshone, and the Arapahoes. Instead, he recommended a different route that would cut west of the Big Horn Mountains. Unfortunately, Bridger's advice went unheeded, and as attacks on emigrant wagon trains increased in 1864, so did pressure to protect them from the Sioux. Appeals to Washington brought military assistance in the form of forts filled with soldiers and cavalry. Parallels between the events that followed and America's experience in Vietnam—from the guerrilla warfare to the hurried exit of U.S. troops at the end of the conflict—are disconcerting.

Red Cloud's War

The first salvo by the Army came in General Connor's savage wanderings through the Powder River in 1865 (see "Ranchester" above). The following year, while treaty negotiations were being held at Fort Laramie, Colonel Henry B. Carrington and a battalion of infantry marched in heading to the Bozeman Trail, where they planned to construct new forts. Red Cloud, a fiery military leader of the Oglala Sioux, grew more and more angry, shouting,

Great Father sends us presents and wants new road, but White Chief goes with soldier, to steal road before Indian says yes or no. . . . White man lies and steals. My lodges were many, but now they are few. The white man wants all. The white man must fight, and the Indian will die where his fathers died.

The treaty was signed by older chiefs and the "Laramie Loafers," who hung around the fort, but not by Red Cloud. He and his warriors stormed out, arriving at Powder River ahead of Col. Carrington.

Carrington was a strange man to direct this massive undertaking. A political appointee with no battlefield experience—let alone experience with guerrilla warfare—he approached the task of building forts and protecting travelers along the Bozeman Trail with a take-no-chances attitude that rankled his trigger-happy men. The troupe left Nebraska with a 30-piece brass band, carriages, and comfortable furnishings, earning the name "Carrington's Overland Circus."

Once finally in the Powder River country, Carrington split his men into three groups, stationing some at Fort Reno near present-day Buffalo (begun the previous year by General Connor) and sending others to build Fort C.F. Smith in Montana. These way stations were to provide military escorts for travelers and havens from Indian attacks. Instead, they themselves came under attack, and Carrington's men nearly became prisoners inside them.

Fort Phil Kearny

In the heart of the Powder River country, Carrington found what seemed a perfect site for a

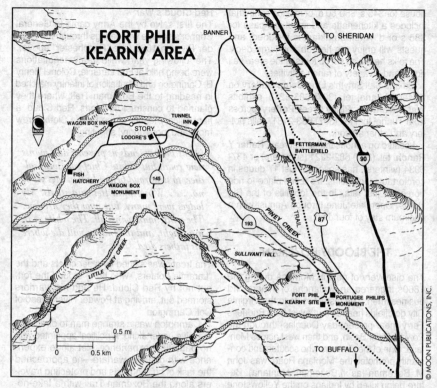

© MOON PUBLICATIONS, INC.

fort along Little Piney Creek: there was good water, grass so thick that horses could barely walk through it, and timber close at hand. His guide, the famed Jim Bridger, pushed instead for a site farther north, away from the center of Sioux country. To Bridger, these "damn paper collar soldiers" seemed bound and determined to get killed. The new garrison—named Fort Phil Kearny for a Civil War general—measured 600 by 800 feet and was entirely enclosed by a heavy log stockade. Big enough for 1,000 men, it never housed anything close to that many. Both Indian attackers and white defenders came to view this as the West's most-hated fort. From the very first day, Carrington found himself harassed by the Sioux; by mid-December, more than 50 raids on the troops and civilians had left 17 military men and 58 civilians dead. Many of the horses and mules were

stolen in the raids, and more than 700 cattle were lost when the Indians created a stampede by driving a herd of buffalo into them. With winter setting in, food and ammunition shortages made conditions worse, and even the nightly band concerts could not maintain morale. Jim Bridger revealed something of even greater concern after one of his scouting trips:

> *Crow chiefs report that it took a half a day's ride to go through the villages of the war parties on Tongue River. The Sioux chiefs said they would not touch the new fort on Powder River [Fort Reno] but would destroy the two new forts, in their hunting grounds, meaning Phil Kearny and C. F. Smith.*

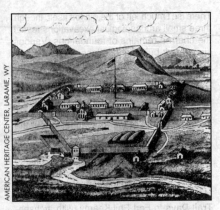

AMERICAN HERITAGE CENTER, LARAMIE, WY

Fort Phil Kearny

Fetterman Fight

Again and again, the Sioux tempted soldiers into traps, drawing them away with attacks on the vital wood wagons (more than 4,000 logs were used in the stockade) and those cutting hay or by stealing stock and then attacking the pursuers. Carrington's caution caused dissension in the ranks, and when a new company of cavalry arrived, led by Capt. William J. Fetterman, the dissension edged on open revolt. Fetterman, like Gen. George A. Custer, had achieved fame for his bravery during the Civil War and, like Custer, would meet an early death. Fetterman viewed the Sioux with reckless disdain, claiming, "I can take 80 men and go to Tongue River through all the Sioux forces." Jim Bridger responded to this boast by telling him, "Your men who fought down South are crazy! They don't know anything about fighting Indians."

On the morning of December 21, 1866, Indians attacked a wood train, and a force of cavalry and infantrymen under Captain Fetterman was sent out. Disobeying orders from Colonel Carrington, Fetterman responded to taunts by Sioux decoys (including young Crazy Horse) by following them into an ambush. Perhaps 2,000 warriors of Red Cloud, High Back Bone, Red Leaf, and Little Wolf suddenly appeared in the tall grass. Within a half-hour, all 81 soldiers had been killed. It was, until Custer's last stand a decade later, the worst annihilation of any American force. Carrington had lost his most experi-

enced fighters. Perhaps 30 Sioux died in the raid. Troops sent out to investigate what had happened found the frozen bodies horribly mutilated. They buried the men in a mass grave.

After the Fetterman Fight, just 119 soldiers remained to guard against several thousand Sioux. Fearing further attacks, Carrington put the fort on full alert and sent messengers to Fort Laramie in a desperate bid for help. John "Portugee" Phillips made the 236-mile ride in four nights of hard riding, struggling through subzero temperatures and blinding blizzards and traveling at night to avoid Indian attacks. In a scene straight out of a Hollywood movie, Phillips staggered into a gala Christmas-night ball with the stunning news. His exhausted horse collapsed and died from pneumonia two weeks later. Because of bad weather, help did not reach Fort Phil Kearny for another two weeks, but the feared Indian attacks never came. Colonel Carrington was reassigned to Fort McPherson in Nebraska—accidentally shooting himself in the foot on the way out—and it took many years to clear his name.

Wagon Box Fight

The tables were turned in the Wagon Box Fight. Woodcutters took the running gear off their wagons to haul logs back to the fort and arranged the wagon boxes in a makeshift fortress filled with ammunition and supplies in case of attack. The attack came on August 2, 1867, when Red Cloud's 3,000 warriors suddenly surrounded 32 woodchoppers and soldiers led by Capt. James Powell. Unbeknownst to Red Cloud, the soldiers were armed with new Springfield rifles that could fire up to 20 rounds a minute. Expecting the soldiers to take time to reload, Red Cloud sent waves of men, only to meet withering gunfire each time. Finally, after six hours of this, soldiers from Fort Phil Kearny arrived with their howitzer and sent the Sioux fleeing. Four soldiers died in the Wagon Box Fight, while estimates of Indian casualties range from six to over a thousand—Sioux warriors removed their dead after a battle, making it impossible to know how many had been killed.

The Fighting Ends

By late 1867, public sentiment had turned against the Army's invasion of Sioux country,

and the Bozeman Trail had become an anachronism, with miners heading to Montana via steamboat up the Missouri River. Besides, the Union Pacific Railroad was well on its way across Wyoming, and the diversion was no longer needed. (Some historians believe this was the primary reason for the forts being built in the first place.) In 1868, the three Bozeman Trail forts were all abandoned. As the soldiers left Fort Phil Kearny, they turned back to see smoke on the horizon. The Sioux were burning it to the ground. Thus ended, at least temporarily, one of the most senseless conflicts in American history. Red Cloud finally returned to Fort Laramie to sign the treaty, having (he thought) forced the government to leave Powder River to the Sioux. Actually the treaty was ambiguous and contradictory, giving them rights to hunt buffalo on the Powder River but saying they would have to live on reservations in Dakota Territory. Six years later, the country would again boil over when another gold rush—this time in the Black Hills—brought General Custer north to fight the Sioux.

The Bozeman Trail Today
The site of Fort Phil Kearny is now a National Historic Landmark and is managed by the Wyoming Division of Parks and Cultural Resources. Entrance costs $1 (free under age 18).

There isn't much left of the old fort itself, though three small archaeological excavations reveal the charred remains of foundations. Various signs mark building locations, the cemetery, and the Bozeman Trail. A fine small **museum** (tel. 307-684-7687 or 684-7629) is open daily 8 a.m.-6 p.m. from mid-May through September and Wed.-Sun. noon-4 p.m. during fall and spring. It is closed Dec.-March. Inside, find an excellent model of the fort, videos about the Bozeman Trail and Fort Phil Kearny, and displays on Indian life. The fort is 17 miles north of Buffalo and 21 miles south of Sheridan off I-90 (take exit 44). Portugee Phillips' ride is noted by a pyramid-shaped monument not far away. The third weekend of June brings **Bozeman Trail Days** to Fort Phil Kearny, with archaeological tours of the fort and nearby battlegrounds, a living history encampment, fife and drum concerts, Indian dancing, and more.

Ruts from the Bozeman Trail are still visible along much of its path, and the battle sites are all marked with monuments of various sorts. Get to the site of the **Wagon Box Fight** by heading a mile south from Story (good road) or driving northwest from Fort Phil Kearny on a winding and rutted road. The **Fetterman Fight** is marked by a stone obelisk on the hilltop where the final stand was made. A three-quarter-mile interpretive trail leads visitors through the battlefield.

BUFFALO

Buffalo (pop. 3,700) is one of those wonderful small towns that seem to define rural America. The "Buffalo bench sitters" hang out each morning where Main Street crosses Clear Creek, and pickup trucks park out front of the local donut shop. Buffalo—the Johnson County seat—is primarily a ranching, oil, and tourism center for the area. The county constitutes the heart of sheep raising in Wyoming; more than 100,000 sheep roam across the sage-covered land here. Although many of the herders now arrive from Mexico, hundreds of Basque shepherds have come over the years and remain an important part of the herding community, giving Buffalo a prominent Basque heritage. There's even a Basque radio program on Sunday mornings. Despite the fact that Buffalo's

Main Street curves along an old bison trail, the town got its name from Buffalo, New York—the name was picked out of a hat.

HISTORY

During Gen. George Crook's 1876 campaign against the Sioux, he had Capt. Edwin Pollock build a supply center along the Powder River and called it Cantonment Reno. It was later renamed **Fort McKinney,** after Lt. John A. McKinney, who had been killed in the Dull Knife Battle. In 1878, Fort McKinney was moved 40 miles north to where the Bozeman Trail crossed Clear Creek. Gradually the new fort took shape, not as one of the stockade-walled structures generally

thought of, but rather as a collection of barracks, mess halls, and two-story houses with board-and-batten exteriors. Soldiers marched from here to South Dakota's Pine Ridge Reservation to put down the Ghost Dance uprising in 1890. More than 150 Sioux and 25 soldiers died at Wounded Knee, the last major battle between Indians and whites in North America.

The establishment of Fort McKinney created an immediate market for all sorts of businesses. Carpenters, blacksmiths, farmers, loggers, merchants, bartenders, and prostitutes arrived and quickly established the town of Buffalo two miles downstream. By 1883, a Cheyenne newspaper noted a dozen saloons and no churches. "Houses of dissipation" seemed more numerous than any other establishment. Much of the barley harvested locally went to supply two breweries. Buffalo had become the largest town in the northern part of Wyoming. This boom suddenly ended in 1894, when the Army declared Fort McKinney excess property and abandoned it. The buildings became the Wyoming Soldiers' and Sailors' Home in 1903 and now house the Veterans' Home of Wyoming. It is still one of the county's largest employers. After WW II, oil and gas exploration and development of the region's vast coal deposits turned Buffalo into an energy center. Today the coal resources of Johnson County remain essentially undeveloped, but substantial amounts of oil and gas are still produced.

Downtown Buffalo has undergone a facelift in recent years as new tourist-oriented businesses move in selling gifts, antiques, Western art, espresso, fly-fishing gear, upscale kids' clothing, and health food.

SIGHTS

Jim Gatchell Memorial Museum
Historic artifacts gathered by druggist Theodore

James Gatchell now make up the core of a collection of some 15,000 articles, making Buffalo's museum one of the finest in the American West. The museum occupies two downtown buildings. Out front are several wagons, including the de rigueur sheepherder's wagon. The front building contains historic photos, a model of Fort Phil Kearny, two videos about Bomber Mountain, and other items. Inside the main building are two floors; downstairs is the standard collection of old junk (including a piece of coral from Maui!) but upstairs is a treasure trove of unusual items, including one of the largest collections of Indian artifacts in Wyoming. Featured are detailed dioramas and displays of items found at the sites of various local battles including the Wagon Box Fight, the Johnson County War, and the Fetterman Fight. Most touching is the flattened horn of bugler Adolph Metzger, the last to die at the Fetterman Fight. The note here says his body was the only one the Indians did not mutilate after the massacre but instead covered it with a buffalo robe out of respect for his valor. Other stories say that after trying to fight off the warriors with his hands and bugle, he was taken captive and tortured to death at the Sioux camp.

Scattered around the room are other surprises: an extensive photographic exhibit on the Powder River, a pair of Cheyenne medicine rattles used in the Dance of Victory after Custer's defeat at Little Big Horn, an arrowhead that belonged to Red Cloud, a cartridge belt made by mountain man Jim Bridger, and the outlaw Tom Horn's spurs and a bridle he braided while awaiting execution. Ask the folks at the museum to point out a rifle probably used by the cavalry at Little Big Horn and a shell from Custer's handgun. Look around and you'll find even more surprises at this most impressive small museum. The museum, on the corner of Main and Fort Streets, tel. (307) 684-9331, costs $2 (free under age 18). A small gift shop sells historical books and old Wyoming license plates. In June, July, and August the museum is

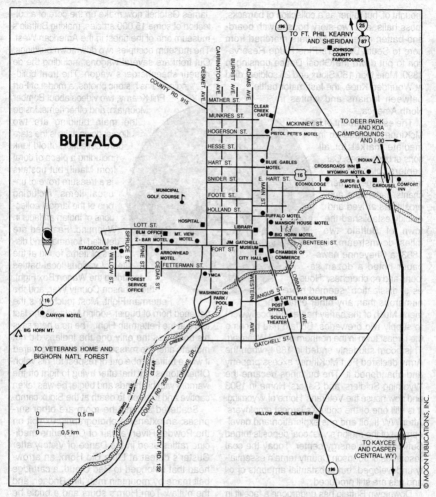

BUFFALO

TO FT. PHIL KEARNY
AND SHERIDAN

JOHNSON
COUNTY
FAIRGROUNDS

TO DEER PARK
AND KOA
CAMPGROUNDS
AND I-90

CLEAR CREEK
CAFE

MCKINNEY ST.

PISTOL PETE'S MOTEL

INDIAN

BLUE GABLES
MOTEL

CROSSROADS INN

WYOMING MOTEL

E. HART ST.

ECONOLODGE

SUPER 8
MOTEL

CAROUSEL

COMFORT
INN

MUNICIPAL
GOLF COURSE

HOSPITAL

BUFFALO MOTEL

MANSION HOUSE MOTEL

LIBRARY

BIG HORN MOTEL

BLM OFFICE

MT. VIEW
MOTEL

Z-BAR MOTEL

JIM GATCHELL
MUSEUM

BENTEEN ST.

STAGECOACH INN

CHAMBER OF
COMMERCE

ARROWHEAD
MOTEL

CITY HALL

FETTERMAN ST.

YMCA

FOREST
SERVICE
OFFICE

WASHINGTON
PARK /
POOL

ANGUS ST.

CATTLE WAR SCULPTURES

CANYON MOTEL

POST
OFFICE

SCULLY
THEATER

BIG HORN MT.

GATCHELL ST.

TO VETERANS HOME AND
BIGHORN NAT'L FOREST

CLEAR CREEK

HIKING TRAIL

WILLOW GROVE CEMETERY

0   0.5 mi

0   0.5 km

TO KAYCEE
AND CASPER
(CENTRAL WY)

© MOON PUBLICATIONS, INC.

DESMET AVE.
CARRINGTON AVE.
BURRITT AVE.
ADAMS AVE.
MATHER ST.
MUNKRES ST.
HOGERSON ST.
HESSE ST.
HART ST.
SNIDER ST.
FOOTE ST.
HOLLAND ST.
LOTT ST.
SPRUCE ST.
PINE ST.
CEDAR ST.
WILLOW ST.
FORT ST.
WESTERN ST.
LOBAN AVE.

COUNTY RD. 915
COUNTY RD. 256
KLONDIKE DR.
COUNTY RD. 132

---

open daily 8 a.m.-8 p.m. (closed July 4). In May, September, and October, it's open Mon.-Fri. 8 a.m.-5 p.m. At other times of the year, call the museum for an appointment or ask at the chamber of commerce.

Petrified Forest

One of the more unusual local sights is a petrified forest on BLM land seven miles south of Buffalo. Take the Red Hills exit from I-90 and follow the road another seven miles to Dry Creek Petrified Forest. An easy three-quarter-mile trail loops through the hot sagebrush country, and markers along the way describe the geological history. Some 60 million years ago, this was a swampy plain dominated by towering metasequoia trees. You can still count the growth rings on the petrified stumps, some of which are over four feet in diameter and 60 million years old.

THE JOHNSON COUNTY WAR

Wyoming's history is a story of constant conflict—between emigrants and Indians, Chinese and white miners, big ranchers and homesteaders, sheepherders and cattlemen. The Powder River has seen more than its share of confrontations; one of the most notorious was the so-called Johnson County War of 1892, the setting for the 1980 box-office megaflop *Heaven's Gate*.

Barons and Grangers
The first white settlers in the Powder River Basin were the "cattle barons," men who owned enormous herds of cattle but who generally resided on the land only part of the year. During the 1880s, more and more homesteaders ("grangers") began to settle here, fencing their spreads and gradually forcing the large cow outfits onto less and less land. The barons tried to force homesteaders off the land, and several Johnson County grangers were found facedown in gullies, shot in the back. Homesteaders retaliated by appropriating cattle that wandered onto their land—and outlaws made off with other stock.

As rustling increased along the Powder River, the big ranchers found little sympathy in nearby Buffalo, the largest town north of the Platte River. Local juries, either sympathetic with or intimidated by cattle rustlers, failed to convict men who were caught, and even the Buffalo sheriff, "Red" Angus, was accused of being in cahoots with rustlers. The cattle barons feared for their lives. The small ranchers and homesteaders in Buffalo were soon openly at odds with the absentee cattle barons based in the largest town south of the Platte—Cheyenne.

The Invasion
In 1892, the small Johnson County ranchers organized their own roundup, an action that proved too much for the powerful Wyoming Stock Growers Association. In a secret meeting, the association proposed a military coup d'état. On April 6, two days after their annual meeting in Cheyenne, a train headed for Douglas with 25 hired Texas gunmen (mostly ex-sheriffs and ex-U.S. marshals) and an equal number of Wyoming men. With them they carried a hit list of 70 suspected rustlers. Cutting the telegraph lines to keep advance word from reaching folks in Johnson County and traveling in darkened railway cars, the "Invaders" headed north, stopping the train near Casper and continuing on horseback.

They first came to the KC Ranch—actually just a couple of cabins—and discovered two of the most notorious rustlers holed up inside, Nate Champion and Nick Ray. In the day-long shootout that followed, Ray died quickly but Champion managed to hold off the Invaders until dusk, when they finally torched the cabin and shot him as he ran for safety. A blood-stained diary found on Champion described his last hours. It ended: "Shooting again. I think they will fire the house this time. It's not night yet. The house is all fired. Goodbye, boys, if I never see you again. Nathan D. Champion."

After this initial success, the Invaders headed on to the friendly TA Ranch, 30 miles north, to rest up for their planned siege of Buffalo. But word got out, and the Invaders suddenly found themselves under attack by a mob of 200 well-armed grangers and rustlers led by Sheriff Red Angus (who was on the hit list). In the shootout that followed, two Texans died. The tables had been turned, and the desperate Invaders faced almost certain annihilation. Meanwhile, word had gotten out to acting governor Amos W. Barber (a supporter of the Invaders), who cabled President Harrison for help. Troops from nearby Fort McKinney arrived before the townsfolk could attack with their tanklike wagon and dynamite bombs. Newspapers around the nation castigated the cattle barons for their effrontery; the *Laramie Sentinel* noted, "of all the fool things the stock association ever did this takes the cake."

Justice Denied
The events that followed made a mockery of the legal system. After being rescued by Army troops, the Invaders were taken to Cheyenne to stand trial. Not surprisingly, two trappers who had happened upon the raid at the KC Ranch mysteriously disappeared until the trial was over, leaving no witnesses for the prosecution. Everyone pleaded not guilty, but when the judge discovered that Johnson County was unable to pay for the prisoners' room and board, he ordered them all released on their own recognizance. After being paid by the barons, the hired Texas gunmen immediately skipped town, never to be seen again. The Wyoming men involved in the raid were released when Johnson County had no more money to prosecute. Many of Wyoming's most prominent citizens—including Barber and Senators Carey and Warren—would later be implicated as supporters of the raid. Johnson County would take years to settle down after the battles of 1892, and for a while the big cattlemen lived in fear for their lives.

BILL NYE ON RUSTLING

Three years ago a guileless tenderfoot came into Wyoming, leading a single Texas steer and carrying a branding iron; now he is the opulent possessor of six hundred head of fine cattle—the ostensible progeny of that one steer. . . . A poor boy can in a few years, with an ordinary Texas steer and a branding iron, get together a band of cattle that would surprise those who figure simply on the ordinary rate of increase. Men soon learn that it is possible and even frequent for a cow wearing a "Z" brand to be the fond and loving mother of a calf wearing the "X" brand, and vice versa. Sometimes a calf will develop a brand that has never been in the family before.

—*19th-century humorist Bill Nye*

Other Sights

Willow Grove Cemetery on the south end of town is an interesting place to explore. Here you will find the graves of rustlers Nate Champion and Nick Ray, Sheriff "Red" Angus, homesteader John Tisdale, and others involved in the Johnson County War. Injured or aged veterans live on the grounds of the **Veterans' Home** (old Fort McKinney) two miles west of Buffalo on U.S. 16. Of the original fort, only an old cavalry stable and the post hospital building are still standing. Check in at the office (tel. 307-684-5511) before sightseeing.

Children (and those who never really grew up) will love the antique **Carousel Park**, tel. (307) 684-7033, on the east end of town behind Col. Bozeman's Restaurant. This is the only carousel in Wyoming and is open daily in the summer and on winter holidays. Just $1 a ride. Included are a dozen custom-carved Wyoming bucking horses. Also here is a 1936 Ferris wheel and a mini golf course. The **Occidental Hotel**, 10 N. Main St., now a made-in-Wyoming gift shop, was the place where Owen Wister's Virginian "got his man." The chamber of

commerce has a walking tour of Buffalo's other historic buildings.

Two three-quarter-lifesize bronze sculptures occupy a small park next to the First National Bank on S. Main Street. Created by local sculptor D. Michael Thomas, they represent combatants in the Johnson County War of 1892. The Johnson County War helped dissuade the Chicago, Burlington, and Quincy Railroad from coming through Buffalo, and for many years Buffalo remained America's largest inland city without a railway. Eventually a spur line was built, connecting Buffalo to Clearmont. Locals called it BC&BM (Buffalo-Clearmont and Back, Maybe) but even it was abandoned in 1946 due to competition from trucking companies. Wyoming Railroad's **Engine 105** now rusts in the city park.

PRACTICALITIES

Lodging

You'll discover plenty of comfortable, exceptionally clean, and friendly motels to choose from in Buffalo, but it's a good idea to reserve well ahead for accommodations during midsummer, when tourists flood the area. See the "Buffalo Accommodations" chart for rates. A couple of recommended places are **Mountain View Motel,** tel. (307) 684-2886, **Z-Bar Motel,** tel. (307) 684-5535 or (800) 341-8000, and **Mansion House Motel,** tel. (307) 684-2218. Be forewarned that motel prices may rise precipitously during the peak summer season, and you may have to pay up to $60 a night. **Cloud Peak Inn B&B,** tel. (307) 684-5794, is a cozy turn-of-the-century home with period antiques and friendly owners. Enjoy a full breakfast and relax on the front porch or in the jacuzzi.

Dude Ranches

Paradise Guest Ranch, tel. (307) 684-7876, is a long-time dude ranch with luxurious log cabins, an outdoor pool, and an indoor jacuzzi. In addition to the main attraction—horseback riding—the ranch has chuck wagon cookouts and special kids' campouts. Open late May to mid-October.

Another popular dude ranch is **Klondike Ranch,** tel. (307) 684-2390, located 15 miles

BUFFALO ACCOMMODATIONS

Note: Accommodations are arranged from least to most expensive. Add a seven percent tax to these rates. Area code is 307.

Buffalo Motel; 350 N. Main St.; tel. 684-2225; $32 s, $36 d

Pistol Pete's Motel; 800 N. Main St.; tel. 684-7453; $34 s, $38 d; indoor pool, open May-Oct.

Z-Bar Motel; 626 Fort St.; tel. 684-5535 or (800) 341-8000; $37 s, $41 d; very nice cabins, kitchenettes $5 extra, AAA approved

Arrowhead Motel; 749 Fort St.; tel. 684-9453 or (800) 824-1719; $38 s or d; kitchenettes $43 s or d; AAA approved

Canyon Motel; 997 Fort St.; tel. 684-2957 or (800) 231-0742; $38 s, $44 d; kitchenettes $45 s or d; AAA approved

Big Horn Motel; 209 N. Main St.; tel. 684-7611; $40 s, $46 d; fridges, open April-Oct.

Mountain View Motel; 585 Fort St.; tel. 684-2881; $40 s, $46 d; cozy cabins, clean and friendly

Blue Gables Motel; 662 N. Main St.; tel. 684-2574; $42 s, 48 d; outdoor pool, cabins, very clean, open April-Oct.

Mansion House Motel; 313 N. Main St.; tel. 684-2218; $45 s, $49 d; turn-of-the-century building, AAA approved

Cloud Peak Inn B&B; 590 N. Burritt; tel. 684-5794; $45-65 s, $55-75 d; turn-of-the-century home, jacuzzi, five guest rooms, shared or private bath, kids okay, full breakfast, AAA approved

Econo Lodge; U.S. 16 E.; tel. 684-2219 or (800) 553-2666; $53 s, $58 d; AAA approved

Triple Three Ranch; three miles northwest of town; tel. 684-2832; $55 s or d; log cabins

Super 8 Motel; U.S. 16 at I-25; tel. 684-2531 or (800) 800-8000; $57 s or d; AAA approved

Comfort Inn; 65 U.S. Hwy. 16 E.; tel. 684-9564 or (800) 228-5150; $60-100 s, $65-100 d; new motel, indoor jacuzzi, continental breakfast, AAA approved

Wyoming Motel; U.S. 16 at I-25; tel. 685-5505 or (800) 666-5505; $62-67 s or d; outdoor pool, kitchenettes $145 (sleeps eight), AAA approved

Crossroads Inn; U.S. 16 W.; tel. 684-2256 or (800) 852-2302; $63 s, $73 d; outdoor pool, AAA approved

HF Bar Ranch; 15 miles west of Buffalo; tel. 684-2487; $140 per person/day including three meals and horseback rides; cozy rustic cabins, swimming pool, open late June-Sept.

---

southwest of Buffalo along Crazy Woman Creek. Horseback riding and fishing keep folks busy, or you can join in the ranch work and help move cattle. The Klondike also offers overnight horseback trips, barbecues, and campfire gatherings. Guests stay in log cabins with private baths and eat in the main lodge. Weekly rates only.

HF Bar Ranch, tel. (307) 684-2487, has 26 comfortably restored cabins—mostly from the 1920s and '30s—on a historic ranch 15 miles west of Buffalo. Guests staying at the dude ranch get two horseback rides per day, access to the outdoor pool, plus all three meals. The ranch also offers guided fishing, skeet shooting, and massages for an extra fee. Open late June to September. In early June, the ranch is a popular place for weddings.

Camping

There's free camping at **Lake DeSmet** eight miles north of town, but the sites can get steaming hot in midsummer. Mostly for the RV crowd. Other nearby public campgrounds ($8-10) are in Bighorn National Forest approximately 15 miles west of Buffalo on U.S. 16. **Big Horn Mountains Campground,** two miles west on U.S.

16, tel. (307) 684-2307 or (800) 684-7628, has tent spaces for $15, RV sites for $18. Showers for noncampers cost $3; open year-round. The friendly folks at **Indian Campground** on U.S. 16 east of town, tel. (307) 684-9601, charge $15 for tents, $18 for RVs in shady spots. Showers for noncampers run $3.50. It's open April-October. Farther out on U.S. 16 is **Deer Park Campground,** tel. (307) 684-5722 or (800) 222-9960, where sites cost $15 for tents, $19 for RVs. They also serve meals and have an outdoor pool and a spa, plus a pleasant creekside trail. The evening ice-cream socials are a favorite. Open May to mid-October. Also along U.S. 16 east of town, the **Buffalo KOA,** tel. (307) 684-5423 or (800) 562-5403, has tent sites for $16.50, and RV spaces for $22. Open mid-April to late October, it boasts an outdoor pool, a jacuzzi, and free pancake breakfasts.

Food
For breakfast, head to the homey **Busy Bee,** 2 N. Main, tel. (307) 684-7544, here since 1928. The Busy Bee sits right along Clear Creek, and on summer mornings the benches out front are often crowded with folks waiting to get in. The Busy Bee's pies are locally famous. **Tom's Main Street Diner,** 41 N. Main St., tel. (307) 684-7444, is another very good place for breakfast. **Deerfield Boutique and Espresso Bar,** 18 N. Main St., tel. (307) 684-2788, has trinkets and clothing in front and lattes in back.

Clear Creek Cafe, 820 N. Main St., tel. (307) 684-7755, has perhaps the nicest atmosphere of any local eatery, and serves pasta, barbecued meats, seafood, chicken, and more. It also has good salads, sandwiches, and burgers for lunch. **The Breadboard,** 107 E. Hart St., tel. (307) 684-2318, has decent subs, soups, and spicy chili for lunch. **Seney's Rexall Drug,** 38 S. Main, tel. (307) 684-7182, houses an old-fashioned soda fountain with thick shakes and malts.

The best local dinner place is **Stagecoach Inn,** 845 Fort St., tel. (307) 684-2507, where the prices are reasonable and the portions substantial. The chicken pot pie special (served on Monday, Tuesday, and Thursday nights) is recommended. A popular family dining place with a good salad bar is **Crossroads Inn** on U.S. 16 east, tel. (307) 684-2256. **Col. Bozeman's,** 675 E. Hart, tel. (307) 684-5555, serves buffalo

steaks, burgers, and Mexican dishes.

When folks are looking for an enjoyable evening away from town, they drive to **Pines Lodge** 14 miles west, tel. (307) 680-8545 or (307) 684-5204, or **South Fork Inn** 17 miles west, tel. (307) 684-9609. Each place has a bar and lounge, along with a standard supper-club menu. Best place for fast food (excellent hickory-smoked fried chicken and ribs) is **Dash Inn,** 620 E. Hart, tel. (307) 684-7930. Get groceries at **Jon's IGA** and **DJ's Thriftway.**

Entertainment
Buffalo has two places to go for live country-western tunes most weekends: **Crossroads Inn,** tel. (307) 684-2256, and the **Century Club,** 14 S. Main, tel. (307) 684-2821. **Scully Theater,** 235 S. Main, tel. (307) 684-9311, is the local movie house. Downstairs from the Scully, **Checkers Sports Bar,** tel. (307) 684-0920, has a small brewery with homemade beer, a big-screen TV, live music or comedy on the weekends, and free Internet terminals. A truly nineties place.

Events
In March, the **Pole Creek Cross-Country Ski Challenge** attracts racers from near and far. **Powder River Roundup Days** in late June or early July features a unique rodeo in which teams rather than individuals compete. The museum's **Living History Days** is held Thurs.-Sun. after the 4th of July and includes Indian dancing, a military drill team, mountain men, horse-drawn wagons, quilting, saddlemaking, Basque dancing, a craft fair, old-time cooking, and more.

On Wednesday nights at 8 p.m. during June and July, the county fairgrounds is the place for the **Buffalo Night Rodeos.** Tuesday evening **All Girls Rodeos** are held from late June to late August. Buffalo's big annual event is the **Johnson County Fair and Rodeo,** held in early August. Call (307) 684-7357 for details. Other events include a **Horseshoe Tournament** in late June and a big **Christmas Parade** on the first Saturday in December.

Recreation
The huge free **outdoor swimming pool** in Washington Park is the largest in the Rocky

Mountains. It has swimming lanes, two diving boards, and a shallow end for tots. Open daily during the summer, this is a great place to play on a hot day. Inside the modern **YMCA,** 101 Klondike Dr., tel. (307) 684-9558, you'll find a pool, a jacuzzi, a weight room, and racquetball and handball courts. Entrance costs $5 for adults, $3 for youths. Rent bikes from **Indian Campground,** on U.S. 16 east of town, tel. (307) 684-9601.

Buffalo's popular **Clear Creek Trail System** makes for a delightful afternoon stroll or bike ride. It follows the creek for 11 miles and is paved to the edge of town. The trail will eventually reach all the way to the foot of the Big Horn Mountains. Buffalo's 18-hole **municipal golf course,** northwest of town, tel. (307) 684-5266, is one of the finest in Wyoming. One hole features a 90-foot vertical drop over 140 yards. Three miles out of town, **Triple Three Ranch,** tel. (307) 684-2832, offers daily horseback rides.

Shopping

Get books on Wyoming from **The Office,** 33 N. Main, tel. (307) 684-2215. Buffalo has two good fishing shops: **Just Gone Fishing,** 777 Fort St., tel. (307) 684-2755, and **The Sports Lure,** 66 S. Main, tel. (307) 684-7682. The latter also sells hiking, skiing, and backpacking gear, as well as topo maps. If you think you're starting to see spots, you may be at **Alabam's Polka Dot Spot,** 421 Fort St., tel. (307) 684-7452, a shop geared to hunters and anglers. Pretty strange. Also in Buffalo, at 15 N. Main, is **Sagewood,** tel. (307) 684-7670, an "earth-friendly" store that sells nature T-shirts, books, and rainforest products. The nicest local galleries are **Margo's Pottery,** 26 N. Main St., tel. (307) 684-9406; **Silver Spur Gallery,** 57 S. Main St., tel. (307) 684-2626; and **Hitching Post Art Gallery,**

51 S. Main Street. **Home Spun Creations,** 5 N. Lobban Ave., tel. (307) 684-5916, sells items from local artisans. **Town Saddlery,** U.S. 16 E., tel. (307) 684-2759, has custom-made tack and saddles.

Information and Services

The **Buffalo Chamber of Commerce** office, 55 N. Main St., tel. (307) 684-5544 or (800) 227-5122, is open Mon.-Sat. 8 a.m.-6 p.m. in summer and Mon.-Fri. 8 a.m.-5 p.m. the rest of the year. Other practicalities include the **Johnson County Public Library** at the intersection of Adams and Lott Streets, tel. (307) 684-7888; the **Buffalo Ranger District Office** of Bighorn National Forest at 300 Spruce, tel. (307) 684-7981; and the BLM's **Buffalo Resource Area Office** at 189 N. Cedar, tel. (307) 684-5586. Get cash from **ATMs** at Buffalo Federal Savings at 106 Fort St., First National Bank at 141 S. Main, the 7-Eleven store at 109 N. Main St., and the Cenex station on U.S. 16 East. Wash clothes at **Tanners Coin Laundry,** 334 N. Main St., tel. (307) 684-2205.

Transportation

Powder River Bus Lines, tel. (800) 442-3682, connects Buffalo with the rest of northern and eastern Wyoming, with onward connections to other parts of the Lower 48. Buses stop at the Action Photo & Video, 327 N. Main Street. Get rental cars at **Northside Car Sales** (Avis), north of Buffalo, tel. (307) 684-5136. The airport in Buffalo does not have scheduled service. Therefore, it was quite a surprise one day in 1979 when a Western Airlines 737 carrying 94 passengers mistakenly landed in Buffalo instead of Sheridan. The pilot has since been "honored" with the celebration of Buffalo's Lowell Ferguson Day (July 31).

BUFFALO VICINITY

LAKE DESMET

Eight miles north of Buffalo is Lake DeSmet, a deep natural lake surrounded by open range country. A stone **monument** to the Belgian Jesuit missionary Father Pierre Jean DeSmet (1801-73) stands along the western shore. DeSmet was one of the few 19th-century men who maintained lifelong friendships with both Indians and whites. The Plains Indians called him "Black Robe" and trusted him with various peacemaking roles at Fort Laramie. But the Indians viewed the lake named for DeSmet with suspicion, as did early settlers, who told of "Smetty the sea monster" who emerged at night from the seemingly bottomless body of water. When first found by DeSmet in 1851, it was a salton lake—the second largest in the west (after Great Salt Lake)—but dams and dikes have increased its size and decreased its salinity. Today, it's a popular place for local boaters. Try your luck at catching one of the mermaids, but you're more likely to pull in a big rainbow trout. Also here are brown trout, crappie, yellow perch, and rock bass. **Lake DeSmet Fishing Derby** is held each Memorial Day weekend and awards over $50,000 in prizes and cash.

You'll find free **camping** just south of the Father DeSmet monument. The area has volleyball nets, picnic tables, and outhouses but no shade or water. **Lake Stop Resort,** tel. (307) 684-9051, rents boats and has a cafe, a bait shop, and cabins. Also here—so the sign claims—is the "world's smallest bar." Just north of the lake is a bed of coal that, in some places, is more than 200 feet thick—second in thickness only to one in Manchuria. No wonder Texaco owns most of the land around Lake DeSmet!

KAYCEE

The town of Kaycee (pop. 290) is named for the nearby KC Ranch and serves as a bentonite, oil, and ranching center. Get on the side roads in spring or fall and you're likely to find yourself behind huge flocks of sheep being herded into or out of the Big Horn Mountains.

Frewen Castle

When the Powder River country was opened to white settlers in the late 1870s, it quickly attracted ranchers and farmers of all types, from homesteaders trying to prove up their 160 acres to wealthy international investors. Two of the most interesting were the English brothers Moreton and Richard Frewen, relatives of Sir Winston Churchill. Coming originally to hunt buffalo, the two saw the lush Powder River area and decided to invest in cattle. Near present-day Kaycee, they erected an elaborate two-story log house, filled it with furniture and fixtures from England, even added an incredible luxury, a telephone. Frewen Castle, as it was soon called, became the center of an enormous spread with at least 60,000 cattle.

Their kingdom attracted English hunting parties and became something of an unofficial dude ranch. (To keep their ladies in the proper spirit, the Frewens set up relay stations to bring hothouse flowers from Denver on galloping horses.) The Frewens' Powder River Cattle Company, Ltd., attracted investments from the British royal family and various lords before reality struck. The cattle did not do as well as expected, competition from surrounding ranchers and rustlers cut into profits, and the disastrous winter of 1886-87 forced the company to the brink of bankruptcy. The Frewens and many other "cattle barons" never really recovered. Today almost nothing remains of Frewen Castle.

Sights

Kaycee's free **Hoofprints of the Past Museum,** tel. (307) 738-2381, is open Sunday 1-5 p.m. and Mon.-Sat. 9 a.m.-7 p.m. Memorial Day to Labor Day, from Labor Day through October Mon.-Sat. 9 a.m.-5 p.m. and Sunday 1-5 p.m. The museum contains items from early settlers, outlaws, and the cattle wars. Look for the wooden potato planter inside. Just south of Kaycee, a marker describes the killing of rustlers Nate Champion and Nick Ray in the

THE WILD BUNCH

Glorified in the 1969 Oscar-winning film *Butch Cassidy and the Sundance Kid,* the Wild Bunch is one of the most famous of all Western outlaw gangs. The Wild Bunch consisted of a constantly changing membership held together by two friends, Robert Parker ("Butch Cassidy") and Harry Longabaugh ("the Sundance Kid"). In 1884, Parker, then a teenager, met up with a local ranch hand and part-time cattle rustler named Mike Cassidy. Rebelling against a strict Mormon upbringing, Parker picked up a few of the master's tricks before getting caught by the law and told to move on. But when he left Utah for Colorado and Wyoming, he took with him his mentor's name, Cassidy. (The "Butch" apparently came later, when he worked in several Rock Springs butcher shops.) Linking up with other outlaws, Cassidy held up the San Miguel Valley Bank of Telluride and then drifted back to horse stealing in Wyoming. Several years later, those horses landed him in the Wyoming State Prison in Laramie. Cassidy was pardoned by the governor after 18 months, reportedly after agreeing not to pursue that line of work in Wyoming anymore. Other places, however, were fair game.

The Gang

If anything, prison made Cassidy more determined than ever to outwit the lawmen. Joining up with Harry Longabaugh—who picked up his Sundance Kid sobriquet while serving time in the Sundance, Wyoming, jail for horse thievery—and Harvey Logan (Kid Curry)—a deadly and fearless Montana fugitive—Cassidy assembled a rogues' gallery of rustlers, drifters, killers, and wanted men soon known as the Wild Bunch. They operated from remote hidden canyons in the west, especially Brown's Park in western Colorado, Bighorn Canyon in Montana, Wyoming's Wind River Valley, and the famous Hole-in-the-Wall southwest of Buffalo, Wyoming—places where entire herds of stolen cattle could be hidden and where the finest horses could be trained for quick getaways.

The Wild Bunch achieved a measure of respect from local ranchers who bought horses and cattle at low prices and found ready workers when the outlaws needed to rest up awhile. For many, Cassidy seemed a modern-day Robin Hood, taking from the rich railroads, banks, mines, and cattle barons while leaving the small folks alone. To this day, locals in Kaycee, Wyoming, still talk fondly of the affable Butch Cassidy.

The gang's activities reached a peak in the late 1890s, with bank robberies in Utah, South Dakota, and Idaho (the latter to pay for a lawyer to clear a gang member on a murder charge). Cassidy—breaking his promise to Wyoming's governor—also led a train robbery in Wilcox, Wyoming, which netted $50,000, but only after he'd blown up the safe with 10 pounds of dynamite, sending money and banknotes in all directions. Within hours, a sheriff's posse was in hot pursuit, and in a gun battle near Casper the sheriff was killed. Somehow, the Wild Bunch managed to slip through the posse's lines for a clean getaway.

In 1900, they struck another Union Pacific train near Tipton, Wyoming (just east of Rock Springs). Amazingly, the same express messenger was present for both robberies; the first time he had refused to open the railcar door and was literally blown out with explosives. The second time the conductor persuaded him to open the door. Perhaps he knew that the safe held only $54; the train carrying $100,000 worth of gold had passed just a few hours before. Then the Wild Bunch was off to Winnemucca, Nevada, where a bank holdup netted them a cool $32,000. After a fling at Fanny Porter's Sporting House in San Antonio, the gang members bought some new hats at a Fort Worth haberdasher and, dressed as dudes, posed for the famous group portrait later used by Pinkerton detectives. Cassidy and two other gang members tried their hands once more at train robbery in 1901, taking at least $40,000 from a dynamited safe in Montana. The law was closing in, however. Of the gang members who stayed behind, all but one died a violent death. For Butch Cassidy and the Sundance Kid, the future lay in South America.

Gringos

In 1901, a trio headed for Argentina: Butch Cassidy, the Sundance Kid, and Etta Place—a strikingly beautiful woman whom Sundance apparently met in Fanny Porter's Sporting House. (Butch later called her "a fine housekeeper, but a whore at heart.") There they settled with their ill-gotten wealth to a quiet life of ranching and traveling occasionally to Buenos Aires, where they stayed in the finest hotels and dressed in formal clothes befitting their new role as bourgeois American settlers. But even in South America, Pinkerton detectives managed to pick up their trail, and, sensing this, the three decided to try their skills in virgin territory. They robbed

(continues on next page)

THE WILD BUNCH
(continued)

three banks in Argentina and a train in Bolivia before Etta Place came down with acute appendicitis. A hurried trip took the trio back to the States, but in Denver, where the operation was performed, the Sundance Kid got in trouble for shooting up his hotel room while drunk. Rather than face the law, he fled to New York, where he and Cassidy again boarded a steamer bound for Argentina. Etta remained behind.

The two outlaws now worked part-time at a Peruvian gold mine, using the work as a cover for their periodic forays into banks, trains, and stores in search of money. For many years, most believed that Butch Cassidy and the Sundance Kid died in a blaze of gunfire at a remote village on the Bolivian-Argentine border in 1909. Today, however, it appears that Cassidy escaped (and perhaps the Kid as

well), using his reported death as a convenient opportunity to change his ways. According to Larry Pointer's *In Search of Butch Cassidy,* Cassidy later fought with Pancho Villa in the Mexican Revolution, met Wyatt Earp in Alaska, and settled down to running a Spokane machine shop, living under the name of William T. Phillips until his death from cancer in 1937. Several Wyoming residents, old friends of the famous outlaw, met him in Lander and Riverton on several occasions before his death. Cassidy reportedly spent considerable time in a fruitless effort to recover buried loot that he had stashed near Mary's Lake in the Wind River Mountains. Today, the Butch and Sundance legends keep growing. Stop by the towns of Rock Springs, Lander, Laramie, Worland, Dubois, Baggs, or Kaycee and you'll be regaled with more tales of their exploits.

The Wild Bunch: Harry Longabaugh (Sundance Kid), Bill Carver, Ben Kilpatrick, Harvey Logan (Kid Curry), and George Parker (Butch Cassidy)

BUFFALO BILL HISTORICAL CENTER

Johnson County War of 1892 (see the special topic). The old **KC Ranch house,** where the two were killed by the Invaders, stood here. The **TA Ranch,** where the Invaders holed up after raiding the KC Ranch, is approximately 30 miles north of here along State 87. Bullet holes are still visible in many of the wonderful old ranch buildings. It is now run as a guest ranch (tel. 307-684-5833).

Ten miles east of Kaycee on State 192 is a marker noting the first buildings in northern Wyoming, constructed in 1834 by Portuguese trapper Antonio Montero. The log stockade and trading post (known as the **Portuguese Houses**) were abandoned around 1839, and nothing remains on the site. The site of old **Fort Reno** (1865-68) is in the same general vicinity; ask in Kaycee for directions. A monument marks

(continues on next page)

the place, and various remains are still present from this little-known fort.

Practicalities and Events

Stay in Kaycee at **Cassidy Inn Motel**, tel. (307) 738-2250, for $26 s, $31 d, or **Siesta Motel**, tel. (307) 738-2291, for $24 s, $30 d. There's free **camping** in the Kaycee town park. Both the **Feed Rack Restaurant** and **Country Inn** offer good all-American food. Events in Kaycee include the **Sheepherders Rodeo and Dog Trials** in the first weekend after July 4th, and the excellent **Deke Latham Memorial PRCA Rodeo** in early September. Kaycee is the smallest town in America with its own PRCA rodeo.

HOLE-IN-THE-WALL COUNTRY

Outlaw Country

The remote country used by the Wild Bunch and other outlaws lies some 30 miles west of Kaycee. Get here by following State 190 for 20 miles to where the pavement ends. At the road junction—maps call this Barnum, but there is no town here—a side road leads to Blue Creek Ranch (private), land once homesteaded by Butch Cassidy and the Sundance Kid. Surrounding you are gorgeous red-walled canyons rising above the Middle Fork of the Powder River. Its waters provide a fine place to fish for rainbow, brook, and brown trout.

Turning right (north) leads you to the **Dull Knife Battlefield**, named for an 1876 incident. General Crook's soldiers surprised Dull Knife's band of Northern Cheyenne in this remote valley. The attack killed at least 40 Cheyenne and ended what whites viewed as a campaign of terror and which the Indians viewed as retaliation for the invasion of their last stronghold.

To reach other area sites, turn left (south) on the graded gravel road that parallels the river. Follow the road five miles, past the Bar C Ranch, and bear right at the signed 4WD side road to **Outlaw Cave**. Beyond the intersection, the road is really only passable in high-clearance vehicles, not 4WD Subarus. The road crosses a three-quarter-mile long stretch of prehistoric **rock cairns** and then tops a knoll. Stop here for impressive views of Hole-in-the-Wall and the country behind it. **Outlaw Cave Camp-**

ground (free but waterless) is two miles beyond this.

From the campground, a quarter-mile path drops 660 feet down to two caves used by the Wild Bunch and other outlaws. One of the caves is little more than a depression in the rocks but the other is room-sized, with posts that were once part of a wall. A corral reputedly used by rustlers is still here. Take your fishing pole down to try for trout. On the other side of the road and up another third of a mile is **Indian Rock Art Cave.** The cave (actually just a rock overhang) contains some of the most unusual Indian rock art in Wyoming, including a large warrior figure, bear claws, and shield designs. A major buffalo jump site (where Indians hunted buffalo by driving them over a cliff) is nearby, along with many tepee rings. The BLM office in Buffalo (tel. 307-684-5586) can provide a useful map and road log of the Outlaw Caves/Hole-in-the-Wall country.

Hole-in-the-Wall

The wealthy Frewen brothers who ranched here in the 19th century named this country after London's Hole-in-the-Wall Tavern. The "Hole" lies at the end of a steep "V" in the red cliffs bordering Buffalo Creek. It was accessible via a narrow trail that cuts up the talus slope and into a funnel-shaped opening that could be blocked with a triangular boulder. The setting was perfect for rustling and as a hideout from the law, especially for gangs such as the Wild Bunch. The cliff was easy to defend and offered a vantage point where sentries could warn of approaching lawmen. Hole-in-the-Wall itself is on public (BLM) land, but much of the surrounding land belongs to ranchers who guard their privacy closely and do not allow access. There are ongoing efforts to gain easements to this famous but almost-unseen place.

Check with the BLM in Buffalo, tel. (307) 684-5586, for authorized outfitters offering tours of the Hole-in-the-Wall area. A unique way to discover the Old West is the **Outlaw Trail Ride** in mid-August. This weeklong trip takes equestrians from the Hole-in-the-Wall country to Thermopolis. You'll need to bring your own horse, bedroll, and gear, but meals are provided for a fee. There is a limit of 100 riders. Call (800) 443-6235 for information on this fascinating not-for-profit adventure.

Western Encounters, tel. (307) 572-1230, offers weeklong horseback trips across various parts of Wyoming including the Hole-in-the-Wall country. The cost is $1,245 per person including horses, meals, equipment, and transport from the company base in Riverton. **Hole in the Wall Country Tours,** tel. (307) 738-2243, leads all-day 4WD tours of Butch Cassidy's old haunts and trips along the Bozeman Trail. Tours depart from the Kaycee Texaco station.

GILLETTE

Campbell County proclaims itself the "Energy Capital of the United States," a title gained by producing more coal and oil than any other county in Wyoming. The county's more than 188 oil fields yield over 25 million barrels per year, while 16 giant strip mines shovel up an eighth of the total U.S. production of coal. At the center of all this is Gillette (pop. 22,000), Wyoming's fourth-largest city.

Gillette isn't known as a tourist destination; its neighborhoods and shopping malls are indistinguishable from those of a thousand other homogenized American cities. Gillette is a young town; the median age in 1980 was less than 27. Interpret this your own way: Gillette actually has an E-Z Street! Despite the lack of any connection to the shaving company, Gillette is jokingly called "Razor City."

HISTORY

When you drive into Gillette, the sense of history permeating much of Wyoming quickly gives way to the raucous present. History is decidedly not Gillette's strong suit, even though the town is nearly a century old. When the Burlington and Missouri route to Sheridan was being planned, it was originally set to go south of the present location, but astute surveyor Edward Gillette discovered a route farther north that saved construction of 30 bridges. Initially, the new company-platted town was to be called "Donkey Town" for its proximity to Donkey Creek, but instead it was named for Gillette. (Edward Gillette later served a term in Washington as a congressman from Wyoming; however, he preferred to live in the more scenic town of Sheridan than in his namesake.) The railroad reached Gillette in 1891, and the town was incorporated the following year. It became a shipping point for local ranchers and homesteaders and grew slowly over the decades.

The Present

Since the late 1960s, Gillette has ridden an enormous growth rocket, powered first by oil and then by coal. Gillette's oil boom really began in the fall of 1967, when a drilling company hit an oil gusher that ignited an enormous fire. Firefighter Red Adair was called in to extinguish the flames, attracting worldwide attention. Hollywood soon followed—John Wayne's *Hellfighters* was based on these events. Other oil companies flooded the area with exploratory rigs, and almost overnight Gillette grew from a sleepy cow town to a major energy center. A frantic scramble for the almighty dollar ensued, with real-estate values quadrupling between 1966 and 1970.

Unlike the rest of Wyoming, where the oil boom of the '70s was quickly followed by the bust of the '80s, Gillette caught the coal wave just as the oil tide was heading back out to sea. With enormous reserves of low-sulfur coal throughout the surrounding countryside, Campbell County quickly became a major player on the energy scene. The city's population nearly tripled in the '80s and continues to grow as coal mining and the Wyodak power plant expand. Today Gillette is the modern version of middle America—shopping malls, spreading suburbia, used-car lots, and fast-food joints. Author Wallace Stegner's description of a California town could fit just as well here: "But mostly it is Main Street, Anywhere, a set used over and over in a hundred B movies, a stroboscopic image pulsing to reassure us by subliminal tricks that though we are nowhere, we are at home."

SIGHTS

The fine **Rockpile Museum,** on U.S. 14/16, tel. (307) 682-5723, is open Mon.-Sat. 9 a.m.-8 p.m. and Sunday 12:30-6:30 p.m June-Aug. and

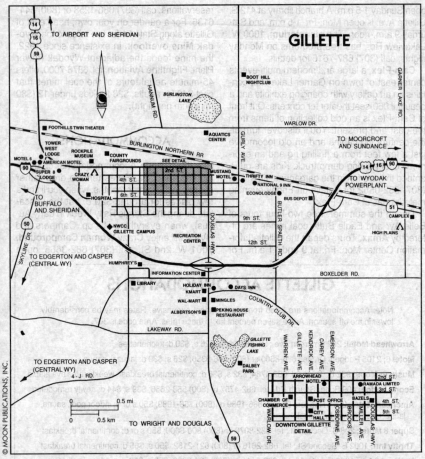

Mon.-Sat. 9 a.m.-5 p.m. the rest of the year. No charge. Out front is a minor local landmark for which the museum was named and a Burlington Northern caboose. This spacious museum contains sheep wagons, a horse-drawn hearse—originally from Montana, its first eight customers died from gunshots—and other wagons, a blacksmith shop, an impressive arrowhead collection, and dozens of elaborate spurs and old rifles. A big board contains a directory of several hundred brands. Be sure to check out the floating rocks from Lake DeSmet. Out front is a tiny one-room schoolhouse that could have served

double duty as a doghouse. The metal building next door has some very strange sandstone rocks.

The **Campbell County Public Library,** 2101 4-J Rd., tel. (307) 682-3223, is one of the finest in the state. Besides a large collection of books about Wyoming, it houses a remarkable collection of art including paintings by Hans Kleiber, Gene Kloss, and Conrad Schwiering. Out front are life-size bronze statues of cowboys and horses. Library hours are Mon.-Thurs. 9 a.m.-9 p.m., Fri.-Sat. 9 a.m.-5 p.m., and Sunday 1-5 p.m. Between September and May, it's also

open Sunday 1-5 p.m. A branch library at 412 S. Gillette Ave. is open Mon.-Fri. 1-5 p.m. and Saturday 9 a.m.-noon. The **planetarium,** 1000 W. Lakeview Rd., has free programs on Monday nights; call (307) 687-7616 for details.

Cam-Plex, a large and modern multi-events center east of town on Garner Lake Rd., contains an art gallery with changing exhibits and a beautiful 960-seat theater for concerts. Out front of Cam-Plex is an odd collection of items from the past and present. You'll discover turn-of-the-century log cabins and an old locomotive just a few feet from a drilling rig and an enormous coal-hauling dump truck. Kids are guaranteed to have fun in the gargantuan tires. Call (307) 682-0552 for details on Friday evening melodramas at Cam-Plex.

During the summer, free two-hour tours of Belle Ayr and Eagle Butte coal mines are offered by **Amax.** Tours depart the Gillette Information Center Mon.-Fri. at 9 and 11 a.m. For reservations, call (307) 686-1258 or (800) 544-6136. For a gander on your own, head east of Gillette along State 51 for five miles to the **Wyodak Mine overlook.** In existence since 1922, the mine feeds the adjacent Wyodak Power Plant. **Flightline Aviation,** tel. 6876-7000, offers 45-minute aerial tours of the coal mines that cost $40 for adults, $20 for kids under 12 ($80 minimum per flight).

ACCOMMODATIONS

See the "Gillette Accommodations" chart for lodging specifics. Rates tend to drop rather sharply in the winter months, when you'll find a few places for around $20 d, but they escalate during the Sturgis Rally Week in early August, when everything fills up. Campers and RVers will enjoy **Crazy Woman Campground,** 1001 W. 2nd St., tel. (307) 682-3665; open

GILLETTE ACCOMMODATIONS

Note: Accommodations are listed from least to most expensive. Rates may be considerably lower in the off-season. Add a seven percent tax to these rates. Area code is 307.

Arrowhead Motel; 202 Emerson Ave.; tel. 686-0909; $26 s, $30 d; kitchenettes

Motel 6; 2105 Rodgers Dr.; tel. 686-8600 or (800) 466-8356; $26 s, $30 d; jacuzzi, sauna

Mustang Motel; 922 E. Third; tel. 682-4784; $32 s, $36 d; continental breakfast, weekly rates avaialable

Econo Lodge; 409 Butler Spaeth Rd.; tel. 682-4757 or (800) 553-2666; $39 s, $44 d; newly remodeled

American Motel; 2011 Rodgers Dr.; tel. 686-1989 or (800) 758-1989; $50 s or d; indoor pool, sauna, jacuzzi, continental breakfast

Super 8 Motel; 208 S. Decker Ct.; tel. 682-8078 or (800) 800-8000; $50 s or d; continental breakfast

Thrifty Inn; 1002 E. Second St.; tel. 682-2616 or (800) 621-2182; $50 s, $65 d; continental breakfast

National 9 Inn; 1020 E. U.S. 16; tel. 682-5111 or (800) 524-9999; $52 s, $59 d; outdoor pool, sauna

Ramada Limited; 608 E. Second St.; tel. 682-9341 or (800) 272-6232; $55 s, $65 d; outdoor pool, continental breakfast

Days Inn; 910 E. Boxelder Rd.; tel. 682-3999 or (800) 325-2525; $55-60 s, $65-70 d; continental breakfast

Best Western Tower West Lodge; 109 N. U.S. 14-16; tel. 686-2210 or (800) 528-1234; $70-82 s, $75-87 d; indoor pool, jacuzzi, sauna, weight room

Holiday Inn; 2009 S. Douglas Hwy.; tel. 686-3000 or (800) 686-3368; $85 s, $93 d; indoor pool, sauna, fitness center, recreation area, AAA approved

Deer Park B&B; 2660 Bishop Rd. (18 miles southeast of Gillette); tel. 682-9832; $75-105 s, $95-125 d; country home, two large guest rooms, private baths, decks, full breakfast, no kids

year-round. It's a pleasant place with genuine shade trees, a rarity in Wyoming's private campgrounds. Also here is a jacuzzi, an outdoor pool, and bike rentals. The rather bleak **High Plains Campground**, tel. (307) 687-7339, is next to Cam-Plex on the east side of town.

Deer Park B&B, tel. (307) 682-9832, is located in the rolling plains south of Gillette and consists of an older home with two spacious guest rooms, each with its own deck from which guests can enjoy the surrounding country. A full breakfast is served.

Skybow Castle Ranch, tel. (307) 682-3228 or (800) 682-3229, is a 3,000-acre working cattle ranch located in the pine forests 15 miles northeast of Gillette. This is a mostly-for-kids place to learn about life on the range with week-long visits that include horseback riding, rodeo events, games, fishing, camping out, sing-alongs, and ranch chores such as moving cattle and feeding goats and lambs. The cost is $800 per kid for a one-week stint.

FOOD

Breakfast
Gillette has a number of interesting eateries, if nothing to knock your socks off. The best breakfasts are probably at **Flying J Restaurant**, 1810 S. Douglas Hwy., tel. (307) 686-0077. **Bazels Restaurant**, 408 S. Douglas Hwy., tel. (307) 686-5149, has retro-'50s diner-style decor, good breakfasts, and substantial portions. Also try **Granny's Kitchen**, 1414 W. U.S. 14/16, tel. (307) 687-1200, for breakfast or lunch. Get cappuccinos, lattes, light breakfasts, and lunches at **Coffee Friends**, 320 S. Gillette Ave., tel. (307) 686-6119.

Ethnic Eateries
Peking House Restaurant, 2701 S. Douglas Hwy., tel. (307) 682-7868, is one of the better Chinese restaurants in Wyoming, with a popular lunchtime buffet. Get pizza and pasta at **Ole's Pizza Parlor**, 114 N. U.S. 14/16, tel. (307) 682-8484. For Mexican food, try **Aunt Chilotta Tacos**, 400 W. 2nd, tel. (307) 682-0610, or **Las Margaritas**, 2107 S. Douglas Hwy., tel. (307) 682-6545.

Lunch and Dinner
Humphrey's Bar & Grill, 408 W. Juniper Lane, tel. (307) 682-0100, is a favorite lunch place for the business crowd with a diverse pub grub menu and Wednesday night ribs. Humphrey's has more than 50 beers on tap, and the small brewery here makes five of them. Unfortunately, the place suffers from a formulaic feel: walls crowded with sporting photos and memorabilia and TVs tuned to all-sports channels.

The big salad bar/dessert bar at **Golden Corral**, 2700 S. Douglas Hwy., tel. (307) 682-9130, makes for a bargain meal. **Bailey's Bar & Grill**, 301 S. Gillette Ave., tel. (307) 686-7667, is a fine place for such homemade lunch and dinner specialties as chicken-fried steak, burgers, and Mexican fare. Great finger food, too. The award-winning **Prime Rib Restaurant**, 1205 S. Douglas Hwy., tel. (307) 682-2944, is another very good place for prime rib ($15-22) and also has a diverse menu that includes steak, pasta, chicken, and seafood. Their wine and champagne list is easily the most extensive in the area. Last, but not least, **Boot Hill Nightclub**, 910 N. Gurley Ave., tel. (307) 682-1600, offers unbeatably priced nightly specials including pork chops, "Rocky Mountain oysters," prime rib, seafood, and steaks.

Get groceries from any of the big chains: Albertson's, Buttery, Decker's, and IGA. **Old World Bakery**, 208 S. Gillette Ave., has doughnuts, sweets, pastries, and freshly baked breads.

OTHER PRACTICALITIES

Entertainment
Head to Gillette City Park on Thursday nights at 8 p.m. during June and July for the **Concerts in the Park** series. Music ranges from bluegrass to classical. The **Powder River Symphony Orchestra**, tel. (307) 686-5767, performs at Cam-Plex in March, May, October, and December.

The state's largest dance hall is **Boot Hill Nightclub**, at 910 N. Gurley Ave., tel. (307) 682-1600. It's a popular place to dance the night away to country music Wed.-Sat. nights. Top-40 and oldies bands play most nights at **Partners Saloon** inside the Tower West Lodge at 109 N. U.S. 14/16, tel. (307) 686-2210. **Kicks Lounge** in the Holiday Inn at 2009 S. Douglas

STRIP MINING

Coal mining has been an important part of the Campbell County economy for many years. The first mines were underground, but once the technology developed to remove the overlying soil, strip mining became feasible. Today, 16 Campbell County strip mines are scattered along an enormous coal seam five miles wide, over 50 miles long, and up to 100 feet thick—enough to last hundreds of years. Together, the 16 mines produce a quarter of the nation's coal, and if Campbell County were a nation it would rank fourth in the world in coal reserves, behind the U.S., Russia, and China! Most of the mines are owned by giant multinational energy companies such as Peabody Coal (Powder River, North Antelope, Caballo, Rawhide, and Rochelle), Amax (Belle Ayr

and Eagle Butte), Kerr-McGee (Jacobs Ranch), Kennecott (Cordero and Antelope), and ARCO (Black Thunder and Coal Creek). Cranking out over 36 million tons per year, the Black Thunder Mine just east of Wright is the largest coal mine in America. The Wyodak Mine is the oldest in the Powder River Basin—it opened in 1922—and feeds one of the world's largest air-cooled power plants (also on the site). You can view the mine from a nearby highway overlook.

Digging the Coal

Powder River Basin mines are heavily mechanized operations with relatively few employees; despite massive increases in production, the number of employees continues to drop. Mining coal here is a relatively simple process, made easier through the use of machinery and blasting equipment that are something beyond gargantuan; all the vehicles seem to be on steroids. Imagine a truck that carries 240 tons of coal—two and a half railroad coal cars' worth—and is powered by a 2,200-horsepower engine. Try changing a flat on it—the tire stands 11 feet tall and weighs four tons! Even this behemoth is dwarfed by the dragline used at the Black Thunder Coal Mine. Its 300-foot boom pulls in a 90-cubic-yard bucket (a typical dump truck holds 12 cubic yards). Powered by electricity,

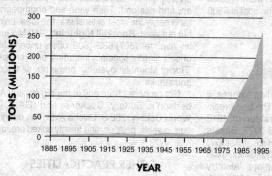

WYOMING COAL PRODUCTION

TONS (MILLIONS)

300
250
200
150
100
50
0

1885 1895 1905 1915 1925 1935 1945 1955 1965 1975 1985 1995

YEAR

Hwy., tel. (307) 686-3000, is the place to go for rock and pop tunes six nights a week and a happy-hour buffet Mon.-Fri. evenings. **Prime Rib Restaurant,** 1205 S. Douglas Hwy., tel. (307) 682-2944, also has occasional live entertainment, as does **Jake's Tavern,** 5201 S. Douglas Hwy., tel. (307) 686-3781. Jake's features happy-hour prices 5-7 p.m. seven days a week. **Mingles,** 2209 S. Douglas Hwy., tel. (307) 686-1222, has half a dozen pool tables, a big-screen TV, and periodic comedy nights.

For movies, head to **Foothills Twin Theatre,** 650 N. U.S. 14/16, tel. (307) 682-6766; **Sky-Hi**

Indoor Theatres, on S. Douglas Hwy., tel. (307) 682-7628; or **Skyline Drive In Theatre,** on S. Douglas Hwy., tel. (307) 674-4532.

Events

Gillette's **4th of July** celebration is the biggest in northeastern Wyoming. In addition to an impressive fireworks show, you'll find a pancake breakfast, a parade, mud volleyball, firehose water fights, and even a Ping-Pong drop (a Ping-Pong drop?). The **National High School Rodeo** will take place at Cam-Plex the third week of July from 1998 through 2000. **Parkfest** brings a

the 3,600-ton machine waddles along like a duck, dragging its power line behind. After blasting loosens the overburden, it is stripped away and dumped into waiting trucks. (Topsoil is stored for use in later reclamation.) Below this overburden lies the deep black coal seam that must be drilled and blasted. Electric shovels scoop up the loosened coal and dump it into the trucks for delivery to crushing and storage facilities. The entire scale of the operation comes into focus

by watching as mile-long, 100-car trains move constantly through the loading facility. Workers can load up to 12 trains in a day—over 130,000 tons.

Environmental Impacts

The strip mining of coal has always been a controversial subject, with environmentalists concerned over the impacts from burning coal in an era of acid rain (97% of Wyoming coal is burned for electricity), global warming, and escalating atmospheric carbon dioxide. They also question whether reclamation will really work on Wyoming's arid lands. The other impacts from mining are equally important: access roads divide up antelope and deer habitat, subdivisions for the workers spread out over the countryside, and wells draw down the water table. Mining companies, however, point with pride to herds of antelope grazing near the coal mines and believe that the land can be restored after the coal is gone.

A visit to the coal mines is an eye-opening odyssey into the Super Bowl of strip mining. No matter what you think about the procedure, a tour of the mines is well worth taking, if only to see the enormous equipment and ponder what burning all this coal will do to the environment.

full day of musical entertainment at Cam-Plex Park the second Saturday of August. The **Campbell County Fair** in mid-August includes livestock judging, arts-and-crafts exhibits, and other old-time favorites. **Cam-Plex,** a large and modern multi-events center east of town on Garner Lake Road, frequently has concerts, cattle shows, rodeos, conventions, and other events. During the summer rodeos take place almost every weekend, the biggest being the **PRCA Rodeo** in late July and early August. The highlight of the PRCA Rodeo is the camel (!) race. **Pari-mutuel horse racing** takes place in June and July at Energy Downs, next to Cam-Plex.

Recreation

Gillette has outstanding recreation facilities. **Campbell County Recreation Center,** 1000 S. Douglas Hwy., tel. (307) 682-5470, houses an indoor pool with a diving well, a 383-foot water slide (summer only), weight rooms, racquetball and squash courts, a gym, and a sauna. The cost is just $2.50 per swim ($1.50 for kids, no

charge for seniors). Free summertime swimming at the pool in **City Park** at Gillette and 10th, tel. (307) 682-1962. There's also a fine indoor **Aquatics Center** for competitive swimming events. Bird watchers should head to **McManamen Park** on W. Warlow Dr., where viewing blinds let you look for ducks and other birds. Roller skaters will enjoy **Razor City Skateland,** 885 Hannum Rd., tel. (307) 682-3529, and bowlers can roll their own at **Camelanes Bowling Center,** 1005 W. 2nd St., tel. (307) 682-4811, or **Frontier Lanes,** 5700 S. Douglas Hwy., tel. (307) 687-0261. Golfers head to **Bell Nob Golf Links,** 1316 Overdale Dr., tel. (307) 686-7069, or **Gillette Golf Course,** 1800 Country Club Rd., tel. (307) 686-4744. **Big Horn Mountain Sports** in Powder Basin Mall, tel. (307) 687-1422, carries a full range of outdoor gear.

Information and Services

The **Gillette Visitors Center,** tel. (307) 686-0040 or (800) 544-6136, is at 1810 S. Douglas Hwy. (next to the Flying J Truckstop at Exit 126)

and is open daily 8 a.m.-6 p.m. June-Sept. and Mon.-Fri. 8 a.m.-5 p.m. the rest of the year. You may want to also try the **Campbell County Chamber of Commerce,** 314 S. Gillette Ave., tel. (307) 682-3673, open Mon.-Fri. 9 a.m.-4:30 p.m. year-round. Get books at **Daniels Books,** 320 S. Gillette Ave., tel. (307) 682-8266. Gillette has the state's fastest-growing junior college (over 900 students), the **Gillette Campus** of Northern Wyoming Community College. Located at 720 W. 8th St., tel. (307) 686-0254, the campus offers a range of classes and degree programs from business to mining. You'll find **ATMs** at banks all over Gillette, including First Interstate Bank, 222 S. Gillette Ave.; Key Bank, 800 E. 7th St.; and Norwest Bank, 500 S. Douglas Highway.

Transportation

Powder River Trailways, 1700 E. U.S. 14/16, tel. (307) 682-0960 or (800) 442-3682, has daily bus service to most other northern and eastern Wyoming towns and connections to other parts of America. (Look for the big Petrolane propane tank to find this easy-to-miss bus station.)

The airport is five miles north of Gillette. **Mesa Airlines/United Express,** tel. (800) 241-6522, has service to Denver and **Skywest/Delta,** tel. (800) 221-1212, offers commuter service to Salt Lake City (via Cody).

Rent cars from **Avis,** tel. (307) 682-8588 or (800) 831-2847; **Enterprise,** tel. (307) 686-5655 or (800) 325-8007; or **Hertz,** tel. (307) 686-0550 or (800) 654-3131. **Yellow Checker Cab,** tel. (307) 686-4090, is the local taxi company.

HEADING SOUTH

Two roads point south from Gillette; more remote State 50 makes a fine bike route. This distinctive red highway was built from scoria. The alternative route, State 59, takes you into the heart of the mixed-grass prairie, with oil pumpjacks, windmills, enormous bales of hay, and thousands of cattle and sheep. Tumbleweeds are plastered against the barbed-wire fences and abandoned farm equipment rusts on hilltops. Amax's Belle Ayr mine stands on the eastern horizon a dozen miles south of town, with flat-topped mesas and nipple-shaped buttes

adding a little spice to the scenery. Far to the west, the Big Horn Mountains rise from the plains. Be sure to pause for a look at the grasses—blue grama is especially pretty when seen up close.

Durham Buffalo Ranch

Approximately 30 miles south of Gillette is Durham Buffalo Ranch, home of the largest private buffalo herd in existence. The Flocchini family owns a 55,000-acre spread here and is dedicated to returning the land to its original state, when bison and other native animals dominated the prairie landscape. Watch for some of the 3,500 head of buffalo along the highway. Herds more than 1,000 times this size once roamed across the land, and this is a rare opportunity to see bison today in a relatively natural setting. Call (307) 939-1271 for tour information (groups only).

Wright

Wyoming's newest town is Wright, right in the center of America's largest low-sulfur coal deposit. Established in 1976, Wright quickly grew to some 1,200 residents. Modern schools, a small shopping mall, and six churches popped up, along with trailer courts and suburban split-level homes on curving streets. Funded partly by Atlantic Richfield Company (ARCO), Wright was built to house workers for nearby coal mines. Pretty weird place. Imagine an enclave of middle-class America plunked down in a setting straight out of *High Plains Drifter.*

On the east end of town off State 387, the small **Wright Centennial Museum,** tel. (307) 464-1222, houses local homestead-era items. Out front is a 70-ton truck that was retired from hauling coal when it was replaced with much larger dump trucks. The museum is open Mon.-Fri. 10 a.m.-5 p.m. from mid-May to mid-October.

The **Latigo Hills Mall** is Wright's focal point, and includes a grocery store, cafe, pizza shop, hardware store/gift shop, library, bank (no ATM), post office, and the **Wright Area Chamber of Commerce,** tel. (307) 464-1312 (open Mon.-Fri. 1-5 p.m.). Get buffalo burgers at **Reno Junction Cafe,** at the junction of State 387 and State 59, tel. (307) 939-1298. The town also has a fine **recreation center** (tel. 307-464-0198) with an indoor pool, racquetball courts, a weight

room, and a gym. Stay at **National 9 Inn,** tel. (307) 464-1510 or (800) 524-9999, where rooms go for $40 s, $45 d; kitchenettes $3 extra. Park RVs at **Sagebluff RV Park,** a mile west of town on State 387, tel. (307) 464-1305. **Powder River Trailways,** tel. (800) 442-3682, has bus service from Wright to other parts of eastern and northern Wyoming.

The annual event here is **Wright Days,** held each August with games, parades, cowboy poetry, and the obligatory rodeo. Gigantic coal strip mines surround Wright; all of them use Paul Bunyan-scale equipment and skeleton crews of employees. Much of this is public land belonging to Thunder Basin National Grassland, meaning enormous revenues for the federal government and severance taxes for the state of Wyoming. The coal trains seem to never end. Stop on the railroad overpass near the dot of a settlement called Bill and you'll see a hundred cars of coal pass every couple of minutes, with empty trains waiting on the sidings. Most of this coal is on its way to electric-generating plants in Texas and the Midwest.

BOB RACE

THE BLACK HILLS

Northeast Wyoming feels quite unlike any other part of the state. South Dakota's Black Hills roll across an arbitrary state line into Wyoming, while the Belle Fourche River (pronounced "bell-FOORSH," French for "Beautiful Fork"—i.e., of the Missouri River) drifts through these hills first heading northeast and then cutting a sudden right angle to the southeast and across the state line. Cattle graze in rich pastures along the river. Nearby, one of the most stunning of all sights—Devils Tower—seems almost alive in its abrupt rise from the surrounding land. South of the Black Hills in Weston County, the country quickly opens into the mixed-grass prairie of the plains. This out-of-the-way part of Wyoming is truly a special place. It's no wonder that the Sioux considered the Black Hills the home of the Great Spirit.

Only 13,000 people live in Crook and Weston Counties, scattered on rural ranches or in the small settlements of Sundance and Hulett in the midst of Wyoming's Black Hills, plus Newcastle, Moorcroft, and Upton along the southern edge. Cattle grazing, bentonite mining, oil wells, and logging provide the jobs.

The Land

The Black Hills stretch in a long ellipse, 125 miles north to south and 65 miles across, rising 3,000 to 4,000 feet above the surrounding plains. South Dakota's Harney Peak, at 7,242 feet, is the tallest mountain in the Black Hills; in fact, it's the tallest peak between the South Dakota-Wyoming line and the Atlantic Ocean. The most famous attraction in this part of Wyoming is Devils Tower, but the Black Hills north of Sundance are captivating, especially in the spring and fall. Most visitors who come to northeast Wyoming do so as part of a trip that includes Yellowstone and various South Dakota sights including Mt. Rushmore and Deadwood.

From a distance, the dark green carpet of ponderosa pine darkens the hills—hence the Sioux name Paha Sapa, meaning "Hills that are Black." The Black Hills are a blend of open meadows, rocky hills crowded with forests of pine and aspen, and valleys lined with bur oak. This is one of the few places you're likely to see native oak trees in Wyoming.

White-tailed deer are abundant throughout the Black Hills, and herds of elk are found southeast of Sundance. Merriam's turkeys are a common sight all through this country. Introduced from New Mexico in 1948, they are now the most widespread game-bird species in northeast Wyoming.

NEWCASTLE

Newcastle (pop. 3,300) sits at the junction of several major roads and serves as a gateway to the Black Hills. Like much of northeast Wyoming, the town's economy is a mixture of energy, ranching, and logging. Every half hour, day and night, traffic backs up on the railroad tracks across Main Street to wait as a hundred soot-black coal cars rumble past bound for midwestern power plants. A Newcastle refinery produces jet fuel for South Dakota's giant Ellsworth Air Force Base, and a natural-gas processing plant sits 25 miles south of town in the midst of the Finn-Shurley fields. Large ranches encompass the town, dotted with oil pumpjacks, windmills, and Herefords. Piles of fresh-cut ponderosa pine surround Newcastle's big sawmill.

HISTORY

The first white settlement of the Newcastle area came in 1875, when Professor Walter P. Jenney and Lt. Col. R.I. Dodge led 432 soldiers and an army of mining engineers, scientists, and mapmakers to a base camp along Beaver Creek. They built the Jenney Stockade, which became a stage station and distribution point along the Cheyenne-Deadwood Trail. Many of the west's most famous characters stopped by en route to Deadwood, including Wild Bill Hickok, Calamity Jane, and Wyatt Earp.

Tubb Town

In 1888, the Chicago, Burlington, and Quincy Railroad announced plans to construct tracks across northeast Wyoming and into Montana. Speculators established Tubb Town, a ramshackle collection of saloons and hotels along the proposed railroad route. All visitors were required to pay a toll upon entrance: "set 'em up for the bunch." The party didn't last long—when the Burlington Railroad decided instead to build a town at present-day Newcastle, Tubb Town faded into history. At Whoopup Canyon (so named because the spring floods came "a-whoopin' through"), a railroad worker attempted to pry the cap off a 25-pound can of black powder. After struggling without success, he decided to try a more forceful approach—using a pickax to punch a hole in the lid. His coworkers found little left to bury.

The Cambria Mines

Coal was discovered in Cambria Canyon in the 1880s, and the coal-mining town of Cambria popped up almost overnight. It became a model community, with a water system, modern homes, three churches, electric lights, and some

THE BLACK HILLS

WYOMING

MONTANA

SOUTH DAKOTA

ALZADA

COLONY TO BELLE FOURCHE, SD
212

BELLE FOURCHE RIVER

112

LOWEST ELEVATION
IN WYOMING
(3,125 ft.)

NEW HAVEN

BLACK HILLS
NATL FOREST

HULETT

ALVA

24

MISSOURI
BUTTES

BEAR LODGE MOUNTAINS

ALADDIN TO
SPEARFISH,
SD

OSHOTO

DEVILS
TOWER
NATL
MONUMENT?

COOK LAKE

111

14

WARREN
PEAK
LOOKOUT

BEULAH

14

REUTER

SUNDANCE

BLACK
HILLS
NATL
FOREST

KEYHOLE STATE PARK

90   14

MOORCROFT

PINE RIDGE

116

MOSKEE

TO
GILLETTE
(POWDER RIVER
COUNTRY)

16

BUCKHORN

INYAN KARA MTN.
(6,368 ft.)

585

UPTON

FOUR CORNERS TO
DEADWOOD, SD

OSAGE

85

TO JEWEL CAVE AND
MT. RUSHMORE, SD

116

NEWCASTLE

450

TO WRIGHT
(CENTRAL WY)

0   10 mi

0   10 km

16

WHOOPUP CANYON

SOUTH DAKOTA

TO LUSK (SOUTHEAST WY)

85

© MOON PUBLICATIONS, INC.

ANNA MILLER MUSEUM

The coal-mining town of Cambria was considered a model community in its time.

of the safest underground mines in the nation. Alcohol was banned, along with bawdy entertainment. At its peak more than 1,500 people lived in Cambria, but when the coal ran out in 1928 the mines were forced to close.

The discovery of coal at Cambria led the Burlington Railroad to establish a townsite as near the mouth of Cambria Canyon as possible, with a spur to the four mines. The town was called Newcastle, after the English coal port of Newcastle-upon-Tyne. At first, the wide-open frontier sensibility of Newcastle contrasted sharply with that of quiet, sedate Cambria. When the new mayor, Frank Mondell (who had established the Cambria mines), decided to get rid of 20 of Newcastle's undesirables, a local hotel owner—fearing that he would lose most of his business—shot the mayor. Mondell (who later served for 26 years as Wyoming's lone congressional representative) carried the bullet in his spine the rest of his life.

After the Cambria mines closed, the town of Newcastle faded, but with the discovery of huge oil deposits nearby in the 1950s it boomed again. By the mid-'50s more than 25,000 people crowded the surrounding countryside. A bust soon followed, only to lead to a similar cycle in the 1970s. Now Newcastle perks along on an economy equal parts oil, coal, logging, and ranching. Folks from Nebraska or Kansas would feel right at home among the quiet streets, staid older homes, pickup trucks, and freight trains.

SIGHTS

Anna Miller Museum
The Newcastle museum at Delaware St. and U.S. 16, tel. (307) 746-4188, is open Mon.-Fri. 9 a.m.-5 p.m. It's housed in the old National Guard Cavalry Barn, a stone structure built in the 1930s by the WPA. Inside is the typical collection of local paraphernalia: items from the Cambria mines, a horse-drawn hearse, a noose (not, however, the one vigilantes used to hang murderer Diamond Slim Clifton from the Newcastle railroad trestle), a model of the giant KB&C ranch, and even a six-legged lamb and a two-headed Hereford calf as a sideshow. Be sure to try a couple of cranks on the old carnival noisemaker. Anna Miller, for whom the museum was named, was a local school superintendent whose husband, Sheriff Billy Miller, was the last white man to die in a battle with the Indians. He was killed in 1903.

Outside the museum is a furnished one-room schoolhouse built in 1890 and the **Jenney Stockade cabin** (built in 1875), the oldest building in the Black Hills. Ask at the museum for directions to the Cheyenne-Deadwood Trail ruts and an Indian petroglyph site in Whoopup Canyon.

Accidental Oil Company
Certainly the most amusing sight around Newcastle is the kitschy Accidental Oil Company. In

1966 (around the time Jed Clampett of television's *Beverly Hillbillies* was "shootin' at some food, and up from the ground came a bubbling crude—oil that is, black gold, Texas tea . . ."), Newcastle rancher Al Smith decided to dig a hole to see how far down it was to oil. Using a pick and shovel, and later dynamite, he reached it at 21 feet. The "world's only hand-dug oil well" is now a small run-down tourist trap along U.S. 16 four miles east of Newcastle. Outside are steam-powered oil rigs and antique pumps. An old oil-storage tank encloses a gift shop, and you can walk down to view the oil-bearing rock under black light. Pure Americana. Accidental Oil, tel. (307) 746-2042, is open daily 9 a.m.-6 p.m. in summer and Mon.-Sat. 9 a.m.-6 p.m. the rest of the year; entrance costs $3 for adults, $2 for kids.

PRACTICALITIES

Accommodations

You'll find nearly a dozen different places to stay in Newcastle (see chart). During Sturgis Rally Week in early August rates at many local motels rise sharply, and the rooms are often booked up almost a year in advance. Two especially well-maintained and quiet places are **Pines Motel,** tel. (307) 746-4334, and **Morgan's Motel,** tel. (307) 746-2715. Also of note is the historic and antique-filled **Flying V Cambria Inn,** tel. (307) 746-2096. The **Horton House B&B,** tel. (307) 756-4366, sits right on the town's main street and was originally built in 1895, though it has been altered over the years. The bed and breakfast has four guest rooms furnished with antiques.

The **EVA—Great Spirit Ranch B&B,** tel. (307) 746-2537, is a modern log home on a 500-acre ranch in the Black Hills 17 miles north of Newcastle. A nice place to get away from it all. For something even more remote, the 18,000-acre **4W Ranch,** tel. (307) 746-2815, is out in the middle of nowhere 50 miles southwest of Newcastle. The accommodations are simple—in a shared-bath bunkhouse or mobile home—but guests get three full meals a day. Not for everyone; most folks come here to "varmint" hunt (shoot prairie dogs.)

Camping

You can pitch a tent for free anywhere on nearby public lands within both Thunder Basin National Grassland (see "Douglas Vicinity" in the

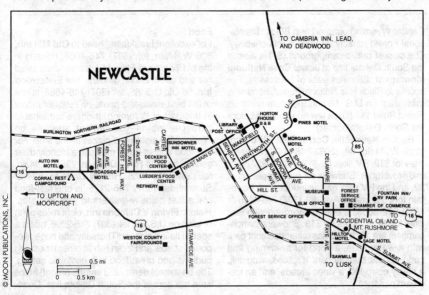

NEWCASTLE ACCOMMODATIONS

Note: Accommodations are listed from least to most expensive. Add a six percent tax to these rates. Area code is 307.

Roadside Motel; 1605 W. Main St.; tel. 746-9640; $26-34 s or d; kitchenettes $36 s or d

Sage Motel; 1227 S. Summit; tel. 746-2724; $28 s, $34 d; AAA approved

Auto Inn Motel; 2503 W. Main; tel. 746-2734; $30 s, $36 d

Pines Motel; 248 E. Wentworth; tel. 746-4334; $30 s, $40 d; kitchenettes $55 s or d; very clean, quiet location, AAA approved

Hilltop Motel; 1121 S. Summit; tel. 746-4494; $32 s, $38 d

Horton House B&B; 17 S. Summit; tel. 746-4366; $32-37 s, $64-74 d; historic home with antiques, four guest rooms, private or shared bath, full breakfast

Morgan's Motel; 205 S. Spokane; tel. 746-2715; $35 s or d; quiet location, nice place, open April-Nov.

Sundowner Inn Motel; 451 W. Main; tel. 746-2796; $38 s or d; outdoor pool, jacuzzi

Flying V Cambria Inn; eight miles north; tel. 746-2096; $39 s, $69 d; historic place, full breakfast, open mid-May through Dec.

Fountain Inn; 3 Seminoe Ave.; tel. 746-4426 or (800) 882-8858; $57 s, $62 d; outdoor pool, water slide, kids' pool, AAA approved

EVA—Great Spirit Ranch B&B; 1262 Beaver Creek Rd. (17 miles north of Newcastle); tel. 746-2537; $50 s, 74 d; new log home, historic 500-acre ranch, two guest rooms, private baths, full breakfast

4W Ranch; 1162 Lynch Rd. (50 miles west of Newcastle); tel. 746-2815; $60 per person/day (includes three meals); working cattle ranch, lodging in bunkhouse or mobile home, shared bath

Central Wyoming chapter) and Black Hills National Forest (described later in this chapter). The closest public campground ($7) is across the South Dakota line at **Jewel Cave National Monument,** 25 miles east of Newcastle. For access to Black Hills National Forest, head nine miles east on U.S. 16 and then turn north up Forest Road 117 (just a few hundred feet before the South Dakota border).

Back in Newcastle, **Corral Rest RV Camp,** 2206 W. Main, tel. (307) 746-2007, has tent sites for $12, RV sites for $17; open mid-April to mid-November. Showers for noncampers cost $2, and the RV park has an indoor pool. **Fountain Inn,** 3 Seminoe Ave., tel. (307) 746-4426 or (800) 882-8858, is open year-round with tent sites for $9, RV sites for $13. Showers for noncampers are $2. It also has an amusement park with a water slide, a pond for swimming and paddle boats, bumper cars, a roller-skating rink, a merry-go-round, a video arcade, and an ice-cream parlor.

Food

For excellent breakfasts, head to **Old Mill Inn,** 500 W. Main, tel. (307) 746-4608, housed in the old Toomey's Flour Mill. It also has a salad bar and all-American dinners. The **Slatewood Inn,** 66 Old U.S. 85, tel. (307) 746-4686, is one of the best steak-and-prime-rib establishments in this part of Wyoming. It offers reasonable barbecue rib all-you-can-eat specials on Wednesday nights and pizzas all the time. For fast food and sit-down meals in a friendly diner setting, head to **Hi-16 Drive In,** 2951 W. Main, tel. (307) 746-4055. **Howdy Drive In,** 834 S. Summit, tel. (307) 746-2176, is one fast-food place that actually delivers to your doorstep. Historic **Flying V Cambria Inn,** eight miles north of town on U.S. 85, tel. (307) 746-2096, offers a special Italian night on Thursday and huge two-pound steaks and fresh fish at other times. Big portions and great food in a nostalgic setting. The best meal deals (and entertainment) in the area are across the South Dakota line. Dead-

wood's gambling casinos have all sorts of discount come-ons including cheap steak dinners. This is where Newcastle folks go for an evening out.

Get groceries at **Decker's Food Center,** 709 W. Main, tel. (307) 746-2779, or **Lueder's Food Center,** 622 W. Main, tel. (307) 746-3511. Decker's has a good bakery.

Entertainment

Head to the **Hy '90s Club** at Railway Ave. and Wakefield St. for country-western or rock tunes. It was formerly the Gay '90s Club—wonder why they changed the name? The **Buckhorn Bar and Grill,** tel. (307) 746-3675, 25 miles north of Newcastle on U.S. 85, is a favorite spot for both travelers and locals. Good food and live country music. The **Dogie,** (as in "Git along, little dogie") 111 W. Main St., tel. (307) 746-2187, is the local movie house.

Events

Newcastle's big local event is the **Weston County Fair,** held in early August. You're likely to find a **rodeo** going on at the fairgrounds most summer weekends.

Information and Services

The **Newcastle Visitor Center,** just west of the intersection of U.S. 16 and 85, tel. (800) 835-0157, is open Mon.-Fri. 9 a.m.-5 p.m. (sometimes on weekends). Be sure to pick up "Beaver Creek: A Trip Through Time," a loop tour of sites in the area; it's filled with delightful descriptions of historical events. The **Weston County Library** is at 23 W. Main, tel. (307) 746-2206. Swim at the high school **pool,** 15 Stampede, tel. (307) 746-2713. Try your fishing skills at **LAK Lake** east of town (named for the Lake, Allenton, and King ranch there), or play a few rounds of golf at **Newcastle Country Club,** 2302 W. Main, tel. (307) 746-2639. The **Bureau of Land Management** office is at 1101 Washington, tel. (307) 746-4453, and the Forest Service's **Elk Mountain Ranger Station** is at 640 S. Summit Ave., tel. (307) 746-2783. Newcastle does not have bus or plane service. For fast cash, First State Bank of Newcastle, 24 N. Sumner Ave., has an **ATM.**

NEWCASTLE VICINITY

Heading North

North of Newcastle, U.S. 85 climbs quickly into the pine-covered Black Hills, providing wide vistas over the town and across the open plains to the south. Eight miles north of Newcastle is **Flying V Cambria Inn,** constructed in 1928 as a resort for and memorial to the Cambria miners and completed just months before the mines closed down for good. It is listed on the National Register of Historic Places. The ghost town of Cambria slowly crumbles on private land nearby.

Another nine miles north is **Red Butte,** a steep-sided sandstone peak rising right along the road like a miniature Devils Tower. A local landmark, it was said to have been used by both Indians and early whites as a lookout. Beyond this, the land begins to open up into an undulating grassy terrain with rich red-black soil. Just a couple more miles up the road is a combination store, cafe (try the chili), and post office at **Four Corners.** The "world's most desolate pay phone" stands alone in front of the store. The graveled Mallo Road heads east from Four Corners, offering a colorful fall drive as the aspens turn a brilliant yellow.

Not far away is the site of the 1878 Canyon Springs robbery on the old Cheyenne-Deadwood Stage Route. A passenger and an outlaw died in the shoot-out, and at least $20,000 (some accounts claim up to $140,000) in gold was taken and buried nearby. Many years later, a local farmer digging potatoes near Red Butte apparently found some of the loot. Packing up his family, he split town without a word.

Heading South

South of Newcastle, U.S. 85 is an arrow aimed at the horizon, pointing across the almost-flat landscape of grass, wind, and antelope. A few bottomland trees line the creeks, and the Cheyenne River etches a narrow line through the land, nearly dry in the late-summer heat. This is the heart of the great mixed-grass prairie that borders eastern Wyoming and reaches into adjacent Nebraska and south into Colorado.

UPTON AREA

On the edge of Upton (pop. 1,000), a sign makes no bones about where you are: the "Best Town on Earth!" Who am I to argue? Like its neighbors—Osage and Newcastle—Upton lies right along the edge of the Black Hills, with ponderosa pines topping the ridge to the north (appropriately named Pine Ridge) and open-range country spreading to the south. The Chicago, Burlington, and Quincy Railroad established a depot here in 1892, and railroad tracks now form Upton's southern border. Beyond this, State 116 climbs over gentle grassy hills through the heart of Thunder Basin National Grassland. It's a high-plains landscape filled with windmills and scattered ranches and grazed by sheep, cattle, antelope, and mule deer. The sky completely dominates the landscape, sending giant white thunderheads over the plains. Upton's limited economy is dependent upon American Colloid's bentonite mine, local ranchers, oil pumping, and coal mining in nearby Campbell County.

Osage

Located halfway between Newcastle and Upton, tiny Osage (pop. 300) has a bar but not much else to show for having once been the center of the oil industry in northeast Wyoming. In 1920, a huge gusher turned the surrounding country into a madhouse of oil prospectors and turned Osage into a tent city of 1,500 people. When the boom inevitably turned to bust, only a core of folks remained in what is now a railroad way station.

Practicalities

If you don't mind in-town, no-shade camping, pitch a tent next to the **Country Market Conoco,** tel. (307) 468-2551, for $4 a night, $10 for RVs. Stay at **Upton Motel,** tel. (307) 468-9282, for $25 s, $30 d (with kitchenettes) or the much nicer **Weston Inn Motel,** tel. (307) 468-2401, for $32 s, $35 d.

The **Stagecoach Inn** is a popular eating spot, and **Upton Drug,** tel. (307) 468-2770, has an old-fashioned soda fountain. Get groceries at **Joe's Food Center,** tel. (307) 468-2372. You can hang out at the public **library** on Pine and 4th Streets, tel. (307) 468-2324.

MOORCROFT

Moorcroft (pop. 800) is a nondescript ranching and oil field town perched within a few miles of popular Keyhole Reservoir. It isn't particularly attractive, but it will do as a stop on the way to somewhere else. Because the famed Texas Trail passed through it, Moorcroft became an important cattle town. Up until the end of WW II, it served as the largest cattle shipping point along the entire Chicago, Burlington, and Quincy Railroad. The local historical stopping place is **Helen Robinson Zimmerschied Western-Texas Trail Museum,** at 200 S. Bighorn, tel. (307) 756-9300. Open Mon.-Fri. noon-4 p.m.; no charge. The name is almost bigger than the museum's collection of local items. Outside are a tepee and a sheep wagon. The main summertime event is **Moorcroft Jubilee Days** in early July.

Practicalities

Lodging is available at the tiny **Wyoming Motel,** 111 W. Converse, tel. (307) 756-3452, for $26 s, 30 d, and the considerably better **Moorcroft Motel,** 214 Yellowstone Ave., tel. (307) 756-3411, where rooms with kitchenettes go for $31 s, $42 d. The nicest place in town is **Cozy Motel,** 219 W. Converse, tel. (307) 756-3486, where rooms are $39 s, $49 d. Get meals at **Donna's Diner,** 203 W. Converse, tel. (307) 756-3422, and groceries from **Joe's Super Valu** on N. Bighorn Ave., tel. (307) 756-3491. Wash clothes at the **Laundry Basket Laundromat** on the west side of town. Moorcroft's **library** is at 105 E. Converse, tel. (307) 756-3232. Drop by **Town Hall,** 104 N. Big Horn, tel. (307) 756-3526, for more about the moors and mores of Moorcroft.

KEYHOLE STATE PARK

Keyhole State Park, tel. (307) 756-3596, surrounds Keyhole Reservoir, a 14,720-acre warm-water lake that backs up water from the Belle Fourche River. (The name comes from the "keyhole" brand, used by a local ranch.) The dam was built in 1952 by the Bureau of Reclamation and supplies irrigation water for South Dakota farmers. Recent drought years

have left a bathtub-ring effect, particularly in late fall. Most of the visitors are locals, but it's an okay place to camp. Pine trees crowd hills to the east while grass and sage grow around the reservoir's western shore. Anglers angle for the biggest walleye and northern pike in the state, bird watchers watch for Merriam's turkeys and white pelicans, and snowmobilers 'bile around in winter. Entrance to the park costs $3 for nonresident vehicles, $2 for Wyoming vehicles. **Camping** costs $4 at eight different state campgrounds along the lake's east and south shores. Nicest are Pats Point and Pronghorn Campgrounds. Get to Keyhole State Park from I-90 by taking the Pine Ridge exit and continuing eight miles north. You'll find a swimming beach here, and the little town of **Pine Haven** (pop. 150) contains **Keyhole Resort,** tel. (307) 756-9529, with a marina (supplies and boat rentals), a cafe, and a motel. Get supplies, booze, and grub from **T.J.'s Bar & Grocery,** tel. (307) 756-9554. **Keyhole Country Club,** tel. (307) 756-3775, has a nine-hole golf course.

SUNDANCE

The quiet country town of Sundance (pop. 1,200) nestles at the foot of Sundance Mountain. The mountain—"Temple of the Sioux"—rises a thousand feet above the town and was an important sacred spot to the various tribes who claimed this land. Sun dances were performed at its base each year. Sundance got its start in 1879, when rancher Albert Hoge set up a trading post here. The town grew slowly until the 1950s, when Sundance Air Base arrived. Since its closing, the town of Sundance has settled into middle age with the old standbys of ranching and logging its economic mainstays, though tourism is increasingly important.

SIGHTS

Crook County Museum

The local museum, tel. (307) 283-3666, is located in the basement of the Crook County Courthouse on Cleveland Street. Hours are Mon.-Fri. 9 a.m.-8 p.m. and Saturday 9 a.m.-4:30 p.m. in the summer and Mon.-Fri. 8 a.m.-5 p.m. the rest of the year. Inside are the usual collection of local paraphernalia such as arrowheads, "period" rooms, wooden wheelchairs, bison skulls, cowboy gear, and a model of Devils Tower. More interesting are the momentos from Harry Longabaugh's visit to the town. Better known as the "Sundance Kid," (see the special topic "The Wild Bunch"), Longabaugh spent 18 months in Sundance's Crook County Jail for horse stealing before being pardoned by the governor in 1889. The museum has the criminal bar docket signed by Longabaugh during his trial and furnishings from the original courthouse. A replica (built in 1983) of the jail that once housed the Sundance Kid stands beside the old stone high school.

Around Sundance

Access to 5,829-foot **Sundance Mountain** is via a dirt road that heads east from State 116 about a half mile south of town. An enjoyable trail leads to the top, gaining 800 feet in elevation along the way. From the top, you're treated with views of the nearby Black Hills and, on clear days, even the Big Horn Mountains 180 miles west. Ask at the visitor center for access information.

Three miles west of the small settlement of **Beulah** (on the South Dakota border, 18 miles east of Sundance) is the **Vore Buffalo Jump,** where Indians drove hundreds of bison into a pit between A.D. 800 and 1600. No developments here. The drive south from Beulah to Buckhorn provides a good taste of the Black Hills canyon country. Follow Sand Creek Road south from the freeway at Beulah, and you can drive for about 30 miles through canyons, the deserted mining town of Moskee, and on to Buckhorn on U.S. 85. In the spring and fall a 4WD may be needed for the muddy conditions, and the route is closed in winter. The Sand Hill Country Club and state fish hatchery at Ranch A are favorites of deer, especially in fall and early winter, when hundreds of deer are visible from the road. There's no hunting here, so you're likely to see a number of trophy animals.

Eleven miles south of Sundance on State 116 is **Inyan Kara Mountain** (an Indian name meaning "Stone-Made Peak"), a 6,368-foot summit that dominates the surrounding country. In 1874, Gen. George A. Custer led a large scientific expedition through this region en route to the Black Hills. Among others, Custer climbed the mountain, carving "G. Custer '74" on a rock near the summit. The inscribed rock is still here, though access to the mountain may be restricted by surrounding ranchers. Ask at the information center or museum for access info.

PRACTICALITIES

Accommodations

Visitors will find four places to stay in Sundance. Be sure to book up to a year ahead if you plan to visit during the Sturgis Rally Week in early August. (Some local motels jack the rates sky high for this event.) Find very nice accommodations at **Bear Lodge Motel,** 218 Cleveland, tel. (307) 283-1611 or (800) 341-8000, with rooms for $42-52 s or d including a jacuzzi. **Arrowhead Motel,**

SUN DANCES

The most spectacular of all Plains Indians religious ceremonies was the sun dance. An annual event, it frequently attracted hundreds or even thousands of tribal onlookers, serving not simply as an important religious service but also as a social and political rally. Native American legends say that it originated centuries ago when a hunter was approached by a buffalo who suddenly spoke to him, offering a cure for sickness. Much later, an eagle came to another young man in a dream, prescribing the complete ceremony. The name is something of a misnomer, since the dance was not a worship of the sun but a highly involved ceremony representing the creation of life and the triumph of good over evil. The specifics varied somewhat between the tribes. A common Native American term for it is "Thirsting Dance," referring to the long periods of dancing without water.

The sun dance was always held in late spring or early summer and led by a young man who spent considerable time learning the complex ceremonial steps from a priest. If he passed the test, the pledger gained immense status in the village as a fearless leader. The festivities lasted up to two weeks, with the main ceremony an intense four-day event. Central to the sun dance were an eagle representation (air), a buffalo head (earth), and a pole connecting the two to signify the sacred Tree of Life. The ceremony took place in a lodge, generally built around a central pole that forked at the top. After the sacred cottonwood tree had been selected by a scouting party, warriors attacked the tree in a furious charge. If it withstood this symbolic assault, the tree was cut down by a respected tribal woman and carried to the sun-dance site, where it was carefully erected. A bundle of brush (to represent an eagle or thunderbird nest) and a buffalo head were placed in the fork of

BOB RACE

the pole. Twelve other poles (the number varied with different tribes) were erected around the central one, with cross beams to the center. (Missionaries would later claim that the 12 poles around the central one were ritualistic representations of Jesus and the 12 apostles.) Brush was then laced around

right next door at 214 Cleveland, tel. (307) 283-3307 or (800) 456-6016, charges $50-62 s or d, and **Deane's Pine View Motel,** 117 N. Eighth St., tel. (307) 283-2262, has cabins for $35-55 s or d, with kitchenettes for $75 (sleep five). Deane's is open April-November. The town's fanciest lodging is the **Best Western Inn at Sundance,** 121 S. 6th, tel. (307) 283-2173 or (800) 238-0965. Rates are $59-70 s, $62-89 d. It has an indoor pool, sauna, and jacuzzi. Located between Sundance and Keyhole Reservoir, **Hawken Guest Ranch,** tel. (307) 756-9319 or

(800) 544-4309, has lodging in cabins for $45 s, $50 d, with horseback rides and evening steak cookouts available. Open May-September.

Camping

You can reserve a spot at the Forest Service's fine **Reuter Campground** ($7), just four miles northwest of Sundance, by calling (800) 280-2267 ($8.25 reservation fee). See "Black Hills National Forest" and "Devils Tower National Forest" below for other public campgrounds. The private **Mountain View Campground,** tel.

the outside to provide partial shade, and a buffalo-skull altar erected at the structure's center.

Supplicants spent four days without food or water, dancing, praying, blowing on eagle-bone whistles, and staring at the buffalo head, the sun, or a sacred doll as they waited for a vision of power. In most tribes, the sun dance also involved self-mutilation. Assistants commonly cut small pieces of skin from the candidates' arms and shoulders as a blood sacrifice to the Great Spirit. (According to several accounts, before the battle at Little Big Horn, Sitting Bull sacrificed 100 pieces of flesh in a sun-dance ceremony, after which a vision told him of the coming destruction of General Custer and his men.) Torture commonly went even further, as assistants cut slices into the back or chest of the dancers and slid bone skewers into the muscle. Thongs would be attached between the skewers and the central pole, while other skewers held heavy buffalo skulls to be dragged behind. Candidates would lean back until the ropes

were taut, jerking as they danced. Eventually the skin and muscle ripped loose and the dancers collapsed on the ground. In some tribes, the dancers were actually lifted off the ground by these tethers.

Whites found the sun dance's torture difficult to understand and thought even less of such sexual aspects of the ceremony as the parading of a giant phallus. When the Indians were forced onto reservations, the sun dance was outlawed, although some tribes continued to practice it secretly. Finally, in the late 1920s, the government relented, and a more sedate version of the dance was resurrected. The traditional blood sacrifice still exists among some tribes but not in Wyoming. Today, the sun dance is performed in separate ceremonies by both the Shoshone and the Arapahoes on the Wind River Reservation. Visitors may watch but cannot take photos or recordings.

The sun dance is now performed primarily as a thanksgiving ceremony, to cure disease, and to pray for the coming year. After several days of preparation, the main ceremony lasts for four days. Without food or water, the dancers move into a trance state that brings visions and power. One authority describes dancers seeing the buffalo head shaking and steam coming out of its nostrils as the power is imparted. On the fourth day, a bucket of water is passed around to signal the end of the sun dance, and that evening more dancing and feasting complete the ceremony.

BOB RACE

(307) 283-2270, 1.5 miles east of town, has tent sites for $13, RV spaces or tepees (d) for $17. An outdoor pool is on site.

Food
Higbee's Cafe, 101 N. 3rd, tel. (307) 283-2165, is open Mon.-Fri. only, cranking out dependably good all-American breakfasts and lunches. For three meals a day with daily specials, head to **Log Cabin Cafe,** 1620 Cleveland, tel. (307) 283-3393. **Aro Restaurant,** 307 Cleveland, tel. (307) 283-2000, has homemade soups and Friday night prime rib; it's probably the best place in town. Get groceries from **Decker's Food Center,** 106 N. Seventh, tel. (307) 283-3155.

Information and Services
The small **Sundance Information Center,** in the rest area at Exit 189 off I-90, tel. (307) 283-2440, is open daily 8 a.m.-7 p.m. from mid-May through September, daily 8 a.m.-5 p.m. in Oc-

tober; it's closed the rest of the year. The Forest Service's new **Bearlodge Ranger District Office** is a mile east of town, tel. (307) 283-1361.

The Sundance **post office** is at 2nd and Main Streets, tel. (307) 283-3939, and the **Crook County Library** is at 414 Main St., tel. (307) 283-1006. Purchase books from **Sundance Books** on N. 3rd St., tel. (307) 283-2713. Get fast cash from an **ATM** inside the Texaco station next to I-90 exit 187, where it intersects U.S. 14. Swim or take a shower at the grade school **pool,** tel. (307) 283-2133; open June-Sept. only. **Country Cottage,** on Cleveland, tel. (307) 283-2450, has locally made gifts as well as frozen yogurt.

Powder River Trailways, tel. (800) 442-3682, has daily service to other parts of eastern and northern Wyoming, plus eastward service to Deadwood and Rapid City, South Dakota. The main event in Sundance is the **Crook County Fair and Rodeo,** which comes to town in early August.

BLACK HILLS NATIONAL FOREST

Black Hills National Forest lies primarily within South Dakota but reaches across the state line around Sundance. It was established in 1897 by President Grover Cleveland after a series of large forest fires had focused attention on the need to protect the timber resource. The Forest Service's very first commercial timber sale was held within the Black Hills, and the area is still a supplier for lumber mills in Hulett and Newcastle. Nearby, South Dakota's Black Hills contain a wide range of justifiably famous sites: the Homestake Gold Mine at Lead, historic Deadwood—now a gambler's mecca—Jewel and Wind Caves, Mt. Rushmore, and an enormous bison herd in Custer State Park. Black Hills National Forest offices are in Sundance, tel. (307) 283-1361, and Newcastle, tel. (307) 746-2783. Pick up a forest map ($3) and information on camping and sights in the area.

Camping
Three year-round campgrounds lie within the Wyoming portion of the forest. **Reuter Campground** ($7) is five miles northwest of Sundance and **Cook Lake Campground** ($6-8) is 16 miles north of Sundance on a tiny forest pond. At both of these you can make advance reservations

(for an $8.25 fee) by calling (800) 280-2267. Free camping is at small **Bearlodge Campground** seven miles west of Aladdin on State 24. You can also camp for free on Forest Service land throughout the Black Hills. Over on the South Dakota side of the line, you'll find more than two dozen additional Forest Service campgrounds.

Scenic Drives
Many gravel roads wind up through the forested hills, and fall colors are brilliant along the aspen-lined stretches of the road just south of Cook Lake. A considerable amount of logging goes on within the ponderosa pine forests here, but it is selective logging, not clearcutting, and hence not as visible. Be sure to stop at **Warren Peak Lookout** eight miles north of Sundance. The road is paved to this point, and you can climb the tower for a magnificent vista and a chance to visit folks at one of the few active fire lookouts remaining in Wyoming. **Grand Canyon Creek,** located southwest of Sundance along County Road 141, offers a long, scenic route into the hills of South Dakota, but be ready for 25 miles of gravel road. There are no hiking trails in the Wyoming portion of Black Hills National Forest.

THE NORTHERN BLACK HILLS

ALADDIN AND VICINITY

Aladdin (pop. 10) was established in the 1870s to supply coal for gold smelters in Lead and Deadwood, South Dakota. During Prohibition, these mines housed moonshine stills. At 3,740 feet, it's the lowest settlement in Wyoming. Don't blink or you'll miss it, but if you do blink turn around and stop for a visit. Aladdin is dominated by the fluorescent red **Aladdin Store,** tel. (307) 896-2226, built in 1896 and operating continuously ever since. Out front is a "liar's bench" for local storytellers; inside is a potbelly stove and an ancient post office with the original boxes. It's worth a visit for a taste of unspoiled Americana. A small antique shop is upstairs with interesting collectibles from the area, and RVs can park in the lot beside the store. A cafe that serves up all-American grub is next door, and across the street is a shady town park. The Aladdin Arena is home to an annual **Bronc Match and Horseshow** each August.

Ten miles northeast of Aladdin is the **lowest point in Wyoming.** From here, the Belle Fourche River drops only another 3,125 feet on its several-thousand-mile descent to the sea via the Missouri and Mississippi Rivers. Just east of Aladdin is the **Tipple Mine Historical Site,** with restored coal-loading chutes and other facilities. Approximately two miles east of Aladdin is a historical marker noting the still-visible tracks left by the party of 110 wagons, 2,000 animals, and 1,000 men led by Gen. George A. Custer in the summer of 1874. Despite the Treaty of 1868 that reaffirmed this as Sioux Indian land, Custer's geologists, scouts, miners, and engineers had come to explore the Black Hills and investigate the rumors of gold. Gold was indeed found by Custer's miners, and when word got out the rush was on. Custer's own rush to judgment at Montana's Little Big Horn had also begun. He and all 268 of his men would die there just two years later.

On the other side of Aladdin, State 24 follows Beaver Creek past 150-foot-tall sandstone cliffs, ridge-top pines, and valley-bottom oaks. Old farmsteads appear, surrounded by fields filled with huge pyramidlike hay piles. The dot of a place called **Alva** (pop. 50) has a few old homes in the midst of the Bear Lodge Mountains but nothing in the way of services. West of Alva the road climbs up into rolling grassy hills with trees in the draws and cattle grazing along the Belle Fourche River.

HULETT AND VICINITY

The tiny logging and ranching town of Hulett (pop. 500) lies right along the Belle Fourche and is just 10 miles north of Devils Tower National Monument. Two lumber mills saw up timber from the adjacent Black Hills National Forest. The side of **Hulett National Bank** has burned-in brands from local cattle ranchers.

Food and Accommodations

For food in Hulett, try **Ponderosa Cafe, Pizza Plus,** or **Little Wrangler Cafe.** The town also has a country grocery store, a bank, a hardware store, and a medical clinic. **Pioneer Motel,** tel. (307) 467-5656, has rooms for $45-50 s or d and is open April-December. **Hulett Motel,** tel. (307) 467-5220, charges $29 s, $39 d, and kitchenettes for $5 more; open all year. Park RVs at **S-A RV Camp,** a not-so-glorified parking lot, for $10; open May-November. Showers cost 25 cents.

Located 10 miles southeast of Hulett, **Diamond L Guest Ranch,** tel. (307) 467-5236 or (800) 851-5909, has room for just 20 guests. The main activity is horseback riding, but you can also join in the chores and pretend to be a real ranch hand or just kick back in the hot tub or play in the swimming pond. Lodging costs $110-120 per person per day, $675-725 per person per week, including meals and horseback riding. A three-day minimum stay is required. In the winter months the ranch is popular with snowmobilers.

Three miles west of Devils Tower, **Lake Guest Ranch,** tel. (307) 467-5908, is a working ranch with 2,000 head of cattle. Guests stay in the lodge or separate cabins and enjoy the chance to ride the range and learn to work

cattle. Weekly all-inclusive rates are $800 per person.

Tumbling T Guest Ranch, tel. (307) 467-5625, is a 3,000-acre ranch just four miles from Devils Tower with horseback riding and fishing. Accommodations are in the main lodge or a modern bunkhouse and cost $60 d per day with breakfast, $900 per person all inclusive for five days. In the winter, guests come here for snowmobiling and cross-country skiing.

Other Practicalities

The town's only library is in the high school. For entertainment, most evenings you'll find folks at the horseshoe pit next to the hardware store, or you can head to **Rodeo Saloon** or **Ponderosa Bar** for a beer with the locals. The big annual event is **Loggers and Ranchers Play Days,** held each September. Horse shows, cookouts, and old farm machinery are on display along with downhome neighborliness. A couple of miles west of Hulett you'll see bison grazing at a private ranch while magnificent Devils Tower looms on the horizon.

Oshoto

West and then south from Hulett is the tiny town of Oshoto (a Native American word meaning "Bad Weather"), accessible only via gravel roads. No services; all that's here is a post office. The Brislawn Cayuse Ranch near Oshoto is one of the last places in America to have pure-blooded Spanish Mustangs—tough, small horses that were the pride of the Wild West.

Alzada and Colony

North from Hulett, State 112 heads to the Montana border settlement of Alzada, cutting across land not unlike the foothills of California's Sierra Nevada. Cottonwoods and oaks fill the draws, and grassy meadows alternate with tree-topped hills. Very scenic, with an abundance of white-tailed deer all the way. The road doesn't really go anywhere most tourists are heading; because of this, it is perfect for cyclists and anyone with an explorer's streak. From Alzada, U.S. 212 cuts southeast across Wyoming and to the South Dakota town of Belle Fourche. Along the way it passes a couple of bentonite mines in the grass-and-sage country around the nothing settlement called Colony. Antelope and cattle abound. Talk about confusion: since there's no post office in Colony, Wyoming, locals have South Dakota addresses on a Montana delivery route! For details on sights to the north, see *Montana Handbook,* by W.C. McRae and Judy Jewell (Moon Publications).

DEVILS TOWER NATIONAL MONUMENT

It's fitting that Devils Tower was used as the contact point for aliens and humans in 1977's *Close Encounters of the Third Kind;* the tower is a strange, otherworldly apparition rising some 1,267 feet above the surrounding plain. The flat-topped tower of rock seems to push out of the earth like an enormous sawed-off stump from Paul Bunyan's forest. From a distance, the tower looks as if it had been scratched by some giant beast, with parallel gouges running up the sides. Up closer, the gouges turn into enormous columns of rock molded into four-, five-, and six-sided shapes. In the setting sun, Devils Tower glows a golden red long after the surrounding hills no longer reflect the sun's rays. As night comes on, the stars and moon outline its bold shape against the horizon. The tower is surrounded by ponderosa pine and bur-oak forests, and the winding Belle Fourche River flows less than a mile away. A large colony of **black-tailed prairie dogs** prospers along the river just inside the park with hundreds of the little critters running around, much to the delight of tourists. You're also likely to see white-tailed deer feeding in the meadows. On top, the tower is a fairly flat oval approximately 300 feet by 180 feet.

Geology

Geologists argue over two similar theories for the creation of Devils Tower; the most widely accepted is that it formed as the core of an ancient volcano. Some 60 million years ago, a mass of molten magma was forced up through the overlying sedimentary rocks. As it cooled and contracted, vertical fractures formed in the

THE LEGEND OF BEAR LODGE

The place we call Devils Tower was known to the Kiowa Indians as Mato Tipila, meaning "Bear Lodge." Many tales are told about the origins of this mystical place, but the best known is that of the Kiowa. Once upon a time, the people camped along a stream that had many bears. Seven sisters and their brother were playing nearby when the boy suddenly turned into a ferocious bear and began chasing the girls. In desperation, the girls climbed on a small rock and prayed, "Rock, take pity on us—rock, save us!" The rock started to grow, pushing them higher and higher as the bear clawed at the sides, trying to get them. Eventually the seven girls were pushed upward into the sky, forming the points of the Big Dipper. The gouges from the bear remain today on the sides of Bear Lodge.

magma, creating long columnar joints—the "scratches" up the side of Devils Tower today. (Some of these columns are as big as 14 feet in diameter!) Eventually, the nearby Belle Fourche River eroded away the surrounding sedimentary rock, leaving the ancient volcanic neck exposed to the elements. Surrounding the 1,000-foot-wide base of Devils Tower is a mass of talus from fallen pieces of columns, but erosion of this very hard igneous rock is almost imperceptible. The four prominent peaks of the **Missouri Buttes,** located four miles northwest of Devils Tower, were formed in the same manner. At 500 to 800 feet in height, they are not as dramatic and lie outside the national monument's boundaries.

HISTORY

Devils Tower was known to Native Americans by a variety of names, most commonly Bear Lodge, Tree Lodge, or Bear's Tepee. Fur trappers and early explorers certainly knew of the existence of Bear Lodge, but it wasn't until 1857 that any note of it was made—an exploration party led by Lt. G.K. Warren saw the rock from a distance. In 1875, Col. Richard I. Dodge finally led a U.S.

Geological Survey party to the formation. Dodge somehow came up with the name Devils Tower, claiming that the Native Americans called it "Bad God's Tower." Despite protests that "Bear Lodge" had long been the aboriginal name, the label Devils Tower stuck.

Establishing the Monument

After the Indians had been driven from their traditional homeland in the 1870s, northeast Wyoming was opened to settlement by whites. Most lands were available to the homesteaders, but the General Land Office prevented developers from gaining this freak of geology. Wyoming already had America's first national park in Yellowstone, and support soon grew to make the tower a second one. After years of effort, President Theodore Roosevelt proclaimed Devils Tower the country's first national monument in 1906. Unfortunately, the final monument was only 1,153 acres in size and excludes the Missouri Buttes.

The First Climb

In the early years of Devils Tower National Monument, the area served as a popular spot for picnics and camping, especially on the Fourth of July, when Independence Day celebrations attracted settlers from the entire region. The most famous of all these came in 1893. Handbills announced that the "unclimb-

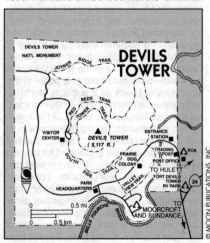

able" tower would be scaled and "On July 4th, 1893, Old Glory will be flung to the breeze from the top of the Tower, 800 feet from the ground by Wm. Rogers." The stunt was well planned. Several days before, two local ranchers, William Rogers and Willard Ripley, drove wooden pegs into a long crack that led to the top and tied the pegs together with strips of wood to make a ladder. They hauled a 12-foot flagpole to the top and returned on July 4 to scale the ladder in front of 800 people. Once on top (it took an hour to climb), Rogers unfurled a flag but a gust of wind blew it off. Wives of the promoters tore it up and sold the pieces as souvenirs (stripes cost 25 cents, stars 50). The climb had been a smashing success.

On July 4, 1895, Mrs. Rogers became the first woman to climb the ladder to the top of Devils Tower, and many other adventurous folks followed over the next several decades. The ladder was last climbed in 1927, but pieces of it are still visible today along the southeast side of the Tower. An iron stairway to the top, proposed by Wyoming's Congressman Mondell as a tourist attraction, was never built.

Developing the Tower

For many years, Devils Tower remained undeveloped, and it was not until 1928 that a bridge was built across the Belle Fourche River to the site. During the Depression, the CCC constructed a log visitor center, new roads, trails, picnic areas, and a campground. Visitation increased as access became easier and more families acquired automobiles. One of the strangest events came in 1941, when George Hopkins—one of the top skydivers in the world—parachuted out of a plane to the top of Devils Tower as a publicity stunt. He had planned to descend on a 1,000 foot rope, but the rope landed on the side of the tower, leaving him stranded on top. Newspapers all over the country headlined his plight. Food and blankets were dropped to him, and for the next six days he spent a lonely vigil on top waiting to be rescued. Finally, Jack Durrance, a mountain climber who had scaled Devils Tower three years before, arrived to lead seven other climbers to the top and help Hopkins down. Many years later, in 1976, *Close Encounters of the Third Kind* was filmed here. Several hun-

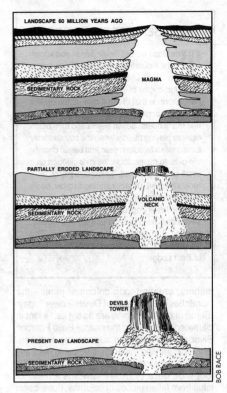

LANDSCAPE 60 MILLION YEARS AGO

SEDIMENTARY ROCK

MAGMA

PARTIALLY ERODED LANDSCAPE

SEDIMENTARY ROCK

VOLCANIC NECK

DEVILS TOWER

PRESENT DAY LANDSCAPE

SEDIMENTARY ROCK

BOB RACE

dred locals appeared in the crowd scenes. When the movie was released the following year, tourism here suddenly hit the stars.

Climbing the Tower

Although Devils Tower was first climbed in 1893 on a wooden ladder, the first ascent using modern rock-climbing techniques was not until 1937. Led by Fritz Wiessner, three New York City climbers made it to the top in a little under five hours. Over the years, as climbing technology has improved and as more people have been attracted to the sport, Devils Tower has become one of the favorite climbing spots in the nation. During the summer you're bound to meet several dozen climbers heading for the base of the tower each morning. More than 40,000 people have reached the top, and the figure grows by 5,000 each year.

Climbing has not been without controversy. Some Indian leaders have called climbing the rock a sacrilege and demanded it be closed, while climbers have trumpeted it as one of the premier crack-climbing areas in the nation. The Park Service came up with a compromise plan in 1995, instituting a voluntary climbing closure for the month of June. Additional regulations were put into place emphasizing clean climbing techniques and restricting access to falcon nesting areas during the breeding season. Be sure to contact the monument for specifics before you climb.

For information on the various routes (at least 120 have been climbed), pick up one of the technical guidebooks in the visitor center: *Devils Tower National Monument—A Climber's Guide,* by Steve Gardiner and Dick Guilmette (Devils Tower Natural History Association), or *Free Climbs of Devils Tower* by Dingus McGee and The Last Pioneer Woman (I somehow suspect these are pseudonyms). Displays in the visitor center and at a kiosk out front describe climbing routes and techniques. Climbing demonstrations are given here each day during the summer. If you're planning to climb Devils Tower, be sure to register at the visitor center.

Those who want to climb Devils Tower but lack the skills or equipment have several options. **Andy Petefish** of Tower Guides is in the area much of the summer and leads climbs. A two-day climbing class and ascent costs around $350-400 per person including equipment. For details, stop by Devils Tower Trading Post or call (307) 467-5659. Other licensed professional climbing guides include **Jackson Hole Mountain Guides** in Jackson, tel. (307) 733-4979; **National Outdoors Leadership School (NOLS)** in Lander, tel. (307) 332-6973; and Susan Scheirbeck of **Slyvan Rocks** in Hill City, South Dakota, tel. (605) 574-2425. Contact the Park Service for others.

Hiking Trails

Four different trails loop through this small national monument, providing fine views of the tower and the surrounding country. Most popular is the 1.5-mile **Tower Trail,** which circles the tower. It's an easy paved path with periodic openings offering impressive views of the tower, along with side paths to see the nearby Missouri Buttes and the Belle Fourche River. Be sure to look through the peep sight to find the old wooden ladder that once went all the way to the top of Devils Tower.

Red Beds/South Side Trail is a three-mile dirt path that also takes off near the visitor center but makes a longer, less-crowded loop around the tower. Along the way you get nice views of the Belle Fourche River and the Red Beds, iron-stained bluffs near the river. A 30-minute side loop, the 1.5-mile **Valley View Trail,** takes you to the prairie dog town and the Belle Fourche River. You'll catch the finest views of Devils Tower from the **Joyner Ridge Trail,** a 1.5-mile path. Views from this hilltop trail are unforgettable, especially at sunrise and sunset.

PRACTICALITIES

Access and Information

Devils Tower is 33 miles northeast of Moorcroft. You enter the park from State 24 seven miles north of its junction with U.S. 14. Entrance fees are $5 for vehicles, $2 for hikers or cyclists, and the passes are good for seven days. Annual passes to the monument cost $30, or you can purchase the Golden Eagle Pass ($25), which lets you into all national parks and monuments. Seniors get in free with a Golden Age Pass (for a one-time fee of $10). The monument is open year-round 24 hours a day, although most of the over 300,000 annual visitors arrive during the summer.

Beyond the entrance station, it is approximately three miles along a paved road to the base of the tower, where you'll find a pleasant old log **visitor center** (tel. 307-467-5501) and a parking lot that overflows on sunny summer days with rock-climbers and gawkers. The center is open daily 8 a.m.-7:45 p.m. from mid-June to Labor Day and daily 8 a.m.-4:45 p.m. April to mid-June and Labor Day to October. The visitor center is closed Nov.-March. Inside, you can watch a six-minute video on the history of Devils Tower, look at ecological displays and photos showing the dozens of climbing routes, and buy books on local lore. **Campfire programs** are held several times a week during the summer at the campground amphitheater, with the standard Park Service fare of talks, tunes, and transparencies. Ask at the visitor center for specifics.

Camping, Food, and More

The Park Service maintains a fine **campground** ($10; open May-Oct.) a half-mile inside the entrance. In midsummer, get a space at the campground in the morning to be sure of having a spot. Just outside the monument are two private campgrounds. The friendlier of the two is **Devils Tower KOA,** tel. (307) 467-5395 or (800) 562-5785, where sites cost $16 for tents, $21 for RVs, and $30 for simple cabins. Facilities include an outdoor pool and are open May to late September. Horseback rides are available here, and if you haven't seen it before, you can watch *Close* *Encounters* on the TV. Most folks stock up on food in nearby towns, but the cafe at KOA serves meals, and a general store has limited supplies. **Devils Tower Trading Post** is directly across the road from the KOA and stocks a few food items, gifts, trinkets, and a fast-food eatery. The other nearby private campground is **Fort Devils Tower RV Park,** tel. (307) 467-5655. Open year-round, with a saloon and supper club for meals. A small **post office,** tel. (307) 467-5937, stands just outside the park entrance gate. Each **4th of July** folks come from miles around to watch a fun fireworks show near Devils Tower.

If the reader thinks he is done, now, and that this book has no moral to it, he is in error. The moral of it is this: If you are of any account, stay at home and make your way by faithful diligence; but if you are "no account," go away from home, and then you will have to work, whether you want to or not. Thus you become a blessing to your friends by ceasing to be a nuisance to them—if the people you go among suffer by the operation.

—Mark Twain in Roughing It

BOOKLIST

DESCRIPTION AND TRAVEL

Anderson, Susan. *Living in Wyoming: Settling for More*. Oakland, CA: Rockridge Press, 1990. A witty and insightful book about the people of Wyoming. Outstanding photos by Zbigniew Bzdak.

Burt, Nathaniel. *Wyoming*. Oakland, CA: Compass American Guides, 1995. Provides a tour of Wyoming and its historical attractions. Photography by Don Pitcher.

DiMunn, Debra. *Ghosts on the Range: Eerie True Tales of Wyoming*. Boulder, CO: Pruett Publishing, 1989. A very popular book with ghost stories from across the state.

Ehrlich, Gretel. *The Solace of Open Spaces*. New York, NY: Viking Penguin Inc., 1985. A stunningly beautiful collection of observations and stories about ranch life in Wyoming from one of America's finest writers.

Hanesworth, Robert D. *Daddy of 'Em All: The Story of Cheyenne Frontier Days*. Cheyenne, WY: Flintlock Publishing Co., 1967. Stories and photos from the early days of Cheyenne's Frontier Days celebration.

Kelsey, Joe. *Wyoming's Wind River Range*. Helena, MT: American Geographic Publishing, 1988. A profusely illustrated and well-written book about Wyoming's finest hiking country.

Kilgore, Gene. *Gene Kilgore's Ranch Vacations*. Santa Fe: John Muir Publications, 1994. The definitive guide to dude and guest ranches in Wyoming and the rest of North America. Includes detailed, up-to-date descriptions of the best places to be a city-slicker cowboy.

Lewis, Dan. *8,000 Miles of Dirt: A Backroad Travel Guide to Wyoming*. Casper, WY: Hawks Book Co., 1992. Describes dozens of the state's most enjoyable backroads in a folksy but not always informative manner. (Example: The chapter on the Outlaw Cave drive doesn't bother to mention its most famous inhabitant, Butch Cassidy!)

Mealey, Catherine E. *The Best of Wyoming*. Laramie, WY: Meadowlark Press, 1990. Contains brief county-by-county descriptions of the state's attractions.

Pence, Mary Lou, and Lola M. Homsher. *The Ghost Towns of Wyoming*. New York, NY: Hastings House, 1956. Describes the state's many historic towns that are slowly fading into the landscape.

Perry, John, and Jane Greverus Perry. *The Sierra Club Guide to the Natural Areas of Idaho, Montana, and Wyoming*. San Francisco, CA: Sierra Club Books, 1988. Information on national parks, national forests, wilderness areas, state parks, wildlife refuges, and other natural areas. Of limited usefulness except as a general description.

Roberts, Phil, David L. Roberts, and Steven L. Roberts. *Wyoming Almanac*. Laramie, WY: Skyline West Press, 1994. Packed with more than 450 pages of Wyoming trivia, including such things as the average market price paid for Wyoming low sulfur and cabooses now used for other purposes. Hard to plow through it all (there's no index), but there are some real gems buried in this avalanche of facts.

Skinner, Holly L. *Only the River Runs Easy: A Historical Portrait of the Upper Green River Valley*. Boulder, CO: Pruett Publishing Co., 1985. An attractive and lovingly written history of the Upper Green River. Excellent.

Stienstra, Tom. *Rocky Mountain Camping*. San Francisco, CA: Foghorn Press, 1989. Describes over 1,200 public and private campgrounds in Wyoming, Colorado, and Montana.

Urbanek, Mae. *Wyoming Place Names*. Missoula, MT: Mountain Press Publishing Co., 1988. An excellent sourcebook for the names of everything from Abiathar Peak to the town of Zenith.

Williamson, Chilton, Jr. *Roughnecking It.* New York, NY: Simon and Schuster, 1982. A funny, insightful, and disturbing portrait of Wyoming during the oil-boom years of the the early 1980s. Gonzo journalism at its best.

Works Projects Administration. *Wyoming: A Guide to its History, Highways, and People.* Lincoln, NE: University of Nebraska Press, 1981. Reprint of a depression-era guide to Wyoming originally printed in 1940, this classic guide still makes fascinating reading.

Wyoming Department of Administration and Fiscal Control. *Wyoming Data Handbook.* Cheyenne, WY: Wyoming Department of Administration and Fiscal Control. A free annual publication jammed with all sorts of technical information about Wyoming. Helpful for folks writing guides to Wyoming.

Wyoming Recreation Commission. *Wyoming: A Guide to Historic Sites.* Basin, WY: Big Horn Publishers, 1988. An excellent collection of descriptions of more than 300 historic sites in Wyoming.

ONWARD TRAVEL

McRae, W.C., and Judy Jewell. *Montana Handbook.* Chico, CA: Moon Publications, 1996. A complete and well-written guide to Wyoming's northern neighbor.

Metzger, Stephen. *Colorado Handbook.* Chico, CA: Moon Publications, 1995.

Weir, Bill, and W.C. McRae. *Utah Handbook.* Chico, CA: Moon Publications, 1997. The definitive guide to Utah.

GEOLOGY, GEOGRAPHY, AND WEATHER

Blackstone, D. L., Jr. *Traveler's Guide to the Geology of Wyoming.* Laramie, WY: Geological Survey of Wyoming, 1988. An excellent overview of Wyoming's geological history and how to see it in today's landscapes.

Brown, Robert Harold. *Wyoming: A Geography.* Boulder, CO: Westview Press, 1980. All sorts of interesting info about Wyoming, from political party affiliations to Indian handicrafts.

Largeson, David R., and Darwin R. Spearing. *Roadside Geology of Wyoming.* Missoula, MT: Mountain Press Publishing Co., 1988. Wyoming is perhaps the most geologically interesting of all the states. This is an invaluable road guide for anyone wanting to know more about geology without resorting to dense textbooks.

McPhee, John. *Rising from the Plains.* New York, NY: The Noonday Press, 1986. A delightful intertwining of the story of Wyoming's complex geology and the life of its preeminent geologist, David Love.

FICTION

Ehrlich, Gretel. *Heart Mountain.* New York, NY: Viking Penguin Inc., 1988. A touching novel about life in the Heart Mountain Relocation Camp near Cody, the forced home for hundreds of Japanese-Americans during WW II.

Nye, Bill. *Bill Nye's Western Humor.* Lincoln, NE: University of Nebraska Press, 1968. A collection of delightfully wry essays by one of America's best-known 19th-century humorists.

Wister, Owen. *The Virginian.* Originally published in 1902 and now available from various publishers. The classic Western novel that established the cowboy hero and the lure of Wyoming.

BIOGRAPHY

Alter, Cecil. J. *Jim Bridger.* Norman, OK: University of Oklahoma Press, 1962. The incredible story of the most famous of all mountain men.

Anonymous. *The Sweet Smell of Sagebrush: A Prisoner's Diary 1903-1912.* Rawlins, WY: Friends of the Old Penitentiary, 1990. This wonderful small volume contains the writings of an "anonymous" criminal (John Kirby) who served four terms in the Rawlins penitentiary

for horse stealing and other crimes. It not only provides descriptions of his many escapades outside the law but also opens a window on the criminal mind.

Olsen, Jack. *Doc: The Rape of the Town of Lovell.* New York, NY: Atheneum, 1989. The true but hard-to-believe story of a respected physician who raped dozens of women in this small, religious town.

Pointer, Larry. *In Search of Butch Cassidy.* Norman, OK: University of Oklahoma Press, 1977. A thoroughly researched book that seems to show that Butch Cassidy's death in South America was a ruse and that he died much later in Seattle.

Sell, Henry Blackman, and Victor Weybright. *Buffalo Bill and the Wild West.* Basin, WY: Big Horn Books, 1979. The authors attempt to sort the incredible true story of William Cody from the legends created by decades of tall tales. Nicely illustrated.

Woods, L. Milton. *Moreton Frewen's Western Adventures.* Boulder, CO: Roberts Rinehart, Inc., 1986. The strange tale of a wealthy British adventurer who made and lost his (and other folks') fortunes in Wyoming.

HIKING AND CLIMBING

Note: See also **Jackson Hole and Grand Teton National Park and** Yellowstone National Park *(below).*

Bach, Orville E., Jr. Hiking the Yellowstone Backcountry. San Francisco, CA: Sierra Club Books, 1979. A pocket-sized volume with descriptions of the park's trails.

Guillmette, Richard, Renée Carrier, and Steve Gardiner. *Devils Tower National Monument: A Climber's Guide.* Devils Tower, WY: Devils Tower Natural History Association, 1995. A detailed guide to one of the most varied and enjoyable rock faces in Wyoming.

Harper, Skip, and Rob Kelman. *The Climbs of Greater Vedauwoo.* Ft. Collins, CO: Heel and Toe Publishers, 1994. A detailed guide to rock-climbing in the Vedauwoos east of Laramie.

Hunger, Bill. *The Hiker's Guide to Wyoming.* Helena, MT: Falcon Press, 1992. A fine, detailed book that describes 75 different hikes in all parts of the state.

Kelsey, Joe. *Climbing and Hiking in the Wind River Mountains.* Evergreen, CO: Chockstone Press, 1994. A thorough and newly updated guide to climbing and hiking in the Winds.

Mitchell, Finis. *Wind River Trails.* Salt Lake City, UT: Wasatch Publications, 1975. A folksy, inexpensive guide by a man who has hiked this country since 1909.

Melius, M. *Cloud Peak Wilderness: Trail Guide, History, and Photo Odyssey.* Pierre, SD: Tensleep Publications, 1993. A complete guide to trails, history, and the environment of the Big Horn's dramatic wilderness country.

Woods, Rebecca. *Walking the Winds: A Hiking & Fishing Guide to Wyoming's Wind River Range.* Jackson, WY: White Willow Publishing, 1994. A useful and up-to-date guide to hiking trails in the Winds.

HISTORY

Baber, D. F. *The Longest Rope.* Caldwell, ID: The Caxton Printers, Ltd., 1953. The fascinating story of the Johnson County War as told by William Walker, the only surviving "rustler" witness of the siege at KC Ranch.

Bille, Ed. *Early Days at Salt Creek and Teapot Dome.* Casper, WY: Mountain States Lithographing Co., 1978. The story of oil boomtimes in Wyoming's most famous oilfields. Many fine old photos.

Brown, Larry K. *The Hog Ranches of Wyoming: Liquor, Lust, and Lies Under Sagebrush Skies.* Glendo, WY: High Plains Press, 1995. A playful book about the saloon-dance hall-brothels that sprang up around Wyoming's frontier forts.

Burt, Struthers. *Powder River: Let 'er Buck.* New York, NY: Rinehart, 1938. A classic book on this famous part of Wyoming by one of the finest writers to come out of the state.

Carlisle, Bill. *Lone Bandit. An Autobiography.* Pasadena, CA: Trails End Publishing Co., 1946. The story of the last of the old Wyoming outlaws, the "gentleman train robber" who later opened a popular Laramie motel.

Cheyenne Centennial Committee. *The Magic City on the Plains: Cheyenne 1867-1967.* Cheyenne, WY: Cheyenne Centennial Committee, 1967. A comprehensive history of Cheyenne.

Coffman, Lloyd W. *Blazing a Wagon Trail to Oregon.* Springfield, OR: Echo Books, 1993. The experience and drama—much told in the participants' own words—of the "great migration," with details on Fort Bridger, Fort Laramie, Independence Rock, and other Wyoming stopping places.

Combs, Barry B. *Westward to Promontory: Building the Union Pacific Across the Plains and Mountains.* New York, NY: Crown Publishers, 1986. How the West was really won. Includes a wonderful collection of historic photos by Andrew J. Russell.

DeVoto, Bernard. *Across the Wide Missouri.* New York, NY: Houghton Mifflin Co., 1947. The Rocky Mountain fur trade and how it shaped American culture. A classic.

Edgar, Bob, and Jack Turnell. *Brand of a Legend.* Greybull, WY: Wolverine Gallery, 1978. The story of one of Wyoming's most famous ranches, the Pitchfork. Includes many of Charles Belden's wonderful old photographs.

Gowans, Fred R., and Eugene E. Campbell. *Fort Bridger, Island in the Wilderness.* Provo, UT: Brigham Young University Press, 1975. An excellent book about the first way station specifically built to serve immigrants on the Oregon Trail.

Gowans, Fred R. *Rocky Mountain Rendezvous: A History of the Fur Trade Rendezvous 1825-1840.* Layton, UT: Peregrine Smith Books, 1985. Describes each of the rendezvous in detail.

Gunderson, Mary Alice. *Devils Tower: Stories in Stone.* Glendo, WY: High Plains Press, 1988. A small book on the history of Devils Tower National Monument.

Haines, Aubrey L. *Journal of a Trapper: Osborne Russell.* Lincoln, NE: University of Nebraska Press, 1955. The fascinating first-person account of a fur trapper from 1834-43. A classic and surprisingly well-written book.

Haines, Aubrey L. *Historic Sites Along the Oregon Trail.* St. Louis, MO: The Patrice Press, 1990. Details many of the interesting places on this historic route.

Hanesworth, Robert D. *Daddy of 'Em All; The Story of Cheyenne Frontier Days.* Cheyenne, WY: Flintlock Publishing Co., 1967. Stories and photos from the early days of Cheyenne's Frontier Days celebration.

Hedgpeth, Don. *Spurs Were A-Jinglin'.* Cody, WY: Northland Press, 1975. Brief text follows the excellent photos by Charles J. Belden of cowboys and ranching in the early parts of this century.

Hill, William E. *The California Trail: Yesterday and Today.* Boulder, CO: Pruett Publishing Company, 1986. Filled with historic photos and drawings of the Oregon and California Trail along with more recent photos from the same places.

Hill, William E. *The Oregon Trail: Yesterday and Today.* Caldwell, ID: The Caxton Printers, Inc., 1986. A historical and pictorial trek along the path of the pioneers. Includes diaries, old photos, and museums along the Oregon Trail.

Homsher, Lola M., ed. *South Pass, 1868; James Chisholm's Journal of the Wyoming Gold Rush.* Lincoln, NE: University of Nebraska Press, 1960. Tales of life in the gold-mining town of South Pass shortly after the first wave of boomers had left. Very interesting.

Junge, Mark. *Wyoming: A Pictorial History.* Norfolk, NE: The Donning Co., 1989. A gorgeous coffee-table book filled with historic black-and-white photos from throughout Wyoming.

Kahin, Sharon, and Laurie Rufe. *In the Shadows of the Rockies: A Photographic History of the Pioneer Experience in Wyoming's Bighorn Basin.* Powell, WY: Northwest Community College, 1983. Outstanding photos and interesting historical quotes on the Bighorn Basin.

Larson, T. A. *History of Wyoming*. Lincoln, NE: University of Nebraska Press, 1978. The definitive tome (663 pages worth) on Wyoming's history, with an emphasis on politics and development rather than on outlaws and Indian wars.

Lavender, David. *Fort Laramie and the Changing Frontier*. Washington, D.C.: U.S. Department of the Interior, National Park Service, 1983. An interesting little book filled with the history of the people who made Fort Laramie a primary center of trade and war in the west. Excellent illustrations, too.

Lindmier, Tom, and Steve Mount. *I See by Your Outfit: Historic Cowboy Gear of the Northern Plains*. Glendo, WY: High Plains Press, 1996. An authorative guide to what *real* cowboys wore. Filled with interesting historic photos.

Madsen, R. Scott. *The Bomber Mountain Crash: A Wyoming Mystery*. Buffalo, WY: Mountain Man Publishing, 1995. A local author untangles the sad tale of the WW II crash of a B-17F Flying Fortress in the Big Horn Mountains. Based upon exhaustive research.

Marcy, Randolph B. *The Prairie Traveler*. New York, NY: Perigee Books, 1859 (reprinted). A telling portrait of life on the frontier as told by a U.S. Army captain. It was considered the essential handbook for travelers.

Mead, Jean. *Casper Country*. Boulder, CO: Pruett Publishing Co., 1987. A profusely illustrated history of Casper.

Mercer, Asa Shinn. *Banditti of the Plains* or *The Cattlemen's Invasion of Wyoming in 1892: the Crowning Infamy of the Ages*. Norman, OK: University of Oklahoma Press, 1954. A reprint of a classic book about the Johnson County War.

Morgan, Dale, ed. *Overland in 1846: Diaries and Letters of the California-Oregon Trail*. Lincoln, NE: University of Nebraska Press, 1963. A two-volume collection of diaries offering many fascinating insights into the lives of the emigrants. Reprinted in 1993.

Mothershead, Harmon Ross. *The Swan Land and Cattle Company, Ltd*. Norman, OK: University of Oklahoma Press, 1971. The story of the most famous of all Wyoming ranches, the million-acre spread begun by Alexander Swan in 1883.

Munkres, Robert L. *Saleratus and Sagebrush: The Oregon Trail Through Wyoming*. Cheyenne, WY: Wyoming State Archives and Historical Department, 1974. This interesting small book offers eyewitness accounts from many travelers along the Oregon Trail.

Murray, Robert A. *The Bozeman Trail: Highway of History*. Boulder, CO: Pruett Publishing Company, 1988. An attractively illustrated history of the West's most violent trail.

Osgood, Ernest Staples. *The Day of the Cattleman*. Chicago, IL: University of Chicago Press, 1929. An authoritative history of the 50 years when cowboys and cattle barons ruled Wyoming and Montana.

Parkman, Francis. *The Oregon Trail*. Boston, MA: Little, Brown and Co., 1886. A classic first-person account of the great westward migration.

Pinkerton, Joan Tregs. *Knights of the Broadax*. Caldwell, ID: The Caxton Printers, Inc., 1981. An account of the life of tie hacks in the upper Wind River country.

Rhode, Robert B. *Booms & Busts on Bitter Creek: A History of Rock Springs, Wyoming*. Boulder, CO: Pruett Publishing Co., 1987. A fine history of one of Wyoming's most turbulent cities.

Sandoval, Judith Hancock. *Historic Ranches of Wyoming*. Casper, WY: Mountain States Lithographing, 1986. Details nearly a hundred of the state's classic old ranches.

Spring, Agnes Wright. *The Cheyenne and Black Hills Stage and Express Routes*. Lincoln, NE: University of Nebraska Press, 1948. Tales from the early days of eastern Wyoming.

Thompson, George A. *Throw Down the Box!* Salt Lake City, UT: Dream Garden Press, 1989. A book about the Gilmer and Salisbury stagecoaches, including its famous Cheyenne and Black Hills branch line.

Thybony, Scott, Robert G. Rosenberg, and Elizabeth Mullett Rosenberg. *The Medicine Bows:*

Wyoming's Mountain Country. Caldwell, ID: The Caxton Printers, Inc., 1985. An outstanding historical account of the Indians, explorers, miners, and tie hacks who called this scenic part of Wyoming home.

Twain, Mark. *Roughing It.* First published in 1872, this is one of the classics of American literature. Samuel Clemens's witty descriptions of the old west seem ageless.

NATIVE AMERICANS

Clark, Ella E., and Margot Edmonds. *Sacagawea of the Lewis and Clark Expedition.* Berkeley, CA: University of California Press, 1979. A fascinating investigation into the truth behind one of the best known women in Wyoming history. Bursts a few bubbles.

Frison, George C. *Prehistoric Hunters of the High Plains.* New York, NY: Academic Press, 1978. The authoritative source on the earliest inhabitants of Wyoming.

Hendry, Mary Helen. *Indian Rock Art in Wyoming.* Lincoln, NE: Augstams Printing, 1983. Detailed descriptions of rock-art sites in the state. Her ages for the rock art are probably too recent, and she intentionally omits locations.

Lowie, Robert. *Indians of the Plains.* New York, NY: The Natural History Press, 1954. Famed anthropologist Robert Lowie presents a detailed picture of life on the plains before the arrival of whites.

Nadeau, Remi. *Fort Laramie and the Sioux Indians.* Englewood Cliffs, NJ: Prentice-Hall, Inc., 1967. A thorough historical account of the impact of Fort Laramie on the high-plains Indians.

Trenholm, Virginia Cole, and Maurine Carley. *The Shoshonis: Sentinels of the Rockies.* Norman, OK: University of Oklahoma Press, 1964. The history of Chief Washakie and the Shoshone tribe.

Trenholm, Virginia Cole. *The Arapahoes, Our People.* Norman, OK: University of Oklahoma Press, 1970. The history of this important Wyoming tribe from prehistory to their forced relocation to the Wind River Reservation.

Urbanek, Mae. *Chief Washakie.* Boulder, CO: Johnson Publishing Co., 1971. The fascinating story of the chief who led the Shoshone people for 60 years while always remaining a friend of whites.

Utley, Robert M. *The Indian Frontier of the American West 1846-1890.* Albuquerque, NM: University of New Mexico Press, 1984. An evenhanded portrayal of a half-century of conflict between Indians and whites.

NATURAL HISTORY

Note: See also **Jackson Hole and Grand Teton National Park** and **Yellowstone National Park** (below).

Baxter, George T., and Michael D. Stone. *Amphibians and Reptiles of Wyoming.* Cheyenne, WY: Wyoming Game and Fish Department, 1985. Everything you wanted to know about the state's snakes, frogs, toads, salamanders, and other cold-blooded critters.

Blair, Neal. *The History of Wildlife Management in Wyoming.* Cheyenne, WY: Wyoming Game and Fish Department, 1987. A large, detailed book covering the time from when the bison blackened the plains to the present.

Clark, Tim W., and Mark R. Stromberg. *Mammals in Wyoming.* Lawrence, KS: University of Kansas Museum of Natural History, 1987. The definitive guide to 117 native or naturalized Wyoming mammals: their identification, distribution, biology, and ecology.

Craighead, Frank J. *Track of the Grizzly.* San Francisco, CA: Sierra Club Books, 1979. The life of grizzlies in Yellowstone, by one of the most famous bear researchers.

Crowe, Douglas M. *Furbearers of Wyoming.* Cheyenne, WY: Wyoming Department of Game and Fish, 1986. A small book describing the state's fur-coated critters, with distribution maps.

Dorn, Robert D. *Vascular Plants of Wyoming.* Cheyenne, WY: Mountain West Publishing Company, 1988. The authoritative key to Wyoming plants; a dense book with few illustrations. For botanists.

Knight, Dennis H. *Mountains and Plains: the Ecology of Wyoming Landscapes.* New Haven, CT: Yale University Press, 1994. The definitive textbook on the ecology of Wyoming. Thorough and well written, but the $40 price may scare you away.

Petersen, David. *Among the Elk.* Flagstaff, AZ: Northland Publishing, 1988. The story of wapiti, with outstanding photos by Alan D. Carey.

JACKSON HOLE AND GRAND TETON NATIONAL PARK

Betts, Robert B. *Along the Ramparts of the Tetons; the Saga of Jackson Hole, Wyoming.* Boulder, CO: Colorado Associated University Press, 1978. A substantial, detailed, and beautifully written book about Jackson Hole's fascinating history.

Burt, Nathaniel. *Jackson Hole Journal.* Norman, OK: University of Oklahoma Press, 1983. Tales of growing up as a dude in Jackson Hole. Contains some very amusing stories.

Carrighar, Sally. *One Day at Teton Marsh.* Lincoln, NE: University of Nebraska Press, 1979. A classic natural history of life in a Jackson Hole marsh. Made into a movie by Walt Disney.

Carter, Tom. *Day Hiking Grand Teton National Park.* Garland, TX: Dayhiking Press, 1993. A pocket-sized guide to 15 day-treks in the park.

Clark, Tim W. *Ecology of Jackson Hole, Wyoming: A Primer.* Salt Lake City, UT: Paragon Press, 1981. An excellent scientific introduction to ecological interrelationships within Jackson Hole.

Duffy, Katy, and Darwin Wile. *Teton Trails.* Moose, WY: Grand Teton Natural History Association, 1995. A fine and inexpensive guide to the hiking trails of Grand Teton National Park.

DuMais, Richard. *50 Ski Tours in Jackson Hole and Yellowstone.* Boulder, CO: High Peak Books, 1990. The finest guide to cross-country skiing in the area.

Hayden, Elizabeth Wied, and Cynthia Nielsen. *Origins, A Guide to the Place Names of Grand Teton National Park and the Surrounding Area.* Moose, WY: Grand Teton Natural History Association, 1988. A guide to the obscure sources for place names in Grand Teton.

Huidekoper, Virginia. *The Early Days in Jackson Hole.* Boulder, CO: Colorado Associated University Press, 1978. Filled with over 100 photos from old-time Jackson Hole.

Johnsgard, Paul A. *Teton Wildlife.* Boulder, CO: Colorado Associated University Press, 1982. A descriptive book by a noted naturalist from the University of Nebraska.

Lawrence, Paul. *Hiking the Teton Backcountry.* San Francisco, CA: Sierra Club Books, 1979. Outdated but still useful guide to trails in Grand Teton National Park.

Love, J.D., and John C. Reed, Jr. *Creation of the Teton Landscape: the Geologic Story of Grand Teton National Park.* Moose, WY: Grand Teton Natural History Association, 1971. A small but authoritatively detailed guide to the geology of Jackson Hole and the Tetons.

Murie, Margaret, and Olaus Murie. *Wapiti Wilderness.* Boulder, CO: Colorado Associated University Press, 1985. The lives of two of America's most-loved conservationists in Jackson Hole and their work with elk.

Ortenburger, Leigh N., and Reynold G. Jackson. *A Complete Guide to the Teton Range.* Palo Alto, CA: self-published, 1990. A very thorough two-volume climbing guide. Available in many Jackson bookstores.

Petzoldt, Paul. *Petzoldt's Teton Trails.* Salt Lake City, UT: Wasatch Publishers, Inc., 1976. An enjoyable small hiking guide by one of the grand old men of mountain climbing.

Raynes, Bert. *Birds of Grand Teton National Park and the Surrounding Area.* Moose, WY: Grand Teton Natural History Association, 1984. A guide to local birds.

Righter, Robert W. *Crucible for Conservation: The Creation of Grand Teton National Park.*

Boulder, CO: Colorado Associated University Press, 1982. The story of how the Tetons were spared through a half-century battle.

Ringholz, Raye C. *Little Town Blues: Voices from the Changing West.* Salt Lake City, UT: Gibbs-Smith Publisher, 1992. This important small book visits several small towns in the west—including Jackson—where the rural qualities and beauty that attract visitors are being inundated by tourism and development. It offers a cautionary note on the consequences of unbridled growth.

Thompson, Edith M., and William Leigh Thompson. *Beaver Dick: The Honor and the Heartbreak.* Laramie, WY: Jelm Mountain Press, 1982. A touching historical biography of Beaver Dick Leigh, one of the first white men to settle in Jackson Hole.

U.S. Department of the Interior, National Park Service. *Grand Teton: Official National Park Handbook.* Washington, D.C.: National Park Service, 1984. An attractive small book about the park and its history.

YELLOWSTONE NATIONAL PARK

Bach, Orville, Jr. *Hiking the Yellowstone Back Country.* San Francisco, CA: Sierra Club Books, 1991. A pocket-sized guide to hiking, canoeing, biking, and skiing in the park.

Bartlett, Richard A. *Yellowstone: A Wilderness Besieged.* Tucson, AZ: University of Arizona Press, 1985. The history of Yellowstone and the fight to prevent its destruction by railroad magnates, concessionaires, and others.

Bryan, Scott. T. *The Geysers of Yellowstone.* Boulder, CO: Colorado Associated University Press, 1979. A complete and detailed guide to more than 400 geysers and other geothermal features in Yellowstone.

Carter, Tom. *Day Hiking Yellowstone.* Garland, TX: Dayhiking Press, 1990. A pocket-sized guide to 20 day treks, coordinated with the Trails Illustrated topographic maps.

Charlton, Robert E. *Yellowstone Fishing Guide: A Comprehensive Guide to Fishing the Lakes and Streams Located in Yellowstone Nation-*

al Park. Portland, OR: Flying Pencil Publications, 1990. A detailed guide to fishing in the park. Leaves no trickle unfished.

Colling, Gene. *The Bicyclist's Guide to Yellowstone National Park.* Helena, MT: Falcon Press Publishing Co., 1984. Includes maps and all you need to know about cycling in America's oldest park.

Fischer, Hank. *Wolf Wars.* Helena, MT: Falcon Press, 1995. A first-person chronicle of the struggle to return wolves to Yellowstone.

Fritz, William J. *Roadside Geology of the Yellowstone Country.* Missoula, MT: Mountain Press Publishing Co., 1985. All the park roads are covered in this easy-to-follow Yellowstone geology primer.

Haines, Aubrey L. *The Yellowstone Story: A History of Our First National Park.* Yellowstone Library and Museum Association, 1977. A definitive two-volume history of the park. Volume one (history up to the park's establishment) is the most interesting.

Henry, Jeff. *Yellowstone Winter Guide,* Niwot, CO: Roberts Rinehart Publishers, 1993. Describes ski trails, winter roads, lodging, snowmobile access, and more.

Hirschmann, Fred. *Yellowstone.* Portland, OR: Graphic Arts Center Publishing, 1982. Exceptional photography.

Janetski, Joel C. *Indians of Yellowstone Park.* Salt Lake City, UT: University of Utah Press, 1987. A general overview of the earliest settlers in Yellowstone and later conflicts with incoming whites.

Krakell, Dean, II. *Downriver: A Yellowstone Journey.* San Francisco, CA: Sierra Club Books, 1987. A extraordinarily moving journey down the magnificent Yellowstone River.

Marschall, Mark C. *Yellowstone Trails: A Hiking Guide.* Yellowstone National Park, WY: The Yellowstone Association, 1995. An excellent, up-to-date, and detailed guidebook to the park's 1,000 miles of hiking trails.

McEneaney, Terry. *Birds of Yellowstone.* Boulder, CO: Roberts Rinehart, 1988. A guide to Yellowstone birds and where to find them.

McNulty, Tim (text), and Pat O'Hara (photos). *Yellowstone National Park: Land of Fire and Falling Water*. San Rafael, CA: Woodlands Press, 1986. A coffee-table book of luscious pictures from the park.

Milstein, Michael. *Wolf: Return to Yellowstone*. Billings, MT: The Billings Gazette, 1995. Describes the extermination of wolves and the controversy over their return to Yellowstone.

Olsen, Ken, Dena Olsen, and Steve and Hazel Scharosch. *Cross-Country Skiing in Yellowstone Country*. Casper, WY: Abacus Enterprises, 1992. Detailed descriptions of 200 miles of ski trails in and near the park, including helpful trail profiles.

Reese, Rick. *Greater Yellowstone: The National Park and Adjacent Wildlands*. Helena, MT: Montana Magazine, 1984. An attractive book with considerable information on ecological conditions in one of the Lower 48's largest intact ecosystems.

Robbins, Jim. *Last Refuge: The Environmental Showdown in Yellowstone and the American West*. New York: William Morrow and Co., 1995. A reporter's eye view of the changing West, incorporating all factions from loggers to Earth Firsters.

Schmidt, Jeremy, and Steven Fuller. *Yellowstone Grand Teton Road Guide*. Jackson, WY: Free Wheeling Travel Guides, 1990. A nicely done pocket-sized guide to the roads of the two parks, with accurate, up-to-date information. Easily the best road guide available.

Schreier, Carl, ed. *Yellowstone: Selected Photographs 1870-1960*. Moose, WY: Homestead Publishing, 1989. An outstanding collection of historic photographs from the park.

Schreier, Carl. *Yellowstone's Geysers, Hot Springs and Fumaroles*. Moose, WY: Homestead Publishing, 1987. An attractive small book filled with color photos and brief descriptions.

Scott, Douglas M., and Suvi A. Scott. *Wildlife of Yellowstone and Grand Teton National Parks*. Salt Lake City, UT: Wheelwright Press, Ltd., 1988. A brief descriptive guide to Yellowstone and Grand Teton critters.

Shaw, Richard J. *Plants of Yellowstone and Grand Teton National Parks*. Salt Lake City, UT: Wheelwright Press, 1981. Photos and descriptions of the most commonly found plants in the park.

Stevens, Lynn. *Wonderland Nomenclature: A History of the Place Names of Yellowstone National Park*. Palmdale, CA: GOSA Press. For the trivia buff: 891 pages listing the origins of all place names in the park.

Varley, John D. *Freshwater Wilderness: Yellowstone Fishes and Their World*. Yellowstone Library and Museum Association, 1983. A lovely book for anglers and those interested in fish.

Whittlesey, Lee H. *Yellowstone Place Names*. Helena, MT: Montana Historical Society Press, 1988. For the Trivial Pursuit enthusiast; detailed descriptions of every possible name from every possible obscure corner of Yellowstone.

Wuerthner, George. *Yellowstone and the Fires of Change*. Salt Lake City, UT: Haggis House Publications, 1988. Good photos and an ecological look at the fires make this perhaps the best book about the fires of '88.

INDEX

Page numbers in **boldface** indicate the primary reference. *Italicized* page numbers indicate information in captions, charts, illustrations, maps, or special topics.

A

Absaroka Beartooth Wilderness: 428, 439
Accidental Oil Company: 536-537
accommodations: 42-45; *see also specific place*
aerial tram (Rendezvous Mountain): 331
Afton: 186-190
Afton Tabernacle: 187
agriculture: 33; *see also specific type of ranching*
airline service: 57
airports: Big Horn County Airport (Greybull) 471; Bozeman 427; Buffalo 521; Cheyenne 80; Cody (Yellowstone Regional Airport) 455; Gillette 532; Jackson Hole 336; Laramie 121; Natrona County Airport (Casper) 221; Riverton 241; Rock Springs 161; Sheridan 505; West Yellowstone 425; Worland 478
Aladdin: 545
Aladdin Store: 545
Alaska Basin: 368
Albany: 129
Albany County Fair: 119-120
Albin: 82
Albin Days: 82
Albright, Horace M.: 349-350, 384
Alcova Hot Springs: 228
Alcova Reservoir: 228
All Girls Rodeos: 520
Almy: 173
Alpine: 192-193, *192*
Alpine Mountain Days: 193
alpine slide (Jackson Hole): 331
Alsop, Tom: 26
Alum Creek: 404
Alva: 545
Alzada: 546
American Heritage Center: 112
Ames Monument: 122
Amphitheater Lake: 359
Amtrak: 59; *see also specific place*
Anchor Dam: 460
Anderson Lodge: 459

Anna Miller Museum: 536
Antelope Butte Ski Area: 492
Anthropology Museum: 113
Applegate Wagon Train: 19
Arapaho Cultural Museum: 260
Arapahoe: 259
Arapaho Indians: 256-258
archaeological sites: Fort Phil Kearny 514; Greybull 473; Medicine Lodge State Park 474-475; Pine Bluffs 81; Spanish Diggings 89; Thermopolis 483
area code: 51
Arlington: 128
art galleries: *see specific place*
Artemesia: *see* sagebrush
Artist Paint Pots: 394
Artist Point: 403
arts and crafts festival (Casper): 219
Arvada: 508
Ashley, William: *294-295*
Aspen Alley: 141-142
Astor, John Jacob: 209-211, *294*
Astorians: 209-211, 282
Atlantic City: 288-289
Atlantic City Mercantile: 288
ATMs: 56; *see also specific place*
Auburn: 190-191
Auburn Fish Hatchery: 190-191
Avalanche Peak: 406
avalanche safety: *344*
Averell, James: 227-228
Aviat, Inc.: 186
Ayres Natural Bridge Park: 207

B

Back Basin: 395
backcountry: on horseback 37; tours 37
backcountry hiking: 36-42; ethics 37-38; etiquette 38; Grand Teton National Park 357-359; safety 38-42; Yellowstone National Park 406-409
Baggs: 143
banking: 56
Bar Nunn: 209

barrel racing: 51
baseball: 231
Basin: 473-474
Battle ghost town: 141
Bear Lodge, Legend of: *547*
Bear River: 178
Bear River State Park: 177-178
bears: *39-42;* Shoshone National Forest 432;
   Teton Wilderness 366; Wind River
   Mountains 273; Yellowstone National Park
   375-376
Beartooth Lake: 439-440
Beartooth Mountains: 439-440
Bear Trap Summer Festival: 219
Beauty Lake: 440
Beauty Pool: 390
Beaver Dick: *351*
beaver fever 38
Bechler River: 408-409
bed and breakfasts: 43; *see also specific
   place*
Bedford: 191
Beehive Geyser: 388
Beery, Wallace: 350
Belle Fourche River: 534
Benton: 24
Benton, Thomas Hart: 278
Bessemer Bend: 224-225
Beulah: 541
bicycling: 58-59; *see also specific place*
Big Boy locomotive: 70
Big Goose Falls: 492
Big Hollow: 129
Big Horn: 509-510
Bighorn Canyon National Recreation Area:
   466-471, *467*
Bighorn Caverns: 468-469
Big Horn County Airport (Greybull): 471
Big Horn County Fair and Bean Festival: 474
Big Horn Equestrian Center: 509
Big Horn Mountain Polka Days: 504
Big Horn Mountains: 487-497, *489*
Bighorn National Forest: 488
bighorn sheep: 251, 264-266, 466
Big Nose George Parrot: *148*
Big Piney: 299
Big Piney Chuck Wagon Days: 299
Big Sandy: 278-279, *279*
Big Springs: 481-482
Bill: 204-205
birds/birdwatching: Casper 220; Downar Bird
   Farm 100; Pathfinder National Wildlife

Refuge 227; Seedskadee National Wildlife
   Refuge; Tensleep Preserve 479
Biscuit Basin: 390
bison: 11-14, 349, 376
Bitch Creek: 368
black bears: *39*
Black Dragons Caldron: 404
blackflies: 56
black-footed ferrets: 86, *126*
Black Hills: 534-550, *535*
Black Hills gold rush: 16
Black Hills National Forest: 544
Black Sand Basin: 390
blacksmithing demonstrations: 284
Blacktail Butte: 356
Blacktail Pond: 399
Blaine, James G.: 380
"Bloody Bozeman": *see* Bozeman Trail
Boars Tusk: 155
Bomber Mountain: 495
Bondurant 300
Bonneville, Capt. Benjamin: 232, *295*
botanic gardens: Cheyenne 69; Torrington 97
Bothwell, A.J.: 227-228
Boulder: 298
Boulder Lake: 298
Boy Scouts: 451
Boysen Powerplant: 486
Boysen State Park: 242-243
Bozeman airport: 427
Bozeman, John M.: 511
Bozeman Trail: 23, 509, 511-514
Bozeman Trail Days: 514
Bozeman Trail Museum: 509
Bradford Brinton Memorial Museum: 510
Bradley Lake: 352-353
brands: *28*
Bretche Creek Ranch: 448
brewpubs: Cheyenne 75; Jackson Hole
   324-325; Laramie 118; Sheridan 503-504
Bridge Bay: 405
Bridger, Jim: 22, 171-172, *174,* 184, 212,
   254, 276, 292, *294,* 379, 397, 449, 512
Bridger-Teton National Forest: 365-367
Bridger Valley: 170-173
Bridger Wilderness: 276-279, *279*
Bright, William: 284
Brink of the Lower Falls: 403
Brink of the Upper Falls: 403
Broken Wheel Ranch: 263
Bronc Match and Horseshow: 545
bronc riding, bareback: 50

bronc riding, saddle: 50
Brooks Lake: 271
Brooks Lake Lodge: 271, 343
brown bears: *39*
brucellosis: 11, 376
Bucking Mule Falls: 492
buffalo: *see* bison
Buffalo: 514-521, *516, 517, 519;* history 514-515; practicalities 518-521; sights 515-518
Buffalo airport: 521
buffalo barbecue (Dubois): 268
Buffalo Bill: 13, 224, *287,* 432, 433-436, 437, 443-445, *449-451,* 500
Buffalo Bill Art Show and Sale: 453-454
Buffalo Bill boyhood home: 443
Buffalo Bill Dam: 432, **437**
Buffalo Bill Historical Center: 443-445
Buffalo Bill Museum: 444
Buffalo Bill Reservoir: 437
Buffalo Days (Gardiner): 427
Buffalo Night Rodeos: 520
Buffalo Ranch: 400
Buffalo Valley Road: 355
Bull Lake: 263
bull riding: 50
Bunsen Peak: 396
Buntline, Ned: 450
Bureau of Indian Affairs (BIA): 260
Bureau of Land Management (BLM): 31, 53
Burlington: 471
Burns, Madam Isabelle: 179
Burt, Struthers: 26, 28, 349-350
bus service: 59-60; *see also specific place*
Byron: 463-464

C
Calamity Jane: *286-287*
Calcite Springs: 401
calf roping: 49-50
calf scramble: 51
California Trail: 18
CallAir Fly-In/Star Valley Aviation Days: 189
CallAir Museum: 186-187
Cambria: 535-536, *536*
Campbell County Fair: 531
Campbell, John: 284
Camp Carlin: 65
camping/campgrounds: 45; *see also specific place*
Camp Monaco: 436
Camp Pilot Butte: 158

Canary, Martha Jane: *see* Calamity Jane
Canyon Village: 402
Carbon ghost town: 127
Carbon County Fair and Rodeo: 150
Carbon County Higher Education Center: 150
Carbon County Museum: 147
Carey Act: 84, 225, 431
Carey, Joseph M.: 25, *27,* 84, 224-225
Carey, Robert: 224
Carlin, William: 123-124
Carlisle, William ("The Lone Bandit"): 146
Carousel Park (Buffalo): 518
Carpenter, Robert E.: 381
Carrigen, Eleanor: 224
Carrington, Col. Henry B.: 26, 511
"Carrington's Overland Circus": 511
Carson, Kit: 212, 278, *294,* 449
Cascade Canyon: 358-359
Casino Night (Hartville): 89
Casper: 209-221, *210, 213, 216-217;* accommodations 216-217; entertainment and events 218-219; food and drink 217-218; history 209-214; information, services, and transportation 221; sights 214-216; recreation and shopping 220-221
Casper College: 214
Casper Events Center: 215
Casper Mountain: 222-224, *222*
Casper Municipal Band concerts: 219
Casper Planetarium: 215
Casper Symphony Orchestra: 219
Casper Troopers Drum and Bugle Corps: 219
Cassidy, Butch: 114, 143, 158, 167, 190, 244, 248-249, 259, 264, 266, 445, 475, 485, **523-524,** 525-526
Castle Gardens: 233-234, 479
Castle Geyser: 389
Castle Rock: 164
Cathedral Group (Teton peaks): 353
"Cattle Kate": 227-228
cattle ranching: 26-29, *28,* 65, 70, 355, *479*
Cedar Mountain: 446
Centennial: 130
Center for Native Arts and Humanities: 259
Central Wyoming College: 241
Central Wyoming Fair and Rodeo: 47, 219
Champion, Nate: 522-524
Chapel of the Transfiguration: 352
Chariot Races (Sheridan): 504

Charles J. Belden Museum: 458
Cheyenne: 24, **62-80**, *64, 68, 71-74;*
    accommodations 71-74; entertainment and
    events 76-78; food 74-76; history 62-66;
    information and services 79-80; sights 66-
    71; recreation 78; shopping 78-79;
    transportation 80
Cheyenne Airport: 80
Cheyenne & Black Hills Stage: *67*
Cheyenne Club: 25, *66*
Cheyenne Depot: 65
Cheyenne Frontier Days: 46, **77-78**
Cheyenne Frontier Days Western Art Show
    and Sale: 77
Cheyenne Gunslingers: 76
Cheyenne Opera House: 64
Cheyenne Symphony Orchestra: 76
Chico Hot Springs: 419, 426
Chief Arapooish: *490*
Chief Bear: 506
Chief Joseph: *378,* 437-438
Chief Standing Bear: *37*
Chief Tall Bull: 450
Chief Washakie: 17, *254,* 255, 257, 263
Chief Washakie Hot Springs: 262
Chief Yellow Hand: 450
Chili Cookoff (Evanston): 177
Chinese Massacre: *158*
Chinese New Year (Evanston): 177
Chinese Spring: 388
Chisholm, James: 16, 24, 63, 272, 283
Chivington, Col. John M.: 15, 257
Chocolate Pots: 394
Christ Episcopal Church: 198
Chromatic Pool: 390
chuck wagon race: 51
chuck wagon shows (Jackson Hole): 326-327
Chugwater: 83
Chugwater Chili Cook-Off: 47, 83
Chugwater museum: 83
Church Buttes: 166
Church of Our Father's House: 260
Church Universal and Triumphant (CUT): 425
Cirque of the Towers: 281-282
Cistern Spring: 395
Clark, Charles Badger, Jr.: *456*
Clarks Fork of the Yellowstone River: 438
Classicfest (Casper): 219
Clay Butte: 439
Clearmont: 507-508
Clepsydra Geyser: 393

Cliff Geyser: 390
climate: 6-8; *see also specific place*
climber's festival: 249
Climbers' Ranch: 360
clinker (scoria): 508
Close Encounters of the Third Kind: 546, 548
Cloud Peak: 495, 497
Cloud Peak Wilderness: 495-497, *496*
Clover-Mist Fire: 440
Clyman, James: *228*
CNL Clothier: 285
coal: 31, 156-157, 179, 204, 526, *530-531,*
    535-536
Cody: 441-456, *442, 447-448, 449-451;*
    accommodations 446-452; Buffalo Bill
    Historical Center 443-445; entertainment
    and events 453-454; food 452-453; history
    441-443; practicalities 455-456; recreation
    454-455; sights 445-446
Cody Firearms Museum: 444
Cody, Isaac: 443, 449
Cody Mural: 446
Cody Nite Rodeo: 453
Cody Old West Show and Auction: 453
Cody Stampede: 46, 453
Cody Wildlife Exhibit: 446
Cody, William F.: *see* "Buffalo Bill"
Cokeville: 184-185
College of Agriculture Research and
    Extension Center: 97
colleges and universities: Carbon County
    Higher Education Center 150; Casper
    College 214; Central Wyoming College
    241; College of Agriculture Research and
    Extension Center 97; Eastern Wyoming
    College 98; Laramie County Community
    College 79-80; Northwest College 461;
    Sheridan College 505; Western Wyoming
    Community College 160
Collins, Lt. Caspar: 211-212
Colony: 546
Colorado Wyoming Association of
    Museums: 53
Colter Bay: 354
Colter Bay Indian Arts Museum: 354
Colter, John: 17, **303-304**, *303,* 379
"Colter Stone": *303*
colt race: 51
Columbia Pool: 408
Committee to Restore Decency to Our
    National Parks: 302

Community Fine Arts Center (Rock Springs): 158
Como Bluff: 123-124
Conger, Patrick H.: 381
Connor Battlefield State Historic Site: 505-506
Connor, Gen. Patrick E.: 506, 511
Continental Divide Snowmobile Trail: 287, 333
Cook, Charles W.: 379
Cooke City: 428-430, *429*
Cooke, Jay: 380
Cooper Mansion: 112
Copperton ghost town: 141
Cora: 274
Cowboy Antiques and Collectibles Show: 453
Cowboy Days (Evanston): 177
Cowboy Poetry & Music Festival (Rock Springs): 161
Cowboy Poetry Roundup (Riverton): 241
Cowboy Round-Up (Big Horn): 510
Cowboy Songs and Range Ballads: 453
Cowboy State Games: 219
Cowboy Village Resort at Togwotee: 343
Cowley: 463
Crazy Horse: 17, 513
Crazy Woman Canyon: 492-493
Crested Pool: 390
Crimson Dawn Museum: 223-224
Crook County Fair and Rodeo: 544
Crook County Museum: 541
Crook, Gen. George: 501, 514
cross-country skiing: 36, Big Horn Mountains 491; Brooks Lake Lodge 343; Cache Creek Canyon (Jackson Hole) 344-345; Casper Mountain 223; Cowboy Village Resort at Togwotee 343; Dubois 269, 270; Evanston 178; Flaming Gorge National Recreation Area 169; Grand Targhee Nordic Center 343; Grand Teton National Park 345, 361-362; Granite Hot Springs 345; Greys River Loop Road 190; Jackson Hole 342; Laramie Mountains 207; Moose-Wilson Road (Jackson Hole) 344; Pinedale 298; Shadow Mountain (Jackson Hole) 345; Sierra Madre 142; Snake River dikes (Jackson Hole) 345; Snowy Range 133; South Pass 287; Spring Creek Resort Nordic Center 342-343; Star Valley 189; Teton Pass 345; Teton Pines Cross-Country Ski Center 342; West

Yellowstone 423-424; Wood River Valley Ski Touring Park 459; Yellowstone Mountain (North Fork Nordic Trails) 436; Yellowstone National Park 411-412
Crowheart: 263
Crowheart Butte: 263
Cub Creek: 366
Cumberland cemetery: 178
Cumberland ghost town: 178
Cunningham Cabin: 355
Cunningham, Pierce: 355
Curt Gowdy State Park: 80-81
Custard's Wagon Train Fight: 212
Custer, George A.: 13, 17, *286*, 449, 450, 514, 542, 545
cutter races: Jackson 327; Saratoga 138; Thayne 191

D
Daisy Geyser: 389
Daniel: 298-299
Dan Speas Fish Hatchery: 225
Dark Cavern Geyser: 394
Dave Johnston Power Plant: 208
Dawes, Henry M.: 380
Days of '49 (Greybull): 472
Days of '47 Celebration (Lyman): 171
Dayton: 506-507
Dayton Days: 507
Deadman's Bar: 356
Death Canyon: 359
deer: 11
Deer Creek Days: 209
Deke Latham Memorial PRCA Rodeo: 525
Depot Square (Evanston): 174-175
Desert Balloon Extravaganza: 161
DeSmet, Father Pierre: 15, 299
DeSmet monument: 522
Devil Canyon: 466-467
Devil's Gate: 229
Devil's Kitchen: 472
Devils Playground: 168
Devils Tower National Monument: 546-550, *547, 548*
Diamondville: 179-182, *180, 181*
Dickinson Park: 281
Dillon ghost town: 141
dinosaurs: 104, 113, 123-124, 473, 483
Disappointment Peak: 359
Discovery Center (Casper): 214
Division of State Parks and Historical Sites: 56

Dixon: 143
Dodge, Col. Richard I.: 535, 547
Dodge, Gen. Grenville M.: 13, 23, 62, 108, 146
dogsledding: 333
Donner Party: 19
Dot Island: 405
Doublet Pool: 388
Douglas: 195-202, *196, 199;* history 195-198; practicalities 198-199; sights 199-202
Douglas Park Cemetery: 198
Douglas Railroad Interpretive Center: 198
Downar Bird Farm: 100
downhill skiing: 36; Antelope Butte Ski Area 492; Grand Targhee Ski Resort 338-340; Hogadon Ski Area 223; Jackson Hole 338; Jackson Hole Ski Resort 340-341; Pine Creek Ski Area 185; Powder Pass Ski Area 492; Snow King Resort 341-342; Snowshoe Hollow Ski Area 189; Snowy Range Ski Area 133; Yellowstone Mountain Ski Area 436
draft-horse pulls: 138
Dragon's Mouth: 404
drag races: 201-202
driving: 57-58, *57;* in winter 60; speed limits 58; Yellowstone National Park 413-414
Dr. Spokes Cyclery & Museum: 215
Dry Creek Petrified Forest: 516-518
Dubois: 264-270, *265*
Dubois Museum: 265
Dubois State Fish Hatchery: 263
dude ranches: 43-45; *see also specific place*
DuFran, Dora: *287*
Dull Knife Battlefield: 525
Dunraven Pass: 402
Durand, Earl: 460-461
Durham Buffalo Ranch: 532

E
Eagles Nest Stage Station: 458
Eagle's Store: 421
East Entrance (Yellowstone National Park): 405-406
Eastern Shoshone Indian Days Powwow and Rodeo: 262
Eastern Shoshone Powwow and Rodeo: 47
Eastern Wyoming College: 98
Echinus Geyser: 395
economy: 31-34
Eddy, John: 494

Eden: 289-290
Edgar, Bob: 445
Edgar, Terry: 445
Edgerton: 231
Edison, Thomas A.: 141
Edness Kimball Wilkins State Park: 220
Ehrlich, Gretel: *437*
Eleanor Lake: 406
Electric Peak: 407
elk: 11
elk antler arch: 186
elk antler auction: 47, 327
Elk Feedground: 192
Elkhart Park: 277-278
Elk Mountain: 127-128
Elk Park: 394
Emblem: 471
Emerald Pool: 390
Emerald Spring: 395
Emerson, Willis George: 138-139
Emigrant Hill: 88
Emigrants' Washtub: 88
Emma Matilda Lake: 354
employment opportunities: 419-420
Encampment: 138-141, *139*
Encampment River Wilderness: 142
Entomology Museum: 113
Esterbrook: 205
Esterbrook Rendezvous: 205
Esther Morris cabin: 285
Ethete: 260
Ethete Celebration: 260
Ethete Community Powwow: 260
Etna: 192
Evanston: 173-178, *175, 176;* history 173-174; practicalities 176-178; sights 174-176
Evanston Rodeo Series: 177
Evansville: 209
events: *see* festivals and events
Everts, Truman: 379-380
Ewing-Snell Historical Site: 470
Excelsior Geyser: 391
Expedition Island: 164
Exum, Glenn: 360
Exum Route: 360

F
Fairy Falls: 393
Fall, Albert: 232
Fall Arts Festival: 47
farmers markets: Casper 218; Cheyenne 75

Farson: 289-290
fauna: 9-14; see also specific animal; specific place
Ferris, Angus: 389
Ferris Mansion: 148
festivals and events: 46-47; Afton 189; Aladdin 545; Albin 82; Alpine 193; Arapahoe 259; Basin 474; Big Horn 510; Big Piney 299; Boysen State Park 242; Bridger Valley 171; Buffalo 520; Casper 219; Cheyenne 76-78; Chugwater 83; Cody 453-454; Crimson Dawn Museum 224; Curt Gowdy State Park 81; Dayton 507; Devils Tower National Monument 550; Dixon 143; Douglas 201-202; Dubois 268; Edgerton and Midwest 231; Encampment and Riverside 140-141; Esterbrook 205; Ethete 260; Evanston 177; Flaming Gorge National Recreation Area 169; Fort Bridger 173; Fort Fetterman 203; Fort Phil Kearny 514; Fort Washakie 262; Gardiner 427; Gillette 530-531; Glendo 91; Glenrock 209; Green River 165; Greybull 472; Guernsey 88; Hartville 89; Hole-in-the-Wall area 525; Hulett 546; Jackson Hole 327-328; Kaycee 525; Kemmerer 181-182; LaGrange 82; Lake DeSmet 522; Lander 249; Laramie 119-120; Legend of Rawhide 103; Lingle 100; Lovell 466; Lusk 103; Medicine Bow 125; Moorcroft 540; Newcastle 539; Outlaw Trail Ride 37; Pine Bluffs 82; Pinedale 297; Powder River 232; Powell 463; Ranchester 506; Rawlins 150; Riverton 240-241; Rock Springs 161; Saratoga 137-138; Sheridan 504; South Pass 284-285, 289; Sundance 544; Ten Sleep 480; Thayne 191; Thermopolis 485; Torrington 100; Wheatland 87; Worland 477-478; Wright 533; Yellowstone National Park 424
Fetterman, Capt. William J.: 513
Fetterman Fight: 513
Fiddler's Lake: 252
Firehole Canyon: 168
Firehole Cascades: 393
Firehole Falls: 393
Firehole Lake: 392
Firehole River: 374, 391, 391
fires: 382-384
First United Methodist Church: 70
fish/fishing: 35-36; see also specific place
Fishing Bridge: 386, 404-405

Fishing Cone Geyser: 386
Fitzpatrick, Thomas: 15, 93, 257, 278, 279, 294
Fitzpatrick Wilderness: 279-280
Five Springs Falls: 490
Flagg Ranch: 354
Flaming Gorge Classic Car Show: 165
Flaming Gorge Dam Visitor Center: 167
Flaming Gorge Days: 165
Flaming Gorge Fishing Derby: 169
Flaming Gorge National Recreation Area: 167-170, 168
flora: 8-9, 8, 10; see also specific flora
Flying V Cambria Inn: 539
Folsom, David E.: 379, 404
Fontenelle Reservoir: 184
food and drink: 45-46; see also specific place
football: 120
forest service: offices 53
Forsling, Neal: 223-224
Fort Bonneville: 299
Fort Bridger: 18, 171-173
Fort Bridger museum: 172
Fort Bridger Rendezvous: 47, 173
Fort Bridger Treaty: 255
Fort Caspar: 214
Fort Caspar museum: 214
Fort C.F. Smith: 466, 511
Fort D.A. Russell: 65-66
Fort D.A. Russell Days: 78
Fort Fetterman: 202-203
Fort Fetterman Days: 201, 203
Fort Fetterman museum: 203
Fort Fred Steele State Park: 143-144
Fort Hat Creek Stage Station: 104
Fort Kearny: 26
Fort Laramie: 15, 18, 295, 449
Fort Laramie National Historical Site: 91-96, 92; history 91-94; practicalities 96; sights 95-96
Fort Laramie (town): 96
Fort Laramie Treaty: 255, 256
Fort Mackenzie: 500-501
Fort Manual Lisa: 441
Fort McKinney: 514-515
Fort Phil Kearny: 509, 511-514, 512, 513
Fort Phil Kearny museum: 514
Fort Reno: 511, 524-525
Fort Russell: 24
Fort Sanders: 24, 107, 116
Fort Stambaugh: 288

Fort Steele: 24
Fort Washakie: 260-262
Fort Wise Treaty: 15
Fort Yellowstone: 381
Fossil Butte National Monument: 182-183
Fossil Country Frontier Museum: 180-181
fossils: 183
Foundation for North American Wild
    Sheep: 446
Fountain Geyser: 393
Fountain Paint Pot: 392
Four Corners: 539
Foxtrotter Horse Show and Sale: 463
Franc, Otto: 441-442
Francis E. Warren Air Force Base: 65, 69
Frank Island: 405
Freedom: 191
Freedom Arms: 191
Freeman, Legh: 24, 25
Fremont Canyon: 228
Fremont County Fair and Rodeo: 240
Frémont, John C.: 179, 227, 278
Fremont Lake: 297
Fremont Peak: 277-278
French Merci Train: 70
Frewen Castle: 522
Frewen, Moreton: 522, 525
Frewen, Richard: 522, 525
Friday: 257
Frontier Days Old West Museum: 69
Frontier Festival: 119, 453
Frontier Index: 24
Frontier Prison: 146-147
Frontier Town: 114-115
Frying Pan Spring: 395-396
fumaroles (Yellowstone National Park): 373

G
galleries: *see specific place*
Gallery 234: 112
gambling: 428
Gannett, Henry: 280
Gannett Peak: 272, **280**
Garden Creek Falls: 224
Gardiner: 425-428, *426*
Gardiner Rodeo: 427
Garland: 464
Gas Hills: 243
gateway towns (Yellowstone National Park):
    420-430, *426, 429*
General Allotment Act: 258

geography: 5-6
Geological Museum: 112-113
geology: Devils Tower 546-547; Wind River
    Canyon 486
Geyser Hill: 388-389
"geyserite" (sinter): 373
geysers: 372-373, *372,* 386-395, 407-408;
    see also specific geyser
ghost towns: Battle 141; Carbon 127;
    Copperton 141; Cumberland 178; Dillon
    141; Hillsboro 468; Kirwin 459; Old Jelm
    132; Piedmont 171; Rambler 141;
    Rudefeha 141; Sunrise 89
Giantess Geyser: 388
Giant Geyser: 389-390
giardia: 38
Gibbon Falls: 394
Gibbon Meadows: 394
Gift of the Waters Pageant: 47, 485
Gillette: 526-533, *527, 528;* history 526;
    practicalities 528-533; sights 526-528
Gillette airport: 532
Gillette, Edward: 526
Glendo Historical Museum: 91
Glendo State Park: 91
Glendo Walleye Fishing Tournament: 91
Glenrock: 207-209
Glenrock Livestock Exchange: 209
Golden Gate: 396
gold-panning demonstrations: 284
golf courses: Afton 189; Buffalo 521; Casper
    220; Cheyenne 78; Cody 454; Dayton 507;
    Douglas 268; Dubois 201; Evanston 178;
    Gillette 531; Glenrock 209; Guernsey 88;
    Jackson Hole 332; Kemmerer 182; Lander
    248; Laramie 120; Lusk 103; Meeteetse
    459; Newcastle 539; Pinedale 297; Rock
    Springs 161; Sheridan 504; Thermopolis
    485; Torrington 99; Wheatland 86
Gollings, Bill: 501
Gooseberry Badlands: 476-477
Goose Egg Ranch: 224-225
Goshen County Fair: 100
government: 34
governor's mansion: 67-69
Gowdy, Curt: 80
Grand Canyon Creek: 544
Grand Canyon of the Yellowstone: *401,*
    402-403
Grand Encampment Museum: 139-140
Grand Geyser: 390

Grand Prismatic Spring: 391, *392*
Grand Targhee Nordic Center: 343
Grand Targhee Ski Resort: 338-340
Grand Teton Music Festival: 47, 328
Grand Teton National Park: 346-364, *346, 347, 348, 358, 363;* geology 346-347; history 349-352; practicalities 360-364; recreation 352-360; wildlife 347-349
Granger: 166
Granger Stage Station: 166
Granite Hot Springs: 300
Grant, Ulysses S.: 380
Grant Village: 386
Grasshopper Glacier: 428
Grassy Lake Road: 354
Gratrix Cabin: 288
Grattan Massacre: 93, 96
Gray Reef Reservoir: 228
Great Arrow: 460
Great Divide Basin: 153
Greater Yellowstone Coalition: 419
Greater Yellowstone Ecosystem: 373-377
Great Fountain Geyser: 392
Great Seal: 34
Great Wyoming Polka & Heritage Festival: 161
Greeley, Horace: 166
Green House: 179
Green River: 162-165, *162, 163,* 170
"Green River Drift": 292
Green River Lakes: 274-276, *275,* 277
Green River Rendezvous Rendezvous Days: 47, 297
Grey, Zane: 253
Greybull: 471-473, *472*
Greybull Livestock Auction: 472
Greybull Museum: 471
Greybull Wildlife Museum: 472
Greyhound: 59; *see also specific place*
Grinnell, Joseph Bird: 384
grizzly bears: *39*
Grizzly Discovery Center: 421
Gros Ventre River: 357
Gros Ventre Slide: 356-357
Gros Ventre Wilderness: 357, 366-367
Grotto Geyser: 389
Grover: 190
Guernsey: 88
Guernsey museum: 88
Guernsey State Park: 89-91
Guernsey State Park Museum: 90-91
guest ranches: *see* dude ranches

H
Haggerty, Ed: 138
Half Moon Lake: 298
Handkerchief Pool: 390
Hanna: 127
Hanna Basin Museum: 127
Hans Kleiber: 506
Happy Days Celebration: 463
"Harlow and Edwards": 123-124
Harold McCracken Research Library: 443
Harry Jackson Studios: 445-446
Hartville: 89
Harvest Festival: 100
Hawk Springs: 100
Hawk Springs State Recreation Area: 100
Hayden, Dr. Ferdinand V.: 207, 380; monument 208
Hayden Valley: 403-404
Hayfield Fight: 466
Haystack Buttes: 168
Headwaters Community Arts and Conference Center: 265
health and safety: 38-42, **56,** 273, *344,* 432
Heart Lake: 408
Heart Mountain: 456
Heart Mountain Relocation Center: 456-458, *457*
Heart Mountain Relocation Center Memorial Association: 458
Hedrick Pond: 355
Helen Robinson Zimmerscheid Western-Texas Trail Museum: 540
Hell Gap: 89
Hell on Wheels Rodeo: 76
Hell's Half Acre: 232
Hermitage Point: 354
Herschler Building: 67
Hickok, James B. (Wild Bill): *287,* 449
Hidden Corral Basin: 367-368
Hidden Falls: 353
High Park Lookout Tower: 488
High Plains Oldtime Country Music Show & Contest: 201
High Uinta Bike Race: 177
High Uinta Wilderness: 169
hiking: 36-37; etiquette 38; *see also specific place*
Hillsboro ghost town: 468
history: 14-30, *16, 19, 21, 25, 27, 28;* cattle ranching 26-29; Native Americans 14-17;

oil industry 30; Oregon Trail 18-20; Overland Trail 22-23; Pony Express 20-22; railroads 23-24; sheep ranching 29-30; statehood 24-26; trappers and explorers 17; *see also specific place*
Hoback Canyon: 300
Hogadon Ski Area: 223
"hog ranches": 93
Hole-in-the-Wall: 475, 525-256
Holladay, Ben: 22
Holy City: 436
Homesteader Museum (Powell): 461
Homestead Museum: 97
Hoodoos: 396
Hoofprints of the Past Museum: 522
Hopkins, George: 548
Horn, Tom: *27*, 29, 198
horse and wagon tours: 37; *see also specific place*
horseback riding: 37; *see also specific place*
Horse Creek: 270
horse racing: Casper 219; Evanston 177; Fort Washakie 262; Gillette 531
horses: 470-471
Horseshoe Tournament: 520
Horsethief Cave: 469
Horsley, Dr. William: 464, 465
hot air balloon rallies: Glendo 91; Riverton 240
hot-air balloon rides: Jackson Hole 332
hotels: 42; *see also specific place*
Hot Lake: 392
hot springs: Yellowstone National Park 373; Yellowstone vicinity 419
Hot Springs County Fair: 485
Hot Springs Historical Museum: 482
Hot Springs State Park: 480-482
Hot Springs Water Park: 482
Hudson: 243
Hulett: 545-546
hunting: 35-36; *see also specific place*
Huston Park Wilderness: 142
Hutton Lake National Wildlife Refuge: 116
Hyattville: 474
hypothermia: 41

I
Icebox Canyon: 400
ice fishing derbies: Curt Gowdy State Park 81; Kemmerer 182; Saratoga 138
ice skating: 332-333
Ice Slough: 251

Imperial Geyser: 393
Independence Rock: 228-229
Indian Bathtubs: 152
Indian Rock Art Cave: 525
Inspiration Point: 353, 402
international climber's festival: 249
internment camp: *see* Heart Mountain Relocation Center
Inyan Kara Mountain: 542
Irma Hotel: 445
Isa Lake: 386
Island Lake: 439-440
Ivinson, Edward: 115
Ivinson Mansion: 115

J
Jackalope Days: 201
jackalopes: *197*
Jackson: 305-338, *306, 307, 308, 312-314, 316, 318, 319, 320, 321, 322;* accommodations 311-321; entertainment 325-327; festivals and events 327-328; food and drink 319-325; information and services 334-335; preservation of *308;* recreation 328-333; shopping 335-336; sights 306-311; snow sports 338-346; transportation 336-337
Jackson, David E.: 302
Jackson Hole: 301-345, *301, 302, 308, 312-314, 316, 318, 319-320, 321, 322; see also* Jackson
Jackson Hole Airport: 336
Jackson Hole Alliance for Responsible Planning: *308*
Jackson Hole Fall Arts Festival: 328
Jackson Hole Land Trust: *308*
Jackson Hole Museum: 308
Jackson Hole Nordic Center: 342
Jackson Hole One-Fly Contest: 328
Jackson Hole Ski Resort: 340-341
Jackson Lake: 349, 353-354
Jackson Lake Dam: 353
Jackson Lake Lodge: 353
Jackson mountain-man rendezvous: 328
Jackson Peak: 277
Jackson rodeo: 328
Jackson Spring Cleanup: 327
Jackson Town Square: 306
Jackson, William H.: 398
jade: *58*, 249
Jim Gatchell Memorial Museum: 515-516

Jay Em: 101
J.C. Penney Home: 180
Jedediah Smith Wilderness: 367
Jeffrey City: 251
Jelm Mountain Observatory: 132
Jenney, Prof. Walter P.: 535
Jenney Stockade cabin: 536
Jenny Lake: 345, 353
Jenny Lake Lodge: 353
Jewel Geyser: 390
John D. Rockefeller, Jr. Memorial Parkway: 354
Johnson County Fair and Rodeo: 520
Johnson County War: 29, 441-442, *479, 517,* 522-524
Johnson Creek Wildlife Habitat Management Area: 123
Johnson, John ("Liver Eating"): 445
Joseph Henry Sharp Garden: 444
Joss House: 175-176

K
kayaking and canoeing: Snake River 330; Yellowstone National Park 418
Kaycee: 522-525
KC Ranch house: 524
Kelly: 305, 356
Kelly Warm Spring: 356
Kemmerer: 179-182, *180, 181*
Kendall dace: 274
Kendall Warm Springs: 274-276
Kendrick, John B.: 499-500
Kendrick Project: 499
Kennaday Peak Lookout: 132
Kepler Cascades: 386
Keyhole Reservoir: 540-541
Keyhole State Park: 540-541
Killpecker Dunes: 155
King's Saddlery: 500
King's Western Museum: 500
Kirwin ghost town: 459
Knott's Berry Farm: 284
Kriendler Gallery of Contemporary Western Art: 444

L
La Barge: 184
Labor Day Powwow: 47, 259
Lacey Act: 375
LaGrange: 82
Lake Alice: 185
Lake DeSmet: 522
Lake DeSmet Fishing Derby: 522

"Lake District": 225-228, *225*
Lake Hattie: 120
Lake Marie: 132
Lake Solitude: 495-497
Lake Yellowstone Hotel: 405
Lamar Valley: 399-400
Lance Creek: 104
land: 5-8, *7*
Lander: 243-250, *245, 246, 247*
Lander, Col. Frederick W.: 299
Lander Cutoff: 18, 185-186, 290, 299
Langford, Nathaniel P.: 359, 380
Laramie: 107-121, *108, 111, 113, 117;* accommodations 116-117; entertainment and events 119-120; food and drink 117-119; history 107-111; information and services 120-121; sights 115-116; sports and recreation 120; transportation 121; University of Wyoming 109-113; Wyoming Territorial Park 113-115
Laramie Airport: 121
Laramie County Community College: 79-80
Laramie County Fair: 78
Laramie Jubilee Days: 119
Laramie Mountains: 205-207, *206*
Laramie Peak Museum: 86
Laramie River Station: 86
LeFors, Joe: *27*
Legend of Rawhide: 47, 103
Legend Rock Petroglyph Site: 459-460
LeHardy Rapids: 404
Leigh, Jenny: *351,* 353
Leigh, Richard ("Beaver Dick"): *351*
Leiter: 508
Lewis and Clark Expedition: 17, *261*
Lewis Falls: 385
Lewis Lake: 385-386
Lewis River Canyon: 385
Lewiston: 289
Liberty Cap: 398
Lincoln, Abraham: 121-122, 380
Lincoln County Courthouse: 181
Lincoln County Fair: 189
Lingle: 100
lingo: *32-33*
Lion Geyser Group: 388
Little America: 166
Little Big Horn, Battle of: 13, 17, 450
Little Britches Rodeo: 191
Little Firehole Meadows: 390
Little Snake River Museum: 143
Little Snake River Valley: 143

Little Snake River Valley Rodeo: 143
livestock markets: Glenrock 209; Greybull 472; Riverton 239; Torrington 97
Living History Days: 520
Lockhart, Caroline: *469*
Lockhart Ranch: 468
Logan, Harvey ("Kid Curry"): *523-524*
Loggers and Ranchers Play Days: 546
logging: 264
Lone Bandit (William Carlisle): 146
Lonesome Lake: 281
Lone Star Geyser: 386-387
Lonetree: 167
Longabaugh, Harry: *see* Sundance Kid
Lookout Mountain: 451
Lost Cabin: 232-233
Loucks, John D.: 497
Louis Lake: 252
Lovell: 464-466
Lovell, Henry Clay: 464
Lower Falls: 402
Lower Geyser Basin: 391-393, *391*
Lusk: 101-103, *102*
Lyman: 170-171
Lysite: 232-233

M
Mackenzie, Gen. Ranald S.: 501
Madison Junction: 393-394
Madison River Canyon: 424
Main Street Historic District (Sheridan): 501
Majors, Alexander: 20-22, 449
Mammoth Hot Springs: 380, 396-399, *397*
Mammoth Hot Springs Hotel: 398
Manila: 168-169
Mansface Rock: 164
Manuse, George ("Big Nose George Parrot"): *148*
Manville: 89
Marbleton: 299
Marsh, Prof. Othniel Charles: 123-124
Martin's Cove: 229-230
Mason, Anthony L.: 464
Mather, Stephen: 384
Maverick Bill: 29
McAuley Store: 288
McKinnon: 167
Meadowlark Lake: 488, 495-497
Medicine Bow: 124-125
Medicine Bow Days: 125
Medicine Bow Mountains: 128-144, *129, 131*
Medicine Bow Museum: 125

Medicine Bow Peak: 132
Medicine Lodge State Park: 474-475
Medicine Wheel: 493-494, *493, 494*
Meeteetse: 458-460
Meeteetse Archives: 458
Meeteetse Mercantile: 458
Menor's Ferry: 352
"Merc": 288
Messick, Alice ("Flaming Mame"): 284
Midsummer's Eve (Crimson Dawn): 224
Midway Geyser Basin: 391, *391*
Midwest: 231
Mills: 209
Miner's Delight: 289
Miner's Delight Inn: 288-289
Minerva Terrace: 397-398
Mini Fair & Rodeo: 82
mining: *530-531*
Minute Man Geyser: 408
Miracle Mile: 226-227
Mirror Lake: 132
Missouri Buttes: 547
ML Ranch: 468
Moe, Tommy: 341
Mokler, Alfred J.: 29-30, 34
Moncrieffe, Malcolm: 509
Moneta: 232
money: 56
Monument Geyser Basin: 394
Monument Hill: 482
Moonlight, Col. Thomas: 94
Moorcroft: 540
Moorcroft Jubilee Days: 540
Moose Falls: 385
Moose Meadows: 368
Moran: 305
Moran Junction: 355
Moran, Thomas: 398
Mormon Row: 356
Mormon Trail: 18
Morning Glory Pool: 389
Morris, Esther Hobart: 67, 284, *285*
mosquitoes: 56
motels: 42-43; *see also specific place*
Mother Featherlegs: 101
mountain biking: *see specific place*
mountain climbing: Devils Tower 548-549; Fremont Peak 277-278; Grand Teton National Park 359-360
mountain man rendezvous: 47; Casper 219; Laramie 119; Riverton 240; *see also* rendezvous

mountain men: *294-295*
mountains: 5-6, *see also specific mountain;
   specific mountain range*
Mountain States Circuit Finals Rodeo: 78
Mountain View: 171
Mt. Haynes: 393
Mt. Helen: 277
Mt. Jackson: 393
Mt. Moran: 355
Mt. Sacagawea: 277
Mt. Washburn: 402
Muddy Gap: 151
Muddy Guard Station: 491
Muddy Medicine Fat Tire Bike Race: 177
Muddy Mountain: 223
mudpots (Yellowstone National Park): 373
Mud Volcano Area: 404
Mule Creek Junction: 104
Mummy Cave: 445
Murie Collection: 356
museum association: 53
Museum of the Mountain Man: 292
Museum of the National Park Ranger: 395
Museum of the Yellowstone: 421
museums: 53; American Heritage Center 112;
   Anna Miller Museum 536; Anthropology
   Museum (University of Wyoming) 113; Big
   Horn County Airport (Greybull) 471;
   Bozeman Trail Museum 509; Bradford
   Brinton Memorial Museum 510; Buffalo Bill
   Dam visitor center 437; Buffalo Bill
   Historical Center 443-445; Buffalo Bill
   Museum 444; CallAir Museum 186-187;
   Carbon county Museum 147; Casper
   Planetarium 215; Charles J. Belden
   Museum 458; Chugwater Museum 83;
   Cody Firearms Museum 444; Cody Wildlife
   Exhibit 446; Colter Bay Indian Arts
   Museum 354; Crook County Museum 541;
   Discovery Center (Casper) 214; Douglas
   Railroad Interpretive Center 198; Dr.
   Spokes Cyclery & Museum 215; Dubois
   Museum 265; Entomology Museum
   (University of Wyoming) 113; Fort Bridger
   museum 172; Fort Caspar museum 214;
   Fort Fetterman museum 203; Fort Phil
   Kearny museum 514; Fossil Country
   Frontier Museum 180-181; Frontier Days
   Old West Museum: 69; Geological Museum
   112-113; Glendo Historical Museum 91;
   Grand Encampment Museum 139-140;
   Greybull Wildlife Museum 472; Grizzly
   Discovery Center 421; Guernsey museum
   88; Guernsey State Park Museum 90-91;
   Hanna Basin Museum 127; Helen
   Robinson Zimmerscheid Western-Texas
   Trail Museum 540; Homesteader Museum
   (Powell) 461; Homestead Museum 97;
   Hoofprints of the Past Museum 522; Hot
   Springs Historical Museum 482-483;
   Jackson Hole Museum 308; Jam Gatchell
   Memorial Museum 515-516; J.C. Penney
   Home 180; King's Western Museum 500;
   Laramie Peak Museum 86; Little Snake
   River Museum 143; Medicine Bow Museum
   125; Meeteetse Archives 458; Murie
   Collection 356; Museum of the Mountain
   Man 292; Museum of the National Park
   Ranger 395; Museum of the Yellowstone
   421; National Bighorn Sheep Interpretive
   Center 264-265; National Museum of
   Wildlife Art 306-308; National U.S.
   Marshals' Museum 114; Nici Self Museum
   130; Nicolaysen Art Museum 214; Norris
   Museum 394; Old West Miniature Village
   and Museum 446; Pathfinder Reservoir
   interpretive center 227; Pioneer Museum
   (Afton) 187; Pioneer Museum (Douglas)
   198; Pioneer Museum (Lander) 244;
   Pioneer Museum (Ten Sleep) 478-479;
   Plains Indian Museum 444-445; Range
   Herbarium (University of Wyoming) 113;
   Riverton Museum 239; Rockpile Museum
   526-527; Rock River Museum 123; Rocky
   Mountain Herbarium (University of
   Wyoming) 113; Salt Creek Museum 231;
   Saratoga Museum 136; Shoshone Tribal
   Cultural Center 260; Sinclair/Parco
   Museum 144; Special Collections
   (Sheridan) 505; Stagecoach Museum 101-
   102; St. Stephens Mission Heritage Center
   259; Sweetwater County Historical
   Museum 164; Tate Mineralogical Museum
   215; Terua P. Williams Botany
   Conservatory (University of Wyoming) 113;
   Teton County Historical Center 308; Texas
   Trail Museum 82; Tom Sun Ranch
   museum 229; Town Hall Museum
   (Meeteetse) 458; Trona Mining Museum
   170; Uinta County Museum 175; University
   Art Museum 112; University of Wyoming
   High Plains Archaeology Field Lab and
   Visitor Center 82; Warren Heritage
   Museum: 69; Washakie County Museum

and Cultural Center 476; Werner Wildlife Museum 215; Western History Center 100; Whitney Gallery of Western Art 444; Wright Centennial Museum 532; Wyoming Children's Nature Center and Museum 116; Wyoming Department of Game and Fish museum 71; Wyoming Dinosaur Center 483; Wyoming Pioneer Home (Thermopolis) 482; Wyoming State Museum 71; Wyoming Transportation Museum and Center 70
Mystic Falls: 390

N

name origins: Absaroka Mountains 441; Bitch Creek 368; Cheyenne 62; Chugwater 83; Grand Tetons 302; Jackson Hole 301-302; Jay Em 101; Medicine Bow 105; Rawlins 145-146; Thermopolis 480; Wyoming 25; "Equality State" 25-26; *see also specific place*
Names Hill: 184
Naramore, Dr. L. Stan: 465
national art show: 268
National Bighorn Sheep Interpretive Center: 264-265
National Elk Refuge: 310-311
national forests: *54-55;* Bridger-Teton National Forest 365-367; offices 53; Targhee National Forest 367-368
National Geographic: 494
National High School Rodeo: 530
National Museum of Wildlife Art: 306-308
National Outdoors Leadership School (NOLS): 248
National Park Mountain: 393-394
national parks: Grand Teton National Park 346-364; offices 53; Yellowstone National Park 369-430
national recreation areas: Bighorn Canyon 466-471, *467;* Flaming Gorge National Recreation Area 167-170, *168*
National U.S. Marshals' Museum: 114
Native Americans: 12-13, 14-17, 253-255, 377-378, *378,* 380; legends 547; *see also specific tribe*
Natrona County Airport: 221
Natural Bridge: 405
Natural Corrals: 155
Natural Trap Cave: 469
Nature Conservancy: 248
Newcastle: 535-539, *537, 538*

New Fork Lake: 274
Nez Percé Indians: *378,* 380
Nici Self Museum: 130
Nicolaysen Art Museum: 214
nightlife: 46; *see also specific place*
Niobrara County Fair: 103
Norris Geyser Basin: 394
Norris Junction: 395-396
Norris Museum: 394
Norris, Philetus W.: 380-381
North Absaroka Wilderness: 440
Northeast Entrance (Yellowstone National Park) 400
Northern Arapahoe Powwow: 259
Northern Arapaho Sun Dance: 260
North Gate Canyon: 134
North Platte River: 134, 136-137, 220, 225-226
Northwest College: 461
Nye, Bill: 6, 25, *110, 518*

O

Oakley, Annie: 451
Obsidian Cliff: 396, *410*
Ocean Lake: 263
oil: 30, 31, 173-174, 203-204, 208, 230-231, 250, 443, 526, 536-537; *see also specific place*
oil well, first: 250
Ojo Caliente: 393
Okie, John B.: 233
Oktoberfest: 78
Old Faithful: 388
Old Faithful Inn: 390
Old Faithful Lodge: 390
Old Jelm ghost town: 132
Old Stone School: 474
Old Timer's Rodeo: 88
Old West Days: 327-328
Old West Miniature Village and Museum: 446
One-Shot Antelope Hunt: 249
Opal Terrace: 398
Open Water Fishing Derby: 182
Oregon Buttes: 282
"Oregon Country": 18
Oregon Trail: 15, 18-20, *19,* 88, *90,* 184, 185-186, 211, 228-229
Oregon Trail Baptist Church: 290
"original-rules baseball": 120
Osage: 540
Oshoto: 546
Osprey Falls: 396

Otto: 471
outdoor recreation: 35-41; see also specific place; specific type of recreation
Outlaw Cave: 525
Outlaw Trail Ride: 37, **485**, 525
Overland Stage Line: 22
Overland Trail: 22-23, 129
Overthrust Belt: 173-174
Owen, William: 359
Oxbow Bend: 354-355

P
Packer, Alferd: 202-203
pack horse races: 268
Pahaska Tepee: 433-436
Paintbrush Canyon: 358-359
Painted Desert: 476-477
Palatte Ranch: 459
Parco (Producers Oil and Refining Company): 144
Park County Fair: 463
Parker, Robert Leroy: see Cassidy, Butch
Parkfest: 530-531
Parting of the Ways monument: 282
Pathfinder National Wildlife Refuge: 227
Pathfinder Reservoir: 227
Pathfinder Reservoir interpretive center: 227
Penney, James Cash: 180
performing arts: see specific place
Periodic Spring: 187-188
Petersen, Frank: 359
Peterson, William: 379
petroglyphs and pictographs: 263-264; Casper 233; Meeteetse 459-460; White Mountain 155
Phelps Lake: 345
Phillips, John ("Portugee"): 513
Phillips, William T.:see Cassidy, Butch
Piedmont ghost town: 171
Pike, George W.: 198-199
Pilot Butte: 159
Pine Bluffs: 81-82
Pine Bluffs Trail Days: 82
Pine Creek Ski Area: 185
Pinedale: 290-298, 291, 293
Pink Cone Geyser: 392
Pinnacle Buttes: 271
Pioneer Days: 249
Pioneer Museums: Afton 187; Douglas 198; Lander 244; Ten Sleep 478-479
Piutes: 22

Place, Etta: 523-524
Plains Complex: 198
Plains Indian Museum: 444-445
Plains Indian Powwow: 47, 453
Plains Indians: 542-543; see also Native Americans
Platte Bridge Encampment: 219
Platte County Court House: 86
Platte County Fair and Rodeo: 87
Platte River Station Stage Bike Race: 219
Platte River Wilderness: 130
Platte Valley Festival of the Arts: 137
Playmill Theatre: 423
Point of Rocks: 153
Poison Spring: 398
Pole Creek: 491
Pole Creek Cross-Country Ski Challenge: 520
Pole Mountain area: 121-122, 121
Pole-Pedal-Paddle Race: 327
politics: 34
Pollock, Capt. Edwin: 514
polo: 509
Polo Ranch: 509
Pony Express: 18, 20-22, 21, 449
Popo Agie Rendezvous: 249
Popo Agie River: 251-252
Popo Agie Wilderness: 280-282
population: 58
Porcelain Basin: 394-395
Porcupine Falls: 492
Porkchop Geyser: 395
Portuguese Houses: 524
Potholes: 353
Potts Hot Springs Basin: 405
Powder Pass Ski Area: 492
Powder River area: 487-533, 489, 490
Powder River Roundup Days: 520
Powder River (town of): 232
Powder River Trailways: 59; see also specific place
Powell: 460-463, 461, 462
Powell, Capt. James: 513
Powell, Maj. John Wesley: 162, 164, 167, 225, 460
powwows: 256-257
prairie dogs: 204, 545
PRCA Rodeo Finals: 46, 219, 531
PRCA rodeos: 201
Prexy's Pasture: 112
prisoner-of-war camp: 196-197

pronghorn antelope: 10-11
Prophet, Elizabeth Clare: 425
Proulx, E. Annie: 507
Pryor Mountain Wild Horse Range: 470-471

Q

Queen Victoria: 451
Quilting in the Tetons: 328

R

Radiator Geyser: 389
radio: 51-53
railroads: 23-24, 108
rail travel: 59; see also specific place
Rainbow Pool: 390
Ralston: 458
Rambler ghost town: 141
Ranch Days Rodeo: 485
Ranchester: 505-506
Ranchester Days: 506
Ranch Tour: 119
Range Herbarium: 113
rattlesnakes: 9-10
Rawhide Buttes: 103
Rawlins: 145-151, 145, 149; history 145-146;
    practicalities 148-151; sights 146-148
Rawlins, Gen. John A.: 145-146
Rawlins Uplift: 148
Ray, Nick: 522-524
Reamer, Robert: 390, 398
Reclamation Act: 225-226, 437
Red Butte: 539
Red Canyon: 282
Red Canyon Overlook Visitor Center: 167
Red Canyon Ranch Preserve: 282
Red Cloud: 15, 211-212, 511, 513, 514
Red Desert: 153-155
Red Desert Round Up: 161
Red Rock Point: 403
Reed, William: 123-124
Register Cliff: 88
Reliance Tipple: 159
rendezvous: Casper 219; Dubois 268;
    Esterbrook 205; Fort Bridger 173; Jackson
    328; Lander 249; Laramie 119; Pinedale
    295, 296, 297; Riverton 240; Saratoga 138;
    West Yellowstone 424
Rendezvous Mountain: 359
reservoirs: Alcova Reservoir 228; Gray Reef
    Reservoir 228; Pathfinder Reservoir 227;
    Seminoe Reservoir 226

Rhinichthys osculus thermalis: see Kendall
    dace
Ripley, Willard: 548
river rafting: Clarks Fork of the Yellowstone
    438; Gardiner/Yellowstone 427; Green
    River 170; North Platte River 134, 220;
    Shoshone River 454; Snake River 193,
    328-330; Wind River 486
Riverside: 138-141, 139
Riverside Geyser: 389
Riverton: 238-242, 238, 240
Riverton Airport: 241
Riverton Arts Center: 241
Riverton Livestock Auction: 239
Riverton Museum: 239
Riverton Museum Folk Festival: 241
Riverton Rendezvous: 240
Riverton rodeos: 241
road conditions: 60
Roaring Mountain: 396
Robber's Roost Stage Station: 104
Rochelle Hills: 204-205
Rock Creek Stage Station: 127, 128
Rockefeller, John D.: 350-352
Rockpile Museum: 526-527
Rock River Museum: 123
Rock Springs: 156-162, 157, 159; history
    156-157; practicalities 160-162; sights
    157-160
Rock Springs airport: 161
Rocky Mountain Herbarium: 113
Rocky Mountain Stage Stop Sled Dog Race:
    181, 189, 193, 249, 268, 289, 297, 327
Rocky Point: 184
rodeo: 47-51; clowns 50-51; history 48;
    modern-day rodeo 48-49; specific events
    49-51
rodeos: 46; Buffalo 520; Casper 219;
    Cheyenne 76-78; Cody 453; Cowley 463;
    Dixon 143; Douglas 201; Encampment
    140; Evanston 177; Fort Washakie 262;
    Jackson 328; Kaycee 525; LaGrange 82;
    Newcastle 539; Old Timer's Rodeo 88;
    Pine Bluffs 82; Platte County Fair and
    Rodeo 87; Ranch Days Rodeo 485;
    Rawlins 150; Riverton 240-241; Sheridan
    504; Sundance 544; Thayne 191
Rogers, William: 548
Rome: 449
Roosevelt Arch: 425
Roosevelt, Theodore: 350, 351

Rosie's Cabin: 355
Ross, Gov. William B.: 26
Ross, Nellie Tayloe: 26
Roundtop Mountain: 485
Rudefeha: 138
Rudefeha ghost town: 141
Rupp, A.G.: 475
Russell, David A.: 65, 250, *294-295, 301,*
    365, *374, 392,* 399
Russell, William H.: 20-22
Russin, Robert: 214-215
Rustic Falls: 396
Rustic Geyser: 408

S
Sacagawea: *261*
Sacagawea Cemetery: 262
Saddle-Peddle-Paddle Triathlon: 138
safety: *see* health and safety
sagebrush: *8*
Salt Creek Days: 231
Salt Creek Museum: 231
Salt Creek Oil Field: 230-231
Sand Creek Massacre: 15, 22, 257
SANTA (Shoshone Arapahoe Nations Transit
    Authority): 59-60; *see also specific place*
Sapphire Pool: 390
Saratoga: 134-138, *135, 136*
Saratoga Museum: 136
Saratoga National Fish Hatchery: 137
Sauger Derby: 477-478
Savage Run Wilderness: 130
Savery: 143
Sawmill Geyser: 390
Sawyer, Col. James: 506
Sawyer Fight: 506
scoria: 508
Scott's Bottom Nature Area: 165
Scout, the: 443
Seedskadee National Wildlife Refuge: 166
Seminoe Reservoir: 226
Seminoe State Park: 226
Senior Pro Rodeo: 201
Shane cabin: 356
Sheep Creek Geological Area: 168
Sheepeater Cliffs: 396
Sheepeater Indians: 377-378
Sheepherder's Fair: 232
Sheepherders Rodeo and Dog Trials: 525
Sheepman's Holiday: 463
Sheep Mountain: 472
sheep ranching: 29-30, *479*

Shell: 474
Shell Canyon: 488-489
Shell Falls: 490
Sheridan: 497-505, *498, 499, 502;*
    accommodations 501-503; food and drink
    503-504; history 497-499; practicalities
    504-505; sights 499-501
Sheridan airport: 505
Sheridan College: 505
Sheridan County Fair: 504
Sheridan County Library: 501
Sheridan County Rodeo: 504
Sheridan, Gen. Philip: 13, 16, 17, 384,
    449-450
Sheridan Inn: 500
Sheridan Wyo Rodeo: 504
Sherman, Gen. William T.: *378*
Shirley Basin: 125-127
Shive, John: 359
Shoshone Arapahoe Nations Transit Authority
    (SANTA): 59-60; *see also specific place*
Shoshone Dam: 437
Shoshone Episcopal Mission: 262
Shoshone Geyser Basin: 407-408
Shoshone Indians: 253-255
Shoshone Lake: 407-408
Shoshone National Forest: 432-441, *433, 434*
Shoshone Point: 386
Shoshone River: 454
Shoshone Tribal Cultural Center: 260
Shoshone Tribal Fair: 262
Shoshoni: 242
Sibley Lake: 491
Sidon Canal: 464
Sierra Madre: 141-143
Sierra Madre Mountain Man Rendezvous: 138
Sierra Madre Winter Carnival: 140
sightseeing must-visits: *52*
Signal Mountain Area: 353
Silex Spring: 392
Silver Cord Cascade: 402
Silver Gate: 428-430, *429*
Simpson, Alan: 350
Simpson, Milward: 350
Sinclair: 144
Sinclair/Parco Museum: 144
Sinks Canyon: *283*
Sinks Canyon State Park: 251-252
sinter: 373
Sitting Bull: 17, 451
skiing: *see* cross-country skiing; downhill skiing
ski races: 327

sleigh rides: 333
Sloans Lake: 78
slot machines: 428
Smith, Al: 537
Smith, Jedediah: *294*
Snake River: 193, 328-330
Snake River Canyon: 193, 329
Snake River Institute: 309-310
snowboarding: 338
"Snow Chi Minh Trail": 106
snowcoach tours: 411
Snow King Resort: 341-342
snowmobiling: 36; Big Horn Mountains 491;
  Casper Mountain 223; Continental Divide
  Snowmobile Trail 287; Dubois 269, 270;
  Flaming Gorge National Recreation Area
  169; Grand Teton National Park 362; Greys
  River Loop Road 190; Jackson Hole 333;
  Keyhole State Park 541; Medicine Bow
  Mountains 133-134; Pinedale 298; Sierra
  Madre 143; Yellowstone National Park 412,
  424
Snowshoe Hollow Ski Area: 189
snowshoeing (Grand Teton National Park):
  333, 362
Snowy Range: 130-134, *131*
Snowy Range Ski Area: 133
Soda Butte: 400
Solitary Geyser: 389
South Buffalo Fork River: 366
South Fork of the Shoshone: 438-439
South Pass: *282*
South Pass City: 282-287, *283, 284*
South Pass gold rush: 283
South Pass Historic Site: 284-285
Spalding, Bishop: 359
Spanish Diggings: 89
Special Collections: 505
Specimen Ridge: 400
speed limit: state 58; Yellowstone National
  Park 414
Spirit Mountain Cave: 446
Split Rock: 230
Sponge Geyser: 388-389
Spotted Horse: 508
Spread Creek: 355
Spring Creek Resort Nordic Center: 342-343
Square Top Mountain: 276
Stagecoach Museum: 101-102
Stage III Community Theatre: 219
St. Andrews Episcopal Church: 288
Star Plunge: 482

Star Valley: 185-193, *187, 188*
State Bath House: 482
state bird: 34
State Bird Farm: 509
State Capitol building: 66-67
state counties: *4;* largest 152; smallest 152
state dinosaur: 34
state facts: *58-59*
state flower: 34
state fossil: 34
statehood: 24-26
state information centers: 51; *see also
  specific place*
state land status: *54-55*
state lowest point: 545
state mammal: 34
state museum association: 53
state nickname: 1, 34
state parks: 53-56, *54-55;* Bear River State
  Park 177-178; Boysen State Park 242-243;
  Buffalo Bill State Park 437; Curt Gowdy
  State Park 80-81; Edness Kimball Wilkins
  State Park 220; Glendo State Park 91;
  Guernsey State Park 89-91; Hot Springs
  State Park 480-482; Keyhole State Park
  540-541; Seminoe State Park 226; Sinks
  Canyon State Park 251-252
state recreation areas: 53-56, *54-55*
state stone: 34
state symbols: 34
state tree: 34
St. Christopher's Chapel of the Big
  Horns: 488
Steady Geyser: 392
Steamboat Geyser: 395
Steamboat Point: 405-406
steer roping: 50
steer wrestling: 49
Stevenson Island: 405
Stevenson, John: 359
St. Joseph's Cemetery: 147
St. Mark's Episcopal Church: 70
St. Mary's Catholic Cathedral: 70
St. Matthew's Cathedral: 116
St. Michael's Mission: 260
stock-car racing: 161
Stockman Livestock Auction: 97
Story: 510-511
Story, Dr. John: 465
Story Fish Hatchery: 510
Story, Nelson: 26
String Lake: 353

St. Stephens Church: 259
St. Stephens Mission: 259
St. Stephens Mission Heritage Center: 259
Sublette, Bill: 19
Sublette County Fair: 299
Sublette Cutoff: 18, 290
Sublette, Milton: *294*
Sublette, Pinckney: 299
Sublette, William: 91, *294*
Sugar Beet Festival: 477
Sugarloaf Recreation Area: 131-132
Sulphur Caldron: 404
Summerfest: 150
Summer Fun Fest and Antique Tractor
    Pull: 87
Summer Institute in Western American
    Studies: 443
Sundance: 541-544
Sundance Kid: 445, 485, 525, *523-524*
Sundance Mountain: 541
sun dances: *542-543*
Sunlight Basin: 437-438, 441
Sunlight Gorge: 438
Sunrise ghost town: 89
Sunset Lake: 390
Super Day: 78
Superior: 159
Swan, Alexander: 70, *84*
Swan Land and Cattle Company: 83, *84*
Swan, Thomas: 70, *84*
Swartz, Ed: 1
Swartz, John: *see* Packer, Alferd
Sweetwater County Fair: 161
Sweetwater County Historical Museum: 164
Sweetwater County Jail: 285
Sweetwater Mines: 282
Sweetwater River Project: 250-251
Swett Ranch: 168
Sybille Wildlife Research Center: 86, 123, *126*
Sylvan Lake: 406
Sylvan Springs Geyser Basin: 394

T
Taggart Lake: 345, 352-353
Tammen, H.H.: 451
TA Ranch: 524
Targhee National Forest: 367-368
Tate Mineralogical Museum: 215
Teapot Dome: 231-232, 499
Ten Sleep: 478-479, *479*
Tensleep Canyon: 479
Ten Sleep Celebration Days: 480

Ten Sleep Fish Hatchery: 479
Tensleep Preserve: 479
Ten Sleep Raid: 29, *479*
Terua P. Williams Botany Conservatory: 113
Teton County Fair: 328
Teton County Historical Center: 308
Teton Pines Cross-Country Ski Center: 342
Teton Science School: 356
Teton Wilderness: 365-366
Texas Trail: 81-82
Texas Trail Museum: 82
Thayne: 191
Thermopolis: 480-486, *481, 484*
Thorofare, the: 409
Thunder Basin National Grassland: 203-205
ticks: 56
tie hacks: *269*
Tipple Mine Historical Site
Titcomb Basin: 277
Togwotee Pass: 271-272
Tollgate Rock: 164
Tom Sun Ranch museum: 229
Tongue River Canyon: 492
Tongue River Cave: 492
torchlight ski parade: 327
Torrington: 96-100, *98, 100*
Torrington Livestock Market: 97
tourism: 31-33
Tour of Heart Mountain: 463
tours: Yellowstone National Park 414,
    427-428; *see also specific place*
Tower Fall: 401
Tower Junction: 399
Town Hall Museum (Meeteetse): 458
Trail End State Historic Site: 499-500
Trail Lake: 280
Trail Town: 445
transportation: 57-60, *57; see also
    specific place*
Trapper Canyon: 475
travelers checks: 56
travertine: 373
Treaty Day Celebration: 262
Treaty of 1851: 15
Treaty of 1868: 94, 545
Triangle X Ranch: 355
Tribal Fish and Game Office (Wind River
    Indian Reservation): 253
trivia: *58-59*
trolley tours: 66
trona: 31, 163-164
Trona Mining Museum: 170

Tubb Town: 535
Turban Geyser: 390
Turn of the Century Days: 181-182
Twain, Mark: *21,* 166, 251, *289, 550*
Two Ocean Creek: 365
Two Ocean Lake: 354

U
Ucross: 507
Uinta County Fair: 177
Uinta County Museum: 175
Undine Falls: 399
Union Pacific Railroad Depot: 70
Union Pass: 270-271
University Art Museum: 112
University of Wyoming: 109-113, *111;* history
   109-111; museums 112-113; visiting
   111-112
University of Wyoming High Plains
   Archaeology Field Lab and Visitor Center: 82
University of Wyoming research and
   extension center: 189
Upper Falls: 402
Upper Geyser Basin: 387-391, *387, 391*
Upton: 540
U.S. Marshals Day & Posse Rendezvous: 119
Ute Mountain Fire Tower: 168

V
Vedauwoo: 122
vegetation: *see* flora
Verendrye, François: 17
Verendrye, Joseph: 17
Veteran: 100
Veterans' Home: 518
Vietnam monument: 446
Virginian Hotel: 125
Virginian, The: 124, 125, 202, 224-225, 368
volcanism: 371-372
Vore Buffalo Jump: 541

W
Waddell, William Bradford: 20-22
Wagon Box Fight: 513
Wahb Springs: 400
Wallop, Sen. Malcolm: 509
Wallop, Sir Oliver H.: 509
Wamsutter: 153
Wapiti: 436
Wapiti Ranger Station: 436
Wapiti Valley: 432-436, *435-436*
War Paint: 253

Warren Air Force Base: 31
Warren, Francis E.: 25, *65,* 84, *158,* 500-501
Warren Heritage Museum: 69
Warren Peak Lookout: 544
Washakie County Fair: 477
Washakie County Museum and Cultural
   Center: 476
Washakie Graveyard: 260-262
Washakie Wilderness: 440-441
Watson, Ella: *see* "Cattle Kate"
Werner Wildlife Museum: 215
West Entrance (Yellowstone National
   Park): 393
Western History Center: 100
Western Wyoming Community College: 160
Weston County Fair: 539
West Thumb: 386
West Thumb Geyser Basin: 386
West Yellowstone: 420-425
West Yellowstone Airport: 425
Wheatland: 84-87, *85, 86*
Whetstone Creek: 366
Whipple House: 69-70
Whirligig Geyser: 394-395
whirling disease: 418
Whiskey Basin: 263-264
Whiskey Basin Habitat Area: 264, 265
Whiskey Gap: 151
Whiskey Mountain Buckskinners Wind River
   Rendezvous: 268
White Dome Geyser: 392
White, Jim: 13
White Mountain Petroglyphs: 155
White Shoshone: *304*
whitewater rafting: *see* river rafting
Whitman, Marcus: 19
Whitney Gallery of Western Art: 444
Wiessner, Fritz: 548
Wigwam Fish Rearing Station: 479
Wild Bill Hickok: *287,* 449
Wild Bunch: *523-524*
Wilderness Act: 276, 365
wildernesses: Absaroka Beartooth
   Wilderness 427, 428, 439; Bridger
   Wilderness 276-279, *279;* Cloud Peak
   Wilderness 495-497, *496;* Encampment
   River Wilderness 142; Gros Ventre
   Wilderness 357, 366-367; High Uinta
   Wilderness 169; Huston Park Wilderness
   142; Jedediah Smith Wilderness 367; North
   Absaroka Wilderness 440; Platte River
   Wilderness 130; Popo Agie Wilderness

280-282; Savage Run Wilderness 130; Teton Wilderness 365-366; Washakie Wilderness 440-441; Winegar Hole Wilderness 367
wild horse race: 51
wild horses: 160, 470-471
wildlife: *see* fauna
wildlife viewing: 9; Alpine 192; Bighorn Canyon National Recreation Area 466; Casper 220; Douglas *204;* Evanston 178; Gillette 532; Grand Teton National Park 347-348; Hulett 546; Hutton Lake National Wildlife Refuge 116; Jackson Hole 310-311; Lander 251; Pathfinder National Wildlife Refuge 227; Seedskadee National Wildlife Refuge 166; Sundance 541; Thermopolis 482; Wheatland 86; Whiskey Basin 264, 265, 266; Yellowstone National Park 374-377, 400
Wild West Winter Carnival (Riverton/Boysen Reservoir): 240, **242-243**
Willow Flats: 353
Willow Grove Cemetery: 518
Willow Lake: 298
Willow Park: 396, 491
Wilson: *304,* 305
Wilson, "Uncle Nick": *304*
Wind River Canyon: 486
Wind River Indian Reservation: 253-264
Wind River Knives: 269
Wind River Mountains: 235-237, *236, 237,* **272-282;** practicalities 273-274
Wind River Mountains Wilderness Areas: *237*
Wind River Visitors Council: 237
windsurfing: Buffalo Bill Reservoir 437; Jackson 330
Winegar Hole Wilderness: 367
Wister, Owen: *124,* 125, 202, 224-225, 368, 518
wolves: 376-377
women's suffrage: 25-26, 109, 283-284
Woodchopper's Jamboree: 47
Woodchoppers Jamboree and Rodeo: 140
Wood River Valley Ski Touring Park: 459
Woods Landing: 132
Worland: 475-478, *477*
Worland airport: 478
Worland, Charlie ("Dad"): 475
"world's most desolate pay phone": 539
World Snowmobile Expo: 424

Wounded Knee Massacre: 17
Wraith Falls: 399
Wright: 532-533
Wright Centennial Museum: 532
Wright Days: 533
Wyoming Children's Nature Center and Museum: 116
Wyoming Cowboys: 120
Wyoming Department of Game and Fish museum: 71
Wyoming Development Company: 84
Wyoming Dinosaur Center: 483
Wyoming Division of Tourism and State Marketing: 51
Wyoming Downs Racetrack: 177
Wyoming Game and Fish Department: 35
Wyoming Geological Survey Building: 113
Wyoming Hereford Ranch: 70
Wyoming High School Rodeo Finals: 201
Wyoming Highway Department: 60
Wyoming Homestay & Outdoor Adventures: 43
Wyoming Outdoor Council: 248
Wyoming Peak: 190
Wyoming Pioneer Home: 482
Wyoming Public Radio: 53
Wyoming State Fair: 47, 201
Wyoming State Flatpick Guitar Contest & Music Festival: 182
Wyoming State Museum: 71
Wyoming State Winter Fair: 249
Wyoming Stock Growers Association: 25, *27,* 29
Wyoming Territorial Park: 113-115
Wyoming Transportation Museum and Center: 70
Wyoming Vietnam Veterans Memorial: 446

Y
Yellowstone Association: 413
Yellowstone Drug Store: 242
Yellowstone fires: *382-384*
Yellowstone Grizzly Foundation: 375-376
Yellowstone Guide: 413
Yellowstone Institute: 400
Yellowstone Jazz Festival: 453
Yellowstone Lake: 404-405
Yellowstone Mountain Ski Area: 436
Yellowstone National Park: 369-430, *371, 374, 378, 379, 382-384, 387, 389, 391, 392, 397, 401, 408, 410, 415, 416, 426,*

429; ecology 373-377; gateway towns 420-430; geology 371-373; history 377-385; practicalities 413-420; touring and recreation 385-412
Yellowstone Park Improvement Company: 381
Yellowstone Regional Airport (Cody): 455

Yellowstone Rendezvous: 424
Yellowstone Today: 413
Yellowtail Wildlife Habitat Management Unit: 468
Young, Brigham: 166

ABOUT THE AUTHOR

Born in Atlanta, Georgia, Don Pitcher grew up all over the East Coast—from Florida to Maine. He moved west to attend college and immediately fell in love with its wide open spaces. Don holds a bachelor's degree in biology from Pacific Union College and a master's degree in fire ecology from the University of California, Berkeley. Once out of school, he traveled north to Alaska to work for the Park Service, the Forest Service, and the Alaska Department of Fish & Game. In 1989, he headed to Wyoming's Teton Wilderness to take part in a grizzly bear habitat study. Don remained in Wyoming to research and write the first edition of this guide and to photograph a second book on the state.

Trained as an ecologist, Don Pitcher's love of travel led him to work on various guidebooks as both a writer and photographer. He is the author of *Washington Handbook* and coauthor of *Alaska-Yukon Handbook* (both Moon Publications), and *Berkeley Inside/Out* (Heyday Books). He has photographed books on Wyoming and Alaska for Compass American Guides, and his photographs have appeared in many books, calendars, magazines, posters, and other publications. Don bases his travels at his Alaska home, where he lives with his wife, Karen Shemet.

MOON TRAVEL HANDBOOKS

THE IDEAL TRAVELING COMPANIONS

Moon Travel Handbooks provide focused, comprehensive coverage of distinct destinations all over the world. Our goal is to give travelers all the background and practical information they'll need for an extraordinary travel experience.

Every Handbook begins with an in-depth essay about the land, the people, their history, art, politics, and social concerns—an entire bookcase of cultural insight and introductory information in one portable volume. We also provide accurate, up-to-date coverage of all the practicalities: language, currency, transportation, accommodations, food, and entertainment. And Moon's maps are legendary, covering not only cities and highways, but parks and trails that are often difficult to find in other sources.

Below are highlights of Moon's North America and Hawaii Travel Handbook series. Our complete list of Handbooks, covering North America and Hawaii, Mexico, Central America and the Caribbean, and Asia and the Pacific, is on the order form on the accompanying pages. To purchase Moon Travel Handbooks, please check your local bookstore or order by phone: (800) 345-5473 Monday-Friday 8 a.m.-5 p.m. PST.

MOON OVER NORTH AMERICA
THE NORTH AMERICA AND HAWAII TRAVEL HANDBOOK SERIES

"Moon's greatest achievements may be the individual state books they offer. . . . Moon not only digs up little-discovered attractions, but also offers thumbnail sketches of the culture and state politics of regions that rarely make national headlines."

—*The Millennium Whole Earth Catalog*

ALASKA-YUKON HANDBOOK
by Deke Castleman and Don Pitcher, 500 pages, **$17.95**
"Exceptionally rich in local culture, history, and reviews of natural attractions. . . . One of the most extensive pocket references. . . . An essential guide!" — *The Midwest Book Review*

ALBERTA AND THE NORTHWEST TERRITORIES
by Nadina Purdon and Andrew Hempstead, 466 pages, **$17.95**
"*Alberta and the Northwest Territories Handbook* provides strong coverage of the most rugged territories in Canada."
—*The Bookwatch*

ARIZONA TRAVELER'S HANDBOOK
by Bill Weir and Robert Blake, 486 pages, **$17.95**
"If you don't own this book already, buy it immediately"
—*Arizona Republic*

ATLANTIC CANADA HANDBOOK
by Nan Drosdick and Mark Morris, 436 pages, **$17.95**
New Brunswick, Nova Scotia, Prince Edward Island,
Newfoundland and Labrador.
"The new *Atlantic Canada* is the best I've seen on the region—
superior maps, travel tips, and cultural essays."
—Peter Aiken, *Providence Journal-Bulletin*

BIG ISLAND OF HAWAII HANDBOOK
by J.D. Bisignani, 349 pages, **$13.95**
"The best general guidebooks available." —*Hawaii Magazine*

BRITISH COLUMBIA HANDBOOK
by Jane King, 375 pages, **$15.95**
"Deftly balances the conventional and the unconventional, for both
city lovers and nature lovers."
—*Reference and Research Book News*

COLORADO HANDBOOK
by Stephen Metzger, 447 pages, **$18.95**
"Hotel rooms in the Aspen area, in the height of winter sports
season, for $20-$30? . . . who but a relentless researcher from
Moon could find it?" —The New York *Daily News*

GEORGIA HANDBOOK
by Kap Stann, 360 pages, **$17.95**
"[a] gold medal winner . . . Anyone who is interested in the South
should get this book." —*Eclectic Book Review*

HAWAII HANDBOOK
by J.D. Bisignani, 1004 pages, **$19.95**
Winner: Grand Excellence and Best Guidebook Awards, Hawaii
Visitors' Bureau
"No one since Michener has told us so much about our 50th
state." —*Playboy*

HONOLULU-WAIKIKI HANDBOOK
by J.D. Bisignani, 365 pages, **$14.95**
"The best general guidebooks available." —*Hawaii Magazine*

IDAHO HANDBOOK
by Don Root, 600 pages, **$18.95**
"It's doubtful that visitors to the Gem State will find a better, more
detailed explanation anywhere."
—*The Salt Lake Tribune*

KAUAI HANDBOOK
by J.D. Bisignani, 330 pages, **$15.95**
"This slender guide is tightly crammed. . . . The information
provided is staggering." —*Hawaii Magazine*

MAUI HANDBOOK
by J.D. Bisignani, 393 pages, **$14.95**
Winner: Best Guidebook Award, Hawaii Visitors' Bureau
"*Maui Handbook* should be in every couple's suitcase. It
intelligently discusses Maui's history and culture, and you can
trust the author's recommendations for best beaches, restaurants,
and excursions." —*Bride's Magazine*

MONTANA HANDBOOK
by W.C. McRae and Judy Jewell, 454 pages, **$17.95**
"Well-organized, engagingly written, tightly edited, and chock-full
of interesting facts about localities, backcountry destinations,
traveler accommodations, and cultural and natural history."
—*Sierra Magazine*

NEVADA HANDBOOK
by Deke Castleman, 473 pages, **$16.95**
"Veteran travel writer Deke Castleman says he covered more
than 10,000 miles in his research for this book and it shows."
—*Nevada Magazine*

NEW MEXICO HANDBOOK
by Stephen Metzger, 320 pages, **$15.95**
"The best current guide and travel book to all of New Mexico"
—New Mexico Book League

NEW YORK HANDBOOK
by Christiane Bird, 615 pages, **$19.95**
Contains voluminous coverage not only of New York City, but also
of myriad destinations along the Hudson River Valley, in the
Adirondack Mountains, around Leatherstocking Country, and
elsewhere throughout the state.

NORTHERN CALIFORNIA HANDBOOK
by Kim Weir, 779 pages, **$19.95**
"That rarest of travel books—both a practical guide to the region
and a map of its soul." —*San Francisco Chronicle*

OREGON HANDBOOK
by Stuart Warren
and Ted Long Ishikawa, 520 pages, **$16.95**
". . . the most definitive tourist guide to the state ever published."
—*The Oregonian*

TENNESSEE HANDBOOK
by Jeff Bradley, 500 pages, **$17.95**
Features nonpareil coverage of Nashville and Memphis, as well as
the Appalachian Trail, Great Smoky Mountains National Park, Civil
War battlefields, and a wide assortment of unusual amusements
off the beaten path.

TEXAS HANDBOOK
by Joe Cummings, 598 pages, **$17.95**
"Reveals a Texas with a diversity of people and culture that is as
breathtaking as that of the land itself."
—*Planet Newspaper,* Australia

"I've read a bunch of Texas guidebooks, and this is the best one."
—Joe Bob Briggs

UTAH HANDBOOK
by Bill Weir and W.C. McRae, 500 pages, **$17.95**
". . . a one-volume, easy to digest, up-to-date, practical, factual
guide to all things Utahan. . . . This is the best handbook of its kind
I've yet encountered." —*The Salt Lake Tribune*

WASHINGTON HANDBOOK
by Don Pitcher, 866 pages, **$19.95**
"Departs from the general guidebook format by offering
information on how to cope with the rainy days and where to take
the children. . . . This is a great book, informational, fun to read,
and a good one to keep." —*Travel Publishing News*

WISCONSIN HANDBOOK
by Thomas Huhti, 400 pages, **$16.95**
Lake Michigan, Lake Superior, and Wisconsin's 65 state parks and
national forests offer unrivaled outdoor recreational opportunities,
from hiking, biking, and water sports to the myriad pleasures of
Door County, the "crown jewel of the Midwest."

WYOMING HANDBOOK
by Don Pitcher, 582 pages, **$17.95**
"Wanna know the real dirt on Calamity Jane, white Indians, and
the tacky Cheyenne gunslingers? All here. And all fun."
—The New York *Daily News*

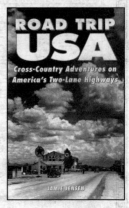

Travel Matters

Smart Reading for the Independent Traveler

Travel Matters is Moon Publications' free newsletter, loaded with specially commissioned travel articles and essays that get at the heart of the travel experience. Every issue includes:

Feature Stories covering a wide array of travel and cultural topics about destinations on and off the beaten path. Past feature stories in *Travel Matters* include Mexican professional wrestling, traveling to the Moon, and why Germans get six weeks vacation and Americans don't.

The Offbeat Path exploring unusual customs and practices from toothfiling ceremonies in Bali to the serving of deep fried bull testicles in a small Colorado bar.

Health Matters, by Dirk Schroeder, author of *Staying Healthy in Asia, Africa, and Latin America,* focusing on the most recent medical findings that affect travelers.

Reviews providing readers with assessments of the latest travel books, videos, multimedia, support materials, and Internet resources.

Travel Q&A, a reader question-and-answer column for travelers written by an international travel agent and world traveler.

To receive a free subscription to *Travel Matters,* call (800) 345-5473, e-mail us at travel@moon.com, or write to us at:

> Moon Publications
> P.O. Box 3040
> Chico, CA 95927-3040

Current and back issues of *Travel Matters* can also be found on our web site at
http://www.moon.com

Please note: Subscribers who live outside of the United States will be charged $7 per year for shipping and handling.

MOON TRAVEL HANDBOOKS

NORTH AMERICA AND HAWAII

Alaska-Yukon Handbook (0897) $17.95
Alberta and the Northwest Territories Handbook (0463) $17.95
Arizona Traveler's Handbook (0714) $17.95
Atlantic Canada Handbook (0072) $17.95
Big Island of Hawaii Handbook (0064) $13.95
British Columbia Handbook (0145) $15.95
Colorado Handbook (0447) $18.95
Georgia Handbook (0390) $17.95
Hawaii Handbook (0005) $19.95
Honolulu-Waikiki Handbook (0587) $14.95
Idaho Handbook (0889) $18.95
Kauai Handbook (0919) $15.95
Maui Handbook (0579) $14.95
Montana Handbook (0498) $17.95
Nevada Handbook (0641) $16.95
New Mexico Handbook (0862) $15.95
New York Handbook (0811) $19.95
Northern California Handbook (3840) $19.95
Oregon Handbook (0102) $16.95
Road Trip USA (0366) $22.50
Tennessee Handbook (0439) $17.95
Texas Handbook (0633) $17.95
Utah Handbook (0870) $17.95
Washington Handbook (0455) $19.95
Wisconsin Handbook (0927) $16.95
Wyoming Handbook (0854) $17.95

ASIA AND THE PACIFIC

Australia Handbook (0722) $21.95
Bali Handbook (0730) $19.95
Bangkok Handbook (0595) $13.95
Fiji Islands Handbook (0382) $13.95
Hong Kong Handbook (0560) $15.95
Indonesia Handbook (0625) $25.00
Japan Handbook (3700) $22.50
Micronesia Handbook (0773) $14.95

Nepal Handbook (0412) $18.95
New Zealand Handbook (0331) $19.95
Outback Australia Handbook (0471) $18.95
Pakistan Handbook (0692). $22.50
Philippines Handbook (0048) $17.95
Singapore Handbook (0781). $15.95
Southeast Asia Handbook (0021). $21.95
South Korea Handbook (0749) $18.95
South Pacific Handbook (0404). $22.95
Tahiti-Polynesia Handbook (0374) $13.95
Thailand Handbook (0420). $19.95
Tibet Handbook (3905) $30.00
Vietnam, Cambodia & Laos Handbook (0293) $18.95

MEXICO

Baja Handbook (0528) $15.95
Cabo Handbook (0285). $14.95
Cancún Handbook (0501) $13.95
Central Mexico Handbook (0234). $15.95
Mexico Handbook (0315). $21.95
Northern Mexico Handbook (0226). $16.95
Pacific Mexico Handbook (0323) $16.95
Puerto Vallarta Handbook (0250). $14.95
Yucatán Peninsula Handbook (0242) $15.95

CENTRAL AMERICA AND THE CARIBBEAN

Belize Handbook (0307) $15.95
Caribbean Handbook (0277). $16.95
Costa Rica Handbook (0358) $19.95
Jamaica Handbook (0706) $15.95

INTERNATIONAL

Egypt Handbook (3891) $18.95
Moon Handbook (0668). $10.00
Moscow-St. Petersburg Handbook (3913) $13.95
Staying Healthy in Asia, Africa, and Latin America (0269) . . . $11.95
The Practical Nomad (0765) $14.95

www.moon.com

WHERE TO BUY MOON TRAVEL HANDBOOKS

BOOKSTORES AND LIBRARIES: Moon Travel Handbooks are sold worldwide. Please contact our sales manager for a list of wholesalers and distributors in your area.

TRAVELERS: We would like to have Moon Travel Handbooks available throughout the world. Please ask your bookstore to write or call us for ordering information. If your bookstore will not order our guides for you, please contact us for a free catalog.

Moon Publications, Inc.
P.O. Box 3040
Chico, CA 95927-3040 U.S.A.
tel.: (800) 345-5473
fax: (916) 345-6751
e-mail: travel@moon.com

IMPORTANT ORDERING INFORMATION

PRICES: All prices are subject to change. We always ship the most current edition. We will let you know if there is a price increase on the book you order.

SHIPPING AND HANDLING OPTIONS: Domestic UPS or USPS first class (allow 10 working days for delivery): $3.50 for the first item, 50 cents for each additional item.

EXCEPTIONS: *Tibet Handbook, Mexico Handbook,* and *Indonesia Handbook* shipping $4.50; $1.00 for each additional *Tibet Handbook, Mexico Handbook,* or *Indonesia Handbook.*

Moonbelt shipping is $1.50 for one, 50 cents for each additional belt.

Add $2.00 for same-day handling.

UPS 2nd Day Air or Printed Airmail requires a special quote.

International Surface Bookrate 8-12 weeks delivery: $3.00 for the first item, $1.00 for each additional item. Note: Moon Publications cannot guarantee international surface bookrate shipping. Moon recommends sending international orders via air mail, which requires a special quote.

FOREIGN ORDERS: Orders that originate outside the U.S.A. must be paid for with an international money order, a check in U.S. currency drawn on a major U.S. bank based in the U.S.A., or Visa or MasterCard.

TELEPHONE ORDERS: We accept Visa or MasterCard payments. Minimum order is US$15. Call in your order: (800) 345-5473, 8 a.m.-5 p.m. Pacific standard time.

ORDER FORM

Prices are subject to change without notice. Be sure to call (800) 345-5473
8 a.m.–5 p.m. PST for current prices and editions, or for the
name of the bookstore nearest you that carries Moon Travel Handbooks.
(See important ordering information on preceding page.)

Name: _____ Date: _____

Street: _____

City: _____ Daytime Phone: _____

QUANTITY	TITLE	PRICE
	Taxable Total	
	Sales Tax (7.25%) for California Residents	
	Shipping & Handling	
	TOTAL	

Ship: ☐ UPS (no P.O. Boxes)   ☐ 1st class   ☐ International surface mail

Ship to: ☐ address above   ☐ other _____

Make checks payable to: **MOON PUBLICATIONS, INC.**, P.O. Box 3040, Chico, CA 95927-3040 U.S.A.
We accept Visa and MasterCard. **To Order**: Call in your Visa or MasterCard number, or send a written order with your Visa or MasterCard number and expiration date clearly written.

Card Number: ☐ **Visa**   ☐ **MasterCard**

☐ ☐ ☐ ☐   ☐ ☐ ☐ ☐   ☐ ☐ ☐ ☐   ☐ ☐ ☐ ☐

Exact Name on Card: _____

Expiration date: _____

Signature: _____

WYOMING HANDBOOK

INCLUDING YELLOWSTONE AND
GRAND TETON NATIONAL PARKS

WYOMING HANDBOOK

INCLUDING YELLOWSTONE AND GRAND TETON NATIONAL PARKS